Essays on Ancient Greek Literature and Culture

Volume 2: Comedy, Herodotus, Hellenistic and Imperial Greek Poetry, the Novels

In this book one of the world's leading Hellenists brings together his many contributions over four decades to our understanding of major genres of Greek literature, above all the Greek novel, but also Attic Comedy, fifth-century historiography, and Hellenistic and Imperial Greek poetry. Many are already essential reading, such as the chapter on the figure of Lycidas in Theocritus' *Idyll* 7, or two chapters on the ancient readership of Greek novels. Discussions of Imperial Greek poetry published three decades ago opened up a world almost entirely neglected by scholars. Several chapters address literary and linguistic issues in Longus' novel *Daphnis and Chloe*, complementing the author's commentary published in 2019; two contribute to a better understanding of the enigmatic *Aethiopica* of Heliodorus; and many explore important questions arising from examination of the form of the Greek novel as a whole. This is the second volume of a planned three-volume collection.

Ewen Bowie is Emeritus E. P. Warren Praelector and Fellow in Classics at Corpus Christi College, Oxford, and Emeritus Professor of Classical Languages and Literature at the University of Oxford. He writes on early Greek poetry; Old Comedy; Hellenistic poetry; and the Greek literature and culture of the Roman Empire. He co-edited volumes on *Philostratus* (Cambridge, 2009) and *Archaic and Classical Choral Song* (2011), edited one on Herodotus (2018), and published a commentary on Longus' *Daphnis and Chloe* (Cambridge, 2019).

Essays on Ancient Greek Literature and Culture

Volume 2

Comedy, Herodotus, Hellenistic and Imperial Greek Poetry, the Novels

EWEN BOWIE
University of Oxford

CAMBRIDGE
UNIVERSITY PRESS

CAMBRIDGE
UNIVERSITY PRESS

Shaftesbury Road, Cambridge CB2 8EA, United Kingdom

One Liberty Plaza, 20th Floor, New York, NY 10006, USA

477 Williamstown Road, Port Melbourne, VIC 3207, Australia

314–321, 3rd Floor, Plot 3, Splendor Forum, Jasola District Centre, New Delhi – 110025, India

103 Penang Road, #05–06/07, Visioncrest Commercial, Singapore 238467

Cambridge University Press is part of Cambridge University Press & Assessment, a department of the University of Cambridge.

We share the University's mission to contribute to society through the pursuit of education, learning and research at the highest international levels of excellence.

www.cambridge.org
Information on this title: www.cambridge.org/9781107058125
DOI: 10.1017/9781107415430

First published 2023

A catalogue record for this publication is available from the British Library.

A Cataloging-in-Publication data record for this book is available from the Library of Congress

ISBN 978-1-107-05812-5 Hardback

Contents

Illustration and Tables

Places of Original Publication

The chapters in this volume were originally published as follows. I am very grateful to the holders of copyright who have given permission for republication in this volume.

1 'Who is Dicaeopolis?', *Journal of Hellenic Studies* 108 (1988) 183–5.

2 '*Marginalia obsceniora*: some problems in Aristophanes' *Wasps*', in E. M. Craik (ed.), *'Owls to Athens': Essays on Classical Subjects Presented to Sir Kenneth Dover*, Oxford, Clarendon Press 1990: 31–8.

3 'Wine in Old Comedy', in O. Murray and M. Tecuşan (eds.), *In Vino Veritas*, London, British School at Rome 1995: 113–25.

4 'Ionian *iambos* and Attic *Komoidia*: father and daughter, or just cousins?', in A. Willi (ed.), *The Language of Greek Comedy*, Oxford, Oxford University Press 2002: 33–50.

5 'Le portrait de Socrate dans les *Nuées* d'Aristophane', in M. Trédé and P. Hoffmann (eds.), *Le rire des anciens: actes du colloque international, Université de Rouen, École normale supérieure, 11–13 janvier 1995*, Paris, Presses de l'École normale supérieure 1998: 53–66.

6 'Aristophanes' *Clouds*: an agonistic note', in C. N. Fernández, J. T. Nápoli, and G. C. Zecchin de Fasano (eds.), *ΑΓΩΝ: Competencia y cooperación de la antigua Grecia a la actualidad. Homenaje a Ana María González de Tobia*, La Plata, EDULP 2015: 95–109.

7 'The Lesson of Book 2', in E. K. Irwin and T. Harrison (eds.), *Interpreting Herodotus*, Oxford, Oxford University Press 2018: 53–74.

8 'Theocritus' Seventh *Idyll*, Philetas and Longus', *Classical Quarterly* 35 (1985) 67–91.

9 'Frame and framed in Theocritus poems 6 and 7', in M. A. Harder, R. F. Regtuit, and G. C. Wakker (eds.), *Theocritus. Hellenistica Groningana* 2, Groningen, Egbert Forsten 1996: 91–100.

10 'The reception of Apollonius Rhodius in imperial Greek literature', in M. A. Harder, R. F. Regtuit, and G. C. Wakker (eds.), *Hellenistica Groningana* 4, Leuven, Peeters 2000: 1–10.

11 'Time and place, narrative and speech in Philicus, Philodamus and Limenius', in A. Faulkner and O. Hodkinson (eds.), *Hymnic Narrative and the Narratology of Greek Hymns*, Leiden and Boston, Brill 2015: 87–118.
12 'Greek Sophists and Greek poetry in the Second Sophistic', in *Aufstieg und Niedergang der römischen Welt* ii 33.1 (1989) 209–58.
13 'Poetry and poets in Asia and Achaia', in S. Walker and A. Cameron (eds.), *The Greek Renaissance in the Roman Empire*, Papers from the Tenth British Museum Classical Colloquium (December 1986), *BICS Suppl.* 55 (1989) 198–205.
14 'Greek poetry in the Antonine Age', in D. A. Russell (ed.), *Antonine Literature*, Oxford, Clarendon Press 1990: 53–90.
15 'Hadrian and Greek poetry', in E. N. Ostenfeld, K. Blomqvist, and L. C. Nevett, (eds.), *Greek Romans, Roman Greeks: Studies in Cultural Interaction*, Aarhus, Aarhus University Press 2002: 172–97.
16 'Denys d'Alexandrie: un poète grec dans l'empire romain', *REA* 106 (2004) 177–85.
17 'Luxury cruisers? Philip's epigrammatists between Greece and Rome', *Aevum Antiquum* 8 (2008) [2012] 223–58.
18 'Doing Doric', in E. Sistakou and A. Rengakos (eds.), *Dialect, Diction, and Style in Greek Literary and Inscribed Epigram.* Trends in Classics Supplementary Volume 43, Berlin and New York, de Gruyter 2016: 3–22.
19 'The novels and the real world', in B. P. Reardon (ed.), *Erotica Antiqua: Acta of the International Conference on the Ancient Novel*, Bangor 1977: 91–6.
20 'The readership of Greek novels in the ancient world', in J. Tatum (ed.), *The Search for the Ancient Novel*, Baltimore and London, Johns Hopkins University Press 1994: 435–59.
21 'Philostratus: writer of fiction', in J. R. Morgan and R. Stoneman (eds.), *Greek Fiction: The Greek Novel in Context*, London, Routledge 1994: 181–99.
22 'Names and a gem: aspects of allusion in the *Aethiopica* of Heliodorus', in D. C. Innes, H. M. Hine, and C. B. R. Pelling (eds.), *Ethics and Rhetoric: Classical Essays for Donald Russell on His Seventy-Fifth Birthday*, Oxford, Clarendon Press 1995: 269–80.
23 'The ancient readers of the Greek novels', in G. Schmeling (ed.), *The Novel in the Ancient World*, Leiden, New York and Köln, Brill 1996: 87–106.

24 'Phoenician games in Heliodorus' *Aethiopica*', in R. L. Hunter (ed.), *Studies in Heliodorus, Cambridge Philological Society Supplementary Vol.* 21, Cambridge, Cambridge Philological Society 1998: 1–18.
25 'The chronology of the earlier Greek novels since B. E. Perry: revisions and precisions', *Ancient Narrative* 2 (2002) 47–63.
26 'The function of mythology in Longus' *Daphnis and Chloe*', in J.-A. López Férez (ed.), *Mitos en la literatura griega helenística e imperial* (Trabajos presentados en el VI Coloquio internacional de Filología griega. Estudios de mitología griega ii, March 1995), Madrid, Ediclas 2003: 361–76.
27 'Metaphor in *Daphnis and Chloe*', in S. J. Harrison, M. Paschalis, and S. Frangoulidis (eds.), *Metaphor and the Ancient Novel. Ancient Narrative. Supplementum* 4, Groningen, Barkhuis Publishing and Groningen University Library 2005: 68–86.
28 'The construction of the classical past in the ancient Greek novels', in S. Eklund (ed.), *Συγχάρματα: Studies in Honour of Jan Fredrik Kindstrand, Acta Universitatis Upsaliensis. Studia Graeca Upsaliensia* 21, Uppsala, Uppsala Universitet 2006: 1–20.
29 'Viewing and listening on the novelist's page', in S. N. Byrne, E. P. Cueva, and J. Alvares (eds.), *Authors, Authority and Interpreters in the Ancient Novel. Essays in Honor of Gareth L. Schmeling, Ancient Narrative Supplementum* 5, Groningen, Barkhuis Publishing and Groningen University Library 2006: 60–82.
30 'Le discours direct dans le *Daphnis et Chloé* de Longus', in B. Pouderon and J. Peigney (eds.), *Discours et débats dans l'ancien roman: actes du colloque de Tours, 21–23 octobre 2004, Collection de la Maison de l'Orient méditerranéen. Série littéraire et philosophique* 36, Lyon, Maison de l'Orient et de la Méditerranée Jean Pouilloux 2006: 27–39.
31 'Pulling the other: Longus and tragedy', in C. Kraus, S. Goldhill, H. P. Foley, and J. Elsner (eds.), *Visualizing the Tragic: Drama, Myth, and Ritual in Greek Art and Literature: Essays in Honour of Froma Zeitlin*, Oxford and New York, Oxford University Press 2007: 338–52.
32 'Links between Antonius Diogenes and Petronius', in M. Paschalis, S. Frangoulidis, S. J. Harrison, and M. Zimmerman (eds.), *The Greek and the Roman Novel: Parallel Readings, Ancient Narrative Supplementum* 8, Groningen, Barkhuis Publishing and Groningen University Library 2007: 121–32.
33 'Literary milieux', in T. Whitmarsh (ed.), *The Cambridge Companion to the Greek and Roman Novel*, Cambridge, Cambridge University Press 2008: 17–38.

34 'The uses of bookishness', in M. Paschalis, S. Panayotakis, and G. Schmeling (eds.), *Readers and Writers in the Ancient Novel, Ancient Narrative Supplementum* 12, Groningen, Barkhuis Publishing and Groningen University Library 2009: 115–26.

35 'Vertus de la campagne, vices de la cité dans le *Daphnis et Chloé* de Longus', in B. Pouderon and C. Bost-Pouderon (eds.), *Passions, vertus et vices dans l'ancien roman: actes du colloque de Tours, 19–21 octobre 2006, organisé par l'université François-Rabelais de Tours et l'UMR 5189, Histoire et Sources des Mondes Antiques*, Lyon, Maison de l'Orient et de la Méditerranée Jean Pouilloux 2009: 13–22.

36 'Socrates' cock and Daphnis' goats. The rarity of vows in the religious practice of the Greek novels', in S. J. Harrison and S. Frangoulidis (eds.), *Narrative, Culture and Genre in the Ancient Novel. Trends in Classics* 4.2 (2012) 225–73.

37 'Caging grasshoppers: Longus' materials for weaving "Reality"', in M. Paschalis and S. Panayotakis (eds.), *The Construction of the Real and Ideal in the Ancient Novel, Ancient Narrative Supplementum* 17, Groningen, Barkhuis Publishing and Groningen University Library 2013: 179–98.

38 'Milesian tales', in T. Whitmarsh and S. Thomson (eds.), *The Romance between Greece and the East*, Cambridge, Cambridge University Press 2013: 243–58.

39 'A land without priests? Religious authority in Longus, *Daphnis and Chloe*', in S. Panayotakis, G. Schmeling, and M. Paschalis (eds.), *Holy Men and Charlatans in the Ancient Novel, Ancient Narrative Supplementum* 19, Groningen, Barkhuis Publishing and Groningen University Library 2015: 69–84.

40 'Poetic elements in the Greek novelists' prose', in M. Biraud and M. Briand (eds.), *Roman grec et poésie. Dialogue des genres et nouveaux enjeux du poétique: actes du colloque international, Nice, 21–22 mars 2013, Collection de la Maison de l'Orient méditerranéen. Série littéraire et philosophique* 56, Lyon, Maison de l'Orient et de la Méditerranée Jean Pouilloux 2017: 97–133.

41 'Captured moments: illustrating Longus' prose', in T. S. Thorsen and S. J. Harrison (eds.), *Dynamics of Ancient Prose: Biographic, Novelistic, Apologetic*, Trends in Classics Supplementary Volume 62, Berlin and Boston, de Gruyter 2018: 195–222.

42 'Λέξεις Λόγγου', in K. Chew, J. R. Morgan, and S. Trzaskoma (eds.), *Literary Currents and Romantic Forms: Essays in Memory of Bryan*

Reardon, *Ancient Narrative Supplementum* 26, Groningen, Barkhuis Publishing and Groningen University Library 2019, 99–112.

43 'Animals, slaves and masters in Longus' *Daphnis and Chloe*', in S. Panayotakis and M. Paschalis (eds.), *Slaves and Masters in the Ancient Novel, Ancient Narrative Supplementum* 23, Groningen, Barkhuis Publishing and Groningen University Library 2019, 107–26.

44 'The demotion of the literary cowherd', in J. Bastick, C. Cusset, and C. Vieilleville (eds.), *Le bouvier dans la poésie hellénistique et le roman grec. Aitia: Regards sur la culture hellénistique au XXIe siècle* 9.1, Lyon, Éditions ENS de Lyon 2019, https://doi.org/10.4000/aitia.3790.

45 'Callimachus and Longus', in J. J. H. Klooster, M. A. Harder, R. F. Regtuit, and G. C. Wakker (eds.), *Callimachus Revisited: New Perspectives in Callimachean Scholarship, Hellenistica Groningana* 24, Leuven, Peeters 2019: 51–64.

46 'Silence in Chariton, Xenophon, Achilles Tatius and Longus', in E. Papadodima (ed.), *Faces of Silence in Ancient Greek Literature*, Trends in Classics Supplementary Volume 100, Berlin and Boston, de Gruyter 2020: 51–72.

Preface

I wish to use this preface, like that of Volume 1, to express my deep gratitude to the many institutions and individuals without whom these volumes could not have seen the light of day, albeit I thank institutions more briefly than there: Corpus Christi, Pembroke, St John's and Merton Colleges, Oxford; the École normale supérieure, Paris; Ormond College, the University of Melbourne; Stanford University; the University of Washington, Seattle; the University of Michigan, Ann Arbor; the Center for Hellenic Studies, Washington, DC; and the University of Crete, Gallos campus, Rethymno. I owe much to the friendship and help of very many colleagues in Europe, the Americas, South Africa, and Australasia who are too numerous to list here. In scanning papers not accessible online I was greatly helped by George Tsimpoukis. Others who have given me assistance of various sorts, whether in writing my introduction or in preparing versions of the papers suitable for submission to Cambridge University Press, and whom I would like particularly to thank here, are: Lucia Athanassaki, Julien du Bouchet, Stephen Harrison, Richard Hunter, Roland Mayer, Silvia Montiglio, John Morgan, Peter Parsons, Janette Reardon, Gareth Schmeling, Tim Whitmarsh, Mary Whitby, and Graciela Zecchin. From Cambridge University Press I would like to express my gratitude to Michael Sharp, Katie Idle, Liz Davey and my indefatigable copy-editor Lesley Hay for their hard work and vigilant eyes in the many stages of production. Finally, the *corpus sanum* and *tranquillitas animi* which are needed for sustained work I owe both to my supportive sons, Orlando and Ben, and, above all, to my wife Lucia.

Editions and Abbreviations

Unless otherwise stated, references to fragments of early elegy and iambus are to M. L. West, *Iambi et Elegi Graeci*, 2nd ed., vol. i Oxford 1989, vol. ii Oxford 1992. References to fragments of Sappho and Alcaeus are to E.-M. Voigt, *Sappho et Alcaeus: Fragmenta*. Amsterdam 1971, whose numeration was followed by D. A. Campbell, *Greek Lyric. Vol. i. Sappho and Alcaeus*. Cambridge MA and London 1982 and G. Liberman, *Alcée. Fragments*. 2 vols. Paris 2002. For fragments of Stesichorus references are given both to *PMGF* and to Finglass (see the abbreviations listed below). Modern works cited by author and date only are listed in the Bibliography. Abbreviations of journal titles are those of *L'Année philologique*. Greek literary and epigraphic texts are generally referred to by the abbreviations of LSJ (H. G. Liddell, R. Scott, H. Stuart Jones, and R. Mackenzie (eds.), *A Greek–English Lexicon*, 9th ed., Oxford 1968. Revised Supplement, ed. P. G. W. Glare, Oxford 1996), with the following exceptions or additions:

adesp.	*adespoton/adespota*
Aes.	Aeschylus
Ag.	*Agamemnon*
ANRW	*Aufstieg und Niedergang der römischen Welt*
ANS	*Ancient Narrative Supplementum*
AR	*Archaeological Reports*
Bacchyl.	Bacchylides
Bull.	*Bulletin épigraphique* in *Revue des Études Grecques*
CA	J. U. Powell, *Collectanea Alexandrina*. Oxford 1922.
CEG	P. A. Hansen, *Carmina Epigraphica Graeca*, 2 vols. Berlin and New York 1983, 1989.
Ch.	Chariton
CHCL	B. M. W. Knox and P. E. Easterling (eds.), *The Cambridge History of Classical Literature*, vol. 2. Cambridge 1985.
D-K	H. Diels (ed.), *Die Fragmente der Vorsokratiker*, 3 vols. 6th ed., revised by W. Kranz. Berlin 1951–2.
EA	*Epigraphica Anatolica*. Bonn 1983–.

EGM	R. L. Fowler, *Early Greek Mythography*, 2 vols. Oxford 2000, 2013.
Eur.	Euripides
FdD	*Fouilles de Delphes*, vol. iii. *Épigraphie*. Paris 1909–.
FGE	D. L. Page, *Further Greek epigrams: epigrams before A.D. 50 from the Greek Anthology and other sources not included in 'Hellenistic epigrams' or 'The Garland of Philip'*, revised and prepared for publication by R. D. Dawe and J. Diggle. Cambridge 1981.
FGrH	F. Jacoby, *Die Fragmente der griechischen Historiker* Leiden, Boston and Köln 1922–.
GCN	*Groningen Colloquia on the Novel*. Groningen 1988–98.
GGM	C. Müller (ed.), *Geographi Graeci Minores*. Paris 1861.
GP	A. S. F. Gow and D. L. Page (eds.), *The Greek Anthology. The Garland of Philip and some contemporary epigrams*, 2 vols. Cambridge 1968.
GVI	W. Peek, *Griechische Vers-Inschriften*, vol. i. *Grab-Epigramme*. Berlin 1955.
HE	A. S. F. Gow and D. L. Page (eds.), *The Greek Anthology: Hellenistic epigrams*, 2 vols. Cambridge 1965.
IAph2007	J. M. Reynolds, C. M. Roueché and G. Bodard (eds.), *Inscriptions of Aphrodisias*, 2007, available at http://insaph.kcl.ac.uk/iaph2007/.
IByzantion	A. Lajtar (ed.), *Die Inschriften von Byzantion. Inschriften griechischer Städte aus Kleinasien*, 58. Bonn 2000.
Id.	*Idyll*
IDidyma	A. Rehm and R. Harder (eds.), *Didyma, vol. ii. Die Inschriften*. Berlin 1958.
IEleus.	K. Clinton (ed.), *Eleusis, the inscriptions on stone: documents of the Sanctuary of the Two Goddesses and public documents of the Deme*, 3 vols. Αθήνα 2005–8.
IEph.	H. Wankel, H. Engelmann, and J. Nollé (eds.), *Die Inschriften von Ephesos*, 7 vols. *Inschriften griechischer Städte aus Kleinasien* 11–17. Bonn 1979–84.

IErythrai u. Klazomenai H. Engelmann and R. Merkelbach (eds.), *Die Inschriften von Erythrai und Klazomenai. Inschriften griechischer Städte aus Kleinasien* 1 and 2. Bonn 1972, 1973.

IGLSyr. L. Jalabert and R. Mouterde (eds.), *Inscriptions grecques et latines de la Syrie.* Paris 1929.

IGUR L. Moretti (ed.), *Inscriptiones Graecae urbis Romae*, 4 vols. Roma 1968–90.

IIlion P. Frisch (ed.), *Die Inschriften von Ilion. Inschriften griechischer Städte aus Kleinasien* 3. Bonn 1975.

IKyzikos E. Schwertheim, *Die Inschriften von Kyzikos und Umgebung, i. Inschriften griechischer Städte aus Kleinasien* 8. Bonn 1980.

IMT Kyz Kapu Dağ M. Barth and J. Stauber (eds.), *Inschriften Mysia & Troas. Mysia, Kyzikene, Kapu Dağ*, nos. 1401–1856. München.

IMT LApollon/Milet. M. Barth and J. Stauber (eds.), *Inschriften Mysia & Troas. Mysia, Lacus Apolloniatis & Miletupolis*, nos. 2150–2417. München.

IMT MittlMakestos M. Barth and J. Stauber (eds.), *Inschriften Mysia & Troas. Mysia, Mittlerer Makestos*, nos. 2501–2578. München.

INikaia S. Şahin, *Katalog der antiken Inschriften des Museums von İznik (Nikaia) / İznik Müzesi antik yazitlar kataloğu. Inschriften griechischer Städte aus Kleinasien* 9–10. Bonn 1979–87.

IOlymp. W. Dittenberger and K. Purgold (eds.), *Die Inschriften von Olympia*, vol. v. Berlin 1896.

IOrop. B. C. Petrakos (ed.), *Hoi epigraphes tou Oropou.* Αθήνα 1997.

IPergam. M. Fraenkel and C. Habicht (eds.), *Die Inschriften von Pergamon. Altertümer von Pergamon* viii.1–3. Berlin 1890–5, 1969.

IPerge S. Şahin (ed.), *Die Inschriften von Perge. Inschriften griechischer Städte aus Kleinasien*, 54. Bonn 1999.

IRT J. M. Reynolds and J. B. Ward-Perkins (eds.), *The Inscriptions of Roman Tripolitania.* Rome and London 1952.

ISelge	J. Nollé and F. Schindle (eds.), *Die Inschriften von Selge. Inschriften griechischer Städte aus Kleinasien* 37. Bonn 1991.
ISmyrna	G. Petzl (ed.), *Die Inschriften von Smyrna.* 3 vols in 2. *Inschriften griechischer Städte aus Kleinasien* 23–4. Bonn 1982, 1990.
K–A	R. Kassel and C. Austin (eds.), *Poetae comici Graeci.* Berlin 1983–2001.
Kaibel	G. Kaibel (ed.), *Epigrammata Graeca ex lapidibus conlecta*. Berlin 1878.
KP	K. Ziegler, W. Sontheimer and Hans Gärtner, *Der Kleine Pauly: Lexikon der Antike*, 5 vols. Stuttgart 1964–75 (paperback München 1979).
LBW	P. Le Bas, W. H. Waddington, and P. Foucart (eds.), *Inscriptions grecques et latines recueillies en Grèce et en Asie Mineure*. Paris 1847–77.
LGPN	P. M. Fraser, E. Matthews, R. Catling, T. Corsten, *et al.*, *A Lexicon of Greek Personal Names*. Oxford 1987–.
LIMC	H. C. Ackermann and J.-R. Gisler (eds.), *Lexicon Iconographicum Mythologiae Classicae.* Zürich 1981–92.
ML	R. Meiggs and D. M. Lewis, *A Selection of Greek Historical Inscriptions to the End of the Fifth Century BC*. Revised ed. Oxford 1988.
PG	J.-P. Migne (ed.), *Patrologia Graeca*. Paris.
PIR[2]	E. Groag, A. Stein, L. Petersen, W. Eck, *et al.* (eds.), *Prosopographia Imperii Romani saec. i, ii, iii*, 2nd ed. Berlin 1933–2015.
PMG	D. L. Page (ed.), *Poetae Melici Graeci*. Oxford 1962.
PMGF	M. Davies (ed.), *Poetarum Melicorum Graecorum Fragmenta*. Vol. i. Oxford 1991.
pr.	preface
RE	A. F. von Pauly *et al.* (eds.), *Real-Encyclopädie der classischen Altertumswissenschaft.* Stuttgart 1893–1970, München 1972–.
RPC	A. M. Burnett, M. Amandry, P. P. Ripollés Alegre, I. Carradice, and M. S. Butcher, *Roman Provincial Coinage*. London and Paris 1992–.

SH	P. J. Parsons and P. H. J. Lloyd-Jones (eds.), *Supplementum Hellenisticum*. 2 vols. Berlin and New York 1983, 2005.
Soph.	Sophocles
Syll.^{3}	W. Dittenberger (ed.), *Sylloge Inscriptionum Graecarum*, 3rd ed. Leipzig 1915–24.
test.	testimonium
tri	trimeter
X.Eph.	Xenophon of Ephesus
Xen.	Xenophon of Athens

Introduction to Volume II: Comedy, Herodotus, Hellenistic and Imperial Greek Poetry, the Novels

1 Fifth-Century Literature

Like many chapters in Volume 1, the original publications of the first nine in Volume 2 evolved directly or indirectly from my Oxford teaching. The first six chapters discuss issues arising from Aristophanes' *Acharnians*, *Wasps* and *Clouds*. I gave tutorials to pupils from Corpus Christi College on the first two plays which (together with *Lysistrata*) were studied for a 'Political Comedy' paper in Honour Moderations from 1968; and for some years I also gave University lectures on *Wasps*, though the publication of MacDowell's excellent Oxford commentary in 1971 rendered these lectures much less important.

Chapter 1, 'Who is Dicaeopolis?' (1988), sets out briefly the case for seeing in the character Dicaeopolis in *Acharnians* not (as often proposed) an *alter ego* of Aristophanes, but his competitor Eupolis, from whose political stance in his comedies Aristophanes circumspectly distances his own.

Chapter 2, '*Marginalia Obsceniora*: Some Problems in Aristophanes' *Wasps*' (1990c), examines passages where I argue that obscene language or sexual elements in the dramatic action have been missed – a subject I thought would be of interest to the honorand of the volume in which it first appeared, Sir Kenneth Dover.

Chapter 3, on the other hand, 'Wine in Old Comedy' (1995a), was catalysed not by my teaching but by a conference in Rome organised by Oswyn Murray that became the volume entitled *In Vino Veritas*. It thus related to my interest in sympotic behaviour that lay behind some chapters in Volume 1, and attempted to document Old Comedy's presentation of alcoholic consumption, both in and outside a sympotic context, and to bring out how different was the perception of the consumption of wine by discerning citizens in a symposium, mixed with water and in moderation, from that by women or slaves, typically neat, indiscriminately, and to deplorable excess.

Chapter 4, 'Ionian *Iambus* and Attic *Komoidia*: Father and Daughter, or Just Cousins?' (2002c), also relates to parts of Volume 1, addressing as it does the question of whether Attic comedy is a direct descendant of Ionian *iambus*. It owes its existence to a Corpus seminar on the language of Attic comedy organised in 2000 by Andreas Willi, and revisits the old problem of its relation to iambic poetry. Comparing three possible hypotheses of dependence, I set out objections to the view of Rosen 1988 according to which Cratinus introduced into Attic comedy certain iambic features which remained characteristic of the genre throughout Old Comedy. Before entering a detailed discussion of several lexical points of contact between *iambus* and comedy, I stressed the substantial differences between the two genres in the matter of length, audience, performers and mode of performance, and in the narrative form of much *iambus*. I argued that these differences counted against a close affiliation of *iambus* and comedy, so that little weight should be given to their superficial lexical overlap, especially prominent in the field of obscenity or *aischrologia*. I also emphasised that in his *Poetics* Aristotle does not suggest any genetic link between *iambus* and comedy. We should rather see such similarities as there are as products of the two independently developed genres in which abuse had a social or political function.

Aristophanes' *Clouds* was one of the half-dozen texts prescribed for a paper on fifth-century Greek literature in the new form of 'Greats', first examined in 1972. From the start, therefore, pupils had the advantage of access to Kenneth Dover's excellent 1968 commentary, and some issues I asked them to consider were ones where I thought it misleading. The question of how close to the 'real' Socrates Aristophanes' 'Socrates' stood is one that I debated with many generations of pupils. When in 1995 a two-centre conference on *Le rire des anciens* was organised in Paris and Rouen, chiefly by Monique Trédé, I took the opportunity to put my thoughts in order in a French version of Chapter 5, stressing the evidence of Aristophanes' *Birds* and of Plato's *Phaedo* that Socrates could plausibly be represented as having Pythagorean connections, and of *Phaedo* that he admitted at some point to having an interest in natural science. These interests may no longer have been important for him in 424/3 BC, but they could well have remained part of his public image. I argued that it was unlikely that an Attic theatre audience, many of whom will have studied with a sophist, could not tell the difference between Socrates and a sophistic teacher of rhetoric, and that it was significant that it was only well into the play, when Aristophanes had established his 'Socrates' as like the 'real' Socrates in several respects, that he started to bring out the role of his stage-figure in teaching rhetoric – a role he gave him because his purpose in *Clouds* was to κωμῳδεῖν, 'make fun of in a comedy', *both* Socrates *and* sophists. The French version was published as 'Le portrait de Socrate dans les *Nuées* d'Aristophane' (1998a) in the conference volume *Le rire des anciens*, edited by Monique Trédé and Philippe Hoffmann. I reworked it in an English version (Chapter 5, 'Socrates in Aristophanes' *Clouds* and the Audience of Attic Comedy', 2007f) given at a series of seminars for teachers of classics in British schools that I helped my wife Lucia Athanassaki to organise in the summer of 2007 at the European Cultural Centre of Delphi. My argument hung to some extent on the socio-economic distribution of spectators in the theatre of Dionysus in Athens, and on that theatre's size: I argued that the costs of theatre-going are likely to have reduced the number of poorer Athenians in a theatre whose capacity was more probably around 11,000 than the 15,000 to 17,000 often suggested, and that a high proportion of these spectators would be from the upper ranges of the zeugite class and above, familiar with sophists, and in many cases actually their pupils.

The last chapter on comedy (Chapter 6, 'Aristophanes *Clouds*: An Agonistic Note', 2015b, wrongly dated to 2016 in Volume 1, 790) was offered to a volume honouring Ana María González de Tobia edited by Claudia Fernández, Juan Tobias Nápoli and Graciela Zecchin. In it I returned to a question I had often discussed with pupils: was Dover right to insist that anachronisms and a change of speaker impossible to stage demonstrated the text of the (second) *Clouds* that we have to be an incomplete revision that was intended as a text only for reading, not for performance? On both counts I argued that Dover's case is not proven.

Chapter 7, 'The Lesson of Book 2' (2018a), is the last in this volume on fifth-century literature. In it I explored one of many questions that fascinated me in reading and – again for a paper on fifth-century literature – teaching Herodotus: is the authorial *persona* of Book 2 radically different from that of his other books, marking it to some extent as a survival from an earlier stage in his development? Jacoby's developmental model was endorsed by Charles Fornara in 1971, and a conference at Columbia, NY, organised by Liz Irwin and Tom Harrison to revisit that book's impact, gave me the incentive to construct an argument for seeing Book 2's authorial *persona* as much closer to that of the rest of his work, and to suggest that Herodotus' use of speeches in historical narrative was not, as Fornara suggested, a momentous innovation, but a technique he owed to narrative elegy, some of it presenting as early as the seventh century an account of conflict between Greeks and non-Greeks in western Asia Minor, and its most recent manifestation a long poem composed by a relative of Herodotus, Panyassis, encompassing a narrative relating not to one but to many Greek cities.

2 Hellenistic Poetry

Chapters 8 to 11 are devoted to Hellenistic poetry. Here too my teaching – tutorials given for Corpus Christi College, first on Theocritus, and later on a Hellenistic poetry paper, and lectures on Theocritus given for the University – was an important stimulus. It was in tutorials that in the late 1970s I developed arguments based on resemblances I saw between Lycidas in *Idyll* 7 and Philetas in Book 2 of Longus, *Daphnis and Chloe*, arguments which led me to propose (Chapter 8, 'Theocritus' Seventh *Idyll*, Philetas and Longus', 1985a) that Lycidas fell into none of the categories listed by Dover in his 1971 commentary – ostensibly a comprehensive list – but into a category he had overlooked: a fictional character from another poet's work. That other poet, I suggested, was Philitas of Cos, whose very influential early Hellenistic poetry is known only from a few fragments and from later allusions and references. Among the many phenomena explained by this hypothesis – and it remains only a hypothesis – are the Coan setting of *Idyll* 7's narrative and the erotodidactic function of Philetas in Longus. The 'Cydonia' given as Lycidas' origin becomes a Cydonia some kilometres north of Mytilene on Lesbos, arguably located in the hill-flanked coastal plain where Longus asks us to imagine the estates on which Daphnis and Chloe pastured their wealthy masters' goats and sheep.

Chapters 9 and 10 owe their existence more to the very congenial workshops on Hellenistic poetry that were organised at Groningen in alternate years from 1992 by Annette Harder, Remco Regtuit and Gerry Wakker. Their friendly atmosphere encouraged frank discussion but discouraged polemic, and many participants continued debate in the nearby tavern *Het paard van Troje* (*The Trojan Horse*: now, alas, demolished). In Chapter 9 ('Frame and Framed in Theocritus Poems 6 and 7', 1996a) I returned to *Idyll* 7, proposing that the change from the unqualified name Amyntas at line 2 to ὁ καλὸς Ἀμύντιχος, 'the lovely dear Amyntas', at line 132 signals a development in the narrator's feelings for Amyntas from friendship to sexual desire. Concerning *Idyll* 6, I suggested that the roles assumed by Daphnis and Damoetas in their quasi-competitive songs – of an unidentified *praeceptor amoris* addressing Polyphemus and of Polyphemus replying – are used by them to disclose to each other their mutual desire, confirmed for the reader by their kiss (line 42) and by their ensuing miniature *fête champêtre*. I noted too that the poem's address to Aratus left it open to him to interpret its exploration of hitherto unconfessed desire as bearing on his own relationship with the poet.

Chapter 10 ('The Reception of Apollonius Rhodius in Imperial Greek Literature', 2000) charted prose writers' references to Apollonius – fewer than might be expected for so prominent a poet – and the extensive exploitation of his language by hexameter poets, above all Dionysius Periegetes.

A different genre, that of the hymn, is explored in Chapter 11 ('Time and Place, Narrative and Speech in Philicus, Philodamus and Limenius', 2015d). In it I compared Philicus' *Demeter* of ca. 275 BC, a poem which, at the time I was writing, I followed all other scholars since its first editor Medea Norsa in classifying as a hymn,[1] with the Delphic paeans of Philodamus (340/339 BC) and Limenius (between 138 and 106/5 BC). I argued that Philicus' poem locates the exchange between Iambē and the inconsolable Demeter not at Eleusis but at Prospalta, where Pausanias attests a cult of Demeter and Persephone, and that it may have proposed a role for that cult in the development of ritual αἰσχρολογία in Attica (cf. Eupolis' chorus in his *Prospaltians*). The interest in Attic cults shown by a Corcyrean domiciled in Alexandria matches Callimachus' decision about the same time to compose his very Attic *Hecalē*. By contrast the Delphic paean of Philodamus is focused chiefly on its place of performance and monumental inscription, albeit setting the arrival of Dionysus at Delphi, where he must be honoured alongside Apollo with cyclic choruses, in a wider geographical frame. Geography is important for the paean of Limenius too, offering as it does a very Athenian version of Apollo's arrival in mainland Greece and his journey to Delphi, a version appropriate for the *Pythais* from Athens by which we know it to have been performed.

3 Imperial Greek Poetry

Chapters 12 to 18 discuss Greek poetry in the Roman imperial period down to the middle of the third century AD. This is a subject that had very little to do with my teaching, and even the Oxford doctoral theses I supervised on imperial Greek literature were focused on prose authors, not poetry. But writing a chapter on later Greek literature for a volume edited and partly written by Kenneth Dover drew my attention to poetry's continuing importance in the period,[2] and I explored different but (inevitably) related aspects of that poetry in three articles whose composition was spread over more years than their publication in 1989 and

[1] I argue against this classification in Bowie forthcoming.

[2] Dover, West, Griffin, and Bowie 1980.

1990 might suggest. Chapter 12 ('Greek Sophists and Greek Poetry in the Second Sophistic', 1989a) aimed at the sort of overview that the editors of *ANRW* encouraged, and brought together the place of poetry in sophists' education; an account of the various poetic genres in which sophists composed, with citation of what we have from the only one of these genres to have survived, epigram; and epigrams on sophists by others. Chapter 13 ('Poetry and Poets in Asia and Achaea', 1989b) resulted from an invitation to contribute to a British Museum Classical Colloquium, *The Greek Renaissance in the Roman Empire*, organised by Susan Walker and Averil Cameron in December 1986. It offered a short sketch of poetic output with special reference to the Roman provinces Achaea and Asia, and with an eye on how far we can differentiate 'professional' poets from virtuoso amateurs. Chapter 14 ('Greek Poetry in the Antonine Age', 1990b), first written for an Oxford seminar organised in Hilary Term 1988 by Donald Russell, attempted a fuller survey of poetry in the reigns of Hadrian, Pius and Marcus. For epigram it drew on both the Greek Anthology (Pollianus and Ammianus for scoptic poems; Rufinus and Strato for erotic) and epigraphy (with examples of Iulia Balbilla's *faux*-Aeolic elegiacs on one of the Memnon colossi). The section on hexameter poetry highlights the poems of Marcellus of Side (again epigraphic texts play an important role) and of Dionysius Periegetes, with some discussion of Pancrates and only a mention of Oppian's *Halieutica*. The final section, on melic poetry, has Mesomedes as its chief exhibit.

Chapter 14 could in principle have discussed Hadrian's own poetry alongside that of his wife's friend Balbilla and of his favourite citharode Mesomedes, but it would then have become too long. Accordingly I devoted another paper (Chapter 15, 'Hadrian and Greek Poetry', 2002e), initially delivered to a conference in Lund on 'Greek Romans, Roman Greeks' organised by Jerker and Karin Blomqvist, entirely to Hadrian and poetry. I discussed his tastes in poetry – a preference for Ennius over Vergil and for Antimachus over Homer; his own surviving poems, with discussion of some dedicatory and sepulchral epigrams, and with a proposal about the nature of the possibly polymetric *Catachannae* mentioned by the *Augustan History*; and poetry composed by people near to him with an eye to his approval, like the *Altar* of the high equestrian official L. Iulius Vestinus (perhaps dateable precisely to 24 January AD 132) and the mysterious inscribed elegiacs from Cordoba in Baetica, signed by 'Arrian the proconsul', pronouncing on the greater appropriateness of the 'gifts of the Muses' to Artemis than of (seemingly) 'the heads of enemies'. This chapter had initially been conceived as part of a projected book on Hadrian's dealings with the Greek world; but the publication in 1997 of Tony Birley's excellent *Hadrian: The Restless Emperor* joined other considerations in leading me to abandon that project.

Scholarly interest in Dionysius Periegetes had been growing since I first mentioned him briefly in the 1980 Dover volume and then wrote my longer account in 1990 – for both of which the most recent text in which his poem could be read was Müller's 1861 *Geographi Graeci Minores*. A conference on him organised by Patrick Counillon in Bordeaux in 2002 was responsible for Chapter 16 ('Denys d'Alexandrie: un poète grec dans l'empire romain', 2004a). Here I argued that Dionysius' poem is not, as sometimes suggested, timeless, but very alert to the impact of Rome and its emperor on peoples it has incorporated into its empire and proud of the Hellenic culture that has spread even beyond that empire's frontiers.

A conference in June 2007 on 'Greek poets in Italy', organised by Josiah Osgood and Alex Sens in Georgetown's *Villa Le Balze* near Fiesole, drew me into a deeper engagement than hitherto with the *Garland of Philip*. The paper I gave there benefited further from close readings of many of the *Garland*'s poets in a graduate seminar I taught in Ann Arbor, Michigan, in the wintry early months of 2010: I am grateful to Silvia Barbantani for then offering it a home in *Aevum Antiquum* (Chapter 17, 'Luxury Cruisers? Philip's Epigrammatists between Greece and Rome', 2012e). I pointed out that Philip's poets share predominantly North Aegean origins, and argued that their mentions of Romans and of visits to Rome should be taken as evidence of these Romans being their 'patrons' much less often than they were by Gow and Page: rather, some at least of these poets were more probably from the propertied Greek elite (as Crinagoras certainly was) and made short visits to Rome either as envoys on behalf of their cities or as tourists, picking out in their poetry its monuments that had Hellenic connections. Only Philodemus seems certainly to have become a long-term resident of Italy, and his contrast of his simple abode with Piso's mansion does not demonstrate him to be financially dependent on him.

The last of the chapters on imperial Greek poetry, Chapter 18 ('Doing Doric', 2016f), was presented to a conference on dialect, diction and style in Greek epigram in Thessaloniki in May 2015, organised by Evina Sistakou and Antonios Rengakos. I argued that, whereas many poets in the *Garland of Philip* never use Doric, several do so to evoke either a Leonidean or Theocritean pastoral world, and sometimes because their subject has a Dorian connection – so Myrinus, Adaeus, Thallus, Erucius of Cyzicus, and Antiphilus of Byzantium. That Cyzicus was originally a colony of Corinth and Byzantium of Megara seems not to be relevant, since Doric appears only rarely in these cities' inscribed poetry. Finally I examined the puzzling case of the five epigrams on Sacerdos of Nicaea preserved in the *Palatine Anthology* (15.4–8), of which three use Doric, two do not. I suggested that more than one poet may have been chosen to compose sepulchral epigrams for this grandiose obelisk-monument of around AD 130, and that the composer of the Doric poems might have been Philostratus' heritage-conscious sophist Memmius Marcus of Byzantium.

4 The Greek Novel

My remaining twenty-eight chapters concern the Greek novel. At an early point in my work on the Greek culture of the Roman Empire I realised the importance of the novels from both a literary and a historical perspective. Already in spring 1965 I gave a talk at Bristol Grammar School in which I enthused about the cinematic technique of the opening of Heliodorus' *Aethiopica*, and I have pleasant memories of reading sceptically Merkelbach's *Roman und Mysterium* in the summer of that year in the garden of St John's College (where I was a Woodhouse Junior Fellow). My interest in the novels was further stimulated (as doubtless was that of many scholars) by the publication in 1967 of B. E. Perry's 1951 Sather lectures, *The Ancient Romances*, and by a sabbatical visit to Oxford in the winter of 1971/2 by Bryan Reardon, whose important 1971 book *Courants littéraires grecs des iième et iiième siècles après J.–C.* rightly gave prominence to the novels. I participated in a small and lively discussion group he established during his visit. Bryan was also the πρῶτος εὑρετής of the International Conference on the Ancient Novel (ICAN), the first of which he organised in Bangor, North Wales, in the hot summer of 1976, with assistance from Gareth Schmeling. Its participants were few enough to be offered generous hospitality in their home by Bryan and his wife Janette. My paper 'The Novels and the Real World' (Chapter 19, 1977) argued that historians of Greek civic culture in the Roman Empire should draw on the novels for details of Greek city life, of the behaviour of its elites, and of the relation between city and country – something Fergus Millar did, quite independently (as far as I know) and very effectively, in March 1981 in his UCL inaugural lecture 'The World of the *Golden Ass*',[3]

[3] Concerning the Greek novels Millar 1981 referred (75 n.59) only to Scarcella 1977 on Xenophon; given its limited circulation the *ICAN Acta* (Reardon (ed.) 1977) are unlikely to have come to his attention.

and that had already to some extent been attempted for Lesbos by Scarcella 1968.[4] My paper was never developed into a full-length article, and this volume reprints it much as it was delivered.

Scholarly interest in the novels was further kindled by the publication in 1983 of Tomas Hägg's *The Novel in Antiquity*,[5] and by the 'Groningen Colloquia on the Novel', organised by Heinz Hofmann, Ben Hijmans and Maaike Zimmerman: they ran from 1986 to the later 1990s, and resulted in nine volumes published between 1988 and 1998. Meanwhile I too had given substantial space to the novels in my portion of the chapter on Greek literature of the Empire in the *Cambridge History of Classical Literature*, written in 1977/8. Its Greek volume, edited by Pat Easterling and Bernard Knox, had gathered many of its contributions by 1980, but was published only in 1985. By then preparations for ICAN 2 were under way, organised by James Tatum at Dartmouth College, NH, in 1989, again a very hot summer – a conference that felicitously coincided with the publication of *Collected Ancient Greek Novels*, edited by Bryan Reardon. This made available in the same volume English translations of the famous five, of novels transmitted in epitomes, and of the major fragments. Its availability further boosted the study of the novels in Anglo-Saxon universities, and in Oxford Stephen Harrison and I were at last able to convince our colleagues in the languages and literature sub-faculty (hitherto cowed by Jasper Griffin's insistence that it would be better for pupils to read Demosthenes) to allow us to construct an ancient novel paper in the Final Honour School – a paper that was very popular from its first examination in 1995 to its last in 2008.

My Dartmouth conference paper (Chapter 20, 'The Readership of Greek Novels in the Ancient World', 1994a) argued against the view of Perry 1967 (to some extent endorsed by Reardon 1971) that the novels were popular literature, written for a 'juvenile' readership and 'for the edification of children and the poor-in-spirit'.[6] Rather, the intertextuality with high literature of the classical period and the level of education it implied pointed to an elite readership, among whom some of the few women to receive such an education were doubtless numbered. I was glad that my arguments were complemented by those of Susan Stephens (1994) based on the high quality of many of the papyri on which fragments of the period's varied and numerous novels are preserved.

[4] Cf. Scarcella 1977, 1981.

[5] An English version of Hägg 1980: it had more impact than the nevertheless important Hägg 1971.

[6] Perry 1967, 5 and 98.

I investigated the problems of the novels' readership more systematically in a 1996 volume edited by Gareth Schmeling (whose insistence that I should write it I should perhaps have resisted more firmly): my Chapter 23 ('The Ancient Readers of the Greek Novels', 1996c) inevitably had some overlap with Chapter 20, but, unlike it, introduced the important distinction between intended and actual readership, and between the early, the 'sophistic', and other known novels. I concluded that the intended and actual readers of 'sophistic' novels were from the educated elite, and that Chariton probably envisaged such readers too, while perhaps writing in such a way that readers might be found further down the social scale: readers of this sort may also have been intended by Xenophon and the other writers of fiction, but in no case *much* further down.

In the 1990s I made five other contributions to understanding the novels. Together with Stephen Harrison, by then himself engaged with the Latin novels, especially that of Apuleius, and invited by Simon Price, I wrote for the *Journal of Roman Studies* a survey article on novel-studies in recent decades, inevitably a topic with a limited shelf-life.[7]

For a collection entitled *Greek Fiction* edited by Richard Stoneman and John Morgan I explored the modes of fictionality in Philostratus' *Heroicus* and *In Honour of Apollonius* (Chapter 21, 'Philostratus: Writer of Fiction', 1994b).

For a volume edited by Doreen Innes, Harry Hine and Christopher Pelling to mark the seventy-fifth birthday of Donald Russell, the distinguished scholar who had done so much to promote the study of imperial Greek literature in Oxford (above all, of course, Longinus, Dio of Prusa, Plutarch and Menander *rhetor*) and who had been crucial in fostering my own interest in it, I wrote a piece on Heliodorus (Chapter 22, 'Names and a Gem: Aspects of Allusion in the *Aethiopica* of Heliodorus', 1995b). The first part explored the effects achieved by Heliodorus in his naming of his characters – among them the unusual name Cnemon from Menander's *Dyscolus* chosen to underline the features of his story that related closely to New Comedy, and the philosophically resonant name Aristippus for his pleasure-seeking father. The second part argued that Heliodorus' detailed description (5.14) of the pastoral 'theatre' represented on the amethyst given to the merchant Nausicles in exchange for Charicleia was calculated to remind readers of Longus, in particular of the scene where Dionysophanes, Clearista and their retinue seated 'as a theatre' spectate Daphnis' goats responding obediently to his panpipe's commands (4.15.2–4). Heliodorus

[7] Bowie and Harrison 1993, not printed in this volume.

invites his readers to contrast the miniature and rustic world of Longus with his own vast and densely populated canvas – and incidentally offers an argument for putting his novel later than that of Longus.[8]

Finally, for a conference organised by Richard Hunter on Heliodorus (the first, to my knowledge, devoted to a single Greek novelist) I wrote a paper initially entitled 'Chains of Imagery in the *Aethiopica*': this became, after a further helpful airing at Harvard, 'Phoenician Games in Heliodorus' *Aethiopica*' (Chapter 24, 1998b). In it I traced the different uses of the term φοῖνιξ/Φοῖνιξ, the cognate adjectives φοινικοῦς and φοινικοβαφής, and verb φοινίττω, running from this last's allusive use to describe Theagenes' blood-stained cheek at the beginning of Book 1 to the revelation at the novel's close that its writer is a Φοῖνιξ, 'Phoenician'. I noted how these uses span the word's range of meanings – crimson, date, palm, Phoenician – and how Phoenicia's importance is augmented by the mysteriously unnamed Tyrian's victory at Delphi and by the description of the ship on which the trio escape as Φοινίκιον … φιλοτέχνημα, 'a Phoenician masterpiece' (5.18), a *mise-en-abyme* of the literary masterpiece which transports the couple from Delphi to Meroe.

Meanwhile for a conference on mythology in Hellenistic and imperial Greek literature, organised in Madrid in 1995 by Juan-Antonio López Férez, I put in order thoughts I had been developing for some time about the role of the inset tales in Books 1, 2, and 3 of *Daphnis and Chloe*, 'The Function of Mythology in Longus' *Daphnis and Chloe*' (Chapter 26, 2003b). I argued that their depictions of male self-assertion and sexual violence are offered not as models which we may expect Daphnis to imitate but as contrasts to his reciprocal and considerate relationship with Chloe. Feedback at that conference and at some other places that I gave the paper had improved it by the time of the *Acta*'s publication in 2003.

The new millennium was marked by the third ICAN, organised at Groningen by Maaike Zimmerman and her team, and by the launch of a website and periodical (which *ab initio* has been available in electronic and printed versions), *Ancient Narrative* (*AN*): to quote Stephen Harrison in the preface to the first printed volume, *Ancient Narrative* 1 (2000–1), it 'offers not only a niche journal for all those interested in Greco-Roman prose fiction and associated literary traditions, but also a "one-stop shop" for contacts, information and bibliography in this important, exciting and still growing

[8] In a paper given in Cambridge in 2018 but not, so far as I know, published, Georg Danek examined passages where it might be thought Longus had read Heliodorus or *vice versa*, and came down in favour of Heliodorus' priority.

academic area. In these functions it both continues and expands the honourable traditions of the *Groningen Colloquia on the Novel* and of the *Petronian Society Newsletter* (the latter of which retains its own sector of the AN website).' For the new venture, which was to carry the torch handed on by the *Groningen Colloquia on the Novel* (of which the last volume, 9, appeared in 1998), Maaike Zimmerman secured the support of Groningen University Library and of Roelf Barkhuis' publishing house. In its second volume (*Ancient Narrative* 2, 2002, which in fact appeared in 2003), I published 'The Chronology of the Earlier Greek Novels since B. E. Perry: Revisions and Precisions' (Chapter 25, 2002a). In this paper, which had benefited from feedback on several occasions, including delivery at the University of Melbourne and (in a French version) at the École normale supérieure, rue d'Ulm, Paris, both institutions where I was a visitor in 2001, I offered arguments for dating Chariton between AD 41 and AD 62, *Ninus* between AD 63 and ca. AD 75, and Xenophon after AD 65. I suggested that the stylistic similarity of *Metiochus and Parthenope* to Chariton might point to proximity in date. I canvassed a date between AD 98 and AD 130 for Antonius Diogenes, who might, like Chariton and the author of the *Ninus*, hail from Aphrodisias. Finally for Achilles Tatius I proposed a date no later than AD 160. My footnotes in this volume take account of some important data from recently published papyri and of the valuable contribution of Henrichs 2011.

The other important development marking the beginning of the third millennium was the institution of a series of biennial Rethymnon International Conferences on the Ancient Novel (RICAN), organised at the University of Crete by Stavros Frangoulidis and Michael Paschalis, thus continuing the regular meetings of scholars engaged with the novels hitherto enabled by the Groningen Colloquia. The first RICAN, on 'Space in the Ancient Novel', took place in May 2001; its *Acta* were published in 2002 as a *Supplementum* to the journal *Ancient Narrative* (*ANS* 1). The second was held in May 2003; its *Acta*, entitled *Metaphor and the Ancient Novel* and edited by Stephen Harrison, Michael Paschalis, and Stavros Frangoulidis, were published in 2005 as *ANS* 4. There ('Metaphor in *Daphnis and Chloe*', Chapter 27 in this volume, 2005b) I attempted a taxonomy of the metaphors in *Daphnis and Chloe* – under the heads symptoms and concomitants of desire (where Longus' metaphors situate his writing unambiguously in the Greek literature of ἔρως, 'desire'); desire in society; anthropomorphisation of the inanimate and of animals; body-parts with a mind of their own; literary and meta-literary activity; and the world of learning.

A year later an invitation to contribute to a volume honouring Jan Fredrik Kindstrand, whom I had known since his years in Oxford writing a thesis on Bion of Borysthenes (DPhil 1976), and who was retiring from his Uppsala chair, induced me to write a paper entitled 'The Construction of the Classical Past in the Ancient Greek Novels' (Chapter 28, 2006a), in which I documented the differences in the five novelists' representation of the Greek past – mythical, archaic, classical and Hellenistic. I distinguished two groups: Xenophon and Longus each offer very little myth or history before the period of the events they narrate; Chariton, Achilles Tatius and Heliodorus, on the other hand, not only use much circumstantial detail to build up a classical or (in Achilles Tatius' case) Hellenistic world in which their story is set, but also give that world temporal depth by exploitation of mythology, and occasionally by introducing events or persons from earlier Greek history. Xenophon's and Achilles Tatius' worlds are such that their similarity with that of readers can almost be taken for granted, with little incentive to ask in what way and to what effect these worlds are to any degree different from their own. Chariton and Heliodorus are different: the more or less determinable historical setting combines with a decidedly contemporary σφραγίς to give readers both a strong sense of Greek cultural continuity and the opportunity to identify features where their contemporary Greek world might be significantly different: the most important such difference is Roman control of the Greek world, which is also strongly hinted at by Longus despite his choice of a timeless, predominantly rural context.

The year 2006 also saw the publication of a volume in honour of Gareth Schmeling: *Authors, Authority and Interpreters in the Ancient Novel*, *ANS* 5. This book brought together papers delivered at a special panel at the 2006 CAMWS meeting in his University at Gainesville and was edited by Shannon Byrne, Edmund Cueva and Jean Alvares. Here, in 'Viewing and Listening on the Novelist's Page' (Chapter 29, 2006d), I explored the ways in which the five novels diverge. Chariton seems well aware of what can be achieved by briefly sketched sound effects, but brief sketches are all we get: he does not suggest that the written word might find it hard to convey varieties of sound. Xenophon is apparently not concerned to communicate sound effects at all. Achilles Tatius offers elaborate rhetoric and sometimes striking imagery in compensation for the written word's inability to render sound. Both Longus and Heliodorus push their readers (in different ways) to reflect on the problem of communicating sound, each offering a different solution. That of Heliodorus for the representation of sung poetry is a striking advance on anything in the earlier novels, apparently learning from (but also upstaging) Philostratus' *Heroicus*.

As well as the biennial RICAN meetings in Crete a series of colloquia, also biennial, was organised by Bernard Pouderon and Cécile Bost-Pouderon in

Tours, and most were attended by some British scholars. To that of October 2004 entitled *Discours et débats dans l'ancien roman* I offered a paper on 'Le discours direct dans le *Daphnis et Chloé* de Longus'. A version not much longer than what I had delivered appeared in the *Acta* (2006b). In this volume Chapter 30, 'Direct Speech in Longus' *Daphnis and Chloe*', is a longer English version in which some omissions and errors have been rectified. I tabulate the number of pieces of direct discourse in each book, the number of sentences in each of these, and the number of words in each sentence. As well as some immediately obvious results – e.g. that the first case of direct discourse is surprisingly late in Book 1 (1.14.1), and is given to Chloe; that the number of speeches, and speakers, rises book by book – I explore some of the effects Longus' artistry achieves: the quasi-stichomythia of Daphnis' internal debate at 3.6 and the stichomythic exchange between him and Chloe at 3.10; the play with vocatives; the differences between emotional reflections expressed in mainly short, paratactic sentences, and the instructions of Philetas, Lycaenion and of the Nymphs, the arguments of Lamon, or the pleas of Gnathon, all articulated in more complex sentences. Unlike Morgan 2021 (a characteristically illuminating analysis from a narratological perspective) I do not bring indirect discourse into my discussion.

In a volume honouring Froma Zeitlin, *Visualizing the Tragic: Drama, Myth, and Ritual in Greek Art and Literature*, edited by Jaś Elsner, Helena Foley, Simon Goldhill and Chris Kraus, I returned to Longus' inset tales in a paper entitled 'Pulling the Other: Longus and Tragedy' (Chapter 31, 2007c). An oral version had benefited from feedback at a *Kyknos* colloquium held at Gregynog in May 2005. After reviewing passages of *Daphnis and Chloe* where intertextuality with one of the three canonical tragedians can be claimed, I suggested that, rather than aiming simply to elevate his prose by exploiting poetic colour, Longus seeks to highlight important features of his own work by contrast with tragedy, and that for this the preface's intertexts with Sophocles' *Antigone* and Euripides' *Hippolytus* are crucial. The latter focuses our attention on the issue of how ἔρως, 'desire', can be appropriately managed, alerting us to differences in its presentation by Longus and by tragedians. I supported this suggestion by returning to the argument of Chapter 26: the mythological world of the inset tales – divine lust leading to destruction or metamorphosis of a young woman who is not herself immortal – is characteristic of a story-type drawn upon by Attic tragedy and more generally by archaic, classical and Hellenistic narrative poetry. In confining the destructive consequences of ἔρως, 'desire', to his inset tales, explicitly described as μῦθοι, 'myths', Longus contrasts the actions of gods and sufferings of mortals in traditional Greek mythology with their handling in his own sort of story. He wants readers to contrast the type of story about ἔρως, 'desire', that he and his novelistic predecessors tell from that preponderant in classical mythology in general and in tragedy in particular. Tragedy never explores stories of mutual and symmetrical desire, nor does it present positive images of female desire, whereas symmetrical desire and a positive image of female ἔρως are crucial to the discourse of the novels. Longus plants a clue to this verdict on tragedy at 4.17.2, where Astylus, expressing surprise at Gnathon's wish to have sex with a goatherd, ὑπεκρίνετο τὴν τραγικὴν δυσωδίαν μυσάττεσθαι, 'acted out revulsion at the foul smell of goats': here the dramatic term ὑπεκρίνετο cues the reader to spot the *double entendre* in τραγικὴν δυσωδίαν, which with the addition of the iota subscript often omitted in imperial Greek epigraphic and papyrus texts becomes τραγικὴν δυσωιδίαν, 'the unpleasant singing of tragedy'.

My other 2007 publication on the novels also returned to a problem I had earlier discussed. In *The Greek and the Roman Novel: Parallel Readings*, *ANS* 8, edited by Michael Paschalis, Stavros Frangoulidis, Stephen Harrison and Maaike Zimmerman (the *Acta* of RICAN 3, held in May 2005), I revisited the date of Τὰ ὑπὲρ Θούλην ἄπιστα in a paper entitled 'Links between Antonius Diogenes and Petronius' (Chapter 32, 2007d). I noted features shared between *The Incredible Things beyond Thule* and the *Satyrica*: their twenty-four-book format, their element of comedy, the location and extent of their characters' travels, and the types of incident they encountered. Of three possibilities – that Antonius Diogenes knew the *Satyrica*, that the author of the *Satyrica* knew Antonius Diogenes, and that both drew on a common source – I saw the first, entailing Antonius Diogenes' knowledge of Latin, as least likely.[9] The second option would place *The Incredible Things beyond Thule* not at the date for which I had argued in Chapter 25 but ca. AD 55, shortly after the publication of Chariton's *Callirhoe* and before that of Petronius' *Satyrica*. As to the third possibility, although on Jensson's hypothesis of a lost Greek original for the *Satyrica* some of the novels' shared features might derive from a Milesian-tale narrative, the pursuit of the hero and his companion by a powerful and vengeful force, the death of the arch-villain, and the location in the bay of Naples and south Italy have no parallel in any known Greek 'low' narratives.

Chapter 33 ('Literary Milieux', 2008d, from *The Cambridge Companion to the Greek and Roman Novel*, edited by Tim Whitmarsh) departs from my general exclusion from these three volumes of pieces written for literary

[9] I might well have concluded differently had I been in a position to read Jolowicz 2021.

histories or *Companions*.[10] It complements other novel chapters in this volume by offering a survey of Greek prose writing in the first to third centuries AD that might have had some impact on the novels, or have been in some way influenced by them. I adopted an admittedly artificial periodisation: 31 BC–AD 50; AD 50–160; AD 160–220; AD 220–270. In the first period, before any known novels, little that might have impinged on a novelist writing in AD 50 can be seen in Dionysius of Halicarnassus, Nicolaus of Damascus or Strabo, or in hexameter poetry: but erotic epigrams, especially those of Rufinus, perhaps composed ca. AD 40–60, apparently in western Asia Minor near the birthplace of the novels, may well have caught a novelist's eye. In AD 50–160 the explosion of sophistic display-rhetoric encouraged fictionality both in declamation and in such imaginative scenarios as those worked out by Dio in his *Euboean*, *Trojan* and *Borysthenitic* speeches (*Orations* 7, 11, and 36). An erotic theme was the mainspring of the *Araspas, Lover of Pantheia*, whether written by Dionysius of Miletus or Caninius Celer, while Plutarch comes near to a mini-novel in his story of the widow's kidnapping of young Bacchon in his Ἐρωτικός, *Tale of Desire*. Moreover many of his *Lives* have cliff-hanging incidents like those in novels. Achilles Tatius' liking for 'scientific' digressions chimes with the popularity of paradoxography – Phlegon's *On Things Miraculous*, and the *Varied Histories* of Pamphila and Favorinus. In the period 160–220 Iamblichus' *Babyloniaca* and Aelian's *Varied History* and *History of Animals* show that the taste for paradoxography continued, while Lucian plays diverse games with fictionality and himself wrote a novel. Pausanias, Athenaeus and Philostratus introduce tales of desire in a way they would not (arguably) have done in a world without novels. Discussion of Heliodorus' relation to other literature dominated my assessment of AD 220–270, though I conceded he might belong a century later.

At the next Tours colloquium (October 2006), published in 2009 as *Passions, vertus et vices dans l'ancien roman*, edited by Bernard Pouderon and Cécile Bost-Pouderon, I presented a paper 'Vertus de la campagne, vices de la cité dans le *Daphnis et Chloé* de Longus' (2009b). I argued that, unlike Dio in his *Euboean Oration* in which the countryside is always presented positively and the city almost wholly negatively, Longus does not make his rustics entirely virtuous or his city-dwellers wholly bad. I differentiated between virtues of ἦθος, 'character', and virtues of πρᾶξις, 'action', illustrating the differences between those of the country and those of the

[10] Another exception is Chapter 39 in Volume 3, 'Xenophon's Influence in Imperial Greece'.

city by an analytical table. I noted especially Longus' presentation of piety and impiety, of deception and of artifice, and of fear and boldness, concluding that the country's vices prompt readers to reflection as much as do its virtues. Chapter 35 in this volume is an English version.

For the RICAN 4 of May 2007, published as *Readers and Writers in the Ancient Novel*, *ANS* 12, edited by Michael Paschalis, Stelios Panayotakis and Gareth Schmeling, I offered a paper entitled 'The Uses of Bookishness' (Chapter 34 in this volume, 2009c). In it I examined some ways in which Greek novels flaunt and make play with their textuality, particularly Antonius Diogenes' *The Incredible Things beyond Thule* and Longus' *Daphnis and Chloe*. I argued that Antonius Diogenes presents recurrent tensions between the textual and the oral and highlights the importance of γράμματα, 'letters', to communication within his narrative, mirroring its writing down on wooden tablets that readers encounter in its frame. I also proposed meta-literary functions both for the name of the Arcadian envoy to Tyre, Κύμβας, 'Cymbas', since one of the meanings Hesychius gives the noun κύμβη is πήρα, 'bag' (i.e. the receptacle in which Paapis carried his magic books), and for the twisting and turning of Mant(in)ias in *P.Oxy.* 4761. Longus apparently follows Antonius Diogenes in (unusually) specifying the number of his work's books, but γράμματα, 'letters', have no role within his narrative (despite being taught to the young couple): that narrative is an entirely oral response by an unnamed exegete to a γραφή in the sense 'painting', and within it tales are told, but nothing is ever written or inscribed, not even in Dionysophanes' *paradeisos* or in his civic world.

For the RICAN 5 of May 2009, published as *ANS* 17 with the title *The Construction of the Real and Ideal in the Ancient Novel*, edited by Michael Paschalis and Stelios Panayotakis, I wrote 'Caging Grasshoppers: Longus' Materials for Weaving "Reality"' (Chapter 37, 2013d). There, after defining 'real' and 'ideal' in relation to character or behaviour and to setting, I noted that, whereas the other four Greek 'ideal' novelists create a realistic background, whether using personal observation or historiography, Longus draws chiefly on literary texts that *themselves* present a fictional world (Homer and Theocritus) or one that is semi-fictional (archaic melic poetry). In 'The Country' I explored Longus' debt to Theocritus' landscape, especially that of *Idyll* 1, advertised by his preface as several steps removed from the real world. I then discussed the relation of 2.32 to Theocritus 1; of 1.17.3 to Sappho and Anacreon *via* Theocritus 11, complicated by the term ἀληθῶς, 'really'; and of the apple at 3.33.4 to Sappho's *epithalamia*, Ibycus, and Theocritus 28. 'The City' explored the literary forebears of Longus' Megacles; 'The Sea' looked at his 'Tyrian' pirates' origins in earlier novels, especially Chariton's; and 'Reality' considered how his use of Thucydides underlines his own fictionality. Overall it is my stress on the fictionality, rather than on the poetic status, of most of Longus' intertexts that differentiated my position from those of Richard Hunter and Maria Pia Pattoni.

Meanwhile an invitation to talk at an Apuleius conference, organised at Rostock in 2008 by Christiane Reitz and Wytse Keulen, offered me the chance to pursue an interest I had developed in the limits on the realism of religion as it is presented in the Greek novels. This paper had further airings at the October 2009 'Colloque roman' at Tours ('Les hommes et les dieux dans l'ancien roman') and to audiences in Ohio State and Notre Dame Universities in spring 2010. Its final version, 'Socrates' Cock and Daphnis' Goats: The Rarity of Vows in the Religious Practice of the Greek Novels' (Chapter 36, 2012f), published in a special number of *Trends in Classics*, edited by Stephen Harrison and Stavros Frangoulidis and entitled *Narrative, Culture and Genre in the Ancient Novel*, benefited greatly from the responses of audiences on all these occasions. In it I explored the religious practice of characters in the five 'ideal' Greek novels, arguing that despite these works' overall presentation of a world that is in many ways 'realistic', their representation of religion diverges from 'reality'. At one end of the spectrum the behaviour of the rustic couple Daphnis and Chloe is almost hyper-religious, and it is only in Longus' novel that we find a full range of traditional religious practices, including vows and libations. In the other four many features correspond to behaviour in the 'real' world – prayers, offerings, sacrifices, feasts and festivals: but libations are sometimes not poured when they might be expected; rituals associated with marriage or burial are omitted or played down; and, most strikingly, the practice of making a vow to a god at critical moments to secure help or rescue, a practice documented in the 'real' world by epigraphy and literature from the archaic period down to at least the third century AD, is wholly absent. Possible reasons for this absence were briefly discussed: is it simply a generally soft-focus and elliptical account of religious behaviour, or is it the avoidance of a device which, if resorted to, would risk short-circuiting characters' peril in cliff-hanging situations?

The year 2009 was also when one of a series of workshops funded by the Arts and Humanities Research Council and hosted, like so many small conferences, by the Corpus Christi College Centre for the Study of Greek and Roman Antiquity, stimulated me to revisit the problem of 'Milesian Tales'. I had first considered evidence and arguments relating to these in Bowie 1996b. Since then, Stephen Harrison had proposed (Harrison 1998) a modified version of Bürger 1892b, suggesting that in this genre an anchor-narrator told of scabrous events in a quasi-ethnographic account of his visits to various places; Gottskálk Jennson had suggested (Jennson 2004) that the *Amores* transmitted as Lucian's pointed to Μιλησιακά in which the key-narrator recounted adventures that were both his own and told to him by others, i.e. just what we find Encolpius doing in the *Satyrica*; and Regine May had argued (May 2010) that the prosimetric ass-papyrus *P.Oxy.* 4762 preserves part of Aristides' Μιλησιακά, '*Milesian Tales*'. After noting these hypotheses I briefly reviewed the impact of Μιλησιακά on the Greek novels. Finally I explored their earlier history, suggesting that just as *Sybaritica*, 'Sybaritic tales', linked to them by Ovid, are shown by Aristophanes' *Wasps* already to be a form of λόγοι, 'stories', circulating in the 420s BC, so too Μιλησιακοὶ λόγοι, 'Milesian stories', may have already been current in Athens by then, linked to Miletus' fame as provider of dildoes (cf. Aristophanes' *Lysistrata*) and as Aspasia's city of origin. The paper (Chapter 38, 2013a) appeared in a volume based on these workshops edited by Tim Whitmarsh and Stuart Thomson, *The Romance between Greece and the East*.

For RICAN 6, held in May 2011 on the topic 'Holy Men/Women and Charlatans in the Ancient Novel', I gave a paper entitled 'A Land without Priests? Religious Authority in Longus, *Daphnis and Chloe*': it was published in the *Acta* of the conference, *ANS* 19, edited by Stelios Panayotakis, Gareth Schmeling and Michael Paschalis. That version (Chapter 39, 2015c), benefited both from discussion at the conference and from comments at a seminar at Harvard, especially those of Albert Henrichs. In it I discussed the absence from Longus of institutionalised community religion and of one of its central elements, priests, who (like priestesses) are found in the other four novels. A reason for this might be that some rural cults ran themselves and thus differed from *polis*-based religion. The only character within the story eligible for description as a holy man is Philetas: he has a very close relationship with Eros, who watches over him. The story's narrator, however, relates in the preface how a shadowy *exegetes* explained the paintings in the Nymph's grove: yet this *exegetes*, on whose say-so the novel's four books are offered, lacks authority. Longus reverses the novelistic trope of supporting his story by a *Beglaubigungsapparat*: instead his *exegetes*' interpretations of the painting's scenes leave the reader quite uncertain about the reality of their world.

Three meetings on the novels took place in 2013. In March a conference was organised at the University of Nice by Michèle Biraud and Michel Briand on the theme 'Roman grec et poésie. Dialogue des genres et nouveaux enjeux du poétique'. At that point I was returning belatedly to my commentary on *Daphnis and Chloe* (Bowie 2019g) and I took the opportunity to set out an analysis of poetic language in the novelists, especially Longus, in a paper entitled 'Poetic Elements in the Greek Novelists' Prose'. In it I presented some preliminary *sondages* which I hoped might help determine how much poetic vocabulary there was in three of our five complete Greek texts, and some indication of its classical and Hellenistic ancestry. I also looked selectively at the lexicon of some poets who were the novelists' near-contemporaries. These *sondages*, represented by eight tables, were not all of the same kind. After reviewing terms in Longus evoking epic, early melic poetry, and epigram, and some Bacchic and other technical terms, I concluded that in Longus many words in the lists of Valley 1926 are not 'simply' poetic but may rather be chosen to trigger some intertextuality, whether with a particular text or with a genre, and that others have no strong claim to be 'poetic' at all. The remaining 'poetic words' that cannot so be explained are not numerous. Longus' prose may be poetic in terms of his Theocritean subject, rhythmical sentences, and preference for coordination over subordination: but the language he uses to do this is predominantly the language of prose. A brief overview of a small selection of potentially 'poetic' words in Achilles Tatius and Heliodorus suggested that they too had only a low proportion of 'poetic' words, a view corroborated by the small number of predominantly 'poetic' words in Marcellus poems from the Via Appia, in the poet(s) of the Sacerdos monument at Nicaea, and in a sample from Ps.-Oppian's *Cynegetica* that are also found in the novelists. I concluded that in this period poets and writers of novelistic prose are still drawing their vocabulary from two different linguistic pools. I had already discussed the poems of Marcellus and of the Sacerdos poet(s) in a paper entitled 'Grandiloquent Epitaphs', together with the epitaph from Syros for six-year-old Nicocrates (*IG* xii 5.677 = *GVI* 272) at a *journée d'étude* in Paris in February 2013, and I revisited others in 'ποῦ κεῖται; Sampling the Linguistic Texture of 2nd and 3rd Century Dactylic Poetry' in a conference on imperial Greek epic at Cambridge in July 2013. The paper published in the *Acta* of the Nice conference (Chapter 40, 2017a) benefited from comments by all these audiences.

In May 2013 the University of Crete hosted RICAN 7, with the topic 'Slaves and Masters in the Ancient Novel'. I gave a paper entitled 'Animals, Slaves and Masters in Longus' *Daphnis and Chloe*', whose first section reworked a paper 'Les animaux dans le *Daphnis and Chloé* de Longus',[11] given to the second Tours colloque organised by Bernard Pouderon in

[11] Bowie 2005a, not reprinted in this volume.

2002 and published by him in 2005 with the title *Lieux, décors et paysages de l'ancien roman des origins à Byzance*. My RICAN paper benefited from comments made in Rethymno and by members of several later audiences: at Brown University, at the Classical Association of South Africa at Cape Town, at the University of Leeds, at the University of Illinois at Urbana-Champaign, at Florida State University, and in the classical seminar at Corpus Christi College, Oxford. It appeared (Chapter 43, 2019b) in the *Acta* of RICAN, edited by Stelios Panayotakis and Michael Paschalis and published as *ANS* 23. After reviewing the roles assigned to animals (often of agents important for the plot), and noting their appearances' frequent intertextuality with Homer, Hesiod, Alcaeus, Sappho and Theocritus, I turned to terms for the master–slave relationship, whose debut comes unexpectedly late in the novel: οἰκέτης, 'house-servant', first at 2.12; δουλεύω, 'I am a slave', first at 2.23; δοῦλος, 'slave', first at 3.31; δέσποινα, 'mistress', first at 3.25; δεσπότης, 'master', first at 3.26. I argued that a significant parallel (hinted at by the comparison between the obedience of Daphnis' goats and that of οἰκέται to their master's command at 4.15.4) should be seen between different relations of dominance – sheep and goats dominated by shepherds and goatherds; slaves and people of low rank dominated by members of Greek city elites – and that this parallel prompts the readers to contemplate the control exercised by Rome over the Greek world and its city elites. Such contemplation is invited by the analogy between Longus' story of a couple suckled by animals and that of Romulus and Remus suckled by a wolf, and by his choice of name for the couple's son, Philopoemen, that of a historical character whom Plutarch says some Roman called 'the last of the Greeks'.

The third novel conference of 2013 was held at the Norwegian University of Science and Technology at Trondheim to commemorate the important work of Tomas Hägg and was organised primarily by Thea S. Thorsen. Its *Acta*, edited by Stephen Harrison and Thea Thorsen, were published in 2018 as Trends in Classics Supplementary Volume 62 with the title *The Dynamics of Ancient Prose: Biographic, Novelistic, Apologetic*. Encouraged by the number of illustrations presented by Hägg 1983, I followed up an interest in illustrated editions of Longus that I had had since discussing them in an unpublished London paper in the 1980s – an interest strong enough to impel me in 1988 to make three trips to London to hear Giles Barber's marvellous Panizzi lectures 'Daphnis and Chloe: The Markets and Metamorphoses of an Unknown Bestseller'. My paper, whose title on publication was 'Captured Moments: Illustrating Longus' Prose' (Chapter 41, 2018c), necessarily made much use of Barber 1989, and it explored

Western European illustrated editions between 1626 (Crispin de Passe the Younger) and 2014 (Karl Lagerfeld's *Moderne Mythologie*), picking out for closer analysis in a table nine printed between 1890 (Raphaël Collin and Eugène-André Champollion) and 1961 (Marc Chagall), editions which are witnesses to the European taste of the last decade of the nineteenth century and the first six decades of the twentieth. That table registered the different scenes in Longus chosen by different illustrators, which I had expected to cluster around a few favourites: but alongside some favourites (Daphnis and Lycaenion, Chloe bathing Daphnis and herself, the couple's wedding night) there are, as it reveals, many chosen by only two artists, some by only one. Other phenomena that emerged from my analysis were that Paris was the pre-eminent location for the production of illustrated editions, and that, unlike Crispin de Passe the Younger in 1626, later artists chose subjects bearing upon the couple's growing understanding of ἔρως, 'desire', much more than ones depicting their few adventures.

Chapter 42 (2019c) had a long gestation. A lean form of the paper was delivered at a symposium entitled 'Greek from Alpha to Omega', organised in Oxford in June 2007 to celebrate the seventieth birthday of Anna Morpurgo Davies; a more developed version at ICAN IV, organised in Lisbon by Marília Futre Pinheiro in 2008. Feedback on both these occasions improved the final version 'Λέξεις Λόγγου', published in a volume assembled to honour Bryan Reardon, *Literary Currents and Romantic Forms: Essays in Memory of Bryan Reardon*, published as *ANS* 26, edited by Kathryn Chew, John Morgan and Stephen Trzaskoma. The paper's first objective was to give a flavour of the post-classical vocabulary in Longus' artistic prose and to determine at what literary level the authors with whom he shares such vocabulary locate him. After noting some *hapax legomena*, and documenting some fifty words and a score of usages first found in post-classical literary texts ranging from Epicurus to Himerius, I concluded that, while these were only a sub-class of the numerous cases of vocabulary and usage that Longus shares with post-classical authors, they showed that, while Longus does himself often Atticise, he does so much less consistently than other Atticising writers of the late second and early third centuries. In some respects, then, his linguistic behaviour could be seen as analogous to that of Chariton, whose vocabulary matches that of several writers of the first century AD. But though writing in a period when Atticism was gaining strength, and may well have been prominent in some places, Chariton does not follow this path: a century and a half later Longus was writing in a world where some lexicographers and sophists both preached and tried to practise hard-core Atticism; but he himself blends Atticist and post-classical usage without apparent concern. I conceded that the data I had marshalled could not establish a firm date for his writing, but suggested they pointed to the 220s or 230s AD.

Chapter 44 (2019h), 'The Demotion of the Literary Cowherd', was elicited by a small colloquium on cowherds/*bouviers* organised at the ENS Lyon by Christophe Cusset in November 2014. In this paper, published in a number of the online journal *Aitia* with the theme *Le bouvier dans la poésie hellénistique et le roman grec*, edited by Jérôme Bastick, Christophe Cusset and Claire Vieilleville, I observed that Longus promotes an αἰπόλος, 'goatherd', to bear the privileged name Daphnis, transferring his canonical role of βουκόλος, 'cowherd', to other herdsmen – something easily done, since all play the syrinx. But Longus' Daphnis does not inherit the capacity of the Theocritean αἰπόλος for singing mellifluous song: whereas Chloe does sing *sola*, Longus' males, including Daphnis, do not, except for the cowherd in the inset tale at 1.27 and Philetas in his recollections at 2.3.2; instead they *tell* μῦθοι, 'myths'. I suggested that Longus might have envisaged his own, often poetic, prose achieving what song had achieved for Theocritus' Polyphemus, and that his elimination of male solo song was part of his programme of refashioning Sappho and Theocritus in prose. I noted that of the three characters to whom, from a Theocritean Daphnis, the status of βουκόλος is transferred, Dorcon twice saves Daphnis, but his understanding of *eros* does not advance the couple's; that of the βουκόλος Philetas does, and his advice is important; Lampis' impact, however, like Dorcon's, is ephemeral, and his character unpleasant. Despite Philetas' positive role, Dorcon's and Lampis' actions may hint that Theocritus was wrong to privilege βουκόλοι, who in Longus can be boisterous and self-assertive, and that a society which gave cowherds free rein would be rougher than one in which standards of behaviour were set by goatherds and shepherds.

Chapter 45 (2019i) was delivered at a colloquium on Callimachus in September 2017 in the *Hellenistica Groningana* series which Jacqueline Klooster has kept alive after Annette Harder's retirement, to the great benefit of the world of Hellenistic scholarship. Its papers were published in 2019 as *Callimachus Revisited: New Perspectives in Callimachean Scholarship*, edited by Jacqueline Klooster, Annette Harder, Remco Regtuit and Gerry Wakker. My paper argued that, unlike all other Greek novelists, Longus shows knowledge of Callimachus' poetry, both the *Aitia* (whence his use of ἀρτιγένειος, twice: 1.15.1 and 4.10.1) and the *Epigrams* (whence the figurative ἕλκος of 1.14.1, near to Longus' first use of ἀρτιγένειος). These strong cases increase the probability that some other words (ἐπτοηθεῖσαι 1.22.2) and themes (e.g. the simultaneous death of two young siblings at 4.24.2, cf. Call. *Anth. Pal.* 7.517; the recondite myth of Branchus, 4.17.6, cf. Call. fr. 229 Pfeiffer) are drawn from Callimachus. In explaining why Callimachus might attract Longus' interest, I proposed that the four-book format of *Daphnis and Chloe*, unique in the novels, might be a further Callimachean intertextuality, calculated to invite readers' reflection on how Longus' work could be read as a series of *Aitia*, that of the cave of the Nymphs (in the preface and Book 4) complementing those of the inset tales of Books 1 to 3.

Chapter 46 (2020b) was delivered to a conference organised by Efi Papadodima in June 2018 at the Academy of Athens on 'Meanings of Silence in Ancient Greek Literature', published by her as *Faces of Silence in Ancient Greek Literature*, Trends in Classics Supplementary Volume 100. My paper, 'Silence in Chariton, Xenophon, Achilles Tatius and Longus', analysed several roles of silence in these novels. On a macro-level, I suggested that the writing of the text was itself a breaking of silence, and when we move from the writer to his narrator Cleitophon's sudden revelation of his love adventures in front of the painting of Europa it prompts us to see the novel's narrative as a whole as breaking silence. A similar choice of speech over silence by Longus' narrator, who does not simply admire silently the painting in the Nymphs' grove but seeks out an *exegetes* to explain it, admits readers to a world from which silence would have excluded them. Moving to characters, I examined situations where the choice between speech and silence is crucial to plot development – most far-reaching in Longus, where the couple's origins must be concealed for four fifths of the narrative to allow them to grow up as simple herdsfolk: both sets of foster-parents keep their babe's origins secret, and first Lamon's decision to break silence (4.18.3), and then Dryas', create turning-points in the plot. In Chariton too the choice between speech and silence repeatedly affects plot development. Silence is often allied with deception, twice with fear. In Chariton, Achilles Tatius and Longus a protagonist's romantic involvement with a third party is crucially suppressed (*Odyssey*-like) in communications between the couple. Next I addressed types of silence closely related to the novels' central theme of *eros*. First, silence in somebody usually voluble is a symptom of *eros*. Second, a *parthenos* like Callirhoe suffers from her passion more acutely because she feels she cannot disclose it. Third, and very different, Achilles Tatius' Cleitophon is advised by Cleinias to conduct his first physical approaches to and attempt to kiss Leucippe in silence, which indeed he does. Fourth, and again different, is the silent awe which a protagonist's dazzling beauty triggers. After analysing these silences, closely linked to the novels' blend of *eros* and adventure, I looked briefly at some *topoi* shared with other genres: 'everybody else was silent, but X began to speak', and 'for a long time X was silent, but eventually began to speak'. I concluded that silence's diverse deployments reveal it, and the terms used for it, as important elements in constructing a narrative well-calculated to engage readers, noting that of these novelists only Longus has an 'unmarked' use of σιωπ- to mean little more than 'he/she stopped speaking'.

The earliest of these papers on the Greek novels (Chapter 19) was written when they still drew little scholarly attention. By the end of the second millennium they had become a hot topic, and the large numbers who had attended the Lisbon conference ICAN IV in 2008 (where I gave a version of Chapter 42) were almost matched by the attendance at ICAN V at Houston in autumn 2015, organised by Edmund Cueva (where I gave a paper on paradoxography in the novels that I have not published). Despite Covid, the programme for ICAN VI at Ghent, organised by Koen De Temmerman, has been on a similar scale, with some 130 speakers. To all who organised the ICAN meetings, and the smaller occasions at Groningen, Rethymno and Tours, I owe a great debt for creating stimulating frameworks in which discussion of the novels could flourish. It has been a privilege to be a foot-soldier in a campaign which has had such an impressive outcome.

1 | Who is Dicaeopolis? (1988)

The name given by Aristophanes to the leading character in his *Acharnians* has given rise to much discussion, and I take the opportunity of the appearance in this *Journal* of another well-documented assessment[1] to put forward briefly, and without a full and independent armoury of footnotes, a solution that contests the *communis opinio* that Dicaeopolis in some sense speaks for and as Aristophanes.

The grounds for this widely held view seem to be (briefly) the following. When Dicaeopolis prepares to plead his case to the Acharnians (366ff.) he refers to what he had himself suffered at Cleon's hands on account of his comedy of the previous year:

> αὐτός τ' ἐμαυτὸν ὑπὸ Κλέωνος ἅπαθον
> ἐπίσταμαι διὰ τὴν πέρυσι κωμωιδίαν.
>
> and what I myself suffered at Cleon's hands
> as a result of last year's Comedy is something I know personally.
>
> Aristophanes, *Acharnians* 377–8

Later, at the start of his long ῥῆσις, 'speech', he asserts that his claims will be δίκαια, 'just' (501), and that Cleon will not bring a διαβολή, 'false accusation', against him on this occasion for abusing the city in the presence of ξένοι, 'non-citizens' (502–3). It seems that the *parabasis* refers to the same incident as these passages when it talks of a διαβολή that the poet insulted the *polis* and *demos* (630–1) and insists that he will continue to present δίκαια, 'just things', in his comedies (655). Since there can be little doubt that in the *parabasis* the poet is talking of his own career and productions,[2] it has often been inferred that at 377–8 the audience was intended to take Dicaeopolis to be speaking for Aristophanes and in the main did so.

Is this inference correct? It is dangerous to allow our knowledge of what is said in the *parabasis* to influence our interpretation of earlier parts of the play, and we should move cautiously in reconstructing the progress of

[1] Foley 1988. For another good discussion see Hubbard 1991, 41–59.
[2] See however MacDowell (Foley 1988, n.3).

the audience's knowledge and expectations as the action of the play proceeds. The first few hundred lines have built up a picture of a peace-loving Athenian (32), antipathetic to Cleon (6), and interested in music and drama (9–16). Though less emphatically rustic than Strepsiades he has marks of ἀγροικία, 'rusticity' (30–1), and hails from a rural deme (33). There is little in this, and nothing in the development of a pugnacious comic 'hero' which is presented up to and including the encounter with the Acharnians, that can have suggested to the audience that this man is especially representative of Aristophanes. Nor, it should be said, have we any evidence that in 425 BC a poet of Old Comedy might be expected to introduce himself in one of his dramas. Admittedly little can be based on an *argumentum ex silentio*, and we know very little indeed about comedies produced before *Acharnians* in 426/5 BC; but nobody has ever suggested that this happened in any earlier play, and when in 424/3 BC Cratinus built the plot of his Πυτίνη, '*Wine-flask*', around a fantastic autobiography it is clear that its 'comic hero' was called Cratinus and not veiled under a *redende Name*.

Only, therefore, at line 377 was the audience suddenly forced to come to terms with an important biographical datum about the play's central character: he was a comic poet, and he had suffered at the hands of Cleon as a result of a comedy produced in the previous year. From being a stereotype with whom many thousands of Athenian males in the audience might readily have identified, the character acquired a *persona* which might be expected to fit one of the comic poets who competed in the Dionysia of 427/6 BC. Would the audience draw the further conclusion that this comic poet was Aristophanes himself? If Aristophanes alone had been the object of some action by Cleon, doubtless they would. But it is only the tenuous reconstruction offered first by our scholia, and then by modern scholars with nothing sounder to turn to, which associates a move by Cleon after the Dionysia of 426/5 BC uniquely with Aristophanes. I suggest that at 377ff. Aristophanes intends not to offer the audience a clear indication that the character in some sense speaks for himself, but to puzzle and tantalise them: the character is identified as representing a comic poet, but nothing, in my view, indicates which comic poet. The unusually late postponement of the use of the character's name might support this view.[3] A personal name might reasonably be expected to clear up the mystery, and the audience will now begin to realise that they have not yet heard one.

[3] Postponement of leading character's names is of course exploited elsewhere, e.g. Strepsiades is first named in *Nu.* 134, Philocleon and Bdelycleon in *V.* 133–4, Trygaeus in *Pax* 190. But in *Ach.* we learn the name even later.

Aristophanes does not keep them in suspense for long. Although nothing further is contributed by the character's declared intention of seeking help from Euripides – the average member of the audience, after all, might imagine that all dramatic poets knew and had dealings with each other – it does give Aristophanes the chance to pull his leading character's name out of his hat: Dicaeopolis (406). It is important for the understanding of this name that it is revealed in the scene between the two poets and not, for example, in one of the early scenes where Dicaeopolis is in the assembly or when, at 496ff., he is putting the case for seeing the Spartans as reasonable people. It is precisely in the context of the imbroglio of the Dionysia of 427/6 BC and his calling on the dramatic poet Euripides that the leading character becomes a named individual. That the audience should at this juncture have sought to interpret that name in the light of his *political* actions is therefore unlikely (and would, I suggest below, have been baffling). Rather, they would have used the name to discover to which of the comic poets of the Dionysia of 427/6 BC the leading character should be related. In the absence of any indication hitherto that the character was Aristophanes, they would only have made that identification now if the name or its components led them to it. That a memory of Pindar's description of Aegina as δικαιόπολις could have gelled with a possible link between Aristophanes and Aegina is an implausible proposal, and has not found much favour since it was proposed fifty years ago by Cyril Bailey.[4] Had they been clairvoyant or gained prior access to texts of the drama, they might have known that Aristophanes would claim in the *parabasis* to offer just comedy and to benefit the city, but it is hardly likely that this claim was made by him alone among competitors at dramatic festivals.[5]

Accordingly, in the absence of a comic poet actually called Dicaeopolis, the name could lead the audience – and would easily lead them – to only one man: Eupolis. Attic names with a component –πολις are not uncommon, but most combine it with a verbal form: e.g. Archepolis or (the name of Eupolis' father) Sosipolis. A combination in which a term of commendation is joined to –πολις is found only in the names Dicaeopolis and Eupolis. The move from the one to the other would therefore easily be made, and would be comparable to the move from Labes to Laches and Κύων (*Kyon*,

[4] Cf. Foley 1988, n.6.

[5] I do not accept that (as suggested by a *Journal* referee) the similarity of phraseology between 497–502 and the *parabasis* demonstrates that the audience would take the passages to refer to the same person. Are we to assume that on hearing the *parabasis* the audience would actually change whatever identification it had already formed at 497ff.?

'dog') to Κλέων (Cleon) in *Wasps*, or to Lysimache from Lysistrata in *Lysistrata* (if that allusion is accepted).[6]

Two objections might readily occur. First, we do not know that Eupolis competed in the Dionysia of 427/6 BC. This must be conceded, but it is highly unlikely that he did not compete regularly after his first production, Προσπάλτιοι, '*Prospaltians*', in 430/29 BC.[7] Secondly, what of the coincidence between Dicaeopolis' references to Cleon and those of the *parabasis*? I have already hinted at how I would resolve this. It is possible that Eupolis' comedy for this festival, like that of Aristophanes, directed some shafts against Cleon (as he certainly did in his Χρυσοῦν γένος, '*Golden race*', of (?) 424 BC, cf. fr. 316 K–A) and that Cleon retaliated against both comedians. Naturally Aristophanes' references in the *parabasis* of *Acharnians* only hint at, and those in later plays suppress, the participation of any other poet than himself in glorious combat with the monstrous politician. But if the hypothesis of an attack by Cleon on both Eupolis and Aristophanes is correct, then the audience of Acharnians will not have been puzzled by the parallelism: Dicaeopolis refers to Cleon's attack on Eupolis, the chorus in the *parabasis* to his attack on Aristophanes. The language is strikingly similar because the nature of the attack was similar. That Dicaeopolis is chosen as a name to suggest a known individual relieves us of the embarrassing problems that have faced those seeking to interpret it as appropriate to the character's policy or conduct.[8] It was never very plausible that Dicaeopolis suggested 'just city'. The leading character may start off expostulating at the corruption of Athenian politics, but at this stage we do not know that his name is Dicaeopolis, and once he has embarked on his private peace-project his interest in making Athens a just (or juster) *polis* evaporates. The alternative meaning 'he who treats his *polis* justly' is even less of a starter: many now agree that Dicaeopolis' implementation of his peace involves selfish πλεονεξία, 'acquisitiveness', almost a polar opposite of δικαιοσύνη, 'justice', in his dealing with his fellow citizens.

It is indeed the case that Aristophanes makes play with the term δίκαιος, 'just'. Dicaeopolis claims that his arguments on behalf of the enemy will be δίκαια (317, 501) – which is conceded by the chorus (561, 562) – and that τρυγῳδία, 'the wine-lees-song', also knows τὸ καλόν, 'what is noble' (500). Likewise in the *parabasis* Aristophanes claims his comic message to be δίκαιον (645, 655). All these claims may be directed to the *polis*, but it

[6] See Lewis 1955, Henderson 1987 xxxviii–xl, Connelly 2007, 62–3.

[7] Eup. *test.* 2a8 K–A. [8] Foley 1988, n.52.

is hard to find a way in which they are especially related to the *polis* and which would elucidate the compound name Dicaeopolis. The final use of τὸ δίκαιον, 'what is just', in the play rather points the audience to the verbal trickery in which Aristophanes has characteristically engaged. In the *parabasis* he proclaims (661) τὸ γὰρ εὖ μετ' ἐμοῦ τὸ δίκαιον ξύμμαχον ἔσται, 'for the "well" and "the just" will be with me as my fellow-fighter'. We are asked to observe the δεξιότης, 'dexterity', of the poet who has given himself and his main character arguments that are δίκαια and has cleverly given his character a name that both fits these arguments and links him indissolubly with τὸ εὖ, 'the well'. A member of the audience who had doubted that Dicaeopolis represented Eupolis could no longer do so. Aristophanes might doubtless have adapted Eupolis' name in some other way, e.g. to Agathopolis (though clearly Sosipolis and Sopolis were excluded if one of these was the name of Eupolis' father). That he adapted it to Δικαιόπολις suits the play made with the concept of τὸ δίκαιον between lines 317 and 655, but this play cannot alone explain the name.

If this suggestion is correct, what follows? First, that we do not need to postulate an unparalleled and undeclared identification of a poet with his main character. Second, that inferences from Dicaeopolis' policies to those of Aristophanes become precarious: instead of finding in the supposed identification an emphatic endorsement by the poet of his character's desire for peace, we find a buffer between the views of the character and those of the poet. A demagogue who objected to the content of Dicaeopolis' speech could be countered on a number of levels: 'Telephus said that'; 'Dicaeopolis said that'; or even 'that's the sort of thing that Eupolis says'. This will have made it easier for Aristophanes to develop Dicaeopolis' case without fear of a come-back from Cleon, but it makes it yet more difficult for us to determine (if we must) where Aristophanes 'himself' stood on the issue of peace. For that, I believe, we must confine ourself to the *parabasis*, where victory rather than peace is what the poet claims to be bringing to Athens, and to a practical argument that I have not seen in modern discussions. Most individuals and states would agree that peace is preferable to war, but some choose war because the conditions attaching to peace are unacceptable. It makes no sense, therefore, to urge the making of peace unless you also make clear on what terms peace is to be made. About terms *Acharnians* says nothing, and because of this, and because of the *parabasis*, cannot be taken as a serious plea for peace.

My suggestion will not be persuasive if no point at all can be suggested in Aristophanes making a character associable with Eupolis urge peace. Had we evidence, for example, that in his plays Eupolis never touched the issue of war and peace, the device would appear arbitrary and humourless. If Eupolis had used his comedies to back the war whole-heartedly there would be some perverse point in turning his stance on its head, but it might be rather forced. As it is, our evidence suggests just what the action of *Acharnians* and the character of Dicaeopolis would lead us to expect, that Eupolis criticised the conduct of the war and focused on some of its damaging or ridiculous concomitants and consequences.

It seems that in Προσπάλτιοι, generally held to be his first play and so produced in 430/429 BC,[9] he attacked Pericles' conduct of the war, a fact that would enhance an audience's appreciation of how Dicaeopolis presents Pericles' role in the outbreak of war (especially *Ach.* 530 ff.). Προσπάλτιοι was also, so far as we know, the only previous comedy with a chorus of demesmen. Its few fragments include a reference to the story of Bellerophon (fr. 259.126), to lameness (fr. 264, cf. for both *Ach.* 427), and to a Thracian lady (fr. 262, cf. *Ach.* 273, spoken by Dicaeopolis). There is also a verbal parallel between Προσπάλτιοι fr. 260.30 and *Ach.* 162 (again spoken by Dicaeopolis).[10] This may all be coincidence, but to me it suggests that in *Acharnians* Aristophanes had at least half an eye on Προσπάλτιοι.

Ταξίαρχοι, '*Brigadiers*', appears to have exploited the contrast between the effeminate and luxury-loving Dionysus and the martinet admiral Phormio. Although Phormio was mentioned in comedy as late as Aristophanes' *Peace* 348, there is much to be said for Wilamowitz's belief that his prominence in Ταξίαρχοι points to that play's production not long after his death in 428 BC.[11] Indeed I know of no reason why it should not actually belong to a festival prior to his death, the Dionysia of 429 BC, or to either festival in 428 BC. It must be conceded, however, that the date is unknown, and hence that any inference is speculative.[12] But if Ταξίαρχοι had been produced between 430/29 BC and 426/5 BC, then the audience might see in Dicaeopolis some elements of Eupolis' Dionysus, and in Lamachus a version of Eupolis' Phormio. It is improbable that in Eupolis' play Phormio was not worsted by Dionysus and martial arts and ideals held up to ridicule.

[9] *PCG* v 442–3 on *Prospaltioi*; Storey 2003, 56, however, thinks it possible *Helots* was his first play.

[10] Fr. 260.30 μέγα στένοι μεντἂν ἀκ[...], 'however the [...] would grumble loudly,' cf. *Ach.* 162–3 ὑποστένοι μεντἂν ὁ θρανίτης λέως ὁ σωσίπολις, 'however the upper-oar people would quietly grumble, the city-saviours', where, as Storey 2003, 54 observes, σωσίπολις can be related to the name that ancient tradition gives to Eupolis' father, Sosipolis (e.g. Suda ε 3567 *s.v.* Εὔπολις). Sidwell 1994, 96 accepts that there is a Eupolidean allusion at *Ach.* 162 and carries the hypothesis of this paper very much further, as again Sidwell 2009.

[11] Wilamowitz 1880, 66.

[12] Storey 2003, 66 and 248 favours 415 BC, following Handley 1982, 24, but conceding that the *communis opinio* puts it ca. 427 BC.

Ἀστράτευτοι, '*Draft-dodgers*', also dealt with contrasts between effeminacy and war (the Suda ε 3657 *s.v.* Εὔπολις gives an alternative title Ἀνδρόγυνοι, '*Men-women*'), and has been placed early by some scholars.[13] The leadership of a campaign involving Minoa in fr. 38 K–A should put the play no earlier than the summer of 427 BC (cf. Th. 3.5.1) and could (but need not) take it later than 424 BC (cf. Th. 4.66.3). The enigmatic reference to Peisander's στρατεία, 'expedition', to the Pactolus (fr. 35 K–A) could conceivably refer to the same abuse of privilege as the envoys' luxurious travel through the plains of the Cayster in *Ach.* 68–71, and Peisander was already a butt of Aristophanes in 427/6 BC (*Babylonians* fr. 84 K–A). Ἀστράτευτοι fr. 41 K–A refers to the keeping of peacocks, a standard present from the Persian king to envoys which we know to have been in the air in 426/5 (*Ach.* 63). All this harmonises with, but cannot demonstrate, a date for Ἀστράτευτοι of 427/6 BC.

It is also necessary to suppose, if my explanation of 377–8 is correct, that at the Dionysia of 427/6 BC Eupolis produced a play which seemed to attack the city's policies. The most economical hypothesis is that this was a play whose theme could be represented as attacking the city's prosecution of the Peloponnesian war (like *Acharnians*, and in this respect different from *Babylonians*) and that it was indeed Ἀστράτευτοι. If either or both Ταξίαρχοι and Ἀστράτευτοι do belong before *Acharnians* (and there can be no doubt about Προσπάλτιοι), then the audience in 426/5 BC will not simply have seen quickly that Dicaeopolis represents Eupolis, but will also have seen the appropriateness of ascribing to him a dislike of the war and a desire for a life of peace. His position will not have been confused with that of Aristophanes.

13 Cf. Storey 2003, 75–6, himself favouring (on very slight evidence) the period 414–411 BC.

2 *Marginalia Obsceniora*: Some Problems in Aristophanes' *Wasps* (1990)

1 Introduction

Wasps is a middle-brow play: so says a slave in its *prologos* (65–6). The claim may be as delusory as those he has just made, that Cleon and Euripides will not be satirised, or as the disclaimers of the revised *Clouds* 534ff. Certainly sexuality and obscenity appear in a number of contexts throughout the play, so that when the last scenes reveal Philocleon to be just as vehement in his pursuit of sexual gratification (1341–87) as he was in his ἔρως, 'desire', for jury-service, we do not feel that this jars with Philocleon's character or with the play as a whole. In this essay I wish to examine some passages where phallic imagery or sexual excitement may have escaped scholars' attention. If my suggestions are accepted, then Aristophanes' characters in *Wasps* repeatedly confront the audience with images of sexuality: one could not say that these images form a pattern, but they prepare the ground for that last scene.

2 Lines 27–8

As MacDowell 1971 saw, the ὅπλα, 'weapons', lost by Cleonymus are not simply his shield but his genitalia. It may be suggested that Xanthias' encouragement to his fellow slave to tell about 'his own', and Sosias' reply, are ambiguous too: τὸ σόν, 'yours', and ἀλλ' ἔστιν μέγα, 'but it is big', can be referred either to his dream or to his ὅπλον, 'weapon'.[1] Ambiguities concerning ὅπλα are an appropriate prelude to Sosias' dream.

3 Lines 31–6

Sosias' dream was of an ἐκκλησία, 'assembly', of sheep, incongruously (as often in dreams) equipped with the sticks and cloaks that seem rather to be the mark of dicasts (*App.prov.* 1.47; cf. Arist. *Ath.* 65.2). They were being

[1] MacDowell 1971, 130 on line 27. The uses of μέγας, 'big', at 56 and 68 have also been proposed as obscene *double entendres*: cf. Killeen 1971; Calder 1970; but cf. the reservations of Stone 1978.

harangued by φάλλαινα πανδοκεύτρια. The many nuances of πανδοκεύτρια, 'hostess to all' or 'innkeeper', cannot be explored here. My focus is on the term φάλλαινα, which from its earliest attestation, now in Aeschylus' Δικτυουλκοί, '*Net-drawers*', means 'whale' or 'sea-monster' (*PSI* 1209.9 = fr. 464.10 Mette = fr. 46a.9 Radt = fr. 46a.9 Sommerstein), although even a fisherman's life cannot have given rise to many occasions for its use. The word's form is likely to have raised other possible interpretations in the audience's mind. The termination -αινα is regularly used to mark the feminine of a noun denoting an animal or (less often) a human being belonging to an ethnic or social group. The audience in the theatre of Dionysus had been hilariously reminded of this in *Clouds* (660–7) at their last dramatic festival, the Dionysia of 424/3:[2] there Aristophanes had made Socrates coin ἀλεκτρύαινα, 'cockess', from ἀλεκτρύων, 'cock'. As that coinage hints, the largest single group of -αινα terms denotes animals: δράκαινα, 'she-snake', λέαινα, 'lioness', σκυλάκαινα, 'female puppy', etc., outnumber such terms as θέαινα, 'goddess', θεράπαινα, 'serving maid', or the apparently new καταπύγαινα, 'a woman keen on anal penetration'. With some exceptions (e.g. ἀμφίσβαινα, 'two-ended serpent') the feminine form implies a masculine, usually in -ων or -ος (but note Σκύθαινα, 'Scythianess', from Σκύθης, 'Scythian', perhaps another comic coinage of Aristophanes, since its first appearance is in *Lys*. 184). Chantraine took the view that an etymological link with φαλλός, 'phallus' / φαλλήν, 'phallic one', was certain, whether there was a pair *φάλλων / φάλλαινα like δράκων, 'snake', / δράκαινα, 'she-snake', or whether φάλλη, feminine of φαλλός, developed the secondary form φάλλαινα.[3]

For my argument the insoluble problem of etymology is less important than the way the audience would take the word. I suggest that in a comic context the feminine form of this rare word would evoke the masculine cognate φαλλός, and could be heard not simply as 'whale' but as 'female φαλλός'. True, a female φαλλός seems self-contradictory. But, as we have seen, dreams combine what is impossible in real life. Moreover, once a φαλλός is detached from the animal or human whose masculinity it marks, almost anything can happen to it, as is well shown by some illustrations in *Greek Homosexuality*.[4] Vase-painters give it wings, legs, or a head: why should not the comic poet make it a female monster on the analogy of a δράκαινα,

[2] The text we have is of course that of the revised version of *Clouds*, but there is no evidence that this scene was the subject of revision.

[3] Chantraine 1968–80, iv 1175, *s.v.*

[4] Dover 1978, 132f. and illustrations R259, a phallus-horse, and R414, a phallus-bird (cf. B494).

'she-snake', especially if, as here, it represents that Cleon on whose monstrosity he loves to dwell (cf. 1032–5, repeated *Peace* 754–7)?

The audience, then, is thrown an image of a ranting female phallus with the voice of a blazing sow. To Xanthias the dream stinks horribly of βύρσης σαπρᾶς, 'rotten hide' (38): hardly the skin of the dream-sow, which on a literal interpretation of ἐμπεπρημένης, 'set on fire', has been burnt but is not rotten, but rather (since a βύρσα is usually of ox-hide) the leather of which stage-phalloi were made (*Clouds* 538), suggested by the larger-than-life φάλλαινα of the dream. The rotten phallus will reappear later, worn by Philocleon, at 1343 ὡς σαπρὸν τὸ σχοινίον, 'what a rotten rope' (cf. 1380).

4 Lines 177–89

Bdelycleon, playing the fall-guy, has thought to put an end to Philocleon's current stratagem by having their family ass brought out of the farm-complex. He thus plays into his father's hands: Philocleon comes out concealed under the ass, like Odysseus (181, 185). On his discovery (played very slowly for maximum effect) his son expostulates:

ὦ μιαρώτατος
ἵν' ὑποδέδυκεν, ὥστ' ἐμοίγ' ἰνδάλλεται
ὁμοιότατος κλητῆρος εἶναι πωλίωι.

O, the pervert,
look where he has crept under, so that to me he seems
to be very like a caller's foal.

Ar. *Wasps* 187–9

First, how was this staged? If Philocleon crawled out from the house under the ass on all fours, he abandoned the Odyssean model, for all painted and plastic representations of the famous scene from the *Odyssey* have Odysseus clinging to the underside of the ram, his head sticking forward.[5] That, surely, is how Aristophanes must have asked his producer Philonides to play this scene, and with a suitable stage-ass they could surely have succeeded (cf. MacDowell on 178).

Second, what is the joke in 189? There is a pun on κλητήρ, 'summons-witness' and 'brayer': MacDowell suggests that this is continued in πωλίωι, 'foal' and 'follower'. The sense 'follower', however, appears only in restricted

[5] See Brommer 1973, 437–9; Fellmann 1972, esp. 79–100.

contexts, and the similarity to a foal is remote if Philocleon is hanging upside-down. Even if this is ignored, the pun hardly justifies the feed-lines that seem to build up towards this εἰκών, 'comparison'.

I propose that Aristophanes wrote ψωλίωι, 'little erect phallus': Bdelycleon expostulates at his father's disgusting behaviour (ὦ μιαρώτατος) and compares him to the erect phallus of a donkey. The size of an equid's phallus will not have been unfamiliar to Attic theatre-goers, and Philocleon's posture under the donkey, hanging with his feet between the donkey's back legs and his flesh-coloured head sticking forward between its front legs, will readily have suggested a large phallus, ἔρυθρον ἐξ ἀκροῦ, 'red-tipped'. It might be thought to be an objection that the hypocoristic form is not otherwise attested, only ψωλή, translated by LSJ *membrum virile praeputio retracto*. But many Aristophanic words, and a number of hypocoristic forms in -ίον, are *hapax legomena*, and ψωλίωι merits consideration.

If this interpretation is correct, the image of the phallus introduced *en passant* by the slaves, and then superimposed upon Cleon, has now been transferred to Cleon's fan Philocleon.

5 Lines 572–3

In establishing the magnitude of his power as a dicast Philocleon, in his half of the *agōn*, recounts how defendants try to conciliate him. One brings on his children, entreats Philocleon like a god, and at 573 asks him to accede to his daughter's plea if he takes pleasure in χοιριδίοις, 'little piggies', here simply slang for female genitalia rather than a pun (there is little relevance in Philocleon liking literal piglets, beyond the maintenance of the sequence of animal images in the play). The suggestion that Philocleon will be allowed sexual access to the girl is not explicit, but is surely there: why else raise the issue of his liking for χοιριδίοις? This is then our first clear indication in the play that Philocleon shares the interest of other 'comic heroes' (and most male Athenians) in heterosexual activity.

What of line 572? Commentators rightly see a pun on ἀρνός / ἄρρενος. But 'If you take pleasure in a lamb's / male's voice, please pity my boy's voice' is rather tame, and if the pleasure is meant to be musical, out of place, since exploitation of vocal and instrumental performers is introduced a little later (579–82). Most damning, however, are the repetition of φωνή, 'voice', and the lack of close parallel with 573. We need something to balance the χοιριδίοιϲ. Read ψωλῆι. For an older Athenian male, interest in χοιριδίοις would of course not exclude homosexual opportunism, and indeed in line

580 Philocleon claims as an advantage the chance to view boys' genitals at a δοκιμασία, 'testing for admission to manhood'. ψωλή is not the most obvious word to describe the son's penis, but I suggest it has been chosen to create a jingle with φωνή, by dittography of which it was then extruded at a relatively early stage in the paradosis (by *P.Oxy.* 1374, of the fifth or sixth century AD).

6 Lines 805–62

Philocleon has accepted his son's suggestion that a domestic court be set up, and Bdelycleon brings out a do-it-yourself kit. A chamber-pot, brazier, some soup, and a cock seem to be sufficient once supplemented by a mock shrine of Lycus, which, however represented (see MacDowell 1971 on 820), offers some visual justification for another joke about Cleonymus' lack of a ὅπλον / penis. The first case Bdelycleon begins to call is that of a Thracian slave-girl who has προσκαύσασα πρώιην τὴν χύτραν, 'scorched her pot the other day'. The effect on Philocleon is immediate and vehement: he complains of the absence of a railing, and rushes off-stage (832–3) to bring back a substitute which he identifies as a χοιροκομεῖον (844). Meanwhile a slave has reported the dog Labes' theft and consumption of a Sicilian cheese, and it is Labes' prosecution by the other κύων, 'Dog', that ultimately (891 ff.) furnishes a trial. The Thracian girl disappears from the script. Why was she introduced at all? The dramatically effective sequence of postponements resulting from the identification of yet more pieces of missing court furniture must indeed be started off by *some* interruption, and the mention of the Thracian girl's culinary clumsiness could be a false trail that leads nowhere. But it does *come* from somewhere, viz. 768 f.: here, in commending the notion of a domestic court, Bdelycleon offers as an example a house-slave who has covertly opened a door, and can be punished by Philocleon by a single ἐπιβολή, correctly seen by MacDowell 1971 as 'a pun: "fine" and "sexual violation"'. Taking his cue from his father's *agōn* speech, Bdelycleon knows that the offer of sexual gratification will not be without influence. Has that been forgotten by 828? I suggest that it has not. Philocleon has been led to suppose that a peccant slave-girl invites sexual violation. He is not the first Aristophanic old man to see Thracian slave-girls as easy game – cf. Dicaeopolis' fantasy as expressed in his phallic song at *Ach.* 263–79. Now Philocleon is confronted with a female slave who has not simply erred but whose error involves a scorched pot – primarily, of course, an expression to be taken literally, but the range of terms for cooking-pots that is also used of female genitalia is considerable, and I believe that the image here offers Philocleon and the audience such a *double entendre*, pointed up by the use of a participle which can also be used of the metaphorical inflammation by erotic passion.[6] It is contemplation of the prospect of 'punishing' the girl that, I suggest, precipitates Philocleon's departure. Until now he has been relatively passive, allowing Bdelycleon to supply the necessary equipment, and some special explanation is needed of why he now rushes off-stage himself.

So much I suggest confidently. I would also propose, more tentatively, that when the Thracian girl is mentioned by Bdelycleon at 828 she actually appears before Philocleon and the audience. On that reconstruction Philocleon hustles her off with him. In either case, his action provokes a comment from Bdelycleon: τί ποτε τὸ χρῆμ'; ὡς δεινὸν ἡ φιλοχωρία, 'What's up? How strange is his love of his place' (834). This φιλοχωρία, 'love of (a) place', is interpreted (where explanation is offered) as an attachment to the place that jury-service is normally conducted. But the cumulative effect of this scene has been to show that it is not the place but its paraphernalia that Philocleon finds important. φιλοχωρία is therefore puzzling and lame. When Philocleon returns, however, it is on his own submission not a χῶρος, 'place', that has been attracting him but a χοῖρος, 'piggy' (844). At 834 Aristophanes surely wrote φιλοχοιρία, 'love of piggies'. Philocleon's 'love of piggies', implied at 573, will be taken primarily in the sexual sense when the girl's mention or display provokes his scuttle off-stage.

He is away a little time (835–43). What is he carrying on his return? Bdelycleon's question 'What is this?' does not show that it is not something the audience can easily identify. And on one level, at least, it is a literal χοιροκομεῖον, 'pig-protector', since only that makes sense as a substitute for a δρύφακτος, 'railing'. But in the only other use of the term in Aristophanes (or indeed in Greek literature before second-century AD lexicographers!) its function seems to be to cover genitals, and although there (*Lys.* 1073) they are the manifestly male genitalia of the Spartan envoys, some pun on the element χοιρο- is surely intended. So too here. On one level the term evokes a railing that has been sacrilegiously plundered from a pen used to keep pigs for Hestia, but on another (that which I suggest that the production 'privileged', to lapse into modern jargon) it is a garment that covered a

[6] For the compound προσκαίω see Xen. *Smp.* 4.23; for the simple verb Ar. *Lys.* 9. For pot-terms cf. Henderson 1975, 143f. Griffith 1988, 33, arguing for an obscene sense for χύτρα, 'pot', at *V.* 938, thought that none of Aristophanes' other uses 'seems to demand a sexual overtone': if my suggestion is correct, it offers support to his interpretation of 938.

girl's χοῖρος, and was thus her last line of defence against sexual violation. The trophy that Philocleon brandishes tells all.

At 847 Philocleon settles down and professes himself in a mood for fining. Delay caused by Bdelycleon going off to get notices and indictments irritates Philocleon, and he explains the irritation by saying (850) ἐγὼ δ' ἀλοκίζειν ἐδεόμην τὸ χωρίον, 'but I wanted to start ploughing my little plot of land'. This is usually explained as a metaphor for entering his vote on his penalty tablet, but MacDowell concedes ambiguity. It is an odd expression to choose, but, if the traditional explanation is right, the oddity may be explained by another *double entendre*, with 'plough' in its frequent sexual sense, and χωρίον a euphemism for the part of the anatomy that is ploughed. Its close similarity in sound to χοιρίον will have reinforced this sense.

That Philocleon is now more interested in sex than dicastics is an important mark of his psychological reorientation. At 852–3 a character starts to run off-stage (οὗτος σύ, ποῖ θεῖς; 'You there, where are you running off to?', 854) to get voting-urns, and is forestalled by the interlocutor's suggestion that two ladles can serve. I set out the lines at issue:

τίς οὑτοσὶ
ὁ πρῶτός ἐστιν;
ἐς κόρακας. ὡς ἄχθομαι,
ὁτιὴ 'πελαθόμην τοὺς καδίσκους ἐκφέρειν.
οὗτος σύ, ποῖ θεῖς;
ἐπὶ καδίσκους.
μηδαμῶς.
ἐγὼ γὰρ εἶχον τούσδε τοὺς ἀρυστίχους.
κάλλιστα τοίνυν. πάντα γὰρ πάρεστι νῶιν
ὅσων δεόμεθα – πλήν γε δὴ τῆς κλεψύδρας.
ἡδὶ δὲ δὴ τίς ἐστιν; οὐχὶ κλεψύδρα;
εὖ γ' ἐκπορίζεις αὐτὰ κἀπιχωρίως.
ἀλλ' ὡς τάχιστα πῦρ τις ἐξενεγκάτω
καὶ μυρρίνας καὶ τὸν λιβανωτὸν ἔνδοθεν,
ὅπως ἂν εὐξώμεσθα πρῶτα τοῖς θεοῖς

Who speaks which line? MacDowell 1971, following Lowe 1962, gives 852b–853 to Bdelycleon, 854a to Philocleon, 854b to Bdelycleon, 854 c–855 to Philocleon, 856–7 to Bdelycleon, 858 to Philocleon, and finally 859–62 to Bdelycleon, on the ground that Bdelycleon is expected to provide all the equipment, while Philocleon is impatient to begin. Philocleon's rush off-stage at 832 (accepted by most editors) breaches the first generalisation, and the interpretation I have offered of 850 counts against the second. In fact impatience is shown rather by Bdelycleon at 824, and here too it is more appropriate that Philocleon should (once again) run off. Bdelycleon, aiming at dignity, is not elsewhere found running in this scene (as Philocleon is at 832). He does, however, tend to address his father by such brusque expressions as οὗτος σύ, 'You there!' (cf. 751 οὗτος, τί βοᾷς, 'You there, why are you shouting'; 1364 ὦ οὗτος οὗτος, 'You there, you there!'). The attribution should therefore be as follows:

851–3 Philocleon. Who is this first one? [Bdelycleon knows what the first case will be] To hell! [Getting up again and moving off-stage: for the phrase in his mouth cf. 982] How irritating, that I have forgotten to bring out the voting-urns!

854a *Bdelycleon*. You there, where are you running off to?

854b *Philocleon*. For voting-urns.

854c–855 *Bdelycleon*. Don't! I already had these ladles.

856 *Philocleon*. Splendid. Then we've got all we need – except, however, the water-clock. [*Philocleon makes a move to rush off again, and is forestalled by his son's remark*]

858 *Bdelycleon*. Then what's this? Isn't it a water-clock?

859 *Philocleon* [*grudgingly*]. Yes, you have laid these things on well and in the spirit of the place.

I am uncertain whether 860 continues Philocleon's remark – he has already uttered a number of prayers with features special to the courts (323 ff., 389 ff.) – or belongs to Bdelycleon and prepares us for 875–84. But the consequences of my proposed attribution for our view of Philocleon are not affected. This scene shows him first rushing off to violate the Thracian girl, then expressing an urge to repeat the experience (850), and finally making two further attempts to get off-stage, presumably for the same purpose, attempts that are forestalled by Bdelycleon. Apart from its inherent amusement (both slapstick and fantasy; for the latter cf. Dicaeopolis' phallic song at *Ach.* 263–79) and its further revelation of the extent of Philocleon's interest in sex, it turns out to be a preview of the scene at the end of the play where Bdelycleon is (significantly for their exchange of roles) far less successful in disentangling his father from the girl who is the object of his lust.

If my proposals are correct, then Philocleon's escapade after the symposium and the slapstick with his aged phallus pick up themes which have been introduced earlier in the play, and which can be added to the other features which show the final scenes to be carefully integrated with the play as a whole.[7]

[7] See Vaio 1971.

7 A Brief Conclusion

Since much of my argument has attempted to show that Philocleon is given many marks of the sort of sexual appetite that the man in the Athenian street would not disavow, it may be appropriate to conclude by offering a defence against the accusation once levelled against him by our honorand. Dover included in his charges against Philocleon the way his daughter extracts the three-obol juror's fee from his mouth at the end of a day in court (607–9). 'This kind of kiss was (naturally enough) known to the Greeks as highly erotic (e.g. *Th.* 130), and the passage is the only one in comedy which dares to hint at the enjoyment of incestuous contacts.'[8] I believe this can be rebutted. The initiative, after all, is taken by Philocleon's daughter, not by him. There is no hint in the language chosen that either party took sexual pleasure in the procedure – Aristophanes could easily have made this clear by using some form of καταγλωττισμός, 'French kiss', or κατεγλωττισμένος, 'lascivious', as (metaphorically, of a tune) at *Th.* 130, but he does not. Moreover, if some hint at incestuous pleasure were detectable, its uniqueness in comedy must be confined to our extant texts: there must be a strong chance that the accusation of incest against Cimon and Elpinice found in Plutarch's *Cimon* 4 derives from a comic poet (not from Stesimbrotus: cf. Jacoby on *FGrH* 107 F4). But I doubt that any suggestion of incest was intended by Aristophanes at 607–9, or that we should see Philocleon as the sort of man who spends his evenings 'running his hand up his daughter's skirt' (Dover 1972, 127). As I have tried to show, other men's daughters were in much greater danger.

[8] Dover 1972, 127. As to the other charges made, Philocleon's recollection of cowardice at Naxos has at least a precedent in a famous quatrain of Archilochus (fr. 5), if not in the characterisation of a 'comic hero', and it might be argued that his urge to go to court so as to κακόν τι ποῆσαι, 'do some harm', is not reprehensible if he believed that those whom he would harm were manifest enemies of the δῆμος, 'people'.

3 | Wine in Old Comedy (1995)

1 Introduction

The poets of Attic Old Comedy present wine as a central constituent of the good life and an important catalyst of well-being, provided that it is correctly used. This is hardly surprising in a form of entertainment which, from the early and mid-fifth century respectively, had played a large and formal part in the Great Dionysia and the Lenaea, two of the Athenians' major festivals in honour of Dionysus. These festivals were themselves characterised by both ceremonial and casual consumption of wine. This is made clear by other evidence,[1] even if we do not wholly accept the report of Philochorus that in the old days Athenian audiences had already consumed food and drink by the time they reached the theatre and continued to do so profusely throughout performances.[2] However some features of the presentation of wine are, if not surprising, at least remarkable, and cohere with many other elements of Old Comedy which show that, like tragedy, it had detached itself almost wholly from its religious context. It is striking, for example, how small a part is played by scenes in which wine is consumed on stage in a way that can be seen as ritual. This in turn will no doubt have made scenes in which wine was in any way ritually consumed all the more effective theatrically and, if I may so express it, theorically, that

[1] Cf. Pickard-Cambridge 1988, 30–4, on the possibility that *stamnoi* with maenadic scenes and then (ca. 440 BC) scenes with stately ladies consecrating wine may be linked with the Lenaea. For an instance of drunken behaviour during the πομπή, 'procession', see D. 19 (*In Midian*).180.

[2] *FGrH* 328 F171 (= Ath. 11.464e–f): λέγει δὲ περὶ τούτων ὁ Φιλόχορος οὑτωσί· "Ἀθηναῖοι τοῖς Διονυσιακοῖς ἀγῶσι τὸ μὲν πρῶτον ἠριστηκότες καὶ πεπωκότες ἐβάδιζον ἐπὶ τὴν θέαν, καὶ ἐστεφανωμένοι ἐθεώρουν·παρὰ δὲ τὸν ἀγῶνα πάντα οἶνος αὐτοῖς ᾠνοχοεῖτο καὶ τραγήματα παρεφέρετο. καὶ τοῖς χοροῖς εἰσιοῦσιν ἐνέχεον πίνειν, καὶ διηγωνισμένοις ὅτ' ἐξεπορεύοντο ἐνέχεον πάλιν, 'Philochorus says the following about them: "During their Dionysiac contests, the Athenians went to the spectacle after having lunched and drunk, and they watched wearing garlands. During the entire competition wine was poured for them and snacks were passed round, and when the choruses entered, they poured wine for them, and after their competition was finished and they were on their way out, they poured wine for them again"'. Cf. Ar. fr. 513 K–A (= 496 Kock) from Ταγηνισταί, '*Friers*'.

is, in relation to the overall agenda of the festival. But that is a by-product and not a reason for the paucity of such scenes, which is perhaps partly to be sought in the dramatists' wish to present scenes that must be perceived as drama and that could not be mistaken for ritual and real life.

2 Dramatic Limitations

Of course, the poet's ability to portray drinking by characters played by actors was constricted by the genre's limitation on their number (whether that limitation was formal or practical).[3] A symposium of typical size could not be played out on the stage by speaking characters. Accordingly, symposia in Old Comedy involving only characters played by actors must be narrated, whether in prospect or retrospect, or take an unusual form.

The narrated symposium is best exemplified by *Wasps*. First Bdelycleon's re-education of Philocleon sets out the normal sympotic pattern; then Philocleon's obtuse perversions anticipate what is later going to happen – off-stage.[4] Finally the disastrous events that actually took place at the party are reported by a slave and corroborated by Philocleon's reappearance on stage, blind-drunk, with a torch in one hand and a naked αὐλητρίς, 'female piper', in the other. The audience does not actually see Philocleon drinking here or in any other part of the play.

A distorted form of the symposium may plausibly be seen in the concluding scenes of some other plays of Aristophanes, where the central character, for whom Whitman's term 'comic hero' is not always appropriate, is launched upon climactic self-indulgence in wine, food and sex. This is a type of scene where the half-imaginary world of the play does overlap with the half-real world of the festival. No doubt many Athenian males in the audience recalled or hoped for some approximation to this ideal in the course of their own private celebrations during the festival.[5] But this sort of drinking is private rather than public and nearer to the secular than to the religious. That is so even if it can be overlaid with elements drawn from religious ritual, as it is in *Acharnians* where Dicaeopolis' competition with Lamachus draws on the ritual not of the Lenaea or Dionysia but

[3] Pickard-Cambridge 1988, 36, 149–53.

[4] Ar. *V.* 1122–1264, on which see Vetta 1976–7. Narrative of sympotic scenes is also found in Ar. fr. 482 K–A (= 466 Kock) from the *Proagon* (422 BC), and fr. 444 K–A (= 430 Kock) from the *Pelargoi* (ca. 400 BC).

[5] Note the interest in conducting an adulterous affair foisted by the chorus on members of the audience of *Birds* (*Av.* 793–6).

of the Anthesteria. Precisely because it involves one single character who drinks, this scene is not sympotic in the normal sense. Its combination of delights, however, can readily be associated with those of the symposium, since in the real world that will have been for many male Athenians one of the most likely contexts in which they might drink and engage in casual sex with αὐλητρίδες 'female pipers'. And Aristophanes does ask his audience to see it as a sort of symposium when he has Dicaeopolis refer to competition with his συμπόται, 'fellow symposiasts' (1135) and commend his situation with the words συμποτικὰ τὰ πράγματα, 'the situation is sympotic' (1142). For Aristophanes, of course, it was both necessary and expedient that this should be a one-man symposium – necessary because he could not use other actors in sufficient number to create a symposium, expedient because it emphasised the unique triumph of his central character.

There were indeed other, non-sympotic forms of drinking which actors might without difficulty portray. But here too the instances – usually representations of drinking in a bad light, as some I later consider show – are fewer than we might expect. The number of drunkards in our texts is remarkably small given that μεθύοντας, 'drunkards', are clearly seen as an important feature of Old Comedy by the writer of the *De comoedia* (who credits Crates with their introduction).[6]

The few cases of religious ritual drinking that might have involved actors seem also to have been kept off-stage. The celebration of the rural Dionysia by Dicaeopolis at *Ach.* 241–79 will in due course involve ritual drinking, but does not do so in the part of the ritual represented to the audience. We have fragments of Aristophanes' *Telmessians* relating to a ritual banquet, but that banquet was narrated, not played out on stage.[7] The one ritual use of wine that is not uncommon in stage-action is for libation – for example at *Peace* 424–38. But there is no indication that this or other libations were followed by drinking, far less finishing the cup ἄμυστιν, 'without taking breath', as urged in a fragment of Cratinus.[8]

[6] Anon. *De comoedia* (*Prolegomena de comoedia* iii) p. 8 = *PCG* iv Crates, *test.* 2a: πρῶτος μεθύοντας ἐν κωμωιδίαι προήγαγεν, 'he was the first to bring drunkards onstage in comedy'. The presence in Old Comedy of drunks may perhaps be corroborated by the vase cited in n.12 below, unless, of course, the conjecture made there about the identity of the φιλοπότης, 'alcoholic', is correct.

[7] Ar. frr. 545–6 K–A.

[8] Cratin. fr. 322 K–A (= 291 Kock), cf. fr. 132 K–A. (= 124 Kock), from his *Nomoi*, a reference to libations to snakes from a golden cup. By contrast Strepsiades denies that he will engage in libations at *Nu.* 426.

There was more scope for ritual drinking by a chorus, whether in a symposium or in a more specifically religious ritual. Twenty-four would have been an unusually large number of participants for an Attic symposium, but not perhaps impossible, and certainly within the known limits for some sorts of ritual banqueting.[9] A poet determined to represent a characteristic Attic symposium might have done so by dividing his χορευταί, 'chorus-men', into two groups of twelve, as was often done for other dramatic ends. But, as far as I know, no such scene was demonstrably created in Old Comedy. We have no title Συμπόται, '*Symposiasts*', or Συμπίνοντες, '*Fellow-drinkers*'. It may be that the accident of survival or the lack of such scenes' dramatic possibilities should be considered as explanations. We do, however, know of two plays entitled Κωμασταί, '*Comasts*', by Ameipsias and Phrynichus. These may have involved choral drinking, but no fragment establishes this. The same is true of Pherecrates' Αὐτόμολοι, '*Deserters*', but in the case of *Deserters* any drinking there may have been is unlikely to have been ritual (see further below, n.14).

One comedy whose title suggests that it might have involved ritual drinking of a more religious sort is Aristophanes' first play, Δαιταλῆς, '*Banqueters*'. The chorus seems to have consisted in θιασῶται, 'members of a religious group', of a cult of Heracles: but on our limited evidence they seem only to have come into the orchestra as a chorus after they had (supposedly) had their ritual δεῖπνον, 'banquet', in the precinct of Heracles.[10] A rather different sort of ritual drinking might also have taken place in one or more of the several plays entitled Σάτυροι, '*Satyrs*' – by Ecphantides, Cratinus, Phrynichus and perhaps Callias – but it is no more than a presumption that satyrs will have engaged in one of their two favourite activities (the other is of course sex).[11] When we turn, however, to comic representations of women engaged in cult, the picture is unambiguous: audiences of comedy were amused by the presentation of women's cults as an excuse for heavy drinking – so, for example, Aristophanes in his *Women at the Thesmophoria* (especially 630–2), in the oath scene of *Lysistrata* (194 ff.), and in his lost Ἀδωνιάζουσαι, '*Women at the festival of Adonis*', and Σκηνὰς λαμβάνουσαι, '*Women in festival-huts*'. The same is likely for the Βάκχαι, '*Bacchants*', of Diocles and Lysippus.

[9] Cf. Bergquist 1990. [10] Cassio 1977, 21–3 and his *test.* h = K–A *test.* iii (a) (*ad finem*).

[11] For a *Satyrs* in 437 BC, probably by Callias, see K–A iv 38 *test.*4; for one by Cratinus in 424 BC (when it was second to Ar. *Eq.*) see *hypothesis* to *Eq.* A5; by Ecphantides, see K–A v, Ecphantides frs. 1 and 2; and by Phrynichus, see K–A vii Phrynichus *test.* 1 = *Suda* φ 763 *s.v.* Φρύνιχος.

3 Sex, Age and Class

This offers a convenient transition to a different approach. I return later to sympotic aspects of drinking, but now I wish to explore how the comic perception of wine and of drinking differs according to the sex, age and class of the drinker. It will emerge that drinking by zeugite males in company is usually perceived as good; that drinking by males of a higher or lower class, or by a zeugite solo (*en Suisse*) can often be seen as bad; that drinking by females is invariably regarded as bad; and the older the women are, the worse it is regarded.

Part of the rationale of these perceptions is that sympotic drinking is kept orderly by the rules of the symposium (when these are contravened, as by Philocleon in *Wasps*, even sympotic drinking is no longer laudable), whereas the other types of drinking are not moderated by that or by any other principle of order. But this is only a partial explanation. Upper-class Athenians, χρηστοί, 'good men', are branded with a penchant for drinking in the opening dialogue between the slaves in *Wasps* 77–80 – they are φιλοπόται, 'fond of drink' – though the categorisation of this as a *νόσος*, 'disease', should not be pressed, since that is required by the poet's intention of presenting Philocleon's addiction to jury-service as a disease. It may be doubted whether there was indeed a greater fondness for drink among the upper classes, but no doubt their symposia were more lavish, and the zeugites who constituted the majority of the spectators in the theatre could interpret more generous provision of wine as reflecting a stronger attachment to its consumption. Moreover the term φιλοπότης seems not to involve very serious criticism. A character in Eupolis' *Cities* used it of Cimon – καλὸς μὲν οὐκ ἦν, φιλοπότης δὲ κἀμελής, 'He was not handsome, but fond of drink and careless' (fr. 221 K–A = 208 Kock) – suggesting an indulgent tut-tutting rather than identification of a grave moral weakness. The same mixture of the positive and negative may be there in its use on an Apulian vase of ca. 380–360 BC to label an old man in a comedy who is tottering home from a party, carrying a torch and wine vessel.[12] There is criticism, not untinged with envy, of the symposia at which the depraved young man in *Banqueters* drank special wine (from Chios) out of imported

[12] See Greifenhagen 1975, who, like other scholars hitherto, took the figure to be a Phlyax: but as Taplin 1993 argues, the comic scenes on South Italian vases of the fourth century – before the composition of Phlyax plays is attested – more probably refer to Attic Old Comedy. We should therefore consider whether the old man on this vase is actually 'Cratinus' in his Πυτίνη, '*Wine-flask*' (see below, p. with nn.40–42).

Laconian vessels and sang rude songs.[13] But this behaviour cannot have been seen as wholly alien, since singing was a part of most symposia, and, as we shall see, the audience was reckoned to be familiar with the features of Chian and other imported wines. More alien, perhaps, were the bibulous habits with which Αὐτόμολοι, '*Deserters*', as a class are charged;[14] or at least they could be perceived as the behaviour of 'the other' by those zeugites who dutifully performed their hoplite service.

Χρηστοί, 'good men', and αὐτόμολοι, 'deserters', are the only groups of male citizens lambasted as φιλοπόται, 'fond of drink'. It is easier to find individual Athenians who are represented as too fond of drink, sometimes with the hint that their drinking was solitary. Alongside Cimon, mentioned above, they include a potter Chaerestratus, suggested by Phrynichus in his *Comasts* (fr. 15 K–A = 15 Kock) to be capable (were he able to tope all day at home) of knocking back 100 κάνθαροι, 'two-handled bowls', of wine daily. Among Aristophanes' dramatic characters Philocleon in his great defence of his lifestyle in the *agōn* claims that if his son does not pour him wine he drinks direct from his ὄνος, 'flagon' (616–7), hinting at solitary and excessive drinking, and preparing the audience for his excesses later in the play.

By contrast citizen women are repeatedly presented as inveterate tipplers and, when given the chance, as consuming wine in excessive quantities or in an unacceptably strong mixture. This perception is of course part of a wider web of fear and suspicion that was interwoven with other emotions in Athenian citizens' attitudes to their womenfolk.[15] It is clearest in *Women at the Thesmophoria*, where one of the charges that the women level against Euripides is that he has portrayed women as bibulous, a charge to which they object not because it is false but because it is true (*Th.* 689ff.). This is not just a joke devised to help along the plot, but a comic stereotype well-documented elsewhere in Aristophanes and other poets of Old Comedy. In Aristophanes we find it in *Lysistrata* (200ff.), produced, like *Women at the Thesmophoria*, in 411 BC. Again, in *Women in festival-huts*,

[13] Ar. fr. 225 K–A (= 216 Kock): ἀλλ᾽ οὐ γὰρ ἔμαθε ταῦτ᾽ ἐμοῦ πέμποντος, ἀλλὰ μᾶλλον πίνειν, ἔπειτ᾽ ᾄδειν κακῶς, Συρακοσίαν τράπεζαν Συβαριτίδας τ᾽ εὐωχίας καὶ 'Χῖον ἐκ Λακαινᾶν', <καὶ κατα>μεθυ<σθῆν᾽> ἡδέως τε καὶ φίλως, '*That*'s not what he learned when I sent him along, but rather to drink, and to sing badly, Syracusan cuisine and Sybaritic feasts, and "Chian wine from Laconian cups", and to get drunk in pleasant and friendly manner'. On Chian, see below n.34.

[14] Pherecr. fr. 34 K–A = 29 Kock: see below, n.28.

[15] The classic treatment remains that of Gould 1980. For a good recent discussion with the previous decade's bibliography see Winkler 1990.

in which women appear to have contested with men the occupation of σκηναί, 'huts' or 'tents', provided for a festival, a woman complains about the loss or breakage of her λήκυθος, 'oil-flask', its capacity comically exaggerated to seven κοτύλαι, 'measures'.[16] Finally at the end of Aristophanes' career, in his *Cocalus*, produced at the Dionysia of 388/7 BC, there was a sung description of an orgy:

ἄλλαι ὑποπρεσβύτεραι γρᾶες Θασίου μέλανος
μεστὸν κεραμευομέναις κοτύλαις μεγάλαις
ἔγχεον ἐς σφέτερον δέμας οὐδένα κόσμον,
ἔρωτι βιαζόμεναι μέλανος οἴνου ἀκράτου

Other, somewhat more elderly crones had got black Thasian,
a vessel-full, and with specially potted large measures
were pouring it into their own bodies, without any ceremony,
compelled by lust for the unmixed black wine.[17]

Other comic poets present the same caricature. It was already there in a play in which Cratinus seems to have parodied Euripides' *Stheneboea*: the heroine drank wine either undiluted or mixed with an equal proportion of water, calling on Bellerophon as she played *kottabos*:

πιεῖν δὲ θάνατος οἶνον ἢν ὕδωρ ἐπῆι.
ἀλλ' ἴσον ἴσωι μάλιστ' ἀκράτου δύο χόας
πίνουσ' ἀπ' ἀγκύλης ἐπονομάζουσ' ἅμα
ἵησι λάταγας τῶι Κορινθίωι πέει.

But it is death to drink wine if water has the upper hand;
but two flagons of unmixed wine, diluted roughly half and half
is what she drinks, and at the same time with bent arm
she throws wine-drops, naming them for the prick from Corinth.[18]

In his play *Tyranny*, exploiting the theme of a state run by women, Pherecrates had a male speaker (probably the κορυφαῖος, 'chorus-leader')

[16] Ar. fr. 487 K–A = 472 Kock: a κοτύλη, 'measure', contained six of the usual dispensing unit, κύαθοι, 'ladels'.

[17] Fr. 364 K–A = 350 Kock: the text, from Ath. 11.478d, is differently restored by different editors: I print that of Henderson 2008. In fr. 365 K–A (= 351 Kock) from the same play a character narrates how vomiting had been precipitated by the consumption of unmixed wine, but it is not certain that the speaker is one of these old ladies. For the charge that women exploited ritual occasions to get drunk cf. *Lys.* 194ff., *Th. passim*, *Ec.* 132ff.

[18] Cratin. fr. 299 K–A (= 273 Kock).

complain that for men the women had had made flat drinking-vessels that held nothing, for themselves deep cups, like wine-ships, so that they could drink as much wine as they could, unmonitored:

> εἶθ᾽ ὅταν τὸν οἶνον αὐτὰς αἰτιώμεθ᾽ ἐκπιεῖν,
> λοιδοροῦνται κὠμνύουσι μὴ ᾽κπιεῖν ἀλλ᾽ ἢ μίαν.
> ἡ δὲ κρείττων ἡ μί᾽ ἐστὶ χιλίων ποτηρίων.
>
> Then when we accuse them of drinking up the wine,
> they start abusing us, and swear they have only drunk one cup:
> but that one outdoes a thousand of our vessels.[19]

Sometimes the charge is directed more specifically against old women. An early use of drunken old women on the comic stage is credited to Phrynichus by Aristophanes in the passage of the revised *Clouds* where he accuses Eupolis of having plagiarised his *Knights* in the *Maricas*:[20]

> Εὔπολις μὲν τὸν Μαρικᾶν πρώτιστον παρείλκυσεν
> ἐκστρέψας τοὺς ἡμετέρους Ἱππέας κακὸς κακῶς,
> προσθεὶς αὐτῷ γραῦν μεθύσην τοῦ κόρδακος οὕνεχ᾽,
> ἣν Φρύνιχος πάλαι πεποίηχ᾽, ἣν τὸ κῆτος ἤσθιεν.
>
> First of all Eupolis dragged Maricas onstage
> disfiguring our *Knights* weakly, weak as he is,
> adding to it a drunken crone for the sake of her lewd dance,
> the one Phrynichus long ago created, the one the sea-monster tried
> to eat.

But, once introduced, the caricature of the drunken old woman was assured of a long stage-existence.[21] Thus in Pherecrates' *Corianno* the eponymous heroine's old nurse, Glyce, comes thirsty from her bath, responds eagerly to the offer of a drink, but vehemently prohibits use of a small κοτυλίσκη, 'little

[19] Pherecr. fr. 152.8–10 K–A (= 143.8–10 Kock). Cf. fr. 207 K–A (= 192 Kock), where Pherecr. is said to have slandered women in connection with taking a Chian cup down from its peg.

[20] Ar. *Nub.* 553–6: cf. Phryn. fr. 77 K–A (= 71 Kock), and for an illustration of an old and ugly woman dancing vigorously and (one would guess) drunkenly, Trendall and Webster 1971, 129 no. iv 12.

[21] The charge is not made in early iambic poetry. Neobule is accused of many things, but not drink, even when old, unless Archil. fr. 42 relates to her. Hipponax's Arete drinks copiously, but no more than her sexual partner: cf. frr. 13–14. Semonides' long list of charges against wives in fr. 7 omits tippling.

measure': it has made her ill, and the bigger one must be used. In another fragment that seems to follow closely on, Glyce is upset by the mixture:

ΓΛΥΚΗ. ὑδαρῆ 'νέχεέν σοι; Α. παντάπασι μὲν οὖν ὕδωρ.
ΓΛΥΚΗ. τί εἰργάσω; πῶς ὦ κατάρατε <δ'>ἐνέχεας;
Β. δύ' ὕδατος, ὦ μάμμη.
　　　　　　　　ΓΛΥΚΗ. τί δ' οἴνου; Β. τέτταρας.
ΓΛΥΚΗ. ἔρρ' ἐς κόρακας. βατράχοισιν οἰνοχοεῖν σ' ἔδει.

GLYCE: 'Has he poured you a watery mixture?' Interlocutor: 'No, it's entirely water.'
GLYCE: [to the wine-pourer] 'What have you done? What proportions did you pour, you cursed creature?'
WINE-POURER: 'Two of water, granny'.
GLYCE: 'And what of wine?'
WINE-POURER: 'Four'.

Two of water to three of wine was the accepted strength, so when the pourer replies 'four' we know that he had indeed meant to give Glyce a stronger mixture. But she is outraged, and would have liked something much stronger:

ΓΛΥΚΗ. ἔρρ' ἐς κόρακας. βατράχοισιν οἰνοχοεῖν σ' ἔδει.
GLYCE: 'Go to hell. You ought to be a wine-pourer to frogs.'[22]

The *Corianno* scene was clearly made all the funnier by Glyce's age. Likewise in Philyllius' *Auge* the drinking (uncondemned) of men and boys is contrasted with the pleasure of old women in plentiful wine:

　　　　　　πάντα γὰρ ἦν
μέστ' ἀνδρῶν <καὶ> μειρακίων
πινόντων, ὁμοῦ † δ' ἄλλων
γραιδίων μεγάλαισιν οἴ-
　　　νου χαίροντα λεπασταῖς.

　　　　　　for everywhere
was full of men and youths
drinking, and together there were others,
old women, enjoying large
　　　flagons of wine.[23]

[22] Pherecr. fr. 76.2–5 K–A (= 70.2–5 Kock), following fr. 75 K–A = 69 Kock. It may also have been in his *Corianno* that Pherecr. had a woman described as ἀνδροκάπραινα καὶ μεθύση καὶ φαρμακίς, 'he-goatess and drunkard, and witch', fr. 186 K–A (= Phot. α 1771). For women's predilection for neat wine cf. Ar. *Lys.* 197, 200–201, *Ec.* 153–5, 1123–4.

[23] Philyll. fr. 5 K–A = fr. 5 Kock.

Another improper use of wine is illustrated by the behaviour of slaves. The line that divides good and bad drinking can be seen in Aristophanes' *Knights*. To escape from their predicament Nicias suggests death by drinking bull's blood, but Demosthenes proposes drinking unmixed wine, as in honour of the ἀγαθὸς δαίμων, 'Good divinity', and praises wine's capacity to nurture human fantasy – a case not of *in vino vera* but of *in vino vana*. In broad daylight he reclines and gets Nicias to steal wine from the house of Demos, where the reviled Paphlagonian, standing for Cleon, is snoring on his back already drunk. Demosthenes has Nicias pour him a large libation, and despite Nicias' urging him to pour it as a libation to the ἀγαθὸς δαίμων he gulps it down himself: then a plan does indeed strike him, that of stealing the Paphlagonian's oracles.[24]

Although there are some elements in this scene that touch on real or comic images of the politicians, such as Nicias' piety and inclination to sobriety, the charge of proclivity to drink is not elsewhere brought against Demosthenes. The similar scene in *Wasps* 19ff., when one of the two slaves may have been drinking, suggests that in *Knights* this penchant for unmixed wine relates to masters' perceptions of their house-slaves. However in the case of Cleon/ the Paphlagonian the charge is repeated later and associated with gluttony: the Paphlagonian ridicules the sausage-seller for waterdrinking, and he in return asks what the Paphlagonian has done for the city by drinking – the Paphlagonian replies that he will gorge himself on tunny, knock back neat wine, and then abuse the generals at drinking – the Paphlagonian replies that he will gorge himself on tunny, knock back neat wine, and then abuse the generals at Pylus.[25] The link with gluttony is important: Cleon's consumption of unmixed wine is an aspect of his excessive consumption in general, and he is not being picked on simply as φιλοπότης. But his declaration that he will drink unmixed wine classes his use of wine with that of Demosthenes (in his dramatic role as a slave) and apart from that of respectable citizens.

4 Citizens and Wine

How then do respectable citizens take their wine? The formal answer 'at the right time and in due quantity' can be given fairly precise content. Drinking during the day is reprehensible. It should happen after a δεῖπνον, 'dinner',

[24] Ar. *Eq*. 80–125.

[25] Ar. *Eq*. 349–58, esp. 353–5: 'ἐμοὶ γὰρ ἀντέθηκας ἀνθρώπων τίν'; ὅστις εὐθὺς | θύννεια θερμὰ καταφαγών, κᾆιτ' ἐπιπιὼν ἀκράτου | οἴνου χοᾶ κασαλβάσω τοὺς ἐν Πύλωι στρατηγούς', 'Then with whom in the world have you compared me? I'll polish off hot tuna straight away, then wash it down with a pitcher of unmixed wine, and whore the generals at Pylus!' For a drunken female slave cf. *Pax* 535.

which in turn belongs at the end of the day, when men's shadows are seven or ten feet long.[26] Indeed the mid-day self-indulgence that brings on sleep can be dismissed as a shortcut to the underworld.[27]

Even worse is the behaviour described in Pherecrates' *Deserters* – presumably but not certainly referring to the eponymous deserters – drinking and getting drunk before the *agora* is full. Its discreditable image is confirmed by Eupolis, who has Alcibiades claim drinking early in the day as his invention, along with the practice of calling for a chamber-pot in mid drinking-bout.[28]

For drinkers at the symposium after a δεῖπνον the sympotic order will allow πίνειν, 'drinking', that does not lead to μεθύειν, 'getting drunk'. Wine will be consumed along with τραγήματα, 'snacks', which will reduce its intoxicating effect and enhance the pleasure of drinking.[29] It will be served by waiters who have been trained, as in Pherecrates' Δουλοδιδάσκαλος, '*Trainer of slaves*', to pour wine through a strainer into a clean κύλιξ, 'cup';[30] who add water in the proportions prescribed by the symposiarch; and who may include οἰνοπόται, 'wine-tasters', whose specific task is to monitor these proportions.[31] Among the games played at symposia is one involving wine itself, *kottabos*, which can almost be used as a metaphor for drinking.[32] Drinking can also lead to proposing riddles, telling μῦθοι, 'myths' or 'stories', and singing, a tradition given less prominence

[26] Ar. *Ec.* 651, cf. fr. 695 K–A = 675 Kock.

[27] Pherecr. 85 K–A = 80 Kock, from Κραπαταλοί, '*Sprats*', with Kock's interpretation (cited by K–A).

[28] Pherecr. 34 K–A = 29 Kock, cf. Eup. 385 K–A = 351 Kock.

[29] Ar. *Ec.* 306, and the mini-symposium set up in Pherecr. *Corianno* fr. 73 K–A = 67 Kock, though here the elegant imitation is deflated by the refusal of beans as bad for the breath. For the distinction between the potentially good activity πίνειν, 'to drink', and the bad μεθύειν, 'to get drunk', cf. Ar. frr. 225 K–A = 216 Kock from *Banqueters*, where πίνειν, 'to drink', accompanied by song, is part of traditional education, and 135 K–A (= Phot. α 2926) from Γῆρας, '*Old Age*', where it is said of a man ὁ δὲ μεθύων ἤμει παρὰ τοὺς ἀρχηγέτας 'but he, drunk, began to vomits beside the statues of the eponymous tribal heroes'; and *Eq.* 1400, where the sausage-seller says the Paphlagonian μεθύων ταῖς πόρναισι λοιδορήσεται, 'drunk, will hurl abuse at whores'. But πίνειν can be used of excessive drinking, as by Philocleon in his parodic *schetliasmos* at *V.* 1253–5.

[30] Pherecr. 45 K–A = 41 Kock.

[31] Cf. Eup. fr. 219 K–A= 205 Kock, from Πόλεις '*Cities*'. On the proportions themselves cf. Eup. 6 K–A. = 8 Kock, Ameipsias 4 K–A = 4 Kock, Hermipp. 24 K–A = 25 Kock (all five of water and two of wine); Diocles 7 K–A = 6 Kock (four and two); Ar. *Eq.* 1187–8 (with van Leeuwen's note) and Cratin. 195 K–A = 183 Kock (three and two); and Cratin. 196 K–A = 184 Kock (equal proportions).

[32] Ar. fr. 960 K–A (= *adesp.* 586 Kock). Cf. Cratin. fr. 124 K–A (= 116 Kock) from his *Nemesis*: τὸν δὲ κότταβον προθέντας συμποτικοῖσι νόμοις, 'and setting up the *kottabos* according to the sympotic rules'; and fr. 299 K–A (= 273 Kock) of Stheneboea's drinking (cf. above, n.18); Hermipp. fr. 48 K–A = 47 Kock.

in comic drama than in archaic song, and mocked in *Banqueters* and by Pheidippides in *Clouds*.[33]

Drink can also lead on to sex. I shall later look more closely at the link set up between wine and sex in *Acharnians*, where it is integral to the purpose of the play. But the link is clear elsewhere too. A fragment of Aristophanes calls wine Ἀφροδίτης γάλα, 'the milk of Aphrodite', and in his second *Women at the Thesmophoria* a character said:

> οἶνον δὲ πίνειν οὐκ ἐάσω Πράμνιον,
> οὐ Χῖον, οὐχὶ Θάσιον, οὐ Πεπαρήθιον,
> οὐδ' ἄλλον ὅστις ἐπεγερεῖ τὸν ἔμβολον.
>
> I shall not allow (? him) to drink Pramnian,
> not Chian, not Thasian, not Peparethian wine,
> nor any other that will rouse the battering-ram.[34]

This passage shows that, just as the Attic theatre audience could be relied upon to distinguish appropriate and inappropriate proportions, so too it was expected to have some, albeit modest, level of connoisseurship. The prized wines were all imported.[35] So too when one of characters promised wines that were not to cause hangovers: Lesbian, Chian, Thasian, Biblian (from Thrace) and Mendaean.[36] Phrynichus (in his Ποάστριαι, '*Grass-cutters*'?) compared Sophocles to wine that was οὐ γλύξις, οὐδ' ὑπόχυτος, ἀλλὰ Πράμνιος, 'not bland or diluted, but Pramnian'. Athenaeus quotes Aristophanes (meaning a character in Aristophanes) who οὐχ ἥδεσθαι Ἀθηναίους φησί, λέγων τὸν Ἀθηναίων δῆμον, οὔτε ποιηταῖς ἥδεσθαι σκληροῖς καὶ ἀστεμφέσιν οὔτε πραμνίοις οἴνοις συνάγουσι τὰς ὀφρῦς τε καὶ τὴν κοιλίαν, ἀλλ' <ἀνθ>οσμίαι καὶ πέπονι νεκταροσταγεῖ, '"the Athenian people", he said, "did not like poets who were tough and unyielding nor Pramnian wines which contracted your eyebrows and belly, but flowery wine and mature nectar-drop"'.[37] Only Dionysus, so far as we know, may perhaps have demanded wine from that island linked to him in the Ariadne myth, Naxos.[38]

33 Ar. Δαιταλῆς, '*Banqueters*', fr. 225 K–A = 216 Kock; *Nu.* 1354–72.

34 Ar. fr. 613 K–A = 596 Kock; 334 = 317 Kock.

35 Cf. Ar. fr. 435 K–A = 423 Kock, ὕρχας οἴνου, jars of wine', from Ὀλκάδες, '*Merchant vessels*'.

36 Philyllius fr. 23 K–A = 24 Kock. For Chian cf. Ar. fr. 546 K–A = 531 Kock, for Mendaean Cratin. fr. 195 K–A = 183 Kock; for Thasian Ar. *Lys.* 196; *Pl.* 1021, fr. 364 K–A = 350 Kock from *Cocalus*, cf. above n.17. Mendaean, Magnesian, Thasian and Chian are all praised at Hermipp. fr. 77 K–A = 82 Kock, while Peparethian is dismissed as fit for enemies.

37 Phryn. fr. 68 K–A = 65 Kock; Ar. fr. 688 K–A = 579 Kock. Note also the term καπνίας, 'smoky', in Cratin. fr. 462 K–A = 334 Kock.

38 Eup. fr. 271 K–A = 253 Kock, from *Taxiarchs* (the speaker is uncertain): δίδου μασᾶσθαι Ναξίας ἀμυγδάλας | οἶνόν τε πίνειν Ναξίων ἀπ' ἀμπέλων, 'Give me Naxian almonds to chew, and wine to drink from Naxian grapes'.

This last comparison may serve to introduce my two final themes, both of which concern the symbolic use of wine, and both of which corroborate the importance of wine as an element in the good life.

5 Wine and Poetic Composition

First I consider the close relation portrayed as linking the drinking of wine and the production of comic poetry. Archilochus (fr. 120) had already proclaimed a link between the consumption of wine and the composition of another form of poetry specially connected with Dionysus, the dithyramb. But it was left to Cratinus, in a magnificent fantasy of self-caricature, to create a dramatic character, Μέθη, 'Drunkenness', and have her contest control of the poet himself with another personification, Κωμωιδία, 'Comedy'. No wonder that the play, Πυτίνη, '*Wine-flask*', won first prize in the Dionysia of 424/3. Cratinus' relationship with Comedy is presented as prior to that with Drunkenness: she had been his wife, abandoned by him when he took up with Drunkenness. But the allegory is complex. Cratinus' attraction to drink is particularised in his weakness for individual wines, represented, since οἶνος, 'wine', is masculine, as young boys:

> νῦν δ' ἢν ἴδηι Μενδαῖον ἡβῶντ' ἀρτίως
> οἰνίσκον, ἕπεται κἀκολουθεῖ καὶ λέγει,
> 'οἴμ' ὡς ἁπαλὸς καὶ λευκός. ἆρ' οἴσει τρία;'
>
> But if he sees a Mendaean, just coming to adolescence,
> a young wine, he follows it and trails after it, and says:
> 'My god! How soft and white he is! Will he take three?'[39]

A similar *double entendre* on the technical terminology of proportions is exploited in the line τὸν δ' ἴσον ἴσωι φέροντ'· ἐγὼ δ' ἐκτήκομαι, 'and another who goes half and half: meanwhile I waste away'.[40] It will have been such scenes as this that gave a cue to ancient biography for its representation of Cratinus as φιλοπότης καὶ παιδικῶν ἡττημένος.[41] Even more influential, and taken up half-seriously by later poets, was one of Cratinus' defences: ὕδωρ

[39] Cratin. fr. 195 K–A = 183 Kock. For the proportions see above n.31.
[40] Cratin. fr. 196 K–A = 195 Kock.
[41] Suda κ 2344 *s.v.* Κρατῖνος: for the possibility that this image was also picked up by a vase-painter see above n.12; cf. Ath. 10.428f = Ar. T55 K–A, asserting that Aristophanes used to compose drunk.

δὲ πίνων οὐδὲν ἂν τέκοι σοφόν, 'if you drink water you could never produce a work of art'.[42]

Clever and theatrically effective though the idea of the *Wine-flask* was, it should not be interpreted as making a serious statement about the relationship between wine and the composition of poetry. It is a jeu d'esprit in which a typical ploy of Old Comedy, the personification of common phenomena in the audience's life, is ingeniously applied to subject-matter that was already firmly at home in the genre: and it is one in which Cratinus would hardly have indulged if he had expected his audience to view fondness for wine as wholly disreputable.

6 Wine, Peace and Plenty

There is a more serious purpose in the second symbolic use of wine, with which I conclude, the occasions where it appears in visions of peace and plenty. Ideal worlds are regularly imagined as providing an amplitude of wine. Admittedly wine plays a smaller role in these than food, and some descriptions of plenty have no reference to wine at all, at least in the form in which they survive.[43] In attempting to explain this I am not sure how much weight should be given to the fact that man can live by food and water, but not by wine alone; how much to the incomparably wider range of foods that an Attic poet can exploit in building up that favourite comic device, a list; and how much to the fact that in Attica of the fifth century and later food shortages could easily occur, whereas domestic production of wine could if necessary meet the demands of the home market. Nevertheless, wine remains important. In a picture of the golden age in Pherecrates' *Persians* a chorus imagines how Zeus will rain smoky wine.[44] His Μεταλλεῖς, '*Miners*', had a long description of the foods on offer in the underworld (thirty-three lines are quoted by Athenaeus) which include four lines on fragrant wine,

[42] Cratin. fr. 203 K–A = 199 Kock (from Nicaenetus *AP* 13.29 = *HE* Nicaenetus 5, cf. Hor. *Epist.* 1.19.1–2): ὕδωρ δὲ πίνων οὐδὲν ἂν τέκοις σοφόν, 'but if you drank water you would not give birth to anything clever'.

[43] Philyll. frr. 12 K–A (= 13 Kock), 18 K–A. (= 19 Kock), 26 K–A (= 27 Kock); Pherecr. fr. 50 K–A (= 45 Kock); Hermipp. fr. 63 K–A (twenty-three lines listing imports mostly of food, none of wine).

[44] Pherecr. fr. 137.6–8 K–A (= 130 Kock) (the fragment has ten lines in all): ὁ Ζεὺς δ' ὕων οἴνωι καπνίαι κατὰ τοῦ κεράμου βαλανεύσει, | ἀπὸ τῶν δὲ τεγῶν ὀχετοὶ βοτρύων μετὰ ναστίσκων πολυτύρων | ὀχετεύσονται θερμῶι σὺν ἔτνει καὶ λειριοπολφανεμώναις, 'Zeus will give a bath to the roof tiles, sending down rain that is smoky wine, and from the roofs will be channeled down channels of grapes with cheese-cakes, along with hot broth and lily rice puddings'.

sloshed out into full cups to all who want it by nubile girls scantily enough clad to show off their elegantly styled pubic hair:[45]

> κόραι δ᾽ ἐν ἀμπεχόναις τριχάπτοις ἀρτίως
> ἡβυλλιῶσαι καὶ τὰ ῥόδα κεκαρμέναι
> πλήρεις κύλικας οἴνου μέλανος ἀνθοσμίου
> ἤντλουν διὰ χώνης τοῖσι βουλομένοις πιεῖν.

> And young girls in fine-spun wraps, just reaching
> the prime of their adolescence and with their roses trimmed,
> were ladling cups of black, fragrant wine
> through a funnel for those who wanted to drink.

In his Ταγηνισταί, '*Friers*', Aristophanes too envisaged starting drinking as soon as we reach the underworld.[46]

More realistically the peaceful life of the Attic countryside involves harvesting grapes and drinking wine.[47] In Aristophanes' Νῆσοι, '*Islands*', it included the bleating of sheep and the sound of 'wine-lees being thrust into a λεκάνη, 'bowl', and ὁ μέν τις ἀμπέλους τρυγῶν ἄν, ὁ δ᾽ ἀμέργων ἐλάας, 'one man harvesting vines, another gathering olives'.[48] But the fullest and most complex elaboration of the intimate relation between wine and the ideal life is offered in his *Acharnians*. Here wine appears time and again as a symbol of the peace that Dicaeopolis seeks, pointed up by occasional illustrations of the abuse of wine which act as foils to the images of its correct use.[49]

The theme is introduced in a low key: in his catalogue of city woes Dicaeopolis complains (35) that ὄξος (*vin ordinaire* / *Tafelwein*),[50] along with charcoal and olive oil, is something he has never before had to buy. By contrast we shortly hear that the Athenian envoys to Persia had been drinking ἄκρατον οἶνον ἡδύν, 'unmixed sweet wine', from crystal and gold cups (73–4). By then there has already been the first mention (at 52 by Amphitheus)

[45] Pherecr. fr. 113.28–31 K–A, quoted by Ath. 6.269b–c.

[46] Ar. fr. 504 K–A (= 488 Kock): for the idea in serious speculation about the afterlife see *PCG ad loc.*

[47] For the link in Attic comedy between ideas of a golden age and the peace and plenty of the countryside see Cassio 1985, 27–33; for Aristophanes' support for peace in the 420s see Athanassaki 2018.

[48] Ar. frr. 402 K–A (= 387 Kock) and 406 K–A (= *adesp.* 437 Kock). Cf. *Peace* 535 τρυγοίπου, προβατίων βληχωμένων, 'a wine-filter, sheep bleating', and 578, and the praise of Attica that emphasizes mid-winter grapes, fr. 581 K–A (= 569 Kock) from the Ὧραι, '*Seasons*'.

[49] See the basic discussions of Newiger 1957, 52–3, 104–6 and 1980, 22–4. In other comedians cf. Hermipp. fr. 48 K–A for a link between *kottabos* and peace; his fr. 55 K–A takes a wine-cup's relegation to its peg as a mark of war.

[50] Only to be drunk when wine of quality is not available: cf. Eup. fr. 355 K–A (= 326 Kock).

of a treaty with Sparta. The term he uses, σπονδαί, is ambiguous, connoting both the treaty's contract and the libations of wine that will seal it. At 178–83 we learn that the Acharnians have caught a whiff of the σπονδαί carried by Amphitheus and have protested at his act – a protest based on the violence that has been done to their vines ἀμπέλων τετμημένων, 'vines cut down'. Again at 232 the enemy's trampling of their vines is chosen as the symbol of his aggression.[51]

The analogy between σπονδαί and wine is entertainingly elaborated at 187–203. The σπονδαί come in three flavours, of five, ten and thirty years. The thirty-year σπονδαί have a bouquet of ambrosia and nectar,[52] and of no need to keep three days of provisions in stock. In Dicaeopolis' mouth they speak to him of freedom of movement. Dicaeopolis' response opens with the ecstatic ὦ Διονύσια, 'O Dionysia', and announces that he will use his freedom of movement to celebrate the rural Dionysia.

When part of that celebration is enacted, Dicaeopolis' hymn to Phales (263–79) does not give first place to drink. The earlier lines of his song focus on casual sex – with boys, with other men's wives and with the Thracian slave-girl of Strymodorus. But he concludes with a parodic vow – ἐὰν μεθ' ἡμῶν ξυμπίῃς, ἐκ κραιπάλης | ἕωθεν εἰρήνης ῥοφήσεις τρύβλιον, 'if you drink with us, you will slurp up a little cup of peace the morning after' (277–8).

It might be fanciful to see the theme of wine given a further subtle twist in the fact that at 420 the first ragged character whom Euripides offers to Dicaeopolis is Oeneus, or in Dicaeopolis' order to his θυμός, 'heart', at 484: οὐκ εἶ καταπιὼν Εὐριπίδην, 'Drink up Euripides and get moving'. But it certainly returns at 499 when Dicaeopolis calls the play a τρυγῳδία, 'wine-lees-song', a term picked up by the *koryphaios*' words χοροῖσιν τρυγικοῖς, 'wine-lee choruses' (628) and by his own τρυγῳδικοῖς χοροῖς, 'wine-lee-song choruses' (886).

The theme of wine is then suspended for several hundred lines. It may be distantly alluded to in the reference to Pericles' laws written like *skolia* (532), songs invariably associated with the symposium, and in the reference to ἀσκοί, 'wine-skins', and κάδοι, 'jars', among the military provisions of 549. But it is not mentioned in the scene with the Megarian, which moves along the axis of the more fundamental necessities of life, food and sex, nor

[51] Cf. Dicaeopolis' point at 512 that his vines have been damaged too.

[52] Cf. Ar. fr. 688 K–A = 579 Kock, cited above at n.37. The thirty-year σπονδαί reappear in *Knights* as beautiful thirty-year-old women offered by the sausage-seller to Demos, but there, despite earlier mentions of σπονδαί (noted by Newiger 1957, 106) they are much less integral to the play and its imagery.

that with the Boeotian, where music leads into food. Perhaps this is partly because wine is too important to the representation of Dicaeopolis' peace to be simply bartered and thus diluted, just as Dicaeopolis refuses to share the σπονδαί with the farmer Dercetes and the παράνυμφος, 'best man', at 1018–36 and 1048–66. When it next appears, at 936, it is again allusively and in a negative context: the συκοφάντης, 'informer', who is to be carried off, is described as a κρατὴρ κακῶν, 'mixing-bowl of evils', and as κύλιξ τὰ πράγματ' ἐγκυκᾶσθαι, 'a cup for stirring up trouble'. Then at 961 we first hear of the competition of the Χόες, 'Cups' – not from Dicaeopolis' perspective, but from that of Lamachus, who wants to buy some thrushes and a Copaic eel for his celebration of this festival.

This sequence of chiefly negative images of wine is gathered together in the choral song at 977–85:

> οὐδέποτ' ἐγὼ Πόλεμον οἴκαδ' ὑποδέξομαι,
> οὐδὲ παρ' ἐμοί ποτε τὸν Ἁρμόδιον ᾄσεται
> ξυγκατακλινείς, ὅτι παροινικὸς ἀνὴρ ἔφυ·
> ὅστις ἐπὶ πάντ' ἀγάθ' ἔχοντας ἐπικωμάσας
> ἠργάσατο πάντα κακά, κἀνέτρεπε κἀξέχει
> κἀμάχετο, καὶ προσέτι πολλὰ προκαλουμένου,
> 'πῖνε, κατάκεισο, λαβὲ τήνδε φιλοτησίαν',
> τὰς χάρακας ἧπτε πολὺ μᾶλλον ἔτι τῶι πυρί,
> ἐξέχει θ' ἡμῶν βίαι τὸν οἶνον ἐκ τῶν ἀμπέλων.

> I will never welcome War into my house,
> nor will he ever sing the Harmodius song,
> reclining beside me, for he is a wine-abuser.
> When we had all the good things, he went on a rampage
> and wrought all kinds of damage, and knocked over, and spilled out,
> and fought; and on top of that, though we kept inviting him
> 'Drink, recline, take this cup of friendship',
> the more he kept setting fire to our vine-poles
> and violently spilling the wine from our vines

It is as a contrast to this abuse of wine that the audience approaches the glorious competitive sequence between Dicaeopolis and Lamachus. At 1000 the herald proclaims the traditional festival competition of the Χόες, 'Pitchers' – the first man to drain his pitcher will get the wine-skin of Ctesiphon. In response Dicaeopolis urges preparation of his banquet, and at 1067 asks for his wine-ladle so that he can pour into it wine for the Χόες. Shortly, at 1085, Dicaeopolis is invited by the Priest of Dionysus to a δεῖπνον, 'banquet', which certainly involves the consumption of wine, even if it is not mentioned at 1090–3, whereas Lamachus has been ordered to remain sober and prepare to resist a Boeotian incursion. The contrasts continue: at 1132–5 Lamachus asks his slave to bring out his breastplate, Dicaeopolis his to bring out τὸν χοᾶ, his 'pitcher', as a breastplate with which he will tank himself up in competition with his συμπόται, 'fellow drinkers'.[53] For him, as we earlier noted συμποτικὰ τὰ πράγματα, 'this is a sympotic situation' (1142). The chorus cues the audience (1143) on the contrast between Lamachus' and Dicaeopolis' lot – Dicaeopolis' is to drink garlanded, and to lie down with a lovely girl and have his thingy rubbed.

When at 1198 Dicaeopolis returns he is supported by two firm-breasted *hetaerae* from whom he requests kisses 'for I was first to drain my cup'. Expertise with wine has been one of the chief symbols of Dicaeopolis' wine-based σπονδαί and has secured him another important symbol of peace, sexual gratification. Now it will also secure him still more wine. For at 1225, just as Lamachus asks to be taken to the doctor Pittalus, so Dicaeopolis asks to be taken to the judges of the *Choes*: 'Where is the βασιλεύς, "king archon"? Give me the wineskin'. He brandishes the cup that he has drained in one (1229) and the chorus tells him to carry off the wine-skin: it will follow celebrating the victory of Dicaeopolis and his wine-skin (1230–4).

7 Conclusions

Together the *Wine-flask* and *Acharnians* show how an individual's indulgence in wine can be heroised. In a non-festive context that of Cratinus may be laughed at, but there is no hint or likelihood that the poet held it up for censure; in a festive context the unadulterated tippling of Dicaeopolis can be presented as an unadulterated good. It is, overall, as an important constituent of the good things of life, though not of its necessities, that wine is presented by Old Comedy. It is a good which in real life or in contexts approximating to it a citizen can be expected to enjoy in moderation and preferably in the company of other citizens, but which slaves and women are likely to abuse.

[53] Cf. in Section 2 on how this scene involves a mini-symposium for Dicaeopolis.

4 | Ionian *Iambus* and Attic *Komoidia*: Father and Daughter, or Just Cousins? (2002)

1 Prelude

Sitting comfortably? 'It were a dark and stormy night'. Spot the genre. Anacreon had said, after all, that it would be a dark and stormy night. When he had seen the clouds on the horizon he had not been able to resist quoting his favourite poet Archilochus:[1]

> Γλαῦχ' ὅρα, βαθὺς γὰρ ἤδη κύμασιν ταράσσεται
> πόντος, ἀμφὶ δ' ἄκρα Γυρέων ὀρθὸν ἵσταται νέφος,
> σῆμα χειμῶνος, κιχάνει δ' ἐξ ἀελπτίης φόβος.
>
> Look Glaucus, to its depths with waves is now stirred up
> the sea, and on the Gyraean heights a cloud stands right above them,
> the sign of a storm, and from the unexpected comes fear.
>
> Archilochus fr. 105

Anacreon hadn't even needed to change the vocative. Bathyllus, after all, had fine grey-green eyes.

But despite his forecast, the next morning had dawned bright and clear. So now they were having an easy voyage back to Athens from Amorgos. It had

[1] No verdict on Archilochus is stated in the fragments of Anacreon, and although Rosenmeyer 1992, 21 and 42 draws attention to the Archilochian side of Anacreon she does not follow it up. Anacreon's interest in Archilochus might be argued for on the basis of some apparent echoes: (*a*) Anacr. fr. 346.(3)8–9 *PMG* δῶρα πάρεστι | Πιερίδων 'there are here the gifts of the Pierian Muses' and Archil. fr. 1.2 Μουσέων ἐρατὸν δῶρον, 'the lovely gift of the Muses'; (*b*) Anacr. fr. 347.1–2 *PMG* καὶ κόμης, ἥ τοι κατ' ἀβρὸν | ἐσκίαζεν αὐχένα, 'and of your hair, which shaded | your soft neck': cf. Archil. fr. 31 ἡ δέ οἱ κόμη | ὤμους κατεσκίαζε καὶ μετάφρενα, 'and her hair | shaded her shoulders and back'; (*c*) Anacr. fr. iamb. 5 (spoken by a woman) κνυζή τις ἤδη καὶ πέπειρα γίνομαι | σὴν διὰ μαργοσύνην 'Now I am become wrinkled and over-ripe | because of your lust': cf. Archil. fr. 196a.26–7 αἰαῖ, πέπειρα, δὶς τόση | [ἄν]θος δ' ἀπερρύηκε παρθενήιον | [κ]αὶ χάρις ἣ πρὶν ἐπῆν. | κόρον γὰρ οὐκ [...], 'Ah! She's over-ripe, twice your age, | and her maidenhood's flower has lost its bloom | as has the charm that she once had. | For she did not [...] satiety'. Note too that the metre of Anacr. fr. iamb. 5 is identical with that of ll. 1 and 2 of the unit used in Archil. fr. 196a, and seems to recur in Anacr. fr. iamb. 7. The metre of Archil. fr. 195 (as we know from Hephaestion) was used for whole poems by Anacr. (fr. 394 *PMG*). The metre of Archil. fr. 105 (trochaic tetrameters catalectic) is used in Anacr. *frr. ia.* 2–4. The polyptoton of Anacr. fr. 359 *PMG* has a precedent only in Archil. fr. 115. For terms of abuse in Anacr. cf. fr. 446 *PMG*, and for discussion of the invective against Artemon in fr. 388 *PMG* see Brown 1983.

been Anacreon's idea to take the chorusmen to Amorgos, get some contact with the Muse of *iambus* by visiting the cities founded by Semonides – and revisit some of these Samian wines that he had come to like at the court of Polycrates and that were only available in Samos and its colonies on Amorgos. Today's journey reminded him of his first trip in an Athenian penteconter – the one Hipparchus, Peisistratus' son, had sent to evacuate him from Samos when Polycrates was assassinated and things began to turn nasty.[2] That was decades ago, and nowadays Anacreon's hairs were all grey, not just some of them. Hipparchus too had been assassinated, and now the leading families of Athens had established an elaborate system of government which persuaded the *demos* that they were running the place.

This voyage wouldn't have happened otherwise. The new form of Dionysia set up in Athens by Cleisthenes and his friends gave hundreds of citizens a chance to sing a dithyramb in huge male-voice choirs, and one of the dithyramb's aristocratic backers had been attracted by Anacreon's idea – an idea he had had on a Tuesday afternoon the previous July, while ruminating on the lack of punch and zap in the Dionysia. Everybody else thought he had just had the eccentric notion of taking off a men's dithyrambic chorus to get some advanced training in peace and quiet on Naxos, which had some rather special Dionysiac associations: fifty men rowing a penteconter, what else could it be but a dithyrambic chorus going off for rehearsals? But Naxos had not been his real destination. First Paros, and then Amorgos, had been the stop-off points, so that he and his singers could pick up a range of iambic metres, tunes, words, and themes different from the few that had survived to the end of the tyranny in Attica. The Pisistratids hadn't been tolerant of abusive poetry, and though they found the story-telling side of the genre entertaining, *iambus* was now much less vigorous than it had been in Solon's Athens, when even Solon himself had used it regularly.

Well, he might have succeeded, but it was perhaps too early to congratulate himself. What a surprise the Athenians would get when he got back! They'd know something unusual was happening at the Dionysia because of the extra day, but not what that something was. Anacreon had sworn to secrecy all fifty oarsmen and the ship's *aulos*-player, so that they were the only Athenian citizens who knew what speech, song, and dance routines he had trained them to perform (after dividing them into two choruses of twenty-four), or what sort of plot he was going to have the remaining two oarsmen act out with each chorus. Had anybody noticed that two of his oarsmen had done some goat-song acting? A pity he hadn't been able to take

[2] Ps.-Pl. *Hipparch.* 228b–c.

one or two more such experienced men without arousing suspicion: as it was the actors, like the *aulos*-player, would have to perform in both dramas. Just as well they had had a bit of experience in these boring dramatic performances they called goat-songs and that had been up and running for a few years. Having only two choruses of twenty-four men competing with each other might also be a bit of a problem, but if the idea caught on he could reasonably hope that more choruses might be trained and allowed to compete next year. Meanwhile there was still the problem of the name: what was he to call them? Bathyllus had suggested *kōmos*-songs, but Anacreon wondered if Bathyllus was pulling his leg – it seemed too much like the sort of late-night singing Anacreon had become notorious for.

Almost there! The ship was making good time along the coast of Attica, despite the spring swell which occasionally threw it about. Perhaps they could start drinking soon, and sing the Archilochian elegy which an old man living in West Paros had claimed was meant to be sung on a boat.[3] Anacreon patted his phallus to make sure it was sitting comfortably. It was a big one, and it would be a shame if it came to harm at this stage, after so many successful performances in Amorgos and Paros. He had had it specially made in Amorgos by the best phallus-maker in town, and he was sure he would be able to work in a procession with a phallus-pole to mark his new creation as specially suited to a festival for Dionysus; and perhaps there would even be an opportunity for a short hymn to Dionysus or Phales that might allow him to play around (not for the first time) with mock cult-titles. Meanwhile there was just time for his late afternoon nap before they made land … zzzz.

2 The Problem

Fiction? Well, of course: but all history is reconstruction, and much that is written about both *iambus* and about the development of comedy is also fiction, though it is not always conscious of being such. And as in Old Comedy, there are some serious arguments buried in my admittedly self-indulgent romp. What I now wish to do in a more sober and scholarly genre is to examine how many similarities there are between early *iambus* and comedy, and what sort of case might be made for saying that comedy in any sense developed – or was developed? – out of *iambus*, or was significantly influenced by *iambus*.

[3] Archil. fr. 4; West 1974, 11.

There are several hypotheses that could be advanced concerning this question.

Either: (1) When Attic comedy developed, late in the sixth or early in the fifth century, one of the genres drawn upon by its creator or creators was Ionian *iambus*. This is the position implied by my μῦθος, 'myth', about Anacreon.

Or: (2) Early comedy did not have the sort of political abuse that we find in both Ionian *iambus* and later comedy, but it was brought in by Cratinus from Ionian *iambus* and was retained by his late-fifth-century successors. This is a crude statement of Rosen's position.[4]

Or: (3) The similarities between Ionian *iambus* and Attic comedy are limited, and those that there are come from a crossing of the abusive and narrative habits of Greeks in many private and public contexts with the political function (in a quite broad sense of political) that each of these two genres acquired.

Any attempt to choose between these positions has to acknowledge the extent of our ignorance. We know very little indeed about Attic comedy before Cratinus. We know rather more about Ionian *iambus*, in the sense that we have quite substantial remains, but it is still debated what sort of performance *iambus* was and what the identifying features of the genre were.[5] I have recently tried to argue that narrative, in the sense of telling things that one claims have happened or narrates as if they had happened, whether to oneself or to others, is an important generic feature of early *iambus*.[6] My conclusions can be summarized as follows: *iambus* was a form of poetry in which a number of identifying features regularly appeared: narrative, speeches embedded in narrative, ψόγος, 'vituperation', either in the narrative frame or in such speeches, self-defence that naturally led to criticism of others, just occasionally reflection or exhortation. Any of these might be addressed to an individual, sometimes to a group. No one of these features needed to be present for a poem to be recognized as (an) *iambus*, and in some metrical types or in some poets certain features may have been commoner than in others, as αἶνοι, 'animal fables', seem to be commoner in Archilochus' epodes than in his other *iambi*. With such an *à la carte* menu for the components of an *iambus*, it may not always have been easy for either poet or audience to perceive immediately when existing patterns were being varied.

[4] Rosen 1988. [5] See e.g. West 1974, 22–39; Carey 1986; Bartol 1993, 61–74.

If my arguments were to be correct, their relevance to this paper's arguments would be to diminish the importance within *iambus* of that element which has most often been seen as linking it closely with comedy, abuse.

Let me turn, then, to a swift and hence very schematic review of the respects in which *iambus* and comedy are similar and are different. Some features I consider may seem very obvious: but the obvious and the elusive have to be taken together in any assessment.

3 *Iambus* and Comedy: Similarities and Differences

(i) Length

To judge from the earliest complete texts to survive, *Acharnians* of 425 BC, *Knights* of 424 BC, and *Clouds* of 423 BC, comedies in the 420s were expected to run to 1200–1500 lines.[7] Perhaps earlier comedies were shorter, but it is hard to imagine that they were less than, say, 700 lines. *Iambi* were of such a length as allowed several to be grouped by Hellenistic editors in a single book.[8] Occasionally we have more precise evidence of length. If we consider the trimeters of Archilochus, the eighteen lines of fr. 24 are almost certainly a complete poem. Archil. fr. 23 seems likely to have been between twenty-two lines (those on our papyrus) and fifty lines. An erotic narrative (fr. 48) addressed to Glaucus extends to at least thirty lines on the papyrus that, by beginning a fresh poem directly underneath, gives a vital clue to its length.[9] If we turn to his epodes, fifty-three lines remain of the first Cologne poem; reconstructions of the lost beginning would add another thirty at the most. The longest trimeter fragment of his rough contemporary Semonides, fr. 7, albeit incomplete, is 117 lines. The longest choliambic fragment yet attested of Hipponax, a century later, is barely half that, but the length of the poem from which it comes is indeterminable (Hippon. fr. 104). The military narratives of Archilochus in tetrameters may have been longer: fr. 91 was certainly more than forty-six lines, but again how many more we do not know.

[6] Bowie 2001b (Chapter 7 in Volume 1).

[7] *Ach.* 1232, *Eq.* 1408, *Nu.* 1510: of course it could be claimed that the greater length of *Nu.* is partly due to our (second) version being a revision – though hardly, as many have thought, a revision not intended for staging: see Bowie 2015b (Chapter 6 in this volume).

[8] It is just possible that the first *iambus* of Hipponax and the first book of his *iambi* were co-extensive, but that is not the inevitable conclusion of citations that are sometimes to the first *iambus* (frr. 2, 3, 6, all in Tzetzes) and sometimes to the first book of *iambi* (frr. 2a, 20, 24, though in all but the first case the text is uncertain). On the length of sympotic poems in general see Bowie 2016b (Chapter 31 in Volume 1).

[9] *P.Oxy.* 2311. Two of these line-beginnings overlap with trimeters quoted by Ath.15.688c.

A quite different sort of criterion may be worth taking into account. The regular address of *iambi* to named individuals, sometimes, in Archilochus' case, to the same individuals as those addressed in his elegies,[10] suggests performance in a sympotic context where all or at least most of the participants were expected to take their turn. That could of course allow a performance as long as the longest speech in Plato's *Symposium*, that of Socrates, which occupies about 450 lines in a modern edition; but the others, at 90 to 200 lines, are probably better guides to what might be acceptable. It seems likely (though it cannot be proved) that the longest archaic *iambus* was some way short of the shortest fifth-century comedy.

(ii) Audience

I have already touched on audience. No doubt, especially for early comedy, a case could be made for informal performance before a small group. But from the time that it became a formal part of a festival in 486 BC, a larger and in principle *polis*-wide audience must be assumed.[11] By contrast the address of *iambi* to individuals points, as I have just suggested, to small groups – groups that were either sympotic or so difficult to distinguish from sympotic that it makes little or no difference for this investigation.

(iii) Performers and Mode of Performance

There is nothing in the poetic texts themselves to suggest that more than one person, far less a group organized as a χορός, 'chorus', ever performed *iambi*. Athenaeus, drawing on the third-century BC writer *On Paeans*, Semus of Delos, does offer a case of performers called *Iambi* who could be choral:

> οἱ αὐτοκάβδαλοι, φησί, καλούμενοι ἐστεφανωμένοι κιττῶι σχεδὸν ἐπέραινον ῥήσεις. ὕστερον δὲ ἴαμβοι ὠνομάσθησαν αὐτοί τε καὶ τὰ ποιήματα αὐτῶν.
>
> The so-called 'Improvisers' (he says) would simply deliver speeches, garlanded with ivy. And later the name *iambi* was given both to them and to their poems.
>
> Semus of Delos, Περὶ παιάνων *ap*. Ath 14.622a–d = *FGrH* 396 F24

[10] Pericles: frr. 13, ?16, 124; Glaucus: frr. 15, 48, 96, 105. For a more detailed investigation of the lengths of sympotic poems see Bowie 2016b (Chapter 32 in Volume 1).

[11] 'In principle' is an important qualification. For the case against supposing an audience drawn equally from all social and economic sections of the city see Sommerstein 1997; Bowie 1998, 58–60 (Chapter 5, 83–7 in this volume).

Details in the description of the other performers whom Athenaeus goes on to mention, ἰθύφαλλοι, 'ithyphallics', and φαλλοφόροι, 'phallus-bearers', show that their performance was indeed choral. But the ῥήσεις, 'speeches', which seem to have been spoken and not sung by the people called *Iambi*, are most easily construed as lines spoken by individual speakers. Even if there were evidence suggesting these *Iambi* to be choral, we would still have no guarantee that the choral nature of the performance described by Semus went back as early as the beginning of the fifth century BC.

In comedy (though again we can only discuss the period when it has become visible) we have a complex mixture of song, recitative, and speech distributed between chorus and actors. Both of these are costumed to distance them from the 'real' world: the actors wear padding and masks, the actors and usually the chorus, at least if male, wear a leather phallus. I don't think there is any convincing evidence for a mask, a phallus, or any other disguising costume being worn by iambic poets or later archaic performers of their *iambi*. A case can and has been made for some part of some *iambi* being sung and/or being accompanied by music;[12] and certainly the metrical pattern of epodes involves combination of sometimes diverse metres, though never building up a system of more than three units. This is very far from the great range of metres and presumably music deployed in comedy.

(iv) Narrative

There are also, of course, similarities. One of these is the vehement abuse directed against individuals, to which I return later. Given, however, that I have been claiming that telling stories is an important generic mark of *iambus*, I should also note that telling stories (sometimes called λόγοι, 'tales') of various sorts can be claimed as another similarity between comedy and *iambus* (though of course it is one that links comedy and *iambus* with almost all other literary genres). Of many possible examples I think of the account of Philocleon's diseased behaviour offered by one of his slaves in the *prologos* of *Wasps* (87–135), or of his outrageous conduct at the symposium (1299–1323): of the marvellous inventions about the unwashed Socrates as ψυχαγωγός, 'summoner up of souls', in *Birds* (1553–64) or the similarly unwashed Cleomenes in *Lysistrata* (274–82). Moreover there is at least one type of story that turns up both in Archilochus' *Epodes* and in Philocleon's conduct at the party, viz. αἶνοι, 'animal fables'. To these too I return shortly.

[12] Bartol 1993.

To me the differences so clearly outweigh the similarities that I would conclude that if hypothesis (1) were to be considered at all it would have to be in the very weakest possible version.

4 Comic Recognition of Iambic Ancestry

Another set of data might, however, shift this conclusion slightly: these are the passages in comedy where the poet has been claimed to make reference to iambographers and *iambi* in a way which presents him as working in the same tradition. Rosen has made these claims, and his argument was largely accepted by Degani.[13] I am sceptical. It is clear, on the one hand, that both the names Archilochus and Hipponax and some of their poems were known to some comic poets and presumably to significant portions of their audiences, and that they were associated with expressions of aggression and abuse. Thus in *Lysistrata* 360–1 the phrase ἔκοψεν ὥσπερ Βουπάλου alludes to Hipponax fr. 120.[14] Five passages of Aristophanes quote Archilochus *verbatim* (in Rosen's words).[15] But it is questionable whether any one of these passages shows the comic poet acknowledging any generic debt to *iambus*.

The second of Aristophanes' allusions to Hipponax illustrates the tenuous nature of Rosen's argument:

Δι. Ἄπολλον – ὅς που Δῆλον ἢ Πυθῶν' ἔχεις
Ξα. ἤλγησεν – οὐκ ἤκουσας;
Δι. οὐκ ἔγωγ', ἐπεὶ
ἴαμβον Ἱππώνακτος ἀνεμιμνῃσκόμην.

Dionysus Apollo – who I think resides in Delos or Pytho
Xanthias He felt pain – did you not hear?
Dionysus No I didn't, for
I was remembering an *iambus* of Hipponax.

Ar. *Ra.* 659–61

Dionysus, tortured by Aeacus, roars out in pain Ἄπολλον. Then, wanting to cover up his suspiciously human reaction, he follows it up with a relative

[13] Rosen 1988; Degani 1993.

[14] εἰ νὴ Δί' ἤδη τὰς γνάθους τούτων τις ἢ δὶς ἢ τρὶς | ἔκοψεν ὥσπερ Βουπάλου, φωνὴν ἂν οὐκ ἂν εἶχον, 'I tell you, if somebody had at this point bashed these women's jaws twice or thrice, like those of Bupalus, they would not be able to speak', *Lys.* 360–1, linked by the *Suda* β 452 *s.v.* Βούπαλος (presumably drawing on a Hellenistic or Graeco-Roman commentary) with Hippon. fr. 120, for which it is the only source: λάβετέ μεο ταἰμάτια, κόψω Βουπάλου τὸν ὀφθαλμόν, 'Take my cloaks, I shall bash Bupalus' eye'.

[15] Rosen 1988, 17: *Ach.* 118–20, *Pax* 298, *Av.* 869, *Lys.* 1257, *Ra.* 704.

clause in ὕμνος κλητικός, 'cletic hymn', style so that he can pass off the whole line as a recollection of an *iambus* of Hipponax. There may be a quite sophisticated joke: the scholiast believes rather that the line was by Ananius, and if that is correct (which we have little chance of determining) then Aristophanes foists a mistake of attribution upon Dionysus. But that only slightly affects the main issue. Rosen argues that 'in choosing a line from Hipponax he [Dionysus] intends to explain away his painful outburst on the grounds that a cry of pain would be appropriate when quoting from that poet. This implies, of course, that the audience would immediately associate the Hipponactean *iambus* with poetic contexts that involved personal attack, exclamations of pain and the like'.[16] But, to judge from allusion in *Lys.* 360–1 to Hipponax fr. 120, Aristophanes was likely to be familiar with lines of Hipponax that had a much more immediate link with the infliction of pain than that which he has Dionysus quote. If the scholiast is to be trusted, the next two lines of Ananius fr. 1 continued the ὕμνος κλητικός routine, and if there was any reference to infliction of pain in the poem it was some way away from the line quoted.[17]

The two passages where 'Aristophanes indicates how conscious he was of his iambographic heritage'[18] are *Peace* 43–8 and *Frogs* 416–30, the entrance of the chorus of mystic initiates. I consider the *Frogs* passage first. As Rosen and commentators note, this passage is probably to be linked with the ritual abuse, γεφυρισμός, 'bridging', which took place during the annual procession to Eleusis, and a little earlier in *Frogs* the chorus had drawn attention to the ritual activity of abuse itself.[19] Rosen claims 'points of diction reminiscent of the iambos':[20]

> Such iambic diction, combined with the fact that the chorus is re-enacting a religious procession that was known to involve abusive αἰσχρολογία, 'filthy language', suggests that Aristophanes had in mind the connection between the literary iambos and its ritual origins.

16 Rosen 1988, 16.

17 Ἄπολλον, ὅς που Δῆλον ἢ Πυθῶν' ἔχεις | ἢ Νάξον ἢ Μίλητον ἢ θείην Κλάρον, | ἵκεο καθ' ἱρὸν ἢ Σκύθας ἀφίξεαι, 'Apollo, who I think resides in Delos or Pytho | or Naxos or Miletus or divine Clarus, | come to your temple – or you will be off to the Scythians!'), Ananius fr. 1, quoted by Σ Ar. *Ra.* 659–61. It is possible that shortly after these lines Apollo was requested to inflict violence on a human enemy of the poet (as I would suspect was the case in Alc. fr. 45): but the absence of violence from the three lines quoted is important.

18 Rosen 1988, 24.

19 χώρει νῦν πᾶς ἀνδρείως | εἰς τοὺς εὐανθεῖς κόλπους | λειμώνων ἐγκρούων | κἀπισκώπτων | καὶ παίζων καὶ χλευάζων, 'Now let everyone go bravely | to the flowery laps | of the meadows, stamping | and deriding | and sporting and mocking', Ar. *Ra.* 372–5. Rosen does not remind us that the metre of that part of the choral song is (apparently) anapaestic, not a metre characteristic of *iambus:* for the identification of the metre see Dover 1993a on 372–82, concluding 'the label "anapaestic" seems appropriate'.

20 Rosen 1988, 25–6.

Rosen goes on to examine the link set up between Eleusinian ritual and comic abuse in the anapaests of *Ra.* 354–71, and concludes:[21]

> The fact, then, that this ψόγος employs diction that has its distinct provenance in the literary Ionian iambos implies that this genre is considered an intermediate, 'poetic' step in the development from ritual ψόγος to comic ψόγος.

As these two passages bring out, Rosen's argument depends heavily on the hypothesis that *iambi* had ritual origins, or at least that Aristophanes and his audience believed that they did. It does not help this argument that the poet seems to make no attempt here to link either comedy or *iambus* with pre-comic and specifically Dionysiac ritual abuse: the ritual abuse to which there seems to be allusion is in the first instance Eleusinian, uttered in the cult not of Dionysus but Demeter.[22] It is true that the metre of the abuse that follows in *Ra.* 385a–394 has been plausibly suggested to be that of 'traditional cult songs',[23] and that the iambic metrical system of 416–30 is very similar to that used similarly for personal abuse by Eupolis fr. 99 K–A. But for somebody sceptical about the hypothesis that Ionian *iambus* had ritual origins the argument is necessarily weak, and must hinge entirely on the strength of the claim that there is 'diction that has its distinct provenance in the literary Ionian iambos'.[24] How convincing is this claim? I consider Rosen's examples.

In Hippon. fr. 114a †ἔξ τίλλοι τις αὐτοῦ τὴν τράμιν †ὑποργάσαι, 'may somebody pluck out his arsehole and (?) knead away at it', 'evidently describes the same activity as the obscene phrase "plucking the anus" (πρωκτὸν τίλλειν, [*Frogs*] 423–4)'.[25] So indeed it does. It might also have been noted that the person who quotes this fragment, the doctor and grammarian Erotianus, who was active in the reign of Nero, also found τράμις, 'arsehole', in Archilochus (fr. 283).[26] It was conjectured by Blaydes that the word was also in Hippon. fr. 51, where the manuscripts of Harpocration have τρόπιν and τρόπην.[27] But all that is common to *iambus* and comedy is

[21] Rosen 1988, 28.

[22] I say 'in the first instance' because the boundaries are not clearly drawn between terms which fit the chorus' role within the play as Eleusinian initiates and their role in the dramatic competition as a chorus honouring Dionysus. For a sensitive exploration of the problem see Dover 1993b and 1993a on 354–71.

[23] Dover 1993a on 385a, citing Fraenkel 1962, 201–2.

[24] Ritual origins are argued for by West 1974, 22–39. The case against is well made by Carey 1986.

[25] Rosen 1988, 25.

[26] Erot. *Lex. Hippocr.* τ 13 (p. 85.7 Nachmanson) is the source for both fragments.

[27] Harp. μ 4 *s.v.* μάλθη, p. 169 Keaney.

reference to the practice and the use of the word τίλλειν, 'pluck'. Rosen also notes ν]ενυχμένωι πρωκτῶ[ι, 'pierced anus' (at Hippon. fr. 104.32), but there the anus is not plucked but pierced (presumably by a penis rather than, as might now happen, by a piece of jewellery). If Aristophanes had wanted to allude unambiguously to Hipponax, or to the iambographers, it would have been better to use the rare word τράμιν. As it is there is the disturbing possibility that both the terms πρωκτός, 'anus', (which appears over thirty times in Aristophanes) and τίλλειν, 'pluck', (nine times in Aristophanes, to say nothing of a dozen uses of this verb's compounds) are so familiar to members of the Attic audience in various imaginable (and perhaps to us unimaginable) contexts that they carry no scent of Ionian *iambus* at all.

Rosen's next word is κύσθος: 'κύσθου at 430 also represents a class of obscene words first found in iambographic diction'.[28] This is indeed the case. Johannes Tzetzes, commenting on the phrase ἄρτι παρατετιλμέναι, 'recently plucked', in *Ra.* 516, explains that this plucking of hair relates to τὸν δορίαλλον, τὸν μύρτον, τὸν χοῖρον, τὸν κύσθον (all slang terms for female genitals) καὶ ὅσα τοιαῦτα ὁ Σώφρων καὶ ὁ Ἱππῶναξ καὶ ἕτεροι λέγουσι, 'and all suchlike words that Sophron and Hipponax and others use'. In his commentary Dover displays a similar degree of scholarly interest in the practice, though of course from a more sophisticated standpoint. It is hard to be sure which term Tzetzes found in which source, but what we can be sure of is that Aristophanes' audience knew κύσθος from other passages in earlier plays (Ar. *Ach.* 782, 789; *Lys.* 1158); and, if they knew what it meant there, they knew it from some register of their everyday speech. It is not easy to infer that they would associate it with iambographers.

Rosen goes on to say that 'The three puns on the proper names have a similar background.' Aristophanes' three puns here are obscene: Σεβῖνον and τὸν Ἱπποβίνου, both suggesting βινῶ, 'I fuck'; and the Attic deme-name Ἀναφλύστιος, 'Anaphlystian', suggesting ἀναφλᾶν 'masturbate' (cf. Ar. *Lys.* 1099 and fr. 37 K–A; Eup. fr. 69 K–A). However, none of the Archilochian punning names listed by Rosen is obscene. They are: Πασιφίλη, 'Friend to all' (fr. 331), suggestive perhaps, but far from obscene; Λεώφιλος, 'Friend to the people' (fr. 115); Ἐρασμονίδης Χαρίλαος, 'Son of a darling, favourite of the people' (fr. 168); and Κηρυκίδης, 'Herald's son' (fr. 185).[29] Of Hipponax's four allegedly punning names one is suggestive, Πανδώρη, 'Giving to all' (fr. 104.48), and two are indeed obscene: Σάννος, 'Prick' (fr. 118.1), and Φλυήσιος in the phrase τὸν Φλυησίων Ἑρμῆν, 'the Phlyasians'

[28] Rosen 1988, 26. [29] On the punning names cf. Bonanno 1980, 65–88.

Hermes' (fr. 47.2), where the *prima facie* ethnic or demotic Φλυησίων might hint at φλᾶν ('masturbate', according to Hesychius).[30] The fourth is neither (Αἰσχυλίδης, fr. 117.9). I do not think it legitimate to extend the field of similarity to all punning names, whether obscene or not: this would allow us to adduce Homeric names like Thersites, Dolon, and Outis / Metis. That Aristophanes uses obscene punning names, and in particular uses Ἀναφλύστιος, might conceivably evoke Hipponax's Φλυήσιος – if we could be sure that this was an invented name, and not a real ethnic, as Ἀναφλύστιος is the demotic of a historical deme in the Attic *phyle* Antiochis. It might also be claimed that the diminutive σάννιον appeared in Eupolis, and might have evoked Hipponax's Σάννος.[31] Like the use of some anatomical terms, however, the obscene punning names in comedy seem to constitute a very weak link with *iambus*.

How much can in fact be done with words? As suggested by the title 'Words Apart', which I initially offered for this paper, I had hoped that a major portion of it might be devoted to an examination of the lexicon of iambographers and comedians. But this is an area where each yard has to be fought over for remarkably little gain, and a preliminary investigation has suggested a (perhaps) surprising lack of coincidence between the two genres. The greatest similarity is not in details but in the overall range of linguistic registers in each. Two examples illustrate the problem. An obscene use of ἀηδονίς, 'nightingale', for the female genitalia was found by Hesychius in Archilochus (fr. 263: Hsch. α 1501, cf. α 1503) and the same sense of ἀηδών, 'nightingale', may appear in *Birds* and (perhaps) *Frogs*.[32] The obscene sense of ἀηδών has not been identified in any other archaic or classical text. Does it follow that its use in *Birds* may evoke the iambographers? The answer must surely be negative. So too with an even rarer word, not obscene, ἄθηλος, 'unweaned'. It is used of a foal in a fragment of Semonides (fr. 5) much quoted by Plutarch, then again of a baby at *Lys*. 881. That these are the word's only attestations constitutes no case for holding that Aristophanes alludes to Semonides. Both words clearly had a use in 'the real world', and that is where Aristophanes and his audiences will have encountered them.

[30] Hsch. φ 567 φλᾶι· θλᾶι, μαλάττει, συντρίβει.

[31] LSJ, following Kock (fr. 440) attribute the word to Eupolis, but the text printed by K–A as fr. 471 makes it clear that οὐρά, 'tail', was the term found in Eupolis by the lexicographers, e.g. Hsch. σ 172: σάννιον· τὸ αἰδοῖον, ἀντὶ τοῦ κέρκιον … τὸ γὰρ αἰδοῖον ἔσθ' ὅτε οὐρὰν ἔλεγον, ὡς Εὔπολις, '*sannion*: the genital, instead of 'little tail' … for sometimes they called the genital 'tail', as does Eupolis'.

[32] *Av*. 203, 208, 659, 664: Dunbar *ad locc.* is canny on the possibility of double entendre at 203 and 208, and does not suggest it at all at 659 and 664. For the Hsch. text see Bossi 1990, 253–6.

If lexicographical investigation is not likely to help reach a solution, where else can we turn? The second passage where in Rosen's view 'Aristophanes indicates how conscious he was of his iambographic heritage' is *Peace* 43–8:

> οὐκοῦν ἂν ἤδη τῶν θεατῶν τις λέγοι
> νεανίας δοκησίσοφος 'τόδε πρᾶγμα τί;
> ὁ κάνθαρος δὲ πρὸς τί;' κᾆιτ' αὐτῶι γ' ἀνὴρ
> Ἰωνικός τίς φησι παρακαθήμενος·
> 'δοκέω μέν, ἐς Κλέωνα τοῦτ' αἰνίσσεται,
> ὡς κεῖνος ἀναιδέως τὴν σπατίλην ἐσθίει.'
>
> So at this point one of the audience might say –
> a would-be-clever young man: 'What is going on here?
> What is the point of the dung-beetle?' And then to him
> there replies an Ionian seated beside him:
> 'It seems to me, this is a riddling reference to Cleon,
> since that fellow shamelessly eats shit.'

Here the slave imagines that an Ionian in the audience suggests that the dung-beetle refers to Cleon, accused of brazen coprophagy. Many suggestions have been made as to why the slave specifies an Ionian.[33] Rosen finds the answer in the link with *iambus*. 'If we ask what the connection is between scatological obscenity and Ionia, the answer must be the Ionian iambos.' Rosen's reasons for this conclusion are the source of the beetle in Aesopic fable (as indicated by *Peace* 127–30) and the mention of dung-beetles at Hippon. fr. 92.7–13. Unfortunately the context in which Hipponax introduces dung-beetles seems to be a scabrous but non-abusive narrative of an unpleasant ritual, perhaps a cure for impotence, to which the narrator is being subjected by a lady whose oral accomplishments included a command of spoken Lydian.[34] The fact that Archilochus used fables in his *Epodes*, which Rosen goes on to discuss, is not perhaps as telling as he wishes. He points to Philocleon's use of fable in *Wasps* (1259, 1401 ff., 1446 ff.) as evidence of 'a fifth-century awareness of the use of fable for invective',[35] and recently Giuseppe Zanetto has again examined the use of fable in *iambus* and in comedy to draw similar conclusions, viz. that in its use of fable comedy was looking back to *iambus*.[36]

[33] As Rosen concedes, Cassio's explanations of the passage, taking the Ionian as an intellectual (Cassio 1981) but also as voicing the probable hostility of an Ionian subject ally towards Cleon (Cassio 1985, 105–6) are 'compelling', which might be taken to show that Rosen's own interpretation is redundant.

[34] Cf. Hippon fr. 78.12, where dung-beetles also figure.

[35] Rosen 1988, 32. [36] Zanetto 2001.

Once more I am sceptical. There is no doubt that fables were circulating in Greece as early as Hesiod, *Works and Days* (202–12), that they were at an early date associated with Aesop, and that Aesop was associated with Ionian Samos, at least by Herodotus (2.134) and presumably by others. It is also clear that in *Wasps* one reason, perhaps the most important, for Philocleon telling fables is that they are thought appropriate to a symposium.[37] I would prefer to conclude that the link between the telling of fables by Archilochus (frr. 174, 185) and by Philocleon in *Wasps* goes no further than the sympotic context of each, and that the supposed Ionian origins of Aesop, together with a known Aesopic fable about a dung-beetle, are enough to explain the choice of an Ionian at *Peace* 43–8.

The case for saying that comic poets were conscious of the importance of *iambus* for comedy is therefore weak. Furthermore, some positive points might be made against it. We have several *parabaseis* in plays of Aristophanes in which the speaker talks about the dramatic poet's career and one that sketches the development of Attic comedy as a whole (*Eq.* 518–40). Neither there nor in possibly parabatic fragments of other poets do we find hints that *iambus* is perceived as important. Secondly, in the passage of his *Poetics* where some similarity between iambographers and comedians is noted, Aristotle never goes beyond noting similarity to claim *influence*. I regard the passage as significant enough to print in full:

> διεσπάσθη δὲ κατὰ τὰ οἰκεῖα ἤθη ἡ ποίησις. οἱ μὲν γὰρ σεμνότεροι τὰς καλὰς ἐμιμοῦντο πράξεις καὶ τὰς τῶν τοιούτων, οἱ δὲ εὐτελέστεροι τὰς τῶν φαύλων, πρῶτον ψόγους ποιοῦντες, ὥσπερ ἕτεροι ὕμνους καὶ ἐγκώμια. τῶν μὲν οὖν πρὸ Ὁμήρου οὐδενὸς ἔχομεν εἰπεῖν τοιοῦτον ποίημα, εἰκὸς δὲ εἶναι πολλούς, ἀπὸ δὲ Ὁμήρου ἀρξαμένοις ἔστιν, οἷον ἐκείνου ὁ Μαργίτης καὶ τὰ τοιαῦτα. ἐν οἷς κατὰ τὸ ἁρμόττον καὶ τὸ ἰαμβεῖον ἦλθε μέτρον – διὸ καὶ ἰαμβεῖον καλεῖται νῦν, ὅτι ἐν τῶι μέτρωι τούτωι ἰάμβιζον ἀλλήλους. καὶ ἐγένοντο τῶν παλαιῶν οἱ μὲν ἡρωικῶν οἱ δὲ ἰάμβων ποιηταί. ὥσπερ δὲ καὶ τὰ σπουδαῖα μάλιστα ποιητὴς Ομηρος ἦς (μόνος γὰρ οὐχ ὅτι εὖ ἀλλὰ καὶ μιμήσεις δραματικὰς ἐποίησεν), οὕτως καὶ τὸ τῆς κωμωιδίας σχῆμα πρῶτος ὑπέδειξεν, οὐ ψόγον ἀλλὰ τὸ γελοῖον δραματοποιήσας. ὁ γὰρ Μαργίτης ἀνάλογον ἔχει, ὥσπερ Ἰλιὰς καὶ ἡ Ὀδύσσεια πρὸς τὰς τραγωιδίας, οὕτω καὶ οὗτος πρὸς τὰς κωμωιδίας. παραφανείσης δὲ τῆς

[37] Cf. *V.* 1258–60: ἢ λόγον ἔλεξας αὐτὸς ἀστεῖόν τινα, | Αἰσωπικὸν γελοῖον ἢ Συβαριτικόν, | ὧν ἔμαθες ἐν τῷ συμποσίῳ. κᾆτ' ἐς γέλων | τὸ πρᾶγμ' ἔτρεψας ..., 'or you yourself have told a witty story, something funny from Aesop or about Sybaris, one of the things you have learned in the symposium. And then you make the incident a laughing matter ...'. For the scene see Vetta 1976–7.

τραγωιδίας καὶ κωμωιδίας οἱ ἐφ' ἑκάτερον τὴν ποίησιν ὁρμῶντες κατὰ τὴν οἰκείαν φύσιν οἱ μὲν ἀντὶ τῶν ἰάμβων κωμωιδοποιοὶ ἐγένοντο, οἱ δὲ ἀντὶ τῶν ἐπῶν τραγωιδοδιδάσκαλοι …

Poetry split up, according to people's personal characters. For the more dignified imitated noble actions, and the actions of people of that sort, whereas those of lesser quality imitated the actions of low people, first composing vituperations, just as the other group composed hymns and encomia. For no poet before Homer can we point to a poem of this sort, but it is plausible that there were many poets, whereas beginning with Homer we can, such as that poet's *Margites* and poems of that sort. In this stage according to the principle of propriety there also developed the iambic trimeter as a metre – which is why it is in fact now called 'iambic trimeter', because it was in this metre that they used to utter *iambi* against each other. And of the ancients some became poets of heroic poems and some of *iambi*. And just as Homer was also pre-eminent as a poet in serious compositions (for he was the only one not simply to compose well but also to compose dramatic imitations) so too he was the first to give a glimpse of the form of comedy, by making a drama of what was laughable and not of vituperation.

For just as the *Iliad* and *Odyssey* stand in relation to tragedies, so does the *Margites* to comedies. But when tragedy and comedy came into being the poets were drawn to each of the two types of poetry according to their own personality, and some, instead of composing *iambi*, became comic poets, while others, instead of composing epic, became tragic playwrights …

Arist. *Po.* 1448b24–49a5

The way Aristotle formulates the relationship between *iambus* and comedy would be very surprising if he thought there was a case for seeing the one as descended from the other. That he did not is further demonstrated by his total silence concerning Ionian *iambus* when a couple of sentences later he alludes (admittedly all too briefly) to the origins of Attic comedy in phallic choral performances.[38] When he returns to its early development a page later he takes it that initially comedy had an ἰαμβικὴ ἰδέα), 'iambic character', but no overarching plots, and that it was an innovation of Crates καθόλου

[38] Arist. *Po.* 1449a9–13: γενομένη <δ'> οὖν ἀπ' ἀρχῆς αὐτοσχεδιαστική, καὶ αὐτὴ (sc. tragedy) καὶ ἡ κωμωιδία, καὶ ἡ μὲν ἀπὸ τῶν ἐξαρχόντων τὸν διθύραμβον, ἡ δὲ ἀπὸ τῶν τὰ φαλλικὰ ἃ ἔτι καὶ νῦν ἐν πολλαῖς τῶν πόλεων διαμένει νομιζόμενα …, 'Although it was to begin with a matter of improvisation, both tragedy itself and comedy, the one developing from those who led the singing of the dithyramb, and the other from those who led the singing of the phallic songs which even now are still performed in many cities … '.

ποιεῖν λόγους καὶ μύθους, 'to construct overall stories and tales' (1449b8–9). Again it would have been very easy for him to say explicitly that pre-Crates comedy was a direct descendant of *iambi*, but instead he limits himself to attribution of an ἰαμβικὴ ἰδέα.[39] Finally he draws a distinction a few pages later between comedy's use of a plot with fictitious names by contrast with the iambographers' compositions which concerned what happened to individuals.[40] Once more he writes as if the two genres had related features rather than the one being descended from or strongly influenced by the other.

5 The Contribution of Cratinus

This is a suitable point to return to the second of the hypotheses that I initially offered as possible explanations of the phenomena, i.e. that early comedy did not have the sort of political abuse that we find in both Ionian

[39] *Po.* 1449a37–b9: ἡ δὲ κωμῳδία διὰ τὸ μὴ σπουδάζεσθαι ἐξ ἀρχῆς ἔλαθεν. καὶ γὰρ χορὸν κωμῳδῶν ὀψέ ποτε ὁ ἄρχων ἔδωκεν, ἀλλ' ἐθελονταὶ ἦσαν. ἤδη δὲ σχήματά τινα αὐτῆς ἐχούσης οἱ λεγόμενοι αὐτῆς ποιηταὶ μνημονεύονται. τίς δὲ πρόσωπα ἀπέδωκεν ἢ προλόγους ἢ πλήθη ὑποκριτῶν καὶ ὅσα τοιαῦτα, ἠγνόηται. τὸ δὲ μύθους ποιεῖν ['Ἐπίχαρμος καὶ Φόρμις] τὸ μὲν ἐξ ἀρχῆς ἐκ Σικελίας ἦλθε, τῶν δὲ Ἀθήνησιν Κράτης πρῶτος ἦρξεν ἀφέμενος τῆς ἰαμβικῆς ἰδέας καθόλου ποιεῖν λόγους καὶ μύθους, '(The development of) comedy has remained obscure, in consequence of its not having been treated seriously from its beginnings. For in fact it was only very late that the *archon* granted a *choros* of comic performers, but they had been volunteers. And it is only when comedy already had some of its features that there is a tradition of those who are said to have been its poets. But who gave it its masks, or prologues, or the numbers of actors, and so on, this has ceased to be known. But as for writing plots [Epicharmus and Phormis], this originally came from Sicily, and of the poets in Athens Crates was first to abandon the iambic character and construct overall stories and plots.' Degani 1993, 5, like Rosen, may go too far in denying abusive comedy to Crates on the basis of this very sketchy point made by Aristotle. Crates fr. 15 K–A (from *Heroes*, according to Poll. 10.175) ῥιπίδι κοπραγωγῷ, 'a dung-bearing fan', has the scatological flavour that Rosen associates with Ionian *iambus* (though neither context nor chronology allows it to be claimed with any confidence as an example of pre-Cratinian political abuse). For other material in Crates that might be claimed (though in my view unconvincingly) to be similar to that of Ionian *iambus* cf. the possible farting Lamia of fr. 20 K–A. Closer to Aristophanic comedy than suggested by Degani is also the sexual play at Crates fr. 43 K–A: πάνυ γάρ ἐστιν ὡρικὰ | τὰ τιτθί' ὥσπερ μῆλα καὶ μιμαίκυλα, 'for her tits are nicely developed, like apples and arbutus-fruits' (perhaps describing a female character in a play) and at fr. 27 K–A (possibly aimed at a real Athenian woman, or rather at her husband): παί|ζει δ' ἐν ἀνδρικοῖς χοροῖσι | τὴν κυνητίνδ' ὥσπερ εἰκός, | τοὺς καλοὺς φιλοῦσα, 'she plays the kissing-game among the men's choruses, as you might expect, kissing the handsome young men'

[40] *Po.* 1451b11–15: ἐπὶ μὲν οὖν τῆς κωμῳδίας ἤδη τοῦτο δῆλον γέγονεν. συστήσαντες γὰρ τὸν μῦθον διὰ τῶν εἰκότων οὕτω τὰ τυχόντα ὀνόματα ὑποτιθέασιν καὶ οὐχ ὥσπερ οἱ ἰαμβοποιοὶ περὶ τῶν καθ' ἕκαστον ποιοῦσιν, 'now in the case of comedy this is immediately clear. For constructing their plot on the basis of the plausible they then attach random names, and do not, like the iambic poets, compose about the circumstances of an individual.'

iambus and later comedy, but that it was brought in by Cratinus from Ionian *iambus* and was retained by his late fifth-century successors – a thesis developed in a chapter of Rosen's book.[41] That hypothesis seems to be completely at variance with the view of Aristotle just quoted that comedy up to Crates had an ἰαμβικὴ ἰδέα, 'iambic character', and some of the points I have made above also count against its plausibility. I do not attempt to demolish it in detail here, not least because, as so often, we lack hard evidence: the ascription of the introduction of political abuse to Cratinus, although suggested by other ancient accounts of comedy,[42] cannot adequately be tested by our surviving material, because we can only guess whether his predecessors did or did not have it, or how serious it was if they did.[43] It cannot be doubted that political abuse did play an important part in the comedies of Cratinus himself, and that in his *Archilochoi* it was very probably linked by Cratinus with Archilochus.[44] What Rosen, despite his claims, has not demonstrated is that Cratinus or any contemporary saw his plays as the *first* comedies to exploit vigorous political abuse, or that 'Cratinus was inspired by specific points of diction associated with iambographic invective'.[45]

6 Conclusion

That leaves me with my third possible hypothesis. The similarities between Ionian *iambus* and Attic comedy are limited, and those that there are come from a crossing of the abusive and narrative habits of Greeks in many

[41] Rosen 1988, 37–58, 'Cratinus'. For Cratinus' contribution to comedy see now Bakola 2010, Storey 2014.

[42] Two different claims need to be distinguished: (1) that of Platonius, *Diff. char.* (*Prolegomena de com.* II, 1, p. 6 Koster = Perusino 1989, 38.1–2 = Cratinus test. 17 K–A) that Cratinus emulated Archilochus in the harshness of his abuse: Κρατῖνος ὁ τῆς παλαιᾶς κωμωιδίας ποιητής, ἅτε δὴ κατὰ τὰς Ἀρχιλόχου ζηλώσεις, αὐστηρὸς μὲν ταῖς λοιδορίαις ἐστίν, 'Cratinus, the poet of Old Comedy, as one might expect in the light of his emulations of Archilochus, was harsh in his abuse': for the problem of ζηλώσεις and a different text cf. Degani 1993, 16 n.33, with the further literature he cites there; (2) that of Anon. *de com.* (*Prolegomena de com.* V, p. 14 Koster = Cratinus test. 19 K–A) that Cratinus ἐπιγενόμενος δὲ ὁ Κρατῖνος … καὶ τῶι χαρίεντι τῆς κωμωιδίας τὸ ὠφέλιμον προστέθεικε τοὺς κακῶς πράττοντας διαβάλλων καὶ ὥσπερ δημοσίαι μάστιγι τῆι κωμωιδίαι κολάζων, 'coming next … (among other innovations) 'attached usefulness to the charm of comedy by lambasting malefactors and punishing them by comedy as if by a public whip'. Combined, these claims would constitute an ancient view that Cratinus' Archilochian abuse was an innovation, but it is important to recall that they are not combined in our sources.

[43] See, however, n.40. [44] This is on the whole well argued by Rosen 1988, 37–58.

[45] Rosen 1988, 47; iambographic diction is again the subject of unsubstantiated claims at pp. 55 and 57.

private and public contexts with the political function that each of these two genres acquired. That seems to me better to explain the phenomena than any other hypothesis.

7 Postlude

Anacreon suddenly woke up. Some noise had abruptly stopped. He began to recall his dreams. Birds, wasps, dung-beetles, gadflies, horsemen, women in assembly, priestesses. Not dreams, nightmares. Thank God he was awake again. He turned to his fellow-oarsman, Magnes, whose parents had given him that name in honour of Anacreon's prayer to Magnesian Artemis that they liked so much.[46] 'Come on, Magnes, let's go over that question-and-answer routine again, and then have some wine.'

[46] Anacr. fr. 348 *PMG*.

5 Socrates in Aristophanes' *Clouds* and the Audience of Attic Comedy (2007)

1 Introduction

It is often held that Aristophanes' portrayal of Socrates in *Clouds* can have borne little resemblance to the historical Socrates of the 420s BC.[1] The version of this view that I shall examine most closely is that offered by Sir Kenneth Dover in the introduction to his 1968 edition of *Clouds*, a version quite widely accepted. There are also other scholars who, both before and after 1968, have argued for the historicity of some features of the Aristophanic Socrates.[2] On the whole I have not tried to restate these scholars' arguments, but have, I hope, approached the problem from a somewhat different angle.

The argument for the Dover-position runs like this:

(i) The picture in *Clouds* conflicts in significant respects from that in Plato and Xenophon. The Socrates of *Clouds* is interested in and teaches natural sciences like astronomy, geology, geography, entomology; he teaches rhetoric and takes fees for doing so; he rejects traditional religion. The Socrates of Plato and Xenophon does none of those things, and is more likely to be a true picture of the historical Socrates.

(ii)
  (a) Since many of these characteristics are indeed those of sophists, the Socrates of *Clouds* is an amalgam of sophistic features and the *komoedia* is aimed not at Socrates but at sophists in general.
  (b) A variation of this would hold that Socrates stands not so much for sophists as for the genus intellectual.

(iii) The humour of this presentation of Socrates worked because the typical member of the audience did not see the difference between Socrates

[1] This paper is an English version of Bowie 1998a, slightly adapted to be suitable for an audience of British academics and school-teachers at the seminars held at, and generously financed by, the European Cultural Centre of Delphi in July 2007.

[2] E.g. Burnet 1911; Taylor 1911; Schmid 1932; Strauss 1965, 3–53; Havelock 1968; Kleve 1983; Edmunds 1985; Zimmermann 1993.

and sophists or intellectuals in general; as for Aristophanes, he may have in some sense known the difference, but did not 'see' it in a strong or active sense 'and if it had been pointed out to him he would not have regarded it as important'.[3]

(iv) Socrates was chosen as the representative of the sophists, despite his differences from them, because he was much better known to an Attic audience than were the sophists, most of whom were not Athenians.

I am not persuaded by all of these arguments, and I hope that it will be of interest to re-examine them. The outcome affects our view of the sorts of invective that were either accepted or effective in fifth-century Athens, as well as our view of the development of Socrates' thought. If the Dover view is correct, a comic poet could expect an audience to be amused and perhaps provoked to criticism by a representation of a prominent fellow citizen that was quite remote from that citizen's real behaviour. It is true that in all of Aristophanes' fifth-century plays many brief passages of personal invective can be argued to make accusations about personal behaviour that are likely to be unfounded and that neither poet nor audience could have been in a position to verify: but when caricatures are presented of individuals active in the public domain they seem to be built upon *some* element of fact. I think here of the Cleon of *Knights* and the very differently constructed Euripides of *Acharnians*, *Women at the Thesmophoria*, and *Frogs*. In *Clouds*, on the view I am challenging, something quite different is supposed to be happening.

2 Socrates and Sophists

Let me start with what seems to me to be a contradiction between points (iii) and (iv). On the one hand the audience did not see the difference between Socrates and sophists; on the other hand Socrates was chosen by Aristophanes as the representative of sophistic thought because he was well known. Socrates certainly seems to have been well known by the year of the production of the first version of *Clouds*, 424/3 BC. As Dover points out,[4] Socrates also seems to have figured in the play which came second in the competition, Ameipsias' *Konnos*, and it would have made little sense for either playwright to give Socrates a part, far less the central role he has in *Clouds*, if he had not been known to a substantial proportion of the

[3] Dover 1968, liii. [4] Dover 1968, li.

audience. If we think that Socrates was better known than visiting sophists, it might be easier to argue that it was of these that the audience was largely ignorant, so that the difference between them and Socrates was not appreciated.

But I think this way out is also closed.

(a) For a start, if Aristophanes is directing his humour and criticism at sophists or intellectuals in general the audience must have *some* conception of who or what these people are for either humour or criticism to be effective. Moreover there are many elements in this play and in other Old Comedies which assume the audience (1) to be familiar with the names of individual thinkers or sophists; (2) to have encountered some thinkers' physical theories; and (3) to be able to recognise certain techniques of rhetoric.

(1) At *Clouds* 361 Prodicus is mentioned with respect for his 'wisdom and judgement', σοφία καὶ γνώμη; and as Dover notes, he appears as a potential source of truth at *Birds* 688ff. and of corruption at Ar. fr. 506 K–A.

Like Albert Henrichs,[5] I would hesitate to infer from *Clouds* 361 that Prodicus was held in popular esteem, or that it was on account of his activity in a literary genre that such esteem was accorded, or was shared by Aristophanes (as proposed by Dover).[6] It is certainly not the only way that lines 358–62 are 'intelligible as comedy'. At least part of the comedy arises from the sharp contrast between the qualities for which Prodicus and Socrates are claimed by the chorus of Clouds to be admirable, impressing upon the audience the dramatic fact that the Clouds do not credit Socrates with σοφία καὶ γνώμη, 'wisdom and judgement'. I think all that can safely be inferred is that Prodicus was someone whom the audience might recognise as plausibly associated with σοφία καὶ γνώμη. I also think that there may be other factors in play: a particular admiration on the part of Aristophanes, a poet fascinated by the behaviour of language, for the sophist who more than all the others made a study of language; and a compliment for his own skill, σοφία, by the poet who in this play is – eventually – going to present his audience with an *agōn* between two λόγοι, 'arguments', modelled on the work of Prodicus for which he had recently, I believe, become famous, his '*Choice of Heracles*' or Ὧραι, '*Seasons*'.

Whatever the correct interpretation of 361, it and other references show that Prodicus was known and could be complimented for his σοφία, 'wisdom'.

[5] Henrichs 1976, 21 n.39. [6] Dover 1968, lv.

At line 830 Socrates is called ὁ Μήλιος, 'the Melian'. Here I would agree with Dover, who thinks that 'there is little doubt that the reference is to Diagoras of Melos, who was regarded, unjustly or not, as impious'.[7] That this reference could be picked up by the audience – or be expected by Aristophanes to be picked up by the audience – suggests that Diagoras is another thinker whose identity and some of whose views are quite widely known.

The characters of Ameipsias' Κόννος (*Konnos*) included not only the music teacher of Socrates, Connus, from whom the play took its name, but also a number of φροντισταί, 'thinkers', whether or not these actually formed the chorus.[8] A character in Athenaeus claims that Ameipsias did not include Protagoras in the chorus, and since he uses Protagoras' absence to argue that he only arrived in Athens for his visit to the house of Callias after the production of Ameipsias' Κόννος and before Eupolis' Κόλακες, '*Flatterers*', of 422/1 BC, he seems to know a text of the Κόννος in which Protagoras did not appear at all.[9] But he certainly had a role in Eupolis' Κόλακες, and there would have been little point in this unless Protagoras had been familiar to a significant proportion of the audience in the later 420s. Likewise with the allusions to Gorgias of Leontini, and to a Philippus who was apparently his pupil, at *Wasps* 421 and *Birds* 35: these allusions are brief, the dramatic action is moving rapidly, so the audience is expected to pick up the allusions quickly.

(2) Whether or not certain physical theories otherwise associated with other thinkers are appropriately ascribed to Socrates in *Clouds*,[10] they are presented in a way that suggests that something in them is familiar to the audience – for example, the features which seem to relate to the views of Diogenes of Apollonia.
(3) Much more striking, however, is Aristophanes' own exploitation of techniques of contemporary rhetoric. This is especially prominent, of course in the *agōn* of *Clouds*, but it is also manifest in that of *Wasps* in 423/2.[11]

(b) Evidence from other sources also suggests that it is unlikely that rhetoric and its teachers were familiar only to a small number in the audience.

[7] Dover 1968, 200. For the evidence for Diagoras' prosecution (and the weakness of the evidence for widespread persecution of 'intellectuals' in late-fifth-century Athens) see Dover 1976.
[8] So Dover 1968, li; Guthrie 1971b, 41 n.1 is scornful of the idea.
[9] Masurius at Ath. 5.218b, in the course of a long speech whose preceding pages have been attacking philosophers and in particular the historical reliability of Plato's dialogues.
[10] See lines 95ff. and 227ff. with Dover 1968, xxxvi. and his notes *ad locc.*
[11] See Murphy 1938.

I wish to look at this from two angles: the extent of the vogue for rhetoric in Athens of the 420s, and the size and social composition of the audience of comedy.

On the first question there is no dispute that among Plato's upper-class friends there was great interest in sophists: but it is hard to believe that interest in sophists stopped there. The people whose ability to participate in debate in the βουλή, 'Council', or ἐκκλησία, 'Assembly', or to prosecute or defend themselves in the courts, would be most enhanced by acquiring rhetorical skills were not from the established political classes but from rather lower down the socio-economic scale – such men indeed as Cleon and the other demagogues who attract the invective of comic poets. Admittedly Cleon is made by Thucydides to criticise the assembly of 427 BC for approaching debates as rhetorical contests in which they are θεαταὶ τῶν λόγων, 'spectators of the speeches',[12] but this in no way precludes the historical Cleon from having studied rhetoric; and the text is valuable as indicating that in 427 BC this charge could, in Thucydides' view, meaningfully be made. 427 BC is also the year in which according to Diodorus Siculus,[13] probably following Timaeus, Gorgias arrived in Athens and stunned the Assembly by his rhetorical skill. It would be nice if this information were reliable, but I doubt the date,[14] and the whole item is precarious.

But the sheer volume of sophists visiting Athens points to a wide diffusion of interest. The visit of Protagoras in ca. 433, which is the dramatic context of Plato's dialogue of that name,[15] may be a special case, but cannot simply be excluded in weighing the evidence: Protagoras, Hippias and Prodicus are imagined as staying with Callias, and when Socrates and Hippocrates arrive they too are assumed by the porter to be sophists (314d–16a). Now the throngs of foreigners and Athenians who have come to hear these three are clearly the *crème de la crème*. But we know the names of many other sophists who came to Athens in the 430s or 420s. It would be improbable that the other names preserved by Plato – Gorgias, Callicles, Polus, Euthydemus, Dionysodorus, Euenus of Paros, Thrasymachus – could give us an exhaustive list – indeed the absence from it of one Athenian, Antiphon, shows that it is not exhaustive. Even these top names seem to have given some lectures that would be affordable by a man at the upper end of the zeugite

[12] 3.38.4. [13] 12.53.1–5. [14] Perhaps a confection based on Th. 3.86.2.

[15] For the date see Morrison 1941. Ath. 5.218b argues for Protagoras' arrival in Athens between the production of Ameipsias' *Konnos* (424/3) and Eupolis' Κόλακες, '*Flatterers*' (422/1), making the unwarranted assumption that his fictional visit to the house of Callias in *Flatterers* is the same as that in the *Protagoras*. Elsewhere, at 11.505f–6a, a speaker in Ath. is aware that the presence of the sons of Pericles who died in the great plague is a problem for this chronology.

class – Prodicus had a δραχμιαία ἐπίδειξις, 'a drachma-lecture', as well as one for which one had to pay fifty drachmas;[16] and we are told by Plato that Callias paid Euenus of Paros five minae, that is 500 drachmas, for the education of his two sons:[17] this presumably involved teaching over some period of time. In his speech *Against the Sophists* Isocrates also suggests that three or four minae, that is three or four hundred drachmae, are the upper range of fees for a course; and later in the same speech he alleges that some sophists charged very low fees to attract a large number of pupils.[18] It seems reasonable to suppose that alongside the big names we encounter in Plato there were many lesser figures aiming at a less exalted market. Now it only takes ten top-ranking sophists and another ten lower down the scale, each with twenty pupils, to create an annual student body of 400; and if Athenian interest in sophists has been alive for at least a decade by 423 BC – and a decade is a conservative estimate – the number of Athenians who had heard a sophist by the time *Clouds* was produced could move up into the thousands.

3 The Athenian Theatre Audience

How large was the audience in the comic theatre, and how did it break down between different economic groups? The first question is one to which some sort of an answer can be given. The theatre of Dionysus as reconstructed by Lycurgus in the later fourth century is estimated to have had a capacity of fourteen to seventeen thousand, a figure proposed by Dörpfeld that seems still to be accepted.[19] The figure given at Plato *Smp.* 175e for the audience of Agathon's first victory in 417/6, πλέον ἢ τριμυρίοις, 'more than thirty thousand', is universally rejected. But although we should imagine a number somewhere around fourteen to seventeen thousand for the Lycurgan theatre, a much smaller number was argued for by Csapo and Goette in Wilson 2007 for the fifth century: as Csapo there argues, Goette demonstrated that the *theatron* of the fifth-century theatre was trapezoidal and suggested that the wooden theatre of the fifth century itself could seat only between 4,000 and 7,000 spectators.[20] That figure may be defended

16 Pl. *Cra.* 384b. 17 *Ap.* 20b9. 18 Isoc. 13.3–4 and 9.

19 E.g. by Pickard-Cambridge 1946, 141, Papastamati-von Moock 2015.

20 Csapo 2007, 97–9. He notes that estimates offered in the decade preceding the writing of his chapter were 3,700 (Dawson 1997); 5,500 (Korres 2002, 540); not more than 7,000 (Goette in personal correspondence with Csapo). Only Moretti 1999–2000, 395 went as high as 10,000 to 15,000. For a statement of the case for a less socio-economically diverse audience of Attic

even after the arguments of Papastamati-von Moock that a Periclean reconstruction of the wooden theatre may have brought it as far up the south slope of the acropolis as the later *diazoma*. For the wooden theatre thus expanded she estimates the number of spectators at between 14,000 and 15,000, which seems far too high.[21] As for the pre-Periclean wooden theatre, on the basis of the drawing in her fig. 18 (p. 71) of a rectangular theatre with twenty-six rows of seats, twenty-seven metres in width east to west,[22] with sides stretching some ten metres south to north,[23] and with a space of 0.41 metres allowed for each spectator (ibid. n.125), I calculate that the southwards facing twenty-six rows will have accommodated around 1,200 spectators, and the eastwards and westwards facing side row each 600, giving an audience of 2,400 overall. Whatever the Cleisthenic ideology of the Διονύσια ἐν ἄστει, 'the Dionysia in the city', being a festival for all Athenians from all demes, only a small proportion of Athenian citizens in the later fifth century can have seen and heard performances either there or at the *Lenaea*.

How this number of spectators broke down is an equally difficult issue. But I am confident that the photograph printed as a frontispiece

drama than usually suggested see Sommerstein 1997. Papastamati-von Moock 2015 uses new evidence of post-holes to argue that the reconstruction of the wooden theatre as part of the Periclean building programme certainly involved the construction of seating as far up the *cavea* as the old road running east-west along the south slope of the acropolis (later the so-called *peripatos*: 9 in fig. 1 on Goette 2007, 117), in particular the post-holes for *ikria* discovered in 2012 in *kerkis* VIII, trench VIII B above the eighteenth row of seating (Papastamati-von Moock 2015, 64–6 with figs. 15 and 16: no. 3 on her fig. 19); but the evidence of wooden seating above that line is the similarity of the cutting in Dörpfeld's west trench ('even those which Dörpfeld shows in the west trench much further north can be related to the Periclean expansion, thus confirming the scale of the Periclean renovation as far as a little south of the late Classical diazoma', 66). The estimate of numbers in the Lycurgan theatre of 14,000 to 17,000 which she endorses (n.157) assumes many rows above the *diazoma* (in what some call the *epitheatron*) and the figure she retains of 10,000 to 12,000 spectators seated below the *diazoma* seems far too high. Before the Periclean reconstruction (? 430s) the capacity will have been even less, with seating perhaps coming up as far as line 7 in fig. 1 on Goette 2007, 117 but not as far as the two wells (there 8) which were still in use for some of the fifth century: cf. Papastamati-von Moock 2015, 63: 'If this supposition holds true, it would mean that the wooden theatre had two phases – an initial one, which went as far as a point near the "old Peripatos", and a second (Periclean) after the mid 5th century BC [rather "about 440/430 BC", 66], during which its planned renovation in stone was not completed and the wooden theatre was either fully renovated with the completion of the stone proedria or was expanded to the north up to the area of the late Classical diazoma, putting the "old Peripatos" out of operation and displacing its function northward to approximately the location of the late Classical diazoma'.

[21] Papastamati-von Moock 2015, 71.

[22] 'a restored breadth of approximately 27 m.', Papastamati-von Moock 2015, 67.

[23] In each case these are the measurements of the uppermost rows of seats: the front rows will have been as much as forty per cent shorter.

and presented as characterising a typical member of a comic audience by Dover in his *Aristophanic Comedy* is wholly misleading – an aged and very rustic shepherd with a lamb on his shoulders. It seems to me that a number of pressures will have combined to make attendance at the theatre more attractive and regular for the more leisured members of the citizen body. For both the Lenaea and the Dionysia more than one day is taken up by dramatic performances – two for the Lenaea, four or five for the Dionysia. Once the theoric fund had been introduced – which some now think to be later than the 420s – the poorer citizen might have the price of his entry to the theatre – two obols for each day – paid by the *polis*. But there was no compensation for his loss of earnings, and any citizen whose livelihood depended on a daily μισθός, 'wage', or on money earned by selling the products of his skill, would have to face a reduction in his income to attend the theatre. The disincentive against doing so would be especially strong for any whose trade might benefit from the great influx into the city from the country that the major festivals encouraged – cobblers, potters, suppliers of fast food; and some of those who came in from the country might have done so more in order to market their produce than to attend the theatre.

The situation of a ζευγίτης (*zeugites*), a man who owned at least one yoke of oxen (i.e. a member of the third Solonian class) would be different; and that difference would increase the nearer the land he owned and income he expected took him to the border-line that divided him from the ἱππεῖς (*hippeis*), those who owned a horse. No doubt at the bottom of the band of *zeugitai* there would be citizens whose land-holding and income were so small that they had no slave to help work the land. But the land can be left for a few days, and livestock can be left in the charge of wives and children: income will not suffer. The higher up the zeugite class we go, the greater the opportunity for the citizen to go to the city for private business, for political activity, and for private and public leisure, since the greater will be the number of that citizen's slaves to whom tasks can be assigned.

How many *zeugitai* were there in the 420s? A crucial passage of Thucydides ought to be able to give us the answer,[24] but of course it too is the subject of argument. Thucydides reports, in indirect speech, how Pericles encouraged the Athenians at the outbreak of the war by listing Athens' formidable resources: these included 13,000 hoplites, not counting the 16,000 in the forts and on the battlements, drawn from the oldest and youngest and from metics who were hoplites. There is a surprising discrepancy here between the numbers apparently of military age (13,000) and

[24] Th. 2.13.6–7.

those outside that age band, which at Athens seems to have been twenty to forty-nine, i.e. the number who are not of military age is high at 16,000. On Gomme's view the metics who were hoplites numbered 4,500 of these 16,000,[25] and the remaining 11,500 were the oldest and youngest of the hoplite class – males between eighteen and nineteen and between fifty and fifty-nine – together with many hoplites of military age (between twenty and forty-nine) who were not suitable for front-line service. For A. H. M. Jones the military age operative for Thucydides' figures was twenty to forty,[26] and on the basis of the figures in Thucydides he concludes that in 431 there were some 20,000 citizen hoplites of military age.[27] Both Gomme's and Jones' interpretation would give a hoplite class of around 26,000 if we include men between eighteen and nineteen and between fifty and fifty-nine. Hansen thinks that the oldest and youngest in Thucydides' figures were drawn from the thetes, and probably from poor metics, as well as from the *zeugitai*, and that the number of oldest and youngest who were citizens from the first three classes did not exceed 4,000.[28] For Richard Duncan-Jones most of the 16,000 were metics.[29] I am persuaded by Hansen, and so would suppose that the hoplites of military age, drawn from the first three classes but mainly from the *zeugitai*, and the oldest and youngest from these same three classes, numbered 13,000 and 4,000 respectively, i.e. 17,000 in all. To reach the total of citizens in the first three classes we must add the thousand or so cavalry attested by Thucydides,[30] whose figure of 1,200 for ἱππεῖς, 'cavalry', including ἱπποτοξόται, 'mounted archers', seems to include 200 thetes.[31] The first three classes, then, number around 18,000 between the ages of eighteen and sixty. One should also take account of boys (known to be present in the theatre audience from *Clouds* 539, *Peace* 50) and of over-sixties. That might raise the numbers from the first three classes who might contemplate attending the theatre to over 20,000.

Of course if Gomme's view were right there would be a much larger pool of potential theatre-goers from the first three classes of citizens – nearer to 27,000.

I would wish to put these data alongside my arguments about the disincentives to attendance encountered by poorer citizens and to infer that most of the places in the theatre –whether we suppose these to be to 3,700, 5,500, 7,000 or 10,000–12,000 – were taken at the Lenaea by citizens from the top three classes, i.e. around 18,000 between the ages of eighteen and

[25] See Gomme 1959, Hansen 1981, 19 with n.2. [26] Jones 1952, 16.
[27] Th. 2.13.6 and 8, Jones 1952, 28 n.42. [28] Hansen 1981, 23.
[29] Duncan-Jones 1983 cited Hansen 1988, n.4 [30] Th. 2.13.8. [31] Hansen 1981, n.13.

fifty-nine and perhaps another 2,000 boys and old men. At the Dionysia the presence of some foreigners and presumably a large number of metics will increase considerably – perhaps to over 25,000 – the number of men from whom the theatre audience might be drawn without taking thetes into account. Of course a thete from a city deme whose economic situation was close to that of poorer *zeugitai* would be more likely to attend than a not-too-well-off *zeugites* from a distant rural deme, and indeed the whole city/country mix is a factor that could have a drastic effect on these estimates. But it is not one which I intend to pursue, since I see even less evidence for constructing an argument than in the issue of economic distribution.

If one concludes that a very high proportion of the audience came from the first three Solonian classes, classes that were in varying degrees leisured classes, able to use substantial blocks of their time as they wished, it becomes very difficult to believe that a sizeable proportion of the spectators, even perhaps the majority, was not familiar with the nature of sophists and the teaching of rhetoric, and did not know quite well that Socrates' activities were different from those of a teacher of rhetoric.

4 The Portrayal of Socrates as a Sophist or 'Intellectual'

I now return to proposition (ii), that Socrates is portrayed as a sophist, or as an 'intellectual'.

It is clear that in one respect at least Socrates is portrayed as a sophist: he offers to teach rhetoric and he is thought to take fees for the instruction he offers.[32] But there are also elements in the portrayal of Socrates in *Clouds* which do not fit the notion that he is being portrayed as a sophist. One is the emphasis on natural science: it is instruction in various sciences that dominates the scenes between Strepsiades' arrival at the *phrontisterion* and the *parabasis* (134–509). Now some men who also taught rhetoric did include natural science among their very wide interests: in Plato's *Protagoras* Hippias is found answering questions περὶ φύσεως καὶ τῶν μετεώρων, 'about nature and the heavens', and there too Protagoras says that other sophists taught λογισμούς τε καὶ ἀστρονομίαν καὶ γεωμετρίαν καὶ μουσικήν, 'calculations and astronomy and geometry and music', whereas he himself does not.[33] But in saying this he glances meaningfully at Hippias, and it seems clear that for most sophists natural science was not central. Guthrie's conclusion

[32] E.g. 98, 245–6. [33] Pl. *Prt.* 315c (cf. *Hp.Ma.* 285b), 316e.

is that 'the aim was to be a good talker and to make debating points, not to acquire a scientific interest in a subject for its own sake'.[34]

Now this may be enough for comic poets to distort their portrayal to maximise humour, and just as *Clouds* includes Prodicus among οἱ μετεωροσοφισταί, 'the experts on the heavens', so Eupolis in *Flatterers* has a character say of Protagoras ἀλαζονευέται περὶ τῶν μετεώρων, τὰ δὲ χαμᾶθεν ἐσθίει, 'he pretends to expertise on the heavens, but he eats things from the ground'.[35] But *Clouds* pushes Socrates much further in the direction of natural science, and in doing so it assimilates him not to sophists but to thinkers περὶ φύσεως, 'about nature', like Anaxagoras, as Socrates himself is made to complain in Plato's *Apology*.[36]

Another interest associated with Socrates in *Clouds* is even less easily seen as contributing to a portrayal of Socrates as a sophist, and that is his involvement with Pythagoreanism. To my mind John Morrison demonstrated that many features of the *phrontisterion* are only explicable by the view that Aristophanes represents Socrates' school as a Pythagorean συνέδριον, 'meeting-house'.[37] Among 'philosophers', only Pythagoreans gathered together to live as a community, and like the inhabitants of the *phrontisterion* had dietetic rules, referred to their master as αὐτός,[38] and were thought of as pale as well as squalid and shoeless. Pheidippides' description of the *phrontisterion*'s inhabitants is as follows:

> τοὺς ὠχριῶντας, τοὺς ἀνυποδήτους λέγεις,
> ὧν ὁ κακοδαίμων Σωκράτης καὶ Χαιρεφῶν.
>
> you mean the pale ones, the unshod,
> who include godforsaken Socrates and Chaerephon.
>
> Aristophanes, *Clouds* 103–4

This is strikingly close to a text admittedly much later, picking out the same features as *Clouds*, where Aeschinas, commenting on how skinny and unkempt Thyomichus has become, says:

> τοιοῦτος πρώαν τις ἀφίκετο Πυθαγορικτάς,
> ὠχρὸς κἀνυπόδητος· Ἀθαναῖος δ' ἔφατ' ἦμεν.
>
> You are like a Pythagorean that turned up just the other day,
> pale and unshod; he claimed to be an Athenian.
>
> Theocritus 14.5–6

[34] Guthrie 1971a, 47. [35] Ar. *Nu.* 360, Eup. fr. 157 K–A. [36] Pl. *Ap.* 19c1–5, 26d6.
[37] Morrison 1958, 203. [38] D.L. 8.46, cf. *Nu.* 123.

The pallor of the inhabitants of the *phrontesterion* must be attributed partly to their Pythagoreanism, partly to the personal appearance of Chaerephon, later in *Clouds* (504) referred to as ἡμιθνής, 'half-dead', rather than to any general tendency of late fifth-century intellectuals to be pale as a result of spending an unusual amount of time indoors: as many of our testimonies show, they did not.

Faced with the difficulty that the ascription neither of scientific nor of Pythagorean interests to Socrates seems to assimilate him to sophists, the proponent of this sort of thesis is tempted to extend the caricature to that of the 'intellectual', i.e. moving from (ii)(a) to (ii)(b).[39] But there are problems here too. The language available to late fifth-century Athenians had no word for 'intellectual', as Dover observes,[40] though it did have specific terms for different classes of abnormal people whom *we* group as intellectuals. Indeed one passage that demonstrates this is actually cited by Dover in making his case. Socrates, commenting on Strepsiades' ignorance of the divine nature of clouds, says:[41]

οὐ γὰρ μὰ Δί' οἶσθ' ὁτιὴ πλείστους αὗται βόσκουσι σοφιστάς,
Θουριομάντεις, ἰατροτέχνας, σφραγιδονυχαργοκομήτας,
κυκλίων τε χορῶν ᾀσματοκάμπτας, ἄνδρας μετεωροφένακας,
οὐδὲν δρῶντας βόσκουσ' ἀργούς, ὅτι ταύτας μουσοποιοῦσιν.

No, for you are unaware that these clouds nourish very many sophists,
Thurian-diviners, men with medical skills, layabouts with long hair and onyx rings,
song-benders for cyclic choruses, men who lie about the heavens –
they nourish layabouts despite their idleness, because they make music about clouds.

Clouds 331–4

Here we should resist interpreting σοφιστάς, 'sophists', as a general term for 'all-purpose-intellectual', of which the chorus would then go on to enumerate certain species (an interpretation that Dover's note on 331 may be arguing for, but his conclusion is not clear to me); for if we do that, we create a list which omits the species of greatest importance for the plot of *Clouds*, the sophist in the specific sense of teacher, particularly of rhetoric. Rather 331–4 gives a list which shows that different species of 'intellectual' can be grouped together, but also shows that they can be differentiated. Furthermore it shows that the 'intellectual' activities expected to evoke

[39] So Dover 1968, xxxv–xxxvi. [40] Dover 1968, xxxv n.1. [41] Dover 1968, liii.

humour cover a wider range than those actually attributed to Socrates in *Clouds*: prophecy, medicine, the composition of songs for cyclic *choroi*. All these activities are in themselves susceptible of comic treatment, and indeed are exploited elsewhere by Aristophanes and other comic poets: but in *Clouds* they are not ascribed to Socrates. If Aristophanes is caricaturing Socrates as an intellectual, he does so selectively. The selection could be random, but it is more likely that some more rational principle is being applied. To me it seems worth investigating further whether that principle is 'conformity to the interests of the historical Socrates'.

5 The Historical Socrates

What were the interests of the historical Socrates? We may now return to proposition (i). There our problem in interpreting Clouds was founded upon the conflict between the picture of *Clouds* and the picture offered by Plato and Xenophon, a conflict where most scholars agreed that Plato and Xenophon must be preferred. I too believe that they must be preferred. But I think it can be argued that a much higher proportion of the picture of Socrates in *Clouds* than is usually allowed makes sense, albeit humorous sense, if seen as caricaturing the Socrates we know from other sources. I happily endorse the pages of an article by Martha Nussbaum where she draws attention to a number of features of Socrates in *Clouds* that chime with our information in Plato and Xenophon and suggest that Aristophanes is indeed giving us a portrait of Socrates:[42] certain physical traits, squalor and asceticism, dreamlike remoteness, education viewed as initiation and practised by stripping away the pupil's assumptions and getting him to recognise his ignorance.

As well as these, however, it can be argued that the two major features which we saw divided Socrates from sophists, an interest in natural science and an association with Pythagoreans, were either genuine features of Socrates or features which could plausibly be attributed to him in 424/3 BC.

The conflict with Plato and Xenophon on the issue of Socrates' interest in natural science is sometimes exaggerated. Whereas Plato's *Apology* vehemently dissociates Socrates from Anaxagoras,[43] elsewhere, in *Phaedo*, Plato (like Xenophon) concedes that in his youth Socrates developed a passionate interest in the writings of Anaxagoras. In *Phaedo* Socrates tells Cebes that in

[42] Nussbaum 1982, esp. 71–6. [43] Pl. *Ap.* 26d6-9.

his youth he became extremely interested in περὶ φύσεως ἱστορίαν, 'natural science';[44] he heard readings from a book of Anaxagoras on the role of νοῦς; he decided that Anaxagoras would tell him what he wanted; and he quickly acquired and read his works.[45] We are then told that he was greatly disappointed in what he found. We are not told how long this period of interest and testing persisted, though the impression is given that it cannot have lasted long. When was this period in Socrates' intellectual development? It could have been as early as, say, 449 BC; but the term νέος, spoken by a man of seventy about to die, could mean anything up to forty in a culture which had no specific term for 'middle-aged', and it does no violence to the phenomena to guess that this interest was in the 430s, when Socrates was still in his thirties, and when Anaxagoras was friendly with Pericles and, ultimately, prosecuted in order to attack Pericles. As Dover himself points out, caricatures of intellectuals are often out of date, and all I want to suggest is that in Athens of the 420s the public image of Socrates, even before its distortion by comic poets, included an association with physical science and Anaxagoras that was based on a historical fact of the 430s.

What of the association of Socrates with Pythagoreanism? Here we have not simply a conflict that has been exaggerated, but no conflict at all. Again the *Phaedo* is a key text. In his death-cell Socrates discusses the nature of the soul with Simmias and Cebes, both of whom are reckoned to be Pythagoreans, pupils of Philolaus of Croton.[46] Of Philolaus' Pythagoreanism there is little doubt, and according to Diogenes Laertius he was the first of the Pythagoreans to write περὶ φύσεως, 'on the natural world'.[47] Phaedo's interlocutor Echecrates can also be claimed as a Pythagorean.[48] Pythagoreans were certainly interested in the nature of the soul and its relation to the body, though the soul's analogy to *harmonia* proposed by Simmias seems to be incompatible with a position otherwise taken by Philolaus.[49] If Plato presents a Socrates who has Pythagorean friends with whom he discusses issues of known interest to Pythagoreans, we should not hesitate to suppose that the historical Socrates had and was known by his contemporaries to have relations with Pythagoreans. I do not want to go further than that. To understand *Clouds* we need not go down the road taken by A. E.

[44] νέος ὢν θαυμαστῶς ὡς ἐπεθύμησα ταύτης τῆς σοφίας ἣν δὴ καλοῦσι περὶ φύσεως ἱστορίαν, 'when I was young I had an extraordinary desire for this wisdom which they call investigation concerning nature', Pl. *Phd.* 96a7–8.

[45] Pl. *Phd.* 96a6ff., 97b8ff., 97d7ff.

[46] Pl. *Phd.* 61d.

[47] D.L. 8.85, quoting a Demetrius, *On homonyms* = D1 Laks–Most, cf. D–K 44A.

[48] D.L. 8.46, Iamb. *VP* 251, 267.

[49] Pl. *Phd* 88b6ff., see Taylor 1983, 221–2.

Taylor and attribute Pythagorean *beliefs* to Socrates.[50] But for the public image of Socrates – and for purposes of the comic poet – *association* with Pythagoreans was sufficient.

That Aristophanes could assume a public image of Socrates which linked him with Pythagoreans and their interest in the soul once separated from the body seems to me to be corroborated by a few lines in his play *Birds*. In a brief song the audience is given a hilarious picture of an unwashed Socrates in a land of ethnographic fantasy, the land of the shadow-feet, conjuring up the souls of the dead – or, as it turns out, half-dead. Peisander the coward went to get his own ψυχή, 'soul', which had abandoned him in mid-life (i.e. from cowardice), but when he had shed the needful sacrificial blood, up came not a conventional twittering ghost but Chaerephon the bat:

πρὸς δὲ τοῖς Σκιάποσιν
λίμνη τις ἔστ', ἄλουτος οὗ
ψυχαγωγεῖ Σωκράτης.
ἔνθα καὶ Πείσανδρος ἦλθε
δεόμενος ψυχὴν ἰδεῖν ἣ
ζῶντ' ἐκεῖνον προὔλιπε,
σφάγι' ἔχων κάμηλον ἀμνόν
τιν', ἧς λαιμοὺς τεμὼν
ὥσπερ οὑδυσσεὺς ἀπῆλθε,
κᾆιτ' ἀνῆλθ' αὐτῶι κάτωθεν
πρὸς τὸ λαῖμα τῆς καμήλου
Χαιρεφῶν ἡ νυκτερίς.

By the Shadowfeet
there is a swamp, where unwashed
Socrates summons up souls.
Peisander in fact went there,
asking to see the soul that
abandoned him when still alive,
bringing as a sacrifice a camel-lamb
and cutting its throat,
like Odysseus he backed off;
and then up from below arose to him,
making for the camel's gore,
Chaerephon the bat.

Aristophanes, *Birds* 1553–64

[50] Taylor 1911.

There is no reason to suppose that the characters in this vignette have been distorted to suit the overall purpose of the play, as can theoretically be argued of the portrayal of Socrates as a Pythagorean in *Clouds*. Socrates has no connection with the plot of *Birds*, even if there had been a brief mention of him as setting a fashion in Athens before the onset of ornithomania – ἐκόμων, ἐπείνων, ἐρρύπων, ἐσωκράτων, 'They grew their hair long, they starved, they were filthy, they were Socratic' (1283) – a mention which may have prepared the audience's mind for the gratuitous foray of 1553–64. But that song must be digested and laughed at by the audience in the time it takes the chorus to sing it: what is needed is immediate recognition of a Socrates interested in the condition of the soul after death, and of a Chaerephon already half-dead.

Where does this leave the portrayal of Socrates in *Clouds*? If my arguments are accepted, the substantial elements of the first half of *Clouds* which represent Socrates as interested in natural science and in Pythagoreanism can be added to those features identified by Nussbaum as portraying a Socrates who does not conflict with that of Plato and Xenophon and who may therefore correspond, as a caricature does to reality, to the historical Socrates of the 420s.

I do not, however, question the virtual unanimity of Plato, Xenophon and other sources that Socrates did not teach rhetoric and did not take fees. Why, then, does Aristophanes present him as doing so? Clearly I do not hold that he simply does not see the difference. Indeed one feature of the play points to his being well aware of the difference. Although Strepsiades goes to the *phrontisterion* to learn rhetoric, he receives no instruction in rhetoric proper until the *agōn*. The topics that occupy the section before the *parabasis* are drawn from natural science, which I have argued to be a legitimate element in caricature of a recognisable Socrates; some of the topics handled between *parabasis* and *agōn* fall within the range that seem to have interested the historical Socrates as well as sophists. When we do get the long delayed *agōn*, the *epideixis* is performed not by Socrates himself but by the two *logoi*: this introduces a certain distance between Socrates and rhetoric, even if the actor playing Socrates now plays the Lesser *Logos*, and may even assume the part of the Lesser *Logos* part in such a way that the audience may think of Socrates as playing it. When the *agōn /epideixis* is over, it may be the Lesser *Logos*, not Socrates, who leads Pheidippides off for his fatal dose of radical education, though there is a textual problem here.[51] Now this in no way exculpates Socrates, *pace* a number of scholars

[51] At 1105–11: see Bowie 2015 (Chapter 6, p. 103 in this volume).

(Murray, Erbse, Schmid, Gelzer),[52] since Socrates is clearly represented as in charge of all that happens in the school and as encouraging Strepsiades. But it might be interpreted as showing Aristophanes' awareness that when he involves Socrates in the teaching of rhetoric for money he is moving away from a caricature that his audience would recognise. Hence, with the exception of the necessarily expounded motive of Strepsiades for seeking out the *phrontisterion*, the picture of that institution and its director is built up to create a Socrates whom the audience can and will indeed recognise. Only when they have accepted that the character on stage is a very funny caricature of Socrates does Aristophanes allow the teaching of rhetoric to proceed.

Of course, like my Aristophanes, I am left with a problem: why did he try to attribute rhetorical expertise to Socrates when he had plenty other material with which to construct a comedy? My answer may seem lame, but to me it has fewer shortcomings than the others I have considered. It is that Aristophanes had two subjects around which he wanted to compose a comedy, and he thought he could combine them. *Clouds* was not the first or last of his plays in which two major themes are interwoven. *Acharnians* and *Lysistrata* deal chiefly with peace, but the former interlaces a long sequence of Euripidean parody, the latter fuses the theme of peace with a satirical treatment of women. *Thesmophoriazousae* combines a focus on Euripides with one on women. In *Clouds* the temptation to have a go at both Socrates and sophists must have been increased by the extent to which their interests and techniques did overlap. It is tempting to think too that there may be some connection with the fact that in the same year Ameipsias' *Konnos* had Socrates as a central character. Did Aristophanes, already intent on a play about the teaching of rhetoric that carried further his satire of political rhetoric in *Acharnians* and *Knights*, hear that Ameipsias planned a comedy about Socrates, and decide to try to up-stage him?

[52] Guthrie 1971b, 49.

6 Aristophanes' *Clouds*: An Agonistic Note (2015)

1 Introduction

The text of *Clouds* which has been transmitted to us by medieval manuscripts is not that of the play that Aristophanes entered in the comic *agōn* at the Dionysia of 424/3 BC but that of a revised version of that comedy. The relation between our revised version and the play performed in 424/3 was discussed in eighteen pages of his introduction to his commentary on *Clouds* by Kenneth Dover.[1] From this characteristically precise, logical and lucid discussion, which took scrupulous account of previous scholarship, some virtual certainties emerged. As maintained by the *hypothesis* that is numbered I by Dover and VI by Nigel Wilson in his Oxford Classical Text of 2007, the play that we have is by and large the play that was produced in 424/3.[2] Major revision was limited to the *parabasis*, the *agōn* between what the *hypothesis* and manuscripts of the play call the Just and the Unjust λόγοι, 'Arguments', and the closing scene of the conflagration of Socrates' school; but minor revisions are likely to have been made throughout the play. A text of the 'First *Clouds*' (as I shall henceforth term the play of 424/3) survived into the Hellenistic period, and this survival gives us good reason to accept the statement of that *hypothesis*; its view that the revised play was not entered in competition was almost certainly based on its absence from the records of victories at the Dionysia and the Lenaea, though Aristophanes' motive for conducting an extensive revision was indeed presumably to enter it in a competition.[3] The play we have contains references to Eupolis' comedy *Maricas* and to Hyperbolus that point to the revision having been made between 420 BC and 417 BC.

1 Dover 1968, lxxx–xcviii. The English version of this paper was published in Fernandez and Zecchin de Fasano 2015, 95–109; a version in Modern Greek appeared in *Ariadne / Αριάδνη* 19 (2013) 49–66.

2 τοῦτο ταὐτόν ἐστι τῶι προτέρωι, 'this is the same as the previous one', Dover 1968, *hypothesis* I = Wilson, N. G. 2007, *hypothesis* VI, line 1.

3 ὡς ἂν δὴ ἀναδίδαξαι μὲν αὐτὸ τοῦ ποιητοῦ προθυμηθέντος, οὐκέτι δὲ τοῦτο δι᾽ ἥνποτε αἰτίαν ποιήσαντος, 'as indeed one might expect if the poet had been keen to produce it again but for some reason or another had not in the end done so', Dover 1968, *hypothesis* I = Wilson, N. G. 2007, *hypothesis* VI, lines 2–3.

Most of these propositions are widely accepted, and I have no wish to challenge them. But two mutually related conclusions seem to me much less certain. One is that (a) if the play was not performed at either of the two great Athenian dramatic festivals it was not performed at all; the second is that (b) the revision was incomplete, and that as it stands the text of the play *could not* be performed. From this second proposition Dover went on to make an observation which would be of great significance if it were correct: 'Ar. allowed an unperformable and incompletely revised version of his play ... to go out of his hands and into circulation as a written text. This text was not a reminder of something seen on the stage but was intended for readers'.[4]

2 A Performance at τὰ κατ' ἀγροὺς Διονύσια?

Much has changed in Hellenists' views of the performance of Attic tragedy and comedy outside the city of Athens since Dover published his commentary in 1968. He himself noted that Aeschines 1.157 was evidence for the performance of comedy in a deme-theatre in the middle of the fourth century,[5] but was sceptical about using this as evidence for earlier practice. But the performance of Attic comedy as well as tragedy in South Italy as early as ca. 400 BC is demonstrated by a number of painted vases, above all the *Telephus* vase, discussed by Taplin 1993 in his ground-breaking book *Comic Angels*; and our greater knowledge of the arrangements for staging plays in the deme-theatre of the Piraeus in the fourth century, explored by Csapo 2007, adds to the admittedly meagre evidence that already pointed to theatrical competitions in deme-theatres in the late fifth century.

That evidence included an inscription from Eleusis, discussed by, *inter alios*, John Gould and David Lewis in their 1968 revision of Pickard-Cambridge's *Dramatic Festivals of Athens*, in which the prize for tragedy went to Sophocles and that for comedy to Aristophanes:[6]

> [Γ]νάθις Τιμοκ[ήδ]ο[ς, Ἀ]ναξανδρίδης Τιμα[γ]όρο
> χορηγôντες κωμωιδοῖς ἐνίκων·
> Ἀριστοφάνης ἐ[δ]ίδασκεν.
> ἑτέρα νίκη τραγωιδοῖς·
> Σοφοκλῆς ἐδίδασκεν

[4] Dover 1968, xcviii.

[5] πρώην ἐν τοῖς κατ' ἀγροὺς Διονυσίοις κωμωιδῶν ὄντων ἐν Κολλυτῶι, 'the other day at the Rural Dionysia when comic players were competing in Collytus'.

[6] Pickard-Cambridge 1988, 87.

Gnathis son of Timocedes and Anaxandrides son of Timagoras
were victorious with the chorus they provided for comic singers:
Aristophanes was the chorus-trainer.
Another victory with tragic singers:
Sophocles was the chorus-trainer.

IG i^3 970 = *IG* ii^2 3090

Unfortunately the date of this inscription is not undisputed, but the victories constitute a *prima facie* case for an *agōn* that took place before the death of Sophocles, and the most recent edition takes 426 BC as its earliest and 406 BC as its latest possible date.[7]

Alongside the theatre in the Piraeus, already in use by 411 BC,[8] a Dionysiac πομπή, 'procession', attested in the Piraeus by Demosthenes 21.10, and the competitions at Eleusis discussed above, epigraphy adds evidence for comedy and perhaps tragedy at Aexone.[9] A dedication of the 440s BC by the χορηγός (*chorēgos*) Socrates, discovered in 1954 at Varkiza, in the deme Anagyrous, commemorates a victory of his chorus in a tragic competition with no less a poet than Euripides, and has been seen by some as a celebration of a victory in a deme-festival. But Wilson was probably right, following Whitehead, to see this as one of several commemorations in demes of victories won by *chorēgoi* in city dramatic festivals.[10] Archaeological evidence adds other theatres in several other demes, including Aphidna, Thoricus and (very recently) Acharnae. The passage of Aeschines quoted above and another in Demosthenes (18.180) add the deme Collytus for fourth-century performances of both comedy and tragedy.

That the theatres in Aphidna and Thoricus were used for the performance of tragedy or comedy in the fifth century remains a matter of speculation, but to my mind the case is strengthened by the evidence presented by Goette in Wilson 2007 for the theatre of Dionysus in Athens having been much smaller than imagined by earlier estimates: as Csapo there

[7] Millis and Olson 2012.

[8] ἐς τὸ πρὸς τῆι Μουνιχίαι Διονυσιακὸν θέατρον ἐλθόντες καὶ θέμενοι τὰ ὅπλα ἐξεκλησίασαν, 'going to the theatre of Dionysus at Munichia and laying down their weapons they held an assembly', Th. 8.93.1.

[9] *choregoi* honoured by *IG* ii^2 1198 of 326/5 BC, 1200 of 317/16 BC and *SEG* 36.186 (312/11 BC). For a thorough discussion of textual and archaeological deme-theatres and suggestions about their uses see Paga 2010.

[10] Wilson 2000, 131–3, Whitehead 1986, 234: Wilson notes however that in Pickard-Cambridge 1988, 361 Gould and Lewis thought that the monument might commemorate a victory in a rural Dionysia. For an illuminating discussion of other deme-commemorations of victories in city festivals see Wilson 2000, 244–52.

argues, Goette demonstrates that the θέατρον, 'spectators' seating', of the fifth-century theatre was trapezoidal and the theatre itself could seat only between 4000 and 7000 spectators.[11] Whatever the Cleisthenic ideology of the Διονύσια ἐν ἄστει, 'City Dionysia', being intended as a festival for all Athenians from all demes, only a small proportion of Athenian citizens can have seen and heard performances either there or at the Lenaea, and the incentive will surely have been considerable for the poets who competed in the two big Athenian festivals also to enter their plays in deme-competitions and achieve wider acclaim. That by the early fourth century several Attic demes had dramatic festivals is also implied by Plato's description of φιλοθεάμονες in his *Republic* (composed around 380 BC but with an indeterminable dramatic date between 432 and 404 BC) as ὥσπερ δὲ ἀπομεμισθωκότες τὰ ὦτα ἐπακοῦσαι πάντων χορῶν περιθέουσι τοῖς Διονυσίοις οὔτε τῶν κατὰ πόλεις οὔτε τῶν κατὰ κώμας ἀπολειπόμενοι, 'but as if they had rented out their ears to listen to all choral performances they run around the Dionysia omitting neither those in cities nor those in villages' (Pl. *Rsp.* 475d).

That the victory-records of the city festivals afforded no evidence of Aristophanes' revised *Clouds* being given a χορός by the *archon* and entered in competition is not, therefore, watertight evidence that it was never performed in Attica. Given the exiguous epigraphic evidence for deme festivals we are very unlikely ever to have a text that shows that it *was* performed in a deme *agōn*, but it would be prudent to admit that we cannot demonstrate that it was not. One might imagine two scenarios: either (a) Aristophanes asks for a χορός, 'chorus', to διδάσκειν, 'produce', a performance of the revised version of *Clouds* at the city Dionysia or Lenaea, and the *archon* refuses to give him one, presumably on the ground that the play was essentially the same as that which had competed in 424/3 (τοῦτο ταὐτόν ἐστι τῶι προτέρωι ..., cf. above n.2) – and at that point Aristophanes decides to enter it in a deme-competition; or (b) he makes that choice of entering it in a deme-competition *ab initio*.

Would either of the above scenarios be precluded by the fact that the text available could not have been performed as it stands?

Here the arguments are of two different sorts, one drawn from anachronism, the other from dramaturgy.

[11] Csapo 2007, 97–9. For a statement of the case for a less socio-economically diverse audience of Attic drama than usually suggested see Sommerstein 1997, Bowie 1998 (Chapter 5 in this volume). For a refutation of part of Goette's argument see Papastamati-von Moock 2015, discussed in Chapter 5, p. 84.

3 Anachronism?

The argument from anachronism is not as strong as represented by Dover. It is clear from the text that has reached us that whereas the *parabasis* proper (518–62) is a new section, in a metre not found elsewhere in extant plays or fragments of Aristophanes (though perhaps more common in Eupolis, hence called by ancient metricians 'Eupolidean'),[12] the following epirrhematic sections of the *parabasis* (563–626) are almost certainly unchanged from 'First *Clouds*'. Thus they assume a *hic et nunc* of 424/3, with a Cleon still alive and active in Athens' political life.

One of their two references to Cleon is unproblematic because it is in a narrative of the past (581–9): the Clouds in their choral *persona* demonstrate their readiness to benefit the city of Athens by recalling the foul weather they had contrived when Cleon was competing for election as one of the ten *stratēgoi* for the year 424/3, elections which should have happened not long before the staging of 'First Clouds', and linking this with eclipses of the sun and moon.[13] Notwithstanding, they say, the Athenians went ahead and elected Cleon. That was as true, and as historically interesting, and as relevant to Aristophanes' own self-representation as a remorseless critic of Cleon, in the years 420–18 as it was when Cleon was still alive.

The second reference is indeed problematic (591–4). The chorus of Clouds continues: if Cleon is found guilty of bribe-taking and embezzlement and punished, the city's fortunes will return to their earlier happy state.

Such prosecution and punishment is clearly impossible after Cleon's death in 422. Should Aristophanes therefore have changed these lines? Simple deletion was not an option, since twenty lines are required in the *epirrhēma* (575–94) to be balanced by twenty in the *antepirrhēma* (607–26). Two related cases suggest that Aristophanes might not have seen an overriding argument for changing the lines.

First, his war against Cleon did not end with Cleon's death: in *Frogs* he has a non-elite character in the underworld call upon Cleon as her προστάτης, 'patron' (*Ra.* 569, followed up in 577). On this analogy from fifteen years later Aristophanes might not have hesitated to leave an anti-Cleon barb in the *epirrhēma* of his revised *Clouds* to entertain his audience.

[12] See Dover 1968, 164–5.

[13] Dover, persuaded by Mayor 1939, perversely doubts any link with the eclipse of the moon on 29 October 425 and of the sun on 21 March 424, certainly within the year during which Cleon will have been seeking election as στρατηγός, 'general', for 424/3, even if not strictly contemporaneous with the elections themselves.

Second, in a play of 423/2, *Wasps*, Aristophanes has his chorus of old, Cleon-loving men anticipate a trial of Laches (ὡς ἔσται Λάχητι νυνί, 'for today Laches will face the music', 240) that is apparently related to his conduct in Sicily. Laches' mission to Sicily ended in 425 BC:[14] if there was a prosecution (and we do not know that there was) it would have happened before the production of *Wasps* at the Lenaea of 423/2.[15] The *hic et nunc* of the chorus in the orchestra is not identical with the *hic et nunc* of the spectators in the *theatron*. What is future to the former can be past to the latter.

4 Dramaturgy

The only point at which Dover argued that the text of our *Clouds* could not be performed as it stands is at 888–92.[16] Strepsiades has brought Pheidippides to Socrates to learn the two Λόγοι, 'Arguments', the Stronger and the Weaker, or if not both, at least the Weaker. Socrates says that Pheidippides will be taught by the Λόγοι themselves, and that he will leave (*prima facie* a stage-direction that the actor playing Socrates will now leave the stage). Only a trimeter and a half spoken by Strepsiades precede two anapaestic dimeters uttered by the κρείττων λόγος, 'Stronger Argument';[17]

14 Laches was sent out to Sicily to aid Leontini in 427/6, Th. 3.86.1: although his fellow στρατηγός Charoeadas was killed, his campaign had some successes (3.90.2, 103.3) before he was succeeded by Pythodorus in 425 (3.115.6). Th. does not tell us why Pythodorus was sent to succeed him, and Laches continued to be prominent in Athenian politics (cf. 5.19.1; 5.24.2; 5.61.2) until his death in the battle of Mantinea (418). Mayor 1939, 48 held that Laches had been re-elected for 426/5 and that his year of office simply ended when he was replaced by Pythodorus in spring of 425.

15 There is no evidence outside *Wasps* and its scholia for a prosecution of Laches. The scholia on line 240 in manuscripts VLh and in the Aldine edition can appeal, *via* a Demetrius (perhaps the pupil of Zenodotus) to Philochorus for the view that his successors Sophocles and Pythodorus were 'also' punished, but their claim that Laches was called back for a trial that is mentioned in *Wasps* 240 is only conjectural (εἰκὸς γοῦν … 'at any rate it is probable …'): I print the text of the scholia as presented in TLG, based Koster's edition, Groningen 1978: ὡς τοῦ Κλέωνος εἰς δίκην ἐπαγαγόντος τὸν Λάχητα τοῦτό φησιν [LhAld], στρατηγῆσαι δὲ [VAld: L and h have γάρ] αὐτόν φησι Δημήτριος ἐπὶ ἄρχοντος Εὐκλέους [VLh] πρὸ τριῶν ἐτῶν εἰς Σικελίαν πεμφθέντα μετὰ νεῶν Λεοντίνοις βοηθήσοντα· οἱ δὲ περὶ τὸν Φιλόχορον διαδέξασθαι αὐτόν φασι Σοφοκλέα καὶ Πυθόδωρον, οὓς καὶ φυγῆι ζημιωθῆναι. εἰκὸς γοῦν μετακληθῆναι αὐτὸν ἐπὶ τὴν κρίσιν, ἧς νῦν ὁ κωμικὸς μνημονεύει [VLhAld], 'He says this on the basis that Cleon had brought Laches to trial [LhAld], but [VAld: L and h have "for"] Demetrius says his post as general was in the archonship of Eucles [VLh] three years before when he was sent to Sicily with a fleet to assist Leontini; and ["but?"] Philochorus and others say that he was succeeded by Sophocles and Pythodorus, who were also punished by exile. At any rate it is probable that he (sc. Laches) was called back for the trial which the comic poet now mentions [VLhAld]'.

16 Dover 1968, xcii–xciii and 208 on line 887.

17 For the allocation of the second half of 887 and the whole of 888, following the scholion on the *Estensis*, see Dover 1968, 208 on line 887.

these are immediately followed by two dimeters uttered by the ἥττων λόγος, 'Weaker Argument':

Σω. αὐτὸς μαθήσεται παρ' αὐτοῖν τοῖν λόγοιν.
    ἐγὼ δ' ἀπέσομαι.
Στ. τοῦτό νυν μέμνησ', ὅπως
    πρὸς πάντα τὰ δίκαι' ἀντιλέγειν δυνήσεται.

ΚΡΕΙΤΤΩΝ ΛΟΓΟΣ
χώρει δευρί, δεῖξον σαυτὸν
τοῖσι θεαταῖς, καίπερ θρασὺς ὤν.

ΗΤΤΩΝ ΛΟΓΟΣ
ἴθ' ὅποι χρήιζεις· πολὺ γὰρ μᾶλλόν σ'
ἐν τοῖς πολλοῖσι λέγων ἀπολῶ.

SOCRATES: He will learn himself from the Arguments themselves.
    I shall make off.
STREPSIADES: Then pay good attention to this, that
    he shall be able to contradict all just propositions.
Stronger Argument: Come here, show yourself
    to the spectators, bold though you are.
Weaker Argument: Go where you like: I shall all the more
    destroy you speaking before a large audience.

Aristophanes, *Clouds* 886–92

Since the actor who has hitherto been playing Socrates is now required to play one of the two *Logoi*, the time available for him to assume his new part is very short: Dover guesses not more than ten seconds.[18] Accordingly Dover follows a marginal note ΧΟΡΟΥ, 'of the chorus', in the *Venetus*, supported by the scholia in the *Venetus* and *Estensis*,[19] and perhaps by ΧΟΡ(ΟΣ),'Chor(us)', in the *Ravennas*, and argues that there was a choral song in 'First *Clouds*' that was removed in the version we have: 'Evidently its content was unsuitable for the revised version; it was therefore removed and, the revision being incomplete, nothing was substituted'.[20]

18 Dover 1968, xciii.

19 These scholia are as follows (I print the TLG text based on Koster's edition, Groningen 1974): (889a alpha) τοῦ χοροῦ τὸ πρόσωπον ἐκλέλοιπεν, ἐπιγραφὴ δὲ φέρεται "χοροῦ". VEBarb RsNp (889a beta) ἐπιγραφὴ ἐνταῦθα φέρεται "χοροῦ", ἐκλέλοιπε μέντοι. ERs (889a alpha) 'The chorus' part has fallen out, but there is transmitted the heading "of a chorus"'. VEBarb RsNp (889a beta) 'The heading "for a chorus" is transmitted here, but it has fallen out'.

20 Dover 1968, xciii.

Dover may be right to resist the idea that here, around 420–418 BC, we have the first instance of a note in a performance text indicating that a choral song *not* in that text was to be included in the actual performance, a phenomenon well-attested in the fourth century, and already found in our texts of *Assembly-women* at 729 and 876. But as he notes, Wilamowitz seems to have taken this note at *Clouds* 889 as our first instance.[21] Even if we give the note a different sense from that which we give it at *Assembly-women* at 729 and 876 and later, it is bold to suppose that knowledge of the text of 'First *Clouds*' at this point in the play had somehow filtered through the commentary and scholiastic tradition to emerge as the marginal note in V. Equally probably, I suggest, an ancient or Byzantine scholar or copyist had followed a similar line of reasoning to Dover's, and had concluded that a choral song was to be expected if not required at this point. Alternatively, as argued by Revermann, the reference to a chorus at this point, going back (in his view) to the metrical scholar Heliodorus, is to be taken as evidence that a choral passage once stood in the text of our revised *Clouds* and has dropped out, a choral passage that may have contained cock-fighting imagery which would explain the scholia's references to that and to the anthropomorphic presentation of the Arguments in our play.[22] It should perhaps also be asked whether the suggestion of the marginal note is not that there should be a choral song here but that the dimeters allocated to the ΔΙΚΑΙΟΣ ΛΟΓΟΣ, 'Just Argument', in the manuscripts should rather be given to the chorus as a form of κατακελευσμός, 'encouragement'.

Given the uncertainty concerning the correct interpretation of the marginal ΧΟΡΟΥ in the *Venetus*, let us return to the text that we have and examine *its* performability. First, we need to think about the use of anapaestic

[21] Wilamowitz, *SPAW* 1921, 738, cited by Dover 1968, xciii n.1. Dover's protestation that 'no inference about fifth-century practice in general can safely be drawn from an incompletely revised play' unfortunately assumes the correctness of his interpretation of one of his main pieces of evidence for incomplete revision.

[22] Revermann 2006, 213–17. The note by the scholiast on 889d in the *Venetus* and *Estensis* 'that he found χοροῦ in his manuscript together with a διπλῆ (<) indicating a change of metre and a κορωνίς (C) indicating the end of a structural unit' does not prove, as claimed by Revermann 2006, 214, that the mark goes back to Heliodorus, to whom the *subscriptio* of the *Venetus* tells us its critical signs and colometry are due. In our text as it stands we have both the end of a structural unit and a change of metre (from iambic trimeters to anapaestic dimeters) and in theory it could be these that Heliodorus' critical signs marked, as indeed the scholiast suggests (I print the text of the scholion on 889d as presented in *TLG*, based on Koster's edition, Groningen 1974): χώρει δευρί ERs: διπλῆ καὶ κορωνὶς ἀποχωρησάντων τῶν ὑποκριτῶν. VEBarb Rs μέλος δὲ τοῦ χοροῦ οὐ κεῖται, ἀλλὰ γέγραπται μὲν ἐν μέσωι "χοροῦ". καὶ ἕπεται ἐν εἰσθέσει ἀναπαιστικὸν < ἀμοιβαῖον> τῶν ὑποκριτῶν, 'Come here ERs: a *diple* and a *coronis*, the actors having withdrawn VEBarb Rs a choral song is not in the text, but there is written in between χοροῦ [of a chorus]. And there follows indented an anapaestic <alternating> song for the actors'.

dimeters, the metre used from 889 to 948. This is a metre of passages usually sung, and so it will have been here, accompanied by instrumental music on an αὐλός, 'pipe'.[23] We have no way of telling whether the musical performance of the actors accompanied by the αὐλητής, 'piper', was preceded (as it sometimes was) by a purely instrumental performance giving the actors the rhythm and tune. Dover's guess of ten seconds may be wide of the mark.

But even if the action moved forward at this rapid pace, how did Aristophanes want us to envisage this cameo-*agōn* by two Arguments? As a piece of entertaining stagecraft the 'abstract' Arguments could have been dressed or kitted-out in various ways to suit their respective roles as the Stronger and the Weaker Argument, and at the same time to evoke the *Virtue* and *Vice* of Prodicus' presumably recently performed or published *Hōrae* in which Heracles chose between the lifestyles offered by these personified abstractions.[24] But how was the audience to imagine Socrates arranging for this show in his generally realistically presented φροντιστήριον, 'Academy'? Just as actors (necessarily) played the Stronger and the Weaker Arguments, so too a realistically-minded spectator will have imagined that two members of the φροντιστήριον assumed the characters of the two Arguments in the confrontation. Given the consistent alignment of Socrates' behaviour and teaching throughout the play with the doctrines of the Weaker (or 'Unjust') Argument,[25] it will surely have seemed very appropriate to Aristophanes to imagine Socrates himself playing that Argument – and if that is how the playwright envisaged the mechanics of the φροντιστήριον performance, why not make the short step towards having the actor who has hitherto been playing Socrates *visibly* assume the part of the Weaker Argument? On this, admittedly very speculative, assumption, the actor who utters Socrates' 'exit-line' ἐγὼ δ' ἀπέσομαι, 'I shall be off' (887a) need change no more than his mask (visibly, on stage, with no need to go inside the *skene*-building to do so) before singing the first lines of the Weaker Argument, 891–2.[26]

Some support for this idea can be found at the end of the cameo-*agōn*. After the defeat of the Stronger Argument and Strepsiades' conversion to

[23] For the importance of the αὐλητής, 'piper', in Athenian dramatic performances see Wilson 2000, 68–9 with further discussions referred to in his n.83.

[24] Xen. *Mem.* 2.1.21–34. That this was a work that has recently come into the public eye is of course conjectural, but the conjecture is supported by the fact that in 424/3 Aristophanes' successful rival Cratinus seems also to have adapted this schema in his Πυτίνη, '*Wineflask*'.

[25] I think the identification precedes this scene (cf. e.g. line 99), whereas Revermann 2006, 222 writes 'from this part of the play onwards Socrates is identified with the weaker argument'.

[26] This hypothesis is of course incompatible with the view that the costume of the 'Weaker Argument' in some way reflected or emblematised a particular lifestyle that differed from that of the stage 'Socrates' himself. As the discussion by Revermann 2006, 209–11 shows, the text offers us virtually no evidence on the costume of either Argument.

the camp of the Weaker (1102–4) a character asks Strepsiades (who has been an internal audience throughout the 212 lines of the performance) whether he wants his son's tutor to be the Stronger Argument or the speaker himself:

> τί δῆτα; πότερα τοῦτον ἀπάγεσθαι λαβὼν
> βούλει τὸν υἱόν, ἢ διδάσκω σοι λέγειν.
>
> Well then? Do you want to choose this one to take away
> your son, or am I the person you want to teach him to speak?
>
> Aristophanes, *Clouds* 1105–6

These two lines, and 1111, ἀμέλει, κομιεῖ τοῦτον σοφιστὴν δέξιον ('Indeed, you will get this boy back a quick-witted sophist'), are given by all the manuscripts to Socrates. Modern editors' allocation of these lines to the Weaker Argument is based on what can be inferred from the remark in the scholia to the *Ravennas* and the *Venetus*, where Pheidippides is described as τῶι ἑτέρωι παραδοθείς. In Dover's words: 'Socrates is off stage, and the part of Right or Wrong has been taken by the actor who played Socrates. There is no time for a change of costume, and no formal grounds for positing a lost choral song between 1104 and 1105. Therefore it is Wrong, not Socrates … who now addresses Strepsiades and takes over Pheidippides … If Socrates is not there, the line can only be spoken by someone else.'

This apparently adamantine logic becomes weaker if we suppose that Socrates has visibly been playing the Weaker Argument, and it offers no explanation of why our chief manuscripts have made an erroneous attribution of speaker. An alternative way to envisage the playing of this scene is that the actor playing the Weaker Argument reveals to, or reminds, the audience that in intra-dramatic terms it has been Socrates himself playing that Argument all along.

5 Conclusions

Neither alleged anachronism nor dramaturgic impossibility can be incontrovertibly demonstrated. The text of *Clouds* that we have could have been performed as it stands. Perhaps, indeed, it was entered and performed in an agonistic deme-festival. Its movement into the transmitted corpus of Aristophanic scripts may therefore have been no different from that of his other plays. Readers of course there were, of many sorts, in Athens of the last quarter of the fifth century BC, but we need not conclude that it was for them that Aristophanes made available a text of his revision of *Clouds*.

7 The Lesson of Book 2 (2018)

1 Introduction

In his admirably judicious, probing and nuanced opening chapter, 'Unitarians, separatists and book II', Charles Fornara made just one statement that has long seemed to me to be uncharacteristically injudicious: 'Most striking of all, and hardly to be explained by the subject-matter, is the *utter absence* in II of the moral or philosophical element, Regenbogen's religious motive, exemplified in I by the Solon-Croesus story, though not by that alone'.[1] This chapter will first explore the ways in which Book 2 might be argued to resist this assessment, and will pick out some features that link it with other parts of Herodotus. It will then draw attention to some elements in Herodotus' presentation already found in archaic and early classical narrative elegy, culminating in the work of Herodotus' relative Panyassis; will briefly notice the differences between Herodotus' work and that of Hecataeus; and will conclude by offering an explanation for the diversity of Herodotus' masterpiece that is so strikingly exemplified by Book 2.

2 A Very Herodotean Helen-*Logos*

One element that seems not to match Fornara's assessment is Herodotus' conclusion to his version of the story of Helen having been not in Troy but in Egypt.[2] That conclusion runs as follows (2.120):

[1] Fornara 1971, 18. The italics of '*utter absence*' are his. This assessment was already questioned by Munson 2001, 5 n.11. I am very grateful to the editors of this volume who invited me to contribute to it and to the conference from which it emerged, and in particular to Liz Irwin for her acute and helpful editorial interventions. I am also grateful to many generations of undergraduate pupils, chiefly at Corpus Christi College, Oxford, with whom I discussed Book 2 once it had become one of the prescribed texts for the main Greek literature paper in the new literature option in the Oxford school of *Literae Humaniores* (first Final Examination June 1972) just after Fornara's book was published. I have also benefited greatly from discussions of Herodotus with many colleagues, especially Oswyn Murray and Detlev Fehling, and with the only person in whose supervision for a doctoral thesis on Herodotus I have been involved, Simon Ubsdell (see Ubsdell 1983). English translations of Herodotus are those of A. D. Godley unless otherwise indicated.

[2] For a subtle and persuasive analysis of Hdt.'s sophisticated treatment of the Helen-*logos* see Irwin 2014, 52–7.

ταῦτα μὲν Αἰγυπτίων οἱ ἱρέες ἔλεγον. ἐγὼ δὲ τῶι λόγωι τῶι περὶ Ἑλένης λεχθέντι καὶ αὐτὸς προστίθεμαι, τάδε ἐπιλεγόμενος· εἰ ἦν Ἑλένη ἐν Ἰλίωι, ἀποδοθῆναι ἂν αὐτὴν τοῖσι Ἕλλησι ἤτοι ἑκόντος γε ἢ ἀέκοντος Ἀλεξάνδρου. οὐ γὰρ δὴ οὕτω γε φρενοβλαβὴς ἦν ὁ Πρίαμος οὐδὲ οἱ ἄλλοι προσήκοντες αὐτῶι, ὥστε τοῖσι σφετέροισι σώμασι καὶ τοῖσι τέκνοισι καὶ τῆι πόλι κινδυνεύειν [ἐβούλοντο], ὅκως Ἀλέξανδρος Ἑλένηι συνοικέηι. εἰ δέ τοι καὶ ἐν τοῖσι πρώτοισι χρόνοισι ταῦτα ἐγίνωσκον, ἐπεὶ πολλοὶ μὲν τῶν ἄλλων Τρώων, ὁκότε συμμίσγοιεν τοῖσι Ἕλλησι, ἀπώλλυντο, αὐτοῦ δὲ Πριάμου οὐκ ἔστι ὅτε οὐ δύο ἢ τρεῖς ἢ καὶ ἔτι πλέους τῶν παίδων μάχης γινομένης ἀπέθνῃσκον (εἰ χρή τι τοῖσι ἐποποιοῖσι χρεώμενον λέγειν), τούτων δὲ τοιούτων συμβαινόντων ἐγὼ μὲν ἔλπομαι, εἰ καὶ αὐτὸς Πρίαμος συνοίκεε Ἑλένηι, ἀποδοῦναι ἂν αὐτὴν τοῖσι Ἀχαιοῖσι, μέλλοντά γε δὴ τῶν παρεόντων κακῶν ἀπαλλαγήσεσθαι. οὐ μὲν οὐδὲ ἡ βασιληίη ἐς Ἀλέξανδρον περιήϊε, ὥστε γέροντος Πριάμου ἐόντος ἐπ᾽ ἐκείνωι τὰ πρήγματα εἶναι, ἀλλὰ Ἕκτωρ καὶ πρεσβύτερος καὶ ἀνὴρ ἐκείνου μᾶλλον ἐὼν ἔμελλε αὐτὴν Πριάμου ἀποθανόντος παραλάμψεσθαι, τὸν οὐ προσῆκε ἀδικέοντι τῶι ἀδελφεῶι ἐπιτρέπειν, καὶ ταῦτα μεγάλων κακῶν δι᾽ αὐτὸν συμβαινόντων ἰδίηι τε αὐτῶι καὶ τοῖσι ἄλλοισι πᾶσι Τρωσί. ἀλλ᾽ οὐ γὰρ εἶχον Ἑλένην ἀποδοῦναι οὐδὲ λέγουσι αὐτοῖσι τὴν ἀληθείην ἐπίστευον οἱ Ἕλληνες, ὡς μὲν ἐγὼ γνώμην ἀποφαίνομαι, τοῦ δαιμονίου παρασκευάζοντος ὅκως πανωλεθρίηι ἀπολόμενοι καταφανὲς τοῦτο τοῖσι ἀνθρώποισι ποιήσωσι, ὡς τῶν μεγάλων ἀδικημάτων μεγάλαι εἰσὶ καὶ αἱ τιμωρίαι παρὰ τῶν θεῶν. καὶ ταῦτα μὲν τῆι ἐμοὶ δοκέει εἴρηται.

1. The Egyptians' priests said this, and I myself believe their story about Helen, for I reason thus: had Helen been in Ilion, then with or without the will of Alexander she would have been given back to the Greeks. 2. For surely Priam was not so mad, or those nearest to him, as to consent to risk their own persons and their children and their city so that Alexander might cohabit with Helen. 3. Even if it were conceded that they were so inclined in the first days, yet when not only many of the Trojans were slain in fighting against the Greeks, but Priam himself lost to death two or three or even more of his sons in every battle (if the poets are to be believed), in this turn of events, had Helen been Priam's own wife, I cannot but think that he would have restored her to the Greeks, if by so doing he could escape from the evils besetting him. 4. Alexander was not even heir to the throne, in which case matters might have been in his hands since Priam was old, but Hector, who was an older and a better man than Alexander, was going to receive the royal power at Priam's death, and ought not have acquiesced in his brother's wrongdoing, especially when that brother was the cause of great calamity to Hector himself and all the rest of the Trojans. 5. But since they did not have Helen there to give back, and since the Greeks would not believe them although they spoke the truth – I am convinced and declare – the divine

> powers provided that the Trojans, perishing in utter destruction, should make this clear to all mankind: that retribution from the gods for terrible wrongdoing is also terrible. This is what I think, and I state it.

This emphatically pronounced judgement follows Herodotus' narrative of Helen's arrival in Egypt, an account which he claims to have been given by Egyptian priests (2.113–15): Helen had come to Egypt with Paris (whom Herodotus calls Alexander, as already at 1.3.1), driven off course by winds; Paris' servants had whistle-blown to the local governor, Thonis; and Thonis had sent a message, presented to the reader in direct speech, to the Pharaoh known to Greeks as Proteus; Proteus' reply, summoning Paris to Memphis, is also in direct speech, as is Proteus' outraged condemnation of Paris, addressing him as ὦ κάκιστε ἀνδρῶν, 'Most evil of men' (2.115.4–5) in a tirade in which he gives Paris three days to leave the country and says that he will keep Helen until her husband, Paris' betrayed host Menelaus, comes to get her. These uses of direct speech and the strong moral stance of Proteus are both very much in the manner of the 'mature', judgmental Herodotus whom the reader knows from Book 1. So too is the insistence on divine retribution for misdeeds which ends the section printed above (2.120.5), though of course it is far from being confined to Book 1 (cf. e.g. 4.205). Between the narrative of Helen's arrival and Proteus' ultimatum comes Herodotus' citation of the *Iliad* (2.116.3) and perhaps of the *Odyssey* (2.116.4–5),[3] and his argument that the *Cypria*'s different version of Paris' trip to Troy, reached already on the third day, shows that poem not to be by Homer (2.116–17). This sophistic play with *Homerkritik* is unlike anything in the rest of Book 2 or elsewhere in his work,[4] though it has some affinities with his exposé of Hecataeus' chronological system a little later in the book (2.143).Yet his display of scholarly virtuosity is seamlessly interwoven with the story Herodotus purports to have got from the priests and with the *ex cathedra* judgement bringing together morality and religion at 2.120.5.

It seems virtually certain to me that the basic outlines of the story that Herodotus credits to the priests are known to him not from them but

[3] Deleted by Schaefer as an interpolation, followed by Hude in his 1908 OCT. Stein (1869–71 vol. 1, xliii–xliv) suggested that at 2.116–17 the two passages from the *Odyssey* (which do not support Hdt.'s main point here) were among several that could be identified as additions by Hdt. at a late stage in composition which he had not had the opportunity properly to integrate in his presentation, a suggestion endorsed by Powell 1936, 76 and Wilson 2015, vol. 1: viii and 191–2.

[4] Quite different are the attribution to Homer or another early poet of the invention of a river Oceanus (2.23) and to Homer and Hesiod of the creation of the Greeks' divine family (2.53.1–2) and the citation of Od. 4.85 on the relation between climate and cattle's horn-growing (4.29). The comment on the authorship of the *Cypria* is, however, in itself similar to the questioning of Homer's authorship of the *Epigonoi* at 4.32. For Hdt.'s *Homerkritik* see Grintser 2018.

from Stesichorus, some of whose poetry was being sung in Attic symposia in the generation before Eupolis and whose *Oresteia* could be assumed by Aristophanes to be familiar to the audience of his *parabasis* in *Peace*.[5] Herodotus' presentation of this Helen-story invites his readers to compare and to contrast the nature of his own predominantly 'scientific' Egyptian *logos* with the hexameter epic of Homer and the epic-like melic of Stesichorus, who, like Homer, had made speeches a major vehicle for the analysis of characters' motivations and for formulations of moral judgements – a feature whose exploitation in prose by Herodotus was characterised by Fornara 1971, 22 as 'a momentous invention'. Herodotus may also, of course, know Euripides' treatment of the story in his Attic tragedy *Helen* of 412 BC, though that supposition would require a later date for Herodotus than many scholars are willing to allow.[6] But from wherever Herodotus has got the bare bones of the story, the flesh he has put on it is distinctly his own: I quote the conclusions reached independently by de Jong 2012, 141:[7]

> The Helen *logos*, said to derive from Egyptian priests, upon closer inspection reveals the hand of Herodotus everywhere. The story pattern of the enquiring king, the motif of incredulity, the principle of divine retribution all occur elsewhere in his work. The story, though presented in two instalments, is in fact a close-knit whole. The handling of rhythm and the repetition of keywords are also typical Herodotean narrative strategies.

It can of course be claimed that the Helen-story was inserted by a 'mature' Herodotus into a draft of Book 2 that had reached its penultimate form, one that perhaps remained closer in texture to the work of Hecataeus, at some time earlier in his intellectual development.[8] Such a claim cannot be formally refuted, but three quite different phenomena much reduce its appeal.

First, some ten chapters after the Helen-*logos*, at 2.134–5, the reader encounters a parallel, pendant *logos* about the Thracian-Greek *hetaera* Rhodopis. It is parallel insofar as the central character in each *logos* is a very beautiful woman whose sexual charm had a far-reaching impact on

[5] Cf. Eup. 148 K–A and 395 K–A, Ar. *Peace* 775–80 and 796–801, which with the *scholia* give us Stesichorus fr. 172–4 Finglass: cf. Bowie 2015a (Chapter 30 in Volume 1). I realise that here I side-step an impassioned debate on Hdt.'s source(s) for his presentation of Proteus and the story of Helen: I have found especially helpful the discussions in Kannicht 1969, 21–48; Lloyd 1988, 46–8; Fehling 1989, 63–4; Austin 1994, 118–36; Nesselrath 1996; the overview by de Jong 2012, 128; Irwin 2014, 42–57.

[6] In favour of such a late date see Irwin 2018.

[7] By 'independently' I mean that I had formulated the overall structure and details of my argument before encountering de Jong's excellent discussion (many other details of which support my position) and I am confident she had no access to my views before writing.

[8] The classic statement of the developmental hypothesis remains Jacoby 1913, succinctly summarised by Fornara 1971, 4.

Greek men – on Menelaus, from the heroic past, who eventually got to Egypt to take Helen home after fighting a war which was the central feature of Homer's epics, and on Charaxus, brother of Sappho, who ransomed the *hetaera* Rhodopis for a large sum and thereby provoked Sappho to compose the only one of her songs to be explicitly mentioned by Herodotus. Although Herodotus seems certainly to be wrong in naming the *hetaera* Rhodopis rather than Doricha, the broad lines of his account have recently received dramatic confirmation with the publication of a poem from the first book of a Hellenistic edition of Sappho's songs in which she addresses a female figure brusquely and enjoins prayers for Charaxus' safe return.[9] The story of Rhodopis is linked to that of Helen not only by its theme but by the epithet ἀοίδιμος, 'famed in song', applied by Herodotus to another beautiful *hetaera* from Naucratis, Archidice,[10] as it is by the Homeric Helen to herself and Paris in the word's only appearance in the *Iliad* (6.358).

The two episodes each illustrate the socially disruptive capacity of human sexual attraction which had been a *motif* since the first pages of the *Enquiry*; but they also, along with one or two other details,[11] serve to link the long Egyptian *logos* with things Greek from which it was in some danger of becoming detached, as Herodotus was surely aware.

Secondly, though the Egyptian geography, ethnography and regal history indisputably have a different overall texture and flavour from other *logoi*, they also share many of Herodotus' recurrent points of reference – the

[9] Herodotus' mistake concerning the name of the *hetaera* was already pointed out by Ath. 13.596c: for a stimulating recent discussion see Nagy 2015; Nagy 2018. For the new Sappho poem concerning Charaxus ('the Brothers song') see Obbink 2014 (*ed. pr.*) and his revised text and discussions by many scholars in Bierl and Lardinois 2016. Already before its discovery Maria Kazanskaya had argued in 2013 (now Kazanskaya 2019) that in the Herodotean sentence Χάραξος δὲ ὡς λυσάμενος Ῥοδῶπιν ἀπενόστησε ἐς Μυτιλήνην, ἐν μέλεϊ Σαπφὼ πολλὰ κατεκερτόμησέ μιν, 'when Charaxus purchased Rhodopis' freedom and returned to Mytilene Sappho heaped much abuse upon μιν [?him? her/] in a song', 2.135.6, the μιν refers not to Charaxus (as most had interpreted it) but to the *hetaera*. For an argument that the 'Brothers' poem on *P.Obbink* (Obbink 2014) also addresses the *hetaera* with whom Charaxus was entangled, see Bowie 2016d (Chapter 33 in Volume 1).

[10] τοῦτο δὲ ὕστερον ταύτης <ἑτέρη> τῆι οὔνομα ἦν Ἀρχιδίκη ἀοίδιμος ἀνὰ τὴν Ἑλλάδα ἐγένετο, ἧσσον δὲ τῆς προτέρης περιλεσχήνευτος, 'and secondly, later than her [sc. Rhodopis], another whose name was Archidice became famed in song throughout Greece, though less gossiped about than the earlier woman', 2.135.5. The historicity of Archidice seems to have been corroborated by the discovery in the *temenos* of Aphrodite at Naucratis of a pottery dedication inscribed on its foot with the name ΑΡ]ΧΕΔΙΚΗ, cf. Hogarth, Edgar and Gutch 1898–9, 56 no. 108, illustrated by Möller 2000, fig. 3d. The MSS of Ath. 13.596d give the form Ἀρχεδίκη, those of Herodotus Ἀρχιδίκη, printed by editors including Wilson 2015.

[11] E.g. other references to Homer, 2.23 and 53 (already noted above n.4) and Hesiod, 2.53; Hecataeus, 2.143; correspondences between Greek and Egyptian divinities, 2.144–6; the embassy of the Eleians concerning their σοφία, 2.160 (see below with n.16).

identification of cleverness in both Greeks and βάρβαροι, 'non-Greeks', of patterns of arbitrary and irrational actions, of brutality, injustice, and megalomania. Reactions both arbitrary and brutal are exemplified in Apries' summary treatment of Patarbemis when, ordered by him to bring Amasis to him, Patarbemis presents himself unaccompanied (2.162.5):

> ὡς δὲ ἀπικέσθαι αὐτὸν πρὸς τὸν Ἀπρίην οὐκ ἄγοντα τὸν Ἄμασιν, οὐδένα λόγον ἑωυτῶι δόντα ἀλλὰ περιθύμως ἔχοντα περιταμεῖν προστάξαι αὐτοῦ τά τε ὦτα καὶ τὴν ῥῖνα.
>
> When he came to Apries without bringing Amasis, engaging in no reflection but overcome by great anger he ordered his ears and nose to be cut off.

Manifest too is an interest in the unavoidable pattern of history and the unpredictability of the course of events, as can be seen again in the case of Apries, who is destined to come to a bad end.[12]

Herodotus also gives recurrent attention to some positive qualities, as in other books. Thus even the Egyptian king Sesostris recognises the importance of ἐλευθερίη, 'freedom', that concept that is central to the other eight books (2.102.4–5):[13]

> ὁτέοισι μέν νυν αὐτῶν ἀλκίμοισι ἐνετύγχανε καὶ δεινῶς μαχομένοισι περὶ τῆς ἐλευθερίης, τούτοισι μὲν στήλας ἐνίστη ἐς τὰς χώρας διὰ γραμμάτων λεγούσας τό τε ἑωυτοῦ οὔνομα καὶ τῆς πάτρης καὶ ὡς δυνάμι τῆι ἑωυτοῦ κατεστρέψατό σφεας· ὅτεων δὲ ἀμαχητὶ καὶ εὐπετέως παρέλαβε τὰς πόλις, τούτοισι δὲ ἐνέγραφε ἐν τῆισι στήληισι κατὰ ταὐτὰ καὶ τοῖσι ἀνδρηίοισι τῶν ἐθνέων γενομένοισι καὶ δὴ καὶ αἰδοῖα γυναικὸς προσενέγραφε, δῆλα βουλόμενος ποιέειν ὡς εἴησαν ἀνάλκιδες.
>
> When those that he (Sesostris) met were valiant men and strove hard for freedom, he set up pillars in their land, the inscription on which showed his own name and his country's, and how he had overcome them with his own power; but when the cities had made no resistance and been easily taken, then he put an inscription on the pillars just as he had done where the nations were brave; but he also drew on them the private parts of a woman, wishing to show clearly that the people were cowardly.

However the Egyptians themselves are observed to be unable to benefit from ἐλευθερίη and to function without a monarchy (2.147.2):[14]

[12] ἔδεε κακῶς γενέσθαι, 'it had to be that disaster should befall him', 2.161.3.

[13] On ἐλευθερίη and other political ideas in Herodotus see esp. Munson 2001.

[14] Tom Harrison draws to my attention the parallel, apparently inevitable, drift towards monarchy in Hdt.'s account of Deioces at 1.96–9.

> ἐλευθερωθέντες Αἰγύπτιοι μετὰ τὸν ἱρέα τοῦ Ἡφαίστου βασιλεύσαντα (οὐδένα γὰρ χρόνον οἷοί τε ἦσαν ἄνευ βασιλέος διαιτᾶσθαι) ἐστήσαντο δυώδεκα βασιλέας, [ἐς] δυώδεκα μοίρας δασάμενοι Αἴγυπτον πᾶσαν.
>
> After the reign of the priest of Hephaestus the Egyptians were made free. But they could never live without a king, so they divided Egypt into twelve districts and set up twelve kings.

That the twelve kings here introduced acted justly for a time is picked out a little later.[15] Justice also marks an anecdote concerning Psammis that is one of those in Book 2 to tie together Egyptian and Greek affairs. The Eleians come to Psammis boasting that their organisation of the Olympic Games shows the height of justice (2.160.1):[16]

> ἐπὶ τοῦτον δὴ τὸν Ψάμμιν βασιλεύοντα Αἰγύπτου ἀπίκοντο Ἠλείων ἄγγελοι, αὐχέοντες δικαιότατα καὶ κάλλιστα τιθέναι τὸν ἐν Ὀλυμπίηι ἀγῶνα πάντων ἀνθρώπων, καὶ δοκέοντες παρὰ ταῦτα οὐδ᾽ ἂν τοὺς σοφωτάτους ἀνθρώπων Αἰγυπτίους οὐδὲν ἐπεξευρεῖν.
>
> While this Psammis was king of Egypt, he was visited by ambassadors from Elis, the Eleians boasting that they had arranged the Olympic games with all the justice and fairness in the world, and claiming that even the Egyptians, although the wisest of all men, could not do better.

Of course Psammis, summoning the wisest of the Egyptians, soon refutes the Eleian envoys.

Just conduct is also attributed earlier in the book to Mycerinus (2.129.1):

> τὸν δὲ τά τε ἱρὰ ἀνοῖξαι καὶ τὸν λεὼν τετρυμένον ἐς τὸ ἔσχατον κακοῦ ἀνεῖναι πρὸς ἔργα τε καὶ θυσίας· δίκας δέ σφι πάντων βασιλέων δικαιοτάτας κρίνειν.
>
> he opened the temples and let the people, ground down to the depth of misery, go to their business and their sacrifices; and he was the most just judge among all the kings.

Here, however, the inevitability of disaster even for this just monarch is flagged up a few lines later in the words κακῶν ἄρξαι, 'begin disasters' (2.129.3):

> ἐόντι δὲ ἠπίωι τῶι Μυκερίνωι κατὰ τοὺς πολιήτας καὶ ταῦτα ἐπιτηδεύοντι πρῶτον κακῶν ἄρξαι τὴν θυγατέρα ἀποθανοῦσαν αὐτοῦ.

[15] τῶν δὲ δυώδεκα βασιλέων δικαιοσύνηι χρεωμένων, ἀνὰ χρόνον ὡς ἔθυσαν ἐν τῶι ἱρῶι τοῦ Ἡφαίστου, 'Now the twelve kings adhered to justice, and when in time they came to sacrifice in Hephaestus' temple', 2.151.1 (here Godley's translation has been modified).

[16] This incident ties in with Herodotus' interest in refuting Greek claims to possess the greatest σοφίη, 'wisdom', cf. 1.60.3 and Munson 2001, 12.

> Though mild toward his people and conducting himself as he did, there came to him first a beginning of disasters, the death of his daughter.

These words κακῶν ἄρξαι, 'there began disasters', slightly vary a locution that Herodotus also uses elsewhere, κακῶν ἀρχή, 'a beginning of disasters' – a phrase that come to him from the *Iliad*'s account of Patroclus' momentous (and disastrous) intervention in the battle for the Achaean ships: the weight given to the concept by the Iliadic intertext helps a reader to see the parallelism between Herodotus' Egyptian story here and his account of the case that was arguably more fateful (certainly for Greeks) of the ships sent by Athens to help the Ionians in their revolt against Persia, where he uses precisely the Iliadic phrase ἀρχὴ κακῶν, 'beginning of disasters'.[17] The form that this particular Herodotean disaster in Egypt takes is the alleged infatuation of Mycerinus with his daughter: she was so traumatised that she strangled herself, a story that Herodotus dismisses as bunk (2.131.1–2), but its inclusion offers a thematic link between this Egyptian narrative and his narratives of incest and other irregular sexual relations in other books,[18] and more broadly with his theme of the impact of sexual desire on the course of history that begins with the first chapters of Book 1, where it is underlined by a possible allusion to what was later the most famous love poem of Sappho, and that is one of several threads running through the whole work, including Book 2.[19]

Thirdly, and finally, very numerous references to Greeks (*passim*), and some to Persians – e.g. to Dareius, contrasting his failure to conquer Scythia with Sesostris' own success (2.110.3) – remind us that Book 2 is part of a wider project to investigate the ἔργα μεγάλα τε καὶ θωμαστά of Greeks and barbarians alike.

[17] αὗται δὲ αἱ νέες ἀρχὴ κακῶν ἐγένοντο Ἕλλησί τε καὶ βαρβάροισι, 'These ships were the beginning of disasters for Greeks and barbarians', 5.97.3: cf. κακοῦ δ' ἄρα οἱ πέλεν ἀρχή, 'and it seems it was the beginning of disaster for him', Il. 11.604 and ἀρχεκάκους in νῆας ἐΐσας | ἀρχεκάκους, αἳ πᾶσι κακὸν Τρώεσσι γένοντο | οἷ τ' αὐτῶι, 'the well-balanced ships, disaster-beginners, that were a disaster for all the Trojans and for him [sc. Paris] himself', Il. 5.82–4. For discussion of Herodotus' use of the phrase see Irwin and Greenwood 2007, index *s.v. archē kakōn*.

[18] E.g. Candaules and Gyges, 1.8–12, Peisistratus, 1.61.2, Periander, 3.48–53, Xerxes first with the wife and then with the daughter of Masistes, 9.108–13.

[19] With ταύτας στάσας κατὰ πρύμνην τῆς νεὸς ὠνέεσθαι τῶν φορτίων τῶν σφι ἦν θυμὸς μάλιστα, 'these women [sc. including the princess Io] stood by the stern of the ship and bought whatever in its cargo most took their fancy', at 1.1.4 cf. Sappho fr. 1.17 κὤττι μοι μαλιστα θέλω γένεσθαι, 'and what I most want to acquire', and 1.26–27 ὄσσα δέ μοι τέλεσσαι | θῦμος ἰμέρρει, 'all the things that my heart longs to be accomplished'. Note also fr. 5.3 κὤττι Ϝῶι θύμωι κε θέλῃ γένεσθαι, 'and whatever he wants in his heart to come about'.

To conclude this very rapid and selective comparison of Book 2 with other parts of Herodotus' *Enquiry*, let me insist that the Egyptian λόγος, 'account', which constitutes the totality of our Book 2 should not be compared with our Book 1 as if on an equal footing with it, nor with our Book 3, but with what Herodotus terms λόγοι, 'accounts', in these books.[20] Of course it is much longer than the Lydian or the Babylonian/Assyrian λόγοι of Book 1 or the Scythian λόγος of Book 4. Herodotus was well aware of this disparity, and he explicitly justifies it, adducing the undoubted plethora of Egyptian wonders and remarkable ἔργα, 'constructions', that are indeed an important part of the explanation for Book 2's length (2.35.1, with my translation):

> ἔρχομαι δὲ περὶ Αἰγύπτου μηκυνέων τὸν λόγον ὅτι πλεῖστα θωμάσια ἔχει καὶ ἔργα λόγου μέζω παρέχεται πρὸς πᾶσαν χώρην. τούτων εἵνεκα πλέω περὶ αὐτῆς εἰρήσεται.
>
> I am proceeding with an extended account (*logos*) concerning Egypt because it has the greatest number of marvellous things and offers constructions of greater note in relation to any other country. These are the reasons why more will be said about it.

3 Herodotus' Other Geographic and Ethnographic λόγοι

If we look at other Herodotean λόγοι that are likewise heavily weighted towards geography and ethnography, there too we find a significantly lower proportion of speech and moral comment than in λόγοι such as the first 130 chapters of our Book 1, where Solon, Croesus and Cyrus are deployed in a very artistic way (as indeed was observed by Fornara in 1971) to convey the messages we have come to associate with the Herodotean *persona* – a proportion much closer to that found in Book 2 (where that lower proportion, both of speech and of the moral comment it is often used to convey, has been put forward as a mark of Book 2's difference from the rest of the work). But in these other λόγοι that are weighted towards geography and ethnography, as in Book 2, we also find numerous links with the persons and themes of other parts of the work, and (again as in Book 2) we do find occasional use of direct speech, almost always in a context where Greeks are involved, and occasional citation of, or reference to, oracles.

[20] For this reason the claim by Fornara 1971, 18, that there is an important difference in structure between Book 2 and Book 1, is misleading.

Thus the section in Book 1 on Persian νόμοι, 'customs' (1.131–40) both lacks speeches and touches on topics similar to those Herodotus addresses in Book 2: religion (1.131–2), food and drink (1.133), sex (1.135), and justice (1.137). Before proceeding from this section to his geography, ethnography and history of the Ionians (1.142–8), Herodotus offers us an exchange between Ionian envoys and Cyrus that is similar to exchanges earlier in Book 1, but the direct speech that enlivens this transitional passage is not in the mouth of Cyrus himself but in that of the αὐλητής, 'piper', whose capture of the fish who had earlier refused to dance for him is told by Cyrus using indirect speech (1.141).

The Ionian and Aeolian geography, ethnography and history that follow are presented without any speech, direct or indirect. Speeches return in Herodotus' narrative of the subjection of the Asian Greeks and Lycians at 1.152: he re-deploys speakers found earlier in the book – Cyrus at 1.153, Cyrus and Croesus at 1.155. Next, however, the narrative of Ionia's subjection or abandonment (1.156–60) offers only indirect speech – Harpagus at 1.164.2, Bias at 1.170.1. Likewise a Delphic oracle is not quoted *verbatim* but given in indirect speech at 1.167.2.

Herodotus' Carian ethnography (1.171–3), predictably without speeches, is separated from the narrative of their subjection (1.175–6), by a Delphic oracle that is cited *verbatim*.

The Assyrian λόγος that begins at 1.178 but at 1.180 zooms in on Babylon has no speeches, no high-sounding moral judgements, and displays many features that reappear in the Egyptian λόγος, including some cross-references that hook it in with other parts of the work – to Egyptian Thebes at 1.182 and to Dareius at 1.183.3. And as in the Egyptian λόγος, Herodotus at one point stresses his dependence on his sources: ἐγὼ μέν μιν οὐκ εἶδον, τὰ δὲ λέγεται ὑπὸ τῶν Χαλδαίων, ταῦτα λέγω, 'I did not see it [sc. the statue], but I tell what is told by the Chaldaeans'.[21]

A similar *assemblage* is found in the partly ethnographic Scythian λόγος in our Book 4. Narrative of action allows the opportunity for one or two direct speeches. First comes that of a Scythian returning home after twenty-eight years that highlights one of the Herodotean *persona*'s chief interests, the nature of dominance and slavery (4.3.3–4), and falls into a genre or form already exemplified in Homer, 'How shall we fight this battle?'. Then we are given the speech of the snake-nymph to Heracles when he

[21] 1.183.3. Not quite, then, a portrayal 'undisturbed by protestations about his dependence on his sources' (Fornara 1971, 19). Note similarly at 4.25.1 ἐμοὶ μὲν οὐ πιστὰ λέγοντες, 'saying things that I do not find credible', concerning the information offered by the Bald People about men with goats' legs.

has wandered off course with the cattle of Geryon (4.9.3–5), significantly in the context of a story about a Greek hero that had been told earlier by at least one poet much given to deploying direct speech, Stesichorus. Indeed a reader of Book 4 who recalls the Helen sequence in our Book 2 may well be provoked to think that in his treatment of Heracles' encounter with a nymph who is a snake from her buttocks down (4.9.1) Herodotus is simultaneously upstaging Homer's narrative of Odysseus' dalliance with Circe and Calypso and Stesichorus' *Geryoneis* with its three-headed but quasi-heroic monster.

Taken together, the ethnographic sections of Books 1 and 4 show that Herodotus, albeit far from slipping into a single formula for presenting ethnography, does exploit direct speech in such sections much less than in his various modes of narrative, and that often when he does so the choice seems to be catalysed by the involvement of a Greek speaker or audience. The pattern of Book 2, then, is not so unusual, even if there is a rather higher proportion of direct speech in the ethnographic part of Book 4 than there is in Book 2 (as well as some indirect speech, e.g. the oracles given to the Metapontines at 4.15.3).

It is also worth recalling that in Book 4, as in Book 2, Herodotus shows an interest in climatic paradox – the northern climate gives rise to phenomena that are the opposite of those found elsewhere (4.28–9).[22] Strikingly, one of the links between the subject-matter of Book 4 and mainland Greece is similar to one such link in Book 2 (2.160) – a reference to Elis: the Eleians need to have mules fathered outside their territory (4.30).

4 Some Conclusions Concerning Book 2

Overall the differences between the texture of Book 2 and that of other geographic and ethnographic *logoi* are not sufficient to demonstrate that these λόγοι were composed by a Herodotus who was at different stages in his intellectual development. The recurrent, albeit infrequent, appearances in all these λόγοι of speeches and oracles, and of links with themes important in other parts of the work, suggest that at least in the work that has been transmitted these predominantly geographic and ethnographic λόγοι have been crafted by the same mind, at a similar stage in its development, as that which shaped the 'historical' narratives of Book 1 and Books 5–9.

[22] Cf. Hp. *Aër.* 18.17ff.

Of course it is quite possible that there were earlier versions of these λόγοι which were not simply predominantly but *exclusively* geographical and ethnographic, but if so we have no way of knowing how unsophisticated and (perhaps) Hecataean or how sophisticated and sophistic they were. To my mind Herodotus has created or chosen versions of these λόγοι that harmonise very well with the remainder of his *Enquiry*.

5 Enrichment of Bare Historical Narrative by Techniques Drawn from Homeric Epic?

I now proceed to raise two rather different but related questions.

One is the following: is it right to suppose that Herodotus elevated a barer and more matter-of-fact narrative and descriptive technique that he found in his comparatively colourless prose-writing predecessors (λογογράφοι, *logographoi*) by adopting techniques he found in Homeric epic – a view that is a corollary of that which suggests that within the text of the *Enquiry* there remains evidence of Herodotus maturing from a less to a more sophisticated presenter of historical narrative?[23] Given the discussion by Dillery 2018, I do not need to say much about Hecataeus, but I do turn briefly to him later. First, however, I would like to point out that not *all* Herodotus' prose predecessors seem to have been as disinclined to combine historical narrative and moral judgements as Hecataeus appears to have been. Consider, for example, the following fragment of Xanthus:[24]

> Ξάνθος ἱστορεῖ Ἄλκιμόν τινα βασιλεῦσαι τῆς ἐκεῖσε χώρας, εὐσεβέστατον καὶ πραιότατον ἄνθρωπον· καὶ ἐπ' αὐτοῦ γενέσθαι εἰρήνην βαθεῖαν καὶ πλοῦτον πολύν, ἀδέως δὲ καὶ ἀνεπιβουλεύτως ζῆν ἕκαστον· εἶτα ἐπειδὴ ἑπτὰ ἔτη ἦν τῶι Ἀλκίμωι, προσελθόντας τοὺς Λυδοὺς παγγενῆ τε καὶ πανδημεὶ προσεύξασθαι, καὶ αἰτῆσαι τῶι Ἀλκίμωι τοιαῦτα ἔτη δοθῆναι ἐς τὸ Λυδῶν ἀγαθόν· ὃ καὶ γέγονε καὶ ἐν εὐποτμίαι τε καὶ εὐδαιμονίαι πολλῆι διῆγον.

> Xanthus reports that a certain Alcimus, a very pious and very gentle man, was king of the land there, and that under him there was profound peace and much wealth, and everyone lived without fear and without plotting;

23 Cf. Fornara 1971, 35: 'Herodotus began to probe into matters in a way that slowed the race of events to a standstill. And this required introducing into "history" in unprecedented fashion a richness of detail which until then was purely the province of the epos. [New paragraph] The parallel is real, for Herodotus, not surprisingly, borrowed some of his methods from Homer. What does Herodotus' "shift of interest" imply if not the desire on his part to achieve something comparable to the *Iliad* in work of prose?'

24 Xanthus *FGrHist* 765 F10 (from the Suda ξ 9 *s.v.* Ξάνθος) (translation adapted from the Suda-online).

> then, when Alcimus was seven[ty?] years old, the whole Lydian people came to him publicly and prayed and sought that such years be given to Alcimus for the good of the Lydians; and this actually happened; and they lived in much good fortune and prosperity.

Herodotus, of course, would probably have done much more with this story, but we are not entitled to assume that Xanthus is simply passing on what he had heard without any elaboration. At the least he chooses to comment on the impact of Alcimus' εὐσέβεια, 'piety', and πραιότης, 'gentleness': what else he *may* have been doing with the story, if anything, is currently beyond our recovery since we do not have its context.

Secondly, however, we should not be setting Herodotus alongside only those of his predecessors whose works were in prose. Narrative of recent or contemporary wars and politics in the early elegists, whether or not in longer, self-standing narrative elegiac poems or perhaps in extended *exempla* adduced to support a *gnōmē*,[25] show how some subjects found in Herodotus had already been treated by his poetic predecessors.[26] The sadly meagre remains of Mimnermus suffice to show that already in the seventh century, perhaps as early as ca. 640,[27] an Ionian poet could choose to narrate wars between his own city, Smyrna, and its expansionist neighbour

[25] I mention this possibility of extended *exempla* because the widely accepted reconstruction of Archilochus' elegiac narrative of Telephus, *P.Oxy.* 4708, first published by Obbink 2005 (with improvements in Obbink 2006a), takes that narrative to be illustrating a *gnōmē* rather than to be self-standing; and although it is apparently a mythical, not a 'historical' narrative, it is possible in principle that fragments of apparently historical elegiac narrative that survive (e.g. Tyrt. frr. 5–7) were also used by their poet to illustrate a *gnōmē*. I remain unconvinced, however, that the traces on the Telephus papyrus have to be restored in such a way as to relate the mythical narrative to a *gnome* that responded to a contemporary military failure on the part of Archilochus and his *hetaeroi*, cf. Bowie 2010b and 2010c (Chapters 15 and 16 in Volume 1): but for a good discussion based on that assumption see Nobili 2009.

[26] I here revisit with a different emphasis, and taking some account of Grethlein 2010, arguments first published in Bowie 1986a (Chapter 1 in Volume 1), developed further (after the publication in 1992 of Simonides' Plataea poem) in Bowie 2001a (Chapter 8 in Volume 1), and again augmented (after the publication in 2005 of Archilochus' elegiac Telephus narrative) in Bowie 2010b and 2010c (Chapters 15 and 16 in Volume 1). For another case of an early narrative elegy, on a subject not historical but mythical (the sack of Troy) by the Argive αὐλητής, 'pipe-player', and elegist Sacadas, see Bowie 2014a (Chapter 28 in Volume 1).

[27] The conventional dating of Mimnermus late in the seventh century is based largely on the poem of Solon apparently addressing and criticising Mimnermus (fr. 6) for his statement that he would welcome death at the age of sixty (Sol. fr. 20: both fragments, and the idea of connecting them, come from D.L. 1.60). That Mimnermus was still alive when Solon presented this sympotic gambit is no more required than that they were (improbably) partying in the same symposium, and Mimnermus' presentation of Smyrna's war with Gyges may rather be of a conflict in his own or the immediately preceding generation. If, with Grethlein 2007, we read ὅς μιν ἴδον not οἵ μιν ἴδον at Mimn. fr. 14.2, Mimnermus was most probably himself of the generation that faced Gyges, i.e. contemporary with Callinus and Archilochus.

Lydia, in a manner reminiscent of Homeric epic. In the case of the poem later circulating with the title *Smyrneis* that narrative had room for a μῦθος (*mythos*), 'speech'(?),[28] Mimn. fr. 13a:[29]

ὣς οἳ πὰρ βασιλῆος, ἐπε[ί ῥ'] ἐ[ν]εδέξατο μῦθ̣ο̣ν̣,
    ἤ[ϊξ]α̣ν κοίληι[ς ἀ]σπίσι φραξάμενοι.

So did they from the king, when he had given his *mythos*,
    speed forth, protecting themselves with their curved shields.

We also know that a poem on the fighting between the Smyrnaeans and Gyges' Lydian forces, most probably also the *Smyrneis*, opened with a proem addressing Muses at some length, Mimn. fr. 13:[30]

Μίμνερμος δέ, ἐλεγεῖα ἐς τὴν μάχην ποιήσας τὴν Σμυρναίων πρὸς Γύγην τε καὶ Λυδούς, φησὶν ἐν τῶι προοιμίωι θυγατέρας Οὐρανοῦ τὰς ἀρχαιοτέρας Μούσας, τούτων δὲ ἄλλας νεωτέρας εἶναι Διὸς παῖδας.

And Mimnermus, composing elegiacs on the battle of the Smyrnaeans against Gyges and the Lydians, says in his prooemion that the older Muses are the daughters of Uranos, and that other Muses, younger than these, are the children of Zeus.

Poetry of Mimnermus about battles with the Lydians also expressed praise of ἀρετή, 'excellence', attributing the basis for the poet's evaluation either to what he had either learned from an earlier generation or seen with his own eyes, Mimn. fr. 14:[31]

οὐ μὲν δὴ κείνου γε μένος καὶ ἀγήνορα θυμὸν
    τοῖον ἐμέο προτέρων πεύθομαι, οἵ μιν ἴδον
Λυδῶν ἱππομάχων πυκινὰς κλονέοντα φάλαγγας
    Ἕρμιον ἂμ πεδίον, φῶτα φερεμμελίην·
τοῦ μὲν ἄρ' οὔ ποτε πάμπαν ἐμέμψατο Παλλὰς Ἀθήνη
    δριμὺ μένος κραδίης, εὖθ' ὅ γ' ἀνὰ προμάχους
σεύαιθ' αἱματόεντος ἐν ὑσμίνηι πολέμοιο,
    πικρὰ βιαζόμενος δυσμενέων βέλεα·
οὐ γάρ τις κείνου δηίων ἔτ' ἀμεινότερος φὼς
    ἔσκεν ἐποίχεσθαι φυλόπιδος κρατερῆς
ἔργον, ὅτ' αὐγῆισιν φέρετ' ὠκέος ἠελίοιο ...

[28] For the range of sense of μῦθος in Homeric poetry see Martin 1989, Chapter 1, esp. 22–6. That 'the fabrication of speeches in prose historians may owe something to Mimnermus and other poets' was noted by Sider 2006, 334.

[29] Cited as from Mimn.'s *Smyrneis* (Μίμνερμ[ος] δ['ἐν] τῆι Σμυρνηίδι) by a commentary on Antimachus, *P.Univ. Mediolan.* 17 col. ii 26 = Antim. p.83 Wyss.

[30] From Paus. 9.29.4.

[31] Stob. 3.7.11. My translation.

Not indeed was that warrior's might and courageous heart
like this, so I have learned from my forebears, who saw him
throwing into confusion the serried squadrons of Lydian cavalrymen
across the plain of the Hermus, a man wielding an ashen spear.
In his case never at all did Pallas Athena reproach
the piercing might of his heart, when among the foremost fighters
he charged in the uproar of bloody war,
forcing his way through the stinging missiles of the foe.
For no one of the enemy was a man better than him
in ranging across the mighty battle-roar's
handiwork, when he was borne like (?) the rays of the swift sun ...

It is not clear whether fr. 14 belongs to the *Smyrneis* or is part of a shorter elegy intended primarily for sympotic performance, but that uncertainty matters little for my argument in this chapter. Narrative of Greeks fighting barbarians, whether in the poet's own generation or in those immediately preceding, did not have to be as austere as what survives from Charon of Lampsacus and was adduced as evidence by Fornara in 1971; nor did they say nothing of their relation to their sources, a feature attributed to Herodotus as the decisive step forward by Fowler a quarter of a century later:[32] citation of sources is something Herodotus could have found in his poetic predecessors.

Did Herodotus know some of the elegiac poetry of Mimnermus? The preservation of a few lines of Mimnermus in the *Theognidea* points to some of his poetry being known in late-fifth-century Athens.[33] It may also be suspected, though it could never be proved, that when Herodotus' Solon bluntly declares a human lifespan to be seventy years at 1.32.2 Herodotus is hinting at the sympotic elegy in which Solon criticised Mimnermus for wishing for a life of sixty years and himself proposed rather a desideratum of eighty years.[34]

Of course Mimnermus' treatment of fighting between Smyrna and Lydia was very probably on a much smaller scale than corresponding parts of Herodotus' Lydian *logos*, even if one continues to believe, as I do, that the *Smyrneis* was a narrative poem of some length, a reconstruction whose fragility has reasonably been emphasised by Jonas Grethlein.[35] Grethlein may also have been right to doubt that our evidence is sufficient to allow

[32] 'Herodotos' discussion of his sources is the unique element in his voiceprint, so far as our evidence goes: we see now that it is an integral part of his self-perception as a historian', Fowler 1996, 86, a conclusion from his careful argumentation at 77–80.

[33] Thgn. 795–6, 1017–22. For late-fifth-century Athens as a likely time and place for the genesis of the core of the *Theognidea* see Bowie 2012a (Chapter 22 in Volume 1).

[34] ἐς γὰρ ἑβδομήκοντα ἔτεα οὖρον τῆς ζόης ἀνθρώπωι προτίθημι, 'for it is up to seventy years that I propose the limit of a lifespan for a human being', 1.32.2. For the relevant poems of Mimn. and Sol. see above n.27.

[35] Grethlein 2010, 291–6 (Appendix).

us to postulate a narrative poem by Tyrtaeus, later entitled *Eunomia* and also composed around 640 BC, with narration both of wars of conquest (or reconquest) of Messenia and of an oracle-seeking *theoria* to Delphi by the kings Theopompus and Polydorus. Nevertheless, whether it was in such a relatively long poem or in a shorter sympotic elegy, Tyrtaeus did offer a generation-based chronological framework of the sort that has sometimes been asserted not to antedate fifth-century prose writing.[36]

By the end of the sixth century there were quite long poems: Xenophanes' on the foundation of Colophon and the emigration of Colophonians to Elea in south Italy is claimed by Diogenes Laertius to have run to 2000 lines. For my argument here it matters little whether this was a hexameter or elegiac poem – in either case a substantial historical narrative was composed by a poet who was also a critical philosopher.[37]

Three further data from the fifth century itself are relevant. First, the publication in 1992 of fragments on Simonides' elegy on Plataea showed that already, it seems, by ca. 478/7 BC, a Greek poet could relate the struggle against Persia to that of Greeks against Trojans, could evoke an image of the chariot of divine justice punishing the Easterner, in this case Troy,[38] and (if the generally accepted supplement is correct) could draw on the rhetoric of freedom and slavery.[39] Herodotus certainly knew some of Simonides' Persian war epigrams (7.228) and he knew a poem or poems of Simonides that praised Eualcides of Eretria.[40] Details of his account of the lead-up to Plataea might suggest that he also knew Simonides' *Plataea* elegy,[41] though it must be kept in mind that the relevant lines of Simonides are very

[36] Cf. αἰχμηταὶ πατέρων ἡμετέρων πατέρες, 'spearmen, the fathers of our fathers', Tyrt. fr. 5.6.

[37] ἐποίησε δὲ καὶ Κολοφῶνος κτίσιν καὶ τὸν εἰς Ἐλέαν τῆς Ἰταλίας ἀποικισμὸν ἔπη δισχίλια ('and he also composed *Foundation of Colophon* and to *The emigration to Elea in Italy*, 2000 lines'), D.L. 9.20. For *ktisis*-poetry cf. Dougherty 1994.

[38]] . θείης ἅρμα καθεῖλε δίκ[ης, 'the chariot of divine justice destroyed (sc. Troy)', Simon. *fr. el.* 11.12.

[39] ἀνδρῶ]ν οἳ Σπάρτ[ηι δούλιον ἦμ]αρ | .....]ἀμυν[] . . [, '[the me]n who from Sparta ...... [the day of slavery] warding off', Simon. *fr. el.* 11.25–6. For discussion of the new Simonides fragments see esp. Boedeker and Sider 2001; Kowerski 2005; Sider 2006; Grethlein 2010, 47–73; Lulli 2011; Sider 2020.

[40] καὶ πολλοὺς αὐτῶν οἱ Πέρσαι φονεύουσι, ἄλλους τε ὀνομαστούς, ἐν δὲ δὴ καὶ Εὐαλκίδην στρατηγέοντα Ἐρετριέων, στεφανηφόρους τε ἀγῶνας ἀναραιρηκότα καὶ ὑπὸ Σιμωνίδεω τοῦ Κηίου πολλὰ αἰνεθέντα, 'and the Persians killed many of them, several men of note, and among these also Eualcides who was leading the Eretrians, a man who had won crown-competitions and had been accorded much praise by Simonides of Ceos', Hdt. 5.102.3. The mention of Eualcides winning competitions suggests that this poem was an *encomion* or *epinicion* (hence it is registered as Simonides fr. 518 *PMG*), but a laudatory elegy or elegies should not be excluded.

[41] E.g. the role of Teisamenus, cf. Munson 2001, 61 n.57.

fragmentary and that editorial decisions about how these lines should be supplemented have been informed by knowledge of Herodotus' narrative.

Secondly, Aeschylus' tragedy Πέρσαι, '*Persians*', of 472, and perhaps Phrynichus' earlier and apparently memorable tragedy Φοίνισσαι, '*Phoenician women*' (note the continued popularity of its lyrics with the imagined jurors of Aristophanes' *Wasps* in 422 BC, *V.* 269), addressed the transgressiveness of Persian expansion west of the Dardanelles, with corollary implications for the transgressiveness of any Greek expansion east.[42]

Thirdly, whereas Mimnermus and Xenophanes had tackled the fortunes in war of single Greek cities in poems that did not exceed 2000 lines, and whereas Simonides may have devoted a single poem to each of a number of key battles,[43] Herodotus' uncle or cousin Panyassis composed an Ἰωνικά, '*Ionian History*', of 7000 lines, and hence several books, that seems certainly to have dealt with the founding of all or several of the Ionian colonies in the eastern Aegean – on this the Suda entry is unambiguous – and may well have handled aspects of the Persian wars, given that the Suda entry seems to derive from some tradition that associated Panyassis with the Persian wars (note καὶ γὰρ ἦν ἐπὶ τῶν Περσικῶν, 'and he was alive during the Persian wars', in the entry that follows):[44]

> Πανύασις, Πολυάρχου, Ἁλικαρνασσεύς, τερατοσκόπος καὶ ποιητὴς ἐπῶν· ὃς σβεσθεῖσαν τὴν ποιητικὴν ἐπανήγαγε ... ἱστόρηται δὲ Πανύασις Ἡροδότου τοῦ ἱστορικοῦ ἐξάδελφος· γέγονε γὰρ Πανύασις Πολυάρχου, ὁ δὲ Ἡρόδοτος Λύξου τοῦ Πολυάρχου ἀδελφοῦ ... ὁ δὲ Πανύασις γέγονε κατὰ τὴν οη′ ὀλυμπιάδα, κατὰ δέ τινας πολλῷ πρεσβύτερος· καὶ γὰρ ἦν ἐπὶ τῶν Περσικῶν. ἀνῃρέθη δὲ ὑπὸ Λυγδάμιδος τοῦ τρίτου τυραννήσαντος

42 I hope to argue in detail for this interpretation of the *Persae* elsewhere. The transgressiveness of Persian invasion of Greek territory is repeatedly stressed by the ghost of Dareius (681–851), especially in his reply to the chorus' question (788–9) 'how will the Persian people now fare best': εἰ μὴ στρατεύοισθ' ἐς τὸν Ἑλλήνων τόπον, 'if you do not campaign into Greek territory'.

43 Artemisium *frr. el.* 1–4: cf. the Suda entry καὶ γέγραπται αὐτῷι Δωρίδι διαλέκτῳι ἡ Καμβύσου καὶ Δαρείου βασιλεία καὶ Ξέρξου ναυμαχία καὶ ἡ ἐπ' Ἀρτεμισίου ναυμαχία δι' ἐλεγείας ἡ δ' ἐν Σαλαμῖνι μελικῶς, 'and he wrote in Doric dialect the reign of Cambyses and Dareius and the sea-battle of Xerxes and the sea-battle at Artemisium in elegiacs, and the sea-battle of Salamis in a melic poem'. The publication of the Artemisium and Plataea fragments in 1992 put an end to attempts to emend away the Suda reference to an account of Artemisium in elegiacs on the grounds that a melic treatment is known (*PMG* fr. 533): West (at *IEG*² ii 114) proposes that the Suda's source read something like γέγραφε δὲ Δωρίδι διαλέκτῳι, κατὰ τὴν Καμβύσου καὶ Δαρείου βασιλείαν, καὶ κατὰ τὴν Ξέρξου τὰς ναυμαχίας τήν τε ἐπ' Ἀρτεμισίου δι' ἐλεγείας τὴν δ' ἐν Σαλαμῖνι μελικῶς, 'and he wrote in Doric dialect, in the time of the reign of Cambyses and Dareius, and in the reign of Xerxes the sea-battle at Artemisium in elegiacs and that at Salamis in a melic poem'. Given the capacity of papyri from Egypt to surprise, we should perhaps retain the possibility that Simonides really did compose an account of the reigns of Cambyses and Dareius – if so, the consequences for our understanding of Herodotus would be considerable.

44 Suda π 248 *s.v.* Πανύασις, my translation.

Ἁλικαρνασσοῦ. ἐν δὲ ποιηταῖς τάττεται μεθ' Ὅμηρον, κατὰ δέ τινας καὶ μετὰ Ἡσίοδον καὶ Ἀντίμαχον. ἔγραψε δὲ καὶ Ἡρακλειάδα ἐν βιβλίοις ιδ', εἰς ἔπη θ', Ἰωνικὰ ἐν πενταμέτρωι, ἔστι δὲ τὰ περὶ Κόδρον καὶ Νηλέα καὶ τὰς Ἰωνικὰς ἀποικίας, εἰς ἔπη ζ'.

Panyassis of Halicarnassus, interpreter of prodigies and dactylic poet, who restored poetry when it had been extinguished ... He is recorded as having been the cousin (*exadelphos*) of the historian Herodotus: for Panyassis was son of Polyarchus, and Herodotus the son of Lyxes the brother of Polyarchus ... Panyassis belongs in the seventy-eighth Olympiad [468–465 BC], and according to some much earlier. For he was alive during the Persian Wars. He was put to death by Lygdamis, the third tyrant of Halicarnassus. Among poets he is ranked after Homer, and according to some after Hesiod and Antimachus. He wrote a *Heracleias* in fourteen books running to 9000 lines, and an *Ionian history*, in pentameters, dealing with Codrus, Neleus and the Ionian colonies, running to 7000 lines.

Thus some part of the impetus that led Herodotus (and perhaps others)[45] to move from the narrower one-city or one-battle focus of the earlier elegiac narratives that we happen to know to a much wider presentation of Greeks' conflict with Lydia and Persia may be due to the poetic work of his uncle or cousin Panyassis.

In the poetry, then, chiefly elegiac, that treated historical themes, there were many features that have been associated with a 'mature' Herodotus – fighting between Greeks and non-Greeks in Asia Minor and in Greece, a moral stance, a broad perspective that transcended the affairs of a single *polis*. Were such features absent from Book 2 (which I have argued they are in any case not) their absence can hardly be explained by the notion that historiography of this complexion had yet to be developed by Herodotus himself.

6 Hecataeus

I now turn briefly to Hecataeus, about whose relation to Herodotus two questions arise that bear on my argument.

First, the sort of moral and political judgements and associated vocabulary discussed earlier (pp. 106–13) are (unsurprisingly) very rarely attested for the periegetic work of Hecataeus. Admittedly we have little more than

[45] Dionysius of Miletus remains a serious candidate.

quite short fragments, and most of these have been transmitted because they preserve geographical details, and might be claimed not to be representative of the lost work as a whole. But they are all we have to go on. So it is worth noting that words of the form δίκαιος, 'just', ἄδικος, 'unjust', δικαίως, 'justly', and ἀδίκως, 'unjustly' occur only once, in a fragment that happens to be quoted by Herodotus concerning the expulsion of the Pelasgians from Attica.[46] Words such as δοῦλος, 'slave', and ἐλεύθερος, 'free', occur only in a fragment drawn from Stephanus of Byzantium where Hecataeus offers an explanation for the name of a city in North Africa, Δούλων πόλις, 'City of Slaves', and where the terms refer simply to civic status.[47] Other judgmental terms like ἤπιος, 'gentle', δυσνομία, 'disorder', and εὐνομία, 'good order' are absent – as, it should be said, is any trace of an investigative method. What evidence we have for how Hecataeus decided what was true and what was false comes not from his periegetic work but from his *Genealogiae*. Here, by contrast with Herodotus' careful distinction between what he gets from autopsy, hearsay and his own judgement,[48] Hecataeus is nowhere preserved as applying any other criterion than 'I think'.[49]

Secondly, given that nothing suggests that Hecataeus approached either category of his material with the Herodotean mixture of system and scepticism, is it right to retain some of Jacoby's views, even in the much-modified

[46] Πελασγοὶ ἐπείτε ἐκ τῆς Ἀττικῆς ὑπὸ Ἀθηναίων ἐξεβλήθησαν, εἴτε ὦν δὴ δικαίως εἴτε ἀδίκως· τοῦτο γὰρ οὐκ ἔχω φράσαι, πλὴν τὰ λεγόμενα, ὅτι Ἑκαταῖος μὲν ὁ Ἡγησάνδρου ἔφησε ἐν τοῖσι λόγοισι λέγων ἀδίκως, 'When the Pelasgians were expelled from Attica by the Athenians – whether in fact justly or unjustly – for this I cannot say, except what is told, that Hecataeus son of Hegesander in his writings said "unjustly"', Hecat. *FGrH* 1 F127 from Hdt. 6.137.2 cf. 4.

[47] Δούλων πόλις· πόλις Λιβύης. Ἑκαταῖος ἐν Περιηγήσει ... καὶ ἐὰν δοῦλος εἰς τὴν πόλιν ταύτην λίθον προσενέγκηι, ἐλεύθερος γίνεται, κἂν ξένος ἦι. ἔστι καὶ ἑτέρα Ἱεροδούλων, ἐν ἧι εἷς μόνος ἐλεύθερός ἐστι, '"City of Slaves": a city in Libya. Hecataeus in his Periegesis ... and if a slave brings a stone to this city he becomes free, even if he is a foreigner. There is also another city of "Sacred Slaves", in which only one man is free', Hecat. *FGrH* 1 F345 from St.Byz. *s.v.* Δούλων πόλις.

[48] Best exemplified by ταῦτα μέν νυν αὐτοὶ Αἰγύπτιοι λέγουσι, ὅσα δὲ οἵ τε ἄλλοι ἄνθρωποι καὶ Αἰγύπτιοι λέγουσι ὁμολογέοντες τοῖσι ἄλλοισι κατὰ ταύτην τὴν χώρην γενέσθαι, ταῦτ᾽ ἤδη φράσω· προσέσται δέ τι αὐτοῖσι καὶ τῆς ἐμῆς ὄψιος ('So far I have recorded what the Egyptians themselves say. I shall now relate what is recorded alike by Egyptians and foreigners, and shall add something of what I myself have seen', transl. A. D. Godley), Hdt. 2.147.1.

[49] Cf. τάδε γράφω, ὥς μοι δοκεῖ ἀληθέα εἶναι ('I write these things, as they *seem* to me to be true'), Hecat. *FGrH* 1 F1 = F1 *EGM*; and καὶ Ἑκατ[αῖ]ος ὁ Μειλήσιός φησιν [οὕ]τως· εἶνα[ι δ]ὲ τ̣ὸν ὄφιν δοκέω οὐ μέγα[ν] ο[ὕ]τως ο[ὔτε.] πε.[..]ιον, ἀλ[λ]ὰ δειν[ό]τερον τῶν ἄλλων ὀφίων, καὶ τού[τ]ου [ἕ]νε[κεν] τὸν Ε[ὐ]ρυσθέα [ἐ]νδέξασθαι ὡς ἀμήχανον ἐ[όν]τα ('and Hecataeus of Miletus says the following: "But I *think* the snake was not so large nor ... but that it was cleverer than other snakes, and this is why Eurystheus declared that it could not be dealt with"'), Hecat. F27b *EGM* (my translation). These passage are discussed by Fowler, who seems to me to go too far in using the term 'revolutionary new method' (Fowler 1996, 71) of Hecataeus' cases of arbitrary 'rationalisation', even suggesting (ibid. 70) that Hecataeus 'had to argue hard for his new method'. So far there is little evidence of his 'arguing' for his method. For a re-examination of 'rationalisation' in ancient historical writing see Hawes 2014.

form in which they were adopted for by Fornara, and to see the long geographic, ethnographic and historical *logos* that is our Book 2 as a survival from a Hecataean period of Herodotus' literary development? Despite points of contact, well-discussed by John Dillery,[50] Hecataeus' Egyptian section must have been on a markedly smaller scale, and was surely less ambitious, than Herodotus Book 2. As was rightly observed by Fornara,[51] Herodotus is very much on show in this book. What he puts on show is a state-of-the-art geography, ethnography and history (this last of course moulded by his very different relation to his Egyptian sources from his relation to his sources in his accounts of Greece and Asia Minor) just as Book 1 can be seen as a sequence of state-of-the-art λόγοι concerning the ἔθνη, 'peoples', of Asia Minor and Mesopotamia. The standards by which he expected his state-of-the-art Book 2 to be judged had very little to do with the work of Hecataeus, by his time almost a century old, and much more to do with 'sophistic' enquiries, debates, catalogues, and histories (in some cases cultural histories) that flourished in Athens and were sometimes on display in the Panhellenic festivals of the last decades of the fifth century BC. That context of philosophical, medical and multifarious sophistic enquiry, augmented in such democratic cities as Athens by forensic oratory and political debate, has already been well explored since 1971 and its implications brought to bear on Herodotus' work.[52] Here I conclude by offering an explanatory model which draws an analogy with just one other prominent figure in that period.

7 The Diversity of Herodotus' *Enquiry*

One of the chief engines driving the developmental hypothesis has been the diversity of Herodotus' geographic and ethnographic material and the difficulty of relating it to his supposedly declared theme, the Persian wars.

First, then, how should we attempt to explain why the work we have is as diverse as it is? Undoubtedly the Herodotus of the 450s and 440s had different interests, different priorities and different favoured modes of presenting his material from that of the 430s and later, but *we* can only *guess* in what

[50] Dillery 2018; see also West 1991.

[51] Fornara 1971, 19.

[52] Above all Ubsdell 1983, esp. 339–99 (= Chapter iii: 'Herodotus and the sophistic movement'). It is unfortunate that this doctoral thesis was not published immediately on completion, but at least the record of its readers in the Bodleian Library shows that many Herodotean scholars have taken the trouble to consult it. For subsequent exploration of Herodotus' sophistic context see Lateiner 1986 and 1989, Thomas 2000.

order Herodotus acquired these interests, priorities or modes, or in what way one might have led to another. The higher our opinion of Herodotus the artist, the less likely we should suppose it to be that his final version (or perhaps even, simply, his last version)[53] would retain substantial features that were no longer in harmony with the way he saw things or wanted to present them. For example, the thought that it might be exciting and self-promoting to write in prose about subjects that included the Persian wars could have plausibly occurred to him in 478, 468, 458, 448 or 438. But neither the origin of this idea nor its relation to his account of parts of the Persian Empire can be extracted from the work we have, because Herodotus has covered his tracks, and has drugged any dogs likely to bark in the night. He has tried to dazzle contemporary and future readers with a range and diversity of themes that are in varying ways and degrees inter-connected. Upon them he has imposed an artistic structure that exploits the expansion first of Lydia, then of Persia, as a device to give shape to his combination of geography, ethnography, and narrative of political and military history[54] – but as has been repeatedly observed by many scholars, the ethnographies are developed on a scale and with a complexity far beyond what is necessary to understand Persian expansion, and that expansion is itself given a far wider coverage than is needed to understand simply the Greco-Persian conflict and no more.

This leads to the second issue, how Herodotus' diverse material should be seen as relating to his stated theme. Here I believe much confusion has arisen through misunderstanding of the emphasis in his proem. The text is well-known:

> Ἡροδότου Ἀλικαρνασσέος ἱστορίης ἀπόδεξις ἥδε, ὡς μήτε τὰ γενόμενα ἐξ ἀνθρώπων τῶι χρόνωι ἐξίτηλα γένηται, μήτε ἔργα μεγάλα τε καὶ θωμαστά, τὰ μὲν Ἕλλησι, τὰ δὲ βαρβάροισι ἀποδεχθέντα, ἀκλέα γένηται, τά τε ἄλλα καὶ δι' ἣν αἰτίην ἐπολέμησαν ἀλλήλοισι.
>
> This is the presentation of the *Enquiry* of Herodotus of Halicarnassus, so that neither shall things that have happened be wiped away from mankind by the passage of time, nor shall great and marvellous achievements, some exhibited by Greeks, others by *barbaroi*, lack renown – among many such, I address in particular the accusations as a result of which they went to war with each other. (my translation)

[53] His statement of an intention to treat something in his Assyrian λόγοι (τῶν ἐν τοῖσι Ἀσσυρίοισι λόγοισι μνήμην ποιήσομαι, 'which I shall mention in my Assyrian *logoi*', 1.184: cf. the less specific statement that he will tell how Nineveh was captured ἐν ἑτέροισι λόγοισι, 'in other *logoi*, at 1.106.2), is usually (and correctly) taken to show that Herodotus did not regard what we have as a final version: cf. Drews 1970.

[54] See Greenwood 2018.

The phrase τά τε ἄλλα καὶ δι᾽ ἣν αἰτίην has often been taken to pick out an overriding theme of the *Enquiry* as a whole, and then made the basis for the claim that Herodotus states the Persian wars to be his theme. But all that he identifies here is the αἰτίη (whether we translate 'cause', 'reason', 'ground', 'complaint' or 'accusation' does not affect my argument) and no scholar has (to my knowledge) tried to insist that the 'cause' or 'complaint' is a *leitmotiv* of all nine books. That the αἰτίη is the key term in this phrase shows that these last nine words of the proem have as their only function the provision of a transition to the first section of what follows (beginning Περσέων μέν νυν …, 'Now of the Persians …'). They do not privilege any subject as a theme of the *Enquiry* as a whole. That leaves us (and all past and future readers) with the preceding words as our only prefatory guide to the work's theme or (more obviously) themes. Thus Herodotus gives himself the broadest of briefs – things that had happened (whether by divine, human or natural agency)[55] and things that had been achieved (which, as the repeated use of ἔργα at later points demonstrates, includes buildings and other artefacts, not simply actions).

This formulation offered in the proem, therefore, might suggest from the start that Herodotus did not regard his material as homogeneous. But he did make a decision to bring it together in a single work with a unifying structure, and in doing so he found a different publication solution from such comparably wide-ranging thinkers as his rough contemporary Hippias, to whom I now turn very briefly for comparison and contrast. That Herodotus might have been contemplating the same sort of questions as to how he might best offer a 'presentation' of his enquiries as Hippias is not at all surprising if we accept that he was fully engaged with sophistic thought and related argumentative procedures and objects of investigation.[56] Here I am not concerned to reinforce that interpretation, but to address the different, albeit related, issue of what 'presentation' options were available to Herodotus.

So far as we can tell Hippias chose to present different sorts of scientific enquiry or moral philosophical exploration in different *types* of written work (which may well have related in ways that we cannot determine to his oral presentations). An exploration of what sorts of activities might secure a young man fame was found in his dialogue Τρωικός, '*Trojan*', with

[55] The translation that is (as far as I can see) universally favoured ('things done by man') which takes ἐξ ἀνθρώπων with τὰ γενόμενα seems to me to be wrong; but even if it is right my argument is not affected.

[56] See above n.52.

Nestor and Neoptolemus as its interlocutors.[57] Poetic virtuosity in elaborating threnodic or consolatory *topoi* presumably marked an elegiac poem with which he is credited.[58] The results of coal-face 'historical' enquiry came out in his Ὀλυμπιονικῶν ἀναγραφή, '*Record of Olympic victors*'.[59] A somewhat Herodotean mixture of enquiry and reflection may have characterised his Ἐθνῶν ὀνομασίαι, '*Names of peoples*', but it had a single defining theme. There might, perhaps, have been a more Herodotean diversity in his shadowy Συναγωγή, '*Collection*', but all we know of it for certain is that it seems to have had the same interest in sexual forwardness as Herodotus, since its only *nominatim* attestation is by Athenaeus, citing it by its title (ἐν τῶι ἐπιγραφομένωι Συναγωγῆι, 'in the book entitled *Collection*') and using it as evidence for a Milesian lady called Thargelia who had thirteen husbands.[60] If, however, the attribution of a quotation by Clement of Alexandria to the *Collection*'s opening is correct, it began with a claim whose references to greatness and to attention to both Greeks and βάρβαροι, 'non-Greeks', are remarkably close to those of Herodotus (Clem.Al. *Strom.* 6.15):[61]

57 ἔστι γάρ μοι περὶ αὐτῶν παγκάλως λόγος συγκείμενος, καὶ ἄλλως εὖ διακείμενος καὶ τοῖς ὀνόμασι· πρόσχημα δέ μοί ἐστι καὶ ἀρχὴ τοιάδε τις τοῦ λόγου. ἐπειδὴ ἡ Τροία ἥλω, λέγει ὁ λόγος ὅτι Νεοπτόλεμος Νέστορα ἔροιτο ποῖά ἐστι καλὰ ἐπιτηδεύματα, ἃ ἄν τις ἐπιτηδεύσας νέος ὢν εὐδοκιμώτατος γένοιτο· μετὰ ταῦτα δὴ λέγων ἐστὶν ὁ Νέστωρ καὶ ὑποτιθέμενος αὐτῷ πάμπολλα νόμιμα καὶ πάγκαλα, 'For I have a very beautiful discourse composed about them, well arranged in its words and also in other respects. And the plan of the discourse, and its beginning, is something like this: After the fall of Troy, the story goes that Neoptolemus asked Nestor what were the sort of noble and beautiful pursuits by whose pursuit a young man would become most famous; so after that we have Nestor speaking and suggesting to him very many lawful and most beautiful pursuits', transl. W. Lamb (adapted), [Pl.] *Hp.Ma.* 286a–b.

58 Generations earlier the Messenians of Sicily had erected at Olympia statues of a chorus of thirty-five boys and their chorus-trainer and piper, who had all been drowned in a shipwreck *en route* to a festival at Rhegium, and in the later fifth century Hippias added an inscribed elegy: τότε δὲ ἐπὶ τῆι ἀπωλείαι τῶν παίδων οἱ Μεσσήνιοι πένθος ἦγον, καὶ ἄλλα τέ σφισιν ἐς τιμὴν αὐτῶν ἐξευρέθη καὶ εἰκόνας ἐς Ὀλυμπίαν ἀνέθεσαν χαλκᾶς, σὺν δὲ αὐτοῖς τὸν διδάσκαλον τοῦ χοροῦ καὶ τὸν αὐλητήν. τὸ μὲν δὴ ἐπίγραμμα ἐδήλου τὸ ἀρχαῖον ἀναθήματα εἶναι τῶν ἐν πορθμῶι Μεσσηνίων· χρόνωι δὲ ὕστερον Ἱππίας ὁ λεγόμενος ὑπὸ Ἑλλήνων γενέσθαι σοφὸς τὰ ἐλεγεῖα ἐπ' αὐτοῖς ἐποίησεν, 'On this occasion the Messenians mourned for the loss of the boys, and one of the honours bestowed upon them was the dedication of bronze statues at Olympia, the group including the trainer of the chorus and the piper. The old inscription declared that the offerings were those of the Messenians at the strait; but afterwards Hippias, called "a wise man" by the Greeks, composed the elegiac verses on them' (transl. Ormerod, adapted), Paus. 5.25.4. On these statues see Kindt 2012, 138–9 (I am grateful to Tom Harrison for drawing this discussion to my attention).

59 Known only from Plu. *Numa* 1.5. See Christesen 2007.

60 Ath. 13.608f = Hippias B44 D–K = D3 Laks–Most.

61 Hippias B6 D–K = D22 Laks–Most, my translation. The location of this fragment near the opening of the *Collection* was proposed (according to D–K *ad loc.*) by Gomperz and is accepted by Laks and Most in their recent Loeb.

τούτων ἴσως εἴρηται τὰ μὲν Ὀρφεῖ, τὰ δὲ Μουσαίωι κατὰ βραχὺ ἄλλωι ἀλλαχοῦ, τὰ δὲ Ἡσιόδωι τὰ δὲ Ὁμήρωι, τὰ δὲ τοῖς ἄλλοις τῶν ποιητῶν, τὰ δὲ ἐν συγγραφαῖς τὰ μὲν Ἕλλησι τὰ δὲ βαρβάροις· ἐγὼ δὲ ἐκ πάντων τούτων τὰ μέγιστα καὶ ὁμόφυλα συνθεὶς τοῦτον καινὸν καὶ πολυειδῆ τὸν λόγον ποιήσομαι.

Of these some have perhaps been stated by Orpheus, and some by Musaeus, briefly and in different places by each, and others by Hesiod, others by Homer, some by others among the poets, others in prose writings, in some cases by Greeks, in others by non-Greeks: and I shall assemble from all these the ones that are the most important, and ones related to these, and shall create the new and diverse work you have here.

Perhaps there were oral performances by Herodotus in (e.g.) the 430s that came nearer to the majority of the written and oral productions of Hippias in dividing his diverse material between different genres or forms; and, if there were, they were no doubt (as is attested for Hippias)[62] tailored to suit different audiences and occasions. But the diversity of Herodotus' material is well disguised in the written masterpiece that survives, and, as I argue above, it is anticipated by the extraordinarily broadly-framed themes set out in the first sentence, the preservation from oblivion of γενόμενα, 'what has happened', and ἔργα μεγάλα καὶ θωμαστά, 'great and marvellous achievements',[63] offering in the key words ἔργα, μεγάλα and θωμαστά a red thread that will carry on through all nine books of strikingly varied subject-matter[64] and impressively diverse treatments.

[62] [Pl.] *Hi.Ma.* 285b–e.

[63] For θωμαστά see especially Munson 2001, 232–66 (her chapter entitled *thoma*) and her excellent discussion earlier at 1–14 of the linkage between Hdt. 1.194 and his preface.

[64] Cf. Ubsdell 1983, 348: 'like Hippias he is clearly aiming at a novel synthesis, a compendium among whose chief attractions is variety of interest'.

8 | Theocritus' Seventh *Idyll*, Philetas and Longus (1985)

Few years pass without an attempt to interpret Theocritus, *Idyll* 7. The poem's narrative and descriptive skill, dramatic subtlety and felicity of language are mercifully more than adequate to survive these scholarly onslaughts, so I have less hesitation in offering my own interpretation.[1] The poem's chief problems seem to me to arise from uncertainty as to: (a) Who is the narrator, and why are we kept waiting until line 21 before we are told that he is called Simichidas? (b) Who, or what sort of man, is the goatherd Lycidas, whom he encounters on his way from town to the harvest festival? Answers to these questions fundamentally affect our interpretation of their exchange of songs, which occupies almost half the *Idyll*, and of Lycidas' gift of his stick to Simichidas; and these interpretations will go far towards interpreting the poem as a whole.

1 The Narrator

The opening lines (1–2) are presented as the reminiscence of an unnamed narrator (ἐγών) of a journey he once made into the country on Cos with two named friends, Eucritus and Amyntas.[2] Ancient readers were familiar with poems where the first person was used at the start of the poem but, as later became clear, did not refer to the poet: e.g. Archilochus fr. 19, where it emerges only later in the *iambus* that the moralising speaker is not Archilochus but Charon the carpenter;[3] or Theocritus' own third

[1] Earlier forms of this paper were delivered to audiences at Queen's University, Belfast (1977); the Edinburgh Branch of the Classical Association (1980); Stanford University (1981); and the Oxford Philological Society (1981): I am grateful to many scholars who contributed to the discussions on these occasions, and to Professor R. G. M. Nisbet, Dr R. S. Padel, Ms P. K. M. Kinchin and Mr Robert Wells for helpful criticisms of a written draft.

[2] Unless the names of these men or of their prospective hosts were meaningful to an ancient reader, his first hint that the setting was in Cos would be the toponym Ἄλεντα (*Halenta*) at the end of the first line (cf. n.45 below), then the references to Clytia and Chalcon in 5 and the description of Burina in 6–9. Further confirmation comes from the tomb of Brasilas (10–11), perhaps from the reference to Philetas without an ethnic (40), and from Lycidas' departure for Pyxa (130–1).

[3] Cf. Arist. *Rh.* 1418b23 ff.

Idyll, where the singer serenading Amaryllis is rapidly manifested as an *ingenu* goatherd and not a sophisticated poet, and where the setting is a dramatised present rather than recollection of the past.[4] In *Id.* 7 it is different. Reminiscence anyway carries a greater implication that the first person will be that of the poet (cf. *Theognidea* 783–8; presumably Archilochus fr. 196a; Hipponax *passim*).[5] As the narration proceeds, pieces of evidence accumulate which suggest to a reader that the first person might indeed be the poet Theocritus, rather, say, than a simple rustic. He has links with town as well as country (1–2). His friends number ἐσθλοί, who claim descent from the founding family of Cos,[6] and enjoy the fruits of a rich country estate (2–6; 143–57). He is himself an ἀοιδός, 'singer' or 'poet', not simply a singing shepherd, but one who can envisage himself in time competing with Sicelidas and Philetas, even if he has not yet reached their standard (37–41). Few contemporary readers of Theocritus would be unaware that the epigrammatist Asclepiades also used the name Sicelidas,[7] or be unfamiliar with the poetry of Philetas of Cos. The narrator's claim that his own poetry's reputation has reached the throne of Zeus (93) can plausibly be taken as a testimony to Ptolemy II Philadelphus' interest in Theocritus' work.[8] Finally the Aratus of the narrator's song (98) can and perhaps should be identified with the addressee of *Id.* 6.[9]

All this suggests that ἐγών, 'I', in line 1 is to be taken as referring to Theocritus. But this impression is undermined at line 21, where Lycidas addresses the narrator as Simichidas, and specific references, as well as his very acquaintance with Lycidas, seem to cast him as in some way a herdsman (36, 92).[10] It appears, then, that Simichidas both is and is not Theocritus, and that his name Simichidas has been deliberately held back to allow the presumption to develop that the narrator is Theocritus himself. When he is identified as Simichidas this must be intended to cause

[4] Note also *Id.* 20, not by Theocritus but by another author of uncertain date, cf. Gow 1952, ii 364 ff.

[5] Reference of the first person to the poet in early iambus has of course been questioned, e.g. by Dover 1964; West 1974, 28 ff.

[6] See Gow 1952, ii 133–4 and scholia *ad loc.* [7] Gow 1952, ii 141 (on 40).

[8] Gow 1952, ii 155 (on 93). [9] Gow 1952, ii 118–20.

[10] βουκολιασδώμεσθα, 'let us be cowherds' (36), can perhaps be explained away as a 'bucolic metaphor' where any poet can be seen as a βουκόλος, 'cowherd', or αἰπόλος, 'goatherd' (cf. van Groningen 1958, 310 ff.). ἀν' ὤρεα βουκολέοντα, 'herding cattle in the mountains' (92), is less susceptible of such treatment.

surprise or puzzlement in the reader, for nowhere else does Theocritus use this name, and it is rare if not unattested elsewhere.[11] It has, however, the same form as that of his interlocutor, Lycidas, so its choice or invention may in part be influenced by that name. To it I now turn.

2 Who Is Lycidas?

A full review of the identifications offered for Lycidas would be a substantial *Forschungsbericht* in itself. I shall here notice only those possibilities which are listed by Dover in his commentary[12] and another which has been proposed since. The former are (I quote):

(i) He was a real Koan goatherd with a genius for poetry.
(ii) He was a real poet who amused himself (or 'dropped out' of urban life) by dressing and behaving as a goatherd.
(iii) He represents a real poet whom Theokritos has chosen to portray as a goatherd.
(iv) He is a wholly imaginary character.

One other possibility, proposed by F. Williams in 1971, is that

(v) He is Apollo, as the reader should see, but the obtuse narrator Simichidas does not.[13]

In assigning Lycidas one of these five identities (or any other) it seems to me that the following criteria must be satisfied:

(1) A Hellenistic reader should be able to identify Lycidas.
(2) Such an identification should be assisted by the proper name, ethnic and description offered by Theocritus at lines 12–19.
(3) It should be intelligible that Simichidas not only recognises Lycidas without difficulty but knows details about him (such as name and ethnic) over and above what is immediately obvious from his appearance.
(4) The identity of Lycidas should be compatible with those features of his meeting with Simichidas which suggest a divine epiphany.

[11] See Gow 1952, ii 127–9. I am more reluctant than Gow to credit the scholiast's Simichidas of Orchomenos. I also doubt that the name Simichidas was as familiar to Theoc.'s contemporaries as the name Sicelidas, and do not see how this is demonstrated by the way it is introduced at line 21 (*ibid.* 129).

[12] Dover 1971, 148–50. [13] Williams 1971.

(5) The identity of Lycidas should be compatible also with the way he and Simichidas behave to each other in the rest of the poem, and in particular with the apparently significant gift of the staff.

(6) The category of being into which Lycidas falls should be intelligible within the practice of ancient poetry.

Since criteria (1) and (2) are not met by Dover's possibility (i),[14] and since criterion (2) (and in particular the phrase ἦς δ' αἰπόλος, 'and he was a goatherd') is not met by his possibilities (ii) and (iii), I would agree with him in rejecting all these. Even less, however, can be said for the version which, following Kühn, he offers of possibility (iv), that 'Lycidas is a symbol of the bucolic world from which Theocritus derived the fundamental ideas for a truly original genre of poetry'.[15] It does not, in my view, meet criteria (1), (2) or (3). Nor does it meet criterion (6): the Greeks had well-established symbols for inspiration, and had Theocritus wanted to symbolise bucolic inspiration he would either have introduced the Muses or Apollo or, if even Hesiod's encounter with the Muses did not make them rural enough,[16] have wheeled on some established deity with more pastoral associations like Hermes or Pan.[17]

Williams' proposal, that Lycidas is Apollo, clearly meets criteria (4) and (6). Since on Williams' development of Giangrande's interpretation,[18] however, Simichidas fails to identify Lycidas as Apollo, problems arise under criteria (2) and (3). Either Simichidas knows a number of personal details about the figure he meets which are clear clues to his identity – but how he can know these is mysterious, and that he fails to draw the obvious conclusions about the identity argues such obtuseness that nothing in his report (including the vital clues) could be taken as reliable – or Simichidas offers the reader biographic details about the figure which are his own invention, and should likewise be untrustworthy guides to his real identity. But since Williams does maintain that the details offered by Simichidas are (unlike his perception of the figure's identity) significant clues, which would meet my criteria (1) and (2), I feel that I must show in what respect they do not. For convenience I retain his order in discussing these 'clues'.

(i) The name Λυκίδας (*Lycidas*). In Williams' view 'Λυκίδας does not merely recall Apollo's title Λύκιος "*Lycian*", but is also formally equivalent to it'.[19]

[14] In particular, no Cydonia has yet been identified on Cos in a literary or epigraphic text.

[15] 150, citing Kühn 1958.

[16] The Muses' gift to Hesiod at *Th.* 29 ff. is certainly recalled by Lycidas' gift to Simichidas and emphasised by the thematic echo at line 44 of *Th.* 27–8. See below and n.51.

[17] Hence there are attractions in the suggestion of Brown 1981 that Lycidas is Pan. But this identification, like that of Williams 1971, fails to meet criteria (1) and (3).

[18] Giangrande 1968.

Unfortunately the phenomenon to which Debrunner, quoted by Williams, draws attention is simply that patronymics in -ιος are of identical meaning with, and were ultimately replaced by, patronymics in -ίδης, -(ι)άδης. Not all names in -ιος are patronymics, and nobody has suggested that Apollo's widespread cult-title Λύκιος (or Λύκειος) denotes the paternity of one Λύκος (*Lycus*). It therefore seems unlikely that Theocritus would expect his readers to reason from Λυκίδας (*Lycidas*) to Λύκιος, 'Lycian', despite the prevalent use of patronymics by Alexandrian poets and his readers' knowledge of many patronymic pairs of the ίδης, (ι)άδης /-ιος.

Indeed the name Lycidas seems to me one very good reason why, despite many hints of a theophany, Theocritus' readers will have been deterred from thinking Lycidas was a god, whether Apollo or any other. For Lycidas is a mortal's name:[20] like most languages Greek had different sets of names for gods, for men and for animals, and it would be extraordinary to find the boundaries crossed. Of course there are links that cross the boundaries. Apollo, Dionysus, Athena have their human eponyms in Apollonius, Dionysius and Athenaeus or Apollodorus, Dionysodorus and Athenodorus. But the mortal name Lycidas shows no sign of being related to Apollo Lykios or Lykeios, nor does it ever appear as one of the range of cult-titles on the divine side of the line – Λύκιος (*Lykios*), Λύκειος (*Lykeios*), Λυκοκτόνος, 'wolf-slayer', and Λυκηγενής, 'wolf-born' or 'Lycian-born'. In choosing the name Lycidas the poet means us to see him as mortal. He may also, of course, intend the name to suggest that this mortal has Apollonian connections, such as an interest in poetry and song, but identity with the god is excluded.

(ii) Κυδωνικὸς ἀνήρ, 'a man from Cydonia', also, in Williams' view, leads to Apollo. Cydonia in Crete was once called Apollonia and, like Crete as a whole, has many Apollonian associations.[21] Suggestive as these associations may be if we already see Lycidas as a god, this interpretation of the phrase

[19] Williams 1971, 138. [20] E.g. Hdt. 9.5, D. 20.131, *Syll.*^{3} 84.5, *IG* vii 1178 (Tanagra).

[21] Williams 1971, 139 with nn.5–7. For some problems in linking Cretan Cydonia with Apollo cf. Brown 1981, 71 (the father of the Cydon who founded it is in fact stated by the scholion on A.R. 4.1492 to have been Hermes, not Apollo, as in the possibly confused entry of St.Byz., our only witness alleging that Cydonia in Crete was once called Apollonia). Brown's own hypothesis, that the ethnic Κυδωνικός, 'Cydonian', leads us, *inter alia*, to the god Pan, is open to the objections to a divine identification for Lycidas offered in the text. Nor am I persuaded by his suggestions that Κυδωνικός might suggest κύων, 'dog', and hence φύλαξ, 'guard' (as Pan is called by Pindar, fr. 95.2 Maehler); nor that it might suggest a quince and hence a carved quince-wood figure of Pan (84–5, but apparently abandoned by 87): on my reading of Brown's proposals we are to understand Lycidas throughout as a carved wayside figure, so it is mysterious how he can walk off at 130 ff. (Proponents of Cretan Cydonia seem incidentally to have missed the possible support of a mountain there called Tityrus, Str. 10.479).

discounts that half of it which describes him as an ἀνήρ, 'man', and so does not meet criterion (1).[22]

(iii) τὰν ἐπὶ Πύξας | εἷρφ' ὁδόν, 'he made his way along the road to Pyxa' (130–1).

The village of Pyxa is asserted by the scholia to have been the location of a shrine of Apollo, hence called Pyxius, and this seems to have been confirmed by the discovery of a sacred calendar attesting a cult of Ἀπόλλων Ὠρομέδων (*Apollon Ōromedōn*). When Lycidas goes off to Pyxa he is departing, on Williams' hypothesis, to his own shrine, like Athena after a similar encounter with a mortal at Od. 7.78 ff. This gives special point to Lycidas' earlier criticism of a builder who tries to build his house as high as the summit of Mount Oromedon (45 f.).[23]

This nexus of associations would certainly be evocative for a reader who came to this part of the poem believing that Lycidas was indeed Apollo. But the reference to Pyxa is too late in the narrative to be a primary clue: it could only have corroborative force. For a reader who has decided that Lycidas is a man, but a man who has special affinity with the Muses, a further link with Apollo also has considerable point: it sets the seal of Apollo's as well as

[22] Brown 1981, 86–7 takes ἄνδρα, 'man', as bringing out 'that the god is a good "man" with the Nymphs (Muses), a ladies' man'. But the 'Theocritean' usage of *Id.* 8 (not usually ascribed to Theocritus) which he offers as a parallel ὦ τράγε, τᾶν λευκᾶν αἰγῶν ἄνερ, 'o billy-goat, husband of the white nanny-goats' (8.49) is different because the genitive αἰγῶν dependent on ἄνερ points the reader to this meaning: I do not see how the Greek ἐσθλὸν σὺν Μοίσαισι ... ἄνδρα could be taken as 'a good man with the Muses' in a sexual sense. Brown (99) also notes that 7.86 αἴθ' ἐπ' ἐμεῦ ζωοῖς ἐναρίθμιος ὤφελες ἦμεν, 'would that in my time you might have been numbered among the living', might be taken as evidence that the singer, Lycidas, is not immortal (since a god would have been a contemporary of Comatas as well as of Simichidas). This point seems to me to have some weight, but I am not convinced by his suggestion that 83–9 are all intended to be part of Tityrus' song: that seems to be excluded by the way in which the line closing Lycidas' (and on Brown's view Tityrus' inset) song is immediately followed by (90) χὣ μὲν τόσσ' εἰπὼν ἀπεπαύσατο, 'and after saying these things he ceased'. This clearly refers to Lycidas.

[23] Williams 1971, 140, 142–3. Brown 1981, 74–5 notes that only the scholiast so far attests an Ἀπόλλων Πύξιος, 'Pyxian Apollo', and that the stone's epithet Φύξιος, 'Phyxian', is not certainly limited to Apollo. Brown's own proposal that ἐπὶ Πύξας should be understood as 'to the tune or accompaniment of boxwoods' requires Theocritus to have coined a form πύξη alongside the regular ἡ πύξος; to have expected his readers to see that 'boxwoods' meant 'panpipes' (Latin *buxus* often means 'flute', cf. *OLD s.v.*, but neither it nor πύξος seems ever to mean 'panpipes', and πύξος nowhere else means even αὐλός, 'pipe') and to have further confused his readers by the use of τάν (sc. ὁδόν?). But τὰν ἐπὶ Πύξας | εἷρφ' ὁδόν can mean only 'he went on the road to Pyxa'. The matter would be unambiguous (if it is not so already) were Theocritus to have written Φύξας; and perhaps he did – the form Φύξιος appears in the scholion on 130/1c (p. 109 Wendel). It might, of course, stem from ancient scholarship and not from the text of *Idyll* 7, but there is some chance that Theocritus wrote Φύξας. On the location of Pyxa cf. n.45. For Oromedon as a cult-title of Apollo see also *IG* xii.5 893 (Tenos, 3rd/2nd c. BC).

the Muses' approval on Lycidas' handing of his baton to Simichidas. I would argue, therefore, that Lycidas' departure for Pyxa tells the reader only that he has Apollonian connections, not that he is Apollo.

(iv) ἦς δ' αἰπόλος, 'and he was a goatherd' (13).

Williams draws attention to Apollo's cult-titles Νόμιος, 'Grazer', and Γαλάξιος, 'Milker', the former traced by Callimachus in his *Hymn to Apollo* to the god's serfdom to Admetus. Unlike Ovid, however, whom Williams also cites,[24] Callimachus does not go so far as to depict Apollo in the absurdity of pastoral attire, and he cannot easily be used to show that Theocritus would have done. Indeed at no point does either Callimachus or Ovid say that Apollo herded goats:[25] Callimachus has him herd the horses of Admetus (*Ap.* 47–9), Ovid *boves*, 'cattle' (*Met.* 2.685). Apollo's link with goats is limited to his protection of them (*Ap.* 50 ff.). The expression ἦς δ' αἰπόλος, therefore, precludes and does not contribute to Williams' identification of Lycidas as Apollo meeting criteria (1) and (2).

3 A Different Tack

If neither Williams' proposal nor any one of Dover's four possibilities meets all my criteria, I must look elsewhere. I suggest that Lycidas belongs to a category which Dover's classification overlooked, though it is perhaps nearest to his (iv). Lycidas is indeed a fictitious character, but not the creation of Theocritus: rather he is a character already created by a writer known to Theocritus and his intended readership.

Part of the evidence for this hypothesis comes from another pastoral work where the characters are also fictitious, the prose novel *Daphnis and Chloe*. Early in the teenage couple's discovery of love Longus introduces a figure who bears an uncanny resemblance to Lycidas:

> τερπομένοις δὲ αὐτοῖς ἐφίσταται πρεσβύτης σισύραν ἐνδεδυμένος,
> καρβατίνας ὑποδεδεμένος, πήραν ἐξηρτημένος, καὶ τὴν πήραν παλαιάν.
> οὗτος πλησίον καθίσας αὐτῶν ὧδε εἶπε.
>
> While they thus delight themselves, there comes up to them an old man,
> clad
> in his rug and a mantle of skins, his carbatins or clouted shoes, his scrip

[24] Williams 1971, 141, Ov. *Met.* 2.680–2. Tibullus 2.3.11 ff. also elaborates a picture of a dishevelled Apollo tending Admetus' cattle, but mentions neither goats nor pastoral garb.

[25] I owe this point to Prof. R. G. M. Nisbet.

hanging at his back, and that indeed a very old one. When he was sate down by them, thus he spoke and told his story.

Longus, *Daphnis and Chloe* 2.3.1 (transl. George Thornley)

The old man introduces himself as one who has often sung to the Nymphs whom Daphnis and Chloe worship, often played the panpipe to Pan, often led his herd of cattle by music alone. His skill on the panpipe and in song likens him to Theocritus' Lycidas (cf. *Id.* 7.28); his herding activities are another link, but that his animals are cattle will have to be explained (cf. below n.38); his σισύρα, a shaggy coat of skins, recalls Lycidas' goatskin garb (15–16); and he is not wearing proper boots, an inference that has been made about Lycidas from his reference to Simichidas' ἀρβυλίδες, 'shoes' (26).[26] One point of clear difference is that Longus' character is old: Lycidas, albeit senior to Simichidas in bearing, is not marked out as old, but rather seems ageless, although his tunic is described as γέρων, 'old', in a way which might be intended to convey age in its wearer too (17).

These features might not be so striking, and could, perhaps, be dismissed as the accoutrements of any pastoral male, were it not for his name, the theme of his discourse and the location of his encounter with Daphnis and Chloe. He introduces himself as Philetas. This is not a common name, and for any educated reader in the late second century AD it must at once have recalled the Hellenistic poet and scholar respected by Callimachus and by Theocritus' Simichidas (40).[27] Many scholars have seen this as an allusion to the Hellenistic poet, and this interpretation is supported by the role Philetas assumes and the story he tells.[28] The role is that of *praeceptor amoris*, 'instructor in love', familiar to us especially from Propertius, whose debt to Philetas is explicit at 3.1.1 *Callimachi Manes et Coi sacra Philitae* ... 'Shades

[26] Gow 1952, ii 139.

[27] The MSS of Longus offer the spelling and accentuation Φιλητᾶς. The MSS of Theoc. 7.40, of Stobaeus, and of most other Greek writers, likewise write Φιλητᾶς or Φιλήτας. The spelling Φιλίτας, which appears in MS A of Athenaeus and in some other writers, is preferred by modern scholars, doubtless correctly, for the Coan scholar-poet, because it is that of a Coan text of 202/1 BC (Paton and Hicks 1891, 10 b 37 and 54 = *IG* xii.4 1.75.111 and 128), cf. *IG* xii.4 1.302.4; note also Φίλιτις in several texts, e.g. *ASAA* n.s. 25–6 (1963), 169 no. ixa 56 (ca. 200 BC). It seems quite likely that the etacistic form Φιλητᾶς (on the analogy of Philemon?) had become established by the second century AD, since it seems to be that known to Augustan poets: it is also that of an inscription of the Roman imperial period, Paton and Hicks 1891, 310. If so, Longus could have written Φιλητᾶς and thought this to be the correct form of the Coan poet's name. It is also possible that he wrote Φιλίτας and that his MS tradition altered that form in the same way as Φιλίτας is assumed to have been corrupted in the *paradosis* of Theocritus and other authors. For a full discussion see now Spanoudakis 2002.

[28] The identification was made at least as early as Reitzenstein 1893, 260 n.1. For other material cf. Cairns 1979, 25 ff. and nn.110 and 112.

of Callimachus and rites of Coan Philitas ...'; and it is a debt that can be argued for elsewhere.[29] The old man's story is also, naturally, about love: he tells how once in his luxuriant garden, at the witching hour of noon, he had a divine encounter – with a boy who turns out to be Eros himself, who in fleeing and rejecting the old man reminds him how he gave him Amaryllis in his youth, and bids him rejoice that he alone among mortals has in his old age seen the boy Eros.[30]

It is improbable that Longus has simply picked on the name Philetas for his old man at random and has clumsily hit on that of a poet who sang, among other things, of love. Daphnis and Chloe has a small cast list, many of the names are chosen for their pastoral associations, and so important a figure as the old man should have been named with care.[31] Why, we must ask, did Longus not choose a name already familiar in the poets' pastoral prosopography, like that of the old man's flame in his youth, Amaryllis, or of his son, whom we shortly discover to be Tityrus?[32] Why not, indeed, if there is some relationship to Theocritus' Lycidas, the name Lycidas? And if the name Philetas is intended to recall the poet, with what purpose? And why is he found not on his native Cos but on a pastoral Lesbos? One further datum which will contribute to answering these questions is Longus' location of his story. It is still disputed just where on Lesbos the action is set. My own view, for which I argue in Appendix 1, is that Daphnis' and Chloe's farms are envisaged by Longus as being on the east coast of the island north of Mytilene, between the modern villages of Pámphyla and Nées Kydoniés. Neither village name is ancient, but we know from Pliny that an island off Lesbos was called Cydonia, and it is clear that the island lay off this coastline (see Appendix 2).[33] Ancient use of the name Cydonia for a village or area on Lesbos itself is not at present attested but seems to me probable (again see Appendix 2).

If my reasoning is correct, then Longus introduces his character Philetas, reminiscent of Lycidas the Κυδωνικὸς ἀνήρ, 'Cydonian man', in a location where we know of a place Cydonia. This increases further the probability that Longus indeed has Lycidas in mind, and prompts consideration of the geographical links of Theocritus' Lycidas. Is a Lesbian connection for him improbable? Far from it. Lycidas' song in *Id.* 7 (52–89) celebrates his love

[29] Hunter 1983, 77 compares Tibullus 1.8.

[30] Longus 2.4–6. For his picture of Eros here Longus also draws on Bion, fr. 13: cf. Hunter 1983, 77; Bowie 2019g *ad loc.*

[31] Longus 2.32. I owe the point about Longus' small cast to M. D. Reeve.

[32] On the names Amaryllis and Tityrus see further below Section 5.

[33] Some scholars, e.g. Gow 1952, ii 135 on 7.12, had noticed this Cydonia but dismissed it.

for Ageanax and prays for a safe voyage for Ageanax to Mytilene (52).[34] Theocritus does not tell us where Ageanax comes from. In theory he might be from any Doric or Aeolic area of the Greek world. But it is most probable that we are expected to think of him as either from Cos (where Lycidas sings his song) or from Lesbos (whither he is bound). The frequency of names in -anax or -anactidas on Lesbos, and particularly in Mytilene,[35] might indicate that he is meant to hail from there. If that is so, the context in which Lycidas fell in love with Ageanax is as likely to be Mytilenean as Coan territory. We must therefore consider seriously the possibility that by Κυδωνικὸς ἀνήρ Theocritus meant a man from Lesbian Cydonia.

Another question now arises. Why did Longus set his pastoral fiction on Lesbos at all? There is, indeed, some chance that it was his own place of birth or residence,[36] and that this influenced him to introduce a pastoral

[34] It is usually assumed that Lycidas' celebratory party takes place wherever Lycidas imagines himself as being (Cos?) and without the presence of Ageanax. There are singular oddities in this scenario. Lycidas celebrates either the departure of Ageanax (which by the normal conventions of ἔρως, 'desire', we might expect to make him miserable or anxious) or his safe arrival at Mytilene – but how he is to know that Ageanax has completed a voyage of 150 or more miles is left obscure. τῆνο κατ' ἆμαρ, 'on that day' (63), seems to refer to his safe arrival, hardly the same day as his departure, and difficult to refer also to the day on which Ageanax might be implied to have granted Lycidas long-withheld favours, and hence little support for the view that Lycidas is rejoicing 'as much for Ageanax's complaisance as for his safety' (Gow 1952, ii 145 on 52–9, cf. *ibid.* 148 on 62. I assume that Gow's '50 miles' (*ibid.* 148 on 63) for the length of Ageanax's voyage is a printing error for 150, though even that would be simply the distance as the crow flies, and a boat would have to travel much further). Matters would be slightly eased if we are intended to imagine the location of Lycidas' song as his native Cydonia, on the above view near enough to Mytilene for the voyage to be completed in a day. But the other oddities remain disturbing. I am tempted to wonder whether the answer lies in the meaning of μεμναμένος (69): the cognate verb μνάομαι is used both in the sense 'remember' (cf. LSJ *s.v.* I) and 'woo' (*ibid.* II, citing Od. 1.39, 11.287, 16.77, 19.529). It would not be untypical of Hellenistic *Gelehrsamkeit* to argue that μεμναμένος should also have this range of meaning and for a learned poet to incorporate an illustrative use in his work. If this speculation is correct, then Ageanax is present and being wooed at the party, and it is a party that takes place after he has arrived at his destination, i.e. Mytilene.

[35] Gow notes names of the form Ageanax/Archeanax from Cos, Smyrna, Miletus and the Troad. For Lesbos cf. in Alcaeus Archeanactidae (fr. 112.24) and Damoanactidas (fr. 296(b); cf. below n.74); Cleanactidae in Alcaeus (fr. 112.3) and Sappho (fr. 98) – all these presumably Mytilenean; and Polyanactidai in Sappho (fr. 99). Later at least two Mytileneans bore the name Lesbonax, the philosopher of the first century BC (cf. *PIR*^{2} L 160) and a sophist of the second (?) century AD, cf. *KP* iii 584–5 *s.n.* Lesbonax (2).

[36] Cf. Cichorius 1922, 321–3, noting the Mytileneans Cn. Pompeius Longus (*IG* xii.2 88, late first century BC?) and A. Pompeius Longus Dionysodorus (*IG* xii.2 249, first century AD?). But Longus is not a rare name (twenty-one Longi are noted by L. Petersen in *PIR*^{2} v 1) and we still lack evidence of the name Longus persisting in Lesbos down to the latter part of the second century AD; nor is there a Longus in the group associated with a Dionysiac cult in Rome whose Lesbian connections are indicated by Pompeia Agrippinilla, cf. Vogliano and Cumont 1933, Merkelbach 1962, 193. That Dionysodorus is an ἀρχιερεύς, 'high priest', does little to strengthen links with a novel in which Dionysus has a significant role, since the office was a mark of social eminence rather than religious devotion, and was concerned with the cult of the emperor in particular. But for a strong case for a link between the Pompeii and Longus see Mason 2018.

tale to an island that had no previous place in literary pastoral. But the kinds of details he uses suggest rather an outsider who knew the island largely from literary sources, and perhaps from the sort of tourist visit his preface asserts.[37] If that is so, then his choice of Lesbos must have been influenced by some other consideration. The most obvious reason will have been that the Mytilenean χώρα has already been given a pastoral colour by some earlier writer in the bucolic tradition. Theocritus' Cydonian Lycidas with his apparently Mytilenean boyfriend Ageanax leads us in the same direction, and requires that such Lesbian pastoral antedate Theocritus.

One hypothesis explains all these phenomena. There was indeed before Theocritus some poetry in which fictional shepherds or goatherds sang and loved. Its setting was the countryside, north of Mytilene. Its characters included, most prominently, a goatherd called Lycidas; also his boyfriend, Ageanax, a shepherd Tityrus, and a cowherd, Daphnis (*Id.* 7.72–3).[38] It was well enough known in Theocritus' time for him to introduce one of its characters by name, trade and ethnic in the sure knowledge that he would be recognised and the allusion appreciated. Its writer's name is supplied by Longus when he transforms the *dramatis personae* in his own pastoral: Philetas.

It has often been conjectured that Philetas wrote bucolic poetry.[39] A text from Antigonus of Carystus has been adduced, inconclusively, and a hexameter papyrus fragment with some pastoral features has been attributed to

[37] Ἐν Λέσβωι θηρῶν ἐν ἄλσει Νυμφῶν θέαμα εἶδον κάλλιστον ὧν εἶδον· εἰκόνος γραφήν, ἱστορίαν ἔρωτος ..., 'When hunting on Lesbos I saw a spectacle in a grove of the Nymphs that was the most beautiful I have seen: the painting of a picture, a story of desire ...' (pr. 1) ... καὶ ἀναζητησάμενος ἐξηγητὴν τῆς εἰκόνος τέτταρας βίβλους ἐξεπονησάμην ... 'and seeking out an expounder of the picture I have laboured to create four books ...' (pr. 3). It is more likely that a writer who says 'When hunting in Lesbos ...' means the reader to think of him as a visitor: a native might be expected to explain that it was his place of birth or residence. It is also more likely that a visitor should require instruction about a picture and local legend than a resident. But it is only a matter of likelihood, and it is always possible to argue that the *topoi* of the preface have more to do with putting the author in a comparable position to his expected audience than with reporting biographic fact. For details which seem to come from literary sources cf. Scarcella 1968, but for evidence of a good knowledge of Lesbos see Mason 1995. One possible motive for a visit to Lesbos would be to receive or give rhetorical instruction as a sophist: we know from Philostr. *VS* 1.22.526 that Dionysius of Miletus taught there early in his career (presumably in the first quarter of the second century AD).

[38] That Longus requires the Philetan cowherd Daphnis to tend goats (balancing Chloe's tending of sheep) explains why his 'Philetas' must, unlike the Philetan Lycidas, be a cowherd.

[39] E.g. Cairns 1979, 25. A significant role for Philetas in the development of bucolic poetry has been argued for by Puelma 1960, 150; against Lohse 1966, 420, without general acceptance.

him, but conjecturally.[40] But we still know very little of the range of the first great Hellenistic poet, doubtless because he was eclipsed by the luminaries of the second generation, and fragments 673–5 in *SH* do not substantially augment the miserable harvest of twenty-six short fragments in Powell's *CA* of 1925 (to which Kuchenmüller 1928 had added four single-word fragments, *SH* 675a–d). We can be sure that love featured in Philetas' poetry, and Hermesianax's vignette of him commemorated by a statue beneath a plane-tree singing of swift-footed Bittis[41] may allude to a scene or scenes in which songs of love were sung ὑπὸ πλατάνωι, 'beneath the plane-tree'. Such a scene may have been the context of fr. 14 Powell (= 8 Spanoudakis = 22 Lightfoot) θρήσασθαι πλατάνωι γραίηι ὕπο, 'to sit beneath an aged plane-tree'; but although plane-trees are more probably rural than urban, they do not allow us to insist on a rural, far less pastoral setting. A little more emerges from four lines describing an alder-tree destined to be a poet's staff:

οὔ μέ τις ἐξ ὀρέων ἀποφώλιος ἀγροιώτης
αἱρήσει κλήθρην, αἱρόμενος μακέλην·
ἀλλ' ἐπέων εἰδὼς κόσμον καὶ πολλὰ μογήσας,
μύθων παντοίων οἶμον ἐπιστάμενος.

No empty-headed rustic shall from the mountains
seize me, an alder-tree, snatching up a mattock.
but one who knows the good ordering of words, who has toiled much,
and who knows the pathway of all manner of speech.
Philetas fr. 10 Powell = 25 Spanoudakis = 8 Lightfoot

This does resemble the staff variously called κορύνα, 'club' or 'staff', and λαγωβόλον, 'hare-hitter', by Theocritus (43 and 128), and it could be that Theocritus is alluding to it. But if this is a complete poem from the Παίγνια,

[40] Antig. 19 (23) Keller (= Philetas, fr. 22 Powell) has been taken as evidence for Philetas' treatment of the Aristaeus legend, but this can only be conjectural. Euphorion fr. 429 *SH* (= *P.Schubart* 7, *P.Berol.* 13873) was argued by Scheibner 1965 to be by Philetas, and goats and sheep appear in lines 25–6. But Carden 1969 showed that Euphorion, fr. 130 Powell almost certainly fits line 48 of the papyrus and that Euphorion is most probably the author, as he is taken to be by *SH*. It seems to me that Philetas could still be the author (line 6 Ὠρομέδον[το]ς, whether the mountain or an alternative name for the giant Eurymedon, would be easier to explain) but in any case mythological material seems to predominate and we are very far from bucolic. Philetas' authorship is not accepted by Spanoudakis 2002, 343.

[41] οἶσθα δὲ καὶ τὸν ἀοιδόν, ὃν Εὐρυπύλου πολιῆται | Κῷοι χάλκειον στῆσαν ὑπὸ πλατάνωι | Βιττίδα μολπάζοντα θοήν, περὶ πάντα Φιλίταν | ῥήματα καὶ πᾶσαν τρυόμενον λαλιήν, 'and you know that even the singer, whom Eurypylus' citizens in Cos set up in bronze beneath the plane-tree, celebrates in song-dance swift Bittis, Philitas, well-honed in all words and every form of speech', Hermesianax 7.75–8 Powell = 3.75–8 Lightfoot. On the statue see Hardie 1997; doubts about a relation to Philetas fr. 14 Powell = 8 Spanoudakis in Spanoudakis 2002, 155–8.

'*Playthings*', it does not offer anything approaching bucolic. It is possible that it is an extract rather than a complete poem, and that the context from which it was taken was bucolic, but that can only be guesswork. Another point of resemblance with *Id.* 7 is offered by a fragment where an unidentifiable individual is described as follows:[42]

> λευγαλέος δὲ χιτὼν πεπινωμένος, ἀμφὶ δ᾽ ἀραιὴ
> ἰξὺς εἴλυται ῥάμμα μελαγκράνινον.
>
> a wretched, dirt-stained tunic, and his (or her?) slim
> waist was girt about with a fastening of black-tufted rushes.
>
> Philetas fr. 17 Powell = Alleged poetical ascriptions 2 Spanoudakis = 30 Lightfoot

This bears some resemblance to Lycidas, but not enough to be useful: this character shows no sign of wearing skins, and Lycidas wears a decent belt, not rushes, to gird a πέπλος, 'robe', not a χιτών, 'tunic'.

Surviving fragments, then, do little if anything to support the inference from Longus and (on my argument) from Theocritus that Philetas wrote some sort of bucolic poetry. Equally they do nothing to refute it. Nor, it must be insisted, does the prominence given by the later tradition to Theocritus' contribution to pastoral. This is entirely consonant with the fact that a major part of Theocritus' poetry is pastoral, and very good pastoral, and with the hypothesis that Philetas, among his many different sorts of poetry, wrote some poems with bucolic settings and *dramatis personae*.[43]

[42] I owe this observation to Mr A. S. Hollis.

[43] Dover 1971 was deterred from accepting his possibility (iii) (which would involve Theocritus 'acknowledging his debt to a particular older poet who developed the idea of bucolic poetry') (a) by the apparent lack of pre-Theocritean bucolic poetry (a dangerous argument from silence – all we can say is that we have no surviving poetry clearly datable before Theocritus that bears the marks of the genre as practised by him) and (b) by the fact that 'the Roman period, which possessed what we do not possess, regarded Theokritos as the inventor of bucolic poetry'. It is not obvious that the Roman period did so regard Theocritus. The life and scholia have no such explicit statement, but simply term Theocritus ὁ τῶν βουκολικῶν ποιητής or ὁ τῶν βουκολικὰ συγγραψάντων ἄριστος (*Scholia in Theocritum vetera*, ed. C. Wendel, Leipzig, 1914, p. 1 (*Prolegomena*) 4, p. 9.6–7). That the writer of the εὕρεσις τῶν βουκολικῶν (ibid. p. 2.4 ff.) looks not to poets earlier than Theocritus but exclusively to cult (Dover 1971, lix) does not seem to me to count for or against the possibility that a poet or poets earlier than Theocritus did write something like bucolic poetry: the writer is trying to offer an *aition* of where bucolic poetry began, not where Theocritus (specifically) looked for his models. (For a brief survey of known pre-Theocritean approaches to bucolic poetry see Dover 1971, lx–lxv; I only saw Halperin 1983 after this article had been drafted.) That Vergil chose Theocritus as his model confirms that he was judged the best bucolic poet, but does not show that he was regarded as the 'inventor': indeed we shall see that there are some details in the *Eclogues* which imply the existence of more Hellenistic bucolic poetry than we have.

Of course a connection has been made between Theocritus' Lycidas and Philetas before,[44] but in forms which have the poet Philetas actually portrayed as Lycidas (Dover's possibility (iii) above). The objections to this view do not hold against the hypothesis I am advancing, that Lycidas was a character in Philetan pastoral. This will emerge, I hope, from the following application of the hypothesis to the poem, as will understanding of a number of hitherto puzzling features of the *Idyll*.

4 Reading *Idyll* 7

That the journey recalled by the narrator takes place on Cos becomes clear to the reader (unless he spots the τὸν Ἄλεντα of 1 as a Coan deme)[45] with the reference to Clytia and Chalcon at 4–5. Why, he may wonder, is the narrator on Cos, an island which does not feature unambiguously in any other of Theocritus' pastoral poems?[46] One possible answer is immediately hinted at with the description of the spring Burina. It had been described by the Coan poet Philetas (fr. 24 Powell = 6 Spanoudakis = 21 Lightfoot): νάσσατο

[44] See Gow 1952, i 130 n.7.

[45] Gow 1952, ii 31 thinks that the use of the article indicates that Theocritus does not intend τὸν Ἄλεντα to refer to the deme Haleis but to a place or river from which the deme took its name. That Haleis in 5.123 is the name of a river in S. Italy and is otherwise attested as a river name is not a good reason for conjecturing that it is a river name in Cos, and it would be odd that the goal of the journey should be stated as a river which plays no later part in the poem. If the article does preclude reading τὸν Ἄλεντα as the name of the deme, then most probably it is the name of the village which gave the deme its name. Although the main centre of population in the deme Haleis has not yet been identified, it is likely to have been in the area of Pyli; cf. Sherwin-White 1978, 59. If Theocritus expects any knowledge of Coan geography in his readers, he can rely on them knowing that Haleis is a deme whose territory is reached about ten km from Cos town, and on placing Phrasidamus' farm near the deme centre, some three to four km into the deme territory and on the foothills of Oromedon (rather than in the flat plain). They may also know that the only deme lying between that of Cos itself and Haleis is the deme Phyxa, whose centre seems to be near Asphendiou, even further up the slopes of Oromedon; they will therefore appreciate that someone bound for Phyxa would have to part from travellers to Haleis by turning left before the territory of the deme Haleis is reached (cf. Sherwin-White 1978, 59 and her map, p. 10; for a map with conjectural deme boundaries, Neppi Modona 1933). Lycidas' departure at 130–1 will therefore make good sense, and his making for Pyxa will corroborate the other indications (e.g. ἐν ὄρει, 'in the hills', 51) that his natural habitat is hill-country.

[46] A reference to a ferry to (?) Calymnos at 1.57 may attest Coan knowledge for the goatherd of *Idyll* 1, as may the reference to the runner Philinus at 2.115 for the lover of *Idyll* 2 (and, less convincingly, the 'Coan oath' of 2.160). But neither poem seems to be intended to be set in Cos, and if the setting of *Idyll* 1 is specific, the west is a stronger candidate. *Idyll* 5 seems clearly set near Sybaris, so if the Haleis of 5.123 is Coan it must be taken as a deliberate fusion of South Italian and Coan background: but it need not be (cf. Gow *ad loc*). I see no good reason for understanding the στομάλιμνον, 'river-mouth lagoon', of 4.23 as a reference to the Coan κώμη, 'village', called Στομαλίμνη attested by Str. 14.657 (again cf. Gow *ad loc.*). Of course, as Robert Wells pointed out to me, Cos is twice mentioned by name in the encomium of Ptolemy, 17.58 and 64.

δ' ἐν προχοῇσι μελαμπέτροιο Βυρίνης, 'and (s)he settled at the outpourings of the black-rocked Burina'. I would suggest that Theocritus' Coan setting and the digressive description of Burina are intended to turn the reader's mind to that poet.[47]

A reader thus prepared will have no difficulty in recognising the goatherd Lycidas of Cydonia as the character of that name and origin known to him from a poem, or poems, by Philetas. He may be surprised to find him on Cos, but will take his transplanting to Cos as part of the compliment to Philetas that Theocritus is paying in setting his whole *Idyll* there. The problematic lines 13–14 now cease to be a difficulty:

ἦς δ' αἰπόλος, οὐδέ κέ τις νιν
ἠγνοίησεν ἰδών, ἐπεὶ αἰπόλωι ἔξοχ' ἐώικει.

and he was a goatherd, nor could one
have mistaken him on seeing him, since he was exceedingly like a goatherd.

Lycidas *was* a goatherd – within the world of Philetan and (now) Theocritean poetry. That this fictitious world strikingly reflects reality is then said with the phrase ἐπεὶ αἰπόλωι ἔξοχ' ἐώικει. In most circumstances, of course, we only find ourselves saying 'he was very like a goatherd' or 'he was the spitting image of a goatherd' when the person of whom this is predicated is *not* a goatherd. Hence, on most interpretations, the problem of reconciling this with ἦς δ' αἰπόλος, 'he *was* a goatherd'. But if Theocritus, as his readers know, is commenting on a created character, the phrase ἐπεὶ αἰπόλωι ἔξοχ' ἐώικει becomes, like the careful detail of his own description, a compliment to the verisimilitude of the creation and to the skill of the creator.[48]

[47] I am persuaded by Zanker 1980 that ancient Burina is correctly identified with the spring which now bears that name, quite high on the slopes of Oromedon five km south-west of the city of Cos and above the Asclepieum, and that it cannot therefore be the same as the spring by which the harvest festival takes place at 131 ff. (as argued by Puelma 1960 and by Arnott 1979). Puelma's argument that if Burina is not on Phrasidamus' farm its mention at 6 ff. lacks point (partly met by Zanker 1980, n.17) is of course fully countered by its role as an allusion to Philetas on my hypothesis. But it may also be relevant that the hillside above the Asclepieum where Burina nestles is clearly visible to travellers to Haleis for the first part of their journey. The repetition of αἴγειροι πτελέαι τε (8 and 136) can also be allowed a function in the poem – to remind the reader of Burina when the harvest festival begins – without insisting that the springs are identical. As indicated in n.45 I doubt the location of the harvest festival on the plain near Linopóti, as suggested by Paton 1891 and adopted by (e.g.) Zanker (see his map p. 377) and Arnott.

[48] Professor Nisbet reminds me of the Hellenistic admiration for ultra-realism in art, of which Theoc. 1.27 ff. offers an example: note especially (1.41) ὁ πρέσβυς, κάμνοντι τὸ κάρτερον ἀνδρὶ ἐοικώς 'the old codger is like a man making the utmost effort', with the following remark (1.42) φαίης κεν γυίων νιν ὅσον σθένος ἐλλοπιεύειν 'you would say he was fishing with all the strength of his limbs'. The hypothesis of Brown 1981 that Lycidas is a cult-statue of Pan would also meet this point, though he does not so exploit it.

When Lycidas speaks he addresses the narrator as Simichidas. The reader who has already recognised Lycidas as a created character will easily conceive an explanation for this. Theocritus himself could hardly, on a walk in the countryside, encounter a fictitious character. He could create another fictitious character who was, like himself and Lycidas, a poet, and send him into the country to encounter Philetas' creation. This created character is clearly linked to Theocritus by the ambiguous first-person narrative presentation, but is also linked to the fictional world of Lycidas by interests shared, acquaintance presumed and, perhaps, the form of his name in -idas. The encounter with Lycidas may embody a further Philetan allusion, viz. to that encounter between Philetas (or a Philetan character) and Eros which has been argued to lie behind the story told by Longus' Philetas.[49]

The way the encounter is developed makes it clear what some of its purposes are. Simichidas opens with straight praise of Lycidas, which can be read as commendation and admiration of Philetas by Theocritus (27–9). He then suggests that he himself is good enough to show Lycidas some tricks (36 τάχ' ὥτερος ἄλλον ὀνασεῖ, 'perhaps one of us will profit the other'): Theocritus both wishes to set his own bucolic creations in the tradition begun by Philetas and to suggest that his own contribution is as worthy of respect. Simichidas does not yet, however, claim to rival Sicelidas or Philetas: by an ironic twist (such as that claimed by Williams for Lycidas' references to Apollo) Simichidas is made to mention Philetas, Lycidas' creator, as in a different class. So, of course, he is – but a different class of reality, not quality. Although this reference could, I must concede, be seen as an obstacle to my hypothesis, it seems to me easily explicable on these lines and precisely the sort of allusive puzzle that Alexandrian readers would expect.

The reference to Sicelidas/Asclepiades may also be intended to create certain expectations in the reader. First, that the songs to be exchanged will be of love, as Asclepiades' surviving epigrams mostly are. Such an expectation might not be created so securely by the mention of Philetas alone, given that poet's wide range, though I would regard it as probable that Philetas presented love in bucolic settings, and that Lycidas' name would itself have turned the reader's mind to the bucolic-erotic parts of Philetas' *oeuvre*. Secondly, if the ascription of *AP* 9.64 to Asclepiades is accepted,[50]

[49] Cf. Cairns 1979, 25–6 and n.112.

[50] *HE* ii 149 on Asclepiades 45 rejects the ascription, apparently because the alternative MS ascriptions are to authors not included in Meleager's garland. Dover 1971, 149 seems to accept the attribution to Asclepiades. Stadtmüller, endorsed by Beckby, accepted the alternative ascription to Archias. See further Sens 2011, 310. Apart from this there are no obvious allusions to Asclepiades in Theoc. 7, but in the absence of all but some of Asclepiades' epigrams there may well be allusions to his poetry that we cannot identify.

then in alluding to a poet who composed an epigram on Hesiod's encounter with the Muses, an epigram which added the detail that this took place in the middle of the day, Theocritus is citing another authority for midday divine encounters and reminding readers that Simichidas' meeting with Lycidas recalls that of Hesiod with the Muses.

That prepares the way for Lycidas' reply to Simichidas. He offers him his κορύνα, 'staff', a clear allusion, as many have seen, to Hesiod's gift from the Muses of a σκῆπτρον … δάφνης ἐριθηλέος ὄζον, 'staff … a branch of a vigorous laurel', a gift which came simultaneously with that of αὐδὴν … θέσπιν, 'god-given … voice'.[51] It may also, as I suggest above, be an allusion to Philetas fr. 10 Powell = 25 Spanoudakis = 8 Lightfoot. But the Hesiodic element in the allusion is driven home by the following line (44):

> πᾶν ἐπ' ἀλαθείαι πεπλασμένον ἐκ Διὸς ἔρνος.
>
> a sapling fashioned entirely upon truth by the gift of Zeus

The combination of πεπλασμένα, things 'fashioned' or 'fictitious', and the truth, is precisely that set out by the Muses at *Theogony* 27–8:

> ἴδμεν ψευδέα πολλὰ λέγειν ἐτύμοισιν ὁμοῖα,
> ἴδμεν δ', εὖτ' ἐθέλωμεν ἀληθέα γηρύσασθαι
>
> we know how to tell many false things that are like the genuine,
> and we know, when we want, how to cry forth true things.

Here, of course, truth and fiction are treated as alternatives. So they usually are. But we have already in *Id.* 7 seen one case where that which *is* within the fictional world has been commended as plausible fiction (13–14). I think the same paradox is being served up in 44: Simichidas is indeed fictional, πεπλασμένον, as a creation of Theocritus, but it is a fiction that (like Philetas' creation of Lycidas) strikes at reality (ἐπ' ἀλαθείαι). In having Lycidas commend Simichidas in comparable terms to those which he, as narrator, has used of Lycidas, Theocritus asserts that his own pastoral creations are as realistic as those of Philetas.

Lycidas' ensuing proclamation of what we think of as the Callimachean ideal of the short poem comes as no surprise in Theocritus. But it is given added point in the mouth of a Philetan character if, as seems likely, Philetas was an early exponent of that ideal.

I would expect the song that Lycidas sings (52–89) to evoke the form, tone and detail of some Philetan poetry, while of course adapting it in Theocritus'

[51] *Th.* 30–3.

own manner to offer the reader provocative *imitatio.* In the absence of substantial fragments of Philetas this hypothesis cannot be tested. As it is, we can only assume that the introduction of Tityrus and Daphnis goes back to Philetas – hence their prominence in Longus – and wonder whether Philetas also told the story of the goatherd Comatas, shut in a chest and fed by a honeycomb (cf. bees in fr. 22 Powell).[52] We might suspect that the mysterious Πτελεατικὸν οἶνον, 'wine of Ptelea' (65), has some connection with the πτελέαι, 'elms', that mark the springs at 8 and 136, the former, Burina, certainly mentioned by Philetas. It may also be significant that the phrase ἔτος ὥριον, 'the year in its springtime' (85), finds its only parallel in Philetas fr. 3 Powell = 10 Spanoudakis = 2 Lightfoot, perhaps from his *Demeter.*[53]

Simichidas' response to Lycidas' song begins πολλὰ μὲν ἄλλα | Νύμφαι κἠμὲ δίδαξαν ἀν' ὤρεα βουκολέοντα | ἐσθλά, 'the Nymphs have taught me too many other good things as I tended flocks in the mountains' (91–3). Lycidas himself gave no explicit credit to the Nymphs, but simply presented his song as a little number that he had worked up in the hills (51). We may be entitled to suppose that Philetas, like Longus, gave the Nymphs an important place as protective deities, and that this is again alluded to in their address at the end of the poem (154). Whether this can be inferred or not, it is important that Simichidas (94–5) offers his song as a γέρας, 'tribute', to Lycidas: in the same way the whole *Idyll* is a γέρας to Philetas.

Simichidas' song should not, of course, highlight Philetan features. And perhaps its complexity and its emphasis on the harsher and more unpleasant side of love are meant to remind the reader of the greater sophistication presumably brought by Theocritus to pastoral and the darker undertones he sometimes used in his pictures.[54]

Lycidas' gift of his stick to Simichidas completes the investiture: the baton has passed from Philetas' creation to that of Theocritus, with full approval of the former. If the Hellenistic reader was expected to recognise Pyxa, Lycidas' destination, as an Apolline shrine, then Philetas was the most obvious source of this information.

[52] On Tityrus see further below, Section 5. Comatas, of course, is the name of a character in *Idyll* 5, cf. below, Section 6.

[53] τῶι οἴμοι πολέω γαίης ὕπερ ἠδὲ θαλάσσης | ἐκ Διὸς ὡραίων ἐρχομένων ἐτέων. | οὐδ' ἀπὸ Μοῖρα κακῶν μελέωι φέρει, ἀλλὰ μένουσιν | ἔμπεδ' ἀεί, καὶ τοῖς ἄλλα προσαυξάνεται, 'so it is, alas, that I range over land and sea, as the years with their seasons are sent by Zeus, nor does Fate take away any from my woes, wretched that I am, but they remain firmly planted for ever, and yet others are added to them' (in line 1 Kuchenmüller proposed τῶι οἴμοι πολέω for the reading τω ου μοι πολέων of the MSS of Stob. 4.40.15). It may also be significant that the only appearance of an αἴγειρος, 'black poplar', and one of the two appearances of πτελέαι, 'elms', in Callimachus are in his Demeter hymn (6.26 and 37), where they (and a πίτυς, 'pine', ὄχναι,'pears', and γλυκύμαλα, 'sweet-apples') are in the desecrated ἄλσος, 'grove'. Another Philetan echo?

[54] E.g. the threatened violence of *Idyll 5.*

The narrator now takes us immediately to the scene of the harvest festival on his host Phrasidamus' farm. The repetition of αἴγειροι πτελέαι τε, 'black poplars and elms', from line 8 associates the water flowing from the Nymphs' cave with that of Burina.[55] The lush description, apart from being melodious and evocative poetry, has been seen as carrying various symbolic meanings.[56] What has not been asked is why a festival of the deity of arable farming should have been chosen by Theocritus for the culmination of a poem whose main characters are pastoral and whose principal theme is pastoral poetry. Most societies, and that of ancient Greece is no exception, are marked by substantial differences between the pastoral and arable-farming communities and ways of life. A god normally associated closely with the one could not easily be taken as a patron of the other. For a reader of Theocritus *Id.* 7 who perceived that the poem was an elaborate compliment to Philetas there would be no puzzle: Philetas' most famous (and perhaps only) long poem in elegiacs was *Demeter*. I would suggest that the festival of Demeter is made so integral a part of Theocritus' poem because he wished to compliment this element in Philetas' *oeuvre* as well as the shorter poems of love in (as I am arguing) a bucolic setting.[57] It may be relevant that Callimachus too picked out Philetas' *Demeter* to compare in some way with his shorter poems.[58]

If my explanation of Lycidas' role in *Id.* 7 is correct, then some light is shed on one or two shadowy problems in Augustan poetry, and (inevitably) some further questions about Philetas are raised.

5 Amaryllis in Vergil's *Eclogues*

Apart from *Id.* 7, the only poem of Theocritus in which the first person is used *ab initio*, without any narrative introduction, is *Id.* 3. It is also the only other poem in which a Tityrus (cf. 7.72) figures: he is asked to tend the goats of the unnamed speaker (3–4: the name may be repeated to ensure that the

[55] Cf. n.47.

[56] E.g. Lasserre 1959, 325, followed by Puelma 1960, 156, Lawall 1967, 102 ff., and Segal 1974, 20–76 = Segal 1981, 148ff.

[57] It may be significant that Theoc. makes no attempt to bridge the gap between arable and pastoral activity by introducing a sacrificial sheep, as does Adaeus, *GP* 2 = *AP* 6.258, influenced by Theoc. 7.155 ff. In deciding to elaborate his festival of Demeter Theocritus may also be influenced by the popularity of her cult on Cos, and in particular by the existence of an important cult centre in the deme Haleis; cf. Sherwin-White 1978, 305–12. As she points out (312), this sanctuary, belonging to the deme, cannot be the private cult of Phrasidamus' family; but it could of course be a reason for Theocritus seeing especial appropriateness in mentioning – or inventing? – that cult. It also seems unlikely that the Haleis cult of Demeter will not have been mentioned in Philetas' *Demeter*.

[58] *Aet.* fr. 1.9 ff. Do 155–7 indicate that Theocritus intends to turn his hand next to an epyllion like the *Demeter*? Call.'s own *Hymn to Demeter*, arguably intended for recitation on Cos, should owe something to Philetas' *Demeter* too; cf. n.53.

reader recognises it, as well as for poetic effect). Amaryllis appears only in *Id.* 3, as the girl whom the speaker serenades, and in *Id.* 4, as a girl now dead but once beloved of Battus, the interlocutor of Corydon. Tityrus and Amaryllis appear twice together in Vergil's *Eclogues.* In *Ecl.* 1 Tityrus is said by Meliboeus to sing of Amaryllis (1–5); this could be a reworking of the *dramatis personae* of *Id.* 3, but one point, shortly to be considered, counts against that. In *Ecl.* 9, however, Amaryllis appears as the beloved of Lycidas (22) and Tityrus as his subordinate, whether son or slave, who is asked to tend his goats in a song (23–5). This doubtless owes something to *Id.* 3.3–4. But it could suggest that Vergil either identifies the speaker of *Id.* 3 as Lycidas or knows bucolic poetry where Lycidas loves Amaryllis. The appearance in Longus of Philetas as the lover of Amaryllis and as a Lycidas-like figure with a son called Tityrus offers an explanation: Philetas' poetry included serenading of Amaryllis by a Lycidas, perhaps in a poem which, like *Id.* 3, used first-person dramatic presentation. Theocritus recalls this in *Id.* 3, Vergil in *Ecl.* 9. In *Ecl.* 1 the next generation, Lycidas' son Tityrus, has symbolically moved into Lycidas' shoes, and in his turn sings of an Amaryllis.

This sequence might seem rashly speculative were it not for one further fact. *Ecl.* 1.5 *formosam resonare doces Amaryllida silvas*, 'you teach the woods to re-echo 'beautiful Amaryllis', was seen long ago, by Leo, to be too close to Longus 2.7.6 to be explicable otherwise than by a direct connection.[59] There the Greek of Philetas' speech runs ἐπήνουν τὴν Ἠχὼ τὸ

[59] Leo 1903, 3 n.1 = Leo 1960, ii. 13 n.1: 'die Übereinstimmung in der Sache ist so auffallend dass man auf eine direkte Beziehung schliessen muss'. My attention was drawn to this observation by Dr R. G. Mayer. The ancestry of *Ecl.* 1 and the influence of the model of Longus 2.3 ff. are of course more complicated than this brief account can set out. For connections with Theoc., Call., and Gallus and the conclusion that the common model must be Philetas cf. DuQuesnay 1981, 38–51, esp. 39–40; Hunter 1983, 79–81. As DuQuesnay and Hunter show (and as had already been drawn to my attention by Ms. P. K. M. Kinchin), there are also themes from this nexus in Propertius 1.18.19–32. Thus the echo-motif of Longus 2.7.6 and *Ecl.* 1. appears as *sed qualiscumque es resonent mihi 'Cynthia' silvae, nec deserta tuo nomine saxa vacent* (Prop. 1.18.31–2); Philetas, in love with Amaryllis, piped πρὸς ταῖς φηγοῖς ἐκείναις, 'by those oaks (*phēgoi*)' (Longus 2.5.3), cf. *sub tegmine fagi*, 'under the shade of a beech (*fāgus*) (*Ecl.* 1.1) and *vos eritis testes … fagus, et Arcadio pinus amica deo*, 'you will be witnesses … beech, and the pine-tree friendly to the Arcadian god' (Prop. 1.18.19–20); and the plights of Philetas in Longus and of Prop. in 1.18 are similar. Prop. 1.18 in turn exploits Call.'s 'Acontius and Cydippe': cf. Cairns 1963 and Hunter 1983, 81, suggesting that Call. may there have drawn on Philetas. I add here a further possible link between *Ecl.* 1 and Longus which should also go back to a common source: at Longus 2.11.3 the progress of Daphnis' and Chloe's experience of love might have continued εἰ μὴ θόρυβος τοιόσδε πᾶσαν τὴν ἀγροικίαν ἐκείνην κατέλαβεν, 'had not the following disturbance descended on that whole countryside', *Ecl.* 1.11–12: Tityrus' enjoyment of *otia* is astonishing, because *undique totis | usque adeo turbatur agris*, 'everywhere there is such a great disturbance in all the countryside'. If these two passages do have a common model we shall have to be cautious about treating confiscations and the plight of Meliboeus as an alien element brought into the pastoral by Vergil.

Ἀμαρυλλίδος ὄνομα μετ᾽ ἐμὲ καλοῦσαν, 'I would praise Echo as she called out the name of Amaryllis after me'. That Longus used Vergil is hard to credit.[60] Vergil did not use Longus, who wrote some two centuries later. A common source must be postulated. Philetas fits the bill.

6 Corydon and *Eclogue* 2

On the basis of correspondences between *Ecl.* 2.31–9 and *Daphnis and Chloe* 2.32–7 'so exact and so numerous that it is hard to believe that they are coincidental' DuQuesnay has argued that they must have a common source and suggested that this source was Philetas.[61] The passage in Longus is that where Philetas the herdsman makes his second entrance, bringing offerings to Pan. Begged by the young people to display his vaunted skill on the panpipe, he sends his son Tityrus to fetch it (Daphnis' own panpipe is too small); Lamon meanwhile tells the myth of Pan and Panpipe and the invention of the panpipe. Then Philetas actually plays; Daphnis and Chloe enact the myth in a ballet; and finally Daphnis plays so well that Philetas presents him with his panpipe. In *Ecl. 2* Corydon imagines that in the woods Alexis might join him in imitating Pan *canendo*, 'in singing', refers to Pan's invention of the panpipe, and then mentions a panpipe presented to him by Damoetas on his death. The certainty of dependence on Philetas has been questioned by Hunter. As DuQuesnay had already noted, there may be a better parallel for *Ecl.* 2.37–8 in the Longan scene where the dying Dorcon hands over his panpipe to Chloe (1.29.2–3); and both Vergil and Longus, Hunter suggests, owe the motif to Theoc. 6.42–3:

> τόσσ᾽ εἰπὼν τὸν Δάφνιν ὁ Δαμοίτας ἐφίλησε·
> χὢ μὲν τῶι σύριγγ᾽, ὃ δὲ τῶι καλὸν αὐλὸν ἔδωκεν.

> With these words Damoetas kissed Daphnis,
> and he gave him his panpipe, and in turn *he* gave him his beautiful pipe.

[60] For a brief review of the knowledge of Latin literature shown by Greek authors of the first two centuries AD see Hunter 1983, 76–7. Williams 1978, 125–34 argues for some cases of anthology poets showing the influence of Latin writing. Fisher 1982 (with bibliography of this question on p. 174 nn.3 and 4) questions the general view that Greeks were indifferent to Latin language and literature, but only substantiates a different view for the later third and the fourth centuries. In recent decades it has become clear that the Greek elite's knowledge of Latin literature was much greater than I suggested in 1985. See esp. Holford-Strevens 1993; Rochette 1997; Adams, Janse and Swain 2002; Adams 2003; with special focus on Longus Hubbard 2006; on Chariton Tilg 2010; on the novels in general Jolowicz 2015 and 2021.

[61] DuQuesnay 1981, 60 with nn.192–200. Cf. Cairns 1979, 27 with n.118, comparing also Tibullus 2.5.31–2.

and to Theoc. 1.128–30, where the dying Daphnis gives his pipes to Pan.[62]

At *Ecl.* 2 Vergil certainly alludes to both these passages of Theocritus. But neither Theocritean passage tells the origin of the panpipe, and Longus 2.32–7 suggests that all three writers knew a passage in Philetas which involved both the panpipe's origin and its gift from one player to another. Further support for this may be found from Propertius (see below Section 8). But the following points about *Ecl.* 2 may also be relevant.

The protagonist of *Ecl.* 2, Corydon, is also one of the two principles of *Ecl.* 1 (his only other appearance is at *Ecl.* 5.86, a back-reference to 2.1). What are his origins? In Theocritus he figures in *Idylls* 4 and 5. In 4 his interlocutor is Battus, whom we have already met as a lover of Amaryllis, and the location seems to be near to Croton. In *Id.* 5 Corydon is not a speaking character but a friend of one of these, Lacon. The other speaking character's name is Comatas; the location near Sybaris might suggest that there is some connection between this and the Comatas of Lycidas' song, whose legend the scholia declare to have been located near Thurii.[63] It is surprising, therefore, to find that in *Ecl.* 7 Corydon is Arcadian. It is also disturbing that Vergil's line describing the shepherds of *Ecl.* 7, Corydon and Thyrsis (3) *ambo florentes aetatibus, Arcades ambo*, 'both in the prime of their youth, both Arcadians', is so close to an epigram of Erucius which opens

Γλαύκων καὶ Κορύδων, οἱ ἐν ὤρεσι βουκολέοντες
Ἀρκάδες ἀμφότεροι …

Glaucus and Corydon, they who graze their cattle in the mountains,
Arcadians both …

Erucius, *GP* 1 = *AP* 6.96

Use by Vergil of Erucius or by Erucius of Vergil is possible, but neither seems to me probable. Rather, as Reitzenstein suggested, we should suppose a common model.[64] Given the reappearance of Corydon in *Ecl.* 2 (where, like Battus in *Id.* 4, he recalls a past affair with Amaryllis, *Ecl.* 2.14 and 52) and the independent

[62] Hunter 1983, 81–2, comparing also Bion *EA* 7–11.

[63] Σ on 78/9, p. 99 Wendel, apparently attributing the story to Lycus of Rhegium, though Λύκος (*Lycus*) is a conjecture: MSS have Λύκιος (*Lykios*). Cf. Gow 1952, ii. 152 on 7.78.

[64] *GP* allows that Vergil may have known the epigram of Erucius (whom they date tentatively to 50–25 BC); but this seems to entail the view that Vergil's relocation of Corydon and the pastoral in Arcadia depended on *a jeu d'esprit* by Erucius. Wilamowitz 1906, 111 n.i judged Erucius to be dependent on Vergil; so too Williams 1978, 126. Hunter 1983, 76–7 thinks this 'not improbable', but he recognises that Greek knowledge of Latin literature at this period is exiguous. For Reitzenstein's view that similarity indicates a common model see Reitzenstein 1893, 131 n.2 (printed on p. 132).

pointers to Philetan material in that *Eclogue*, I conjecture that Philetas is the source of the name Corydon and perhaps even of his Arcadian setting. Theocritus will have resettled him in South Italy, perhaps in order to bring him into association with Comatas.[65] On this supposition *Ecl.* 2 draws on Philetas for a Corydon who receives from another singer a panpipe, a gift which prompts the tale of Panpipe and (Arcadian) Pan. The use of the gift-motif by Philetas will be another reason for its exploitation by Theocritus in *Id.* 7.66.[66]

7 Lycinna

Propertius in Book 3 (whose opening poem begins *Callimachi Manes et Coi sacra Philitae, in vestrum, quaeso, me sinite ire nemus*, 'Shades of Callimachus and rites of Coan Philetas, allow me, I pray, to enter your grove') builds a poem (15) around his girlfriend's jealousy for a lady who instructed him in love during his innocent youth. She was strongly attracted to him, for she sought no reward:

> illa rudis animos per noctes conscia primas
> imbuit, heu nullis capta Lycinna datis!

> She shared our explorations and in these first nights my untaught spirit
> she initiated, ah!, Lycinna – ensnared by no gifts!
> Prop. 3.15.5–6

[65] I would also take the mysterious appearance of Comatas in Id. 7 within Lycidas' song (78–89) as a *prima facie* indication that Comatas figured in Philetas – presumably, in view of Id. 5 and the Σ on 7.78/9 (cf. n.63), in a South Italian setting. If this, and my other speculative suggestions, were correct, then Philetas' pastoral poetry would be associated with three areas of the Greek world (Lesbos, Arcadia and S. Italy), but given the range of geographical interest shown by other Hellenistic poets this is no objection. That Philetas should depict a peaceful pastoral landscape in S. Italy ca. 290 BC is less surprising than Theoc.'s location of *Idylls* 4 and 5 in an area that had been devastated by war since Rome's confrontation with Tarentum in 282 BC and the consequent invasion of Pyrrhus. I would see the precedent of S. Italian pastoral by Philetas as making Theocritus' choice of setting more intelligible. For an additional reason which may have led Philetas to Comatas and South Italy see below n.75.

[66] If the above is correct, it follows that Vergil's influential choice of Arcadia as a chief constituent of his pastoral landscape, apparent first in *Ecl.* 7 and further elaborated in *Ecl.* 10, was prompted not merely by Arcadia's associations with Pan and the primitive life but by its pedigree as a pastoral landscape in earlier poetry, that of Philetas. The location would thus be less innovative than on most accounts (e.g. Rosenmeyer 1969, 232–46; Coleman 1977, 22 and on *Ecl.* 7.4). A case has also been made for Gallus' part in the location of pastoral in Arcadia by D. F. Kennedy in a paper delivered to the Gallus colloquium at Liverpool on 23 April 1983, later published as Kennedy 1987. That Gallus may have so exploited Arcadia counts neither for nor against my suggestion that Philetas did.

Lycinna's role is exactly that of the older woman who seduces Daphnis in Longus' novel and offers him the practical instruction that complements Philetas' λόγος.[67] That woman is called Λυκαίνιον (*Lykainion*), a diminutive of Λύκη (*Lykē*), as is Lycinna. Λύκη appears as the name of a *hetaera*, as does Lycaena.[68] It could be that both Propertius and Longus hit independently on a suitable name for an experienced woman. But the closeness of situation and of name rather suggests a common source: conjecturally, Philetas.

8 Propertius 3.3

In the third poem of a programmatic group at the beginning of Book 3 Propertius recalls a dream or vision in which he has a divine encounter with Apollo and the Muses. The scene is both Helicon and Castalia, involving a confusion which need not concern us here. Apollo warns him off epic themes, and shows him an untrodden path to a cave whose accoutrements include *calami, Pan Tegeaee, tui*, 'the reeds, Pan of Tegea, that are yours' (30); there too are the nine Muses, one of whom, Calliope, repeats Apollo's advice and directs Propertius to love-poetry and the role of *praeceptor amoris*, 'instructor in love' (49–50). The poem concludes:

> talia Calliope, lymphisque a fonte petitis
> ora Philitea nostra rigavit aqua.
>
> Such were Calliope's words, and taking the nymphs' liquid from the spring
> she irrigated our mouth with Philetan water.
>
> Prop.3.3.51–2

The debt of this poem to Hesiod's interview with the Muses on Helicon and Callimachus' admonitions from Apollo is clear enough. But the last couplet reminds us that there are as important debts to Philetas. On the evidence of *Id. 7* and Longus I would conjecture them to be as follows:

(a) A divine encounter, perhaps with Apollo (evoked by Simichidas' encounter with Lycidas, and by that of Longus' Philetas with Eros).
(b) The message 'small is beautiful'; cf. *Id.* 7.45–8.

[67] Longus 3.15.1ff.
[68] Λύκη as the name of a *hetaera*, Ath. 13.567e–f (citing the comedians Timocles and Amphis); Lycaena, Luc. *DMeretr.* 12.1. Lycinna is elusive as a real name in the Greek world: it does not appear in Fisk or Pape-Benseler, nor in the indices of *CIL* vi. In the Packard epigraphy database only *IEph* 3492 = *SEG* 32.1187 from Metropolis (Ionia), *SEG* 34.530 from Atrax (Thessaly).

(c) Whereas (a) and (b) could be derived from Callimachus alone, but need not be, the *spelunca*, 'cave', of 3.3.27 cannot.

The prominence of a cave of the Nymphs in Longus, a cave that is the source of a stream, and the importance of the spring Burina in *Id.* 7, make Philetas a likely source. In Longus' cave, where ἐκ πηγῆς ἀναβλύζον ὕδωρ ῥεῖθρον ἐποίει χεόμενον, 'from a spring water bubbling up created a stream that flowed forth': and there are dedications of γαυλοὶ καὶ αὐλοὶ πλάγιοι καὶ σύριγγες καὶ καλαύροπες, 'milk-pails and transverse pipes and panpipes and crooks' (1.4.3).[69] In Theocritus likewise ἱερὸν ὕδωρ Νυμφᾶν ἐξ ἄντροιο κατειβόμενον κελάρυζε, 'sacred water of the Nymphs babbled as it flowed down from a cave' (7.136–7). That Theocritus presently seems to name these nymphs as Castalian (7.148) has long been a problem;[70] one explanation is the possible introduction of Castalian nymphs by Philetas – these would then be one reason for Propertius' fusion of Helicon and Castalia in 3.3.

Longus' cave is set in a luxuriant grove dedicated to the Nymphs.[71] Theocritus' spring is also in a grove (135 ff.), and so is Propertius', to judge from 3.3.13, *ex arbore*, 'from a tree', and 26 *muscoso*, 'mossy'; related too is 3.1.2 *in vestrum, quaeso, me sinite ire nemus*, 'allow me, I pray, to enter your grove'.

(d) The alternative to epic is the poetry of love: tales of lovers pernoctating on doorsteps (3.3.47; cf. *Id.* 7.122), advice to other would-be-lovers (3.3.49–50; cf. the role of Philetas in Longus and the stance of Simichidas

[69] The panpipes are a common element to the divine-encounter nexus (associated with a cave of the Nymphs and precepts about poetry) and the symbolic-gift nexus argued for in Section 6 above: on my hypothesis, two Philetan scenes and not just one. It is of course possible that only one Philetan scene is involved, and that I am wrong in tracing to Philetas some of the constituents which require us to suppose two. Note that Prop. 3.3.1 (*visus eram molli recubans Heliconis in umbra*, 'I seemed to be lying in the soft shade of Helicon') has been suggested (by DuQuesnay 1981, 40) to belong with *Ecl.* 1.4 (*lentus in umbra*, 'relaxed in the shade') and Propertius 1.18.21 (*sub umbras*, 'beneath your shade') in alluding to Gallus and Philetas (cf. above n.59). Another possible verbal link (but perhaps too trivial to be significant) is *Ecl.* 1.23 *sic parvis componere magna solebam*, 'in this way I used to compare great things with small'; cf. Prop. 3.3.5 *parvaque tam magnis admoram fontibus ora*, 'and I had brought my small mouth close to great springs'; Longus 2.33.2 (a Philetan context, cf. Section 6 above) ἡ δὲ (sc. σῦριγξ) ἦν μικρὰ πρὸς μεγάλην τέχνην οἷα ἐν παιδὸς στόματι ἐμπνεομένη, 'and it (sc. the panpipe) was small in comparison with his great skill, as might be expected of one being blown in the mouth of a boy'.

[70] See Gow 1952, ii on 7.148.

[71] Pr. 1 ... ἐν ἄλσει Νυμφῶν ... θέαμα εἶδον κάλλιστον ὧν εἶδον· εἰκόνος γραφήν, ἱστορίαν ἔρωτος. καλὸν μὲν καὶ τὸ ἄλσος, πολύδενδρον, ἀνθηρόν, κατάρρυτον· μία πηγὴ πάντα ἔτρεφε, καὶ τὰ ἄνθη καὶ τὰ δένδρα, '... in a grove of the Nymphs ... I saw a spectacle that was the most beautiful I have seen: the painting of an image, a narration of love. The grove was beautiful too – with many trees, full of flowers, running with water: a single spring nurtured everything, both the flowers and the trees'.

vis-à-vis Aratus in *Id.* 7.122 ff.). Such love may have a rural context, indicated by the presence at the cave of Pan's pipes as well as Venus' doves (3.3.30–2).[72]

9 Conclusions

Many of the correspondences adduced above are individually open to explanation by coincidence in an area where *topoi* are finite and often recur. Taken together they are less easy to explain away, and to me they seem to corroborate the hypothesis of Philetan pastoral poetry where there were characters called Lycidas, Tityrus and Amaryllis, where declaration and narrative of love played a part, and where the poet or one of his characters met a protective deity and received advice, whether on love-poetry, or the relation between love and poetry. I shall pursue only one of the many questions about Philetas' contribution which may now be asked. Why, if my hypothesis is correct, did Philetas set at least some of his pastoral scenes on Lesbos?

The answer that I would conjecturally offer is that Philetas was influenced by Lesbos' reputation in the world of poetry. His native Cos had little or no poetic pedigree. Lesbos laid claim to the birthplace of Homer and the head of Orpheus; its poet Terpander was credited with a fundamental role in the development of Greek music; and, perhaps most significant of all, Sappho and Alcaeus were already being read and admired in Philetas' scholarly world. Sappho had done most of all these to associate Lesbian poetry with love, a central theme for Philetas; but she was not perhaps an obvious model for a male poet singing either *propria persona* or through the mouths of male characters. Alcaeus of Mytilene, by contrast, must have been known in the ancient world for love-poetry to boys, of which we have only wretched traces.[73] One of these is in Horace, who makes Alcaeus sing of

> Liberum et Musas Veneremque et illi
> semper haerentem puerum canebat
> et Lycum nigris oculis nigroque
> crine decorum.
>
> Bacchus and the Muses and Venus and her
> boy that ever clings to her – of these he would sing,

[72] Hubaux 1953 has also argued that similarities between Prop. 3.16.11–20 and Longus 3.5.4 point to a common source in Philetas. I am persuaded by Hunter 1983 that they are rather to be explained by use of *topoi* (more widely attested) than by a common ancestor.

[73] Cf. Page 1955, 294–9.

and Lycus, whose black eyes and black
hair gave him charm.

Hor. *Carm.* 1.32.9–12

We also have scraps of a poem by Alcaeus which seems to have been a *propempticon*, and whose treatment of the melting of winter into spring seems to have influenced another well-known ode of Horace, *Solvitur acris hiems*, 'Harsh winter is being dissolved' (*Carm.* 1.4).[74] That ode also uses the name Lycidas (*tenerum Lycidan*, 'tender Lycidas', 19) for an attractive boy, so that there is some possibility that in Alcaeus too a Lycidas figured as a παῖς καλός, 'beautiful boy'. I would suggest that either the boy Lycus, certainly attested for Alcaeus, or Lycidas, conceivably Alcaic, prompted Philetas to choose the name for his pastoral character.[75] Alcaeus' various contexts, some presumably in the city of Mytilene, others in the distant countryside where he lurked as an exile,[76] may have suggested the landscape north of Mytilene as a suitable setting. If there were echoes and allusions to Alcaeus in Philetas' poetry, he will have expected his readers to recognise them with as little difficulty as readers of Theocritus with a full text of Philetas might have recognised the goatherd Lycidas from Cydonia who loved Ageanax of Mytilene.

[74] Fr. 286(a) cf. Page 1955, 289–90, and Nisbet and Hubbard 1970, 58 on 1.4. The theme of spring's arrival seems also to have been treated in an erotic context by Alc. in fr. 296(b), too scrappy to make it clear whether the Damoanactidas addressed is an ἐραστής, 'lover', or ἐρώμενος, 'beloved'. If the latter, then Alc.'s Damoanactidas may have some part in the ancestry of Lycidas' ἐρώμενος Ageanax. The reputation of Alc. as a poet of pederastic love in Theocritus' generation is demonstrated, as Robert Wells has pointed out to me, by Theoc. *Id.* 29 and 30.

[75] In considering why Philetas chose Lycidas as the name of a pastoral character one further factor may have been relevant, viz. his debt to Lycus of Rhegium for the story of Comatas (if it is correctly argued above that Philetas told that story, and correctly asserted by the scholiast that it was to be found in Lycus; cf. above n.63). We may note that this Comatas story was in some way associated with a cave of the nymphs (Σ Theoc. 7.78/9b) and that Lycus had an interest in unusual springs and rivers (cf. *FGrHist* 570 F7–F11, F14) which was not confined to the Western Mediterranean (F14 cites one in India = Plin. *Nat.* 13.17). It is possible that Pliny derived his notice about the spring in the island Cydonea that flowed only in spring (cf. Appendix 2) from Lycus (though he is not cited among the sources for Books 2 or 5). If this were so, then it might also be that Philetas was indebted to Lycus for local colour about Lycidas' Cydonian haunts as well as for the Comatas story. To choose the name Lycidas would thus be a compliment to a contemporary currently influential in Alexandria (cf. Spoerri 1975) as well as an evocation of Alcaeus.

[76] Especially fr. 130B.17 ff. For the probable location of the sanctuary at which Alc. watched beauty contests cf. Stella 1956, 322–3, followed by Robert 1960, 300 ff. They place it at Messon/Messa, some five km north of the site of Pyrrha at the NE end of the gulf of Kalloni. For a recent discussion, taking account of the evidence of *P. CG inv.* 105, frs. 1–4, see Pirenne-Delforge and Pironti 2014. A further (but, I should guess, minor) factor drawing the attention of a Coan poet to Lesbos could have been the legend according to which Cos was colonised from Lesbos by Macareus' son Neander after Deucalion's flood (D.S. 5.81.8). For Alc.'s exile see also Bowie 2007a (Chapter 10 in volume 1).

Appendix 1: Where Does Longus Set *Daphnis and Chloe*?

Since Longus probably envisaged readers chiefly in the Greek East, few of whom could be expected to have first-hand knowledge of Lesbos, and since many features of Greek novels are unreal, it is tempting to suppose that he formed only a vague conception of his work's setting, e.g. 'some distance from Mytilene in the direction of Methymna'. But right at its beginning he presents his readers with a precise figure for the distance from Mytilene of the farm on which Daphnis grows up:

> ταύτης τῆς πόλεως τῆς Μιτυλήνης ὅσον ἀπὸ σταδίων διακοσίων ἀγρὸς ἦν ἀνδρὸς εὐδαίμονος, κτῆμα κάλλιστον.
> εἴκοσιν **V** διακοσίων **F**[77]
>
> from this city, Mytilene, about 200 stades distant was the estate of a prosperous man, a most beautiful property.
>
> Longus, *Daphnis and Chloe* 1.1.2

Later we have figures for the distance which separates Daphnis' farm from Chloe's (ten stades, 3.5.4); which Chloe is carried prisoner by the Methymnans (ten stades, 2.25.1); which separates Philetas' farm from that of Daphnis (ten stades, 2.33.2); which lies between Methymna and the point at which Methymnan forces meet those of Mytilene (100 stades, 3.2.2); and which lies between Methymna and the point to which the Mytilenean general finally advances (ten stades, 3.2.4). Although these figures must generate suspicion, since they are all ten stades or multiples thereof, Longus' apparent familiarity with many details of the Lesbian landscape has encouraged scholars to exploit them in determining his setting. The possibilities are as follows:

(i) We may read διακοσίων at 1.1.2 with **F**. This allows two locations:

(a) Somewhere in the area of Mandamadhos and Aghios Stephanos, as argued for by Mason 1979. The arguments against this location have been well set out by Green 1982. The landscape does not fit that depicted by Longus, there is neither perennial river nor half-moon bay, and (crucially) the ancient boundary between Mytilene and Methymna (on the Mytilenean side of which both young persons' farms lie) seems to have run some distance south of this area, between it and Mytilene. Green's paper makes it clear that Mason's proposal must be rejected.

[77] For the MSS designated by **F** and **V** and their relationship see Reeve 1982, v–xiv.

(b) Green's own suggestion (Green 1982) is that the scene is set in the gulf of Kalloni 'near the site of ancient Pyrrha', at the modern village of Achladeri, which by existing routes is the requisite thirty-seven km from Mytilene. To me this also seems to encounter insuperable objections:

(1) The general impression conveyed by Longus' narrative is that the 'sea' is open sea, not a gulf whose head is at most six kilometres from Daphnis and Chloe's playground and whose other shore is never more than eight from that on which they are located. This impression is, of course, subjective. But it is reinforced by an objective detail. At 3.21.1 a fishing vessel hurries past, its crew rowing because there is no wind, ἠπείγοντο γὰρ νεαλεῖς ἰχθῦς εἰς τὴν πόλιν διασώσασθαι τῶν τινι πλουσίων, 'they were hurrying to bring fresh fish to the city in good condition for one of the rich men'.

If the boat is going SW to NE up the gulf, then for fish to reach Methymna or (the more natural interpretation of εἰς τὴν πόλιν) Mytilene it will have to be unloaded and carried by land, either nineteen km to Methymna or thirty-seven km to Mytilene. If it is travelling NE to SW, then it has a long coastal circumnavigation of over 150 km ahead of it. Neither of these prospects is suggested by, or indeed is easily compatible with, Longus' description of the boat's haste and purpose.

The same impression of a shore stretching from Methymna to Mytilene is given by the narrative of the Methymnan *jeunesse doree*'s boating holiday (2.12 ff.) and the military reprisals which their treatment by the κωμῆται, 'villagers', provoked (2.20.1 ff.). Longus tells how the Methymnan youths launched a boat and sailed along Mytilenean territory. He does not suggest that they had to travel eighteen km from the city of Methymna to the gulf of Kalloni to do this, and the fullness with which he describes their various activities (2.12.2–5) suggests they had holidayed for several days before the unfortunate incident when a peasant stole their rope (2.13.1). This is not easily reconciled with a location of Daphnis' and Chloe's farms two or three kilometres from the Methymnan – Mytilenean border; and when Longus then says that they 'sailed along the coast for thirty stades' (2.13.2) this distance reads most naturally as referring to their day's journey after they had lost their rope, not (as Green 1982, 212 n.22) to their whole journey since its outset – it would be hard to compress the varied activities of 2.12.3–5 into a coastal trip of 5.58 km! Likewise when the Methymnans have believed the fabrications of their upper-class louts and resolved that they must be avenged, their general orders a fleet of ten ships to be launched and the next day εὐθύς, 'immediately', puts to sea (2.19.3–20.1). Nothing here suggests that a journey by land of eighteen km to a point very near the Mytilenean border is required before a naval squadron, based in the gulf of Kalloni, can be launched and manned.

(2) The location near ancient Pyrrha raises serious problems. Longus offers little explicit indication of *when* the events of the story should be envisaged as taking place, and we are doubtless meant to imagine the timeless universe of folk-tale. But the fact that Methymna and Mytilene are independent to the extent of possessing and deploying military forces points to the classical period, a period to which so much of the literature of the second-century Greek world harked back, and in which at least one other novel, Chariton's, was unambiguously set. If a reader did form the impression that the setting was in the classical period, then he would also be likely to know that in the fifth and fourth centuries Pyrrha was independent, and that the immediate environment of Pyrrha could not have been within even the outlying estates of a Mytilenean aristocrat. That Longus does envisage an independent Pyrrha is made clear by 1.28.2, where the pirates who kill Dorcon and kidnap Daphnis are described as either Τύριοι (**V**) or Πύρριοι (**F**). Since they are then described as wishing to *seem* to be barbarians, Τύριοι can hardly be right, and M. D. Reeve was surely correct to read Πυρραῖοι: as with the Methymnan incident, Longus is careful to draw his instruments of action from within the carefully insulated world of Lesbos.

Even if we do not read Πυρραῖοι at 1.28.2 and assume that Longus envisages a post-classical Lesbos in which Pyrrha is no longer an independent city, we should note that in Strabo's time (the nadir of Aegean fortunes) ἡ δὲ Πύρρα κατέστραπται, τὸ δὲ προάστειον οἰκεῖται καὶ ἔχει λιμένα, 'and Pyrrha has been sacked, but the suburbs are inhabited and have a harbour' (Str. 13.618). It is unlikely that the density of population fell sharply between the beginning of the first and the end of the second century AD, so a writer with a good knowledge of the island and an intention of providing accurate detail would be unlikely to pick the site of Pyrrha for a rural paradise.[78]

Accordingly it seems that neither of the two locations which could be supposed if we read διακοσίων is suitable.

(ii) We may read εἴκοσιν, 'twenty', at 1.1.2 with **V**.

This also allows two possibilities, a site on the gulf of Yera or one on the east-facing coast north of Mytilene. The former is open to the sorts of objection brought above against a site on the gulf of Kalloni. Therefore I

[78] I later decided that Τύριοι was more likely to be the correct reading, see Bowie 2019g, 155–6. For an account of Pyrrha see Paraskevaidis 1963; Paraskevaidis thinks the city's *acme* to have been in the Hellenistic period, arguing from the nearby temple at Messon/Messa, and notes that a basilica at Achladeri and the fact that Pyrrha had one of Lesbos' five bishoprics point to its being a place of some importance in the early Christian period (Paraskevaidis 1963, 411). Kondis 1978, 344–6 gives greater weight to the notices of Str. and Plin. *Nat.* 5.39.139 *ex his Pyrrha hausta est mari*, 'of these (sc. cities) Pyrrha has been swallowed up by the sea', and concludes (346) that Pyrrhan territory was administered by Mytilene.

have earlier taken the view that the area twenty stades north from Mytilene on the island's east coast is what Longus envisaged. But there are problems with this too. The proximity to Mytilene is hard to reconcile with two data offered by Longus. First, when the Methymnans raid the countryside around Daphnis' and Chloe's farms, there is no 'immediate military response' (Mason 1979, 160), and only when people coming in from the countryside report what has happened is action taken (3.3.1; cf. Green 1982, 212 n.17). Of course it does not suit Longus' narrative to have Mytilenean action at this point – he wishes to follow up the miraculous rescue of Chloe – but if we lay stress on this factor we begin to undermine the assumption that Longus is conscientiously realistic in matters of topography. It might, indeed, be insisted that the headland of Kará Tepé obscures the view of much of the bay that runs between twenty and forty stades (3.7 and 7.4 km) north of Mytilene, just south of Pámphyla (see Figure 1). But although it must have prevented people in the main population area of Mytilene seeing anything of events in that bay, they *could* have been seen from the acropolis, and it seems to me now that this incident makes it hard to believe that Longus envisages a location so close to the city.

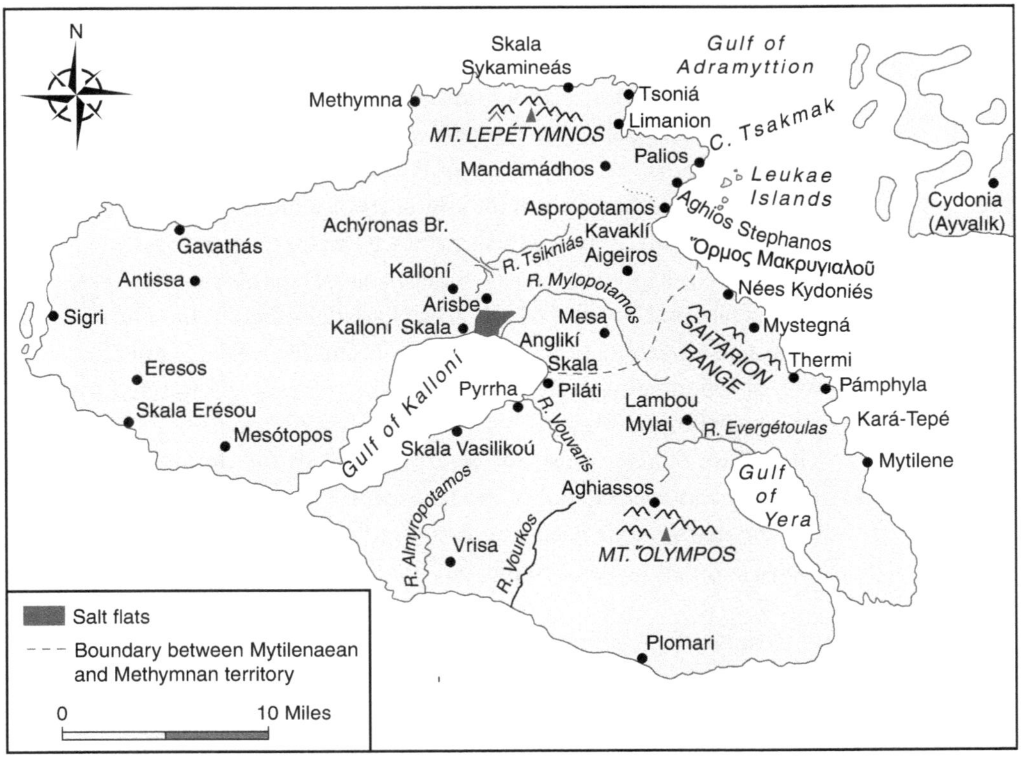

Figure 1 Lesbos

The second point is perhaps conclusive. When towards the end of the story Daphnis and Chloe leave the country for the city (4.33.2), they set off at dawn, travel in a horse-drawn carriage, yet arrive at a time when they can slip into the city unnoticed in darkness. Even allowing for elaborate leave-taking (4.33.2), frequent stops *en route* and deliberate delay to ensure nocturnal arrival, it is hard to see how the distance could have been a mere twenty or thirty stades (3.7 or 5.5 km).

If precise application neither of 200 stades nor of 20 stades gives us a location compatible with other data in the work, there remain two courses open to us: either the figures in the MSS are both corrupt, or Longus is using them to give an appearance of precision which is not matched by any careful consideration of where precisely these figures take one. Either explanation is possible, but a number of factors suggest the second.

First, Longus' regular recourse to round numbers that are multiples of ten. Secondly, his readiness in non-topographical matters to offer circumstantial rationalisation that is sheer invention: e.g. 1.12.5, Daphnis has to think of an explanation – attack by a wolf – in case somebody notices the absence of the goat which is to be sacrificed; 1.20.2, we are told how Dorcon came by a wolf-pelt; he is not simply presented to us as having access to one. Thirdly, the difficulty in reconciling *all* Longus' topographical data whatever the figure at 1.1.2 was supposed to be. Thus, if we choose a site on the gulfs of Yera or Kalloni on the ground that only into these do rivers flow which would have enough water for Daphnis to swim in during summer months (i.e. the Evergetoulas and the Vouvaris; cf. Green 1982, 212–3 nn.22–3), then we run into the sorts of difficulty set out at (i) (b) (1) above. Conversely, if we seek a site at any point on the east coast, our choice must ignore the implication of Longus having Daphnis swim in 'rivers'. But the very fact that 'rivers' (1.23.2; 2.24.2) are described in the plural should perhaps be a warning to us that Longus' brand of realism is not one which involves topographical precision: no plain in Lesbos is watered by more than one perennial stream.

It follows that we must not seek precision in the distances offered by the MSS or in every detail of the landscape.[79] We may still, however, take the view that Longus has some first-hand knowledge of the landscape of Lesbos, and that he has a rough, but not precise, notion of where his novel

[79] Cf. Bowie 1977, 4 (Chapter 19, in this volume). It is perhaps worth noting that mistakes over the most basic details can be made even by modern novelists who appear to take great pains over a realistic setting. From a novelist educated at Oxford, Rachel Billington, I note: 'Gordon and I were walking back from dinner at the Mitre … we walked down the Broad. Just as we reached Queen's College …' (*A Woman's Age*, Penguin edition, 1981, 135).

is set. The pointers towards where this is are to my mind clear. It is between Mytilene and Methymna (not therefore on the east coast south of Mytilene). It is a fair distance from the city of Mytilene (see (ii) above), though it is also some way south of the Methymna – Mytilene border (see (i) (b) (1) above). Pasture, hunting country, and arable land – including vineyards and orchards – are to be found close together. There is a stretch of coast, along which boats pass towards Mytilene (see (i) (b) (1)), and it contains at least one half-moon bay (2.25.2); but there is likely to be more than one, since in describing the fishing boat's passage Longus draws attention to the echo of the rowers' song perceived by Daphnis and Chloe when the singers passed a half-moon bay,[80] and gives no hint that Daphnis and Chloe are at that moment off their normal playground and ten to twenty stades further along the coast (which is the location of the bay of 2.25.2; cf. 2.25.1).

If the above features of Longus' landscape are accepted as being significant, then the coast between Pámphyla and Nées Kydoniés must be where Longus sets his story: not too near to Pámphyla, given the implications of 3.3.1 and 4.33.2 (see (ii) above), nor yet right on the border (see (i) (b) (1) above). Of the only two bays that have a pronounced half-moon shape, one, below the village of Mystegná, is quite large (about 1000 metres from promontory to promontory) the other, about 3.5 km (twenty stades) further north, below Nées Kydoniés, is much smaller (about 300 metres from promontory to promontory). If we believe that Longus had some picture of the east coast of Lesbos in his mind, then we must conclude that he envisaged the main setting of the action (and the echo-sequence of 3.21.3) in the half-moon bay of Mystegná; Chloe's farm a bit further north (he gives the round number of ten stades, 3.5.4); and the halting-place of the Methymnan raiding squadron as the bay of Nées Kydoniés (again the round number of ten stades further north, 2.25.1). The distance between Mystegná and Mytilene is ca. seventeen km. If we accept either twenty or two hundred stades as the distance offered by Longus, then the latter is more easily intelligible as a careless guess for a substantial distance from town. For those who find this to be incompatible with the many elements of realism in Longus' descriptions, and who accept my interpretation of the other topographical indications, there remains the easy course of taking both MS readings as corruptions of 100, ἕκατον.

[80] ἐπεὶ δὲ ἄκραι τινὶ ὑποδραμόντες εἰς κόλπον μηνοειδῆ καὶ κοῖλον εἰσήλασαν, μείζων μὲν ἠκούετο βοή, σαφῆ δὲ ἐξέπιπτεν εἰς τὴν ὕλην τὰ τῶν κελευστῶν ᾄσματα, 'and when running close beneath a headland they propelled the boat into a hollow, moon-shaped bay, their cries were heard louder, and the songs of their time-keepers were borne clearly into the wood', Longus 3.21.3.

Appendix 2: Where Is Cydonia?

The name Kydona is currently attached to a small island off the northern promontory bounding the bay below the village of Nées Kydoniés. However, neither that toponym nor the village name seems to be antique. Plin. *Nat.* 2.106.232, however, tells of a hot spring: *in Cydonea insula ante Lesbum fons calidus vere tantum fluit*, 'on Cydonea, an island off Lesbos, a hot spring flows only in springtime'; and at 5.39.140 (his notice on Lesbos) he writes *insulae adpositae Sandalium, Leucae V. ex iis Cydonea cum fonte calido*, 'adjacent islands are Sandalium and the five White Islands: one of these is Cydonea, with a hot spring'. This makes it clear that Cydonia was one of the five islands whose nearest point on Lesbos is a promontory two-thirds of the way from Aghios Stephanos to Palios, though they are clearly visible from as far down the coast as the promontory north of the bay below Mystegná. The assignation of a hot spring also excludes the small island at present called Kydona, since that is flat and (as far as I could determine in a visit early in April 1984) waterless; indeed at present it is so small that it seems unlikely ever to have been inhabited.[81]

I know of no evidence which determines which of the five White Islands was anciently called Cydonia. I would guess it to be the present Nísos Panagías, but I have not yet been able to visit the islands to investigate whether the Panagía is associated with an intermittent hot spring. Although it seems certain that the present settlement of Nées Kydoniés is recent, it is possible that a village or area on the coastline of Lesbos was associated with the island in antiquity and bore the same name. If only the island bore the name in antiquity, then at least we can be sure from its citation in Pliny that its spring had attracted attention, and that it was known to local tourists and to some genres of literature. This would be sufficient for a learned poet to locate a shepherd Lycidas on the island, doubtless not neglecting its miraculous spring,[82] and to bring him into association with Mytilenean territory and persons.

The reasons for suggesting that in antiquity a village or area on this coastline of Lesbos bore the name Cydonia are these. The present Nées Kydoniés is (I presume) a settlement of Greeks expelled from Asia Minor in the exchange of populations in 1923. Their mainland settlement was

[81] Kondis 1978 marks Kydona island / Cydonea as the site of a mineral bath from ca. 480 BC to the fourth century AD (figs 22–8), but I can find no evidence for this in his text nor have I discovered any elsewhere. I am tempted to wonder whether this classification is based on Pliny's notice about the hot spring and nothing more.

[82] Cf. above n.75.

Kydonia, now Ayvalık (simply a Turkish translation, 'Quincy'); its history as a city goes back only to 1773, though the Greek settlements from which it developed seem to have been founded in the seventeenth century.[83] Why was the name Kydonia given to the new city? It is possible that the identity of its name and that of the island is coincidental. It is also possible, and perhaps more probable, that it took its name from the island. But since the island can never have sustained a large population (whether it is one of the five Leucae as argued above or, even more, that currently called Kydona), it is most likely that the name Kydonia was brought by the settlers from Lesbos (as too in the ancient Lesbian settlement of the Peraea toponyms were carried, e.g. Pyrrha). One would therefore expect it to have been associated with an area of the coastline facing the Peraea. If that is so, then there is also a high probability of a causal connection between the attachment of the name Cydonia to this area and to the island. Which came first would involve even more guesswork than I have already indulged in.[84]

[83] See Kondis 1978, 73.

[84] Further valuable work by Hugh Mason (e.g. Mason 1995, 2018) has greatly strengthened the case for thinking that Longus had a good knowledge of Lesbos.

9 Frame and Framed in Theocritus Poems 6 and 7 (1996)

1 *Idyll* 6

The sixth *Idyll* of Theocritus is as neglected as the seventh is overgrazed. Its forty-six lines make it Theocritus' shortest pastoral poem. It is sometimes treated as little more than a delightful miniature, a scene constructed to allow the display of ideal pastoral song. It is certainly well-crafted as well as small. The opening five lines, setting the bucolic scene, are exactly balanced by five closing lines (42–6). They introduce the reader, rapidly and economically, to the two singers, Daphnis ὁ βουκόλος, 'the cowherd', and another herdsman, also apparently a βουκόλος and perhaps tending the same herd. In the noonday heat they relax by a spring and Daphnis proposes a singing contest. As its proposer, he sings first, and the opening of his song soon shows that he is playing the role of a friend of Polyphemus, a *praeceptor amoris*, 'instructor in love', advising him how to handle Galatea – a Galatea who, the singer insists, does really feel ἔρως, 'desire', for Polyphemus. A single line of transition (20) takes us into the response of Damoetas. Exact symmetry is avoided both in length and in role: Damoetas sings as Polyphemus himself, a naive Polyphemus who hopes that his show of indifference to Galatea will bring her to his bed, and concludes by expressing his conviction that he can be attractive – a point that matches the closure of Daphnis' song (34–40 ~ 19). Then in the five closing lines Damoetas kisses Daphnis, gives him his σῦριγξ, 'panpipe', and in exchange gets Damoetas' αὐλός, 'pipe'; they play on each other's instruments while their heifers dance on the soft grass. Neither was victor, and they were unconquered.

Has their world changed, or does the end take them back to the beginning, and to the possibility that a similar scene might take place tomorrow, and tomorrow, and tomorrow? The crucial question, I think, is how we are to interpret ἐφίλησε, 'he kissed'. Andrew Gow (1952), often short on literary exegesis, and writing at a time when there might have been problems in making public his own homosexual orientation, is totally silent. Sir Kenneth Dover (1978, 142–5), whose judgement in these matters one must respect and who can rarely be accused of suppressing or ignoring sexuality, offers no commentary. Gregory Hutchinson (1988, 184 with n.67) pronounces that the kiss has no sexual role. Yet he offers no parallel to kissing in the pastoral world as a simple mark of non-sexual affection or an expression of *joie de vivre*, and I cannot help suspecting that their interpretation is influenced by the prevalence in Western European culture of cheek-pecking/kissing – performed with aplomb in France and Italy but often with embarrassment in the Anglo-Saxon world – or even by the practice of hand-kissing rather commoner in Eastern Europe.[1] Hutchinson (1988, 184 n.67) indeed draws attention to occasions in Greek and Latin literature where kissing is a mark of deep but non-sexual emotion, either in response to a great service (Soph. *OC* 1131) or (in his other cases) in a context of reunion (Od. 16.6; Hor. *Carm*. 1.26). These passages suggest that at the least the act of Damoetas in kissing Daphnis expresses strong emotion. None brings the practice close to mere ceremonial. This might, indeed, be held of some later instances: Quintus of Smyrna has contestants in wrestling (4.271) and boxing (4.380) kiss to mark their friendship after their bout is decided, and Longus has Dionysophanes' messenger kiss Daphnis in response to his generous gift of pastoral presents (4.6.2).[2] The bearing of these passages on Theocritus is hard to assess. Both authors may be affected by Roman practices of the second century AD and later, while the kiss that Longus has bestowed on his Daphnis may both allude to the very line of Theocritus 6 under consideration and be intended to prepare the reader for overt sexual attentions from the urban parasite Gnathon some paragraphs later. But it must be emphasised that the Hellenistic pastoral corpus itself represents kissing only in sexual situations.[3] Of these even *Id*. 27.7 (καλόν σοι δαμάλας φιλέειν, οὐκ ἄζυγα κώραν, 'it would be good for you to kiss calves, not an unyoked girl') has, in context, the role of a sexual kiss. Damoetas' action, then, is at the very least emotional, but most probably to be read as sexual.

It is surely right, therefore, to interpret the poem as one in which the conclusion shows us the two cowherds displaying their mutual desire, as Lawall, Gutzwiller and Cairns have read it.[4] On Lawall's interpretation (1967, 67–9) this kiss marks a re-establishment of harmony between two herdsmen whom the reader has taken to be lovers, and whose love has been

[1] Polyphemus presents kissing Galatea's hand as an inferior substitute for kissing her lips (11.55). For an illuminating discussion of kissing in modern Europe see Frijhoff 1991.

[2] I am grateful to Dr. Hans Bernsdorff for drawing my attention at the workshop to the collection of these and other passages by Sittl 1890, 38. Cf. too Plu. *Sept. sap. conv*. 3 = *Mor*. 148c.

[3] 2.126; 3.19–20; 5.132, 135; 11.55–6; 20.1–4, 31–2, 36, 38, 42, 45; 23.40, 42; 27.2, 6; 27.7.

[4] Alan Griffiths suggested in discussion that the exchange of instruments might be seen as an allusion to the homosexual practice known as δὸς λάβε (cf. Griffiths 1970, 36): if so, that clearly corroborates the sexual reading of the poem's conclusion.

interrupted by slight contention, signalled by ἔρισδεν, 'made the challenge', in 5. Gutzwiller (1991, 126) follows Lawall in inferring a quarrel. This reading seems to me to lay too much weight on ἔρισδεν – which can after all signal simple competition – and to take too little account of their apparently harmonious occupation of the same *locus amoenus* and assembling of their herds. Cairns (1972, 194–5) does not make it clear whether he thinks we should take Daphnis and Damoetas as lovers from the beginning of the poem, and is more interested in the relation between the role played by them in their songs and their respective parts in their own erotic world: 'The true situation of Polyphemus and Galatea, and its anticipated happy ending, are hinted at by the allotment and nature of the two songs and by what follows them. Daphnis the beloved delivers the komos on behalf of Galatea, and Damoitas the lover sings the qualified refusal of Polyphemus. The two songs are judged equal, and are the prelude to the love-making of the bucolic singers.'

I think it is important for our reading of the poem that we do not know from the start that Daphnis and Damoetas are lovers. We are indeed given hints. One of them is at the age when young men are at their most attractive – the down is just beginning to grow on his cheeks (cf. Il. 24.438), which is the sense of πυρρός (see Gow 1952 *ad loc.*); the other is slightly older, which (*pace* Hutchinson) is enough to make him a potential ἐραστής, 'lover', and the younger herdsman his ἐρώμενος, 'beloved'.[5] There is no clear indication, however, that they already enjoy this relationship, and indeed the reader might be in some doubt as to which of the two is described by which term. Cairns (1972, 195) takes ὁ μὲν πυρρός to be Daphnis, and Damoetas to be the older, i.e. ὁ μέν picks up the nearer of the two terms. That is probably how the adjectives should be taken, and we can see confirmation in Damoetas' initiative in kissing. But Theocritus could be describing the two youths in the order in which we have met them, with Damoetas ὁ πυρρός, and hence the younger.

The reader may be influenced by associations generated by the names. Even if this poem was not composed after *Id.* 1, Daphnis is a name associated with ἔρως, 'desire', in earlier poetry by Stesichorus.[6] The ill-fated love of the βούτας, 'cowherd', Daphnis for Xenea is alluded to in *Id.* 7.73–7 in a way

[5] For archaic and classical examples of lovers close in age see Dover 1978, 86–7.

[6] Fr. 279 *PMGF* = Ael. *VH* 10.18. Whether this is by the 'second' (fourth-century) Stesichorus, as held e.g. West 1970, 206, or by the sixth-century poet, is of little importance for the connotations of the name in Theocritus. For a defence of its attribution to Stesichorus see Bowie 2012b (Chapter 23 in Volume 1).

that might be argued to imply familiarity. *Id.* 1 too seems to expect a reader to associate Daphnis with some sort of ἔρως, even if the precise nature of his ailment is never made clear in the poem. Thus a reader encountering a cowherd Daphnis in *Id.* 6 would expect him to be susceptible to ἔρως. The name Damoetas is less evocative, at least for us. I have often suspected that it was not so unusual, and hence was neutral, for Theocritus. There are sparse attestations of the name in Aetolia, not an area in which Theocritus elsewhere shows any interest (unless in 1.57 we read Καλυδωνίωι)[7] and in Epirus.[8] But its chief locus is clearly Thessaly, as Gow (1952 *ad loc.*) noticed.[9] That was less interesting before the recent publication of the papyrus fragments of a poem of Simonides expressing love or strong affection for the Thessalian aristocrat Echecratidas, a poem that seems in some way to be echoed in *Idyll* 7.[10] At the risk of being ridiculed as speculative and in the certainty of advancing a guess that may never be confirmed, I hazard the conjecture that Damoetas was a name that came to Theocritus from Thessaly, and in particular from the poetry of Simonides, either poetry composed for the family of Larisa that included Antiochus, Echecratidas and Dyseris, for the Aleuadae of Larisa, or for the Creondae and Scopadae of Crannon.[11]

This might, then, be another indication that a reader is expected to take Daphnis as a potential ἐραστής and Damoetas as a potential ἐρώμενος. That Daphnis then speaks for the ἐρωμένη, 'beloved', Galatea, would then introduce some tension – but only some: Galatea does, he insists, feel ἔρως for Polyphemus.

More important, however, than allocation of conventional roles of pursuer and pursued is Daphnis' choice of a song about ἔρως at all. We know from reading of other herdsmen's songs that they are very likely to be about ἔρως, but that they need not have been so, and each requires and deserves

[7] *IG* ix.1^2 1.17.52 and 72 (ca. 262–236 BC, a man from Naupactus); 1.137.46 and 78 (ca. 130–120 BC, Calydon). For these and the following attestations of the name Damoetas I am grateful to Mrs. E. Matthews and the *LGPN*.

[8] Cabanes 1976, 534 no. 1.18 (370–68 BC, Dodona); 536 no. 2.9 (370–344 BC, Dodona); 581 no. 56.10 (ca. 170 BC, Dodona); *SEG* 35.665A.14 (167 BC).

[9] Gow noted three instances. The tally is now much longer: *IG* ix.2 1060 (second/first c. BC, Sykyrium); 32.2 (?end of second century AD, Hypata); 549.10 (late first c. BC/early first c. AD), *SEG* 13.390.6 = 33.460.6 (197–186 BC), *SEG* 26.672.11 (200–190 BC) – all from Larisa; *CID* ii 86.7 (331 BC, a man from Thessaly).

[10] Cf. Hunter 1993; Bowie 2009a, 132–4 (Chapter 13, 312–14 in Volume 1).

[11] See Gow 1952 on 16.34–9, where Theocritus recalls the importance to these patrons of the poetic fame conferred by Simonides. Cf. Wilamowitz 1913, 142. Note Aleuas ὁ πυρρός, Arist. fr. 455, cf. Ael. *NA* 8.11.

a particular explanation. The reader of Daphnis' song is entitled to wonder whether Daphnis has a particular reason to sing of erotic tactics.

Damoetas too could have sung of something other than love. The expectation that it will balance that of Daphnis does indeed set some limitations to the subjects or treatments he might appropriately adopt for his song. But he could have sung of some non-erotic relationship that contrasted with that of Galatea and Polyphemus (just as the goatherd's cup with its three vignettes, only one of them involving love, balances Thyrsis' song of ἔρως in *Id.* 1). Or he could have sung, like Simichidas in *Id.* 7, of a love whose character and object were quite different from that sung of by the first singer. That Damoetas chooses to take up the relationship between Galatea and Polyphemus is in itself significant; and we learn more from his ascription to Polyphemus of an indifference that is a cover for his continued interest in Galatea (25–6).

When Damoetas kisses Daphnis at 42 the role-playing songs suddenly fall into a new pattern. From one perspective they have been read simply as songs about distant mythological figures. Now they can also be read as expressions of emotions that are a guide to those of the singers. This is not a poem in which we hear much about Polyphemus and Galatea and little about Daphnis and Damoetas, but one in which our knowledge of Daphnis and Damoetas draws on the feelings and strategies that they attribute to Polyphemus and Galatea. Read this way, the poem begins with only the *possibility* of ἔρως. The herdsmen test out each other's reactions to a lover who is reluctant to come out. Daphnis' assurance that Galatea really does feel ἔρως for Polyphemus, and Damoetas' that Polyphemus' indifference is a feigned indifference, offers reassurance to the other that his desires are reciprocated, and that declaration of them will not incur rebuff and humiliation. That Damoetas is the one who moves the action on by initiating a kiss is perhaps of minor significance. The important message of the songs is that the desires are reciprocal, whatever appearance of indifference may have been given by either party; and that message is restated in the last lines, where the mutual ἔρως is felt no longer by Polyphemus and Galatea but by Damoetas and Daphnis. The strategy of covertly declaring a sexual interest by disguising it as that of a third party is doubtless not uncommon in the real world; but I am not a sexologist, and can only offer a parallel from art, viz. the duet sung by the hero and heroine of Gilbert and Sullivan's *Ruddigore*, beginning 'I know a youth who loves a pretty maid'.

So far, then, I have argued that the poem's interest lies not so much in any tension or complementarity between the content of the songs and the situation of their singers, but in the way that this content makes their exchange dynamic and not static, an action rather than a tableau, an action which reaches its τέλος, 'completion', in 41–5.

But we should not stop there. Like 11 and 13, *Id.* 6 is addressed to an individual, presumably to a friend. For this poetic trope the model here is less the epistle, as sometimes suggested, than the early sympotic song, whether lyric or elegiac, so often evoked in Theocritus. It is usually thought that the talk of the power of love in *Id.* 13 and of poetry's capacity to heal it in *Id.* 11 bear upon the personal predicament of their addressee Nicias. What of *Id.* 6? The most obvious hypothesis is that Theocritus wants his addressee to understand the inhibitions sometimes felt by ἐρασταί in making a declaration to their ἐρώμενος and that Theocritus himself stands to Aratus in that role of inhibited ἐραστής (or, conceivably, even ἐρώμενος). This point was seen by Ott, but as far as I can recall I have reached this conclusion independently.[12]

2 *Idyll* 7

This hypothesis both affects and is affected by a reading of *Id.* 7. In *Id.* 7 we again encounter an Aratus, as the friend of Simichidas whose interest in the young (or not so young) Philinus the song of Simichidas purports to address.

First, the bearing of *Id.* 7 on *Id.* 6. If in *Id.* 7 Aratus stands to Philinus as ἐραστής to ἐρώμενος, does this count against interpreting the Aratus of *Id.* 6 as a potential ἐρώμενος? We could, of course, deny the identity of the Arati since that of *Id.* 7 is within the song of Simichidas, who is at least to some degree a fictional character. But that Simichidas also in some way reflects Theocritus himself, and in a small corpus of poems the disjunction of the two appearances of an Aratus becomes implausible. So I would accept the view that the Aratus of *Id.* 6 is the same as that of *Id.* 7, and suggest either (as did Ott) that we are to suppose that the Aratus of *Id.* 6 is a couple of years younger than that of *Id.* 7 – a hypothesis that would fit the likely order of composition of these two poems – or that a shift from the role of ἐραστής to ἐρώμενος is in itself unproblematic.[13]

[12] Ott 1969, 70 n.207: 'Aratus bekommt Theokrits Liebe zu ihm and seine eigene Koketterie durch die Blume, am Exemplum von Polyphemos und Galatea vorgehalten; natürlich steckt ein gutes Stück scherzhafter Selbstironie, wenn sich Theokrit sich dem Kyklops vergleicht (cf. 11); als positives Beispiel dient die Einmutigkeit von Daphnis und Damoetas. Dass sie nicht erotisch dargestellt ist, muss als Delikatesse des Werbenden gelten, der seine Wünsche nicht in Worter fasst.'

[13] Cf. Dover 1978, 86–7.

But the more interesting question is the bearing of my reading of *Id.* 6 on our reading of *Id.* 7. I shall make no attempt to sketch the numerous conflicting lines of interpretation that have been offered of *Id.* 7. Let me focus rather on an element in all that I have encountered – including my own discussion in 1985a – that now seems to me unsatisfactory. The journey to the harvest festival at Haleis, in the middle of which Simichidas' encounter and exchange with Lycidas are set, concludes appropriately enough with a long and lush description of the *locus amoenus* in which the celebration takes place. The festival has been interpreted by Lawall (1967, 102) as an 'allegory of poetic inspiration' in which the fruits in some way stand for the Theocritean poetry whose collection Lawall takes this poem to conclude and celebrate. I find this notion difficult, but do not regard it as one that need be refuted in order to justify further probing.

What seems to me positively to demand such further probing is the point well made by Pearce (1987, 276–87): when Greek writers of poetry or prose present an encounter with a divinity of the sort upon which Simichidas' encounter with Lycidas appears to be modelled, that encounter is regularly followed by some consequential action – in many cases taking the form of more facile or impressive composition of literary works. Pearce also holds (1987, esp. 296, 300), as have most interpreters, that the *locus amoenus* of 7.132–57 must be of great importance for the poem's overall interpretation. However I am not persuaded by his view that Simichidas' encounter with Lycidas has made him receptive to the intimations of divinity regularly present in a *locus amoenus*, and that consequently he is now enabled to compose a true βουκολικὰ ἀοιδά, 'bucolic song', which the reader can see to be different from his earlier song with its urban features (96–127). The chief arguments against this view are the following. First, both Lycidas (49) and Simichidas (36, 92) seem to regard the song Simichidas sings earlier as a representative βουκολικὰ ἀοιδά, and Lycidas' apparently approving gift of his λαγωβόλον, 'stick', to Simichidas (126) is hard to understand if he judges the song to fall short. Secondly, what Theocritus gives us in 132–57 is not presented to us as something in a sung register but as part of Simichidas' narrative on the same level as what had gone before. It might also, thirdly, be doubted whether, despite the presence of *loci amoeni* in Theocritean pastoral, the *topos* was sufficiently pastoral to be offered as a palmary example of inspired bucolic. So neither Pearce's view, nor that of Lawall, nor any other I have encountered, seems to me to offer an action of sufficient moment to constitute an adequate consequence of the divine encounter.

My own – necessarily tentative – solution starts with one change that *can* be observed between the opening and closing sections of the poem. In lines 1–2 Theocritus' two party-going companions, Eucritus and Amyntas, are introduced neutrally, and neither is given an epithet. As is sometimes remarked, they seem to fade into the background during the exchange between Lycidas and Simichidas, though we are not entitled to suppose that in some sense they are not there at all. When they come back into focus we are presented with what seems to me a striking change:

> αὐτὰρ ἐγών τε καὶ Εὔκριτος ἐς Φρασιδάμω
> στραφθέντες χὡ καλὸς Ἀμύντιχος ἔν τε βαθείαις
> ἁδείας σχοίνοιο χαμευνίσιν ἐκλίνθημες
> ἔν τε νεοτμάτοισι γεγαθότες οἰναρέοισι.
>
> but I and Eucritus towards Phrasidamus' farm
> turned, and the beautiful Amyntas too, and on deep
> couches of sweet rush lay reclined,
> happily, and in fresh-stripped vine-leaves.
>
> Theoc. 7.131–4

Amyntas, earlier described simply as the third member of the group, has now been given the hypocoristic name-form Amyntichus and the erotic epithet καλός, 'beautiful'. That this epithet is to be taken erotically is supported by the vast majority of the other Theocritean contexts in which it is used of a person, and by the fact that we have just been reading – and the poem's four characters have been hearing – songs about love. And how have these songs presented love? Lycidas has fantasised about the joys of a *fête champêtre* generically similar to the party at the end of the poem, a *fête champêtre* marking the safe arrival of Ageanax at Mytilene that is conditional upon him saving his lover Lycidas from the fire of Aphrodite. Whether this party is to happen at Ageanax's point of arrival, as I still believe, or at another place, presumably on Cos, that he has left, it is a party celebrating an erotic conquest as much as a safe arrival.[14] We are not told, of course, how Eucritus and Amyntas respond to this song – our attention is all on Simichidas. His song, as has often been analysed, differs in many ways from that of Lycidas. But it retains the theme of love. Pan and the Erotes are asked to bring Philinus into his lover Aratus' arms (98–119). Philinus is then briefly warned that his prime is passing (120–1).[15] Then Simichidas changes his tack, and, like Daphnis in poem 6, takes on the role of *praeceptor amoris* and counsels Aratus to adopt indifference.

[14] Of course the images of erotic conquest and steering a ship safely into port can readily fuse: cf., as so often in this poem, Archil. fr. 196a, in this case 23–4 σχήσω γὰρ ἐς ποη[φόρους] [κ]ήπους, 'I shall steer into the grassy gardens'.

[15] Again with a possible allusion to Archil. fr. 196a, viz. 26–8.

Is this just an example of a different style of song from that of Lycidas? Recalling the interaction between songs and frame in *Id.* 6, we should ask what, if at all, the song can tell us about Simichidas' *own* sexual interests. Of course, like Daphnis' and Damoetas' songs, it is ostensibly about another couple's affair. More difficult for my suggestion, perhaps, Simichidas professes at an early stage to be interested in a girl, Myrto, and his statement that the Erotes have sneezed on him seems to imply that he is happy in his relationship with her. But things may not be so simple. First, of course, an affair with a girl does not establish that Simichidas' orientation is exclusively heterosexual (cf. *Id.* 2.150). Second, it is not made wholly clear that this affair *is* proceeding successfully: Simichidas' luck in love, symbolised by the Erotes' sneeze, may simply consist in his having discovered a person who excites his ἔρως. We may infer that, unlike the ἔρως of Aratus, it has gone well, but we may infer incorrectly. But even if that inference is correct, the role of Simichidas' opening mention of Myrto can be taken in more than one way. Part of the function, of course, is precisely to stand as a contrast to the situation of Aratus. But as the only autobiographical element in the song it may be there to serve the same purpose as *Id.* 6.26, where Polyphemus is made to claim ἀλλ' ἄλλαν τινὰ φαμὶ γυναῖκ' ἔχεν, 'but I claim to have another woman': i.e. it may be there to heighten the sexual interest of the true object of Simichidas' ἔρως. If my suggestion that Amyntas is that object is correct, then the reader is to suppose that, as Simichidas' song proceeds, Amyntas is made aware of the persistence with which Simichidas and his friend Aratus pursue their ἐρώμενοι (102–19: note the first person plurals 122–6); to take note of the ephemeral nature of youths' sexual attraction for older men (120–1); and to ponder the prospect that Simichidas himself, as he advises Aratus, will decide that the game is not worth the candle and lose interest.

The song of Lycidas can now also be seen to have a dynamic function in the poem. That song has celebrated the joys of a *fête champêtre* that is associated with an erotic conquest. It may be seen as directing the thoughts both of the potential ἐραστής Simichidas and the potential ἐρώμενος Amyntas. When the narrator starts to describe the *Thalysia* that Lycidas' party anticipates, it is natural for a reader, primed by two songs of love, to ask whether this party too celebrates an erotic victory. I suggest that the change in description to χὠ καλὸς Ἀμύντιχος tells the reader, subtly but adequately, that Simichidas exploits the *locus amoenus* to woo Amyntas. The length and lushness of the description of that *locus amoenus* is to be explained, in dramatic terms, by its importance as the setting of that wooing. Seduction is, of course, regularly associated with various forms of *locus amoenus*. Sometimes it is only the flowery meadow of *Iliad* 14, the *Homeric Hymn to Demeter* and the Cologne Archilochus.[16] Sometimes the *locus* has a wider range of attractive features, as in Sappho fr. 2. Plato's *Phaedrus* 229–30 may also be relevant: there the *locus amoenus* is a catalyst not just for eloquence in general but for eloquence in the matter of love, and in putting the case for granting erotic favours. In Theocritus himself a more elaborate description of a *locus amoenus* is associated both with attempted seduction (Polyphemus' description of his ἄντρον, *Id.* 11.44–8) and with successful rape (the description of the spring where the Nymphs are smitten by desire for Hylas, *Id.* 13.39–49). In Theocritus *Id.* 7 the description of a *locus amoenus* is also the description of a symposium, and here too Theocritus and his readers would know the many sympotic scenes in archaic poems where an essential feature of the symposium was ἔρως.[17] In particular the song of Lycidas would have reminded readers of the love poetry of Simonides, and of the journey to an island where the poet might enjoy the charms of the young Echecratidas.

In suggesting that the journey of Simichidas to the *Thalysia* is also an erotic journey, which brings Simichidas and Amyntas together, and that the two songs prepare the way for that conclusion, I have probably taken readers much further than most are prepared to go.[18] So I feel I cannot lose much by a final and even more conjectural throw. Whence the name Amyntas? It is especially associated with Macedonia, and after Alexander's conquests it was not uncommon in many parts of the Greek world. Curiously, however, it seems not yet to be attested in Cos, the ostensible setting of *Id.* 7. Like Damoetas, however, it is well-attested in Thessaly.[19] The form Amyntichus is also attested at Magnesia and Oeanthea.[20] Did Amyntas come from the love poetry of Simonides?

[16] Cf. Bremer 1975 and Slings in Bremer et al. 1987, 45 on Archil. fr. 196a.28.

[17] Of course the majority of archaic love poetry was composed for *performance* in a sympotic setting, but even those poems where love and a sympotic setting are explicitly linked are numerous: e.g. Thgn. 237–54, *Theognidea* 983–8, 993–1002, Simon. fr. 22. See further Bowie 1993b (Chapter 5 in Volume 1).

[18] During discussion at the workshop Kathryn Gutzwiller suggested to me that if a form of my hypothesis were to be acceptable it should cast the otherwise superfluous Eucritus as Amyntas' suitor. After initial enthusiasm for that solution I have reverted to my original position: the rhetoric of 95–127 is in Simichidas' mouth, as is the crucial characterisation of Amyntas as καλὸς Ἀμύντιχος and (of course) the description of the *locus amoenus*. Moreover it is to changes in *his* emotions and situation that the reader might be expected to be alert.

[19] *IG* ix.2 15.5 and 19.3 (Hypata); 207.1 (Melitea); 234.159 (Pharsalus); 262 (Cierium); 287a9 (Gomphi); 1290 (Pythium); 1296.12 (Azorus); 1321.9 (Halmyrus).

[20] *IG* ix.2 1111.7–8 (ca. 130–126 BC); *IG* ix.1^2 3.706.B18–19 (ca. 280 BC).

10 The Reception of Apollonius Rhodius in Imperial Greek Literature (2000)

1 Sophistic Prose

When around AD 140 the Stoic Apollonius of Chalcedon was setting off for Rome to take up the position of philosophy tutor to the future emperor Marcus,[1] escorted by a swarm of pupils, Demonax, Lucian's witty scourge of ostentation, allegedly quipped: προσέρχεται Ἀπολλώνιος καὶ οἱ Ἀργόναυται αὐτοῦ, 'Here comes Apollonius and his Argonauts'.[2] Given our other evidence of Apollonius of Chalcedon's reputation for acquiring money, the joke seems to consist in comparing his trip to Rome with Jason's mission to Colchis to get the golden fleece. This anecdote told by Lucian suggests that for Demonax and his audience Apollonius' poem was both well-known and the obvious literary source for knowledge of the Argonautic legend.

One or two other allusions support that impression. In *On dancing*, a work of AD 163 or 164, Lucian lists pantomime themes drawn from Thessaly: τὸν Πελίαν, τὸν Ἰάσονα, τὴν Ἄλκηστιν, τὸν τῶν πεντήκοντα νέων στόλον, τὴν Ἀργώ, τὴν λάλον αὐτῆς τρόπιν, τὰ ἐν Λήμνωι, τὸν Αἰήτην, τὸν Μηδείας ὄνειρον, τὸν Ἀψύρτου σπαραγμὸν καὶ τὰ ἐν τῶι παράπλωι γενόμενα, 'Pelias, Jason, Alcestis, the expedition of fifty young men, the Argo, its talking keel (cf. A.R. 4.580–91), the events in Lemnos, Aeetes, Medea's dream (cf. A.R. 3.616–82), the dismemberment of Apsyrtus, and what happened in the journey along the coast.'[3] Apollonius is presumably the source for these episodes, and Lucian again alludes to the miracle of the Argo's talking keel in *The dream or cock*.[4] It also seems likely that there is an allusion to the Argonauts carrying the Argo across the desert in the episode in *True histories* where the narrator and his fellow sailors, faced with an impenetrable forest towering out of the sea, hoist their boat to tree-top level and simply

[1] See SHA *Pius* 10.4, and for other testimony *PIR*² A 929. Cf. Champlin 1980, 42–3; Birley 2000, 62–3.

[2] Luc. *Demon.* 31.

[3] Luc. *Salt.* 52–3.

[4] καίτοι τί ἂν ἐποίησας, εἰ σοὶ τῆς Ἀργοῦς τρόπις ἐλάλησεν, 'but what would you have done if the keel of the Argo had talked to you', Luc. *Gall.* 2: cf. A.R. 1.524, 4.580–3, though the myth could also be known from Apollod. 1.9.16.

sail across the foliage.[5] One scene not integral to the story of the Argonauts themselves is also ingeniously alluded to, that of Eros and Ganymede playing with knuckle-bones: in *Dialogues of the gods* Zeus offers Ganymede the prospect of playing at knuckle-bones with Eros.[6]

About the same time in the second century Pausanias twice draws on Apollonius Book 1. At 2.12.6 (composed around 160 AD) he cites A.R. 1.115–7 in support of his view that Dionysus, not Ceisus son of Temenus, was father of Phlias.[7] Again at 8.4.3 (composed between AD 175 and 180) Pausanias seems to allude to Apollonius when he says that ποιηταὶ καλοῦσιν Ἀφειδάντειον κλῆρον τὴν Τεγέαν, 'poets call Tegea "the lot of Apheidas"': the phrase Ἀφειδάντειον κλῆρον τὴν Τεγέαν appears at A.R. 1.162. At other places it is possible that Pausanias consulted Apollonius: perhaps for the names of the daughters of Pelias, where – in the context of the story that Medea persuaded them to cut Pelias up and casserole him – he notes that none of the poetic texts ὅσα γε ἐπελεξάμεθα ἡμεῖς, 'at least those we have consulted', offers names for the daughters (*contra* the painter Micon).[8]

Again in the early 190s the way that Apollonius is used by Athenaeus shows that he expects familiarity in his readers.[9] At the opening of Book 13 (555b) his speaker, about to catalogue τίνες λόγοι περὶ αὐτοῦ τοῦ ἔρωτος καὶ τῶν ἐρωτικῶν ἐλέχθησαν, cites without attribution or even any hint at its source the opening of Book 3:

[5] Luc. *VH* 2.42 cf. A.R. 4.1370–92, comparing especially 1376 ὑψόθεν ἀνθέμενοι ψαμαθώδεος ἔνδοθι γαίης | οἴσομεν, 'we shall lift (sc. the ship) on high and carry it to the midst of the sandy land', and 1385–6 νῆα … ἄγεσθε | ἀνθεμένους ὤμοισι, 'you have carried the ship, lifting it up on your shoulders', with Lucian's καὶ δὴ ἐδόκει ἡμῖν ἀναθεμένους τὴν ναῦν ἐπὶ τὴν κομὴν τῶν δένδρων … ὑπερβιβάσαι, 'and so we decided to lift the ship up and transport it over the foliage of the trees'. I am grateful to David Sansone for drawing my attention to this in the workshop discussion.

[6] ἔχεις κἀνταῦθα τὸν συμπαιξόμενόν σοι τουτονὶ τὸν Ἔρωτα καὶ ἀστραγάλους μάλα πολλούς, 'Here too you have Eros here to be your playmate, and a huge number of knuckle-bones', Luc. *DDeor*, 10.3, cf. A.R. 3.114–27.

[7] Φλίαντα δέ … Κείσου μὲν παῖδα εἶναι τοῦ Τημένου κατὰ δὴ τὸν τῶν Ἀργείων λόγον οὐδὲ ἀρχὴν ἔγωγε προσίεμαι, Διονύσου δὲ οἶδα καλούμενον καὶ τῶν πλευσάντων ἐπὶ τῆς Ἀργοῦς καὶ τοῦτον γενέσθαι λεγόμενον. ὁμολογεῖ δέ μοι καὶ τοῦ Ῥοδίου ποιητοῦ τὰ ἔπη 'Φλίας αὖτ' ἐπὶ τοῖσιν Ἀραιθυρέηθεν ἵκανεν, | ἔνθ' ἀφνειὸς ἔναιε Διωνύσοιο ἕκατι | πατρὸς ἑοῦ, πηγῇσιν ἐφέστιος Ἀσωποῖο (A.R. 1.115–7), 'and that Phlias was the son of Ceisus the son of Temenus, as in fact the Argives say, I do not even begin to accept, but I know that he is called the son of Dionysus and that he too was said to have been one of those who sailed on the Argo. I am corroborated by the verses of the poet of Rhodes: "After them there came in his turn Phlias from Araethyrea, where he dwelt in a house by the springs of the Asopus, wealthy thanks to his father Dionysus."'

[8] Paus. 8.11.2–3.

[9] Ath. also cites hexameters from Apollonius' *Foundation of Naucratis* 7.283f–4a = *CA* frr.7–9; refers to his prose monograph *On Archilochus* 10.451d; and knows a work *On feasts* by an Apollonius (5.191f), probably not the poet of Rhodes, *FGrH* 661 F2.

Εἰ δ' ἄγε νῦν, Ἐρατώ, πάρ θ' ἵστασο καί μοι ἐνίσπω ...

Come now, Erato, stand beside me and relate to me ...

Moving on into the first decades of the third century we find another writer with a selective interest in the history of literature, Philostratus, certainly showing and probably assuming knowledge of Apollonius. This is not in his *Lives of the sophists* or his work *In honour of Apollonius of Tyana*, but in the first set of Εἰκόνες, '*Paintings*' (I take the author of these three works to be the same).[10] *Painting* 2.15 depicts Glaucus prophesying to the Argonauts, the scene described by Apollonius at 1.1310–28. Some details may, but need not, be drawn from elsewhere in Apollonius – the keel from 1.524 and 4.580–3 (cf. n.4 above), Tiphys from 1.105–14.

The author of the second set of *Imagines*, arguably the nephew of the older Philostratus, makes even more use of Apollonius. *Painting* 8. Ἀθύροντες, '*Players*', is of Eros and Ganymede playing dice in the palace of Zeus. The account of their game (8.1, 402 Kayser) closely follows Apollonius 3.117–27, while Aphrodite's ruse of bribing Eros with a ball (8.3, 403 Kayser) follows 3.131–42. Philostratus explicitly links the incidents with the arrival of the Argo and its fifty heroes at Colchis. Apollonius is again used for *Painting* 11, *Argo or Aeetes*. The depiction of the serpent drugged and lulled to sleep (11.1, 411 Kayser) draws on 4.139–66, while that of Aeetes λαμπάδιόν τε τῆι δεξιᾶι αἰωροῦντα, 'and holding a torch aloft in his right hand' (11.4, 412 Kayser) may evoke 4.222–3 σκαιῆι μέν ῥ' ἐνὶ χειρὶ σάκος δινωτὸν ἀείρων, | τῆι δ' ἑτέρηι πεύκην περιμήκεα, 'In his left hand he raised up his circling shield, and in the other a torch of great length'.

2 Critics, Scholars, Philosophers and Aristides

My anecdote about Apollonius of Chalcedon induced me to plunge *in medias res*. But if we go back to the first century AD we have further clear indications of the importance of Apollonius' poem, in 'Longinus' Περὶ ὕψους, '*On the sublime*'. Contrasting poems that display ὕψος, 'sublimity', with those that are no more than technically perfect, the author asks:

> ἆρ' οὖν Ὅμηρος ἂν μᾶλλον ἢ Ἀπολλώνιος ἐθέλοις γενέσθαι; τί δέ; Ἐρατοσθένης ἐν τῆι Ἠριγόνηι (διὰ πάντων γὰρ ἀμώμητον τὸ ποιημάτιον) Ἀρχιλόχου ... ἆρα δὴ μείζων ποιητής;

[10] See Bowie 2009e (Chapter 23 in Volume 3).

Would you rather be Homer or Apollonius? Is the Eratosthenes of that flawless little poem *Erigone* ... a greater poet than Archilochus ...?

'Longinus' 33.5 (transl. D. A. Russell)

'Longinus' certainly purports to have read Apollonius and pondered the reasons why he is inferior to Homer, and he expects his readers to have done so too.

Another witness even less easy to date than 'Longinus' is the mythographer Apollodorus, whom I assume to be writing late in the first or early in the second century AD. The *Library*'s account of the Argonauts' expedition seems to use Apollonius as its chief source (1.9.16–27), but he is not the only source, and at one point Apollonius is specifically cited (2.284–98) for a variant concerning the pursuit of the Harpies by Zetes and Calais:

Ἀπολλώνιος δὲ ἐν τοῖς Ἀργοναύταις ἕως Στροφάδων νήσων φησὶν αὐτὰς διωχθῆναι καὶ μηδὲν παθεῖν, δούσας ὅρκον τὸν Φινέα μηκέτι ἀδικῆσαι.

But Apollonius in his *Argonauts* says that they were pursued as far as the Strophades islands and that they were not harmed, once they had sworn that they would no longer persecute Phineus.

Apollod. 1.9.21

It may be that in the second half of the first century AD knowledge of Apollonius was also shown by the voluminous Alexandrian scholar Pamphilus. The notes of sources that precede all but four of the tales in the *Metamorphoses* of Antoninus Liberalis seem in one case (the story of Battus) to make Pamphilus refer to Apollonius, but not apparently to the *Argonautica*:

ἱστορεῖ Νίκανδρος Ἑτεροιουμένων α′ καὶ Ἡσίοδος ἐν Μεγάλαις Ἠοίαις καὶ Διδύμαρχος Μεταμορφωσέων γ′ καὶ Ἀντίγονος ἐν ταῖς Ἀλλοιώσεσι καὶ Ἀπολλώνιος ἐν Ἐπιγράμμασιν, ὥς φησι Πάμφιλος ἐν α′.

Nicander tells the story in the first book of his *Transformations* and Hesiod in his *Great Ehoeae* and Didymarchus in the third book of his *Metamorphoses* and Antigonus in his *Shape-changes* and Apollonius in his *Epigrams*, according to Pamphilus in his first book.

Antoninus Liberalis 23

Sakolowski[11] wanted to emend ἐν Ἐπιγράμμασιν to ἐν ἔπεσιν, 'in his epic', but the story does not, of course, appear in the *Argonautica*, and mere mention of characters like Argos who do can hardly have been the basis for

[11] Sakolowski 1893, 52.

claiming a source for the Battus story in Apollonius' epic. The existence of epigrams by Apollonius is *a priori* likely, and one may survive in the elegiac distich attacking Callimachus, a distich that its source, *AP* 11.275, ascribes to Ἀπολλωνίου γραμματικοῦ, 'By Apollonius the scholar'.[12] Although the possibility of a collection of epigrams by Apollonius is not often discussed (nothing, for example, in Cameron 1995) such a collection may indeed have existed and may have been available to a chalcenteric scholar working in Alexandria.

By contrast with the authors considered above – all of whom are in some degree professional historians or interpreters of literature – there are many others of this period who neither quote Apollonius by name nor show any sign of familiarity.

So far as we can tell Apollonius does not attract the attention of philosophers. From the late first and very early second centuries Apollonius seems neither to be cited by name nor alluded to by Dio of Prusa,[13] by Plutarch,[14] or by their common pupil Favorinus.[15] Nor at any point does the great sophist Aelius Aristides name Apollonius, and where he refers to Medea or to the Argonauts he seems not to be drawing on Apollonius' poem. Thus at 38.15 Keil he refers to Medea's flight through Thessaly[16] and at 46.29 Keil to the expedition of the Argonauts, claiming that Argo started from Corinth: there is no ground to see this as dissociating his version from that of Apollonius in particular. Accordingly when he refers to the chariot of Poseidon in his *Isthmian oration: to Poseidon* he may, as suggested by Behr, be influenced by Apollonius,[17] but the case for seeing influence is weak:

> ἀτεχνῶς ὥσπερ ἐν ἁρματηλασίας, εἴ πως ἦν ἰδεῖν ἀνθρώποις οὖσι φερόμενον τὸ Ποσειδῶνος ἅρμα ...
>
> exactly as in chariot races, if somehow it were possible for us mortals to see the chariot of Poseidon being borne along ...
>
> Aelius Aristides 46.31 Keil

[12] *FGE* 17 on 'Apollonius of Rhodes? I'.

[13] For Medea's ἔρως, 'desire' (66.2), ἐπῳδαί, 'spells' (66.16), and child-murder (74.8) Dio probably uses the Euripidean *Medea*, not Apollonius. Jason's physical attractions at 8.27, the dragon, bulls and ointment of 16.10, and the sowing of the dragon's teeth at 23.4 could, but need not, derive from Apollonius.

[14] This contrasts with fifteen quotations from or allusions to Aratus, fourteen quotations from or allusions to Callimachus, and two quotations from or allusions to Theocritus, see Helmbold and O'Neil 1959.

[15] At [Dio] 37.13–15 (i.e. Favorinus) the discussion of the first Isthmian games and Jason's dedication of the Argo to Poseidon does not draw on Apollonius.

[16] Keil compares Σ Ar. *Nu.* 749.

[17] Behr 1981, 424 n.60.

οἷος δ' Ἴσθμιον εἶσι Ποσειδάων ἐς ἀγῶνα,
ἅρμασιν ἐμβεβαώς ...

And like Poseidon when he goes to his Isthmian Games,
mounted on his chariot ...

A.R. 3.1240–1

If Aristides has no occasion or wish to mention Apollonius it is not surprising that his less erudite contemporary Maximus of Tyre also makes no reference either. But that of course does not mean that he had not read Apollonius. The emperor Marcus, not surprisingly, neither cites nor alludes to Apollonius in his *Meditations*, but in a letter written to Marcus around AD 163 Fronto analyses the proem of Book 1 in a way that implied that his addressee was familiar with the text.[18]

3 The Novelists

It is perhaps also surprising how little use of Apollonius is made by the novelists. On the one hand the typical story-pattern of the novels, with its emphasis on sudden falling in love, erotic suffering and exotic travels, clearly takes a similar form to, and could be claimed to be influenced by, that of Apollonius.[19] On the other hand specific borrowings or allusions are rare. In Chariton only 1.1.15 seems secure: τότε δὲ Χαιρέας ἀπὸ τῶν γυμνασίων ἐβάδιζεν στίλβων ὥσπερ ἀστήρ, 'At that point Chaereas was walking from the gymnasia, shimmering like a star', blends A.R. 1.774 βῆ δ' ἴμεναι προτὶ ἄστυ, φαεινῷ ἀστέρι ἶσος, 'and he went on his way to the city, just like a brilliant star', with Theoc. 2.79–80: στήθεα δὲ στίλβοντα πολὺ πλέον ἢ τύ, Σελάνα, | ὡς ἀπὸ γυμνασίοιο καλὸν πόνον ἄρτι λιπόντων, 'and their chests were shimmering much more than you do, Moon, seeing as they had recently left the fair toil of the gymnasium'. Brioso Sánchez has also argued for influence of A.R. 1.238–59 on the scene of the departure of Chaereas' expedition from Syracuse to find Callirhoe (3.5),[20] but I doubt if the parallels are close enough to support such a conclusion: rather both authors are manipulating some obvious features of a departure scene, some of which are already there in Thucydides 6.32.1–2 (which may indeed have influenced Chariton). There is none of the detail which later secures Apollonius as a model for the departure scene at Quintus of Smyrna 14.369–98.[21]

[18] *Ad M. Antoninum de orationibus* 2 = ii 101 Haines.
[19] For recognition of this cf. Heiserman 1977, 13–29; Reardon 1991, 129; Ruiz Montero 1996, 55–7.
[20] Brioso Sánchez 1989.
[21] See Vian 1954; 1959; Carvounis 2019 *ad loc.*

In Achilles Tatius' description of the παρθένοι, 'maidens', playing by the sea in the painting of Europa one detail seems to be drawn from Apollonius' description of Medea's ἀμφίπολοι, 'attendants': τὸ ζῶσμα μέχρι γόνατος ἀνεῖλκε τὸν χιτῶνα, 'their belts pulled up their tunic to their knees', seems to rework A.R. 3.874–5 ἂν δὲ χιτῶνας | λεπταλέους λευκῆς ἐπιγουνίδος ἄχρις ἄειρον, 'and they lifted up their delicate tunics as far as their white thighs'.[22]

Longus has Daphnis play a herding tune at 4.15.2 – ἐπέπνευσε τὸ νόμιον, 'he blew the grazing tune' – but there is only a slight chance that he is here influenced by Apollonius' comparison of Orpheus (1.575–8) to a shepherd leading his flock by καλὰ μελιζόμενος νόμιον μέλος, 'playing beautifully a grazing tune' – not least because there is a possible relationship with νόμιον ἐξηκούετο μέλος, 'a grazing tune could be heard', at Alciphron 2.9.[23]

I have noticed no other echoes of Apollonius in the novelists, though there are likely to be some, and there are many places where the novelist plays with the same *topoi* as the poet. Apollonius' description of Medea's falling in love with Jason deploys similar details to the novelists and both show knowledge of Sappho and Euripides,[24] but no lexical detail clinches use of Apollonius by a novelist. Another possible case might have been when the hero is reduced to despair. Despair is of course a natural reaction to inability to master a problem and afflicts heroes in traditional epic too (e.g. Odysseus weeps at Od. 5.82). In the novels we find heroes succumbing despair and tears, e.g. Xenophon of Ephesus 2.1.1–6; Achilles Tatius 4.10.5 and (less straightforwardly) 3.11.1; Longus 2.22, 3.27.1 and 4.28.2 (cf. Chloe's tears at 4.27.1). But none of these treatments shows any direct influence of Jason's ἀμηχανίη, 'helplessness', at A.R. 1.1286–9 or 3.422–4.

4 Poetry

The position in poetry of the first two centuries is, perhaps predictably, rather different. I have not found echoes of Apollonius in literary epigram, nor in the quasi-Homeric epic narrative of the Hadrianic poet from Alexandria, Pancrates. But the tradition of didactic poetry represented by Dionysius of Alexandria in the 130s AD and by the two poems ascribed

[22] 1.1.7, see Whitmarsh 2020, 126.

[23] See Hunter 1983, 8–9.

[24] For Longus see Bowie 2019g, 122–3. Perhaps the case for Leucippe's presentation at Ach. Tat. 2.29 is stronger, cf. Whitmarsh 2020, 242: 'The episode shows general similarities to A.R. 3.616–64, where Medea grapples alone with her turbulent feelings: like Medea, Leucippe must choose whether to stay with an oppressive parent or cut ties and elope with a lover'.

to Oppian,[25] composed respectively late in the second and early in the third century AD, saw itself to some degree as the heir of Hellenistic principles of τέχνη and refinement. It is therefore not surprising that these poets allude repeatedly to Apollonius. Dionysius clearly knew the canonical Hellenistic poets well, as is demonstrated by his reworking of phrases from Callimachus and Aratus, and his allusions begin with his own first three lines.[26] They can extend to a whole line.[27] But for his Περιήγησις τῆς οἰκουμένης, '*Description of the inhabited world*', he may have been especially drawn to Apollonius by the latter's descriptions of landscapes and seascapes traversed by the Argonauts. Thus of the thirty-seven borrowings or re-workings of Apollonius registered by Tsavari for the first 450 lines of Dionysius only six are from the third book, and, of these six, three might be questioned.[28]. The allusions to Apollonius continue in the Oppians and are even more prominent in the *Posthomerica* of Quintus of Smyrna, written at some time in the third century AD. As Vian demonstrated, Quintus makes much use of Apollonius.[29] All this is rather different from allusions in prose writing. The poets turn to Apollonius (as they all still turn to Homer) for a word or phrase whose reuse in a new setting can add depth and learning to their own poetry, and often it is important that the word reappears in the same *sedes*. Here Apollonius is not in competition with poets at large, far less prose writers, but simply with other canonical dactylic poets.

[25] The *Halieutica*, '*On fishing*', composed by a Cilician late in the second century AD, and the *Cynegetica*, '*On hunting*', also transmitted as by Oppian but composed by a citizen of Apamea in Syria in the reign of Caracalla (AD 212–217) to whom it is dedicated.

[26] ἀρχόμενος ... μνήσομαι 1–3 ~ A.R. 1.1–2. For Dionysius' use of Apollonius see Hunter 2002 and 2003 (repr. in Hunter 2008), noting that 'Other than the Homeric poems, the *Argonautica* is in fact probably the most important poetic model for Dionysius' (Hunter 2008, 723). For much more detail see Lightfoot 2014, esp. 48–60 on his lexicon (where 'debts to Apollonius are especially marked', p. 48) and 60–74 on his metre (less influenced by A.R.), and the many places noted in her index p. 559.

[27] D.P. 315 Ῥιπαίοις ἐν ὄρεσσι διάνδιχα μορμύρουσι, 'in the Rhipaean mountains they thunder in two directions', ~ A.R. 4.287 Ῥιπαίοις ἐν ὄρεσσιν ἀπόπροθι μορμύροισιν, 'they thunder far off in the Rhipaean mountains'.

[28] Tsavari 1990: D.P. 4 ἐστεφάνωται, 'is encircled as by a garland', ~ A.R. 3.1214 ἐστεφάνωντο, 'encircled like a garland'; 144 εἰν ἁλὶ πέτρας, 'rocks in the sea' ~ A.R. 3.1294 εἰν ἁλὶ πέτρῃ, 'a rock in the sea'. But more dubious are 46 ἔσω ... αἴης, 'to within the land', ~ A.R. 3.311 εἴσω χθόνος; 128 ἐπιπροβέβηκε, 'juts forward towards' ~ A.R. 3.665 ἐπιπρομολοῦσ', 'advancing towards'; 141 Ἥρης ἐννεσίῃσιν, 'at the bidding of Hera', ~ A.R. 3.818 or Call. *Dian.* 108; τόθι, 'there', 179, 300, 563, 635, 764, 1138 ~ A.R. 3.577 or Call. *Iov.* 32.

[29] See Vian 1954, 30–51 and 235–54; 1959 *passim* (the passages are listed in his index on p. 262); and, for a thorough discussion of themes and motifs taken from Apollonius by Quintus, Triphiodorus and Nonnus, Vian 2001; for A.R. 2.1047–89 as a model for Quintus 11.258–61 see Greensmith 2020, 332–3; for 14.369–98 see Carvounis 2019 *ad loc.* For Oppian's *Halieutica* see Kneebone 2020, esp. 196–200, 224–5, 361–4, 375–6; for Nonnus' *Paraphrasis* see Massimilla 2016 (with a useful review of discussions of Hellenistic elements in the *Dionysiaca* at 251 n.10).

5 Readers in Egypt; Commentators

Alongside and contrasting with this very uneven evidence of interest in Apollonius in literary texts we have ample testimony both to his being read in Egypt and to scholarly work on the poem. The Egyptian readers are attested by the papyri. The great majority – twenty-six or twenty-seven – of the thirty-four papyri used by Vian 1974 are from the first three centuries AD. Some have scholia, e.g. the second-century papyrus *P.Oxy.* 2694 (Vian's Π^{16}) with 2.917–53 and 4.317–22, 416–61, 468–512 (see also Vian's Π^{7}).[30]

Some such readers wanted or were at least offered commentaries. We know of a commentary by Theon of Alexandria in the second half of the first century BC and a text accompanied by a commentary by Lucillus of Tarrha in the second half of the first century AD. Probably during the second century more work was done by an Irenaeus of whom criticisms survive in the scholia (on 1.1299; 2.123–9e; 2.992; 2.1015b). These criticisms were voiced in a commentary (*hypomnēma*) by one Sophocleius, who apparently based his work on the commentary of Theon.[31]

It is also clear that Apollonius' *Argonautica* was used by commentators on other poets. It is cited six times in the Homeric scholia (1.88 at Il. 1.72; 2.248 at Il. 17.415; 2.822 at Il. 16.8b1; 2.956 at Il. 14.164 c; 4.337 at Il. 23.141; 4.1700 at Il. 16.861). As well as these references to Apollonius in the Homeric scholia, he was drawn upon for a commentary on Aratus by a scholar called Achilles: 1.496–8 is carefully attributed to Book 1 of Apollonius' *Argonautica* at Achilles 3.17–22 Maass.[32] This might have a bearing upon Apollonius' use by novelists: the jury is still out, but it is possible that Achilles the commentator on Aratus is also the novelist of that name.[33]

6 Conclusions

Apollonius, then, was recognised as an author of importance who attracted the attention of scholars and writers engaged with mythography or literature. A further testimony to his prominence might be argued to rest in the fact that no Greek poet tried to supersede him by a reworking of the

[30] See Vian 1974, lxxxviii–xc and 1980, xv. Cf. the five papyri (all from Book 1) published by Wartenberg 1997 and one by Gonis 1997.

[31] On all this see Vian 1974, xli.

[32] Edited by Maass 1898, Di Maria 1996.

[33] See Whitmarsh 2020, 3–4, pointing out, however, that the astronomer Achilles is nowhere given the name Tatius.

Argonautic legend until the late antique Orphic *Argonautica*. Is it surprising that he did not attract more attention from authors who were themselves engaged in the production of literature – poets or novelists – or from philosophy and sophistic rhetoric? I began to reflect on this issue thinking that it was surprising, but perhaps I was wrong.

First, although Apollonius was the obvious source for parts of the Argonautic legend, he was not the only source. Elements of the story could derive from other literary texts or from local traditions; and for some Greeks (not to say non-Greeks), depictions in paintings might have been their only access to parts of the story. Arrian's remarks in his *Periplus Ponti Euxini* illustrate the importance of local traditions. At section 9 (p.110.14–22 Roos) he discusses fragments of the anchor of the Argo still displayed in the 130s AD at Phasis – the only record, he says, of the μῦθοι, 'myths', concerning Jason. If he regards Apollonius' poem as the palmary rendition of these myths, he abstains from saying so, even in this highly literary composition addressed to an emperor with a taste for Hellenistic poetry. Again in section 25 (128.13–15 Roos) he identifies the Cyaneae with the rocks which οἱ ποιηταί, 'the poets', say πλαγκτὰς πάλαι εἶναι, καὶ διὰ τούτων πρώτην ναῦν περᾶσαι τὴν Ἀργώ, 'they were once wandering, and through them they say the Argo was the first ship to sail'. No hint that 'poets' above all signifies Apollonius. Perhaps it does, just as when Arrian's junior the lexicographer Pollux (Polydeuces) of Naucratis cites terms from Theocritus (5.86 citing *Id.* 6.10; 1.229 citing *Id.* 13.41) he ascribes the words' usage to οἱ ποιηταί. Pollux, incidentally, seems at no point to cite Apollonius.

Another text of the same period illustrates a related point. Galen's περὶ κράσεων, '*On temperaments*' iii 658 Kühn (= p.93.22 Helmreich) says καὶ τὸ τῆς Μηδείας δὲ φάρμακον τοιοῦτον ἦν, 'and Medea's drug was of this sort'. Where did he hear or read about Medea's φάρμακον? Does it make sense to ask to which literary text he refers?

Second, any attempt to use Jason and Medea as examples of lovers, for instance, or to compose a sequel to the *Argonautica*, would have been discouraged by the even better known disasters that befell their relationship and by these disasters' handling by Euripides in his *Medea*. Hence many of the passages that *are* cited do not come from the part of the text, Book 3, that moderns read with greatest enthusiasm. In choosing to compose a prequel to that Euripidean tragedy Apollonius had set limits to the reception of his own poem.

11 | Time and Place, Narrative and Speech in Philicus, Philodamus and Limenius (2015)

1 Introduction

My three chosen subjects may seem unlikely bedfellows: two poets whose epigraphically preserved hymns were composed for performance in the sanctuary of Apollo at Delphi, Philodamus of Scarpheia and Limenius of Athens; and composing between them chronologically, but treated before them in my discussion, a scholarly figure from the Alexandrian Pleiad, Philicus of Corcyra, of whose hymn to Demeter a third century BC papyrus preserves sixty-two lines in various degrees of legibility. Yet their works are all 'hymns', and their diversity will cast some light on the difference that can be found between species of the capacious form.

My discussion of Philicus will bring out how prominent speeches seem to have been in his hymn, and how its spatial focus was concentrated on three demes of Attica associated with the cult of Demeter and Persephone, Eleusis, Halimous and above all (I propose) Prospalta, a focus that seems to have been matched by his otherwise surprising choice of Attic dialect for his medium. Philicus' apparent choice of Prospalta for the dramatically presented entry and ῥῆσις, 'speech', of the old woman from Halimous, Iambē, may, I suggest, have related to his use of his hymn to offer an alternative explanation for the origins of αἰσχρολογία, 'abusive language', in the cult of Demeter, and perhaps for its place in Attic comedy.

By contrast the hymns of Philodamus and Limenius, performed and then inscribed for timeless readers in the sanctuary of Apollo at Delphi, sweep their audiences and viewers along on the whirlwind journeys through Greece performed by the *fama* and by the persons of the hymned divinities – Dionysus in the case of Philodamus, Apollo in that of Limenius – journeys that end at the navel of the world where the performance and inscription were created, and in Limenius' poem a journey that is paralleled by the movement from Athens to Delphi of the *Pythais* that performs it. Again by contrast with Philicus, whose poem seems to have had a possibly slender narrative frame within which very substantial aetiological speeches were set, the primary level of utterance chosen by Philodamus is invocation, to which narrative of the god's birth, movements and instructions to mortals is subordinated by a relative pronoun. Limenius has roughly equal proportions of invocation and narrative. Within these narratives we never hear unambiguously inset speech, though Philodamus offers some cases where singers of the paean and singers who inhabit his subordinate narrative may be singing from the same hymn sheet.

2 Philicus

Although Philicus falls chronologically between Philodamus and Limenius, the very different nature of his hymn prompts considering him first.[1] Philicus was a priest of Dionysus in the reign of Ptolemy Philadelphus and probably an early president of the guild of Dionysiac *technitae*, with whom he marches in the great procession of the penteteric *Ptolemaea* that fell in 279/278 BC, 275/274 BC or 271/270 BC and whose description by Callixeinus of Rhodes is preserved by Athenaeus.[2] As is shown by the metre of fragment 677 *SH* (printed below), his name is Philicus, not Philiscus, the form which is found in the manuscripts of the Suda and is unfortunately printed by Olson in his Loeb edition of Athenaeus.[3] The Suda entry suggests that Philicus was chiefly known for the composition of tragedies:

> Φιλίσκος, Κερκυραῖος, Φιλώτου υἱός, τραγικὸς καὶ ἱερεὺς τοῦ Διονύσου ἐπὶ τοῦ Φιλαδέλφου Πτολεμαίου γεγονώς. καὶ ἀπ᾽αὐτοῦ τὸ Φιλίσκιον μέτρον προσηγορεύθη, ἐπείπερ αὐτῶι ἐνεδαψιλεύετο. ἔστι δὲ τῆς δευτέρας τάξεως τῶν τραγικῶν, οἵτινές εἰσιν ζʹ καὶ ἐκλήθησαν Πλειάς. αἱ δὲ τραγωιδίαι αὐτοῦ εἶσι μβʹ.
>
> Philiscus of Corcyra, son of Philotas, tragedian and priest of Dionysus active under Ptolemy Philadelphus. And the Philiscian meter was named after him, since he indulged in it liberally. He is among the second group of tragedians, who are seven and were nicknamed the 'Pleiad'. His tragedies number forty-two.[4]

[1] For careful and perceptive discussions of the poem, first published by Norsa 1927, see Brown 1990; Furley 2009; Giuseppetti 2012. A valuable re-edition of the fragments of Philicus, with introduction and commentary, is offered by Provenzale 2009. I am grateful to Prof. J. Danielewicz for drawing my attention to this thesis. Philicus makes no appearance at all in Bouchon, Brillet-Dubois and Le Meur Weissman 2012.

[2] Ath. 5.196a and 198b–c = Callixeinus, *FGrH* 627 F2. On the date cf. Rice 1983, 182–7; Provenzale 2009, 43.

[3] Olson 2006, 456 (Ath.5.198b), Suda φ 358, cf. Snell, *TrGF* 104. On the form of the name see Provenzale 2009, 36–7.

[4] The translation is that of Chad Schroeder in the Suda on line. Käppel's figure of twenty-four in *Brill's New Pauly s.v.* Philicus is presumably a misprint.

It is to Hephaestion, possibly the Hephaestion who was tutor to the Roman emperor Verus[5] and hence was writing his metrical handbook in the middle of the second century AD, that we owe what is certainly the opening line of a hymn specified by the line itself as addressed to Demeter, Persephone and Clymenus. Here by 'Clymenus' Philicus means Hades, who received cult under this euphemistic title at Hermione in the Argolid:[6]

> τῆι χθονίηι μυστικὰ Δήμητρί τε καὶ Φερσεφόνηι καὶ Κλυμένωι τὰ δῶρα
>
> To Demeter of the nether world, and Persephone, and Clymenus, the gifts which concern their mysteries
>
> Philicus fr. 676 *SH*

As this line exemplifies, Philicus' hymn was composed in choriambic hexameters catalectic – clever, challenging and innovative,[7] though, as Hephaestion pointed out, not quite so innovative as Philicus implies in another boastful line from the hymn:

> καινογράφου συνθέσεως τῆς Φιλίκου, γραμματικοί, δῶρα φέρω πρὸς ὑμᾶς

[5] SHA *Vita Veri* 2.5. It is just possible (though the chronology is tight) that this is the same as the Hephaestion who wrote Περὶ τοῦ παρ' Ἀνακρέοντι λυγίνου στεφάνου, '*On the withy garland in Anacreon*', attacked by Democritus in Ath. 15.673e as having stolen his solution to this problem and also having plagiarised the peripatetic philosopher Adrastus.

[6] Φίλικος δὲ ὁ Κερκυραῖος, εἷς ὢν τῆς Πλειάδος, ἑξαμέτρωι συνέθηκεν ὅλον ποίημα 'τῆι χθονίηι μυστικὰ Δήμητρί τε καὶ Φερσεφόνηι καὶ Κλυμένωι τὰ δῶρα'. τοῦτο δὲ καὶ ἀλαζονεύεται εὑρηκέναι Φίλικος λέγων 'καινογράφου συνθέσεως τῆς Φιλίκου, γραμματικοί, δῶρα φέρω πρὸς ὑμᾶς'· ψεύδεται δέ· πρὸ γὰρ αὐτοῦ Σιμμίας ὁ Ῥόδιος ἐχρήσατο 'λεύσσετε τὸν γᾶς τε βαθυστέρνου ἄνακτ' Ἀκμονίδαν τ' ἄλλυδις ἑδράσαντα', πλὴν εἰ μὴ ἄρα ὁ Φίλικος οὐχ ὡς πρῶτος εὑρηκὼς τὸ μέτρον λέγει, ἀλλ' ὡς πρῶτος τούτωι τῶι μέτρωι τὰ ὅλα ποιήματα γράψας, 'Philicus of Corcyra, one of the Pleiad, composed a whole poem in the (sc. choriambic) hexameter: "To Demeter of the nether world, and Persephone, and Clymenus, the gifts which concern their mysteries". And Philicus actually claims falsely to have invented this metre, saying "I bring gifts to you, philologists, of Philicus' innovatively written composition". He is lying. For before him Simmias of Rhodes used it in his *Axe*: "Phocian Epeius has offered a gift to the virile goddess Athena, so as to honour her strong counsel", and in his *Wings*: "Behold the lord of the deep-bosomed earth and one who established the heaven elsewhere" – unless perhaps Philicus is speaking on the basis not that he was the first to invent the metre but that he was the first to compose whole poems in it', Heph. 9.4 p. 30 Consbruch, on Philicus' use of the choriambic hexameter.

[7] If, as Hephaestion thinks possible, Philicus is claiming to be the first to use this metre for a whole poem, this may show that his *Demeter* precedes Callimachus' *Branchus* composed in choriambic pentameters catalectic and opening (fr. 229 Pfeiffer) Δαίμονες εὐυμνότατοι, Φοῖβέ τε καὶ Ζεῦ, Διδύμων γενάρχα, 'Divine beings most deserving of hymns, Phoebus and Zeus, founders of Didyma'. I am grateful to Prof. J. Danielewicz for drawing my attention to the relation between the two poems and between Philicus fr. 2.61 βοτάνη δῶρον, ὀκνηρᾶς ἐλάφου δ̣ί̣αιτα, 'there is grass as a gift, a timorous deer's diet' and χ̣λ̣ω̣ρὴν̣ β̣ο̣τ̣άνην νέμο̣ι̣τ̣ο̣, 'may (sc. flocks) graze on green fodder', in Call. fr. 229.4 Pfeiffer = 182.4 Asper.

I bring gifts to you, philologists, of Philicus' innovatively written composition

Philicus fr. 677 *SH*

Part of this line is said by the scholiast on Hephaestion to have been in Philicus' *prooemium*,[8] and though Richard Stoneman has suggested that it might be from the end of the poem,[9] I incline to accept the scholiast, and to reflect that Hephaestion may well not have made his way very far into a text that will have been distinctly rebarbative even when it was complete. Fr. 677 *SH*, then, should come later in the *prooemium*, which in that case would tell us that this *prooemium* was not just a one-liner, but something more substantial.

We have no idea, I believe, how long the poem was, but it is improbable that it exceeded the 495 lines of the *Homeric Hymn to Demeter*, which Philicus certainly knew,[10] and it may have been nearer in length to the 326 lines of Callimachus' *Hymn to Delos*. It seems likely from Philicus' giving Hades the name Κλύμενος that Philicus knew, and may have expected some readers to know, the hymn of Lasus to Demeter as she was worshipped in his own city Hermione, beginning:

Δάματρα μέλπω Κόραν τε Κλυμένοι' ἄλοχον
Μελιβοίαν ὕμνον ἀναγνέων
Αἰολίδ' ἄμ βαρύβρομον ἁρμονίαν

I dance and sing Demeter and her Daughter, wife of Clymenus,
Meliboea, raising up a hymn
in the deep-booming Aeolian harmony

Lasus fr. 702 *PMG*[11]

One of several possible reasons for Lasus' hymn catching the eye of Philicus might have been that it was asigmatic, as Heraclides Ponticus had pointed out three generations earlier.[12] But Philicus had quite enough to contend with in the straitjacket of choriambic hexameters, and he did not emulate

[8] Σ ACD to p. 31.1 (p. 140.14).

[9] Cited by *SH* p. 321. Accepted by Giuseppetti 2012, 117 (with doxography in n.64).

[10] Richardson 1974, 70 with n.4.

[11] Quoted by Ath. 14.624e–f and (the first line only) 10.455c. For the cult see Prauscello 2013, and for Call.'s use of the *epiclesis* Clymenus in *Hecale* fr. 285 Pfeiffer = 100 Hollis = 277 Asper see Giuseppetti 2011.

[12] Ath. 10.455c, cf. Eustathius Il. 1335.52. For retaining the manuscript reading Μελιβοίαν (as against Hartung's emendation to μελιβόαν, 'honey-voiced') and for a persuasive argument for the likelihood of an *epiclesis Meliboea* in the chthonic cult of Demeter and Persephone at Hermione see Prauscello 2011.

Lasus' asigmatism. Nor could he have begun with a straightforward use of Lasus' performative term μέλπω, which comprises both singing and dancing, since it is virtually certain that Philicus did not intend his hymn for dancing, or even for singing, but rather for reading by the 'scholars', γραμματικοί, to whom his *prooemium* says it is a gift – though of course he could have used the word μέλπω to contribute to the mimetic fiction that his poem was being performed, in a manner analogous to that of Callimachus in *Hymns* 2 and 5.

So much by way of contextualisation. I now print what is essentially the text of *SH* fr. 680 with a very select set of textual points in footnotes and some improvements suggested by William Furley.[13] I have not re-examined the papyrus, but have consulted the photograph in Provenzale 2009, 138; Provenzale's apparatus offers all readings and conjectures known to her, but since she and Furley 2009 were published in the same year neither was able to benefit from the other.

fr. 678 *SH* (papyrus fr. 1)	].χρην̣[
(= fr. 3 Provenzale)	
fr. 679 *SH* (papyrus fr. 2)	]ρσ. [
(= fr. 4 Provenzale)	]σανη.[
	]ταιναρ [

fr. 680 *SH* (papyrus fr. 3)	]νδε̣ θυγατ̣ρὸς [
(= fr. 5 Provenzale)	[μη]τέρα[14] παῖς οὐκ[
[	ἅρμ]α̣ κ̣ατειλισσομέ[νων δρακόντων[15]
[	]π̣ο̣υ δὲ μετήλλα[ξε[16]
[	ἁρπ]άσ̣ματα ληιστὴν . ν̣[
[	] λαμπάδας ὑληδ.[
[	]ὧς τε χιτὼν ἀμπ[εχόνη[17]
[	]α̣σα δὲ τουσ̣ ε̣ξα.[[18]
[	]τῶιδε κόρη[.] .ψα[19]
[	]α τύχην οὔτε γάμ̣[ους[20]
[	].ματος εἰπεῖν ἀναλυ[
[	]. σ̣ην οὐρανὸν ἐνδε[
[	] ἀλύο̣υ̣σ̣[α] δρο̣μ̣ο̣υ[

[13] Furley 2009.

[14] μη]τέρα Vogliano.

[15] Furley 2009 *exempli gratia*, cf. Orph. *H.* 40.13.

[16] μετήλλα[ξε Körte 1931.

[17] ὧς τε Körte 1931; ἀμπ[εχόνη Furley 2009.

[18] ἇσ]ασα δὲ τοὺς ἐξαμ[έτρους στενάζει Gallavotti 1931.

[19] τῶιδε Furley 2009.

[20] γάμ[ους Gallavotti 1951.

[ ]νιδαι τọι̣άδ' ἔπη̣[
[π]οδε̣ς̣ οὐκ εἴδ̣[ε]τ̣ε̣[
[ ]ε[. .]ο ημ... γ
[ ].ν[.]μοι τ̣ε̣[

fr. 4 col. i]νυ.[
[ ]ο χανοῦσ̣[
[σ]υ̣μμ[ιγ]ε̣[ς] ἔρριπτο χύδ[ην
[ ]μασι θερμὴ δ' ἐπέκαεν α[ὐγή[21]
[ ]δε μύθου προλαβοῦσα θ̣[εά
[ν]ικηφόρον οἰωνὸν ἔκρινον
[κλ]υ̣θι λιτὰς μητρόθεν αὐταδέλφους
[ ]ι̣ς ὁμόσπλαγχνον ἔθρεψα κύπριν
[ποθ]ε̣ινὴ γάλα σοι, μητρὶ δ' ἐγὼ σύναιμος
[μ]εγάλας κοινοπάτωρ λοχεύει
[μεγ]άλαυχόν τε βίαν ἔτικτεν
[ ]μοιριδία πρᾶσις,[22] ἐμοὶ δὲ πείθειν
[τούτ]ο̣υ[23] μετέχειν, μηδὲ μόνημ με τοὐμόν

fr.4 col.ii+fr.5] . . . εις ἀ̣π̣ι̣θ̣ήσασα[24] λόγοις, αἱ δὲ θεαὶ σ̣ε κ̣[
[γ]ὰρ ἐσ[ηγ]γέ̣λ̣μεθα τιμὴν μί' ἐγὼ σὺγ Χάρ[ισιν] σ̣τ̣ε̣λ̣ο̣[ῦσαι
[διέ]σ̣χιστο μ̣έ̣ν,[25] ἄλλας δὲ σὺ τιμὰς ἀνελοῦ π̣α̣ρ' ἡ̣μῶν
[ ]α̣ καὶ μ̣[εί]ζο̣ν̣ας ἀντ' οὐ μεγάλης, ἃς διελοῦσα λέξω.
[οὐδενὶ μὲν γὰρ πλέον] ἢ σοὶ δ̣ά̣σ̣ε̣τ̣α̣ι̣ τις φίλος, α<ἰ>εὶ δὲ πλέον
φιλήσω
[ ]ν̣ ὥρ̣α̣σ̣ι̣ν̣ Ἐ̣λ̣ευσῖνάδε[26] μυστηλασίαις ἰάκχων
[ ]τε π̣ο̣λ̣λ̣[ὴ] π̣ολὺν ἐγδεξαμένη τὸμ παρὰ κῦμα ν̣η̣σ̣τη̣ν̣
[ ]μ̣η̣τ̣ι̣ μυ[ρ]η̣ρ̣ούς, τροφίμη, σοι λιπανοῦσι κλῶνας
[ ]λ̣[.]ς̣ δ̣ι̣χ[α] κ̣ρ̣ηναῖον ἑκάστης ἓν ὕδωρ ὁρισθέν
[το]υ̣τ̣ου δ[ιθρό]ν̣ου[27] σοῖς προσανήσεις δακρύοισι πηγήν
[κα]λει̣τ̣αι βασ[ί]λεια κρήνη
[τῶ]νδε λόγων τείσομεν ἔργα κρείσσω
[πρὶ]ν ἐλέγξαι προλαβεῖν ἀπ[ί]στους
[κλάδ]ο̣ν ἱκτῆρα φέρουσι μὲν νῦν
[ ] . . δε πάλιν χέονται

[21] α[ὐγή Furley 2009, ἀγρούς Gallavotti 1951.
[22] The papyrus has κτησις with the correction πρασις written above the line. Lobel (reported by Gallavotti) conjectured πᾶσις.
[23] τούτ]ο̣υ Körte 1931.
[24] εις ἀπιθήσασα Körte 1931.
[25] διέ]σ̣χιστο μ̣έ̣ν Furley 2009.
[26] Or, as Norsa 1927 observed, Ἐ̣λ̣ευσῖνα δὲ.
[27] το]ύ̣του δ[ιθρό]ν̣ου Furley 2009.

[θ]υ̣ομένην[28] σῆι τελετὴν ἑορτῆι
[ ]ζη̣λοτύπωι κρατῆσαι
[ἀλλ’ αἰρομένη σκ]η̣π̣τρον[29] ἄγου Φερσεφόνην ὑπ’ ἄσ̣τ̣ρ̣α
[ ] . δ̣ε̣σιν ἡγησαμένης οὐθὲν ἐμοῦ σφαλήσει
α̣[ ]υ̣ πεύκας ἀνελοῦ, λῦε βαρεῖαν ὀφρύν.’
ἡ μὲν [ἔ]ληγεν·[σ]υ̣ν̣έ̣φ[ήπτοντ]ο̣[30] δ̣ὲ Νύμφαι τε δικαίας Χάρι̣τ̣έ̣ς τε πειθοῦς
πᾶς δὲ γυναικῶν ἀ[νάριθμός τε π]έριξ[31] θ’ ἑσμὸς ἐθώπευσε πέδον μετώποις
φυλλοβολῆσαι δ[ὲ] θ̣εὰν̣ [χερσ]ὶ[ν ἀ]ν̣έσχον[32] τὰ μόνα ζώφυτα γῆς ἀκ̣άρπου,
τὴν δὲ γεραιὰν παρ[άπλαγ]τον μὲν ὀρείοις Ἁλιμοῦς ἤθεσι, καιρίαν δέ,
ἒ̣κ τινος ἔστειλε τύχ[ης· τοῖσι δὲ][33] σεμνοῖς ὁ γελοῖος λόγος ἆρ’ ἀκερδή<ς>;
σ̣τᾶσα γὰρ ἐφθέγξατ’[ἄφαρ θα]ρ̣σ̣αλέον καὶ μέγα· μὴ βάλλετε χόρτον αἰγῶν,
οὐ τόδε πεινῶντι θεῶ̣ι̣ [φάρ]μ̣α̣κον, ἀλλ’ ἀμβροσία γαστρὸς ἔρεισμα λεπτῆς.
καὶ σὺ δὲ τῆς Ἀτθίδος, ὦ δα̣[ῖμ]ον̣, Ἰάμβης ἐπάκουσον βραχύ μού τι κέρδος·
εἰμὶ δ’ ἀπαίδευτα χέα[σ’ ὡς ἄ]ν̣[34] ἀ̣π̣οικοῦσα λάλος δημότις· αἱ θεαὶ μέν
αιδεθε[..][35]σοι κύλικας κα̣[ὶ τελ]έ̣σ̣αι σ̣τ̣έμ̣ματα καὶ [β]απτὸν ὕδω[ρ]ἐν ὑγρῶ̣ι̣
ἐγ δὲ γυναικῶν π̣[έλεται], ἦν̣,[36] βοτάνη δῶρον, ὀκνηρᾶς ἐλάφου δί̣αιτα,
οὐθὲν ἐμοὶ τῶνδε [μέτεστιν][37]γ̣έρα̣ς̣. ἀλλ’ εἰ χαλάσ̣ε̣ι̣ς̣ π[έ]νθος ἐγὼ δὲ λύσω

fr. 3]this of the daughter[
mot]her child not[
chariot of] writhing [snakes
]and where (she?) has gone away to[
clo?]thes predator
]torches wood[
like a] tunic her [wrap
]..........[
] to him the girl[
] fortune nor marr[iage
] to speak[

[28] θ]υ̣ομένην Furley 2009.
[29] ἀλλ’ αἰρομένη Furley 2009; σκ]ῆπτρον Körte 1931.
[30] [σ]υν̣έ̣φ[ήπτοντ] Furley 2009.
[31] ἀ[νάριθμός τε π] Furley 2009.
[32] [χερσ]ὶ[ν Furley 2009; ἀ]ν̣έσχον Gallavotti 1951.
[33] [καί ποτε] Furley 2009.
[34] εἶμι δ’ ἀπαίδευτα χέα[ι πολλὸ]ν ἀποικοῦσ’ Latte 1954; δαρ]ο̣ν̣ Furley 2009.
[35] αἵδ’ ἔθεσαν Lloyd-Jones and Parsons 1983; but Provenzale 2009, 27 denies that σα can be read.
[36] ἦν̣ Furley 2009.
[37] μέτεστιν Furley 2009 following Vogliano.

] heaven [
] wandering at a run[
] words such as these[
f]eet; did you not see[
… …
] to me [

fr. 4 col. i] … [
] gaping[
]was thrown without order[
]and the hot beam was burning upon[
]and the g[oddess], beginning to speak first,[
]I judged it an omen of victory[
list]en to prayers that are from a sister from the same mother
]in the same womb I nurtured Cypris
I was desir]able [when I gave my] milk to you, and I, of the same stock as your mother
us?]mighty ladies a common father begat
]and she gave birth to mighty-boasting violence
]a destined possession; and for me to persuade
]to have a share in this, and not from me alone my[

fr. 4 col. ii + fr. 5
]not failing to hearken to these words, and the goddesses [will reward?] you
]for we, I alone, with the Graces, have been announced as to give honour[
]have been apportioned, but you should accept other honours from us
]and greater ones in return for what is a small one – these I shall tell you in detail.
[for to none will] a friend accord [more] than to you, and I shall love more and more
]in the season(?) to Eleusis with the mystic coursings of the Iacchoi
]large [ ] welcoming the faster by the wave in large numbers
they] will swell out for you, nurturing one, perfumed branches
]a single fountain water marked out for each
[by] this two-throned [precinct] with your tears you will send up a spring
will be ca]lled the royal fountain
]than these words we shall accord in honour more powerful deeds
]do not prematurely take them as untrustworthy before testing
the branches]of supplication they bear now
th]ese again will pour forth

to be perfor]med as a ritual at your festival
]zealous ... overcome
[taking up the sceptre] bring Persephone up to where there are stars
]with me leading you shall not go wrong at all.
but] pick up the torches, relax your heavy brow.'
She ceased, and the Nymphs and Graces [joined in] just Persuasion,
and whole swarm of women in a circle about her caressed the ground with their foreheads
and gathered the only living growth from the cropless earth to cast as foliage upon the goddess
But Halimous despatched the old woman, who had lost her way in the mountain haunts, but arrived at a good time
as a result of some chance: for solemn occasions can an amusing tale be unprofitable?[38]
For she stood and uttered at once in a bold, loud voice: 'Do not throw goat-fodder:
it is not this that is [a remedy] for a starving god, but ambrosia is the support for such a delicate stomach.
But you, divine one, should give ear to Attic Iambē's little benefit;
I am one who has poured out unschooled words, as well might a chatterer living in a distant deme: these goddesses
here []for you cups and garlands and water drawn in a fresh stream;
and from the women, look!, there is grass as a gift, a timorous deer's diet.
None of these things do I have for my gift: but if you loosen up your grieving, then I shall release ...'

Given that so much of this poem is lost and that so many surviving lines are fragmentary, it would be unwise to offer negative statements of the form 'Philicus did not ...'. Thus we should not press the fact that in what is preserved we have no attempt closely to tie the hymn to even a fictional performance context, nor anything that is unambiguously a narrative of Persephone's abduction.[39] One might guess that there was indeed such a narrative, and that some move was made to set it in mythic time, but it

[38] In favour of taking σεμνοῖς as referring not to people but to occasions or modes of speech see Fantuzzi 2007, 63, also suggesting attractively that this is a meta-literary reference to the serio-comic texture of Philicus' *Demeter* (noticed, he argues, by the composer of the epigram on Philicus 980 *SH* = *P.Hamburg* 312 recto = Provenzale 2009 *test.* 7). I am less confident than he, however, that the lost lines contained αἰσχρολογία too shocking to be found in a high-style poem.

[39] ταιναρ.. [at fr. 679.3 may be a reference to Taenarum as an entrance to the underworld, but we cannot be sure it was actually part of an abduction-narrative.

can only be a guess, and for all we know such events could have been narrated not in the poet's voice but in yet another character speech. Equally one might wish to guess that Philicus did not in fact build in any link, near the beginning of the hymn or elsewhere, to a particular festival in a specific place at a particular time of year, but again this would be a guess, and it might be quite wrong.

What is undeniable is that in the surviving portion there are only two sequences of narrative, one of them at least short. The very lacunose fr. 680 lines 1–21 may indeed be narrative in the poet's voice, a narrative of Demeter's searching for Persephone (cf. ἀλύουσα, 'wandering', line 13) and of the dire ecological consequences of her bitterness (line 21, θερμὴ δ' ἐπέκαεν α[ὐγή, 'and the hot beam was burning upon …'); but our remains are too fragmentary to exclude the possibility that some of this narrative is within a character's speech. Certainly at line 22 a female character is described as μύθου προλαβοῦσα, 'beginning to speak', and her long speech, aetiologically predicting cult of Demeter, only ends twenty-nine lines later at line 51 (ἡ μὲν [ἔ]ληγεν ..).[40] Five and a half lines then narrate the placatory response of nymphs and mortal women and the timely arrival from the deme Halimous of Ἰάμβη (Iambē), an old woman. In the middle of line 56 she shouts brusquely, perhaps even boorishly, dismissing the nymphs' and women's offering of, perhaps, dry twigs (κλῶνας?) and announcing that she has something to help matters. The papyrus breaks off before we discover just what her remedy was, but presumably it was both entertaining and in some way related to ritual αἰσχρολογία.

In the lines that we have, then, fragmentary and constituting an uncertain proportion of the poem, speech dominates; it is the principle means of conveying aetiological data and of putting flesh on the poem's skeleton.

How attentive was Philicus to evocation of place? Full knowledge of the poem, especially of the parts before what survives, would almost certainly allow a more confident answer. But I note that his specification of Halimous as the deme of Iambē shows Philicus keen to provide some topographical detail. If we accept Stoneman's attractive supplement in 54 πα[ράπλαγ]τον μὲν ὀρείοις … ἤθεσι, 'who had strayed from her path in mountain haunts',[41] then we can avoid the improbability that the scholar Philicus, working in Alexandria but originating in the Greek island of Corcyra, was unaware

[40] For the problems in identifying this speaker see Gallavotti 1931 (Demeter); Körte 1931 and Gallavotti 1951 (Peitho); Page 1941, 405 (Dione); Latte 1954 (Tethys); Brown 1990: 181–3 (Rhea); Furley 2009 (Aphrodite).

[41] Printed in her text by Provenzale 2009: her apparatus (p. 25) presents other possibilities, discussed in her commentary (p. 114).

that the Attic deme Halimous was on the coast.[42] But we still have to explain why Iambē found herself in the hills at all. Her origin in Halimous presumably associated her with the cult of Demeter and Persephone which is registered there by Pausanias (1.31.1, printed here): but what is the geographical setting of the poem's action to which chance so opportunely brings her? That setting cannot plausibly be either Eleusis (as seems to be assumed by most scholars)[43] or Athens itself, each of which Iambē could quite easily reach from Halimous without straying into mountains (though admittedly if she were on her way from Halimous to Eleusis she might, if impatient or injudicious, attempt to cut across the hill near Perama). But scholars looking at Pausanias seem not to have noticed that precisely the same section of his book on Attica also records another Attic cult of Demeter and Korē, in the deme Prospalta, situated south of present-day Markopoulo at Kalyvia Kouvara, now called Kalyvia Thorikou:[44]

> δῆμοι δὲ οἱ μικροὶ τῆς Ἀττικῆς, ὡς ἔτυχεν ἕκαστος οἰκισθείς, τάδε ἐς μνήμην παρείχοντο· Ἀλιμουσίοις <μὲν> Θεσμοφόρου Δήμητρος καὶ Κόρης ἐστὶν ἱερόν, ἐν Ζωστῆρι <δὲ> ἐπὶ θαλάσσης καὶ βωμὸς Ἀθηνᾶς καὶ Ἀπόλλωνος καὶ Ἀρτέμιδος καὶ Λητοῦς. τεκεῖν μὲν οὖν Λητὼ τοὺς παῖδας ἐνταῦθα οὔ φασι, λύσασθαι δὲ τὸν ζωστῆρα ὡς τεξομένην, καὶ τῶι χωρίωι διὰ τοῦτο γενέσθαι τὸ ὄνομα. Προσπαλτίοις δέ ἐστι καὶ τούτοις Κόρης καὶ Δήμητρος ἱερόν, Ἀναγυρασίοις δὲ Μητρὸς θεῶν ἱερόν.
>
> The small demes of Attica, each founded in its own way, offered the following for the record. The people of Halimous have a sanctuary of Demeter Thesmophoros and Korē; and at Zoster on the sea there is also an altar of Athena, Apollo, Artemis and Leto. That Leto gave birth to her children here is not what they claim, but that she loosened her girdle in order to give birth, and that the place got its name because of this. As for the Prospaltians, they too have a sanctuary of Korē and Demeter, and the people of Anagyrous a sanctuary of the Mother of the Gods.
>
> Paus. 1.31.1

To reach Prospalta from Halimous without a long detour a traveller would have to climb over the shoulder of Mount Hymettus: the ridge of Hymettus runs north-south, coming ever closer to the coast, all the way down to Cape Zoster,

[42] Furley 2009, 494–5 unfortunately misreports my Lampeter paper as having proposed that Philicus' knowledge of Attic geography was 'decidedly faulty'.

[43] E.g. Körte 1931, 449; Page 1941, 404 (by implication in his phrase 'Eleusinian mysteries'; Latte 1954, 12 ('Immerhin muß man annehmen, daß Ort der folgenden Handlung (Eleusis) und die Situation der schweigenden Demeter mit genügender Deutlichkeit vorher angegeben war'); Provenzale 2009, 90–100; Giuseppetti 2012, 120–1.

[44] There remains some uncertainty about its precise location: cf. Humphreys 2007, 65.

and becoming lower the further south it goes: it only becomes low enough for a relatively easy crossing to the Mesogeia at Halae Aexonides, where the current motor road climbs over from Voula, south-east of Glyphada, towards Markopoulo and the new airport. Recently a tunnel was contemplated further north to take traffic inland from near Halimous, but it was never built. So a necessarily hilly journey from Halimous to Prospalta could well explain Iambē's mountain aberration. Did Philicus, then, set his story in the deme Prospalta, and had it some connection with the cult of Demeter and Korē there?

One further point in favour of Philicus having located the encounter with Iambē in some deme other than Eleusis is the mismatch between the topographical details of his poem and what we know of the topography of Eleusis.[45] Philicus seems to specify two springs, πηγαί, one associated with Demeter, one with Persephone (39–40) and one of these will be called 'the royal spring', κα]λεῖ̣ται βασ[ί]λεια κρήνη (41). At Eleusis there was a Παρθένιον φρέαρ, 'Maiden's well', by which Demeter sat when she reached Eleusis (*h. Dem.* 99), and some scholars think it is the same well as is called 'Fair dances', Καλλίχορος or Καλλίχορον, at *h.Dem.* 272.[46] The term φρέαρ, 'well', does not appear in our fragments of Philicus' *Hymn*, and the Homeric hymn's φρέαρ was already there when Demeter arrived, and so was not the product of her tears. Nor is it attractive to identify Philicus' two springs with the two salt-water channels at Eleusis called Ῥειτοί, 'Streams', mentioned by Pausanias:[47] each of these was indeed linked with Demeter and Persephone respectively, but there is an important difference between a spring and a salt-water channel. I conclude that there is some case for thinking that Philicus located the encounter with Iambē not at Eleusis but at Prospalta. Certainly lines 35–7 refer to rituals performed at Eleusis. But I propose that in the lacunose beginning of line 38 the speaker's promises shifted to what would be established at Prospalta: that shift could have been briefly indicated by a '(but) here'.

If this were so, then it is tempting to suppose that there is a link with the chorus of what seems to have been Eupolis' first play, Προσπάλτιοι (*Prospaltioi*), whose choice of Prospaltians for what was probably his first comic chorus rightly seemed puzzling to Ian Storey. Storey speculated that

[45] I am very grateful to Richard Seaford for pointing this out to me and for discussing the whole issue.

[46] See Richardson 1974, 326–8.

[47] Paus. 1.38.1, cf. Th. 2.19.2, Hsch. ρ 202 *s.v.* Ῥειτοί. This identification of the κρηναῖον ... ὕδωρ, 'water from a fountain-house' (39) was suggested by Latte 1954, 16 and followed tentatively by Lloyd-Jones and Parsons 1983, 326, who wondered if the springs of lines 40 and 41 were the same or were Parthenius, Callichorus, or Anthius; Furley 2009, 493 takes the κρηναῖον ... ὕδωρ,' fountain water' (39), to be the Ῥειτοί, 'Springs', and the πηγή, spring', created by Demeter's tears perhaps to be the 'Maiden's well' of *h.Dem.* 99.

Eupolis' choice of Προσπάλτιοι was because Prospalta was his own deme.[48] That is possible: we have as yet no hard evidence on which was Eupolis' deme. But those who accept my argument about the relation between the fictional dramatic character Dicaeopolis in Aristophanes' *Acharnians* and the real comic poet Eupolis will suppose it to have been Cholleidae.[49] If that is so, there must have been another reason why Eupolis chose the deme Prospalta to provide the chorus of his first play. A local tradition of iambic αἰσχρολογία would not be a bad explanation – an explanation which invites the question (currently unanswerable) whether Philicus' poem was a voyage into Attic dramatic as well as Attic religious history, a poem that offered an unconventional view of the mythical origins of comedy and its generic αἰσχρολογία.[50] Such an agenda in his *Demeter* would also make especially pointful his strongly dramatic construction of the poem: speeches, characters interacting, and apparently very little narrative – just what one might expect from a poet whose principle compositions were tragedies.[51] It looks as if a full text of Philicus' *Demeter* might have been just as interesting and playfully allusive as Callimachus' *Hymns*, *Aitia* and similarly Attic *Hecale*,[52] and we might wonder whether the wanderings of Iambē on remote mountain paths or the pure springs of Demeter's tears had a self-referential metapoetic function within this undoubtedly innovative composition.[53]

48 Storey 2003, 53: 'we must conclude that Eupolis' deme is not known for certain; much would be explained if it were Prospalta'; 239: 'All in all it seems an out-of-the-way and not especially prominent deme to have supplied a comic chorus, unless it were Eupolis' own deme. What would be so distinctive or funny about it, unless the humour lies in the "backwoods" nature of the people?' My hypothesis offers an answer to this question.

49 Bowie 1988 (Chapter 1 in this volume), cf. Ar. *Ach.* 408 Δικαιόπολις καλεῖ σε Χολλείδης ἐγώ, 'I, Dicaeopolis of Cholleidae, am calling you'.

50 Brown 1990, 187 with n.3 notes the scholion on Ar. *Th.* 86 δεκάτηι (sc. Πυανεψίωνος) ἐν Ἁλιμοῦντι Θεσμοφόρια ἄγεται, 'on the tenth (sc. of Pyanepsion) Thesmophoria are celebrated in Halimous', and the evidence of [Apollod.] *Bibl.* 1.5.1 that Iambē was an *aition* for αἰσχρολογία at the *Thesmophoria*; he seems to conclude that Philicus is offering an *aition* for the *Thesmophoria* at Halimous.

51 Nicholas Richardson has pointed out to me that there were other places in Attica with cults of Demeter and Persephone, and that it might be wrong to privilege Prospalta. The coincidence of Prospalta's separation from Halimous by mountainous territory and its choice by Eupolis for his *Prospaltians* seems to me nevertheless to make this deme an especially strong candidate.

52 Prof. J. Danielewicz kindly allows me to mention some possible allusions he has noticed: μὴ βάλλετε χόρτον αἰγῶν, 'Do not throw goat-fodder' (54), to μὴ βάλλετε, κοῦροι Ἀχαιῶν, 'Do not cast your weapons, youths of the Achaeans' (Il. 3.82); γαστρὸς ἔρεισμα λεπτῆς, 'the support of a delicate stomach' (57) to 'Ἑλλάδος ἔρεισμα, κλειναὶ Ἀθᾶναι, 'the support of Hellas, glorious Athens' (Pi. fr. 76.3 S-M); and (comically) ἐλάφου δίαιτα, 'the diet of a deer' (61) to the technical δίαιτα τῶν ἀνθρώπων, 'men's diet', in Hp. *Aër.* 1.19.

53 I am grateful to Tim Whitmarsh for allowing me to refer to this suggestion which he made during a discussion of this chapter's section on Philicus at Corpus Christi College, Oxford. Note too the epithet λεπτή, 'delicate', of a divine stomach (57). If Gallavotti's supplement in line 8 ἑξαμ[έτρους στενάζει] ('laments in hexameters', see n.18 above) were correct it would offer another (rather different) case of self-referentiality.

3 Philodamus

[Δεῦρ' ἄνα[54] Δ]ιθύραμβε Βάκχ'
ε[ὔιε, ταῦρε, κ]ι̣σ̣σ̣ο̣χαῖ-
τα, Βρόμι', ἠρινα[ῖς ἵκου]
[ταῖσδ'] ἱεραῖς ἐν ὥραις·
Εὐοῖ ὦ Ἰό[βακχ' ὦ ἰὲ Παιά]ν·
[ὃ]ν Θήβαις ποτ' ἐν εὐίαις
Ζη[νὶ γείνατο] καλλίπαις Θυώνα,
πάντες δ' [ἀθά]νατοι [χ]όρευ-
σαν, πάντες δὲ βροτοὶ χ[άρεν]
[σαῖσι], Βάκχιε, γένναις.
Ἰὲ Παιάν, ἴθι σωτήρ,
[εὔφρων τάνδε] πόλιν φύλασσ'
εὐαίωνι σὺν [ὄλβωι.]

[Hither lord, D]ithyrambus, Bacchus
[greeted with 'Euoi', bull, i]vy-tressed,
Roarer, come in [these] spring
times that are holy –
Euoi, O Iobacchus, O Ie Paean –
whom in Thebes, once, where 'Euoi' is cried,
Thyone of fair children [bore] to Zeus,
and all the [imm]ortals [d]anced,
and all mortals r[ejoiced]
[at your] birth, Bacchian.
Ie Paean, come, saviour,
benignly preserve this city
with a blessed era of prosperity.

Ἦν,[55] τότε βακχίαζε μὲν
χθὼ[ν μεγαλώνυμός] τε Κά-
δμου Μινυᾶν τε κόλπ[ος ...]
[..]ωα τε καλλίκαρπος·
Εὐοῖ ὦ Ἰόβ[ακχ' ὦ ἰὲ] Παιάν·
πᾶσα δ' ὑμνοβρύης χόρευ-
ε̣ν̣ [Δελφῶ]ν ἱερὰ μάκαιρα χώρα·
αὐτὸς δ' ἀστε[ρόεν δ]έμας
φαίνων Δελφίσι σὺν κόραι[ς
[Παρν]ασσοῦ πτύχας ἔστας.
Ἰὲ Παιάν, ἴθι σω[τή]ρ,
εὔφρων [τάνδε] πόλιν φύλασσ'
εὐαίωνι σὺν ὄλβωι.

Lo, on that day there was bacchic dance
in the mighty-famed land of Ca-
dmus, and the vale of the Minyans, and [..
[..] oa fair in crops –
Euoi, O Iobacchus, O Ie Paean –
and, brimming with hymns, was dancing
all Delphi's holy, blessed land.
And you yourself, your starry body
displaying, with Delphian girls
stood on the folds of [Parn]assus.
Ie Paean, come, saviour,
benignly preserve this city
with a blessed era of prosperity.

[Νυκτ]ιφαὲς[56] δὲ χειρὶ πάλ-
λων σ̣[έλ]ας ἐνθέοις [σὺν οἴσ-]
τροις ἔμολες μυχοὺς [Ἐλε]υ-
σῖνος ἀν' [ἀνθεμώ]δεις·
Εὐοῖ ὦ Ἰόβακχ' ὦ ἰ[ὲ Παι]άν·
[ἔθνος ἔνθ'] ἅπαν Ἑλλάδος
γᾶς ἀ[μφ' ἐ]νναέταις [φίλοις]
ἐπ[όπ]τ̣αις

And in your hand brandishing your [night]-
lighting flame, with god-possessed frenzy
you went to the vales of [Eleu-]
sis rich in flowers –
Euoi, O Iobacchus, O Ie Paean –
where the whole people of Hellas'
land, alongside [your own] native
witnesses

[54] *CA* pp. 165–9, *SEG* 32.552. The supplement [Δεῦρ' ἄνα] goes back to Weil 1895, and is plausible whether one takes ἄνα as 'come on!' or as vocative of ἄναξ, 'Lord!': cf. Furley and Bremer 2001, ii 58.

[55] Ἆν Vollgraff 1926.

[56] Diels proposed [Νυκτι]φαές for Weil 1895's [ἀστρο]φαὲς ... δ[έρ]ας: σ̣[έλ]ας was proposed by Vollgraff 1926.

ὀργίων ὁσ[ίων Ἴ]ακ-
χον [κλείει σ]ε̣· βροτοῖς πόνων
ὤιξ[ας δ' ὅρ]μ̣ον [ἄμοχθον.][57]
Ἰὲ Παιάν, ἴθι σωτή[ρ,
ε[ὔφρων] τάνδε [πόλιν φύλα]σσ'
εὐαίωνι σὺν ὄλβωι.

of the ho[ly] mysteries, calls upon you
as Iacchus: for mortals from their pains
you op[ened a ha]ven [without toils].
Ie Paean, come, saviour,
benignly preserve this city
with a blessed era of prosperity.

[Παννυχίσιν] δὲ καὶ χοροῖς
γ[… … … …]αις
[… … … … . .]εκγ
[… … … … …]ς
… .
… .

[In all-night festivals] and dances

[… .] υθ … υρ[
. λ . . το … ν[… .]
Ἰὲ] Παι[άν, ἴθι σωτήρ]
εὔφρω[ν τάνδε] π̣ό̣[λιν] φύλασ[σ']
[ε]ὐ[αίωνι σὺν ὄλβωι].

Ie Paean, come, saviour,
benignly preserve this city
with a blessed era of prosperity.

[Ἔ]ν[θεν ἀ]π'[58] ὀλβίας χθονὸς
Θεσ̣[σαλίας] ἔκελσας ἄ-
στη τέμενός τ' Ὀλύμπι[ον],
[Πιερ]ίαν τε κλειτάν·
Εὐοῖ ὦ Ἰόβακχ' [ὦ ἰὲ Παι]άν·
Μοῦσαι [δ'] αὐτίκα παρθένοι
κ[ισσῶι] στε[ψ]άμεναι κύκλωι σε πᾶσαι
μ[έλψαν] ἀθάνα[τον] ἐς ἀεὶ
Παιᾶν' εὐκλέα τ' ὀ[πὶ κλέο]υ-
σαι· [κα]τᾶρξε δ' Ἀπόλλων.
Ἰὲ Παιά[ν, ἴθι σ]ωτήρ,
[εὔ]φρων τ[άνδε] πόλιν φύλ[ασσ'
εὐαίωνι σὺν ὄλβωι.

From that prosperous land
you voyaged to The[ssaly's]
cities and to the holy precinct of Olympus
and [Pier]ia the renowned –
Euoi, O Iobacchus, [O Ie Pae]an –
and the Muses forthwith, the maidens,
crowned themselves with ivy and in a circle
d[anced and sang] around you: 'immortal
forever Paean and renowned' they hymned
with their voice; and Apollo led their song.
Ie Paean, come, saviour
benignly preserve this city
with a blessed era of prosperity.

….σευ . θ . ετ̣αστ . τιμ … … . .
ισορι
….κανεξ̣εσι πυθοχρη̣[στ … .
.] ἰαχὰν …]
…νεαι

…] pronounced by the Pythian[ ] cry

[57] ἄμοχθον Vallois 1931, ἄλυπον Weil 1895.
[58] ἀπ' Vollgraff 1926, ἐπ' Weil 1895.

εὐοῖ ὦ Ἰόβακχ᾽ [ὦ ἰὲ Παιὰ]ν	Euoi, O Iobacchus, O Ie Paean –
. . . εμι . . . . λε . .δαιδ . . . . . .πις	torch (?)
[	
… … . .]νφο[	
[	
παλ	
ρων φιλ	
ων προφη[	prophet[
νομοθετ[	lawmak[er?]
παλλ . κ̣[	
ωσ[	
[	
[	
[	
ναπεμπε̣[	send
οισέβου[σι	who revere
ωσδυσαντ̣[	
σ̣ιν εχρθθπο̣[	
ε χώραν ελ̣ε	land
[… … …]	
πατρωι [… … . . .]	ancestral
Ἰ[ε̣ Παιάν, ἴθι] σωτήρ,	Ie Paean, come, saviour
[εὔφρων] τάνδε πόλιν φύλ[ασ]σ᾽	benignly preserve this city
εὐαίωνι σ[ὺ]ν ὄλβ[ωι.]	with a blessed era of prosperity.
Ἐκτελέσαι δὲ πρᾶξιν Ἀμ-	To bring to completion the work
φικτύονας θ[εὸς] κελεύ-	the god commands the Amphictyons
ει τάχος, ὡ[ς Ἑ]κ̣αβόλος[59]	with speed, so the Far-shooter
μῆνιι̣ ε[. .][60] κατάσχηι.	may restrain his wrath –
Εὐοῖ ὦ [Ἰόβ]ακχ᾽ ὦ ἰὲ Παιάν·	Euoi, O Iobacchus, O Ie Paean –
δε[ῖξαι] δ᾽ ἐγ ξενίοις ἐτεί-	and to put on show in yearly welcoming
οις θεῶν ἱερῶι γένει συναίμωι	of gods, for the holy race, this
τόνδ᾽ ὕμνον, θυσ̣ίαν δὲ φαί-	hymn for his brother, and to present a sacrifice
νει[ν] σὺν Ἑλλάδος ὀλβίας	together with prosperous Hellas'
πα[νδ]ήμοις ἱκετείαις.	people-wide supplications.
Ἰὲ Παιάν, ἴθι σωτήρ,	Ie Paean, come, saviour

59 [Ἑ]κ̣αβόλος Roussel [ἐπ]άβολος Weil 1895.

60 μῆνιι̣ ἐ[κὰς] Marcovich 1975 μῆνιι̣ ἐ[ὴν Furley and Bremer 2001.

εὔ[φρ]ων τάνδε πόλιν φύλασσ’	benignly preserve this city
εὐαίωνι σὺν ὄλβωι.	with a blessed era of prosperity.
Ὦ μάκαρ ὀλβία τε κεί-	O blessed and prosperous is that
νων γεν̣[εὰ] βροτῶν, ἀγή-	generation of mortals, which will
ρων ἀμίαντον ἃ κτίσηι	establish an unageing, unpollutable
ναὸ[ν ἄ]ν̣ακ̣[τι] Φοίβωι	temple for the [lo]rd Phoebus –
Εὐοῖ ὦ Ἰόβακχ’ ὦ ἰὲ Π[αιάν].	Euoi, O Iobacchus, O Ie Paean –
χρύσεον χρυσέοις τύποις	golden with golden images
πα[… … …]ν̣ θ̣εαι ’γκύκλοῦ[νται][61]	[the Paean?] the goddesses encircle
κ̣ω̣[… … …]δογ, κόμαν	[ ] his hair
δ’ ἀργαίνοντ’ ἐλεφαντί[ναν	gleaming in ivory
ἐν] δ’ αὐτόχθονι κόσμωι.	and with an indigenous adornment.
Ἰὲ Παιάν, ἴθι [σωτήρ,]	Ie Paean, come, saviour
εὔφρων τάνδε πόλιν φύλασσ’	benignly preserve this city
εὐαί[ωνι] σὺν ὄλβωι.	with a blessed era of prosperity.
Πυθιάσιν δὲ πενθετή-	And for the penteteric Pythiads
ροις [π]ροπό[λοις] ἔταξε Βάκ-	he has instructed his ministers
χου θυσίαν χορῶν τε πο̣[λ-]	that a sacrifice to Bacchus and for many
[λῶν] κυκλίαν ἅμιλλαν	choruses a circular competition –
(Εὐοῖ ὦ Ἰ[ό]βακχ’ [ὦ ἰὲ Παι]ὰν)	Euoi, O Iobacchus, O Ie Paean –
τεύχειν, ἁλιοφεγ̣γ[έ]σ[ι]ν	shall be created, and like the rays of the rising
δ’ἀ[ντ]ο[λαῖς][62]ἶσον ἁβρὸν ἄγαλμα Βάκχο[υ]	sun a delicate statue of Bacchus
ἐν [ζεύγει][63]χρυσέων λεόν-	in a chariot drawn by golden li-
των στῆσα[ι], ζαθέωι τε τ[εῦ-]	ons shall be set up, and for the most godly
ξαι θεῶι πρέπον ἄντρον.	god shall be created a suitable grotto.
Ἰὲ Παιά[ν, ἴθι σω]τήρ,	Ie Paean, come, saviour
εὔφρων τάνδε πόλ[ιν φ]ύλασσ’	benignly preserve this city
εὐα[ίωνι] σὺν ὄλβωι.	with a blessed era of prosperity.
Ἀλλὰ δέχεσθε Βακχ[ια]σ̣	Come then, welcome the Bacchants’
[τὰ]ν Δι[ό]νυσ[ον, ἐν δ’ ἀγυι-]	Dionys[us, and in the streets]
α̣ῖς ἅμα σὺγ [χορ]οῖσ]ι κ[ι-]	together with choruses with ivy in their
[κλήισκετε] κισσ[οχ]αίταις	tresses call upon him –
Ε[ὐοῖ ὦ Ἰ]όβακχ’ ὦ ἰὲ [Παιὰν]	Euoi, O Iobacchus, O Ie Paean –
πᾶσαν [Ἑλ]λάδ’ ἀν’ ὀ[λβίαν	throughout all of prosperous Hellas

[61] ’γκύκλοῦ[νται] Vollgraff 1926.

[62] ἀ[ντ]ο[λαῖς] Vollgraff 1926, ἀ[ρχ]ο[ύσαις] Weil 1895.

[63] ζεύγει Vollgraff 1926.

παν . . . .ετε . . πολ . . υ . .σ̣τα . .[64]	
ν̣ας . .ρεπι	
λω̣. . . . .ν. . .ιο.ε. . . κυκλι[	
[Χαῖρ'[65] ἄ]να[ξ] ὑγιείας.	[Hail! L]ord of health.
Ἰὲ Πα[ιάν, ἴ]θι σω[τήρ·	Ie Paean, come, saviour
εὔφρων] τάνδε πόλιν φύλασσ'	benignly preserve this city
[εὐαίωνι σὺν ὄλβωι.]	with a blessed era of prosperity.

The Delphic paean for Dionysus by Philodamus, from the Ozolian Locrian city of Scarpheia, is a poem that has been much more discussed than that of Philicus in recent decades.[66] I have chosen it as a palmary example of a paean that is a cult song rather than a literary production, though in using this distinction I agree with those scholars who question it.[67] The paean is known to us because the *stēlē* on which it was inscribed, at some date in the fourth century, was later used for re-paving the Sacred Way in Delphi. Much of it is well preserved, but the central stanzas which might have answered some questions are not. We now seem to have a firm date for its first performance, not because we know anything of Philodamus himself, but because the office of the Delphic eponymous magistrate in charge of arrangements, Etymondas, can be dated to 340/339 BC. At this date the temple of Apollo, destroyed in 373 BC, had not yet been completely rebuilt, and one of the divine commands the paean seeks to reinforce is the acceleration of that work of rebuilding.

But the more important divine instruction is to offer cult to Dionysus, by singing *this* hymn, the paean of Philodamus, in the late spring festival, the Theoxenia; by setting up an ἀγών, 'competition', of κύκλιοι χοροί, 'circular choruses' (i.e. dithyrambs), within the framework of the penteteric summer festival, the Pythia; by erecting a statue of Dionysus in a chariot drawn by golden lions; and by building him an ἄντρον, 'cave'. This substantially extends the role of Dionysus in Delphi. In the archaic and high classical period Dionysus had been worshipped by dithyrambs chiefly during

64 Vollgraff 1926 and Sokolowski 1936 restore this line to include a reference to the worshippers proceeding to Athens.

65 Χαῖρ' Vollgraff 1926.

66 Especially illuminating is the discussion of Clay 1996, *inter alia* carrying further the observations of Käppel 1992 that Philodamus was influenced by the *Homeric hymn to Apollo* and arguing persuasively that it was his model for the paean. For other discussions since the *editio princeps* of Weil 1895 see Furley and Bremer 2001, ii 52–3; since 2001 note Vamvouri Ruffy 2004, 187–206; Bertazzoli 2009; Calame 2009; Marcos Macedo 2010: 268–86. The stone has been re-read by Pascale Brillet-Dubois and Richard Bouchon, who are preparing a new edition and commentary.

67 E.g. Brown 1990: 174–5.

the winter months while Apollo was absent among the Hyperboreans.[68] Now, as well as being given an important place on the West pediment of the reconstructed temple, equipollent to the place of Apollo on the East pediment, Dionysus' apparently growing importance was to be formalised by the promotion to a place in the calendar both of the Theoxenia and of the summer Pythia's ἀγὼν μουσικός, 'musical competition', of the genre particularly associated with his cult, dithyramb.

The 'paean' itself emblematises this promotion by addressing Dionysus in a form particularly associated with Apollo and Asclepius, blending Dionysiac and Apolline cult-titles, emphasising their kinship as brothers, presenting Apollo as issuing the orders for his brother's worship, and modelling itself on the *Homeric hymn to Apollo*.[69]

4 Time and Place, Speech and Narrative in Philodamus

The paean repeatedly anchors its performance in the *hic et nunc*: the *hic* is the *polis* of Delphi, the *nunc* is its spring festival, the Theoxenia, described poetically, to avoid the technical term, in 3–4, as ἠρινα[ῖς ἱκοῦ | ταῖσδ'] ἱεραῖς ἐν ὥραις, '[come in these] spring times that are holy', and in 110–12 (following κελεύει, 'commands', 106–7) ... δε[ῖξαι δ' ἐγ ξενίοις ἐτεί|οις θεῶν ἱερῶι γένει συναίμωι | τόνδ' ὕμνον, 'to put on show in yearly welcoming of gods, for the holy race, this hymn for his brother'. It must be admitted that the deictic ταῖσδ', 'these', of line 4 is a supplement: ταῖς, 'the', or σαῖς, 'your', would also be possible. But the τάνδε, 'this', of the three-line *ephymnion* that closes each thirteen-line stanza is secure in several places: Ἰὲ Παιάν, ἴθι σωτήρ, | εὔφρων τάνδε πόλιν φύλασσ'| εὐαίωνι σὺν ὄλβωι, 'Ie Paian, come, saviour, | benignly preserve this city | with a blessed era of prosperity'. These deictics will continue to constitute *deixis ad oculos* in any Delphic Theoxenia in which τόνδ' ὕμνον, 'this hymn', is sung, and indeed both this τόνδε, 'this', and the τάνδε, 'this', in the phrase τάνδε πόλιν, 'this city', will maintain the same deictic function for a viewer reading the text inscribed in the sanctuary.[70]

But though Delphi is prayed to be the destination of Dionysus now, his initial arrival there in mythical time is only achieved after an extended narrative of his birth and of his welcome as a god by the established dwellers

[68] Cf. Ba. 16.5–11 S–M; Plu. *De E Delph*. 9 = *Mor.* 388d–9c.
[69] Cf. Clay 1996 and above n.66.
[70] For the importance of the act of inscription see LeVen 2014, chapter 7, esp. p. 316.

on Olympus and by mortals in other parts of Greece. This narrative is, characteristically of hymns, introduced by a relative pronoun at lines 6–7:[71] ὃν Θήβαις ποτ᾽ ἐν εὐίαις | Ζη[νὶ] γείνατο καλλίπαις Θυώνα, 'whom in Thebes, once, where "Euoi" is cried, Thyone of the fair children bore to Zeus'. It presents to its audience first the celebrations conducted among the gods (lines 8–10); next those in Thebes, Orchomenus and Euboea (lines 14–17); then, probably, at the Delphi of *illud tempus*, if we accept the supplement [Δελφῶ]ν in lines 19–20: χόρευ|εν [[Δελφῶ]ν ἱερὰ μάκαιρα χώρα, 'Delphi's holy, blessed land was dancing'. At this point we have so far only heard the responses to Dionysus' birth. Then (at line 21) we hear how 'he himself displaying his starry body with the Delphic girls stood on the folds of Parnassus', girls who are the mythical models of the Thyiades: lines 21–3 αὐτὸς δ᾽ ἀστερόεν δέμας | φαίνων Δελφίσι σὺν κόραις | Παρν]ασσοῦ πτύχας ἔστας. Dionysus then went to Eleusis, taking his place in its cult as Iacchus; to somewhere whose identity the loss of the fourth stanza has obscured; then via the cities of Thessaly to Olympus and Pieria, where the Muses in a cyclic song-dance (lines 59–60 κύκλωι σε πᾶσαι | μ[έλψαν, 'all sang and danced around you in a circle') and 'Apollo led their song' (62 [κα]τᾶρξε δ᾽ Ἀπόλλων). This widespread celebration in earth and on Olympus can be read as justification for augmentation of Dionysiac celebration in Delphi, and the cyclic song-dance of Apollo and the Muses offers a divine model both for the prescribed dithyrambic ἀγών and indeed, of course, for 'this hymn' itself, even if its performance will probably not have been cyclic.

As almost always in cult hymns the discourse of the frame is not narrative but address; the dominant mode is imperative. The first *secure* imperatives are in the *ephymnion*, 11–13: Ἰὲ Παιάν, ἴθι σωτήρ | εὔφρων τάνδε πόλιν φύλασσ᾽| εὐαίωνι σὺν ὄλβωι, 'Ie Paian, come, saviour, | benignly preserve this city | with a blessed era of prosperity'. But the imperative ἱκοῦ or ἱκέο, 'come!', is an uncontroversial supplement at lines 3–4, ἠρινα[ῖς ἱκοῦ | ταῖσδ᾽] ἱεραῖς ἐν ὥραις, 'come in these spring times that are holy'. The first two words were suggested by the text's first editor, Weil, to have been Δεῦρ᾽ ἄνα, 'Hither, lord', but they could have been Δεῦρ᾽ ἴθι, 'Come hither'.

The narrative and descriptive tenses introduced by ὃν ... ποτ᾽, 'whom ... once', in line 6 continue into the uncharted wastes of stanzas 6, 7 and 8; punctuated and anchored by the address of the *ephymnion*, and by at least one other address at lines 35–6: [κλείει σ]ε· βροτοῖς πόνων | ὤιξ[ας ὅρ]μον ἄμοχθον, 'calls upon you: for mortals you opened a haven from their pains that is without toil'. When we return to *terra firma* in the much

[71] For this hymnic feature the discussion of Norden 1913, 168–76, remains fundamental.

better preserved stanza 9, the present tense of κελεύει, 'he commands', is no longer to be understood as part of the extended narrative introduced by ὅν ... ποτ'. We are no longer *in illo tempore*. The same communication of a command, now in the aorist, is given near the start of stanza 11: line 132 ἔταξε, 'he instructed'. The instructions set out in detail in stanzas 9 and 11 are syntactically dependent on these two verbs of command. Between stanzas 9 and 11 there is one, 10, which opens with a *makarismos*, and on it too depend instructions, or perhaps a description of what singers and audience already knew to be the plan for the decoration of the temple of Apollo. The final, twelfth stanza reverts to imperatives with the surprising δέχεσθε, 'welcome' (line 144), an imperative addressed not to the god but to the Delphians.

To recapitulate, then, the only recurrent use of verbs in narrative tenses is within the account of Dionysus' birth and reception, introduced by the ὅν ... ποτ', 'whom ... once', of lines 6–7; there are one or two encapsulated in the *makarismos*; and the only first-order narrative verbs are κελεύει and ἔταξε.

This recipe is not unusual in paeans either inscribed or 'literary', but of course it is in varying degrees different from what we find in Homeric hymns or the hymns of Callimachus. The subordinate role of narrative and the primary role of 'address' – which is also the stance of the *meshymnion* that constitutes line 5 of every stanza – may be one of the main reasons (perhaps *the* main reason) why within the narrative we find little or no direct speech – contrast the extensive and varied play with direct speech in Homeric hymns, Bacchylides' dithyrambs, Callimachus' hymns, and the hymn of Philicus discussed above.

In their translation Furley and Bremer put inverted commas round 'Forever immortal and famous Paian!' in their sentence 'proclaiming you to be "Forever immortal and famous Paian!"': the Greek, however, is less decisively in favour of treating this as a quotation in *oratio recta*: μ[έλψαν] ἀθάνα[το]ν ἐς ἀεὶ | Παιᾶν' εὐκλέα τ' ὀ[πὶ κλέο]υ|σαι, lines 60–2. Indeed to me the case seems to be equally strong for taking the following words in line 62 [κα]τᾶρξε δ' Ἀπόλλων, 'and Apollo led the song', as leading into what becomes *both* the paean's *ephymnion and* the words with which Apollo led off his cyclic chorus, Ἰὲ Παιάν, ἴθι σωτήρ, | εὔφρων τάνδε πόλιν φύλασσ'| εὐαίωνι σὺν ὄλβωι, even if that interpretation requires τάνδε πόλιν, 'this city', momentarily to acquire the reference of the 'city' of the gods, Olympus. As observed by José Marcos, at this point in the paean the song of the Muses and of the chorus is the same, the barriers between myth and performance collapse, and the singing of these words by the Muses legitimises the chorus' own innovation of hymning Dionysus as Paian.[72]

The other place in their translation where Furley and Bremer use inverted commas (as well as to begin and end the whole paean) is in the twelfth and last stanza: here they render lines 145–9 'and call upon him in your streets with dances performed by people with ivy in their hair who sing "Euhoi, o io Bakchos, o ie Paian!" all over blessed Hellas ….' The Greek runs: Ἀλλὰ δέχεσθε Βακχ[ια]| [σ̣τὰ]ν Δι[ό]νυσ[ον, ἐν δ' ἀγυι]| α̣ἷς ἅμα σὺγ [χοροῖσ]ι κ[ι]| [κλήισκετε] κισσ[οχ]αίταις | Ε[ὐοῖ ὦ 'Ι]όβακχ' ὦ ἰὲ [Παιὰν] | πᾶσαν [Ἑλ]λάδ' ἀν' ὀ[λβίαν. It seems to me that we can take this *meshymnion*, now heard for the twelfth time, *both* as the *meshymnion* we have grown to love (or hate) *and* as an internal accusative after κ[ι-]|[κλήισκετε]: 'summon him with the call "Euhoi, o io Bakchos, o ie Paian"'. Even if this slight modification is not accepted, we are not dealing with a fully blown case of direct speech: this is not a sentence with a verb, it is no more than an invocation.

Overall, then, there are no clear cases where characters mentioned within the song, whether that song takes the form of prayer, of praise or of narrative subordinated by an introductory relative pronoun, are unambiguously given embedded utterances.

This matches what we find in other cult hymns. The only two cases of embedded utterances I have found in Furley and Bremer are:

(i) The anonymous Epidaurian hymn to the mother of the gods of the fourth or third centuries BC, their hymn 6.2,[73] in which she is addressed (by Zeus?): 'Μάτηρ, ἄπιθ' εἰς θεούς,| καὶ μὴ κατ' ὄρη π̣λ̣α̣ν̣[ῶ],| μή σε χαροποὶ λέον|τες ἢ πολιοὶ λύκοι'·|'καὶ οὐκ ἄπειμι εἰς θεούς,| ἂν μὴ τὰ μέρη λάβω,| τὸ μὲν ἥμισυ οὐρανῶ,| τὸ δὲ ἥμισυ γαίας,| πόντω τὸ τρίτον μέρος·| χοὔτως ἀπελεύσομαι', 'Mother, be off to the gods! Don't wander over the hills in case the ravening lions or timber-wolves [get] you …' and she answers: 'I won't go off to the gods unless I receive my share: a half of sky above and a half of the earth and, third, a half of the sea. Only then will I go.'

(ii) In the dactylic hexameter section (F) of the set of inscriptions which give us the paean of Isyllus.[74] Here the encounter of Isyllus' son with Asclepius involves a short appeal by the boy and a long reply by Asclepius. Since this is in the hexameter section, not in the melic paean, it is not a counter-example.

[72] Marcos Macedo 2010, 282–3.

[73] Furley and Bremer 2001, i 214–24 (where lines 15–24 of their text = *IG* iv^2.1 131.12–17); ii 167–75.

[74] *IG* iv^2.1 128.

Finally a brief mention of the granting of privileges at Delphi not only to Philodamus but also to his two brothers. As Jenny Strauss Clay reports, Dirk Obbink made the attractive suggestion that the brothers of Philodamus were equal partners in the production of the paean, and she suggests herself their roles were perhaps those of χορηγός, 'chorus-leader', διδάσκαλος, 'trainer', and κιθαριστής '*cithara*-player' (this last presumably Philodamus himself).[75] But as is clear from the *Pythais* inscription of two centuries later (discussed below), there were several important roles that might be played by the poet's brothers, and all we can confidently exclude is the curious suggestion that they jointly composed the paean.[76] It is also now clear, after a new reading of the stone, that on it no causal connection is explicitly set out between the composition of the hymn and the granting of the Delphic privileges.[77]

5 Limenius

Πα]ι̣ὰν δὲ καὶ π[ροσό]διον εἰς τ[ὸν θεὸν ὃ ἐπό]η̣σε[ν καὶ
προσεκιθάρισε]ν Λιμήνι[ος Θ]ο̣ίνο[υ Ἀθηναῖος.

The paean and prosodion to t[he god which was compos]ed [and accompanied on the cithara] by [the Athenian] Limenius, son of [Th]oenu[s].

[Ἴ]τ' ἐπὶ τηλέσκοπον τάνδε Παρ[νασί]αν [φιλόχορον]
δικόρυφον κλειτύν, ὕμνων κα̣[τά]ρχ[εσθ' ἐμῶν,[78]
Πιερίδες, αἳ νιφοβόλους πέτρας ναίεθ' [Ἑλι]κωνίδ̣[ας·]
μέλπετε δὲ Πύθιον χ[ρ]υσοχαίταν ἕ[κα]τον εὐλύραν
Φοῖβον, ὃν ἔτικτε Λα̣τὼ μάκαιρα πα[ρὰ λίμναι] κλυτᾶι,
χερσὶ γλαυκᾶς ἐλαίας θιγοῦσ̣'[ὄζον ἐν ἀγωνίαι]ς ἐριθα[λῆ.]
πᾶ[ς δὲ γ]άθησε πόλος οὐράνιος [ἀννέφελος ἀγλαός,]
ν̣ηνέμους δ' ἔσχεν αἰθὴρ ἀε[λλῶν ταχυπετ]εῖς [δρ]όμους, λῆξε δὲ βα-
ρύβρομον Νη[ρέως ζαμενὲς ο]ἶδμ' ἠδὲ μέγας Ὠκεανός,
ὃς πέριξ [γᾶν ὑγραῖς ἀγ]κάλαις ἀμπέχει.

[75] Clay 1996, 87 n.9.

[76] Oddly put forward by Vamvouri Ruffy 2004 and espoused by Marcos Macedo 2010.

[77] I am grateful to Pascale Brillet and Richard Bouchon for allowing me to refer to this important new information given in a paper by Pascale Brillet on Philodamus' poem delivered to a symposium held at Stanford University on 25 and 26 April 2014.

[78] The postponement of δ' in the phrase κα̣[τά]ρχ[ετε δ' ἐμῶν], 'and begin my ...', which is usually supplemented, is unsatisfactory; the middle κα̣[τά]ρχ[εσθ', 'begin', is as well attested as the active, and indeed more often in religious contexts, cf. LSJ s.v. II.2.

τότε λιπὼν Κυνθίαν νῆσον ἐ[πέβα θεὸ]ς πρω[τό]καρ-
πον κλυτὰν Ἀτθίδ' ἐπὶ γαλ[όφωι πρῶνι] Τριτωνίδος·
μελίπνοον δὲ Λίβυς αὐδὰγ χέω[ν λωτὸς ἀνέ-
μελ]πεν [ἁ]δεῖαν ὄπα μειγνύμενος αἰόλ[οις κιθάρι]ο[ς
μέλεσιν, ἅ]μα δ' ἴαχεν πετροκατοίκητος ἀχ[ὼ Παιὰν ἰὲ Παιάν·(?)]
[ὁ] δὲ γέγαθ', ὅτι νόωι δεξάμενος ἀμβρόταν
Δι̣[ὸς ἐπέγνω φρέ]ν'· ἀνθ' ὧν ἐκείνας ἀπ' ἀρ-
χᾶς Παιήονα κικλήισκ[ομεν ἅπας] λα̣ὸς α[ὐτο]χθόνων
ἠδὲ Βάκχου μέγας θυρσοπλὴ[ξ ἑσμὸς ἱ]ε-
ρὸς τεχνιτῶν ἔνοικος πόλει Κεκροπία̣.
ἀλ̣[λὰ χρησμ]ωιδὸν ὃς ἔχεις τρίποδα, βαῖν' ἐπὶ θεοστιβ[έα
τάνδε Π]αρνασίαν δειράδα φιλένθεον.
ἀμφὶ πλόκ[αμον σὺ δ' οἰ]νῶ[πα] δάφνας κλάδον
πλεξάμενος ἀπ[λέτους θεμελίους] ἀμβρόται χειρὶ σύ-
ρων, ἄναξ, Γ[ᾶς πελώρωι συναντᾶις[79] τ]έραι.
ἀλλὰ Λατοῦς ἐρατογ[λέφαρον ἔρνος ἀγρία]ν παῖδα Γᾶ[ς]
τ' ἔπεφνες ἰοῖς, ὁ[μοίως τε Τιτυὸν ὅτε] πόθον ἔσχε μα̣τρὸς [φίλας ?]
[. .]θῆρα κατέκτ[α]ς οσ[. . . .
[...σ]ύριγμ' ἀπε[υν]ῶν[. . .

εἶτ'] ἐφρούρε[ις δὲ Γᾶ[ς ἱερόν, ὦναξ, παρ' ὀμφαλόν, ὁ βάρ-]
βαρος Ἄρης ὅτε [τε]ὸν μαντόσ[υνον οὐ σεβίζων ἕδος]
[πολυκυθ]ὲς λη<ι>ζόμενος, ὤλεθ' ὑγρᾶι χι[όνος ἐν ζάλαι.]
[ἀλλ', ὦ Φοῖβε,] σῶιζε θεό-
κτιστον Παλλάδος [ἄστυ καὶ
λαὸν κλεινόν, σύν] τε θεά,
τόξων δεσπότι Κρησίω[ν]
κυνῶ[ν τ' Ἄρτεμις, ἠδὲ Λα-
τὼ] κυδίστα̣· καὶ ναέτας
Δελφῶν τ[ημελεῖθ' ἅμα τέ-
κνοις συμ]βίοις δώμα̣σιν ἀ-
πταίστους, Βάκχου [θ' ἱερονί-
καισιν εὐμε]νεῖς μόλετε
προσπόλοισ[ι], τάν τε δορί-
σ̣[τεπτον κάρτεϊ] Ῥωμαίω[ν]
ἀρχὰν αὔξετ' ἀγηράτωι
θάλλ̣[ουσαν φερε]νίκαν.

[Co]me to this slope seen from far off, Parnassus, friend to dances,
with twin peaks, lead off my hymns,
Pierian goddesses, who dwell on the snow-struck crags of Helicon,

[79] The imperfect συνήντας, 'you confronted', would fit the narrative better.

and sing and dance the Pythian with golden tresses, the far-shooter,
fine with the lyre,
Phoebus, whom blessed Leto bore by the famous [lake], clutching
with her hands a grey olive's ever-green [shoot in her labour-pain]s.
And the whole vault of the heavens rejoiced [cloudless and gleaming]
and the bright air kept windless the swift-flying paths of its storms,
and there ceased
the deep-roaring, powerful surge of Nereus, and mighty Ocean,
who enfolds the earth all around in his liquid embrace. Then leaving
the Cynthian island the god set foot upon the first land to bear crops,
renowned Attica, on Tritonis' headland crowned with earth; and the
African reed poured forth its honey-strained voice mingled with
c[ithara's shi]mmering
[tunes]; and at the same time there called out the rock-settled one,
Echo, ['Paean, Ie Paean'(?)].
And he rejoiced because he took in with his mind the immortal
[thought] of Zeus, and [recognised it]. For these reasons from that
starting point
we call upon 'Paeeon', we [the whole] people of those who are natives
and Bacchus' mighty sacred swarm, struck by his thyrsus,
of artists, dwelling in the city of Cecrops. But you who control the
tripod where [oracles] are sung, come to this god-trodden
ridge of Parnassus that loves divine possession.
And about your wine-dark locks you bound a shoot of laurel
And dragging along im[mense foundation-stones] with your
immortal hand,
Lord, you joined battle with the gigantic monster of the Earth.
But you, [offspring] of Leto with desire [in your eyes], slew both the
[savage] child
of Earth with your arrows, and l[ikewise Tityus, when] he conceived a
longing for your mother
you killed the wild beast[...........]
a hissing from its lair[...........]
Then you stood guard by the Earth's holy navel, O Lord, when the bar-
barian's war-force, failing to revere your oracle and plundering your
seat
with its many treasures, perished in the wet hail of a snowstorm.
[But come, Phoebus], keep safe Pallas' god-
founded [city and its
famous people, and together with you] the goddess,
mistress of Cretan bows
and of dogs, Artemis, and Le-
to of greatest fame; and [protect]

the dwellers in Delphi together with their
children, their wives, their homes
unshaken, and to the sacred victors,
attendants of Bacchus, come
benignly, and augment the spear-
garlanded empire of Rome with power
that ages not so that it
flourishes and wins victories.

My third section offers a brief discussion of Limenius because his poem and its associated epigraphic documents combine to offer information of a sort available neither for the hymn of Philicus nor for the paean of Philodamus.[80]

The text of Limenius' poem (printed above) has been preserved on the south wall of the Athenian Treasury at Delphi, alongside another paean by a poet and musician whose name has been convincingly argued by Bélis to be Ἀθήναιος, 'Athenaeus' – as against earlier interpretations of the stone's ΑΘΗΝΑΙΟΣ which took it to be the ethnic Ἀθηναῖος, 'Athenian'.[81] Both paeans were argued by Bélis to have been performed in 128 BC;[82] Furley and Bremer argued for performance at the successive Pythaids of 138 BC and 128 BC;[83] Rutherford assigned the paean of Athenaeus to 128/7 BC and that of Limenius to 106/5 BC.[84]

The texts are inscribed close to those of official documents relating to administration of *Pythaides* sent in 138/7, 128/7, 106/5 and 98/97 BC.[85] Both poems are accompanied by musical notation, which has encouraged attempts at re-creation.[86] Its superscription identifies its composer and citharistic accompanist as an Athenian Limenius, son of Thoenus. The father's name comes not from this text, where only Θ]ọίνο[υ can be read, but from one of the *Pythais* documents which names Limenius, son of Thoenus, as one of the seven κιθαρισταί, '*cithara*-players', who took part in the *Pythais* of 128 BC, the archonship of Dionysius.[87] As Furley and

[80] *FdD* iii 2.138. For discussions between Weil and Reinach 1909–13 and 2000 see Furley and Bremer 2001, ii 84–85; since 2001 Vamvouri Ruffy 2004, 171–9 (cf. already Vamvouri 1998).

[81] Bélis 1992, 53–4, noting that one of the *choros* of 128 BC is named as Ἀθήναιος Ἀθηναίου', Athenaeus son of Athenaeus', *FdD* iii.2 no. 47 line 19.

[82] Bélis 1988; Bélis 1992, 140–1; Bélis 2001.

[83] Furley and Bremer 2001, i 129–31.

[84] Rutherford 2004, 76 (following Schröder 1999).

[85] *FdD* iii.2 nos 11, 47, 48 and 49. For brief but illuminating discussions of the nature of *Pythaides* see Rutherford 2004, 76–81, and further Rutherford 2013.

[86] References and links in Furley and Bremer 2001; Hagel and Harrauer 2005 (with a CD).

[87] *FdD* iii.2 no. 47 line 23.

Bremer rightly insist, it is only barely conceivable that these are not the same κιθαριστής.[88] One could add that the name is extremely unusual – nobody else of that name from Attica or anywhere else in the published volumes of *LGPN*, though one or two names quite close to Limenius turn up in the imperial period. The name of his father, Thoenus – also the name of a brother who, like Limenius, was one of the κιθαρισταί on the *Pythais* – is more common, but it is very likely this is the same father and son Thoenus whom we know in 131 BC from the deme Atene, way down near Sunium.[89]

Both Limenius and brother Thoenus are professional musicians, members of the Athenian chapter of the Dionysiac *technitae*.[90] They are only two of a huge number of performers which the document shows to have taken part in the *Pythais* of 128/7 BC; thirty-nine people to sing the paean itself (τοὺς ἀισομένους τὸν παιᾶνα εἰς τὸν θεόν, 'those who are to sing the paean to the god');[91] two auletes; seven citharists; one aulode; either two or three citharodes; eight comic performers (κωμωιδοί); two tragic performers (τραγωιδοί); one κωμικός, 'comic actor'. Three of the singers also figure in the list as χοροδιδάσκαλοι τῶν Πυθαϊστῶν, 'chorus-trainers of the *Pythaistae*'.

In my view Limenius was not a bad wordsmith, commendable for much more than his striking neologism πετροκατοίκητος, 'rock-settled' (line 15);[92] and although there are many similarities to the closely contemporary paean of Athenaeus, the forty-seven surviving lines of Limenius' poem are more interesting than the twenty-five of that of Athenaeus.[93] Like the poem of Athenaeus, that of Limenius uses no refrain, neither meshymnic nor epiphthegmatic. It is widely thought that the first thirty-three lines in a cretic-paeonic metre are the paean proper, and the last fourteen lines, in an aeolic metre, are what is termed π[ροσό]διον (*prosodion*), 'processional hymn', in the superscription.[94] But even in this last section there is no refrain, and indeed in neither section do we certainly hear Ἰὲ Παιάν, 'Ie Paean'.[95] It is of course possible that the choir was trained to intersperse paeanic utterances that were not included in the inscribed text.

[88] Furley and Bremer 2001, i 129 n.103; so too Stefanis 1988, 284 no. 1553.

[89] *LGPN* ii 1994 *s.n.* Θοῖνος, cf. Stefanis 1988, 223 no. 1223.

[90] On the Dionysiac *technitai* in this period see Le Guen 2001, Aneziri 2003.

[91] *FdD* iii.2 no. 47 line 9.

[92] If, of course, it *is* a neologism. That it can be accommodated in a hexameter opens the possibility that Limenius found it in a lost epic mentioning Athens.

[93] For some good points about the poem's structure, especially its relation of past to present, see Marcos Macedo 2010, 221–31.

[94] Furley and Bremer 2001; Rutherford 2004, 81; Marcos Macedo 2010, 224–5.

[95] Unless, with Pöhlmann 1970, one restores the end of line 15 (his line 17), where the line-length is uncertain, as ἀχ[ώ παιάν ἰὲ παιάν], 'ech[o paian ie paian', a supplement printed by Powell 1936; Bélis 1992; and Rutherford 2004, 81; but not noticed by Furley and Bremer 2001, i 92–100.

The paean gives no strong sense of performance at a particular time – Limenius says nothing explicit about the season of the year, unlike Alcaeus in the 580s BC[96] and Philodamus in 340/39 BC. The epithet νιφοβόλους, 'snow-struck', given to the πέτρας, 'crags', of Helicon (line 3) may point to performance in spring rather than high summer, but need not pick out a feature of these rocks' present condition (compare the snow on Parnassus in line 17 of Athenaeus' paean). Nor is there any reference to the divine sign, lightning observed over Mount Parnes in Attica, that presumably had catalysed the sending of the *Pythais*.

On the other hand three horizontal spatial axes stand out, converging upon Delphi, identified as the place of performance by the deictic τάν[δ]ε, 'this', in the command of the first two lines – [Ἴ]τ' ἐπὶ τηλέσκοπον τάν[δ]ε Πα[ρνασί]αν [φιλόχορον] | δικόρυφον κλειτύν, 'Come to this slope seen from far off, Parnassus, friend to dances, with twin peaks' – and again in the parallel invocation to Apollo at lines 21–2, βαῖν' ἐπὶ θεοστιβ[έα | τάνδε Π]αρνασίαν δειράδα φιλένθεον, 'come to this god-trodden ridge of Parnassus that loves divine possession'. These axes are: (a) the movement of the Heliconian Muses to Delphi to lead the paean's performance (ὕμνων κ[ατά]ρχ[ετε δ' ἐμῶν, 'lead off my hymns', line 2); (b) the movement of Apollo from his birth on Delos to his arrival at Delphi, where he destroys the Pytho and then the invading Gauls; (c) the movement of the Pythaist chorus from Athens to Delphi, a movement implicit in the performance that the audience is hearing and that later readers of the texts on the wall of the Athenian treasury are reading.

The shortest journey is that of the Muses. Though they are in some sense, perhaps by origin, Pierian,[97] their current home is taken to be Mount Helicon, which will have been prominently visible on the Pythaists' left for the central section of their journey to Delphi, and which, as the Dionysiac *technitai* will have known very well, was closely associated with the Muses in the festival of the *Mouseia* which was now being regularly celebrated at Thespiae.[98] The longest journey is that of Apollo. Six lines (5–10) draw us into the miraculous moment of his birth on Delos: Delos had been administered by Athens for some forty years, since 166 BC, and the island's Athenian credentials are enhanced by the innovative detail that it was an olive tree, not a palm, that Leto clutched when in labour (line 6).[99] At the same time

[96] Alc. fr. 307, cf. Furley and Bremer 2001, ii 1; Bowie 2009a, 120–1 (Chapter 13, 300 in Volume 1).

[97] Cf. Hes. *Th.* 53 with West *ad loc.*

[98] For the reorganisation of the Thespian *Mouseia* late in the third century BC see Knoepfler 1996; for their late-Hellenistic and Roman development Robinson 2012.

[99] As an anonymous referee points out, earlier writing does refer to a sacred olive tree on Delos (Hdt. 4.34.2, Eur. *IT* 1100, Call. *Del.* 262 and fr. 94), but not as a support for Leto in labour.

Limenius extends the impact of Apollo's birth to the whole world – even the surrounding Ocean, increasingly familiar to the Greek world of the later second century BC, was hushed. The next ten lines, 11–20, take Apollo to Attica. Here Limenius naturally follows the Atheno-centric view, first found in Aes. *Eu.* 9–10, that Apollo made his mainland Greek landfall not in Boeotia but Attica. On this view his journey from Athens was the mythical model for that of the *Pythais* itself,[100] and as has been noticed, this bolsters the Athenian claim to the special favour of Pythian Apollo.[101] Here the response of Echo is presented as an etymology for the cult title Παιήων, 'Paeēon', and Apollo's pleasure when he visited Athens is made the basis of his cult there, offered by the whole autochthonous λαός, 'people' (lines 18–19) and by the great swarm of Dionysiac *technitai* resident in Athens. By this doublet Limenius endorses the right of the Pythaists to represent the Athenian people as a whole, and glosses over the fact that by 128 BC many of these professionals were not autochthonous Athenians.

Apollo's journey from Athens to Delphi is not narrated: it can be inferred from the journey of the Pythaists that imitates it.[102] Instead Apollo is now, at lines 21–2, asked to come in a paradeigmatic cletic imperative, ἀ[λλὰ χρησμ]ωιδὸν ὃς ἔχεις τρίποδα, βαῖν', 'But you who control the tripod where [oracles] are sung, come', which might be seen to operate in the same way as the meshymnic invocations of Philodamus, and at the least offers a brief change of perspective from the narrative tenses that go before and after. More narrative of the god's arrival certainly follows: his encounter with the Pytho at lines 23–5 (cf. Athenaeus' paean lines 19–22) leads into an apostrophe congratulating him on his victory. Like Athenaeus, Limenius at line 30 mentions the monster's hissing, [σύ]ριγμ',[103] though he first teases his audience with a verb of quite different sense but similar sound, σύρων, 'dragging', used at lines 24–5 of Apollo himself. Given the fame attaching to the νόμος Πυθικός, 'Pythian nome', still well known to Pollux in the late second century AD, and given the fact that this auletic nome represented different stages in the struggle between Apollo and Pytho, it must have been a great temptation for a musician to recall the music of that nome at this point of the narrative, and I recommend those interested in trying to recover something of the νόμος Πυθικός to ponder the musical accompaniment to these lines.

[100] See Sommerstein in his commentary on Aes. *Eu. ad loc.*, citing Ephorus *FGrH* 70 F31(b) = Str. 9.422. This may also be a version that is represented on the pediment of the temple of Apollo at Delphi built by the Alcmaeonids, cf. Athanassaki 2011, 249–52.

[101] Vamvouri 1998, 49 ff.; Furley and Bremer 2001, ii 96.

[102] A correspondence also noted by Rutherford 2004, 81.

[103] Athenaeus lines 21–2, *h.Ap.* 360–2.

Apollo's next achievement, lines 27–9, *may* have been the killing of Tityus, though in Strabo's reworking of Ephorus this achievement is set during his journey from Athens to Delphi.

As in Athenaeus' paean, the final manifestation of Apollo's divine power is the destruction of the Gallic invaders of 278 BC. The last lines shift from cretic-paeonics to glyconics to sing the prayer that Apollo, Artemis and Leto preserve Athens, the inhabitants of Delphi, the Dionysiac *technitae* and the Roman Empire.

The singers have an almost equal amount of narrative and imperative verbs. Within narrative there is no speech, direct or even indirect.

6 Brief Conclusions

Despite using a melic metre Philicus presents his hymn in a very different way from the paean poets, Philodamus and Limenius. His exploitation of speech follows a Greek narrative habit that we see already in the *Iliad*, *Odyssey* and *Homeric hymns* and that is prominent in much melic poetry – e.g. in Stesichorus, in Pindar's *epinicia* and in Bacchylides' *epinicia* and dithyrambs – but is rare in Pindar's paeans and in surviving cult hymns. His interest in the cults of old Greece matches that of contemporary poet-scholars with Alexandrian connections, Callimachus and Apollonius, and the interest I have suggested in the origins of Attic comedy is also found in his fellow-member of the Pleiad, Lycophron of Chalcis. If I am right to propose a focus on the cult of Demeter and Korē at Prospalta rather than, or at least alongside, the big names of Eleusis and Halimous, this chimes with Callimachus' preference for the off-beat and marginal over the central and well-trodden.

In Philodamus and Limenius the framework is one of appeal, prayer and exhortation, and the audience and reader are shifted into narrative by a relative pronoun. Within this assemblage of appeal, prayer, exhortation and narrative almost the only voice that can be heard is that of the singing chorus. Speech in the mouths of others is hard to establish, and if it is there the utterances are attributable *both* to these others (Philodamus' Muses; perhaps Limenius' Echo) *and* at the same moment to the chorus. It is as if the chorus' urgent need to hold the attention of the god cannot be imperilled by another potentially distracting voice. These poets' spatial horizons, however, are much broader than those of Philicus. Whereas Philicus' *Demeter* seems (like Callimachus' *Hecale* to which it is often compared) to have confined its universe to a few Attic demes, and may indeed have set its action in just one deme, both Philodamus and Limenius ask their audiences and readers to sweep across the Greek world, in the former's poem tracking the news of Dionysus' birth and the spread of his cult, in the latter's the path of Apollo to Delphi where the paean is to be performed and inscribed.

12 Greek Sophists and Greek Poetry in the Second Sophistic (1989)

1 Introduction

The role of poetry and poets in Greek society of the Second Sophistic is easy to underestimate. Sophists and philosophers had undoubtedly seized the intellectual high ground, and their medium of communication was almost wholly prose. So too are the other great genres whose texts edified and entertained readers throughout the Hellenised Eastern Mediterranean and in many cities of the Latin West – historiography and the novel. Yet it is wrong to see this world as one where poetry, sole literary queen in the archaic period and still dominant in the fifth century BC, has surrendered all her powers and functions to prose and ekes out a servile existence as her handmaiden. Much poetry was written in the period, and the capacity to write it was respected, even if its quality was rarely high. I have attempted to sketch outlines of its place in the intellectual history of the period elsewhere.[1] Here I wish to focus on the place of poetry in the cultural universe of the sophists. This question has two aspects. The one to which I give most attention comprises the poems actually composed by sophists and the conclusions they permit about their view of poetry. But first I consider briefly the other aspect, which has often been discussed, the way in which sophists use and react to poetry in their prose works.

2 Poetic Rhetoric

When Nicagoras of Athens called tragedy 'the mother of the sophists', Hippodromus of Larissa capped the remark by calling Homer their father: so we are told by his contemporary Philostratus, who goes on to say that Hippodromus also called Homer the φωνή, 'voice', of sophists, Archilochus their πνεῦμα, 'breath' (*VS* 2.27.620). The verdicts may exaggerate in their attempt to coin a striking aphorism, but they are correct to assert a close relationship between sophistic rhetoric and classical poetry.

[1] Bowie 1989b, 1990b (Chapters 13 and 14 in this volume).

This relationship took a variety of forms. In the realm of εὕρεσις/*inventio*, 'discovery of material', poetry often supplied the subject of a declamation, e. g. Dio's Τρωικὸς λόγος, '*Trojan oration*' (*Or.* 11) and Aristides' πρεσβευτικὸς λόγος, '*Speech for an envoy* (to Achilles)' (16 L–B), or ideas for handling its arguments. The poets were drawn upon for vocabulary and figures, and exploited by quotation or allusion. Part of the purpose of this was to exploit the authority of the classical past through the medium of the authors whom all πεπαιδευμένοι, 'educated men', had read at school,[2] and to offer such an audience the pleasant *frisson* of recognition. Quotation from a poet could also be used to back up a point. In these respects the poets were used no differently from classical prose authors. But quotation from poetry could also contribute to stylistic level: Hermogenes Περὶ ἰδεῶν, '*On ideas*' (2.4, 331 and 334 Rabe) observed that citations from the poets conferred γλυκύτης, 'sweetness', and poetic vocabulary, combined with the rhythmical and intoned delivery that some speakers affected, could assimilate declamatory rhetoric to sung poetry.

One might suppose that in all this there is evidence of nothing other than a high respect for poetry and its power. Occasionally, however, we find suggestions in our texts that prose rhetoric is consciously competing with poetry, and some scholars have concluded that prose was not simply the dominant literary medium of the sophistic period, but that some of its exponents wished to displace poetry and to arrogate every field for prose. This last judgement is almost certainly wrong: but before attempting to revise it I wish briefly to expand some of the general points I have already made.

First, the phenomenon of quotation from and allusion to the classical poets. The foundations for a study of this were laid by Schmid's work *Der Atticismus*.[3] Schmid offers lists of words drawn from the poets by Dio of Prusa (i 148–54), Lucian (i 313–52), Aristides (ii 187–213), Aelian (iii 178–228) and Philostratus (iv 266–337). The extent and manner of Lucian's quotation of, and allusion to, the poets (as likewise to prose-writers) was tabulated and assessed by Householder,[4] and a useful but less full and analytic list is included in the *index nominum* of Macleod.[5] His knowledge and use of Homer was exhaustively investigated by Bouquiaux-Simone.[6] A brief

[2] See North 1952; Morgan 1998; Cribiore 1996, 2001b.

[3] Schmid 1887–96.

[4] Householder 1941, 41, where table 1 arranges quotations by Lucian in order of frequency, and 44, where table 1a gives the frequency of quotation in fourteen imperial texts: Aelian, Marcus Aurelius, scholia on Aristophanes, Athenaeus, Demetrius, Dio, Dionysius of Halicarnassus, Longinus, Lucian, Maximus, Pausanias, Plutarch, Pollux, and *Rhetores graeci* (ed. Spengel).

[5] Macleod 1987.

[6] Bouquiaux-Simone 1968.

note and discussion of Favorinus' use of the poets was offered by Barigazzi,[7] and figures for Aristides' quotations from the poets by Behr.[8] A thorough investigation of the knowledge and exploitation of Homer by Dio of Prusa, Maximus of Tyre and Aelius Aristides was conducted by Kindstrand; Maximus' range of knowledge and use of the poets has been discussed by Trapp.[9]

Although there are individual variations, the broad picture is similar for all these writers. Homer leads the field by far, and the *Iliad* is more often exploited than the *Odyssey*, even by Dio despite his recurrent adoption of an Odyssean *persona*.[10] Euripides comes second. Thereafter Hesiod, Pindar, Aeschylus, Sophocles, Aristophanes and Menander may be found (not always in the same order of frequency) before we reach a dozen other poets who are only occasionally quoted.

The variations are not such as to suggest that works quoted or alluded to by sophists in their declamatory work (Dio, Favorinus, Maximus, Aristides' *Orations*) or in writing variously related (Lucian, Aristides' *Sacred Tales*, Aelian, Philostratus) are significantly different from the range available to other writers of the period.[11] Occasionally there are notable deviations. Aristides seems to be especially fond of Aeschylus and Pindar, whereas Lucian's citations of Sophocles and Aeschylus fall behind those of Euripides even further than the norm, and he quotes remarkably little Aristophanes for one who both claims to draw upon him (*Bis acc.* 32) and has been shown to do so for themes and structures.[12]

Unsurprising is the neglect, almost total, of writers later than Menander. Three times (or four if we add the disputed epigram *AP* 11.400 = 41 Macleod) Lucian parades his knowledge of the much-quoted lines 2–4 of Aratus' Φαινόμενα, '*Celestial phenomena*'; a passage of his Ἔρωτες, '*Loves*', quotes Callimachus; three passages allude to or seem to recall Apollonius' *Argonautica*; and one passage alludes to Nicander.[13] Of these only Aratus is cited by either Dio (line 2 at *Or.* 74.15) or Aristides (line 2 at *Orr.* 43.26, 45.30; line 33 countered at *Or.* 43.8). Lucian mocks Euphorion and

[7] Barigazzi 1966, 66.

[8] Behr 1968, 11 with nn.28 and 29, cf. Schmid 1887–96, ii 295–7. For Aristides' quotation of early poetry see Gkourogiannis 1999; Bowie 2008c (Chapter 20 in Volume 3).

[9] Kindstrand 1973; Trapp 1986.

[10] For Dio's reception of early melic, elegiac and iambic poetry see Bowie 2016i (Chapter 40 in Volume 3).

[11] For Philostr.'s quotation of and allusion to classical poetry in *VA* see Bowie 2009d (Chapter 22 in Volume 3).

[12] Anderson 1976a, and for Luc.'s limitations 1976b.

[13] Call. is cited by seven of Householder's fourteen texts, Theoc. by only five.

Parthenius alongside Callimachus in *How to write history* (57), but there is only one dubious sign that he had read them.[14] He does, however, show knowledge of a poet of the generation before his own, Mesomedes.[15] None of these three writers betrays acquaintance with Theocritus, though it is clear that Longus expected him to be familiar to his readership. It is therefore no surprise that Dio's very selective reading list (*Or.* 18.12), proposing Homer, Euripides and Menander, and allowing lyric, elegy, iambus and dithyrambs only to gentlemen of leisure, does not hint at value in more recent poetry as it does in oratory. Perhaps, had we more Polemo than we do, he would have shown a distinctly wider command of the poets: after all, Philostratus credits him with the aphorism τὰ μὲν τῶν καταλογάδην ὤμοις δεῖν ἐκφέρειν, τὰ δὲ τῶν ποιητῶν ἁμάξαις, 'one should bring out the works of prose-writers in backpacks, but those of the poets in wagon-loads' (*VS* 1.25.539). But perhaps not.

The second point on which I wish to dwell is the movement of rhetoric towards poetry. This had long been a contentious issue. In the fifth century BC Gorgias had set out to displace poetry by prose rhetoric, and in doing so had adopted poetic vocabulary, *schemata*, and rhythms.[16] The fashion can be traced through Asianic orators of the Hellenistic period like Hegesias and the anonymous writer of Antiochus of Commagene's edicts to a number of Philostratus' sophists, as Norden did. Some critics saw danger in taking the practice too far. Demetrius' Περὶ ἑρμηνείας, '*On eloquence*', 112 counselled moderation in *mimesis* of poetry; the author of Περὶ ὕψους, '*On the sublime*', insisted (15.2 and 8) that its goal was different from that of prose.

Criticism was directed in particular against rhythms and delivery. Such is Dio's criticism of rhythmical perorations in his *Alexandrian Oration* (32.68) and Lucian's ironic advice for a would-be-sophist (*Rh.pr.* 19): 'and if you ever think the time has come to sing, then let your whole speech become song and music.' Lucian also tells us that Demonax mocked τῶν ... μελῶν τὸ ἐπικεκλασμένον, 'the corrupted tunes/limbs' of Favorinus (*Demon.* 12), while Philostratus alludes sarcastically to Favorinus' musical perorations: ἔθελγε δὲ αὐτοὺς τοῦ λόγου καὶ τὸ ἐπὶ πᾶσιν, ὃ ἐκεῖνοι μὲν ᾠδὴν ἐκάλουν, ἐγὼ δὲ φιλοτιμίαν, 'and they were also charmed by his epilogue, which they called "song", but I call self-promotion' (*VS* 1.8.492) – a habit that is indeed

[14] *AP* 6.164 = Macleod 1987, no. 4 (dubious because in line 3 the dedicator calls himself Lucillius): cf. Parthenius *ap.* Gell. 13.2 beginning Γλαύκωι καὶ Νηρῆϊ καὶ Ἰνώωι Μελικέρτηι (fr. 30 Martini = *SH* 647 = 36 Lightfoot).

[15] With Ποδάγρα, '*Gout*', 129–32, cf. Mesomedes 2.1–6 Heitsch = 10.1–6 Horna.

[16] Norden 1898, 30–41; Burgess 1902, 166–9.

discernible in Favorinus' *Corinthian*.[17] In the same vein Philostratus savagely criticises Varus of Laodicea for degrading his delivery ἣν εἶχεν εὐφωνίαν αἰσχύνων καμπαῖς ᾀσμάτων, αἷς κἂν ὑπορχήσαιτό τις τῶν ἀσελγεστέρων, 'befouling such vocal gifts as he had by suggestive pieces of song to which someone from the demi-monde might actually dance' (*VS* 2.28.620). But he is not always dismissive: many of his quotations from sophists whom he admires are rhythmical, as Norden noted, and it is in praise not blame that Philostratus records of Hadrianus of Tyre that people ἠκροῶντο ... ὥσπερ εὐστομούσης ἀηδόνος, 'listened to him like a nightingale in fine voice', and that he astonished audiences by καὶ τοὺς πεζῆι τε καὶ ξὺν ὠιδῆι ῥυθμούς, 'his rhythms both in prose and in sung passages' (*VS* 2.10.589).

The taste for rhythmical prose, then, was not universal, and its critics recognised the different demands of prose and verse. Nor do the many features that a sophistic shared with a dramatic performance entitle one to conclude that rhetoric is consciously moving into the shoes of drama. In arguing for this view Schmid (i 40–1) greatly exaggerated the lack of contemporary dramatic performances, and was clearly unaware of the chiefly epigraphic evidence for dramatic competitions and the thriving guild of the artists of Dionysus.[18]

In one area, it is true, we find the sophist Aristides claiming to offer prose where tradition prescribed poetry, and that is in his prose hymns. But it is clear that this genre is not as innovative as he pretends.[19] Prose *encomia* of the gods were already a category of competition in μουσικοὶ ἀγῶνες, 'musical competitions', and had a place in cult.[20] Rules for their composition are to be found in Quintilian (3.7.7–8) and in the rhetorical writer Alexander son of Numenius, already active in AD 130 when he composed a consolation

[17] i.e. [D.Chr.] 37: cf. Barigazzi 1966, 71–2; Amato 1995. On rhythm see Norden 1898, i 376; Goggin 1951.

[18] See Jones 1993. For the development of the synods of Dionysiac artists in the Hellenistic period see Le Guen 2001; Aneziri 2003: their further growth in the Roman Empire was a major factor in maintaining theatrical performances.

[19] See Boulanger 1923, 303 ff.; Russell 1990a.

[20] As were other ἐγκώμια: cf. from Oropus *IOrop.* 520 = *IG* vii 414.8, attesting the victory of a σοφιστής (dated to 366–38 BC); *IOrop.* 521.8, an ἐγκώ[μιο]ν εἰς τ[ὸν θ]εὸ[ν κ]αταλογάδην, '*encomium* to the god in prose', ca. 85 BC; *IG* vii 416.1 possibly recording an ἐγκωμιογράφος; *IG* vii 418.2 = *IOrop.* 524, an ἐγκώμιον καταλογάδην; *IG* vii 420 = *IOrop.* 528 (both these in the second quarter of the first century BC). Roesch 2007–9 no. 178 = *IG* vii 1773.12–13 attests an ἐγκώμιον to the Muses for the *Mouseia* at Thespiae, but its date is probably later than the 160s, and it might be argued that this item entered the competition as a result of Aristides' development of the genre. Prose encomia of emperors are now attested for the Σεβαστά, '*Augustan Games*', at Naples as early as AD 94, see Bowie 2019f (Chapter 46 in Volume 3). The delivery of prose *encomia* in cult was the task of θεολόγοι, 'Speakers of the divine': cf. Pleket 1965.

to Hadrian on the death of Antinous (iii 4–6 Spengel = ix 331–9 Walz). The main constituents of Aristides' prose hymns are those of a traditional verse hymn – invocation, narration of powers and exploits, and, usually last, a prayer. But his dismissal of the poets' claims to have a monopoly on composition of hymns, above all in the Εἰς Σάραπιν, '*To Sarapis*' (*Or.* 45.1–14 Keil, cf. *Or.* 37.8 Keil) is chiefly a rhetorical foil to his own prose performance, and should not hastily be taken as evidence for a serious attempt to create a prose hymn that would actually displace the verse form.[21] The poets are allowed to maintain the composition of hymns: indeed they have advantages over a prose speaker, and greater licence which makes for easier composition (*Or.* 45.13 Keil). The recurrent comparison and contrast with poets in Aristides' hymns can be simply explained: whereas epideictic oratory in general was closer to poetry than other forms of rhetoric, only the hymn was co-extensive with an established classical genre of poetry and was still actively practised as a poetic form.

Aristides' practice, like his programmatic remarks in the '*To Sarapis*', shows that he knew that an orator's techniques must be different from a poet's. Furthermore, it is notable that the vocabulary of the hymns is no more poetical than Aristides' norm (Boulanger 1923, 313), although perhaps certain figures of speech (e.g. vocative addresses) are commoner. The distinction is still maintained by Menander a century later. The first treatise ascribed to Menander observes that poetry is due greater licence than prose,[22] and can be more expansive;[23] it can also attempt a genre of hymn that is closed to prose, the φυσικός, 'On nature'.[24]

Although, therefore, sophistic rhetoric displays certain poetic features, the frontiers between it and poetry remain discernible, and it is far from annexing poetry's entire territory. Many poetic genres, indeed, are not replicated in prose: tragedy, which is still being composed, and the many forms of epigram, now as vigorous as ever. Others, like epic, continue despite the development of prose genres distantly related, historiography and the novel. Lucian's humorous dialogues owe something to Old Comedy, but their composition can hardly have threatened the position of Comedy in dramatic festivals. Here, of course, a traditional context secured a traditional form. By a similar token the genre that contested with the hymn the strongest claim to be the heir of archaic melic poetry, κιθαρῳδία, singing to

21 For a good analysis of the programmatic section of the *To Sarapis* see Russell 1990a, 201–6.

22 Russell and Wilson 1981, sections 333.31–334.5, cf. 334.20–1, 335.19–20.

23 338.28 on μῦθοι, 'myths', cf. 340.20

24 336.29–30.

the accompaniment of the *cithara*, flourished in the mouth of Mesomedes without any conceivable threat from the most musical of sophists.[25]

3 Sophists as Poets: Aristides and Philostratus

The limitations which sophists recognised when their prose rhetoric entered the domain of poetry might be argued to show that they still allowed it an independent role. That may also be inferred from the scattered but unambiguous evidence that sophists composed poetry in a number of genres – epic, tragedy, lyric poetry and epigram. I here attempt to present a full review of sophists' poetry, classified principally by genre, although I group together the productions of any individual who composed in more than one genre.

I begin with the genre which has been taken as a prime example of prose's annexation of poetry and with the individual whose theoretical observations and actual prose creations have been most influential, Aristides and the hymn. Aristides seems in fact to have composed more hymns in verse than in prose, though their total bulk was certainly less. We learn from the *Sacred Tales* that, under divine command, he composed over a dozen verse hymns, some of which were performed by a chorus of ὑμνῳδοί, 'hymn-singers'.[26] The first was not long, comprising a single system of strophe, antistrophe and epode (*Or.* 50.31 Keil), and it is likely enough that the remainder were of comparable length – certainly those which he prided himself on having composed in his head while walking or riding in his carriage (*Or.* 50.41 Keil). This brevity coheres with his assertion in his prose hymn to Sarapis that two strophes or periods are enough to complete a poet's hymn or paean (*Or.* 45.3 Keil). Yet it is worth noticing that when the god first proposed composition to him he claims to have regarded it as a challenge which his lack of previous experience rendered him inadequate to meet.

With the encouragement of various divinities Aristides' hymns multiplied. That first, composed at the beginning of his illness during his visit to Rome in AD 144, was a paean to Apollo: a dream indicated that Aristides should compose it, and even provided him with the first line that evoked a classical melic poet he knew well, Pindar:[27]

[25] For κιθαρῳδία's importance in the imperial period see Power 2010; on Mesomedes see further Bowie 1990b (Chapter 14 in this volume); for a good edition, with introduction and commentary, Regenauer 2016.

[26] For Aristides' account of his illness in his *Sacred Tales* see Behr 1968; Petsalis-Diomidis 2010; Israelowich 2012; Downie 2013.

[27] Pi. *O.* 2.1. Aristides' line is Heitsch 1963–4, ii 42 no. S2.3.

> φορμίγγων ἄνακτα Παιᾶνα κληΐσω
>
> I shall sing of the lord of lyres, of the Healer

Only when Aristides had completed the paean did someone tell him that it was the day of the *Ludi Apollinares*, '*Apolline Games*' (July 13th): the hand of Apollo was clearly at work (*Or.* 50.31 Keil). Aristides also saw it in his subsequent weathering of storms to arrive safely at two Apolline sanctuaries, first Delos and then Miletus (50.32 Keil), and in his own refusal to sail on from Delos within two days which spared him and his fellow-travellers exposure to an even worse tempest: and he compared this reward for his paean to Simonides' fabled salvation by the Dioscuri (*Or.* 50.36–7 Keil).[28]

Some time later (AD 145–6 on Behr's reckoning) Asclepius Sotēr instructed Aristides διατρίβειν ἐν ᾄσμασι καὶ μέλεσι, 'to busy himself with songs and tunes', and to maintain a chorus of boys (*Or.* 50.38 Keil). He still maintained a chorus of boys twenty years later, for on January 25th of the year 166 he dreamed that they were singing part of a classical hymn (*Or.* 47.30 Keil).[29] Their task in his waking life, however, was to sing Aristides' compositions. This Aristides' doctor, Theodotus, prescribed as a remedy for his asphyxia, and their performance duly brought relief. These hymns were initially addressed to Asclepius and, together with paeans to Apollo, continued to form the greatest part of Aristides' poetic output (cf. *Or.* 50.41 Keil); but so highly did the god rate them that he commanded Aristides to compose hymns to other gods too, like Pan, Hecate and Achelous (*Or.* 50.38–9 Keil). There followed a dream in which Athena made him a present of the first line of a hymn in her honour:

> Ἕπεσθε Περγάμωι, νέοι
>
> Come with me to Pergamum, young men

and another for Dionysus in which Aristides was transported by a song whose refrain ran

> χαῖρ', ὦ ἄνα Κισσεῦ, Διόνυσε
>
> Hail, Ivy-lord, Dionysus![30]

In this dream he was bidden address Dionysus as Λύσιος, 'Releaser', and in a later one as Οὐλοκόμης, 'Curly-locks'. Zeus also sent such a dream, and in another Aristides sang fluently of Hermes.

[28] Cf. Cic. *De or.* 2.86, Quint. 11.2.11, Simon. fr. 510 *PMG*, Slater 1971; on Simonides Molyneux 1992; Rawles 2018.

[29] Heitsch 1963–4, i 165, no. 47. [30] Both are Heitsch 1963–4, ii 42 no. S2.4.

For some reason the 'Goddesses of Smyrna', the Νεμέσεις (*Nemeseis*), did not communicate by dream: but Aristides thought that he recalled his τροφεύς, 'foster-father', observing that they should not be neglected, and we are meant to understand that he wrote a hymn to them (*Or.* 50.41 Keil). His sense of obligation to them is corroborated by a marble altar at Omer Köy, probably from the hill Aşar Kale, argued by Robert to be the hill of Atys where Aristides erected altars, north of his estate Laneium and near the sanctuary of Zeus Olympius (*Or.* 49.41 Keil).[31] The altar bears the following inscription:

Δίκηι
καὶ Νεμέσει
Ἀριστείδης

To Justice
and Nemesis
Aristides (dedicated this)[32]

Mortal third parties continued to play a part. An unnamed man from Thasos or Macedon at the Asclepieum, not even a friend of Aristides, dreamed that he was singing a paean by the sophist with the refrain

ἰὴ Παιὰν Ἥρακλες Ἀσκλήπιε

Iē Healer Heracles Asclepius!

It seems that Aristides then composed a complete hymn, to which he later referred in his prose hymn to Heracles of AD 166 (*Or.* 40.21 Keil) as well as in his *Sacred Tales* (*Or.* 50.39–42 Keil).[33]

All or most of these hymns, except the first, seem to have been privately performed by Aristides' chorus of boys whenever his ailments required (cf. *Or.* 50.38 Keil). More elaboration attended the ten public performances which he tells us he staged, some with a chorus of boys – presumably his regulars – and some with a chorus of men (*Or.* 50.43–4 Keil, dated by Behr to August 147). They will surely have taken place in the small theatre that stands at the East end of the Asclepieum

[31] Robert 1937, 216–20 with pl. xiii; *IMT MittlMakestos* 2509; Puech 2002, 139 no. 41.

[32] This area has preserved a dedication to another god not mentioned in this part of the *Sacred Tale*, Sarapis: in the village of Gökcedere a fragmentary text was copied, probably also from Aşar Kale, reading (κ)αὶ Σαράπιδι Ἀριστείδης, 'and to Serapis, Aristides'. Robert 1937, 218–9 plausibly suggested that this was a dedication to Isis and Serapis, in whose sanctuary at Smyrna Aristides sacrificed in AD 149 (*Or.* 49.48–9 Keil); cf. Puech 2002, 139 no. 42, noting similarity of letter-forms to the dedication to Hera discussed shortly p. 226.

[33] Heitsch 1963–4, ii 41 no. S2.1.

courtyard's North range (cf. *Or.* 48.30 Keil). Here too Aristides was given signs of divine intervention. The Asclepieum's distinguished benefactor L. Cuspius Pactumeius Rufinus, who had held the ordinary consulate in AD 142,[34] visited the shrine earlier in the day than was his habit, just as the first performance was imminent, and took this coincidence as evidence that the god had invited him. When one ᾆισμα, 'song', was omitted from the last performance, a dream demanded that be sung too, and was duly heeded.

It sounds from this as if each occasion involved the singing of several hymns. Aristides certainly viewed the sequence as a significant contribution to the cultural life of the Asclepieum, for he decided to commemorate it by the dedication of a tripod (the traditional form of monument to a choregic victory) inscribed with an epigram, predictably in elegiacs. He gives us the first couplet of his intended version:[35]

ποιητὴς ἀέθλων τε βραβεὺς αὐτός τε χορηγὸς
  σοὶ τόδ' ἔθηκεν ἄναξ μνῆμα χοροστασίης.

A poet, both umpire of contests and himself *choregos*,
  dedicated this to you, lord, as a memorial to his setting up a chorus
Aristides *Or.* 50.45 Keil

A second couplet, which he does not quote, contained his name and an acknowledgement of Asclepius' patronage. The four-line poem, however, was never inscribed, for at dawn on the day of the dedication Aristides dreamed that he was about to offer the tripod to Zeus with the more fulsome couplet:

οὐκ ἀφανὴς Ἕλλησιν Ἀριστείδης ἀνέθηκεν
  μύθων ἀενάων κύδιμος ἡνίοχος.

One not obscure among the Greeks, Aristides, dedicated (this),
  the glorious charioteer of ever-flowing tales.
Aristides *Or.* 50.45 Keil

On consultation with the priest and νεωκόροι, 'temple attendants', he dedicated the tripod to Zeus Asclepius, but hedged his bet by making another

[34] See *PIR*² C 1637; Habicht 1969, 9 ff.; Halfmann 1979, no. 66. Aristid. also mentions him at *Or.* 50.28, 83–4, 107.

[35] This and the following poem are Heitsch 1963–4, ii 42, no. S2.5. Aristides' language suggests that in a mini-competition he played ἀγωνοθέτης, 'competition-organiser', as well as competitor, ranking the different performances of his choruses in order.

dedication with the same epigram to Zeus Olympius, i.e. in the sanctuary near his estates north of Hadrianoutherae.[36]

All these hymns seem to belong in the years 144–6, which are likely also to have seen the composition of his prose hymn to Dionysus. Late in the summer of AD 148, shortly before the death of his foster-father Zosimus, he obtained striking relief from his illness by composing a song, presumably but not necessarily a hymn, about the union of Coronis and Apollo and the birth of Asclepius (*Or.* 47.73 Keil): he tells us he made the στροφή, 'stanza', as long as he could – almost penance, one might think, for his dismissal of poets in the εἰς Σάραπιν for achieving completion in one or two στροφαί, 'stanzas' – but unfortunately does not quote any of what must have been one of his most substantial poems.

The latest anecdote in the *Sacred Tales* concerns the tenth year of Aristides' illness, shortly after the winter solstice of AD 152. Promised cure by a vision, he set off for the Asclepieum at Poemanenum, and on the twentymile journey, whose torch-lit prolongation into the hours of darkness must have given it the character of a religious procession, he composed many songs to Asclepius Sotēr and to the river Aesēpus, the Nymphs and Artemis Thermaea,[37] praying for release and recovery (51.2–4 Keil).

Such is the picture Aristides gives us of his melic *oeuvre*. Motivation and performance bulk larger than content, and it is sad that we have nothing longer than a single line, even if our literary judgement of a complete poem might well have been unfavourable.

We have a slightly longer fragment of a hexameter poem to Asclepius that (in AD 146 on Behr's reckoning) Aristides dreamed was being sung by schoolchildren in Alexandria and was presumably, therefore, a hymn rather than straight narrative:

> πολλοὺς δ' ἐκ θανάτοιο ἐρύσατο δερκομένοιο
> ἀστραφέεσσι πύλῃσιν ἐπ' αὐτῇσιν βεβαῶτας
> Ἀΐδεω …
>
> and many he saved from death that looked upon them
> as at the immoveable gates themselves they stood
> of Hades …
>
> Aristides *Or.* 49.4 Keil[38]

[36] See Robert 1937, 211 ff.

[37] For a prose dedication by Aristides to Asclepius from Pamphyla in Lesbos, perhaps associable with a visit to the spa and cult centre of Artemis Thermaea a few miles north, cf. Charitonidis 1960, no. 33 with pl. 118; *Bull.* 1970, 422; Robert 1980a, 718; Puech 2002, 139 no. 43.

[38] Heitsch 1963–4, ii 41, no. S2.2.

He goes on to say that they were virtually the first of his ἔπη, 'hexameters', to Asclepius, suggesting that there were others, unless he means that they were the first of his poems (in general) to the god. This is possible, and does not conflict with his story about composition of a hymn to Apollo in Rome, since his inexperience there is specific to melic poetry. This hexameter poem surely post-dates not only his journey to Egypt (AD 141) but his illness, and so falls between AD 144 and 146.

Two (perhaps three) more poems are added by epigraphy.

One is an elegiac couplet for a statue of Hera dedicated – along with at least one other statue of a god, to judge from its phraseology – at Hadrianoutherae:

> καὶ τήνδ' Ἀργείην Διὸς αἰγιόχοι[ο] σ[ύνευνον]
> εἵσατ' Ἀριστείδης ἐν δαπέδοισι [θεοῦ].

> This statue too of the Argive goddess, wife of aegis-bearing Zeus,
> did Aristides set up on the floors [of the goddess].[39]

The second gift of epigraphy is more substantial, an eighteen-line poem which, despite many lacunae, is manifestly addressed to Asclepius, and on the basis of its biographical references was argued persuasively by Herzog to be composed by Aristides towards the end of his life, after his speech before the imperial family at Smyrna in AD 176.[40] Herzog's arguments have found general acceptance, but it must be remembered that the attribution to Aristides is conjectural. Moreover his classification of the work as a hymn should be questioned. This poem too is in elegiacs, so it is unlikely that it was ever performed by Aristides' choruses. Their hymns will have been either in lyric metres or hexameters, also regular for hymns, and indeed used for one composed in AD 166/7 and preserved on a stone from Pergamum.[41]

[39] Wiegand 1904, 280 with fig. 15: cf. Robert 1937, 211; Herzog 1934, 767 (rejecting the supplement θεοῦ); *IMT MittlMakestos* 2549; Merkelbach-Stauber 2001, 08/06/01 p.96; Puech 2002, 138–9 no. 40 (cf. my n.32 on the dedication to Sarapis). So far as we know Aristides composed neither a prose nor a verse hymn for Hera.

[40] The best text is to be found in Habicht 1969, 144–5, no. 145, following the proposals of Herzog 1934 and 1941). For discussion see Jones 2004; Petsalis-Diomidis 2010, 117–8 with photograph (fig. 25).

[41] *IPergam.* ii 324. We do indeed have one or two elegiac hymns, e.g. Callin. fr. 3, Sol. fr. 13, Thgn. 1–18, 757 ff., 773 ff.; but these are hymns within the genre of sympotic elegy. For a 'real' elegiac hymn by one Isidorus from Egypt in the first century BC see *SEG* 8.549, 551. Hellenistic poets also created literary versions, notably Call. *Lav.Pall*: cf. also Posidippus, *SH* 705, and the discussion by Bulloch 1985, 31–8. I doubt if the eight-line poem quoted by Ael. *NA* 11.4, narrating the miraculous power of Demeter at Hermione and concluding with a prayer, should be classified as hymn rather than an epigram: for a text see *FGE* 30–31 (with discussion), *SH* 206. The identity and date of the Aristocles whom Aelian cites as witness and whom he means us to take as the author is unknown: he could even be the late-second-century sophist Ti. Claudius Aristocles of Pergamon (Philostr. *VS* 2.3, *PIR*² C 789), but such an identification is too speculative to justify the poem's inclusion in a list of sophistic poetry.

Our text in elegiac couplets is rather to be taken as an extended dedicatory epigram, admittedly with hymnic features, probably accompanying some object dedicated, most likely a statue of Asclepius.[42] That would have been clear from the opening, but unfortunately it is lost, and as the following text (that of Habicht based on Herzog) shows, the sense often depends heavily on supplements. Since a number of these are open to objections I have attempted to indicate them in my translation:

[κληθεὶς ἐν νυξίν τε καὶ ἤμασι πολλ]άκι [παῦσας]
    [τειρόμενον νούσωι καρφαλ]έῃι κραδίην.
[εἰν ἁλὶ δὲ πρόφρων μου] κήδεαι οὐδ᾽ ἐσ[ορᾶις με]
    [δεινὰ βιαζόμενον] πήμασι λευγαλ[έοις],
[ἀλλ᾽ ἀδεῶς μὲν πέμψας], ὅτε πλώοντά με Δ[ήλωι]
    [ἴσχες ἅμ᾽ Αἰγαῖον τ᾽ οἶδ]μα καταστόρεσας,
[ῥύσαο δ᾽ αὖ ναυηγό]ν, ὅτε στροφάλιγγι βαρεί[ηι]
    [κῦμα τρόπει μι]κρῆι, στῆσας ὑφ᾽ ἡμετέρηι,
[πρήυνας δ᾽ ἀνέ]μους, ὅτ᾽ ἐπ᾽ ἄνδρασι μαίνετ᾽ ἀ[ήτης]
    [αἰνὴν ἀμ]φ᾽ αὐτοῖς αἶσαν ἄγων θανάτου.
[ἐκ δ᾽ ἀλέη]ς με σάωσας ἀεικέος ἔκ τε ῥο[άων]
    [χειμε]ρίων ποταμῶν ἔκ τ᾽ ἀνέμοιο βίη[ς].
[αὐτὸς δ᾽] Αὐσονίων ἕταρον ποιήσας ἀν[άκτων]
    [καὶ κλέ]ος ἐκ πολίων ἐσθλὸν ἔνευσ[ας ἄγειν]
[εὐλογίηι ζ]αθεῆς Βειθύνιδος ἔνδοθι [χώρης]
    [καὶ γῆν θεσπ]εσίην σὴν ἀνὰ Τευθρ[ανίην].
[ἀνθ᾽ ὧν σὸν τιμ]ῶ τε καὶ ἅζομαι οὔν[ομα, Σῶτερ],
    [κληίζων χω]ρῆς πε[ίρ]ατ᾽ [ἐς ἡμεδαπῆς].

[when called upon by night and day you have of]ten [stopped]
    my heart's [torment by parch]ing [disease].
[And at sea you zealously] care for me and do not neg[lect]
    [me when I am being dreadfully oppressed] by dire pains
[but you escorted me safely] when I was sailing to D[elos]
    [and you preserved me and] quelled the [Aegean] swell,
[and you also saved me in shipwreck], when with a whirlwind
    dire you ranged [a wave] against our small [keel],
[and you calmed the] winds, when the blast raged against men

[42] Herzog's reason for denying that the genre is dedicatory epigram seems simply to have been the poem's length, Herzog 1934, 756. But for parallels cf. the poems of Glaucus discussed below (pp. 246–55) and Kaibel 818 = *IG* xii.5 229 from Paros, a dedication of a statue to Persephone (note the opening σο[ὶ τ]ό[δ᾽] ἄγαλμα, θεά, 'to you, goddess, this gift') in more than twenty-four lines, and 831 = *IG* xiv 1003, from Rome, for an offering to Heracles (lines 3–4 τοι τόδ᾽ ἄγαλμα ... θῆκα) in fourteen lines. Both these poems move from record of dedication to prayers for future blessings: the former is described by its author as a ὕμνος (23), the latter ends with the invocatory σὲ ... κλήιζομεν Ἡράκλεες.

bringing about them the [dread] fate of death.
You have saved me from deadly heat and from the stre[ams]
[of wint]ry rivers and from the violence of the wind.
[You have yourself] made me the companion of the Italian lords
and have granted that I should get noble [glo]ry from cities
[by my gift for words] within the godly territory of Bithynia
[and] throughout your [div]ine land of Teuthras.
[For these favours I honou]r and revere your na[me, Saviour,]
[calling you to] the boundaries of our land.

Finally we may note a brief address to the river god Meles found near the river at Smyrna:

ὑμνῶ θεὸν Μέλητα {ποταμόν}, τὸν σωτῆρά μου,
παντός με λοιμοῦ καὶ κακοῦ πεπαυμένον.

I sing of the god Meles {the river}, my saviour,
who spared me from every plague and ill.[43]

Herzog conjectured that this might be by Aristides, but given the presence of his name in several other dedications, and his apparent attention to detail in the inscription of the long piece from Pergamum (with *Lesezeichen* and an *iota* adscript added later in a different hand), this couplet with its unhappily interpolated or unmetrical ποταμόν and the dubious syntax of πεπαυμένον is surely unlikely to have been composed and inscribed by the sophist.

Aristides' poetic activity was, it is manifest, intimately connected with his illness and his attempts to cure it. He represents his verse hymns as produced by divine command and as vehicles of the god's healing powers and of his own gratitude. But that does not entitle us to argue that he only composed verse under compulsion,[44] and that it was to prose that he always turned when he had a free choice of media. Some prose hymns too are responses to a divine request (cf. *Orr.* 37.1, 38.1, 40.1, and 41.1 Keil), and Aristides' conviction that gods required him to compose poetry surely reflects some inner drive to do so, and to do so with distinction. The most telling incident is perhaps his arrangement of the choral competition in which one of his own compositions was guaranteed victory. He could thus satisfy his craving for recognition as an outstanding artist with words, a recognition that his illness had imperilled in the world of sophistic declamation. It is perhaps

[43] *ISmyrna* 766 = *IGR* iv 1389: cf. Herzog 1934, 768–9, proposing a text slightly different from Kaibel 1030; for the *Lesezeichen* in the Pergamum text see Herzog and the photograph in Habicht 1969, pl. 40.

[44] As did Mesk 1927, 672.

relevant that the great classical writers whom he dreams visited him numbered Sophocles as well as Plato (*Or.* 50.57–61 Keil).

There is, of course, an oddity in his turning to the composition of verse hymns after his démarche in favour of prose in the εἰς Σάραπιν, '*To Sarapis*', which probably belongs early, perhaps as early as AD 141. But that was a rhetorical manoeuvre, and the chronology, although in some respects precarious, demonstrates clearly that, after he fell ill, verse and prose hymns were being composed over the same period and to the same divinities.[45] The most significant difference between the two was that the prose hymn was intended for ἐπίδειξις, 'display rhetoric', one of the weapons in Aristides' sophistic armoury, whereas the verse hymn was for performance in the context of cult, an area of second-century Greek society where tradition remained powerful. Similarly the traditional form of the dedicatory or commemorative epigram was one to which Aristides adhered and for which he seems to have made no attempt to develop a prose substitute.

Other sophists had no special reason to engage in the composition of hymns. Although we know of many occasions, both cultic and competitive, for which hymns were required, and a number of hymns survive,[46] there is only one explicit reference that I know to a hymn for performance composed by another sophist, the Olympic hymn by Glaucus of Marathon (see below Section 7).

The form of the hymn, however, was bound to attract sophists, who will have studied classical hymns with a view to the construction of prose *encomia*.[47] Hence it is no surprise that we find hymn-like pieces composed by

[45] Only four gods receive hymns in both media: Asclepius, Athena, Dionysus, and Heracles. In verse alone Aristides hymned Apollo, Pan, Hecate, Achelous, the Nemeseis, the river Aesepus, the Nymphs, Artemis Thermaea; in prose alone the Asclepiadae, Zeus, the Aegean Sea, Sarapis, Poseidon, and the Well at the Asclepieum. The prose hymns to Dionysus, the Asclepiadae and Athena have been argued to belong to AD 147–53 (cf. Mesk 1927, 664 ff.), with the last dated by its subscription to the date when Aristides was thirty-five years and one month old, i.e. AD 153 (perhaps a response to his success in obtaining immunity: cf. 50.75–6 Keil).

[46] Hymns will have been required for singing by the ὑμνῳδοί for whom we have evidence in connection with the imperial cult at Pergamum, *IPergam.* 374 = *IGR* iv 353, *IEph.* 17.53–63, 18d.16 ff., 19.65 and 145; at Ephesus *IEph.* 267, 296.34 and 23, 275, 645, 742, 790, 892.19, 921, 925a, 1002, 1004, 1061, 1600, 1604, 2446, 3081–8, 3247, 3801, 4336 (note the possible [ὑμνο] γράφος, '[hymn] writer', *IEph.* 1149); at Smyrna *ISmyrna* 594 = *IGR* iv 1398. For ὑμνῳδοί, 'hymn-singers', of Artemis at Ephesus see *IEph.* 645. It is likely that hymns were composed by C. Cornelius Secundus Proculus, who was honoured both as τὸν τῶν μελῶν ποιητήν, 'the melic poet', and as προφήτην τοῦ Σμινθέως, 'expounder of (Apollo) Smintheus', *IGR* iv 6 = *IG* xii.2.519, from Methymna on Lesbos. For surviving hymns cf. Heitsch 1963–4, i 165–99 nos. 48–59; ii 42–3, no. S3, 44 no. S5. For further discussion of ὑμνῳδοί and of hymns at Curium, Panamara and Clarus see Bowie 2022b.

[47] Men. Rh. *Treatise* 1.333 ff.

Philostratus himself for his *Heroicus*. The first, according to the vintner who is the dialogue's principal speaker, is a hymn to Thetis sung in times past by Thessalians coming to sacrifice at Achilles' tomb in the Troad as instructed by the oracle at Dodona.[48] The hymn was to be sung before they landed at dawn:

Θέτι κυανέα, Θέτι Πηλεία,
τὸν μέγαν ἃ τέκες υἱὸν Ἀχιλλέα,
τοῦ θνατὰ μὲν ὅσον φύσις ἤνεγκε,
Τροία λάχε· σᾶς δ' ὅσον ἀθανάτου
γενεᾶς πάϊς ἔσπασε, Πόντος ἔχει.
βαῖνε πρὸς αἰπὺν τόνδε κολωνὸν
μετ' Ἀχιλλέως ἔμπυρα,
βαῖν' ἀδάκρυτος μετὰ Θεσσαλίας,
Θέτι κυανέα, Θέτι Πηλεία.

Dark blue Thetis, Thetis wife of Peleus,
who gave birth to your mighty son, Achilles,
whose portion that mortal nature produced
was allotted to Troy, but the portion which your son
drew from your immortal ancestry, that the Black Sea has.
Come to this steep hill
to the burnt offerings for Achilles,
come without tears together with Thessaly,
dark blue Thetis, Thetis wife of Peleus.

Philostratus, *Heroicus* 53.10 = 68.1–9 De Lannoy

The second is presented as one of the songs sung by Achilles and Helen as they party on Λευκὴ νῆσος, 'White Island', to which Achilles was supposed to have been conveyed, and where Achilles, says the vintner, has become much given to poetry now that he has ceased warring. As a man of letters Philostratus prefers to offer us not one of the songs he mentions that they sing of their mutual love – a tempting theme for an epideictic poet – but one on Homer, which was known to the ghost of Protesilaus and which travellers had heard Achilles singing on White Island only the year before:

Ἀχώ, περὶ μυρίον ὕδωρ
μεγάλου ναίοισα πέρα Πόντου,
ψάλλει σε λύρα διὰ χειρὸς ἐμᾶς·
σὺ δὲ θεῖον Ὅμηρον ἄειδέ μοι

[48] For this sacred pilgrimage see Rutherford 2009, 2013. For *Her.* see Beschorner 1999; Grossardt 2006; Hodkinson 2011.

κλέος ἀνέρων,
κλέος ἁμετέρων πόνων
δι' ὃν οὐ θάνον,
δι' ὃν ἔστι μοι
Πάτροκλος, δι' ὃν ἀθανάτοις ἴσος
Αἴας ἐμός,
δι' ὃν ἁ δορίληπτος ἀειδομένα σοφοῖς
κλέος ἤρατο κοὐ πέσε Τροία.

Echo, who dwell by boundless waters
beyond the mighty Black Sea,
you resound from the lyre in my hand:
sing to me of divine Homer,
the renown of men,
the renown of my labours,
through whom I have not died,
through whom I have
Patroclus, through whom I have, equal to the immortals,
my friend Ajax,
through whom the spear-taken city, sung by skilled men,
has won renown, and has not fallen, Troy.

Philostratus, *Heroicus* 55.3 = 72.20–73.4 De Lannoy

Despite titillating allusion, they are not distinguished pieces, at least on the basis of their words alone. Even if we allow for the intention that the second should complement the first, the decision to couch it in the form of a prayer to Echo is not wholly happy. Nor can their basically anapaestic rhythms (with some other *cola*, including one *apocroton*, in the second song) have greatly taxed Philostratus' metrical expertise. But anapaests were used for actual hymns,[49] and, in combination with *apocrota*, were also popular with the second century AD citharode Mesomedes, whom we know Caracalla to have admired. It may therefore be that we should envisage a sung performance within a text otherwise recited – plausibly, indeed, recited to Caracalla on the occasion of his visit to Troy in AD 214.[50] Had we

[49] Cf. Heitsch 1963–4, i 165 no. 47; 168 no. 51; 176–9 no. 58; ii 44 no. S5; West 1982, 170–1. West 1982 may be right (176) to suggest that in the second hymn Philostr. is trying to recreate 'the ancient style', but the *apokroton* counts against that, and the contrast proposed below seems to me more likely.

[50] So Münscher 1907, 497 ff., 501 ff. (holding that the *Her.* is not by the biographer); Anderson 1986, 241 with n.3. Solmsen 1940 and Anderson 1986, 254 take the view (also my own) that the *Her.* is by the same hand as the *VA* and *VS*; Solmsen argues that it was written between AD 217 and 219 (cf. also *RE* xx.1 [1941] 154), after the related passage in the *VA* and, like it, reflects Caracalla's interest in Troy. For Caracalla's admiration for Mesomedes see D.C. 77.13.7.

heard his own recitation we would be in a better position to know whether Philostratus is making a clever point in giving the second song, heard only last year, a different and more complex metrical structure than the first, 'archaic', piece, but that does seem likely. He certainly seems to want us to reflect on the songs' characteristics, since the Phoenician interlocutor compliments Achilles on a song worthy of himself and of Homer, and comments that brevity is a mark of quality in songs to be accompanied by the lyre (cf. Aristid. *Or.* 45.3 Keil). The Phoenician also proceeds to pronounce on an old literary controversy in a typically Philostratean manner, to take the songs as evidence of the antiquity of poetry's repute and virtuosity, allowing the vintner to agree, and to offer a further testimony in a hexameter epigram which he alleges that Heracles inscribed by the crucified body of the centaur Asbolus. This too must be Philostratus' composition, cleverly combining the sepulchral and dedicatory genres:

Ἄσβολος οὔτε θεῶν τρομέων ὄπιν οὔτ' ἀνθρώπων,
ὀξυκόμοιο κρεμαστὸς ἀπ' εὐλιπέος κατὰ πεύκης
ἄγκειμαι μέγα δεῖπνον ἀμετροβίοις κοράκεσσιν.

I, Asbolus, who feared the wrath of neither gods nor men,
hung here from a resiny pine with prickly leaves
am dedicated, a great feast for crows of countless years.
Philostratus, *Heroicus* 55.5 = 73.11–13 De Lannoy

The opportunity to hint at the fancy that Achilles was the πρῶτος εὑρετής, 'inventor', of melic poetry, and Heracles of epigram, was doubtless one motive for the inclusion of these pieces. But they also show that Philostratus regarded poetry as εὐδόκιμόν τε καὶ σοφόν, 'distinguished and wise' (the Phoenician's words, endorsed by the vintner, *Her.* 55.4), and we may infer that he found poetic composition enough of a challenge to want to try his hand.

It seems likely that in the same way Philostratus planted an epigram of his own composition in his work on Apollonius. In a passage allegedly derived from Damis he reports how in Cissia his hero discovered the tombs of a group of Eretrians deported by Dareius in the Persian wars. One of these bore a four-line epigram, also found in the *Greek Anthology*, where it is ascribed to Plato:

οἵδε ποτ' Αἰγαίοιο βαθύρροον οἶδμα πλέοντες
Ἐκβατάνων πεδίῳι κείμεθ' ἐνὶ μεσάτωι.
χαῖρε κλυτή ποτε πατρὶς Ἐρέτρια, χαίρετ' Ἀθῆναι,
γείτονες Εὐβοίης, χαῖρε θάλασσα φίλη.

> We, who once sailed the deep-flowing surge of the
> Aegean, lie in the midst of Ecbatana's plain.
> Farewell, once-famed native land, Eretria, farewell Athens
> neighbour to Euboea, farewell the sea we loved.
>
> Philostratus, *VA* 1.24 = *AP* 7.256

The episode is a manifest fiction, based on anecdotes of Herodotus (6.119) and Plato (*Lg.* 3.698b, *Mx.* 240a). The question of the poem's authorship is complicated by the existence of a two-line poem on the same subject, likewise ascribed to Plato in the *Anthology* (*AP* 7.259). Page convincingly argued that neither epigram can be a copy of a classical inscription, and concluded that they are literary pieces of Hellenistic date.[51] Perhaps we can go further. *AP* 7.259 was already known to, and ascribed to Plato by, Diogenes Laertius (3.33), and we may reasonably guess that it was so known to Philostratus and his readers. It is only in the *Anthology*, however, that *AP* 7.256 is ascribed to Plato, probably by analogy with the two-line poem: since it is not quoted by Diogenes Laertius among Plato's epigrams it is unlikely that in his day it was attributed to Plato, and its attribution to him in the *Anthology* counts against its having been by a well-known Hellenistic poet. It is improbable, however, that Philostratus would present his readers with an anonymous poem unless it was indeed a recognisable text by a well-known author: hence it is almost certainly his own creation, a reworking of the two-line poem. Unfortunately in his pursuit of *variatio* he switched the scene from Susa (which is indeed in Cissia) to Ecbatana (which is not): but in other respects he was successful, and he would have been satisfied that his *mimesis* had struck Page as exhibiting 'the simplicity, dignity and high poetic quality characteristic of epitaphs from the classical period'.

4 The Novelists as Poets

It is but a short step from Philostratus' work on Apollonius to the full-blown novel. Here too we find prose-writers playing the game of inserting poetry into their narrative, although only a hymn in Heliodorus seems to be introduced primarily to display the writer's virtuosity: the other texts, chiefly oracles, are deployed simply to mimic reality.

[51] *FGE* 171–3 on 'Plato' 11 and 12. For the Eretrians in Cissia see Penella 1974; Anderson 1986, 204–6; for Philostr.'s literary game here, Gyselinck and Demoen 2009; for the fictitious nature of Damis, Bowie 1978 (Chapter 4 in Volume 3), esp. 1663 ff.

Three of our surviving novels are traditionally considered 'sophistic', and although we have no evidence that Longus was ever a sophist, Achilles Tatius is denominated a ῥήτωρ, '*rhetor*', by a late source (Thomas Magister, *Ecloga nominum et verborum Atticorum s.v.* ἀναβαίνω), and a case can be made for Heliodorus too having practised as a sophist. Although Longus, like the less mannered Chariton, nowhere embellishes his prose with poetic texts of his own composition,[52] both Achilles and Heliodorus do.

The only verses in Achilles, and four of six texts in Heliodorus, are oracles. They are parodies of the oracles familiar to every Greek, and they add realism to the religious texture of the novels,[53] while linking them with classical historiography, their most obvious godparent, where oracles are often quoted (above all by Herodotus). Achilles Tatius was not the first to exploit an oracle in this way, since Xenophon of Ephesus (who can hardly have been a practising sophist) had offered his readers an Apolline oracle from Clarus in nine hexameters, the regular metre for oracles (1.6.2). Achilles too uses hexameters, and there is nothing unusual in the inelegant riddling of his oracle or in the way it is received. Its role in his plot is to occasion an embassy from Byzantium to Tyre which can be exploited by the dastardly Callisthenes to abduct the object of his lust:

> νῆσός τις <πόλις > ἔστι φυτώνυμον αἷμα λαχοῦσα,
> ἰσθμὸν ὁμοῦ καὶ πορθμὸν ἐπ᾽ ἠπείροιο φέρουσα,
> [ἔνθ᾽ ἀπ᾽ ἐμῆς ἔσθ᾽ αἷμα ὁμοῦ καὶ Κέκροπος αἷμα·]
> ἔνθ᾽ Ἥφαιστος ἔχων χαίρει γλαυκῶπιν Ἀθήνην·
> κεῖθι θυηπολίην σε φέρειν κέλομαι Ἡρακλεῖ.
>
> There is an island city whose blood bears the name of a tree,
> leading both an isthmus and a sea-passage to the mainland,
> [where there is both blood from my land and blood of Cecrops]:
> where Hephaestus rejoices to hold grey-eyed Athena:
> there I bid you bring a sacrifice to Heracles.
>
> Achilles Tatius 2.14.1 = *AP* 14.34[54]

Achilles does not leave his reader puzzled for long: a character is made to explicate the text, setting off a paradoxographic excursus.

[52] Chariton does, however, constantly quote classical texts *verbatim*, above all the *Iliad*, to give heroic colour to his narrative. Cf. Morgan 2008, 219 with discussions cited in his n.2.

[53] For limits to that realism, however, see Bowie 2012f (Chapter 36 in this volume).

[54] The *Anthology* (into which the oracle was presumably gathered for its riddling rather than poetic qualities) has a line between the second and third of the text offered by the MSS of Achilles. It is probably an interpolation, since it is even more unintelligible than the others, and is not explained by Achilles in the subsequent narrative: see further Whitmarsh 2020, 215–6 *ad loc.*

Heliodorus, characteristically, is much more complex in his exploitation of oracles. These come in two pairs, the first, predictably, in Calasiris' description of his visit to Delphi. When he first goes to the temple and offers a prayer (though he puts no specific question) the Pythia utters:

ἴχνος ἀειράμενος ἀπ᾽ ἐυστάχυος παρὰ Νείλου
    φεύγεις μοιράων νήματ᾽ ἐρισθενέων.
τέτλαθι, σοὶ γὰρ ἐγὼ κυαναύλακος Αἰγύπτοιο
    αἶψα πέδον δώσω· νῦν δ᾽ ἐμὸς ἔσσο φίλος.

You have raised your tread from the corn-rich land by the Nile
    and flee the threads of the all-powerful Fates.
Be strong, for to you the plain of dark-furrowed Egypt
    I soon shall give: but for now be my friend.

Heliodorus 2.26.5

Later in his Delphic narrative, at the point when sacrifice is being offered to Neoptolemus, Calasiris tells how a second oracle was delivered that caused consternation and puzzlement in the crowd:

τὴν χάριν ἐν πρώτοις αὐτὰρ κλέος ὕστατ᾽ ἔχουσαν
    φράζεσθ᾽, ὦ Δελφοί, τόν τε θεᾶς γενέτην·
οἳ νηὸν προλιπόντες ἐμὸν καὶ κῦμα τεμόντες
    ἵξοντ᾽ ἠελίου πρὸς χθόνα κυανέην,
τῆι περ ἀριστοβίων μέγ᾽ ἀέθλιον ἐξάψονται
    λευκὸν ἐπὶ κροτάφων στέμμα μελαινομένων.

She who has charm for her beginning, but glory for her end,
    be your mark, Delphians, and he born of a goddess:
leaving my temple and cutting through the waves
    they shall reach the dark land of the sun;
and there they shall don a great prize for their good lives,
    a white chaplet upon their darkening temples.

Heliodorus 2.35.5

Heliodorus has framed his oracles with the ambiguity that was *de rigueur* but with an elegance that Achilles lacks: nor does it require too clever a reader to see the punning references in the first couplet to Charicleia and Theagenes. That Heliodorus takes neither oracles nor their poetry entirely seriously is shown by another pair much later in his story. Charicleia suddenly recalls a dream in which Calasiris has appeared to her and has uttered a couplet (also gathered into the *Anthology*) concerning the magic stone *Pantarbē*:

παντάρβην φορέουσα πυρὸς μὴ τάρβει ἐρωήν,
ῥηΐδι᾽ ὡς Μοίραις χἄ τ᾽ ἀδόκητα πέλει.

If you wear the Frightall, be not frightened by the force of fire,
since for the Fates even the unexpected comes easily.
Heliodorus 8.11.2 = *AP* 9.480

Charicleia's dream reminds Theagenes that he has also been given a χρησμός, 'oracle', by a vision of Calasiris, so that he too is 'demonstrated to be a poet by the act of recollection':

Αἰθιόπων εἰς γαῖαν ἀφίξεαι ἄμμιγα κούρῃ
δεσμῶν Ἀρσακέων αὔριον ἐκπροφυγών.

You shall reach the land of the Ethiopians together with the girl
escaping tomorrow the chains of Arsacē.
Heliodorus 8.11.3

Theagenes' remark that he is demonstrated to be a poet looks like a dig at oracular poetry: neither couplet could be said to have high poetic quality, nor did Heliodorus expect it to be detected in them. But Heliodorus also plays a literary game. With a very few exceptions Delphic oracles reported by other sources are in hexameters.[55] All those of Heliodorus are in elegiac couplets, the standard metre for epideictic epigram, marking them out as literary miniatures rather than simple mirrors of life.

This handling of oracles helps us to understand the most elaborate of Heliodorus' poetic emblems, a hymn that is similar and apparently related to that of Philostratus' *Heroicus*. In Book 3 of the *Aethiopica* Calasiris is about to continue his description of the spectacular procession of Thessalian Aenianes when, by a typically Heliodoran trick, Cnemon interrupts him and demands a rendering of the hymn sung by the two girl-choruses so that he may not only see but actually hear what is happening.[56] The hymn was an opportunity for Heliodorus to display his virtuosity in a different genre, and was striking enough to catch the eye of one of the compilers of the *Greek Anthology*, where it appears among the Ἐπιδεικτικά, '*Epideictic poems*':

τὰν Θέτιν ἀείδω, χρυσοέθειρα Θέτιν,
Νηρέος ἀθανάταν εἰναλίοιο κόραν
τὰν Διὸς ἐννεσίῃ Πηλέϊ γημαμέναν
τὰν ἁλὸς ἀγλαΐαν ἁμετέραν Παφίην,

[55] As are those in X.Eph. and Ach. Tat. The others in elegiacs are to be found in D. Chr. 31.97, Ath. 13.602b, *AP* 14.74, 75: see Parke and Wormell 1956, ii p. xxii, n.3.

[56] On Hld.'s game here see further Bowie 2006b (Chapter 29 in this volume).

ἃ τὸν δουρομανῆ τόν τ᾽ Ἄρεα πτολέμων
Ἑλλάδος ἀστεροπὰν ἐξέτεκεν λαγόνων
δῖον Ἀχιλλῆα, τοῦ κλέος οὐράνιον,
τῶι ὕπο Πύρρα τέκεν παῖδα Νεοπτόλεμον,
περσέπολιν Τρώων, ῥυσίπολιν Δαναῶν.
ἱλήκοις ἥρως ἄμμι Νεοπτόλεμε,
ὄλβιε Πυθιάδι νῦν χθονὶ κευθόμενε,
δέχνυσο δ᾽ εὐμενέων τάνδε θυηπολίην,
πᾶν δ᾽ ἀπέρυκε δέος ἁμετέρας πόλιος.
τὰν Θέτιν ἀείδω, χρυσοέθειρα Θέτιν.

Of Thetis I sing, golden-locked Thetis,
immortal daughter of Nereus, lord of the brine,
who married Peleus at the behest of Zeus,
the glory of the brine, our own Paphian goddess.
He of the mad spear, the War-god of wars,
the lightning bolt of Hellas, was born from her loins,
God-like Achilles, whose renown reached heaven,
to whom Pyrrha bore their son Neoptolemus,
city-sacker for the Trojans, city-saver for the Greeks.
be gracious to us, hero Neoptolemus,
blessed one now buried in Pythian soil,
and receive with favour this sacrifice,
and ward off all fear from our city.
Of Thetis I sing, golden-locked Thetis.

Heliodorus 3.2.4 = *AP* 9.485

The hymn is written entirely in pentameters, with only a few substitutions of spondee for dactyl in their first half (including two in line 10, clearly for special effect) and should be read as a *tour de force*. Stichic pentameters are rare, and Heliodorus perhaps wishes to allude to Philip's five-line poem in which each successive pentameter has one more spondee (*AP* 13.1 = *GP* 62), and where the opening words are Χαῖρε, θεὰ Παφίη, 'Hail, Goddess of Paphos!' (cf. ἁμετέραν Παφίην, 'our own Paphian goddess', in the hymn, line 4).

That Heliodorus also knows the hymns of Philostratus, or Philostratus knows his, seems an almost certain conclusion from the similarity of their first and last lines, and that is one reason for taking account of this poem here. The other is that (as has already been said) Heliodorus has been thought to be a sophist, not simply by reason of his manner and style, which since Rohde has been classified as 'sophistic', but also because he may be identical with Philostratus' sophist, Heliodorus 'the Arab' (*VS* 2.32.626). This is not the place to rehearse the controversy over the date and identity of the novelist.[57] If he is a fourth-century figure, his poem must be seen as a response to those of Philostratus. So too it may be if he is Philostratus' sophist, whom the biographer encountered on an embassy to Caracalla in AD 213 and reports to have been spending his old age in Rome at the time of his own writing the *Lives*: the composition of the novel might belong to his later years, after he had become familiar with Philostratus' *Heroicus*. A third possibility is that Heliodorus had already composed his novel in the earlier part of his career, and that it was known to Philostratus when he composed the *Heroicus*. Only arguments from likelihood exclude this last hypothesis. Allusion in the somewhat straight-faced and archaistic *Heroicus* to the *avant-garde* genre of the novel is less probable than exploitation by the highly allusive and complex Heliodorus of a Philostratean dialogue. Moreover Heliodorus' metrical form might be explained as a deliberate attempt to upstage, whereas the metres of Philostratus are, as remarked above, not untypical of hymns.

Heliodorus' hymn has brought us back to melic poetry. There is only one other piece of evidence that a sophist attempted a melic genre, and that concerns the sophist from Larissa who attracted adverse comment by his singsong delivery, Hippodromus. His λυρικοὶ νόμοι, 'lyric nomes', were still being sung more than a decade after his death, at the time Philostratus composed *Lives of the Sophists* (*VS* 2.27.620). Perhaps these were the sort of citharodic performances in which Mesomedes excelled in Hadrian's reign.[58] Another melic poet, Hermocrates of Rhodes, is also mentioned by Aristides as present at the Pergamum Asclepieum, where a number of sophists were to be found, but he was not himself a sophist (*Or.* 50.23 Keil). Other examples of sophistic poetry take us away from melic compositions. Scopelianus of Clazomenae, we are told by Philostratus (*VS* 1.21.518), composed in all poetic genres. Presumably these included melic, but it is for epic and dramatic poetry that he is specifically praised. He composed an epic *Gigantias*, '*Battle of the giants*', and in tragedy rivalled his teacher Nicetes (who was also, therefore, a tragedian).[59]

[57] For an outline see Bowie 1985b, 696 and 883–4 (bibliography, to which add Lightfoot 1988). Since Bowersock 1994 the majority of scholars have favoured a fourth-century date.

[58] For the link between the *cithara* and νόμοι, 'nomes', cf. Lucillius, *AP* 11.133 on the μελογράφος, 'song-/tune-writer', Eutychides (fictional? cf. Floridi 2014, 329–30). For other such singer-poets cf. P. Aelius Agathemerus, κιθαρωιδὸς καὶ μελοποιός, 'citharode and song-/tune-composer', from late-second-century Ephesus, *ISmyrna* 659 = *IGR* iv 1432; M. Sempronius Nicocrates – rather lower in the social scale, since later in life he traded in εὔμορφοι γυναῖκες, 'beautiful women', *GVI* 1049 = Kaibel 613.

[59] For the imperial popularity of *Gigantiads* cf. the work ascribed to a Dionysius, for which the edition of Benaissa 2018, following his 2011 *editio princeps* of *P.Oxy.* 5103, supersedes Heitsch 1963–4, i 60–77 and Livrea 1973. For the remote possibility that the Tiberian *rhetor* Apollonides may have composed a tragedy as well as epigrams see *GP* ii 148 n.2 (cf. my n.75); on his epigrams see Bowie 2012e (Chapter 17 in this volume).

5 Sophists as Poets: Epigram

Three epigraphic examples may be added to those quarried from literature, but the uncertain poetic status of their authors' limits their value. From the right leg of one of the Memnon colossi we have a poem of three couplets (dated after AD 205 by Bernand) signed by one Falernus who calls himself poet and sophist:[60]

ἐγὼ σοφιστὴ[ς] ὢν
[Μέμν]ων οἶδε λαλεῖν ὅσον ῥήτωρ, οἶδέ τε σιγᾶν
  εἰδὼς καὶ φωνῆς νεῦρα καὶ ἡσυχίας.
[κα]ὶ γὰρ ἰδὼν Ἠῶ τὴν μητέρα τὴν κροκόπεπλον
  [ἤχη]σεν λιγυρῆς ἡδύτερον λαλίης.
τ]αῦτα Φάλερνος ἔγραψε ποητὴς ἠδὲ σοφισ[τὴς]
  [ἀξ]ία καὶ Μουσῶν, ἀξία καὶ Χαρίτων.

I, being a sophist
Memnon knows how to speak as much as a *rhetor*, and knows how to
  be silent, skilled in the sinews of both speech and silence:
for when he saw Dawn, his mother, in her saffron-robe,
  he called out more sweetly than clear speech.
This was written by Falernus, poet and sophist,
  lines worthy of the Muses, worthy of the Graces.

The appellation 'poet' presumably refers to something more than simply this poem, but it could be that he only wrote epigrams.[61] It is unlikely that anything he wrote was at all good. More conjecturally, a tablet apparently from Egypt mentions a M. Decrius Decrianus as a poet of epic and melic who competed in local festivals.[62] This might just be the same man as a sophist Decrianus from Patrae who figures in Lucian's *Ass* (2) but he need not be, and indeed Lucian's sophist could be quite fictitious. Finally an epigraphic text from Iasus honours one A. Mussius Aper for τὴν ἐν ῥητορικῆι καὶ ποιητικῆι καὶ τῆι λοιπῆι πάσηι σοφίαι ποικιλωτάτην καὶ ἀσύνκριτον μεγαλοφυιείαν, 'his very varied and incomparable talent in rhetoric, poetry and all other wisdom', and seems to belong to the first century AD.[63]

[60] Kaibel 994 = Bernand 1960, no. 61. For the inscriptions on the Memnon colossus see Rosenmeyer 2018 (120–1 on Falernus); on this and two other two-word signatures of Falernus see Puech 2002, 241–2 nos. 110–12.

[61] Note that D.L. 5.61 describes Strato as ποιητὴς ἐπιγραμμάτων, 'poet of epigrams'.

[62] *SEG* 18.716. See Fraser 1959 for text and discussion.

[63] *IIasos* 94; the dating emerges from *IIasos* 105.

The six lines by Falernus, poet and sophist, were in the much-practised genre of epigram, as were some of the poems of Aristides and Philostratus; and the novelists' oracles, particularly those of Heliodorus, have displayed epigrammatic features. It is in fact the genre into which most of the poetry composed by sophists falls, and the reasons are obvious. The practical routines of daily life required dedicatory, commemorative and sepulchral epigrams in civic and private contexts, and they were commissioned by men and women from almost all levels of society. Consequently they were composed by individuals of many degrees of competence and professionalism. It cannot tell us much about a sophist's attitude to poetry as a whole that he writes his own epigrams rather than commissioning them from a friend – although it becomes of interest when an epigraphic text is so commissioned: but epigrams are undeniably poetry, and in some sophistic hands were developed into substantial poems, as indeed we have already seen in the case of Aristides' poetic 'hymn'. They are certainly important to an assessment of poetry's place in the sophistic world. In a few cases, those of Herodes Atticus and Flavius Glaucus of Marathon, and perhaps Lucian and Aelian, we have enough poems by a single hand to form more than a superficial impression of a poet's goals and style, although none of our figures is a virtuoso epigrammatist like the Augustan *rhetor* Marcus Argentarius.

6 Herodes Atticus

As chronology invites, and as Herodes himself would certainly have wished, his poems will be considered first.[64] None of them is likely to antedate AD 160, so they are works of his often unhappy sixties and seventies. Four of the six poems are at least in part a response to bereavement or separation and share a melancholy tone. The three longer poems all display a straining for effect which, endemic though it was in the genre, might well have been exaggerated by Herodes' declamatory career; in compensation, however, two of the three depart from generic expectations in an interesting way.

The most successful was found on the gate of the estate at Marathon initially constructed when the estate was given as a bridal gift from Herodes to Regilla about AD 143: the epigram itself must have been inscribed later, after Regilla's death at the end of the 150s:[65]

[64] For several of the poems discussed below see Skenteri 2005; for Herodes' relations with Athens Tobin 1997, Strazdins 2023.

[65] Geagan 1964; Ameling 1983, ii 117–20 no. 99. For discussion see Tobin 1997, 242–9; Galli 2002, 134–8; Gleason 2010, 135–42; Strazdins 2023.

'ἆ μάκαρ, ὅστις ἔδειμε νέην πόλιν, οὔν[ο]μα δ' αὐτὴν
  Ῥηγίλλ̣ης καλέων ζώει ἀγαλλόμενος.'
'ζώω δ' ἀχ̣[ν]ύμενος τό μοι οἰκία ταῦτα τέτυκται
  νόσφι] φίλης ἀλόχου καὶ δόμος ἡμιτέλης.
ὥς ἄρα τοι θνητοῖσι θεοὶ βιοτὴν κεράσαντ[ες]
  χά[ρ]ματά τ' ἠδ' ἀνίας γείτονας ἀμφὶς ἔχο̣[υν]'.

'Blessed is he who built a new city, and, giving it the name of
  Regilla, lives rejoicing in it.'
'But I live in sorrow that I have had these dwellings fashioned
  without my dear wife, and that my house is half-complete;
so it is, you see, that for mortals gods have blended life
  and gave as neighbours on either side both joys and woes.'

SEG 23.121

The opening phrase may echo archaic elegy,[66] though the first couplet also evokes a building inscription, like those on the arch of Hadrian at Athens which this gate imitates. The texture of archaic elegy is maintained in the mixture of autobiography and maxim found in the last four lines, but the dialogue form which articulates them to the first two smacks of sepulchral epigram, appropriate to the mention of Regilla's death, though Herodes may well have known archaic elegies which used it too. The last line echoes a famous passage of the *Iliad* (24.525–30) and perhaps a metaphor in Aeschylus' *Agamemnon* (1004). The author's play with genres and verbal allusiveness come off, and alongside this complexity the poem's clarity of expression gives it a simple dignity. Although we cannot be certain that it was composed by Herodes himself, all these features point in his direction.

Less felicitous is another six-line poem on the death of yet a third of Herodes' children or τρόφιμοι, 'foster-children':[67]

Ἡρώδης οἷ τήνδε κόμην οὐ πάντα ἐνιαυτόν
    οὔτε κόμην θρέψας οὔτε σὲ παῖδα φίλον
μηνὶ τρίτωι κείρας ὑπὸ κεύθεσι θήκατο γαίης
    Ἡρώδης, δεύσας ἄκρα κόμης δάκρυσι·
σῆμ' ἔτυμον παίδων ψυχαῖς τρισίν, ὥς ποτε σῶμα
    δέξεσθ' ἐν θήκαις ὑμετέροιο πατρός.

Herodes, alas, dedicates this hair – not for a whole year growing
    his hair, nor your hair, dear child,

[66] Cf. Thgn. 1013, 1173, drawing no doubt on the ὦ μάκαρ of Il. 3.182.

[67] Peek 1942 [1951], 136–9 (an important discussion), no. 306; Follet 1977, 53–4 (linking it with Polydeucion's death); Peek 1980 no. 356; *SEG* 26.290; Ameling 1983, ii 143 no. 140.

cutting in the third month did he place you in the earth's depths,
Herodes, wetting the ends of his hair with tears:
a veridical sign to the three souls of his children, that one day
you will receive the body of your father in your tombs.

GVI 1613

Although modern appreciation has been blunted by the difficulty of identifying which child or τρόφιμος, 'foster-child', of Herodes is the occasion of the poem, even a fully informed reader would find the phrasing convoluted. The attempt to link Herodes' mark of mourning and the third-month ritual of the *Apatouria* (if that is indeed referred to) is forced; and the redeployment of Herodes' hair to catch his tears is inelegant if clever. Again we cannot insist on Herodean authorship, but it is not unlikely.

Our third long poem is unfortunately preserved in so fragmentary a condition that we cannot be sure whether it was in hexameters or elegiac couplets. The remaining ten line-beginnings on a stone plaque from Eleusis show that it proclaimed and commemorated the friendship of Herodes and his pupil the emperor Lucius Verus, recalling their conversation and contrasting the emperor's practical career that took him to face the enemy with Herodes' quieter life in his homeland, Attica. The enemy mentioned is probably the Parthian, the date between AD 162 and Verus' return in AD 165. In the following text I adopt Peek's supplements:[68]

[ἐν τρι]ọδω καὶ τῆιδε[
λέσχηι τερπέσθην κα[
ἔνθ' ἀνέμων σκέπας ῆ̣[
πῆξαν τ' ἀσπασίως[
ἀλλ' ὁ μὲν ἐν πάτρηι[
τῶι δ' ἔρ̣γ̣ων πρηκτὴρ[
ἀμφὶ δέ μιν π̣όλεμ̣[
εἰρωτῶν ὃς ἔτλη Γ̣[
Ἡρώδης Β̣ῆ̣ρ̣ον κρ[
πολλῶν καὶ μεγά[λων

[in this] meeting-place too [by the palace of dear Demeter]
the two of them enjoyed talking a[nd]
where there was a shelter from the winds[]
and they built pleasingly []
but he in his native land []
but for his friend a doer of deeds []

[68] Peek 1942, 154 ff. = Clinton 1972 = Ameling 1983, ii 177 no. 186.

and about him wa[r's cloud and dread din of battle]
asking, who dared P[arthian?]
Herodes (verb) Verus []
for many great [kindnesses making some return]

Herodes' authorship is only conjectural, but it receives some support from the poem's allusions, not just to Homer (with line 3 cf. Od. 5.443 etc.) but to the more recherché Callimachus: line 4's λέσχηι τερπέσθην, 'the two of them enjoyed talking', echoes his famous epigram for Heraclitus, 2.3 Pfeiffer = *HE* 34.3. If Peek's tentative suggestion for the end of the last pentameter is correct, the inscription must have been associated in some way with a mark of Herodes' gratitude to Verus. The most obvious such mark would be the erection of a statue, and if that were so this poem would be an example of the sort of extended dedicatory epigram which we shall shortly see to have been well represented in Eleusis of the third century. But the stone on which the poem was inscribed does not seem to have been a statue base, but rather some sort of plaque. Furthermore two of the themes of the poem are among those which a century later Menander prescribed as appropriate to a *propempticon*: ἐπὶ τούτοις ἅπασιν ἀξιώσεις αὐτὸν μεμνῆσθαι τῆς πάλαι συνηθείας, τῆς εὐνοίας, τῆς φιλίας, 'Finally you will ask him to remember old acquaintance, kindness, and friendship' (cf. our lines 4–6); and διάγραφε τὴν ὁδὸν καὶ τὴν γῆν δι' ἧς πορεύεται, 'describe the route and the country through which he travels' (cf. our lines 9–10).[69] We also find Statius, two generations earlier, elaborating a similar contrast between Maecius Celer's travels (*tu rapidum Euphraten et regia Bactra*, 'you the fast-flowing Euphrates and Bactrian palaces') and his own literary activities (*ast ego* ..., 'but I ...') in the *propempticon* of *Silvae* 2.3 (136–43). It is interesting that the friendship theme is one that Menander sees as appropriate to a speech made on the departure of an equal, whereas in lines 8–10 we can see *encomium* (prescribed by Menander for sending off a superior): such ambiguity between equality and deference was characteristic of the great sophists' relations with emperors. A sophist who practised a century before Menander is quite likely to have formulated rules similar to his for the composition of *propemptica*, and we may see them in operation here. The stone would then preserve the text of a poem that Herodes had composed – and perhaps declaimed – to mark Verus' departure from Athens to the East.

These three poems show that Herodes saw poetry as appropriate for certain sorts of commemorative text and (if we accept his authorship) was not

[69] Men. Rh. *Treatise* 2.395–9, with the notes of Russell and Wilson 1981. The passages cited are at 398.26–8 and 30.

reluctant to put his own products on view. We also know, however, that for commemorative poetry he turned on occasion to a professional poet. This is shown by Marcellus of Side's two signed poems erected at the Triopeum on the *Via Attica* on Regilla's suburban estate.[70] So too, it must be conceded, is the superiority of Marcellus' poetry over that by Herodes himself or others whom he commissioned.

The remaining poems are too short to be much of a test of a writer's skill or to betray his idiosyncrasies, but it is likely enough that they were composed by Herodes. One at least of the monuments to Herodes' dead foster-sons Achilles, Memnon and Polydeucion bore metrical inscriptions. Thus a herm of Polydeucion found at Cephisia and put up after his death towards AD 173 preceded a prose imprecation with:

ἥρως Πολυδευκίων
ταῖσδέ ποτ' ἐν τριό-
δοις σὺν σοὶ ἐπε-
στρεφόμην

hero Polydeucion,
once in these
crossways
I spent time with you.[71]

IG ii² 13194

Polydeucion's name required the aeolic colon – – ᴗ ᴗ – ᴗ –, and each of the other two lines is a hemiepes (– ᴗ ᴗ – ᴗ ᴗ –), so the metrical system more probably reflects necessity than gratuitous virtuosity.[72]

More striking, perhaps, than the existence of these few verse texts is the great preponderance of short prose inscriptions commemorating these τρόφιμοι, 'foster-children'. I should guess that this is indeed a mark of Herodes' attachment to and pre-eminence in prose rhetoric, and that in hands other than those of a *rhetor* more of these would have been verse.

[70] *IG* xiv 1389 = Kaibel 1046 = *IGUR* 1155 = Ameling 1983, ii 153 no. 146: for discussion Wilamowitz 1928 remains fundamental. See also Peek 1979; Davies and Pomeroy 2012; Bowie 1990b, 66–70 (Chapter 14, 295–8 in this volume) and 2019d (Chapter 44 in Volume 3). On Regilla's death see Pomeroy 2007.

[71] Kaibel 1090; Ameling 1983, ii 163 no. 158: cf. Philostr. *VS* 2.1.558–9.
For the date of Polydeucion's death cf. Follet 1977, with doubts by Holford-Strevens 1988, 102 n.67. On the cult of Polydeucion, and on Herodes' other τρόφιμοι, 'foster-children', see Jansen 2008; Strazdins 2023.

[72] Kaibel 1091 is unlikely to have been, as there restored, metrical, cf. Ameling 1983, ii 172, no. 177; Ameling 1983, ii 164 no. 163 could, but need not, be metrical.

Two elegiac couplets belong to Herodes' very last years. One is a dedicatory couplet for a statue of Asclepius set up in the Asclepieum at Eleusis, perhaps after his illness at Oricum, and if so in AD 175:[73]

μύστην Ἡρώδης Ἀσκληπιὸν [ε]ἵσατο Δηοῖ
  νοῦσον ἀλεξή[σ]αντ' ἀντιχαρ[ι]ζόμενος.

Herodes dedicated to Demeter the initiate Asclepius
  in gratitude for his driving away disease.

IG ii² 4781 = *IEleus.* 498

A final witness to Herodes' gifts in epigram may be found in the epitaph which marked the tomb constructed by the Athenians two years later in the Panathenaic stadium:[74]

Ἀττικοῦ Ἡρώδης Μαραθώνιος, οὗ τάδε πάντα,
κεῖται τῶιδε τάφωι, πάντοθεν εὐδόκιμος.

Atticus' son Herodes of Marathon, who created all this,
  lies here in this tomb, renowned everywhere.

GVI 391

A man so careful of his fame would be unlikely to leave his sepulchral epitaph to another; though since Athenians disregarded his wish to be buried at Marathon, they may equally have discarded a Herodean epigram. But the poem's classical brevity and allusion to Antimachus of Colophon[75] might be thought to point to Herodes.

Herodes' poems are a curious mixture that reflects his classicising ideals. They sometimes achieve a clean simplicity, but more often their richness of allusion to earlier poetry makes them top heavy, and when strained conceits are aimed at they come near to foundering.

73 *SEG* 1.55; Ameling 1983, ii 211 no. 191, linking it with Herodes' illness at Oricum on his return from Sirmium (Philostr. *VS* 2.1.562).

74 Philostr. *VS* 2.1.566 = Ameling 1983, ii 211 no. 192: cf. Tobin 1993; Rife 2008; Strazdins 2023.

75 Fr. 53.1–2 Wyss = 131 Matthews ἔστι δέ τις Νέμεσις μεγάλη θεός, ἣ τάδε πάντα | πρὸς μακάρων ἔλαχεν, 'There is a mighty god, Nemesis, who has been allotted all this by the blessed ones'. Cf. Rife 2008, 113; Matthews 1996, 313–21, esp. 319, suggesting τάδε πάντα means 'everything here on earth'. For Herodes' possible interest in the cult of Nemesis at Rhamnous see *IG* ii² 13208 with Strazdins 2022. By contrast the long elegiac poem commemorating Herodes' return to Attica and Marathon, ca. AD 175, *IG* ii² 3606, is marked by too many infelicities of style and oddities of grammar to be easily ascribed to Herodes himself, and its recurrent presentation of him as an almost divine benefactor would involve a stance too arrogant even for Herodes. For a text and discussion see Ameling 1983, ii 205–11 no. 190; English translation Oliver 1970, 34: see also Wilamowitz 1928, 223–8; Tobin 1997, 272–5; Skenteri 2005, 86–110; Strazdins 2023.

Before turning to the poems of Glaucus, brief consideration should be given to a text associated with a pupil of Herodes and apparently influenced by him. We know from Philostratus that one of Herodes' favourite pupils was Flavius Amphicles of Chalcis in Euboea.[76] A six-line elegiac sepulchral epigram on a herm from Chalcis in Euboea commemorates a dead youth Amphicles, long thought to be that pupil of Herodes, and the accompanying curse resembles those erected in various places by Herodes, so that he himself has been thought to be the poet. Robert 1978a showed finally that this Amphicles could not be Herodes' pupil. Rather the pupil Amphicles, probably the archon of the Panhellenion in AD 177–81 or 181–5,[77] is the composer of the poem, while its subject is his son; the curse which follows (and which also appears on other stones, but without the epigram) marks him as a clone of Herodes. So too does the poem, not inelegant but somewhat forced in its conceits:[78]

χαῖρον ἐγὼ λοετροῖσι καὶ | εἰσέτι τοῖσδ' ἐσορῶμαι
  Ἀμφικλέης, χώρου | δεσπόσυνος φιλίου.
ναὶ μὴν καὶ γένεος φερε|κυδέος ἐξ ὑπάτων με
  δέρκεο, Πειεριδῶν οὔποτε λησάμενον·
κρατὶ δ' ἐπηιώρηντ' ὄπι|θεν κομόωσαι ἔθειραι·
  οὐ γὰρ ἔκερσ' ἥβα, ἀλ|λὰ πότμος προλαβών.

I used to enjoy these baths, and still I look upon them,
  Amphicles, master of a place dear to me;
Yes indeed, from a glory-winning lineage of consuls,
  behold me, never forgetful of the Muses;
and upon my head the luxuriant locks flowed behind,
  for it was not manhood that cut them, but fate, who got there first.

IG xii.9 1179

7 T. Flavius Glaucus of Marathon

When we turn to Philostratus' own generation we encounter a figure who was at once – as he tells us in a prose text[79] – a poet, *rhetor* and philosopher, T. Flavius Glaucus of Marathon. His poems reveal much about his

[76] Philostr. *VS* 2.8.578, 10.585, *PIR*² F 201: cf. Jones 1968; Robert 1978a.

[77] *IG* ii² 2957, Oliver 1970, 103–4 no. 15, cf. 133.

[78] Ameling 1983, ii 225 no. 212; Puech 2002, 47–64, no. 5.

[79] *IG* ii² 3704.12. A masterly elucidation of the texts relating to T. Flavius Glaucus and Sarapion is to be found in Oliver 1949, with important revisions by Follet 1976. On Sarapion see Bowie 2006d (Chapter 16 in Volume 3).

illustrious ancestry, which included a homonymous procurator of Cyprus (his paternal grandfather) and the sophist Isaeus (a maternal great-great-grandfather); the same text in which he proclaims himself a poet shows that another ancestor was the Sarapion of Plutarch's *Sympotic Questions*, also a poet and philosopher. Perhaps memory of that ancestor played a part in influencing our Glaucus to try his hand at poetry as well as philosophy and rhetoric. His rhetorical distinction may not have been great – certainly he is not given a mention, far less a *Life*, by Philostratus, although the biographer does commend the εὐφωνία, 'fine voice', of his uncle (also named Glaucus) displayed in the office of hierophant at Eleusis (*VS* 2.20.600–1) and registers another uncle, Callaeschrus, as a pupil of Chrestus of Byzantium (*VS* 2.11.591).

It is in fact to honour relatives who held the highest offices in the cult at Eleusis that T. Flavius Glaucus composed several of his poems. The longest and best was for a statue of his maternal grandmother Isidotē who, as ἱεροφάντις (*hierophantis*), had initiated Marcus and Commodus in AD 176. The statue was set up after her death, but the poem has more features of an anathematic than a sepulchral epigram. It is not signed, but since the statue was put up by Glaucus, by his brother Callaeschrus, and by their mother Eunicē, Oliver is surely right to insist that the poem must be by the poet of the family, Glaucus:[80]

ἀγαθῆι τύχηι
πυροφόρου Δήμητρος ὑπείροχον ἱεροφάντιν
πολλὸν ἐπ' εὐσεβίηι κῦδος ἀειραμένην
Ἑλλάδος εὐρυχόρου πρῶτον γένος Ἀντολίης τε
ἔγγονον Εἰσαίου τοῦ σοφίας ὑπάτου,
ὃς δὴ καὶ βασιλῆος ἀμύμονος Ἁδριανοῖο
μουσάων ἀγαθὴν εἶχε διδασκαλίην·
Εἰσαίου δὲ θύγατρα μεγαινήτοιο καὶ αὐτοῦ
ἔξοχον ἔν τ' ἀρεταῖς ἔν τε σαοφροσύναις,
ἣν καὶ ἀμειβομένη Δηὼ μακάρων ἐπὶ νήσσους
ἤγαγε παντοίης ἐκτὸς ἐπωδυνίης·
δῶκε δέ οἱ θάνατον γλυκερώτερον ἡδέο[ς] ὕπνου
πάγχυ καὶ Ἀργείων φέρτερον ἠιθέων,
ἥ τε καὶ Ἀντωνῖνον ὁμοῦ Κομμόδωι βασιλῆας
ἀρχομένη τελετῶν ἔστεφε μυστιπόλους.
τὴν μὲν ἄρα ψήφωι μὲν Ἄρηι φίλη θέτο βουλή,
εἰκόνα δ' ἠγαθέην ἐκτελέσαντο νέην
Εὐνίκη τε φίλη θυγάτηρ υἷές τε θυγατρός

[80] Oliver 1949, 248–50 no. 1 (citing earlier editions); Puech 2002, 270–83, no. 123.

Ζωιλίδαι μητρὸς μητέρα θεσπεσίην
Κάλλαισχρος καὶ Γλαῦκος ἐν εἰκόνι κυδαίνοντες,
ἣν καὶ Δημήτηρ ὤπασεν ἀθανάτοις.

Corn-bearing Demeter's surpassing *hierophantis*
who acquired much honour for her piety,
first in family in Hellas with broad dancing-places and the East,
grand-daughter of Isaeus, the first minister of learning,
who indeed gave the blameless emperor Hadrian
his excellent schooling in the Muses;
and daughter of Isaeus who also was himself greatly praised,
outstanding both in her virtues and in her chaste ways,
whom indeed in reward Deo to the Isles of the blessed
led, away from any sort of pain,
and gave her a death sweeter than gentle sleep,
and in every way better than that of the Argive youths; she
who to Antoninus, together with Commodus, the emperors
gave initiates' crowns, presiding over the mysteries –
she whom the Council dear to Ares has voted be honoured,
and whose statue new and most holy was provided
by Eunicē, her dear daughter, and her daughter's sons
the scions of Zoilus, for their mother's divine mother,
whom they, Callaeschrus and Glaucus, honour in her portrait,
whom Demeter herself took to the immortals.

IG ii^2 3632 = *IEleus.* 502

This poem is relatively successful. The abundant genealogical information that it seeks to convey is set off by decoration which draws effectively on traditional poetic language. Glaucus can be felicitously allusive. In lines 11–12, where the greater sweetness of death than sleep may indeed, as Oliver suggests, hint at Plato's *Apology* 40 c–e, there is also a possible allusion to the *Odyssey* that would suggest death to be Isidotē's natural home; and while φέρτερον in line 11 may allude to *Iliad* 6.156–8, spoken precisely by the Lycian hero Glaucus as he narrates his genealogy, that does not exclude allusion in Ἀργείων φέρτερον ἠιθέων to the famous anecdote of Cleobis and Biton, the paradigms of a good death.[81] There are also hints that

[81] For Pl. *Ap.* and Il. 6 see Oliver 1949, 249–50 (missing the Glaucus link). His denial of a reference to Cleobis and Biton is rightly rejected by Follet 1976, 265 n.2. That the family had an interest in Platonic philosophy emerges not only from the specific statement about the poet's uncle Callaeschrus in *IG* ii^2 3709 (discussed below) but from his name, that of Critias' father. γλυκερώτερον in line 11 evokes Od. 9.27–8 οὔ τοι ἐγώ γε | ἧς γαίης δύναμαι γλυκερώτερον ἄλλο ἰδέσθαι, 'I cannot set eyes on anything sweeter than one's own land'. In line 3 πρώτη should probably be read for πρῶτον.

Glaucus knows Marcellus' poem on the heroisation of Regilla, book-texts of which must surely have been available in Marathon and Athens as well as the inscribed text on the *Via Appia*.[82]

Similarities of thought and language are to be found in another text from Eleusis intended for a statue of the daughter of Glaucus' brother, another Callaeschrus. The fourteen hexameters, however, are more subservient to the exposition of genealogy, and although they must be by the same poet, they are less impressive:[83]

μυστιπόλοι Δήμητρος, ἐμεῖό τις ἱερὴ ἔστω
μνημοσύνη Δηοῦς παρ' ἀνακτόρωι· οὔνομα μέν μο[ι]
[Εὐ]νείκη, τίκτεν δὲ Θάλειά με κυδήεσσα
πατρὶ φίλωι Καλλαίσχρωι ἀγακλεῖ, τοῦ δ' ἄρ[α μήτηρ]
Εὐνείκη. τῆς δ' αὖτε σαόφρων ἱεροφ[άντις]
ἦεν ἀπ' Εἰσαίοιο φερώνυμος Ἀντολί[ηθεν]
[Ε]ἰσιδότη, τοῦ κῦδος ἀμύμονο[ς ....]
ῥητήρων· πάππος δ' ἄρ' ἐμεῦ πέλεν [...... .]
Ζωίλος, ὃς δοιοῖσιν ἀδελφειοῖς φρόν[ει ἶσα],
τῶι μὲν ἀπ' αἰγλήεντος ἀνακτόρου ἱερο[φάντηι]
Γλαύκωι· ἀτὰρ σοφίης ἡγήτορι – τὴν <δ>ὲ Πλά[τωνος]
δρέψατο – Καλλαίσχρωι περιωνύμωι : οὐ μὲν ἐμεῖο
[τηλ]οῦ συνκλήτοιο πέλει γένος· ἀνχόθι γάρ μο[ι]
[.... ἀνε]ψιαδῶν ἕπεται κλέος Αὐσονίηθεν.
vac.

Celebrants of Demeter, let me have some sacred
memorial by the temple of Demeter. My name is
Eunicē, and glorious Thaleia bore me
to my dear father Callaeschrus, much-famed, whose mother
was Eunicē – and hers in turn the chaste *hierophantis*
who took her name from Isaeus from the East,
Isidotē, from him who, blameless, had the glory [and kingship]
of orators; and my grandfather was [from Marathon],
Zoilus, whose mind was [like] that of his two brothers,
one the hierophant at the glittering temple

[82] E.g. with ἀμύμονος in line 5 cf. Marcellus A 13; with the thought of line 9, Marcellus A 9–10.

[83] Oliver 1949, 250–2 no. 2; Puech 2002, 270–83, no. 12; Follet 1976, 263–4, whose supplements should be preferred to those of earlier editors: thus in line 6, since Isidotē does not get her name from the East, I reject Graindor's Ἀντολί[ης τε] in favour of her Ἀντολί[ηθεν] with Εἰσαίοιο (as Αὐσονίηθεν appears to go with [ἀνε]ψιαδῶν in line 14) – for Αὐσονίηθεν Follet notes a parallel in [Opp.] *C.* 1.43, of AD 212–17; at line 7 the supposed parallel with *IG* ii^{2} 3632 has deluded, and no satisfactory syntax is offered by Graindor's Ἀδριανοῖο. I am tempted by ἠδ' ὑπατεία, 'and first place', cf. *IG* ii^{2} 3632.5 σοφίας ὑπάτου, but Follet saw traces of MONE–AK.

Glaucus, and the other a wisdom – and it was Plato's that he
reaped – renowned Callaeschrus. Nor is my
family far from the senate; for close to me
follows the [divine] fame of my cousins from Italy.

IG ii^2 3709 = *IEleus.* 659

The Glaucus here called 'the prince of wisdom', the poet's uncle, was also honoured. His poem is no more than a sepulchral epigram (there is no mention of a memorial), and its effects are to some extent dictated by that genre: but again the point is made (cf. *IG* ii^2 3632.11–12) that death is a good, not an evil, a point that Oliver rightly traces to the Platonic writings which the deceased's brother Callaeschrus studied:[84]

γηραλέην ψυχὴν ἐπ' ἀκμαίωι σώματι Γλαῦκος
  καὶ κάλλει κεράσας κρείττονα σωφροσύνην
ὄργια πᾶσιν ἔφαινε βροτοῖς φαεσίμβροτα Δηοῦς
  εἰνάετες, δεκάτωι δ' ἦλθε πρὸς ἀθανάτους.
ἦ καλὸν ἐκ μακάρων μυστήριον, οὐ μόνον εἶναι
  τὸν θάνατον θνητοῖς οὐ κακὸν ἀλλ' ἀγαθόν.

Glaucus blended an aged soul with a body in its prime
  and with beauty, modesty, that is its better;
and to all men he displayed the man-lighting mysteries of Deo
  for nine years, and in the tenth joined the immortals.
Indeed it is a fair secret revealed by the blessed, that
  not only is death for mortals no evil, but it is a good.

IG ii^2 3661 = *IEleus.* 646

A statue was also put up at Eleusis by the sister of Glaucus the hierophant, and aunt of the poet, to honour her husband. As before, the authorship of Glaucus the poet is conjectural, but highly likely. The text is much more fragmentary than that of the three poems already considered, and the husband's name is lost, but he was certainly both eponymous archon and hierophant, and may himself have been a sophist:[85]

[84] Oliver 1949, 252–3 no. 3; *GVI* 879; Puech 2002, 270–83, no. 124; Follet 1976, 262–3 (dating Glaucus' period as hierophant to 215/6–225/6, allowing a possible error of five years).

[85] Oliver 1949, 253–4 no. 4; Follet 1976, 265–7; Puech 2002, 100–15 no. 21. The husband may be the Apollonius honoured in *IG* ii^2 3811 and therefore the sophist of Philostratus *VS* 2.20: see below n.90. Against, and favouring identification with P. Aelius Apollonius of *IG* ii^2 3688 and 3764 (her nos. 23 and 24) see Puech 2002, 105–15. Oliver (following Wilhelm) had restored the lady's name as [Eury]alē, but Follet 1976, 266 with nn.3 and 4 makes a good case for [Myrt]alē, accepted by Puech 2002, 100–16 no. 22.

ἀγ]λαὰ δέξατο δῶρα
[ ]φρονέοντα λόγον
]την καὶ ἐπώνυμον ἀρχήν
]μυστικὸν ἡγεμόνα
[ ]αντα πρὶν ἀνδράσιν ἱερὰ φαίνειν
[τίμησεν ψ]ήφωι πατρὶς ἀγασσαμένη·
[εἰκόνα δὲ] στῆσεν χαλκήλατον ἥ ποτε νύμφη
[Μυρτ?]άλη εἰσοθέωι σεμνὸν ἄγαλμα πόσει.
[ἡ δ'] ἦν Γλαύκου μὲν θυγάτηρ, ὃς ἄριστος ἐτύχθη
ἱππήων, βυθίην Κύπρον ἐπιτροπέων,
Γλαύκου δὲ γνωτὴ θεοειδέος, ὅς τε καὶ αὐτός
ἱεροφαντήσας ᾤχετ' ἐς ἀθανάτους.

[----] received splendid gifts
[----]-minded speech
[----] and the eponymous archonship
[-----] leader of the initiates
[.....] before displaying the mysteries to men
his native land voted to honour him in its admiration;
[and a portrait] forged in bronze was put up by his bride
[Myrt?]alē, a proud statue to her godlike husband.
[And she] was daughter of Glaucus, who was the best
of knights, procurator of deep-sea Cyprus,
and sibling of god-shaped Glaucus, who himself has also
displayed the mysteries and departed to the immortals.

IG ii^2 3662 = *IEleus.* 649

Two shorter epigraphic poems take us away from Eleusis to the other great sanctuaries of Greece, Olympia and Delphi. There is little doubt about authorship (though equally no mark of individuality) concerning a couplet for Glaucus' own statue at Olympia, proclaiming that he had sung the ὕμνος, 'hymn', at Olympia:[86]

ἀγαθῆι [τύχ]ηι.
Κεκροπ[ίδ]ης ὅδε | Γλαῦκος, Ὀλύμπιον | ὕμνον ἀείσας, |
εἵδρυμαι βουλῆς | ψήφωι Ὀλυμπιάδος.

With good fortune
Here Cecrops' scion, Glaucus, who sang the Olympic hymn,
I stand, by vote of the Council of the Olympia.

IOlymp. 457

[86] Oliver 1949, 254 no. 5; Puech 2002, 281–2 no. 126.

Some sung performance, this time by a chorus, may also be attested by a very scrappy text from Delphi, but although the name Glaucus appears in it both attribution and meaning are doubtful.[87]

Our epigraphic haul can be supplemented, admittedly with appropriate reservations, from the *Greek Anthology*. Five poems in the *Palatine Anthology* and one in the *Planudean* are attributed to a Glaucus, and of these one (*AP* 7.285) is given by a marginal note to a Glaucus of Nicopolis, to whom modern scholars also generally assign *AP* 9.341 and 12.44.[88] Of the other three one has the rubric Γλαύκου Ἀθηναίου, 'By Glaucus the Athenian' (*AP* 9.774), and a marginal note says that the following poem (*AP* 9.775) is by the same hand. Both are *ecphraseis* of works of art, as is *APl.* 111, so that the latter has generally been given to Glaucus 'the Athenian'. That he is our poet T. Flavius Glaucus, as proposed by Oliver, is likely enough.[89]

The epigrams are these:

> Ἁ βάκχα Παρία μέν, ἐνεψύχωσε δ᾽ ὁ γλύπτας
> τὸν λίθον· ἀνθρώισκει δ᾽ ὡς βρομιαζομένα.
> ὦ Σκόπα, ἁ θεοποιὸς <ἄπιστον> ἐμήσατο τέχνα
> θαῦμα χιμαιροφόνον θυιάδα μαινομέναν.

> The bacchant is Parian, but the sculptor has breathed life into
> the stone, and she leaps up like one rapt by Bromius.
> O Scopas, your art, that fashions gods, has wrought
> a miracle, a goat-slaying maenad in her frenzy.

AP 9.774

The next poem has been thought by ancient and modern commentators alike to describe no bacchant, but Antiope about to be seduced by Zeus:

> Ἡ βάκχη Κρονίδην Σάτυρον θέτο· εἶς δὲ χορείαν
> θρώισκει μαινομένων ὡς βρομιαζόμενος.

[87] Bousquet 1959, 180–2 no. 6, attributed tentatively to Glaucus by Follet 1976, 267; Puech 2002, 282–3 no. 127 is cautious.

[88] So Jacobs 1813–17, followed by Oliver 1949, 255–6; *HE* ii 286–7 on Glaucus 1–3.

[89] Cf. Oliver 1949, 255–6; Stadtmüller 1894–1906, ii p. xxii, also noted similarity of expression between 9.774.3 and *APl.* 111.5. Oliver's arguments seem to have been unknown to the Budé editors of *Anthologie Grecque* 9.774–5 (viii, Paris 1974) and 16.111 (xiii, Paris 1980), and to *HE* ii, 286–7 and *GP* ii, 457–8, where the three epigrams of Glaucus the Athenian are Glaucus 1–3, and the editors are suitably cautious in assessing their claim to be from the *Garland of Philip* (as they could not be if Glaucus is our third-century poet); they also, perhaps rightly, doubt (*GP* ii, 458) that *AP* 9.775 = Glaucus 2 is by the author of 9.774 = Glaucus 1. Oliver's attribution of *IG* ii^2 3816 to Glaucus is entirely speculative.

The bacchant has made Cronus' son a satyr; into the dance
of the frenzied he leaps, like one rapt by Bromius.

AP 9.775

The third is on a painting of Philoctetes by Parrhasius:

Καὶ τὸν ἀπὸ Τρηχῖνος ἰδὼν πολυώδυνον ἥρω
τόνδε Φιλοκτήτην ἔγραφε Παρράσιος·
ἔν τε γὰρ ὀφθαλμοῖς ἐσκληκόσι κωφὸν ὑποικεῖ
δάκρυ, καὶ ὁ τρύχων ἐντὸς ἔνεστι πόνος.
ζωιογράφων ὦ λῷιστε, σὺ μὲν σοφός, ἀλλ' ἀναπαῦσαι
ἄνδρα πόνων ἤδη τὸν πολύμοχθον ἔδει.

Him too, the hero from Trachis, seeing in his many
agonies, this Philoctetes Parrhasius painted:
for in his eyes drained-dry there mutely dwells
a tear, and the wasting pain is deep within him.
O best of painters, you are indeed skilled, but to release
the man from his pains was by now the long-sufferer's due.

APl. 111

The surviving selection of Glaucus' poetry marks him as a poet of some significance in his age, as indeed preservation by the *Anthology* might be thought to indicate. Without knowing anything of his rhetorical activity we cannot form a view on their mutual relation, and although Oliver notes that a sophistic contemporary, Philostratus, composed prose *ecphraseis* of works of art, that cannot be taken as a sophistic streak in Glaucus, for epigrammatists had been playing this game for centuries. More significant, perhaps, is the association of the majority of his known poems with Eleusis: other memorials from Eleusis employ verse, and it may be that it was Glaucus' family's association with the cult that provoked him to the composition of these substantial verse texts.

A further pair of poems from Eleusis also stands a slight chance of being by Glaucus. They honour a hierophant named Apollonius: he too was a sophist, and is widely agreed to be the Apollonius given a *Life* by Philostratus (*VS* 2.20). His career makes him highly eligible to be the unnamed husband of Glaucus' aunt, honoured by the statue and text discussed above (pp. 250–1), although Oliver was hesitant. If he is, however, then Glaucus is quite likely to have been asked to compose the poems even though this monument was not erected by Apollonius' widow (Glaucus' aunt) but partly by Apollonius himself, partly by his children; and whether he is or is not, the fact that the first poem makes him speak in the first person also introduces the possibility that he composed that poem himself, and that it then deserves attention as the poetic work of another sophist.[90] The poems are these:

ὦ μύσται, τότε μ' εἴδετ' ἀνακτόρου ἐκ προφανέντα
    νυξὶν ἐν ἀργενναῖς, νῦν δὲ μεθημέριον,
ἐκ προγόνων ῥητῆρα λόγοις ἐναγώνιον αἰεί·
    τῶν ἀποπαυσάμενος θέσφατα νῦν ἰάχω.
οὔνομα δ' ὅστις ἐγὼ μὴ δίζεο· θεσμὸς ἐκεῖνο
    μυστικὸς ὤιχετ' ἄγων εἰς ἅλα πορφυρέην.
ἀλλ' ὅταν εἰς μακάρων ἔλθω καὶ μόρσιμον ἦμαρ,
    λέξουσιν τότε δὴ πάντες ὅσοις μέλομαι.
        vac.

Initiates, erstwhile you saw me appearing from the
    temple in blazing nights, and then by day,
ever contesting in speech as an orator like my fathers:
    from this I have ceased and now cry out holy utterances.
What name is mine, do not ask: that law
    of the mysteries has borne it off into the purple sea.
But when I come to the land of the blessed and my doomed day then
    shall it be spoken by all to whom I am dear.

IG ii^2 3811.1–8 = *IEleus.* 637.1–8

The point of the opening lines seems to be that for a time the subject combined a career as a sophist with the post of hierophant, probably as successor to Glaucus the poet's uncle and so from no earlier than ca. AD 220.[91] As alluded to in these lines, the rule of hieronymy required the hierophant to shed his own given name on taking up office: thereafter he would be known as (e.g.) P. Aelius Hierophantes until his death. It was therefore only after this hierophant's death that his children added a poem to identify him:[92]

[90] *IG* ii^2 3811: Puech 2002, no. 21; *IEleus.* 637, cf. 3812. *IG* ii^2 3811.11–12 (= lines 3–4 of the second poem) establish that this father's or son's name was also Apollonius: he was identified by Oliver 1967, 334 –5 with the Apollonius son of Apollonius mentioned in a letter of Commodus, Geagan 1967, 187–93, and a member of his *consilium* ca. 182/183, but Follet 1976, 267–72 argued for identification with P. Aelius Apollonius of *IG* ii^2 3688 and 3764 (Puech nos. 23 and 24) who had a homonymous son, and was followed by Puech 2002, 109–16, noting 116 n.1 that Oliver's identification is ruled out by the peregrine status of the member of Commodus' *consilium*.

[91] See Follet 1976, 268, followed by Puech 2002, who in her helpful summary of the career of this P. Aelius Apollonius of Pallene (116 n.2) suggests he became hierophant ca. AD 225.

[92] Like Follet 1976, 268 n.4, I accept the supplements of Philios, except for line 5: there in 1989 I accepted his ἔχων, but am persuaded by Puech 2002, 101 that Keil's ὁμοῦ is syntactically possible and better suits what was seen by Keil and Clinton.

νῦν ἤδη παῖδες κλυτὸν ὄνομα πατρὸς ἀρίστου
φαίνομεν, ὃ ζωὸς κρύψεν ἁλὸς πελάγ[ει]·
οὗτος Ἀπολλώνιος ἀοίδιμος, ὃν φ[ίλος υἱὸς]
σημαίνει μυσταῖς οὔνομα πατ[ρὸς ὁμοῦ],
σὺν δὲ Ποσειδάωνι φερώνυμος εὐπα[τέρεια].
vac.

Now is the time when by his children their glorious father's name
is revealed, which in life he hid in the briny sea:
this is celebrated Apollonius, whom his [dear son]
points out to initiates, son of a fat[her like him] in name,
and with him, bearing a name for Poseidon, his well-born daughter.
IG ii^2 3811.9–13 = *IEleus.* 637.9–13

8 Aelian of Praeneste

From the same generation as the poems honouring Eleusinian dignitaries, though perhaps a few years earlier, is a group of epigrams inscribed on a pair of herms of Homer and Menander, found in Rome outside the *Porta Trigemina*. On each herm are three poems about the poet it represents. Of those on Homer the first is known from the *Anthology* as a poem of Antipater of Sidon, here changed to suit its function on the herm and to remove a phrase which marked it as sepulchral. In the second Homer reveals his name and country 'for the sake of Aelian', and it has generally been concluded that the herms and their poems adorned a *villa suburbana* of Philostratus' sophist Claudius Aelianus of Praeneste, author of the *On the nature of animals* and *Diverse history*, and that five of the poems, and the changes to the first on Homer, are actually Aelian's work. There is some slender support for this view in the assertion by Ligorio that the herms were found in the villa of Claudius Valerius Aelianus of Praeneste, then called Casale di Valeriano, but it cannot be given much weight. The quality of the poetry (however we rate it) hardly counts either way, and caution is counselled by the large number of known Aeliani. But the identification receives further support from the extensive use of Menander by Aelian in his *Rustic letters*, while probable plagiarism there from possibly contemporary Alciphron offers a parallel for the herm's silent borrowing from Antipater.[93]

[93] Kaibel 1084, 1085 = *IG* xiv 1188, 1183 = *IGUR* iv 1532, 1526. The Antipater poem is *AP* 7.6 = *HE* Antipater 9, cf. *HE* ii, pp. 2 and 41. On Aelian see Philostr. *VS* 2.31; *PIR*^{2} C 769 (silent on the epigrams); Bowie 1985b, 680–2; Smith 2014. For Aelian's use of Menander cf. esp. *Epp.* 13–16 and Thyresson 1964; Smith 2014, 29–46: on the programme of *Rustic Letters* Hodkinson 2013. For less ambitious poems on herms from the late second or early third century cf. *IGR* iv 413, 415–6 (Pergamum).

Without knowing how the herms were originally placed we cannot be sure which group of poems was intended to be read first (if either), but since those on Menander refer to Homer, but not *vice versa*, it is likely that the poem Aelian meant his guests to read first was his adaptation of Antipater. The first is preceded by the name Ὅμηρος, 'Homer', identifying the now lost portrait-head:

Ὅμηρος
(a) ἡρώων κάρυκα ἀρετᾶς μακάρων τε προφήταν,
Ἑλλάνων δόξης δεύτερον ἀέλιον,
Μουσέων φέγγος, Ὅμηρον, ἀγήρατον στόμα κόσμου
παντός, ὁρᾶις τοῦτον, δαίδαλον ἀρχέτυπον.

Herald of the heroes' valour, and prophet of the blessed,
a second sun for the renown of the Greeks,
Light of the Muses, Homer, the ageless voice of the
universe in its entirety – him you see here, a crafted likeness.
IG xiv 1188.1–5 = *IGUR* iv 1533.1–5

The phrase Ἑλλάνων δόξης has replaced Antipater's Ἑλλάνων βιοτᾶι, 'for the life of the Greeks', perhaps because Aelian thinks of himself and many of his guests as Roman and not Greek. The last phrase, replacing ἁλιρροθία, ξεῖνε, κέκευθε κόνις, 'the sea-beaten dust, stranger, conceals', is clever in its juxtaposition of ἀρχέτυπον, suggesting a statue that is both close to the original and early in the history of statuary, and δαίδαλον, both commending its workmanship and evoking the first sculptor, Daedalus. Antipater's poem certainly survives the transplants.

The remaining poems have aroused widespread scorn, but (with the exception of the very flat (b)) they perhaps deserve some praise for the cleverness with which each works out its conceit: this is just the sort of verse one might expect a declaimer to produce:

(b) οὐχ ἔθος ἐστὶν ἐμοὶ φράζειν γένος οὐδ' ὄνομ' αὐτό,
νῦν δ' ἕνεκ' Αἰλιανοῦ πάντα σοφῶς ἐρέωι·
πατρίς μοι χθὼν πᾶσα, τὸ δ' οὔνομά φασιν Ὅμηρον·
ἐστὶ δὲ Μουσάων, οὐκ ἐμὸν οὐδὲν ἔπος.

It is not my habit to reveal my ancestry, nor my name itself,
but now, for Aelianus' sake, I shall tell all with skill:
My country is the whole world, and my name, they say, Homer,
and my poetry is the Muses', not a word my own.
IG xiv 1188.6–9 = *IGUR* iv 1533.6–9

The speaker of the first poem might have been either the villa's owner or Homer, who certainly speaks in the second. In the third the speaker becomes a spectator, whether Aelian or a guest:

(c) εἰ μὲν θνητὸς ἔφυς, πῶς ἀθάνατόν σε ἐποίησαν
Μοῦσαι, καὶ Μοιρῶν νῆμα ἀνέκλωσαν, ἄναξ;
εἰ δ' ἦσθα ἀθάνατος, πῶς ἐν θνητοῖς σε ἀριθμοῦσιν;
οὐ μὰ σὲ ταῦτ' ἐχρῆν, σεμνὲ ποιητά, φρονεῖν·
ἀλλ' ἔγνων τὸ ἀληθές· ἐπεὶ τὸ σαφὲς διαφεύγει,
ἄνθρωπόν φασιν, θεῖέ, σε, Ὅμηρε, πέλειν.

If you were born mortal, how did they make you immortal,
the Muses, and respin the thread of the Fates, lord?
But if you were immortal, how do they count you among mortals?
By your divinity, proud poet, they should not have thought thus.
But I have recognised the truth – for the clear path is elusive –
they say you are, divine Homer, a man.
IG xiv 1188.10–15 = *IGUR* iv 1533.10–15

The poet's own attachment to the view that Homer was divine is implied by the vocative of line 2 and the oath of line 4, so we know that line 6, which we have been warned will be obscure, must retain an element of divinity: and so it does, in the vocative phrase, though we are left uncertain how that is meant to balance or combine with the statement of his humanity.

The three poems on Menander are livelier, though the first and third turn on a conceit, the latter somewhat forced. Their arrangement parallels that of those on Homer – first apparently spoken by an observer, then one by the poet-herm, finally one spoken by the owner-epigrammatist. Unfortunately there is a problem with the text of all three. The surviving stone is broken on the left, and, although a full text was offered by Fulvio Orsini in a manuscript dated 18th March 1567, Kaibel in *IG* xiv, following Maffei, decided that it was unreliable and printed a text whose supplements for the first halves of the lines depart from Orsini's text. Maffei and Kaibel were almost certainly right, and the texts I print follow those of *IG* xiv in all but one detail, not those printed earlier by Kaibel.[94]

[94] For earlier editions and discussions see Kaibel in *IG* xiv, p. 313 on 1183. In line 7 (line 3 of the second poem) the proposal [φησὶν δὲ α] is stilted (and the *scriptio plena* of δέ suspect, cf. lines 9 and 11) and I revert to Orsini's [οὕνεκα]: I doubt if this is excluded by line length, and the parallel of the second Homeric poem strongly favours a restoration which has the whole quatrain spoken by Menander.

[Μέ]νανδρος
vacat

(a) [οὐ φθόνος ἦ]ν στῆσαι σὺν Ἔρωτι φίλωι σε, Μένανδ[ρε],
[οὔ ζώων γ'] ἐτέλεις ὄργια τερπνὰ θεοῦ·
[δῆλος δὲ εἶ] φορέων αἰεὶ θεόν, ὁππότε καὶ νῦν
[εἰκόνα σ]ὴν κατιδὼν αὐτίκα πᾶς σε φιλεῖ.

I was not reluctant to put you beside your dear Eros, Menander,
the god whose joyful mysteries you celebrated when alive;
but you always had that god [clearly] upon you, since even now
everyone who sees your [portrait] loves you.

vac.

(b) [φαιδρὸν ἑ]ταῖρον Ἔρωτος ὁρᾶις, Σειρῆνα θεάτρων
[κλωσὶ Μ]ένανδρον ἀεὶ κρᾶτα πυκαζόμενον·
[οὕνεκ' ἄρ' ἀ]νθρώπους ἱλαρὸν βίον ἐξεδίδαξα,
[ἐμπλήσας] σκηνὴν δράμασι πᾶσι γάμων.

It is the [radiant] companion of Eros whom you see, the theatres' Siren,
Menander here, his head always garlanded [with sprigs]:
[because] I taught men a cheerful life
filling the stage with all marriage's dramas.

vac.

(c) [οὐκ ἄλλως] ἔστησα κατ' ὀφθαλμούς σε, Μένανδ[ρε],
[γείτον' Ὁ]μηρείης, φίλτατέ μοι, κεφαλῆς,
[εἰ σέ γε δεύτ]ερα ἔταξε σοφὸς κρείνειν μετ' ἐκεῖνον
γραμματι]κὸς κλεινὸς πρόσθεν Ἀριστοφάνης.

Not idly have I put you in our sight, Menander,
to be the neighbour, my dearest one, of the head of Homer,
if indeed you were given the second place after him by a
skilled [scholar] before me, the famous Aristophanes.

IG xiv 1183 = *IGUR* iv 1526

Although these three poems cannot comfortably be read as a dialogue, they are held together by the response of φιλία, 'friendship', that Menander's close understanding of Eros elicits – from everybody, in the first poem, and from the epigrammatist in the third. The warmth of the epigrammatist's feelings for Menander in the first two poems becomes explicit in the third, and is perhaps reflected in the pairing of the two herms: as we are told, Aristophanes of Byzantium put Menander *second* to Homer, but the pairing of the herms suggests equality with the great poet whom the epigrammatist venerates, but does not claim to love, an equality justified by the divine association that Menander is accorded in the first and claims in the second. None of them may be a great poem, the language is trite and the versification can be faulted, but together they create a pleasing and intellectually stimulating ensemble that would mark out the herms' owner-poet as a discerning man of letters and not a mere dilettante, far less a Trimalchio.

9 Sophists as Poets of Occasional Epigrams

The review of dedicatory epigrams may now be concluded by considering a few poems which are their authors' only known compositions. Close in date to the epigrams of Herodes and Amphicles, some time between AD 163 and 169, is the epigram by the sophist Hadrianus of Tyre for a statue honouring Cn. Claudius Severns in the *temenos* of the temple of Artemis at Ephesus.[95] Groag correctly identified the addressee as Cn. Claudius Severus (*consul II ordinarius* in AD 173) and the poet as the sophist, though the view that the latter is the emperor Hadrian was still held by Page (in *FGE*). Despite elevated expressions the eight elegiac lines move largely in the world of doggerel and cliché:

παντοίης ἀ[ρετ]ῆ[ς σ]ταθμήν, ῥ̣[υσί]πτολιν ἄνδρα
  ἔξοχον Ἑ[λ]λήνων, πρόκριτον Αὐσονίων,
κλεινοῦ Κοδράτοιο φίλον πατέρ', ὧι βασίλειον
  Ἁρμονίη θάλαμον πῆξατ' ἐπ' εὐγαμίηι,
Ἁδριανὸς Μούσαισι μέλων ἀνέθηκε Σεουῆρον
  εἰκὼ χαλκείην οὕνεκα προστασίης.
ὑ[μῖν] δ̣', ἄνδρες Ἴωνες, ἀγάλματα καλὸν ὁρᾶσθαι
  [ἑσταότ' Ἀ]ρτέμ[ιδος πλου]σίωι ἐν τεμένει.

The canon of all manner of excellence, a man who saves his city
  outstanding among Greeks, foremost among Ausonians,
the dear father of renowned Quadratus, for whom royal was the
  bridal-chamber Harmonia fashioned, to give him a fine marriage,
Severns, has been dedicated by Hadrianus, dear to the Muses,
  a bronze portrait-statue on account of his protection.
But for you, men of Ionia, it is a fine thing to see statues
  [standing in the rich] precinct [of Artemis].

IEph. 1539

[95] Kaibel 888a = Keil 1953, 13–15 = *FGE* 566–8 = Merkelbach and Stauber 03/02/28 Ephesos. For further discussion see Bowersock 1969, 83; Syme 1968, 102–3 = 1979, 690; Halfmann 1979, 180–1; Puech 2002, 284–8 no. 128.

Less pretentious is a slightly earlier quatrain from Athens honouring the sophist Lollianus. It was for a statue erected in Athens by his pupils with the sanction of the Council and People – perhaps, as Kaibel suggested, the statue in the *agora* mentioned by Philostratus (*VS* 1.23.527): presumably it is not earlier than his appointment to the civic chair of rhetoric at Athens (as its first holder) around AD 140, and so falls in the reign of Pius. The lines will not have been by Lollianus, but they are almost certainly by pupils whom he schooled in sophistic rhetoric:[96]

ἀμφότερον ῥητῆρα δικῶν μελέτῃσί τε ἄρι|στον
   Λολλιανὸν πληθὺς εὐγενέων ἑτάρων.
εἰ δὲ θέλεις τίνες εἰσὶ δαήμεναι, οὔνομα πατρὸς
   καὶ πάτρης αὐτῶν τε οὔνομα δίσκος ἔχει.

On both counts, a pleader of suits and best in declamations,
   Lollianus was honoured by his crowd of noble comrades.
And if you wish to learn who they are, the name of their father,
   of their country, and their own, the disc displays.

IG ii^2 4211

A similar move to honour their teacher was made in early-third-century Ephesus by the pupils of Soterus, a man whom Philostratus (*VS* 2.23.605) dismissed as one of the Greeks' ἀθύρματα, 'playthings', in contrast to real sophists like Damianus, but whom the city of Ephesus, as the text asserts, twice invited to come from Athens, and, when he did so, established in a civic chair of rhetoric with a salary of 10,000 drachmae. The verses were presumably composed by one of his pupils who are listed:[97]

δίς με σοφιστὴν πρῶτον Ἀθήνηθεν καλέσαντο
   Σώτηρον βουλῆς δόγμασιν Ἀνδροκλίδαι·
πρώτωι δὲ ἀντ' ἀρετῆς τε βίου σοφίης τε λόγο[ιο]
   ὥρισαν ἐν τιμαῖς μυρί[α] δῶρα τελεῖν.

I am the first sophist to be called twice from Athens,
   I, Soterus, by the decree of the Council of Androclus' sons;
and to me first, in recognition of my virtuous life and skilled speech,
   did they resolve to pay ten thousand gifts as my meed.

IEph. 1548

[96] Kaibel 877: cf. *PIR*^{2} H 203; Puech 2002, 327–30, no. 149.
[97] Kaibel 877^a, Merkelbach and Stauber 03/02/31 Ephesos: cf. Keil 1953, 15–18; Puech 2002, 455–8 no. 243.

These short, functional epigrams have little to commend them as poetry. Much punchier is the pair of trimeters which survives in the *Appendix Planudea* (322) and which was presumably composed by the *rhetor* and πυρφόρος, 'fire-carrier', Licinnius Firmus for a statue of his father who held the same office:[98]

> Φίρμος με Φίρμον, πυρφόρος τὸν πυρφόρον,
> ὁ παῖς ὁ ῥήτωρ τὸν πατέρα τὸν ῥήτορα
>
> Firmus honours Firmus, a *purphoros* the *purphoros*,
> a son who is a *rhetor* his father who is a *rhetor*.
>
> *APlan.* 322

Another genre of epigram, the erotic, is disappointingly represented in our surviving evidence for sophistic poetry. This does not show that it was less popular than the dedicatory epigram, since it naturally missed the epigraphic bus which has conveyed us so many of the latter. At least one *rhetor* of the period before the Second Sophistic had been an effective composer of erotic (and of scoptic) epigram, Marcus Argentarius, the poet of thirty-seven pieces in *The Garland of Philip* who seems to be identical with a *rhetor* of the Augustan period known to the elder Seneca.[99] Given that many good examples of the genre were being composed in the second half of the first century and in the reign of Hadrian by Rufinus and Strato,[100] it is likely that some sophists will have attempted it. They certainly did in the Latin West, for in his *Apologia* (9) Apuleius quotes two of his own erotic epigrams (of six and twelve lines) addressed to slaves of his friend Scribonius Laetus under the pseudonyms of Critias and Charinus.

From the Greek world proper, however, our only examples are a couple of poems of which one is ascribed to a sophist Dionysius by the Palatine manuscript and the other to a Dionysius, plausibly the same, by the *Appendix Barberino-Vaticanus*.[101] Although identification of this Dionysius is perilous, the label sophist should take him to our period, which metrical licence

[98] For Athenians with the name Firmus who were πυρφόροι, 'fire-bearers', see *IG* ii^2 3563: cf. Peek 1974, 142; Puech 2002, 247–8; for other Firmi see Follet 1976, 253.

[99] See *GP* ii 166 ff. on their lines 1301–1508, and for a rewarding exploration of some poems see Sens 2007, 384–90; Gagné and Höschele 2009. Apollonides too, with thirty-one poems in *GP*, may have been a *rhetor*, see *GP* ii 147 ff. on their lines 1125–1294, but the identification is hazardous. For further discussion of these and other poets in *GP* see Bowie 2012e (Chapter 17 in this volume).

[100] I accept the arguments of Cameron 1982 for the dating of Rufinus and Strato, on whom see further Bowie 1990b (Chapter 14 in this volume). For Rufinus see now Höschele 2006; for Strato Steinbichler 1998, Floridi 2007.

[101] See *FGE* 44–5.

supports. He might be the Hadrianic Aelius Dionysius of Halicarnassus descended from the Augustan critic, but this man is known only as a γραμματικός, 'grammarian', not a sophist, and there is a sporting chance that the two poems are by the much greater figure Dionysius of Miletus.[102] The composition of erotic epigrams would perhaps make more intelligible the ascription to Dionysius of an apparently novelistic work 'Araspas the lover of Pantheia' and the vigour with which Philostratus denies that ascription, insisting that Dionysius οὐκ ἐρωτικήν ποτε αἰτίαν ἔλαβεν, 'never faced any erotic accusation'.[103]

The poems are certainly by ancient standards harmless, if elegant, pieces:

ἡ τὰ ῥόδα, ῥοδόεσσαν ἔχεις χάριν. ἀλλὰ τί πωλεῖς;
ἢ τὰ ῥόδ', ἢ σαυτήν, ἠὲ συναμφότερα;

You with the roses, rosy is your charm: but what do you sell?
The roses, or yourself, or both together?

AP 5.81[104]

ὦ σοβαρὴ βαλάνισσα, τί μ' οὕτως ἔκπυρα λούεις;
πρὶν μ' ἀποδύσασθαι, τοῦ πυρὸς αἰσθάνομαι.

Provocative bath-girl, why do you give me so fiery a bath?
Before undressing I can feel your fire.

AP 5.82

The remaining genre of epigram popular in the period is the scoptic. It had been exploited with verve by Lucillius, Nicarchus and Ammianus, but none of these virtuoso composers is known to have been a sophist.[105] On a more casual level many cultured Greeks must have tossed off a few scoptic epigrams, and the fact that one or two examples by sophists are preserved does not indicate that they took their composition very seriously. Furthermore the genre's conventional objects and techniques of invective are adhered to as much by declamatory sophists as by the leading

[102] On Aelius Dionysius see *PIR*² A 169; on the sophist of Miletus, now known to be called Ti. Claudius Flavianus Dionysius, see Philostratus *VS* 1.22; *PIR*² D 105; Bowie 1997c (Chapter 10 in Volume 3); Puech 2002, 229–32 nos 98–9. On *grammatici* see Bowie 2022e (Chapter 47 in Volume 3).

[103] Both details at *VS* 1.22.524.

[104] I print the text as corrected by Cameron 1980b: for line 2 the MS has the unmetrical word-order σαυτὴν ἢ τὰ ῥόδα ἠὲ συναμφότερα.

[105] On Greek scoptic epigram in the imperial period see Nisbet 2003; on Nicarchus, Schatzmann 2012; on Lucillius, Floridi 2014.

exponents mentioned above. When a sophist composes a scoptic epigram he is an epigrammatist, not a sophist, and the following poems show no trace of their authors' principal literary activity – supposing, that is, that we do indeed know their authors. The ascription of poems in the anthology is often precarious, and when generic features bulk so large as they do in scoptic epigram the attribution of an individual poem is sometimes little more than an act of faith.

With that *caveat* we may first approach two poems ascribed to an Antiochus, probably Philostratus' sophist from Aegeae, P. Anteius Antiochus, who heard Dionysius of Miletus in Ephesus and must have flourished under Pius and Marcus.[106] The first merits some commendation for the wit of its attack on its victim's psychic deformity:

Ψυχὴν μὲν γράψαι χαλεπόν, μορφὴν δὲ χαράξαι
ῥάιδιον· ἀλλ' ἐπὶ σοὶ τοὔμπαλιν ἀμφότερον.
τῆς μὲν γὰρ ψυχῆς τὸ διάστροφον ἔξω ἄγουσα
ἐν τοῖς φαινομένοις ἡ Φύσις εἰργάσατο.
τὸν δ' ἐπὶ τῆς μορφῆς θόρυβον καὶ σώματος ὕβριν
πῶς ἄν τις γράψαι, μηδ' ἐσιδεῖν ἐθέλων;

To portray the mind is hard, to carve the outward appearance
easy; but in your case both are the reverse.
For by bringing your mind's distortion out into the open
Nature has wrought it among the things that are manifest.
But the confusion in your appearance and outrage in your body
– who could portray it when he couldn't even bear to look at it?
AP 11.412

The second takes us to the theme of sophistic declamation and (a common target) the performer's inadequacy, though this does not require that it be written by a sophist:

Βήσας, εἰ φρένας εἶχεν, ἀπήγχετο· νῦν δ' ὑπ' ἀνοίας
καὶ ζῆι καὶ πλουτεῖ, καὶ μετὰ τὴν πάροδον.

If Besas had any sense, he would have hung himself: as it is, by his
idiocy he lives and grows wealthy, even after his performance.
AP 11.422

The last word, πάροδον, 'coming onto (a stage)', is technical term for a rhetorical ἐπίδειξις, 'display'. The sophist lurking in the name Βήσας, 'Besas',

[106] Philostr. *VS* 2.4: cf. *PIR*[2] A 730; Robert 1977, 119–29; Puech 2002, 68–74 no. 10.

cannot be identified, unless this is a corruption for Βύζας, 'Byzas', and the poet is hitting at Marcus of Byzantium who claimed descent from that city's founder Byzas.[107]

10 Lucian

The greatest scoptic sophist, Lucian, might be expected to be the most significant sophistic poet of the scoptic epigram, and that could indeed have been so. However the *Anthology*'s general problems of ascription are here exacerbated by the easy confusion of the names Lucillius and Lucianus, compounded by the idleness of a scribe who was content to write ΛΟΥΚΙΑ to indicate attribution to Lucian and even ΛΟΥΚΙ for one or the other. Thus few if any of the sixty-three epigrams variously assigned to Lucian can be treated as his with confidence, even if we may have reason to believe that a considerable number of these are his. This is extremely vexing, since in Lucian we have a man who certainly trained as a *rhetor* and very probably started his career giving conventional sophistic displays, but who then turned his gift for elegant and humorous prose to new ends. He shares with conventional sophistic his use of the epideictic medium and his almost total preference for prose. But even if only a dozen of the epigrams were his, they would show (along with his parodic verse) that Lucian did not simply write the odd verse (like Antiochus) but that he stands nearer to the persistent, if not professional, epigrammatist like his *Doppelgänger* Lucillius. One reason may be that, of course, the stance of scoptic epigrams chimes with that of much of Lucian's prose works, so that their composition is a more obvious way of extending his literary persona than it could be for a straight sophist. This in turn adds problems to ascription: a feature may look Lucianic, and even be paralleled in his prose work, but simply be characteristic of the verse genre.[108] Given the uncertainty of ascription and the eccentricity of Lucian's sophistic credentials, a full examination of the epigrams would not be justified here: I shall limit myself to one epigram whose date, at least, seems to favour Lucianic authorship, and to a few more which bear upon sophistic culture.

[107] For Marcus see Philostr. *VS* 1.24.528; Puech 2002, 344–5; for the name Byzas on Thasos cf. Robert, *Bull.* 1973 no. 142.

[108] For a useful discussion of problems of ascription (both generally and poem by poem) see Baldwin 1975. The basic problems are set out by Macleod 1987, pref. xviii, and discussed, along with several poems, by Nisbet 2003, 165–81; for discussion of some poems see Gómez Cárdo 2008.

The first, a mock epitaph on Lollianus, unusual in being ascribed only to Lucian in our manuscripts. The victim is almost certainly Philostratus' sophist from Ephesus (*VS* 1.23) whose career extended from the reign of Hadrian to that of Pius, and whom we have earlier seen honoured in Athens by a statue with a four-line epigram. Presumably the scoptic poem was directed at an Athenian audience (though its identical length is not much of an argument for seeing it as a response to the honorific epigram, as suggested by Baldwin 1975, 328) and was necessarily composed after Lollianus' death. Its mock-epic address to Cyllenian Hermes, cleverly alluding both to the *Odyssey* and to conventions of sepulchral epigram, may perhaps show knowledge of a dedication to Hermes in Athens by a Lollianus whom Follet speculated might be our sophist.[109]

εἰπέ μοι εἰρομένωι, Κυλλήνιε, πῶς κατέβαινεν
    Λολλιανοῦ ψυχὴ δῶμα τὸ Φερσεφόνης;
θαῦμα μέν, εἰ σιγῶσα· τυχὸν δέ τι καὶ σὲ διδάσκειν
    ἤθελε· φεῦ, κείνου καὶ νέκυν ἀντιάσαι.

Tell me, in answer to my question, Cyllenian Hermes, how did
    Lollianus' soul go down to the house of Persephone?
A miracle, if in silence: and perhaps teaching even you something
    was its wish. My god, to think of meeting him, even as a corpse!
AP 11.274 = Macleod 35

Two other couplets relate directly to sophists. One is in a sequence given to Lucian by the Palatine and Planudean manuscripts and variously ascribed to Lucillius, Ammianus and Lucian by moderns:

Θαυμάζειν μοι ἔπεισιν, ὅπως Βύτος ἐστὶ σοφιστής,
    οὔτε λόγον κοινὸν οὔτε λογισμὸν ἔχων.

It occurs to me to be surprised that Bytus is a sophist,
    when he shares neither language with us nor reason.[110]
AP 11.435 = Macleod 58

[109] For εἰπέ μοι εἰρομένωι cf. Od. 13.263, 24.114 (in the second *Nekuia*!): εἰπέ alone is common in epitaphs, e.g. *GVI* 1872. For Cyllenian Hermes cf. Od. 24.1, *GVI* 1090. For a dedication by a Lollianus in archaising letters, *IG* ii^2 4742, cf. Follet 1976, 194: his name Lollianus Asclepiades almost certainly excludes identification with the sophist.

[110] Bytus is not simply uncommon (so Baldwin 1975, 331) but as far as I know unattested. Is Lucian punning on βυττός (= γυναικὸς αἰδοῖον, Hesychius β 1353 *s.v.*) and attacking the eunuch Favorinus (cf. *Demon.* 12)?

Less enigmatic is the following poem in the sequence:

> Θᾶττον ἔην λευκοὺς κόρακας πτηνάς τε χελώνας
> εὑρεῖν ἢ δόκιμον ῥήτορα Καππαδόκην.
>
> It would be easier to find white crows and winged tortoises
> than a *rhetor* of repute from Cappadocia.
>
> *AP* 11.436 = Macleod 59

This might be a dangerous line of attack for Lucian from Commagenian Samosata, but regional or racial prejudice is easily tapped, and Cappadocians had evoked hostility as early as an epigram attributed to Demodocus (*AP* 11.237). In the Second Sophistic Greeks from Cappadocia might be sniped at for their accent, as Herodes' pupil Pausanias of Caesarea was criticised by Philostratus.[111] Like Lollianus, Pausanias held a chair at Athens, though perhaps not before the 180s: but it is there he must have studied with Herodes, and he may well be the target of this couplet.

So far we have been dealing in the main with first-order poetry – that is, poetry which was composed to be read (or heard) and judged as a representative of its genre. Naturally any poetry of this period will be self-conscious, and in the hymns of Philostratus and Heliodorus we were already moving towards second-order poetry, where the author is creating an imitation of a particular form of poem rather than simply an example. This was even clearer in the novelists' oracles, where a parodic element became prominent. In Lucian we have a writer whose first-order poetry, the scoptic epigrams, was slight in comparison to his second-order compositions whose main objective is the humour of parody. I do not wish to review these in detail: Lucian is far from being a neglected author, and the effects achieved by the verse parodies embedded in his primarily prose works (e.g. *Menippus* or *Descent into Hades*, and *Zeus the tragic ranter*) can only be assessed by looking at each work as a whole. Often, moreover, quotation and pastiche are interlaced to achieve similar results. I therefore offer only a couple of examples of the game Lucian plays, examples where his own compositions rather than quotations are deployed.

In the underworld scene of the Ἀληθῆ διηγήματα, '*True histories*', Homer is made to have composed an epic whose first line is all that Lucian can recall, since he has lost the book-text the author had given him:[112]

[111] *VS* 2.13.593–4 (cf. by contrast *VA* 1.7!).

[112] For commentary on *VH* see Georgiadou and Larmour 1998; for a good discussion Ní Mheallaigh 2014, 206–60.

νῦν δέ μοι ἔννεπε, Μοῦσα, μάχην νεκύων ἡρώων

Now tell me, Muse, of the battle of the heroes' corpses

Lucian, *VH* 2.24

Later, on his departure, Lucian asks Homer to draft a commemorative couplet: this he inscribes on a beryl *stēlē* by the harbour. One might expect from the term δίστιχον, 'distich', that we are going to get elegiacs, but of course Homer's metre was the hexameter:

Λουκιανὸς τάδε πάντα φίλος μακάρεσσι θεοῖσιν
εἶδέ τε καὶ πάλιν ἦλθε φίλην ἐς πατρίδα γαῖαν.

Lucian, dear to the blessed gods,
saw all this and went back again to his dear native land.

Lucian, *VH* 2.28

The parody of traditional literary language and contemporary life (we may recall the scores of texts on the Memnon colossus) is typical of Lucian's satire. A very different exploitation of verse is to be found in the Ποδάγρα, '*Gout*', which, although long suspect, has been firmly ascribed to Lucian by his most recent editor.[113] Although parodic, it is self-contained and somewhat neglected, and a brief account is appropriate here.

The Ποδάγρα is a mock-tragedy in 334 lines: its brevity may partly reflect contemporary practice – as far as I know we are simply ignorant about the length of Greek tragedies of the period – but it is quite long enough to run through an amusing range of the well-known conventions of tragedy, and to bombard the reader with phrases from earlier poetry, particularly tragic. The basis of the humour lies in the absurdity of the scenario and the incongruity between it and the tragic language and postures in which it unfolds. It opens with a man afflicted by gout apostrophising and cursing the goddess Gout. A chorus of her votaries enters, hymning her in *Bacchae*-like anacreontics and ionics: after paratragic problems of mutual recognition the chorus narrates their divinity's birth in another hymn (this time in anapaests) then explains in Sotadeans how their mystery rites take the form of attacks of gout. Recognising that he is already an initiate, the gouty man joins them in a third hymn (anapaests) to announce Gout's epiphany. In a long speech she asserts her invincibility, despite divine and mortal attempts at cures, and elicits another hymn (again anapaests). A messenger, like his mistress lamed by gout, and hence un-tragically slow, reports opposition to

[113] Macleod 1987, 1–16, no. 69: cf. Macleod 1967, 319–55. For a brief discussion see Whitmarsh 2013, 183–5.

her dominion by two doctors. They appear, introduce themselves as Syrians from Damascus, and after a verbal confrontation are thrown into torments by the Pains which Gout summons and unleashes. They repent and are forgiven, and the chorus concludes with a list of mythological *exempla* showing the folly of opposing gods (in miuric dactylic hexameters), and with moralising reflections (in anapaests) of the sort we find in our MSS at the end of some plays of Euripides.

The piece shows Lucian to have been as dexterous in the production of funny and parodic poetry as he was in that sort of prose. To some extent its parody exploits the same range of reading in classical poetry that is required for full appreciation of the prose writing of Lucian and other writers of the Second Sophistic. But his decision to write a verse-spoof shows in itself that for Lucian poetry remained an effective literary medium, and some of the parody ties in with contemporary rather than classical poetry. Alongside verbal allusions to the fifth-century Attic dramatists his readers were expected to recognise one to Mesomedes,[114] and in his display of metrical virtuosity they were expected to enjoy the blend of paroemiacs and *apocrota*, also characteristic of Mesomedes and contemporary *citharoedia*, as well as the allusions to Euripides' *Bacchae* in the anacreontics and to hymn-poetry in the anapaests.[115] We should remember, too, that tragedies on classical themes were still being written and performed: had we examples of the tragic poetry of Nicetes or Scopelianus we might be better able to appreciate the structural features of this short work, and taken together with it they would have made it easier for us to accept that for sophists too the composition of tragedy was a serious literary activity.

11 Conclusion

The second-order poetry of Lucian, wholly dependent upon the reader's knowledge of classical texts, has brought us back to the theme of my second section, contemporary prose's exploitation of poetry. But I hope that the number and (sometimes) quality of other sophistic poems reviewed has shown that poetry was not simply regarded as a dead form from the past whose corpse could provide spoils, but a living medium of literary expression where traditional themes and language could be reworked as they were in prose.

[114] See n.15. [115] For analysis of the metres see Macleod 1987, 15–16.

As always in our perception of antiquity we are blinkered by the accidents of survival. Epigrams dominate the reconstructed corpus of sophistic poetry, but only in the commemorative or sepulchral genres may we suppose what we have to be at all representative, and here the mannered productions of Herodes and Aelian seem to bear marks of sophistic taste that those of Glaucus do not. In Glaucus it is not his rhetorical career that informs his poems but his pride in ancestry and in high Eleusinian office, pride that he shares with non-sophistic members of the elite. Our few traces of scoptic and erotic epigram may be entirely misleading, not least because those that do survive were probably transmitted by the anthology of Diogenianus, compiled around AD 150–160,[116] and therefore too early for the majority of Philostratus' heroes: had any sophists of the late Antonine or Severan period been dab hands at scoptic or erotic epigram, we would be unlikely ever to know.

In other genres we may perhaps conclude that composition of any poetry was the exception rather than the rule. Many sophists, like Fronto, it seems, in the West,[117] may never have penned a line. Nicetes and Scopelianus may well be in a small minority in their composition of tragedies, but these lost works could have been as good as any sophistic prose that has survived. Scopelianus' *Gigantias* is our only trace of a sophist's epic: perhaps this is chance, but much hexameter poetry by contemporary writers not known to be sophists has survived, so the case of epic is perhaps different from that of tragedy. Here is a genre that was still achieving popularity and occasionally distinction, but it required long hours of composition and virtuoso skills as well as the mixture of flair and *paideia* that can generate an epigram or even a tragedy. These requirements may not have been easily compatible with a sophistic career, and it may be significant that our one example of sophistic epic dates from early in Philostratus' Second Sophistic: the demands – and prizes – of successful declamation may not have been so obvious to Scopelianus as to a sophist a century later. Then even Aristides, who hardly taught and whose illness created a sort of leisure, seems not to have put his hand to an epic. As for his hymns, they are an oddity, the result more of his psychological and physical ailments than an urge to excel as a poet. But that urge played a part, and their composition alongside his prose hymns is an important indication that melic poetry still had some prestige. Had they survived they too might have given us a favourable impression of sophistic poetry, more favourable, at any rate, than the even shorter, almost miniature, hymns of Philostratus and Heliodorus.

[116] See Sakolowski 1893. [117] See Champlin 1980, 52–4.

13 Poetry and Poets in Asia and Achaea (1989)

1 Introduction

It is generally agreed that Greek poetry in the Roman Empire was of little consequence. Thus in her *Short History of Greek Literature* Jacqueline de Romilly notes that 'only two names deserve mention, and they come very late in the period, Quintus of Smyrna and Nonnus of Panopolis'.[1] Even the larger scale *Cambridge History of Classical Literature*, stopping in the middle of the third century, allows only a little over five pages in which Glen Bowersock was able to offer a short discussion of some epigrammatists, Mesomedes and the didactic poems ascribed to Oppian, and to mention the name Babrius. 'The bulk of the surviving Greek literature of the Imperial age is in prose and implies limited interest in traditional verse forms', suggested Bowersock; 'even decent versifiers like Aelius Aristides preferred to write hymns in prose'.[2] I cannot evade some responsibility for the shape of *The Cambridge History of Classical Literature*, and I confess that I once shared this view. Now I wonder if it is so straightforward, and in this brief paper I should like to ask, although I can only begin to answer, a number of related questions. Was contemporary poetry of as little account in the Greek society of the first three centuries of the empire as these remarks suggest? Is there a measurable difference between the rest of the Greek world and the provinces where, from about AD 70, the sophistic fashion flourished most, Achaea and Asia? If so, is it a real difference, attributable to a preference for prose over poetry, or is it partly the product of our dependence on Philostratus for our view of the period?

In this investigation I shall look at poetry partly by genre. But I shall also employ from time to time – and hope to develop elsewhere – a crude distinction between amateur poets, whose literary interests are principally in other forms of writing or do not exist at all, and professional poets, people known to us, and proud to be widely known, as poets. Within the ranks of the professionals there are two species. One is the true professional,

[1] De Romilly 1985, 191.

[2] Bowersock 1985, 649 = 1989, 89. Note the even harsher verdict of Habicht 1985, 130 (writing of the second century): 'poetry was dead'.

sometimes a man commissioned to compose a sepulchral or dedicatory epigram,[3] more often the composer of poems for competition at festivals, festivals that increased in number and elaboration in the first and second centuries AD.[4] We have many records of names and victories, and several honours from the Dionysiac *technitae* and from cities, for this species of poet, but hardly anything of their poetry.[5] The second species, whom I shall call semi-professional, is the poet who is not known to have entered competitions, to which his chosen genre might well be inappropriate, but whose main literary commitment is to the production of poetry. It is this sort of poet, so far as we can tell, that produced the poetry with greatest claims to quality and long life.

2 Epigram

One genre, epigram, in fact needs no apology, and it is tempting to set it aside as little more than part of the intellectual furniture of the πεπαιδευμένος, the 'educated man'. Yet to set aside epigram would be to distort the overall picture, since Greek epigrams of the period are so numerous, are often of high quality, and are composed by poets from all three classes, amateurs, semi-professionals and professionals.

Greek epigram's preferred form is the elegiac couplet, and it reaches us in two rarely overlapping channels, the poems preserved in the *Anthology* and those set up on stone throughout the Greek world and even in non-Hellenic parts of the empire. There is still much work to be done on the imperial epigrammatists of the *Anthology*. Some have had more attention than others: Crinagoras, Argentarius, Maccius, and Honestus benefited from Gow and Page's *Garland of Philip*; Lucillius from work by Louis Robert; Rufinus from Page's edition, even if Page failed to date him correctly to the first century, where his *termini* appear to be AD 60–80.[6] But there are others whose

[3] For example, the Dionysius of Magnesia who composed and signed a fine eighteen-line epitaph for Socratea of Paros, *IG* xii.5 310 = *GVI* 1871 (second century AD).

[4] A good example in Achaea is offered by the *Mouseia* at Thespiae, the evidence for which is assembled and discussed by Schachter, 1986, 147–79. For the late Hellenistic development of the sanctuary and festival see Knoepfler 1996; Robinson 2012. For Asia see the important discussion of Mitchell 1990.

[5] For a possible exception see the text from Curium in Cyprus cited below p. 277. Much more is now understood about the guilds of *technitai* since Le Guen 2001, Aneziri 2003.

[6] See *GP* and *FGE;* on Lucillius Robert 1968; Nisbet 2004; Floridi 2014; on Rufinus Page 1978, but for dating Cameron 1982; Robert 1982. For a nuanced study of Rufinus see Höschele 2006. On the earlier progress of studies in epigrammatic, as in other Hellenistic and imperial Greek poetry, the surveys of Keydell (see below n.40) remain invaluable.

poems are rewarding, not least Strato of Sardis, probably from the period around AD 120–30.[7] As for the vast and constantly increasing body of epigraphic poems, work has hardly even started, but it is clear that some are just as good as those that entered the *Anthology*.[8]

The status of epigrammatic poetry is less easy to assess than its volume and occasional quality. So far as I know we have no honours to epigrammatic poets from cities, and only rarely is somebody referred to as 'the epigrammatic poet', as is Strato by Diogenes Laertius (5.61). But we do know that Lucillius opened his second book with an epigram thanking Nero for financial support (acknowledging χαλκός, 'bronze', rather than – perhaps pointedly – χρυσός, 'gold');[9] and there are other indications, such as the career of Martial in the Latin-speaking world,[10] that epigram was respectable and recognised in a way that writing of novels was not.

It can be said at once that Asia and Achaea are here no different from the rest of the empire. Men with literary reputations at stake are happy to sign epigrams inscribed on stone, like that of Arrian from Cordoba in the 120s, or the sophist Hadrianus of Tyre's epigram on Claudius Severus at Ephesus in the third quarter of the century.[11] Similarly T. Flavius Glaucus of Marathon, who calls himself ποιητὴς καὶ ῥήτωρ καὶ φιλόσοφος, 'poet and *rhetor* and philosopher', clearly took pride in the series of epigrams honouring his relatives collected and discussed by Oliver, even if Glaucus makes no explicit claim to write the poems.[12]

[7] For analysis see now Steinbichler 1998; for an excellent edition and commentary Floridi 2007. Strato's poems are almost all to be found in *AP* 12, but it is the satirical epigram *AP* 11.117 which ties Strato to the reign of Hadrian, as argued (in my view convincingly) by Cameron 1982, 168–70. It is less clear that the relation with the *Corpus Priapeorum*, suggested by Buchheit 1962, 109ff. (cf. Cameron 1982, 171), requires a date earlier than AD 117 for the amatory poems: in Bowie 1990b, 56–7 (Chapter 14 in this volume) I argue briefly that they belong in the 120s. For pre-1980 work on Strato see *CHCL* i 861–2.

[8] Much work has indeed been done, above all by W. Peek and L. Robert, but still more remains, and can hardly proceed until a full and well-indexed corpus is available. Given the prospect of continual accessions, it would most conveniently be assembled on computer, but I know of no plans for such a project. For texts of epigraphic poems East of the Aegean scholars are now indebted to Merkelbach and Stauber 1998–2004; for commentary on a selection of sepulchral epigrams, many of them imperial, to Hunter 2022.

[9] Μοῦσαι Ὀλυμπιάδες, κοῦραι Διός, οὐκ ἂν ἐσώθην, | εἰ μή μοι Καῖσαρ χαλκὸν ἔδωκε Νέρων, 'Olympian Muses, daughters of Zeus, I would not have survived if Nero Caesar had not given me bronze', *AP* 9.572.7–8.

[10] See Sullivan 1993.

[11] For Arrian's poem see the bibliography in Stadter 1980, 195 n.61, and his discussion *ibid.* 10–11 and 52–3; for that of Hadrianus of Tyre see Groag 1902, 261; Kaibel 888a; Keil 1953, 13–15; *SEG* 13.505; *IEph* 1539; *FGE* 566–8 (wrongly ascribing it to the Emperor Hadrian), Puech 2002, 284–8.

[12] *IG* ii² 3704.12, see Oliver 1949, 243–58, further discussion in Bowie 1989a (Chapter 12 in this volume). Although there is no outright signature, for Glaucus' identity cf. *IG* ii² 3632.26–7 (= *IEleus.* 502.26–7). Note also the signed epigram of Dionysius of Magnesia from Paros, above n.3.

Another indication of the prestige of epigram is offered by the collections known to have been compiled (and there were doubtless more): the *Garland* of Philip (either ca. AD 40 or more probably ca. AD 60); under Hadrian, Strato's collection of his own erotic poetry and four books of the epigrams of Herennius Philo of Byblus; then under Hadrian or Pius the anthology of Diogenianus of Heracleia, most probably, as the Suda suggests, Heracleia Salbace in Caria.[13]

Finally the contemporary assessment of epigram may be judged by the way the form was extended and adapted. The elegiac metre can be used for unusual purposes or with unusual dialect. The invocation to Asclepius from Pergamum, ascribed by Herzog and Habicht to Aelius Aristides and called by them a hymn,[14] lies somewhere between an elegiac hymn like Callimachus, *Hymn* 5, and an anathematic epigram. The set of elegiac poems by Julia Balbilla inscribed on the Memnon colossus at the time of the visit of Hadrian and Sabina in November 130 employ a crude version of Aeolic dialect to present their author as a latter-day Sappho: her reputation would be higher if an anthology had given us only the best of these, but they have undeniable pretensions.[15]

In another direction, the epigram – or poems that are developed from epigrams – could be composed in metres other than elegiac. In the Latin world Martial wrote many non-elegiac epigrams, and Statius, Greek in his origins, developed the epigram into occasional poems in varied metres in his *Silvae*.[16] We should assume that the *lyrica doctissima*, 'most learned lyrics', written by Vestricius Spurinna in both languages, were similar, poems to be recited and read, not to be sung.[17] The emperor Hadrian's own poetry was in a variety of metres, as Dio and surviving examples attest.[18] The best, in my view, in his hendecasyllabic dedication of ἀκροθίνια, 'first fruits', to Eros at Thespiae:[19]

13 Gow and Page held that the *Garland of Philip* was published ca. AD 40, but Cameron 1980a argued for publication under Nero, a date I accept in my discussion of Philip's *Garland* (Bowie 2012e, Chapter 17 in this volume). We know of Philo's poems from the *Violarium* of Eudocia. For Diogenianus' Ἐπιγραμμάτων ἀνθολόγιον, 'Anthology of epigrams', see the Suda δ 1140 *s.v.* Διογενειανός; Sakolowski 1893, 1–58.

14 Herzog 1934; Habicht 1969, n.145; Bowie 1989a (Chapter 12 in this volume).

15 The best texts remain A. and E. Bernand 1960, 80–98, nos. 28–31: for discussions of Balbilla see West 1978, 106–8; Bowie 1990b, 61–3 and 2002e (Chapters 14 and 15 in this volume); Brennan 1998; Rosenmeyer 2008 and 2018b.

16 An important advance in understanding the *Silvae* was made by Hardie 1983. For their relation to epigram see his chapter 8, 'Epigram and ekphrasis'.

17 Plin. *Ep.* 3.1.7.

18 D.C. 69.3.1. For Hadrian's poetry see Bowie 2002e (Chapter 15 in this volume).

19 *IG* vii 1828 = Kaibel 811 = *FGE* 565–6.

ὦ παῖ τοξότα Κύπριδος λιγείης
Θεσπιαῖς Ἑλικωνίαισι ναίων
Ναρκισσοῦ παρὰ κῆπον ἀνθέοντα,
ἱλήκοις· τὸ δέ τοι δίδωσι δέξο
ἀκροθείνιον Ἁδριανὸς ἄρκτου,
ἣν αὐτὸς κάνεν ἱππόθεν τυχήσας.
σὺ δ᾽ αὐτῶι χάριν ἀντὶ τοῦ σαόφρων
πνέοις Οὐρανίας ἀπ᾽ Ἀφροδίτης.

O archer child of clear-voiced Aphrodite,
dwelling in Heliconian Thespiae
by the blooming garden of Narcissus,
be gracious, and accept what Hadrian offers,
the spoils of his hunt, a she-bear
which he slew himself with a cast from horseback.
And in exchange for this may you chastely
breathe favour upon him from heavenly Aphrodite.

As shown by Robert, the spoils are those of Hadrian's hunt in Mysia during his Asian tour of AD 123–4. It is likely that it was in that visit he first encountered Antinous, and this may be one reason why the god to whom he chose to dedicate the symbol of successful hunting was Eros. But another will have been the prestige of the two cults at Thespiae, that of Eros and that of the Muses, and of the literary productions the festival of the Muses encouraged.[20]

Another adaptation of the epigrammatic form is found in the Βωμός, '*Altar*', of Vestinus. Although this poem could belong to the time when L. Iulius Vestinus was head of the Alexandrian Museum, on Pflaum's view around AD 130, and so could have been composed during Hadrian's visit to Egypt in that year, references in the text to Attica and Boeotia seem to corroborate the indication of the acrostic that the poem belongs to mainland Greece. The date might be AD 131–2. The acrostic runs ΟΛΥΜΠΙΕ ΠΟΛΛΟΙΣ ΕΤΕΣΙ ΘΥΣΕΙΑΣ 'Olympian may you sacrifice for many years!' The references in the text come in lines 17–22:

σὺ δ᾽, ὦ πιὼν κρήνηθεν, ἣν
ἶνις κόλαψε Γοργόνος,
θύοις τ᾽ ἐπισπένδοις τ᾽ ἐμοὶ
ὑμηττιάδων πολὺ λαροτέρην
σπονδὴν ἄδην ...

[20] For the link with the Mysian hunt see Robert 1978b, 440–1; Bowie 2002e, 180–1 (Chapter 15 in this volume, 331–3); for Thespiae above n.4; for the cult of Eros, Schachter 1981, 217–9.

May you, who have drunk from the spring which
the scion of the Gorgon carved out with his hoof,
offer sacrifice and pour libations upon me –
far sweeter than that of the daughters of Hymettus
this libation poured unceasingly …

I would like to see this altar of Vestinus – its altar shape achieved by playing about with metrical units of different length in imitation of the *Altar* of the Hellenistic poet Dosiadas – as a literary analogue to the hundred or more small altars set up in Athens in association with the dedication of the Olympieum in AD 131/2. That a man already high in the imperial service, later to be *ab epistulis graecis*, 'secretary for Greek correspondence', chose (or was chosen) to contribute to the ceremonies in this way – while the sophist M. Antonius Polemo, we are told, delivered an epideictic oration – tells us something about the status of this sort of poetry at the time.[21]

Another mark of the respectability of polymetric epigrams may be seen in Diogenes Laertius' collection of epigrams entitled Πάμμετρος, '*Verse in every metre*'.[22] We may have a low view of Diogenes as a writer of prose, as a historian of philosophy, and indeed as a poet. But he thought it appropriate both to make such a collection and to draw on it liberally in his *Lives*.

3 Hexameter and Melic Poetry

When we turn to other genres it is equally clear that poets and their products were respected, even if not accorded the adulation lavished on sophists. An epic poet might be rewarded by an emperor with σίτησις, 'eating rights', at the Alexandrian Museum, as was Pancrates by Hadrian.[23] The poet Marcellus of Side had his forty-two book *Medical Books* lodged in libraries in Rome by order of Hadrian and Pius: so says his own epigram, rounding off the hexameter work's bulk to forty books and calling it

[21] For this poem see further Bowie 2002e, 185–9 (Chapter 15 in this volume, 338–42); for it and other Greek 'figure poems' Luz 2010; Kwapisz 2014. The text is preserved in *AP* 15 (where it is no. 25) and codex Y of the Greek bucolic poets (the fourteenth-century *Vaticanus Graecus* 434). Y and the *index vetus* to the Palatine manuscript of *AP* ascribe it Βησαντίνου, 'of Vesantinus', conjectured by Haeberlin to be a corruption of Βηστίνου, 'of Vestinus'. If so, then identification with the Hadrianic *ab epistulis*, L. lulius Vestinus is plausible: on his scholarly activity see the Suda ο 835 *s.v.* Οὐηστῖνος; on his career *IG* xiv 1085; Bowie 1982 and 2013e (Chapters 6 and 32 in Volume 3). For other testimonia cf. *PIR*² I 623; Pflaum 1960–1, no. 105.

[22] D.L. 7.31.

[23] For the honour to Pancrates see Ath. 15.677d–f. For the fragments of his poem on the lion hunt of Hadrian and Antinous see Heitsch 1963, i 51–4; Bowie 1990b, 81–3 (Chapter 14 in this volume, 310–12); Höschele 2018.

Chironides, '*Sagas of Chiron*'. Perhaps its section on lycanthropy was more exciting than the surviving portion, 101 lines listing the fish that can be used to make medicines.[24]

But it should be said that although these lines are tedious, two other hexameter poems by Marcellus are among the best of the period. These are the two poems of fifty-nine and thirty-nine lines respectively, commissioned by Herodes Atticus after the death of his wife Regilla (AD 160 or 161) for display on her estate by the third milestone of the via Appia. In one the women of Rome are urged to offer cult to Regilla's statue, giving Marcellus the opportunity to open with a formula suggesting a hymn. The second prays to Athena and to the Nemesis of Rhamnous to punish anybody attempting to encroach on Herodes' estate either by cultivation or by the construction of tombs. The poems are at once a functional exploitation of poetry for purposes incorporating poetry's traditional role and a virtuoso demonstration of the poet's skill. They are analogous to Aelius Aristides' hymn save that his is in elegiacs, Marcellus' poems in hexameters. But they are of much higher quality, and have an interesting balance of Homeric and Callimachean features. Perhaps the short poem and different subject made it easier to write well, or Marcellus' skills as a poet had advanced since his *Chironides*, which ought to belong late in Hadrian's and early in Pius' reign. Herodes did not make a mistake in commissioning the pieces from Marcellus, and Marcellus need not have been ashamed to sign the pieces, as he did.[25]

In another genre the melic poet Mesomedes was given a salary by Hadrian, which Pius halved, and was still so admired by Caracalla that he constructed a cenotaph for him.[26] I would take Pancrates, Marcellus and Mesomedes to fall within my class of semi-professionals, but for all we know Mesomedes may have entered competitions in κιθαρωιδία, 'singing to the accompaniment of the *cithara*'.[27]

[24] The epigram is *AP* 7.158. The fragment on fish-medicines is most easily found in Heitsch 1963–4, ii 16–22; for a section on lycanthropy see the Suda μ 205 *s.v.* Μάρκελλος: Μάρκελλος Σιδήτης, ἰατρός, ἐπὶ Μάρκου Ἀντωνίνου. οὗτος ἔγραψε δι' ἐπῶν ἡρωϊκῶν βιβλία ἰατρικὰ δύο καὶ μ', ἐν οἷς καὶ περὶ λυκανθρώπου, 'Marcellus of Side, a doctor, in the time of Marcus Antoninus. He wrote *Medical Books* in hexameters, forty-two, in which he also wrote about a lycanthrope'.

[25] The poems are *IG* xiv 1389 = *IGUR* iii 1155, cf. *SEG* 29.999. The discussion of Wilamowitz 1928 remains important, although he misses some Callimachean features. That *Chironides* belongs in the 130s I infer from the epigram's claim that both Hadrian and Pius secured its accession to Roman libraries: publication was presumably serial. For further discussion of his work see Bowie 1990b, 66–9 (Chapter 14 in this volume); 2019d (Chapter 44 in Volume 3); of the poems for Regilla Peek 1979; Skenteri 2005; Davies and Pomeroy 2012.

[26] SHA *Pius* 7.8 for the salary, and for Hadrian's patronage Whitmarsh 2004; D.C. 77.13.7 for the cenotaph, which admittedly he attributes to Caracalla's own learning of *citharoedia*.

[27] For the high value set on *citharoedia* in this period see Power 2010. Mesomedes is now much better understood after the commentary of Regenauer 2016.

4 Honours and Patronage

Honours bestowed by cities also cover a number of genres. Another *citharoedos*, the man who composed a hymn to Antinous at Curium in metres akin to those of Mesomedes, was perhaps of sufficient status to be sent on an embassy to Hadrian by his city. Presumably the embassy conveyed condolence for Antinous' death – or congratulation on his apotheosis – and a copy of the hymn itself.[28] We may recall that the epigrammatist Crinagoras was entrusted by Mytilene with important missions, though it was hardly Crinagoras' status as a poet that gained him this role.[29]

We also find cities honouring tragic poets. Our best instance is of a poet who was not limited to tragedy, and it is unclear just which of the genres he practiced impressed the city. In AD 127 Halicarnassus honoured the poet from Aphrodisias C. Iulius Longianus. Longianus had given ποιημάτων παντοδαπῶν ἐπιδείξεις ποικίλας, 'varied displays of poetry of every sort', which entertained the old and improved the young.[30] In return for these displays he received citizenship of Halicarnassus, the greatest honours the laws provided for, and bronze statues to be erected in the most distinguished parts of the city, including the τέμενος, 'sanctuary', of the Muses and the ephebes' gymnasium παρὰ τὸν παλαιὸν Ἡρόδοτον, 'beside Herodotus of old'. It was also decided to lodge his books in the libraries so that the young might be educated by them as by the classics. An associated decree of the Dionysiac *technitae* gives us the date of AD 127 – that decree itself was passed on March 27th – and the information that Longianus was a tragic poet.[31]

Honours also went to hexameter poets who composed both epic and didactic verse. The widest spread of acclaim is attested for L. Septimius Nestor of Laranda in the time of Septimius Severus: he was honoured with statues at Ostia, Paphus, Ephesus, and Cyzicus – this last appropriately accompanied by a six-line epigram. His works included *Metamorphoseis*, a lipogrammatic *Iliad*, an *Alexandrias* (presumably celebrating Alexander Severus), and two didactic works, *Alexicepus* and *Panaceia*.[32]

[28] See *IKourion* 104, published by Mitford 1971; for improvements and a good discussion, Lebek 1973. I now think that the text's πρεσβευτής was not the poet but another person involved in the performance and/or inscription. In Bowie 2022b I suggest that the poet and composer was indeed Mesomedes himself, a view now also taken by Pöhlmann 2019.

[29] For Crinagoras see Bowie 2012e (Chapter 17 in this volume); Ypsilanti 2018.

[30] *MAMA* viii 418(a) and (b), from Aphrodisias = *IAph2007* 12.27(i) and (ii).

[31] *MAMA* viii 418 (c) = *IAph2007* 12.27 (iii).

[32] The evidence was conveniently summarised by Keydell in *KP* iv (1975), col. 82 *s.v.* Nestor 3. The Ephesus text is now *IEph.* 3067. For an important discussion of Nestor see Ma 2007.

Three centuries earlier the Athenians had honoured Nicanor, friend of Augustus, as νέος Ὅμηρος, 'a new Homer', though perhaps rather because he had bought back Salamis for Athens than because of the quality of his verse.[33] The same epithet was applied at Side to its citizen P. Aelius Pompeianus Paeon,[34] though it is not clear that epic was among his fields. Two elegiac epigrams appear on the statue of Memnon, probably about AD 130, one on behalf of a Mettius but signed by Paeon, the other speaking for Paeon himself. It is the same Paeon who appears in a decree of the Dionysiac guild from Nysa ca. AD 142, described (lines 3 and 61) as ποιητὴς πλειστονείκης, μελοποιὸς καὶ ῥαψωιδὸς θεοῦ Ἁδριανοῦ, 'poet with numerous victories, song-maker and rhapsode of the god Hadrian'. This description shows that he was indeed a professional, but a professional interesting enough to be taken to Egypt by a Mettius, perhaps governor of Pamphylia ca. AD 129, and so perhaps there to catch the ear of Hadrian and commend to him his Sidetan compatriot Marcellus.[35] A variant of the title 'new Homer' was applied to another medical poet, Heraclitus of Rhodiapolis, ἰατρικῶν ποιημάτων Ὅμηρον, 'Homer of medical poems'. He too had been honoured by the Dionysiac technitae, by the Areopagus and the Epicureans at Athens, and by Alexandria and Rhodes. He gave copies of his prose works and poems alike to Rhodiapolis, Alexandria, Athens and Rhodes.[36]

5 Poets and Sophists

As well as receiving honour from emperors and cities, poets clearly moved in the same circles as sophists. The friends of Plutarch include the Athenian poet and Stoic philosopher Sarapion. His victory in a competition where choruses of all the tribes were financed by Balbilla's brother C. Iulius Antiochus Philopappus is the occasion for his *Sympotic questions* 1.10; and to him Plutarch dedicated his dialogue on the E at Delphi.[37]

[33] See Bowersock 1965, 96. [34] Bean 1965, no. 107.

[35] The Memnon texts are Bernand 1960, nos. 11 and 12; that from Nysa is now *IEph.* 22 (= *SEG* 4.418). On the career of Paeon (comparing Nicanor and Heraclitus) see Robert 1980, 16–18, associating Paeon's Memnon texts with Hadrian's visit in AD 130 and not with Mettius, prefect of Egypt in AD 89–91. For the Mettius who governed Pamphylia ca. 130–1 see Eck 1983, 171 n.415. Robert takes ῥαψωιδός to mean composer of epic poems. For a fuller discussion of Paeon see Bowie 1990b, 65–6 (Chapter 14 in this volume); Rosenmeyer 2018a. For a suggestion that Paeon might be the author of the poem on Rome ascribed by Stobaeus to Melinno see West 2013, 365, n.28.

[36] *TAM* ii 910 = *IGR* iii 733: cf. Robert 1980b, 14; İplikçioğlu 2014.

[37] Plut, *QC* 1.10.1 = *Mor.* 628a, *De E Delph.* 1 = *Mor.* 384d. On Philopappus see Baslez 1992a.

That choruses of all the tribes competed shows that Sarapion's victory had been in dithyramb, still an important cultural form in Athens.[38] Another Athenian, T. Flavius Glaucus of Marathon, ποιητὴς καὶ ῥήτωρ καὶ φιλόσοφος, 'poet and *rhetor* and philosopher', claims as his great-grandfather a (Q. Statius) Sarapion who may be this Sarapion's son: his descent makes Glaucus the kin of asiarchs, ὑπατικοί, 'men of consular rank', and of the sophist Isaeus.[39]

Indeed sophists themselves composed poetry more demanding than epigram. Nicetes of Smyrna and his pupil Scopelianus of Clazomenae composed tragedies: it is hard to see where these can have been performed other than in agonistic festivals. Scopelianus also attempted every branch of poetry, including epic, in which genre Philostratus mentions a *Gigantias*. Hippodromus composed lyric νόμοι, 'nomes', which were still sung in the 220s AD, and Philostratus himself included quasi-melic pieces in his *Heroicus*.[40] I say 'quasi-melic' because although their metres recall Mesomedes and the pieces are presented as songs, they appear in a text that was designed for reading or recitation. Or should we suppose that at the first performance Philostratus did sing them? The sophist Aelius Aristides was likewise encouraged to compose melic poetry as therapy, and his acquaintance at the Pergamene Asclepieum included the melic poet Hermocrates of Rhodes. He also mentions one Metrodorus who must have been a professional poet, since Aristides dreamt that he was engaged in the competition for poets at Smyrna, but there is no evidence that Metrodorus visited the Asclepieum.[41]

There is in all this plenty to show that poets were not honoured to the same degree as sophists: it may be significant that we have as yet no text honouring a poet from the Asclepieum, and that Lucian's satirical targets, although they include poetry at large, do not include arguably identifiable contemporary poets as they do philosophers and sophists – contrast one of his models, Aristophanes. It also seems that there is little difference between the centres of sophistic activity and other places, as least so far as concerns the honouring of poets by contemporaries.

[38] For the importance of choral performances as markers of Greek identity and for Sarapion see Bowie 2006c (Chapter 16 in Volume 3); for Sarapion and his descendants see Oliver 1936; Geagan 1991; Kapetanopoulos 1994; Follet 2001; for dithyramb in the Roman period see Shear 2013.

[39] *IG* ii^2 3704, mentioned p. 272 with n.12; *testimonia* and discussion in Puech 2002, 270–83.

[40] Philostr. *VS* 1.21.518, 2.27.620; *Her.* 53.10 (p. 68 de Lannoy), 55.3 (pp. 72–3 de Lannoy).

[41] Composition as therapy, Aristid. 47.73 Keil. He was not alone in receiving such instructions: cf. Galen vi 46 Kühn. For Hermocrates see Aristid. *Or.* 50.23 Keil; for Metrodorus *Or.* 47.42 Keil.

6 Hexameter Survivors

If we adopt a different perspective, however, and evaluate poetry by the admittedly dubious criterion of its survival, a different pattern stands out. The most important Greek poem to have survived from the first two centuries of the empire –and indeed to have survived in a very large number of manuscripts – is the *Periegesis*, '*Guide to the world*', of Dionysius of Alexandria. Doubtless it was its usefulness as a geographical text that preserved it, but its 1187 hexameters contain much good writing, and it is now undeservedly neglected.[42] It is one of a number of didactic poems to have been produced outside Asia and Achaea. The same Dionysius is credited with a Λιθι(α)κά, 'The science of stones', and we have a prose paraphrase of an Ἰξευτικά, '*Hunting with bird-lime*', that is probably his too.[43] We have already encountered didactic poetry by Marcellus of Side, under Hadrian and Pius; by Heraclitus of Rhodiapolis, later in the second century, and by Nestor of Laranda, under the Severi. The first century AD had produced the five-book astronomical poem of Dorotheus of Sidon, dated by the most recent editor of its remains (in an Arabic translation) to AD 25–75.[44] The writer of *Apotelesmatika*, claiming to be Manetho, is shown by his horoscope to have been born in AD 80.[45] The remaining 2000 or so lines are not much read. The author's attempt to secure the paternity of Manetho suggests that they were written in an Eastern province.

It is in this context of continuous production of didactic poetry in the Eastern Mediterranean that we should place the two poems ascribed to an Oppian. One writer, from Anazarbus or Corycus in Cilicia, dedicated his *Halieutica*, '*On catching fish*', to Marcus and Commodus, so between AD 177 and 180.[46] The other, from Apamea on the Orontes, dedicated his four-book *Cynegetica* to Caracalla, probably after AD 211, certainly before his death in 217.[47] They do not appear in a vacuum, but stand in a tradition

[42] When this chapter was first published Dionysius had still be read in *GGM* ii 103–76. Since then there have been several editions, some with translations, notably Tsavari 1990; Jacob 1990; Brodersen 1994; Amato 2005; Lightfoot 2014. For other discussions of aspects of Dionysius see Counillon 1981; Jacob 1981; Bowie 1990b, 70–80 (Chapter 14 in this volume, 299–308), 2004a (Chapter 16 in this volume); Hunter 2003, 2004; and other papers in *REA* 2004.

[43] For the Λιθι(α)κά see *GGM* ii p. xxvi. The paraphrase of the Ἰξευτικά was edited by Garzya 1963: he discusses title and authorship in Garzya 1957. An Ἰξευτικά in two books was also written half a century later by Oppian of Cilicia according to the Suda *s.n.* ο 452.

[44] Pingree 1976. [45] Neugebauer and van Hosen 1959, 92.

[46] Fajen 1999 argues for the narrower limits 177–78. For discussion see Kneebone 2008, 2017, 2020.

[47] Text, Papathamopoulos 2003; for brief discussion and bibliography to ca. 1980 see Bowersock in *CHCL* 653–4 and 862–3; more recently Whitby 2007, Kneebone in the online *OCD* (2016).

that goes back to the Hellenistic period and that was alive if not entirely well through the first two centuries AD. It may be coincidence that all these poems were written outside Asia and Achaea, even if some of their poets were honoured there too. But it might also be suggested that a career as a sophist left little room for such laborious and learned writing, whereas, for example, the museum at Alexandria might encourage it.

Epic may be a similar case. We have indeed seen the sophist Scopelianus composing a Γιγαντιάς, '*War with the Giants*', and the same theme was attempted by a Dionysius: we have fragments of both his Γιγαντιάς and his Βασσαρικά, '*Tales of Dionysiac worshippers*', clearly from the same pen, the most recent (published 2011) showing he must antedate the early second century.[48] A scholiast on Dionysius Periegetes (427) attributes him to Samos, and we have nothing to contradict this. But the contribution of more Easterly provinces is greater. From Egypt we know, as well as Pancrates (n.23), an epic poet Areius from the Alexandrian Museum who inscribed or had inscribed a dreadful Homeric cento on the Memnon colossus, probably about AD 130.[49] In Egypt we also know of one M. Decrius Decrianus, who in a dedication made after a victory in a competition describes himself as ἐπῶν καὶ μελῶν ποιητής, 'epic and melic poet'.[50] Peisander, who wrote Θεογαμίαι, '*Weddings of the gods*', in sixty books, and his father Nestor, already mentioned,[51] were from Laranda in Lycaonia. When we begin to have complete texts, Triphiodorus' *Capture of Troy*, probably written in the third century and after Nestor, is from Egypt;[52] so too later Colluthus and the stupendous Nonnus of Panopolis.[53] Only Quintus, composer of a fourteen-book *Posthomerica*, '*The story after Homer*', that probably falls in time between Oppian and Triphiodorus, is from the Aegean, securely (or so he presents himself) tied to Smyrna.[54] We may recall that the new Homer under Augustus, Nicanor, started life in Syrian Hierapolis.

[48] The edition of Benaissa 2018, following his 2011 *editio princeps* of *P.Oxy.* 5103, supersedes Heitsch 1963–4, 60–77, and Livrea 1973.

[49] Bernand 1960, no. 37: cf. Rosenmeyer 2018a.

[50] Fraser 1959.

[51] See n.32.

[52] For his date see now Miguelez-Cavero 2013, 6, following Vian 1986 in putting him after both Nestor, whose lipogrammatic *Iliad* may have inspired his lipogrammatic *Odyssey*, and Quintus. The *terminus ante quem* is *P.Oxy.* 2946 dated by Rea 1972 to the third or fourth century.

[53] A good introduction to the earlier bibliography on these poets remains that in Keydell's articles in *KP*, and his full bibliographical surveys in *Bursians Jahresberichte* are reprinted in Keydell 1982.

[54] Among several recent studies of Quintus note especially Baumbach, Bär and Dümmler 2007; Maciver 2012; Greensmith 2020.

7 Conclusions

Briefly to conclude. Poetry and poets enjoyed some esteem in the first three centuries of the empire. It was modest by comparison with that accorded to sophists and philosophers, but not negligible. And if we had *Lives of the Poets* as well as *Lives of the Sophists* they would have something to tell us. In epic and didactic poetry, however, it seems that the contribution of Asia and Achaea is strikingly small, and one factor may be the dominance of sophistic rhetoric, a dominance that affected large-scale productions whereas it did not discourage melic and epigrammatic poetry.[55]

[55] Aspects of this chapter's subject are treated in greater detail in Bowie 1989a, 1990b, and 2002e (Chapters 12, 14 and 15 in this volume).

14 Greek Poetry in the Antonine Age (1990)

1 Introduction

Although the Antonine Age produced much less Greek poetry than prose, there is still far more than can be assessed adequately in a single chapter, and to help me in my task I focus on a shorter period, the reigns of Hadrian, Pius, and Marcus. Even here I must be selective, but I make no apology for including the reign of Hadrian, since so many of the poets of the period AD 117–80 flourished under him, some indeed as a direct result of his interest.

2 Epigram

I discuss the poets of this period by genre (although some operate in more than one) and begin with epigram, a form that retained its popularity century after century while that of others waxed and waned. It remained popular for a number of reasons: any πεπαιδευένος, 'well-educated person', knew hexameter and elegiac models that could suggest words and ideas, and did not need to be a professional poet to write metrically for a few lines. Moreover epigrams were short enough to risk on a readership of friends, or on a convivial gathering, and continued to have a function in public life – particularly for epitaphs, but also for dedicatory, honorific, and commemorative inscriptions. Thousands of such functional epigrams composed in this period all over the Greek-speaking world survive on stone, betraying various levels of skill and education, while a few, mostly by established writers of prose or poetry, were gathered into ancient anthologies. Although many of the former are doubtless by local professional poets, very few are signed or precisely dated, and much more preliminary work needs to be done before a history of Roman imperial epigram could be written.[1] Later I

[1] Kaibel 1878 and *GVI* (1955) remain basic, but the former is desperately obsolete, and of the latter only the first volume – epitaphs – has appeared. Many of the hundreds of epigrams to be published, or republished, since 1878 were worked on by Louis Robert, and his views, scattered through his voluminous writings, must always be taken seriously. The accessibility of inscribed epigram east of the Aegean has been greatly enhanced by the publication of Merkelbach–Stauber 1998–2004. Only a few poems either epigraphically transmitted or from the *Palatine*

shall pick out a few examples. But first I wish to look at the poems that survive in a manuscript tradition, since they are sometimes numerous enough to guide us to the characteristic features of an individual or generation.

To judge from what survives in the *Palatine Anthology*, the most favoured type of literary epigram in the latter part of the first century AD had been the satirical, developed in Greek by Lucillius and Nicarchus and carried to its limits in Latin by Martial.[2] The only poem attributed to Trajan in the anthology is in this genre, and we know of at least one by Hadrian.[3] It continued to flourish in his reign in the hands of two Greeks whose connections are with the province Asia, Ammianus and Pollianus. One of Pollianus' most interesting poems disparages derivative, Homerising narrative epic and enrols its author in the freer and less imitative tradition of elegy:

τοὺς κυκλίους τούτους, τοὺς αὐτὰρ ἔπειτα λέγοντας,
　　μισῶ, λωποδύτας ἀλλοτρίων ἐπέων.
καὶ διὰ τοῦτ᾽ ἐλέγοις προσέχω πλέον᾽· οὐδὲν ἔχω γὰρ
　　Παρθενίου κλέπτειν ἢ πάλι Καλλιμάχου.
θηρὶ μὲν οὐατόεντι γενοίμην, εἴ ποτε γράψω,
　　εἴκελος, ἐκ ποταμῶν χλωρὰ χελιδόνια.
οἱ δ᾽ οὕτως τὸν Ὅμηρον ἀναιδῶς λωποδυτοῦσιν,
　　ὥστε γράφειν ἤδη μῆνιν ἄειδε, θεά.

These cyclic poets, those poets who say 'But then …',
　　I hate them, plunderers of others' lines.
and so I am more attached to elegies: for I have nothing
　　to steal from Parthenius, or yet Callimachus.
Like 'the long-eared beast' may I become, if ever
　　I write 'from the rivers, green celandine'.
But they plunder Homer so shamelessly
　　As even to write 'Sing, goddess, of the wrath'.

Pollianus, *AP* 11.130

Anthology figure in *FGE*, and the notes in Beckby's and in the Budé edition (which in 1990 still lacked Books 10 and 12) are very selective. Robert 1968 is invaluable on Lucillius; Setti 1892 (on Lucian) and Page 1978 (on Rufinus) were our only modern commentaries on a *corpus* of an anthology poet of the imperial period until González Rincón 1996 (Strato); Sider 1997 (Philodemus); Steinbichler 1998 (Strato); Höschele 2006 (Rufinus); Giannuzzi 2007 (Strato); Floridi 2007 (Strato), 2014 (Lucillius); and Ypsilanti 2018 (Crinagoras). For a brief account of the popularity of epigram and other genres with particular reference to the Roman provinces of Asia and Achaea, see Bowie 1989b (Chapter 13 in this volume).

2 Cf. Laurens 1965; Robert 1968; Nisbet 2003; Floridi 2007; for Nicarchus, Schatzmann 2012.

3 Trajan: *AP* 11.418, cf. *FGE* 560–1. Hadrian: *AP* 9.137, cf. *FGE* 564–5.

We shall see when we turn to hexameter poetry that Pollianus was swimming with the tide: indeed he could have expected the approval of Hadrian, who wrote a sepulchral epigram for Parthenius' tomb.[4] By contrast Ammianus' readiness to attack not simply the rhetorical pretensions of sophists (e.g. *AP* 11.147, 150, 152) but the judicial integrity of Hadrian's friend M. Antonius Polemo (*AP* 11.180, 181) was not calculated to elicit imperial favour.[5]

Both these poets, of whom Ammianus is demonstrably from the province Asia, are well represented in the eleventh book of the *Anthology* and offer interesting sidelights on Antonine culture. There are, however, few individual traits in their poems, since the stance of the scoptic epigrammatist imposes a uniformity of tone and theme. This too impedes any attempt to determine which epigrams in Book 11 are by Lucian: we can be confident that several of the sixty-three that have at various times been given to him are indeed his, but the ascription of each poem is precarious, and in this context it is sufficient to note that his engagement with the genre takes its popularity at least into the AD 150s.[6]

Another pointer to the popularity of satirical epigram is the anthology of Diogenianus, arguably the first stage in the transmission of all these scoptic poets (and a few others less well represented) to the *Palatine Anthology* where we find them. Sakolowski argued for its composition around AD 150, though if Lucian's epigrams did indeed pass through this intermediary a slightly later date is more likely. The Diogenianus who compiled it is most probably a learned doctor from Heracleia Salbace in Caria, though the Suda also alleges a homonym from Heracleia Pontica: both, according to the Suda, flourished under Hadrian, but this dating may stem merely from a reference to events of his reign which should be treated as no more than a *terminus post quem*.[7] Whatever the exact date of compilation and identity of the compiler, the anthology seems to have been one of scoptic and sympotic

[4] *IG* xiv 1089 = *GVI* 2050 = *FGE* Hadrian 7. On Pollianus see Nisbet 2003, 183–94. For another Callimachean démarche by Pollianus see *AP* 11.127.

[5] On Ammianus see Nisbet 2003, 134–64; Schulte 2004.

[6] For a discussion, both general and particular, of the attribution of Lucian's epigrams see Baldwin 1975; Nisbet 2003, 165–81. For a probable candidate for his mockery (and scoptic epigrams by his contemporary Antiochus of Aegeae) see Bowie 1989a, 250–3 (Chapter 12, 263–4 in this volume).

[7] Cf. Sakolowski 1893, 1–93. Sakolowski and others put Diogenianus' anthology as late as AD 150 or even the reign of Marcus. We have a *terminus post quem* in the notice in *EM* 34.5 that Hadrian's name Aelius was mentioned in Diogenianus' Χρονικά, 'Chronicles' (perhaps also Aelia Capitolina, but that part of the entry may not be from Diogenianus): and this may indeed be the source of the Suda's dating.

epigrams. It can thus be used to show that their vogue persisted from the reign of Nero right through to that of Pius, perhaps even Marcus. Whether it then declined we cannot say, since the absence of a comparable third-century anthology may have robbed us of a further wave of poets.

The second century also saw one gifted composer of erotic epigrams, Strato of Sardis. These had been popular in the first century BC, and some of their writers can be allocated to the first half of the first century AD. But they probably received a boost from Rufinus, who seems to have published a collection of his amatory epigrams not later than ca. AD 80, and perhaps as early as AD 40. The *terminus ante quem* follows from his influence on Martial, persuasively argued for by Cameron, who rebutted Page's case for putting Rufinus as late as AD 400. The earlier limit is given by Rufinus' absence from the *Garland of Philip*, usually thought to have been collected about AD 40, though Cameron sets it under Nero.[8]

Rufinus seems to have influenced Strato, and both (like Ammianus and Pollianus) were from the province Asia. Rufinus hailed from within a day's journey of Ephesus, which he knows well, and both Ephesus and Smyrna are within Strato's geographical horizons.[9] But whereas Rufinus' poems are all of heterosexual love, Strato writes exclusively about boys. The reasons could be literary: Rufinus had come near to exhausting the available moves in poetry about girls, so Strato turns his pen to the obvious alternative. But another factor surely operates too. Cameron's chronology led him to put Strato's collection, the *Musa puerilis*, a little earlier than AD 117. This is because he accepted Buchheit's suggestion that Strato's two introductory poems influenced those set at the opening of the *Corpus Priapeorum*, dated by Buchheit shortly after Martial.[10] But we have no precise *terminus ante*

[8] Cameron 1982 and Robert 1982b simultaneously argued against Rufinus' dating by Page 1978. For the date of the *Garland of Philip* see *GP* xlv–xlix; Cameron 1982; Bowersock 1985. For Rufinus see Gärtner 2006, Höschele 2006.

[9] One of the Rufinus' poems, 1 Page = *AP* 5.9, shows a good knowledge of Ephesus, but makes clear that his home was not there but somewhere no more than a day's journey away. A number of cities might be considered, but Smyrna is not unlikely for a man well versed in earlier poetry and writing sensitively himself. It is accordingly tempting to conjecture that he was an ancestor of the later sophist Claudius Rufinus, στρατηγός, 'general' (i.e. chief magistrate), at Smyrna at the end of the second century, teacher of Hermocrates of Phocaea and perhaps the dedicatee of Book 9 of Phrynichus' *Praeparatio sophistica* (Philostr. *VS* 2.25.608; *PIR*[2] C 998). For Strato's home, Sardis, cf. *AP* 12 *pr*.; for his horizons, *AP* 12.193, 202, 226.

[10] Cameron 1982, 171; Buchheit 1962, 109 ff. Clarke 1984 argues that Strato must antedate the domination of Roman coinage in Asia on the grounds that the equivalence of 20 drachmae to a stater is implied by *AP* 12.239. I doubt if the implication is necessary: the progression 5–10–20 may be the only point, with a *further* escalation in the second line's introduction of χρυσοῦς, 'a stater'.

quem for the *Corpus Priapeorum*: ca. AD 120 or 130 would be just as likely as ca. AD 110; and one of Strato's satirical epigrams seems to belong in or close to Hadrian's reign, since it is arguably aimed at Artemidorus Capito, a doctor whose edition of Hippocrates we know from Galen to have earned approval by Hadrian.[11] It is probable, then, that Strato's collection was published when Hadrian was already emperor, and some chance that it falls in the period of his two tours of the province Asia, AD 123–4 and AD 129, by the latter of which, if not earlier, Hadrian's relationship with the Bithynian Antinous must have been widely known. It can hardly be a coincidence that Strato's decision to cultivate the pederastic Muse was made under a philhellenic emperor whose homosexual tastes were on public display. It is unfortunate that his subject has alienated so many generations of critics, for he is not simply a prolific poet (about 458 lines in Book 12 are his) but a good one, ready with both wit and passion, and as deserving of a modern edition as Rufinus.[12]

One or two amatory epigrams by other second-century figures may lurk in the *Palatine Anthology*,[13] and it is interesting to find the Platonic philosopher and sophist Apuleius composing some in Latin Africa (*Apol.* 9). The survivals in the anthology may only be the tip of an iceberg, and as with satirical epigram the absence of a collection later in the second or in the third century may have been crucial.

With dedicatory epigrams and poems commemorating the dead or (less often) the living, we move to poetry whose surviving examples on stone greatly outnumber those anthologised in antiquity. It is hard to discern major exponents, and only broad changes in practice stand out (such as the growing preference for hexameters over elegiacs).[14] As I have already said, much more work needs to be done before a synthetic study of this material could be attempted, and my few examples are necessarily unrepresentative.

Few epitaphs on stone can be securely and precisely dated, and even fewer are signed. We know that an elegiac couplet on the sarcophagus of Iulius Hermes at Thessalonica (*GVI* 385) belongs to AD 119, and another from Saitta in Lydia (*GVI* 516) to AD 175, but the poems themselves are unremarkable. More interesting is a signed eighteen-line elegiac epitaph,

[11] *AP* 11.117, cf. Galen xv 21 Kühn, Cameron 1982, 168–71. Clarke 1984, 215–16 is over-sceptical about this identification.

[12] On Strato see Maxwell-Stuart 1972; González Rincón 1996; Steinbichler 1998; Giannuzzi 2007; and for other work up to 2006 the excellent edition and commentary of Floridi 2007.

[13] Dionysius the sophist, *AP* 5.81, 82, cf. *FGE* 44; Fronto, *AP* 12.174, 233, cf. *FGE* 115.

[14] Cf. Wifstrand 1933, 155–77. For a concise but full account of the fortunes of various metres in the imperial period see West 1982, 162–85.

probably of the second century, commemorating a young woman, Socratea of Paros, who died from haemorrhage while giving birth to her third child at the age of twenty-six.[15] The poem blends these details with sonorous poetic language and is a fine piece of work: unusually, it is signed, by an otherwise unknown Dionysius of Magnesia, who may even be the person who carefully checked and emended the stonecutter's text.

It is frustrating that we have no idea what other verses Dionysius composed that encouraged him to sign himself as ποιητής, 'poet'. His work compares well with two epitaphs by Antiphon of Athens on whom we do happen to have further information. The epitaphs are for brothers from Acharnae, Ti. Flavius Diophantus and Glaucias, whose deaths fell close together soon after AD 131/2. The poet who signed their epitaphs, Antiphon, himself an Athenian, also appears in the records of a competition at Thespiae: he was victor in the προσόδιον, 'processional song' (as its poet), and in New Comedy (both as poet and as actor): he is, therefore, a professional.[16] The epitaphs are rather mechanical, although judgement of the first is impeded by the loss of more than half of each line. The second runs:

καὶ τόνδ' Ἠλύσιός τε δόμος καὶ χ[ῶρος ἀμείνων]
    Γλαυκίου υἷα μιῆς δεύτερον [ἐκ γενεῆς]
Ζηνὸς ἐνὶ προὔχοντα χοροστασί[ησιν ἔδεκτο],
    αὐτοκασιγνήτωι ξύνδρομ[ον ἀρτιθανεῖ].
ἀλλ' ἐπὶ καὶ τῶι στῆσε πόλις τόδ[ε πὰρ μακάρεσσαι]
    λάινον ἀτμήτου σᾶμα θε[οῖσι κόμης].

This man too the Elysian mansion and a [better place] received,
    a son of Glaucias, the second from a single family,
as he showed his prowess in the choral dances for Zeus,
    speeding to join his own brother [who had lately died.]
But for him too the city raised this memorial [before the blessed gods]
    in stone to mark his unshorn [hair].

15 *GVI* 1871 = Kaibel 218 = *IG* xii.5 310. I note some other datable epitaphs: *IG* vii. 118 = Kaibel 858, six elegiac lines for a dead Diogenes at Megara, probably post 126/7 (cf. *IG* ii² 3734); IG ii 3743 = Kaibel 963, six elegiac lines for the statue-base of a dead Athenian ephebe Philotimus, dated by the archonship of T. Aur. Philemon to 158/9; *MAMA* ix 79 = Kaibel 375 = *GVI* 607, from Çavdarhisar in the Aezanitis, an elegiac couplet for the tomb of a horseman Menogenes who died in a plague, so probably AD 165 or shortly after; *GVI* 1613, six elegiac lines by Herodes Atticus on one of his children or τρόφιμοι, 'foster-children', probably of the 160s; *IG* xii.9 1179, six elegiac lines for Amphicles of Chalcis by his homonymous father, probably of the 170s. I discuss these last two, and the poems of Flavius Glaucus of Marathon, some of them epitaphs, and all probably later than AD 180, in Bowie 1989a, 232–43 (Chapter 12, 246–55 in this volume).

16 *IG* ii² 3963–4 = *GVI* 2025. The victories are attested by *IG* vii 1773 (Thespiae).

Dedicatory poems that can be dated are more numerous,[17] but many of them are dull and flat: unlike epitaphs, they rarely have a place for pathos, and usually add little ornament to their catalogue of the basic facts attending a dedication or the erection of an honorific statue. Thus there is little rewarding in the series of short poems (an elegiac couplet, or two or three trimeters) on herms honouring Athenian *kosmetai*, many of them dated.[18] The longer the poem, the greater the scope, even if it is not always exploited: the sophist Hadrianus of Tyre's eight elegiac lines for a statue at Ephesus honouring Cn. Claudius Severus (between AD 163 and 169) are no more inspiring than the four for a statue of the sophist Hordeonius Lollianus in Athens of the 140s.[19] But once there is a story to tell the poetry acquires more life. Thus a group of three poems associated with Eleusis, honouring the hierophant Iulius (?) Heraclides, escapes banality by highlighting his successful preservation of the ἄρρητα, 'secret cult objects', from the Costoboci in their invasion of AD 171. I cite one which should precede AD 176, since it makes no mention of the hierophant's initiation of Marcus in that year.[20]

μνῆ]μα τόδ' ὑψιφανὲς Δη[οῦ]ς [ζ]α[κόρ]οιο δέδορκας,
    μυρίον ἐν σοφίηι κῦδος ἐνεγκαμένου,
ὃς τελέτας ἀνέφηνε καὶ ὄργια πάννυχα μύσταις,
    Εὐμόλπου προχέων ἱμερόεσσαν ὄπα.
ὃς καὶ δυσμενέων μόθον οὐ τρέσεν, ἀλλ' ἐσάωσεν
    ἄχραντα ἀρρήτων θέσμια Κεκροπίδαις.
ἆ μάκαρ, ὃν καὶ δῆμος ἐπεστεφάνωσε γεραίρων ...

You behold here the lofty memorial of Demeter's attendant,
    the winner of measureless renown in wisdom,
who displayed mysteries and night-long rituals to initiates,
    pouring forth the lovely voice of Eumolpus:
who also feared not the enemies' battle-din, but saved
    untainted the secret ritual objects for the sons of Cecrops.
Ah! blessed is he, whom the People also crowned in honour ...

[17] For a dedication whose date is unusually secure see the six-line elegiac dedication of a statue of Hadrian at Syros, *IG* xii *suppl.* 239, dated by the accompanying prose text to AD 134/5 (*trib. pot.* XIX).

[18] e.g. *IG* ii² 3744 = Kaibel 964, under Hadrian or Pius; *IG* ii² 3740 = Kaibel 959 of 142/3 and 2055 = Kaibel 960 of 145/6.

[19] For Hadrianus see Kaibel 888a = *IEph.* 1539 = *FGE* 566–8 (wrongly ascribing it to the emperor Hadrian); Puech 2002, 284–8; for Lollianus Kaibel 877 = *IG* ii² 4211; Puech 2002, 327–30. On both see Bowie 1989a, 247–8 (Chapter 12, 259–60 in this volume).

[20] *IG* ii² 3639 = Kaibel 97a (p. 518) = *I Eleus.* 515, on the road from Eleusis to Athens; cf. from Eleusis the four elegiacs in *ASAA* 22–3 (1959–60) 421–7, and *IG* ii² 3411 = *I Eleus.* 516, eight or ten elegiacs mentioning both the rescue of the ἄρρητα and Marcus' initiation, hence after AD 176.

This poem neatly sets off conventional praise of hierophants against Iulius' special achievement. Another Eleusinian poem went too far: of the twelve elegiacs for a statue of the ἱεροφάντις, 'woman hierophant', who initiated Hadrian (so probably about AD 130), eight focus on that initiation, and four of these list great figures whom she did not initiate! Excessive too, in a number of ways, are the thirty-eight elegiacs from Marathon (there were once more) commemorating the return of Herodes Atticus, probably in 174/5. But they may serve to remind us that epigram could be developed in the direction of other genres – here the hymn[21] – and that some poems we find on stone were intended – perhaps primarily – for recitation.

The standard elegiac, hexameter, or trimeter epigram can also be made more interesting by the choice of a recherché metre. Thus Hadrian used hendecasyllables in his dedication of a bear's ἀκροθίνια, 'best offerings', to the god Eros at Thespiae in AD 124, and his civil servant L. Iulius Vestinus combined several metres to construct his Βωμός, '*Altar*', a poem composed in lines of varying length to give the shape of an altar – to Hadrian himself, perhaps in AD 131/2.[22] His polymetric virtuosity also reflects contemporary taste in recitations, a medium which will have bulked large in an Antonine Greek's perception of poetry. Our best understanding of live poetic performance is actually furnished by a poet with a Greek background who wrote in Latin, Statius, though there are some traces in Book 11 of the *Palatine Anthology*.[23] But a text from Athens, perhaps as early as the first century AD but possibly from the second, honours a poet from Pergamum who had been given Athenian citizenship, Q. Pompeius Capito, for his virtuosity in extemporising 'in every rhythm and metre' as well as for his moral dignity.[24]

Before leaving epigram I cite some examples from a series of commemorative poems (of the sort parodied by Lucian in *True Histories* 2.28), many of which have the advantage of being both signed and dated, although only a few can be commended as poetry, viz. the bizarre collection inscribed

[21] The ἱεροφάντις, *IG* ii² 3575 = *I Eleus.* 454; Herodes, *IG* ii² 3606, cf. Ameling 1983 ii 205–11, no. 190; Skenteri 2005; an English translation in Oliver 1970, 34. For dedicatory epigrams that have also acquired hymnic features, cf. the inscribed poem of Aristides, Habicht 1969, 144–5, no. 145, and pp. 296–8 in this chapter on Marcellus.

[22] Hadrian's dedication, *IG* vii 1828 = Kaibel 811 = *FGE* 5; Vestinus' Βωμός, *AP* 15.25. I discuss these in Bowie 2002e (Chapter 15 in this volume), and Vestinus' career in 2013e, 253–5 (Chapter 32 in Volume 3).

[23] See Hardie 1983; Coleman 1988. Note also C. Iulius Longianus of Aphrodisias who was honoured at Halicarnassus by statues one of which was 'next to old Herodotus', for ποιημάτων παντοδαπῶν ἐπιδείξεις ποικίλας, 'varied displays of poetry of every sort', although he seems chiefly to have been a tragedian, *MAMA* viii 418(a) and (b), from Aphrodisias = *IAph2007* 12.27(i) and (ii): see more fully Bowie 1989a (Chapter 13, 277 in this volume).

[24] *IG* ii² 3800, discussed by Hardie 1983, 22 and 83–4.

on the legs of one of the Memnon colossi by Roman tourists. Not surprisingly the most ambitious are by an associate of Hadrian, Julia Balbilla. Her four poems of between seven and eighteen lines clothe elegiac couplets in a superficially Aeolic dialect and are precisely dated to the visit of the imperial party on 19–21 November of the year 130.[25]

Julia Balbilla was granddaughter of the last king of Commagene, C. Iulius Antiochus Epiphanes, and, it seems, of Ti. Claudius Balbillus, prefect of Egypt in AD 55. Her brother, C. Iulius Antiochus Philopappus, was the addressee of Plutarch's essay *How to distinguish a flatterer from a friend*, and the builder (about AD 114–16) of the impressive mausoleum which still crowns the hill of the Muses in Athens.[26] From this and from his archonship in 87/8 it seems that Athens was Philopappus' principal residence, and Balbilla may well have lived in Athens too; but apart from the poems on Memnon's thigh we have no trace of her existence. We may guess – but it is only a guess – that she had accompanied Hadrian since he left Athens in AD 129, though her visit to Memnon with Sabina hints that she was chiefly the empress' companion, perhaps her answer to Hadrian's Antinous.

None of Balbilla's verse is great poetry, and some is atrocious. The two best epigrams commemorate Memnon singing for Sabina on 20 November at the first hour and again for Hadrian at the second:

Αὔως καὶ γεράρω, Μέμνον, πάι Τιθώνοιο,
    Θηβάας θάσσων ἄντα Δίος πόλιος,
ἢ Ἀμένωθ, βασίλευ Αἰγύπτιε, τὼς ἐνέποισιν
    ἴρηες μύθων τῶν παλάων ἴδριες,
χαῖρε, καὶ αὐδάσαις πρόφρων ἀσπάσδε[ο κ]αὔτ[αν]
    τὰν σέμναν ἄλοχον κοιράνω Ἀδριάνω.
γλῶσσαν μέν τοι τμᾶξε [κ]αὶ ὤατα βάρβαρος ἄνηρ,
    Καμβύσαις ἄθεος· τῶ ῥα λύγρωι θανάτωι
δῶκέν τοι ποίναν τῶτωι ἄκ[ρωι] ἄορι πλάγεις
    τῶι νήλας Ἆπιν κάκτανε τὸν θέϊον.
ἀλλ' ἔγω οὐ δοκίμωμι σέθεν τόδ' ὄλεσθ' ἂν ἄγαλμα,
    ψύχαν δ' ἀθανάταν λοῖπον ἔσωθα νόω.
εὐσέβεες γὰρ ἔμοι γένεται πάπποι τ' ἐγένοντο,
    Βάλβιλλός τ' ὀ σόφος κἀντίοχος βασίλευς,
Βάλβιλλος γενέταις μᾶτρος βασιλήϊδος ἄμμας,
    τῶ πάτερος δὲ πάτηρ Ἀντίοχος βασίλευς·

[25] For the date and text of the poems see Bernand 1960, 80–98, nos. 28–31. For their dialect Hodot 1990. Much has been written since the interesting discussion of Balbilla by West 1978, notably Brennan 1998; Rosenmeyer 2008, 141–68, 2018a, 2018b; Di Marzio 2019, identifying in Bernand no. 31 the acrostic ΕΦΗ Ω ΚΑΕ, 'He said "O Cae(sar)"'.

[26] On Philopappus and his ancestry cf. *PIR*[2] I 161; Baslez 1992a. On the monument Kleiner 1983.

κήνων ἐκ γενέας κἄγω λόχον αἶμα τὸ κᾶλον,
Βαλβίλλας δ᾽ ἔμεθεν γρόπτα τάδ᾽ εὐσέβε[ος].

Memnon, son of Dawn and of revered Tithonus, sitting before the Theban city of Zeus, or Amenoth, Egyptian king, as the priests who know the ancient tales relate, hail! – and may you be keen to welcome by your cry the august wife too of the lord Hadrian. Your tongue and ears were cut by a barbarian, the godless Cambyses; hence by his wretched death he paid the penalty, smitten by the same sword with which in his ruthlessness he slew the divine Apis. But I do not judge that this statue of yours could perish, and I perceive within me that your soul shall be immortal.[27] For pious were my parents and grandparents, Balbillus the wise and Antiochus the king, Balbillus the parent of my royal mother, and Antiochus the king, father of my father. From their line do I too draw my noble blood, and these are the writings of Balbilla the pious.

Bernand 1960, no. 29

The poem for Hadrian has an identifying rubric – 'By Julia Balbilla: when Hadrian Augustus heard Memnon':

Μέμνονα πυνθανόμαν Αἰγύπτιον ἀλίω αὔγαι
αἰθόμενον φώνην Θηβαΐ<κ>ω 'πυ λίθω.
Ἀδρίανον δ᾽ ἐσίδων τὸν παμβασίληα πρὶν αὔγας
ἀελίω χαίρην εἶπέ <F>οι ὡς δύνατον.
Τίταν δ᾽ ὄττ᾽ ἐλάων λεύκοισι δι᾽ αἴθερος ἴπποις
ἐν σκίαι ὠράων δεύτερον ἆχε μέτρον,
ὠς χάλκοιο τύπεντος ἴη Μέμνων πάλιν αὔδαν
ὀξύτονον · χαίρων καὶ τρίτον ἆχον ἴη.
κοίρανος Ἀδρίανος τοτ᾽ ἄλις δ᾽ ἀσπασσατο καὔτος
Μέμνονα κἀν στάλαι κάλλιπεν ὀψιγόνοις
γρόππατα σαμμαίνοντά τ᾽ ὄσ᾽ εὔϊδε κὤσσ᾽ ἐσάκουσε
δῆλον παῖσι δ᾽ ἔγεντ᾽ ὤς <F>ε φίλισι θέοι.

I had been told that Memnon the Egyptian, warmed by the ray of the sun, spoke from his Theban stone. And when he saw Hadrian, king of all, before the rays of the sun, he greeted him as best he could. But when Titan, driving through the sky with his white horses, held the second measure of the hours in shadow, Memnon again uttered a sharp-toned cry as of bronze being struck: in greeting he also uttered a third call. Then the lord Hadrian himself also offered ample greetings to Memnon, and on the monument left for posterity verses marking all that he had

[27] For the improvement to Bernand's text at 1. 12, giving 'I perceive within me' (ἔσωθα νόω) instead of 'I have saved with my mind' (ἔσωσα νόω), see West 1977, 120.

seen and all he had heard. And it was made clear to all that the gods loved him.

Bernand 1960, no. 28

Of the other verses on Memnon some are clearly the work of amateurs who would have been well advised to restrain their Muse, others are by men who call themselves poets, and can sometimes do better. Thus Gallus Marianus, a Hadrianic ἐπιστράτηγος, 'regional governor', of the Thebaid, attempted his own hexameters:

Θήβης ἐν πεδίοισι [παρα]ὶ βα[θ]υδινήεντ[α]
Νεῖλον ἀναπλώσας [σῆς ἔ]κλυ[ε], Μέμνον, ἀϋτῆς
[Γάλ]λος ἐπιτροπ[έω]ν Θηβηΐδος ἠμαθ[οέσσ]ης
[θεινο]μ[έ]νων χαλκῶι ἰκέλη[ς ……]ΑΔΕΙΑ.. μῦθος.
Πηλεΐων ἐδάμ[ασσε τ]ὸν Ἠὼ(ς) τίκτε ποτ' υἷα.
Ὁπποῖον γὰρ ἐνὶ Τ[ροίῃ Σιμ]όεντος ἐ[π' ὄχ]θαις
ἔβραχε τεύχ[εα κείν]ου, ὅτ' ἐν [κονίηι]σι τάνυστο,
τοῖο[ν] νῦν [κ]τυ[πέ]ει λίθος ἄσπετος ἐγγ[ύθι] Ν[είλο]υ.

In the plain of Thebes by the deep-swirling Nile Gallus, custodian of the sandy Thebaid, sailed up and heard your voice, Memnon, like the bronze of men being struck … the tale. The scion of Peleus overpowered the son whom Dawn bore; for even as the armour of Memnon clanged at Troy on the banks of the Simoïs, when he sprawled in the dust, so too does the marvellous stone ring out near the Nile.

Bernand 1960, no. 36

This is not bad for an amateur. We also have traces of professional poets. A poem in trimeters (but including at least one scazon!) was composed by a companion to a στρατηγός, 'Commissioner', of two *nomes* who visited Memnon with his wife on 5 September 122 (as he noted in a prose graffito):

Φουνεισουλανὸς ἐνθαδεὶ [Χα]ρείσιος
στρατηγὸς Ἑρμωνθιός τε [καὶ] Λάτων πάτρης,
ἄγων δάμαρτα Φουλβίαν, ἀκήκοεν
σοῦ, Μέμνον, ἠχήσαντος, ἡν[ίχ' ἡ] μήτηρ
ἡ σὴ χυθεῖσα σὸν δέμας ἀπ … . . φει
θύσας δὲ καὶ σπείσας τε ΚΑΡΤ … .
τοῦτ' αὐτὸς ἠΰτησεν εἰς σεῖ[ο κλέος]·
λάλον μὲν Ἀργὼ παῖς ἐ[ὼν … .]
λάλον δὲ φηγὸν τὴν Διὸ[ς …]
σὲ δ' αὐτὸν ὄσσοις μοῦνον ἐδ[ράκην ἐμοῖς]
ὡς αὐτὸς ἠχεῖς καὶ βοήν τιν[… .]
τοῦτον δέ σοι χάραξε τὸν στίχο[ν …]
ὃς εἶπε ταὐτῶι φίλτατος τ[… … .

> Here Funisulanus Charisius, *strategos* of Hermonthis and the land of Lato, accompanied by his wife Fulvia heard you calling, Memnon, when your mother spread herself [over?] your body. After offering sacrifice and libation he uttered this himself to your glory: 'That the Argo talked I was told as a child, and that the oak of Zeus [at Dodona] talked: but you alone have I seen with my own eyes, how you yourself called out and uttered a cry.' This verse was inscribed for you by the dearest friend who was in his company, T[–]
>
> Bernand 1960, no. 19

Funisulanus seems to have felt less competent to compose a poem than his friend, but that does not prove that the latter was a professional poet. Such, however, was the writer of four lines (probably Hadrianic) signed 'By Areius the Homeric poet from the Museum when he heard': the lines are appropriately made up of Homeric phrases:

> ὢ πόποι, ἦ μέγα θαῦμα τόδ᾽ ὀφ[θαλμοῖσιν ὁρῶμαι]·
> ἦ μάλα τις θεὸς ἔνδον, οἳ οὐρανὸν εὐρὺν ἔχουσιν,
> ἤϋσεν φωνήν· κατὰ δ᾽ ἔσχεθε λαὸν ἅπαντα.
> οὐ γάρ πως ἂν θνητὸς ἀνὴρ τάδε μηχανόωιτο.
>
> Ἀρείου Ὁμηρικοῦ ποιητοῦ ἐκ Μουσείου ἀκούσαντος.
>
> Ah me! this is indeed a great wonder that I see with my eyes! Indeed some god within, of those who inhabit the broad heavens, has uttered his cry, and has hushed the whole people. For in no way could a mortal man have devised this.
>
> By Areius, a Homeric poet from the Museum, when he heard.[28]
>
> Bernand 1960, no. 37

Two other epigrams by a professional poet may be associated with Hadrian's visit to Memnon in AD 130. They are by Paeon of Side, and in one he writes on behalf of himself:

> αὐδήεντα σε, Μέμνον, ἐγὼ Παϊὼν ὁ Σιδήτης
> τὸ πρὶν ἐπυνθανόμην, νῦν δὲ παρὼν ἔμαθον.
>
> Your talking, Memnon, was before known to me, Paeon of Side,
> by repute, but now I have been here to learn for myself.
>
> Bernand 1960 no. 12

The other he writes for a Mettius:[29]

> εἰ καὶ λωβητῆρες ἐλυμήναντο δέμας σόν,
> ἀλλὰ σύ γ᾽ αὐδήεις, ὡς κλύον αὐτὸς ἐγώ,
> Μέττιος, ὦ Μέμνον· Παϊὼν τάδ᾽ ἔγραψε Σιδήτης.

[28] For discussion see Rosenmeyer 2018a, 134–8.

[29] *PIR*² M 568 rather than M 572, cf. Robert 1980b, 17–21.

> Even if vandals have defaced your body, yet you still have your voice, Memnon, as I, Mettius, heard for myself. This was written by Paeon of Side.
>
> Bernand 1960 no. 11

The contrast between learning by proxy and in person was clearly one that was traditional in Memnon-poems (cf. Bernand nos. 19 and 28) – did Roman tourists bring Herodotus Book 2 as bedtime reading? – and is here handled somewhat crudely. The three lines composed for Mettius (two hexameters sandwiching a pentameter) are rather better, reworking the *topos* of the contrast between a perishable mortal body and imperishable words, used for example by Callimachus in his epitaph on Heraclitus:[30] applied to Memnon's stone body and non-mortal voice it gives a pleasing conceit.

We can fill out some details of Paeon's career as a professional poet. As L. Robert saw, he is surely that P. Aelius Pompeianus Paeon of Side whom we already know from a decree of the World Guild of Dionysiac Artists' meeting in Ephesus about AD 142. Paeon was both the proposer of this decree to honour T. Aelius Alcibiades of Nysa and (as often) one of the envoys commissioned to carry copies of the decree to Alcibiades and to his city Nysa. Paeon is there described as a citizen of Tarsus and Rhodes as well as of Side, and as [ποιη]τοῦ πλειστονίκου, μελοποιοῦ καὶ ῥαψ[ωιδοῦ, θε]οῦ Ἀδριανοῦ θεολόγου ναῶν τῶν ἐν Π[εργαμωι], 'a poet with many victories, and composer of songs and a rhapsode, speaker of the divine of the god Hadrian in the temples at Pergamum'.[31] His involvement with the Dionysiac Guild and the epithet πλειστονίκης show him to be a professional rather than a dabbling member of the upper classes. As μελοποιός he will have composed hymns, as ῥαψωιδός hexameter poetry. That he wrote some hexameter poetry seems also to follow from his honour at Side as 'the new Homer'.[32]

3 Hexameter Poetry

I now turn to other hexameter poets, beginning with one of the best of the period, Marcellus, who was also from Side. His work is comparatively well preserved: 101 didactic hexameters, and perhaps an epigram, survive in

[30] Call. *Epigr.* 2 Pfeiffer = *HE* 34.

[31] *IEph* 22 = *SEG* 4.418, cf. Robert 1938, 45 ff., Robert 1980b. For the place of θεολόγοι in imperial cult see Pleket 1965. West 2013, 365, n.28 takes [θε]οῦ Ἀδριανοῦ with μελοποιοῦ καὶ ῥαψ[ωιδοῦ], which seems to me less probable.

[32] Bean 1965, no. 107.

manuscript tradition; two hexameter poems, of fifty-nine and thirty-nine lines respectively, on stone. But they are a small fraction of a voluminous production. The Suda knows an Ἰατρικά, '*Healings*', in forty-two books which included a section on lycanthropy. This must be the same as the epigram's *Chironides*, here given forty books (presumably a rounding-off of forty-two). This epigram, conceivably by Marcellus himself, also tells us that both Hadrian and Pius had the books 'dedicated' in Rome, i.e. acquired by the imperial libraries:

> Μαρκέλλου τόδε σῆμα περικλυτοῦ ἰητῆρος,
> φωτὸς κυδίστοιο τετιμένου ἀθανάτοισιν,
> οὗ βίβλους ἀνέθηκεν ἐϋκτιμένῃ ἐνὶ Ῥώμῃ
> Ἀδριανὸς προτέρων προφερέστερος ἡγεμονήων,
> καὶ πάϊς Ἀδριανοῖο μέγ' ἔξοχος Ἀντωνῖνος,
> ὄφρα καὶ ἐσσομένοισι μετ' ἀνδράσι κῦδος ἄροιτο
> εἵνεκεν εὐεπίης, τήν οἱ πόρε Φοῖβος Ἀπόλλων,
> ἡρώῳ μέλψαντι μέτρῳ θεραπήϊα νούσων
> βίβλοις ἐν πινυταῖς Χειρωνίσι τεσσαράκοντα.
>
> This is the tomb of the renowned doctor Marcellus, a most glorious mortal honoured by the gods, whose books were dedicated in well-built Rome by Hadrian, foremost of our leaders of yore, and Hadrian's son the outstanding Antoninus; so that he might win glory among future men too for the eloquence which Phoebus Apollo gave him, when he sang the remedies of diseases in heroic verse, in forty sage books, the *Chironides*.
>
> *AP* 7.158

Hadrian's discovery of Marcellus could be independent of his patronage of Paeon – we saw that his eye was somehow caught by Artemidorus Capito's edition of Hippocrates – but probably the favour acquired by the one led to the introduction of the other. Which first, we cannot say: but that it was in Hadrian's later years that he arranged for Marcellus' books to be lodged in Rome's libraries follows from Pius' involvement – presumably the work was still being written when Hadrian gave it his *imprimatur*.

Marcellus' other surviving work supports the attribution of his *Chironides* to the 130s. Two signed poems on stone, commissioned by Herodes Atticus after the death of his wife Regilla late in the 150s, have been found on her estate off the Via Appia near the third milestone, an estate which she had brought to Herodes in her dowry and where – conjecturally in his consulate of AD 143 – he had consecrated a temple to the then recently dead and deified Faustina.

The first is an elegant and allusive dedication of a statue of Regilla to which the women of Rome are urged to offer cult, giving Marcellus the opportunity to open his extended dedicatory epigram with a formula that suggests a hymn:[33]

Δεῦρ᾽ ἴτε, Θυβριάδες, νηὸν ποτὶ τόνδε γυναῖκες
Ῥηγίλλης ἕδος ἀμφὶ θυοσκόα ἱρὰ φέρουσαι.

Come hither to this temple, ladies of Tiber,
bearing sacred objects of sacrifice about Regilla's seat.

IG xiv 1389.1–2

He goes on to describe the heroising of Regilla, a reward from Zeus, and her son's elevation to the patriciate, a consolation from Pius to Herodes. Their ancestry (30–40) brings him back to cult, 40–50:

σὺ δ᾽, <ε>ἰ φίλον, ἱερὰ ῥέξαι
καὶ θῦσαι· θυέων ἀτὰρ οὐκ ἀέκοντος ἀνάγκη,
ε<ὖ> δέ τοι εὐσεβέεσσι καὶ ἡρώων ἀλεγίζειν.
οὐ μὲγ γὰρ θνητή, ἀτὰρ οὐδὲ θέαινα τέτυκται·
τοὔνεκεν οὔτε νεὼν ἱερὸν λάχεν οὔτε τι τύμβον,
οὐδὲ γέρα θνητοῖς, ἀτὰρ οὐδὲ θεοῖσιν ὅμοια.
σῆμα μέν οἱ νηῶι ἴκελον δήμωι ἐν Ἀθήνης,
ψυχὴ δὲ σκῆπτρον Ῥαδαμάνθυος ἀμφιπολεύει.
τοῦτο δὲ Φαυστείνηι κεχαρισμένον ἧσται ἄγαλμα
δήμωι ἐνὶ Τριόπεω, ἵνα οἱ πάρος εὐρέες ἀγροί
καὶ χορὸς ἡμερίδων καὶ ἐλαιήεντες ἄρουραι.

but do you, if you will, perform ritual
and sacrifice: yet of sacrifice there is no need from the unwilling
but it is well for the reverent to heed heroes too.
For she is not mortal, yet neither is she a goddess:
hence she has been given neither temple nor any tomb,
nor honours like those of mortals, yet not like those of gods.
There is a memorial to her like a temple in a deme of Athena
but her soul attends the sceptre of Rhadamanthys.
But this statue, pleasing to Faustina, has been set up

[33] The text is *IG* xiv 1389 = *IGUR* iii 1155: cf. *SEG* 29.999. For a full discussion of Marcellus see Arena and Cassia 2015. A basic discussion remains that of Wilamowitz 1928, though he overstresses Homeric/Hesiodic and misses Hellenistic features. See also Peek 1979; Ameling 1983; Davies and Pomeroy 2012; Bowie 2019d (Chapter 44 in Volume 3); and on Regilla Pomeroy 2007. For epigrams with hymnic features cf. this chapter n.21.

> in the deme of Triopas, where before were her broad fields
> and a chorus of tended vines, and olive groves.
>
> *IG* xiv 1389.40–50

The second poem is a prayer to Athena and to the Nemesis of Rhamnus to punish any encroachment on Herodes' estate, whether for cultivation or burial: its stern curses contrast sharply with the first poem's emollient tone. Although both have many Homerisms, the influence of Hellenistic poetry is also apparent, and these examples of Marcellus' mature work are a pleasure to read.

Less so the fragment of his *Chironides*. In dealing with the medicine that can be manufactured from fish, Marcellus catalogues the finny tribe with tedious monotony:

> εὖ δὲ καὶ εἰναλίων ἐδάην φύσιν ἰήτειραν
> <σχ>ήμασι παντοίοισιν ἐμὸν νόον ἐξερεείνων,
> ὡς αὐτός τ' ἐνόησα καὶ ἄλλων μῦθον ἄκουσα·
> ὧν τοι ἐγὼ πληθὺν ἠδ' οὔνομα πᾶν ἀγορεύσω.
> βένθεα χητώεντα πολυσκοπέλοιο θαλάσσης
> ἰχθύες ἀμφινέμονται ἀπείριτοι ἀργινόεντες
> παμμέλανες περκνοί τε καὶ αἰόλον εἶδος ἔχοντες.

> And well too have I learned the healing properties of the creatures of the sea, searching out my mind in manifold ways, both as I have observed myself and have heard told by others: of these shall I tell you the whole multitude and every name. The monstrous depths of the crag-strewn sea are the abode of countless fish, all-black, dusky, or glittering.[34]
>
> Heitsch 1963–4, ii no. lxiii.1–7

Thirty-three lines follow in which names of fish are ingeniously accommodated to the hexameter.

Marcellus' medical poem was not unique. At some time in the second century Rhodiapolis honoured its son Heraclitus as the ἰατρικῶν ποιημάτων Ὅμηρον, 'Homer of medical poetry', and as πρῶτον ἀπ' αἰῶνος ἰατρὸν καὶ συνγραφέα καὶ ποιητὴν ἔργων ἰατρικῆς καὶ φιλοσοφίας, 'first in all history to be a doctor, a historian, and a poet of medical and philosophical works'.

[34] For a higher estimation of Marcellus' artistry in this work see Overduin 2018. To bibliography in Heitsch 1963–4, ii 16 add Effe 1977, 196 ff. Effe considers the fragment to be from a different work from the Ἰατρικά, surely unnecessarily. It is long enough to show that Marcellus' work is in some way related to the popular medical/paradoxographical *Koiranides* of disputed date. Keydell 1941 showed that Marcellus did not directly use the *Koiranides*, and Heitsch 1963 that they did not use Marcellus: so a common source is likely, contrary to the view of Wellmann 1934 that Marcellus was versifying the *Koiranides*.

His statue was erected in the theatre to commemorate his *paideia*, and he was also honoured by Alexandria, Rhodes, and Athens (where his backers included the Areopagus and the Garden of Epicurus), and by the World Guild of Dionysiac Artists.[35] Unlike Marcellus, Heraclitus' horizons are those of the Eastern Mediterranean: he gave copies of his prose- and verse-works to his own city and to Alexandria, Rhodes, and Athens, but not, it seems, to Rome.

Marcellus and Heraclitus are but two of a number of poets who show that Greek didactic poetry flourished in the Antonine age.[36] We also have the incomplete remains (totalling over 2000 lines) of an astrological poem attributed by tradition to Manetho and indeed professing to be addressed to a king Ptolemy. Three of the six surviving books seem to belong together (Books 1, 3, and 6) and the horoscope given in one of them places the writer's birth in AD 80.[37] It is likely, then, that the writer was active in our period.

More interesting than these, however, and transmitted complete, is Dionysius of Alexandria's *Guide to the inhabited world*.[38] It stands in the Hellenistic didactic tradition which aimed both to instruct and to please, and to do so within a small compass. To reduce a description of the whole world to 1187 hexameters inevitably involves vast omission and extreme brevity in describing what is admitted: but for mere catalogues with only occasional descriptive epithets there were precedents in the *Iliad*'s 'Catalogue of Ships' and in the *Theogony*, and by careful signposting of new sections and by cross-references Dionysius succeeds in setting out a description that gives readers an intelligible picture of the world, even if it would not allow

[35] *TAM* ii 910 = *IGR* iii 733: cf. Robert 1980b, 14; İplikçioğlu 2014. A temple of Asclepius and Hygieia dedicated by Heraclitus (who was their priest) is mentioned in the honorific inscription, and fragments remain of its dedication: *TAM* ii 906 = *IGR* iii 732.

[36] It had been lively too in the first century: witness a didactic elegiac poem in 174 lines dedicated to Nero by his court physician Andromachus (Heitsch 1963–4, ii. no. lxii) and the long astronomical work of Dorotheus of Sidon, of the 80s AD, which survives only in Arabic translation, ed. Pingree 1976.

[37] The Ἀποτελεσματικά were edited by Koechly in 1851 and 1858. He thought the earlier sections Severan, the later fourth-century or later, and was followed by Schmid-Stahlin ii. 2. 974 and E. Berneker in *KP* iii.953 (despite Garnett 1895): cf. Neugebauer and van Hoesen 1959, 92, no. L80, demonstrating a birth-date of 28 (or 27) May, AD 80, for the writer of 3.738–50. *P. Oxy.* 2546 (ed. J. Rea 1966) and *P.Amsterdam Inv.* no. 56 are both third-century and both have fragments of Book 4. Lopilato 1998 takes Books 2, 3 and 6 to be written ca. AD 120 and the six-book text to have been assembled in the Severan period.

[38] Before 1990 the most recent edition of Dionysius was that of C. Müller in *GGM* ii 103–76: for a note of fifty-six MSS not used by Müller see Livadaras 1964. Tsavari 1990 and Jacob 1990 were the first modern editions, followed by Brodersen 1994; Amato 2005. The first major commentary is Lightfoot 2014. For discussion see her bibliography, including the works cited below, and Jacob 1981; Christian 1984.

them to construct an accurate map. Dionysius takes his didactic purpose seriously, notwithstanding his reliance on outdated geographical models, and to achieve it he exploits a variety of traditional poetic techniques.

For example, he first uses the invocation of the Muses as a source of knowledge to make the transition from his treatment of the encircling Ocean (1–57) to the Mediterranean (58–168):

> ὑμεῖς δ', ὦ Μοῦσαι, σκολιὰς ἐνέποιτε κελεύθους,
> ἀρξάμεναι στοιχηδὸν ἀφ' ἑσπέρου Ὠκεανοῖο·
> ἔνθα τε καὶ στῆλαι περὶ τέρμασιν Ἡρακλῆος
> ἑστᾶσιν, μέγα θαῦμα, παρ' ἐσχατόωντα Γάδειρα.
>
> But you, O Muses, tell its twisting paths
> beginning in order from the western Ocean
> where near the boundaries the pillars of Heracles
> stand, a mighty wonder, by furthest Gades.
>
> Dionysius, *Periegesis* 62–5

Again, the sections on the Mediterranean, Africa (169–268), and Europe (269–446) are rounded off by six mythologically rich lines on Delphi (441–6), invoking Apollo and again the Muse, while also echoing the Homeric hymn to Apollo and Apollonius Rhodius:[39]

> ἀλλ' ὁ μὲν ἱλήκοι· σὺ δέ μοι, Διός, ἔννεπε, Μοῦσα,
> νήσων πασάων ἱερὸν πόρον ...
>
> But may he show favour; and you, Muse, daughter of Zeus, tell me
> the sacred way of all the islands ...
>
> Dionysius, *Periegesis* 447–8

Dionysius enhances the articulatory effect of this second invocation by opening the following section on islands (450–619) with seven lines (450–6) on Gades. We are thus taken back to the western point of departure that opened the description of the Mediterranean, Africa (174 ff.) and Europe (281 ff.). This is both didactically convenient and also appropriate under an emperor (see below) whose *patria*, Italica, was near Gades, and whose adoptive mother and patron Plotina was actually from that city.

The third invocation to the Muses (650–1) signals the transition from Dionysius' general introduction to the shape of Asia to his catalogue of its

[39] Cf. *h.Ap.* 165, A.R. 2. 708. For the importance of Apollonius for Dionysius see the *apparatus fontium* in Tsavari 1990; Bowie 2000a (Chapter 10 in this volume); Hunter 2003, 2004; Lightfoot 2014.

peoples, so numerous that the Asian section alone (620–1152) balances in number of lines (as Dionysius suggests the land mass does in reality) those on the Mediterranean, Africa, Europe, and the Islands taken together (58–619). But Dionysius does not open and close his poem with the Muses. In his businesslike broaching of his theme he gives himself a higher profile, recalling perhaps both Hesiod's *Theogony* and the Homeric hymn to Apollo:[40]

> ἀρχόμενος γαῖάν τε καὶ εὐρέα πόντον ἀείδειν
> καὶ ποταμοὺς πόλιάς τε καὶ ἀνδρῶν ἄκριτα φῦλα
> μνήσομαι Ὠκεανοῖο βαθυρρόου ...
>
> In beginning to sing of the earth and broad sea
> and of rivers and cities and the countless tribes of men
> I shall talk of the deep-flowing Ocean ...
>
> Dionysius, *Periegesis* 1–3

At the poem's close, after a brief account of Dionysus' Indian expedition which introduces the eastern pillars of Dionysus (1164–5) to balance the western pillars of Heracles (63–4), he notes that he has talked of the most significant peoples of the earth but acknowledges mortal incapacity to enumerate all its inhabitants: only the gods who created the world and man in his various forms could do that (1166–80). Then he takes an emotional leave of his theme, again evoking a Homeric hymn in words and posture:[41]

> ὑμεῖς δ' ἤπειροί τε καὶ εἰν ἁλὶ χαίρετε, νῆσοι,
> ὕδατά τ' Ὠκεανοῖο καὶ ἱερὰ χεύματα πόντου
> καὶ ποταμοὶ κρῆναί τε καὶ οὔρεα βησσήεντα.
> ἤδη γὰρ πάσης μὲν ἐπέδραμον οἶδμα θαλάσσης,
> ἤδη δ' ἠπείρων σκολιὸν πόρον· ἀλλά μοι ὕμνων
> αὐτῶν ἐκ μακάρων ἀντάξιος εἴη ἀμοιβή.
>
> But you, continents, and sea-girt isles, farewell
> and waters of Ocean and the holy streams of the deep
> and rivers and streams and gladed mountains.
> For now I have sped over the swell of every sea,
> now the twisting way of the continents: but may my hymns
> bring me a fitting reward from the blessed ones themselves.
>
> Dionysius, *Periegesis* 1182–7

[40] Hes. *Th.* 1, *h.Ap.* 1.

[41] Cf. *h.Ap.* 166 (and the echo of 165 at Dionysius 47).

The Callimachean didactic poem is at the same time a hymn, its composer a celebrant as well as expounder of his material. That didactic aim is occasionally stressed, not without emphasis on Dionysius' own powers, as in the transition from the Mediterranean to Africa:

τοίη μὲν μορφὴ κυαναυγέος Ἀμφιτρίτης·
νῦν δέ τοι ἠπείρου μυθήσομαι εἶδος ἁπάσης,
ὄφρα καὶ οὐκ ἐσιδὼν περ ἔχοις εὔφραστον ὀπωπήν·
ἐκ τοῦ δ' ἂν γεραρός τε καὶ αἰδοιέστερος εἴης,
ἀνδρὶ παρ' ἀγνώσσοντι πιφαυσκόμενος τὰ ἕκαστα.

Such is the shape of blue-glancing Amphitrite:
but now I shall expound the form of every continent,
so that even without seeing them you may have a distinct view,
and thus may be honoured and more respected
when you utter everything in the presence of one who is ignorant.

Dionysius, *Periegesis* 169–73

Similarly the transition from north to south Asia:

ῥηιδίως δ' ἄν τοι λοιπὸν πόρον αὐδήσαιμι
γαιάων Ἀσίης· ὁ δέ τοι λόγος ἐν φρεσὶν ἔστω,
μηδ' ἀνέμοις φορέοιτο πονηθέντων χάρις ἔργων.
εἰ γάρ μοι σάφα τήνδε καταφράσσαιο κέλευθον,
ἦ τάχα κἂν ἄλλοισιν ἐπισταμένως ἀγορεύοις.

Easily might I tell the remaining path
of the lands of Asia: and let the account stay in your mind
nor let the charm of the work I have laboured on be carried off by the winds.
For if you have clearly understood this way of mine
then with knowledge you may readily tell others.[42]

Dionysius, *Periegesis* 881–4

The χάρις, 'charm', that will assist the reader to remember the work is enhanced by carefully deployed purple passages. Mention of the African Nomads near the beginning of the African section allows nine lines elaborating the *topos* of their pre-agricultural way of life (186–94): this is balanced by a passage towards its end where the Egyptians are extolled as inventors of civilisation, agriculture, and astronomy (232–7). The frozen, barren wastes

[42] Cf. Nicander, *Ther.* 1–4 (ῥεῖά κέ τοι ... φωνήσαιμι, 'Easily could I voice ... to you') and 4–7 (the respect his reader will gain among rustic peers).

of Scythia, on whose inhabitants Dionysius expostulates σχέτλιοι, οἳ περὶ κεῖνον ἐνοίκια χῶρον ἔχουσιν, 'Impossible people, who have their dwellings in that country' (668), provoke an ecphrasis (664–78), later balanced by an even longer account of the riches of Arabia, whose aromatic treasures derive from Dionysus' release there from Zeus' thigh (927–53).

Many similar expansions, some of them introducing mythology, others natural history, endow the geographical framework with variety and allow a more lively or emotional tone. They must have enhanced the poem's eligibility for use as a school-reader through whose line-by-line explication *grammatici* could introduce pupils not only to geography but to central features of history and myth.

Some techniques are perhaps overworked. The pathetic triple repetition of a place-name is exploited four times. But at least three of these are carefully chosen. First Carthage:

τοῖς δ' ἔπι Καρχηδὼν πολυήρατον ἀμπέχει ὅρμον,
Καρχηδών, Λιβύων μέν, ἀτὰρ πρότερον Φοινίκων,
Καρχηδών, ἣν μῦθος ὑπαὶ βοῒ μετρηθῆναι.

After these Carthage embraces its lovely anchorage,
Carthage, city of Africans, before of Phoenicians,
Carthage, which legend tells was measured by an ox-hide.

Dionysius, *Periegesis* 195–7

Next comes the Tiber:

τοῖς δ' ἔπι μέρμερον ἔθνος ἀγανῶν ἐστι Λατίνων,
γαῖαν ναιετάοντες ἐπήρατον, ἧς διὰ μέσσης
Θύμβρις ἑλισσόμενος καθαρὸν ῥόον εἰς ἅλα βάλλει,
Θύμβρις ἐϋρρείτης, ποταμῶν βασιλεύτατος ἄλλων
Θύμβρις, ὃς ἱμερτὴν ἀποτέμνεται ἄνδιχα Ῥώμην,
Ῥώμην τιμήεσσαν, ἐμῶν μέγαν οἶκον ἀνάκτων,
μητέρα πασάων πολίων, ἀφνειὸν ἔδεθλον.

After these is the dread people of the noble Latins,
dwelling in a lovely country, through whose midst
Tiber wending about casts its pure stream into the brine,
Tiber fair-flowing, most royal of other rivers,
Tiber, which cuts in twain beloved Rome,
Rome the honoured, mighty dwelling of my lords,
mother of all cities, wealthy shrine.

Dionysius, *Periegesis* 350–6

Then the river Rhebas:

ἄγχι δὲ Βίθυνοι λιπαρὴν χθόνα ναιετάουσι
Ῥήβας ἔνθ' ἐρατεινὸν ἐπιπροΐησι ῥέεθρον,
Ῥήβας, ὃς Πόντοιο παρὰ στομάτεσσιν ὁδεύει,
Ῥήβας, οὗ κάλλιστον ἐπὶ χθονὶ σύρεται ὕδωρ.

And nearby the Bithynians inhabit a rich land
where the Rhebas casts forth its delightful stream,
Rhebas, who marches beside the mouths of the Pontus,
Rhebas, whose water is the fairest that sweeps the earth.

Dionysius, *Periegesis* 793–6

Soon after we encounter the final example, Troy. Phrygia Minor, we are told,

κεῖται ὑπὸ ζαθέης πόδας Ἴδης,
Ἴλιον ἠνεμόεσσαν ὑπὸ πλευρῇσιν ἔχουσα,
Ἴλιον ἀγλαὸν ἄστυ παλαιγενέων ἡρώων,
Ἴλιον, ἣν ἐπόλισσε Ποσειδάων καὶ Ἀπόλλων,
Ἴλιον, ἣν ἀλάπαξαν Ἀθηναίη τε καὶ Ἥρη,
Ξάνθωι ἔπ' εὐρυρέοντι καὶ Ἰδαίωι Σιμόεντι.

lies at holy Ida's feet;
Ilion the windy is set beneath its flanks,
Ilion, glorious city of heroes of long ago,
Ilion, which Poseidon and Apollo built,
Ilion, which Athena and Hera destroyed,
upon the broad-flowing Xanthus and Idaean Simoïs.

Dionysius, *Periegesis* 815–19

The importance of Carthage, Rome, and Troy are clear: here are two great empires which had to fall to give way to the third, Rome; and, just as Troy might seem to be the only begetter of Greek narrative epic, so it is possible that Dionysius from learned Alexandria knew how important Carthage was to the Latin epic tradition. Moreover, it is interesting that he is ready to hail the imperial house as ἐμῶν … ἀνάκτων, 'my lords': we may contrast his compatriot Appian a generation later for whom the Ptolemies were τοῖς ἐμοῖς βασιλεῦσι, 'my kings.'[43]

Not surprisingly, this praise of Rome and the Tiber comes at the midpoint of the European section (269–446). It is linked to the later admiration of Ilion by the conjunction of city and river, and Ilion comes as close to

[43] App. *pr.* 39.

the mid-point of the Asian section as the major division between north and south Asia allows. The use of this emotive technique a mere nineteen lines earlier to describe the Rhebas is puzzling, and I suspect that it is to be explained as a tribute to the Bithynian origin of Antinous.

I have so far focused entirely upon the poem to the neglect of the poet. This reflects the apparent anonymity adopted by the writer. Despite occasional intrusions in the first person, the poet seems to tell us almost nothing of himself. The closest we come to his personality is an outburst against travel in a Hesiodic vein[44] that leads into a further praise of the power of the Muses:

> ῥεῖα δέ τοι καὶ τήνδε καταγράψαιμι θάλασσαν,
> οὐ μὲν ἰδὼν ἀπάνευθε πόρους, οὐ νηὶ περήσας·
> οὐ γάρ μοι βίος ἐστὶ μελαινάων ἐπὶ νηῶν,
> οὐδέ μοι ἐμπορίη πατρώιος, οὐδ᾽ ἐπὶ Γάγγην
> ἔρχομαι, οἷά τε πολλοί, Ἐρυθραίου διὰ πόντου,
> ψυχῆς οὐκ ἀλέγοντες, ἵν᾽ ἄσπετον ὄλβον ἕλωνται,
> οὐδὲ μὲν Ὑρκανίοις ἐπιμίσγομαι, οὐδ᾽ ἐρεείνω
> Καυκασίας κνημῖδας Ἐρυθραίων Ἀριηνῶν·
> ἀλλά με Μουσάων φορέει νόος, αἵτε δύνανται
> νόσφιν ἀλημοσύνης πολλὴν ἅλα μετρήσασθαι,
> οὔρεά τ᾽ ἤπειρόν τε καὶ αἰθερίην ὁδὸν ἄστρων.
>
> And easily might I describe for you this sea too (sc. the Caspian)
> though I have not seen its paths from afar nor crossed it by ship,
> for my life is not spent on black ships,
> nor do I inherit commerce from my father, nor to the Ganges
> do I go, like many, across the Red Sea
> heedless of their lives, that they may get unspeakable wealth,
> nor do I have dealings with Hyrcanians, nor do I seek out
> the Caucasian ridges of the Red Arianians:
> but I am borne by the mind of the Muses, who are able
> without wandering to measure the great brine
> and mountains and continent and the ethereal path of stars.
>
> Dionysius, *Periegesis* 707–17

This disclaimer can hardly refer only to travel to the further reaches of Asia, as Bernays (1905, 3) wished, generally framed as it is, and followed by descriptions not only of the Far East but of the much more accessible regions of Asia Minor and Syria. Rather it emphatically dissociates the author from the investigative explorer such as Herodotus, Megasthenes, or

[44] Hes. *Op*. 640–62, cf. also Thgn. 249–50.

Posidonius and sets him in a purely literary and scholarly tradition. But neither it nor other utterances in the poem helped to locate the poet in time and place until in 1884 Leue published his discovery of two acrostics.[45]

The first comes early in the poem (109–33), and is associated with the sea named by sailors after Pharos (115) and with the first of the only two extended similes in the poem (123–6): it runs

ΕΠΗ ΔΙΟΝΥΣΙΟΥ ΤΩΝ ΕΝΤΟΣ ΦΑΡΟΥ[46]

The verses of Dionysius, of those who live within Pharos

This confirms the statement of the *Life* of Dionysius in a fourteenth-century Chigi manuscript in the Vatican that Dionysius was from Alexandria, a statement we would otherwise have no good reason to prefer to others in scholia and lexicographers.[47]

The second is some 400 lines later, at 513–32, coextensive with Dionysius' description of the islands of the Aegean and marked at its close by the second extended simile of the poem:

ΘΕΟΣ ΕΡΜΗΣ ΕΠΙ ΑΔΡΙΑΝΟΥ[48]

The god Hermes in the reign of Hadrian

The acrostic signature is in the didactic tradition: compare Nicander's signature in *Theriaca*, 345–53, and that of another Dionysius, son of Calliphon, in his iambic geographical poem '*A record of Greece*'.[49] We also know from Vestinus' Βωμός, '*Altar*', that acrostics were in vogue under Hadrian. Although it took seventeen centuries for a scholar to detect them, we must assume that Dionysius imagined his contemporaries would be quicker off the mark. The second acrostic fixes him certainly under Hadrian, and the reference to the god Hermes is probably to Antinous, which would put the lines' composition between AD 130 and 138.[50]

[45] Leue 1884. The further acrostics seen by Leue 1925, at 135–7 (οἶς) and 254–9 (τεχνοῖ) are not convincing, cf. Counillon 1981, himself proposing στένη at 307–11: it is not clear what this acrostic is meant to communicate to the reader.

[46] The opening word of 110 in all MSS is μακρόν, giving EMH: Nauck 1889, 325, proposed to emend μακρόν to πολλόν, and ΕΠΗ gives an easily intelligible sense which EMH does not (unless we understand it to stand for ἐμὴ πατρίς, as has been proposed).

[47] *Vita Chisiana* ed. Colonna 1957.

[48] In *GGM* Müller printed the reading of most MSS, Εὐρώπης δ' ἤτοι: to get the η of ΕΡΜΗΣ the reading of A, ἤτοι δ' Εὐρώπης, is required.

[49] Διονυσίου τοῦ Καλλιφῶντος ἀναγραφὴ τῆς Ἑλλάδος, lines 1–23 in *GGM* i 238.

[50] Counillon 1981.

Conjecture may go further. Müller had already observed a notice in an eleventh century excerptor of the Ravenna geographer concerning a description of Sybaris by a Dionysius who was librarian at Rome for twenty years and composed a hexameter *Periegesis*. A Dionysius of Alexandria, son of Glaucus, is registered in the Suda as having held an imperial post *a bibliothecis*, 'In charge of libraries', as well as being *ab epistulis*, 'In charge of correspondence', and likewise of embassies and rescripts. But this Dionysius is there stated to have flourished from Nero to Trajan, and to have succeeded his teacher Chaeremon, in Alexandria, presumably as head of the Museum. Not, therefore, our writer: but conceivably his father, for manuscripts of the *Periegesis* call the writer Dionysius son of Dionysius, and Klotz argued that Guido's puzzling description of his Dionysius as *Ionicus* reflects a source where Dionysius was styled Διονυσίου, 'son of Dionysius', and where the geographer was stated to be the librarian's son.[51] It is a precarious foundation, but could be right. Upon it would be constructed the following scenario. The elder Dionysius, son of Glaucus, succeeds Chaeremon as head of the Museum when Chaeremon goes to Rome to teach Nero philosophy, about AD 50. Through his former teacher's influence this Dionysius is himself called to Rome under Nero and holds the procuratorial posts listed in the Suda – perhaps totalling twenty years, rather than spending twenty years a *bibliothecis* alone. His son Dionysius the Periegete may know Rome from his childhood and feel attachment to the imperial house (cf. 350–6 quoted above). But on his father's retirement from imperial service under Trajan he returns to their πατρίς, 'native land', Alexandria.

We cannot estimate when Dionysius' poem began to acquire the vogue it enjoyed from late antiquity, when it was translated by Avienus (or Avienius) and Priscus into Latin, through to Byzantium, the Middle Ages and early modern Europe, where it continued to be a textbook in schools and Universities until the eighteenth century.[52] The total silence on Dionysius in other second-century writers does not prove neglect, any more than does the silence on Lucian everywhere except in an Arabic translation of

[51] Guido's comment (chapter 25 p. 466.3 in the Pinder–Parthey edn. of the Ravenna geographer; also printed in *GGM* ii xvi): 'de qua Sybari refert Iuvenalis satiricus, latius tamen Dionysius Ionicus, qui Romae bibliothecarius per annos fuit viginti et orbem metro heroico graeco carmine descripsit' (there follows a rendering of Dionysius 378). The relationship between the librarian and geographer was suggested by Bernays 1905, 23–4, argued for by Klotz 1909 (apparently unaware of Bernays' work), and accepted by Gärtner in *KP s.n.* Dionysius no. 30. For the librarian see Bowie 2013e, 249–50 (Chapter 32 in Volume 3).

[52] For the use of Dionysius as a school text cf. Jacob 1981, 56 ff. It was edited (and adapted) by Edward Wells in an Oxford edition of 1704 apparently intended to teach geography in the University.

Galen. It would have been interesting to know whether Dionysius' prayer for reward from the 'blessed ones' duly received attention from Hadrian. The least that Dionysius must have hoped for, if he did not already have it, was membership of the Alexandrian Museum. If his father was indeed Dionysius son of Glaucus, he may already be a member of the Museum aspiring to higher things.

A word should be said about the other works that may be ascribed to Dionysius. The *Life* mentioned above (n.47) attributes to him a Λιθιακά or Λιθικά, *On stones*, and says this attribution is accepted because the work has the style of the *Periegesis*. One might add in its favour that in the *Periegesis* Dionysius mentions stones as the most noteworthy product of a number of regions.[53] Only two fragments survive. Other works, the *Life* notes, were ascribed to Dionysius by some and denied by others: Διοσημίαι, '*Signs from heaven*', a Γιγαντίας (*Gigantias*), '*War with the Giants*', and Ὀρνιθιακά (*Ornithiaka*), '*Bird lore*': the Βασσαρικά (*Bassarika*), '*Tales of Dionysiac worshippers*', by reason of its stylistic roughness, was generally ascribed to Dionysius of Samos.[54]

We now have some papyrus fragments of the Βασσαρικά (once at least fourteen books) and Γιγαντιάς (once at least seventeen). The former, more voluminous, are more different from the *Periegesis* than genre alone can explain, and both look like the work of the same hand. One of the papyrus fragments of the Γιγαντιάς is dated to the second half of the second century, and, like Dionysius Periegetes, both seem to know Nicander and be known to Quintus. That they are by our Dionysius is not perhaps as absurd as Livrea insists,[55] but more probably they are by another. A poem on giants, however, would not be out of place in Dionysius' lifetime, since one is ascribed by Philostratus to the Flavian and Trajanic sophist Scopelianus of Clazomenae.[56]

The Ὀρνιθιακά or Ἰξευτικά, '*On bird-catching*', are not preserved, but a prose paraphrase gives us a fair idea of the content of its three books. Fabulous behaviour, and indeed fabulous birds, place the work near to that

[53] Electrum, 213, 317–19; crystal, 724; crystal and iaspis, 781–2; beryl, 1011–12. For the fragments of the Λιθιακά see *GGM* xxvi: one actually quoted by a scholiast on *Periegesis* 714, the other (referring to Book 2) by Maximus on Dionysius the Areopagite *De myst. theol.* chapter 2.

[54] Cf. Eustathius in *GGM* ii. 215.6–14.

[55] For the fragments Heitsch 1963–4 i, 60–77 (no. xix) was superseded by the edition of Livrea 1973, which includes *P.Oxy.* 2815, and both now by Benaissa 2018, following his 2011 *editio princeps* of *P.Oxy.* 5103; for Quintus of Smyrna's probable knowledge of the Βασσαρικά and Γιγαντιάς see Wifstrand 1933, 178–80, and *prolegomena* to Livrea 1973, 10 ff. Livrea emphatically rejects identification with the Periegete, as does Keydell implicitly (in *KP s.n.* Dionysius no. 13) and Lesky 1966, 816 n.3 explicitly.

[56] Philostr. *VS* 1.21.518.

of Aelian, while there are traces of what must have been purple passages of poetry, such as descriptions of cliffs and canyons echoing the song of the swan.[57] The mixture of solid information and θαύματα, 'marvels', makes ascription to the periegete attractive, as does the poet's claim to derive his knowledge from Apollo,[58] but we are in no position to make a serious judgement.

All this hexameter poetry seems to belong in a Hesiodic and Callimachean tradition. This continued to flourish into the third century. At the end of our period, between AD 177 and 180, a Cilician poet, Oppian, dedicated his Ἁλιευτικά (*Halieutika*), 'On catching fish', in five books to Marcus and Commodus, and some forty years later a Syrian poet whose work has been transmitted under the same name dedicated his four-book Κυνηγετικά (*Cynegetika*), 'On hunting', to Caracalla. Admittedly their scale was greater, following (though not in metre) Callimachus' four books of *Aitia* rather than Aratus' *Phaenomena*, but their blend of learning and entertainment establishes them as successors to the didactic Dionysii.[59]

Epic narrating the deeds of kings and heroes is less well represented. Clearly mythological epic was written: fragments of a *Bassarica* and a *Gigantias* by a Dionysius have already been mentioned, as has Areius the Homeric poet from the Museum at Alexandria.[60] The *Gigantias* of Scopelianus and the prolific Severan father and son from Lycaonian Laranda, Septimius Nestor and Septimius Peisander, fall respectively before and after our period, but hint that the production of mythological epic was continuous in the three centuries preceding our first text to survive complete, the *Posthomerica* of Quintus of Smyrna, whose fourteen books belong after the *Halieutica* of

[57] The prose paraphrase is edited by Garzya 1955 and as a Teubner text (with *index verborum*) by Garzya 1963; again by Papathomopoulos 1976. Title and authorship are discussed by Garzya 1957, who shows that the ascription to Oppian in one group of manuscripts is conjectural and should be discarded in the light of clear ascription to a Dionysius at 1.1 (πανθ' ὅσα περὶ πτηνῶν τῶι ποιητῆι Διονυσίωι συγγέγραπται, 'everything that the poet Dionysius wrote about winged creatures') and 3.25 (Διονύσιος δ' αὐτὰ παρὰ τοῦ τῆς Λητοῦς Ἀπόλλωνος διδαχθῆναί φησιν, 'and Dionysius says that he was taught these things by Apollo son of Leto'). Garzya also argues that on the analogy of Oppian's works the title should have been Ἰξευτικά and that the titles περὶ ὀρνίθων/ὀρνιθιακά, are unfounded (apparently neglecting the latter title's mention in the *Vita Chisiana* and by Eustathius, *GGM* ii 215. 6–14); and that the paraphrased work may have used Oppian's Ἰξευτικά (five books according to the Oppian *Life*, but only two in the Suda), though he seems also (mysteriously) to allow that both it and the Λιθι(α)κά could be by the Periegete. For the swan's song echoed see 2.20.

[58] See 3.25, already quoted n.57.

[59] On the Oppians see Bowersock 1985; on the *Halieutica* Fajen 1999; Kneebone 2020; on the *Cynegetica* Bartley 2003; Whitby 2007; Agosta 2009.

[60] Note too M. Decrius Decrianus, ἐπῶν καὶ μελῶν ποιητής, 'composer of epic and melic poetry', on a tablet published by Fraser 1959.

Oppian and before the *Fall of Troy* by Triphiodorus, so probably between AD 200 and 250.[61]

Narration of the deeds of emperors, however, seems not to have been much favoured. A poem on the reigning emperor(s) is attested as a subject for competition at the *Mouseia* at Thespiae, and entries cannot have run to great length.[62] So too the only example to survive from the second century, by the Egyptian Pancrates, can hardly have been a full-length epic. One fragment and some information about its author have long been known from Athenaeus of Naucratis (15.677d–f). In a long discourse on garlands his character Ulpianus expounds the origin of the Alexandrian garland called 'Antinoeios'. Pancrates, an ἐπιχώριος, 'man from the region', drew Hadrian's attention to the red lotus while the emperor was visiting Alexandria, saying it ought to be so called because it had shot up from the ground when it drank the blood of the Moorish lion slain by Antinous in a hunt near Alexandria. Ulpian quotes a description of the lotus in four lines which echo Homer's description of the flowers that sprang up during Hera's seduction of Zeus. A second-century papyrus published in 1911 gave us forty hexameters, of which thirty are almost complete, in which Hadrian casts his spear at the lion and misses – deliberately, to test Antinous' mettle, and doubtless because he is familiar with the conventions of the Homeric duel. The lion attacks Antinous; then the clip fades, with clear traces of the lion's inevitable death at the hands of Hadrian. Hadrian's rescue of Antinous is predictable, and the successful outcome of the hunt is confirmed by Athenaeus' description and by the *tondi* on the Arch of Constantine which originally decorated a Hadrianic hunting-monument. A few line-ends and beginnings were contributed by another second-century papyrus published in 1927: they seem to come from Pancrates' opening and his description of the party assembling for the hunt.[63]

[61] For concise accounts of the Septimii and Quintus see R. Keydell *s.nn.* in *KP* iv (1975), 59. For the Septimii see Ma 2007; for Quintus see Baumbach, Bär, and Dümmler 2007; Bär 2009; Maciver 2012; Greensmith 2020.

[62] See *IG* vii 1773 = Roesch 2007–9, no. 178, of ca. AD 150–60, and *SEG* 3.334, of ca. AD 150–60 or after AD 169, attesting an epic poem honouring the emperor (as well as one honouring the Muses) as a subject for competition at the *Mouseia* at Thespiae: for details cf. Schachter 1986, 176–8. Poems honouring members of the imperial family (Augustus, Livia, Claudius, Vespasian, and Titus) are attested by the new evidence for the *Sebasta* at Naples; cf. a hexameter poem on the apotheosis of Poppaea by *P.Oxy.* 5105 (ed. P. Schubert; third century).

[63] The fragments are in Heitsch 1963–4, i 51–3 (no. xv). For analysis of poetic echoes see F. Stoessl in *RE* xxxvi.2 *s.n.* Pankrates no. 5, 615–19; good discussion by Höschele 2018. The tondos on the arch of Constantine were attributed to a Hadrianic hunting-monument by Bieber 1911, and their bearing on the hunt in Pancrates noted by Hoffa 1912. On that monument see Maull 1955.

The fragments pretty certainly come from the poem of Pancrates, as the Oxyrhynchus fragment's first editor, Hunt, saw. It is turgid stuff, prodigal with simile and exploiting echoes of Homer and the Hesiodic *Shield* to build up a heroic encounter between Hadrian and the lion that recalls conflicts of Heracles and of Zeus with the Giants:

τοῖ]ον ἐφεζόμενος δαμασήν[ο]ρα μίμνε λέοντα
Ἀ]ντίνοος λαιῆι μὲν ἔχων ῥυτῆρα χαλωόν,
δεξιτερῆι δ' ἔγχος κεκορυθμένο[ν] ἐξ ἀδάμαντος.
πρῶτος δ' Ἀδριανὸς προιεὶς χαλκήρεον ἔγχος
οὔτασεν, οὐδὲ δάμασσεν, ἑκὼν γὰρ ἀπήμβροτε σ[ίντου·
ε]ὐστοχίης γὰρ πάμπαν ἐβούλετο πειρηθῆναι
Ἀ]ργειφοντιάδαο μεγηράτ[ου Ἀντι]νόοιο.
θ]ὴρ δὲ τυπεὶς ἔτι μᾶλλον [ὀ]ρίνετο, ποσσὶ δ' ἄμυσσ[ε
γαῖαν τρηχαλ[έ]η[ν] θυμούμ][ε]νος, ἐκ δὲ κονίη
ὡ[ς ν]έφ[ος] ἱσταμένη φ[άος ἤ]χλυεν ἠελίοιο.
μαίνετο δ' ὡς ὅτε κῦμ[α] πολυκλύστο[ι]ο θαλάσσης
Στρυ[μ]ονίου κ[α]τόπισθεν ἐγειρομένου Ζεφύρ[οιο.
ῥί]μ[φα δ' ἐ]π' ἀμφοτέροισιν ἐπώρορε ...

Mounted on such a horse did Antinous await the man-slaying lion holding the restraining rein in his left hand and in his right a spear headed with steel. First Hadrian cast his bronze-tipped spear, and wounded the beast without vanquishing it, for he deliberately missed the [predator?]: for he wished fully to test the aim of Argus-slayer Hermes, the lovely Antinous. But wounded the beast grew even more excited, and in his wrath tore at the rough ground with his paws, and the dust hung like a cloud and darkened the light of the sun; and he raged as does the wave of the thundering sea as the west wind from Strymon blows up behind it. Swiftly he lunged at them both ...[64]

This is not the stuff of poetic immortality, but it did secure Pancrates membership of the Alexandrian Museum, and both his poem and his person were remembered for at least a century. It was probably composed in the immediate aftermath of the hunt, early in September 130, before the fatal trip up the Nile which was already under way in October, since it is hard to think that Pancrates risked this theme when Antinous was already dead: if one believes he did, then the first months of 131 remain open.[65]

[64] *P.Oxy.* 1085, fr. 2 col. ii.3–15.

[65] Weber (who did not know the papyrus fragments) thought that the hunt took place after Antinous' death, as (less intelligibly) did Sijpesteijn 1969; that is also argued forcefully by Höschele 2018: *contra* Follet 1968; Lambert 1984, 257 n.7. For a lively account of the events see Lambert 1984, 118–20, 153–4.

There may be more than this to the person of Pancrates. When the first papyrus was published Radermacher drew attention to the story in the Paris magical papyrus that an Egyptian from Heliopolis, Pachrates, had demonstrated to Hadrian a magical sacrifice with astounding properties: and in his *Philopseudes* Lucian tells of an Egyptian wizard Pancrates.[66] Though some vehemently distinguish the two, perhaps the hexameter poet who was honoured by membership of the Museum was the same as the wizard.

4 Melic Poetry

I conclude with a brief glance at melic poetry – not simply such poems as the epigrams we have seen in metres that for archaic and classical Greece were melic, but poetry that was actually sung, such as Paeon of Side's description μελοποιός, 'melic poet', implies. Like recitations of poetry, singing of various kinds of text must have bulked much larger in the experience of a second-century Greek than it does in our surviving witnesses. I look first at poetry that was certainly, or probably, choral.

Choirs sang *prosodia* in competitions and (in the framework of cult) hymns in honour of the Roman emperor and his household and of long-established divinities like Asclepius. The first two categories will clearly have required new compositions, but apart from one recent discovery our knowledge is limited to the names of victors in competitions and of ὑμνῳδοί, 'hymn-singers', and ὑμνογράφοι, 'composers of hymns'.[67] In worshipping traditional gods traditional texts will still have been sung,[68] but alongside these some new hymns were composed. One of these, a paean to Asclepius by Diophantus of Sphettus, probably the prytanis of AD 167/8, is chiefly

[66] Luc. *Philops.* 34, cf. Radermacher 1916; Ogden 2004, 2007.

[67] Of victors in the *prosodion* at Thespiae we know Antiphon of Athens (cf. in this chapter n.16) who shared a victory between AD 150 and 160 with a Thespian, Eumaron son of Alexander (*IG* vii 1773 = Roesch 2007–9, 178); Eumaron is the sole victor recorded in a competition of the years AD 150–60, or after AD 169 (*SEG* 3.334 = 2007–9, 177); two victors, Vipsanius Philoxenus of Thespiae and Callitychides of Thebes, are recorded for a competition which must fall between AD 161 and 169 or AD 176 and 180 (*SEG* 3.344.3–5 = Roesch 2007–9, 179): they also between them took prizes for the (hexameter) poem and (prose) encomia on the emperors and on the Muses. Cf. n.62 and Bowie 2019f (Chapter 46 in Volume 3). For ὑμνογράφοι see (perhaps) L. Sertorius of Daldis and Ephesus (*IEph* 1149.5–9); at Clarus note Nedymianus, ὑμνογράφου διὰ βίου, 'hymn-writer for life', from Laodicea at Lycum in AD 132/3, *IGR* iv 1587.14–15; for the young choirs from many cities who sang hymns during *theoriae* to Clarus see Rutherford 2013; Ferrary 2014; Bowie 2022b; for ὑμνῳδοί cf. Bowie 1989a, 221, n.27 (Chapter 12, 229 with n.46 in this volume).

[68] The practice of singing 'classics' seems to be secured by the re-inscription of Sophocles' 'Paean to Asclepius', *IG* ii^2 4510, and the inclusion of that ascribed by Ath. 15.702a to Ariphron of Sicyon in the sequence of verse texts on *IG* ii^2 4533 (late second or early third century) – both from the Athens Asclepieium.

written in *apocrota*, and so, like the hymn to Antinous discussed below, was perhaps intended to be sung by a citharode and not by a choir.[69]

If that is so, our few choral fragments from hymns to traditional gods are, ironically, from the verse hymns to various deities composed by the great exponent of the prose hymn, Aelius Aristides. They belong to the first decade of his illness, AD 144–153, and were composed at the command of divinities, chiefly Asclepius, to assist his cure: and Aristides indeed claims that their performance by a chorus of boys brought relief.[70] This chorus, which he seems still to have maintained as late as AD 166, was presumably modelled to some extent on the ὑμνῳδοί attached to the cult of Artemis at Ephesus and to the imperial cult in Pergamum, Ephesus, and (from AD 123) Smyrna.

Although no hymn to an emperor survives, a hymn to Antinous has been discovered in the shrine of Apollo Hylatas at Curium in Cyprus, apparently inscribed by a citharode chosen to serve on an embassy, perhaps consolatory, to Hadrian.[71] It is not clear how this song was performed. It seems to begin with a first-person-plural verb, but thereafter the singer refers to himself in the singular and claims to have mounted a choral performance (1. 7). Moreover the metre, *apocrota* combined with paroemiacs, was a favourite with the citharode Mesomedes,[72] and might therefore suggest solo performances. Either, then, as Lebek proposed, the inscribed text was sung by the citharode alone, to be followed by a choral song; or, as some believe archaic κιθαρωιδία was performed, the chorus merely danced while the citharode sang.

When we turn to solo performance it is clear that song accompanied by the *cithara* is in vogue,[73] and we are fortunate to have substantial remains of one of its leading exponents, perhaps its doyen, Mesomedes. He seems to

[69] *IG* ii² 4514, ten + ten *apokrota* followed by four hexameters: on possible aspects of its performance cf. Melfi 2010, 322. Of the hymns quoted in literary sources or found on papyrus collected in Heitsch 1963–4, i 155 ff., most are in hexameters, and none can be securely dated to our period.

[70] Aristid. *Hieroi Logoi* 4 (= 50 Keil).38. For a fuller discussion see Bowie 1989a, 214–20 (Chapter 12, 221–9 in this volume).

[71] First published by Mitford 1971, no. 104. For discussion and identification of the metre see Lebek 1973. I now think that the πρεσβευτής, 'ambassador' or 'legate', of the text was not the poet but another person involved in the performance and/or inscription. I suggest in Bowie 2022b that the poet and composer was indeed Mesomedes himself; so too independently Pöhlmann 2019.

[72] Cf. West 1982, 172–3: the *apocroton is* ⏑ ⏑ – ⏑ ⏑ – ⏑ ⏑ – ⏑ –, the pareomiac ⏑ ⏑ – ⏑ ⏑ – ⏑ ⏑ – –.

[73] A number of melic poets are known of whose compositions we cannot say whether they were citharodic, for choirs, or for some other sort of solo performance. These include the λυρικοὶ νόμοι, 'lyric nomes', of the sophist Hippodromus (Philostr. VS 2.27.620); the μέλη, 'songs', of Paeon; and the poetry of the Hermocrates of Rhodes encountered by Aristides at Pergamum ca. AD 145, Aristid. *Hieroi Logoi* 4 (= 50 K) 23. The varied talents of Q. Pompeius Capito and C. Iulius Longianus of Aphrodisias, honoured in AD 127 (above n.22), presumably included melic compositions, and C. Cornelius Secundus Proculus honoured at Methymna (*IGR* iv 6 = *IG* xii.2 519) as poet of μέλη, 'songs', may just belong in our period.

span the reigns of Hadrian and Pius. The Suda asserts that he was a citharode from Crete and Hadrian's freedman – presumably, then, his full name was P. Aelius Mesomedes – and μάλιστα φίλος, 'a close friend'. Eusebius put Mesomedes' floruit in AD 144, and the *Augustan History* has the emperor Pius reduce the salary of the *lyricus* – a salary presumably granted to him by Hadrian. Among 'various works' the Suda ascribes a *Praise of Antinous*, which, for good or ill, has not survived. But as well as two poems preserved in the Palatine and Planudean anthologies, thirteen, originally from a single corpus, have been transmitted in various manuscripts, four of these with musical notation (which at least another two seem once to have had).[74]

The poems with musical notation are *prooemia* to the Muse (1a Heitsch = 1 Pöhlmann), and to Calliope and Apollo (1b Heitsch = 2 Pöhlmann: both = 9 Horna); and hymns to the Sun (2.7–25 Heitsch = 4 Pöhlmann) and to Nemesis (4). Another *prooemium* with no trace of musical notation precedes the hymn to the Sun (2.1–6 Heitsch = 3 Pöhlmann: both = 10 Horna). These three *prooemia* are not distinctive poetry, and it has been suggested[75] that they are earlier than Mesomedes and that he simply set the first two to new music.

There is much more to the hymn to Nemesis (3 Heitsch = 5 Pöhlmann = 11 Horna), which mixes the paroemiac with the *apocroton*:[76]

Νέμεσι πτερόεσσα βίου ῥοπά,
κυανῶπι θεά, θύγατερ Δίκας,
ἃ κοῦφα φρυάγματα θνατῶν
ἐπέχεις ἀδάμαντι χαλινῶι,
ἔχθουσα δ᾽ ὕβριν ὀλοὰν βροτῶν
μέλανα φθόνον ἐκτὸς ἐλαύνεις·
ὑπὸ σὸν τροχὸν ἄστατον ἀστιβῆ
χαροπὰ μερόπων στρέφεται τύχα,
λήθουσα δὲ πὰρ πόδα βαίνεις,
γαυρούμενον αὐχένα κλίνεις.
ὑπὸ πῆχυν ἀεὶ βίοτον μετρεῖς,
νεύεις δ᾽ ὑπὸ κόλπον ὄφρυν ἀεί

[74] Suda μ 668, SHA *Pius* 7.8. For texts see Heitsch 1963–4, ii 24–32. To his bibliography add Pöhlmann 1970, 12–31, who rightly argues that Heitsch 1a and 1b and 2.1–6 are separate poems, discusses transmission, and print the texts with their musical notation. For a good discussion see Whitmarsh 2004; for a full re-evaluation of Mesomedes see Regenauer 2016.

[75] By Maas and Wilamowitz, cf. Pöhlmann 1970, 28. For discussion of the music for the hymn to the Sun see Barker 2002, 122.

[76] Cf. n.72. The plural 'we sing' at 16 is not a good basis for the view of Wilamowitz 1921 that 1–15 were sung by a solo performer and 16–20 by a chorus. For the hymn to Isis (5 Heitsch = 6 Regenauer) see Gordon 2020, 32–4.

ζυγὸν μετὰ χεῖρα κρατοῦσα.
ἵλαθι μάκαιρα δικασπόλε
Νέμεσι πτερόεσσα βίου ῥοπά.
Νέμεσιν θεὸν ἄιδομεν ἀφθίταν,
Νίκην τανυσίπτερον ὀμβρίμαν
νημερτέα καὶ πάρεδρον Δίκας,
ἃ τὰν μεγαλανορίαν βροτῶν
νεμεσῶσα φέρεις κατὰ Ταρτάρου.

Nemesis, winged balancer of life,
dark-faced goddess, daughter of Justice,
you who restrain with adamantine bridles
the frivolous insolences of mortals,
and spurning the destructive violence of mankind
drive out black envy!
Beneath your unceasing, traceless orbit
is spun the grey fortune of man
and unnoticed you walk in his tracks,
you bend the neck that is proud.
Beneath your arm you ever measure out life
and ever do you lower your eye to your bosom
as you control the scales in your hand.
Be gracious, blessed dealer of justice,
Nemesis, winged balancer of life.
Nemesis the deathless goddess we sing,
Victory with slender wings, all-powerful
infallible, and the assistant to Justice,
you who in displeasure at the pride of men
carry it down into Tartarus.

This hymn is traditional in thought and language and retains a sombre tone throughout. Equally serious are the hymns to Isis (5 Heitsch = 2 Horna) and the powers of the universe, perhaps Nature (4 Heitsch = 1 Horna). A lighter tone is struck in a hymn to the Adriatic (6 Heitsch = 3 Horna), composed in the same metre as that to Nemesis.

In a different genre a poem of some charm, composed in proceleusmatics, tells the fable of the rustic and the swan (10 Heitsch = 7 Horna).[77]

κύκνον ἐνὶ ποταμῶι
κάτεχεν ἄτερ βρόχου

[77] A more conventional metre for telling fables is to be found in the choliambic collection of Babrius, almost certainly from the last quarter of the first century AD, best consulted in Perry 1965, with discussion of date at xlvii–lii.

παγόδετον ὕδωρ·
ὃν ἄμουσος ἰδών
αἰπόλος ἀγρότας
ἔθελε διολέσαι,
κεφαλὰν λιγύθρουν
τῶι σταχυοτόμωι
δρεπάνωι θερίσας.
κατὰ δ' ὑδατοπαγοῦς
βαῖνε κελεύθου
βήμασι κούφοις,
Τιτὰν δὲ κύκνωι
πυρόεντι βολᾶι
σύμμαχος ἐφάνη·
γίγνετο μὲν ὑγρόν
πάλι ποταμὸς ὕδωρ·
ἔπεσεν ὁ βούτας,
ὁ δὲ κύκνος ἀνέθορε
κἄμπτατο χαίρων.

A swan in a river
was caught without a snare
by the ice-bound water:
a rustic goatherd
no friend of the Muse
saw it and wanted to kill,
harvesting with his sickle
for cutting ears of corn,
the head that sings sweetly.
Along the frozen path
of water he walked
with light steps,
and to the swan's aid the Sun
with his fiery dart
appeared as an ally:
once more the river
became flowing water:
the oxherd fell
and the swan leapt up
and flew off rejoicing.

Although Mesomedes is careless in some matters – is this a goatherd, an oxherd, or a reaper? – his language is often allusive as well as economical, and even without the music this swan-song makes a favourable impression. Less so two ingenious poems on sundials (7 Heitsch = 4 Horna; 8 Heitsch = 5 Horna) and one on the chimaera (12 Heitsch = 12 Horna). But two more deserve quotation. That on a mosquito (11 Heitsch = 8 Horna) has the wit of a *chreia*:

ἐλέφαντος ἐπ' οὔατι κώνωψ
πτερὸν οὐ πτερὸν ἵστατο σείων,
φάτο δ' ἄφρονα μῦθον· ἀφίπταμαι,
βάρος οὐ γὰρ ἐμὸν δύνασαι φέρειν.
ὃ δ' ἔλεξε γέλωτος ὑφ' ἁδονᾶι·
ἀλλ' οὔτ' ἐδάην ὅτ' ἐφιπτάθης
οὔθ' ἡνίκ' ἀφίπτασαι, κώνωψ.

On an elephant's ear a mosquito
settled flapping its wing (no wing, to be sure)
and uttered the foolish remark: off I fly
for my weight is much more than your frame can endure;
and the elephant pleasantly laughed his reply:
but I didn't detect when you flew onto me
nor when you flew off, dear mosquito.

A lusher texture, reminiscent of erotic epigram,[78] pervades the set-piece description of a sponge (9 Heitsch = 6 Horna):

ἄνθος τόδε σοι βυθίων πετρῶν
πολύτρητον ἁλὸς παλάμαις φέρω
σμήνεσσι πανείκελον Ἀτθίδων
ἅτε κηρὸν Ὑμήττιον ἐκ πετρῶν,
ὧι Γλαῦκος ἐν ὕδασι τέρπεται.
Τρίτωνος ὅδ' ἐστὶ χαμεύνα,
τούτωι παρὰ κύμασι παρθένοι
παίζουσιν, ἀγάλματα Νηρέως,
πώλων ὅδ' ἀφρώδε' ἀθυ<ρμάτ>ων
Ἐνοσίχθονος ἄσθματα λούει.
τοῦτον τάμε νηχόμενος δύτας
ἁλὸς ὕδασιν ἄτρομος ἐργάτας,
ἵνα σὸν κατὰ χιονέων μελῶν
λύσηι μετὰ νύκτα, γύναι καλά,
κάματον τὸν ἐρωτοπαλαισμάτων.

78 No doubt love-songs formed a prolific genre of their own, but we have little evidence of its forms. Later we hear of a poet Celsus who devoted himself to such ὠιδαί, Philostr. *Ep.* 71.

This flower I bring to you in my hands
with many holes from the deep rocks of the sea
the very image of a beehive, like a honeycomb
on Hymettus from the crags of Attica
which gives Glaucus pleasure in his waters.
This is the mattress of Triton,
with this by the waves do maidens
play, the pride of Nereus,
this washes the foamy panting
of colts, the playthings of Poseidon.
This was cut by a swimming diver
a fearless labourer in the waters of the brine
that from your snowy limbs
you might part, when night is over, fair lady,
the tiredness of love's wrestlings.[79]

The survival of Mesomedes' songs and music shows that he appealed not simply to his patron Hadrian but to a wider public. He is surely the tip of an iceberg. There must have been many citharodes whose songs gave pleasure to Antonine Greeks: κιθαρωιδία figured in the *Mouseia* at Thespiae, and slightly later a Severan text from Smyrna documents a citharode's victories in over twenty-five competitions in seventeen Greek cities and in Rome.[80]

The popularity of Mesomedes' rhythms has even left its mark on Lucian, whose mock-tragedy Ποδάγρα (*Podagra*), '*Gout*', follows him in mixing *apocrota* with paroemiacs for a 'choral' passage (87–111). We need not doubt Cassius Dio's story that Caracalla constructed a cenotaph for him, and may note that he expected his readers to recognise Mesomedes as τῶι τ οὺς κιθαρωιδικοὺς νόμους συγγράψαντι 'the man who composed citharodic nomes'.[81]

[79] The translation assumes Ἀτθίδων in 3 (Wilamowitz 1921, 601). The general sense of the last line seems certain; I print and translate τὸν ἐρωτοπαλαισμάτων (*conj.* D. A. Russell, *exempli gratia*) for τῶν ἐρωτικῶν ὀμμάτων.

[80] At the *Mouseia*, *SEG* 3.334.30 (= Roesch 2007–9, 179.30) and perhaps *IG* vii 1773.28 (= Roesch 2007–9, 178.28), cf. Schachter 1986, 177 n.5. The Smyrna text is *IGR* iv 1432 = *ISmyrna* 659, the citharode C. Antonius Septimius Publius; his victories are in Rome, Smyrna, Puteoli, Naples, Actium, Argos, Nemea, Pergamum, Delphi, Ephesus, Epidaurus, Athens, Sardis, Tralles, Miletus, Rhodes, Sparta, and Mantinea (he does not list minor *agones*). He also gives credit (22–7) to his φωνασκός, 'voice-trainer', P. Aelius Agathemerus, himself a κιθαρωιδὸν ἱερονίκην καὶ μελοποιὸν ἔνδοξον, 'citharode victorious at sacred games and famous song-composer'. Note too that it is an illusion of κιθαρωιδία that Philostratus tries to create by his compositions for his *Heroicus* of ca. AD 215 (208 Kayser = 53 Lannoy, 213 Kayser = 72–3 Lannoy), cf. Bowie 1989a, 222–3 (Chapter 12, 230–2 in this volume). For a valuable account of κιθαρωιδία from its beginnings to the imperial period see Power 2010.

[81] D.C. 77.13.7, cf. Suda μ 668 *s.n.* Μεσομήδης.

5 Conclusion

I have offered a sketch, not a history: whether our material will ever allow the latter to be written is doubtful. We can be more confident in positive than in negative generalisations. Various species of epigram flourished, and some commemorative poems on stone grew into poems longer and grander than classical epigram. Some hexameter poems followed, and fewer seem to have flouted, Callimachean precepts, but our picture may be skewed by the greater capacity for survival of apparently useful didactic poetry. I have said almost nothing of dramatic poetry, but new tragedies and comedies were written and performed in competitions.[82] In melic poetry it is song accompanied by the *cithara* that seems to hold centre-stage, but again we are frustrated by the lack of examples of other melic texts we know to have existed. To explain why so little poetry survives from a period from which we have so much prose would require another paper. Quality is not the only factor, and poets of the Antonine Age deserve some congratulation for carrying the flag through an era in which prose had seized the literary high-ground.

[82] E.g. the *Mouseia* at Thespiae, see the texts cited in nn.62 and 67. Of imperial Greek tragedies a few trimeters may survive if the five iambics in Stob. iv. 22 (i) 3, 4 (p. 494 Hense) belong to the Tiberian epigrammatist Apollonides: cf. *GP* ii 148 n.2. On drama in the imperial period see Jones 1993; Bowie 2022a.

15 | Hadrian and Greek Poetry (2002)

1 Introduction

The section of *FGE* containing epigrams by imperial Romans has twelve composed by emperors. On Page's attribution, these comprise two by Germanicus, one possibly by Tiberius, one by Trajan, seven by Hadrian and one by Julian.[1] Even once we have subtracted the poem inscribed on a statue base in Ephesus by the sophist Hadrianus of Tyre, a poem that Page mistakenly attributed to the emperor,[2] Hadrian's surviving output places him clearly in a unique class. If he was not the 'Greekest' Roman of them all, he was certainly in this matter, as in many other things, the most Hellenic Roman emperor of them all. Of course an interest in Greek poetry and writing Greek poems are only two criteria on which the Hellenism of a person originating from the Latin-speaking West might be judged. They do, however, merit inclusion in any attempt to explore this broad and complex subject.

In this paper, then, I shall first look at Hadrian's tastes in established Greek poetry – those canonical texts which he liked and those which he did not. Then I shall examine briefly the poetry that he himself composed. Finally I shall consider some examples of Greek poetry composed by some of his friends or close associates. I shall regularly stray from Greek into Latin texts, because, symptomatically of this period, Hadrian and his friends of western origin showed equal facility in both, though it is unlikely that many πεπαιδευμένοι, 'educated men', brought up in the Greek language and culture were even competent in Latin in this period.[3]

[1] *FGE* 555–73. Of those ascribed by Page to others which are also given to Hadrian in the tradition, *AP* 9.17 (where the Corrector, having written Γερμανικοῦ Καίσαρος, 'by Germanicus Caesar', then added Ἀδριανοῦ, 'by Hadrian', in the margin) is argued forcefully by Page to be by Germanicus. *AP* 9.387, of which a Latin translation is ascribed to Germanicus in the *Anthologia Latina (PLM* iv 102), has the ascription Ἀδριανοῦ Καίσαρος, 'by Hadrian Caesar', then qualified by the Corrector οἱ δὲ Γερμανικοῦ, Ἡσύχιος δὲ εἰς Τιβέριον Καίσαρα ἀναφέρει αὐτόν, 'but some say it is by Germanicus, and Hesychius ascribes it to Tiberius Caesar'. Page ascribes it to Tiberius, and its translation to Germanicus: the tone of exultation in which Roman control of Thessaly is described should be added to the arguments against Hadrianic authorship. Other recent, but less full, discussions of these and other poems are to be found in Fein 1994; Birley 1997.

[2] *IEph* 1539 = Kaibel 888a, *FGE* Hadrian 6. For discussion and further references see Bowie 1989a, 247 (Chapter 12, 259 in this volume).

[3] For the substantial evidence against this view see Jolowicz 2021.

2 Hadrian's Poetic Tastes

First, then, what was Hadrian's own taste in poetry? The answer of the ancient tradition is clear: he wished to dethrone established classics. So, after noting Hadrian's preference in Latin literature for Cato over Cicero, for Ennius over Vergil, and for Coelius Antipater over Sallust, the *Historia Augusta* says:

> amavit praeterea genus vetustum dicendi … Ciceroni Catonem, Vergilio Ennium, Salustio Coelium praetulit, eademque iactantia de Homero et Platone iudicavit.
>
> Moreover he liked an archaic style. He preferred Cato to Cicero, Ennius to Vergil, Coelius (sc. Antipater) to Sallust; and he uttered the same pretentious verdicts on Homer and Plato.[4]

I take it that this means that Hadrian preferred other writers in the same genre, and that would also seem to be suggested by Cassius Dio's related remark, talking of his envy:

> καὶ οὕτω γε τῆι φύσει τοιοῦτος ἦν ὥστε μὴ μόνον τοῖς ζῶσιν ἀλλὰ καὶ τοῖς τελευτήσασι φθονεῖν· τὸν γοῦν Ὅμηρον καταλύων Ἀντίμαχον ἀντ' αὐτοῦ ἐσῆγεν, οὗ μηδὲ τὸ ὄνομα πολλοὶ πρότερον ἠπίσταντο.
>
> And he was so strongly of this natural bent that he envied not only the living but even the dead: for example he tried to unseat Homer and introduce Antimachus in his place, a poet whose very name was hitherto unknown to many.
>
> Cassius Dio 69.4.6

In fact, as will be noted, Hadrian rewarded at least one Homerising poet, Pancrates, and I am inclined to dismiss Dio's assertions as silly gossip, as I have tried to demonstrate are the earlier parts of his chapter about Apollodorus of Damascus.[5] That Hadrian tried to persuade members of his entourage that the *Thebais* of Antimachus was a better poem than Homer's *Iliad*, or tried to replace Homer by Antimachus in libraries or school curricula, is barely credible, although Antimachus had been given qualified approval by Domitian's professor of rhetoric, Quintilian, and was later read

[4] SHA *Hadr.* 16.6. Presumably the alternative to Plato was Xenophon, especially popular in the imperial period (cf. Bowie 2016g, Chapter 39 in Volume 3) and emulated by Hadrian's friend Arrian, on whom see below.

[5] Bowie 1997c (Chapter 10 in Volume 3). Note however the reservations of Jones 1997, 527–30.

in second century Oxyrhynchus.[6] But no doubt there was some truth in this claim. Part of the explanation may lie in the poetry of Hadrian that allegedly emulated Antimachus (this is discussed shortly), and part in the fact that, as we can infer from a comparison mounted by Plutarch in his *Timoleon* between the poet Antimachus and the painter Dionysius on the one hand, and Homer and the painter Nicomachus on the other, in the early second century AD comparison of Homer with Antimachus was an established literary critical game.[7]

3 Hadrian's Poetry

Another contribution to our understanding of Hadrian's liking for Antimachus is to be found in the Greek poetry he himself wrote. First, there is no evidence that he wrote any long poems. That is hardly surprising, since he had many other calls on his time, but some equally busy emperors did write poems of some length. According to Suetonius, Augustus was responsible not only for epigrams – composed like all good epigrams in the bath – but also for a one-book work *Sicilia* and a tragedy *Ajax*. We also know that Domitian wrote a *Bellum Capitolinum*, '*The war for the Capitol*'.[8] It may be significant, therefore, that the positive evidence for Hadrian's poetic activity is different. According to Dio, as well as prose compositions ἐν ἔπεσι ποιήματα παντοδαπὰ καταλέλοιπε, 'in verse he left poems of all sorts'.[9] Dio does not say whether these were in Greek or in Latin, but since he has just been talking about Hadrian's devotion to letters in either language, and since poems by Hadrian in both languages are preserved, I infer that he means in both languages.

The surviving poems are not only short but deploy considerable variety of metre. The Latin poems are in hexameters, Anacreontics, and a metre which alternates iambic dimeters and Aristophaneans; the Greek are in elegiacs and hendecasyllables.

[6] Quint. 10.1.53. For the remains of Antimachus see the editions of Wyss 1936; Matthews 1996; second-century readers in Oxyrhynchus, *P.Oxy.* 2516, 2518. Given that genre is the basis of Dio's comparison the claim must relate to the *Thebais* (as Wyss test. 31, followed by F. J. Williams on Antimachus in Hornblower and Spawforth 2003, 106) and not to the *Lyde*, whose merits were the subject of hot poetic debate in the third century BC (see Cameron 1995, esp. 303–38) or the *Artemis* (about which we know nothing, but its title is not that of an epic) as suggested by Birley 1997, 171.

[7] Plu. *Tim.* 36.3. [8] Suet. *Aug.* 85, Mart. 5.5.7. [9] D.C. 69.3.1.

The production of different sorts of poem in a variety of metres puts Hadrian in a tradition that can be traced back through Hellenistic poetry as far as Archilochus. It is a tradition one branch of which was represented in Hadrian's youth by the Latin *Silvae*, '*Woods*', of Statius, published between AD 93 and 96 (i.e. when Hadrian was between seventeen and twenty). In AD 104 (when Hadrian was already twenty-eight) the younger Pliny praised the elderly Arrius Antoninus for epigrams that rivalled those of Callimachus, and *mimiambi*, 'iambic mimes', that rivalled those of Herodas, while he himself embarked upon some translations into Latin of Arrius' Greek epigrams. He then sent a friend a *libellus*, 'slim volume', of Latin hendecasyllables that he had composed while travelling, bathing, or dining.[10] A year or two earlier he had talked of the *lyrica doctissima*, 'most learned lyric poems', written by Vestricius Spurinna for relaxation in both Latin and Greek, and later, in AD 107, he was putting together a book of poetry in various genres and metres.[11] In the Greek world a Pergamene who had been honoured with Athenian citizenship, Q. Pompeius Capito, was commemorated, perhaps before the end of the first century, as extemporising παντὶ μέτρωι καὶ ῥυθμῶι, 'in every rhythm and metre'.[12] The composition of short poems in various metres and in either language was a trend already vigorous in Hadrian's twenties, and not one that he had set.

That Hadrian had a special interest in some 'post-classical' poetry and poets may also be argued on the basis of his decision to restore the tomb of Parthenius of Nicaea and furnish it with a new sepulchral epigram. The text of that epigram is extremely uncertain, and unfortunately the stone on which it was inscribed, which was situated near Rome, perhaps at Tivoli, has long been lost. It seems, however, to allude to Parthenius' poetry of mourning for his dead lady Arete.[13] That theme might itself recall the *Lyde*, which Antimachus allegedly composed to console himself after the death of his wife of that name.[14] Parthenius himself seems generally to have been

[10] Arrius, Plin. *Ep.* 4.3; 4.18; 5.15; Pliny's hendecasyllables, 4.14, cf. 7.4.

[11] For the *lyrica* of Vestricius Spurinna *utraque lingua*, 'in each language', see *Ep.* 3.1.7; for Pliny's own *liber, et opusculis varius et metris*, 'book diverse both in its composition and its metres', *Ep.* 8.21.4. For a review of Latin polymetric poetry in the second century see Steinmetz 1982.

[12] *IG* ii^2 3800: see Hardie 1983, 22, 83–4. Note also C. Iulius Longianus of Aphrodisias, honoured at Halicarnassus for ποιημάτων παντοδαπῶν ἐπιδείξεις ποικίλας, 'diverse performances of all manner of poems', *MAMA* viii 418(b)2–3 = *IAph2007*, 12.27(ii) 2–3: see further Bowie 1989b, 202 (Chapter 13, 277 in this volume).

[13] *IG* xiv 1089 = Kaibel 2050. For a further attempt to establish a text see *FGE* Hadrian 7. For discussion of Hadrian and Parthenius see also Fein 1994, 48–9, with bibliography; Lightfoot 1999, 82–4 (and T 4).

[14] Ps.-Plu. *Consol. ad Apoll.* 9 = *Mor.* 106b.

neglected after Vergil and Propertius, whose echoes may be a tribute as much to Parthenius' patron Gallus as to Parthenius. He is not mentioned by Ovid or by Quintilian, and that Tiberius liked Parthenius, Euphorion and Rhianus and wrote poems in imitation of theirs, as well as ensuring that their poems and statues were in public libraries, is recorded by Suetonius as an aspect of Tiberius' unusual taste – perhaps with a glance at imperial taste in his own time, the 120s.[15] One element in Parthenius' literary output seems to have been unrestrained criticism of Homer, as we know from an epigram by Erucius whose target is certainly a Parthenius and is conjecturally this one.[16] Hadrian's interest in Parthenius may be not unrelated to Parthenius' attack on Horner, and it is doubtless partly in response to imperial taste that another epigram, by the Asian poet Pollianus, praises poetry in the elegiac tradition of Callimachus and Parthenius and vilifies imitators of Homer who plagiarise Homeric phraseology.[17] Later in the second century Parthenius is mentioned in the company of Callimachus and Euphorion by Lucian, and his 'Elegies' are referred to by Artemidorus.[18]

Such an attack on 'theft' is not, of course, an attack on Homer himself. Nor do I think there is a serious attack on Homer in Hadrian's own epigram which purports to be for the tomb of Archilochus:

> Ἀρχιλόχου τόδε σῆμα, τὸν ἐς λυσσῶντας ἰάμβους
> ἤγαγε Μαιονίδηι Μοῦσα χαριζομένη.

> This is the monument of Archilochus, whom into raging iambics
> the Muse diverted, as a favour to Homer.[19]

A nice point is made in complimenting Archilochus: as an epic poet he would have been a serious rival to Homer. But Homer is not thereby dethroned. We might, however, see the composition of such an epigram as one of the starting points for Dio's exaggeration.

A final candidate for an epigram that purports to relate to a tomb is the single line:

[15] Suet. *Tib.* 70.

[16] *AP* 7.377 = *GP* Erucius 13, with full discussion of the identity of the Parthenius attacked.

[17] *AP* 11.130. For text, translation and brief discussion see Bowie 1990b, 54–5 (Chapter 14, 284 in this volume); Nisbet 2003, 183–94.

[18] Luc. *Hist. Conscr.* 56; for his 'Elegies' as a source of recondite stories (along with Lycophron and Heraclides Ponticus) Artem. 4.63; cf. further Lightfoot 1999, 82–4.

[19] *AP* 7.674 = *FGE* Hadrian 2. Although Page is right to insist that this poem may not be a reply to *AP* 7.352 on Archilochus (perhaps by Meleager, see *HE* Meleager 132) which ends Πιερίδες, τί κόρηισιν ἐφ' ὑβριστῆρας ἰάμβους ἐτράπετ', οὐχ ὁσίωι φωτὶ χαριζόμεναι; 'Muses, why did you turn his violent *iambi* against girls, doing a favour to an impious man?', it undoubtedly shows knowledge of it.

τῶι ναοῖς βρίθοντι πόση σπάνις ἔπλετο τύμβου.

For one so heavy with temples what scarcity was shown by his tomb!

Appian cites the line in his account of Pompey's death. After recounting his murder, he says that someone buried him, and that someone else composed an epigram for the tomb – then goes on to narrate how in his day Hadrian cleared the tomb of encroaching sand-dunes and re-erected its statues of Pompey. Xiphilinus' epitome of Cassius Dio, however, claims that during Hadrian's visit to Egypt (i.e. autumn of 130) he performed a sacrifice to Pompey, uttered this line, and restored Pompey's monument.[20] Hadrian's enthusiasm for restoring dilapidated constructions, of which we may already have seen an example in the case of Parthenius' tomb, is well attested by other cases throughout the empire.[21] It is surprising that Appian, who originated precisely from Alexandria, was wrong when in citing the line he said 'and someone else inscribed the epigram …'. But it is conceivable that he was working from memory of a personal visit, and was not aware that the epigram was Hadrian's simply because it was not signed, whereas Dio was drawing on a narrative which (like that of the *Augustan History*) had access to a collection or selection of Hadrian's poetry.

Just what the epigram's composer meant is also unclear. The Budé notes point out the difficulty in the usual translation 'weighed down by temples': we have no other evidence of Pompey receiving divine honours in the form of a temple. Unless Hadrian is confused on the pre-history of the imperial cult, he is more likely to mean 'who was so generous with temples', a quality in which of course Hadrian could well see himself as similar to the great Pompey.[22]

20 τὸ δὲ λοιπὸν σῶμά τις ἔθαψεν ἐπὶ τῆς ἠϊόνος καὶ τάφον ἤγειρεν εὐτελῆ· καὶ ἐπίγραμμα ἄλλος ἐπέγραψε …, 'the body itself somebody buried on the shore and erected a simple tomb: and somebody else inscribed the epigram …', App. *BC* 2.86; μετὰ ταῦτα ἐς Αἴγυπτον παριὼν καὶ ἐνήγισε τῶι Πομπηίωι· πρὸς ὃν καὶ τουτὶ τὸ ἔπος ἀπορρῖψαι λέγεται, 'after this he went round to Egypt and performed a hero-sacrifice to Pompey – to whom he is also said to have uttered the following verse', D.C. (= Xiphilinus) 69.11.1. Cf. SHA *Hadr.* 14.4 *peragrata Arabia Pelusium venit et Pompeii tumulum magnificentius exstruxit*, 'after touring Arabia he reached Pelusium and built up Pompey's grave-mound in a more imposing fashion'. The line also appears at *AP* 9.402 ascribed to Hadrian. For discussion see the notes in Waltz et al. 1974 (and for the complex authorship of *AP* 9.359–827 see their intro. vii–x); Pekáry 1970, 195–8; *FGE* Hadrian 4; Fein 1994, 55–6; Birley 1997, 235–7.

21 Note his addition of a στήλη, *stele*, to Epaminondas' tomb at Mantinea and the composition of an epigram for it, Paus. 8.11.8; his attention to Alcibiades' tomb at Melissa, where he commissioned a statue of Alcibiades in Parian marble and instituted an annual sacrifice of an ox, Ath. 13.574f; and his refurbishment of Ajax's tomb in the Troad, Philostr. *Her.* 8.1.

22 Waltz et al. 1974 cite Od. 6.159 ἐέδνοισι βρίσας, 'having weighed you down with bridal gifts' as a parallel for this sense: it perhaps counts in favour of the traditional translation that this sense only appears with the aorist, and the present tense seems always to have the sense 'be heavy with'. However their alternative proposal, that Hadrian alludes to a verse initially composed about Alexander, is unsupported speculation: see Boatwright 2000, 140–2.

A declamatory epigram that is not overtly sepulchral, although its source claims that it was, is a hexameter three-liner ascribed to Hadrian in a Bodleian manuscript and first published by Bühler twenty years ago. It expresses envy of Achilles for the publicity given him by Homer. I accept Bühler's strong arguments against Hadrianic authorship.[23]

What, then, of Hadrian's alleged attempt to exalt Antimachus? As well as Hadrian's disinclination to emulate Homer, one particular work may have given rise to this claim. According to the *Augustan History*, Hadrian *Catachannas libros obscurissimos Antimachum imitando scripsit*, 'wrote most obscure books (called) Catachannae in imitation of Antimachus'.[24] The manuscripts are corrupt, but as Bernhardy saw in 1847, their readings (*catacannas*, *catacaimos*, *catacaymos*) should render the same word that we find in a letter of Fronto, where it is the name of a tree he saw about AD 140 in the garden of a *villa suburbana* owned by Hadrian's friend Q. Pompeius Falco, his colleague in the consulate of AD 108 and proconsul of Asia during his visit there in AD 123/4. It was an unusual tree 'bearing on a single stock shoots of almost every tree'.[25] There must be some connection between Hadrian's books of poetry and Fronto's pet name (*suum nomen*) for this tree. Was this tree already flourishing when Hadrian composed his poetry, so that he gave the name as a title to a heterogeneous, probably polymetric collection? That cannot be excluded. But another possibility is more attractive. The word should be Greek, and the nearest attested (as is noted in the *OLD*)

[23] Bühler 1978. The epigram runs: ὄλβιε Πηλέος υἱέ, τεῆς τάχα χειρὸς ἀέθλους | ἄλλος ἀνὴρ ῥέξειε,τυχεῖν δ᾽ οὐκ ἔστι καμόντα | τοσσαύτης σάλπιγγος ἀεὶ ζώοντος Ὁμήρου, 'Blessed son of Peleus, another man might perhaps accomplish the achievements of your arm, but on death could not get so great a trumpet as the ever-living Homer'. The superscription in *codex Bodl. Grabianus* 30 f.33 (in which it was found) runs Ἀδριανοῦστί(χοι) καίσαρος εἰς τὸν Ἀχιλλέως τάφον, 'lines of Hadrian Caesaron the tomb of Achilles', which Bühler compared with that at *AP* 9.387 in its citation by the Venetus scholiast at the end of Book 24 of the *Iliad* (Σ *Ven. Hom*. p. 532 de Villoison): Ἀδριανοῦ Καίσαρος εἰς τὸν Ἕκτορος τάφον, 'by Hadrian Caesar on the tomb of Hector'. Bühler argued for a post-Nonnan composition on the grounds of the similarity between line 3 and the ending of Nonn. *D*. 25.269 σάλπιγγος Ὁμήρου, 'the trumpet of Homer'.

[24] SHA *Hadr*. 16.2.

[25] *anno abhinc tertio me commemini cum patre meo a vindemia redeuntem in agrum Pompei Falconis devertere; ibi me videre arborem multorum ramorum, quam ille suum nomen catachannam nominabat. sed illa arbor mira et nova visa est mihi in uno trunco omnium ferme germina* <*arborum ferens*> ..., 'Three years ago I remember turning aside with my father to the estate of Pompeius Falco when on our way home from the vintage; and that I saw there a tree with many branches, which he called by its special name '*catachanna*'. But it seemed to me a new and extraordinary tree, bearing as it did upon its single trunk shoots of almost every kind of tree ...', Fronto 2.6 = i 141 Haines = 29.7 van den Hout, a letter written in AD 143. The link with the tree in Fronto was already seen by F. Orioli, cited by Mai 1823, 106: cf. Cantarelli 1898, 157. For discussion of the *Catachannae*, see also Schanz–Hosius iii[3] 8; Bardon 1956, 414–5; Fein 1994, 42–3; Birley 1997, 171.

is Καταχῆναι, which happens to be the title of a Comedy,[26] while the singular καταχήνη means 'mockery'. I suggest that Καταχῆναι meant 'Mockeries', on the analogy of titles like Ἴαμβοι, '*Iambi*', and Σίλλοι, 'Lampoons', and that Hadrian's book was a collection comprising satirical poems in various metres: on this hypothesis Pompeius Falco then named his tree in allusion–perhaps overtly mocking allusion, if the name was given after Hadrian's death in AD 138 – to the emperor's heterogeneous collection. By AD 163, the date of the word's next surviving appearance in another letter of Fronto, the name of the tree is well enough known to be used as an analogy for a style of rhetoric with strikingly diverse constituents.[27]

Nothing in all this, however, helps us to understand the assertion that the collection imitated Antimachus. This poet from Colophon is remembered chiefly as the composer of a hexameter *Thebais* and an elegiac *Lyde*. These can never have circulated in a single *volumen*. It is possible that there were papyrus books of Antimachus that had copies both of the elegiac *Lyde* and of some short poems from other genres or in other metres (as we now know that Simonides' elegiac narrative of the battle of Plataea could be read on the same roll as some shorter sympotic elegies),[28] but that is unlikely to have been the basis of a perception of Antimachus as the author of a diverse and polymetric book. We do know of another Antimachus, a melic and apparently comic poet who was attacked by Aristophanes for ill-treatment of his comic chorus:[29] but it is unlikely that his name, far less his poetry, was familiar to anyone in the early second century other than scholars working on Aristophanes. The Antimachean element in Hadrian's collection remains obscure.

It remains possible that the *Catachannae* were not in fact satirical but simply diverse. If so they might have included the mock epitaph on Archilochus already discussed. They might also have contained the many erotic poems that Apuleius recalls having read from Hadrian's pen and that were known to the *Augustan History*, but of which no other trace

[26] Καταχήναις, *IG* xiv 1097.8 = *IGUR* i 216.8 (which at the time of the publication of *IG* xiv was in the Villa Albani) records victors at Athenian festivals in certain archon years in the second half of the fifth century, see Millis and Olson 2012, 225–8; where identifiable the category of competition is comedy.

[27] *Ad Marcum Antoninum de orationibus* 2 = ii 102 Haines: *confusam eam ego eloquentiam, catachannae ritu partim pineis nucibus Catonis partim Senecae mollibus et febriculosis prunulis insitam, subvertendam censeo radicitus, immo vero, Plautino ut utar verbo, exradicitus*, 'For as to that hybrid eloquence of the catachanna procedure, grafted partly with Cato's pine-nuts, partly with Seneca's soft and feverish plums, I vote that it be plucked up by the roots, indeed, to use a Plautine expression, root by root'.

[28] Parsons 1992: cf. Boedeker and Sider 2001, Sider 2020. [29] Ar. *Ach.* 1150–2.

remains.[30] Whether they were diverse or only satirical, it is possible that they included one of the epigrams attributed to him in the *Anthology*, *AP* 9.137, according to the *Anthology* rubric a reply to a starving γραμματικός, 'schoolteacher/scholar'. *AP* first offers, as γραμματικοῦ τινὸς ἡμιξήρου πρὸς Ἀδριανὸν τὸν βασιλέα, '(the poem) of a half-starved *grammaticus* to the emperor Hadrian':

ἥμισύ μου τέθνηκε, τὸ δ' ἥμισυ λιμὸς ἐλέγχει·
σῶσόν μου, βασιλεῦ, μουσικὸν ἡμίτονον.

Half of me is dead and half succumbs to the logic of starvation:
save, my emperor, a semitone of this man of the Muses.

AP then continues πρὸς ὃν ὁ βασιλεὺς Ἀδριανὸς ἀπεκρίνατο, 'to whom the emperor Hadrian answered':

ἀμφοτέρους ἀδικεῖς καὶ Πλουτέα καὶ Φαέθοντα·
τὸν μὲν ἔτ' εἰσορόων, τοῦ δ' ἀπολειπόμενος.

You wrong both Pluto and the sun,
still seeing one and missing your rendezvous with the other.[31]

However the close relation between the two couplets raises problems about their authorship. It is possible that in a sympotic context a γραμματικός had indeed uttered a couplet that made a bid for financial support, but it is also conceivable that a real exchange that took place in 'prose' was later encapsulated in pithy verse. In that case the composition of the first couplet could well be by the author of the second; and this draws attention to the more unsettling possibility that neither couplet is in fact by Hadrian, but that a third party composed both couplets as a pair.

A further candidate for inclusion in the *Catachannae* is the well-known riposte to Florus, presumably the historian. According to the *Augustan History*, Florus had sent Hadrian a poem:

[30] *Ipsius etiam divi Hadriani multa id genus legere me memini*, 'I also recall that I read many of this sort of poem (i.e. what Apuleius has just called *lasciva*, 'lubricious') by the god Hadrian himself', Apul. *Apol.* 11, in the context of Hadrian's epitaph for Voconius Romanus: cf. SHA *Hadr.* 14.9 *nam et de suis dilectis multa versibus composuit*, 'for he also composed many works in verse about the objects of his love'. The phrase that follows in the MSS, *amatoria carmina scripsit*, 'he wrote love-poems', is usually deleted as being a gloss.

[31] *FGE* Hadrian 3. Compare the incident narrated by Macrobius when Augustus eventually wrote an epigram in reply to a Greek poet who had been pestering him with epigrams whenever he walked down from the Palatine, Macr. *Sat.* 2.4.31.

ego nolo Caesar esse
ambulare per Britannos
<latitare per Pelasgos>[32]
Scythicas pati pruinas.

I don't want to be a Caesar
want to walk among the Britons
<want to lurk among the Hellenes>
or endure the frosts of Russia.

In reply Hadrian sent the following lines picking up each of those in Florus' stanza:

ego nolo Florus esse
ambulare per tabernas
latitare per popinas
culices pati rutundos

I don't want to be a Florus
want to stroll among the taverns
want to lurk among the bistros
or endure the plump mosquitoes.[33]

It is not likely that Florus was trying to be rude or seriously critical – Favorinus had had the last word on attempting to compete with the emperor in wit or erudition when he said: *non recte suadetis, familiares, qui non patimini me illum doctiorem omnibus credere, qui habet triginta legiones*, 'You give me bad advice, friends, in not allowing me to believe the man who has thirty legions to be more learned than everyone else'.[34] Florus does in fact offer a clearer reflection of the imperial ideology of *patientia*, 'endurance', than any other poem of the reign, and of course gives Hadrian an opportunity to dissociate himself from the life of self-indulgence in which Juvenal represents Rome's governing class as totally immersed. Hadrian also achieved pungent wit, perhaps including bilingual puns: Florus can be

[32] Birley 1997, 143, discussing these poems, suggests that the people in the missing line should relate to Hadrian's tour of the Rhine and upper Danube in AD 121, hence he supplements *<latitare per Sugambros>* (as Steinmetz 1989, 274 n.10) or *Batavos* (he also suggests, unmetrically, *Germanos*). But *latitare* demands rather some people among whom Hadrian seemed to withdraw from other activities: hence my preference for supplementing *Pelasgos*.

[33] SHA *Hadr.* 16.3–4: for discussion (including the identity of this Florus) and bibliography see Herrmann 1950; Steinmetz 1989, 274–5; Fein 1994, 53; Birley 1997, 143.

[34] SHA *Hadr.* 15.13: for the broader context of Favorinus' confrontations with Hadrian see Bowie 1997c (Chapter 10 in Volume 3).

heard or read as φλαῦρος, 'bad, worthless, trivial', and *culices* might suggest the Greek κύλικες, also suitably described as *rutundos*, 'round' (though of course a Greek accusative would be κύλικας).[35]

If this exchange did appear in the *Catachannae* alongside Greek poems, then this was a bilingual collection. That would not be an unprecedented innovation. We have no knowledge of such a practice in the late Republican or Augustan period. Latin poets had indeed included translations of Greek poems in collections: already Lutatius Catulus, then Catullus with poems 51 and 66 translating (and developing) Sappho and Callimachus respectively. But it does not seem that Catullus' *lepidum novum libellum*, 'elegant new book', included texts of the Greek poems translated. However we have noted that Vestricius Spurinna was credited by Pliny with *lyrica doctissima utraque lingua* (n.11); later in the second century AD the letters of Fronto included Greek letters and the *Attic Nights* of Aulus Gellius had extensive quotations of Greek. The survival of a number of poems in each language whose preservation might have been assisted by such a collection also supports the hypothesis that it existed.

So much for the *Catachannae*. Hadrian's remaining extant poems belong in what both the *Palatine Anthology* and the Suda call (τὰ) ἀναθήματα, 'dedications'.[36] The context in which we learn that title is a ten-line epigram accompanying a dedication by Trajan to Zeus Casius, on Mount Casius in Syria, during the preliminaries to the Parthian war, presumably during the winter of AD 113/14. Although the corrector has added an ascription Τραιανοῦ Καίσαρος, 'by Trajan Caesar', the original ascription of the *Anthology* and of the Suda to Hadrian should be accepted. Trajan's literary skills were limited, and it is probable that the epigram came to the *Anthology* and the Suda *via* the *Parthica* of Arrian.[37] Since both Arrian and Hadrian were involved in Trajan's Parthian expedition and Arrian seems to have become close to Hadrian, Arrian's authority, if it is behind the tradition, is certainly to be preferred:

> Ζηνὶ τόδ' Αἰνεάδης Κασίωι Τραϊανὸς ἄγαλμα,
> κοίρανος ἀνθρώπων κοιράνωι ἀθανάτων,
> ἄνθετο, δοιὰ δέπα πολυδαίδαλα, καὶ βοὸς οὔρου
> ἀσκητὸν χρυσῶι παμφανόωντι κέρας,
> ἔξαιτα προτέρης ἀπὸ ληΐδος, ἦμος ἀτειρὴς

[35] Both *calices* and *culices* are found in the manuscript tradition: see Fein 1994, 53 n.74.

[36] *AP* 6.332 gives the heading Ἀδριανοῦ ἐν τοῖς ἀναθήμασιν; the Suda κ 454 *s.v.* Κάσιον ὄρος refers a quotation from the epigram to ἐπιγράμματα ἐν τοῖς ἀναθήμασιν Ἀδριανοῦ. For good arguments for accepting this title see *FGE* Hadrian 1.

[37] The Suda entry (quoting only the first two lines) was attributed to Arr. *Parth.* by Roos 1912, 33, and included by him in his Teubner (Roos 1968) as fr. 36, though not admitted as a secure fragment by Jacoby in his commentary in *FGrH* iid p. 575.

πέρσεν ὑπερθύμους ὧι ὑπὸ δουρὶ Γέτας.
ἀλλὰ σύ οἱ καὶ τήνδε, Κελαινεφές, ἐγγυάλιξον
κρῆναι ἐϋκλειῶς δῆριν Ἀχαιμενίην,
ὄφρα τοι εἰσορόωντι διάνδιχα θυμὸν ἰαίνηι
δοιά, τὰ μὲν Γετέων σκῦλα, τὰ δ' Ἀρσακιδέων.

Trajan, Aeneas' son, dedicated this image to Casian Zeus,
the lord of men to the lord of the immortals,
a pair of much-decorated cups, and from an aurochs
a horn adorned with all-shining gold,
set aside from previous booty, when tireless
he destroyed the over-proud Getae with his spear:
but do you promise to him, dark-clouded one, this
conflict too to accomplish gloriously against the Achaemenids,
so that as you gaze on them your heart may be doubly warmed
by a pair, the spoils of the Getae and of the Arsacids.
AP 6.332

The epigram is neat in its concise inclusion of the chief relevant facts, and in the way it holds back to the last line the identification of the finely-wrought mixing bowls and gilded ox-horn[38] as Getic spoils, so that they can balance the hoped-for Arsacid spoils also mentioned in that line. It is not a great poem, but its tropes may help us with another shortly.

One dedicatory poem that rises decisively above the ordinary is the elegant hendecasyllabic epigram preserved on stone from Thespiae:

ὦ παῖ τοξότα Κύπριδος λιγείης
Θεσπιαῖς Ἑλικωνίαισι ναίων
Ναρκισσοῦ παρὰ κῆπον ἀνθέοντα,
ἱλήκοις· τὸ δέ τοι δίδωσι δέξο
ἀκροθείνιον Ἁδριανὸς ἄρκτου,
ἣν αὐτὸς κάνεν ἱππόθεν τυχήσας.
σὺ δ' αὐτῶι χάριν ἀντὶ τοῦ σαόφρων
πνέοις Οὐρανίας ἀπ' Ἀφροδίτης.

O archer child of clear-voiced Aphrodite,
dwelling in Heliconian Thespiae
by the blooming garden of Narcissus,

[38] The horns of sacrificial animals were regularly gilded, cf. Pl. *Alc.* 2 149c; but the horn here offered along with two cups should be a drinking horn, the use of which Greek perceptions associated with Thracians and Getae: so Theopompus (*FGrH* 115 F38) *ap.* Ath. 11.476d–e attributes their use to Paeonians, D.S. 21.12.5 to Getae (in a third century BC context). For the gilding of such horns see Krausse 1996, 146ff. (I am grateful to Susanne Ebbinghaus for these references).

be gracious, and accept what Hadrian offers you,
the best offering of his hunt, a bear,
which he slew himself with a cast from horseback.
And may you, in exchange for this, chastely
breathe favour upon him from Heavenly Aphrodite.[39]

The bear is unlikely to be one hunted down in the relatively tame country around Thespiae. Rather it is almost certainly, as Louis Robert argued,[40] the one that he slew during a famous hunt in Mysia – a hunt which allowed one of the cities he established there to be named Hadrianoutherae, 'Hadrian's hunts': both the killing of the bear and the city's foundation passed into the *Augustan History*.[41] One of the cities in this group, Stratoniceia, could still be termed 'recently created' in AD 127,[42] so that both the hunt and foundation of Hadrianoutherae should fall during Hadrian's long visit to Asia Minor in AD 123–4.[43] One of a series of coins of Hadrianoutherae commemorating the hunt shows Hadrian on horseback casting his javelin, precisely the manoeuvre of the poem.[44] In September 124 Hadrian travelled by sea from Asia to Achaea, and there, based in Athens, spent the last months of AD 124 and the first half of AD 125.[45] From Athens he could easily have visited Thespiae, perhaps at a time when one of its two great four-yearly festivals, the *Mouseia* or *Erotidia*, was being celebrated.[46]

[39] *IG* vii 1828 = Roesch 2007–9, 270 = Kaibel 811 = *FGE* Hadrian 5. For a full and illuminating discussion see Gamberale 1993.

[40] Robert 1978b, 440ff. = Robert 1987, 136ff.

[41] SHA *Hadr.* 20.13; D.C. 69.10.2 also mentions the foundation.

[42] ἄρτι γεινομένηι in Hadrian's letter to Stratoniceia from Rome dated 1 March AD 127, *IGR* iv 1156a.8–9 = *Syll.*³ 837.8–9 = Oliver 1989, 79–81: see J. and L. Robert 1948, 80–4.

[43] Hadrian's movements in Bithynia and in *provincia Asia* during the years 123 and 124 cannot be determined with precision, but we now know that he was in Ephesus on 29 August 124, the date of the letter sent to Oenoanda published by Wörrle 1988 (*SEG* 38.1462): other indications are compatible with the hypothesis that he was touring cities in the north-west part of the province in the first half of AD 124, cf. Halfmann 1986, 199–201; Bowie 2012g, 2012h (Chapters 27 and 28 in Volume 3).

[44] Imhoof-Blumer 1911, 10–11 pl. 1, von Fritze 1913, nos. 558 (*RPC* iii 1625: bear's head on obverse), 564 (*RPC* iii 1626: Hadrian on horseback casting javelin at bear, as also 1624, where animal is a lion: not in von Fritze), 565–7 (*RPC* iii 1629 bear's head on reverse), 569–70 (*RPC* iii 1631: bear's head on reverse and legend ΑΔΡΙΑΝΟΥΘΗΡΑ) with plates ix 17, 22, 23, 25. Cf. *RPC* iii 1632: Antinous ΗΡΩΣ ΑΓΑΘΟΣ on obverse, legend ΑΔΡΙΑΝΟΥΘΗΡΑ on reverse.

[45] Halfmann 1986, 201–3.

[46] Cf. Wörrle 1988, 231–3. For the bulk of the inscriptions see Jamot 1895; for more recent discoveries Plassart 1926; J. & L. Robert *Bull.* 1978, no. 215; Moretti 1981. Clearly there was a revival in the second century AD, probably due to Hadrian, and the *Mouseia* are now called μεγάλα Τραιάνηα Ἀδριάνηα Σεβαστῆα Μουσῆα, 'the great Trajanic Hadrianic Augustan *Mouseia*', Jamot 1895, no.16 = Roesch 2007–9, no. 177. For a collection of the evidence, see Schachter 1986; for a republication of all the inscriptions Roesch 2007–9 nos 161–85; for the festival in the Hellenistic period Knoepfler 1992; Robinson 2012.

The belief that the bear is the one slain in Mysia entails the supposition that the head was preserved in the imperial baggage-train until a suitable dedicatee was found. This is not perhaps as absurd as it may sound. It seems to be just what we have seen Trajan doing with an aurochs-horn that was booty from his Dacian campaigns. That must have been kept for some seven years (from AD 106 to 113/14), whereas the bear's head might have had to be kept for no more than a few months in the calendar year 124.[47] But the choice of dedication to Eros ought perhaps to have prompted more thought. What connection is there between a successfully hunted bear and love? The metaphor of hunting is common in love-poetry,[48] and in Roman art Erotes are represented hunting – as they are on the frieze of the 'Piazza d'Oro' in Hadrian's villa at Tivoli, part of the villa that seems likely to have been built around AD 125.[49] But neither of these facts seems sufficient to explain this dedication at Thespiae. I would guess – but of course it must be only a guess – that Hadrian had met Antinous during his passage through Bithynia in AD 123/4, and that Antinous was already a companion in Hadrian's favourite sport of hunting, as we know that he later was from the lion-hunt in Egypt mentioned by Athenaeus, written up in hexameters by Pancrates,[50] and commemorated on one of the Hadrianic tondos from the Arch of Constantine.[51]

I turn now to two more epitaphs. First, one in Latin which also ties in with Hadrian's interest in hunting. Cassius Dio, in an account of Hadrian's enthusiasm for hunting, says that when his favourite horse Borysthenes, 'died, he built him a tomb, erected a memorial and inscribed epitaphs'.[52] A stone was found in Provence that offers just such an epigram, which oddly was also found in a single manuscript, but both are now lost.[53] Neither source assigned it an author, but its first editor, Pierre Pithou, was probably

[47] Fein 1994, 55 (with n.186) exaggerates the interval in describing it as 'rund ein Jahr', and metamorphoses the bear into a lion. For the question whether the bear's head (Robert 1978b) or skin (as most others have supposed) was dedicated see Gamberale 1993, 1099, noting the regular offering of the skin in hunters' dedications in the *Anthology* but the bear's head on the Hadrianic tondo on the arch of Constantine (cf. below n.51).

[48] E.g. Thgn. 949–50 = 1078c–d, *AP* 12.146 = *HE* Rhianus 5: cf. Aymard 1951, 129ff.; Barringer 2001; Paschalis 2005.

[49] See Conti 1970, 18ff. with plates ix–xiii, and on the date his p. 10.

[50] Ath. 15.677d–f, Heitsch 1963–4, i 51–3 no. xv: see Bowie 1990b, 81–3 (Chapter 14, 310 in this volume); Höschele 2018.

[51] For discussion and illustrations of the tondos see L'Orange and van Gerkan 1939; Aymard 1951, 527–37 with plates 35 and 37–9; Maull 1955; Elsner 2000. For Hadrian's interest in hunting, see also Anderson 1985, 105ff.

[52] ἀποθανόντι γὰρ αὐτῶι καὶ τάφον κατεσκεύασε καὶ στήλην ἔστησε καὶ ἐπιγράμματα ἐπέγραψεν, D.C. 69.10.2.

[53] *CIL* xii 1122 = *CLE* ii 1522: cf. Schizzerotto 1968, 276–83; Stadter 1980, 209 n.5; Fein 1994, 50 with n.165; Birley 1997, 144–5.

correct in suggesting that it was by Hadrian.[54] It may be a forgery, but in favour of its authenticity is the unusual metre, which alternates iambic dimeters catalectic and Aristophaneans.[55]

Borysthenes Alanus
Caesareus veredus
per aequor et paludes
et tumulos Etruscos
volare qui solebat
Pannonicos in apros
nec ullus insequentem
dente aper albicanti
ausus fuit nocere
– ut solet evenire –[56]
vel <si> extimam saliva[m]
sparsit ab ore caudam:
sed integer iuventa
inviolatus artus
die sua peremptus
hoc situs est in agro.

Borysthenes, from Alan lands,
the stallion of Caesar,
who across the plain and marshes
and the mounds of Etruria
was wont to fly
after Pannonian boars,
nor ever as he pursued
did a boar dare injure him
with white-flashing tusk
– as it often happens –
even if he sprayed its tail's tip
with saliva from his mouth;
but in the full flower of youth,
with his limbs unmauled,
carried off in his due time,
he is laid to rest in this land.

[54] Pithou 1590, 145 and addendum 465.

[55] A number of modem scholars have accepted Hadrianic authorship (Bücheler in *CLE*; Bardon 1968, 419–20; Fein 1994, 50) but it is doubted by Cameron 1980c, 172 n.8. For full discussion of the poem see Vinchesi 1988.

[56] Both sense and metre suggest that this line should follow *ausus fuit nocere* and not, as in the Renaissance copies, *sparsit ab ore caudam*.

The date should be AD 121 or 122, when Hadrian was passing through Gaul *en route* to and from Britain. The reference to Borysthenes' death is mysterious. How did he die? If we think ahead to AD 130, when one reconstruction of events would involve Hadrian drowning Antinous, perhaps as some sort of sacrifice,[57] while he was still *integer iuventa inviolatus artus*, we may wonder whether this was, as it were, a prequel to that turning point in Hadrian's life.

The last sepulchral epigram I want to discuss is a poem whose authorship is uncertain. It is an epitaph from Rome:[58]

> ὁ κλεινὸς ἶνις βασιλέως Ἀμάζασπος,
> ὁ Μιθριδάτου βασιλέως κασίγνητος,
> ὧι γαῖα πατρ<ὶ>ς Κασπίας παρὰ κλήιθ̣ρας,
> Ἴβηρ Ἴβηρος ἐνθαδὶ τετάρχυται
> πόλιν παρ᾽ ἱρήν, ἣν ἔδειμε Νικάτωρ
> ἐλαιόθηλον ἀμφὶ Μυγδόνος νᾶμα,
> θάν<ε>ν δ᾽ ὀπαδὸς Αὐσόνων ἁγητ<ῆ>ρι
> μολὼν ἄνακτ̣ι̣ <Π>αρθικὴν ἐφ᾽ ὑσμίνην,
> πρίν περ παλάξ̣αι χεῖρα δηίωι λύθρωι,
> ἴφθιμον αἰαῖ χεῖρα δουρὶ κα<ὶ τ>όξ̣ω<ι>
> καὶ φασγάνου κνώδοντι, πεζὸς ἱππ̣[εύς τε]·
> ὁ δ᾽ αὐτὸς ἶσος παρθένοισιν αἰδοίαις.
>
> The glorious scion of a king, Amazaspus,
> the brother of king Mithridates,
> whose native land was by the Caspian gates,
> an Iberian, son of Iberian, here is buried
> by the sacred city, which Nicator built,
> burgeoning with olives, by Mygdon's stream;
> and he died a squire to the Ausonians' leader
> going for his lord (?) to the Parthian conflict,
> before even he stained his hand with enemy gore,
> a hand ever mighty with spear and bow
> and the blade of his sword, on foot and horse.
> But he himself was like unto modest maidens.

This poem commemorates the brother of an Eastern client king, Mithridates of Iberia: its subject, Amazaspus, accompanied a Roman emperor on Parthian expedition and died at Nisibis, i.e. Antiocheia Mygdonia, 'before

[57] For a full discussion of a problem to which we are unlikely ever to have a definitive answer see Lambert 1984, 128–42.

[58] *IG* xiv 2139 = Kaibel 728 = *GVI* 722 = *IGUR* 1151.

even he had stained his hand with enemy gore'. The emperor must be Trajan, the context his Parthian campaign of AD 114–17, when Nisibis was conquered, lost to an insurrection, and then reconquered. Perhaps Amazaspus was killed in the insurrection, or perhaps he was simply carried off by one of those virulent Eastern Anatolian tummy bugs. Oddly the stone talks as if it has been set up in Nisibis (ἐνθαδί, 'here') but it was copied by Fulvio Orsini in Rome: Mommsen conjectured that Amazaspus was ultimately cremated, not inhumed, and that his bones were taken to Rome where the epigram, originally intended for a tomb at Nisibis, was reused. Moretti conjectured that the bones were taken to Rome under Pius, but as far as I can discover Nisibis was then no longer under Roman control. The puzzle remains. Odd too is the metre, choliambics (or 'scazons'), usually used for invective or scabrous narrative, and a strange choice for an epitaph, even if, as we have seen, scazons were being written ten years earlier in Rome, as they were by Arrius Antoninus, maternal grandfather of the emperor Pius, in imitation of Herodas.[59] On grounds of the metre and of the ornate language I would infer that the epigram on Amazaspus comes from the pen of a litterateur who happened to be in Trajan's company during the Parthian expedition, and (to judge from the last line comparing him to 'modest maidens') one who was not unaware of the Eastern prince's personal charm. Further conjecture is of course irresponsible, but we should recall that Hadrian was himself on the expedition; that during it he composed, as we have seen, at least one 'official' epigram (the poem for the dedication to Zeus Casius); and that he had a penchant for wily metres, not to mention handsome orientals. That the poem was by Hadrian, and had been included by him in a collection which circulated on a roll or in a codex, would offer an explanation of how a text was available to be inscribed in Rome. The pathos brought out in description of the modest prince's death before he had even contributed to the campaign might also suit the attitude to the campaign of the emperor who rapidly gave up almost all that Trajan had conquered; and if the stone was erected in a public place in Rome during Hadrian's principate, then it might be seen as a reminder of the cost to Rome and her friends of the policy of expansion.

I have left to last in this section the Latin poem attributed to Hadrian that has excited most interest, his 'Farewell to life':

[59] The other epitaphs in *GVI* in scazons are 187, a one-liner from Rome of the first to second century AD; 246, of the second or third century AD from Traiana Augusta, whose metre may have something to do with its subject having been a writer of mimes; 538, of the same period from Amorgos, home of the archaic iambographer Semonides; and 1935, a very long and affected poem from second-century Alexandria whose choice of metre is unlikely to be casual.

animula vagula blandula
hospes comesque corporis
quae nunc abibis in loca?
pallidula rigida nubila
nec ut soles dabis iocos.

Little soul, little wanderer, little charmer
body's guest and companion,
to what places will you set out for now?
To darkling, cold and gloomy ones
– and you won't make your usual jokes.

The *Augustan History* ascribes the poem to Hadrian on his death-bed, and a number of leading scholars have defended its authenticity vigorously, in recent years notably Cameron and Birley.[60] It is secured for Hadrian neither by the apparent echo of Ennius, a poet favoured not only by Hadrian but also by the likes of Gellius and Fronto, nor by Cameron's observation that it is too good to have been composed by the author of the *Augustan History*. If we accept that author's claim that it was uttered by Hadrian *moriens*, 'on his death-bed', then the likelihood of its authenticity becomes minimal – those authentic poems of Hadrian that survived did so because he included them in a collection that he himself circulated, whereas *ex hypothesi* the 'Farewell' poem must depend on a supposed third-party witness. Add to that the tendency of many cultures to fabricate impressive – and characteristic – 'last words', and one must conclude that scepticism is legitimate. The poem may well have been composed in or not long after AD 138, but more probably by another than by Hadrian.

So much for Hadrian's own poetry. Some of what survives is rewarding, and if his *Catachannae* had survived complete they would tell us much more of his literary tastes and qualities.

4 Some Poems by Hadrian's Friends

I conclude this chapter with a brief consideration of two poems by friends and associates of Hadrian that display some connections with his own.

60 SHA *Hadr.* 25.9; Cameron 1980; Birley 1994 (with extensive bibliography, to which should be added Bejarano 1975). The text and translation I print are those of Birley, who (like Bejarano) accepts the conjecture of Sajdak 1914–15, 153–4, of *nubila* for MS *nudula*. Sajdak saw in *nubila* an echo of Ennius' description of the underworld. The lines which, following Ribbeck, he took to be by Ennius, *Acherunsia templa alta Orci pallida leti nubila tenebris loca*, quoted by Cic. *Tusc.* 1.48 without ascription, are denied to Ennius by Jocelyn 1967, 256 (on fr. 35, from the *Andromacha*): perhaps correctly, but they are certainly from early Latin poetry, and their quotation by Cicero raises the probability that they would be known to Hadrian.

First, an epigram which was probably composed by one of those Greek πεπαιδευμένοι, 'educated men', who enjoyed an equestrian career under Hadrian, L. Iulius Vestinus. In Book 15 of the Palatine Anthology and alongside the bucolic poets in a Vatican manuscript of the fourteenth century is preserved a poem which both purports to be 'spoken' by an altar and when written out forms an altar's shape.

Ὀλὸς οὔ με λιβρὸς ἱρῶν
Λιβάδεσσιν οἷα κάλχη
Ὑποφοινίῃσι τέγγει·
Μαύλιες δ' ὕπερθε πέτρης Ναξίης θοούμεναι
Παμάτων φείδοντο Πανός· οὐ στροβίλωι λιγνύι
Ἰξὸς εὐώδης μελαίνει τρεχνέων με Νυσίων.
Ἐς γὰρ βωμὸν ὁρῇις με μήτε γλούρου
Πλίνθοις μήτ' Ἀλύβης παγέντα βώλοις,
Οὐδ' ὃν Κυνθογενὴς ἔτευξε φύτλη
Λαβόντε μηκάδων κέρα
Λισσαῖσιν ἀμφὶ δειράσιν
Ὅσσαι νέμονται Κυνθίαις,
Ἰσόρροπος πέλοιτό μοι·
Σὺν οὐρανοῦ γὰρ ἐκγόνοις
Εἰνάς μ' ἔτευξε γηγενής,
Τάων ἀείζωιον τέχνην
Ἔνευσε πάλμυς ἀφθίτων.
Σὺ δ', ὦ πιὼν κρήνηθεν, ἣν
Ἶνις κόλαψε Γοργόνος,
Θύοις τ' ἐπισπένδοις τ' ἐμοὶ
Ὑμηττιάδων πολὺ λαροτέρην
Σπονδὴν ἄδην. ἴθι δὴ θαρσέων
Ἐς ἐμὴν τεῦξιν· καθαρὸς γὰρ ἐγὼ
Ἰὸν ἱέντων τεράων, οἷα κέκευθ' ἐκεῖνος,
Ἀμφὶ Νέαις Θρηικίαις ὃν σχεδόθεν Μυρίνης
Σοί, Τριπάτωρ, πορφυρέου φὼρ ἀνέθηκε κριοῦ.

Not me does the black ink of rites
like the murex with droplets
tinged with crimson moisten,
and knives being sharpened above a stone from Naxos
spared the possessions of Pan: not with twists of smoke
does fine-fragrant gum blacken me from Nysian saplings.
For you behold an altar neither with golden
bricks constructed nor with clods from Alybe,
nor that which the Cynthian-born stock made

taking horns of bleaters
that graze around about
the Cynthian ridges precipitous
would be my counterpart.
For with Uranus' daughters
the earth-born nine made me
to whose craft eternal life
was granted by immortals' emir.
But you, drinker from a spring
which Gorgon's scion sculpted
may you sacrifice and pour
much sweeter than the girls of Hymettus
a libation in plenty. Come now with courage
to encounter me. For I am pure
of monsters that shoot forth poison, such as that which
near to Thracian Neae, nor far from Myrine
to you, three-fathered one, the red ram's thief dedicated.

The Palatine codex does not ascribe an author, but the *index vetus* of the Anthology and the Vatican manuscript both give the poem to Βησαντίνου, 'Besantinus'.[61] The conjecture of Haeberlin 1887 that this is a corruption of 'Vestinus' is generally accepted, but it is important to remember that it is only a conjecture. Certainly several factors point to Hadrian's principate: the poem's metrical diversity, necessary to the attempt to present on a page the shape of an altar in imitation of the *Altar* of Dosiadas, probably of the second century BC (*AP* 15.26); its recondite language and mythological allusions; and the acrostic, a trick also used in the contemporary hexameter *Periegesis* by Dionysius of Alexandria.[62] But the most powerful argument comes from the content of the acrostic. The first letters of each line read:

Ὀλύμπιε, πολλοῖς ἔτεσι θυσείας

Olympian, may you sacrifice for many years

We can conclude that the addressee was someone who both performed sacrifices and yet had the title Olympian. Hadrian is perhaps the only individual who matches this description. In his titulature Ὀλύμπιος appears

[61] *AP* 15.25. The Palatine Anthology is preserved in the late-tenth-century manuscript *Palatinus* 23 + *Paris. suppl. gr.* 384; the Vatican MS has the *siglum* Y in Gallavotti's edition of Theocritus (Rome 1946, 3rd edn 1993). For a brief account of the collection of *technopaignia* see Gow 1952, 552. For editions with discussion see Haeberlin 1887; Luz 2010; Kwapisz 2013.

[62] D.P. 109–33 and 513–32, see Bowie 1990b, 77 (Chapter 14, 306 in this volume) with further references at n.38.

from AD 128/9, but it may be possible to narrow down still further the probable date of the poem's composition within the years between AD 128 and Hadrian's death in AD 138. Although the initial adoption of the title 'Olympian' in AD 128/9, apparently while Hadrian was at Athens, remains one possible occasion,[63] a more attractive one is the final dedication of the completed temple of Olympian Zeus in Athens, late in AD 131 or early in AD 132.

A third possibility is the visit of Hadrian to Egypt between August AD 130 and spring of AD 131. This should be considered a candidate because L. Iulius Vestinus may have been in a procuratorial post in Egypt about that time: some discussion of him and of his family is now necessary.

Vestinus is known chiefly from two sources. The Suda reports his epitome of Pamphilus' Γλῶσσαι, '*Rare words*', and selections of words from Demosthenes, Thucydides and Isocrates,[64] and some other book titles are attested elsewhere. An inscription from Rome gives us his career:[65] he was 'ἀρχιερεύς, 'high priest', of Alexandria and all Egypt and superintendent of the Museum, *procurator* in charge of the Latin and Greek libraries at Rome, *a studiis* (in charge of education) of the emperor Hadrian and *ab epistulis* (in charge of correspondence) of the same emperor'. The chronology of Vestinus' appointments cannot be precisely established, and Pflaum's suggestion that his Egyptian posts (which he plausibly argues were held concurrently, as they were already under Claudius by Claudius Balbillus)[66] fell about AD 130 and his post *ab epistulis* towards AD 138 may put them all too late.[67] But if Pflaum's chronology is right, L. Iulius Vestinus may actually have been in charge of the Museum when Hadrian visited Egypt in 130, and as ἀρχιερεύς would have been the highest official of the imperial cult in Egypt. It might seem appropriate that abstruse Alexandrian learning and

[63] For the evidence see Weber 1907, 209ff., Birley 1997, 220.

[64] Suda o 835 *s.v* Οὐηστῖνος, Ἰούλιος χρηματίσας, σοφιστής. Ἐπιτομὴν τῶν Παμφίλου Γλωσσῶν βιβλία ϛδ΄, Ἐκλογὴν ὀνομάτων ἐκ τῶν Δημοσθένους βιβλίων, Ἐκλογὴν ἐκ τῶν Θουκυδίδου, Ἰσαίου, Ἰσοκράτους καὶ Θρασυμάχου τοῦ ῥήτορος καὶ τῶν ἄλλων ῥητόρων, 'Vestinus, who went under the name Iulius, a sophist: (he wrote) an *Epitome of the "Rare Words" of Pamphilus*, 94 books, *A Selection of Words from the Books of Demosthenes, A Selection from those of Thucydides, Isaeus, Isocrates, and the rhetor Thrasymachus and other rhetors*'.

[65] *IG* xiv 1085 = *OGIS* 679 = *IGR* i 136 = *IGUR* 62, cf. *PIR*[2] 623 (Stein–Petersen); Pflaum 1960–1, no. 105; Bowie 1982, 40f. (Chapter 6 in Volume 3); Fein 1994, 267–9: ἀρχιερεῖ Ἀλεξανδρείας καὶ Αἰγύ|πτου πάσης Λευκίωι Ἰουλίωι Οὐηστί|νωι καὶ ἐπιστάτηι τοῦ Μουσείου καὶ | ἐπὶ τῶν ἐν Ῥώμηι βιβλιοθηκῶν Ῥωμαι|κῶν τε καὶ Ἑλληνικῶν καὶ ἐπὶ τῆς παι|δείας Ἀδριανοῦ τοῦ Αὐτοκράτορος καὶ ἐπι|στολεῖ τοῦ αὐτοῦ Αὐτοκράτορος [. . . . .]

[66] See Pflaum 1960–1, no.105

[67] Birley 1997, 142 with n.2, puts Vestinus' move to the post of *ab epistulis* early in the 120s, immediately after Suetonius: as he says, there is no evidence either way. For further discussion see Bowie 2013e (Chapter 32 in Volume 3).

grateful piety should be combined in a poem purportedly composed for inscription on an altar upon which the emperor was exhorted to sacrifice. Its virtuosity might even have been one factor in persuading Hadrian to promote Vestinus from his Egyptian post to those in Rome, and thence finally to that of *ab epistulis* – a move made before him by Dionysius of Alexandria, father of the Periegete who also fancied acrostics.[68]

But the appointment of the head of the Museum was itself imperial,[69] so Vestinus must have come to an emperor's attention before it was made. Indeed he is almost certainly from a family from Vienne in Narbonensien Gaul already well entrenched in the Roman elite, with an ancestor, perhaps his grandfather, L. Julius Vestinus, prefect of Egypt under Nero (59–62 AD) and a M. Vestinus Atticus, perhaps the prefect's son, rising to the consulate in AD 65, only to lose Nero's favour and be forced to suicide in that very year.[70] Moreover the poem itself has no hint of an Alexandrian geographical context, but does have pointers to Attica, Boeotia and the Aegean. In the Callimachean tradition these features are of course quite compatible with composition in Alexandria, but the mode of address to the unnamed reader whom the acrostic identifies as Hadrian tips the balance (17–22): its reference to drinking from Hippocrene on Helicon, created by the hoof of Pegasus, together with the reference to the honey-bees of Hymettus, best suits publication in a mainland Greek context, and points to one of Hadrian's visits to Athens and neighbouring parts of Greece, whether in AD 128/9 or in AD 131/2. That he had earlier visited Thespiae near Helicon we have already seen from his poem to Eros. This visit was most probably in AD 124, but it need not have been forgotten four or even eight years later: and indeed Hadrian may well have returned to Thespiae again, perhaps even to attend the Μουσεῖα Ἀδριανεῖα which were celebrated in his honour in the month Demetrius, apparently the equivalent to the Attic Pyanepsion, i.e. October/November.

In choosing between AD 128/9 and AD 131/2 one factor points us to AD 131/2. With the consecration of the Olympieum in AD 131/2 and the simultaneous founding of the Panhellenion is associated an extraordinary crop of almost one hundred small altars (a high proportion of them carved from Hymettus marble) set up in Athens to Hadrian as σωτὴρ καὶ κτίστης, 'saviour and founder', and (invariably) Ὀλύμπιος, 'Olympian'.[71] Such altars are

[68] See Bowie 1982, 77–8 (Chapter 6 in Volume 3); Fein 1994, 269–70.

[69] Strabo 17.794. On the high-priest's functions cf. Rigsby 1985.

[70] *PIR* [2] I 622 and 624.

[71] Benjamin 1963, 57–86. On the Panhellenion see Spawforth and Walker 1985 and 1986; Jones 1996.

indeed found elsewhere before 131/2 (though not before AD 128/9 with the title Ὀλύμπιος) but the address Ὀλύμπιε would most aptly reflect the ceremonies in Athens in AD 131/2, at which another leading πεπαιδευμένος, the sophist and grandee from Laodicea *ad Lycum* who had based himself in Smyrna, M. Antonius Polemo, was chosen by Hadrian to deliver the oration to celebrate the inauguration of the finally completed temple of Olympian Zeus.[72] The formula 'for many years' also suggested to Buffière that a birthday might be an appropriate occasion for the poem.[73] If that guess is correct, then an exact date emerges: 24th January AD 132, Hadrian's fifty-sixth birthday.

This date and indeed the Athenian context can only be attractive possibilities. But wherever and whenever the poem was composed, it presumably presented an image of Hadrian that his equestrian official Vestinus had some reason to think was welcome to the emperor: as sacrificer, Hadrian stands in the tradition of Greek piety, as the implied reader of the poem he is assumed to belong to the connoisseurs of recondite Hellenistic poetry. Several of the rare words in Vestinus' *Altar* had also been used by Dosiadas in his:[74] πάλμυς, 'emir', had been used by Lycophron, probably taking it from Hipponax; ἶνις, 'scion', was a tragic word also exploited by Lycophron and, of course, the epigram on Amazaspus.[75]

Another dedicatory epigram from Cordoba that can be plausibly claimed to be by one of Hadrian's friends in the governing class was published in 1971. Signed by 'Arrianus, proconsul', it relates to a dedication to Artemis:

> κρέσσονά σοι χρυσοῖο καὶ ἀργύ̣ρου ἄμβροτα δῶρα
> Ἄρτεμι, καὶ θήρης πολλὸν ἀρειότ[ερα]
> Μουσάων. ἐ[χ]θρῶ̣ν̣ δ̣ὲ̣ καρήατα δῶρα κομί[ζ]ειν
> εἰς θεὸν οὐχ ὁσίη δαίστορας ἀλλοτρίων.
>
> Ἀρριανὸς ἀνθύπατος

[72] A L. Vestinus was one of the magnates who contributed sums of money to the reconstruction of buildings in Smyrna in AD 123/4, a project for which Polemo extracted assistance in kind – marble columns from the imperial quarries – from Hadrian, as attested by *IGR* iv 1431.11 = *ISmyrna* 595.11, on which see Bowie 2012g (Chapter 27 in Volume 3). Given the procurator Vestinus' presence in Athens, Rome and Egypt (where he may have monitored the despatch of the six porphyry columns of *ISmyrna* 595.43) it is surely likely that he is also the benefactor recorded in Smyrna.

[73] Buffière 1970, 138 n.1.

[74] Φώρ, 'thief' (Vestinus 26, Dosiadas 16); (ἔ)τευξε, 'constructed' (Vestinus 9, Dosiadas 3); ἶνις, 'scion' (Vestinus 19, Dosiadas 17); ἰός, 'poison' (Vestinus 24, Dosiadas 13); others echo similar words: Τριπάτωρ, 'Three-fathered' (Vestinus 26), ἀπάτωρ, 'fatherless' (Dosiadas 7); ἀείζωιον, 'living for ever' (Vestinus 16), δίζωιος, 'with two lives' (Dosiadas 17).

[75] πάλμυς Hipponax frr. 3 and 38.1 etc., Lyc. 691; ἶνις Lyc. 570.

Better than gold and silver, immortal gifts for you,
Artemis, and far finer than the catch
are those of the Muses: but to bring as gifts their enemies' heads
to the god is not right for those who feast on others' property.[76]
Arrian Proconsul

Given the interest in hunting displayed by the philosopher and historian Arrian in his Xenophontic *Cynegeticus* it is likely that this poem is by him, though attribution as well as interpretation have been much disputed since its first publication. The insistence on the superiority of literary creations to other artefacts and to ἀκροθίνια, 'best offerings', of animals, as well as being a *locus communis* of dedicatory epigram,[77] blends Arrian's belief in the primacy of λόγοι (expressed pugnaciously in his *Anabasis* 1.12) with a Stoic view he may have learned from Epictetus, i.e. that man is not master of anything outside him. It may be, as Bosworth suggests, that the reference to gold and silver is to be connected with the Celtic practice that Arrian in his *Cynegetica* tells us he adopted, of setting aside money for each animal killed, money which he then used to finance an annual sacrifice to Artemis,[78] though the reference to precious metals and to hunted animals could simply be to characteristic objects of dedication.

It is much harder to know what is being said in the second couplet. However best sense is given by reading (as above) (e.g.) ἐ̣[χ]θρῶ̣ν and καρήατα in the third line: ἐ̣[χ]θρῶ̣ν is not required by, but is compatible with, the traces, and the stone's dative καρήατι has not been accommodated in any plausible reconstruction of the couplet, requiring as it does the male dedicant to be carrying gifts (of water?) on his head in a mode that ancient practice and iconography seem to restrict to females. 'Heads', however, are regularly the objects of dedication, whether those of sacrificial or of hunted animals. It is less clear that ἐ̣[χ]θρῶ̣ν, 'of their enemies' is right, although Bosworth has made an attractive case for referring this term to predatory or destructive animals, above all to the rabbit which wreaked havoc in Spain and southern France. This interpretation involves taking δαίστορας ἀλλοτρίων, 'feasters on others' property', in apposition to καρήατα, 'heads', whereas it might rather be expected to be in apposition to ἐ̣[χ]θρῶ̣ν, and hence in the genitive. Moreover the assertion that such dedications are οὐχ ὁσίη, 'not religiously acceptable', chimes better with a depreciatory

[76] *SEG* 26.1215, *ed. pr.* Tovar 1971. For bibliography to ca. 1990 see Bosworth 1993; more recent *SEG* 46.1368*bis*.

[77] Bosworth 1993, n.72 compares *AP* 6.321 and 325 by the Julio-Claudian poet Leonides of Alexandria = *FGE* Leonides 1 and 4.

[78] *Cyn.* 34–35.1; Bosworth 1993, 239.

description of the dedicator than of the dedication. Perhaps Arrian is saying that regular consumption of animals who really belong to Artemis makes dedication of no more than their heads an act of impiety, but if so he was reversing the standard perceptions of Greco-Roman sacrifice.

Whatever the nuances, the issues of sacrifice are debated. That the debater is indeed the philosopher and historian has been doubted, most recently on the grounds that the lettering on the stone is of the third century AD,[79] but like many scholars I accept the identity. Arrian's tenure of the proconsulate of Baetica was not previously known, but can be fitted into the years before his consulate, probably ca. AD 124/5. The poem is thus almost certainly earlier than that of Vestinus, which plays with the same notion of the superiority of the Muses' creations to real objects (in Vestinus' poem altars of animal horns, lines 8–12). Although Arrian's poem was inscribed in Spain we must allow for the probability that Arrian circulated a text which Vestinus could have seen – it is unlikely in the literature-oriented Greek world of the 120s that Arrian would have restricted the readership of an epigrammatic composition to the inhabitants of an overwhelmingly Latin-speaking city in a western province.

More striking is a possible link with Hadrian's epigram composed for Trajan's dedication to Zeus Casius. That had been a dedication of silver cups and a gilded animal horn plundered from Rome's enemies, the Dacians: could it be to this that the mysterious 'enemies' in Arrian's poem alludes? In the case of the Casius epigram a literary text almost certainly circulated in Hadrian's reign, but it is probable that Arrian was himself in the Roman expeditionary force when the epigram was composed in AD 113/4. It is possible that Arrian alludes to that epigram, composed by Hadrian on Trajan's behalf, and that the phrase ἐ[χ]θρῶ̣ν̣ δ̣ὲ καρήατα means not 'enemies' [own] heads' but 'heads belonging to enemies': Arrian would be suggesting that spoils both of the hunt and of war are of questionable appropriateness as dedications.

5 Conclusion

Arrian and Vestinus are but two of a number of cases where Hadrian's interests – admittedly, in the former case, chiefly his interest in hunting – can be seen to have an impact on poetry composed by others.[80] In the context

[79] Beltran Fortes 1992. If the lettering is indeed third-century (which Birley 1997, 337 n.16 doubts), one might postulate the recutting of an inscription originally set up by a figure who was by then famous.

[80] I have explored other cases in Bowie 1990b (Chapter 14 in this volume).

of a book entitled *Greek Romans, Roman Greeks* they are as significant for their careers as for their literary output. Vestinus was a westerner of Narbonensian ancestry who divided his procuratorial career between the East and the largest Greek city of the empire, Rome, and his literary works of which we know were all in Greek. Arrian was from a family well-established in the elite of Nicomedia, though possibly of Italian descent.[81] His Latin linguistic skills must have been considerable to administer Baetica as *proconsul*, perhaps even to execute his duties as suffect consul in Rome (probably in AD 129), and he sent Hadrian reports from the Black Sea in Latin as well as in Greek.[82] Yet his substantial philosophical and historical writing was all in Greek. Though things must still have seemed different to many members of the Greek city elites, here were men for whom, as for Hadrian, the question 'Are you Roman or Greek?' would have been one to which it was impossible to give a simple answer.

[81] On Arrian's Bithynian context see Bowie 2014d (Chapter 36 in Volume 3).

[82] Arr. *Peripl. M. Eux.* 6.2, 10.1.

16 | Dionysius of Alexandria: A Greek Poet in the Roman Empire (2004)

1 Introduction

Literary works vary according to the degree to which their form or content is marked by the historical context in which they are written and the position therein occupied by their author.[*] The poem of Dionysius of Alexandria is generally considered to be at that end of the spectrum where one can only discern a minimal impact of the contemporary political situation on the work. Its apparent indifference to the Greco-Roman world of the 130s AD is such that at least one scholar has been tempted to see it as an (almost timeless?) manual, helping Greek readers of canonical texts to locate the places and peoples they encountered during their reading: 'Anders als heute stand also nicht der praktische Nutzen der Geographie im Vordergrund, sondern ihr Wert für das Verständnis der Literatur ...';[1] or else: 'Nennt auch er eine ganze Reihe von Orten, die in Homers Ilias und Odyssee, im Mythos vom Indienzug des Gottes Dionysos oder in der Sage von den Fahrten der Argonauten zu und dann mit dem Goldenen Vlies von Bedeutung sind; auch die historisch wichtigen, aber längst untergegangene Reiche etwa der Perser (1063 ff.) oder der Seleukiden (920) erwähnt er – dies alles zum Nutzen eben der literarischen Bildung seiner Lesenschaft'.[2]

Dionysius, however, took to pains to establish himself in the reader's mind as a poet writing in a precise and identifiable time and place. It is well known that the two great acrostics of the poem identify him on the one hand as a certain Dionysius who is one of the people who live below Pharos (109–33) and on the other hand register the appearance of a deity named Hermes during the reign of Hadrian (513–32). If 'Hermes' is Antinous, an

[*] This chapter was originally published in French with the title 'Denys d'Alexandrie: un poète grec dans l'empire romain' in *REA* 106: 177–85.

[1] 'Unlike today, then, it was not the practical usefulness of geography that took precedence, but its value for the understanding of literature', Brodersen 1994, 12.

[2] 'He also names a whole sequence of places that are important in Homer's *Iliad* and *Odyssey*, in the myth of Dionysus' Indian expedition, or in the saga of the journey of the Argonauts for, and then with, the Golden Fleece; he also mentions the historically important, but long since disappeared empires of the Persians (1063 ff.) or of the Seleucids (920) – all this precisely for the benefit of the literary culture of his readership', Brodersen 1994, 12–13.

identification that I still think plausible,[3] this poet is writing after October 130 and is unaware that the life of Hadrian will end in AD 138.[4] Brodersen concluded,[5] relying on the lack of any reference to Hadrian in the section on Egypt, even in the passage where Dionysius mentions the *aubade* of Memnon (249), that the composition of the poem must have predated the visit of the emperor to Egypt, and to Memnon in November 130. However, one could argue that Dionysius' decision to mention Memnon at all makes more sense if a visit by Hadrian is known to him, as it will have been to other members of the imperial entourage.

One might expect a very brief description of the emperor: but that we do not get, and, except in the second acrostic, no Roman emperor is named, and only Trajan is even mentioned, in the context of Roman victory over Parthia, Αὐσονίου βασιλῆος ἐπεπρήϋνεν ἀκωκή, 'the spear-point of the Ausonian king tamed them' (1052). By contrast, Dionysius takes time to offer us a small portrait of himself as a new Hesiod, a poet who does not need to travel in this Roman world because the Muses – or the Alexandrian Museum – provide him with all the information he needs (707–17). In addition, there are indeed some allusions to contemporary events. Are we right, then, to rally to a perspective that makes the poem as a whole a work of timeless scholarship, rather than a work alert to political issues and to the contemporary world? I shall undoubtedly yield on the 'rather than' – there is a dimension of timelessness in its aspirations. But it can also be maintained that the poem has some moral and even political messages, messages which should be far from surprising in didactic poetry in the manner of Hesiod and Apollonius.[6]

2 The March of History

Although the *Periegesis* is a geographical work in substance as well as in form, Dionysius, like Strabo before him, offers his reader a certain number of historical insights. Their position and order of appearance are significant.

Our first encounter with the human race is the brief mention of the ἀρειμανέων Ἀριμασπῶν, 'war-mad Arimaspes' (31), located at the northernmost point of the Ocean, in a harsh and unenviable climate. Next we meet the Italians in Liguria:

[3] Bowie 1990b, 77 (Chapter 14, 306 in this volume), cf. Counillon 1981.

[4] For the date of Antinous' death see Birley 1997, 247.

[5] Brodersen 1994, 11. [6] For the political element in Apollonius see Mori 2008.

> ἔνθ' Ἰταλῶν υἷῆες ἐπ' ἠπείροιο νέμονται,
> ἐκ Διὸς Αὐσονιῆες, ἀεὶ μέγα κοιρανέοντες,
> ἀρξάμενοι βορέηθεν ἔσω Λευκὴν ἐπὶ πέτρην.
>
> Then the sons of the Italians range over the mainland,
> Ausonians, descended from Zeus, for ever holding great power,
> beginning from the north right down to the White Rock.
>
> Dionysius Periegetes 77–9

The contrast between these two passages is striking. The Arimaspes are entitled only to one adjective, and their location marks them as distant and disadvantaged. They are thus a foil for the three-line description of the Italians, the first ethnic group to receive close attention, whose location is given as Italy as a whole – which will later be described in detail and with praise – and who are presented as wielding a power which is μέγα, 'great', and is theirs ἀεί, 'for ever'. Something of this contrast reappears in lines 97 and 98 between the Dalmatians who are bellicose (97) and the Italians' peninsula (98–9), not so characterised.

In the remainder of the section on the Ocean, there is a brief mention of the Pamphylians (127) and the ἄσπετα φῦλα ... Ἀσίδος αἴης, 'countless peoples of the Asian land' (138), and finally a short description of the Cimmerians of cold Crimea in the section's penultimate line (168), a conclusion which balances the mention of the Arimaspes at its beginning. But the most important human presence in this section on the Ocean is that of Dionysius himself, spelt out in the acrostic of lines 109 to 133 spanning the Eastern Mediterranean and part of the Aegean. By the end of this section, therefore, we have encountered three types of humanity: non-Greeks, far distant and plunged in the darkness of barbarism; Italians, forever all-powerful; and a Greek from Alexandria who confirms his poetry's impression of Callimachean erudition and virtuoso versification by the panache with which he accomplishes a very Hellenistic *tour de force* – an acrostic-signature.

3 Africa

Of the three continents he distinguishes, Dionysius chooses first to describe Λιβύη, 'Africa', and he decides to start by following its Mediterranean coast from West to East. Whichever way he had chosen to proceed would have entailed different consequences and opportunities. Among the advantages of the choice he made Dionysius perhaps counted the possibility of developing the model for which I will now argue.[7]

Our first detailed ethnographic description, in this section as well as in the poem as a whole, is that of the Νομάδες, 'Numidians', among whom he includes Μασαισύλιοί, 'Masaesylii', and Μασυλῆες, 'Masyleis'. The description's eight lines (186–94) offer much more detail than the brief mention of the Italians in lines 77–9, and present a vivid and successful picture of these peoples' pre-agricultural way of life: adults and children are hunter-gatherers, ignorant of the plough and the wheel, of cattle and of agriculture.

Placing these lines near the beginning of his account of Africa allows Dionysius to follow a sequence in which the advance of human civilisation matches his geographic progress Eastward. Right after these Nomads we encounter Carthage:

> τοῖς δ' ἐπὶ Καρχηδὼν πολυήρατον ἀμπέχει ὅρμον,
> Καρχηδών, Λιβύων μέν, ἀτὰρ πρότερον Φοινίκων,
> Καρχηδών, ἣν μῦθος ὑπαὶ βοῒ μετρηθῆναι.
>
> After them Carthage embraces its much-desired harbour,
> Carthage, now African, but previously Phoenician,
> Carthage, which myth has it was measured out by an ox.
>
> Dionysius Periegetes 195–7

This lively and enthusiastic sketch of Carthage, enhanced by the first of the poem's several triple (and sometimes quadruple) *epanalepses*, grabs our attention. What do we discover, and what do we not discover? The reference to its harbour and its beginnings as a Phoenician city reminds us of the importance of navigation and trade in the Greeks' image of the Phoenicians (cf. 906–9). The myth of the territory's measurement tells us that, unlike the Nomads, this society used oxen – and also reminds us of the Phoenicians' reputation for resorting to cunning. The silence over all the events that occurred after the city's foundation is deafening. Hardly anybody in the second century AD among the acquaintances of Dionysius, or indeed among the readers whom he might expect, would have been completely unaware of the wars between Carthage and Rome, of the destruction of Carthage by the Romans in 146 BC, of its Augustan *colonia* and its rebirth as a great Roman city where Latin had become the dominant language. Several readings are possible, but in my opinion the most likely is that we are expected

[7] One may add the mention of Γάδειρα (*Gades*, Cadiz) near the beginning of the poem (11). This was the birthplace Hadrian's mother Matidia: cf. Birley 1997, 253.

to see that the emergence of a mighty, eternal empire from Italy cut short the development of an African city which had made important contributions to civilisation.

This reading is perhaps reinforced by the following two historical observations. First, very briefly, in verses 204–5, the city called Neapolis by Dionysius (a name also noted by Scylax, Strabo and Ptolemy),[8] although in the 130s all but scholars must have known it under the name of Lepcis Magna, another major Roman city in the province of *Africa proconsularis*, which had been elevated by Trajan to the rank of *colonia* – *colonia Ulpia Traiana fidelis.*[9] Dionysius marks Neapolis as a neighbour of the Λωτοφάγοι, 'Lotus-eaters', and therefore linked to Odysseus' wanderings (206–7). But this mythical setting does not necessarily obliterate a reader's potential awareness of contemporary references. Moreover, the contemporary world is brought under the reader's nose by the lines that follow on the deserted houses of the Nasamones, now wiped off the world-map:

> οὓς Διὸς οὐκ ἀλέγοντας[10] ἀπώλεσεν Αὐσονὶς αἰχμή.
>
> whom, paying no heed to Zeus, the Italian spear destroyed.
>
> Dionysius Periegetes 210

The elimination of the Nasamones took place in AD 85–6: a punitive expedition by the army of the Roman emperor Domitian.[11] Dionysius certainly expects his reader to apply the principle of complementarity often evident in the Hellenistic poems that are his chief models, and to supplement this stage of destruction in reading the passage devoted to Carthage itself. If we compare them, the pictures presented of Carthage, Lepcis and the Nasamones recall different aspects of 'Romanisation', a process that Dionysius follows from an instance some 280 years before his time to a much more recent example, barely fifty years in the past when he wrote. But we know that this is a process that will be with us ἀεί, 'for ever' (78). When will it end? Who will be the next victim? It should be remembered that the city of Alexandria was not always peaceful.[12]

The reader hastily passes Cyrene (with brief mention of its Spartan origins, 213) and other peoples, before being blocked by the Nile at line 228. At

[8] Scyl. 109, 110; Str. 14.634; Ptol. *Geog.* 4.3.3. [9] *IRT* 284, 353.

[10] The phrase οὐκ ἀλέγοντας assimilates the Nasamones to the lawless Cyclopes of Od. 9.275.

[11] His *bon mot* Νασαμῶνας ἐκώλυσα εἶναι, 'I stopped the Nasamones' existence', is preserved by D.C. 67.4.6 (from Zonaras 11.19 Boissevain = iii 59 Dindorf).

[12] Cf. D.Chr. *Or.* 32.

232–7, we have a *laudatio* of the race that lives beside that river, inventors of the plough, of agriculture and of astronomy. The Egyptians – all the more effectively because they are not named, although recognisable by all – provide the summit of technical progress traced from the Nomads through the Phoenicians of Carthage. Then many details – for example Memnon and Peleus – give Egypt a Greek appearance. Thus ends the section on Africa, which invites us to ponder the relationship between Roman domination – which can inflict sudden and unforeseen destruction – and the acme of Greco-Egyptian culture.

4 The Poet's Values

What were the values of this learned poet whom the text presents to us? He prefers: (1) mild climates to harsh; (2) peace to war; (3) justice to arbitrary punishment; and, perhaps more ambiguously (4) civilisation, knowledge, and science to a primitive and ignorant lifestyle.

(1) The appalling climatic conditions faced by the Scythians (664–78) are set out in part to explain their nomadism, but Dionysius expands on the horrors of extreme cold as a subject meriting treatment in itself.

(2) As we saw earlier, the first people mentioned in the section on the Ocean are marked out as ἀρειμανέων, 'war-mad' (ἀρειμανέων Ἀριμασπῶν, 31).[13] For Dionysius, war and madness go hand in hand. He uses the adjective only one other time, in connection with the Germans who, like the Britons, live near the icy course of the Northern Ocean

Βρετανοὶ
λευκά τε φῦλα νέμονται ἀρειμανέων Γερμανῶν,
Ἑρκυνίου δρυμοῖο παραθρώσκοντες ὀρόγκους

Britons
and the white tribes of war-mad Germans range,
leaping through the mountains of the Hyrcanian forest.
Dionysius Periegetes 284–6

A similar link with Ares is invented for the Sarmatians/Sauromatae, ἐσθλὸν ἐνυαλίου γένος Ἄρεος, 'a noble race of Ares, god of war' (654). Good warriors are repeatedly presented as scary.

[13] For the rare ἀρειμανέων cf. its application to the Gauls by the elegiac poet Simylus (in the same *sedes*), cited by Plu. *Rom.* 17.7.

(3) For Dionysius' preference for justice we can think of the Nasamones (209) and Sybaris (372 –4).[14]

(4) The Massagetae (740–6) are men whom Dionysius would not wish to meet either one of his friends or himself – they are both unique for their hostility towards strangers and (this is the explanation, γάρ) they feast not on wheat and wine, but on milk mixed with horse-blood. We have already seen the contrast between the pre-agricultural Nomads (186–94) and the highly inventive Egyptians (232–7). The Chinese also arouse Dionysius' admiration: they have gone beyond the use of leather and wool, and weave clothes in dazzling and fresh colours with what must be silk, even if Dionysius' description of the origin of this material suggests rather cotton (752–8).

For Dionysius, therefore, just and peaceful men, living in a mild climate and in a technologically advanced society, are more admirable than a bellicose, under-developed or unjust people. He leaves it to his reader to decide where to place Greeks and Romans respectively according to this set of criteria.

5 Greek, Roman, or Greco-Roman?

To almost any contemporary Greek speaker an important characteristic of the world described by Dionysius was that almost half of this world was ruled by Rome, the remainder not. Despite the references to the great and eternal reign of the 'Ausonians', to the destruction inflicted by them on the Nasamones, to their supremacy imposed on the Parthians, and to Rome as ἐμῶν μέγαν οἶκον ἀνάκτων, | μητέρα πασάων πολίων, 'the mighty home of my lords, | the mother of all cities' (355–6), this fundamental division is never recognised. For some near-contemporaries, the empire was bounded by great rivers. For Dio of Prusa, the Danube marks the border between Rome and the Getae;[15] for Tacitus, *mari Oceano aut longinquis amnibus saeptum imperium*, 'the empire is hedged about by the sea of the Ocean or by long rivers';[16] for Aelius Aristides, Ares ἐπὶ ταῖς ὄχθαις τῶν ἔξω ποταμῶν χορεύει τὴν ἄπαυστον χορείαν, 'dances his dance without rest on the banks of the outer rivers'.[17] Dionysius, by contrast, often draws attention to the

[14] Like the Nasamones their behaviour provoked the anger of Zeus (in this case the Olympian, not the Roman emperor), Διὸς μέγα χωσαμένοιο.

[15] D.Chr. *Or.* 12.16–20.

[16] Tac. *Ann.* 1.9, cf. 2.61 *Romani imperi, quod nunc rubrum ad mare patescit*, 'the Roman empire, which now stretches uninterrupted to the Persian Gulf'.

[17] Aristid. *Or.* 26.105 Keil, where I have emended the MS reading ἔξω τῶν ποταμῶν, 'outside the rivers', to τῶν ἔξω ποταμῶν.

way in which a river divides a territory – for example the Tiber (354) – but he never notes this fact for the three great border rivers of the empire, the Rhine, the Danube, and the Euphrates. The same is true of his mention of the Red Sea and the Nile cataracts, which are seen by Aelius Aristides as borders.[18]

On the other hand, Dionysius constantly reminds us of (a) the Greek *diaspora*, (b) the power and demise of previous empires, and (c) the bond constituted by Greek religion:

(a) The toponym Canopus is linked to the name of Menelaus' pilot, originally from Amyclae in Laconia (13); Cyrene is reported as a Spartan foundation (213); Alexandria is praised as a Μακηδόνιον πτολίεθρον, 'Macedonian city' (254); the river Eridanus river (the Po) is associated with the Greek myth of Phaethon and the Heliads (289–91); the Tauri of the Black Sea with Achilles' δρόμος, 'running track' (306). Although the Tiber Valley itself is ceded to the Latins (350), the men between these and the Etruscans are identified as Pelasgians (347–8), presumably Evander's Arcadians, and Dionysius' choice of identifying the cities of the Bay of Naples by the siren Parthenope (357–8) reminds us of their strongly Hellenic ancestry. As for the Romans themselves, they are always 'Ausonians': Αὐσονιῆες (78, 333, 467), Αὐσόνιοι (98, 1052), Αὐσονὶς αἰχμή, 'the Ausonian spear' (210) or ἄκρη, 'peninsula' (339), and their country is Αὐσονίη, 'Ausonia' (366, 383, 472). The name's mythological origin is the son of Odysseus and Circe.[19] From line 472 these Ausonians disappear from the text, only to reappear once, in 1052. But places Greek continue to occupy centre stage. I give only three examples. When mentioning Sinope, Dionysius reminds us that this Milesian colony took its name from of one of the daughters of the Boeotian river Asopus (775); introducing Selge, he recalls that it was a Spartan foundation (859–60); and he expands his notice on Tarsus with a reference to the Greek myth of Bellerophon (868–71).

(b) The Persians are distinguished from other peoples of Asia by their royal race and from all other peoples by the unheard-of wealth they acquired when they conquered Lydia and sacked Sardis:

[18] ἐρυθρά τε θάλαττα καὶ Νείλου καταρράκται καὶ λίμνη Μαιῶτις, ἃ τοῖς πρότερον ἐν πέρασι γῆς ἠκούετο, ἴσα καὶ αὐλῆς ἑρκία τῆιδε τῆι πόλει, 'the Persian Gulf and the Nile's cataracts and Lake Maeotis, which were previously talked of as at the ends of the earth, are now like courtyard walls for this city', Aristid. *Or.* 26.28

[19] Servius on *Aen.* 8.328, Σ *Aen.* 3.171.

μοῦνοι γάρ τ' Ἀσίης βασιλεύτατον ἔθνος ἔχουσι,
μοῦνοι δ' ἄσπετον ὄλβον ἐνὶ μεγάροισιν ἔθεντο,
ὁππότε Μηιονίην καὶ Σάρδιας ἐξαλάπαξαν.

For they alone have the most royal race of Asia,
they alone have stored away unspeakable wealth in their palaces,
when they sacked Maeonia and Sardis.

Dionysius Periegetes 1056–8

These lines sum up the greatness and decline of the empire controlled by Lydia – a region that some 200 lines earlier (830–45) Dionysius had ranked among the most fortunate by enthusiastically flagging its gold, the singing swans of the Maeander marshlands, and its beautiful young women dancing in Dionysiac choruses. But by evoking the greatness of the Persian Empire these lines also remind readers of its fall. It is also possible that the brief mention of Babylon (980, 1005–13), fortified by Semiramis with invincible walls (1005–6), is calculated in part to remind the reader how this empire too had disappeared, however invincible the walls were hoped to be. As for the end of the Persian Empire, this is implicit in the mentions of Alexandria – first, allusively, in line 13, next with more detail in lines 254–9 – then in the Seleucid toponyms of lines 918–20, and finally, towards the end of the poem, when Dionysius briefly describes the immense and inaccessible rock Aornis (1149–51). This rock is only known in connection with the oriental conquests of Alexander,[20] although Dionysius may be confusing a Bactrian with an Indian site. Even if the poet nowhere mentions these conquests explicitly, the mention of the rock Aornis is certainly intended to awaken thoughts of the Macedonian expansion of the Greek world, introduced first by Canopus' mention in line 13, and to remind us that the Macedonians carried Greek government and the Greek language much further East even than Rome. The following lines could perhaps confirm this idea: Dionysius describes a sacred place beside the Ganges where rituals are performed commemorating the military conquest of Dionysus and his Λῆναι, 'Maenads'. This episode, and the main part of the poem, then end with the erection by Dionysus of two columns at the ends of the earth and his celebratory return to the mighty course of the Theban river Ismenus (1161–5).

What is Dionysius doing? On the one hand, he locates the story on a timeless mythological level. But the Indian expedition of Dionysus was sometimes considered a harbinger of Alexander's, and its triumphant conclusion,

[20] D.S. 11.85, Plu. *Alex.* 58, [Plu.] *Reg. imp. ap.* 25 = *Mor.* 181c.

like the return of the protagonist to the Greek city which Alexander sacked, also reminds readers of *his* Eastern conquests. Furthermore, Dionysius thus situates his poem in the context of Greek religion with its Olympian pantheon. Dionysius mentions almost all the Greek gods in his poem, although usually only once, as if to make sure they are not forgotten. A whole troop of gods is mentioned in connection with Troy – built by Poseidon and Apollo, destroyed by Athena and Hera (817–8): Hera was also mentioned at 141, Poseidon reappears at 917. Soon after, Artemis appears as the divinity of Ephesus (827), designated by her epithet Ἰοχέαιρα, 'Arrow-shooter' (cf. Il. 21.480 where, as here, this epithet alone identifies the goddess). At 853 Aphrodite is introduced by her matronymic Διωναίη, 'daughter of Dione', in connection with her cult at Aspendus; Ares we have already met at lines 653–4 in connection with the Sauromatae. Hephaestus and Demeter are honoured with a place in the second acrostic (513–32), the former as the god of Lemnos (522), the latter in connection with Thasos (523).[21] Hermes is absent only until we have deciphered the second acrostic. In contrast to these almost passing mentions, Zeus and Dionysus are each entitled to multiple appearances. For Zeus, king of the gods, this is easily explained. But why Dionysus? Brodersen suggested that the poet knew of Hadrian's interest in Dionysus, but such an interest does not stand out in Hadrian's religious activities. The answer is certainly the same as for the mention of Apollo in the first line of the epic which was one of Dionysius' chief models, the *Argonautica* of Apollonius of Rhodes: Dionysius felt a special bond with the god to whom he owed his name. This explains well the exuberance with which Dionysiac mythology and rituals are narrated, frequently and in passages of disproportionate length.[22]

6 Conclusion

To what extent can these observations help to define the position taken by Dionysius' poem towards the Roman world of the 130s? It is a poem that embeds itself firmly in the Greek cultural tradition, not only through its complex reinvestment of the language and themes of earlier hexametric poetry – Homer, Hesiod, Apollonius of Rhodes, Nicander – but also through its frame of reference. Roman power based in Italy is admittedly

[21] The mention of Attic river Ilissus (423) might also allude to Demeter, and the Chalybes (768–71) to Hephaestus.

[22] 700–5, 830–45, 939–53, 1142–4, 1160–5.

mentioned, and its capacity for retaliation and destruction is emphasised rather than concealed. But despite the epithet phrase μέγα κοιρανέοντες, 'holding great power' (78), its spatial extent is not explored, and the idea that it is ἐκ Διός … ἀεί, 'of divine origin … eternal' (78), is undermined by the occasional mention of other empires that collapsed. What seems to be both more solid and much larger is a Greek world whose history dates back to the Trojan War, and which has left its mark on other ἔθνη ranging from Tartessus/Cadiz in the West to the Indus to the East, and from the Black Sea to the Nile. The glimpses of Greek myths and history that Dionysius on occasion offers closely resemble those found in Greek novels, another genre of literature remarkably silent on Rome and the Romans: they choose episodes that even a modestly educated person would recognise immediately, and in Dionysius these details on which he zooms in seem to me to have the dual function of embellishing the poem and of offering the reader a means of relating it to other more familiar subjects. They contribute to the arachnid network of Hellenism which, like his Chinese who emulate spiders (757), Dionysius, weaving his many diverse threads, reveals as covering the whole world.

17 Luxury Cruisers? Philip's Epigrammatists between Greece and Rome (2012)

1 Introduction

This paper discusses some of the poets in the *Garland of Philip*, Greek epigrammatists, or epigrammatists writing in Greek, in the long century from the 60s BC to the 50s AD. The phrase 'luxury cruiser' is intended to open up a number of issues. Thinking of one, colloquial sense of 'cruiser', I wondered whether the epigrams gave any evidence of their poets seeing Rome and Italy as a goal for the pursuit of high-quality, or at least highly-priced, consumer commodities, not excluding sexual conquests: how far could their erotic poetry be fitted into any model of this sort? But I also wanted to see whether any of these Greeks could be seen to be approaching a visit to Italy as high-class and more cultural tourism: are they rich Greeks swanning round Italy in a Hellenic cruising mode, keen to present themselves as Hellenes and especially interested in Italian and Roman appropriation of Greek culture? And if there turned out to be evidence for their membership of local elites, how far is it a reason for questioning or modifying one predominant model offered by scholars and historians for these poets' relationship with prominent Romans, that of client and patron?

My discussion of Crinagoras here shares much with some other work where I compare Crinagoras' career and production with those of two other literary figures from first century BC Mytilene, Theophanes and Potamon:[1] it seems to me important to discuss him both in that Mytilenean context and in the context of other Greek epigrammatic poets, as is attempted here.

[1] Bowie 2011b (Chapter 26 in Volume 3). This chapter has benefited from discussion with the graduate students at the University of Michigan, Ann Arbor, who participated in a seminar on the *Garland of Philip* I ran in the first months of 2010, and from feedback at a conference organised in Florence by Georgetown University in 2007. I was also stimulated by the oral version, delivered at a conference in Bonn in 2006, of Whitmarsh 2011, though that written version only appeared when this chapter was already in proof for *Aevum Antiquum*. I would certainly have made some points differently had I read that version, and doubtless I would have approached Crinagoras differently if I had had the benefit of using Ypsilanti 2018. Among Philip's poets whom I do not discuss is Archias, earlier than even Philodemus: on him see Penzel 2006. The whole issue of the relations between Greek intellectuals and Roman patrons is well discussed by Bady 2021.

Most of Philip's *Garland* poets do indeed share interesting features with Crinagoras. The origins assigned to them in the *Anthology* and occasional flashes of local colour in their poems associate them with the northern Aegean and the Propontis, i.e. with Macedonia, above all Thessalonica, with the Thracian coastline between Thessalonica and the Dardanelles, and with Byzantium and Nicaea.[2] Only a few poems bring their readers south down the eastern coast of the Aegean into *provincia Asia* and as far south as Samos and Rhodes, and of all these epigrams not many offer unambiguous indications of travel to Rome and Italy.

Section 2 will discuss these indications, and evidence for relations with Romans who might be considered to be 'patrons'. Section 3 explores the epigrammatists' various modes of self-presentation as self-consciously Greek poets writing in and primarily for a Greek world.

2 Italy, Rome and the Caesars

My key exhibits in this section are few: Aemilianus, Antipater of Thessalonica, Antiphilus of Byzantium, Apollonides of Nicaea, Crinagoras of Mytilene, Diodorus of Sardis, Erucius (perhaps of Cyzicus), Honestus (probably of Corinth), Lollius Bassus, Macedonius of Thessalonica, Philip of Thessalonica himself, Philodemus of Gadara, and (Antonius?) Thallus of Miletus. Some of these poets make at most only a slight contribution, but for convenience I shall review all in alphabetical order, both here and in the following section. It would of course be helpful to be able to examine them in chronological order, but about some poets too little is known to achieve this goal, about others nothing at all. I set out a tentative chronology in the Appendix.

Aemilianus

Of this Nicaean poet's three epigrams one (*GP* 3 = *AP* 9.756) is a four-liner on Praxiteles' marble *Sileni*. If this is the sculpture owned by Asinius Pollio,[3] it can be added to the dossier of works of art seen by one of our poets in Rome (discussed shortly in connection with Antipater).

[2] For the Greek culture of Bithynia in the first two centuries AD, and for Nicaea's predominance, see Bowie 2014d (Chapter 36 in Volume 3), 2022c.

[3] Plin. *Nat.* 36.23, cf. *GP* ii 16.

Antipater (active ca. 12–1 BC)

Antipater's poetry illustrates more than any other's the functioning of 'patronage'. Like Philodemus, discussed below, he had a 'patron' among the Calpurnii Pisones, Piso the Pontifex, consul in 15 BC, the son of Philodemus' Piso, and the father of the Gaius celebrated by Apollonides *GP* 26 = *AP* 10.19.[4] In 11 BC Piso's eventual victory over the Bessi earned him *ornamenta triumphalia*, 'triumphal honours', a *supplicatio*, 'ritual thanksgiving',[5] and a work by Antipater celebrating his campaign which may have been either a poem or a prose history: a six-line epigram composed to accompany this work's presentation to Piso (*GP* 1 = *AP* 9.428), establishes Thessalonica as Antipater's origin. Several other epigrams show Antipater treating Piso as his *patronus*, epigrams that flattered him and accompanied presents suitable for a martial hero. *GP* 41 = *AP* 6.335 came with a Macedonian καυσία, the broad-brimmed white felt hat regularly worn by Macedonian kings, among them Alexander himself; *GP* 42 = *AP* 9.552 accompanied a sword that was apparently claimed once to have belonged to Alexander.[6] It is reasonable to suppose that both these were gifts from Antipater to Piso, as is explicitly the case with the candle given at the Saturnalia and accompanied by *GP* 45 = *AP* 6.249,[7] and with the birthday-present book accompanied by *GP* 31 = *AP* 9.93, a volume he claims to have fashioned (πονησάμενος) in a single night. The gift of the antique sword suggests that Antipater himself was not poor. Antipater also, however, composed poems to go with others' gifts to Piso: *GP* 44 = *AP* 9.541 to go with a gift of a pair of bowls by The(i)ogenes; *GP* 43 = *AP* 6.241 to go with a helmet seemingly given by Pylaemenes, son of the Galatian king Amyntas, and perhaps to be associated with an appointment of Piso as *legatus Galatiae*, 'legate of Galatia'.[8] Both The(i)ogenes[9] and Pylaemenes take us into the circle of Augustus, and it is not surprising to find two poems for

[4] See p. 364.

[5] D.C. 54.34. 5–7. Gow–Page's notion that Piso was awarded a triumph betrays misunderstanding of the Augustan context. For the problem of correctly assigning epigrams to Antipater of Thessalonica and Antipater of Sidon see Argentieri 2003.

[6] The scepticism of *GP* ii 53 is excessive: the issue is not whether this could really have been Alexander's but whether it could have been claimed to have been.

[7] On this poem see Plastira 1982.

[8] As *GP* ii 54 remark, the ἐκ of ἐκ Πυλαιμένεος (3) could be used either of a former owner or of a donor, but the latter seems much more likely, and they are surely right to see in Pylaemenes not the Paphlagonian of Il. 2.851 but, following Cichorius 1922, 328–9, the son of the Galatian tetrarch Amyntas. For Piso in Galatia see Syme 1986, 332–3, castigating *GP*.

[9] If he is the *mathematicus*, 'astrologer', Theogenes who predicted greatness for Octavian at Apollonia (Suet. *Aug.* 94.12), as guessed by Brunck and made probable by the bowls' astronomical decoration.

Gaius Caesar, probably composed around 1 BC, *GP* 46 = *AP* 9.59 and *GP* 47 = *AP* 9.297. Some of these poems were very probably composed in the East, especially those relating to Piso's Thracian campaigns. But at least three poems suggest that Antipater spent some time in Italy. *GP* 40 = *AP* 10.25 is a poem addressed to Phoebus in Cephallenia, praying for a good voyage to Asia for Piso in his *navis longa*, 'warship', and for Antipater following as his *comes*, 'companion'. The date is likely to be around 10–8 BC.[10] The couplet *GP* 29 = *APl.* 143 asks the reader to imagine – ἴδε, 'see!' – a painting of Medea contemplating infanticide: this is probably the painting by Timomachus that had been in Rome in the temple of Venus Genetrix since soon after that temple's dedication in 46 BC.[11] The poem on the pantomime Bathyllus (*GP* 78 = *APl.* (A) 290), praised for his effect on Italian audiences, is a third that surely belongs in an Italian and probably Roman context.[12]

Given these poems' implications, the house of Piso in which stood the statue of Dionysus which speaks the first couplet of *GP* 30 = *APl.* (A) 184 should be taken to be his house in Rome. Ann Kuttner has made the exciting suggestion that some of Antipater's poems should be interpreted as responses to statues and a tree in the portico and garden-complex associated with the theatre of Pompey. The strongest case is that for the epigram on the nine women poets, *GP* 19 = *AP* 9.206 to be read as an 'ekphrastic address' to nine statues of poetesses attested as there, with others, by Tatian.[13] These nine will have been pendants to the nine statues of the Muses that we know from other evidence to have been there, and to which the last two lines of *GP* 19 = *AP* 9.206 may allude.[14] Kuttner rightly insists (against the weaker reading of *GP* ii 36) that the deictic τάσδε, 'these', that opens the first line, followed by ἴδε, 'behold', in line 7, establishes these as 'images before which the poet stands'. Alongside this very attractive case she also proposed a possible reference to these same Muses in *GP* 90 = *APl.* (A) 220, and further references to a plane-tree in the garden of this complex in the plane-tree poems of Antonius Thallus, *GP* 5 = *AP* 9.220, and Antipater, *GP* 35 = *AP* 9.231.[15]

[10] Cichorius 1922, 326.

[11] For the epigrams on Timomachus' *Medea* see Gutzwiller 2004, Gurd 2007. It is hard to tell from his phraseology at *De aud. poet.* 3 = *Mor.* 18a whether Plutarch had himself seen the painting.

[12] *GP* 107 = *AP* 7.692 on the death of the Pergamene pancratiast Glycon also refers to his winning in Italian contests, but this does not require the poet's presence in Italy. As *GP* ii 104 note, the reference to Glycon by Horace in *Ep.* 1.1.30 suggests Glycon was still alive when that book was completed in 20 BC.

[13] *Ad Graecos* 33. The proposal was already made by Whittaker 1982, 61.

[14] Kuttner 1999, 361. On *GP* 19 see also Gosetti-Murrayjohn 2006.

[15] Kuttner 1999, 363 and 364–5.

A sceptic might wish to protest that there is no hint in any of the poems of the Pompeian location – the only clearly Pompeian connection in Antipater's surviving oeuvre is *GP* 16 = *AP* 7.185, a sepulchral poem on an African slave of a Pompeia whom Cichorius had simply conjectured to be the daughter of Sextus Pompeius and mother-in-law of Piso the Pontifex.[16] It is an attractive and plausible enough conjecture, but the name Pompeius is too common for much to be hung on it. As to the overlap between Tatian's fifteen names of women poets and Antipater's nine, we must reckon with the possibility that both draw on a canon of nine women poets constructed to balance that of the nine lyric poets (found in *AP* 9.184 and 571) and that Tatian's list might indeed catalogue fifteen who were commemorated by sculptures in the Pompeian complex whereas Antipater's nine do not.[17]

That said, the *Medea* poem already mentioned (*GP* 29 = *APl.* 143) does indeed seem to stem from observation of a painting in Rome, and Kuttner has pointed to other Roman monuments to which epigrams may refer – Niobids (*GP* 22 = *AP* 7.530), the cows on the Palatine that could have provoked Antipater's contribution to the Myron's cow series (*GP* 84 = *AP* 9.728), and perhaps the Apollo of Onatas (*GP* 83 = *AP* 9.238).[18] She would add *GP* 9 = *AP* 6.208, a description of a painting apparently by Aristomenes of Thasos, in which three citizen women, once *hetaerae*, 'courtesans', make offerings to Aphrodite in gratitude for having each found a husband. But although this painting could well be imagined to have been transplanted to a Roman temple of Venus there is no evidence that it ever was: Antipater may know it from a Greek sanctuary.[19]

If there is a case for some of Antipater's epigrams responding to Pompey's theatre and to some other Roman sites that displayed Greek works of art, then one or two further possibilities might be considered tentatively.

Several male poets are commemorated by Antipater: Homer (*GP* 72 = *APl.* 296), Alcman (*GP* 12 = *AP* 7.18), Stesichorus (*GP* 74 = *AP* 7.75), Pindar (*GP* 75 = *APl.* (A) 305) and Aeschylus (*GP* 13 = *AP* 7.79). Some of these might be candidates for statues or paintings in Pompey's theatre. But only that on Pindar, addressing him in the second person, is a strong claimant (as the lemma in the Planudean collection indicates: εἰς εἰκόνα Πινδάρου, 'on a statue

[16] Cichorius 1922, 330 and 340.

[17] For the view that there were in all fourteen statues of women poets, of whom Antipater picked out nine to correspond to the nine Muses, see Geiger 2021.

[18] But if Antipater saw this in Rome it was surely a copy, since the bronze original was in Pergamum, Paus. 8.42.7.

[19] It is also possible (no more) that the scene of Leander's crossing, Hero's tower, and their tomb (*GP* 11 = *AP* 7.666) represents a painting (see *GP* ii 29) seen by Antipater in Rome.

of Pindar'); that on Homer, reviewing rival birthplaces, is a close second. The epigram on Alcman makes specific reference to the appearance of his tomb (and reworks a similar poem of Leonidas),[20] while those on Stesichorus and Aeschylus identify where they were buried. One might guess that Antipater breathed new life into the conventional poem on tombs of great men by picking poets with whose statues Piso and other potential readers were familiar from Pompey's theatre, but it would be no more than a guess.

Second stand trees. Was the plane-tree alone? The speaking laurel (*GP* 27 = *AP* 9.282) locates itself specifically near a river whose source, adjacent to a wood, is implied not to be distant: this is not compatible with a location in Pompey's theatre, but might fit the area of *Lucus Egeriae*. Less specific are the complaining walnut tree (*GP* 106 = *AP* 9.3) and the monitory poplar (*GP* 81 = *AP* 9.706): the former's reference to attacks by passing children perhaps excludes a Pompeian setting, but the latter's reference simply to a 'passer-by' (παρερχόμενος, line 1) does not. If, as seems possible, Antipater had a sequence of tree-poems, it would be hard to claim a Pompeian context for all of them; but it is conceivable that a reader located in Rome would be inclined to associate all with a number of Roman settings.

Finally, the unusual evocation of another product of human τέχνη, 'skill', a watermill (*GP* 82 = *AP* 9.418). We know from Strabo that Mithridates had built a watermill at Cabira, presumably seen by Pompey's troops; Vitruvius describes such mills' construction; and by Pliny's time they are in use in Italy.[21] That Pompey should have put one on show in some relation to the water-system of his theatre would be far from surprising.

That Antipater visited Rome and composed several poems there should be accepted. But how much time he spent there, whether as Piso's guest or *proprio motu*, remains uncertain, and we cannot tell if he was allowed to participate in Piso's notorious binge-drinking.[22] But some at least of the opulent environment and artistic display in which Antipater found himself filters into his poems. Without the knowledge of a philosophical commitment such as gives Philodemus' stay in Rome and Italy a seriousness that may outweigh hints that he was lured by the high life of Rome and the bay of Naples, the profile of Antipater as it is conveyed by the poetry alone might suggest that he is more of a 'luxury cruiser' than Philodemus, albeit one with a strong interest in high Hellenic culture. But our lack of other testimony on Antipater makes such a verdict extremely precarious.

[20] *AP* 7.19 = Leonidas *HE* 57. [21] Str. 12.556, Vitr. 10.5.2, Plin. *Nat.* 18.197.
[22] Sen. *Ep.* 83.14, Plin. *Nat.* 14.145, Suet. *Tib.* 42.

Antiphilus (active ca. 33–53 AD)

Antiphilus' activity seems to be almost half a century later than that of Antipater; his city of origin Byzantium; his range of reference predominantly the Propontis, the Dardanelles and mainland Greece as far south as the Euboean Euripus.[23] His date seems to be secured by *GP* 6 = *AP* 9.178, probably a response to Nero's speech in the Roman senate in AD 53 which secured the restoration of the status of *civitas libera*, 'free city', to Rhodes.[24] More probably this adds Rhodes, not Rome, to Antiphilus' geographical range. But a visit to Rome is indeed indicated by a poem on Timomachus' *Medea*, *GP* 48 = *APl.* 136, eight lines as against the single couplet by Antipater (see earlier with n.9), and a visit to Italy by *GP* 3 = *AP* 7.379, praising the huge mole that formed the harbour of Dicaearcheia/Puteoli. There is no reason to agree with *GP* that such a poem would be unlikely after work on the development of Ostia started in AD 42: but if the Sabinus of *GP* 40 = *AP* 9.306 is the Poppaeus Sabinus whose career took him to Macedonia – and this identification is quite uncertain – then it, at least, must have been composed before Sabinus' death in AD 34.[25] This would spread Antiphilus' epigrammatic activity over at least two decades (ca. AD 33–53).

Within his oeuvre, however, there is no hint of his appreciation of the luxury or elegance of life in Rome and Italy; he may, after all, only have made a single visit. But as the discussion of Hellenism in the third section of this paper indicates, his epigrams project their poet as a Greek, and cater to an audience steeped in Greek culture, to a greater degree than those of any other of my poets. That of course does not establish that they were conceived only or even primarily for a Greek audience. But for the moment I am inclined to classify Antiphilus as a highly cultured Hellenic cruiser rather than as a Greek whose defining characteristic is seeking pleasure or patronage in Italy.

Apollonides of Nicaea (active ?ca. 10 BC–AD 10)

Apollonides' Nicaean origin is conjectural: it depends on whether he is the same man as the writer of a commentary on Timon of Phlius dedicated to Tiberius Caesar, known from Diogenes Laertius.[26] Although Apollonides

[23] For the rare toponyms Pytheion and Triton in *GP* 11 see Robert 1979.

[24] Tac. *Ann.* 12.53, cf. *IG* xii 1.2 lines 12–14 and the discussion in *GP* ii 120. For the bearing (or not) of *GP* 6 on Nero's self-identification with Helios see Champlin 2003, 281.

[25] Macedonia, Tac. *Ann.* 1.80; death, ibid. 6.49.

[26] D.L. 9.109. The identification was proposed by Bowersock 1965, 134, with a useful assessment of Tiberius' philhellenism. The Stoic Apollonides of Smyrna mentioned in Plu. *Cat. Min.* 65.6 and 69, and canvassed by Herrmann 1951, is surely too early.

honours eminent Romans with poems, there is no sign that he went to Italy, and where we find local colour it is Aegean, as in the two of his several poems on drowning, one of a Milesian Diphilus off Andros (*GP* 7 = *AP* 7.631) and the other of a Samian Menoetius between Syros and Delos (*GP* 8 = *AP* 7.642). A visit to Rhodes during or after Tiberius' long stay there (6 BC–AD 2) seems likely from a poem about the eagle that alighted on the roof of Tiberius' house (*GP* 23 = *AP* 9.287), but the story's appearance in Suetonius (*Tib.* 14) shows that it travelled, and it thus does not prove Apollonides' own presence in Rhodes. He is unusual, however, in showing knowledge of Cercaphus son of Helios both there and in another poem, *GP* 28 = *APl.* (B) 49. This latter poem compares Leon, a descendant of Cercaphus, to Cinyras, Ganymede and Paris, and may well be taken as evidence of the obvious fact that travel to Italy was not needed to find handsome boys, though we cannot tell from the poem whether this is a young person who has really aroused Apollonides' passion, or whether the poet is rather offering traditional Hellenic praise of the son of a host, friend or even potential 'patron'. That the latter is possible is a salutary reminder that forms of patronage were as important within Greek society as they were between Greeks and Romans or Italians.

Apart from his eagle-poem (*GP* 23 = *AP* 9.287), Apollonides has three other epigrams that might show him seeking patronage from highly placed Romans. The sea-girt temple of Aphrodite celebrated by *GP* 25 (= *AP* 9.791) is credited to a Postumus, plausibly argued by Cichorius, followed by *GP*, to be C. Vibius Postumus, proconsul of Asia AD 13–15.[27] The father of the Gaius whose first shave is commemorated in *GP* 26 (= *AP* 10.19) has been argued, also by Cichorius,[28] to be L. Calpurnius Piso Frugi the Pontifex, consul 15 BC, also at some time after 8 BC proconsul of Asia. This same Piso was also 'patron' to Antipater (see above), and Apollonides' claim that his 'elegies' are no worse gifts to Gaius than the family's gifts of gold clearly implies a close relationship of some sort with the Calpurnii Pisones.[29] Cichorius suggested that the Laelius whose astonishment at the river Eurotas seemingly provoked him to become a poet in the enigmatic poem *GP* 21 = *AP* 9.280 was D. Laelius Balbus, *cos.* 6 BC, perhaps passing through Laconia *en route* to a post as proconsul of Asia 'in den ersten Jahre n.Chr.'.[30] Both that post and the journey are conjectural, though Laelius'

[27] Cichorius 1922, 336. [28] Cichorius 1922, 337–41.

[29] For the analogy of Horace's relations to his 'patrons' note Murray 1985, 47 and Barchiesi 1996, 28. For the fate of the Gaius in question see Syme 1987, 197.

[30] Cichorius 1922, 336–7.

consular status is secured by Apollonides' punning phrase ὕπατον κλέος, 'highest/consular renown' (line 1). We can only guess whether Apollonides got as far south as Sparta and witnessed the supposed occasion himself.

None of these poems helps establish Apollonides' level in society to the point where we could refine the term 'patron'. All this makes it very hard to evaluate his poem (*GP* 20 = *AP* 7.233) about Aelius, a high-ranking military Roman officer (Apollonides uses the term πρόμος, 'leader') who fell on his sword rather than die of disease.

Crinagoras (active ca. 47–?10 BC)

Crinagoras, son of Callippus, of Mytilene is one of the earliest and at the same time one of the best documented of Philip's poets. He served on an embassy from Mytilene to Caesar in 47 BC and 45 BC, and was again a legate to Augustus in Spain in 26–5 BC. In 47 BC he seems still to have been in his twenties, and he may possibly have lived until at least AD 13 – a date based on the identification of the Selene who has just died in *GP* 18 = *AP* 7.633 with Cleopatra Selene (who died not earlier than AD 11),[31] and of the campaign of a Germanicus in GP 26 = *AP* 9.283 with that of Germanicus in AD 13.[32] But both identifications are very precarious, and for Syme 'nothing precludes Drusus' Alpine campaign of 15 BC' being the subject of *GP* 26 = *AP* 9.283.[33] Crinagoras' youth at the time of the first two embassies is consonant with the fact that on the second of these he is named seventh out of eight, whereas a man who must have been his relation, Phaenias son of Phaenias son of Callippus, is listed second to Potamon. From his many years of contact with powerful Romans fifty-one epigrams of Crinagoras have been transmitted *via* the *Garland* of Philip, though of these the only poem that can be dated with complete confidence is *GP* 10 = *AP* 6.161, celebrating the first cutting of Marcellus' beard when he returned from the Cantabrian war in 25 BC at the age of eighteen.[34]

This poem, however, is one of several that demonstrate Crinagoras to be directing some of his epigrams to the *domus Augusta*, 'house of Augustus'. Another early poem is *GP* 29 = *AP* 9.149, apparently composed on the edge of the Pyrenees to celebrate the waters that Augustus resorted to in 25 BC as a cure for his grave illness, perhaps already on the prescription of Antonius

[31] *GP* ii 225–6. [32] *GP* ii 234. [33] Syme 1986, 347.
[34] For the participation of Tiberius and Marcellus in this war cf. D.C. 53.2.

Musa, who saved his life in 23 BC.[35] They were thereafter called 'The Waters of Augustus'.[36] The assault of *GP* ii 238 on the poem's quality is excessive. *GP* 28 = *APl.* 61 celebrates the victories of a Nero on the Rhine and the Araxes – certainly Tiberius Claudius Nero, probably in 16 BC, though conceivably as late as 9 BC.[37] It too is straightforwardly encomiastic. But in two other epigrams Crinagoras takes the opportunity to confront young members of Augustus' family with major figures of Greek culture. *GP* 11 = *AP* 9.545 is a six-liner to accompany the gift to Marcellus of a copy of Callimachus' *Hecale*; its second couplet brings together the eponym of the Attic deme, Hecale, the name of the greatest Attic hero, Theseus, and the historically resonant toponym Marathon. The ephebic Theseus is held up as an exemplar for the ephebic Marcellus,[38] and the τορευτὸν ἔπος, 'chiselled verse', of Callimachus in hexameters is hinted to be a model for the elegiac verse of Crinagoras himself. Crinagoras' chiselling includes a Homeric lengthening of the epsilon at the end of Μάρκελλε before the combination of mute plus liquid at the beginning of κλεινοῦ (as *GP* note, 'highly abnormal').[39] The emphasis on Hecale's warm hospitality may prompt reflections on the relations between Crinagoras and Marcellus: are these a mirror-image reversal, with the ageing Crinagoras (now perhaps approaching fifty) enjoying the luxury of the young Marcellus' house in Rome, or does he expect the young Marcellus to visit his own modest abode, as Philodemus had earlier invited his patron Piso?[40]

Similarly *GP* 7 = *AP* 9.239 is written to go with a gift of an edition of Anacreon in five books to an Antonia, perhaps Antonia Minor,[41] daughter of the triumvir Antonius and Octavia, on some special occasion. The choice of a canonical Greek poet, famous for the poetry of wine, love and

[35] Suet. *Aug.* 81, D.C. 53.25. Note that Musa's brother Euphorbus was doctor to Iuba of Mauretania, whose marriage to Cleopatra Selene is celebrated by Crinagoras 25 = *AP* 9.235, apparently in '20 BC or a little earlier', *GP* ii 233.

[36] Ptol. *Geog.* 2.7.9 shows that Ὕδατα Αὔγουστα, 'Augustan waters', became the name of the Tarbellian city that grew up there: cf. Mysian Hadrianoutherae.

[37] *GP* ii 239, following the preference of Cichorius 1922, 313 for 16 BC. That Tiberius' Armenian campaign, integral to the poem (even if Ἀρμενίην, 'Armenian' in line 3 is an emendation), was in 20 BC favours the earlier date. The hint of *GP* ii 248 that *GP* 38 = *AP* 9.240 was also composed in connection with this campaign is elaborated by Chaumont 1992.

[38] Similarly Tatum 1997, 493, though I do not share his view (n.69) that Crinagoras was straightforwardly a 'court poet'.

[39] *GP* ii 221.

[40] Philodemus *GP* 23 = *AP* 11.44. The term καλιήν, 'hut' (Crinagoras line 3) stands close to καλιάδα, 'hut', in Philodemus' opening line.

[41] For the identification, and discussion of possible occasions, see *GP* ii 217. For an argument linking several of Crinagoras' poems with Octavia see Mayer forthcoming.

the symposium, in what may well be the standard Alexandrian edition,[42] aligns Crinagoras with earlier sympotic poets and gives him a place in a distinguished Greek tradition. That Anacreon was recorded to have performed at the court of Polycrates in Samos and to have been patronised by the Peisistratids may have coloured Crinagoras' self-presentation, at least in this poem. The switch from elegiacs into iambic trimeters in lines 3–4, which seems certain even though our text of these lines is corrupt, shows both Crinagoras' virtuosity and his awareness that Anacreon composed in iambic and elegiac as well as in melic metres.

Both these poems accompanying gifts can well belong in or shortly after 25 BC. Indeed they might be seen as pendants for gifts on the same occasion to the siblings who were both children of Octavia.

Our next poems associated with the *domus Augusta* are that for the young Tiberius, *GP* 28 = *APl.* 61, which could belong as well in 16 BC as in 9 BC, and another poem for an Antonia, *GP* 12 = *AP* 6.244, a prayer to Zeus and Hera to secure a gentle birth. Once again this Antonia is likely to be Antonia Minor, and the birth to be that of Germanicus in 15 BC or Livilla in 13 BC.[43] A prayer to Zeus and Hera is not so markedly Hellenic as evocation of Callimachus or Anacreon (a Roman reader could easily transpose to Jupiter and Juno) but together with the rest of Crinagoras' oeuvre it shows him representing not a Greco-Roman but a Hellenic culture. Together the two epigrams might support the idea that Crinagoras was in Rome around 16–15 BC. He need not have stayed there uninterruptedly since 25 BC. Syme pontificated: 'Crinagoras remained thereafter [sc. after 26/25 BC] at Rome for a number of years, operating as a court poet.'[44] Perhaps not: Crinagoras surely had interests in Mytilene to attend to. It is tempting to suppose that he might have decided to travel again to Rome for the celebration of the Secular Games from 31 May to 2 June 17 BC, perhaps in the hope (which our witnesses' silence does not prove to have been vain) that he too might be asked to compose poetry for the occasion.

The importance of Athens and Attica in Greek culture, hinted at in the poem presented as accompanying a gift of Callimachus' *Hecale* to

[42] Fragments are quoted from Books 1, 2 and 3, but none from a book with a higher number. That is far from proving that the standard Alexandrian edition was in three books, and one in which Anacreon's poetry was distributed between five books, just like those of Alcman and Ibycus, is quite probable. For discussion of Alexandrian editions of melic poets and their antecedents see Hadjimichael 2019.

[43] See *GP* ii 221 following Cichorius 1888, 58. *GP* 6 = *AP* 6.345, a birthday poem, was also guessed by Cichorius 1888, 57 to be for Antonia: Cameron 1980d suggested rather the elder Julia.

[44] Syme 1986, 346.

Marcellus, resurfaces in several other epigrams. *GP* 35 = *AP* 11.42 takes the form of an encouragement to a stay-at-home to visit Attica in order to be initiated in the mysteries of Demeter. It emphasises the antiquity of Athens and of Eleusinian mysteries by identifying Attica by the epithet Κεκροπίης, 'of Cecrops', (line 3).[45] *GP* 8 = *AP* 6.100 purports to accompany a dedication by Antiphanes son of Antiphanes of a torch won in a torch-race in a festival in honour of Prometheus. Torch-races were not unique to Athens,[46] but their association with Prometheus is undoubtedly Athenian. The occasion may of course be a real one, and the epigram may have been composed for inscription, but Crinagoras' decision to compose it links his poetry with a major festival in a city that, despite the devastations of the previous century, remained of prime cultural importance in the Greek world.[47]

Athens' political history also gets a sideways glance with a mention of the hero of Marathon, Aeschylus' brother Cynegeirus, in the first line of *GP* 21 = *AP* 7.741 (on which see further below), and with a praise of a Milesian trumpet-victor called Demosthenes (*GP* 13 = *AP* 6.350) in terms which at the same time evoke the impassioned oratory in the *genus grande*, 'grand style', of the fourth-century BC Athenian politician: Δημόσθενες, οὔ ποτε κώδων | χάλκεος ἤχησεν πλειότερῳ στόματι, lines 5–6, 'Demosthenes, never was there a bronze bell that rang with a fuller voice'. Athens' cultural importance is implicitly celebrated in the couplet praising an unnamed actor for his roles in plays of Menander, *GP* 49 = *AP* 9.234.

The poetic voice of Crinagoras, then, is strongly Hellenic. That Greek frame of reference is given geographical specificity in his request to a friend, the geographer Menippus, for a guide to the Aegean islands and to Corcyra for a sea-journey to Italy he is about to undertake. I cite the epigram (*GP* 32 = *AP* 9.559) in full:

πλοῦς μοι ἐπ' Ἰταλίην ἐντύνεται· ἐς γὰρ ἑταίρους
  στέλλομαι, ὧν ἤδη δηρὸν ἄπειμι χρόνον.
διφέω δ' ἡγητῆρα περίπλοον, ὅς μ' ἐπὶ νήσους
  Κύκλαδας ἀρχαίην τ' ἄξει ἐπὶ Σχερίην.
σύν τί μοι ἀλλά, Μένιππε, λάβευ φίλος, ἵστορα κύκλον
  γράψας, ὦ πάσης ἴδρι γεωγραφίης.

[45] The evocation of age-old Greek traditions is backed up by the Hesiodic abjuration of sailing in lines 1–2 (cf. esp. Hes. *Op.* 650: οὔτε τι ναυτιλίης σεσοφισμένος οὔτε τι νηῶν. | οὐ γάρ πώ ποτε νηΐ γ' ἐπέπλων εὐρέα πόντον: 'neither in any degree skilled in sailing, nor in any degree in ships. For never yet have I sailed over the broad sea'), and by the rare Homeric infinitive ἐπιβήμεναι, 'to set foot upon', in line 3, noted by *GP* ii 245. For the Eleusinian mysteries as emblematic of Greek culture cf. Ch. 5.4.4.

[46] See *GP* ii 218.

[47] For the Augustan promotion of Athens as a site of Greek culture see Spawforth 2011.

A sea-voyage to Italy is being prepared. For to my friends
  am I setting off, from whom I have now been away for so long a time;
and I am looking for a guide to coastal sailing, which will take me
  to the island Cyclades and to ancient Scheria.
Please, Menippus, give me some help, my friend: a historical circuit
  is what you should write, omniscient as you are in geography.

The poem asks the distinguished geographer Menippus of Pergamum, otherwise known as the writer of a Three-book Περιπλοῦς τῆς ἐντὸς θαλλάσσης, '*Guide to the Mediterranean Sea*',[48] to provide Crinagoras with a custom-built guide for his voyage from Mytilene to Italy (presumably following the route Corinth–Corcyra–Brundisium). As *GP* note, the reference to friends in Italy whom he has long not seen better fits his embassy of 27 or 26 BC than that of 45 BC.[49] But it does not follow that the 'occasion must then be the Third Embassy': Crinagoras clearly maintained contact with the imperial house long after 27/26 BC, and he may well have revisited Rome from time to time: and there is no mention of the fact that the embassy's target, Augustus, is at this time in Spain, not Italy. Here ἀρχαίη Σχερίη ('ancient Scheria'), the island of the Phaeacians traditionally identified with Corcyra,[50] follows closely upon the Cyclades in a manner that is geographically curious, but intelligible given the way the latter were emblematic of Aegean culture centred in Delos.[51] Crinagoras relates himself both to a Greek cultural background and to his 'friends' (hinted, perhaps, to be important) in Rome.

Those who know the poet will infer from his mention of the Cyclades that this was a journey starting in Lesbos. But Mytilene and Lesbos are remarkably absent from the surviving poems. Lesbos appears by name only in *GP* 16 = *AP* 7.376, an elegant and emotional sepulchral epigram for the death of the perfect young Seleucus in furthest Spain. Despite the poem's stress on Seleucus' youth, he may be one of the envoys of 26/5 BC, as seemed likely to Gow–Page in the light of his articulacy and virtue – μύθοισι καὶ ἤθεσι … ἄρτιος, 'perfect in his speech and in his character'; or perhaps he simply accompanied the envoys as an aide, a research assistant, or a relative. Whoever he is (indeed whether or not he was a real person), Crinagoras effectively brings out the sadness of the death of an ephebic Greek in a distant land that has only been brought into Greek horizons by Roman conquest.[52]

[48] On Menippus see González Ponce 1993. [49] *GP* ii 243.
[50] Cf. the specification of Corcyra as Phaeacian in *GP* 31.7 = *AP* 9.516.7.
[51] One may compare, two centuries later, Aristid. 44.11–12 Keil.
[52] The pathetic trope of the foreign death begins with Agamemnon's threat concerning Chryseis in Homer Il. 1.30: πρίν μιν καὶ γῆρας ἔπεισιν, | ἡμετέρωι ἐνὶ οἴκωι, ἐν Ἄργεϊ, τηλόθι πάτρης, 'before that shall old age overtake her in my house, in Argos, far from her native land'.

Crinagoras was ready to celebrate the members of the imperial family who claimed the credit for such conquests (cf. *GP* 28 = *APl.* 61, discussed earlier), and he was ready to praise a Roman legionary who saved his legion's eagle despite being on the point of death from his wounds, even comparing him to iconic Greek heroes like Othryadas and Cynegeirus (*GP* 21 = *AP* 7.741, already mentioned). But in *GP* 37 = *AP* 9.284 he was also prepared to express his unhappiness at the resettlement of Corinth, city of the Bacchiadae, by Italian *libertini*, 'sons of freedmen', under the *lex Iulia* of 44 BC, something he may have become aware of on his journey to the West in 26/25 BC.[53]

A couple of poems which may be read as gross flattery could equally be seen as a humorous scepticism on the matter of the emperor's divinity. In *GP* 23 = *AP* 9.224 the speaking voice is that of a goat whose milk's quality ensures that it accompanies Caesar even aboard ship: 'Before long', it says, 'I shall come even to the stars; for the man to whom I gave my udder is not at all inferior to the Aegis-bearer'. In *GP* 24 = *AP* 9.652 a parrot trained to utter the greeting 'Caesar!' escapes and teaches the trick to wild birds, who vie to be the first 'to utter a greeting to the god' (δαίμονι χαῖρ' ἐνέπειν, line 5). I doubt if it is right to see these poems as a product of time-serving flattery. Both poems belong in a tradition of poems on pet animals (exemplified, as it happens, by some inscribed epitaphs from Lesbos)[54] and the goat-poem's play with the possibility of divinisation recalls the Callimachean *Lock of Berenice*, probably as well known to some readers in Augustan Rome as its Catullan translation. The leading men of Greco-Roman society who received divine honours – and these included Crinagoras' older Mytilenean contemporary Theophanes,[55] as well as Caesar Augustus – did not always regard the procedure with utter seriousness. We may recall from a century later Vespasian's alleged dying remark *Vae! Ut puto, deus fio*, 'Alas! I think I am becoming a god'.

Diodorus ('the younger') of Sardis (active ?ca. 20–9 BC)

A similar figure is cut by Diodorus of Sardis. Epitaphic poems relate to Nicaea (*GP* 10 = *AP* 7.701) and Nicomedia (*GP* 6 = *AP* 7.627); dedicatory poems involve the Heraeum on Samos (*GP* 3 = *AP* 6.243), the Carpathian sea, and the Boeotian Cabiri (*GP* 4 = *AP* 6.245). The dedicator at the Heraeum bears

[53] So Cichorius 1888, 51ff., castigated by *GP* ii 247 n.1, who think, like Mommsen, that the poem should belong shortly after 44 BC. For emendations and interpretations see Borthwick 1971; Giangrande 1975.

[54] *IG* xii.2 458 and 459. [55] *IG* xii.2 163: cf. Bowie 2011b (Chapter 26 in Volume 3).

[56] Cichorius 1922, 299; *GP* ii 265.

a Roman name, Maximus, too common to justify even a guess at identification. But two poems give surer results. One (*GP* 8 = *AP* 9.405) celebrates the physical and moral qualities of a Drusus, the other (*GP* 1 = *AP* 9.219) compares to Achilles a Nero who has just returned to Rome 'a youth who still has the down of a freshly grown beard' (κοῦρος ἔτ' ἀρτιγένειον ἔχων χνόον, line 5). Again following Cichorius, Gow–Page argue persuasively that the Nero is the later emperor Tiberius, but they associate the poem not with his return from Armenia in 20 BC (as did Cichorius), but with his return from Spain aged seventeen or eighteen in 24 BC.[56] They take Drusus to be his brother who died in 9 BC. It is then only a guess, however, that, in the words of Gow–Page, 'It is likely that Diodorus lived in Rome in this period and was acquainted with the eminent persons whom he praises, Drusus ... and Tiberius'.[57] Not much support for this guess comes from a sepulchral epigram for a lady from Tarentum, Paula (*GP* 9 = *AP* 7.700): Tarentum is too far from Rome, too near to other centres of Greek culture.

Erucius (active ?ca. 30 BC)

Other poets are marginal for other reasons. Erucius has a Roman name, but his décor is entirely and quite insistently Greek, and the ethnic 'Cyzicene' attached to *GP* 12 = *AP* 7.230 may or may not be supported by a pathos-rich epitaph on a woman who died in Cyzicus (*GP* 6 = *AP* 7.368) – a woman born in Athens, then captured and taken to Rome, presumably in the Sullan sack of Athens in 86 BC that still pained Pausanias in the later second century AD. It may be more likely that Erucius is an Italian immigrant in Cyzicus, composing around 30 BC, than a Greek from Cyzicus with Roman citizenship, but nothing shows him to be composing Greek poetry *in* Italy.

Honestus (active ca. AD 14–37)

The same must be said of Honestus, attested by poems both in the *Anthology* and inscribed on bases for statues of the Muses at Thespiae. Honestus also composed a poem (*GP* 21) for the base of a statue of Augusta (Σεβαστή), persuasively identified as Livia, wife of Augustus, to be set up alongside those of the Muses. Unless Honestus was responsible for commissioning the whole sequence of statues, both of the Muses and of Livia (which is improbable), the wish to honour Livia is not Honestus' own but that of

[57] *GP* ii 270, again following Cichorius 1922, 301.

[58] The bases are currently displayed in the forecourt of the archaeological museum of Thebes.

whoever did indeed commission the ensemble.[58] Nor do Honestus' poems show evidence of contacts outside the triangle Corinth–Sicyon–Thespiae. His Roman name, a *cognomen* used as an ὄνομα, might suggest that he is a settler in the Roman *colonia* at Corinth: but there are of course other possibilities. That he was 'one of those who sought or enjoyed patronage at the imperial court'[59] is a claim that cannot be made with any confidence.

Lollius Bassus (active ca. AD 19)

That same phrase is used by Gow-Page of Lollius Bassus, an even more shadowy figure, and again more probably Italian than Greek.[60] His epigram on the death of Germanicus (*GP* 5 = *AP* 7.391), however deplorable as poetry, may well reflect genuine feeling – we may think of the reactions to the death of Gaius, about which we now know much more – but neither it nor the epigram on the world empire of Rome, founded by Aeneas (*GP* 6 = *AP* 9.236), give solid support the view that he 'sought or enjoyed patronage at the imperial court'. Another poem (*GP* 3 = *AP* 7.372), commemorating a Theban Atymnius who died at Tarentum, may indicate that at some point Lollius Bassus was in South Italy, but if this was so, we cannot tell why, nor whither he was bound.

Macedonius (date uncertain)

Much stronger Italian colour is exuded by one of the three surviving epigrams of Macedonius, *GP* 3 = *AP* 11.27, on the three cities Sorrento, Pollenza and Asti, producers of pottery wine-containers. Macedonius may, like Philip, be from Thessalonica (as claimed by the lemma to *GP* 1 = *AP* 11.39), and he could be the Macedonius whom an inscribed paean in first century AD Athens identifies as its author:[61] if so, we are dealing with a virtuoso or semi-professional poet, and one who to all appearances is indeed Greek. So does *GP* 3 attest a Greek touring and toping in Italy? The praise of the three Italian cities can hardly do this: precisely the same three are

[59] *GP* ii 301. For powerful arguments that Honestus comes from a Roman settler family in Corinth, and that the lady honoured as Σεβαστή is indeed Livia, see Jones 2004.

[60] *GP* ii 192.

[61] For the text see *CA*, Furley and Bremer 2001; for inscribed paeans in the first and second centuries AD see Bowie 2006c (Chapter 16 in Volume 3), Melfi 2010. The text is *IG* ii [2] 4473, headed Μακε[δόνιος] ἐποίη[σεν], cf. ii 3784 [Μακε]δόνιος ἐποίει and *SEG* 30.166.

picked out by the elder Pliny as well known for the production of drinking cups,[62] and the considerable distance separating Sorrento on the bay of Naples from the northern cities whose products were needed for the fine wines of Piedmont shows that the poem is not a traveller's *capriccio*. Italian wine and vessels were exported to Achaea and Macedonia, and Macedonius may never have sailed west across the Adriatic.

Philodemus (active ca. 70–40 BC)

With Philodemus we move into much better documented territory. Of all Philip's poets Philodemus is the one whose residence in Italy, whose relations with a 'patron' (in his case L. Calpurnius Piso, *cos.* 58), and whose philosophical and literary activities are best attested by far.[63] His poetry, however, bears scant traces of all this, which may be a warning to us how little we are entitled to expect from the other poets' works about their lives as a whole. Although Philodemus' erotic poetry represents him as a 'cruiser' *par excellence*, indefatigable in his pursuit of sexual pleasure (a point not brought out by *GP*), we have no way of judging how far any of these images of the self-indulgent life corresponds to his real world. Philippson supposed that his extraordinarily prolific philosophical writing, requiring long hours of labour and reflecting a serious morality, followed a period of youthful dissipation which he abandoned at the age of 37.[64] Gow and Page, showing a better understanding of the operations of genre, opine that it is more likely that the 'two very different styles of composition' ran in parallel both earlier and later.[65]

It is easier to be sure that in some sense Philodemus' relation with Piso is that of client and patron.[66] But is it a predominantly economic relationship, in which Philodemus is dependent on Piso, or is Piso rather the social agent for Philodemus' various modes of communication with philhellenic

[62] *Samia etiam nunc in esculentis laudatur. retinet hanc nobilitatem et Arretium in Italia, et calcium tantum Surrentum, Asta, Pollentia*, 'In the matter of table-ware Samian pottery is still commended; a reputation for this is also retained by Arezzo in Italy, and, simply for cups, by Sorrento, Asti, and Pollenza', Plin. Nat. 35.160, cited by *GP*, who also note Martial 13.110, 14.102.

[63] For Philodemus' life see Sider 1997, 3–24. *P.Oxy.* 3724 adds the first lines of several more epigrams, but since they are not in *AP* we cannot be sure that they were in the *Garland* of Philip.

[64] *RE* xix.2 (1938) on Philodemos (5), 2446 and 2448, using *GP* 17 (= *AP* 9.41) and 18 (= *AP* 5.112).

[65] *GP* ii 373. For a nuanced account, attempting to reconcile serious philosophy and continued partying, see Sider 1997, 18.

[66] A reasoned case for seeing the relationship as one of patronage (invoking the criteria of Saller 1982) is put by Sider 1997, 5–6 n.11.

Roman society of (roughly) the period 70 to 40 BC? In *GP* 23 (= *AP* 11.44) he represents himself as a poor poet inviting Piso to his simple abode and openly encouraging him to confer approval and support. That he was able to leave Gadara in order to study Epicureanism with Zeno in Athens establishes that Philodemus was no pauper.[67] On the other hand, the richer Roman senators of the first century BC were vastly more wealthy than almost any individual among the elites of the Greek cities. So the very rich can stand in a relationship of patronage to the modestly rich: to view it from a different perspective, gifts and hospitality offered by the very rich to the modestly rich can reinforce the hierarchy within the upper orders of Greek and Roman society (as it can of many others).

Philip (active as a poet ca. AD 37–9)

It is fitting that only towards the conclusion of this section should I address the garland-weaver himself, necessarily junior to the majority of his chosen poets. Assessment of his movements is complicated by a general problem affecting several poems: Philip enjoys reworking poems of his contributors, and such a reworking of a theme that might otherwise point to an Italian visit cannot of course do so. Thus Antiphilus' poem on the gigantic mole at Puteoli (*GP* 3 = *AP* 7.379) is reworked by Philip in *GP* 57 = *AP* 9.708; and his poem on Timomachus' *Medea* (*GP* 48 = *APl.* 136) seems to be reworked by Philip in *GP* 70 = *APl.* 137: neither can therefore reveal Philip in Campania or Rome. The *rostra* of *GP* 2 = *AP* 6.236, dedicated after Actium, look more promising: but *rostra* were dedicated both in Rome and at Actium itself,[68] and since *GP* 7= *AP* 6.251 is a prayer for a good sea-voyage to Actium it is very likely that Philip saw the *rostra* there. The eleven lines of iambic trimeters commemorating an old woman healed by a miraculous spring on Etna, *GP* 6 = *AP* 6.203, would take Philip to Sicily, but *GP* doubt Philip's authorship, preferring the manuscript's alternative ascription to an otherwise unknown Lacon.[69]

This leaves *GP* 4 = *AP* 9.285 as the best candidate for a poem demonstrating Philip's presence in Rome. The epigram celebrates the use of elephants,

[67] And as noted by Sider 1997, 16, adducing Cic. *De fin.* 1.20.65, a humble dwelling is the conventional hallmark of the professional Epicurean. If the anecdote (preserved in *Suda* τ 634 *s.v.* τιμῶνται = T 8 Sider) about confiscation of his property after a period of residence in Himera has any historical basis, then at that stage in his life (whatever it was) Philodemus owned property worth confiscating.

[68] D.C. 51.1.3; 19.2.

[69] *GP* ii 369.

once instruments of war, to draw the chariot of 'divine Caesar', associated with εἰρήνη, 'peace' (5) and εὐνομίη, 'good order' (6). Identification of the 'Caesar' and consequent dating are problematic, but the ostentatious use of elephants is only attested, and only probable, for ceremonies in Rome itself.[70]

If the elephant-car (*GP* 4 = *AP* 9.285) secures Philip's presence in Rome, then two other poems are likely also to have been composed in Rome, though neither formally need have been. *GP* 6 = *AP* 9.778 commemorates the gift of a tapestry to the emperor by a queen almost certain (by slight emendation) to be Cyprus, wife of Herod Agrippa, a gift securely dated to the summer of 39 AD.[71] *GP* 3 = *AP* 6.240 prays for the recovery from illness of an emperor, most probably Gaius in October or November 37 AD.[72]

Philip's reworking (in *GP* 31 = *AP* 7.234) of Apollonides' epigram on the suicide of a Roman officer (*GP* 20 = *AP* 7.233) may be put alongside his praise of 'peace' and 'good order' as evidence that he presented himself as endorsing the imperial virtues claimed by Rome. But like many of his contributors, he may not have been in Italy for long, and the world that the majority of his poems communicates is a strongly Greek world, as will be seen in Section 3.

Thallus (active ?ca. AD 18)

Thallus is another of Philip's poets whose epigrams touch on the imperial house and on Italy, but who may well neither have been patronised by the one nor visited the other. *GP* 2 (= *AP* 6.235) is probably, as Gow–Page argue, in praise of Germanicus, but it could well have been composed during his time in the East. The quasi-epitaphic commemoration (*GP* 4 =

[70] The conclusion of *GP* ii 332, following but modifying Cichorius 1922, 344–6, that the emperor is deified and so dead, and that the limits are 14–41 AD, surprises me: insistence on 'peace' and 'good order' seem to me rather to point to a living emperor (cf. *GP* 2 = *AP* 6.236) and use of elephants for Drusilla's birthday extravaganza (D.C. 59.13.8) in 38/9 AD shows they were not confined to funerary processions (such as those of Augustus and Livia, as Suet. *Cl.* 11).

[71] Jos. *AJ* 18.247ff., cf. Cichorius 1922, 351–4, followed 'throughout' by *GP* ii 333–4. Their conclusion, however, that the *Garland* itself, containing poems so flattering to Gaius, must have been published before Gaius' death in 41 AD, is false: *GP* 6 = *AP* 9.778 may have been circulating on its own, or as part of a small book of epigrams praising the imperial house and its members (e.g. *GP* 4 = *AP* 9.285 on the elephants) in the years 39–41 AD, and then given a second life rather later in Philip's *Garland* (which seems to have included Antiphilus *GP* 6 = *AP* 9.178 of 53 AD, see on Antiphilus p. 363).

[72] So *GP* ii 331–2 following Cichorius 1922, 347 and adducing D.C. 59.8, Suet. *Cal.* 14, and Philo *Leg. ad Gaium* 356 for widespread concern at the still-popular Caesar's illness.

AP 7.373) of two Milesians who died in Italy, perhaps athletes, could easily have been composed for a readership in Miletus itself, where three of the Palatine manuscript's *lemmata* locate Thallus.[73]

3 The Greek World of Philip's Poets

Hard evidence of these epigrammatists composing in Rome and Italy and choosing what they encountered there for their subjects has proved to be scanty. Philodemus was certainly a long-term resident, while Crinagoras and others made visits whose number and duration is hard to determine. Even in these cases explicit reference to things Roman or Italian is rare. In the case of Antipater a much larger number of poems *may* be responses to objects he saw in Rome; but the arguments, however attractive, are fragile, and it remains true of Antipater too that explicit identification of Roman or Italian contexts or subject-matter has yet to be demonstrated. That a poem responded, therefore, to what might be seen in Pompey's theatre (for example), might have been clear to a recipient of the poem on its first airing in Rome, be that recipient a friend or a 'patron', but would be less clear to readers of whatever collection of his own poems Antipater himself put together and circulated in Thessalonica and perhaps in Rome and other cultural centres (Athens? Smyrna? Alexandria?). By the time some of these had been taken by Philip into his alphabetically arranged *Garland* their supposed original Roman focus might have been far from apparent and need not have been relevant to their appreciation as epigrammatic poetry.

By contrast the Greek 'wallpaper' of the *Garland*'s poets is omnipresent. Subjects range over literary and historical figures, over works of art and their creators, and over places with names resonant in Greek history, all in some way significant for Greeks' constructions of their cultural identity. I review the evidence in alphabetical order of the poets' names.

Adaeus

In this perhaps Macedonian poet's ten poems one (*GP* 2 = *AP* 6.258) presents a Greek with the rare name Crethon sacrificing to Demeter; three are on the death and fame respectively of Euripides (*GP* 3 = *AP* 7.51), Philip II

[73] *GP* 1 = *AP* 6.91; *GP* 4 = *AP* 7.373, *GP* 5 = *AP* 9.220. Cichorius 1922, 356 accepts Milesian origin and proposed on the basis of the name Antonius (Ἀντωνίου Θάλλου) in the *lemma* of *GP* 3 = *AP* 7.188 that he had received Roman citizenship from Antonia Minor; but if Thallus is from the highest levels of society the *gentilicium* could go back to the triumvir M. Antonius. Note at Didyma Μάρκου Ἀντωνίου Ἀπολλωνίου of 41/40 BC (*IDidyma* 317).

(*GP* 4 = *AP* 7.58) and Alexander (*GP* 5 = *AP* 7.240). Two seem to work specifically with the Greek world of Macedon, one on an otherwise unknown hero Polypregmon at Potidaea (*GP* 6 = *AP* 7.694), another on a Peucestes (a name that inevitably evokes that of Alexander's companion) who drinks neat wine from the horns of a bull he killed with his Paeonian spear near Doberus in Eastern Macedonia (*GP* 7 = *AP* 9.300). A poem recognising Artemis' aid to a whelping bitch (*GP* 8 = *AP* 9.303) and another on a beryl carved by the Greek artist Tryphon (*GP* 9 = *AP* 9.544) bring to eight the total of markedly Greek subjects in the ten extant poems.

Aemilianus

Aemilianus' epigram on Praxiteles' marble *Sileni* (*GP* 3 = *AP* 9.756) was noted in Section 2 as a work of art possibly seen in Rome. But both the sculptor and his subject are of course Greek.

Antipater

Here we have a much larger corpus of 115 poems. Some set contemporaries with Greek names in a Hellenic cultural background: *GP* 3 = *AP* 11.24, elevating a cup-bearer named Helicon by references to the Boeotian mountain and to Hesiod; *GP* 4 = *AP* 9.517, relating a piper Glaphyrus to Apollo, Athena, Marsyas and Hypnus; and *GP* 78 = *APl.* (A) 290, expanding on the Theban origins of the Dionysus whose madness the pantomime Pylades brilliantly represented.[74]

Epigrams on Greek works of art, some already addressed from a different perspective in Section 2, are numerous: Aristomenes' painting of three women dedicating to Aphrodite (*GP* 9 = *AP* 6.208); Bithynian Cythera's marble statue of Aphrodite (*GP* 10 = *AP* 6.209); the *Niobids* (*GP* 86 = *APl.* (A) 131, *GP* 87 = *APl.* (A) 133 and perhaps *GP* 22 = *AP* 7.530); Timomachus' *Medea* (*GP* 29 = *APl.* (A) 143); Piso's *Dionysus* (*GP* 30 = *APl.* (A) 184); Onatas' bronze *Apollo* (*GP* 83 = *AP* 9.238); Myron's *Cow* (*GP* 84 = *AP* 9.728); and Theogenes' bowls (*GP* 44 = *AP* 9.541). But there are many more: the Νῖκαι, '*Victories*', ridden by divinities (*GP* 46 = *AP* 9.59); a picture of Hades by the fourth-century BC painter Nicias (*GP* 85 = *AP* 9.792); statues of an armed Aphrodite at Sparta (*GP* 88 = *APl.* 176) and of a bound Eros (*GP* 89 = *APl.* (A) 197). The poem on statues of three Muses (*GP* 90 = *APl.*

[74] Also the theme of the only surviving poem of Boethus, on whose possibly Tarsian identity see *GP* ii 209.

(A) 220) ascribes them to three different sculptors of the sixth century BC, Aristocles, Ageladas and Aristomenes.

Some of these works of art had a place in Greek cult as well as in the history of Greek art. Cultic too, but hardly to be claimed as bearing on art, is the horned altar dedicated to Athena by Seleucus (*GP* 39 = *AP* 6.10).[75] There are also dedications by Greek rustics: a spear to Heracles (*GP* 32 = *AP* 6.93) and fowling gear to Pan (*GP* 54 = *AP* 6.109).

Another dimension of the Hellenic world is introduced by two poems on the great temple of Artemis at Ephesus (*GP* 91 = *AP* 9.58, *GP* 92 = *AP* 9.790); one on an unspecified seaside temple of Aphrodite (*GP* 93 = *AP* 9.143); and epigrams on the decline of Amphipolis (*GP* 50 = *AP* 7.705) and Delos (*GP* 94 = *AP* 9.550 and *GP* 113 = *AP* 9.408).

Antipater's numerous ἐπιτυμβίδια, 'sepulchral epigrams', for (it seems) contemporaries include one for a homonymous orator of Athenian or Egyptian (presumably Greek-Egyptian!) descent (*GP* 49 = *AP* 7.369); another for an athlete struck by lightning returning home from Olympia (*GP* 62 = *AP* 7.390); and a third for the Pergamene pancratiast Glycon (*GP* 107 = *AP* 7.692).[76] Of two other celebrations of contemporary Greek athletes, one, on the *stadiodromos* who won in the category παῖδες, 'boys', Menecles, stresses his city Tarsus' foundation by Argive Perseus (*GP* 79 = *AP* 9.557); like that for a Milesian Olympic victor in boxing, Nicophon (*GP* 110 = *AP* 6.256), it is perhaps for an honorific statue. Also for statues were the epigrams on portraits of Greek poets already discussed – *GP* 72 = *APl.* (A) 286 on Homer's birthplace; *GP* 73 = *AP* 7.15 on Sappho; *GP* 75 = *APl.* (A) 305 on Pindar) – though one of these also refers to the poet's tomb, i.e. that on Stesichorus (*GP* 74 = *AP* 7.75). Sepulchral or quasi-sepulchral epigrams add several iconic figures from the Greek past to Antipater's gallery: Themistocles (*GP* 115 = *AP* 7.236);[77] Socrates (*GP* 76 = *AP* 7.629);[78] and Diogenes (*GP* 77 = *AP* 7.65). Aristophanes makes his entry *via* a poem on an edition of his plays (βίβλοι, 'books'), foregrounding *Acharnians* (*GP* 103 = *AP* 9.41).

Antipater's poems that have survived into the *Greek Anthology* thus offer a miniature and selective tour of the major components of Greek culture's claims to importance: politics, poetry, philosophy, sculpture, painting, athletics. One might guess that a complete text of Antipater would have been less selective. Poems for Piso certainly had their place, and probably some

[75] On the text of *GP* 39.4 = *AP* 6.10.4 see de Vries 1970.

[76] But also, it must be noted, one for an Italian named Egerius, *GP* 63 = *AP* 7.367.

[77] As *GP* ii 110 note, all the epigrams in *AP* on Themistocles are by Philippan poets.

of the art works were to be seen not in Greece but in Rome. But a resident of Rome who was lured by these to peruse Antipater's βίβλος, 'book', or βίβλοι, 'books', would have been drawn into a world that was overwhelmingly Greek.

Antiphanes

Antiphanes' ten surviving poems show that this predominance is not inevitable. Unless weight is given to references to Aphrodite as from Cythera (*GP* 1 = *AP* 6.88),[79] to Hymen and Hades (*GP* 3 = *AP* 9.245), or to metaphorical Nymphs, Bacchus and Ares (*GP* 5 = *AP* 9.258),[80] Antiphanes' only presentation of Greek culture is negative, his attack on fans of Callimachus and Erinna (*GP* 9 = *AP* 11.322).

Antiphilus

Antiphilus of Byzantium's fifty-three poems, however, have an even greater density of Hellenic reference than those of Antipater. In some these references are simply geographical: the Euboean Euripus (*GP* 5 = *AP* 9.73); the strait between Thasos and the Thracian mainland (*GP* 22 = *AP* 9.242). One links geography and cult: *GP* 11 = *AP* 10.17 on a journey to Pytheion.[81] Three epigrams touch diversely on the cult of Demeter: a ploughman's dedication to Demeter (*GP* 15 = *AP* 6.95), a wine-amphora inappropriately filled with Demeter's grain (*GP* 22 = *AP* 6.257), and a blind man to whom Demeter and Persephone have restored sight (*GP* 39 = *AP* 9.298). Others link Greek geography and mythology, like that on the tomb of Protesilaus (*GP* 23 = *AP* 7.141). The Greek mythological heritage and its literary and artistic vehicles are frequently exploited: the feuding sons of Oedipus in *GP* 27 = *AP* 7.399;[82] the *Iliad* and *Odyssey* (*GP* 36 = *AP* 9.192, perhaps, as suggested by *GP*, on a sculptured representation like the Archelaus relief);[83] a painting of the Trojan horse (*GP* 35 = *AP* 9.156); Timomachus' *Medea* (*GP*

[78] *GP* ii 79 suggest 'On the tomb of Socrates', but εἰς σέ τις ἀθρῶν, 'somebody looking at you', in the first line suggests rather a portrait statue.

[79] But for a possible allusion to Alcman fr. 50b *PMGF* see Nannini 1982.

[80] Cf. Bromios in *GP* 6 = *AP* 9.409.

[81] For the attractive suggestion that this poem may have been fashioned by Antiphilus to stand at the beginning of a collection of his epigrams (with *GP* 16 = *AP* 6.199 at its end) cf. Höschele 2007, 361–2.

[82] On the theme see Aricò 1972.

[83] *GP* ii 137.

48 = *APl.* (A) 36); a painting of Leda and the swan (*GP* 13 = *AP* 5.307); and one of Perseus and Andromeda (*GP* 49 = *APl.* 147), perhaps that by Nicias.[84] Greek history supplies Leonidas (*GP* 38 = *AP* 9.274) and Alexander's spear (*GP* 21 = *AP* 6.97).

Antistius

Of four surviving epigrams of Antistius, guessed by Cichorius to be the grandee *e primoribus Macedoniae*, 'from among the leading men in Macedonia', convicted of *maiestas*, 'treason', in 21 AD,[85] three have strong Greek colour: one on three Greek athletes drowned respectively in the Ionian and in the Carpathian seas, and sailing between Greece and Sicily (*GP* 2 = *AP* 7.366); one on a boy who dances in a θίασος, a group of dancers honouring Dionysus (*GP* 3 = *AP* 11.40);[86] and one spoken by a figure of Priapus protecting the fields and sheds of a Greek with the rare name Phricon (*GP* 4 = *APl.* 243). The fourth (*GP* 1 = *AP* 6.23) on a Gallus who scared off a lion by beating the drum of his divine mistress, the Magna Mater, 'Great Mother', has less claim to be Greek.

Apollonides of (?) Nicaea

Of Apollonides' thirty surviving epigrams at least six take the reader into the world of Greek religion: dedications to Artemis by a fisherman (*GP* 1 = *AP* 6.105); to unnamed gods by a poor farmer (*GP* 2 = *AP* 6.238) and by a bee-keeper (*GP* 3 = *AP* 6.239); a seaside temple of Aphrodite (*GP* 25 = *AP* 9.791); a kneeling statue of Priapus by the sculptor Phyromachus of the early third century BC (*GP* 30 = *APl.* 239); a spring sacred to Nymphs (*GP* 17 = *AP* 9.257). Poseidon is also prayed to in an epitaph on the drowned fisherman Glenis (*GP* 9 = *AP* 7.69). Apollonides' other poems on drowned men mark their Hellenic ambience by personal names – Aristomenes (*GP* 10 = *AP* 9.271); Melitaea and Dio (*GP* 14 = *AP* 9.228) – and sometimes also by location: Miletus and Andros (*GP* 7 = *AP* 7.631); Samos, Syros and Delos (*GP* 8 = *AP* 7.642). The mythological rarity represented by the sons of Cercaphus has already been noted (*GP* 23 = *AP* 9.287 and 28 = *APl.* (B) 49,

[84] *GP* ii 143, citing Plin. *Nat.* 35.132. For both paintings see Neutsch 1938.

[85] Cichorius 1922, pp. 360–1, cf. Tac. *Ann.* 3.38.

[86] On the importance for Greek self-definition of χοροί, 'choruses', and χορεύειν, 'dance in a chorus', see Bowie 2006c (Chapter 16 in Volume 3).

cf. p. 364); the run-of-the-mill Ganymede, Paris and Cinyras figure in the same poem, and Heracles in *GP* 29 = *APl.* (B) 50. Apollonides also offers a historical rarity, the underwater swimmer Scyllis or Scyllus of Scione who cut the anchor-ropes of Xerxes' fleet off Pelion (*GP* 24 = *AP* 9.296),[87] as well as historical commonplaces like Cretan archers (*GP* 19 = *AP* 9.265). When Romans are introduced it is mostly against a Greek background: Laelius at Sparta (*GP* 21 = *AP* 9.280); the eagle visiting Rhodes during Tiberius' residence (*GP* 23 = *AP* 9.287); and the Postumus who built the temple of Aphrodite (*GP* 25 = *AP* 9.791).

Argentarius

Whether because he is an Italian writing in Italy,[88] or because his amatory and satirical epigrams greatly outnumber his dedicatory and sepulchral compositions, Argentarius' thirty-seven poems have rather less Greek colour. A witty ἐρωτικόν, 'amatory poem', advertises a preference for sex over reading Hesiod (*GP* 15 = *AP* 9.161),[89] and the choice of Antigone for the name of one of his several ἐρώμεναι, 'girl-friends' (*GP* 3 = *AP* 5.63, *GP* 13 = *AP* 5.128, and *GP* 34 = *AP* 11.320) savours of iconoclasm.[90] But Greek colour is far from absent; witness dedications of clothing to Artemis by a woman who has given birth (*GP* 17 = *AP* 6.201); of riding gear to Poseidon by an Isthmian victor (*GP* 18 = *AP* 6.246); and of a flagon to Aphrodite by Marcus Argentarius himself (*GP* 23 = *AP* 6.248). Greek gods are to be found both new (Sarapis in *GP* 16 = *AP* 9.286) and old: Priapus as the god protecting both seafarers in *GP* 28 = *AP* 10.4 and crops in *GP* 37 = *APl.* (A) 241); Dionysus solo (*GP* 27 = *AP* 11.26) and with Aphrodite (*GP* 29 = *AP* 10.18); Ino (*GP* 31 = *AP* 7.384); Semele (*GP* 25 = *AP* 9.246); Eros engraved on a seal-stone (*GP* 35 = *AP* 9.221); and Heracles introduced to support a *double entendre* on Hebe (*GP* 33 = *AP* 9.554). Not surprisingly, then, one of the two ἐπιτυμβίδια, 'sepulchral epigrams', brings in the Aegean (*GP* 19 = *AP* 7.374). The Libyan sea of *GP* 20 = *AP* 7.395 does not diminish the Hellenic flavour of the victim's name Callaeschrus: that this name and several motifs are drawn from Leonidas (*AP* 7.273 = *HE* 62) does not

[87] Cf. Paus. 10.19.1–2; Plin. *Nat.* 35.139; Frost 1968.

[88] I accept the persuasive identification with the *rhetor* known from the elder Seneca, cf. *GP* ii 166. Cf. Nisbet 1978, pp. 5–7. Among discussions of Argentarius before *GP* note especially Small 1951.

[89] For a nuanced reading see Gagné and Höschele 2009.

[90] On *GP* 3 = *AP* 5.63 see Baldwin 1988; Ricks 1991.

count against registering Argentarius' epigram among those which show an apparently Italian poet succeeding in creating, when he wants, very much the same Hellenic world as his Greek contemporaries.

Automedon

Automedon's dozen poems show much knowledge of the Greek world but little enthusiasm. *GP* 5 = *AP* 11.319 criticises Athens for selling citizenship (one can become Erechtheus, Cecrops, Codrus or even Triptolemus);[91] *GP* 4 = *AP* 11.50 sets a few axioms about marriage above Epicurean physics; *GP* 6 = *AP* 11.324 satirises a predatory warden of a temple of Apollo;[92] *GP* 8 = *AP* 11.346, deploying an enigmatic but apparently figurative reference to Cyzicus and the Samothracian Cabiri, pokes fun at a fraudulent banker with the Greek name Polycarpus. The seemingly laudatory poem on the Greek *rhetor* Nicetes, *GP* 3 = *AP* 10.23,[93] is the only indication of admiration for things Greek,[94] but that fact may be down to a decision by Automedon to tread the under-worked path of satirical epigram.[95]

Lollius Bassus

If Bassus is of Italian origin (which would be more likely, but still not certain, if we were sure his *nomen* was Lollius), he shows as much penchant for Greek topics as Philip's poets of Greek origin. Of his dozen poems two handle Thermopylae (*GP* 2 = *AP* 7.243 and *GP* 7 = *AP* 9.279, which also shows knowledge of the Spartan battle in the Thyreatis ca. 545 BC);[96] one addresses Nauplius' beacon-trick that wrecked the Greek fleet returning from Troy off Cape Caphereus (*GP* 8 = *AP* 9.289); one a sculpture of Niobe (*GP* 4 = *AP* 7.386). These are well-worn epigrammatic subjects: a real occasion may have sparked an epitaph for a Theban, Atymnius, who died at Tarentum (*GP* 3 = *AP* 7.372). Rome and not Greece is the engine of

[91] See the important contextualising discussion by Robert 1982a.

[92] The *nomen* Arrius, if identifying a real person, could suggest a member of a Greek city elite who already in Automedon's day had Roman citizenship, or of an Italian settler family that had integrated in a Greek city.

[93] Discussed by Borthwick 1971 and 1972; Casson 1992.

[94] Unless *GP* 12 = *AP* 7.534 for the shipwrecked Cleonicus, with its complimentary epithet λιπαρήν, 'gleaming', for Thasos, is believed to be by Automedon: but see Gow 1952, ii 548.

[95] On the imperial development of satirical epigram see Nisbet 2003.

[96] Cf. Paus. 2.38.5.

the poem on the Trojan refugee Aeneas' founding of Rome, destined to be κόσμου παντὸς ἄνασσα πόλις, 'the city that is mistress of the whole world', (*GP* 6 = *AP* 9.236), as in some sense it is also of the poem on the death of (a?) Germanicus (*GP* 5 = *AP* 7.391).

Bianor

The twenty-two poems of Bianor, twice denominated Bithynian in the *Palatinus*, are less strongly Hellenica. Bianor knows his mythology, e.g. the crow as Apollo's bird in *GP* 11 = *AP* 9.272; the undying feud of Oedipus' sons in *GP* 6 = *AP* 7.396.[97] He also knows his Herodotus: two poems are on Arion and the dolphin (*GP* 15 = *AP* 9.308) and on a sculpture representing them, *GP* 22 = *APl.* (A) 276), surprisingly the only epigrams on this subject in the *Anthology*.[98] He crafts a poem on a lightning-strike on Euripides' tomb (*GP* 1 = *AP* 7.49), an incident known otherwise from Plutarch, who also locates it Macedonia.[99] To the East Bianor's horizons extend to Sardis, whose devastation by an earthquake in AD 17 (*GP* 16 = *AP* 9.423) he compares to the well-known destruction of the Achaean cities Bura and Helice in 373–2 BC,[100] and to Egypt, where he locates not just a poem on snakes (*GP* 18 = *AP* 10.22), but also one on river-savvy wolves (*GP* 9 = *AP* 9.252). None of his several water-related poems (*GP* 3 = *AP* 7.388, *GP* 8 = *AP* 9.227, *GP* 13 = *AP* 9.278, *GP* 14 = *AP* 9.295, *GP* 20 = *AP* 11.248) specifies the Aegean, as some of these poets most probably would have.[101]

Crinagoras

The Hellenic aspect of Crinagoras' epigrams has been discussed on pp. 367–9.

Diocles

A dedication to Pan (*GP* 2 = *AP* 6.186) and metonymic use of Ares for war and Nereus for the sea (*GP* 3 = *AP* 9.109), both poems where the *Palatinus*

[97] On the theme cf. Antiphilus *GP* 27 = *AP* 7.399 with Aricò 1972.
[98] There is, however, one among the epigrams of Posidippus preserved on the Milan papyrus, 37 AB.
[99] More specifically Arethusa, Plu. *Lyc.* 31.
[100] Ovid *Met.* 15.293–4, Str. 8.359 and 384, Paus. 7.25, 2 and 5. For a defence of the text see Giangrande 1990.
[101] Though not, it must be admitted, Antiphilus *GP* 30 = *AP* 9.14, a poem that reworks Bianor *GP* 8 = *AP* 9.227: on both poems see Guidorizzi 1979.

give Diocles the name Iulius, cannot take us far; but one can expect little more in the four extant poems of a man who may be the Diocles of Carystus known from the elder Seneca.[102]

Diodorus

The eighteen poems of (a) Diodorus yield much more.[103] Five, perhaps a group, purport to be epitaphs for great Greeks: *GP* 11 = *AP* 7.235 and *GP* 14 = *AP* 7.74 for Themistocles (both specifying Magnesia); *GP* 13 = *AP* 7.40 for Aeschylus; *GP* 12 = *AP* 7.38 for Aristophanes; and *GP* 15 = *AP* 7.370 for Menander. Other, perhaps 'real' epitaphic poems relate to Nicaea (*GP* 10 = *AP* 7.701), Nicomedia (*GP* 6 = *AP* 7.627), Lesbos (*GP* 16 = *AP* 6.348), and Tarentum (*GP* 9 = *AP* 7.700). Dedicatory poems involve the Heraeum on Samos (*GP* 3 = *AP* 6.243) and the Carpathian sea and the Boeotian Cabiri (*GP* 4 = *AP* 6.245). A poem on the Pharos (*GP* 17 = *AP* 9.60) and on a miniature painting of an Arsinoe on glass (*GP* 18 = *AP* 9.776) may reveal Diodorus picking up themes from Posidippus, and suggest a context in a *provincia Asia* that was as aware of its Hellenistic traditions (Arsinoe may Cleopatra's sister, who lived in Ephesus between her display in Caesar's triumph and her murder in 41 BC)[104] as of the classical past. Against this background, the three poems for Roman eminences (*GP* 1 = *AP* 9.219 for 'Nero'; *GP* 8 = *AP* 9.405 for 'Drusus'; *GP* 3 = *AP* 6.243 on the dedication at the Heraeum by a Maximus) contribute less to Diodorus' profile, though the names of the drowned men in *GP* 5 = *AP* 7.264, Aegeus and Labeo, make it clear that his poetry has room both for the Greek and the Roman world.[105]

Erucius

Whether Greek or Italian, one poet or two, the author(s) of the fourteen epigrams in *GP* were doubtless city-dwellers: but it is a Greek countryside that stands out in the poems. Pan appears in *GP* 1 = *AP* 6.96 (receiving a

[102] Sen. *Con.* 1.25 etc., cf. RE v 801: if his full name is Iulius Diocles he could be either an imperial freedman or a member of the Carystus elite who acquired citizenship.

[103] On the problems of ascription respectively to Diodorus Zonas, to a younger Diodorus of Sardis, historian, poet and friend of Strabo (13.627–8), and to a *grammaticus* Diodorus of Tarsus see *GP* ii 264.

[104] Cichorius 1922, 320–3; *GP* ii 275–6.

[105] Gow–Page do not comment on the names. That they travel with ἑταῖροι, 'companions', perhaps to be taken as *comites*, 'members of a governor's staff', may suggest that Labeo was a Roman on official business, Aegeus perhaps a Greek φίλος, 'friend'.

sacrifice from two Arcadians); in *GP* 2 = *AP* 9.237 (where he himself pours a libation to a statue of Heracles); and in *GP* 4 = *AP* 9.824 (where he promises to aid hunters who call for his help). In *GP* 5 = *AP* 6.255 a cowherd dedicates a bull's horn;[106] *GP* 7 = *AP* 7.174 is an epitaph for another struck by lightning; *GP* 9 = *AP* 9.233 addresses a woodcutter poisoned by a spider; *GP* 3 = *AP* 9.558 describes a billy-goat whose snorts prompted the dogs to drive off a wolf from the herd. Atypically, then, the statue of Priapus described in *GP* 14 = *APl.* (A) 242 has a city setting, Lampsacus, and it is cities – Athens, Rome, Cyzicus – that mark the stages in the life of the woman whose epitaph is offered by *GP* 6 = *AP* 7.368 (cf. in Section 2, p. 371). Greek literature is treated in an encomiastic poem on Sophocles' tomb (*GP* 11 = *AP* 7.36),[107] and in a vituperative and sustained attack on the allegedly anti-Homeric elegist Parthenius, surely that of Nicaea (*GP* 13 = *AP* 7.377). Classical Greek history is represented by the well-worn anecdote of the Spartan mother killing her battle-fleeing son (*GP* 12 = *AP* 7.230), and may be glimpsed in the location chosen for the drowning of Satyrus (*GP* 8 = *AP* 7.397), Mycale.[108] The Hellenic fabric of Erucius (or the Erucii) is all-pervasive.

Euenus

Across eleven epigrams Euenus' Hellenism is located partly in books, whether those attacked by worms (*GP* 1 = *AP* 9.251) or those of Homer which secure Troy's immortality because she will 'rest in the mouths of all Hellenes' (πάντων δ᾽ Ἑλλήνων κείσομαι ἐν στόμασιν: *GP* 2 = *AP* 9.62), partly in sculpture: there are two poems on Myron's cow (*GP* 8 and 9 = *AP* 9.717 and 718), two on Praxiteles' Cnidian Aphrodite (*GP* 10 and 11 = *APl.* (A) 165 and 166). Only *GP* 4 = *AP* 9.602, on a girl who changed sex on her wedding night, specifies a Greek location, Chalcis, if *GP* is right so to take the name Χαλκίς in the seventh line (the place name would then balance 'Thebes' at the opening of the line): but metonymic Bacchus and Nymphs (*GP* 6 = *AP* 11.49),[109] and a mythologically allusive description of a swallow as 'Attic maiden' (*GP* 5 = *AP* 9.122), demand Hellenically complicit readers. This last chimes more with the Athenian than the Sicilian origin variously offered by *lemmata*, but cannot confirm it.

[106] Cf. Giangrande 1975.

[107] Cf. Borthwick 1971.

[108] It is reasonable to suppose that the poem is a literary exercise on a favourite theme, though *GP* ii 283, following *GVI* 1808, think it might be for a real inscription.

[109] But this poem is a strong candidate for composition by the fifth-century Euenus of Paros: see *GP* ii 289.

Tullius Geminus

If Tullius Geminus is indeed the *cos. suff.* of AD 46 and then *legatus Aug. pro pr.* of Moesia in the early 50s AD, as seems likely,[110] we have a clear case of a poet whose Hellenism has everything to do with his poetic *persona* and nothing to do with his personal origins. Five are ecphrastic poems on works of art: two (*GP* 8 and 9 = *AP* 6.260 and *APl.* (A) 205) on the statue of Eros given to Phryne by Praxiteles and dedicated by her to Eros at Thespiae; one on Lysippus' *Heracles* (*GP* 7 = *APl.* 103); another on Polygnotus' representation (probably a painting) of Salmoneus (*GP* 6 = *APl.* (A) 30); and finally one (*GP* 5 = *AP* 9.740), predictably, on Myron's *Cow*. *GP* 4 = *AP* 9.707 has the great Macedonian river Strymon pour forth a self-descriptive ecphrasis. Two key moments in Greek history are picked out: an epitaph for Themistocles, spoken by the Athenian leader himself, mentions Hellas, Salamis and Xerxes (*GP* 1 = *AP* 7.73); a monument for Chaeronea packs into *its* speech references to Cecrops, Philip, Marathon, Salamis, Macedonia and Demosthenes (*GP* 2 = *AP* 9.288). Only the couplet spoken by a παλίουρος, 'thorn-bush' (*GP* 3 = *AP* 9.414), seems to have no message about the poet's esteem for Greek culture.[111]

Honestus

Like Geminus, Honestus seems likely to be of Roman origin, very probably from Corinth (see in Section 2, p. 372), but his commission to write poems for sculptures of the Muses, Thamyris and Livia Augusta at Thespiae (*GP* 10–21) helpfully pins down one location where he worked. Not surprisingly, then, most of his *Anthology* epigrams have a Boeotian bias: there are poems on Thebes (*GP* 6 = *AP* 9.250), on the diverse fates of characters in Theban myth (*GP* 3 = *AP* 9.216), and on the Corinthian spring Peirene and the Heliconian Hippocrene (*GP* 4 = *AP* 9.225). Helicon is also used metonymically for the πόνος, 'labour', of poetic composition (*GP* 5 = *AP* 9.230);[112] *GP* 8 = *AP* 11.32 takes the reader across the Corinthian gulf to Corinth's near neighbour Sicyon, praised as the origin of satyr drama.[113]

[110] Cichorius 1922, 359–60, followed by *GP* ii 295.

[111] Unless the thorn-bush that is a 'guardian of fruitful plants' (τὴν φορίμων φύλακα) is a metaphor for the military power of Rome that protects Greek culture.

[112] The Muses of *GP* 21 (for the statue of Livia) are also 'Heliconian'.

[113] On this poem and his epigram on a statue of Thamyris (*GP* 20) as revealing Honestus' 'interest in recondite themes of early poetic and musical history' see Power 2010, 207–8 n.54 (noting also the Amphion myth in *GP* 3 = *AP* 9.216 and *GP* 6 = *AP* 9.250).

Maccius

The name of the poet, whether Maccius or Maecius, and his two uses of Cornelius as the name of his ἐρώμενος, 'boy-friend' (*GP* 2 = *AP* 5.117; *GP* 3 = *AP* 9.411), suggest he was working in an environment at least partly Roman or Italian. But like Marcus Argentarius, whose name also points to a Roman ambience, Maccius has many Greek 'genre' poems. These include two epigrams on works of art, a *Pan* (*GP* 9 = *AP* 9.249), and a *Bound Eros* (*GP* 11 = *APl.* (A) 198) – a suitable subject for the opening of a collection of ἐρωτικά – and two dedicatory poems: to Priapus by fishermen (*GP* 7 = *AP* 6.89), and to Isthmian Poseidon by Stratius, presumably a victor (*GP* 8 = *AP* 6.233). Very Greek, yet unparalleled in the *Anthology*, is a poem inviting Dionysus to join in grape-pressing in return for an offering of cakes and a she-goat (*GP* 10 = *AP* 9.403).

Macedonius

Of the three surviving poems, one on Italian towns that produced wine-vessels (*GP* 3 = *AP* 11.27, discussed in Section 2, p. 372) is balanced by one wholly Greek, on a hunter Codrus and his goddess Artemis (*GP* 2 = *AP* 9.275).

Myrinus

Both of Myrinus' two invective poems – a mock-dedication to Priapus by 'the Paphian's' effeminate Statyllius (*GP* 2 = *AP* 6.254) and that vilifying an old whore (*GP* 4 = *AP* 11.67) with its references to Lais, Hecuba, Sisyphus and Deucalion – have a strong Greek colour. So too his other two epigrams, rustic vignettes in which a herdsman Diotimus offers gifts to Arcadian Pans (*GP* 1 = *AP* 6.108),[114] and Eros, watching the flocks of a Thyrsis who has been lulled to sleep by mid-day wine, risks abduction by wild beasts (*GP* 3 = *AP* 7.703).

Parmenion

Of Parmenion's fifteen short epigrams only one, that on Alexander (*GP* 5 = *AP* 7.239), exploits the poet's apparently Macedonian origin. Two couplets

[114] *GP* are silent on Myrinus' choice of the name Diotimus. Albeit not uncommon, its appearance in an Arcadian setting may remind some readers of the Mantinean Diotima of Plato's *Symposium*.

on Zeus and Danaë (*GP* 1 and 2 = *AP* 5.33 and 34) play with Greek mythology. *Ecphraseis* of Polyclitus' *Hera* in the Argive Heraeum (*GP* 14 = *APl.* (A) 216) and of Pheidias' *Nemesis* at Rhamnous (*GP* 15 = *APl.* (A) 222) may suggest a visit to Achaea, or simply an interest in contributing to the corpus of such ecphrastic poems – though that on the Argive *Hera* is unique, and that on the *Nemesis* perhaps the first of three to survive.

Philip of Thessalonica

With the eighty-nine poems of Philip himself one has an even wider spectrum than for Antipater, and since many rework themes of poets in his *Garland*, some *déjà vu* is predictable. Inscription of Philip's work in a Greek literary tradition begins with the opening of his *Garland*, imitating that of Meleager (*GP* 1 = *AP* 4.2). Other literary figures to receive homage are (by implication) Homer (*GP* 33 = *AP* 7.385, on the tomb of Protesilaus: cf. Antiphilus *GP* 23 = *AP* 7.141) and Hipponax (*GP* 34 = *AP* 7.405, in simple trimeters). But the trail-breakers of Alexandrian scholarship are lampooned in *GP* 60 = *AP* 11.321 (cf. Antiphanes *GP* 9 = *AP* 11.322), on γραμματικοί, 'grammarians', as 'puppies of Zenodotus and soldiers of Callimachus'. They are also associated with recondite Aristarchan scholarship in *GP* 61 = *AP* 11.347.

Several poems are ecphrases of sculptures or paintings.[115] The paintings are a *Medea*, perhaps that of Timomachus (*GP* 70 = *APl.* (A) 137),[116] to which a poem addressing a swallow nesting on a painting of Medea (*GP* 71 = *APl.* (A) 141) may have been a pendant; and perhaps a representation of Erotes with Olympian gods' weapons (*GP* 74 = *APl.* (A) 215). The sculptures are a bronze *Eurotas* (*GP* 63 = *AP* 9.709), probably that of Eutychidas (ca. 300 BC);[117] a *Horse* by Lysippus (*GP* 64 = *AP* 9.777); Pheidias' *Zeus* at Olympia (*GP* 67 = *APl.* (A) 81); a *Heracles* in which the hero recites his labours (*GP* 68 = *APl.* (A) 93) and another is which he is said to be stripped of his weapons by Eros (*GP* 69 = *APl.* (A) 104);[118] and, perhaps, an *Aphrodite* in armour (*GP* 72 = *APl.* (A) 177).

Philip also devotes trimeter epigrams to statues of contemporary athletes: a six-times Isthmian wrestling-victor from Sinope, Damostratus

[115] But probably not, despite the many such he included by his contributors, a poem on Myron's cow, *GP* 9 = *AP* 9.742, rejected by *GP* ii 371.
[116] See Gutzwiller 2004; Gurd 2007.
[117] Plin. *Nat.* 34.78: cf. Männlein-Robert 2004.
[118] Cf. Geminus 7 *GP* = *APl.* (A) 103.

(*GP* 65 = *APl.* (A) 25), otherwise unknown, and a pancratiast from Laodicea, Heras, victorious at Smyrna, Pergamum, Delphi, Corinth (i.e. at the *Isthmia*), Olympia, Argos and Actium (*GP* 66 = *APl.* (A) 52): Heras is attested elsewhere as an Olympic victor in AD 25.

Divine statues are also implicitly the protagonists in the humorous dialogues between a passer-by and Hermes (*GP* 73 = *APl.* (A) 193), in one case, and with Priapus (*GP* 75 = *APl.* (A) 240), in another; and they are the recipients of dedications in a substantial series of epigrams. The majority of these are rural: by fishermen to Hermes (*GP* 8 = *AP* 6.5) and to Poseidon (*GP* 10 and 12 = *AP* 6.38 and 90); by a fieldworker and a ploughman to Demeter (*GP* 9 and 19 = *AP* 6.36 and 104); by a goatherd to Pan (*GP* 15 = *AP* 6.99); by a fruit-grower to Priapus (*GP* 17 = *AP* 6.102); by a hunter to Pan (*GP* 20 = *AP* 6.107). But some claim urban crafts: by a scribe to the Muses (*GP* 11 = *AP* 6.62); by a goldsmith to Hermes (*GP* 13 = *AP* 6.92); by a meat-griller to Hephaestus (*GP* 16 = *AP* 6.101); and by a carpenter and a weaver to Athena (*GP* 18 and 22 = *AP* 6.103 and 247). All present individuals with Greek names dedicating to established Greek gods. Only a thank-offering to Isis for a safe voyage combined with a prayer to escape poverty (*GP* 21 = *AP* 6.231) moves towards the margins of classical Greek religion.

Only one of Philip's half dozen epitaphic poems locates its subject's death: that on Damis (*GP* 30 = *AP* 9.26), drowned in the Icarian sea. But though here and elsewhere he is less ready than some of his contributors to offer a specific Greek location, the Hellenic fabric of his own *oeuvre* (unless his choice for what to put in his *Garland* was bizarrely unrepresentative) is firmly established by its exploitation of the Greek literary, religious and artistic heritage and of contemporary Greek athletic achievement. Poems relating to Rome, Italy and the Caesars (discussed in Section 2, pp. 374–5) had an important role, but they constitute hardly ten per cent of what we have.

Philodemus

Though only twenty-nine of his poems (roughly a third of the number of Philip's that survive) are extant, Philodemus nevertheless has a telling range of Hellenic reference. A joke-poem about several girls called Demo for whom 'Philodemus' was fated to fall (*GP* 6 = *AP* 5.115) distributes them between Paphos, Samos, Nysa and the Argolid.[119] His twenty-one ἐρωτικά,

[119] The Demo of *GP* 16 = *AP* 12.173 may be imagined as one of these, or as yet another.

'amatory poems' (*GP* 1–18, 25, 27 and 30), are liberally sprinkled with girls' names, all but one Greek: the exception (*GP* 12 = *AP* 5.306) is the explicitly Italian (Ὀπική) Flora, whose inability to sing the songs of Sappho is compensated for by her rapidly enumerated physical features and sexual skills, and whose appeal for the poet is compared to Andromeda's for Perseus. Greek mythology also supplies the Phaeacians and Bromius of the invitation to Piso (*GP* 23 = *AP* 11.44), just as Greek vineyards supply the occasion with Chian wine for the celebration of Epicurus' birthday to which he is invited; Chian and Mytilenean wines reappear (alongside Syrian frankincense) in *GP* 21 = *AP* 11.34. An ecphrastic epigram on a statue with a head of Pan, a torso of Heracles and legs of Hermes (*GP* 29 = *APl.* (A) 234) matches no known cult or work of art, but a prayer to Poseidon, Leucothea and Melicertes for a safe voyage to the Piraeus (*GP* 19 = *AP* 6.329) introduces one of the period's major Greek cults.[120] Were it not for the invitation to Piso and the talented Flora a reader would never guess that Philodemus was long-term resident on the bay of Naples, and even these poems do not exclude a Greek setting.

Polemon, Quintus, Secundus, Scaevola and Serapion

The dozen epigrams of these scantily represented poets offer a few poems whose Hellenic features chime with those already found. Polemo (*GP* 3 = *AP* 5.68) has a prayer to Eros. Secundus (*GP* 4 = *APl.* (A) 214) describes a painting or sculpture of Erotes; his *GP* 2 = *AP* 9.260 speaks as Lais lamenting her senescence. Sabinus 2 = *AP* 6.158 (reworking Leonidas *AP* 6.154) is a dedication to Pan, the Nymphs and Dionysus. Quintus 1 = *AP* 6.230 is a dedication by a Bithynian fisherman to Apollo with a prayer that he live out his years without disease.[121] Scaevola *GP* 1 = *AP* 9.217, in the voice of a goatherd, tells she-goats to stop leaping about and scrapping by a statue of ὑλιβάτην … Νόμιον, 'the mountain-climbing god of grazing', i.e. Pan.

[120] Perhaps achieving its point by bathos: the major cult is at the Isthmus, the west wind (Ζέφυρε) requires the ship to approach Piraeus from the west – so the πλατὺ κῦμα, 'broad sea', of line 5 is the short haul from the Isthmus to Piraeus. The geographically wrong, and puzzling, epithet 'Thracian' for the Zephyr alerts readers to Philodemus' game. The cult of Cybele, backdrop for the unsympathetic epitaph for the effeminate Gallus (*GP* 26 = *AP* 7.222), would hardly be seen as especially Hellenic.

[121] *Pace GP* ii 403, it is this prayer, and not the coastal position of Apollo's cult, that explains why *he* is the recipient of the fisherman's dedication.

Thallus

While one of Antonius (?) Thallus' five poems celebrates a Caesar's birthday (*GP* 2 = *AP* 6.235, discussed in Section 2, p. 375) and another has been argued to describe a plane-tree in Rome (*GP* 5 = *AP* 9.220),[122] two are markedly Hellenic. The quasi-epitaphic commemoration (*GP* 4 = *AP* 7.373) of two Milesians who died in Italy, perhaps athletes, has already been touched on: here full weight should be given to the encomiastic phrase in the sixth line, ἀστέρας ... Ἑλλάδι λαμπομένους, 'stars ... shining upon Hellas'. In the other pertinent poem (*GP* 1 = *AP* 6.9), nine warriors with Greek names dedicate different items of weaponry to Ares. If Thallus' Caesar is indeed Germanicus, his date is one at which no Greek city's warriors expected to fight for it and very few Greeks indeed were fighting for Rome either as legionaries or *auxilia*.[123] If the laudatory tone of *GP* 4 is also seen in *GP* 1, then it is the Greek past that is the object of admiration.

Zonas

Finally, the much earlier Diodorus Zonas, from the period of the Mithridatic wars.[124] His nine poems have several rural dedications: of fruits to Priapus by a fruit-warden (*GP* 1 = *AP* 6.22); of crops to Demeter and the Ὧραι, 'Seasons', by an arable-farmer (*GP* 2 = *AP* 6.98); by a hunter of a wolf-skin and his killer staff to Pan (*GP* 3 = *AP* 6.106). Pan also appears as a protector of bees (*GP* 6 = *AP* 9.226) and as a voyeuristic admirer of a bathing Daphnis (*GP* 8 = *AP* 9.556).[125] Zonas' only shipwreck poem (*GP* 5 = *AP* 7.404) has an unspecified Aegean location.

Conclusions to Section 3

The majority of Philip's poets come across as highly conscious of their place in a Greek world and a Greek literary and artistic tradition. There are exceptions, like Antiphanes and Antistius, which show that this Hellenism is not an unbreakable generic law. But it can certainly be argued that the rules of the genre had been established in the third to first centuries BC, by poets including many of those represented by Meleager's selection in his *Garland*, and that Philip's poets were simply continuing to write epigram according to these

[122] Kuttner 1999: cf. p. 395. [123] See Bowie 2014c (Chapter 35 in Volume 3).
[124] See *GP* ii 264, citing Str. 13.627–8.
[125] For Pan as Daphnis' lover see Glaucus *GP* 3 = *AP* 9.341.

rules. And indeed some of the important Hellenic resonances occur in types of epigram that had been established early in the Hellenistic development of the genre, by such poets as Anyte, Nossis and Posidippus, i.e. Greek rustic scenes and depictions of Greek works of art. Moreover the extent to which poets of apparently Roman or Italian origin – Lollius Bassus, Erucius, Honestus, Tullius Geminus – present the same density of Hellenic colour as those who are apparently Greek poets shows that a major factor is generic expectation. That said, the smallish number of poems, by only a small number of these poets, that take up Roman or Italian subjects or are directed to Roman friends shows that the genre was capable of morphing in response to the new configuration of the Mediterranean world. It is then legitimate to ask why there are not more such poems, and to observe that they become no more frequent in the later decades of the period covered by the *Garland*, ca. 70 BC to ca. AD 53. My tentative answer would be that the 'freezing' of Greek epigram in its Hellenistic shape was an early symptom of the literary effort to create an autonomous Greek world, much of it built on re-creations of the Greek past, that we encounter in full flow in the period of the second sophistic. Chariton's *Callirhoe* was most probably published before Philip assembled his *Garland*,[126] and the first of Philostratus' sophists, Nicetes of Smyrna, is already active under Nero.

4 Overall Conclusions

The cruise has perhaps been too long, but we have seen the cities and glimpsed the *mentalité* of many men. Much more than the brief glimpses the material allows would be needed to build up a secure case. But some often-repeated views begin to look less well-founded. The claim that a poet 'sought or enjoyed patronage at the imperial court' should be advanced less often than it is by Gow and Page. The notion that several of these people spent long periods in Rome – and hence were bound to meet each other there – should be deployed with more caution than it was by Bowersock in 1965. Nor does his characterisation of the poets of Philip's *Garland* any longer seem quite right: 'It was natural that, when Philip of Thessalonica assembled a garland of Greek verse in the reign of Gaius, he drew from the works of poets *at the imperial court* [my italics] under Augustus and Tiberius as under Gaius himself'.[127] Many of these poets came into contact from time to time with highly placed Romans, but their life rarely revolved around them: Philodemus may to some extent be an exception. Many or

[126] See Bowie 2002a (Chapter 25 in this volume); Tilg 2010.

perhaps most may have been, indeed are likely to have been, members of local Greek elites with property and power in their own *polis* and even province, concerns that spread over the whole region of the Aegean, especially its northern waters and shores, and in some cases a strong sense of Hellenic identity that comes out visibly in the analysis of Section 3. When visiting the West they may have been cultivated and cultural tourists rather than 'luxury cruisers', and sometimes, as is documented for Crinagoras, their chief purpose in Italy and Rome may have been business, not pleasure.

Appendix: A Preliminary Chronology of Philip's Poets

Diodorus Zonas	active during Mithridatic wars
Philodemus	?70–ca. 40 BC
(Q. Mucius?) Scaevola	50s BC[a]
Crinagoras	ca. 47–ca. 10 BC (or later?)
Erucius	ca. 30 BC
Diodorus (the younger) of Sardis	ca. 20–ca. 9 BC
Antipater of Thessalonica	ca. 12–ca. 1 BC
Apollonides of Nicaea	ca. 10 BC–ca. AD 10
Antistius	ca. 10 BC–ca. AD 21
Sabinus	?ca. AD 10[b]
Bianor	ca. AD 17
Antonius Thallus	ca. AD 18
Lollius Bassus	ca. AD 19
King Polemo (?II)	ca. AD 37–63
Antiphilus of Byzantium	AD 33–53
Tullius Geminus	*cos. suff.* AD 46; *leg. Aug. Moesiae* early 50s AD
Philip of Thessalonica	active as poet AD 37–9

[a] Cf. *GP* ii 406.

[b] If this Sabinus is the friend of Ovid, *Am.* 2.18.27, *Pont.* 4.16.15. Given the possible presence of Tullius Geminus in the *Garland* he could equally be Poppaeus Sabinus, who was in Macedonia in AD 14 (cf. Tac. *Ann.* 1.80) and who died in AD 34 (*ibid.* 6.49).

Undateable poets: Adaeus,[128] Aemilianus of Nicaea,[129] Antiphanes of Macedon, Automedon, Euenus, Maccius, Myrinus, Parmenio, Quintus, Secundus.

[127] Bowersock 1965, 141.

[128] Unless he is the *rhetor* known from Sen. *Con.* 9.1.12 etc.

[129] Unless he is the *rhetor* known from Sen. *Con.* 10.34.25.

18 | Doing Doric (2016)

1 Introduction

This paper has two parts. In the longer, first part I offer some observations on the use of Doric by poets whose work has been transmitted initially *via* the *Garland of Philip* and then *via* the *Anthology*. In the second and shorter part I consider the case of five poems from a sepulchral monument in Nicaea, poems not read by modern epigraphists but preserved by Book 15 of the *Anthology*.

2 The *Garland of Philip*

Some of Philip's poets, especially those of the middle and latter part of the first century BC, have no truck with Doric. This is no surprise in Philodemus, whom neither his Gadarene origin nor his Italian residence, whether in Rome or on the Bay of Naples, would have given an incentive to compose any of his twenty-nine surviving epigrams in Doric. Nor is it a surprise in the fifteen poems of Parmenion and Diodorus of Sardis respectively, despite the Spartans at Thermopylae being the subject of Parmenion *GP* 10 = *AP* 9.304 and a Tarentine setting being that of Diodorus *GP* 9 = *AP* 7.700. But if it is right to think that Honestus was domiciled in Corinth it is somewhat surprising that none of his twenty-two poems shows any sign of Doric,[1] and also perhaps surprising that Crinagoras, despite his Mytilenean origin, adhered throughout his fifty-one surviving poems to Attic-Ionic.[2] Less can be argued on the basis of poets of whose epigrams only very few survive, but for what it is worth I note that there is no Doric in the single surviving epigrams of Apollonius, Automedon, Boethus, Diotimus, Etruscus, Quintus, Scaevola or Serapion; in the two epigrams of Sabinus; in the three of Macedonius, Maeandrius or Polemo; or in the four of Diocles or Secundus.

[1] For Honestus see Jones 2004, 93–6; Bowie 2012e, 236 (Chapter 17, 386 in this volume).

[2] But for the absence of local dialect features from the works of both Theophanes and Crinagoras see Bowie 2011b, esp. 195 (Chapter 26 in Volume 3).

In certain poets who did choose Doric for *some* of their surviving poems it might be argued that the dialect is chosen either when there is a thematic or contextual trigger in the poem, or when the poem follows or refashions the work of an earlier poet strongly associated with Doric.

Thus several poems using Doric evoke either a Leonidean or a Theocritean pastoral world, and their poets may be choosing to use Doric so as to stress that aspect of a poem. Of Myrinus' four transmitted epigrams it is only that on Thyrsis asleep that uses Doric:

> Θύρσις ὁ κωμήτης, ὁ τὰ νυμφικὰ μῆλα νομεύων,
> Θύρσις ὁ συρίζων Πανὸς ἴσον δόνακι,
> ἔνδιος οἰνοπότης σκιερὰν ὑπὸ τὰν πίτυν εὕδει·
> φρουρεῖ δ' αὐτὸς ἑλὼν ποίμνια βάκτρον Ἔρως.
> ἆ Νύμφαι, Νύμφαι, διεγείρατε τὸν λυκοθαρσῆ
> βοσκόν, μὴ θηρῶν κύρμα γένηται Ἔρως.
>
> Thyrsis the rustic, who pastures the Nymphs' sheep,
> Thyrsis whose piping equals Pan's reed,
> the noon wine-bibber, is under the shady pine, asleep,
> and Eros himself has taken a crook and guards his flocks.
> – oh Nymphs! Nymphs! Wake up the wolf-bold
> herdsman, lest the beasts' prey should be Eros.

Myrinus *GP* 3 = *AP* 7.703

Of Thallus' poems it is just one, on the pleasures of sex under a plane-tree entwined with a vine, his only surviving treatment of a rural (though not properly pastoral) scene, that is also his only epigram to exploit Doric:

> Ἁ χλοερὰ πλατάνιστος ἴδ' ὡς ἔκρυψε φιλεύντων
> ὄργια τὰν ἱερὰν φυλλάδα τεινομένα·
> ἀμφὶ δ' ἄρ' ἀκρεμόνεσσιν ἑοῖς κεχαρισμένος ὥραις
> ἡμερίδος λαρῆς βότρυς ἀποκρέμαται.
> οὕτως, ὦ πλατάνιστε, φύοις· χλοερὰ δ' ἀπὸ σεῖο
> φυλλὰς ἀεὶ κεύθοι τοὺς Παφίης ἑτάρους.
>
> The green plane-tree – see how it has hid the lovers'
> rites, stretching out its sacred foliage:
> and around its own branches, a delight to the Seasons,
> a sweet tended vine's bunch dangles down.
> So may you grow, plane-tree, and may your growth
> of green foliage ever conceal the Paphian's companions.

Thallus *GP* 5 = *AP* 9.220

Another example is Adaeus' epigram for a dedication by Crethon to Demeter 'characteristic of the imitators of Leonidas' (*GP ad loc.*), 'in the Leonidean manner':[3]

Τὰν ὄιν, ὦ Δάματερ Ἐπόγμιε, τάν τ' ἀκέρωτον
μόσχον καὶ τροχιὰν ἐν κανέωι φθοΐδα
σοὶ ταύτας ἐφ' ἅλωος, ἐφ' ἇι πολὺν ἔβρασεν ἄντλον
Κρήθων καὶ λιπαρὰν εἶδε γεωμορίαν,
ἱρεύει, πολύσωρε· σὺ δὲ Κρήθωνος ἄρουραν
πᾶν ἔτος εὔκριθον καὶ πολύπυρον ἄνοις.

The ewe, Demeter of the Furrow, and the hornless
calf, and the wheel-cake in its basket,
to you, on this threshing-floor, where a rich pile
he has winnowed, and seen a brilliant harvest, Crethon
consecrates, o many-heaped one! May you make Crethon's plough-land
fine in barley and plentiful in wheat every year.

Adaeus *GP* 2 = *AP* 6.258

The name Crethon is already in Adaeus' model, Leonidas:

αὕτα ἐπὶ Κρήθωνος ἐγὼ λίθος, οὔνομα κείνου
δηλοῦσα· Κρήθων δ' ἐγχθόνιος σποδιά.
ὁ πρὶν καὶ Γύγηι παρισεύμενος ὄλβον, ὁ τὸ πρὶν
βουπάμων, ὁ πρὶν πλούσιος αἰπολίοις,
ὁ πρίν – τί πλείω μυθεῦμ' ἔτι; πᾶσι μακαρτός,
φεῦ, γαίης ὅσσης ὅσσον ἔχει μόριον.

Here upon Crethon stand I, a stone, and his name
I display; but Crethon's in the earth, he's ash.
He who before equated his prosperity even with Gyges, who before
was cattle-rich, who before was wealthy in flocks,
who before – why do I say more? Blessed in every way
alas! of so much land how small a piece he has!

Leonidas *HE* 75 = *AP* 7.740

But as *GP* noted Adaeus is also influenced by Theocritus 7.154–7.[4]

Both such a pastoral setting *and* Doric subjects seem to have been relevant to Erucius' decisions to use Doric. Of his fourteen transmitted poems

[3] Cf. Magnelli 2007, 178.

[4] οἷον δὴ τόκα πῶμα διεκρανάσατε, Νύμφαι, | βωμῶι πὰρ Δάματρος ἀλωίδος; ἇς ἐπὶ σωρῶι | αὖτις ἐγὼ πάξαιμι μέγα πτύον, ἁ δὲ γελάσσαι | δράγματα καὶ μάκωνας ἐν ἀμφοτέραισιν ἔχοισα, 'such was once the drink that your fountain poured forth, Nymphs, by the altar of Demeter of the threshing-floor: on whose heap may I again plant a mighty winnowing-fan, and may she laugh, holding sheaves and poppies in both hands'.

Erucius chooses Doric for no less than eight, in four of these apparently for its pastoral associations; and of those for which he did not choose to use any Doric two were virtually excluded by their subject matter – an epigram on an Athenian woman who died at Cyzicus which begins programmatically with her ethnic Ἀτθίς, *GP* 6 = *AP* 7.368,[5] and another on the Athenian poet Sophocles, *GP* 11 = *AP* 7.36. The poems with some Doric have almost all a pastoral setting:

Two oxherds sacrifice to Pan:[6]

Γλαύκων καὶ Κορύδων, οἱ ἐν οὔρεσι βουκολέοντες,
Ἀρκάδες ἀμφότεροι, τὸν κεραὸν δαμάλην
Πανὶ φιλωρείται Κυλληνίωι αὐερύσαντες
ἔρρεξαν καί οἱ δωδεκάδωρα κέρα
ἅλωι μακροτένοντι ποτὶ πλατάνιστον ἔπαξαν
εὐρεῖαν, νομίωι καλὸν ἄγαλμα θεῶι.

Glaucon and Corydon, who herd cattle in the mountains,
Arcadians both, took the horned calf
for Pan, the mountain-loving Cyllenian, drew back its head,
and slaughtered it; and its twelve-palmed horns
they pinned with a long-tapered nail to a plane-tree
that stood broad, a fair ornament for the god of pastures.

Erucius *GP* 1 = *AP* 6.96

Dogs frighten off wolves:

Ὁ τράγος ὁ Κλήσωνος ὅλαν διὰ πάννυχον ὄρφναν
αἶγας ἀκοιμάτους θῆκε φριμασσόμενος –
ὀδμὰ γάρ μιν ἔτυψε λύκου χιμαροσφακτῆρος
τηλόθε πετραίαν αὖλιν ἀνερχομένου –
μέσφα κύνες κοίτας ἀνεγέρμονες ἐπτοίασαν
θῆρα μέγαν· τραγίνους δ' ὕπνος ἔμυσε κόρας.

Clyson's billy-goat throughout all the dark night
kept the nanny-goats awake with his snorting –
for the scent of a she-goat-slaying wolf had struck him
as it made its way up from afar to the rock-built fold –
until the dogs, aroused from their rest, scared off
the great beast, and sleep closed the goats' eyes.

Erucius *GP* 3 = *AP* 9.558

5 Merkelbach-Stauber 2001, 08/01/36 = *GVI* 806.

6 The Doric forms are φιλωρείται (3) and ἅλωι, ποτὶ, and ἔπαξαν (5). For a succinct and judicious statement of the debated relationship between this poem and the *Arcades ambo* of Vergil, *Ecl.* 7.1–5 see Clausen 1994.

Pan promises success to hunters. The dialect is very Doric, the subject reworks a poem of Leonidas:

Εὔστοχα θηροβολεῖτε, κυναγέται, οἱ ποτὶ ταύταν
    Πανὸς ὀρειώτα νισσόμενοι σκοπιάν,
αἴτε λίνοις βαίνοιτε πεποιθότες, αἴτε σιδάρωι,
    αἴτε καὶ ἰξευταὶ λαθροβόλωι δόνακι·
κἀμέ τις ὑμείων ἐπιβωσάτω· οἶδά ποτ' ἄγραν
    κοσμεῖν καὶ λόγχαν καὶ λίνα καὶ καλάμους.

May you hit your target, huntsmen, who to this
    peak of mountain-dwelling Pan come,
whether you advance trusting in nets, or in iron,
    or indeed are fowlers with a stealthy-striking rod;
and let each of you call upon me: I know how to set
    the foot-trap, and spear, and nets, and reeds.

Erucius *GP* 4 = *AP* 9.824

The Leonidas poem is clearly Erucius' model, but Erucius has eight Doricisms in his six lines (κυναγέται, ποτὶ, ταύταν, ὀρειώτα, σιδάρωι, ἐπιβωσάτω, ποτ'(ί), λόγχαν), Leonidas only one in his four (βόασον, line 3):

Εὐάγρει, λαγόθηρα, καὶ εἰ πετεεινὰ διώκων
    ἰξευτὴς ἥκεις τοῦθ' ὑπὸ δισσὸν ὄρος,
κἀμὲ τὸν ὑλωρὸν ἀπὸ κρημνοῖο βόασον
    Πᾶνα· συναγρεύω καὶ κυσὶ καὶ καλάμοις.

Good hunting, hare-chaser, or if pursuing winged things
    you come with lime to beneath this twin peak,
and from a crag call upon me, the forest-watcher,
    Pan: I shall join your hunt with dogs and reeds.

Leonidas *HE* 29 = *AP* 9.337

An epitaph for a cowherd, is marked by light Doric:

Οὐκέτι συρίγγων νόμιον μέλος ἀγχόθι ταύτας
    ἁρμόζηι βλωθρᾶς, Θηρίμαχε, πλατάνου·
οὐδέ σευ ἐκ καλάμων κεραοὶ βόες ἁδὺ μέλισμα
    δέξονται σκιερᾶι πὰρ δρυῒ κεκλιμένου.
ὤλεσε γὰρ πρηστήρ σε κεραύνιος· αἱ δ' ἐπὶ μάνδραν
    ὀψὲ βόες νιφετῶι σπερχόμεναι κατέβαν.

No more do you fashion your pastoral tune near this
    tall plane-tree, Beast-fighter,

nor will the horned cattle listen to the sweet tuning from your reeds
as you recline beside a shady oak.
For a lightning bolt destroyed you: and to their byre
your cows came down late, hurried by snow.

Erucius *GP* 7 = *AP* 7.174

Two other poems seem to use Doric not only because of their pastoral setting but also because their speaker is Dorian. One, on a statue of Heracles about which an unnamed interlocutor asks a cowherd, is noted by *GP* as exhibiting a 'severer Doric dialect':

'Βουκόλε, πρὸς τῶ Πανός, ὁ φήγινος, εἰπέ, κολοσσὸς
οὗτος, ὅτωι σπένδεις τὸ γλάγος, ἔστι τίνος;'
'Τῶ λειοντοπάλα Τιρυνθίω· οὐδὲ τὰ τόξα,
νήπιε, καὶ σκυτάλην ἀγριέλαιον ὁρῇς'.
'Χαίροις, Ἀλκείδα δαμαληφάγε, καὶ τάδε φρούρει
αὔλια κὴξ ὀλίγων μυριόβοια τίθει'.

'Cowherd, in Pan's name tell me, the oak statue
here, for whom you pour your libation of milk – whose is it?'
'The Tirythian lion-wrestler's: do you not even see his bow,
you idiot, and his club of wild-olive?'
'Hail, calf-eating Alcides, and guard these
byres, and from few make their cattle countless'.

Erucius *GP* 2 = *AP* 9.237

The second is both pastoral and at the same time a vehicle for the thoughts of an Ambraciot dedicator: it uses several Doric forms despite touches of epic colour:[7]

Τοῦτο Σάων τὸ δίπαχυ κόλον κέρας Ὠμβρακιώτας
βουμολγὸς ταύρου κλάσσεν ἀτιμαγέλου,
ὁππότε μιν κνημούς τε κατὰ λασίους τε χαράδρας
ἐξερέων ποταμοῦ φράσσατ' ἐπ' ἀιόνι
ψυχόμενον χηλάς τε καὶ ἰξύας· αὐτὰρ ὃ βούτεω
ἀντίος ἐκ παγέων ἵεθ'· ὁ δὲ ῥοπάλωι
γυρὸν ἀπεκράνιξε βοὸς κέρας, ἐκ δέ μιν αἰπᾶς
ἀχράδος εὐμύκωι πᾶξε παρὰ κλισίαι.

This docked horn of two cubits Saon the Ambraciot,
the cow-milker, broke off from a bull that scorned his herd,

[7] Epic colour noted by *GP* ii 282. For a defence of the Palatinus' αὐτᾶς and a rejection of *GP*'s emendation αἰπᾶς see Giangrande 1975, 41–2.

after he had sought it out along the ridges and shaggy torrent-beds
and spotted it on a river's bank
cooling its hooves and flanks. But right for the cowherd
it lunged from the stream – and he with his club
de-headed the curved horn from the ox's head, and on a tall
pear tree fixed it, beside his fine-lowing byre.

Erucius *GP* 5 = *AP* 6.255

The remaining poem of Erucius to use Doric seems to do so exclusively because of its Dorian subject: a Spartan mother castigates and kills her son who had fled from the battlefield (i.e. he was a τρέσας, 'deserter'). The Doric appears both in the description and in the mother's words that are quoted:

Ἁνίκ' ἀπὸ πτολέμου τρέσσαντά σε δέξατο μάτηρ,
πάντα τὸν ὁπλιστὰν κόσμον ὀλωλεκότα,
αὐτά τοι φονίαν, Δαμάτριε, αὐτίκα λόγχαν
εἶπε διὰ πλατέων ὠσαμένα λαγόνων·
'Κάτθανε, μηδ' ἐχέτω Σπάρτα ψόγον· οὐ γὰρ ἐκείνα
ἤμπλακεν, εἰ δειλοὺς τοὐμὸν ἔθρεψε γάλα'.

When you fled battle and your mother received you
after you had lost all your hoplite gear,
it was she herself, Damatrios, who forthwith a deadly spear
thrust through your broad flanks, with the words
'Die, and may Sparta bear no blame: for it is not
she who erred, if it was cowards my milk nourished'.

Erucius *GP* 12 = *AP* 7.230

By contrast I can see no obvious explanation for the choice of Doric in an epigram in which a Gallus dedicates his kit to Cybele:

Γάλλος ὁ χαιτάεις, ὁ νεήτομος, ὡπὸ Τυμώλου
Λύδιος ὀρχηστὰς μάκρ' ὀλολυζόμενος,
τᾶι παρὰ Σαγγαρίωι τάδε Ματέρι τύμπαν' ἀγαυᾶι
θήκατο καὶ μάστιν τὰν πολυαστράγαλον
ταῦτά τ' ὀρειχάλκου λάλα κύμβαλα καὶ μυρόεντα
βόστρυχον, ἐκ λύσσας ἄρτ' ἀναπαυσάμενος.

The long-haired Gallus, gelded young, the one from Tmolus,
the Lydian dancer whose shrieks carry far,
has dedicated to the noble Mother by the Sangarius
these timbrels and scourge with many knuckle-bones
and these chattering copper cymbals and a perfumed
lock, having just now entered rest after frenzy.

Erucius *GP* 10 = *AP* 6.234

Since Erucius' origin is Cyzicus it might seem probable that his choice of dialect related to the city's claims to have been originally an ἀποικία, 'colony', of Corinth, though the city was later refounded by Miletus. Epigraphically preserved epigrams from Cyzicus do indeed use some Doric, though neither extensively nor consistently, and its proportion diminishes slightly between the Hellenistic and imperial periods. But even what seems to be our earliest case, from the third or second or first century BC, an iambic trimeter epitaph for Menecrates, has only three or four Doric forms in eight lines other than the personal name of his father, Matrodorus.[8] From the second or first centuries BC an elegiac poem for Maeandria surprisingly has twelve Doric forms in ten lines,[9] whereas one for Menander has only two in six lines.[10] A first century AD epitaph for Alexander from Alexandria has only two Doric forms in eight lines,[11] while the elaborate and ambitious acrostic poem for Apollonides, of the first or second century AD, two in its ten lines – the first (ἁ …) required by the acrostic, and the second (ποτί) perhaps following suit: the remaining nine and a half lines are consistently Attic-Ionic.[12] Likewise two imperial epigrams from Cyzicene territory for statues of poets eschew Doric – though of course that both statues are of epic poets may have been sufficient reason for their epigrammatists to maintain Attic-Ionic. That for Homer's statue is short and simple:[13]

ἡρώων κλέα πολλὰ καὶ Ἰλιακοῦ πολέμοιο
κοσμήσας ὁ θεοῖς ἶσος Ὅμηρος ὅδε.

The man who the heroes' many deeds of renown and the war for Ilium
arrayed, the man equal to the gods, Homer, is before you.

IMT Kyz Kapu Dağ 1425

The other, much later, is for the poet Nestor of Laranda:[14]

ἡ βουλή{ι} τείμεσσεν ἀγασσαμένη τὸν ἀοιδόν
Νέστορα καὶ μολπῆς εἵνεκα καὶ βιοτοῦ·

[8] Merkelbach-Stauber 2001, 08/01/47 = *GVI* 1792 = *IKyzikos* 520: [τᾶς] Ἀφροδίτας ναός (1), ἐτερπόμαν (3), Ματροδώρου (8): ναός, regular in Attic tragedy, might well not be perceived as Doric. For the special case of personal names see Sens 2004, 73 with n.38.

[9] Merkelbach-Stauber 2001, 08/01/45 (assigning to the late Hellenistic period) = *GVI* 1585 (assigning to the second or first century BC) = *IKyzikos* 516: Φερσεφόνα (1), θνατοὺς ἁλικίαν θεμένα (2), τᾷ (3), ἀλλοδαπὰν (5), δεικνυμένα (6), γενόμαν … λειπομένα (8), Φερσεφόνας (9), Λάθας λουσαμένα (10).

[10] Merkelbach-Stauber 2001, 08/01/46 = *GVI* 1552 = *IKyzikos* 519 τὰν (1), ἀνδρολέταν (6).

[11] Merkelbach-Stauber 2001, 08/01/33 = *GVI* 1816 = *IKyzikos* 492: δμαθεὶς (1), Λάθας (2)

[12] Merkelbach-Stauber 2001, 08/01/34 = *GVI* 1610 = *IKyzikos* 494: ἁ … ποτὶ (1).

[13] Merkelbach-Stauber 2001, 08/01/04.

[14] *CIG* 3671 = Merkelbach-Stauber 2001, 08/01/07. On Nestor of Laranda see Ma 2007.

[ε]ἰκόνα <δ’> ἐξετέλεσσεν καὶ εἵσατο πατρίδος ἄρχων
Κορνοῦτος θαλερῆς ἐν τ<ε>μένεσσ<ι> Κόρης·
ὄφρα καὶ ὀψίγον<ο>ί περ ἐν ἄστεϊ παῖδες ἔχοιεν
σῆμα φιλοξενίας καὶ δέλεαρ σοφίης.

The Council honoured in admiration the bard
Nestor, both for his singing and his lifestyle.
The image was made and set up by the fine city's archon
Cornutus in the precincts of Korē,
so that children in later generations too might have
a marker of friendly action and a lure to wisdom.

IMT Kyz Kapu Dağ 1451

If there is a pattern to be discerned at all, it is one which reveals a decline in Doric by the late first century BC.[15] Erucius' choice, then, was not determined by his Cyzicene origin.

But similar choices to those of Erucius of Cyzicus may also be seen in the epigrams of Antiphilus of Byzantium,[16] who seems to eschew Doric for paradoxography, but uses it in a Leonidean dedication by the rustic Parmis, a γατόμος, 'ploughman' (line 6), whereas in his other Leonidean dedications by tradesmen he does not:[17]

Βουστρόφον, ἀκροσίδαρον, ἀπειλητῆρα μύωπα
καὶ πήραν μέτρου σιτοδόκον σπορίμου
γαμψόν τε δρέπανον, σταχυητόμον ὅπλον ἀρούρης,
καὶ παλιουροφόρον, χεῖρα θέρευς, τρίνακα
καὶ τρητοὺς ποδεῶνας ὁ γατόμος ἄνθετο Δηοῖ,
Πάρμις, ἀνιηρῶν παυσάμενος καμάτων.

His ox-turning, iron-tipped, threatening goad,
and wallet that held corn in the measure to be sown,
and curved sickle, ear-cutting tool of the field,
and fork that casts back to the wind, the harvest's hand,

[15] I set aside the sporadically Doric poems describing mythological scenes represented on columns of the early second century BC temple of Apollonis, mother of Attalus and Eumenes of Pergamum: it seems clear that the nineteen poems, constituting Book Three of the *Palatine Anthology*, are late, perhaps as late as Nonnus, cf. Demoen 1988, Cameron 1993, 148.

[16] *GP* ii 117 rightly see his geographical references as confirming the ethnic 'Byzantine' attached to twenty-four poems, though they miss the *mise-en-scène* of Elaeous at *GP* 23 (= *AP* 7.141). See also Robert 1979.

[17] On these other dedications see Ypsilanti 2006. For an interesting proposal that Antiphilus *GP* 11 (= *AP* 10.17) was a programmatic first poem in an Antiphilan collection and 16 (= *AP* 6.199) an epilogue see Höschele 2007, 360–1.

and pierced funnels – the ploughman dedicated to Dēo,
Parmis, when he retired from his painful toils.

Antiphilus *GP* 15 = *AP* 6.95

This reworks a Leonidas poem which is also a dedication by a rustic Parmis, Leonidas *HE* 66 (= *AP* 7.504), where the *Palatinus* has Doric ὀλοάν (line 6) and παλλομένα (line 8) but *HE* (and other editors) print Ionic ὀλοήν and παλλομένη.

Antiphilus also uses Doric for the several poems with arguably Doric themes. One of these immortalises the moment when Nero gave freedom to the Dorian island of Rhodes:

Ὡς πάρος Ἀελίου, νῦν Καίσαρος ἁ Ῥόδος εἰμὶ
νᾶσος, ἴσον δ' αὐχῶ φέγγος ἀπ' ἀμφοτέρων·
ἤδη σβεννυμέναν με νέα κατεφώτισεν ἀκτίς,
Ἅλιε, καὶ παρὰ σὸν φέγγος ἔλαμψε Νέρων.
πῶς εἴπω, τίνι μᾶλλον ὀφείλομαι; ὃς μὲν ἔδειξεν
ἐξ ἁλός, ὃς δ' ἤδη ῥύσατο δυομέναν;

Just as before I was the island of the Sun, so now I, Rhodes, am Caesar's,
and I boast an equal light from both:
when I was already being extinguished a new beam lit me up,
Sun, and alongside your light shone Nero.
How can I put it? To which of you do I owe more? To the one displayed me
from the sea, or the other saved me when I was already sinking?

Antiphilus *GP* 6 = *AP* 9.178

Another describes a painting of Leda and the swan, and here the choice of dialect may be a response to the very explicitly Spartan setting:

Χεῦμα μὲν Εὐρώταο Λακωνικόν, ἁ δ' ἀκάλυπτος
Λήδα χὠ κύκνωι κρυπτόμενος Κρονίδας.
οἵ δέ με τὸν δυσέρωτα καταίθετε. καὶ τί γένωμαι;
ὄρνεον. εἰ γὰρ Ζεὺς κύκνος, ἐγὼ κόρυδος.

The stream is the Eurotas, in Laconia, the unclothed woman
Leda, the male concealed as a swan, Zeus.
You inflame my fragile passion – just what am I to become?
A bird. If Zeus is a swan, then I am a lark.[18]

Antiphilus *GP* 13 = *AP* 5.307

[18] *GP* see this as an adaptation of the 'proverbial phrase' comparing the singing of larks and swans, *AP* 9.380.1 and Dioscorides *HE* 36.5–6 (= *AP* 11.195.5–6). Konstan 2008, 296–7 suggests that Antiphilus' point is that like Zeus he will be a singing bird – not indeed a swan, but 'at all events' a lark. This still lacks force, and I suggest there may also be a pun – with itacism κόρυδος can sound like κόρη δός, 'Give, girl'.

The Trojan horse of Antiphilus *GP* 35 (= *AP* 9.156) is a more precarious case. The *Palatinus* reads ὅλα in line 4 and μάταν in line 5, both of which *GP* print; the Planudean reads ὅλη and μάτην. Homer had Menelaus describe the Trojan horse filled with the best of the Argives (Od. 4.271–3), which may be enough to explain the Doricisms.[19]

Δέρκεο τὸν Τροίας δεκέτη λόχον, εἴσιδε πῶλον
εὐόπλου Δαναῶν ἔγκυον ἡσυχίης.
τεκταίνει μὲν Ἐπειός, Ἀθηναίη δὲ κελεύει
ἔργον, ὑπὲκ νώτου δ᾽ Ἑλλὰς ὅλα δύεται.
ἦ ῥα μάταν ἀπόλοντο τόσος στρατός, εἰ πρὸς Ἄρηα
ἦν δόλος Ἀτρείδαις ἐσθλότερος πολέμου.

Behold the tenth-year ambush of Troy, behold the filly
pregnant with Greeks' well-armed silence.
The carpenter is Epeius, and Athena commands
the work, and up into its back all Greece enters.
In vain did so large an army perish, if for Ares
the Atreidae found guile better than battle.

The Doric of a poem on the corpse of Leonidas is much more pervasive, though at line 6 the Palatine has Ionic ἐλευθερίης where the Planudean has ἐλευθερίας:

'Πορφυρέαν τοι τάνδε, Λεωνίδα, ὤπασε χλαῖναν
Ξέρξης ταρβήσας ἔργα τεᾶς ἀρετᾶς.'
'οὐ δέχομαι· προδόταις αὕτα χάρις· ἀσπὶς ἔχοι με
καὶ νέκυν· ὁ πλοῦτος δ᾽ οὐκ ἐμὸν ἐντάφιον.'
'ἀλλ᾽ ἔθανες. τί τοσόνδε καὶ ἐν νεκύεσσιν ἀπεχθὴς
Πέρσαις;' 'οὐ θνάισκει ζᾶλος ἐλευθερίας.'

'This purple cloak, Leonidas, is given you
by Xerxes, in fear of your valour's deeds.'
'I do not take it. This is a favour to traitors. May a shield cover me
even as a corpse. Wealth is not my shroud.'
'But you have died. Why, when dead, so hostile
to Persians?' 'Love of freedom never dies.'

Antiphilus *GP* 38 = *AP* 9.294

[19] Or perhaps Antiphilus has been reading the Ἰλίου πέρσις, '*Sack of Troy*', of Stesichorus, a well-known poem, or that of the Argive poet Sacadas, still known to Ath. 13.610c some 150 years after Antiphilus, cf. Bowie 2014a (Chapter 28 in Volume 1).

Similarly another epigram has six instances of Doric in eight lines in describing Timomachus' *Medea*, perhaps gesturing to the myth's location in Corinth:[20]

Τὰν ὀλοὰν Μήδειαν ὅτ' ἔγραφε Τιμομάχου χεὶρ
ζάλωι καὶ τέκνοις ἀντιμεθελκομέναν,
μυρίον ἄρατο μόχθον, ἵν' ἤθεα δισσὰ χαράξηι,
ὧν τὸ μὲν εἰς ὀργὰν νεῦε, τὸ δ' εἰς ἔλεον.
ἄμφω δ' ἐπλήρωσεν· ὅρα τύπον· ἐν γὰρ ἀπειλᾶι
δάκρυον, ἐν δ' ἐλέωι θυμὸς ἀναστρέφεται.
ἀρκεῖ δ' ἁ μέλλησις, ἔφα σοφός· αἷμα δὲ τέκνων
ἔπρεπε Μηδείηι, κοὐ χερὶ Τιμομάχου

When Timomachus' hand painted murderous Medea
by her jealousy and her children pulled to and fro,
he took on a huge task, to sculpt the two sides of her character,
of which one inclined to anger, the other to pity,
and achieved both: see the image – for in her threat
a tear lurks, and in her pity, anger.
'Intent suffices', said the sage: the children's blood
fitted Medea, not Timomachus' hand.

Antiphilus *GP* 48 = *APl.* (A) 136

Another ecphrasis weaves some Doric into its description of a painting of Perseus and Andromeda, presumably because Perseus is a hero of Argive descent:

Αἰθιόπων ἁ βῶλος· ὁ δὲ πτερόεις τὰ πέδιλα
Περσεύς· ἁ δὲ λίθωι πρόσδετος Ἀνδρομέδα·
ἁ προτομὰ Γοργοῦς λιθοδερκέος· ἆθλον ἔρωτος
κῆτος· Κασσιόπας ἁ λάλος εὐτεκνία.
χὰ μὲν ἀπὸ σκοπέλοιο χαλᾶι πόδ' ἀνηθάδι νάρκαι
νωθρόν· ὁ δὲ μναστὴρ νυμφοκομεῖ τὸ γέρας.

The soil is Ethiopian; the man with winged sandals
Perseus; the woman tied to the rock Andromeda;
the head, a petrifying Gorgon's; love's ordeal
a sea-monster; Cassiopeia's, the big-mouthed child-pride.
She loosens her legs from the crag, numb with
now-familiar torpor; her suitor scoops his bridal prize.

Antiphilus *GP* 49 = *APl.* (A) 147

[20] For a discussion of this and the three other epigrams on Timomachus' *Medea* see Gurd 2007.

But this explanation does not work for Antiphilus' poem on the *Iliad* and *Odyssey*, unless the prominence of 'Argives' in the *Iliad* is relevant:

Αἱ βίβλοι, τίνες ἐστέ; τί κεύθετε; 'Θυγατέρες μὲν
 Μαιονίδου, μύθων δ' ἵστορες Ἰλιακῶν·
ἁ μία μὲν μηνιθμὸν Ἀχιλλέος ἔργα τε χειρὸς
 Ἑκτορέας δεκέτους τ' ἄθλα λέγει πολέμου·
ἁ δ' ἑτέρα μόχθον τὸν Ὀδυσσέος ἀμφί τε λέκτροις
 χηρείοις ἀγαθᾶς δάκρυα Πηνελόπας'.
'Ἵλατε σὺν Μούσαισι· μεθ' ὑμετέρας γὰρ ἀοιδὰς
 εἶπεν ἔχειν αἰὼν ἕνδεκα Πιερίδας'.

'Books, who are you? What have you within?'
 'Homer's daughters, tellers of the tales of Troy.
One tells of Achilles' wrath and the deeds of
 Hector's hand, and ordeals of a ten-year war,
the other Odysseus' toil and the tears of
 noble Penelope over her widowed bed'.
'Be gracious, with the Muses: for after your songs
 Time has said it has eleven Pierians'.

Antiphilus *GP* 36 = *AP* 9.192

I find Antiphilus' choice of Doric here as puzzling as that of Argentarius for *his* only Doric epigram out of his thirty-seven surviving poems, describing a carving of Eros on a σφραγίς, 'seal':

Αὐγάζω τὸν ἄφυκτον ἐπὶ σφραγῖδος Ἔρωτα
 χερσὶ λεοντείαν ἁνιοχεῦντα βίαν,
ὡς τᾶι μὲν μάστιγα κατ' αὐχένος, ἇι δὲ χαλινοὺς
 εὐθύνει· πολλὰ δ' ἀμφιτέθηλε χάρις.
φρίσσω τὸν βροτολοιγόν· ὁ γὰρ καὶ θῆρα δαμάζων
 ἄγριον οὐδ' ὀλίγον φείσεται ἁμερίων.

I behold on the seal inescapable Eros
 reining in a mighty lion with his hands,
with one guiding the whip to its neck, with
 the other the bit: much grace blooms all around.
I shudder at the man-destroyer: for he who tames
 even a wild beast will not spare mortals at all.

Argentarius *GP* 35 = *AP* 9.221

As suggested by Kathryn Gutzwiller in the discussion at the Thessaloniki conference, the best explanation for this unusual move by Argentarius is that the recipient of the poem, perhaps also recipient or existing owner of the seal, had a Dorian connection.

In the case of Antiphilus we might perhaps expect Doric to be his dialect of choice, since Byzantium was, and sometimes remembered that it was, a Megarian colony. But in fact Byzantium's inscribed epigrams are resolutely Attic-Ionic, and by the imperial period we find Doric only in occasional personal names like Asclapiadas, or in the names of offices like that of the *ἱερομνάμων*, a magistrate in charge of religious matters.[21] A nice example of an inscribed epigram of the early first century AD ('or shortly after') is the following poem with some literary aspirations but no scent of Doric, presumably composed for the sculpture of a dolphin on a nymphaeum:

[τόν με κυ]βιστητῆρα τὸν ἐξ ἁλὸς οὐκέτι Νηρεὺς
    [ποιμαίνει]· χέρσονδ' ὧδε μετωικισάμην·
[ἤλλαγμ]αι Νύμφας Νηρηΐσι καὶ πεπέδημαι
    [νάματος ἀ]λλοτρίου τερπνοτέραις σταγόσιν·
[χαίροιτ' εἰ]ς κόλποιο μυχοὺς εὐίχθυες ἄγραι·
    [.......]ς χέρσωι πόντον ἀναινόμεθα.

A diver from the sea, I no longer have Nereus
    [as my shepherd]: I have moved house to here on land.
[I have exchang]ed the Nereids for Nymphs, and am tied
    to the pleasanter droplets of another's [stream].
[Farewell] hunts rich in fish into the gulf's depths:
    [content with?] dry land we reject the sea.

IByzantion 10

3 Sacerdos of Nicaea

Against this background of poets composing during the century or so before the reign of Nero I turn to five splendid poems from Nicaea. We might approach these epigrams of Nicaea with no special expectation that *they* would be Doric. Indeed there is only one other poem which uses some Doric in the currently known epigraphy of Nicaea, an epitaph for a weaver called Myrmex:

[....] σου χθὼν ἥδε [..........]κεύθει
    [Μ]ύρμηξ, ἱστεῶνος πρόστατα καλλιπέπλου·
[σᾶι τ]έχναι γὰρ ἔφυς [.....] ἔξοχος ἄλλων
    [κ]αὶ δόκιμος βιοτᾶι καὶ φρενὶ πιστότατος·
[οὔ] σε μάταν μύρμηκος ἐπώνυμον ἔφρασαν [ἄ]ν[δρες].

[21] *IByzantion* 30.

[. . . .] this earth [. . . . .]holds
Ant, guardian of the fair-clothed loom
For in your skill you were [ ] above others
and approved in your lifestyle and most trusted for your character;
not for nothing did men give you the name of the ant.

IByzantion 103

More telling, perhaps, is the fact that of the thirty-one surviving epigrams of Apollonides, who seems to be from Nicaea, not one uses Doric, even though *GP* 21 (= *AP* 9.280) has a Spartan setting and *GP* 28 (= *APl.* (B) 49) is set in Rhodes. One might add that Doric is not used by Diodorus *GP* 10 (= *AP* 7.701) in his poem for Diomedes of Nicaea; but since Diodorus seems never to have used Doric anyway not much weight can be placed on this detail. Overall, however, Nicaea seems very rarely to exhibit Doric either in its 'literary' or in its other inscribed epigrams.

It is therefore surprising that Doric is on show in no less than three of the five poems on the grandiose funeral monument of a Nicaean who is there referred to only by his ὄνομα, 'name', in Roman terms his *cognomen*, Sacerdos. Its five elegiac epigrams are transmitted by Book 15 of the *Palatine Anthology*, where the poems are numbers 4 to 8.[22] A note by J tells us that *AP* 15.4 was an ἐπιτύμβιον ἐν Νικαίαι πλησίον τῆς λίμνης ἐν τῶι ὀβελίσκωι, 'a sepulchral epigram at Nicaea near the lake on the obelisk'. The writer of this note, suggested by Cameron to be Constantine of Rhodes and perhaps to be getting his information from Alexander, metropolitan of Nicaea in the tenth century,[23] evidently uses the term '*the* obelisk' because this was the architectural form of Sacerdos' tomb. It must have been similar to the obelisk of Cassius Philiscus, some five kilometres out of town away from the lake, and erected ca. AD 120.[24] I have discussed these poems recently elsewhere,[25] but for convenience I also print both texts and translations here:

αὔχησον, Νίκαια, τὸν οὐρανομάκεα τύμβον
καὶ τὰν ἀελίωι γείτονα πυραμίδα,
ἃ τὸν ἐνὶ ζωιοῖς βεβοαμένον ἱεροφάνταν
κρύπτει ἀμετρήτωι σάματι θαπτόμενον.
ἔστι Σακέρδωτος τόσον ἠρίον, ἔστι Σεουήρας
μνᾶμα τόδ', ὧι γείτων οὐρανός, οὐκ Ἀίδας.

[22] Merkelbach-Stauber 2001, 09/05/04, 05, 06, 07 and 08 (on their pp. 159–63).
[23] Cameron 1993, 316.
[24] *INikaia* 85: Γ. Κάσσιος Φιλίσ|κος, Γ. Κασ|σίου Ἀσκληπιοδότου υἱός,| ζήσας ἔτη πγ'. Cf. Bekker-Nielsen 2008, 112.
[25] Bowie 2014d, 42–5 (Chapter 36 in Volume 3).

Boast, Nicaea, of the tomb as tall as heaven
and the pyramid that is neighbour to the sun,
which hides the hierophant renowned among mortals
buried in its measureless monument.
This is the great sepulchre of Sacerdos, of Severa is
this memorial, to which heaven, not Hades, is neighbour.

AP 15.4

οὐράνιον τὸ μνᾶμα καὶ ἁ χρυσήλατος ἀκτὶς
ἀνδρὸς ἴσον βιότωι καὶ τάφον εὑραμένου
ἄστροις γειτονέοντα· φέρει δ᾿ ὅσον οὔτινα τύμβος
ἀνέρα, τὸν τελετᾶς οὐρανίδος ζάκορον,
τὸν πάτραν ἐριποῦσαν ἀπὸ χθονὸς ὑψώσαντα,
τὸν φρενός, ἧι γλώσσας, ἄκρα λαχόντα γέρα·
ὧι πέρι δηρίσαντο καὶ ἁ νέκυν ἐν πυρὶ θεῖσα,
Ἀτθὶς χἀ κόλποις ὀστέα δεξαμένα.

The heavenly memorial and the ray of beaten gold
matches the life of a man who found even his burial
neighbouring the stars: the tomb harbours
a peerless man, sacristan of the heavenly mystery,
who raised up his fallen country from the ground,
who attained the highest honours for mind as for tongue,
over whom the land fought that set his body on a pyre,
Attica, and that which took his bones to its bosom.

AP 15.5

τοῦτο Σακέρδωτος μεγάλου μέγα σῆμα τέτυκται
παμφαές, Ἀσκανίης ἄστρον ἐπιχθόνιον,
ἀκτίνων ἀντωπόν· ὁ δ᾿ ἥσυχος ἔνδοθι δαίμων
κεῖται ὁ καὶ πάτρηι δεξιτερὴν τανύσας
κεκλιμένηι καὶ στέμμα περὶ κροτάφοισιν ἀνάψας
ἱερὸν ἐκ πατρὸς παιδὶ νεαζόμενον,
ὃν πάτρη μὲν ἔδεκτο φίλον νέκυν, ἥγνισε δ᾿ Ἀτθὶς
πυρκαϊῆι, σέβεται δ᾿ Ἑλλὰς ἅπασα πόλις.

This is the great monument of great Sacerdos,
shining everywhere, the earthly star of Ascania,
its face to the sun: but inside in peace the spirit
rests, who stretched out his hand to his country
in collapse, and tied a sacred fillet on the head
of a son when it was rejuvenated by a father,

whose dear body his country received, Attica
    sanctified on a pyre, and every Greek city reveres.

AP 15.6

ἁ πάτρα Νίκαια, πατὴρ δέ μοι ὀργιοφάντας
    οὐρανοῦ, αὐτὰρ ἐγὼ κλαρονόμος τελετᾶς·
οὗτος ὁ καὶ σεισθεῖσαν ἐμὰν πόλιν ἐξ ἀίδαο
    ῥυσάμενος δώροις Αὐσονίοιο Διός·
θνάισκω δ᾽ Ἀσκανίας μὲν ἀπόπροθεν ἠδ᾽ ἐπὶ γαίας
    Ἀτθίδος ἀρχεγόνου πυρκαϊᾶς ἐπέβαν.
μνᾶμα δέ μοι περίσαμον ὁμώνυμος εὕρατο πάππωι
    παῖς ἐμός· ἁ δ᾽ Ἀρετὰ λεύσσει ἐς ἀμφοτέρους.

My country is Nicaea, my father displayer of the
    holy objects of heaven, and I the heir of his office.
I am the man who also saved from Hades his city
    shaken by earthquakes, by the gifts of Ausonian Zeus.
I died far from Ascania, and in the Attic land,
    whence my family came, I mounted the pyre.
My famed memorial was devised by one who has his grandfather's name,
    my son: excellence looks upon both of them.

AP 15.7

εἷς γάμος ἀμφοτέρων, ξυνὸς βίος, οὐδὲ θανόντων
    μνήμονες ἀλλήλων ἔσχον ἀποικεσίην·
καὶ σεῦ μὲν τελεταί τε καὶ ἄρρενος ἔργα, Σακέρδως,
    κηρύξει βίοτον πάντας ἐς ἠελίους·
αὐτὰρ ἐμὲ Σευουήραν ἀνήρ, τέκος, ἤθεα, κάλλος
    τῆς πρὶν Πηνελόπης θήσει ἀοιδοτέρην.

One marriage united both, a shared life, and
    not even dead did they part, thinking of each other.
And your offices and manly deeds, Sacerdos,
    will proclaim your life each day the sun rises;
me, Severa, my husband, child, character, beauty,
    will make more hymned than Penelope of old.

AP 15.8

One surprising feature of these five poems commemorating Sacerdos is that neither his father nor the homonymous son who erected the obelisk is named. But the riddling phrase that closes one covertly reveals their names:

μνᾶμα δέ μοι περίσαμον ὁμώνυμος εὕρατο πάππωι
    παῖς ἐμός· ἁ δ' Ἀρετὰ λεύσσει ἐς ἀμφοτέρους.

My famed memorial was devised by one who has his grandfather's name,
    my son: excellence looks upon both of them.

AP 15.7.7–8

Not many Greek names mean 'virtuous' (in Bithynia ἀγαθός, for example, is used only as part of a compound personal name),[26] but the name Chrestus does (of course with the shift of accent from χρηστός, 'good', to Χρῆστος that is regularly found when nouns or adjectives are used as personal names). The father of Sacerdos is therefore none other than a man well attested in Nicaean epigraphy, C. Cassius Chrestus, who died aged fifty-eight.[27] The Sacerdos of the tomb-obelisk thus had as his full Roman name C. Cassius Sacerdos: he will have taken on the position of ἀρχιερεὺς καὶ σεβαστοφάντης, 'high-priest and sebastophant', on his father's death, perhaps around AD 90, and seems himself to have died around AD 130. He joins Cassius Asclepiodotus, Cassius Philiscus and (a century later) the historian Cassius Dio Cocceianus as a distinguished member of one of the leading families in imperial Nicaea, the Cassii.

We do not know Sacerdos was doing in Attica when he died. Merkelbach suggested he was there for the ceremonies attending establishment of the Panhellenion in AD 131/2,[28] but there is no hint of that in the poetic texts. His presence in Attica may equally have related to his intellectual and rhetorical eminence, picked out in the second poem in the attributive phrase τὸν φρενὸς ἧι γλώσσας ἄκρα λαχόντα γέρα, 'who attained the highest honours for mind as for tongue' (*AP* 15.5.6)?[29] Nothing helps answer these questions as yet. Unfortunately the name of Sacerdos' wife, Severa, is too common to be diagnostic either for her place of origin or her status in society, but certainly admits a relationship with some of the top families in western Asia Minor.

[26] But it does appear as a name in other provinces, e.g. in Egypt, Baillet 1920–6, no. 1742.

[27] C. Cassius Chrestus is described on his late-first-century sarcophagus, found outside Nicaea's East (Lefke) gate (for whose reconstruction between AD 70 and 81 he was responsible, *INikaia* 25), as πρέσβυ[ς καὶ] (or πρεσβύ̣[τερος]) | ἀρχιερεὺς καὶ σεβαστοφάντης | ἐτῶν νη', '[president and]' (or 'the elder') 'high-priest and sebastophant, fifty-eight', *INikaia* 116.

[28] Merkelbach 1987, repeated Merkelbach-Stauber 2001, 159.

[29] In this line the *Palatinus* reads ἤ, 'or', giving the feeble sense 'who attained the highest honours for mind or for tongue'. Merkelbach-Stauber 2001, 160 translate ἤ 'und'. I print and translate ἧι, 'just as', which may of course have been indistinguishable from ἤ in the epigraphic text copied at Nicaea given the rarity with which *iota* subscript is written.

One mark of Sacerdos' παιδεία, 'culture', may be the Doric dialect that was chosen for three of the five poems. Like Byzantium, Astacus, on the gulf of Nicomedia and a little west of Nicaea, claimed foundation by Megara,[30] and the poet may be gesturing towards the Dorian origins of parts of his and Sacerdos' region. The identity of that poet cannot be resolved – indeed it cannot be assumed that the same epigrammatist was responsible for all five poems. Sacerdos was grand enough for more than one poet to have been approached, and the practice of inscribing poems by more than one poet on the same monument is a very old one.[31] That said, it is possible that the poet responsible for the poems that use Doric might be the sophist Memmius Marcus, a member of the governing class of Byzantium and a man whose *floruit* is Hadrianic.[32] Among the anecdotes reported by Philostratus is one concerning his visit to Megara and his successful intervention to quell Megarian hostility to Athenians, allegedly stemming from Pericles' Megarian decree of the fifth century BC.[33] Memmius Marcus was clearly conscious of Byzantium's foundation by Megara – indeed he traced his family's origin to the founder Byzas.[34] As one might expect, and as the poets collected by Philip of Thessalonica in his *Garland* exemplify, the intellectual links between the cities of the northern Aegean, the Propontis and north-western Asia Minor (i.e. Bithynia and Mysia) were sometimes closer than their links with Attica or with the great cities of *provincia Asia*.[35] Marcus might well have had connections with the elite of Nicaea.

[30] Bekker-Nielsen 2008, 28 n.3. Note also the Doric form γυνά in *INikaia* 225 Ὀλυμπιὰς Διονυσίου γυνὰ ἐτῶν σε' χαῖρε, of which Robert *Bull.* 1980 no. 562 wrote that the woman must have come from the southern shore of the gulf of Nicomedia, around Pylae, which was Byzantine territory.

[31] Cf. the story about a competition between Aeschylus and Simonides for a ἐλεγεῖον to commemorate the battle of Marathon, with Bowie 2010d, 215–7 (Chapter 17 in Volume 1, 462–3); more generally on epigram competitions Petrovic 2009, 203–12.

[32] ἠγάσθη αὐτὸν καὶ Ἀδριανὸς ὁ αὐτοκράτωρ πρεσβεύοντα ὑπὲρ Βυζαντίων, ἐπιτηδειότατος τῶν πάλαι βασιλέων γενόμενος ἀρετὰς αὐξῆσαι, 'when he went on an embassy on behalf of Byzantium he was admired too by the emperor Hadrian, who was the most well-adapted of the kings of old to cultivate virtues', Philostr. *VS* 1.24.529–30. For a good discussion distinguishing the (Memmius) Marcus noted as magistrate on coins representing Pius and then later as ἥρως (i.e. after his death) on coins representing Annia Lucilla (i.e. pre-169) from the Memmius Marcus, his son, on coins of Marcus and Commodus, see Puech 2002, 344–5.

[33] Philostr. *VS* 1.24.529. [34] Philostr. *VS* 1.24.528.

[35] On the economic basis for this network see Gren 1941.

The other sophist from Byzantium who makes it into Philostratus' selective series of biographies is called Chrestus.[36] This Chrestus lived at least a generation after our grandee commemorated at Nicaea, Sacerdos, son and father of a Chrestus. But his name raises the possibility that there was some connection between the families located in Byzantium and Nicaea respectively. It will not only be in the fictional world of Achilles Tatius that a member of the Byzantine elite married somebody of their own class from another city.

[36] Philostr. *VS* 2.11.590–2. That Chrestus had been a pupil of Herodes, and that the Athenians wanted the emperor to appoint him as successor to Hadrianus of Tyre in the imperial chair at Athens, suggests a *floruit* in the 170s and early 180s.

19 The Novels and the Real World (1977)

1 Introduction

The Greek novels' presentation of the real world deserves attention from the social and economic historian. It also bears on two literary questions. First, what sort of change of attitude is involved, and how big a step is being taken, when a Greek prose-writer offers fiction instead of historical fact? Secondly, any general theory about the literary objectives of the novels must take into account how carefully the writers try to give the impression that they are presenting a real rather than a fairy-tale or science-fiction world.

2 Truth and Fiction in Poetry and Prose

The relation of the novelist's subject-matter to the real world should be seen in a perspective stretching back to the earliest Greek poetry. There (e.g. in Archilochus) it is not easy to distinguish sincere, veridical and functional utterances (which must be understood as such to be effective) from formally similar utterances which are not in fact trying to tell the truth or to precipitate action. In epic narrative details must have been assumed to be invented even if outlines were taken as historical. Hesiod (*Th.* 27–8) knows that poets can sing both truth and falsehood; Stesichorus can replace the *fable convenue* with a better (fr. 192 *PMGF* = 91a and c Finglass). Poetry also tackles subjects like recent wars where historicity might be expected but no difference of approach is evident.

The choice of prose for narrative of myth by Hecataeus introduces no guarantee of truth, for his competitive scepticism had no scientific basis and is no advance on Stesichorus. Even with Herodotus, who in certain areas is indeed aware of the importance of knowing the truth (and of recognising what can be known), there remains much in his prose narrative that he could hardly have sworn to be the whole truth. Thucydides explicitly asserts accurate reporting of events, but his note on speeches shows that for these he must have fabricated details, if not generalities, of debates, and have concentrated points made by several speakers in the mouths of one speaker or a pair of speakers. Invention must also have played a part in providing details for such narratives as the escape from Plataea (3.20ff.) or the battle in the bay of Syracuse (7.69.3ff.). Hellenistic historians continue to rely on fiction for exciting episodes, but are less important as models for the novelists' era than Herodotus and Thucydides.

Given the mixture of true with formally similar but fictitious utterances in the classical historians there is not so great a difference in a narrative beginning (Ch. 1.1) πάθος ἐρωτικὸν ἐν Συρακούσσαις γενόμενον διηγήσομαι, 'I shall narrate something brought about by love that happened in Syracuse' – a narrative in which the author can, even if he clearly does not expect to, be taken to be treating the real world of γενόμενα, 'things that happened'.

Thus the mixture of truth and fiction in both poetic and prose narrative (rather than a correlation of prose with fact and poetry with fiction that is sometimes assumed) will have assisted the use of prose for a primarily fictional narrative, as will the formal similarity between statements about true and fictional γενόμενα.

3 Novelistic 'Realism'

There are two ways the novelists set about giving the impression that their subject *is* drawn from the real world. One is to give an explicitly historical setting, such as the Polycratean Samos which the reader will know from Herodotus for the (now fragmentary) *Metiochus and Parthenope*, or the Syracuse known from Thucydides for Chariton's plot. Although chronology cannot be pressed, the latter slips in details to bolster credibility (e.g. 1.1.1; 1.11.6): the reader can treat the story as one which *might* have happened, but which eluded the classical historians, The second technique (sometimes incompatible with the first) is to present a convincing reflection of the contemporary world: this is done with such care that the novels merit treatment as evidence for Greco-Roman society,

4 Members of the Greek Elite

Two examples will be pursued. First the local *princeps civitatis*, 'leading man of his city' (or even *provinciae*, 'of his province'), who with his family bulks large in the novels: not a fairy-tale prince, but a life-like member of the elite of the Greek East well documented by literary and epigraphic texts. Dionysophanes is an ἀνὴρ εὐδαίμων, 'prosperous man', with an estate whose mixed farming corresponds to that shown on inscriptions from Lesbos of the late third century AD,[1] and a παράδεισος which could be a 'jardin arabe' (so Grimal 1969) or simply an orchard seen through romanticising eyes.

Chariton's Dionysius and Achilles' Melite have similar estates, to which visits of inspection are natural (in a lavish style recalling Philostratus' notice on Polemo, *VS* 1.24.532) and on which luxurious *villae rusticae* may be expected. The novelists also portray the interdependence of a nabob's ostentation and his city's prestige, albeit their leading figures, and especially their hero and heroine, are regarded as superior creatures. The contemporary cultural scale is likewise reflected in the superiority of Hellene to barbarian: this is clear in Xenophon and Heliodorus, while Achilles Tatius' avoidance of the *topos* may be seen as corroboration of his Egyptian connections. Most striking, however, is Chariton's emphasis on *paideia*, 'education', as an attribute of his heroes and as a feature to be seen as essentially Hellenic: this too fits the cultural boom of the second sophistic and should be taken into account in reckoning Chariton's date.

5 Landscape

Secondly, landscape and geography. I begin with Longus. The selective and sometimes inconsistent description of Lesbos suggested to Scarcella that it was the product of an idealising literary tradition and not the personal observation of an inhabitant.[2] Yet this does not show the author was not aiming at realism (and some details impugned can be defended). If neither the author (as he seems to me to show by the way he has to have the painting explained, according to his preface) nor most intended readers are natives of Lesbos, then what the author must attempt is to give a *plausible* picture. This explains the agreement with other imperial writers on the prominence of viticulture: neither author nor readers may know what the inscriptions mentioned make clear for the late third-century Lesbos, that then olives were at least as important, as presumably they had always been.[3] Likewise all ancient communities had some pasture land: to set Daphnis and Chloe in Mytilenean pastures (even if it *may* be a response to a literary tradition) is compatible with the reader's conception of a real Lesbos, and over-detailed concentration on aspects of the pastoral environment would have lost more realism than it gained.

1 *IG* xii.2 76–80.

2 Scarcella 1968.

3 Olives grow alongside other trees in Dionysophanes' *paradeisos* (Longus 4.2.2), but they are not mentioned as part of his productive estate.

The upper class urban attitude to the countryside also appears in Xenophon: Scarcella brought out in his paper to *ICAN* 1976 how the countryside was seen as forests and pastures, a place of violence, desolation and death.[4] Recently Dr. Stephen Mitchell argued a similar attitude in the city aristocrat from quite different but contemporary sources:[5] Aristides' journeys give the impression of frantic dashes between havens of urban refuge in a countryside he feared and did not understand, and Galen shows that its starving peasants must often eat roots as substitutes for cereals carried off to city landlords. Xenophon's omission of cultivated land offers a sidelight on the city view: fields could be suppressed in the memories of a city-dweller, prone to see the country as the paradise familiar from elegant literature or simply as range of forests for hunting (allegedly what took Longus to the grove which had the painting of his tale, *pr.* 1). Both characters and landscape, then, are seen selectively, but realistically, from the point of view of a rich city-dweller.

6 Plausibility and Conclusion

Lack of realism is often asserted of plot, particularly in Achilles. Yet individual incidents are plausible, even if their cumulation may stretch credulity (and Achilles is careful to explain how the most implausible appearances can be saved). Brigands may be melodramatic, but they did exist even in the peaceful second century,[6] as they always had in certain areas. Pirates are less easy to document, but in the reign of Augustus they were still a problem in the Hellespont (*IGR* iv 219), and again by the end of the second century in Rhodes (*SEG* 41.661.17–18). Capture by brigands may have been a rarity, and by pirates only a fear, for Greeks, but the statistical rarity of hijacking today does not make its exploitation in a story unrealistic: and in Egypt Achilles' βουκόλοι, 'Herdsmen', are, notoriously, attested by a historian, Dio.[7]

If it is accepted that these novelists aim at realistic portrayal of the contemporary world (which is less true of Heliodorus, and hardly at all, as far as we can see, of Antonius Diogenes), then material in their works remains to be exploited by the historian (e.g. on the pattern of Scarcella 1968, 1977 and 1981 on Longus and Xenophon), material that will be especially valuable for society's attitudes. It should also be pertinent to literary evaluations of the characters in the novels as points of reference for significant aspects of the *Zeitgeist*.

[4] Scarcella 1977. For his full awareness that the novels do not simply give a mirror image of society see Scarcella 1981.

[5] Developed in Mitchell 1993, i 165–70.

[6] *Dig.* 48.36.1 for Asia under Hadrian; *BGU* 312 for Egypt under Pius.

[7] For the *longue durée* of βουκόλοι see Rutherford 2000.

20 The Readership of Greek Novels in the Ancient World (1994)

1 Introduction

Widely divergent opinions have been expressed on the readership either envisaged or achieved by ancient novelists for their works – a divergence largely the result of an almost total lack of evidence on the second of these two related issues.* In an ideal world, it would be desirable to approach the questions of intended and actual readerships separately, and also to build up evidence and argument for each of the known novels independently, moving from conclusions concerning the readership of each to a general theory about overall readership. But of the arguments about intended and actual readership, more converge than conflict; what might count as evidence for either the intended or the actual readership of any one novel is exiguous; and most arguments that hold for one are applicable to all or many. Accordingly, I shall attempt to discuss the general issue first, and shall only mark out an argument as limited to either intended or actual readership when that limitation is significant.

There remains, of course, a problem in defining the category 'novel' and in deciding how that category should be subdivided. I include in the category the five 'ideal' novels extant in complete texts (Chariton, Xenophon, Achilles Tatius, Longus, and Heliodorus); related works known from Photius (Iamblichus' *Babyloniaca*), and papyrus fragments (the most important are the *Phoenicica* of Lollianus, *Ninus*, *Metiochus and Parthenope*, *Iolaus*, *Sesonchosis*, *Chione*, *Calligone*, and one that may concern a character Herpyllis); and finally fictional works in which sexual relationships play a much less central role, the Ἄπιστα ὑπὲρ Θούλην, '*Incredible things beyond Thule*', of Antonius Diogenes, and the *Metamorphoses*, which I believe to be by Lucian. Only the accident that we have no Greek text or fragment of Apollonius, King of Tyre excludes it from the list. Both Lucian's *Verae historiae* and the Ps.-Callisthenes *Alexander* seem to me to belong to different, albeit related, genres.

* This chapter was presented as a paper at a London seminar and at the *colloque international* at the École normale supérieure, Paris, 17–19 December 1987; a version of the latter appeared as Bowie 1992.

2 Juvenile Readers?

Within the genre one broad division has often been assumed, principally in considering the novels extant in full texts: to wit, between the 'first novels' and those that display manifest sophistic influences – Achilles Tatius, Heliodorus, and Longus.[1] It was chiefly on the 'first novels' that one of the most dismissive modern verdicts was pronounced by a scholar who has contributed greatly to our understanding of the genre. In his book *The Ancient Romances*, B. E. Perry opines that

> the form itself … was … confined, in Graeco-Roman antiquity, to a narrow range of uses, tending either to become stereotyped as melodrama for the edification of children and the poor-in-spirit, or employed by intellectuals on isolated occasions for the ostensible purpose of satire or parody … The novel appears first on a low and disrespectable level of literature, adapted to the taste and understanding of uncultivated or frivolous-minded people.[2]

Later in the same work, Perry develops the hypothesis of a juvenile readership with particular reference to Chariton:

> It is probable that Chariton's romance was well known in the second century after Christ and that it was read by many people, particularly, we may suspect, by young people of both sexes. There is such a thing as juvenile literature even in our own highly sophisticated age; and in ancient times the ideal novel must have catered to that obscure but far-flung literary market long before it became adapted in some measure to the taste and outlook of mature or educated minds.[3]

Perry also confidently asserts a juvenile readership for the Ninus romance.[4] Admittedly, he concedes that 'in Daphnis and Chloe the novel approached the top level of literary quality for its time',[5] but it is not clear whether in doing so he intends to exempt Longus from his general condemnation.

[1] E.g. Hägg 1983, 94. Although I take issue with Hägg on a number of points, his chapter 3, 'The Social Background and the First Readers of the Novel', 81–108, is an excellent account of the problem of readership. So too, with conclusions much closer to my own, is that of Müller 1981, esp. the section 'Der antike Romanleser' (392–6). There are also good discussions by Schmeling 1974, 27–33; 1980, 131–8. I have not found much that I can both understand and assent to in Levin 1977.

[2] Perry 1967, 5.

[3] Perry 1967, 98. The low opinion of Chariton goes back at least as far as Rohde. Perry himself was able to discern merit in the work; cf. Perry 1930. For still more sympathetic approaches to his artistry, see Hägg 1971; Reardon 1982; Connors 2002; Smith 2007; Tilg 2010; De Temmerman 2014; Lefteratou 2018.

[4] Perry 1967, 164: 'an obscure Greek romancer addressing himself to juvenile readers'. The idea of teenage readership goes back to Gilbert Highet, but he added an important qualification: 'They are meant for the young, or those who wish they were still young' (Highet 1949, 165).

[5] Perry 1967, 7.

Assertion of a juvenile or intellectually underdeveloped readership is an old ploy in dealing with literature about whose qualities one has doubts or whose claims to be taken seriously one wishes to undermine. Strabo had tried to explain the mythological content of early poetry as geared to an immature age: later the same lessons could be taught by history or philosophy. In the fifth century AD, Macrobius dismissed the novels of Petronius and Apuleius as *argumenta fictis casibus referta*, 'plots packed with invented situations' and as mere *nutricum cunae*, 'nurses' cradles'.[6] In modern discussions of the novel, the notion of a young readership seems partly to derive from the age of the typical lovers – a curious argument rapidly scotched by Tomas Hägg[7] – and partly from the sentimentality of the narrative, an equally unsatisfactory consideration to which I return below.

3 Female Readers?

I doubt if there is much more to be said for the view, which goes back at least as far as Rohde, and to which Hägg himself gave some support, that many of the readers – and even some of the authors – were women.[8]

One line of argument asks us to consider the presentation of women in the novels. Hägg notes the strength of characters like Chariton's Callirhoe, by contrast with his Chaereas and Achilles Tatius' Melite, but on the other hand takes the view that the ideal of womanhood held up is a male product. More recently, Brigitte Egger has argued persuasively that the images of women presented by the novelists are reconcilable with the aspirations of women in the Greco-Roman world.[9] It is also the case, however, that these images correspond to male views of women and their social role in the period. Egger's arguments, therefore, have removed any obstacle that the novels' presentation of women might have constituted to a hypothesis of a female readership, but they do not, I think, render that presentation a testimony to female rather than male readership. To my eye there remain hints that a male rather than female readership was the primary constituency envisaged by the novelists. In Longus' work the introductory tale's reference to hunting in Lesbos – which could so easily have been cast differently – sets up a situation that would have been familiar to a male member of the

[6] Str. 1.19–20; Macrob. *Somnium Scipionis* 1.2.7ff. [7] Hägg 1983, 96.

[8] Hägg 1983, 95–6, more cautiously than the caption to his illustration on p. 97, which reads 'The cover girl – a woman novelist in her hour of inspiration?'

[9] Egger 1988.

Greek upper classes at first hand, but would not have been so to a female. The sexual forwardness of some experienced Greek women – Achilles Tatius' Melite, and even more, Longus' Lycaenion, who gives Daphnis practical instruction in sex – is hardly what the heads of Greek οἶκοι, 'households', would be happy to commend to their wives and daughters. It also seems to me more likely that the long debate in Achilles Tatius 2.36–8 on the respective delights for a male of homosexual and heterosexual activity was intended more for a male than a female reader, though of course I accept the judgment of a female colleague that it has its fascination for women too.[10]

A *prima facie* more fruitful area of investigation is the level of women's education. One of our novelists, Antonius Diogenes, is said by Photius (our only evidence for the novel's plot) actually to have dedicated his work to his sister Isidora, whom he described as φιλομαθῶς ἐχούσηι, 'keen on learning'.[11] Can this be taken as evidence that for Diogenes and his readers it was entirely natural to suppose that his work might find female readers φιλομαθῶς ἐχούσας? Unfortunately, even the text is not straightforward. The prefatory letter to Isidora was included in or preceded by another letter addressed to one Faustinus, which raises questions about the immediacy of Isidora's presumed access to literary texts. It then emerges from Photius' account that the letter to Isidora cited another from Balagrus to his wife Phila, daughter of Antipater, telling of the discovery of the tablets bearing the text of the Ἄπιστα, '*Incredible things beyond Thule*', during Alexander's sack of Tyre. This bogus 'authentication' (like the list of authorities prefaced to each book) stands in provocative contradiction to the posture Diogenes took up in the letter to Faustinus himself, that he was a poet of Old Comedy and the fabricator of things false and incredible. It seems, then, that Isidora has a number of functions. She stands for a female reader, avid for information, who may accept at face value what Faustinus (admittedly on cue!) is to take as a spoof; her pairing with Faustinus (conceivably her husband?) may have a literary role as a foreshadowing of the wife-husband pair Balagrus and Phila and the brother-sister pair Mantineas and Dercyllis. Doubtless she would not be so used by Diogenes unless such a class of reader was conceivable. But unfortunately her use cannot tell us how numerous or typical such readers might be.

[10] Women: Ach. Tat. 5.11ff., Longus 3.15–19; homosexuality: Ach. Tat. 2.36–8. On attitudes to homosexuality see MacMullen 1982.

[11] Phot. *Bibl.* 111a30–b31. For my interpretation of Antonius Diogenes' prefatory letters I am indebted to the commentary of Stephens and Winkler 1995. On bogus authentication see now Ní Mheallaigh 2008.

Evidence from other quarters can at least give some indication of what level of education might be expected for some women in the first three centuries AD, but it is not a precise indication, and like all aspects of the whole debate on literacy it leaves wide margins of uncertainty.[12] Even on a pessimistic view it is likely that many women achieved some basic literacy (but always in much smaller numbers than men)[13] that would enable them to read the text of a novel.

But for most of the novels it is not simply the ability to read the text that is at issue; indeed, the regular practice of reading aloud by slaves to owners means that the ability to read is not in itself a condition of 'readership' in a broader sense. What is at issue is the ability to pick up novelists' allusions to earlier literature and to respond to these allusions in the intended direction. It may be that *Ninus*, *Chione*, and Iamblichus' *Babyloniaca* made as few demands on the reader's educational attainments as Xenophon of Ephesus, although without a complete text it is impossible to tell. But even of the 'early' novels it is probable that *Metiochus and Parthenope* (with its allusions to Herodotus and archaic writers like Ibycus and Anaximenes), and certain that Chariton, required a well-read reader to appreciate the force of the quotations and allusions. Those in Chariton's work include Homer, Sappho, Euripides, Herodotus, Thucydides, Xenophon, the orators, Menander, Apollonius, and Theocritus.[14] The range of allusion in the three 'sophistic' novelists is even wider (I discuss those of Longus below). Moreover, Chariton, like the 'sophistic' novelists, has characters deploy rhetoric in a way he surely expected his readers to admire. What we must ask, therefore,

[12] For the problem of literacy in the Roman Empire, see Harris 1989, with a brief but trenchant discussion of the readership of novels at 227–8, and Humphrey 1991. Earlier works I found helpful include Duncan-Jones 1977 and Harris 1983). The problem of female literacy is discussed by Pomeroy 1977, 51 and 1981, esp. 309ff.; Cole 1981. An inscription from Teos of the second century BC attests the education of girls as well as boys for the first three levels; *Syll.*[3] 578. Texts from Pergamum show that some παρθένοι, 'unmarried girls', studied epic, elegiac and lyric poetry, reading, and καλλιγραφία, 'elegant writing', see Hepding 1910, esp. 436, no. 20, Robert 1937, 58–9. We also know of a *gymnasiarchus* from Dorylaum who was in charge of women, *MDAI(A)* 22 (1897) 480–1. For a dossier of letters about the education in second-century AD Egypt of a girl named Heraidous see *P.Giessen* 80–5, and cf. Préaux 1929, esp. 772–8.

[13] Wesseling 1988, 71 no. 25.

[14] Molinié, in his Bude edition of Chariton, notes thirty-one citations of twentyeight different passages of Homer (p. 12 and footnotes): cf. Papanikolaou 1973, 14–16. For allusions to Sappho, see 1.1.13, 1.1.15; to Sophocles, 3.8.8 (cf. Papanikolaou 1973, 16); to Menander, 1.4.2, 1.4.3, 1.7. 1, 2. 1.5 (cf. also Papanikolaou 1973, 23–4); to Apollonius 1.774–80, and Theoc. 2. 79–80; see 1.1.5. The historians are evoked constantly (cf. Papanikolaou 1973, 16–22); the orators occasionally (ibid. 22–3). For Chariton's knowledge and use of Xenophon (with important observations on his use of earlier literature in general) see Trzaskoma 2011; 2018.

is how many women had an education that familiarised them with a range of texts wider than such central authors as Homer and Euripides, and with the basic moves of rhetoric.

Certainly many women with grammatical (as it were, secondary) and some with rhetorical and even philosophical education are attested at many periods of Greek culture. But the proportion of the female population educated to these various levels is clearly smaller than that of the male population: we gain the impression that among women, they are very much exceptions, and that, if anything, there are fewer in the period than before. At the level of tertiary education the world that we see through Dio, Plutarch, Gellius, Lucian, Aristides, Athenaeus, Philostratus, the world of sophistic declamations, philosophical lectures and intellectual *conversazioni*, is almost entirely a male world. All Lucian's targets,[15] all Philostratus' sophists, all the learned acquaintances of Aristides and Gellius are men.

There are, indeed, some remarkable exceptions, women who composed either prose works or poetry. In the former category stands Pamphila, daughter of a *grammaticus* from Egypt, probably Alexandria, and resident at Epidaurus. The Suda gives her thirty-three books of Ἱστορικὰ ὑπομνήματα, '*Historical essays*', several epitomes, and a work Περὶ ἀφροδισίων, '*On sex*'. Photius had access to an eight-book edition in whose preface Pamphila claimed that her knowledge derived from conversations with her husband (whose side she had not left in their thirteen years of marriage) and with his many intellectual friends, as well as from her own reading of books. One wonders if the preface to the book on sex was as explicit. It is tempting to suppose that Photius' and the Suda's dating to Nero may derive from the dedication of one of her works.[16] As in the case of some other educated women attested on inscriptions, it is significant that Pamphila is herself from a family in the education industry, and so could receive her schooling in-house.[17]

Our other two prose writers are linked to another religious and cultural centre of old Greece, Delphi. Plutarch believed that girls should be

[15] Note however mention of women with cultural ambitions at Luc. *Merc. Cond.* 39.

[16] See the Suda, τ 139 *s.v.* Παμφίλη; Phot. *Bibl. cod.* 175, esp. 119b16–25, 38–40; cf. Lefkowitz and Fant 1992, 168, no. 219. The authenticity of the work Περὶ ἀφροδισίων is doubted by Holford-Strevens 1988, 21 n.13, but the name Pamphila does not seem to me in itself sufficiently suggestive to father the treatise. For other such works ascribed to ἑταῖραι, 'courtesans' (Astyanassa and Elephantine), and to Philaenis from the fourth century BC (with a scrap surviving on *P.Oxy.* 39 [1972]: no. 2891), cf. Lefkowitz and Fant 1992, 348 n.25. An overall account of literature produced by women in antiquity is offered by Snyder 1989.

[17] Cf. from Sparta, Aur. Oppia and her daughter Heraclia, *IG* v.1 598 (= *SEG* 11.814), 599. From Apollonia ad Rhyndacum in Mysia, Magnilla, daughter of Magnus and wife of Menius, all three philosophers, *IGR* iv 125 = *IMT LApollon/Milet* 2365.

educated and had a wife who was: he addressed to her the *consolatio* on the death of their two-year-old daughter Timoxena, and she herself composed a work Περὶ φιλοκοσμίας, '*On Love of Self-Adornment*', that she addressed to one Aristylla.[18] Both women would have been expected to read the works dedicated to them. Education was also expected of the Eurydice for whom, along with her bridegroom Pollianus, he composed the *Advice on Marriage*, and of the priestess Clea, dedicatee of both the *Fine Deeds of Women* and (a much more intellectually taxing work) the essay *Isis and Osiris*.[19] It is also from Delphi that we have our only evidence in the high empire of a woman delivering lectures. Early in the second century, perhaps at the Pythia of AD 115 and AD 119, Aufria, whose ethnic name is unfortunately lost, was honoured, first by Delphian citizenship and then by the erection of statues, for her display of παιδεία, 'learning', in λόγους τε πολ[λοὺς καὶ κ]αλοὺς καὶ ἡδί[στους], 'many fine and very pleasing discourses'.[20] More than two centuries later, Sosipatra was sufficiently expert in philosophy (which she taught in her home in Pergamum) to be written up by Eunapius at about the time Hypatia was establishing her reputation in Alexandria. But Sosipatra proves the rule – her educators, who predicted that she would have a mind οὐ κατὰ γυναῖκα καὶ ἄνθρωπον ... μόνον, 'not like that of a woman or a mortal ... only', are not human but demons or heroes.[21]

In poetry the *Greek Anthology* offers no imperial successors to the Hellenistic women poets Erinna and Nossis. But the works of three are inscribed on the Memnon Colossus. The most eminent and voluminous is Balbilla, sister of Antiochus Philopappus and granddaughter of the last

[18] For the *Consolatio*, *Mor.* 608b. For the work of his wife (also called Timoxena), Περὶ φιλοκοσμίας, *Mor.* 145a: the Lamprias catalogue ascribes a work with this title (no. 113) to Plutarch, and Wilamowitz 1962, 655 thought him to have written it himself and ascribed it to his wife – I think it plausible enough that she wrote it and that it was to be found among a collection of Plutarch's own writings.

[19] For the dedication of the *Praecepta conjugalia* see *Mor.* 138a, with Eurydice addressed at 145a, 145e; dedications to Clea are at *Mor.* 242e, 351c.

[20] The honorific degree was published in *FdD* iii 4.79 by G. Colin, whose dating and interpretation I follow. The missing ethnic name (or *cognomen*?) at 3–4 Αὐφρίαν [. . . .]νήν could be, e.g., [Βιθυ]νήν. Note an addressee of a work of Plutarch Περὶ φιλίας called Βιθυνός, Lamprias Catalogue no. 83.

[21] Eun. *VS* 466ff.(= p. 398ff. in the Loeb edn). There is a late and presumably apocryphal tradition that claimed female pupils for Plato: Lastheneia of Mantinea, D.L. 3.46; Axiothea of Phlius, *ibid.*, and Them. *Or.* 23.295c. For women who seem to have been drawn to philosophy by fathers or husbands, note Aristippus' daughter and pupil, Arete of Cyrene (also claimed as teacher of her own son Aristippus by D.L. 2.86); Crates' wife, Hipparchia, *ibid.*, 6.96–8, Magnilla, above n.17; and the five daughters of Diodorus Cronus and the wife of Epicurus' pupil Leontes, Clem. Al., *Strom.* 4.19. For pseudepigrapha attributed to Pythagorean women, cf. DK i 448, 50a, and Thesleff 1965; an excerpt in Lefkowitz and Fant 1992, no. 208; see also *P.Oxy.* 52 (1984) no. 3656 'Philosophical biography'.

king of Commagene, who commemorated the visit of Hadrian and Sabina to the colossus in November AD 130 in four elegiac poems written in pseudo-Sapphic dialect. The colossus also preserves the works of two (clearly amateur) women poets, Caecilia Trebulla and Damo.[22]

Julia Balbilla clearly moved at the highest social level, and here we may also document more women with serious intellectual interests. These are suggested for Trajan's wife Plotina by her interest in the succession to the headship of the Garden of Epicurus at Athens.[23] The empress Julia Domna notoriously professed an interest in literature of various kinds.[24]

These cases establish only that a number of women in the upper crust of Greco-Roman society were able both to read and to compose literature. They cannot help determine what proportion of women in the upper classes of the Greek cities were potential readers. We are taken further down the social scale by the case of Hermione, who died in Egypt ca. AD 200, described on her mummy portrait as γραμματική, *grammatiké*: but it is not clear whether she is simply being credited with literacy or actually taught γράμματα, 'letters'. Much later, we hear of Eusebius' use for copying of κόραι, 'girls', at a lower social level, perhaps even slaves, but not demonstrably girls who would themselves spend time reading.[25]

Overall, the small tally of women who make a contribution to literary history of the imperial Greek world seems to me to strengthen the case for doubting that many women who received a rhetorical education were equipped to appreciate Chariton or the sophistic novelists. But it must be conceded that the evidence is desperately short, and that no confident judgement can be made.

The suggestions of a juvenile or female audience both reflect the reluctance of scholars to concede that novels had the same audience as other literary works. The same reluctance moves Hägg to consider audiences in villages listening to recitations by scribes, or slow readers helped along by pictures. Hägg supports the hypothesis of reading by scribes with the argument that it accounts better for 'the wider circulation of the novel than itinerant story-tellers'. I do not find the grounds or the conclusion very

[22] See Bernand 1960, nos. 28–31, 83, and 92–4. For Balbilla see Bowie 1990b, 61–3 (Chapter 14, 291–3 in this volume, with references to later discussions at n.25).

[23] For Plotina's interest in the Epicurean succession, see *IG* ii^2 1099 = *ILS* 7784 = *Syll.*^{3} 834 = Martin 1982, no. 12.

[24] On Julia Domna see Bowersock 1969, 101–9, Flinterman 1995. To elite women with intellectual interests can be added the dedicatee of Nicomachus of Gerasa's *Harmonicum Enchiridion*, 2–3.

[25] See Cole 1981, suggesting that Hermione might have been a secretary and comparing for female scribes the κόραις εἰς καλλιγραφίαν ἠκημέναις mentioned by Eus. *Hist.* 6.23.

convincing: it would be more attractive if we had evidence of scribes in the Greco-Roman world acting in this way (presumably for a fee?), but as far as I know we do not, and the furthest that I am happy to go is to endorse Bryan Reardon's suggestion that there may have been 'small reading circles' along with the more prevalent habit of individual reading.[26]

The notion of a 'wider circulation' also needs examination. It goes together with the view that the novel, at least in its early manifestations, was a 'popular' form.[27] But although 'popular' is a reasonable label to attach to the earliest quasi-novel, the *Dream of Nectanebus*, translated from Egyptian and attested on a papyrus of the second century BC, and might just suit the sentimental and clumsy Xenophon of Ephesus (if we could be sure we had a text whose paternity he would acknowledge), it does not seem to me appropriate to Chariton (far less to the three sophistic novelists), unless by 'popular' we mean 'likely to attract a readership among the educated bourgeoisie'.[28] We must also question Hägg's ascription of 'wider circulation'. Our papyri of novels are vastly outnumbered by those of Homer and Euripides of the same period,[29] and no one novelist is represented by as many papyri from the period as Hesiod or Callimachus. Hägg also argues that what appears to be an illustrated novel text of the second century AD shows that the early novels were intended for readers who found the act of reading difficult. The notion that illustration was to help inexperienced readers is very speculative, and we must remember that we have a fragment of an illustrated Homer, too.[30] I would be ready to give greater weight to Hägg's observation

[26] Hägg 1983, 93; Reardon 1982, 15. The idea of 'recitations in private circles' is supported by Hägg by reference to the narrative technique of the non-sophistic novels (foreshadowings, regular plot summaries). Appropriate as these are to a work recited bit by bit, they also suit works that are so read by an individual, as modern literature demonstrates. For the proposal that reading by one woman to others accompanied weaving see West 2003.

[27] The term '*populaire*' was perhaps rather loosely used by Reardon 1971, 323. He tells me (*per litteras*) that he meant literature aimed at people without critical standards or a wider background of reading, and was in any case discussing the early novels.

[28] Note Chariton's somewhat dismissive reference to τό ... δημωδέστερον πλῆθος, 'the more demotic crowd', 3.2.15.

[29] Cf. Harris, *Ancient Literacy*, 228 n. 274; Pack 1965 (now superseded by the Mertens-Pack Online database); Willis 1968. The opposite conclusion might be advocated on the basis of our papyrus texts: a number of these are fragments of elegant, and therefore relatively expensive, books. *P.Oxy.* 42.3012 (Antonius Diogenes) is from a handsomely set out book roll. *PSI* viii no. 981 (the Calligone fragment) 'conveys the impression of a most luxurious edition' (Stephens and Winkler 1995, 271). The two Berlin fragments of the *Ninus* romance (*P.Berol.* 6926) are from the same well-made book roll. These indications point to prosperous readers. Cf. the persuasive arguments of Stephens 1994, and for a balanced and authoritative account Henrichs 2011.

[30] München Staatsbibliothek, *Papyrus Graecus* 128 (fourth century AD): see Weitzmann 1959, 32ff., arguing for a cycle of illustrations as early as the Hellenistic period.

that some novels are in codices, not rolls, but the proportion is very small – four codices against about forty rolls, one of these codices being as late as circa AD 550 – and does little to support Hägg's suggestions.[31]

4 The Novels and Other Literary Texts

There are indeed, overall, a number of points which could support the notion that the readership of the novel may have spilled over from the class of παπαιδευμένοι who read other literary works to reach a slightly wider circle. I am not persuaded, however, that the *typical* reader envisaged by Chariton or Xenophon (far less by the sophistic novelists) was significantly different from the sort that we assume for the *Lives* and *Moralia* of Plutarch, for the historians, or for Lucian, or from the sort of people who attended lectures and epideictic performances by philosophers and sophists. The reasons for thinking that they are different are more often left unstated than explicitly presented, but I suspect they are basically four.

First, the theme of love and the sentimentality of its treatment mark off the novels from these other works.[32] Yet this cannot carry the argument very far. Love, and love treated sentimentally, is a central motif in New Comedy, a genre that was attracting both audiences and readers from the educated classes in the second century. Note how much New Comedy is quoted by Plutarch.[33] Love is also, of course, much exploited by Hellenistic poets whose readership at any time has generally (and perhaps too confidently)

[31] Hägg 1983, 93. The four codices are of Achilles Tatius (ca. AD 150), Lollianus (ca. AD 175), *Sesonchosis* (ca. AD 300), and Heliodorus (ca. AD 550). My figures are drawn from those used by Stephens to illustrate her paper on which Stephens 1994 is based (figures at p. 494). The most obvious conclusion is that which she draws there – that the novels are on the same footing as classical texts.

[32] For a useful review of inferences from the sentimentality of the novels to a particular class of reader, see Schmeling 1980, 131–8. Schmeling's position had by then changed slightly from that formulated in Schmeling 1974, where he suggested (cf. 30–4) that writers came from the middle classes and spoke to an audience of the middle classes. In writing in 1980 on Xenophon, Schmeling wished rather to see the readership 'as a sentimental group, i.e. one which suspends its intellectual judgments and appreciation for reality and adopts a view that events in life are simple, rather than as a middle-class audience' (p. 133). On p. 137, however, Schmeling again endorses Scobie's view of the audience as 'middle-class readers who enjoy reading fiction which mirrors their own ideals and unfulfilled longings' (Scobie 1973, 96).

[33] Helmbold and O'Neill 1959: around fifty for Menander (p. 50), six for Philemon (p. 54). So too Lucian alludes regularly to New Comedy, cf. Householder 1941). Again, the evidence of papyri, which have so greatly augmented the twentieth century's knowledge of New Comedy, is telling: cf. the figures for Menander in Willis 1968, 212, 229.

been reckoned to be from the best-educated classes. Even historians in the second century exploit the love interest; witness the story of Stratonice in Appian's *Syriace*.[34] This is hardly surprising, given the popularity of Xenophon in the second century and the treatment in his *Cyropaedia* of the story of Araspas and Pantheia.[35]

The second argument is related, and invokes the generally low quality of the novels. This too seems to me to be a poor argument. Even where the quality is low, as it certainly is in Xenophon of Ephesus and from time to time in Achilles Tatius, that actually tells us little about their intended or actual audience. And those critics who condemn all the exponents of the genre have done so with historical hindsight, aware of the ways in which the modern world has developed the novel and contrasting the ancient genre to its predictable disadvantage.

Third, there is the absence of an ancient name for the genre. A balanced and representative view is that of Hägg:

> The novel is a whole class of literature, and a prolific one at that, lacking a learned designation of its own. The main reason for this, besides their postclassical start, seems to be that early novels, like early Christian writings, were not regarded as literature by literary theorists and critics. There is no positive evidence for the acceptance in such quarters even of the sophisticated novels of imperial times, in spite of the obvious stylistic ambitions of their authors. Novels were most probably also read in highbrow circles, but they were not acknowledged or seriously discussed.[36]

Since generic classification was principally the work of Alexandrian scholarship in the Hellenistic period (as Hägg earlier noted), it is not at all surprising that a later genre went without a label. Some parallel, though I concede it is not a close one, can be found in the fact that neither the prose hymn developed by Aristides nor the satirical dialogue or narrative developed by Lucian acquired a special name.[37] It is doubtless because Hägg sees the weakness of this argument that he attempts to bolster it by adducing another, the silence of ancient authors. To this argument, the fourth, I now turn, but again I doubt if it should be given so much weight as it has been.

[34] App. *Syr.* 308–27, and note too Plu. *Ant.* with Swain 1992.

[35] For Xenophon's popularity see Münscher 1920, Bowie 2016g (Chapter 39 in Volume 3); for the *Cyropaedia*, see Tatum 1989, Gera 1993.

[36] Hägg 1983, 3–4.

[37] For Aristides' use of prose for hymns, cf. his hymn to Sarapis, *Or.* 45.1–5 Keil, with Bowersock 1985, 659–60, and Russell 1990a. Wesseling 1988, 69 compares the omission of lyric poetry in Arist. *Poetics* – which would not be surprising in that curiously slanted work, but is not strictly correct, since he does mention dithyramb (1449a11).

5 Silence and Chronology

Consider chronology. Our earliest attestation of the genre remains fragments of the *Ninus* romance. This is certainly not later than AD 101, as is shown by the accounts on the verso of the papyrus, and palaeographic arguments suggest that the text was written not later than AD 50 and perhaps as early as 50 BC. The work's composition has been attributed to the early date of 100 BC, chiefly to bring it back nearer to such works as Xenophon's *Cyropaedia*, but neither that nor other reasons offered are compelling.[38] *Ninus* and two other fragments apart,[39] thirty-eight papyri so far bring us no earlier than the second century AD, and indeed are more numerous for the second half of the second and for the third century. It is partly on the slippery ground of development of the genre, partly because of his relative immunity to Atticism, that some scholars have dated Chariton as early as the first century BC.[40] But Atticism surely reached different places at different times, and in Asia it may have been resisted longer than in Rome or Athens. I have never been persuaded that a date earlier than AD 50 is mandatory, and I am attracted by arguments of Marie-Françoise Baslez and Christopher Jones that would put him as late as the reign of Hadrian.[41] Chariton's earliest papyrus published so far dates to the middle second century. Both the language and the classicising historical context for its love story link *Metiochus and Parthenope* with *Chaereas and Callirhoe*, and a date in the first century AD has been asserted as the date of the work's composition.[42] Perhaps that is right, but again the papyri are from the second century.

When we begin to get non-papyrological evidence for dates, it all takes us well into the second century. Xenophon, in some ways associable with Chariton, mentions the local office of eirenarch first known under Trajan.

[38] Perry 1967, 153, asserting also the relevance of the decline of drama on the stage after Terence, as if the fashions of Latin Rome were a guide to those of the cities of the Eastern Mediterranean, where in fact drama did not disappear from the repertory of city entertainment until late antiquity: cf. Jones 1993.

[39] Powell 1936, no. 18, and the Tithraustes papyrus, Grenfell and Hunt 1908, no. 868 = Pack 1965, no. 2630, written in the first century BC but not certainly novelistic.

[40] For a tabulation of the novels' chronology, see Bowie 1985b, 684, with brief citation of evidence for the date of individual novelists in the bibliographical appendix, 879–86. For the linguistic arguments for an early date for Chariton, see Papanikolaou 1973, with a summing up on 160–3: his dating to the first century BC was accepted by Dihle; cf. below, n.42. A more precise definition of the linguistic habits of Chariton has been constructed by Ruiz Montero 1991. For more support for a first-century date for Chariton see Bowie 2002a (Chapter 25 in this volume); Tilg 2010; Henrichs 2011.

[41] Baslez 1992b, 204; Jones 1992a.

[42] For the dating of *Metiochus and Parthenope* see Dihle 1978 and 1989, 147.

Iamblichus' claim to have predicted Verus' Parthian victory puts him after AD 165, perhaps by a decade or two. Lucian's *Metamorphoses* probably belongs between AD 155 and 180, and, to note a by-product of the novel, Philostratus' *Apollonius* was published about AD 230. I believe Heliodorus belongs there as well, and indeed that the author of the *Aethiopica* may be Heliodorus the Arab of Philostratus' *Lives of the Sophists*, but this is still *sub iudice*, and a late-fourth-century date for Heliodorus could yet be proved.[43] The papyri tell a similar story. Apart from three antedating AD 100, their distribution when allocated to twenty-five-year spans is as follows:[44]

ca. AD 150	15
ca. AD 175	2
ca. AD 200	7
ca. AD 225	1
ca. AD 250	7
ca. AD 275	0
ca. AD 300	4
ca. AD 550/600	3

The production of the genre could therefore cover as short a span as the years AD 60–AD 230, with a concentration in the second half of the second century and first half of the third, and only *Ninus* and two other lost works certainly antedating AD 100.

Why this insistence on chronology? It will be useful later, but for the moment the point is this: where should we *expect* to hear about novels and novelists? Of works on literary theory they come too late for Demetrius, for Dionysius of Halicarnassus, perhaps even for Longinus (though he would be unlikely to seek examples of sublimity from Chariton or Xenophon). Chronology alone would permit the technical writers on rhetoric to notice the novels, but are novels a suitable authority for the points these writers want to make? They would indeed have provided them with examples of rhetorical schemata, but not backed up by a context in a well-known and respected classical text. Absence from their citations shows the novels never acquired the status of classics, but there is a substantial middle ground between that and the total neglect and contempt that is alleged. Perhaps when we encounter a list of suggested reading, such as Dio of Prusa *Or.* 18, the absence of novels might be thought more significant, but even there the

[43] For eirenarchs see Rife 2002. On the date of Heliodorus, see below, n.55.

[44] Again I am indebted to Susan Stephens' table.

established constituents of an educational curriculum are clearly not conceived as forming the totality of 'serious literature', and it is observable that the only genre of which modern representatives are admitted is oratory, the very skill the addressee seeks to acquire.

When we turn to non-technical works, in other literary genres, the argument from silence becomes precarious. For a start, as in the rhetorical handbooks, the vast bulk of quotation and allusion is deliberately from works of the classical period, and references to contemporary writing are a rarity. If Plutarch mentions his eminent contemporary Favorinus only five times in the *Moralia* and not at all in the *Lives*, should we expect him to mention novels or novelists if he knew them? Again, Plutarch knows a contemporary poet, Sarapion of Athens, and even gives him a part in the dialogue *On the Pythian Oracles*, but he quotes none of his or any other contemporary's poetry.[45] Finally, it is clear that Plutarch's chief circle of Greek acquaintance is from Achaea, though there are some Asian friends, like Menemachus of Sardis, whereas hints in our texts suggest that the novel chiefly flourished east of the Aegean. That might also explain the silence of Gellius. Lamentably, we have no Plutarch or Gellius for a city in Asia Minor. Aristides, Galen, and Artemidorus are all silent on the novel, but given the broad spectrum of cultural activities to which they do allude the novel's absence can hardly be attributed to its falling below their intellectual sights. It must simply be chance that it escaped Galen, Artemidorus, and the *Sacred Tales* of Aelius Aristides, while the formal speeches of the last naturally draw only on classical writers.

Lucian is a different matter. It is true that he names no novelist, nor does he show explicit awareness of the genre of ideal romance, but in judging the first of these points we should recall that Lucian himself was thought to have passed unnoticed by contemporary writers until it was recently observed that he lurked in an Arabic translation of a work of Galen.[46] In judging the second, we must also assess the exploitation of themes related to those of the novel in the *Toxaris* and *Philopseudes*, the relationship of *Verae historiae* to Antonius Diogenes' *Incredible things beyond Thule*, and finally the fact that Lucian himself seems to have composed a novelistic work, the *Metamorphoses*, which survives in Photius' epitome and in the abridged version Λούκιος ἢ ὄνος, '*Lucius* or *The ass*', which has been

[45] Plu. *Quaest. Conv.* 1.10 = *Mor.* 628a, *De Pyth. or.* 5 = *Mor.* 396d ff. For Sarapion see Oliver 1949, 243ff.; Flacelière 1951; chapter 13, 278–9 in this volume.

[46] Strohmaier 1976.

transmitted among Lucian's works.[47] That Lucian knew only romances in which travel dominated and was unfamiliar with the sentimental 'ideal' romance is highly improbable.[48]

When we reach Philostratus, it is no longer a matter of explaining silence but assessing whether two references are indeed to novels. The first candidate is *Epistle* 66:

> Χαρίτωνι,
> Μεμνήσεσθαι τῶν σῶν λόγων οἴει τοὺς Ἕλληνας, ἐπειδὰν τελευτήσῃς. οἱ δὲ μηδὲν ὄντες, ὁπότε εἰσιν, τίνες ἂν εἶεν ὁπότε οὐκ εἰσίν;
>
> To Chariton
> You think that the Greeks will remember your words when you are dead; but those who are nobodies while they exist, what will they be when they exist not?
>
> (trans. Benner and Fobes)

There is no good reason to doubt that the addressee is the novelist. The reference to λόγοι, 'writings', shows that he is a literary figure, and one can see why Philostratus might have thought that depreciation of a writer in a recent and innovative genre would make good copy. On the other hand, Philostratus' dismissal of Chariton cannot be used to support the view that novels were in general regarded as trash by sophists. Such seems to be Perry's view: 'The writing of that kind of romance in prose, at least in the early stages of its development, was left to authors who were nobodies (as Philostratus says of Chariton).'[49] It would be equally unwise to generalise from Philostratus' criticism of Plutarch for attacking sophists (*Ep.* 73 *ad fin.*). Rather, Philostratus' letter indicates that by his time novels and their creators had a claim to belong to the world of λόγοι, and that Philostratus might expect his cultivated readers to recognise both the individual and his genre.

The second Philostratean passage is less straightforward. In his life of Dionysius of Miletus, Philostratus impugns the ascription to Dionysius of a work called ὁ Ἀράσπας ὁ τῆς Πανθείας ἐρῶν, '*Araspas in Love with Pantheia*', and asserts that it was by his enemy, the τεχνογράφος, 'writer of rhetorical

[47] On the *Toxaris* and *Philopseudes* see Anderson 1976c, 12–33; on *Toxaris* Ní Mheallaigh 2014, 39–71; on *Philopseudes* Ogden 2007.

[48] See Anderson 1976c, on Lucian's links with novels, observing (89) 'Lucian knew the Ideal Romance but opted out of writing it'.

[49] Perry 1967, 89. Anderson 1986, 276 thinks Philostratus is drawing a distinction between the jejune style of Chariton and such contemporary work as that of Heliodorus: perhaps. For Philostratus himself drawing on Ach. Tat. see Lehmann 1910, 50–68, Whitmarsh 2020, 13 with n.62; on Longus in the Εἰκόνες, '*Paintings*', Bowie 2019g, 20 (also proposing knowledge of Longus by [Opp.] *Cynegetica*).

handbooks', Celer.[50] Both men were rhetors who made it to the rank of *ab epistulis Graecis*, but Philostratus manifestly has a lower opinion of Celer, giving him no *Life* of his own and (in this same passage) criticising his capacity for μελέτη, 'declamation'. What was the work in question? It could have been a declamation, as Anderson, for example, takes it to be. But since it is mentioned by Philostratus in the context of Dionysius' blameless life, unmarred by any ἐρωτικὴ αἰτία, 'charge of sexual misconduct', something more seems to be indicated, and I share Perry's view that this was a novel.[51] It is less easy to follow Perry in his view – which he actually presents falsely as a statement by Philostratus – that Celer ascribed the book to Dionysius in order to disgrace him. Philostratus does not suggest that there is anything disgraceful about the work, although he does by implication suggest that it might be adduced as evidence by anyone wanting to draw attention to the author's erotic proclivities. He denies it to Dionysius not on moral but on stylistic grounds: it did not display Dionysius' rhythms, his ἑρμηνεία, 'style', or his ἐνθυμήματα, 'modes of reasoning'.

If the work was a novel, then we learn that a novel could be written in the middle of the second century by a rhetor who had come near to the top of his profession – it matters little whether it was Dionysius or Celer – and could be read carefully enough by Philostratus around AD 240 for him to form a stylistic judgment. That should not surprise anyone who has read Philostratus' *In honour of Apollonius*, a work that in a number of ways resembles the novels, particularly those of Achilles Tatius and Heliodorus. It has also been suggested that the *Metamorphoses* reported by Photius were composed by one of Philostratus' sophists, Hadrianus of Tyre, appointed to the imperial chair of rhetoric in Athens ca. AD 176, and that the work was then parodied in the extant *Lucius* or *The Ass* by one of the Thessalian sophists, Flavius Phylax and Flavius Phoenix, the latter also given a brief *Life* by Philostratus.[52] The proposal has not received much scholarly assent, and is certainly not my own view of these works' genesis.

In the second half of the third century, Porphyrius of Tyre knew the *Incredible things beyond Thule* of Diogenes and drew on them for his life of Pythagoras,[53] but this is clearly a special case, since he would have been

[50] *VS* 1.22.524. [51] Anderson 1976c, 29; Perry 1967, 169.

[52] van Thiel 1971, 37ff. For Hadrianus see Philostr. *VS* 2.10; Puech 2002, 284–8; for Phoenix, *VS* 2.22; *PIR*^{2} F 199; Puech 2002, 384–5 (and for Phylax 385–6). Arguments against van Thiel's position are put by Anderson 1976c, 35ff.

[53] Porph. *VP* 10, 32; cf. Burkert 1972, 99 n.9 (= 88 of the 1962 German edition). For Antonius Diogenes, including a discussion of his use of Porphyry, see Schmedt 2020.

drawn to the work not as novelistic entertainment but as a repository of Pythagorean lore.

Thereafter there is indeed silence on the novel for over half a century, until the 360s AD. But that period is one for which our literary texts are very much fewer than for the preceding centuries. Then Julian offers two pieces of evidence. First, writing from Antioch about January of AD 363 to the ἀρχιερεύς, 'high-priest', of Asia, Theodorus, whom he had appointed to oversee cults in the Greek East, Julian clearly refers to novels as a category of literature to be avoided (along with iambic poetry and Old Comedy):

> ὅσα δέ ἐστιν ἐν ἱστορίας εἴδει παρὰ τοῖς ἔμπροσθεν ἀπηγγελμένα πλάσματα παραιτητέον, ἐρωτικὰς ὑποθέσεις καὶ πάντα ἁπλῶς τὰ τοιαῦτα.
>
> We must eschew the fictions reported in the form of history by earlier writers, love-themes and all that sort of stuff.[54]

This could, at a pinch, refer to Herodotus or Xenophon, but the term ἐρωτικὰς ὑποθέσεις, 'love-themes', points rather to works in which love was a central theme, not incidental decoration, and I share the view that Julian is here referring to novels. If he is, then it is of interest that he treats them as a genre produced by earlier and not by contemporary writers.

That should be borne in mind when we consider the second piece of evidence in Julian, his description in his *Orations* 1 and 3 of Sapor's siege of Nisibis in AD 350. There are, notoriously, close parallels between this and Heliodorus' description of a siege of Syene in the *Aethiopica* 9.3ff. That the parallels show the use of one writer by the other is widely agreed, but not so which used which. The controversy cannot be pursued in detail here. I have myself been disposed to accept the view of Szepessy and Maróth that Heliodorus is prior; Szepessy in particular seems to have shown that Julian's picture of the siege does not cohere with the eyewitness account of Ephraim of Nisibis.[55] Discussion with John Morgan in the course of the 1989 ICAN at Dartmouth persuaded me that the question remains open. But if Julian were to be shown to be using Heliodorus, he would emerge as a reader of novels himself (something his epistolary remark suggests rather than excludes), and Heliodorus would have to antedate AD 357.

With the final triumph of Christianity, the world changed in a number of important ways, and evidence from the fifth century and later cannot be

[54] Jul. *Ep.* 63 = Bidez 1960, *Ep.* 89b, p. 169.

[55] See Szepessy 1976; Maróth 1979; Lightfoot 1988. For further arguments (in my view inconclusive) for Heliodorus' use of Julian see Bowersock 1994.

deployed to identify the first readers of novels. But it is convenient to notice here how the novels gradually join the mainstream of the classical tradition.

Diverse witnesses attest some knowledge of the novels in the first half of the fifth century. Around AD 400 the physician Theodorus Priscianus recommended the reading of erotic novels as a cure for impotence: he specifies Iamblichus and Herodian, the latter name perhaps a corruption of Heliodorus.[56] Presumably it was another motive that led the church historian Socrates Scholasticus to know of Heliodorus, whom he asserts to have become a bishop of Trikka in Thessaly.[57] It may also have been in the fifth century that Aristaenetus composed his collection of love letters, which appear to show a knowledge of Xenophon of Ephesus. Toward the end of the same century, Musaeus' epyllion *Hero and Leander* draws certainly on Achilles Tatius and perhaps on Chariton, and shortly after Nonnus certainly knows Achilles Tatius and very probably Longus.[58]

Two of these names recur among the three novelists with entries in the Suda – Xenophon, Iamblichus, and Achilles Tatius – entries that probably stem from the fifth- or sixth-century lexicon of Hesychius of Alexandria. But it would be rash to insist that only these three were known to Hesychius. Certainly neither Heliodorus nor Chariton had been wholly forgotten in Egypt, since we have a fragment of a parchment codex of Heliodorus copied about AD 550, and the parchment codex of ca. 600 transported by Wilcken to Hamburg, only to be destroyed by fire before much had been transcribed, contained texts of Chariton and of the *Chione* romance.[59]

[56] Theodorus Priscianus, *Euporista* 2.11.34 (133 Rose): *uti sane lectionibus animum ad delicias petrahentibus. ut sunt ... aut Herodiani aut Syri Iamblichi, vel ceteris suaviter amatorias fabulas describentibus*, 'by all means use reading matter that turns the mind to pleasures. Such are ... those of Herodian or the Syrian Iamblichus, or the other writings that sweetly describe erotic stories'. Although an unknown novelist, Herodianus, cannot be excluded, the hazards of transmission make it more likely that Heliodorus is meant (cf. the grouping of Iamblichus, Achilles Tatius, and Heliodorus by Phot. *Bibl. Cod.* 94, 73b). Our Latin version of Theodorus was translated by him from a work he originally wrote in Greek; it would be dangerous to assert on its basis that he knew Latin translations of the two novelists he cites, but the cases of *Apollonius, King of Tyre* (and, in a related genre, Dictys) shows that they may have existed.

[57] Socrates, *Hist. Eccl.* 5.22.

[58] For the possible influence of Xenophon on Aristaenetus, see Gärtner 1967; Schmeling 1980, 141; of Ach. Tat., Lehmann 1910, 5–12. For a much fuller documentation of knowledge of Ach. Tat. in the fourth century and later see Whitmarsh 2020, 13–16. Schmeling 1980, 141–6 also argues for the influence of Xenophon on the Ps.-Clementine *Recognitions* and on the apocryphal *Acts*; so too for several novels Bremmer 1998. For Ach. Tat. in Musaeus, see Lehmann 1910, 12–25; Kost 1971, 29ff.; Dümmler 2012; Montiglio 2020b, 8–12, 76–7, 81–2, 84–5, 87–8, 90, 93. Orsini 1968, xv–xvii, also asserts the influence of Chariton 1.4–7, but I doubt if the parallels are close enough. For Nonnus see Miguelez-Cavero 2016; Bowie 2019g, 20; Whitmarsh 2020, 14.

[59] The Heliodorus parchment was published by Gronewald 1979.

A different selection was known to Photius in the second half of the ninth century: Antonius Diogenes, the *Metamorphoses* that Photius ascribes to Lucius of Patrae, and Iamblichus, Achilles Tatius, and Heliodorus, whom he groups together.[60] The *Palatine Anthology* also ascribes either to Photius, or to his friend and contemporary Leon the philosopher, an epigram on Achilles Tatius (9.203) that seems to be intended for the frontispiece of an edition.

In the second half of the eleventh century Michael Psellus wrote a *synkrisis* of Achilles Tatius and Heliodorus. That is also the date of our earliest medieval manuscript of Heliodorus.[61] Finally, in the twelfth century, four novels were composed that showed knowledge of and admiration for the sophistic novels of the high empire, particularly Achilles Tatius and Heliodorus, though Longus' *Daphnis and Chloe* was also familiar to Theodorus Prodromus, author of *Rhodanthe and Dosicles*, and to Nicetes Eugenianus, author of *Drosilla and Charicles*.[62] These, like Constantine Manasses' now fragmentary *Aristandros and Callithea*, were in verse, while Eustathius Macrembolites' *Hysmine and Hysminias* was in prose. Knowledge of another text, that of Xenophon, is shown by the twelfth-century commentator Gregory of Corinth, who refers to Achilles, Xenophon, and τὰ ἄλλα ἐρωτικά, 'the other writings about love'.[63] The late thirteenth century saw the transcription of the novels of Chariton and Xenophon into the manuscript that is the only medieval witness to their texts and is one of two chief witnesses to the texts of Longus and Achilles Tatius. Investigation of the ownership and location of these and of the more numerous manuscripts of Heliodorus would make an important contribution to our understanding of the novels' readership in this period. This is not, however, the place for that investigation.

I return again to late antiquity. Before a brief foray into the geographical spread of the novels' readers, I will attempt to summarise what has been argued concerning their intellectual level. I hope I have shown that there are insufficient grounds for denying that the novel was known in intellectual circles. If this is accepted, then the positive indications in the novels that an educated readership is expected, and in particular the relation to sophistic

[60] Heliodorus, *Cod.* 73; Achilles Tatius, *Cod.* 87; Iamblichus, *Cod.* 94 (compared with Achilles Tatius and Heliodorus at 73b); *Metamorphoses*, *Cod.* 129; Antonius Diogenes, *Cod.* 166.

[61] For a text and good discussion of the epigram see Whitmarsh 2020, 15–16. Cf. Michael Psellus, *De op. daem.* 48ff.; Dyck 1986.

[62] For bibliography on the Byzantine novels see Hägg 1983, 240–1, and Beaton 1989. For knowledge of Longus, cf. Reeve 1982, v n.5, Burton 2012.

[63] Gregory of Corinth in *Rh.* vii 1236.

products of the novels of Longus, Achilles Tatius, and Heliodorus, should be taken as evidence that their writers were steeped in sophistic literature, if not practising sophists themselves, as the titles in their manuscripts claim for Achilles Tatius and Longus. It should also be taken as evidence that their readership overlapped with the educated classes who attended the lectures of sophists and philosophers and who read poetry, history, and occasionally philosophy. Chariton is just as allusive, and his novel's relative immunity to Atticism and to sophistic elaboration should not be attributed to unambitious literary objectives. In *Metiochus and Parthenope* we also have a historical context that would evoke nostalgia in educated readers brought up on Herodotus. For this novel we may also have, in evidence from the visual arts, a possible corroboration of the postulate of an educated readership, as well as some evidence for an aspect I have so far neglected, the novel's geographical reach.

6 The Visual Arts and Geographical Reach

Two mosaics from Daphne, the suburb of Syrian Antioch, depict Metiochus and Parthenope; in one both lovers are clearly labelled, in the other only the tag identifying Metiochus survives. The house in which they were found is not among the most opulent, but it is not small, and certainly does not belong to the poor in spirit or in worldly goods. It was dated by its excavators, who called it 'the house of the man of letters', to the Severan period (AD 193–235). That the mosaics illustrate the novel, rather than some other literary treatment of the story, might be suggested by the presence in the same house of a mosaic whose subject can be identified as Ninus contemplating a portrait, presumably of Semiramis: the identification is established by a mosaic of the same subject labelled ΝΙΝΟΣ, 'Ninos', from nearby Alexandria *ad Issum* (Iskenderun).[64] We thus seem to have a pair of illustrations of novels used in the same way as the numerous mosaic floors in all the other houses at Daphne deployed standard mythological themes, and it is tempting to think that here, at least, in the very place where Philostratus had his conversations with Gordian, a well-to-do Antiochene was a fancier

[64] Levi 1947, i 117–19, ii 2 pl. 20, 107; cf. Levi 1944. For the chronology see the table in Levi 1947, ii 625; for the mosaic from Alexandria *ad Issum*, i 118. There is a good discussion of the problem of interpreting the mosaics by Maehler 1976; see also Quet 1992, arguing that one of the Metiochus-Parthenope mosaics does indeed depict a stage performance. For the linking of novel-writing with the writing of mime, cf. Epiphanius, *Adv. haer.* 1.33.8 (*PG* xli 568), bracketing Philistion and Antonius Diogenes.

of novels; and not of the sophistic novel, but of the supposedly less pretentious *Parthenope* and even less advanced *Ninus*.

Before succumbing to this temptation, however, another piece of evidence from the Syrian region must be weighed. As Doro Levi noted in his full publication of the Antioch mosaics, Ninus and Metiochus are linked by Lucian.[65] Here, however, they are introduced as examples not of characters in a novel, but of characters in a theatrical performance. Attacking the sophist who is the pamphlet's ostensible victim, Lucian makes the sophist's tongue say of the stages that preceded his activity as a primary teacher:

> ἐγώ σε, ὦ ἀχάριστε, πένητα καὶ ἄπορον παραλαβοῦσα καὶ βίου δεόμενον, τὰ μὲν πρῶτα ἐν τοῖς θεάτροις εὐδοκιμεῖν ἐποίησα, νῦν μὲν Νίνον, νῦν δὲ Μητίοχον, εἶτα μετὰ μικρὸν Ἀχιλλέα τιθεῖσα ...
>
> I found you, thankless creature, poor and destitute and without a livelihood, and first secured you a reputation in theatres, making you now Ninus, now Metiochus, and then a little later Achilles ...
>
> Lucian, *Pseudologista* 25

That the activity is represented as more disreputable than elementary teaching excludes the possibility that the reference is to declamation.[66] Nor is the supposition that it refers to recitations from novels consonant with the clearly *dramatic* role being alleged. Most probably, then, it is indeed a reference to drama, and in particular mime, whether involving plots influenced by the novel or plots that themselves influenced the novel.[67] This cannot be certain, but at least doubt is cast on the hypothesis that the Daphne mosaics illustrate novels, though it cannot be disproved.

If it were the case that these mosaics did illustrate novels, however, they would constitute a large proportion of our knowledge of the geographical spread of the readership. Our other data are too scanty to allow anything but the most precarious inferences, and it would be unwise to use them to limit readership to a particular quarter of the Greek-speaking world, or to suggest that one type of novel found favour in one part, another in another.

[65] *Pseudol.* 25. [66] As suggested e.g. by Müller 1981, 393.

[67] Both Parthenope (as noted by Müller 1981, 393) and Achilles were also characters in pantomime; cf. Luc. *Salt.* 2 and 54 (Parthenope) and 46 (Achilles). This helps establish Parthenope as a suitable subject for mime too, but the *Pseudol.*'s attack on the victim's tongue shows that it, at least, cannot refer to pantomime. For links between Ach. Tat. and the mime, and the suggestion that a papyrus fragment has a mime of Leucippe and Cleitophon, see Mignogna 1996a and 1996b; for the relation between mime and the novels Bréchet, Videau and Webb 2013; Webb 2013; Whitmarsh 2020, 29 and 226.

There is, for instance, no easily interpreted distinction in Egyptian papyri between the sophistic novels and what are often seen as 'the popular type of novel'.[68] We have papyri of the *Ninus*, Chariton's *Chaereas and Callirhoe*, *Parthenope and Metiochus* (if that was of the 'popular' sort); of stories involving Iolaus and Sesonchosis; and of Antonius Diogenes' *Incredible things beyond Thule* and Lollianus' *Phoenicica*. But we do not as yet have papyri of Xenophon of Ephesus, Lucian's *Metamorphoses*, or Iamblichus' *Babyloniaca*. This last is admittedly a borderline case: from some points of view 'popular', it does have 'sophistic features'. Within the triad of developed novels, both Achilles Tatius and Heliodorus have appeared on papyri – Achilles Tatius now on no fewer than seven[69] – but not (so far) Longus. It might be tempting to argue that Longus was as widely read elsewhere, but not in Egypt, as members of the first category; and to explain Achilles' and Heliodorus' appearance on Egyptian papyri on the grounds that Achilles is a local author – from Alexandria – who gives his novel much local colour, and that this also abounds in Heliodorus. But I doubt if the evidence from papyri is voluminous enough to justify this distinction, and would register no surprise if a papyrus of Longus were to be published.

No help can be sought from the writers from the third to the fourth centuries whom I argued above show knowledge of novels; Lucian, Philostratus, Porphyry, and Julian were not tied to one part of the empire, but traversed many of its provinces, eastern and western alike, and knew Italy too. That the Greek novel was as well known in Rome as in the Greek East is likely for the second to fourth centuries, and virtually certain for the first. Even if Persius' half-line *post prandia Callirhoen do* (1.134) does not refer to Chariton's work (I have some doubts that it does), Petronius' *Satyrica* shows that in the sixties AD he at least knew some form of the Greek novel.[70]

Nor is the geographical setting of a novel's story a reliable guide to the location of readers, since the exotic ambience of Babylon or Egypt must have been more fascinating to an Aegean or Anatolian city-dweller than to a civil servant in Mesopotamia or the Fayum. But something can perhaps be made of the origins boasted by the writers themselves. Iamblichus and Lucian both claim to have grown up with Aramaic as their mother tongue, Iamblichus in an unspecified part of Syria, Lucian in Commagenian

[68] Hägg 1983, 3.

[69] See Henrichs 2011. The latest to be published (in 2009) was *P.Oxy*. 4948, of 2.37.8–10 and 38.4, dated to the third century.

[70] For the question of Petronius' debt to the Greek novel see Bowie 2007d (Chapter 32 in this volume).

Samosata. Heliodorus belongs to the same general area, coming from Emesa, now Homs. But at least one of these, Lucian, had his literary career in Ionia, Achaea, and the West; and if Heliodorus of Homs is the same as the sophist Heliodorus the Arab in Philostratus, he too went West, holding the post of *advocatus fisci* and living in retirement in Rome.[71] Iamblichus may have been working on his novel in the Near East, but we cannot safely assume that he was. Achilles Tatius was an Alexandrian, according to the Suda, and he certainly offers detailed descriptions of both Alexandria and up-country Egypt. On the other hand, Byzantium, Tyre, and Ephesus are important in his plot, and although papyri show he had many Egyptian readers we would be rash to exclude others in the sophistic centres too.

It is western Asia Minor to which the claimed πατρίδες, 'native cities', of Chariton and Xenophon take us, Aphrodisias and Ephesus respectively: were the Lollianus who wrote the *Phoenicica* to be identified with Philostratus' sophist, he too had Ephesus as his πατρίς, but that identification is not easy.[72] That another of the apparently early novels, *Metiochus and Parthenope*, sets important scenes on Samos and in the Thracian Chersonese might be taken, along with the origins of Chariton and Xenophon, to indicate that this stage of the genre at least it flourished chiefly in western Asia Minor: this was Hägg's conclusion,[73] and I would like to offer a further possible argument.

Where was the *Ninus* romance conceived? On the analogy of Iamblichus, with his Babylonian setting, and in the light of the Antioch mosaics, a Near Eastern context might be tempting. But there is no evidence that the author is trying to glorify Ninus as a national hero.[74] There is, on the other hand, a city in western Asia Minor with a special interest in Ninus: Aphrodisias, which gave him a place in its foundation legend and commemorated Ninus and Semiramis on reliefs. That one of our other early novels was written by a man claiming to be from Aphrodisias, Chariton, may be sheer coincidence, but I am not the only person to have been tempted by the thought that a city whose chief deity was Aphrodite may have been a suitable nursery for the early novel.[75]

[71] Aramaic mother tongue: for Iamblichus, the *scholium* in manuscript A at the beginning of Phot. *Cod.* 94; for Lucian, *Bis acc.* 27. For the sophist Heliodorus, cf. Philostr. *VS* 2.32. The view that he may be identical with the novelist has also been advanced by G. W. Bowersock and C. P. Jones in Bowersock 1974, 38.

[72] For a stylistic argument against the identification see Reeve 1971.

[73] Hägg 1983, 98.

[74] Cf. the forceful rhetoric of Perry 1967, 164.

[75] For reliefs of Ninus and Semiramis from Aphrodisias see Erim 1986, 20–1. I am grateful to Dr. Charlotte Roueché, who had independently developed the same idea, for discussion of the evidence.

Finally, I turn to the particular case of Longus' *Daphnis and Chloe*, the work whose problems were in fact responsible for my attempting this study in the first place. It might of course be argued that *Daphnis and Chloe* is so different from the other novels that a different class of reader might legitimately be postulated. Indeed, Richard Hunter in his excellent study comes near to excluding it from the genre entirely.[76] But there are enough shared features to justify its classification with the others, and I shall proceed on the hypothesis that Longus knew other examples more typical of the genre, such as the works of Chariton, Xenophon, and Achilles Tatius.[77]

That the educated classes of *provincia Asia* were indeed foremost among the intended readership of novels in general would certainly suit what little can be inferred about the readership of *Daphnis and Chloe*. That readership is expected to recognise the names of the chief cities of Lesbos – Mytilene, Methymna, perhaps Pyrrha – and to know something of its landscape, but not to know it well. A native of Lesbos would be puzzled by a number of features Longus attributes to his scene. The city of Mytilene is said to be distinguished by canals and bridges. So far excavation has revealed only one canal, separating the island on which the acropolis is built from the mainland, and over the canal only one bridge.[78] Perhaps, of course, the plural is rhetorical. The same argument certainly has to be used to deal with the plural rivers in which Daphnis bathed, since few parts of Lesbos have one perpetual stream deep enough to swim in, and none has two. But there are other ways in which Longus' topography does not fit, as I have tried to show elsewhere,[79] and it seems best to conclude that Longus does not expect readers to demand a depiction of Lesbos that is *both* realistic *and* accurate. This conclusion could accommodate readers familiar with Lesbos but not expecting accuracy or realism in a novel. On the other hand, Longus makes so many gestures toward topographic exactitude that it is easier to infer that his readers were expected to know Lesbos from geographers and other literary sources, but not by close personal acquaintance, and to enjoy recognising what they knew. Indeed, the sort of acquaintance that Longus as narrator seems to claim – that acquired on a hunting or tourist trip – is what

[76] Hunter 1983.

[77] For the unity of the genre, see Müller 1981, 387–92. For Longus' knowledge of earlier novels see Bowie 2019g, 5–6.

[78] Longus 1.1: in 1994 I owed the information about the archaeological evidence to Prof. E. H. Williams of the University of British Columbia, who had recently been excavating in Mytilene. Since then the existence of two bridges has been established, see Karydis and Kiel 2000, Bowie 2019g, 100.

[79] For the rivers in which Daphnis bathes see Longus 1.23.2, 2.24.2; cf. Bowie 1985a, 89 (Chapter 8, 160 in this volume).

I would set as the maximum expected in a reader, and perhaps as much as Longus had himself.[80]

That Longus' readers should know Lesbos principally from their reading but might possibly be expected to have made a tourist visit suits a geographical catchment area of *provincia Asia*, within which indeed the island was included for administrative purposes. Lesbos was never a sophistic centre like Pergamum, Smyrna, or Ephesus, but some sophists must have gone there to perform, and Dionysius of Miletus, the man to whom Philostratus denies the work on Araspas and Panthea, taught there in his youth before moving down the coast and up-market to Ephesus.[81] We do not know whether all his pupils were from Lesbos or some went there from overseas. We can also detect some links with the religious and sophistic centre, Pergamum, adumbrated by Louis Robert.[82]

If we return from the geographical to the intellectual horizons of Longus' readers we are taken firmly into the educated class. Knowledge of Alcaeus is necessary to appreciate Longus' picture of a Lesbian winter with its ice and *silvae laborantes*, knowledge of Sappho to appreciate the apple ἐπ' αὐτοῖς ἄκροις ἀκρότατον, 'on the very topmost branches the topmost', that Daphnis plucked and placed in Chloe's bosom. Allusions to Theocritus are naturally numerous, and there is also, I have argued, allusion to Philetas.[83]

The four-book structure might also be allusive. Clearly the scale of the work is largely a function of the miniature plot and landscape, but Longus cannot have been ignorant of the historiographic model chosen by Chariton and Xenophon, and he himself moves into a para-Thucydidean mode in narrating the πόλεμος, 'war', between Methymna and Mytilene.[84] But whereas Thucydides wrote eight books and Herodotus nine, one historian of the late fifth century had a penchant for shorter works, usually in two books, sometimes in three or perhaps four, and that was Hellanicus of Lesbos.[85] Is one facet of Longus' Lesbian setting an evocation of that

[80] For Longus' possible origin in Lesbos see Hunter 1983, 2–3 (overestimating the accuracy of Longus' picture). For the attractive suggestion of Mason that Longus has some connection with the family of M. Pompeius Macrinus Neos Theophanes (*cos.* AD 115) see Bowie 2019g, 19 n.46, 275.

[81] Philostr. *VS* 1.22.526.

[82] Robert 1980a, 1–9.

[83] For the apple, Longus 3.33–4; Bowie 2013d (Chapter 37 in this volume); for Philetas see Hunter 1983, 59–83; Bowie 1985a, esp. 74–86 (Chapter 8 in this volume); for Longus' exploitation of earlier poetry and prose see Bowie 2019g, 2–6; of Theocritus, Bowie 2021b; of Callimachus Bowie 2019i (Chapter 45 in this volume).

[84] 2.19.3ff., 3.1–2: cf. Hunter 1983, 4 n.18; Cueva 1998; Trzaskoma 2005; and for details Bowie 2019g *ad locc.*

[85] Cf. the evidence collected by Jacoby in *FGrH* 4 Hellanikos von Lesbos.

historian? I have no verbal echoes to point to, and given our scanty remains of Hellanicus I do not expect to find any, but if there *is* any sort of allusion here to Hellanicus, it argues an expectation of readers, some of whom have a very good knowledge of classical literature. Indeed, many of the authors to whom Longus alludes indicate a higher level of education than would follow from allusions to more accessible texts like the *Odyssey*, Herodotus, or New Comedy. The range and exploitation of Longus' allusion is admirably discussed by Richard Hunter in his monograph, and I am sure he is right to insist 'that in the majority of cases … an echo of earlier literature invests a scene with a layer of meaning which would be difficult otherwise to fit into the artificially simple narrative; it allows the author to direct a reader's reaction without in fact having to intrude directly into the narrative'.[86] This requires readers who are mature, alert, and well-educated. The case cannot be made so forcefully for the sort of allusion we find in the non-sophistic novels, but I hope that the evidence and arguments contemplated soberly have shown that an educated readership for these too should not be excluded, and that the hypothesis of a readership, either intended or actual, that centred on women, juveniles, and 'the poor in spirit' has little to recommend it.

[86] Hunter 1983, 59.

21 Philostratus: Writer of Fiction (1994)

1 Introduction

'You think that the Greeks will remember your words when you are dead. But those who are nobodies when they are alive, what can they be when they are not?'[1] With this epigrammatic letter, addressed to a Chariton who is most probably the novelist, Philostratus seems to dismiss his literary activity as worthless, and the text has been used to support the thesis that the writing of romantic fiction was despised by respectable creators of high literature. Whether or not it can sustain this weight, we should hesitate before concluding that it is the fictionality of Chariton's writing that the sophist expects his readers to find unacceptable. After all, if a librarian were required to keep all Philostratus' works on the same shelf, and were permitted only the categories of 'non-fiction' and 'fiction', the decision would be hard to make. In what follows I attempt a brief exploration of the territory of the fictional in Philostratus' writing, bearing in mind that the most important landmark in contemporary fictional writing as a whole was undoubtedly the romantic novel.

There are indeed two works where 'non-fiction' is preponderant, the *Gymnasticus* and the *Lives of the Sophists*, both works which give a historical account of two important features of contemporary Greek culture. But even in these, and especially in the latter, that account is often thick with anecdotes in which it is hard to know what is drawn from reliable tradition and what from the moulding of Philostratus' imagination.[2]

[1] Philostr. *Ep.* 66. I attribute to the second of the Suda's Philostrati, whose literary activity falls in the period AD 213–38, the *Lives of the Sophists*, *The Story of Apollonius*, the *Gymnasticus*, the *Letters*, the *Heroicus* and the first set of *Pictures*. The authorship of the last two is contested. For the problem (and different solutions to it) see Anderson 1986, 291–6; Bowersock 1969, 2–4; Münscher 1907, 515–57; Solmsen 1940, 556–72 and 1941. On the attribution of the *Letters* to the writer of the *Lives* and the *Apollonius* see Fobes in Benner and Fobes 1949, 387–94. My chapter was not able to take account of the recent and thorough investigation of the *Apollonius* by Flinterman 1993 (English edn 1995). For a recent account see Miles 2017.

[2] The reliability of the *Lives* is debated, but even if much can be defended (as by Swain 1991) a residue of fiction remains.

2 The *Letters*

In another group of works fictionality operates on a different level. The *Letters* contain a few, like that to Chariton with which I began, 'addressed' to dead men whose names will be recognised by Philostratus' readers: *Ep.* 67 to Philemon, *Ep.* 72 to an Antoninus who is probably Caracalla. We should no more read them as 'real' letters than we should read as 'real' the request to Julia Domna in *Ep.* 73 (which could indeed in other respects be a 'real' letter) to argue Plutarch out of his disapproval of sophists. But most are *Love Letters*, as the Suda and almost all manuscripts entitle the collection as a whole, manipulating common erotic themes and addressed in the main to an unnamed woman or boy. Those with named addressees (e.g. *Ep.* 45 to Diodorus) are no more likely than the rest to be intended to flatter or persuade real people. Their rhetorical elaborations of the predicaments, emotions and physical sensations of a lover stand close to the monologues given by the novelists to their heroes and heroines. One example will suffice:

> καὶ τίς ὁ καινὸς ἐμπρησμός; κινδυνεύω, αἰτῶ ὕδωρ, κοιμίζει δὲ οὐδείς, ὅτι τὸ σβεστήριον ἐς ταύτην τὴν φλόγα ἀπορώτατον, εἴτε ἐκ πηγῆς κομίζοι τις, εἴτε ἐκ ποταμοῦ λαμβάνοι. καὶ γὰρ αὐτὸ τὸ ὕδωρ ὑπὸ ἔρωτος κάιεται.
>
> And what is this new sort of combustion? In my peril I beg for water: but nobody lays it to rest, for the extinguisher for this flame is most ineffective, whether one brought it from a spring or took it from a river. For the water itself is burned by love.[3]
>
> Philostratus, *Ep.* 11

Such facility in the creation of verbal responses appropriate to particular situations occasions no surprise in a man who himself delivered διαλέξεις 'discourses', and μελέται, 'declamations', as a practising sophist.[4] The former might involve anecdotes which could be fictional, the latter required the sophist's speech to assume and exploit a set of circumstances which to him and his audience were equally unreal, whether based on an episode in classical Greek history or on an imaginary and improbable legal dispute. We have only one or perhaps two of Philostratus' *Discourses*, and none of the *Declamations* attested by the Suda. But some of the latter, like the letters,

[3] For the rhetorical question cf. e.g. Longus 1.14 and 18; for the conceit of fire and water, id. 1.23.2. For the *Letters*' treatment of love see Walker 1992, Goldhill 2009, Schmitz 2017. For their place in epistolography, Rosenmeyer 2001, Drago and Hodkinson 2023.

[4] For the difference between the informal and usually prefatory discourse and the full-blown declamation see Russell 1983, 77–84.

might have blended fiction and love, since we know of several declamations by other sophists which did: e.g. Onomarchus' speech for a man in love with a statue,[5] or Choricius' pair which plays off the speech of a young man claiming as his prize for valour the right to marry the pretty girl he loves against that of his miserly father who has lined up a rich but ugly bride for him.[6]

3 The *Pictures*

Third in this group would stand the first of the two sets of Εἰκόνες, *Pictures*, if we could be sure they were by this Philostratus. Here we find deployed another rhetorical skill that is also much exploited in the more sophistic novels, detailed and evocative description of a scene or object. The Εἰκόνες purport to describe a set of paintings in a gallery at Naples, chiefly mythological in subject, and naturally Philostratus chooses scenes and techniques of rendering them with which his readers will be familiar from the paintings that decorated their public and private buildings. That he is actually describing a set of paintings that he saw is a possible but unnecessary conclusion, and it would cohere better with his other literary activity to suppose that here too is a set of fictional entities.[7]

Such incursions into the fictive are of course very different in intent and in effect from that of a writer of extended narrative fiction. But that Philostratus made them should deter us from overestimating the gap that separates his literary activity from that of the novelists. Once the remaining two works are considered that gap will be seen to be quite narrow.

4 The *Heroicus*

The shorter work (though longer than *Daphnis and Chloe*) is the dialogue Ἡρωϊκός, '*Of Heroes*'. Its major speaker had been born into the elite of his Greek city Elaeous on the Thracian Chersonese, but had been robbed of most of his ancestral estates when orphaned; now he is contentedly cultivating

[5] Philostr. *VS* 2.18.598–9. [6] *Or.* 20 in Foerster and Richtsteig 1929.

[7] For a bibliography of the prolonged debate over whether the set of pictures is real or invented see Anderson, 1986, 277 n.4; more fully Kalinka and Schönberger 1968, 26–37; Bougot 1991; Baumann 2011; Bachmann 2018.

the one that is left, chiefly planted with vines, across the Dardanelles from Troy. His interlocutor is a Phoenician, storm-bound on a sea-voyage that had already lasted thirty-five days since Phoenicia and Egypt. Soon the vintner discloses that his farming is aided by the hero of Trojan legend, Protesilaus. They move to the *locus amoenus* of the vineyard and once he has combated the Phoenician's scepticism by cataloguing documented discoveries of gigantic skeletons (interpreted as those of mythological heroes) the vintner gives a detailed account of the activities and appearance of a ghostly Protesilaus. Stories of miraculous powers of reward and punishment exercised by Protesilaus and other heroes finally convince the interlocutor, whose role thereafter is to assure the vintner how exciting his stories are, and to ask for more. Some space is devoted to the assault on Telephus' kingdom of Mysia, omitted by Homer, and a number of other corrections and supplementations of Homer's account are offered without any clear structure, until two-fifths of the way through the work (chapter 26) the vintner settles down to describing the appearance, character and achievements of the major Greek and Trojan heroes, including a sustained rehabilitation of Palamedes. This sequence – obvious enough for our medieval manuscripts to pick out the section on each hero by writing his name in the margin as a subtitle – is punctuated by appetite-whetting anticipations of The Truth about Achilles, a narrative on a much larger scale that eventually begins at chapter 45, about three-quarters of the way through the dialogue. This section on Achilles also tells us more than Homer about Patroclus and Neoptolemus before we are given an account of cult offered by Thessalians at Achilles' tomb and stories of sailors who have heard Achilles and Helen singing to each other of their mutual love on an island in the Black Sea.[8] This move away from information gleaned from the ghost of Protesilaus prepares for a tempestuous ending, an account of an Amazon raid on the island's reputedly rich shrine, a raid which ended in disaster when a divine madness drove their horses to trample and savage the Amazons and a supernatural storm destroyed their ships.

There are two levels of fiction here. First, the frame. Both the vintner from the Chersonese and the Phoenician sailor are anonymous and unlikely to bear any relation to individuals in Philostratus' own world. But of course the fictional dialogue had a long and respectable ancestry in Greek prose, and although most writers maintained Plato's normal practice of giving speakers the names of historical characters who might plausibly be supposed to

[8] On this *theoria* see Rutherford 2009. For *Her.* see Beschorner 1999; Grossardt 2006; Hodkinson 2011.

have met on some such occasion to discuss such topics, his later and less common technique of using unnamed speakers was also taken up. It was a form of fiction common in imperial Greek writing,[9] and Philostratus will probably have known the dialogues of Lucian and Athenaeus, certainly those of Plutarch and Dio. Indeed Dio's *Euboean Tale*, not itself a dialogue, may have been one of Philostratus' sources for the idea of a cultivated traveller brought face to face with a contented rustic living in tune with nature.

The second level of fiction lies in the material that provides the bulk of the work, the accounts of Homeric heroes' appearance, character and actions that supplement and sometimes correct the narrative of the Homeric poems. This caters to the same sort of reading public that pored over commentaries on the Homeric poems to resolve omissions, uncertainties and contradictions in the poet's story. Like such commentaries, it assumes that behind the surviving poems there lies a set of historical characters and events about which more can be discovered. But here, in calling a fictional witness who claims privileged access to these, Philostratus invites readers to treat his solutions to questions about the Trojan war as his own creations. The possibility that there had been such an encounter, that there was a peasant in the Chersonese who communed with the ghost of Protesilaus, that this ghost could indeed offer a keen Trojan war-correspondent a series of journalistic scoops – all this permits the reader a self-indulgent *frisson* of satisfaction. With one part of her mind she knows that it is all Philostratean illusion, with another she can toy with the notion that this source might really provide extra information that only the privileged readers of this work can share.

It is partly to corroborate this second inclination that Philostratus frames his narrative of the Homeric heroes in material of a rather different stamp. His opening with tales of gigantic skeletons, some at least of which a reader will have found 'attested' in other texts and some of whose reputed findspots she will perhaps have visited, helps to erode the scepticism not only of the fictional interlocutor but of the real-life reader too. His closing tale of a hero's punishment of a sacrilegious attack fits a pattern widespread in Greek religious thought and could be accepted as credible even by highly educated pagans of the second and third centuries AD.

The combination of a claim to a reliable channel of information and framing in plausible material shows that Philostratus has some interest in presenting his fiction as truth. The first technique is used in various forms to achieve a similar end by some of the romantic novelists and, much closer

[9] See Oikonomopoulou 2007; Klotz and Oikonomopoulou 2011.

to Philostratus in his subject matter, by the Dictys story, which we know from fragments to have circulated in Greek as well as in the Latin version preserved in manuscripts.[10] Nearest among the former is Iamblichus' claim to have derived the story of his *Babylonian Tale* from a 'Babylonian' captured in Trajan's Parthian wars. More remote but still analogous are Longus' presentation of the story of Daphnis and Chloe as a local exegete's interpretation of paintings seen in a shrine of the nymphs by the narrator while hunting on Lesbos, and Achilles Tatius' presentation of his story as told to the narrator by one of its principals, the love-sick Cleitophon of Tyre, in the shrine of Astarte at Sidon (both, of course, Phoenician cities). Achilles' opening shares what may be only a superficial similarity with the *Heroicus* in having the interlocutor a sailor and the narrator in effect the chief participant in the reported action (since the vintner is simply a mouthpiece for Protesilaus). A variant on these techniques of authentication was to be found in Antonius Diogenes' *The Incredible beyond Thule:* this story, he claimed, was written down by one of its leading actors, Deinias, on tablets buried in his and his beloved Dercyllis' grave at Tyre, there to be discovered during the city's siege by Alexander the Great.[11] This is surely related to the opening claim of Dictys' Trojan narrative that its author was taken to Troy by Idomeneus and Meriones for the express purpose of compiling a history of the war. Wooden tablets bearing this history were buried beside him in his grave in Crete and discovered when it was opened in the thirteenth year of the Roman emperor Nero. Nero commissioned a Greek translation of the original Phoenician and lodged it in his library; from this our Latin text claims to have been translated. Philostratus is doing something similar to these in the *Heroicus*, a similarity he may wish to draw to our attention by identifying his sailor as Phoenician.

The framing of the far-fetched by the credible also has a number of analogies in the novels, though it can take different forms and none of these is so manifestly close. One is to anchor the narrative in an explicit and familiar historical context: the family of Hermocrates after the Athenian defeat at Syracuse provides Chariton with his heroine Callirhoe, the court of Polycrates ties the story of Metiochus and Parthenope to historical 'reality'. More generally the novelist may adopt the historiographic pose so well analysed in Heliodorus by John Morgan.[12]

[10] *P.Tebt.* 268 (published 1907), *P.Oxy.* 2539 (published 1966) and 4943–4 (published 2009).

[11] See the scholiast on Phot. *Cod.* 94 (Iamblichus); Longus, *pr.* 1–3; A.T. 1.1–3; Phot. *Cod.* 166, 111a20–b31. Note too the claims of the *History of Apollonius King of Tyre*, version b, chapter 51, and of X.Eph. 5.15.2. For an excellent discussion of pseudo-documentarism see Ní Mheallaigh 2008.

[12] Morgan 1982.

In some significant elements of his technique, then, Philostratus in the *Heroicus* stands close to the novelists. Other details exemplify some shared interests. Such is the recurrent insistence on the heroes' physical beauty, with especial attention to their hair-styles (e.g. Menelaus 29.5, Hector 37.3, Aeneas 38.3). There are also occasional erotic episodes, like Agamemnon's lust for Cassandra (31.4) and an Amazon's for a captive youth; or Achilles and Polyxena falling in love at the ransoming of Hector's body, so that she deserted to kill herself on Achilles' tomb, a 'correction' of tradition (51.2–6); and finally Achilles and Helen sharing an immortal love on the White Island (54). Yet other details show preoccupations similar to those of the sophistic novelists: the pictorial creation of vivid and memorable scenes, like the ship fired and allowed to drift out to sea at dawn in commemoration of the drowned Locrian Ajax (31.8–9).

There are also, of course, features common to many types of literature, like the short speeches employed to give a further dimension to heroes' characters: Idomeneus, Ajax and Agamemnon at Aulis (30.2–3), or the contrary recommendations and ensuing dispute of Palamedes and Odysseus after a solar eclipse (33.6–14). Finally there are elements that set Philostratus apart from the novelists, attributable sometimes to the difference in subject matter, sometimes to different habits of writing. The heroes are quick with repartee, a facility that ranges them with Philostratus' sophists rather than with novelistic characters. Thus at 33.44–6:

> εἰπόντος γοῦν ποτε πρὸς αὐτὸν Ἀχιλλέως 'ὦ Παλάμηδες, ἀγροικότερος φαίνηι τοῖς πολλοῖς, ὅτι μὴ πέπασαι τὸν θεραπεύσοντα', 'τί οὖν, ὦ Ἀχιλλεῦ, ταῦτα;' ἔφη, τὼ χεῖρε ἄμφω προτείνας. διδόντων δὲ αὐτῶι τῶν Ἀχαιῶν ἐκ δασμοῦ χρήματα καὶ κελευόντων αὐτὸν πλουτεῖν, 'οὐ λαμβάνω', ἔφη, 'κἀγὼ γὰρ ὑμᾶς κελεύω πένεσθαι καὶ οὐ πείθεσθε.'
>
> Once Achilles said to him: 'Palamedes, you seem rather uncultivated to the majority, because you don't have somebody to attend you.' 'Then what are these, Achilles?', he said, holding out both hands. And when the Achaeans offered him wealth from the division of spoils and urged him to be rich, he replied: 'I am not taking it: for I urge you to be poor and you ignore me.'
>
> Philostr. *Her.* 33.44–6

Such exchanges are clearly influenced by the sort of intellectual, and particularly philosophical, biographies we have in Lucian's *Demonax* and Philostratus' own *Lives*, but they are not confined to the proto-Cynic Palamedes. Even Achilles spits *bons mots*:

> ‘τραῦμα δέ, ὦ Ἀχιλλεῦ, ποῖον μάλιστά σε ἐλύπησεν;’ ἦ δ’ ὅς. ‘ὃ ἐτρώθην ὑπὸ τοῦ Ἕκτορος.’ ‘καὶ μὴν ὑπ’ αὐτοῦ γε οὐκ ἐτρώθης’, ὁ Αἴας ἔφη. ‘νὴ Δία κεφαλήν’, ὁ Ἀχιλλεὺς εἶπε, ‘τάς τε χεῖρας· σὲ μὲν γὰρ κεφαλὴν ἐμαυτοῦ ἡγοῦμαι, Πάτροκλος δέ μοι χεῖρες ἦν.’
>
> ‘What wound was it, Achilles, that gave you most pain?’
> ‘That inflicted by Hector.’
> ‘But you were not wounded by Hector’, said Ajax.
> ‘Oh yes I was’, said Achilles, ‘in the head and in the arms: for I consider you my own head, and Patroclus was my arms.’
>
> Philostr. *Her.* 48.22

The *Heroicus*, then, lures the reader through a landscape where some of the illusions will be familiar from incursions into the romantic novel but many will not. Yet illusions they are: this can hardly be doubted. For the remaining and longest work the boundaries between fact and fiction are much more contentious.

5 *In Honour of Apollonius*

A Severan reader encountering the work *In honour of Apollonius of Tyana* in a library or bookshop would have been prudent to suspend judgement about genre and factuality until much of the work had been read. Its scale alone must have puzzled. The title (if original) might suggest biography. But most biographies were in one book – more often the thirty or so modern pages of Lucian's *Alexander* or Diogenes Laertius' *Plato* than the seventy of the latter's *Epicurus*. The eight books of the work on Apollonius (344 Teubner pages) might rather recall the proto-novelistic *Cyropaedia* of Xenophon, a historical monograph like those of Thucydides or historians of Alexander,[13] or the genre that has debts to all of these, the ideal novel (both Chariton's and Achilles' are in eight books).

The narrative proper only begins (at 1.4) after a triad of oblique openings redolent of a sophistic προλαλιά, ‘prefatory discourse’. The first gives a brief sketch of the archaic sage Pythagoras. The second notes Apollonius' resemblance to Pythagoras and adumbrates a defence against the charge that his powers were those of a μάγος, ‘*magos*’. The third sets out as the writer's

[13] This sort of length seems common in Alexander-histories, though the precise total of eight books can be claimed only tentatively for Chares of Mytilene (*FGrH* 125) and with certainty for the work of Dio of Prusa *On the Virtues of Alexander* (Suda δ 1240 *s.v.* Δίων).

goal an account accurate in chronology and characterisation, based on oral and written sources, including letters of Apollonius. It is in this connection that Philostratus claims (1.3) to have used not only a work by Maximus of Aegeae on Apollonius' residence there as a young man, and a four-book work by Moeragenes, dismissed with such venom that it must have been the standard work Philostratus sought to supersede, but a hitherto unknown memoir drafted by one Damis of Nineveh, brought to his attention by Julia Domna. We later read in more detail (1.18–19) how Apollonius resolved to travel to Mesopotamia and India to consort with *magoi* and Brahmans, and *en route* at Nineveh acquired Damis as a disciple. Damis joined him for the duration of his travels and compiled a notebook of ἐκφατνίσματα, 'tit-bits', which professed to include all that Apollonius had said, even casual remarks; and, to combat any suspicion that he had invented this journal written by a man whose Greek was mediocre ἅτε παιδευθεὶς ἐν βαρβάροις, 'since he had been educated among people who did not speak Greek' (*VA* 1.19), he reports an anonymous criticism of it and Damis' spirited defence.

From this point the narrative is constructed around a series of exchanges of Apollonius with Damis and with others that display his formidable moral and intellectual strength. He has many sides: the ascetic philosopher who blends Socratic and cynic with predominantly neo-Pythagorean stances; the encyclopaedic sage who knows that eunuchs can feel sexual desire (1.33, 36) and can discourse on animal behaviour (2.14–16); the philhellene who secures the rights of descendants of Eretrians transplanted to Cissia by Dareius (1.23–4);[14] the literary scholar who knows obscure poems composed by one Damophyle of Perge (surely bogus) in the tradition of Sappho (1.30) and later criticises Dio of Prusa's rhetorical style (5.40). In Book 2 the journey to India introduces the staples of ethnography and paradoxography – mountains, rivers, strange plants and diet – and Apollonius talks philosophy and aesthetics with the Indian king Phraotes who is fluent in Greek. Book 3 takes him to a Brahman community presided over by the sage Iarchas, then quickly back to the Mediterranean. Book 4 starts with visits to Greek cities of Ionia and Achaea in which Apollonius combines the sharp reforming tongue of a Stoic or Cynic philosopher with a readiness to offer political advice characteristic of a sophist.[15] Thence to Italy, where he corresponds with a Musonius Rufus supposedly in exile and survives confrontations with Nero and his praetorian praefect Tigellinus.

[14] For further marks of Hellenism see Anderson 1986, 129–30.

[15] For many other details in which Apollonius resembles sophists of the *Lives* cf. Anderson 1986, 125–7.

The fifth book first takes him to Spain, then Egypt, again linking him with prominent historical figures. In Spain these are Vindex and Galba, while at Alexandria Apollonius, Dio of Prusa and the Stoic Euphrates advise Vespasian in his choice between monarchy and democracy and Apollonius gives his blessing to the imperial rule he has recommended. A journey to Ethiopian sages replays some of the Indian themes while establishing that the Indian Brahmans were superior. Then, for the finale in Book 8, Philostratus offers a confrontation with Domitian much more serious than that with Nero, involving a major trial scene and Apollonius' miraculous escape from prison. He ends with the conflicting stories of Apollonius' death or apotheosis.

I have cited more detail from the first book than the remaining seven because it is in reading it that the reader will form his preliminary judgement of the character of the work. He may of course revise that judgement, and as different sorts of material are brought in by Philostratus some revision would certainly be appropriate. How would he assess it once the colophon of the last roll had been reached?

Some features might have inclined a reader to see the work as novelistic, though none of these is unique to the novel. Scale has already been mentioned, pointing to novels, *Cyropaedia* and perhaps Alexander-histories. More diagnostic of the novel might be the form of the title – not *The Life of Apollonius* but *The Stories of Apollonius of Tyana*, like a novelist's *The Story of Chaereas and Callirhoe*.[16] Even more indicative is the elaborate construction of convincing 'testimony' constituted by the journals of Damis (cf. p. 452). Of course real historians have prefaces which discuss their handling of their sources, and again histories of Alexander present a closer analogy, appealing to contemporary accounts by companions (cf. Arr. *An.* 1.1.1) or claiming to be based on diaries. But 'Damis' more closely resembles the 'witnesses' claimed by the novels, and might suggest to the reader that both he and the material that he authenticates partake of the fictional.[17] A third feature linking the *Apollonius* with both novels and Alexander-histories is the vast extent and variety of the hero's travels.

[16] For a more detailed discussion of this point see Bowie 1978, 1665 with n.48 (Chapter 4 in Volume 3). Boter 2015, however, demonstrated that the correct title of the work was not τὰ εἰς τὸν Τυανέα Ἀπολλώνιον but simply εἰς τὸν Τυανέα Ἀπολλώνιον, '*In honour of Apollonius of Tyana*', so this argument (though only this) for a novelistic colour to the work must now be discounted.

[17] See Bowie 1978, 1653–71 (Chapter 4 in Volume 3). Anderson 1986, 155–73 attempts to reinstate a real Damis and to establish the existence of some written source claiming to be by that Damis, but he seems to concede that that source need not be by a companion of Apollonius called Damis.

These adumbrations would be countered by some marked differences from the novel. Three stand out, and of these the first two can be briefly stated. First, between Cadiz and the Ganges there are no pirates or brigands to threaten Apollonius' travels. Even Longus gets pirates into his pastoral dream-world, and Philostratus would not have been short of *bons mots* with which Apollonius in his present incarnation might brow-beat pirate kings. But Philostratus distances him from that novelistic *topos*. Instead pirates are given a second-order cameo appearance in Apollonius' account to the Brahman Iarchas of a previous incarnation: as an Egyptian helmsman he had deceived pirates into letting his ship escape (3.24). The double-dealings with pirates and the role of a non-Greek helmsman of a merchant ship can be read as a parody of the novelistic topic,[18] while the over-the-top detail that he lived in a wretched hut on Proteus' island of Pharos adds to the attractions of a humorous reading.

Second, there are none of the independent sub-plots to which the novelists resort in varying degrees. Everything narrated in some way involves the central character. This is not odd in a hagiographic work, but its difference from the practice of the novelists would soon be observed. It is a related feature that although the novels are episodic, they have a unity which is a property of their narrative structure, whereas the work *In honour of Apollonius* has only the unity imposed on it by the consistency of a central character, and its shape is that of a life rather than a plot.[19]

The third and most important difference concerns the power at the heart of the novels, ἔρως, *eros*. Philostratus' hero is no lover but an ascetic sage, his constant companion not a beautiful girl whom he worships as the object of his desire but a middle-brow Hellenised Syrian whom he often puts down as the target of his repartee. Philostratus gives him a vow of chastity at an early age and vehemently rejects charges of an erotic peccadillo (1.13). Writing for a readership familiar with Plato's *Phaedrus*,[20] Philostratus could well have chosen to sound some erotic overtones in Apollonius' didactic relationship to Damis, or in Apollonius' pursuit of wisdom and truth, but he does neither.[21]

When ἔρως, 'love' or 'desire', intrudes it is wholly negative. At 1.10 Apollonius divines the sinful state of the richest man in Cilicia who has

[18] The closest analogy is at Hld. 5.20–2. [19] I owe this point to John Morgan.

[20] For knowledge of the *Phaedrus* in writers of the second and early third century see Trapp 1990.

[21] It is true that Philostratus uses ἐρᾶν, 'to love' or 'to desire, of non-sexual admiration (e.g. 1.20 Damis is Apollonius' ἐραστής, 'lover'; 4.1 of Apollonius' relationship with Smyrna), but this is a common Second Sophistic use of the verb.

been offering prodigal sacrifices to Asclepius at Aegeae: he turns out to have conceived a passion for his stepdaughter and to be flagrantly cohabiting with her. Philostratus follows this tale and its moral (1.11) with that of how the ephebic Apollonius aroused the lust of a Roman governor who was ὑβριστὴς ἄνθρωπος καὶ κακὸς τὰ ἐρωτικά, 'a violent man and sexually depraved' (1.12). Apollonius sends him packing (μαίνηι ... ὦ κάθαρμα, 'You are out of your mind, you scum'), and within three days he has been summarily executed for conspiring with Archelaus of Cappadocia against Rome. Both these incidents were probably already in the tradition, since they are credited to Maximus of Aegeae, but Philostratus' decision to select from what was presumably a fuller narrative by Maximus shows his interest in establishing early in his work the polarity between Apollonius of Tyana and such characters as Apollonius of Tyre. Apollonius' contempt for sexual passion reappears when he asserts eunuchs' susceptibility to it at 1.33, an assertion borne out by the incident narrated at 1.36.

Another negative example decorates the sessions with Brahmans: Apollonius drives out a demon who for two years had possessed an eighteen-year-old youth (3.28). The demon was the ghost of a man who had died in battle, and whose wife (whom he still loved) had married another man after only three days: disgusted with heterosexual passion he had become infatuated with the boy. A pendant, the famous 'Bride of Corinth', varies the themes of the Greek journeys of Book 4. A handsome pupil of Demetrius the Cynic (hence appropriately given the name Menippus) was about to marry a rich Phoenician woman who had fallen in love with and seduced him. His conquest is seen as diminishing his claim to be a philosopher – τὴν μὲν γὰρ ἄλλην φιλοσοφίαν ἔρρωτο, τῶν δὲ ἐρωτικῶν ἥττητο 'in other respects his philosophy was securely founded, but he was susceptible to sexual passion' (4.25). Apollonius can tell that she is an Ἔμπουσα (he has had experience of one *en route* to India, 2.4), one of those vampires who ἐρῶσι ... καὶ ἀφροδισίων μέν, σαρκῶν δὲ μάλιστα ἀνθρώπων ἐρῶσι, καὶ παλεύουσι τοῖς ἀφροδισίοις, οὓς ἂν ἐθέλωσι δαίσασθαι, 'experience lust, and they lust for sex, but above all for human flesh, and they use sex to entice those on whom they wish to feast'. Apollonius challenges, unmasks and (it is implied) dismisses the vampire at the wedding itself. Vampire and riches vanish into thin air. Philostratus avers that the outlines of the story are widely known, but that he has taken the details and the link with Menippus from Damis. These details, like the implicitly Damis-attested ghost in India, should be treated as Philostratean invention, and together the stories present ἔρως both heterosexual and homosexual as a dangerous power to be feared and mistrusted. Unlike Apuleius in his *Metamorphoses*, where such images are balanced by diverse positive examples, Philostratus never invites us to see a benign element in ἔρως.[22] His only positive example is the love of Polyxena for Achilles, the subject of one of the five questions Achilles' ghost agrees to answer in the miniaturised *Heroicus* of 4.16; and although represented as noble, this love drives her to suicide on his tomb.

The same perspective is maintained in the second half of the work, though there it is given less prominence. Travelling up the Nile they encounter an Egyptian youth Timasion who is a replay of Menippus. In Naucratis, the sex-capital of literary Egypt, he had rejected the advances of his stepmother: Apollonius is supernaturally aware of his story, praises his virtuous conduct (especially impressive because Timasion conceded that he was a fan of Aphrodite) and welcomed him to his following (6.3). Further on, in Ethiopia, just south of the obligatory cataracts of the Nile, a satyr's φάσμα, 'ghost', has been pestering village women and has killed two whom it especially desired: Apollonius uses wine to cure it of its lust, tricking it into drinking itself to sleep (6.27). Again sexual desire involves a desire to kill. Philostratus seeks to corroborate the reality of satyrs and their lust by citing a story of one of his contemporaries in Lemnos whose mother was said to be visited by a satyr. No word here of the lady's murder: Philostratus seems to be taking up a popular belief but developing a version for his Ethiopian sequence which casts ἔρως in the worst possible light. A few pages later (6.40) the futility of ἔρως is brought out by the story of the youth in love with the Aphrodite of Cnidus, a well-known tale whose association with Apollonius Philostratus can only expect his readers to take as a *jeu d'esprit*.[23] Apollonius' characterisation of normal sexual relations here (with which the young man's passion is contrasted) is their only favourable recognition in the whole work.

It is hardly surprising, then, that some pertinent ἐρωτικά, 'matters concerning ἔρως', are omitted. The affair between Titus and Berenice, given due coverage by Philostratus' contemporary Cassius Dio of Nicaea (66.15.3–4), cannot be mentioned. It would have cast a cloud over the sunny picture we are given of Titus (6.29–33). More telling is the total silence on a passion Apollonius allegedly felt for Alexander Peloplaton's mother, a society beauty whom the *Lives of the Sophists* reports as rejecting all lovers except the handsome sage (*VS* 2.5.570). That anecdote was admittedly published later

[22] For a similarly negative presentation of ἔρως in Philostr. *VS* see Bowie 2019e (Chapter 45 in Volume 3).

[23] Cf. Luc. *Im.* 4, (Ps.?)-Luc. *Am.* 15–16; note too its use as a topic for declamation Philostr. *VS* 2.18.

than the *In honour of Apollonius*, but it cannot be held that it was unknown to Philostratus when he wrote it, since he somewhat mendaciously refers to the *Apollonius* for the story's refutation. Rather the character and narrative constructed by Philostratus for Apollonius could not tolerate anything but a wholly negative view of ἔρως, even a view presented for refutation.

Philostratus' handling of ἔρως in the *In honour of Apollonius*, then, so different from that of the *Heroicus* and the *Letters*, would check any reader's inclination to assimilate the work to a romantic novel. Instead it would reassert the work's status as a laudatory biography of an ascetic philosopher endowed with supernatural powers and claiming a special relationship with the divine. When the *In honour of Apollonius* was written, probably in the second decade of the third century, the only obvious pagan model for such a work would be biographies of Pythagoras, precisely the guru whom Philostratus delineates in his opening sentences and on whom his Apollonius most models himself. Similarities between the *In honour of Apollonius* and the later lives of Pythagoras by Porphyry and Iamblichus suggest that several details in the former are drawn from earlier Pythagorean biography. A Christian reader can of course see many similarities with the Gospels, but these are not so close as to require the supposition that Philostratus knew of and drew upon them.[24]

A feature which the *Apollonius* shares with works on Pythagoras and on Jesus of Nazareth is that it concerns a figure in whose historicity many readers believed. By the time Philostratus wrote many local traditions were already well established, associating Apollonius with miracles in mainland Greece, Ionia, Cilicia and Syria.[25] That of Apollonius' vision at Ephesus of Domitian's simultaneous murder in Rome was famous enough to be written up by Cassius Dio (67.18). Some readers might know the previous literary works to which Philostratus refers and from which he must draw much: that on Apollonius' youth by Maximus of Aegeae; Moeragenes' work in four books which seems already to have represented Apollonius as both a philosopher and a μάγος, 'a man with supernatural powers'; and a collection of letters of Apollonius to cities and individuals whose dominant theme seems to have been vituperative correction of their addressees' moral failure and degeneracy.[26] All this establishes a presumption shared by writer

[24] So rightly Anderson 1986, 144; for the convergences see Petzke 1970. On the relation of the *Apollonius* to biographies of Pythagoras see Anderson 1986, 136–7 with nn.7–9 and p. 301 (re-establishing the case for identifying the δόξαι, '*Beliefs*', of Pythagoras brought by Apollonius from the cave of Trophonius at Lebadeia with the *Life of Pythagoras* attributed to him by the Suda).

[25] See especially Dzielska 1986, with my review in *JRS* 79 (1989) 252–4.

[26] On these works and Philostratus' relation to them see Bowie 1978, 1671–9 (Chapter 4 in Volume 3), and on Moeragenes Raynor 1984 and Edwards 1991.

and reader that there is a set of historical facts concerning Apollonius on which Philostratus may draw. He may select well or ill, he may elaborate without warrant, but he and his readers would agree that his story has a historical core. In this respect too it clearly both differs from the novels, whose attempts to integrate themselves with historical events are never more than an author's ploy, and it resembles the *Heroicus*, where Homer's account of the Trojan war forms a historical core and the ghost of Protesilaus plays the role of Damis.

The *Apollonius* emerges as a literary hybrid, something *sui generis* that resists reduction to other genres. But if the principal stock is would-be-historical biography and the novelistic features have been grafted on, what is the point of these grafts? I do not imagine that I can track down Philostratus' literary objectives. We can only speculate on possible attractions, and in doing so we must remember the general enthusiasm for experimenting with literary form that marks Greek literature of the period.[27]

At the most basic level Philostratus may simply wish to expand the story. The motive for this might be partly to create a monumental tribute to Apollonius, partly to establish his work as definitive and clearly fuller (as well as more correct) than the four books of Moeragenes. The expansion to eight books results in the scale which I have earlier suggested might be read as a novelistic feature. But what material should be exploited to achieve this expansion, and how can it be presented as a historically reliable accretion? Without texts of Maximus and Moeragenes any identification of Philostratean additions is inevitably speculative. Moeragenes is attested by Origen to have narrated confrontations between Apollonius, the Stoic Euphrates and an Epicurean,[28] but the exchanges with Demetrius, Musonius and Dio of Prusa are a development of this element in the tradition that we can probably lay at Philostratus' door. He could have found many models in *Lives* of philosophers. So too the sequence of confrontations with temporal powers – Roman governors, oriental monarchs and finally the evil emperors Nero and Domitian and the good emperors Vespasian and Titus. These developments not only consolidate the image of a high-principled philosopher speaking his mind fearlessly but establish Apollonius as an important political actor on a historical world stage rather than a small-time wizard in the shadowy local traditions of the Aegean and Syria.

The exchanges with Vardanes and Phraotes, with the Indian Brahmans and the Ethiopian Gymnosophists, have the advantage not only of

[27] Still fundamental is Reardon 1971, 'Le nouveau', 233–405.
[28] Origenes *Cels.* 6.41 = Philostr. ii 110.4 Kayser.

generating more entertaining copy but of extending Apollonius' power and manifest traces of Hellenism even wider than the power of Rome. Although the Indian journey has often been defended as historical, in my view it is a fiction, and the only doubt is whether it was already in the tradition by the time of Moeragenes.[29] If it was, Moeragenes had already embarked on a development which assimilates Apollonius to globe-trotting couples in novels and to Alexander the Great, and Philostratus needed simply to take this further, and should probably still be seen as the inventor of the Ethiopian trip. The point of stressing the Ethiopian Naked Sages' inferiority to Brahmans might then be to devalue the Ethiopian world created by Heliodorus.[30] If neither the Indian nor the Ethiopian travels were in Moeragenes, then Philostratus' decision to invent them is more momentous. But he may have reckoned the colour they imparted to be more that of Alexander-history than of the novels: so much might be argued from the explicit reference to Alexander at several points in the Indian travels (2.9–10, 12, 24, 42–3). In that case he would be developing a fictitious account which did not consistently parade its fictionality by alluding to the novels but dissimulated it by aping historical writing.

In this context it is appropriate to pay a final visit to Damis. If some of the *prima facie* novelistic features might not have evoked novels at all, and if Philostratus sets out chiefly to construct a monument to Apollonius grander and longer-lasting than the ἡρῷον, 'hero's shrine', built for him at Tyana by Caracalla, then why does he play the apparently novelistic card of an allegedly privileged source? Again part of the answer may be that it is not specific to the novel – witness the Dictys story. Another may be that Philostratus was pleased with the literary effect of such elaborate construction of convincing 'testimony' in the *Heroicus*. But neither the writer of the Dictys nor Philostratus in casting the *Heroicus* expected to be taken *au pied de la lettre*. Their works may not be read as Fiction, but they will be read as fiction. If I am right to maintain that Damis was invented, and invented by Philostratus, did his introduction not risk exposing his construction as something as insubstantial as the riches offered to Menippus by his vampire bride at Corinth? That risk was there, but perhaps he thought it worth taking. Over and above the patterns and themes that he may have drawn from the novelists he may have learned a

[29] See Bowie 1978, 1674–6 (Chapter 4 in Volume 3), and for discussion of and references to bibliography on Gymnosophists Bowie 2016h.

[30] This would of course require an early-third-century date for the *Aethiopica*: others hold that the evidence favours the second half of the fourth century.

deeper literary lesson: the pleasure of playing with the ontological status of a narrative.[31]

It is a corollary of our uncertainty about the seriousness with which Philostratus wheels on Damis that he seems to block our attempts to discern what he draws from this 'source'. Sometimes we are given clear indications that something is 'derived from' Damis, or is drawn from other traditions, or represents Philostratus' own investigations (εὗρον, 'I have discovered', e.g. 1.25, 4.22).[32] At others we are left uncertain, and Philostratus wilfully complicates the status of his narrative by introducing events with λέγουσι, 'they say', where 'they' are not some unspecified oral or written sources but Apollonius, Damis and their companions of the moment. Thus in Spain, after reporting the phenomenon of tides and the topography of the isles of the blest with a 'they say' which is apparently unspecific (e.g. φασί 5.3), Philostratus proceeds to note trees that ἰδεῖν … φασίν, 'they say that they saw' (5.5) and to tell us that φασὶ δὲ καὶ τὸν ποταμὸν ἀναπλῶσαι τὸν Βαῖτιν, 'they say that they also sailed up the river Baetis' (5.6).[33] Yet the only eye-witness who can claim to have 'seen' is Damis, unless we are to suppose a group of ethnographic letters of Apollonius rather different from those that 'survive'. Philostratus is teasing us. He repeatedly gives his narrative ethnographic colour, and 'they say that they saw' is a discernibly ethnographic formula. He does not scruple to use it despite the confusion it creates as to the source of the material, and he must know it will again strain our belief in Damis.

With some justification, Philostratus may hope to have his wedding cake and eat it. The sober and sceptical reader who wants a good but credible story will welcome the apparently reliable source that Philostratus claims Damis to be; the more sophisticated connoisseur of literary technique will interpret the 'notebooks' of Damis as a covert admission of fictionality. My conclusion is close to that I offered for the *Heroicus*. It leaves Philostratus as a borrower from and even a contributor to the techniques of fiction, and perhaps suggests that he saw Chariton not as a member of a despised club but as a rival in his own.

[31] Within the known novels the game nearest to this is played by Antonius Diogenes, with a preface which at one part claimed numerous sources and in another aligned him with writers of fiction: see Phot. *Cod.* 166, 111a30–40. On Antonius Diogenes see further Bowie 2007d and 2009c (Chapters 32 and 34 in this volume).

[32] Anderson 1986, 155–73 offers a thorough analysis and is right to protest against wholesale foisting upon Damis of material not explicitly attributed to him by Philostratus.

[33] Anderson 1986, 161–2 weakens his argument by failing to distinguish these different senses of 'they say'. For an analysis of Philostr.'s presentation of his sources in *VS* see Bowie 2022d.

22 Names and a Gem: Aspects of Allusion in the *Aethiopica* of Heliodorus (1995)

1 Introduction

Names can evoke a vast range of associations. Dropped into the calm flow of a narrative they set up ripples which persist long after they have first splashed into the reader's awareness. Any classicists reading a novel with a character named Donald Russell would expect him to be learned, helpful, and companionable, with a nice sense of humour. A novelist who then constructed a quite different character would challenge readers by a constant play between his construction and their expectation. Inventing (or borrowing) names for characters is one trick open to novelists (and to Athenian comic poets, as Antiphanes reminded his audience)[1] that is largely denied to genres that work with traditional myths. Thus whereas writers (who are most often poets) drawing on a mythological tradition can exploit the ethical qualities which that tradition associates with certain characters (e.g. *sit Medea ferox*),[2] others with freely invented plots and *dramatis personae* can create expectations of character and behaviour by a telling choice of names – though here too a tradition can establish expectations, as for the servile name Davus in New Comedy.[3] The first part of this discussion explores the way in which Heliodorus, a novelist who draws on a wide range of sophisticated literary tricks, exploits the potential of names to create expectations, partly simply to entertain the reader by offering a character or actions that defeat these expectations, partly to force the reader's attention on the all-important ethical qualities of his principal characters. The second part of my discussion considers a different rhetorical technique for using subordinate elements of a narrative to throw its main features into greater relief.

[1] Antiph. fr. 189 K–A = 191 Kock. [2] Hor. *Ars* 123. [3] Hor. *Sat.* 2.7.2.

2 Allusive Names

I wish to examine first the names chosen by Heliodorus for the important sub-plot that constitutes the story of Cnemon. Cnemon is introduced early in the main narrative, as a young Athenian captive quartered with the loving couple Charicleia and Theagenes when they too have been captured by the Egyptian bandit Thyamis (1.7). Cnemon is later to provide a naive and enthusiastic audience for the priest Calasiris' long narrative of the couple's story-so-far. But his immediate function is to postpone the impatient reader's comprehension of the couple's identity and origins, offering instead an explanation of his own presence. As John Morgan has superbly shown, the characters and actions of Cnemon's story act as a foil to the main narrative. After Cnemon has told his story it becomes increasingly clear from Heliodorus' authorial narrative of the couple's adventures in Egypt that they have very different ethical qualities from the characters in Cnemon's Athenian tale (as indeed has been hinted in their brief appearances and utterances before it). I quote Morgan's summary of his view:[4]

> It provides a prolonged portrait of perverted, immoral, simply bad love, which, by being placed programmatically at the start of the whole novel, will inform and structure the reader's appreciation of the true love of the central characters, and at the same time provide points of reference for some of the hostile elements that threaten their love, notably the Persian princess Arsake … Between them, the negative love of the *novella* and the positive love of the novel form a framework of moral values, the expression and reinforcement of which is the fundamental *raison d'être* of the *Aithiopika*.

Morgan goes on to illustrate this by a well-documented series of polarities: Charicleia and Theagenes display a love that is mutual, altruistic, faithful, lifelong, and spontaneous; the sexual relations of the Athenians in Cnemon's story are unreciprocated, egocentric, promiscuous, ephemeral, and mercenary.

Why does Heliodorus set this story of Cnemon in Athens? Partly, no doubt, because Attic literature of the classical period was, next to Homer, the core of the educational syllabus, and re-creation of the social, political, and architectural milieu of fifth- and fourth-century Athens was a game enthusiastically played by many genres of imperial Greek literature, not least those that betray the influence of rhetorical training. Heliodorus is

[4] Morgan 1989b, 107.

doing his bit (not always accurately) to satisfy the Greeks' interest in the Athenian past when he presents a Panathenaic procession; public dining in the Prytaneum (both 1.10); an accusation before the ἐκκλησία, 'assembly'; enrolment in a φράτρα, 'phratry' and in a φύλη, 'tribe' (1.13); and Demaenete hurling herself to her death into a βόθρος, 'pit', in the Academy where the polemarchs sacrificed to the heroes (1.17).[5] But this evocation of classical Athens cannot be the whole explanation. There are other classical sites that had become theme-parks by the imperial period which go quite unmentioned – Olympia and Sparta are the most obvious – and there are other cities, like Pergamum, Smyrna, or Ephesus, which would have made a plausible setting and had an interesting classical past to evoke.

The explanation, I suggest, is rather to be found in the plot and characters of Cnemon's story. They recall the less edifying side of New Comedy, a genre well-populated with pimps, *hetaerae*, merchants, slave-girls, and ingenuous young men who are too easily led astray, and a genre whose plays were chiefly written for the Attic theatre and typically set in Athens. New Comedy was also the first genre in Greek literature to exploit at length the story-pattern in which boy meets girl, they fall in love, and are eventually married – the pattern that had been developed by the addition of travels, trials, and temptations to become the stereotypical novel. That the Greek novel numbered New Comedy among its ancestors was certainly obvious to Heliodorus. It is clear, too, that the extreme attachment to chastity with which Heliodorus burdens his loving couple, and his story's religious and mystical colouring, take them and it still further from New Comedy than earlier novels went. Chariton's heroine Callirhoe, who is prepared to marry Dionysius of Miletus in order to secure the future of her unborn child by the hero Chaereas, would stand more easily on the comic stage than Charicleia; so too Achilles Tatius' Cleitophon, who succumbs to the advances of the Ephesian matron Melite. I would suggest, therefore, that Cnemon's story reminds us of certain aspects of the novel's inheritance from New Comedy in order that their condemnatory presentation may establish this novel's healthy distance from it. Heliodorus is suggesting that this was one sort of literature from which the novel developed and which some other novelists had incorporated (novelists like Lucian in his *Metamorphoses*): he himself gives it a subordinate role, only as a counter-plot against which the true love of Theagenes and Charicleia can be measured.

[5] It may be an aspect of Heliodorus' exclusive focus on heterosexual love that he does not reveal, as does Paus. 1.29.15, that these heroes were the homosexual pair Harmodius and Aristogeiton.

Heliodorus offers a pointer to this interpretation in the name of the story's chief character and narrator. Cnemon is not a common name. In literature it seems to appear only three times outside Heliodorus. Its debut is in Menander's *Dyscolus* as the name of the cantankerous old man who gives the play its name. It is revived ca. AD 160 by Lucian in his *Dialogues of the Dead* (18 MacLeod) as a suitable name for a deceased misanthrope (who had made his will before dying, so was presumably not young). It is exploited again by Aelian in two pairs of his '*Letters of Farmers*', Ἀγροικικαὶ ἐπιστολαί, 13–16, written ca. AD 220. Two of these are sent to a misanthropic Cnemon living near a shrine of Pan in the deme Phyle, the other two are his replies; Aelian's character is manifestly drawn from Menander's play, and indeed the reader of the *Letters* is meant to think of them as identical. On the evidence we have, then, the chief literary text that the name Cnemon would evoke is one from New Comedy.[6] Unlike many another name given to young men in New Comedy, Cnemon's absence from other literary texts means that Heliodorus can be sure of its associations for almost any reader. Furthermore, the age and character of Cnemon in Menander's play offers Heliodorus the chance to set up an amusing conflict with readers' expectations – Cnemon is a malleable youth, easily interested in sex, rather than an aged misanthrope.

Once he has the name Cnemon, Heliodorus can build another sort of literary joke around it, making Calasiris bamboozle young Cnemon by a deliciously *ad hominem* quotation of Homer (whom he claims to have been Egyptian) as evidence for the possibility of identifying gods by the way they move their feet and shins:

[6] I am grateful to Elaine Matthews for providing me with material from the database of the *Lexicon of Greek Personal Names* for the names Cnemon, Thisbe, Nausicles, Nausicleia, and Charicleia, and for the warning that for certain areas (including Syria and Egypt) it is incomplete. So far that database has no 'real-life' use of Cnemon. Apart from the instances cited in my text, Cnemon appears (a) in Ammonius (ca. AD 500), *In Aristotelis librum de interpretatione*, ed. A. Busse in *GAG* iv (part v) (Berlin, 1889), 114.29–31 = 93r: οὐ γὰρ δὴ περὶ ὧν μηδεμίαν ἔχομεν ἢ ἐκ πείρας ἢ ἐκ μαρτυρίας γνῶσιν, εἰ μὴ τοῦ Κνήμονος ἢ τοῦ Τίμωνος εἴημεν μισανθρωπότεροι, τολμήσομεν ἀποφαίνεσθαι, 'for to be sure, we shall not be so bold as to make statements about things concerning which we have no knowledge either from experience or from testimony, unless we were more misanthropic than Cnemon or Timon'. For the name Cnemon Ammonius must know either Menander's *Dyscolus* or Aelian, probably the former; (b) in an ostracon of the 4th or 5th c. which bears lists of names, almost all others of which are mythological and most are Homeric, Crum 1902, 83, no. 525, with the sequence ΘΑΑΗ- | ΚΡΕΩΝ ΚΝΗΜΩΝ ΛΩ– | ΠΕΛΟΨ ΠΡΟΙΤΟΣ | ΠΗΛΕ–. A similar list, but without Cnemon, is found in *P.Bouriant*, no. 1, most accessible in Ziebarth 1913, no. 46. The compiler of the list on the ostracon could be drawing on either Menander or Heliodorus.

ἴχνια γὰρ μετόπισθε ποδῶν ἠδὲ κνημάων
ῥεῖ᾽ ἔγνων ἀπιόντος· ἀρίγνωτοι δὲ θεοί περ ...

for readily did they recognize the tracks of his feet and shins as he departed, for the gods are easily recognized ...[7]

The reader is surely meant to be amused by the dexterity of Calasiris (i.e. Heliodorus) in dragging in (by the back heels!) the only line of Homer with the phonemes κνημάων. But this joke can hardly be the motive for giving the young man the name Cnemon. It helps, however, to remind the reader of Cnemon's Comic origins.

We are told Cnemon's name right at the beginning of his story (1.8). Almost immediately we also learn the name of his father, Aristippus. Although a much commoner name than Cnemon, its best-known bearer was Socrates' pupil from Cyrene who followed a very different philosophical path from Plato and made ἡδονή, 'pleasure', the τέλος, 'goal'. Aristippus is generally treated unsympathetically by Plato, Xenophon, and later philosophers in other schools. He was said to have had the famous *hetaera* Lais as his mistress, and, when offered the choice of three *hetaerae* by the tyrant Dionysius, walked off with all three. His works included one addressed to Lais; among his pupils was a man called Aethiops, a detail that might well have caught the eye of our writer of the *Aethiopica*.[8] In a novel with a strong Neoplatonic colouring the reader of Cnemon's story is both amused and has her expectation of its contents directed by the discovery that one of the principal members of its pleasure-seeking Athenian circle – and the father of a young man who at this stage in the narrative may be expected to turn out as crabbed as his Menandrean eponym – bears the name Aristippus.

The two men's names, Cnemon and Aristippus, are set off against two women's names which take the reader away from Athens and evoke a complex of erotic associations. The more important of the two is borne by the slave-girl whose collusion with Cnemon's stepmother was responsible for Cnemon's and his father's exile from Athens, and whose appearance in Egypt creates the opportunity for both readers and characters to believe that Charicleia has been murdered. The name of this girl – who, it turns out, was killed by mistake for Charicleia – is Thisbe. In classical Greece Thisbe is the name not of a person but of a place in Boeotia. By Ovid's time it is enjoying in the Latin-speaking West its most famous use in literature, as the name of one of a pair of ill-starred lovers, and his *Metamorphoses* offer

[7] Quoted at 3.12.2. [8] Details in D.L. 2.67, 74, 84, 86.

the fullest version of the story that moderns know best from *A Midsummer Night's Dream*.[9] It is set in Babylon. The couple, of outstanding beauty, live in adjacent houses and fall in love with the boy/girl next door. Parents impede, so they arrange a tryst under a mulberry tree by Ninus' tomb. Thisbe arrives too soon, sees a lion and flees into a cave, leaving a veil which is stained by the blood of the lion's prey. When Pyramus sees it he thinks she has been killed by the lion and he kills himself, his blood staining the mulberry, so that henceforth its fruit is red, not white. She returns and follows suit. Ovid elaborates both suicides with appropriate rhetoric.

Ovid is thought to be using a Hellenistic Greek original.[10] It is surely from this Hellenistic source that Heliodorus has also drawn his recherché name Thisbe. Like Cnemon, the name Thisbe is rare in the Greek world in both literary and documentary contexts. Other than Heliodorus only three extant Greek writers use it: the epigrammatist Metrodorus (early in the fourth century AD) has it as the name of a playful and attractive παρθένος, along with commoner names of girls, in one of his arithmetical puzzle-poems (*AP* 14.116.6). Later, in the second half of the fifth century, Nicolaus of Myra tells, and Nonnus implies, a version of the love of Pyramus for Thisbe in which the crisis arises from Thisbe's pregnancy and the lovers are metamorphosed into a river and a spring respectively.[11] That version is already implied by mosaics from Antioch of the early third century AD, where, as in Nonnus, Pyramus and Thisbe are juxtaposed with Alpheus and Arethusa.[12] A conflation of the two stories appears on a mosaic floor of the second half of the third century AD from the House of Dionysus at Nea Paphos: Pyramus is given the iconography of a river-god, but the scene has the big cat (looking more like a panther than a lion), garment, and blood of Ovid's narrative.[13] The love-unto-death of Pyramus and Thisbe is clearly the chief literary association of the personal name Thisbe in the imperial Greek world, from a Greek epigram at Ostia, whose poet (probably first century AD) compares the lifelong love of a dead couple to that of Thisbe and P[yramus],[14] to the late fifth century AD. The story was also

[9] Ov. *Met.* 4.55–166, see also Servius Auct. on Virg. *Ecl.* 6.22, Hyginus, *Fab.* 242.5.2–3.

[10] H. Gärtner in *KP s.v.* Thisbe, Bomer 1976, 33–6 on Ov. *Met.* 4.55ff.; but Ovid's version is argued to be his own by Holzberg 1988. For a proposal that Ovid used a local Cilician myth see Knox 1989.

[11] Nicol., *Rh.* i 271.21–8 Walz; Nonn. *D.* 6.346–55.

[12] Levi 1947, i 109–10, ii, pl. xviiic: the mosaic, from the House of the Porticoes, portrays four heads to which the names are attached (now *IGLSyr* iii.2 1122).

[13] Nikolaou 1963, 56ff., esp. 64–5, and 1967, 100ff. A good coloured illustration in Karageorghis 1981, 190 pl. 148; full discussion and illustrations in Kondoleon 1994, 148–56.

[14] *IG* xiv 930.12: οὐ φιλία Θίσβης καὶ Π[υράμου], 'not the love of Thisbe and P[yramus]'.

well known in the Latin West, as is attested, for example, by a wall-painting at Pompeii.[15] In the West Thisbe is also widely used as a real name in the early imperial period, chiefly for slaves. At least one of these occurrences must be credited to knowledge of the Ovidian story, since we find a *libertus* named Pyramus and his wife, also a *liberta*, named Thisbenis (?): it may be assumed that the names were given to the slaves when purchased by or born in the household of a whimsical reader of Ovid.[16] In the Greek East, however, Thisbe does not establish itself as a common personal name: so far (cf. n.6) I have found only three instances: (i) Thisbe is the name of a slave enfranchised at Delphi ca. AD 90–100; (ii) an Aelia Thisbe at Ancyra; (iii) a Thisbe in Aezani in northern Phrygia.[17] In Thisbe, then, Heliodorus has found another name which would for most Greek readers have definite literary associations, associations likely to be untrammelled by encounters with its use in real life.

The first association would be that of an oriental setting, clearly a favourite with novelists. Our earliest novelistic text to be preserved on papyrus, the Ninus romance, is set partly in Babylon, and in one fragment (fragment A)[18] it seems that marriage between Ninus and his beloved has for the moment been vetoed. It is also to Babylon that Chariton's Callirhoe was taken so that the Persian king could decide whether she belonged to the Milesian Greek Dionysius or the Persian satrap Mithridates (4.6ff.), and where Callirhoe faces yet another suitor; and of course Babylon was the starting-point of Iamblichus' *Babyloniaca*.[19] The second set of associations is with the overpowering love that Thisbe and Pyramus feel for each other, love that leads each to suicide rather than live without the other.

The first of these associations is picked up in the main narrative when Theagenes is to be dispatched to the Persian king as a present (5.9). Of the second set of associations that of lifelong and overriding love is of course

[15] For the Pompeian painting and other attestations of the story see Kondoleon 1994, 148–56.

[16] *CIL* ix 1830 (Beneventum): *C. Herennius | C. l. Pyramus fe|cit sibi et | Herenniae Thisbe|ni coniugi suae et | Herenniae Faventinae | Lauro et Quintae suis*, 'C. Herennius, freedman of Gaius, Pyramus, made (this) for himself and his wife Herennia Thisbenis and Herennia Faventina, Laurus, and Quinta, their children'. For another clearly libertine case cf. *CIL* xi 1434 =*ILS* 1667 (Pisa, early second cent AD): *D. M. | M. Ulpio Aug. lib. | Vernae | ab epistulis| Latinis | Vibia Thisbe | uxor | infelicissima*, 'To the shades. For M. Ulpius Verna, freedman of Augustus, secretary for Latin letters, Vibia Thisbe his most unhappy wife (built this).' There are six more instances of Thisbe in *CIL* ix, and sixteen from Rome in *CIL* vi.

[17] Delphi, *FdD* iii.6.123.5 and 12, where the other women are called Alcippe and Nico; Ancyra, Bosch 1967, 188, no. 148; Aezani, *CIG* 3846 = LBW 964 = *MAMA* ix list 185 P2.

[18] For a translation see Sandy 1989a; text and trans. in Stephens and Winkler 1995. For date cf. Bowie 2002a (Chapter 25 in this volume).

[19] Iamb. *Bab.* ed. Habrich, 2ff., trans. Reardon 1989, 785.

fundamental to the presentation of Charicleia and Theagenes. But there is also a constant threat that one of the lovers will commit suicide. It is already there at 1.2, where Charicleia gazes at the bloodstained and almost dead Theagenes and promises she will kill herself with a sword if he dies – a scene that recalls, among other antecedents, the death of Pyramus. The appearance of the name Thisbe at 1.11 thus reminds the reader of danger that the love of Theagenes and Charicleia, unlike that of this Thisbe, may lead them to suicide rather than to the 'right' ending of the story. When both Thisbe and Charicleia are concealed in a cave, so that we are invited to compare and contrast their qualities, we recall the cave of the Pyramus story. When Theagenes thinks that the body of Charicleia has been discovered in the cave he delivers rhetorical last words, like Pyramus, before seeking his sword to stab himself precisely as the tale of Thisbe has threatened that he might: just in the nick of time Cnemon stops him and tells him that Charicleia is in fact alive (2.1).

The use of Thisbe's name, therefore, helps to underline some of the positive themes of Heliodorus' story and to remind us, time and again, of how the world from which Cnemon comes is different from that of Charicleia and Theagenes. Moreover, like the name Cnemon, its function within the sub-plot retains an element of humorous incongruity – the inconstant Thisbe bears the name of a famous paradigm of the committed lover.

A supporting role in this reader manipulation may be played by Thisbe's friend and workmate, the *hetaera* Arsinoe. It may of course be that the Ptolemaic queens of that name extruded other associations from a reader's mind, especially in a novel where much of the action is played out in Egypt. If so, perhaps the name is chosen simply as a historical joke. But imperial Greek readers could also have known a story in Antoninus Liberalis (39) taken from the *Leontion* of Hermesianax: a Phoenician fell in love with Arsinoe, a princess of Salamis in Cyprus, but both she and her parents rejected him; he starved himself to death, and when she gloated over his unhappy end from a window she was turned to stone by Aphrodite. This might, then, be another carefully chosen name for an *hetaera* who helps Thisbe to dupe Demaenete – with consequences fatal for Demaenete and disastrous for Cnemon and his father – and who belongs to a set of characters with the wrong view of love. Again there is some entertaining incongruity in a name associated with real and fairy-tale princesses being borne by a *demi-mondaine* from Athens.

I now turn briefly from the story of Cnemon to the main narrative. I begin with a name chosen chiefly for its humorous effect, that of the bandit leader's henchman called Thermouthis (1.30 etc.). When Cnemon attempts to lose him, by the comic technique of feigning diarrhoea, Thermouthis is in fact killed off by a snake-bite (2.20.2). Although his is indeed an Egyptian name, readers of Aelian will have recalled that *thermouthis* was also the name of an Egyptian snake.[20]

Heliodorus uses three other names that have a genuine Egyptian ring. Two of these, given to Calasiris' sons, Thyamis and Petosiris, seem to be chosen simply to impart Egyptian décor. But that of Calasiris himself has associations that are, like his character, more complex. The term καλάσιρις was known to readers of Herodotus as the name both of an Egyptian warrior class and of a linen garment worn by Egyptian priests, not unsuitable for the vegetarian priest in Heliodorus.[21] But Calasiris may have further resonances. As a priest with a special channel of communication to the divine he may be seen as an Egyptian version of Calchas, prominent of course in the opening scene of the *Iliad*, some lines of which (1.46–7), describing Apollo's descent from Olympus, are echoed right at the beginning of the *Aethiopica* (1.2.5). The name may also recall the Indian naked sage Calanus, who followed Alexander back from India and, when he fell ill in Persia, had himself burned alive on a huge pyre, refusing to say farewell to Alexander because he would greet him in Babylon (where Alexander in fact later died).[22] Allusion to a prophet and to a guru well established in Greek literary traditions enhances Calasiris' own claim to a similar status.

Alongside these names which are, I argue, evocative of other literature, there are many which are either unremarkable[23] or are chosen as straightforwardly appropriate to their bearer.[24] Among the latter, the names Charicleia and Theagenes were presumably chosen with special care. The chief criterion was clearly the sense of the component Greek terms, as is brought out by the spontaneous oracle at 2.35. That spells out for the reader that the name Charicleia starts with χάρις, 'grace', and will end with κλέος, 'glory'. Theagenes is descended from Thetis through Achilles, as Calasiris states (2.34) and as the hymn to Thetis at 3.2 emphasises. There the significance of Theagenes' name may end.[25]

[20] Ael. *NA* 10.31. [21] Hdt. 2.81, 164. [22] Arr. *An.* 7.2.4, 3.1, 18.6.

[23] E.g. Anticles (2.10), Charias and Teledemus; Demaenete; Isias of Chemmis.

[24] E.g. the Ethiopian priest Sisimithres, anagram of Isis and Mithres. For Heliodorus' convincing choice of Persian names (Orondates, Arsace, Mitranes, Bagoas) and largely unambitious attempt at Ethiopian names (Sisimithres, Persinna, Hydaspes, Hermonias: only Meroebus carries Ethiopian colour) see Morgan 1982, 247.

[25] But it is worth asking whether an author with some interest in the allegorical interpretation of Homer (cf. above with n.7) might have chosen the name Theagenes to evoke the sixth-century BC Greek from Rhegium who was the first to interpret Homer allegorically and to investigate his life and works: cf. Pfeiffer 1968, 9–11.

One might dismiss as a simple *redende Name* the name given to the merchant Nausicles, who lives by sea-borne trade. But here too there is a nice nuance. Nausicles' daughter can without surprise be called Nausicleia: but once she is given that name, this father and daughter invite reading as a contrast to the father and daughter who also share name-forms, Charicles and Charicleia, while the name Nausicleia also kindles recollections of the *Odyssey*'s Nausicaa. These recollections underline the lack of commitment and staying power of Cnemon, who jumps at the offer of Nausicleia's hand instead of honouring his undertaking to escort Charicleia until Theagenes is found (6.7–8). How different was the behaviour of the traveller who did not allow potential marriage to Nausicaa to deflect him from his commitment to return to Penelope, and who is a prototype in different ways for both Theagenes and Charicleia! To achieve these effects Heliodorus has given his merchant a name widely used in real life: but Nausicleia, though plausible enough, is only once attested, and has probably been invented by Heliodorus for his literary purpose.[26]

3 An Allusive Gem

Nausicles offers a convenient transition to a rather different type of intertextual allusion. When Calasiris is at last reunited with Charicleia, now in the possession of the merchant Nausicles, who has claimed (with her connivance) that she is his lost chattel Thisbe, Nausicles hints that a ransom should be paid to him for her restoration. In one of his puzzling performances of apparently magical tricks Calasiris pretends to conjure out of the fire a ring set with an amethyst[27] – in fact it is one of the opulent tokens with which the infant Charicleia had been dispatched from Ethiopia. Heliodorus describes the jewel in detail and offers learned explanations of the sources of amethysts and of the meaning of the name (5.13). The scene that is engraved on it is allowed half a page of virtuoso description (5.14). It is described first as a μίμημα ζώιων, 'imitation of animals': its γραφή, 'depiction', is of a shepherd-boy, playing on transverse αὐλοί, 'pipes', to his flock; his sheep graze to the music and their lambs gambol in circles round the rocks on which he

[26] A Nausicleia at Thera, *IG* xii.3 873/1824 and suppl. p. 328. *LGPN* ii (1994) records thirteen instances of Nausicles for Athens, and its data base none of Nausicleia (but cf. n.6, and note that women's names are much less well documented by epigraphy than men's).

[27] Cf. his pretence to exercise magic arts when Theagenes and Charicleia suffer from lovesickness at Delphi, 3.16–17, 4.5, and, for the problem of interpreting his character, Sandy 1982; Winkler 1982; more recently Kim 2017; Kruchió 2017.

stands, giving the effect of a pastoral theatre. Such *ecphraseis* have long been seen as a favourite constituent of the sophistic novels: characteristically, and above all in Heliodorus, they make an important contribution to the reader's interpretation, offering a μίμημα, 'imitation', which not only displays the writer's rhetorical skill but invites the reader to relate the scene or object in some way to the main narrative.[28]

What is the jewel's contribution here? Set against the very different and exotic landscape around the village of Chemmis,[29] where crocodiles scuttle across the tracks, this miniature works partly to offer the sort of contrast with which Homeric pastoral similes point up Iliadic battle narrative. The apparently untroubled and relaxed shepherd-boy himself contrasts with the anxious central characters. But the subject-matter is *so* alien to that of the *Aethiopica* that some deeper explanation is called for. It is not hard to see, even if (to my knowledge) modern scholars have not yet suggested it. Any reader of our corpus of ancient novels must surely be tempted to think that Heliodorus is alluding to that literary miniature, the Ποιμενικὰ τὰ κατὰ Δάφνιν καὶ Χλόην, '*The pastoral tale of Daphnis and Chloe*',[30] usually simply referred to as *Daphnis and Chloe*. That work itself begins with an *ecphrasis* of a γραφή, 'painting', its hero is a herding boy, and at least two of Heliodorus' phrases recall expressions in Longus. Heliodorus' phrase ἀρνείων ἁπαλὰ σκιρτήματα, 'the lissom gambols of lambs' (5.14.3), recalls Longus' σκιρτήματα ποιμνίων ἀρτιγεννήτων, 'the gambols of new-born sheep' (1.9.1). His reference to the ποιμενικὸν θεάτρον (ibid.) reminds us of the scene towards Longus' denouement where Lamon proclaims Daphnis' skill to Dionysophanes and Cleariste. Cleariste wants to test the claim that Daphnis has made his goats μουσικάς, so Daphnis makes his human audience sit down like that in a theatre – καθίσας ὥσπερ θέατρον (4.19.2) – and plays to his goats on a syrinx. They respond to different tunes in different ways – cf. Heliodorus' sentence 'they (sc. the sheep) were obedient, as it seemed, and were content to be grazed to the panpipe's musical signals' (5.14.2).[31] Earlier Daphnis' goats are said to lie down as if listening to his panpipe tunes (1.13.4).

[28] Rommel 1923; Bartsch 1989, who mentions the jewel only briefly, noting the animation of the scene (123) and the jewel's contribution to the advancement of the plot (149). Dubel 1990 has a good discussion of the description of the jewel and its emphasis on craftsmanship, but draws no conclusions from its subject's difference from the rest of the novel.

[29] I shall discuss elsewhere the implications for the novel's interpretation of Heliodorus' choice of the name Chemmis for the village where so many strands of the first half of his story are drawn together.

[30] The text of **V**. That of **F** is ποιμενικὰ περὶ Δάφνιν καὶ Χλόην.

[31] The ability of the skilled herder to control grazing animals by music alone appears also at Longus 1.27.2, 28.3, 29.3.

The image of the θέατρον, 'theatre', is of course one much exploited by Heliodorus, who often describes characters within his narrative either as themselves a θέατρον or as playing as if to a θέατρον.[32] If, as I am arguing, there is an allusion to Longus here, the theatrical analogy is an element which encourages us to recall the text in which the allusive description is set. We are invited to contrast the huge Aida-like stage across which Heliodorus has his characters process with the miniature and enclosed world of Longus. Such a comparison may cause us to reflect that, despite the virtuosity displayed by Longus in his mimesis of his confined pastoral universe, only the grand operatic stage created by Heliodorus really deserves comparison with the theatre.

The narrative setting also allows us to see the gem as standing for a literary work. Calasiris, who often seems to play the role of the author in the first half of the work, has here decided to exchange an item of great value for Charicleia (who has sometimes been seen by scholars as emblematic of the work Charicleia in which she has the leading role). A jewel evoking another novel is judged by Calasiris to be worth less than his Charicleia. Heliodorus has crafted an appropriate assertion of his own work's pre-eminence in the novelistic tradition and given it prominence in a pivotal scene near the mid-point of his novel.

[32] See esp. the excellent discussion of Bartsch 1989, 129–41.

23 The Ancient Readers of the Greek Novels (1996)

1 Introduction

As Cleitophon begins to fall passionately in love with Leucippe in Achilles Tatius' novel, he hits on a stratagem for catching glimpses of her in the part of his parental home that had been set aside for her and her mother when they arrived as refugees from Byzantium (1.6.6, cf. 5.1). He takes a book and perambulates the house in such a way that from time to time, facing the doorway behind which Leucippe is to be found, he can raise his eyes from the book over which he is bent and glimpse his beloved. Achilles does not tell us what sort of a book it was, and we are free to suppose that it might be precisely the sort of book that he has written and that we are reading. The uncertainty left by this brief mention of a (presumably) literary text, the only such mention in our extant corpus of Greek novels whether complete, summarised or fragmentary, is an appropriate metaphor for the obscurity attaching to the readership of these works in the ancient Greek world. The issue has been alive since Rohde, and has been much debated since Perry's Sather lectures were published in 1967, particularly over the last decade.[1] Yet although some more evidence has been gathered and arguments and distinctions have been refined, the subject is still one where the best that can be offered is plausible inference and not proof.

The lack of what can reasonably be termed evidence is at the heart of our problem. Hence it is possible for some scholars to hold that the novel developed in the late Hellenistic period precisely as a literature designed for a new category of reader, men and women who were literate but not intellectual, residents of huge Hellenistic cities whose *déracinement* encouraged them to identify with the often isolated characters in the novels and to find meaning for their own lives in the pattern of their adventures, and for others to hold that the texts were primarily produced for and read by the same social and intellectual elite who read Plutarch and historians or

[1] Hägg 1983 and 1994; Wesseling 1988; Treu 1989; Harris 1989; Bowie 1985b and 1994a (Chapter 20 in this volume); Stephens 1994.

attended philosophy lectures. The following discussion will necessarily traverse ground already much trodden by both these groups (the latter of which has included me) and the most my reader can hope for is a map with clearer definition of important features, not one in which 'The Answer' is unambiguously marked.

A definition that must be essayed at the outset is that of the novels themselves. Are we dealing with a single genre, or should the 'ideal' romances, in which a pair of heterosexual lovers is central and chastity esteemed, be seen as different from a more lubricious form apparently represented by Lollianus' Φοινικικά, '*Phoenician tales*', and the Iolaus story, and should yet a third type be seen in the twenty-four-book Τὰ ὑπὲρ Θούλην ἄπιστα, '*The incredible things beyond Thule*', of Antonius Diogenes, in which the central couple are brother and sister, not lovers, and extensive and fantastic travel is a more important element than love? In the absence of ancient literary theory we are again denied any demonstrable conclusion. But we may argue that both Lollianus and Antonius Diogenes read more effectively if they are taken to involve some parody of the 'ideal' romance, and that any propositions about readership should take account both of generic links and of diversity between individual specimens.[2]

A similar question must be addressed concerning the relation between the novels that have been argued to be less ambitious and that in most cases also seem to be earlier (*Ninus*, *Parthenope and Metiochus*, Chariton's *Chaereas and Callirhoe*, Xenophon's *Anthia and Habrocomes* and arguably the supposed Greek original of *Apollonius king of Tyre*) and those by common consent described as 'sophistic' (Achilles Tatius' *Leucippe and Cleitophon*, Longus' *Daphnis and Chloe* and Heliodorus' *Charicleia and Theagenes*). Can a conclusion about readership reached for the one group be expected to hold in any degree for the other? Again the sorts of intertextuality with the earlier works that have been detected in the sophistic novels do something to hold the two groups together. At the least the readers of the sophistic novels are, it seems, expected to know what the stereotypical features of the earlier novels were, and to admire the adroitness with which the sophistic novelist handles them: such features are the pirates, perhaps even Phoenician pirates, that invade Longus' pastoral Lesbos, or the sort of story implied as gripping by the responses of Cnemon to Calasiris' narrative in Heliodorus.[3]

[2] On this see now Henrichs 2011, 313–18.

[3] Longus 1.28.1, where Τύριοι, the reading of **V**, should be retained, see Bowie 2019g, 155–6: **F** has Πύρριοι, emended by Young to Πυρραῖοι, which was accepted by Reeve 1982. For Cnemon as a simple-minded audience see Winkler 1982.

A final preliminary: it is clear that an investigation should consistently distinguish between actual and intended readers, and that the sorts of result we might in principle expect in trying to establish these two categories are likely to be different. If we had comprehensive data on *actual* readership in the ancient world (though of course we have almost no data at all) we would be able to draw up an inventory of all individuals who actually read novels and allocate them to different groups by criteria of income, geographical location, and level of education, and come up with some hardandfast generalisations. But the question of an author's 'intended readership' is much more slippery. Some authors of certain sorts of work (intermediate Greek language-teaching manuals; travelguides to Disneyworld) have a very precise category of reader in mind; authors of other sorts of work (histories of the Second World War; crime fiction; 'soft' pornography) might be thought often to have a much looser conception of their intended readership: at the time they start writing they may envisage four or five possible categories, in the course of composing their work they may admit a further two, and if pressed by an interviewer might concede that certain other categories might also furnish appropriate readers. Finally (of my selective list, though not of course of any possible list) there are some authors who (like musicians and like pictorial or plastic artists) may claim to have no regard to prospective audiences at all, and may explain their creativity in terms of some inner compulsion, or (with less mystification) as adoption of a fashion: *semper ego auditor tantum*?[4]

This last point abuts on an issue that has often been closely bound up with that of readership, viz. the reasons for the development of this post-classical genre. Perry saw its genesis as a response to the reading needs of late Hellenistic man, and Tomas Hägg has recently suggested that such positions as my own which do not connect readership with the emergence of the genre are for that reason flawed.[5] I am not embarrassed that my view of a predominantly intellectual readership takes us back to 'square one' on the question of origins. The hard question we have to ask is this: did the writers of either the first novels (of which we are statistically unlikely to have any examples in our selective remains) or of their immediate successors (by which I mean *Ninus*, *Parthenope and Metiochus*, *Chaereas and Callirhoe* and *Anthia and Habrocomes*) have any idea, whether inchoate or clear, of the sort of reader for whom they were writing, and did the *way* that they wrote take account systematically of that envisaged readership? Like so many of the fundamental questions in this enquiry, it is probably

[4] 'Am I always to be only a listener?', Juv. 1.1.

[5] Hägg 1994, 52–3.

unanswerable. But we can exclude, at the one end of the spectrum, extensive consumer research resulting in the designer-novel; and we might equally wish to exclude an extreme form of the *semper ego auditor tantum*? approach. We should be ready to admit familiarity with the sorts of literature that have proved to go down well in the (necessarily) limited environment of the writer,[6] but we might also be wise to admit an impulse to try out a new formula in an age when all the established genres were already overcrowded with past masters and contemporary aspirants. A scribbler in a city of Egypt, Syria or Asia Minor might thereby hit on a recipe that was to catch the attention of certain sorts of reader all over the Eastern Mediterranean (just as a Jewish mystic from Nazareth hit on a winning religious formula) but we may doubt that he could have had good reason to believe that this was what he was doing. And unless we endorse some relatively strong form of the 'designer-text' hypothesis, we should beware of claiming too close a link between the reasons for which the first novels were written and their intended readership.

If we are to insist that some link must be supposed between the reasons for writing novels and their earliest readers, another *caveat* should perhaps be entered at this point. Like Hägg, I have seen hints in the earliest extant novels that suggest that not only *Callirhoe* (which explicitly purports to be by a man from Aphrodisias) but also *Ninus*, and perhaps *Parthenope*, were composed or intended for a readership in Western Asia Minor.[7] Recently Bowersock has also claimed Antonius Diogenes, persuasively if unprovably, for Chariton's city Aphrodisias.[8] These novels' presumptive predecessors may of course have been written elsewhere, but in an era when most works must have had a geographically restricted circulation it is at least *more likely* that such predecessors should also be associated with Western Asia Minor. Now whether or not the picture of Hellenistic man as suffering a sense of loss and isolation as a result of the breakdown of the society and shared values of the classical *polis* is a correct diagnosis of inhabitants of huge cities like Antioch and Alexandria,[9] it is hardly applicable even to

[6] On contemporary Greek literary activity see Bowie 2008d (Chapter 33 in this volume).

[7] Hägg 1994, 70 n.32; Bowie 1994a, 450–2 (Chapter 20, 440 in this volume).

[8] Bowersock 1994, 38–41.

[9] Scepticism concerning the applicability of this *mentalité* to Hellenistic Athens has already been voiced by Gruen 1993. Note Gruen's conclusion (drawn admittedly from evidence that is chiefly for the third century BC): 'Civic spirit had not evaporated in the Hellenistic age. The polis held its place as a centre of allegiance and a source of pride. Hellenistic individuals were not all driven to seek inner solace or to reach out longingly to the cosmos. They could still find support in the familiar institutions of the polis' (354). Note too the arguments (not all cogent) of Martin 1994, 117, that 'neither the Hellenistic idea nor ideal can be held to value in any way an individualistic view of the self'. I am grateful to Mark Golden for drawing my attention to these discussions.

the biggest cities of Western Asia Minor. Although this too is treacherous ground, the citizen population of Pergamum in the high Roman Empire is put by Galen at 40,000, with guesses that this implies a total population of between 160,000 and 200,000, and that the Hellenistic city was substantially smaller.[10] Ephesus and Smyrna may well have been of the same order. We are not here in a different world from that of fifthcentury Athens or Syracuse, the former with at least 20,000 citizens in the first three Solonian classes in 432/1 BC, and arguably a total male citizen population over 30,000.[11] Of the remainder of the reputedly 500 cities of *provincia Asia* very few can have been as large as classical Athens, and the vast majority were on the same small scale as the classical *polis*. A recent estimate allows few cities more than 25,000 inhabitants and puts the majority in the range between 5,000 and 15,000.[12] All these cities about which we know anything, large and small, seem to have been highly conscious of their identities in the Hellenistic and Roman period, to have elaborated traditions which authorised that identity, and sometimes to have enjoyed benefactions whose founders were in varying degrees careful to use their benefaction to create a structure in which all but the lowest echelons of the citizen body were given a place.[13] Things were no doubt different in Antioch on the Orontes and Alexandria, both cities created *de novo* and from very heterogeneous populations: the latter's free residents in the middle of the first century BC are numbered at 300,000 by Diodorus Siculus, from which a population of ca. 500,000 has been inferred.[14] Scholars who ascribe isolation and *déracinement* to Hellenistic man are doubtless influenced by our image of these two huge cities, but any who hold that the novel may have been first written in Western Asia Minor must reckon with a different sort of environment. Indeed the enthusiasm for true or forged traditions and for local history

[10] Magie 1950, 585 and n.50 on 1446. Gal. *De cogn. curand. animi morbis* 9 (= v 49 Kühn) attests 40,000 citizens for Pergamum, totalling 120,000 with wives and slaves: from this a total population of between 180,000 and 200,000 is estimated by Mitchell 1993, i 244, while Radt 1988, 175 estimated 160,000 for the later second century AD and only ca. 25,000 to 40,000 for the Attalid period. It was thought by Magie 1950 i 585, ii 1446, n.50 (and others have followed him) that the inscription published by Keil 1930 = *IEph.* 951 attested 40,000 citizens as entertained by Aur. Varanus at Ephesus late in the second century AD: but as pointed out by Warden and Bagnall 1988, comparing Plin. *Ep.* 10.116, the text's χειλίους τεσσαράκοντα credits Varanus with entertaining not 40,000 but 1,040 citizens over eleven days.

[11] For interpretations of the key passage, Th. 2.13.6, see Gomme 1927, 1933, 1956, 33–9 and 1959; Jones 1957, 161–80; Hansen 1981: cf. Bowie 1998a (Chapter 5, 85–6 in this volume).

[12] Mitchell 1993, i 244.

[13] The closest and most illuminating studies of such benefactions concern those of C. Vibius Salutaris at Ephesus in AD 104 by Rogers 1991 and of C. Iulius Demosthenes at Oenoanda in AD 124 by Wörrle 1988. For discussion of interest in local foundation legends cf. Strubbe 1984–6.

[14] D.S. 17.52; Bowman 1986, 208.

that characterises these cities might more appropriately be associated with precisely that orientation in *Parthenope* and *Callirhoe*.

After these preliminaries I return to the main theme of this chapter, and attempt to outline the state of the question (as I see it) under six heads.

2 Possible Readers

(A1) The 'Sophistic' Novels: Intended Readership

This seems now to be a relatively uncontested aspect of the problem. Tomas Hägg is happy to allow that Achilles Tatius, Longus and Heliodorus were themselves highly educated and envisaged similarly educated readers as the primary readership of their works. The argument is based on the frequency and subtlety of intertextuality with earlier literature, some of it more recondite than the stuff of basic secondary educational curricula.[15] At the same time it may be reasonable to insist (as Hägg does for Chariton)[16] that in the 'sophistic' novels too 'narrative suspense, emotional impact, the escapist function were there for all', and that their writers *may* have envisaged a few less highly educated readers who would turn to them for these and would not find the more complicated narrative structure of Heliodorus or the Atticising Greek of all three an obstacle to understanding. We must remember, however, that quite a high level of education must be assumed in a prospective reader of Atticising Greek – an education acquired by studying classical texts in one's youth and reinforced by encounters with these texts or with their imperial written or spoken imitators in adult life.

(A2) The 'Sophistic' Novels: Actual Readership

Paradoxically, we are little better off for evidence of actual readers of the big three than of other species of the genre. True, we have eight papyri of Achilles Tatius, one of the first half of the second century (*P.Oxy.* 3836) and the other eight from the third.[17] But we have only one of Heliodorus, and

[15] Bowie 1994a, 438, 451–3 (Chapter 20 in this volume, 420, 436–7).

[16] Hägg 1994, 54.

[17] Six were listed by Garnaud 1991, xxiii–xxv: three from Oxyrhynchus, one from Hermoupolis and the others of unknown provenance. The tally now stands at eight, with two more from Oxyrhynchus, from six rolls and two codices, representing seven different editions (i.e. two are from the same edition), cf. Henrichs 2011, 306 with n.17; Bowie 2002a, updated as Chapter 25 in this volume, 525 with nn.67–70.

that as late as the sixth century,[18] and still none of Longus. We know, then, that some Greek speakers in Oxyrhynchus and in other parts of Egypt read or thought they might like to read Achilles Tatius in the first half of the second and in the third centuries. The format of the book and the type of writing do not mark off these papyri from those of high literary texts,[19] the numbers of novel papyri remain smaller than those of the most read of such high literary texts, and it remains tempting to infer that their readers are indeed the same as the readers of these texts. It is also tempting to ascribe the greater popularity of Achilles Tatius (if a mere eight papyri can attest 'popularity' of any sort) to the Alexandrian origin claimed for him by the Suda and to the prominence of Egypt in his narrative. But then Heliodorus also sets the largest single section of his narrative in Egypt, and so far he has no known readers in Egypt before the sixth century.

He does, however, have a possible reader in the emperor Julian. Julian's account of the siege of Nisibis in AD 350, to be found in his *Orations* 1 and 3 of AD 357, is either influenced by Heliodorus' narrative of the siege of Syene or influences it.[20] Proof of a date in the later fourth century for Heliodorus would compel the latter conclusion, but so far this has not been forthcoming, and I still regard the issue as open, with a greater readiness to believe that Julian read Heliodorus than *vice versa*. If so, our first known reader of Heliodorus is indeed highly educated, even if he is one who in a letter of AD 363 to the ἀρχιερεύς, 'high-priest', of Asia proscribed the reading of erotic fiction.[21]

A further fourth-century reader for Heliodorus has been enticingly proposed by Bowersock.[22] In the *Augustan History*'s life of Aurelian his successortobe Tacitus, praising his achievements, lists the Seres among the peoples he

[18] Gronewald 1979, 19–21.

[19] See Stephens 1994, 412–14, though note the slightly different emphasis of Treu 1989, 190–1, who allocates the novel papyri to the middle and bottom part of a scale running from luxurious to simple. What is important, however, is that the novel papyri 'in the aggregate look different both from the early New Testament material and from unskilled productions', Stephens 1994, 413.

[20] For the evidence and arguments see Bowie 1994a, 446 with n.54 (Chapter 20, 434 with n.55 in this volume); Chuvin 1991, 321–5; Bowersock 1994, 149–60.

[21] *Ep.* 89, p. 169 Bidez, cf. Bowie 1994a, 446. The case for use of Julian by Heliodorus and against a third-century date was reaffirmed by Bowersock 1994, 149–60. Much turns on whether the description of the siege works at Nisibis by the Syriac term *talâla* (plural of *tall*) assimilates them to or differentiates them from the χώματα, 'earthworks', of Heliodorus 9.3–4. I am not competent to pronounce. But even if the terms describe the same phenomenon, that simply removes an argument for seeing Julian as dependent on Heliodorus and does not constitute an argument for the reverse relation. Heliodorus' interest in cataphracts (Bowersock 1994, 157–60) does indeed match their fourth-century prominence, but the armed cavalryman goes back at least as far as Crassus' debacle at Carrhae in 53 BC (as of course Bowersock concedes).

[22] Bowersock 1994, 150–60.

conquered alongside the Blemmyes and the people of Aksum, *Exomitae*.[23] Bowersock has suggested that the idea of associating the Seres with these African peoples came to the historian from reading Heliodorus' account of envoys sent to Hydaspes by his allies (10.25–7), and notes that an earlier list of Aurelian's conquests, in the description of his triumph mentions Blemmyes, the people of Aksum, and a giraffe offered by the latter (but no Seres):[24] a giraffe also figures in the Ethiopian king Hydaspes' triumphal parade at Meroe (10.27). The suggestion is attractive but its foundations precarious. Giraffes could be found in other Latin texts by the writer of the *Augustan History*,[25] and the bizarre location of the Seres, as Bowersock himself notes, was already offered by Lucan (10.292–3). Their conjunction in the *Augustan History*, written in the last two decades of the fourth century, *may* arise from its author's familiarity with Heliodorus' work (presumably the Greek text: we have no hint that there was ever a Latin translation) but it need not.

The first man, therefore, to show certain knowledge of Heliodorus is Socrates Scholasticus, whose history of the church, written in Constantinople and stopping at AD 439, alleges that he became bishop of Trikka in Thessaly.[26] Although eschewing Atticism himself, Socrates undoubtedly belongs to the highly educated elite, and defended Christians' reading of pagan literature. That he actually read Heliodorus, we have no proof. There is even less support for his reading rather earlier in the fifth century by the doctor Theodorus Priscianus, who prescribed the reading of erotic novels as a cure for impotence. He names Iamblichus and Herodian: in the absence of a known novelist Herodian it might be that the name is a corruption of Heliodorus, with whom Iamblichus and Achilles Tatius are grouped by Photius.[27]

Between its second-century composition and this mention by Photius in the latter half of the ninth century influence of Achilles Tatius' *Leucippe and Cleitophon* has been detected in three fifth-century texts: Musaeus' *Hero and Leander* (? ca. AD 470), Aristaenetus' erotic *Letters* and Nonnus' *Dionysiaca*.[28] Musaeus is a learned poet, well deserving the epithet

[23] SHA *Aurel.* 41.10. [24] SHA *Aurel.* 33.4. [25] E.g. Varro *Ling.* 5.100, Plin. *Nat.* 8.69.

[26] *Hist. eccl.* 5.22

[27] Theodorus Priscianus, *Euporista* 2.11.34 (133 Rose), a Latin translation by Theodorus of his own Greek text; Phot. *Bibl. Cod.* 94, 73b: cf. Bowie 1994a, 457 n.55 (Chapter 20, 435 n.56 in this volume).

[28] Ach. Tat. 1.4 is the chief model for expressions in Musaeus 58, 92, 96, cf. Orsini 1968, vi–xvii; Kost 1971, 29–30. For his importance for Musaeus see Dümmler 2012; Montiglio 2020b, 8–12; for details Montiglio 2020b, 76–7, 81–2, 84–5, 87–8, 90, 93. For knowledge of Ach. Tat. in the fourth century and later see Whitmarsh 2020, 13–16; for Aristaenetus, Mazal 1971; for Nonnus, Miguélez-Cavero 2016. For possible knowledge of Longus by Philostr., [Opp.] *C.*, Hld., Aristaenetus and Nonnus see Bowie 2019g, 20–1.

γραμματικός, 'grammarian', given him by his manuscripts. The second- and third-century owners of papyri of Achilles Tatius may indeed not have been so learned, but given the similarity of their books to those of high literature, we have no warrant for supposing that they were from a significantly less-educated stratum.

(B1) The 'Early' Novels: Intended Readership

Of all the issues discussed in this chapter this is perhaps the one most fought over and least susceptible of a confident answer. The early novels' sentimentality and preference for simpler forms of narrative have led scholars to suppose they were aimed at some class other than the readers of high literary texts – whether women, children, or simply a lower social and cultural level of reader. The alleged silence concerning novels in higher literary genres has reinforced this position, but of course it bears not on intended but actual readers, and is discussed below under (B2). In an earlier discussion I have drawn attention to the limited number of women likely to have been educated to a level at which they could both read literary texts with ease and appreciate allusions in them to earlier literature, and have stressed that the importance of such allusions in Chariton (and their presence in *Metiochus and Parthenope*) points rather to the same sort of reader who read classical texts and contemporary writers such as Plutarch.[29]

Tomas Hägg has recently advanced important criticisms of these arguments and restated the case for a wider audience – not simply, that is, a wider readership, but aural access to novels by audiences who either lacked literacy or found it tedious to activate, and who listened while another read aloud.

Many of Hägg's points have considerable force. It is fair, for example, to insist that the survival of positive evidence for certain sorts of readers cannot establish the non-existence of other sorts of reader for whom our surviving witnesses would be unlikely to offer testimony. It is also fair to insist that a work may be intended to entertain on several levels, or may actually do so, and that 'the narrative suspense, the emotional impact, the escapist function were there for all, the rhetorical and classicizing embellishment for some',[30] and so that Chariton may have had several different audiences in mind.

[29] For discussion of literary influences on and allusions in Chariton see the excellent article of Hunter 1994; for citation in the novelists in general Fusillo 1990a.

[30] Hägg 1994, 54.

Some other points made by Hägg strike me as less convincing. In support of a female readership he lays stress on 'the early novels' preoccupation with women' – particularly evident in *Callirhoe* and *Parthenope* – and with 'psychology, sentiments and private life'. The problem remains that a considerable interest in all these subjects can well be supposed of a male readership, and certainly the classical Greek male poet who has often seemed to critics ancient and modern to have shown especial interest in women's psychology, Euripides, composed and produced his plays for audiences that were predominantly or – in my view – wholly male. It is one thing to demonstrate, as Hägg rightly judges that Egger 1988 has, that novel heroines are described in a way that would make them suitable objects of identification for women in the Roman Empire, relatively more emancipated than those of classical Greece, and another to show that a novelist had such women in mind as a significant element in his readership.

Another point seen by Hägg to support a 'partly, some would say predominantly, female audience' is the phenomenon that the early novels' heroines are 'sympathetically drawn and altogether more alive than their pale husbands and lovers'.[31] It is perhaps dangerous to claim this for the shadowy Parthenope (and on present evidence the claim could not be extended to Semiramis), though it is certainly true of Callirhoe and Anthia: but it is also, unfortunately, true of Charicleia in Heliodorus' *Aethiopica*, a work that Hägg agrees to envisage a predominantly male readership. An explanation for the relative weakness of the hero and strength of the heroine in terms of the novels' internal dynamics that applies to the genre as a whole has recently been offered by David Konstan and if accepted would make an explanation in terms of prospective readers redundant.[32]

Hägg's main arguments, however, are drawn from the style and form of the early novels, on the basis of which he had already in 1971 formulated his hypothesis that the early novels were intended for 'oral' delivery.[33] The four key features are these:

(i) Stereotyped linking phrases between episodes which summarise preceding action in a clause with the particle μέν and begin the new action with a δέ clause. As examples Hägg notes Chariton 4.2.1 and Xenophon 2.14.1. As Hägg points out, however, these devices are found throughout Greek

[31] Hägg 1994, at n.43.

[32] Konstan 1994, esp. 3–59. Konstan himself suggests (78) that the presence of implied male and female audiences within the novel may be Chariton's way of suggesting a complex readership for his work.

[33] Hägg 1971a chapter 7, and the oral hypothesis at 332.

narrative prose, and their presence in such texts as that of Thucydides makes it hard to associate their use with intended oral performance, even if they may originally have been welcomed into Greek narrative at a time when that was oral (our earliest instances are of course in Homer).

(ii) Recapitulations of earlier events, in Xenophon mostly in indirect speech (Hägg notes 3.3.1), in Chariton either in a character's words or reflections (e.g. 2.5.10, 8.7.8) or in his own authorial voice – above all 5.1.1–2, but also more briefly, and combined with foreshadowing, at 8.1.1.

(iii) Foreshadowing (of which 8.1.1 is but one example). Hägg concludes that 'This whole apparatus of repetitive material must have some kind of functional explanation', and he finds this explanation in the hypothesis that the novels were intended for 'people who had not yet moved definitely from orality to literacy', i.e. for 'inexperienced readers', or for 'listeners'.[34] Of course it may be wrong to suppose that all these features – and others that Hägg goes on to consider, (iv) and (v) below – are correctly to be subjected to the same explanation. The δέ transitions, for example, might, as I suggest above, be there for a different reason. As to Chariton's recapitulations at the beginnings of books, Hägg himself notes the relevance of the appearance of such recapitulations in our manuscripts of Xenophon's *Anabasis* (at the beginnings of Books 2, 3, 4, 5 and 7), recapitulations which Chariton and his readers probably had in their texts. At least part of their function, then, may be to corroborate Chariton's historiographic pose; another is to reinforce the sense of closure with which Chariton clearly seeks to mark the ends of his books.[35]

I would suggest too that the most striking example of recapitulation, that which occupies seventeen lines in the Budé text at 5.1.1, may serve the same function as was presumably served by the interpolated summaries in Xenophon, i.e. to offer orientation to readers who had access only to the roll or rolls which began with that book-opening and not to earlier rolls. Chariton may have felt a particular need to place such a full recapitulation at the beginning of book five. In literary terms, it is the midpoint of the work. From a codicological point of view (if this technical term can be transferred to a discussion of *volumina*) the chances that book five would begin on a new roll must be high. On the one hand our extant and attested novels (Xenophon and Longus excepted) are too long to fit on one roll (not

[34] Hägg 1994 at n.50.

[35] On the historiographical frame see esp. Hunter 1994, 1056–64; on closure at bookends, 1064 with n.43.

surprisingly the beginning of an Oxyrhynchus papyrus roll of Antonius Diogenes was also the beginning of a book, probably Book 4).[36] On the other hand more than one book of a novel *could* be accommodated on a roll, as the fragments of Lollianus, spanning three books, show. Chariton's 150 Budé pages would certainly exceed one roll, but could be comfortably divided between two. A weaker form of this argument could be offered in terms of where a reader who had access to a complete set of rolls of Chariton's novel might most likely pause. The format of division into books encourages such pauses to be at the end of books, so that a reader resuming the reading of the work after a pause (of minutes? hours? days?) might welcome a reminder of the storysofar at the beginning of a book.

The stronger version of this explanation cannot be offered for 8.1 (unless we were to suppose that Chariton envisaged each book occupying a separate roll, which I would not). Here, however, the function must be taken alongside that of the foreshadowing which immediately follows (8.1.2–5). Now it must be agreed that if Chariton did envisage 'inexperienced' readers, or listeners who lacked the opportunity to remind themselves of how the story had developed, both the recapitulation and the foreshadowing could have a specific function in relation to them. However it is also clear that the way in which such foreshadowing raises the dramatic temperature can be as rewarding for experienced as for 'inexperienced' readers. It is not only 'inexperienced' readers whom suspense and increased expectations encourage to continue reading. Moreover the terminology of this case of foreshadowing, with its apparent allusion to the *catharsis* theory of Aristotle's *Poetics*,[37] seems to be aimed to some extent at a well-educated reader.

These recapitulations and foreshadowings may, then, be an indication that Chariton envisaged 'inexperienced' readers, but it is not an unambiguous indication. It might also be observed that if Hägg's model of an individual reading aloud to a group is adopted, we lose one constraint which may have generated recapitulations in genuinely oral performances, i.e. the lack of opportunity (in theory always open to a solo reader) to go back to check what has happened in earlier parts of the text: an individual reading aloud to others can always be asked to go back and check (as many parents must know!). Moreover we should remember that such checking is much harder

[36] *P.Oxy.* 3012 ed. Parsons 1974. One, perhaps two, further papyrus fragments of Antonius Diogenes, *P.Oxy.* 4760 and 4761, were published by Parsons 2006a and 2006b; a further fragment, *P.Oxy.* 5354, by Parsons 2018. For a text of Photius' summary and all fragments with an excellent introduction and commentary see Schmedt 2020.

[37] καθάρσιον γάρ ἐστι, 'for it is something that will purge', 8.1.4: cf. Hunter 1994, 1070.

for users of rolls than for users of codices: thus even for a solo reader, of whatever level of experience, recapitulations have a useful function.

(iv) Hägg also adduces in favour of an 'inexperienced' readership the stereotypical phraseology that is especially noticeable in Xenophon and the stereotypical scenes, motifs and plots that characterise the whole genre. That the latter mark even the 'sophistic' novels naturally weakens their force as indicators of inexperienced readers, and since many 'high' genres of ancient Greek literature also have stereotypical scenes and motifs I doubt if they can be given much weight. The stereotypical phraseology of Xenophon is another matter: perhaps Hägg's explanation should be considered seriously, but it must compete with the more common view that such phraseology is part of a broader limitation in Xenophon's literary skills,[38] or that they are consciously evoking them.[39] Even if the explanation is to be linked to features of 'oral' narrative, it remains possible that these are present either because the early novels are successors of oral narratives or that they are consciously evoking them.[40]

(B2) The 'Early' Novels: Actual Readership

In the Greek world the papyri are again our first witnesses. Our earliest Greek evidence for the 'ideal' romance remains the *Ninus* fragments: the two Berlin fragments (*P.Berol.* 6926) were written on a papyrus whose verso bears accounts of AD 101, while the hand of the novel text itself seems to belong around AD 75.[41] Our four papyri of Chariton stretch unevenly from the mid-second century (*P.Michaelides* 1, *P.Fayum* 1) through the third (*P. Oxy.* 1019 + 2948) to Wilcken's codex of ca. 600. The *Chione* story that was also on that ill-fated codex also looks like an 'early' novel. The other work in this group, *Parthenope and Metiochus*, is represented by two papyrus rolls, both late second century, and by an ostracon (*O.Bodl.* 2175). Once again it is worth stressing that the books here represented are similar to the texts of classical authors. It has been claimed that the ostracon is different: Kurt Treu, whose scholarly integrity was never compromised by his DDR environment in Berlin, took the ostracon as one of the few pieces of evidence for

[38] See also Zanetto 1990.

[39] For oral features in Xenophon and Chariton see Scobie 1983, 32–5; in Xenophon, O'Sullivan 1995, 2014; for a sympathetic analysis of Xenophon, Tagliabue 2017.

[40] For oral features in Xenophon and Chariton see Scobie 1983, 32–5.

[41] Stephens and Winkler 1995, 31. Further discussion of the papyri of the novels in Bowie 2002a (Chapter 25 in this volume); Henrichs 2011.

the impact of the novel on classes lower than the educated elite.[42] Perhaps he was right, but ostraca were used for a wide range of purposes, high and low, and the appearance of a literary text on an ostracon does not establish that its owner was of a lower social class. That is certainly unlikely to have been true of the owner of the ostracon which preserved Sappho fr. 2, who must have had a taste and a capacity to read difficult Lesbian poetry. The person who copied (or had copied) part of *Parthenope* onto an ostracon need have belonged to a social group no different from that to which those who owned papyrus rolls belonged.

There may also, however, be evidence that the early novels were known in the Latin world, evidence that may antedate the *Ninus* fragments. Niklas Holzberg has argued that Ovid's version of the Pyramus and Thisbe story in *Metamorphoses* (4.55–166) parodies the literary conventions both of New Comedy and of the 'ideal' novel: the setting in adjacent houses and love between members of the families that occupy them are to be recognised as taking off New Comedy, while the flight from city to country and the decision to commit suicide on misleading evidence of a partner's death hint at the novel, with its exploitation of *Scheintod*, its impulsive and easily overwrought hero and heroine, and their commitment to a love unto death.[43] The idea is an attractive one, but suicide-decisions on mistaken grounds are also found in earlier mythology, and although the fact that Ovid's couple dies can be seen as an unexpected reversal of the novel's convention whereby they improbably survive all manner of perils, it can also be argued to give so different a flavour to the story that any allusion to novels becomes difficult to pick up. I regard the case as not proven. But if Holzberg were right, then we would have not just our earliest hard *terminus ante quem* for the composition of novels (the first years of our era) but evidence that its readers in the Latin West included both Ovid and (on Ovid's calculation) those people whom he expected to entertain with his *Metamorphoses* – the one a poet as *doctus* as any and the others people of substance and culture.

Again, if Holzberg were right, then the case would be strengthened for seeing Persius' halfline *post prandia Callirhoen do*, 'after dinner I present *Callirhoe*' (1.134), as alluding to recitation from a novel, our *Chaereas and Callirhoe*.[44] It need hardly be said that both the audience of a recitation such

[42] Treu 1989, 192. Treu's terms are 'Kreisen eines mittleren Bildungshöhe' and 'auf soziale Unterschichten'.

[43] Holzberg 1988.

[44] It is still debated whether Persius' reference is to the novel: it is so interpreted by Smith 2007, 2, Tilg 2010, Henrichs 2011, 311, all giving Chariton a Neronian date. See further Bowie 2002a (Chapter 25 in this volume).

as the *eques Romanus*, 'Roman knight', Persius imagines and the readership he is likely to have conceived for his rebarbative satires (composed in the years immediately preceding his death in AD 62) belong well up the economic and cultural scale.

If doubts remain about Ovid and Persius, it is harder to maintain them for Petronius. Although Petronius parodies the *Odyssey* and, from time to time, other established genres, his *Satyrica* arguably (if again unprovably) also either parodies the ideal romance, with the pair Encolpius and Giton a deformation of that genre's hero and heroine, or draws on a Greek comic version of the genre (like the *Iolaus*) that does.[45] In either case a Roman of the writing classes in the reign of Nero emerges as a fancier of one or other sort of Greek novel, and as a writer who expects *his* readers to appreciate the parody.

Our next candidates for witnesses to knowledge of the early novels are from the Severan period. Two mosaics from a substantial house in Antioch's hillsuburb, Daphne, depict Metiochus and Parthenope, clearly identified by name; a third depicts Ninus looking at a portrait, identifiable by its similarity to a mosaic portrait from nearby Alexandria ad Issum labelled 'Ninus'. However, since Lucian links Ninus and Metiochus as (it seems) characters in some form of theatrical performance, and since one of the two mosaics of Metiochus and Parthenope depicts them standing on a level surface most plausibly interpreted as a stage, it is perhaps more likely that the owner of the house knew the three characters from theatrical performances, presumably mimes, than from reading novels.[46] If, however, the novels played a part in his interest, we have here a man from the propertied classes who could, like Petronius' Trimalchio, be deficient in education, but is more likely to belong to the well-educated.

It is one of this man's best-educated contemporaries, Philostratus, who affords us what is probably our first glimpse of Chariton outside Egypt. In *Letter* 66 he attacks a Chariton whose claim to distinction in λόγοι, 'words' or 'letters', makes him hard to dissociate from the novelist:

[45] For Petronius' relation to Greek novels see Jensson 2004, Bowie 2007d (Chapter 32 in this volume).

[46] For a fuller discussion Bowie 1994a, 448–9 (Chapter 20, 437–8 in this volume). The Daphne mosaics are published by Levi 1947, i 117–19, ii pll. xx, cvii f.; cf. Levi 1944, 420–8; that from Alexandria ad Issum is discussed on p. 118. See further Maehler 1976; Quet 1992. The Lucian text is *Pseudol.* 25. On Lucian and pantomime see Lada Richards 2007. That plots or characters might appear both in the mime and the novel may contribute to the linking of Antonius Diogenes and the mime composer Philistion by Epiph. *Adv. haer.* 1.33.8 = *PG* xli 568, cf. below (C2). For the relation between mime and the novels see Chapter 20, n.67.

> Χαρίτωνι
> Μεμνήσεσθαι τῶν σῶν λόγων οἴει τοῦς Ἕλληνας ἐπειδὰν τελευτήσῃς. οἱ δὲ μηδὲν ὄντες, ὁπότε εἰσιν, τίνες ἂν εἶεν ὁπότε οὐκ εἰσιν;
>
> To Chariton
> You think that the Greeks will remember your words when you are dead; but those who are nobodies when they are alive, what will they be when they are dead?

As in his similarly critical reference to Plutarch in *Letter* 73, addressed to Julia Domna,[47] Philostratus treats as if alive a writer who is long dead. As he must see, his claim that Chariton will not be remembered is falsified both by his very mention of him and by his assumption that his readers will know who this person is. We may infer that Philostratus expected these readers to share a low literary evaluation of Chariton – though even that inference may be questioned – but we must also conclude that they were expected to know enough about Chariton to understand why it was witty to write in these dismissive terms about him.

(C1) Other Novels: Intended Readership

Antonius Diogenes is said by Photius to have written a preface in which he dedicated his twenty-four-book τὰ ὑπὲρ Θούλην ἄπιστα, '*The incredible world beyond Thule*' to his sister Isidora. But this dedication was made in a letter not to Isidora herself but in one to a Faustinus (perhaps her husband, so Antonius Diogenes' brother-in-law) and at least one of her functions may be to stand for the avid but gullible reader who will take Antonius' elaboratedly authenticated and encyclopedic information at face value, contrary to his indication to Faustinus that he is a fabricator of the fantastic in the tradition of Old Comedy.[48] The more plausible target remains the male reader to whom the term Old Comedy was meaningful and who was familiar enough with encyclopedic writers given to citing their sources (in the manner of the Elder Pliny) to appreciate literary humour at their expense.

The *Metamorphoses* which Photius took to be by Lucius of Patrae, and which (with some other scholars) I think likely to be the work of Lucian, had a lower moral tone than either Antonius Diogenes or the apparently

[47] πεῖθε δὴ καὶ σύ, ὦ βασίλεια, τὸν θαρσαλεώτερον τοῦ Ἑλληνικοῦ Πλούταρχον μὴ ἄχθεσθαι τοῖς σοφισταῖς, μηδὲ ἐς διαβολὰς καθίστασθαι τοῦ Γοργίου, 'So you should also, my queen, persuade the man who is bolder than Greeks should be, Plutarch, not to be irritated by the sophists, nor to embark on slandering Gorgias'.

[48] Phot. *Bibl. Cod.* 166, 111a30, p. 147.32–42 Henry and more fully Bowie 1994a, 437–8 (Chapter 20, 421 in this volume); on Faustinus Bowie 2002a (Chapter 25 in this volume, 524 with n.66).

typical 'ideal' novels and, as far as can be told from Photius' epitome, showed no sign of these works' recurrent urge to purvey recondite knowledge. We might, therefore, more readily suppose that its author envisaged a rather lower level of readership, and certainly less elevated than we know it actually got (below C2). The similarity of some of its narrative to Milesian tales (signalled by Apuleius in the prologue of his Latin adaptation) may entitle us to recall Plutarch's story of the copy of Aristides' Μιλήσιακά, '*Milesian Tales*', allegedly found in a Roman's kit after the battle of Carrhae,[49] and the fact that Aristides' work was translated into Latin by Sisenna, probably the historian who was *praetor* in 78 BC.[50] Reading of *Milesian Tales* might be lambasted as immoral (as it is by Arrian's Epictetus[51] as well as by Plutarch) but both Plutarch and Arrian expect their readers to know the work, and its Latin translator was of praetorian rank. Lucian, or whoever may be the author of the *Metamorphoses*, may have expected some less-educated readers, but he is unlikely to have excluded πεπαιδευμένοι.

It may be right to group Lollianus' Φοινικικά and the prosimetric Iolaus with the *Metamorphoses*. Sensationalism and a coarser treatment of sex certainly separate them from the 'ideal' novels, and Lollianus' failure to avoid hiatus may corroborate a tentative inference that here we come nearer than elsewhere to a work written for a readers who, though literate, were not from the well-educated elite.[52]

(C2) Other Novels: Actual Readership

For two, rather different novels in this broad category we have some indication of actual readership. For Egypt three, or possibly four, papyri, two of the second or third century, the other two no earlier than AD 200, attest readers (or would-be readers) of Antonius Diogenes.[53] Rather earlier it may

[49] Plu. *Crass.* 32.4–6. On *Milesian tales* see Bowie 2013c (Chapter 38 in this volume).

[50] Ov. *Tr.* 2.443–4 cf. 413–14. [51] Arr. *Epict.* 4.9.6.

[52] For the sensationalism cf. Winkler 1980; for the relation to Apuleius, Jones 1980; for hiatus see Reeve 1971. For a reassessment of Lollianus see Henrichs 2011, 313–18.

[53] *PSI* 1177 (no earlier than AD 200); *P.Oxy.* 3012, from a very handsomely set out book roll (Stephens) and assigned to second/third century by its editor Parsons 1974, as is *P.Oxy.* 4760 (Parsons 2006a). *P.Oxy.* 4761, dated to the third century by Parsons 2006b, may also be by Antonius Diogenes. *P.Mich.* inv. 5 (a magician's speech) was claimed for Antonius Diogenes by Reyhl 1969, 14–20, but is accepted neither by Fusillo 1990b nor by Stephens and Winkler 1995. Likewise *P.Dubl.* C 3 (second-century): see Stephens and Winkler 1995, 158–72 for text, commentary, and discussion of whether this fragment is from Antonius Diogenes (with his heroine Dercyllis) or from a novel with a female character Herpyllis. It is now held that the relevant traces in the papyrus cannot be read as Dercyllis.

be that Lucian read Antonius Diogenes and exploited some of his ideas in his *True Histories*. So Photius thought (*Bibliotheca*, Codex 166), but the relationship has been forcefully challenged by Morgan (1985), and at the least the absence of Antonius Diogenes' name from Lucian's text might be taken to indicate that he could not rely on his readers to recognise that author or his work. By the middle of the third century, however, Antonius Diogenes is being used by Porphyrius of Tyre in his *Life of Pythagoras*.[54] In the second half of the fourth century Epiphanius brackets him with the writer of mimes, Philistion, as a byword for incredible invention.[55] Soon after, Servius refers to him when commenting on the reference to Thule by Vergil at *Georgics* 1.30;[56] and about the same time Synesius of Cyrene refers to Thule as a place about which untestable fictions circulate, a reference easiest understood if he expects his readers to recognise a particular work (and has knowledge of it himself). The final testimony before Photius is that of John the Lydian in his work *On Months*.[57]

Although of course (as always) this documentation of readers (only one of them dismissive) drawn from the educated classes cannot show that other and less well-educated people did not read Antonius Diogenes, it at least demonstrates that he *was* known among these classes. It is unfortunate that the papyri of the *Iolaus* narrative and of Lollianus cannot securely establish to what class their readers belonged.

For the *Metamorphoses* of Lucius we can be certain only of two readers before Photius: the compiler of the epitome that has been transmitted in the works of Lucian, and the Platonist philosopher who was the nearest thing in Latin culture to a Greek sophist, Apuleius of Madaurus.[58] Of course they cannot be seen as typical readers, since each had a special purpose, to create a new literary work on the basis of the *Metamorphoses*. But it is of some relevance to the question of whether the novels were known or 'recognised' in elevated literary circles that Apuleius should have encountered the *Metamorphoses* at all; and it might be argued that the perception of the compiler of the epitome, entitled Λούκιος ἢ Ὄνος, that there were certain

[54] Porph. *VP* 10–17, 32–47, 54–5, cf. Reyhl 1969. [55] *Adv. haer.* 1.33.8 = *PG* xli 568.

[56] Stephens and Winkler 1995 *ad loc.* suggest that Servius' ascription of wonders concerning Thule to Sammonicus may indicate that Servius' knowledge of Antonius came to him *via* Sammonicus. If so Serenus Sammonicus (murdered AD 212) rather than Servius becomes his earliest known Latin reader. For the suggestion that Antonius Diogenes antedates and was read by Petronius see Bowie 2007d (Chapter 32 in this volume).

[57] Lyd. *De mensibus* 3.5, 4.42 (with specific ref. to Book 13). [58] See esp. Harrison 2000.

readers for whom the full-length *Metamorphoses* was too long or complicated, offers some support to the view that the *Metamorphoses* was being tackled by readers with greater pretensions, as well as to the view that there were other potential readers lower down the cultural scale for whom it was too challenging.

3 Conclusions

What conclusions can be drawn from the evidence and arguments set out above?

As to the 'sophistic' novels, I would conclude that they were principally intended for and chiefly read by well-educated readers. Less-educated readers may in fact have attempted them, and some may have persevered, though their level of appreciation of the texts must have been different from that of the former group.

Of our surviving 'early' novels that of Chariton comes closest to the 'sophistic' novel in its exploitation of allusion to classical texts (*Metiochus and Parthenope* may not have been far behind) and I would not doubt that Chariton aimed at, and reached, well-educated readers. It is also possible that he both expected and got less-educated readers, but the nature of our evidence is such that we cannot expect these readers to be documented even in the haphazardly selective way that our more elevated readers are documented, and the argument must depend on indications within Chariton's text, indications that are susceptible of different explanations.

The different character of Xenophon's work – the fact that it is not similarly dependent on allusion to classical literature, its stereotyped phrases, and its unsophisticated and sometimes clumsy use of stereotyped motifs – may point to a rather lower level of reader, but not, I suspect, dramatically lower; and any scholar who holds that we have only an epitome of a longer original may postulate that that original was better fashioned and aimed at a more exacting class of reader than the supposed epitome. I remain sceptical about the hypothesis that novels might have been read aloud to an illiterate audience or 'inexperienced' readers,[59] but if any of our extant complete texts was intended or exploited for this purpose Xenophon's work is a better candidate than Chariton's.

[59] *Contra* S. West 2003.

Of other novels Antonius Diogenes' twenty-four books seem intended rather for the light relief of the πεπαιδευμένοι than for the bafflement of simple readers, and there is adequate evidence that he was indeed read by πεπαιδευμένοι. I suspect – but we are back with guesswork – that Lucian destined his *Metamorphoses* for the same class of reader as his other works, but that the epitome Λούκιος ἢ Ὄνος may be going for a slightly different market, one for which Lollianus and the author of the *Iolaus* were also catering. I would be reluctant, however, to come far down the economic scale, or to shift the principal target group from adult male either to female or to juvenile readers. Of the diverse novels considered one might well expect an example of any category to have been in Cleitophon's hands in that early scene in Achilles Tatius: but, had the reader been Leucippe and not Cleitophon, I would be as surprised to learn that it was from the last and most lubricious class as that it was one of the more learned and allusive texts that Achilles himself writes. More likely, if Leucippe had been presented reading a novel at all, that of Xenophon, or, if Leucippe were as educated as Parthenope or Charicleia (which Achilles does not tell us that she is!) that of Chariton.

24 Phoenician Games in Heliodorus' *Aethiopica* (1998)

1 Introduction

This paper looks at two related chains of images in Heliodorus' *Aethiopica*, a work rich in a range of literary features that might be called 'imagery'. One feature eligible for the term 'image' is the striking, almost cinematically depicted scene, as an example of which the opening tableau is the most often cited. This aspect of Heliodorus' literary technique has deservedly had ample attention.[1] Another concerns the novelist's use of similes and metaphors, examined in a useful chapter by Feuillâtre:[2] but his twenty pages are more of a survey than an analysis, and do not begin to offer the meticulous treatment accorded four years earlier to Aristophanes by Taillardat 1962. More remarkably, perhaps, the imagery based on terms drawn from the stage was already being discussed more than a hundred years ago by Walden 1894. I think much more work is waiting to be done on simile and metaphor in Heliodorus. One interesting feature is the way in which Heliodorus sustains the impact of metaphorical uses of words or of similes by interweaving these with literal uses. A second is a related phenomenon, the way in which much of his metaphorical universe not only functions effectively within its immediate context but reflects much more broadly the major themes of the tale he is telling.[3] I do not attempt any such analysis here, but I mention these phenomena because their presence in the work may offer some support to the suggestions that I make.

These suggestions concern neither metaphors nor similes but words that seem to me to have a symbolic function – to carry a further layer of meaning for the narrative over and above their sense in their immediate context. I do not expect to persuade everybody that they do, but I hope that exploration of the question will be rewarding.

[1] For example by Bartsch 1989, 109–77. I am extremely grateful to audiences in the Universities of Cambridge, Montpellier, Stanford, Harvard, Princeton and Fribourg, and to Prof. Glenn Most, for stimulating comment on and discussion of earlier drafts of this paper.

[2] Feuillâtre 1966, Pt 2, chapter 2, 74–93, entitled 'Un style imagé'.

[3] For a stimulating discussion of the issues raised by related images see Mossman 1996, esp. 58–61.

It has been suggested to me that the close reading of the text of Heliodorus which the following hypothesis implies is not the way that Heliodorus' early readers are likely to have approached either his or other novels. No doubt his first readers approached the *Aethiopica* in a variety of ways, and it is likely enough that some read fast and inattentively. But although we are lamentably ill-informed about the novels' early readership, one can argue (as I have elsewhere)[4] that at least the sophistic novels were directed to and read by members of the intellectual elite; and though the presence of allusions to earlier literature (for which I shall also be arguing in what follows) is one prop of such an argument, it is not the only one. Richard Hunter demonstrated in 1983 that in the case of Longus 'an echo of earlier literature invests a scene with a layer of meaning which would otherwise be difficult to fit into a simple narrative'.[5] Such echoes are more readily observed by careful than by hasty readers, and can only be observed by those whose education or leisure has made them familiar with that earlier literature. We know, too, that professional expounders of classical literature wrote, and may presume that some of the leisured elite read, commentaries and essays whose points depended on very close attention to texts. Of course these texts were almost all from the classical period. Poets predominated, above all Homer. But 'Longinus' expected his readers to take points about a number of prose authors, the latest of whom is Amphicrates, of the first century BC, and himself wrote a monograph on Xenophon.[6] It is not unlikely that a reader trained to think carefully about metaphors and similes in poets, orators and historians should also be alive to their power in prose fiction.

2 φοῖνιξ (*phoenix*)

We cannot be sure with what conception of its title and author a reader approached the *Aethiopica*. Hefti argued that the form was more probably Τὰ περὶ Θεαγένην καὶ Χαρίκλειαν, 'The story of Theagenes and Charicleia', than one which revealed the destination of the lovers by the term Αἰθιοπικά (*Aethiopica*).[7] For what follows it would make a significant difference whether Heliodorus expected the work's title and his personal name, without an ethnic, to appear at the beginning and to be on a slip attached to each roll, or whether

[4] Bowie 1994a, 1996c (Chapters 20 and 23 in this volume). [5] Hunter 1983, 59.

[6] Gorgias, 3.2; Herodotus, 43.1, cf. 13.2; Xenophon, 4.4, etc.; Demosthenes is quoted ten times, Plato nine times, Timaeus twice in 4; Callisthenes, Cleitarchus and Amphicrates are adduced at 3.2 (and the last also at 4.4). For 'Longinus' work on Xenophon, 8.1.

[7] Hefti 1950, 179. On the form of novels' titles see Whitmarsh 2005b.

he expected to be described there as in the last sentence of the transmitted text of the work, ἀνὴρ Φοῖνιξ Ἐμισηνός, 'a Phoenician man from Emesa'.[8]

That said, let us begin where readers of rolls are required and of codices are encouraged to begin, with the much-discussed beach scene at the opening of Book 1. Heliodorus writes of the stricken Theagenes:

> ἤνθει δὲ καὶ ἐν τούτοις ἀνδρείωι τῶι κάλλει, καὶ ἡ παρειὰ καταρρέοντι τῶι αἵματι φοινιττομένη λευκότητι πλέον ἀντέλαμπεν.
>
> even in this condition he bloomed with a manly beauty, and his cheek, growing crimson (φοινιττομένη, *phoenittomenē*) by the blood that flowed down it, gleamed with a greater contrasting whiteness.
>
> Hld. 1.2.3

The image of white stained by crimson seems to recall a well-known passage in the *Iliad* (of which 1.46–7 is of course about to be evoked by the description of Charicleia's rattling weapons at 1.2.5). The passage is the wounding of Menelaus by Paris, compared by Homer (Il. 4.141–5) to ivory stained with crimson:

> ὡς δ' ὅτε τις ἐλέφαντα γυνὴ φοίνικι μιαίνηι
> Μηιονὶς ἠδὲ Κάειρα, παρήιον ἔμμεναι ἵππων ...
>
> As when some woman stains ivory with crimson,
> a woman from Maeonia or Caria, for it to be a cheek-piece for horses ...
>
> Il. 4.141–2

A reader whose memory of that passage is triggered will call to mind not just the phenomenon of reddening, τὸ φοινίττεσθαι (*phoenittesthai*), but also the red dye, the φοῖνιξ (*phoenix*), which is necessary to the process of staining. He may also recall that the Homeric artefact was a παρήιον, 'cheek-piece', and note how Heliodorus has transferred the image to Theagenes' manly παρειά, 'cheek'.[9]

[8] *P.Colon.* inv. 3328, fragments of a papyrus codex of Lollianus' *Phoenicica*, assigned to the end of the second century AD by Stephens and Winkler 1995, 329–30, has a subscription at the end of Book 1 (ibid. 329) of the form Λολλιανοῦ Φοινικικά, and apparently had a similar subscription at the end of Book 2 (B.1 *recto* 22–4, ibid. 340). Hefti 1950 also argued that the *sphragis* was an addition and not to be credited to Heliodorus: the arguments against this offered by Morgan 1978, 622–7 are persuasive.

[9] It is possible that Hld. is also influenced here by the phrase used by Plu. to describe Alexander's complexion (*Alex.* 4.3): ἦν δὲ λευκός, ὥς φασιν, ἡ δὲ λευκότης ἐπεφοίνισσεν αὐτοῦ περὶ τὸ στῆθος μάλιστα καὶ τὸ πρόσωπον, 'his complexion was white, they say, but his whiteness had a crimson shade, especially on his chest and his face', though I cannot see that any sort of allusion is intended. Hld.'s knowledge of Plu.'s *Alex.* may also be indicated by his use of the name Sisimithres (*Alex.* 58.4), though that also appears in other accounts (e.g. Str. 12.517).

Later in Book 1 we are twice reminded of this image of the wounded Theagenes. First, when Charicleia contemplates her reply to the noble robber Thyamis' proposal of marriage she is unusually flushed: καὶ γὰρ πεφοίνικτο τὴν παρειὰν ὑπὸ τῶν ἐνθυμημάτων πλέον ἢ σύνηθες, 'for as a result of her ponderings her cheek had a more crimson colour (*pephoenikto*) than usual' (Hld. 1.21.3). The reason for the presence of both παρειά and πλέον (as well as parts of φοινίττεσθαι) in both passages may of course be that in the second Heliodorus is unconsciously recalling the first: but we have many indications of his careful writing that make this less likely than that Heliodorus is consciously reminding his readers of the earlier passage.

Second, towards the end of Book 1, in the description of the attack on Thyamis' island base that balances the battle that never was in the opening chapters, we again encounter something turned crimson by blood, when the wounded are described as αἵματι τὴν λίμνην φοινιττόντων ..., 'making the marsh crimson (*phoenittontōn*) with their blood ...' (Hld. 1.30.3). We leave Book 1, then, with a well-established perception of φοῖνιξ (*phoenix*) and its cognates in its meaning 'crimson' and associated with blood.

A quite different sense of φοῖνιξ (*phoenix*) is introduced in Book 2. At 2.23 Calasiris, shortly to be named for the first time (2.24.5), is about to tell Cnemon his story. He insists, in one of his many Odysseus-modes, that they first take some food (2.23.4), and they eat his habitual vegetarian fare of nuts, figs, freshly-picked dates and suchlike: τῶν τε καρύων καὶ σύκων ἀρτιδρεπῶν τε φοινίκων, 'nuts, figs and freshly-picked dates' (Hld. 2.23.5). By attaching the epithet ἀρτιδρεπῶν, 'freshly-picked', to the dates φοινίκων (*phoenikōn*) Heliodorus gives them more emphasis than the nuts and figs, and, I suggest, prepares our minds for further appearances of φοίνικες (*phoenikes*) of the palmary variety. A second-time reader may also notice that Calasiris' story is being nourished by Phoenician τροφή, 'sustenance' (2.23.4).

Book 3 brings back to us the crimson image established in Book 1. It reappears twice in the same chapter, 3.3. The fifty ephebes who accompanied Theagenes to Delphi wear boots with crimson straps, and Theagenes himself wears a crimson mantle: κρηπὶς μὲν αὐτοῖς ἱμάντι φοινικῶι διάπλοκος ὑπὲρ ἀστραγάλων ἐσφίγγετο, 'their boots had interlaced crimson straps and were tied tightly above their ankles', and ἀπὸ γυμνῆς τῆς κεφαλῆς πομπεύων φοινικοβαφῆ χλαμύδα καθειμένος, 'he processed with bare head and a flowing crimson cloak' (Hld. 3.3.2 and 5).

It will not cause surprise that when φοῖνιξ (*phoenix*) returns, as we surely knew that it would, in Book 4, it is again in the botanical sense of Book 2. This time, however, the term is not used for the fruit, but for the branch, φοίνικος (*phoenīkos*) ἔρνος, held out in Charicleia's right hand when, in Calasiris' narrative, she allays the reader's and Cnemon's fear by suddenly appearing to perform her appointed role at the *Pythia*: τῆι λαιᾶι μὲν ἡμμένον πυρφοροῦσα λαμπάδιον, θατέραι δὲ φοίνικος ἔρνος προβεβλημένη, 'in her left hand carrying the flame of a lighted torch, and in her other hand holding out a shoot of palm' (Hld. 4.1.2). This palm-shoot is the prize of victory which Theagenes shortly gets from her at the very moment of defeating the Arcadian Ormenus in the hoplite race (4.4.2), showing himself more than characteristically street-wise by surreptitiously kissing her hand. The mark of victory peculiar to the Pythian Games was a garland of laurel, as Heliodorus and most of his readers surely knew. But, as we learn from a discussion in Plutarch,[10] the palm-shoot was a symbol of victory at all agonistic festivals, and, as Heliodorus and his readers could have known from their reading of classical texts, both laurel and palm are associated with sites of the cult of Apollo.[11] So in this Delphic context Heliodorus could have chosen to have Charicleia hold either a laurel-garland or a palm-shoot. The palm-shoot offers him at least two gains. The greater of these is to create another unit in his sequence of phoenix images: but, by putting a φοίνικος (*phoenīkos*) ἔρνος in the hand of the young maiden who has fallen in love with a handsome stranger at the shrine of Apollo at Delphi, Heliodorus also links his scene with Book 6 of the *Odyssey*, and his heroine Charicleia with Nausicaa, who is there compared by Odysseus to a φοίνικος ἔρνος, 'young palm-shoot', which he had seen at Delos Ἀπόλλωνος παρὰ βωμῶι, 'beside the altar of Apollo' (Od. 6.162–3).[12] It is one of a sequence of intertextualities which persistently invite us to question how like, and how unlike, the Odyssey this story is going to be.[13]

A small detail in the description of Theagenes' race may also make its contribution. His competitor, as mentioned, is an Arcadian called Ormenus.

[10] *Quaest. Graec.* 8.4 = *Mor.* 723a–24f. For the place of the laurel in Delphic myth see Sourvinou-Inwood 1991, 192–216.

[11] Laurel and palm together at Eur. *Hec.* 458–61, Call. *Ap.* 1–4. For the palm alone cf. Hom. *h.Ap.* 117, *h.Del.* 210, Thgn. 6. Some readers might even know of the importance of the palm and laurel from personal visits to Delos or Delphi, but Hld. could not assume that for a reader, nor should we for him.

[12] In the discussion after this paper's delivery at the Laurence Seminar in Cambridge it was helpfully suggested that there might be a link with the iconographic meaning 'marriage' established by Sourvinou-Inwood 1991, 99–143 for the conjunction of palm-tree and altar on works of art of the archaic and classical period. I have not been able to find any evidence that this conjunction retained this meaning in art of the imperial period.

[13] Charicleia's mirror image, Nausicleia, is also of course evocative of Nausicaa: see Bowie 1995b, 278 (Chapter 22, 470 in this volume).

As John Morgan noted,[14] this would be an appropriate name for a runner if it means 'speeding', but I do not know of any support for that translation. The name is far from common.[15] The name Ormenus, and the patronymic Ormenidas, appear four times in the *Iliad*. Twice Ormenus is the name given to a Trojan who is cast as mere spear-fodder (Il. 8.274, 12.187). More interesting, however, is the patronymic Ormenidas used of Amyntor, father of Achilles' tutor Phoenix (whose relationship to Achilles bears some resemblance to the relationship of Calasiris to his descendant Theagenes). Amyntor has a negative image in the *Iliad* – he prefers a concubine to his wife, Phoenix's mother, and curses Phoenix when on that mother's supplication he sleeps with the concubine (Il. 9.448–61). This is the world of self-seeking sexual intrigue represented in the *Aethiopica* by Cnemon, Demainete and Arsace.[16] He is also the victim of a theft – from him was stolen the boar's tusk helmet that eventually is worn by Odysseus in the *Doloneia* (10.266–71). We hear nothing of Amyntor's father Ormenus: like Theagenes, he must have been a Thessalian. But by choosing the name Ormenus for the Arcadian with a run-on part Heliodorus succeeds in reminding us of another Phoenix, a Calasiris-like figure, and of the wiles of Odysseus to whom Calasiris also owes many traits.

The *Odyssey* too uses the name Ormenus. When Eumaeus tells Odysseus his life-story,[17] it begins with a description of the prosperous island Syriē, ruled by his father, Ctesius son of Ormenus, then moves on to tell how as a boy he was kidnapped by his Sidonian nanny, herself seduced by tricksy Phoenician merchants. Again the name Ormenus takes the reader to a Phoenician connection against which Heliodorus' own narrative can be read. In particular it reminds us of the disreputable status of Phoenicians in canonical Greek texts, a status from which we soon find Heliodorus promoting them.

Calasiris proceeds with his tale. Hurrying to the temple at Delphi to seek guidance from Apollo on how to help Charicleia and Theagenes to elope, Calasiris had met a group of people holding a banquet in honour of Heracles: ἔλεγον δὴ οὖν εἶναι μὲν Φοίνικες Τύριοι τέχνην δὲ ἔμποροι 'Now they said that they were Phoenicians (*Phoenikes*) from Tyre, and were

[14] Morgan 1989a, 426 n.103. [15] Not in the *LGPN* vols i or ii.

[16] See Morgan 1982, Bowie 1995b (Chapter 22 in this volume).

[17] Od. 15.403–84, a narrative shortly to be recalled by the description of the Phoenician boat on which Calasiris and his wards escape from Delphi as ὁλκάδα μυριοφόρον, 'a cargo ship whose capacity was measured in tens of thousands', at 4.16.6: cf. the description of the Phoenicians of Od. 15.416 as μύρι' ἄγοντες ἀθύρματα, 'bringing tens of thousands of playthings'.

merchants by profession' (4.16.5). It turns out that the party was to celebrate the wrestling victory of a young Tyrian in the Pythian games. Calasiris joined their festivities, though τῶν ... ἐξ ἔθους ἀπογευσάμενος, 'tasting his habitual food'[18] (which we may remember includes φοίνικες, 'dates', 2.23.5), and elicited the offer of a passage on their boat. By now we are not surprised to discover ethnic Φοίνικες (*Phoenikes*) in the story, although it is surprising that these Phoenicians have been upgraded from the role of pirates, standard in almost all literature since the *Odyssey*, to that of respectable if chrematistic merchants. It is a nice literary reversal, complementing the paradox (in a novel written in Greek) that the city of Tyre has been announced as the victor's city in a contest of Hellenes (νικῶσαν τὴν Τύρον ἐν Ἕλλησιν ἀναγορεύσαντος).[19] It is also characteristic of Heliodorus' light touch that he mentions the garland that the Tyrian had won (στέφανος, 4.16.6) but says nothing of the palm-shoot (φοίνικας [*phoenikos*] ἔρνος) that he must also be presumed to have been given.

Another trick Heliodorus plays is never to name this wrestling victor, although he predictably falls in love with Charicleia, seeks to marry her and stays in Calasiris' story until their vessel is overpowered by real pirates (this time apparently non-Phoenician) and the Phoenicians scramble to save their lives in a dinghy (5.25.3). At that point the unnamed Phoenician disappears from the tale as suddenly as he had been brought into it. At least one reader is left puzzled by the anonymity of this character, referred to repeatedly simply as the Tyrian merchant (e.g. 5.19.1, 5.22.6) or the Phoenician (e.g. 5.20.1) – a character rather more important to the story than other unnamed individuals like the lover of Isias of Chemmis (6.3.1–3, cf. below). Of course the Phoenician who seduced Eumaeus' nanny is given no name in Homer (*Odyssey* 15.420), but that in itself seems an insufficient ground for Heliodorus' decision. Closer to home, perhaps, is a text that Heliodorus has already evoked in Book 2, Philostratus' *Heroicus*. That dialogue is conducted between an unnamed vintner and an unnamed Phoenician from the area of Tyre and Sidon, detained at the Dardanelles (as Heliodorus' Phoenician will be at Zacynthos) by weather unsuitable for sailing. The hymn that the vintner reports as sung by Thessalians coming

[18] 4.16.5.

[19] As was kindly pointed out to me in discussion of this paper at Harvard, we have epigraphic documentation of an embassy from Tyre to Delphi in the first century BC claiming a kinship relationship between the two cities, *SEG* 2.330 (= Curty 1995, no. 12). This would be likely enough to be known to the elite of Tyre in the third century AD, and not impossibly to a priest at Emesa, but Heliodorus could not have expected it to be familiar to a significant number of his readers.

to sacrifice at Achilles' tomb in the Troad seems likely to be the model for the hymn of the Thessalian Ainianians who have come to honour Achilles' son Neoptolemos at Delphi (Heliodorus 3.2.4), and Philostratus' play with an internal narrator and audience may also have caught Heliodorus' eye.[20] The anonymity of Heliodorus' Phoenician might then have been expected to turn the reader's attention to Philostratus' *Heroicus*. Once there, another Phoenician connection awaits. One of the few contemporary references in the *Heroicus* is to the athlete T. Aurelius Helix, who after an initial wrestling victory at Olympia entered in the next Olympic games for both wrestling and *pankration*: nearly banned by the Eleian organisers from both events, he was reluctantly allowed to claim victory in the *pankration*.[21] We know Helix's origin from Philostratus' *Gymnasticus*, though there he is not given a city: he is simply a Φοῖνιξ (*Phoenix*), a Phoenician.[22] We have no evidence that he competed at the Pythian games, nor does it matter whether he did. As the only Phoenician athlete to be noticed by literary texts of the early third century he is somebody whose renown might be known both to Heliodorus and to his readers. Indeed it seems, as will be argued by Christopher Jones, that it is with this wrestler that an athlete labelled Helix on a mosaic at Ostia should be identified.[23] It is tempting to suppose that, in giving his unnamed Phoenician a wrestling victory at the *Pythia*, Heliodorus is compensating for the wrestling victory denied to T. Aurelius Helix by the Eleians.

Heliodorus' luctatory Phoenician also alerts us for a further and more significant involvement of Φοίνικες (*Phoenīkes*) than their bloody, botanical and ethnic appearances had so far intimated. Thus forearmed, a reader might be glad to discover that when (at 5.5.2) Theagenes and Charicleia agree on passwords whereby they might recognise each other – in a sequence in which, unusually, the author is himself filling in details of the story-so-far, cf. 5.4.3 – Charicleia chooses the word λαμπάς, 'torch', and Theagenes the word φοῖνιξ (*phoenix*). Since a λαμπάδιον, 'torch', was what Charicleia held in her left hand when she gave Theagenes a φοίνικος ἔρνος, 'palm-shoot', with her right (4.4.2, cf. 4.1.2 already discussed) we should certainly associate these passwords with that moment of modulated erotic excitement, and so think of the password φοῖνιξ (*phoenix*) as a φοίνικος

[20] For Philostr.'s exploitation of his internal audience see Bowie 1994b, 183 (Chapter 21, 447–8 in this volume); for the hymns Bowie 1989a, 221–2 and 228–9 (Chapter 12, 230–1, 236–8 in this volume); Hunter 1998a, 53–5.

[21] Philostratus, *Her.* 15 (16.23ff. de Lannoy): cf. D.C. 79.10.2, Stein in *PIR*² A 1520.

[22] Philostratus, *Gymn.* 46 Jüthner (287.19–22 Kayser).

[23] I am grateful to Christopher Jones for drawing my attention to this mosaic: for his discussion see Jones 1998. It comes from the so-called *caupona di Alexander*, and was published in Calza, Becatti *et al.* 1953, 153.

ἔρνος, 'palm-shoot': but if we simply translate the Greek and think of φοῖνιξ as palm we are cutting down its resonances. We might also reflect that it is extremely odd that the lovers should think that they will need such passwords. They have already agreed on the name ὁ Πυθικός for Theagenes and ἡ Πυθιάς for Charicleia (both meaning 'Pythian') as the signature of any graffiti they might inscribe to mark the direction of their journey (5.5.1). Moreover, when in the extraordinary scene outside the walls of Memphis Theagenes fails to recognise Charicleia in her beggarly disguise (7.7.7), so that she has both to address him as 'ὦ Πύθιε', 'Pythian', and to ask him οὐδὲ τοῦ λαμπαδίου μέμνησαι, 'do you not even remember the torch', the reader is surely as surprised as she is. I find it hard to resist the conclusion that the password device is introduced more for the reader's benefit than for that of the couple, and that Theagenes' failure to recognise Charicleia is forced on Heliodorus by his adoption of this device for other reasons. I suggest that the chief reason is his wish to foreground the term φοῖνιξ (phoenix).

A little later in Book 5 Heliodorus reintroduces the sense 'crimson' when he notes the paleness of the shade of red in the Iberian or British amethyst by contrast with that from Ethiopia: ἡ μὲν γὰρ ἀδρανεῖ τῶι ἄνθει φοινίσσεται, 'for its bloom of crimson is pale and weak' (Hld. 5.13.3).[24]

It is only a page or two later in Book 5 that the arrival of the Phoenician boat at Zacynthos is made the occasion for some words of high praise: the boat has been ἐκπεπονημένη, 'crafted', with a view both to μέγεθος, 'size', and κάλλος, 'beauty', making it recognisably a Φοινίκιον … φιλοτέχνημα, 'a work of Phoenician craftsmanship':

> οἱ δὲ τῆς νήσου περὶ τὸν ὅρμον οἰκοῦντες ἀπέχοντα οὐ πολὺ τῆς πόλεως καθάπερ ἐπί τι παράδοξον τὴν θέαν τὴν ἡμετέραν συνέρρεον, ἀγάμενοι μὲν ὡς ἐφαίνοντο καὶ τὸ τῆς ὁλκάδος εὐάγωγον εἰς κάλλος τε ἅμα καὶ μέγεθος αἱρόμενον ἐκπεπονημένης, Φοινίκιον τὸ φιλοτέχνημα γνωρίζειν λέγοντες, πλέον δὲ θαυμάζοντες ὡς παραλόγωι τῆι τύχηι χρησαμένους εὔδιόν τε καὶ ἀπήμονα πλοῦν ἐν χειμερίωι τῆι ὥραι καὶ Πλειάδων ἤδη δυομένων ἀνύσαντας.
>
> Those who lived around the island's harbour, not far from the city, gathered together to the spectacle we afforded as if to something unexpected, admiring, as it seemed, the manoeuvrability of the merchant vessel which had been crafted with an eye to beauty and at the same time size, saying that they recognized the masterpiece as Phoenician, and expressing greater wonder that as a result of enjoying unpredictable good luck we had completed our voyage unharmed and in fine weather at a stormy time of the year when the Pleiads were already setting.
>
> Hld. 5.18.2

[24] The excellent translation of Morgan 1989a.

ἐκπονεῖν, 'to craft', is rare in the novelists: twice in Longus, and otherwise only here. Longus' first use is in his preface, where he describes the creation of his work in the terms τέτταρας βίβλους ἐξεπονησάμην, 'I crafted four books' (*pr.* 3). In a context already marked out as pastoral this word certainly recalls Lycidas' description of his song as one which, he claims, ἐξεπόνασα, 'I crafted', in Theocritus 7.50–1, a claim joined with a request for aesthetic approval:

> ὅρη, φίλος, εἴ τοι ἀρέσκει
> τοῦθ' ὅτι πρᾶν ἐν ὅρει τὸ μελύδριον ἐξεπόνασα.
>
> See, friend, if you are pleased
> by this little song that I crafted the other day on the hillside.

Longus' second use of the verb describes Philetas' labours on his garden (2.3.3):

> κῆπός ἐστί μοι τῶν ἐμῶν χειρῶν, ὃν ἐξ οὗ νέμειν διὰ γῆρας ἐπαυσάμην ἐξεπονησάμην, ὅσα ὧραι φύουσι πάντα ἔχων ἐν αὐτῶι καθ' ὥραν ἑκάστην.
>
> I have a garden, my own handiwork, which since I stopped herding because of my old age I have crafted: everything that the seasons bring forth, it has in it in each season.

Longus' use of the same form of the verb as in the preface, ἐξεπονησάμην, 'I crafted', encourages us to see Philetas' garden, in which Eros makes a guest appearance, as a *mise-en-abyme* of the four-book work as a whole, a creation upon which πόνος, 'toil', has been lavished and which is as a result perennially fruitful. When Heliodorus, whom I have argued elsewhere to have known Longus,[25] uses ἐκπεπονημένης of a Phoenician ship complimented on its beauty, size and manageability, one is naturally tempted to see this human creation too as a *mise-en-abyme*: the fates of Theagenes and Charicleia are conveyed by a work that possesses not just κάλλος, 'beauty', but, unlike that of Longus, μέγεθος, 'size',[26] and is εὐάγωγον ('manoeuvrable') in the hands of a pilot whom the reader will ultimately discover to be Phoenician. That it is reasonable to succumb to that temptation is confirmed by the Zacynthians' recognition of the ship as Φοινίκιον φιλοτέχνημα. The unusual term φιλοτέχνημα, a 'superb work of craftsmanship', is more

[25] Bowie 1995b (Chapter 22 in this volume). For further discussion of Longus' ἐξεπονησάμην see Bowie 2019g *ad locc.*

[26] Note that Hld. has also commented on the size and beauty of the amethyst which also stands for a literary work (see p. 501).

appropriately used of a literary creation than of a ship.[27] Like Philetas' garden in Longus, which admirably bears fruit in every season, this φιλοτέχνημα of Heliodorus causes admiration (θαυμάσαντες) because of its unpredictable good fortune in making a safe journey in fine weather from the port of Delphi to Zacynthos despite the stormy season of the year. This παράλογος τύχη, 'unpredictable good fortune', is also, perhaps, metonymic for the whole story of the couple's adventures: the phrase joins a number of hints given by the author that his couple's tale will indeed have the generically requisite happy ending. This may well be recognised by an alert reader, who has just been reminded by the somewhat contrived phrase Φοινίκιον τὸ φιλοτέχνημα γνωρίζειν λέγοντες, 'saying that they recognized the masterpiece as Phoenician', that recognition is to be a recurrent issue in this as in so many other novels.

As we proceed further through Books 5 and 6 we may settle down with the expectation that Φοίνικες (*Phoenikes*) are to be understood as Phoenicians (as at 5.25.3). But Heliodorus has another trick up his sleeve. The party that leaves Chemmis to try to find Theagenes encounters the lover of Isias taking her a φοινικόπτερον (*phoenikopteros*), 'flamingo' (6.3.2–3). When this unnamed friend of Nausicles explains his mission, Nausicles tartly remarks that he is lucky that Isias had not asked him to get her a φοῖνιξ, 'phoenix':

> φοινικόπτερον ἀλλ' οὐκ αὐτόν σοι τὸν φοίνικα τὸν ἐξ Αἰθιόπων ἢ Ἰνδῶν ὡς ἡμᾶς ἀφικνούμενον ὄρνιν ...
>
> 'a flamingo and not the phoenix itself, the bird which comes to us from the Ethiopians or Indians ... '
>
> Hld. 6.3.3

Heliodorus could of course have made Isias ask for all manner of love-gifts. The choice of the φοινικόπτερος, 'flamingo', is, I suggest, to give an opportunity for Nausicles' comment, and that in turn completes the set of the chief meanings of the Greek word φοῖνιξ (*phoenix*) – 'crimson', 'palm', 'Phoenician', and now 'phoenix'. Heliodorus thus reminds us that Phoenicians are not the only sort of φοῖνιξ.

He also reminds us, by his suggestion that the phoenix comes from the Ethiopians or Indians, that Ethiopia – to which Isias' lover might have had

[27] The word is used by Cicero of a masterpiece of sculpture at *Ad Att.* 13.40.1. It also appears in a maritime context in Aristid. 44.13 Keil, describing the Aegean's pleasing mixture of sea and islands. Otherwise before Christian writers it is confined to four appearances in D.S., who uses it rather to mean 'trick' (3.37.6, 4.11.6, 4.76.5, 15.18.4); one in Men. Rh. 402.9 and Choricius 13.35 (399.3 F–R).

to travel to find a phoenix – is still a long, long way away. Herodotus' story (2.73.3) had been that the phoenix came from Arabia, an area located suggestively near Phoenicia itself. Achilles Tatius makes his general in Book 3 give an account of the phoenix that mentions only Ethiopia as its place of birth and upbringing: like Herodotus, Achilles Tatius makes Heliopolis in Egypt the goal of the bird's journey when it brings its father for burial, encased in a ball of myrrh, but unlike Herodotus is explicit in associating the phoenix with the sun.[28] Lucian in his *On the death of Peregrinus* (28) ascribes to his vilified charlatan the wish to be called no longer Proteus but Phoenix, τὸ Ἰνδικὸν ὄρνεον, 'the Indian bird', because it climbs onto a funeral pyre in extreme old age.[29] Philostratus in his *In honour of Apollonius* (3.49), whether or not independently, has his Indian Brahman Iarchas appropriate the phoenix for India.[30] Heliodorus here combines the traditions of predecessors in the writing of prose fiction, Achilles Tatius, Lucian and Philostratus – the phoenix may come from India or Ethiopia, the same disjunction of origins as is offered for the sort of amethyst produced by Calasiris at 5.14: but he probably does not expect us to forget the Herodotean association with Arabia that is thus being denied. He may well also expect his reader to recall that for Achilles Tatius the phoenix was specifically associated with the Sun God.

The phoenix may also evoke another set of associations. The peripatetic philosopher Alexander of Aphrodisias, in his treatise Περὶ εἱμερμάνης, 'On Fate', dedicated to Severus and Caracalla between AD 198 and 209, also knows a tradition that makes the phoenix Ethiopian.[31] He scoffs at the Stoic position that makes the truly virtuous man, i.e. ὁ σοφός, 'the sage', ὥσπερ τι παράδοξον ζῶιον καὶ παρὰ φύσιν σπανιώτερον τοῦ φοίνικος τοῦ παρ' Αἰθίοψιν, 'like some unexpected creature contrary to nature, rarer than

[28] αὐχεῖ δὲ τὸν Ἥλιον δεσπότην, καὶ ἡ κεφαλὴ μαρτυρεῖ, 'it vaunts the sun as its lord, and its head corroborates this', Ach. Tat. 3.25.2; and ἱερέων δὲ παῖδες Ἡλίου τὸν ὄρνιν τὸν νεκρὸν παραλαβόντες θάπτουσι. ζῶν μὲν οὖν Αἰθίοψ ἐστὶ τῆι τροφῆι, ἀποθανὼν δὲ Αἰγύπτιος γίνεται τῆι ταφῆι, 'And the children of the priests of the sun receive the bird and bury it. So in life it is an Ethiopian by nature, but in death it becomes an Egyptian by its burial', Ach. Tat. 3.25.7.

[29] I know of no earlier ascription of the phoenix to India, but an earlier tradition and common source must be a possibility. Equally, however, Philostr. could have read Luc., and each could have his reason for making an Indian connection – Luc. influenced by the self-immolation of the Indian Calanus (25, cf. 39), Philostr. because he is looking for material subverting classical versions to ascribe to Iarchas.

[30] The chapter is close to that (3.46) discussing the magical qualities of the stone παντάρβη (*pantarbe*), also taken over and adapted by Hld. Philostr. *Ep.* 8 also associates the phoenix with India. For the various ancient views cf. Hubaux and Leroy 1939.

[31] Perhaps he and Achilles Tatius are drawing on a common tradition not elsewhere attested, but it seems to me as likely that Alexander, hailing from the city of Chariton, and, very probably, of Antonius Diogenes (see Bowersock 1994, 39) had actually read Ach. Tat.'s novel.

the phoenix of the Ethiopians'.[32] The comparison itself is not Alexander's own: the comparison of the rare sage with the phoenix was already made by Seneca, and presumably goes back even earlier.[33] It is therefore not unlikely that Heliodorus was familiar with this comparison of a sage to the phoenix. A reader may only see its full possible significance much later, but for the moment the only sage on parade is Calasiris (whose name may owe something to the self-immolating Indian sage Calanus). When in Book 7 Calasiris unexpectedly dies in Memphis, his now pious children at his bedside (7.11.3–4), we may feel that he too, a priest whose travels took him from Ethiopia and who received burial from his progeny in an Egyptian holy city, has something of the phoenix in him.

But Books 7, 8 and 9 have no explicit mentions of any species of φοῖνιξ: we may begin to wonder if, like Calasiris, they have been killed off by the author so that the couple may be left to find their own destinies. Book 10 will falsify any such presumption, but the phoenix may also make a veiled appearance in Book 7. The conflict of the brothers Thyamis and Petosiris outside the walls of Memphis (7.4–7) clearly recalls the single combat between Eteocles and Polyneices (just as the pursuit round its walls recalls that of Hector by Achilles in *Iliad* 22).[34] Of the dramatic treatments of the Theban brothers' combat, the Hellenistic and Greco-Roman reader was much more familiar with that of Euripides than that of Aeschylus:[35] and that Euripidean play was entitled (from its chorus) *Phoenissae*, '*Phoenician women*'. A nice touch, even if it does no more than hint at the importance of Phoenicians in Greek literature.[36]

In Book 10 φοίνικες return in force. The horsemen carrying news of Hydaspes' victory to Meroe ride through the city τάς τε κεφαλὰς τῷ Νειλώιωι λωτῶι καταστέψαντες καὶ φοινίκων πτόρθους ταῖς χερσὶ κατασείοντες, 'their heads garlanded with the Nile lotus and waving palm branches' (Hld.10.3.2). These are not φοίνικος ἔρνη, 'palm-shoots', as in Book 4, but φοινίκων πτόρθους, 'palm branches'. Heliodorus follows this up with a

[32] *De Fato* 28 (199.17 Bruns = *SVF* iii 165 no. 658). For the date, *ibid.* 2 (164.14 Bruns); Sharples 1983, 180.

[33] *Ep.* 42.1. I am grateful to George Boys-Stones for discussion of the relevant Stoic texts.

[34] So, e.g., Morgan 1989a, 492 n.169.

[35] Thus, according to Helmbold and O'Neil 1959, Plutarch cites or alludes to Aes. *Septem* seven times, Eur. *Phoenissae* thirty-four times. Householder 1941 notes only one Lucianic allusion to Aes. *Th.*, four to Eur. *Ph.*. On the popularity of the *Ph.* in the imperial period see Cribiore 2001a; Bowie 2022a.

[36] There might, indeed, be more. The speech of Iocasta that opens *Ph.* is addressed to the sun, and reminds the audience of the genealogy of Oedipus and the story of his exposure as a child whose presence in the royal household is predicted to cause trouble: the intertextuality might thus invite us to see the story of Charicleia's birth and disposal as a variant on a canonical myth.

description of the area around Meroe in which he especially commends its φοίνικές τε ὑπερμήκεις καὶ τὴν βάλανον εὔστομοί τε καὶ ὑπέρογκοι, 'ultra-tall palms bearing ultra-heavy, mouthwatering dates' (10.5.2).

The φοίνικος ἔρνη, 'palm-shoots', duly make their appearance in the next chapter among the principal components of the huge and environmentally friendly canopy that covers the pavilion erected for the sacrificial ritual:

> σχήματος τετραπλεύρου γωνίαν ἑκάστην ἑνὸς καλάμου, κίονος δίκην, ἐρείδοντος καὶ κατὰ τὰς ἄκρας εἰς ἁψῖδα περιαγομένου καὶ τοῖς ἄλλοις ἅμα φοινίκων ἔρνεσι συμπίπτοντος καὶ τὸ ὑποκείμενον ὀροφοῦντο.
>
> a single reed supporting each corner of a rectangular structure like a column and bent round at its tip to form an arch, joining the others and together with palmshoots roofing over the space beneath.
>
> Hld. 10.6.2

Just at the moment Theagenes and Charicleia seem to be destined for imminent death our minds are taken back by the mention of palm-shoots to the first time they kissed (4.1.2, 4.4.2).

There is then a remission until, almost half-way through the book, the term φοινίττειν (*phoenittein*), 'to make crimson', is used to describe the blush of Meroëbus when he colours at the prospect of marriage to Charicleia:

> ὁ δὴ Μερόηβος πρὸς τὴν ἀκοὴν τῆς νύμφης ὑφ' ἡδονῆς τε ἅμα καὶ αἰδοῦς οὐδὲ ἐν μελαίνῃ τῆι χροιᾶι διέλαθε φοινιχθείς, οἱονεὶ πυρὸς αἰθάλην τοῦ ἐρυθήματος ἐπιδραμόντος.
>
> At the mention of the 'bride' Meroëbus, in pleasure and at the same time embarrassment, went visibly crimson even with his black skin-colour, the blush running across his face like a flame running over soot.
>
> Hld. 10.24.2

The circumstances of this blush assimilate it to Charicleia's at 1.21.3 when she answered Thyamis' proposal of marriage, while its comparison to a flame running over soot – οἱονεὶ πυρὸς αἰθάλην τοῦ ἐρυθήματος ἐπιδραμόντος – can be argued to invert the image of red blood on a white cheek with which, at 1.2.3, this whole sequence began. This image had already been recalled earlier in Book 10, when Charicleia's ebony birthmark was said to 'stain' her ivory left arm: καὶ ἦν τις ὥσπερ ἔβενος περίδρομος ἐλέφαντα τὸν βραχίονα μιαίνων, 'and there was a sort of ebony ring staining her ivory arm' (Hld. 10.15.2). That contrast between red and white finally recurs in the description of the silks brought as gifts by the Chinese (in the chapter immediately after Meroëbus' blush) τὴν μὲν φοινικοβαφῆ, τὴν δὲ λευκοτάτην ἐσθῆτα προσκομίζοντες, 'bringing some garments dyed crimson, some brilliant white' (Hld. 10.25.2). Here the adjective φοινικοβαφῆ (*phoenīkobaphē*), 'dyed crimson', picks up its use of Theagenes' cloak at 3.3.5.

This concentration of φοῖνιξ terms in Book 10 thus helps to create an impression of closure. It also prepares us for Heliodorus' last throw, when – if we accept that this *sphragis* belongs to the text – he signs off as ἀνὴρ Φοῖνιξ Ἐμισηνός, 'a Phoenician man from Emesa'. Only now do we realise why the writer has been juggling so persistently with various senses of φοῖνιξ, and even the comparison of the phoenix to a σοφός, 'sage', may have some relevance to the framing of our text.

3 Torches and Illumination

Parallel to this φοῖνιξ (*phoenix*) sequence runs another. At 5.5.2 the φοῖνιξ (*phoenix*) was chosen as a symbol by Theagenes, just as its colour had been first associated with him in 1.2.3 and again with his cloak in 3.3.5. Charicleia's chosen symbol was a λαμπάδιον, 'torch'. A λαμπάδιον, 'torch', λαμπάδες, 'torches', and λαμπάδιον πῦρ, 'the fire of torches', first enter the story associated, as very commonly, with weddings. Thyamis thinks that his dream of the Iseum full of torches relates to deflowering Charicleia: καὶ τὸν νεὼν τῆς Ἴσιδος ἐπερχόμενος λαμπαδίωι πυρὶ τὸν ὅλον ἐδόκει καταλάμπεσθαι, 'And coming to the temple of Isis he thought that it was entirely lit up with the flames of torches' (Hld. 1.18.4). This dream is recalled by him a little later: ἐνθύμιον αὐτῶι τὸ ὄναρ γίνεται καθ' ὃ τὴν Ἶσιν ἑώρα καὶ τὸν νεὼν ἅπαντα λαμπάδων καὶ θυσιῶν ἀνάμεστον, 'he took thought of the dream in which he had seen Isis and her whole temple full of torches and sacrifices' (Hld. 1.30.4). Shortly thereafter Theagenes presents the conflagration in which he thinks Charicleia has perished as a wretched substitute for marriage-torches: ἀλλὰ πυρός, οἴμοι, γέγονας ἀνάλωμα, τοιαύτας ἐπί σοι λαμπάδας ἀντὶ τῶν νυμφικῶν τοῦ δαίμονος ἅψαντος, 'But fire, alas, has consumed you – these are the sort of torches, instead of bridal torches, that the divinity has lit' (Hld. 2.1.3). Again, when Theagenes and Cnemon think they have found Charicleia's body, Cnemon throws his torch to the ground and extinguishes it: 'ὦ Ζεῦ, τί τοῦτο; ἀπόλωλαμεν· ἀνῄρηται Χαρίκλεια'· καὶ τό τε λαμπάδιον εἰς τὴν γῆν καταβαλὼν ἀπέσβεσε, '"O Zeus, what is this? We are lost! Charicleia has perished!", and he threw the torch to the ground and extinguished it' (Hld. 2.3.3). Two books later Charicles recalls the death of his own daughter in a fire as an extinction of her bridal torches: 'τὴν πρώτην μοι καὶ γνησίαν, ὡς ἴστε, θυγατέρα ταῖς νυμφικαῖς λαμπάσι συναπέσβεσε', '"(ill fortune) has extinguished my first and natural daughter together with her bridal torches"' (Hld. 4.19.8).

Alongside these cases stands Charicleia's handing of the ritual torch to Theagenes at 3.5.4–6.1, an act which is simultaneous with and symbolic of their sudden falling in love: the torch is first called a δᾶις, 'torch', or πῦρ, 'fire':

> 'ὁ δὲ Χαρικλῆς τὴν μὲν σπονδὴν αὑτῶι προσήκειν ἔλεγε "τὸν βωμὸν δὲ ὁ τῆς θεωρίας ἄρχων ἁπτέτω παρὰ τῆς ζακόρου τὴν δᾶιδα κομισάμενος. τοῦτο γὰρ ἔθος ὁ πάτριος διαγινώσκει νόμος". ταῦτα εἶπε, καὶ ὁ μὲν ἔσπενδε, τὸ δὲ πῦρ Θεαγένης ἐλάμβανεν. ὅτε, φίλε Κνήμων, καὶ ὅτι θεῖον ἡ ψυχὴ καὶ συγγενὲς ἄνωθεν τοῖς ἔργοις ἐπιστούμεθα. ὁμοῦ τε γὰρ ἀλλήλους ἑώρων οἱ νέοι καὶ ἤρων, ὥσπερ τῆς ψύχης ἐκ πρώτης ἐντεύξεως τὸ ὅμοιον ἐπιγνούσης καὶ πρὸς τὸ κατ' ἀξίαν οἰκεῖον προσδραμούσης. πρῶτον μὲν γὰρ ἀθρόον τι καὶ ἐπτοημένον ἔστησαν καὶ τὴν δᾶιδα ὀλκότερον ἡ μὲν ἐνεχείριζεν ὁ δὲ ὑπεδέχετο ...'
>
> 'Charicles said that the libations were his prerogative, but "Let the altar be lit by the leader of the sacred embassy when he has been given the torch by the priestess. For this is the custom that our ancestral laws determine". After saying this he began to pour the libations, and Theagenes moved to take the flame. Then it was, dear Cnemon, that we received confirmation from what happened that the soul is divine and has a kinship from its origins: for at the same moment the young people saw each other and fell in love, as when a soul recognises its like at a first encounter and rushes towards what is rightly its own. Now first they stood still in a state of overwhelming excitement, and very reluctantly she put the torch into his hand, and he took it from her ...'
>
> Hld. 3.5.3–5

Finally the torch is called a λαμπάδιον, 'little torch': ἐπεὶ δὲ ὀψέ ποτε καὶ ὥσπερ βιαίως τῆς κόρης ἀποσπώμενος ὁ Θεαγένης ὑπέθηκέ τε τὸ λαμπάδιον καὶ τὸν βωμὸν ἀνῆψεν, 'and when at long last and almost by force Theagenes wrenched the torch from the girl and put it to the altar and lit it' (Hld. 3.6.1). The torch so firmly etched upon the reader's vision here is evoked in the description of the virginal Charicleia holding a torch in her left hand and the palm-shoot in her right (4.1.2, already cited); and that in turn is recalled, as we have seen, at 5.5.2, in Charicleia's choice of λαμπάς, 'torch', as a password, a password that she actually uses in the recognition at 7.7.7.

When λαμπάδες reappear in the next chapter they are less obviously related to nuptials: καὶ ὑπὸ λάμπασιν ἡμμέναις ἐπὶ τὸν νεὼν τῆς Ἴσιδος κατήγετο ὁ πρεσβύτης, 'and to the accompaniment of lighted torches the old man was escorted to the temple of Isis' (Hld. 7.8.5). This is the procession which escorts Calasiris back into Memphis after the reconciliation of Thyamis and Petosiris and almost immediately after the recognition at 7.7.7. As the procession formed, Heliodorus had directed our attention to the reunited Theagenes and Charicleia:

> ἐφ᾽ ἅπασι τὸ ἐρωτικὸν μέρος τοῦ δράματος ἡ Χαρίκλεια καὶ ὁ Θεαγένης ἐπήκμαζεν, ὡραῖοι καὶ χαρίεντες οὕτω νέοι παρ᾽ ἐλπίδα πᾶσαν ἀλλήλους ἀπειληφότες καὶ πλέον τῶν ἄλλων εἰς τὴν ἐφ᾽ ἑαυτοὺς θέαν τὴν πόλιν ἐπιστρέφοντες.
>
> To crown everything, the love element in the drama – Charicleia and Theagenes – was at its peak, young people so charming and in the full bloom of their youth, who contrary to all expectation had found each other again and were turning the city's gaze upon themselves more than on any of the others.
>
> Hld. 7.8.2

In this situation

> τοῦ μὲν ἐφηβεύοντος τῆς πόλεως καὶ εἰς ἄνδρας ἄρτι παραλλάττοντος τῶι Θεαγένει προστρέχοντος ... τὸ δὲ παρθενεῦον τοῦ ἄστεως καὶ νυμφῶνας ἤδη φανταζόμενον τὴν Χαρίκλειαν περιεῖπε ...
>
> while those of ephebic age in the city and just making the transition to manhood rushed to Theagenes ... those in the town who were virgins and were already imagining their bridal chambers escorted Charicleia ...
>
> Hld. 7.8.3

Heliodorus seems to be raising his reader's expectations that the reunion of Theagenes and Charicleia will shortly be followed by their marriage; and that the remains of Book 7 and Book 8 may whisk them away for a trouble-free wedding in Ethiopia. Does he expect his reader to know that this novel does not, like those of Chariton and Achilles Tatius, have only eight books, but also a ninth and tenth? We should perhaps see 7.8 as a false move towards closure, in which the λαμπάδες, 'torches', have a part to play.

The torch is switched on again at 9.9.4–5. Here Heliodorus is explaining the mystic meaning of the flooding of Egypt by the Nile: the land is Isis, longing for her absent husband Osiris, represented by the Nile's waters. Φυσικοί, 'natural scientists', and θεολόγοι, 'theologians', do not disclose the hidden meanings in this mystery to the profane, but give them a foretaste in the form of a myth, whereas τοὺς ... ἐποπτικωτέρους καὶ ἀνακτόρων ἐντὸς τῆι πυρφόρωι τῶν ὄντων λαμπάδι φανότερον τελούντων, 'those who have reached the higher grade of mystic and are within the shrine they initiate more clearly with the fire-bearing torch of truth' (Hld. 9.9.5). Although the torch is here intriguingly linked to the sexual union of Isis and Osiris (9.9.4), and, as John Morgan notes, may recall the torchlit ceremonies of the Isiac mysteries[37] – thus picking up the torchlit Iseum of 1.18 and 1.30 – its chief function in this passage is as a symbol of elucidation and interpretation.

The end is near. As Book 10 proceeds, the identities of Charicleia and of Theagenes are confirmed, Hydaspes is urged by Persinna to allow the couple to wed, and Sisimithres breaks into fluent Ethiopian to sanction the abolition of human sacrifice. The gods, he explains, have brought about this chain of events: 'νῦν τὴν κορωνίδα τῶν ἀγαθῶν καὶ ὥσπερ λαμπάδιον τοῦ δράματος τὸν νυμφίον τουτονὶ τὸν ξένον νεανίαν ἀναφήναντες', '"now (the gods) have revealed the young stranger as the girl's bridegroom, the last words of their blessings and as it were the culminating torch of the drama"' (Hld. 10.39.2). κορωνίς (*korōnis*), the technical term for the symbol used in written texts to close sections of a work or whole literary works, forces us to the realisation that we are at the end of a literary text; λαμπάδιον δράματος, 'culminating torch of the drama', reminds us how often the story has been framed as a theatrical performance. The meaning of λαμπάδιον here is obscure and contested. I find it hard to believe, as suggested by Rattenbury-Lumb, that this is a reference to a particular type of mask representing a young woman (cf. Poll. 4.151). A more plausible link with dramatic performances was proposed by Geoffrey Arnott.[38] What does seem to be difficult to resist is that this λαμπάδιον, 'torch', reminds us of the torch so closely associated with Charicleia, and chosen by her as her password; and that the bridal connotations that have so frequently been associated with λαμπάς or λαμπάδιον earlier in the text still have some force here. But we have also seen the torch to be associated with correct interpretation (9.9.5). What within Heliodorus' story is Charicleia's wedding, formally and finally solemnised by Hydaspes in the next few lines (10.41.3), is for readers a completion of their long and slow process of understanding.

What, then, of the linking of the torch and the φοῖνιξ in Charicleia's hands at Delphi? I am tempted to see the torch as a symbol not only of Charicleia the character but of Charicleia the book we have been reading. The book has initiated us in the mysteries of divinity, fate and love. It is then not surprising that the light of understanding which the torch thus symbolises has been imparted to it by an author whose role is complementary to that of his text, just as the torch and the φοῖνιξ (*phoenix*), are held in Charicleia's left and right hands, and as Charicleia and Theagenes, the torch and the φοῖνιξ (*phoenix*) are complementary. It then completes our understanding of these symbols that in the last words of our book we discover that its author is also a Φοῖνιξ.

[37] Morgan 1989a, 544 n.206. [38] Arnott 1965.

25 The Chronology of the Earlier Greek Novels since B. E. Perry: Revisions and Precisions (2002)

This paper first revisits the problem of the chronology of the earlier Greek novels. The texts at issue are the *Ninus* romance, the *Chaereas and Callirhoe* of Chariton, the *Ephesiaca* of Xenophon, and the *Metiochus and Parthenope* romance. I then add some observations on the dates of Antonius Diogenes and Achilles Tatius, and on the geographical location of the Greek novels' genesis.[1]

1 Chariton, *Ninus* and *Metiochus and Parthenope*

For Chariton[2] and for *Metiochus and Parthenope* we are given firm *termini ante quem* by papyri, in each case of some time in the second century AD. The Michaelides papyrus of Chariton, *P.Michael.* 1, is dated to the second century; *P.Fayum* 1 has been dated by Cavallo to the first half of the second century.[3] The Berlin fragments of *Metiochus and Parthenope*, *P.Berol.* 7927+9588+21179, were also written in the second century, a more recently published fragment, *P.Mich.* 3402, in the third.[4] The *terminus ante quem* given by the principal *Ninus* papyrus (*P.Berol.* 6926, with fragments A and B) is half a century earlier: unless its writer broke the regular habit of first using a roll of papyrus on the side on which the fibres ran horizontally, the *recto*, somewhat easing the movement of writing, and instead chose to use

[1] Versions of this paper were given at the École normale supérieure, rue d'Ulm, Paris, and at Melbourne and Göteborg Universities; a penultimate version was pre-circulated and discussed at the novel panel during the New Orleans meeting of the APA in January 2003. I benefited greatly from discussions on these occasions, and particularly from the critique offered by Antonio Stramaglia at the APA panel. For the dates of *Ninus* and *Metiochus and Parthenope* see now López Martínez 2019, Fernandez-Garrido 2021.

[2] For authoritative discussions of the date of Chariton see Ruiz Montero 1994, 1008–12; Reardon 1996, 309–35; a strong case for a Neronian date is made by Tilg 2010, 92–126.

[3] Cavallo 1996, 16, 25 pl. 7, 38, accepted by Henrichs 2011, 310 n.37 (with a list of other Chariton papyri); Reardon 2004, xxii assigns it to the late second century.

[4] Alvares and Renner 2001. It is possible, but no more, that the *Panionis* fragment published by Parsons 2007, *P.Oxy.* 4811, and with it the *Staphylos* fragment (*PSI* 1220; Stephens and Winkler 1995, 429–37), which seems to be from the same second-century roll or copy, belong to *Metiochus and Parthenope*: see Parsons 2010, 44–9, Henrichs 2011, 313 n.53.

the *verso* (where the fibres ran vertically) the text of the *Ninus* on the *recto* of *P.Berol.* 6296 is earlier than the tax documents written on its *verso*; and these documents are of the years AD 100/101 (fragment A) and AD 101/102 (fragment B). The hand is comparable to others dated to AD 60–90,[5] and is assigned by Susan Stephens to ca. AD 75.[6] Thus *Ninus* cannot possibly have been composed later than AD 100, and was most probably composed earlier than ca. AD 75. This chronology also follows from the other known papyrus of the *Ninus*, fragment C, from Oxyrhynchus (*PSI* 1305), described by Stephens as 'assignable also to the last half of the first century CE'.[7]

How much earlier? Here we run out of evidence, and have to start guessing. Most scholars guess 'early', and in any case earlier than Chariton's work. I quote Gerald Sandy, in the Anglophone bible of the Greek novels, Bryan Reardon's *Collected Ancient Greek Novels*:

> On the basis of this *terminus ante quem*, as well as on the basis of palaeography and the author's literary style, papyrologists have established that fragments A and B were written down sometime between 100 BC and AD 100. This chronology annihilated the then prevailing view of Rohde that the Greek romances were a product of the Second Sophistic, the period of renewed Greek literary activity during the second and early third centuries AD.[8]

This statement seems to elide the views of literary historians and papyrologists. Now, at any rate, papyrologists are saying ca. AD 75: as far as I know no papyrologist would support an early first-century AD date for our papyrus text, far less the first century BC. And of course if *Ninus were* composed around AD 60–75, it would fall *within* the Second Sophistic as defined by Philostratus (who, after all, invented it!), since Philostratus' first imperial sophist is Nicetes, already prominent in Smyrna when Nero referred his dispute with a λογιστής, 'finance commissioner' (Verginius?) Rufus to the court of Rufus himself, by then (AD 67–8) on an imperial appointment in Gaul.[9] Nicetes was heard ca. AD 79 by the younger Pliny in Rome, whither his reputation in Asia for flowery rhetoric had already permeated by the dramatic date of Tacitus' *Dialogus*, i.e. ca. AD 75.[10]

So the case for a significantly earlier date for the composition of *Ninus* must rest on what Sandy called 'the author's literary style'. That had already been stressed by Lesky:[11]

[5] Roberts 1956, plates 11a and 11b. [6] Stephens and Winkler 1995, 31.
[7] Stephens and Winkler 1995, 63; so too Cavallo 1996, 31: cf. Bastianini 2010.
[8] Sandy 1989a, 803. [9] Philostr. *VS* 1.19.512. [10] Plin. *Ep.* 6.6.3, cf. Tac. *Dial.* 15.3.
[11] Lesky 1966, 861.

> The affinity with historiography, and linguistical details, such as the pronounced dread of hiatus, recommend an early date, probably the second century BC.

There is consensus here, and authority: Bryan Reardon's view in 1991[12] endorsed that of Gerald Sandy.

What are the props of this inclination to set the composition of the *Ninus* a century or more before the papyrus? 'The affinity with historiography' can count for little: the 'historiographical manner' is equally strong in Chariton, and a version of it is vigorous in Heliodorus, as was well analysed by John Morgan in 1982.[13] The simplicity of the style may be one feature implied by Sandy to be significant: it cannot be denied – though it should not be exaggerated – but it would not suffice to detach the date of *Ninus* from that of Chariton, for whom an early dating in the sequence of novels was first proposed precisely on stylistic grounds. If we try to appeal to more precise or objective stylistic criteria, the case of Chariton should give us pause. On the basis of his linguistic analysis of Chariton Papanikolaou concluded, and persuaded Albrecht Dihle – or did Dihle persuade Papanikolaou? – that Chariton's relative immunity to Atticism required a dating as early as the first century BC. But a wider examination of Chariton's language, by Ruiz Montero and Hernández Lara, has shown how much he shares with first-century AD writers – Philo, Josephus and Plutarch.[14]

The fragments of *Ninus* are not extensive enough for a telling analysis such as has been done for Chariton. But for what it is worth, the writer of the *Ninus* does indeed avoid *hiatus*, as Reeve noted in 1971,[15] though from this Reeve drew the opposite conclusion to Lesky. He also seems to seek out favoured clausulae and Attic vocabulary, with some exceptions.[16] These exceptions had been adduced by Dihle in 1978 in his discussion of the *Metiochus and Parthenope* fragment[17] – non-Atticist features that he argued to put *Ninus* in the same pre-Atticising world as the one in which he wished to locate Chariton and the *Metiochus and Parthenope* romance. They are not wholly convincing, as the following discussion attempts to show:

ναυτιλία A.III 20–1. But ναυτιλία is used twice in this sense 'sea journey' in Heliodorus (6.6.3, 7.14.8) and at another place in the sense 'sailing' (5.27.3). Its use in the novelists, not admittedly an Attic use, is likely to be drawn from Herodotus (cf. Hdt. 1.1.1, 1.163.1).

[12] 'The romance itself probably goes back at least to the 1st century BC.': Reardon 1991, 10 n.14.
[13] Morgan 1982. [14] Papanikolaou 1973; Ruiz Montero 1991; Hernández Lara 1994.
[15] Reeve 1971, 536–8. [16] Stephens and Winkler 1995, 31. [17] Dihle 1978, 55.

ἤμην A.III 38 for Attic ἦν. Again the *Ninus* does not stand alone. Xenophon of Ephesus, not surprisingly, has συνήμην 3.2.9, ἤμην 5.1.6. Neither Chariton nor Heliodorus has ἤμην, but Achilles Tatius has it three times (3.22.3, 4.1.2, 5.1.4). In Longus it appears at 4.28.3, and is offered by **V** at 2.7.4, where **F** has ἦν; παρήμην is the reading of both **F** and **V** at 2.5.3.

κόρη A.IV 20. Again this is indeed a non-Attic word, but it is one that is repeatedly used by most novelists to describe their heroine – Xenophon, Achilles Tatius, Longus and Heliodorus. Chariton is unusual in using it only twice: 1.3.1, of Callirhoe shortly after her marriage, and 3.8.3, of her beauty before she gave birth to her child, οὐκέτι κόρης ἀλλὰ γυναικὸς ἀκμὴν προσλαβοῦσα, 'acquiring the bloom that was no longer that of a girl, but of a woman'), but this is chiefly because his Callirhoe is not a κόρη for most of his story.

ἐντός with genitive A.IV 23:

ἡ γὰρ παρθέν[ος ἐντὸς τ]ῆς γυ- ναικωνίτιδ[ος ζῶσα ο]ὐκ ...

For the maiden, living inside the women's quarters, did not ...

Here ἐντός, in any case a supplement, is not, as Dihle suggested, a simple equivalent for ἐν with the dative. Here and in general ἐντός means not 'in' but 'inside', as it does in the one place where Longus uses it at 2.25.2 ἄκρας ... ἐπεκτεινομένης μηνοειδῶς, ἧς ἐντὸς ἡ θάλασσα γαληνότερον τῶν λιμένων ὅρμον εἰργάζετο, 'a headland ... stretching round crescent-like, inside which the sea created an anchorage calmer than harbours'.

ἐρυθαίνω, not ἐρυθραίνω, 'I make to blush', A.IV 35. Like ἐντός, this is a supplement, but a fairly secure one: there seems to be no room for a ρ. The form ἐρυθαίνω without a ρ is indeed poetic and not Attic, and favoured, for example, by Apollonius Rhodius (e.g. 1.791) and by Leonidas (*AP* 9.322.5 = *HE* 25.5, line 2117). Neither form appears in the other novelists, who use ἐρυθριῶ. But the poetic form ἐρυθαίνω did creep into at least one second-century writer who was careful: Arrian in one of his meteorological fragments uses ἐρυθαίνεται, 'turns red';[18] and it is also offered as a way one might describe cheeks by Pollux 2.87.

θέρειος, 'of summer', and not Attic θερινός is used at B.II 13. However Longus used both θέρειος[19] and Attic θερινός, if we accept Courier's reading at 1.17.4 of χλωρότερον τὸ πρόσωπον ἦν πόας θερινῆς, 'her face was paler than grass in summer', based on the superscript θε above the και of καιρινῆς, 'seasonal', in **F**. The form that the author of *Ninus* needs for his purpose and

[18] Arr. *Scripta minora*, p.191.27 Roos = Stob.1.31.8.

[19] 3.24.1 καιναὶ τέρψεις καὶ θέρειοι, 'new pleasures, those of summer'.

uses is a comparative: πολὺ θερειότερος τῆς ὥρας ἐπιπεσὼν νότος ..., 'an unseasonably summery south wind blew up and ....' Even if he had remembered, unlike Longus, that θερινός is not Attic, he might have been deterred from using θερινός by discovering that this form had no attested comparative or superlative.

πλὴν ἀλλά, 'except however', cited by Dihle, is not read in modern editions of the papyrus.

θηρίον refers to a war-elephant at B.III 18, 24: cf. Plb. 11.1.2. But it is not clear that at B.III 18 and 24 the term is meant to be technical (as it appears to be in Plb.): these beasts have already been referred to as ἐλέφαντες, 'elephants' at B.III 11.

What we are finding in *Ninus*, I think, is careful writing that shares some features with other genres that are more single-minded in their Atticising, but writing that looks to a wider range of models that, not surprisingly, includes the godfather of novel-writing, Herodotus. These features allow a date for the composition of the novel much nearer to that of the papyrus: although I see no particular reason to put it as late as, say, ca. AD 90, I think that the widespread inclination to date it substantially earlier has little objective basis, and I do not see how we can exclude a date as late as the 60s AD. It has been suggested that the lapse of some twenty years between postulated composition of *Ninus* in the 60s and apparent copying of our papyrus no later than ca. AD 90 is too short a span for a text composed (most probably, see below) in Aphrodisias to reach the place it was copied (perhaps Karanis). We do not even begin to have data which would allow us to estimate the average time for a text composed in Rome or Asia Minor to reach cities in Egypt, and no doubt there was considerable variation between one case and another. At one extreme we can note the elegiacs by Cornelius Gallus discovered at Qasr Ibrîm, composed probably in the 50s or 40s BC, and found in a context that belongs most probably to the late 20s BC.[20] It is, of course, a special case, given Gallus' Egyptian connections: but it suffices to demonstrate that it would be unwise to insist on a lapse of (e.g.) four or more decades before a text composed elsewhere might be found written on an Egyptian papyrus.

Another point that does not bear on dating may nevertheless be worth noticing. The author of *Ninus* has hit on a key term which appears in two other novels, those of Chariton and Heliodorus, ἀστάθμητος, 'unstable'. It is

[20] Anderson, Parsons and Nisbet 1979, esp. 128: 'If we accept (1), we shall date the Gallus-papyrus *c.* 50 BC–*c.* 20 BC If we accept (2), we shall date it *c.* 50 BC–AD 25. The balance of evidence favours (1)'.

combined with ἀτέκμαρτος, 'incalculable', at A.III 28–9. The author of *Ninus* may have found these two words within four lines of each other in a speech by the Syracusan Hermocrates in Thucydides: at 4.62.4 τὸ … ἀστάθμητον τοῦ μέλλοντος, 'the instability of what is to come'; and at 4.63.1 διὰ τὸ ἀτέκμαρτον δέος, 'because of the fear of the incalculable'. These phrases well bring out a generic feature of the novelistic world – neither characters nor readers can be sure what the couple's fate will be. Chariton uses ἀστάθμητος once, though in a slightly different sense;[21] Heliodorus uses it three times.[22]

I react similarly to Dihle's linguistic arguments for the date of the *Metiochus and Parthenope*, though I do so more selectively.

Dihle noted σήμερον, not Attic τήμερον, for 'today' at I.31. Chariton has σήμερον five times (1.1.11, 14.10; 5.7.5; 6.5.3; 7.5.8); Achilles Tatius has σήμερον once (8.8.7), τήμερον once (5.26.7); Longus has only τήμερον, once (2.4.1); Heliodorus has σήμερον twice (3.14.1; 4.2.3) and τήμερον fifteen times. If one supposes that the sophistic novelists were consistent then we should blame their copyists for the occasional appearance in them of σήμερον, and we should suppose that Longus and Heliodorus, at least, and perhaps Achilles Tatius, wrote τήμερον. Equally it seems probable from its five appearances that Chariton wrote σήμερον; perhaps so too did the author of *Ninus*, but a single case has to be treated with caution.[23]

I.25 τὸ εὐθαρσές, 'of good courage': as Dihle noted, the form is used by Xenophon – whom Dihle then dismisses as a forerunner of the *koine*.[24] Xenophon was also, however, an important model for several types of writing in the second century AD[25] – Arrian had a go at almost all of them – and Heliodorus has εὐθαρσέστερον, 'more self-confident', at 10.18.2. The use of τὸ εὐθαρσές by the author of *Metiochus and Parthenope* does not help the case for the first century BC date.

Nor does the author's use of βρέφος, 'baby', at I.48. True, βρέφος never appears in Attic prose. But the novelists use the word frequently, usually of young babies, but once, as here, of Eros – Achilles Tatius at 1.2.1. The other

[21] 6.4.5, of Callirhoe imagined by the Persian king: στῆθος ἀστάθμητον, 'her breast in confusion', or στῆθος ἀσταθμήτου πλῆρες, 'her breast full of confusion' (the text is uncertain).

[22] 5.4.7 ἐπεὶ δὲ ἀστάθμητόν τι τὸ ἀνθρώπειον, 'but since the human condition is something unstable'; 6.7.3 ἀσταθμητότατον τύχης ἀνθρωπίνης κίνημα, 'most unstable motion of human fortune'; 6.9.3 οὐκ ἐννοήσεις ἄνθρωπος οὖσα, πρᾶγμα ἀστάθμητον …; 'Do you not understand that you are human, a thing unstable …?'

[23] For τήμερον as Attic see Moeris τ 6; Poll. 1.66 allows either. For the problem of σήμερον and τήμερον in Comedy see Arnott 2002, 209–10. For the extent of Longus' Atticism Bowie 2019g, 17–19 and index; Bowie 2019c (Chapter 42 in this volume).

[24] *Ages.* 11.10, *Eq.mag.* 4.12, *HG* 7.1.9.

[25] For Xen.'s impact on imperial Greek literature see Bowie 2016g (Chapter 39 in Volume 3).

appearances of βρέφος are in Chariton – five times, twice of the child the pregnant Callirhoe is carrying (2.11.4, 3.2.13) and thrice of the same child after his birth (3.8.6, 7; 5.10.8); at Achilles Tatius 1.10.1; in Longus at 1.2.1, 3.1, and 6.1 (of the exposed babies); and at Heliodorus 9.11.5–6. I find it hard to see βρέφος as contributing to the case for an early date.

Then consider the adverb παντελῶς, 'entirely', qualifying an adjective at I.53. Not Attic, notes Dihle: but he admits a few exceptions in Plato and Xenophon, e.g. *R.* 502d7 παντελῶς ἀληθής. This shows that the author has a broad conception of Attic models, not that he antedates Atticism.

Finally at II.43 παρηρτημένον. This verb is not, indeed, attested in classical Attic. But its use by Plutarch, Lucian, and the arch-Atticiser Aelian surely exculpates our author from careless slumming.[26]

Again, as with *Ninus*, I think Dihle has overestimated the factors that might count against locating the writer in a period when Atticism was gaining strength, and I suggest that the novelists' awareness of their literary ancestry and their consequent readiness to draw on Plato, Xenophon and even Herodotus need to be thrown into the scales.[27]

A further piece of evidence might help us in dating *Metiochus and Parthenope*. A short text on an ostracon in the collection of the Bodleian Library, Oxford, *O.Bodl.* II 2175, was argued by Gronewald to be a part of the novel: he suggested that the words (lines 2–4) Παρ|[θ]ενόπη, καὶ τοῦ σοῦ | [Μ]ητιόχου λήσμων | [ε]ἶ; 'Parthenope, are you forgetful even of your Metiochus?' might be from a letter.[28] Stephens and Winkler noted that they could as well be from a soliloquy, but that 'since the characters from the novel were popular subjects for theatrical performance, the ostracon is just as likely to be a derivative composition, perhaps related to rhetorical exercise, or a quotation of a famous line from a stage performance'.[29] On any interpretation the ostracon seems to imply the existence of a *Metiochus and Parthenope* narrative. It was perhaps because they rated the chance of this being from the actual text of the novel as low that Stephens and Winkler did not discuss the date of the ostracon, saying no more than that it was 'from the Roman period'.[30] But as Stephens and Winkler were going to press Stramaglia suggested in a conference in Cassino that the ostracon was written in the first decades of the first century AD, citing the support of

[26] Plu. *Ant.* 4.3; Luc. *Peregr.* 15; Ael. *NA* 1.2, 5.3; also Ps.-Plu. *Vit. Dem.* = *Mor.* 844e.

[27] For the influence of Hdt.'s language on Longus see the index entries in Bowie 2019g, 329.

[28] Gronewald 1977.

[29] Stephens and Winkler 1995, 93. For a full discussion of the literary kind and context to which the ostracon might be assigned see Stramaglia 1996, 120–7.

[30] Stephens and Winkler 1995, 93.

Cavallo.[31] However Cavallo had also said that he could see parallels to the hand in which the ostracon was written over a period running from the first century BC to as late as AD 66.[32] Dirk Obbink has very kindly examined the ostracon and has stressed that this sort of hand is extremely difficult to date: he has suggested that it could well have been written as late as the second half of the first century AD. It is unfortunate that Cavallo's phrase '*i primi decenni*' has attracted more attention than his other suggested *termini* of first century BC–AD 66. Even supposing that this text *is* from the novel, it seems clear that a date in the 60s AD would do no violence to the evidence, such as it is. But the ostracon offers no significant support for a date of composition in the first century BC.

Where, then, do I put *Metiochus and Parthenope*? Close to Chariton, probably but not certainly. Where then Chariton? I am no longer persuaded by the case put by Marie-Françoise Baslez for a Flavian or Hadrianic date, which is partly based on the perception of the Euphrates as a frontier between Rome and Parthia, i.e. within the novel the Greek world and the Persian, and partly on the Armenian route taken by Mithridates at Chariton 5.2.1.[33] Nor am I now persuaded by that of Christopher Jones for the same date on the grounds of the similarity between Chariton's Dionysius of Miletus and the sophist of that name known from epigraphy, Cassius Dio and Philostratus' *Lives*[34] – a similarity that I concede, but that I take to be clear evidence that Chariton's fictional character must antedate the distinguished Milesian of the same name, unless he were prepared to cause great offence to a man with some influence in *provincia Asia*. I am also unpersuaded by the arguments of Cueva that Chariton uses Plutarch and so belongs early in the second century.[35] So I tentatively accept the reference of Persius *Sat.* 1.134 *post prandia Callirhoen do*, 'after dinner I present *Callirhoe*', to our author's *Callirhoe*, and hence the hypothesis of the work's publication by the early 60s AD.[36]

Another detail might offer a little support. Chariton gives the name Chaereas to his hero who sets the disasters of the novel in train by an act of

[31] Stramaglia 1996, 123 referring to Cavallo ('*per verba*') as dating it 'ai primi decenni del I d.C.'

[32] Stramaglia 1996, 123, n.129: 'Cavallo *per verba*, adducendo riscontri (spècialmente per il *my*) che si collocano in un arco cronologico compreso fra PBerol inv. 13045 (Pack² 2102) = *PGP* 2.2, 15 (I a.C.); e POxy 246 = *GLH* ² 10c (66 d.C.)'.

[33] Baslez 1992b. [34] Jones 1992a. [35] Cueva 1996, 2000, 2004.

[36] Smith 2007, 2, and Henrichs 2011, 311 also favour a Neronian date, and hold that Persius is referring to Chariton's *Callirhoe*. Others think Persius' *Callirhoe* was a quite different work, e.g. poetry (Whitmarsh 2005b, 590 n.14).

violence, and who to some extent redeems himself by gathering Greek mercenaries to fight heroically against the Persian king. Why? Chaereas is not a very common name, though it is borne by an Athenian in Thucydides.[37] In the forties AD, however, it was in the headlines. It was the name of the man who as a centurion in AD 14 had been an *adulescens animi ferox*, 'a youth with a proud spirit',[38] and who twenty-seven years later, now a tribune of the *cohors praetoria*, 'praetorian cohort', had been so persistently insulted by the emperor Gaius that he assassinated him on 24 January AD 41: he was called Cassius Chaerea – in Greek sources Κάσσιος Χαιρέας. The act was remembered in the Greek world as it was in the Roman:[39] the phrase *adulescens animi ferox* well describes Chariton's young Chaereas. This is not to say that the use of the name Chaereas in New Comedy (e.g. by Menander in *Dyscolus*, *Aspis*, *Koneazomenai* and at least one other play) plays no part in Chariton's choice of name. But although Chaereas is an *adulescens* in love, there are more strands to his character than are intimated by these ancestors in New Comedy: those of a propensity to violent actions and a readiness to seek a military career are better explained by the mid-first-century historical figure Cassius Chaerea.

That events at Rome and affecting the empire should be known to an author from Aphrodisias is no surprise. In the Julio-Claudian period Aphrodisias and its elite were strengthening their links with the ruling family in Rome.[40] Aphrodisias could also be the πατρίς, 'home country', of the author of *Ninus*, an idea that has occurred independently, I think, to me and to Stephens and Winkler. I think it is unlikely that the author of *Ninus* is Chariton himself: the papyrus text of *Ninus* twice has οἶσθας, 'you know' (e.g. A.II 22) whereas Chariton's manuscript always has Attic οἶσθα;[41] as we have seen, at A.III 38 *Ninus* has ἤμην, 'I was', for Attic ἦν, Chariton does not; and Chariton's very selective use of κόρη does not quite match the case in *Ninus*. So perhaps we should imagine two Julio-Claudian novel writers in Aphrodisias, not one. Of these Chariton, on the above, admittedly very precarious argument, should be writing between AD 41 and AD 61.

37 Th. 8.74.1 and 3, 86.3. 38 Tac. *An.* 1.32.

39 Plu. *De superst.* 11 = *Mor.* 170e; J. *AJ* 19.32–114; Paus. 9.27.4 (but omitting his name); D.C. exc. 59.29.

40 Cf. the presence of the obscure Ti. Claudius Drusus in the Sebasteion reliefs from Aphrodisias, as noted by Smith 1987, 95, or his hypothesis that one or more of the commissioners of the North Portico, Menander, Eusebes and Attalis Apphion, had seen the Augustan series of reliefs in Rome in the *Porticus ad nationes*, Smith 1988, 75. Note also the important figure C. Iulius Zoilus, with Smith 1993; and for a full publication of the Sebasteion Smith 2013.

41 For οἶσθας and οἶσθα in Comedy see Arnott 2002, 203–4.

Is *Ninus* before or after Chariton? The more confident claim I make is that we have no good ground for putting him before, certainly no good stylistic ground. Less confidently, I hazard a possible reason for putting *Ninus* later. King Ninus' expedition into the wintry wilds of Armenia constitutes a colourfully handled section of our fragments. Chariton too had taken his love-struck satrap Mithridates through Armenia to get to Babylon,[42] but without dwelling on the problems of this route. But since Chariton had written, if we place him before AD 61, campaigning in Armenia had been in the news. Early in Nero's reign war between Rome and Parthia had again broken out, with control of Armenia the chief objective, and the campaigns of Corbulo in AD 58 and subsequent years figure prominently in Tacitus' and Cassius Dio's accounts of that period.[43] Armenia is the principal battle-ground. Of course Armenia had been a similar *casus belli* in the late Republic, involving campaigns by Lucullus and Pompeius, and again in the Augustan period. But if we put Chariton in the forties or fifties AD, and if we suppose that the author of *Ninus* is writing not far removed in time or place from Chariton, then the years from AD 58 to 63 offer themselves as a time when Armenian campaigns might be an especially attractive subject for prose fiction rooted in recognisable historical landscapes.

That is speculation enough. But let me be even bolder (and hence more vulnerable). It is often thought that the account of the campaigns in Tacitus and Dio goes back to the memoirs of Corbulo himself: these can hardly antedate AD 63, nor can they have been written after his death in AD 66. If it were precisely the publication of these memoirs that suggested campaigning in Armenia to the author of *Ninus* (but of course that may not have been what triggered the fiction), then a date after AD 63 would follow. We would then have a chronology that put Chariton's publication of his novel a few years before the composition of the *Ninus*. Rome's claimed successes in Armenia were certainly known in Aphrodisias around AD 60, as is clear from the Sebasteion relief which shows Nero supporting a defeated Armenia who is slumping and eroticised,[44] a feature that might be thought interesting for an exploration of the genesis of the erotic novel.

[42] 5.2.1: cf. Baslez 1992b. [43] Tac. *An.* Books 12–15; D.C. Books 60–3.

[44] Smith 1987, 117–20 with Plates xvi and xvii; 2013, 140–3 C 8 with fig. 88 and Plates 58–9.

2 Xenophon of Ephesus

I say less about our other early novelist, Xenophon of Ephesus. Like almost all scholars before James O'Sullivan's book,[45] and like some since, I adhere to the view that Xenophon draws on Chariton, and not Chariton on Xenophon. But with no papyri so far discovered Xenophon is even more difficult to date. One detail, however, is often adduced: the mention of ὁ τῆς εἰρήνης τῆς ἐν Κιλικίας προεστώς, 'the officer in charge of peace in Cilicia' (2.13.3: cf. 3.9.5). This office, held by the character Perilaus, a member of the elite of Tarsus, has been seen to be the same as that of εἰρηνάρχης or εἰρήναρχος, 'peace-magistrate', frequently attested in the epigraphy of Roman Asia Minor.[46] The earliest such attestations are currently from the reign of Trajan. That does not, however, compel a dating of Xenophon after AD 98. We have no right to suppose that our earliest epigraphic testimony is exactly contemporary with the first institution of such an office, and in any case only seven of these inscriptions are from Cilicia,[47] whose mountainous regions were much more fertile ground for brigandage than the environs of Smyrna, Miletus or even Ancyra. Xenophon could well be writing some time earlier than AD 98.[48]

One detail remains to be exploited. When Habrocomes lodges near Syracuse with an old fisherman, Aegialeus, he discovers that his host had eloped from Sparta as a youth with his beloved Thelxinoe, and that his love for her had been so constant that recently, on her death, he had not buried her but kept her body in a back room of his small house (5.1.4–9). Aegialeus takes Habrocomes to show him the body: τὸ δὲ σῶμα αὐτῆς ἐτέθαπτο ταφῆι

[45] O'Sullivan 1995: cf. Schmeling 1996, Morgan 1996b.

[46] Of 139 cases in the Packard epigraphy database 131 are from Asia Minor. The two epigraphic attestations of the office's existence before the reign of Hadrian are from Ancyra (Latinius Alexander, whose pre-Hadrianic tenure of the office is known from a later text honouring his daughter Latinia Cleopatra, *IGR* iii 208 = Bosch 1967, 141 no. 117), and from Sebastopolis in Caria, with the adjective εἰρηναρχικός, *BCH* 9 (1995) 347 no. 30 = Robert 1937, 339–41, a text dated to AD 116/17. For a full discussion see Rife 2002.

[47] See Rife 2002, 107–8 listing 123 literary and (chiefly) epigraphic texts referring to the office. None is from epigraphically ill-attested Tarsus, but six are from the Cilician mountainous region to its north and west, Bean and Mitford 1970 nos. 9, 14, 19, 20, 21, and 23; one from a Cilician coastal site, Heberdey and Wilhelm 1896, 146, no. 249, honouring a νέος, 'young man', Hieronymus, as eirenarch at Syedra, a maritime city on the Pamphylian-Cilician border.

[48] On the question of the priority of Chariton and Xenophon see Whitmarsh 2013, 35–48, seeing a stronger intertextual case for Chariton using Xenophon than *vice versa*: so too Konstan 2009. Tagliabue 2017, 213–15 thinks the issue insoluble on present evidence. Coleman 2011 argues attractively that Xenophon's bringing Habrocomes to Nuceria fits the period between Stabiae's destruction by the eruption of Vesuvius in AD 79 and its resurgence under Pius.

Αἰγυπτίαι, 'and her body had been buried with an Egyptian burial'. It is worth asking whether this burial of Thelxinoe, apparently by embalming, takes its inspiration from the embalming of Poppaea by Nero, an event of the year AD 65 reported by Tacitus: *corpus non igni abolitum, ut Romanus mos, sed regum exterorum consuetudine differtum odoribus conditur tumuloque Iuliorum infertur*, 'her body was not consumed by fire, as is the Roman custom, but in the manner of foreign kings it was laid to rest packed with scents and borne into the tumulus of the Iulii'.[49]

What has emerged from this discussion of the early novels? They all seem likely to have been composed within a few decades: Chariton between AD 41 and 62, *Ninus* between AD 63 and ca. 75, Xenophon after AD 65, *Metiochus and Parthenope* less firmly dated, but pulled by its stylistic similarity to Chariton into the same temporal ambience. That ambience may also be geographically circumscribed: Chariton and the author of *Ninus* both working in Aphrodisias, Xenophon (if indeed he is from Ephesus) some ninety miles away, in a city that had links of various sorts with Aphrodisias.[50] It may therefore be no accident that the setting of some important scenes in *Metiochus and Parthenope* was Samos, the closest of the major Aegean islands to Ephesus and Aphrodisias. Persius shows that Chariton was soon known in Rome; the papyri and perhaps the ostracon that it did not take more than a generation for all but Xenophon to become known to Greek readers in Egypt, presumably *via* Alexandria, a city that had connections of many sorts with Ephesus.

3 Antonius Diogenes

It should not, then, be very surprising that the two writers who constitute what seems to be the next generation of novelists should also be linked respectively to Aphrodisias (Antonius Diogenes) and to Alexandria and Ephesus (Achilles Tatius).

Antonius Diogenes' work, Τὰ ὑπὲρ Θούλην ἄπιστα, '*The incredible things beyond Thule*', is a quirky variant on the story of boy-girl love presented by the texts already mentioned, not a straightforward example of it.[51] However the case for his place of origin being Aphrodisias is a strong one: Bowersock pointed out that only in the epigraphy of Aphrodisias do we have so far an

[49] Tac. *An.* 16.6.

[50] For arguments in favour of the novel's genesis in south-west Asia Minor see Bremmer 1998; Bowie 2004c (Chapter 14 in Volume 3).

[51] For an important new edition of Antonius Diogenes with discussion of his date see Schmedt 2020.

example of the conjunction of the Roman *nomen* Antonius with the Greek name Diogenes.[52] One case is L. Antonius Claudius Dometinus Diogenes, whose impressive statue from the Odeon at Aphrodisias is well known.[53] This prominent figure in early third-century Aphrodisias cannot himself be the novelist, one of whose papyri is dated to the second century, and indeed by one authority to perhaps the first half of the second century,[54] and two of whose papyri are dated ca. AD 200.[55] But the man whose statue we have could well have had our novelist as father or grandfather; and, as Bowersock pointed out, a more recently discovered text, an inscription on a sarcophagus, attests a Flavius Antonius Diogenes, demonstrating that at least one member of the family acquired Roman citizenship in the Flavian period.[56]

If we take AD 200 as a certain *terminus ante quem*, and ca. AD 150 as a possible *terminus ante quem*, have we any clues to how much earlier Antonius Diogenes actually wrote? Photius believed his work to be one of the sources of Lucian's *True histories*, and although John Morgan brought strong arguments against that view,[57] I don't think he showed that it must be wrong. If Photius was right, then Antonius' work was in circulation by no later than ca. AD 160.

But he could well be writing much earlier. Again geographical focus might be relevant. Thule, flaunted in Antonius Diogenes' title and important in his plot, had been brought to the Greek world's attention by Pytheas of Massalia, whence come several of the fifteen or so mentions of Thule in Strabo, as does at least one of those in the elder Pliny.[58] Then Thule seems to disappear from Greek literary consciousness: it figures in the technical work of Geminus, *Introduction to astronomy*, ca. AD 50, but is not mentioned in substantial *corpora* of the middle and later first century AD, those of Philo, Josephus or Plutarch, despite Plutarch's introduction in a Delphic dialogue of a fellow intellectual who had been to Britain and made a dedication to the Ocean, the *grammaticus* Demetrius of Tarsus.[59] The second

[52] Bowersock 1994, 38–40.

[53] *PIR* C 853: for the statue see Inan and Alföldi-Rosenbaum 1979; Zanker 1995, 245 Plate 135.

[54] *P.Oxy.* 4760 is dated to the second century, and perhaps the first half of the second century, by Del Corso 2010, 251, cf. Del Corso 2006, 95–6. Of the other papyri *P.Oxy.* 3012 is assigned to the late second or early third century, *PSI* 1177 to the early third century, *P.Oxy.* 4761 (which may be Antonius Diogenes) to the second half of the third century: cf. Del Corso 2010, 251.

[55] Another papyrus is dated ca. AD 150, *P.Mich.* inv. 5, cf. Stephens and Winkler 1995, 173–7, but is now thought not to be attributable to Antonius Diogenes.

[56] The sarcophagus was published by Jones and Smith 1994: cf. *SEG* 44.866.

[57] Morgan 1985. [58] Plin. *Nat* 2.187: cf. 4.104. [59] Plu. *De def. orac.* 2 = *Mor.* 410a.

century is different: Thule is mentioned by Dionysius of Alexandria, the Periegete, writing between AD 130 and 138;[60] by Vettius Valens,[61] writing between AD 152 and 162; by Ptolemy in his *Geography*,[62] written ca. AD 160, and by Aelius Herodianus,[63] writing between AD 161 and 180, who reports its summer days as lasting twenty hours out of twenty-four.

A nexus of events may have played a part in wider knowledge of Thule. First, the Roman expedition that reached and reported back on Thule while Agricola was governor of Britain: it took place in one of the years AD 80–3. Second, the publication by Tacitus early in AD 98 of his *Agricola*, mentioning that achievement.[64] Third, I suggest, the exploitation of Thule by Antonius Diogenes in Τὰ ὑπὲρ Θούλην ἄπιστα. I conjecture – but it can only be speculation – that Antonius Diogenes' attention was drawn to Thule by the expedition and the publicity given to it by Tacitus, and that in turn he is responsible for Thule's no fewer than seven lines in the *Periegesis* of Dionysius, a popularising, not a scientific work. Again all very precarious: but if correct, a date between AD 98 and AD 130 would follow.[65]

That date is in turn supported by Bowersock's proposal that the Faustinus to whom Antonius dedicated his work is the same as the patron of Martial and dedicatee of the third and fourth books of his epigrams. That suggested to Bowersock that Antonius' work belonged 'in the time of Domitian or a little later'.[66] Taking this together with the argument from the attention given to Thule we might tentatively put it in the decade following AD 98.

[60] D.P. 580–6. For his date cf. Bowie 1990b, 77 (Chapter 14, 305 in this volume); Counillon 1981. For Dionysius' perspective on the Roman Empire see Bowie 2004a (Chapter 16 in this volume); for discussion of all aspects of Dionysius see Lightfoot 2014.

[61] Vett.Val. 9 p.9.11 [62] 2.3.14, 2.6.22, 8.3.3. [63] *De prosodia catholica* 3.1 p. 319.9 Lentz.

[64] Tac. *Agr.* 10.

[65] For arguments that would put Antonius Diogenes much earlier, in the 50s AD, see Bowie 2007d (Chapter 32 in this volume). For a suggestion that the geographical range of his novel was in part a response to the sculptured reliefs of the Julio-Claudian Sebasteion at Aphrodisias see Bowie 2017c (Chapter 42 in Volume 3).

[66] Bowersock 1994, 37–8, followed by Stramaglia 1999, 97–100 and 2000, 15. For Martial's Faustinus cf. *PIR* ² F 127. The dedication by Antonius Diogenes is attested by Phot. *Cod.* 166, 111a, p.147.32–42 Henry: γράφει Φαυστίνωι ὅτι τε συνταττει περὶ τῶν ὑπὲρ Θούλην ἀπίστων, 'he writes to Faustinus that he is composing a work about the incredible things beyond Thule'. That Faustini were also to be found in Aphrodisias is shown by *IAphr2007* 4.118, a statue-base which Joyce Reynolds dated cautiously by its lettering to the second century AD: its text has her husband (unknown) honouring Iulia Faustina: Ἰουλίαν Φαυ[- *v.*]|στεῖναν τὴ[ν]| γυναῖκα-| *vac.* αὐτοῦ *vac.*

4 Achilles Tatius

The next in sequence is most probably Achilles Tatius. Two of their six papyri were dated by Stephens and Winkler around AD 150: *P.Oxy.* 3836[67] and *P.Mediolan.* 124.[68] The Milan papyrus was dated more cautiously to the end of the second century by Vogliano and Conca, but then to the late third century by Cavallo, thus leaving *P.Oxy.* 3836 as crucial evidence for a second-century text of Achilles Tatius.[69] Parsons 1989a allowed a mid- to late-second-century date. Stephens' date of around AD 150 was of course not precise, and she was choosing between rough dates of AD 175 and AD 150.[70] Immediately after the publication of Stephens and Winkler 1995 Cavallo pronounced in favour of a date in the first half of the second century AD, a verdict whose precision was doubted by Henrichs.[71] But even a date a few years before AD 175 would make it unlikely that we should see the βουκόλοι, 'Herdsfolk', of Achilles Tatius as a reflection of historical trouble with the βουκόλοι recorded by Cassius Dio for the year AD 172,[72] or that Laplace was correct to put the novel in the last quarter of the second century.[73] Although that is the earliest appearance of βουκόλοι in Roman imperial historiography, it is clear that they had been a thorn in the flesh of urban authorities since the Ptolemaic period.[74]

An argument for dating may be tentatively constructed on the basis of Achilles Tatius' use of the name Pantheia for the wife of Sostratus and mother of Leucippe.[75] This he will have done partly because of its lineage in erotic fiction. Xenophon's *Cyropaedia* had told the story of Araspas' infatuation with Pantheia, of Pantheia's faithfulness to her absent husband, and of her eventual suicide upon his corpse when he was killed in battle.[76]

[67] Published by Parsons 1989a.

[68] Published by Vogliano 1938: cf. Conca 1969. The number of papyri of Achilles Tatius now known stands at eight: cf. Henrichs 2011, 306 with n.17.

[69] Cavallo 1996, 16, 24 pl. 6, and 37–8: cf. Henrichs 2011, 308. Henrichs 2011, 312 n.44 rightly criticised my putting Achilles Tatius after AD 150 in *OCD*^{3}, though his reference to the 2003 reprint masks the date of the article (mid-1990s, for publication in 1996): the version of my Achilles Tatius article in the online *OCD*, published 2016, runs 'shown by papyri to be circulating by the mid-2nd cent. CE, it probably dates from the preceding decades'.

[70] The other two papyri from Oxyrhynchus, 3837 and 4948, are dated to the third century: see Parsons 1989b; Obbink and Trnka-Amrhein 2009.

[71] Cavallo 1996, 16, 36; Henrichs 2011, 308–9 with n.29.

[72] D.C. 72.4.1. The connection was proposed by Schwartz 1967, accepted e.g. by Bertrand 1988.

[73] Laplace 2007, 1–19. [74] See Rutherford 2000. [75] 1.3.6, 2.28.1 etc.

[76] X. *Cyr.* 5.1–17, 6.1.31–47, 7.3.2–15.

This seminal tale of love had been re-worked some time in the 120s–140s AD in a piece variously ascribed to the sophist Dionysius of Miletus and to his younger contemporary, the writer of rhetorical Τέχναι, *Technical treatises*, and holder of the imperial post *ab epistulis graecis*, 'Secretary for Greek correspondence', Caninius Celer.[77] Celer was mentioned as *ab epistulis graecis* by Aelius Aristides in an incident of January AD 148,[78] but the date of his *Araspas the lover of Pantheia* cannot be fixed. However unless it was satirical in a way that would have been perilous for its author, it was surely written before the Eastern provinces were titillated by reports of an affair between the emperor Lucius Verus and a *hetaera* from Smyrna also called Pantheia. I am inclined to draw the same conclusion for Achilles Tatius, which would allow us to import more precision than the papyrus data allow and set *Leucippe and Cleitophon* firmly before AD 164. When Achilles Tatius chose the name Pantheia for the conventionally moral mother of Leucippe, it was a name that connoted marital fidelity. By the time Apuleius wrote his *Metamorphoses*, almost certainly well after AD 164, the name's associations had broadened, and to its tang of erotic fiction had been added a whiff of Roman imperial misdemeanour – just as a name that might have evoked Augustinian saintliness in a work of fiction composed around 1990, Monica, will for a while continue to have added piquancy in a fictional text. Thus the name chosen by Apuleius for one of his lustful witches, Pantheia,[79] resonates on the level both of ideal and of satirical erotic fiction.

Another detail might support a pre-160 date suggested by the papyrus. The Alexandrian coinage in the reign of Pius breaks with earlier practice by representing a number of mythological subjects. Among these is the scene of Andromeda being liberated by Perseus.[80] This is one of two scenes which were apparently represented in a pair of paintings at the temple of Zeus Casius at Pelusium, viewed and interpreted by the characters of Achilles Tatius (3.6–8). That this painting was among the famous sights for tourists in Alexandria is of course sufficient to explain its appearance in both

[77] Philostr. *VS* 1.22.524. [78] *Or.* 50 (= *Sacred Tales* 4).57. [79] Apul. *Met.* 1.12 etc.

[80] My attention was drawn to the coins and to their possible link with the paintings in Achilles Tatius by Angelo Geissen in paper delivered to a colloquium on 'Coinage and identity in the Roman provinces' held in Oxford in September 2002. Milne 1933, 57 nos 2421 and 2422 recorded drachmae in the Ashmolean Museum collection with reverses depicting Perseus and Andromeda, minted in AD 160/161 (year ΚΔ, i.e. twenty-four, of Pius' reign): now *RPC* iv.4 temporary number 13952. This detail was not included in the published version of his paper, Geissen 2005.

Achilles Tatius and on coins. But if other indications point to a date some time before AD 160 for the novel, the myth's appearance on coins of the years AD 160/161 is perhaps not mere coincidence. Did the novelist react to the coins? Did the mint-master react to the novel?

5 Some Conclusions

What follows from these proposals for our understanding of the genre as a whole? It may be significant not simply that the context of the novel's birth becomes not the late Hellenistic Greek world but the Roman Empire, but that it becomes the earlier decades of the cultural renaissance that begins at the same time as, and is strongly influenced by, Philostratus' Second Sophistic. The background to the writers' own lives is not one of political chaos and uncertainty, one in which the reversals of fortune might be fancied once more to make Greek political units (of whatever size) the controlling powers of the Eastern Mediterranean, but one in which it has become progressively clearer in the three or four generations since Actium that Roman dominance was there to stay. That the novels, like declamations and much historiography, took readers and audiences out of this world has invited various historical explanations which I do not wish to debate again here. That the universe into which the novels took readers was one of strong personal emotions was of course not new in Greek literature (and their attention to the self has contemporary parallels in the philosophical writing of Plutarch and then Arrian). But that the principal emotion in this genre was ἔρως, 'desire', and persistent and idealistic ἔρως at that, cannot be fully (or even partly?) explained by changing social or political contexts. Perhaps Perry's 'Tuesday afternoon in July' suggestion was right after all. But not any July. A July in a decade when Greek rhetorical activity and Greek literary compositions of related sorts were attracting more and more writers and readers, speakers and audiences, and when the imperative to display *paideia* was becoming ever stronger; and a hot July in the booming city of Aphrodisias, presided over by its great cult of Aphrodite. The writer or writers of Aphrodisias hit on a winning formula. But if they had been playing with a literary experiment in a more remote city, Perinthus or Oenoanda or Tyana, would it ever have spread? Or would our twentieth- and twenty-first-century houses, bookshops and libraries be dominated by a quite different literary invention?

26 The Function of Mythology in Longus' *Daphnis and Chloe* (2003)

1 Introduction

The place of myth in Longus' *Daphnis and Chloe* is quite different from its place in other Greek novels. The most important single reason for this difference is that from the start Longus presents his miniature, pastoral romance as standing much closer to a traditional μῦθος, 'myth', than other writers of prose fiction set their narratives.

The other writers of 'ideal' romances furnished them with a discernibly historical setting, even if it is less easy to pin down the date at which we are to imagine the action of Xenophon or Achilles unfolding than it is that of the *Ninus and Semiramis*, of the *Metiochus and Parthenope*, or of the narratives of Chariton and Heliodorus.[1] The same is true of the twenty-four-book *Incredible things beyond Thule* of Antonius Diogenes, despite all its elements of magic and unreality, and of texts at the other end of the spectrum like Lollianus' *Phoenicica* and the Lucianic *Ass*.

The setting of Longus' *Daphnis and Chloe* is less clear cut.[2] True, the *ego*-narrative of the preface, like that of Achilles Tatius, suggests to the reader that the story presumed to follow in the rest of the papyrus roll will be a story not simply told to the writer in time contemporary with that writer's activity, but a story whose events, like those of Cleitophon's story in Achilles, are also set in that contemporary time. But the writer's description of a painting dedicated in a grotto sacred to the Nymphs (*pr.* 2) very rapidly calls any such assumption into question, The painting's scenes – women giving birth, children who had been exposed, sheep and goats feeding them and shepherds finding them – might in principle be located in any era. But tales of children being fed by animals and adopted by herdsmen are more numerous in mythological than in historical narratives: suckling by animals appears in the myths of Telephus, Melampus and Aegisthus.[3] On the other hand such fostering does figure in stories that Herodotus presents as

[1] For Chariton and Heliodorus see Jones 1992b; Hunter 1994; Morgan 1982.
[2] For a thorough review of recent discussions of the *prooemium* and inset tales see Wouters 1994.
[3] Hyginus *fab.* 87, Ael. *VH* 12.42: cf. Calder 1983.

historical – the rearing of Cyrus and the experiment of Psammetichus.[4] So these scenes, at least, may leave the reader undecided whether their explanation is more likely to emerge in a mythological or an historical context.

The remaining scenes mentioned offer little to resolve this uncertainty: 'young people trysting, an incursion of pirates, an invasion of enemies'. If the following phrase 'many other things and all of them concerning *eros*' is taken to be part of this sentence, as it is by Reeve 1982, then these three scenes, taken together and glossed as πάντα ἐρωτικά, 'all concerning *eros*', would locate the subject matter in the area of novelistic writing for any reader already acquainted with examples of such works, and that in turn would lead her to expect the context of 'an incursion of pirates, an invasion of enemies' to be the context habitual in such writing, i.e. historical. Perhaps by the eighty-fourth word of the preface, then, the matter is settled. Our reader is embarked on a tale set in a historical context. But I doubt if the signals given by the exposure and fostering themes are so easily overridden. Without the cue 'many other things and all of them concerning *eros*' only the 'incursion of pirates' points more to history than myth; and even myth harbours examples of piracy, whether in the *Odyssey* or in the myth of Dionysus and the Tyrrhenian pirates.[5] That cue 'many other things and all of them concerning *eros*' only *invites* a novelistic reading, it does not compel it: again, plenty 'things … concerning *eros*' in myth. So I would conclude rather that the preface leaves the reader uncertain whether to expect a mythical or an historical context.

The same uncertainty persists when the narrative itself begins. Mytilene, its canals spanned by bridges of white marble (1.1.1) suggests a city of the Hellenistic or Greco-Roman period; the names of the goatherd and his wife, Lamon and Myrtale, have no mythical resonance. But again the *Odyssey* boasts cities, that of Alcinous splendid enough to arouse Odysseus' admiration (Od. 7.43–5). It is, I think, only with the couple's decision to name the exposed boy Daphnis that our interpretation seems finally to be closed: ὡς δ' ἂν καὶ τοὔνομα τοῦ παιδίου ποιμενικὸν δοκοίη, Δάφνιν αὐτὸν ἔγνωσαν καλεῖν, 'and so that even his name might seem to be pastoral, they decided to call him Daphnis' (1.3.2). Longus here throws down a hermeneutic clue for the educated reader. For the rustic couple the name Daphnis has *already* pastoral associations. They are thus located in a time *after* a famous pastoral Daphnis: and the reader is expected to think of the Daphnis whose woes were sung by Thyrsis in Theocritus *Idyll* 1, of whom Lycidas imagines

[4] 1.108.2–119, 2.2.2.

[5] Od. 3.73, 16.426, 17.425; *h.Bacch.* (7).

Tityrus singing in Theocritus *Idyll* 7.73–7, about whose encounter with Damoetas Theocritus *Idyll* 6 may also tell. For the characters of Theocritus *Idylls* 1 and 7 that Daphnis belonged to a pastoral mythology, a mythology already treated in a higher genre of poetry by a Stesichorus whom I am content to see as the great Stesichorus of Himera.[6] Longus' brief sentence identifies his goatherd as belonging to a generation for whom that Daphnis is also remote and mythical, as well as prompting his reader to prepare for further Theocritean allusions.

From this point a reader settles down to interpret the story as set broadly in the historical past, though the introduction of Theocritean allusion complicates her reading by offering a choice between the 'ideal' (and unreal) and the 'real', as well as between 'mythical' and 'historical'. Certain features pull a reading towards the ideal and unreal: the extreme naivety of Daphnis and Chloe; the apparent isolation of their small pastoral community from the city of Mytilene, no more than forty kilometres away; the recurrent allusions to the poetic world of Theocritus. But other features anchor the narrative in the 'real' – by which I mean no more, of course, than the fictitiously real. Among these features I include the cowherd Dorcon, who is sexually attracted to Chloe, and who knows what that attraction is and how to satisfy it;[7] the sudden incursion of pirates – the reader must by now have heavily discounted any such realisation of the preface's picture – which eliminates Dorcon and occasions Daphnis and Chloe to bathe together and become aware of each other's bodies;[8] the vintage-scene at the opening of Book 2; and the holiday-cruise of the Methymnan *jeunesse dorée* which sets off a train of events culminating in a small-scale Thucydidean war between Mytilene and Methymna.[9] By the end of the fourth and final book we seem to be unambiguously in a historical and real context, a Mytilene with an elite bearing traditional names like Megacles and discharging the traditional obligations of euergetism, χορηγίαι, 'financing of choruses', and τριηραρχίαι, 'commanding (i.e. financing) of triremes'.[10] Even here, however, the unreal retains a voice: Daphnis and Chloe continue to herd for the rest of their life – whereas elsewhere we are led to suppose that even in Daphnisland only young people herd, and that in later life women manage households while men dig, plough, sow and reap. Not only do they

[6] Stesich. fr. 279 *PMGF* = 323 Finglass. There is not space here for me to offer my arguments against the view that this fragment (preserved by Ael. *VH* 10.18) is not by the sixth-century Stesichorus. For such an attribution see Lehnus 1975; Bowie 2012b (Chapter 23 in Volume 1); further discussion Rutherford 2015.

[7] 1.15–21, 29. [8] 1.28–32. [9] 2.12–3.2. [10] 4.35.3.

continue herding, they have children who replicate themselves, a son whom they have fostered by a goat and a younger daughter whom they entrust to a sheep, and who are given names Philopoemen and Agele, names far more redolent of goats than those of the storied couple.[11]

This, then, is the texture of Longus' main narrative. The distance Longus places between its universe and that of mythology is further defined by the manner in which characters make paradeigmatic use of myth just as historical and real-life or realistic characters do. The three principal uses of myth are in the three tales of males' domination of females at 1.27.2–4, 2.34 and 3.23.1–4 – told respectively by Daphnis, by Lamon and then again by Daphnis. But there are also two outliers: the speeches of Dorcon and Daphnis in their competition at 1.16.1–5, and the illustrations of the birth and miracles of Dionysus in the temple set in Dionysophanes' garden at 4.3.2. I set aside from the 'myths' in *Daphnis and Chloe* the story told by Philetas of his encounter with the boy Eros in his garden: it has some mythical features, and its function might be argued to have a bearing on that of the inset mythical tales, but it is presented as an account of an event roughly contemporary with the main action, narrated by a principal participant, and these features mark it as non-mythical.

The speeches of Dorcon and Daphnis in their beauty competition at 1.16.1–5 are entertaining chiefly as a miniaturised *controversia* that is surprising in a rustic and specifically bucolic setting. The claims of Dorcon play up to that transposition. His superiority to Daphnis is commensurate with that of his cattle over Daphnis' goats. He compares his white complexion to milk and his reddish-blond hair to corn ripe for harvesting, whereas Daphnis is 'black like a wolf'. His twice repeated point that Daphnis was fostered by an animal is answered by Daphnis with the claim that Zeus too was fostered by a goat, and that his association with goats makes him no more malodorous than it does Pan. As for his having no beard, neither does Dionysus, who is superior to satyrs who do. These learned precedents come surprisingly from Daphnis, even when we recall that Daphnis and Chloe had been taught by their pastoral foster parents to read and write (1.8.1): nothing had led us to expect that a goatherd whose foster-parents did not even recognise the standard iconography of the boy Eros (1.8.2) would have such a command of even basic mythology, or would be able to allude to the suckling of Zeus by Amaltheia. Nevertheless, once we have

[11] 4.39. For the resonance of the name Philopoemen see Bowie 2019b (Chapter 43 in this volume); Bowie 2019g *ad loc.*

heard these arguments, we cannot simply forget them. Hard though they are to reconcile with his persistent inability to recognise love and all his works, they add a streak of the mythologically learned sophist to our conception of Daphnis.

2 The First Inset Tale

That prepares us for the first of the three major mythological *exempla*. Longus uses this first *exemplum* to close his leisurely *ecphrasis* of the hot summer which exacerbates the couple's mutual but still undiagnosed desires. It immediately follows the episode in which Daphnis, apparently by now conscious of some of the things he would like to do, if not why, thrusts his hands into Chloe's bosom to extract a fugitive cicada – an episode which, like many, tests the extent of the young people's sexual innocence.[12]

The telling of the story is occasioned by the call of a wood-pigeon: 'There delighted them one day a wood-pigeon which sang a pastoral song from the forest, and when Chloe wanted to learn what it was saying Daphnis instructed her, acting as the story-teller of the oft-told tale' (1.27.1).

That concise introductory sentence sets up many expectations. Its opening word, ἔτερψεν, 'there delighted them', adds the song to the list of their summer pleasures (the τοιάσδε τέρψεις, 'such pleasures as these', of 1.28.1): we may reasonably expect the story itself to be, like Longus' own, a κτῆμα τερπνόν, 'pleasant possession' (*pr.* 3). This expectation is reinforced by his description of Daphnis' telling as 'instructing' – we expect a *mis-enabyme* of Longus' four-book work – and by his enigmatic qualification of the bird's song as βουκολικόν, 'pastoral'. It turns out to be 'pastoral' not simply because it is being heard by shepherds but because it tells a story of herding. That it is likely not simply to be 'pleasant' but to be concerned with ἔρως, 'love' or 'desire', is perhaps suggested by the frequent appearance of the pigeon as a symbol of love.[13] We may well expect Daphnis to use it in a covert way to engage in some ostensibly innocent sexual contact with Chloe, just as he had used the cicada and the episode in which he ἐδίδασκεν, 'taught her', to play the pan-pipe that immediately preceded it (1.24.4).

The terms used to describe Daphnis' activity as a narrator are also important. The verb μυθολογῶ, 'I tell a myth', recurs twice as a description of Daphnis' telling of the third tale, that of Echo (3.22.4, 23.5); μυθολόγημα,

[12] 1.26: and for the extent of reader's complicity, cf. Goldhill 1995.
[13] Cf. Chalk 1960, 40 n.61.

'a myth told', is the noun applied to Lamon's tale of Syrinx (2.35.1). Knowledge of all μυθολογία ἐρωτική, 'mythology to do with love or desire', is also ascribed to Gnathon at 4.17.3 – a knowledge of myths of ἔρως which in his case has been acquired in city *symposia*, and which he knows how to apply as *exempla* to persuade Daphnis to succumb to his advances. The use of the verb μυθολογῶ at 1.27.1 leaves us in no doubt that Daphnis is telling a μῦθος, and may encourage us to expect his use of it to be exemplary.

It is less certain that this μῦθος is, as Daphnis claims, a much-told story. The story is not told elsewhere in surviving texts, and Longus is as likely to be inventing it as he is to be vying with another well-known version.[14] Telling a μῦθος was one of the standard rhetorical *progymnasmata*.

Contrary to what I have suggested would have been a reader's expectations, the story is neither explicitly about love nor is it manifestly 'pleasant':

> ἦν παρθένος, παρθένε, οὕτω καλὴ καὶ ἔνεμε βοῦς πολλὰς οὕτως ἐν ὕληι. ἦν δὲ ἄρα καὶ ὠιδικὴ καὶ ἐτέρποντο αἱ βόες αὐτῆς τῆι μουσικῆι, καὶ ἔνεμεν οὔτε καλαύροπος πληγῆι οὔτε κέντρου προσβολῆι, ἀλλὰ καθίσασα ὑπὸ πίτυν καὶ στεφανωσαμένη πίτυϊ ἦιδε Πᾶνα καὶ τὴν Πίτυν, καὶ αἱ βόες τῆι φωνῆι παρέμενον. παῖς οὐ μακρὰν νέμων βοῦς, καὶ αὐτὸς καλὸς καὶ ὠιδικὸς ὡς ἡ παρθένος, φιλονεικήσας πρὸς τὴν μελωιδίαν, μείζονα ὡς ἀνήρ, ἡδεῖαν ὡς παῖς φωνὴν ἀντεπεδείξατο, καὶ τῶν βοῶν ὀκτὼ τὰς ἀρίστας ἐς τὴν ἰδίαν ἀγέλην θέλξας ἀπεβουκόλησεν. ἄχθεται ἡ παρθένος τῆι βλάβηι τῆς ἀγέλης, τῆι ἥττηι τῆς ὠιδῆς, καὶ εὔχεται τοῖς θεοῖς ὄρνις γενέσθαι πρὶν οἴκαδε ἀφικέσθαι. πείθονται οἱ θεοὶ καὶ ποιοῦσι τήνδε τὴν ὄρνιν, ὄρειον ὡς ἡ παρθένος, μουσικὴν ὡς ἐκείνη. καὶ ἔτι νῦν ἄιδουσα μηνύει τὴν συμφοράν, ὅτι βοῦς ζητεῖ πεπλανημένας.
>
> Once there was a maid, maid, as beautiful as you, and she pastured her many cows, as you pasture, in a wood. Now it seems she was also a singer, and her cows enjoyed her music, and she would pasture them without the blow of a stick or the prod of a goad – she would sit down under a pine and wearing a garland of pine would sing of Pan and Pitys, and the cows would stay close to her voice. A boy pasturing cows not far away, he too handsome, and a singer like the maid, moved to rivalry with her song gave a competing display of his voice which was louder, since he was a man, but sweet, since he was a boy: and in pastoral rivalry he charmed her eight best cows into his own. The girl is distressed at the loss to her herd, at her defeat in song, and prays to the gods to be turned into a bird before she reaches home. The gods assent and make her into this bird, a hill-dweller like the girl, musical like her. And to this day she uses her song to proclaim her misfortune, singing that she is searching for her strayed cows.
>
> Longus, *Daphnis and Chloe* 1.27.2–4

[14] As suggested by Schönberger 1989 *ad loc.*

That the myth was one of metamorphosis might superficially support the expectation of something 'pleasant', since telling μῦθοι of metamorphosis was reckoned by rhetors to contribute sweetness.[15]

The juxtaposition παρθένος, παρθένε, 'a maid, maid', followed by the numerous details in which the girl resembles Chloe – for example Phatta's pine garland –[16] and the παῖς, 'boy', resembles Daphnis, suggests that Daphnis expects Chloe to learn something from Phatta's fate. The most obvious lesson is that Daphnis as a male is stronger than she,[17] and that competing with him could have an unpleasant outcome. The effect is increased by the fact that neither girl nor boy is given a name. That the girl was turned into a φάττα, 'dove', may allow the inference that this was her human name, but we are not told this. By making both the girl and her musical rival cowherds Daphnis may hint that the cowherd Dorcon is a threat to Chloe in a way that he himself, a goatherd, never is. The detail that Phatta's cows respond to music prepares Chloe and the reader for Dorcon's instructions to Chloe that will save Daphnis from the pirates (1.29.2).[18]

But there are clear limits to any parallel between the boy and girl and Daphnis and Chloe. They herd larger quadrupeds, cows, and show no signs of love for each other; and it is hard to read the annexation of the cows as an allegory of rape or seduction, even though the term ἀποβουκολῶ, 'I entice away a herd', is used elsewhere of quasi-erotic enticement.[19] The girl, unlike Chloe, seems to be aware of love, since she sings of Pan and Pitys. This story within Daphnis' tale is explicitly of love, like the later μῦθος of Pan's love for Syrinx and Echo, and like them and Phatta's own story it ends in unhappy metamorphosis: Boreas and Pan were rivals for the nymph Pitys' love, her preference for Boreas led Pan to violence which resulted in her death, and she was turned into a pine-tree.[20] The reader can see Pitys' relation to Chloe, attractive both to Daphnis and to Dorcon, but Daphnis need not be supposed to see this, nor need even know what Phatta's song said happened between Pan and Pitys: he might, for all we are told, simply be picking out those elements in the 'oft-told tale' which made sense to him in his (as yet) innocent condition.

[15] For γλυκύτης, 'sweetness', see Hermog. Id. 2.4.18–20 Rabe (= ii 357.6 Spengel); for tales of metamorphosis Men.Rh. iii 393.1–5 Spengel.

[16] 1.27.2: cf. already Chloe's pine-garland 1.24.1–2. [17] Cf. 1.28.2, 2.9.1.

[18] The bird φάττα is said by Porph. *Abst.* 4.16 to be sacred to Persephone, for whose Attic name Phersephatta he gives an ingenious but improbable etymology παρὰ τὸ φέρβειν τὴν φάτταν, 'from feeding the dove'. But Longus' story has no obvious link with Persephone, and in telling it he avoids the term for a young girl κόρη that was also a name for Persephone.

[19] Luc. *Bis Acc.* 13.

[20] Cf. 2.7.6, 39.3, *Gp.* 2.10, Luc. *DDeor.* 2.4 (where the story is grouped with that of Echo), Nonn. 42.259ff.; in Latin literature Prop. 1.18.20.

One further lesson may be offered by Phatta's prayer. So far in Longus' story only Dryas has prayed to a god (1.6.1); Dorcon has sacrificed a goat, but Daphnis and Chloe were not themselves involved (1.12.5). The introduction of a prayer, and one quickly answered, into the inset tale prepares characters and readers for Daphnis and Chloe's own resort to prayer when trouble comes.[21]

So something is taught, something may even be learned. But the lessons concern male dominance and religion, not the workings of ἔρως – these only the reader glimpses through the window of Phatta's song from an angle closed off to the characters in the story. And indeed whether anything at all is learned we cannot be sure, for Longus closes the tale with an abrupt transition to autumn and no indication of Chloe's response to the story she has been told.

3 The Second Inset Tale

The second tale is told towards the end of Book 2 (2.34), about as far from the end of the book as the tale of Phatta is from the end of Book 1. The first tale was followed immediately by Daphnis' seizure by pirates and his escape as a result of Chloe playing the panpipe given her by the dying Dorcon, thus attracting his plundered cows off the pirates' boat and back to land. The second tale closely follows Chloe's capture by the Methymnans and her release as a result of Pan's miraculous intervention. The couple and their families immediately celebrate by sacrificing their best she-goat to the nymphs; the next day they sacrifice the leading he-goat to Pan, Philetas joins the ensuing celebration, and while his son Tityrus runs off to fetch his σῦριγξ, 'panpipe', so that he can demonstrate his skill, second to Pan's, Daphnis' father Lamon expounds τὸν περὶ τῆς σύριγγος … μῦθον, 'the myth of the panpipe (*syrinx*)'.

Lamon offers this μῦθος as one which was sung to him by a Sicilian goatherd for a fee of a goat and a panpipe. Sicilian goatherds are as intrusive in Lesbos as the Tyrian pirates who carried off Daphnis, and Longus' unusual breach of plausibility marks a literary allusion, chiefly, if not wholly, to the poetry of Theocritus. We are not to understand the goatherd to be Theocritus himself (he was, after all, no goatherd) but rather to be the Pan-fearing and unnamed goatherd of Theocritus *Idyll* 1, who persuaded Thyrsis to sing his tale of Daphnis for the reward of a splendid cup and three milkings of a goat.[22] The panpipe which here replaces the cup is a thematically appropriate payment,

[21] 2.20.3, 21.3. For further possible links to the novel's themes see Kossaifi 2012.

[22] Theoc. 1.23–60.

and it too has a model within Thyrsis' song, when the dying Daphnis hands his pipe to Pan.[23] That Lamon's story has a similar pedigree to one about the mythical Daphnis may add to our inclination to relate it to Chloe. The detail of a panpipe passing from one herdsman to another prepares us for the episode's conclusion, when Philetas bestows his man-sized panpipe on Daphnis, thus freeing Daphnis to dedicate his own small panpipe to Pan.

The tale is almost exactly the same length as that of Phatta. It runs:

> ἡ σῦριγξ αὕτη τὸ ἀρχαῖον οὐκ ἦν ὄργανον ἀλλὰ παρθένος καλὴ καὶ τὴν φωνὴν μουσική· αἶγας ἔνεμεν, Νύμφαις συνέπαιζεν, ᾖδεν οἷον νῦν. Πάν, ταύτης νεμούσης παιζούσης ἀιδούσης, προσελθὼν ἔπειθεν ἐς ὅ τι ἔχρῃζε, καὶ ἐπηγγέλλετο τὰς αἶγας πάσας θήσειν διδυμοτόκους. ἡ δὲ ἐγέλα τὸν ἔρωτα αὐτοῦ, οὐδὲ ἐραστὴν ἔφη δέξεσθαι μήτε τράγον μήτε ἄνθρωπον ὁλόκληρον. ὁρμᾶι διώκειν ὁ Πὰν πρὸς βίαν· ἡ Σῦριγξ ἔφευγε καὶ τὸν Πᾶνα καὶ τὴν βίαν· φεύγουσα κάμνουσα ἐς δόνακας κρύπτεται, εἰς ἕλος ἀφανίζεται. Πὰν τοὺς δόνακας ὀργῆι τεμών, τὴν κόρην οὐχ εὑρών, τὸ πάθος μαθών, τὸ ὄργανον νοεῖ, καὶ τοὺς καλάμους ἐμπνεῖ κηρῶι συνδήσας ἀνίσους, καθ' ὅ τι καὶ ὁ ἔρως ἄνισος αὐτοῖς· καὶ ἡ τότε παρθένος καλὴ νῦν ἐστι σῦριγξ μουσική.
>
> This panpipe (*syrinx*) in olden days was not an instrument but a maid, beautiful and with a tuneful voice. She would pasture her goats, she would play with the Nymphs, she would sing as she does now. While she was pasturing, playing, singing, Pan approached her and tried to cajole her into doing what he wanted, and promised to make all her goats have twin kids.[24] But she laughed at his love, and said that she would not take a lover who was not entirely either a goat or a man. Pan lunged in pursuit to force her. Syrinx ran away from Pan and force. Running away, getting tired, she hides among reeds, she disappears into a marsh. Pan, cutting the reeds in anger, not finding the girl, understanding what had happened, devises the instrument and blows into the reeds, binding together reeds of unequal length just as their love had been unequal. And she who was then a fair maid is now a tuneful Syrinx.[25]
>
> Longus, *Daphnis and Chloe* 2.34

[23] Theoc. 1.128–30, cf. also the gift of pipes at 6.43. However the similarity between this scene and Verg. *Ecl.* 2 – where Corydon refers to Pan's invention of the panpipe, and then to a panpipe presented by Damoetas to him on his death – has suggested that both draw on Philetas, cf. DuQuesnay 1981, 60 with nn.192–200, Bowie 1985a, 82 (Chapter 8, 149–50 in this volume).

[24] Perhaps recalling the goat promised to Thyrsis for milking, Theoc. 1.25. The power to make goats bear twins is credited to Pan by Philip *AP* 6.99 = *GP* 15, cf. Call. *Ap.* 54 (ewes), but is an obvious symbol of pastoral plenty: cf. [Theoc.] 8.45.

[25] The aetiological tale of Pan and Syrinx is also told by Ach. Tat. 8.6.7–11, who attaches it to a cave at Ephesus. The accounts are close, and if there is any dependence that of Longus on Ach. Tat.'s fuller narrative is more likely, *pace* Rohde 1914, 536 n.1.

The tale makes several contributions to the narrative. First, it reinforces the perception of Pan's power displayed in the preceding account of his miraculous intervention, and transfers it to the sexual sphere: the violence of his pursuit of Syrinx drove her to self-destruction. Secondly, it carries further the lesson of Daphnis' own inset tale at 1.27, that males are stronger than females. That tale had invited its hearer, Chloe, to compare herself to the cow-girl metamorphosed into a wood pigeon, who herself sang of Pan's fatal pursuit of Pitys. Here Pan's violence has become the main theme, and one effect of this tale's relation to the first is to invite both Chloe and readers to ask whether Chloe (whom by now readers know will be the subject of a μῦθος, 2.27.2) risks not simply subordination to her fellow herdsman, like the cow-girl, but destruction as a result of resisting male sexual violence.

The reader's answer must surely be negative. Syrinx may resemble Chloe, but she is also different in that she moves freely among divinities, Pan and the Nymphs, and may be thought of as a Nymph herself. Daphnis may resemble Pan, but he is entirely human, despite his goatish upbringing, and neither earlier nor later in the story is it ever hinted that he might try to rape Chloe. Of course there is never any need to, for the love of Daphnis and Chloe for each other is reciprocal, ἴσος, 'equal', not ἄνισος, 'unequal'.

It is important, then, that this is not a tale told by Daphnis to Chloe, which might underline his superiority, but a tale told to them both, even if Longus underlines the male perspective of the tale by putting it in the mouth of Daphnis' father and not Chloe's.

It is even more important how Daphnis and Chloe respond to the tale. After its telling Longus invites readers to admire it, having Philetas compliment it as a μῦθον ᾠδῆς γλυκύτερον, 'a myth sweeter than song'. Longus thus takes an opportunity neglected after his other inset tales, but much exploited by other writers telling tales within tales.[26] The term ᾠδή, 'song', draws attention to the verse-like impression given by Longus' short and chiefly asyndetic cola, a style which invited intoned delivery and was condemned as 'song' in contemporary sophistic oratory.[27] Then Philetas gives a virtuoso performance on his large panpipe (it has now been delivered) followed by a pantomimic representation by Dryas of different elements in the vintage (thus recalling the opening scene of Book 2). Daphnis and Chloe realise as rapidly as does the reader that now that all other main characters have performed it is their turn: what will they do? They leap up and give a pantomime performance of the myth of Syrinx, but one which is significantly different from Lamon's tale:

[26] Cf. Pl. *Phdr.* 257c1–2; Hld. 3.4.4; Theoc. (of inset songs) 1.146–8, 15.144–6.

[27] Cf. D.Chr. 32.68; Luc. *Demon.* 12; Philostr. *VS* 1.8.492, 2.28.620.

> ὁ μὲν ἱκέτευε πείθων, ἡ δὲ ἀμελοῦσα ἐμειδία· ὁ μὲν ἐδίωκε καὶ ἐπ' ἄκρων τῶν ὀνύχων ἔτρεχε τὰς χηλὰς μιμούμενος, ἡ δὲ ἐνέφαινε τὴν κάμνουσαν ἐν τῇ φυγῇ. ἔπειτα Χλόη μὲν εἰς τὴν ὕλην ὡς εἰς ἕλος κρύπτεται, Δάφνις δὲ λαβὼν τὴν Φιλητᾶ σύριγγα τὴν μεγάλην ἐσύρισε γοερὸν ὡς ἐρῶν, ἐρωτικὸν ὡς πείθων, ἀνακλητικὸν ὡς ἐπιζητῶν.
>
> He pleaded with her, cajoling, but she smiled and paid no attention. He pursued her and ran on the tips of his toes, imitating hooves; she gave the appearance of the Nymph growing tired in her attempt to escape. Then Chloe hid herself in the wood as if in a marsh, and Daphnis took Philetas' panpipe, the big one, and played a plaintive tune of desire, a lover's tune of cajoling, a tune of a searcher calling her back.
>
> Longus, *Daphnis and Chloe* 2.37.1–3

The ballet suppresses the violence of Pan's sexual pursuit and of his cutting of the reeds into which Syrinx has been transformed, and moderates the laughter of Syrinx's scorn to a smile. Some interpreters have been tempted by the notion that in their innocence the young couple have missed the integral element of violence. To me this seems an unpersuasive reading. Their meeting with Philetas near the beginning of the book has considerably advanced their theoretical understanding of the nature of Eros, even if they have not been able to work out how to put theory into practice. Both Lamon's tale and Longus' account of their ballet identifies Pan's stimulus as ἔρως.[28] Moreover, shortly after the ballet, when Daphnis and Chloe exchange oaths in the Nymphs' cave, Chloe extracts from Daphnis a second oath because she knows, she says, that Pan is ἐρωτικός, 'given to ἔρως, and ἄπιστος 'inconstant', that he had experienced ἔρως for Pitys and Syrinx, and that he persistently harasses Nymphs, so that he might fail to punish Daphnis if he too were promiscuous.[29] As well as reminding us that Daphnis and Chloe's love is wholly reciprocal, this exchange of oaths provides the reader with evidence that their bowdlerisation of the tale of Syrinx was not due to naive inattention or a fit of absence of mind. They have become aware of the phenomenon of male importunity in sexual matters, and, to the extent that they are ready to make the tale of Pan and Syrinx briefly their own, they are at one in eliminating its harsher side.

Taken together with the first tale this carefully contextualised tale of Syrinx establishes a clear gulf between the human desires of Daphnis and Chloe and the self-assertive lust of the god Pan.

[28] ἔρωτα, 'love' or 'desire' … ἐραστήν, 'lover', 2.34.2: ἔρως, 'love', 2.34.3; ἐρῶν, 'desiring', … ἐρωτικόν, 'expressing desire', 2.37.3.

[29] 2.39.2–4.

4 The Third Inset Tale

The third tale comes in the second half of Book 3, not quite so near its end as the others stand in their books. Daphnis has at last been taught how to make love by Lycaenion (3.18–19) and has returned to Chloe, but is afraid to go further than kissing her because of Lycaenion's warning that she will weep and bleed. It is spring (3.24.1) and Longus brings round a headland a boat whose rowers' chant is echoed by the crescent-shaped gulf (3.21). The naive Chloe wonders if the echo comes from another as yet unseen boat (3.22.3), and Daphnis kisses her and begins μυθολογεῖν τὸν μῦθον, 'to tell her the tale', of Echo, asking a μισθός, 'fee', of another ten kisses εἰ διδάξειε, 'if he gives her this instruction'. His μῦθος goes thus:

> Νυμφῶν, ὦ κόρη, πολὺ γένος, Μελίαι καὶ Δρυάδες καὶ Ἕλειοι· πᾶσαι καλαί, πᾶσαι μουσικαί. [καὶ] μιᾶς τούτων θυγάτηρ Ἠχὼ γίνεται, θνητὴ μὲν ὡς ἐκ πατρὸς θνητοῦ, καλὴ δὲ ὡς ἐκ μητρὸς καλῆς. τρέφεται μὲν ὑπὸ Νυμφῶν, παιδεύεται δὲ ὑπὸ Μουσῶν συρίζειν, αὐλεῖν, τὰ πρὸς λύραν, τὰ πρὸς κιθάραν, πᾶσαν ᾠδήν, ὥστε καὶ παρθενίας εἰς ἄνθος ἀκμάσασα ταῖς Νύμφαις συνεχόρευε, ταῖς Μούσαις συνῇδεν· ἄρρενας δὲ ἔφευγε πάντας, καὶ ἀνθρώπους καὶ θεούς, φιλοῦσα τὴν παρθενίαν· ὁ Πὰν ὀργίζεται τῆι κόρηι, τῆς μουσικῆς φθονῶν, τοῦ κάλλους μὴ τυχών, καὶ μανίαν ἐμβάλλει τοῖς ποιμέσι καὶ τοῖς αἰπόλοις. οἱ δὲ ὥσπερ κύνες ἢ λύκοι διασπῶσιν αὐτὴν καὶ ῥίπτουσιν εἰς πᾶσαν τὴν γῆν ἔτι ἄιδοντα τὰ μέλη. καὶ τὰ μέλη Γῆ χαριζομένη Νύμφαις ἔκρυψε πάντα καὶ ἐτήρησε τὴν μουσικὴν καὶ γνώμηι Μουσῶν ἀφίησι φωνὴν καὶ μιμεῖται πάντα καθάπερ τότε ἡ κόρη, θεούς, ἀνθρώπους, ὄργανα, θηρία· μιμεῖται καὶ αὐτὸν συρίττοντα τὸν Πᾶνα. ὁ δὲ ἀκούσας ἀναπηδᾶι καὶ διώκει κατὰ τῶν ὀρῶν, οὐκ ἐρῶν τυχεῖν ἀλλ' ἢ τοῦ μαθεῖν τίς ἐστιν ὁ λανθάνων μαθητής.

> Of the Nymphs, young girl, there are many kinds, Ash-nymphs, Oak-nymphs, Marsh-nymphs, all beautiful, all tuneful. One of these had a daughter Echo, mortal since she was of a mortal father, beautiful since she was of a beautiful mother. She was fostered by the Nymphs, she was instructed by the Muses to play the panpipe, to play the pipe, accompanying the lyre, accompanying the cithara, every sort of song. And as she matured into the flower of maidenhood she would also dance with the Nymphs, she would sing with the Muses. And she shunned all males, both men and gods, because she cherished her maidenhood. Pan is angry with the girl, envying her tunefulness, unable to possess her beauty, and strikes madness into the shepherds and goatherds. They, like dogs or wolves, tear her apart and scatter her still singing limbs over the whole earth; and Earth, out of kindness to the Nymphs, hid all her limbs, and preserved her

> tunefulness, and by decree of the Muses has a voice and imitates everything just as the girl once did, gods, men, instruments, beasts. She imitates too Pan himself playing his panpipe, and when he hears it he leaps up and pursues it over the hills, desiring nothing more than to discover who is his invisible pupil.
>
> Longus, *Daphnis and Chloe* 3.23

This is without question a tale in which the violence of Pan again plays a major role, as it did in the allusion to Pitys in the first tale and in the second's story of Syrinx. But the motive is not only sexual: like the cowboy in the story of Phatta, Pan is jealous of Echo's musical gifts, so this third story combines the motives for male self-assertion presented in the two earlier tales. It is difficult to read it as a further warning to Chloe or premonition to the reader that Daphnis' relationship to Chloe might degenerate into violence or envy. Both have already had examples of Pan's violence in satisfying his sexual appetite in the first and second tales, and no change in Daphnis has been perceived. Both have also seen that the Pan of the Mytilenean χώρα, 'countryside', has the welfare of the couple at heart, and that in their story his anger is directed against their enemies. Moreover the difference between Echo and Chloe is clearly set out from the start: Echo is daughter of a nymph, Chloe is a mortal girl – the opening carefully juxtaposes, for contrast, the terms Νυμφῶν, 'Of the Nymphs', and ὦ κόρη, 'young girl'. True, once we learn that Echo had a mortal father, she too is termed κόρη (3.23.3), but by then we have established a conception of her as different from Chloe. She differs in other respects too: she rejects all men, whereas Chloe let the dying Dorcon kiss her and would let Daphnis do much more if only she knew how. Her first action when Daphnis finishes telling the story is not, of course, to run away home, but give him not simply the ten promised kisses but many more (3.23.5). Chloe is musical, but her skill is less than that of Daphnis (1.24.4), and it never excites his jealousy.

A related reading of the second and third tales might interpret them as a warning to Chloe not to attach too great importance to her virginity. In support of this it might be noted that, when Moschus treats Pan's love for Echo in a short and witty poem,[30] his Echo loves a satyr: Longus very probably knew this poem, and might be ostentatiously changing the story to one where Echo was too attached to her virginity. But this reading also founders on the absence of any indication that Chloe sets great store by her virginity.

[30] Moschus fr. 2 Gow.

It seems to me rather that two contributions are made to the work by this tale. First, the difference between the mutual and reciprocal desires of Daphnis and Chloe and the extreme form of sexual passion exemplified by Pan is once more emphasised. Second, the role of Daphnis as a teacher of Chloe is restated. We have known since Daphnis lost his virginity to Lycaenion that the story cannot progress until he has the courage to put his lesson into practice with Chloe, and we have discovered that he lacks that courage. That he is prepared to maintain the stance of her teacher, as he had earlier been in playing the panpipe (1.24.4) and in telling her the story of Phatta, and particularly an instructor in a tale of ἔρως, reassures us that the story will not grind to a halt but that he is likely in the end to teach her how to make love.

5 Interpreting the Inset Tales

What, then, have the three tales done for the reader? They have established a pattern of domination of females by males, a pattern which in the case of Pan takes the form of violent sexual pursuit. That pattern is one which contrasts with the behaviour of Daphnis and Chloe so far in Longus' story, and which at no point earlier or later is imitated by them. Attempts have indeed been made to suggest that they offer important *analogies* to Daphnis and Chloe.

Before briefly considering two of these, I shall even more briefly take account of the Dionysiac myths that adorn the temple of Dionysus in the garden of Dionysophanes in Book 4:

> εἶχε δὲ καὶ ἔνδοθεν ὁ νεὼς Διονυσιακὰς γραφάς· Σεμέλην τίκτουσαν, Ἀριάδνην καθεύδουσαν, Λυκοῦργον δεδεμένον, Πενθέα διαιρούμενον· ἦσαν καὶ Ἰνδοὶ νικώμενοι καὶ Τυρρηνοὶ μεταμορφούμενοι· πανταχοῦ Σάτυροι <πατοῦντες>, πανταχοῦ Βάκχαι χορεύουσαι· οὐδὲ ὁ Πὰν ἠμέλητο· ἐκαθέζετο δὲ καὶ αὐτὸς συρίζων ἐπὶ πέτρας, ὅμοιος ἐνδιδόντι κοινὸν μέλος καὶ τοῖς πατοῦσι καὶ ταῖς χορευούσαις.
>
> And the temple also had within it Dionysiac paintings: Semele giving birth, Ariadne sleeping, Lycurgus bound, Pentheus being torn apart. There were both Indians being vanquished and Tyrrhenians being transformed. Everywhere Satyrs <treading grapes>, everywhere Bacchants dancing. Nor had Pan been neglected, but he sat on a rock and himself played the panpipe, giving a similar tune for the treaders and the dancers alike.
>
> Longus, *Daphnis and Chloe* 4.3.2

We should note first that these myths are alluded to, with extreme concision, not narrated, and that Longus therefore offers us no encouragement to take them as exemplary. There are indeed phrases or themes that recall what readers have encountered earlier in the story: the Tyrrhenian pirates recall Pan's miracle that saved Chloe (2.25–9); the grape-treading recalls the opening of Book 2 (1–2), where Chloe had been compared to a Bacchant and the treaders to satyrs (2.2.2); Pan's not being neglected may remind us of the couple's initial neglect of him (cf. 2.23.4); and his panpiping recalls the several occasions where humans played the panpipe. But it is hard to extract a pattern from these recollections. It is also hard to assess how much significance to attach to the violence entailed by some of the actions of Dionysus that are portrayed. The main features of Dionysiac myth being as they were, it would have required a deliberate exclusion of these and a focus on less central myths to illustrate the power of the god without actions in which violence was implicit. The one sexual episode, the sleeping Ariadne, is one where no violence is involved, and indeed is a scene that seems often to be used to symbolise eternal happiness. The god to whom violent action is ascribed in the main narrative and violent sexual pursuit in the inset tales, Pan, is here a relaxed source of celebratory music. I would accept the suggestion that the Dionysiac paintings do something to remind us of the power of the gods, sometimes exercised with destructive violence, but not that they offer violence as the principal model of divine interaction with human beings or as in any way necessarily linked with sexuality.

I return, then, to the interpretation of the inset tales. First, John Morgan has suggested that an important element common to the three tales was that in each the creation of something worthwhile and beautiful was preceded by loss and destruction: the reader is to infer that the successful love-making and marriage of Daphnis and Chloe can only happen after the loss of her innocence.[31] Attractive as this hypothesis may be, it does not persuade me. It is surely important that what is created out of the destruction of Phatta, Syrinx and Echo is something musical (as Morgan himself notes, and as was well stressed by Hunter).[32] Now although music is important to Daphnis and Chloe, she has no more stake in it than he, and the consummation of their love in the last chapters is a sexual act and not the playing of a musical duet. I find it hard to move from the creation of 'musical beauty'

[31] Morgan 1994, 70 and 76–7.

[32] Morgan 1994, 70; Hunter 1983, 53. For the importance of music in *Daphnis and Chloe* see further Maritz 1991; Montiglio 2012.

to the notion that 'violence and loss are necessary preconditions for the creation of true harmony', whether that harmony is to be taken generally or to be sought in the relationship achieved by Daphnis and Chloe by the end of the fourth book.

Another point which seems to me to be an obstacle to Morgan's interpretation also counts heavily against that of Winkler, so I shall now consider that interpretation too. In Winkler's view Chloe starts off as ready to take the sexual initiative as Daphnis, if not readier: but, as the conventional patterns of city culture begin to trap the couple, she shifts into a subordinate position. At the same time the sexual act towards which the couple is heading involves violence by the male to the female, a violence which is alluded to by Lycaenion in her prediction that Chloe will weep and bleed (3.19.3), a prediction recalled to the reader by the presence of Lycaenion at the wedding and by the last sentence's reference to what she had taught Daphnis (4.40.3), and alluded to by Longus' description of the singing of the ὑμέναιον as being performed σκληρᾶι καὶ ἀπηνεῖ τῆι φωνῆι, καθάπερ τριαίναις γῆν ἀναρρηγνύντες, οὐχ ὑμέναιον ᾄδοντες, 'in a harsh and stern voice, as if they were breaking up the earth with forks, not singing a wedding-song'.[33]

The difficulties with this position seem to me to be as follows. Chloe does indeed fall behind Daphnis, especially in her understanding of the nature of ἔρως, but it is an inevitable requirement of the story Longus has chosen to tell that one of the two acquires practical skills from a third party, and it is intelligible on many grounds why Longus should make that one Daphnis, not Chloe. In other respects Chloe does not seem to me to fade. As to the last chapters, Lycaenion's presence at what is almost a curtain call is hardly surprising. Dorcon, who had lusted after Chloe and had achieved a kiss from her in his last moments, would have been there if he had been alive; and since he is not, his relatives are (4.38.2). Longus' identification of what Daphnis does with Chloe as what Lycaenion had taught him is (*inter alia*) a simple way of emphasising that this is not going to be another false start in the couple's erotic progress, as well as giving credit where credit is due – and indeed credit Lycaenion had specifically requested Daphnis to remember (3.19.3). If Longus had thought it important that the reader should recall Lycaenion's prediction of blood and weeping I hold that he would have had to give rather clearer indications. As it is, the description of the way the ὑμέναιον is sung can only fancifully be seen as an allusion to that prediction. The simpler, and surely sufficient, explanation is that we are being

[33] Cf. Winkler 1990, 101–26. For a more exhaustive and characteristically provocative response to Winkler's interpretation see Goldhill 1995, esp. 30–45.

reminded, as so often throughout the work, how much cruder rustic ways are than those of the city – the ὑμέναιος sounds not like the polished rhetorical composition one might be trained to put together by a city *rhetor* but like one of the worksongs of which Longus has just given us an example.[34]

But the crucial point against Winkler, which is also one which seems to me to count against Morgan, is that the nature of male sexual violence exhibited by Pan is quite different from such physical force as may be involved in the penetration of Chloe by Daphnis. The violence of Pan is a combination of exercising force to impose his sexual desire when persuasion fails and inflicting violent destruction on the objects of that desire, Syrinx and Echo. Whatever Daphnis may have to do when the last scene fades is highly unlikely to require him to impose his desire by force – he is not likely even to need persuasion; and although Chloe's virginity will be lost, nothing else will, far less her life, as we are assured by the preceding vignette of Daphnis and Chloe herding their animals and children into the sunset.

For me, then, it is not easy to draw a moral about the need for destruction or loss to precede sexual fulfilment, nor about the necessarily violent nature of male sexuality destined to affect even Daphnis and Chloe.

But another moral there may be. To see it, we need to bear two points in mind. First, as we have known since Pan's intervention to save Chloe from the Methymnans, it is the intention of Eros to make a μῦθος of Chloe: Pan calls Chloe παρθένον ἐξ ἧς Ἔρως μῦθον ποιῆσαι θέλει, 'a maiden out of whom Eros wishes to make a myth' (2.27.2). As I have argued in my 'Introduction', Longus leaves us in doubt as to whether his main narrative is to be read as 'history' or 'myth', and this statement by Pan counter-balances a number of indications that had hitherto pointed rather to history. Secondly, Longus is much given to balance, not simply in his sentence structures but in the work as a whole. We have had three myths, one towards the end of each of the first three books: surely we expect a fourth. Why do we not get one? The answer, surely, is that we do. The marriage and sexual union of Daphnis and Chloe come just at the point in Book 4 where we might expect a fourth inset tale. But just as Pan has moved from a cameo role in the first tale to a leading role in the second and third, so the ἔργα, 'acts', of Eros have moved in Book 4 from the inset tales to the narrative frame. And like the events of the three inset tales, the ἔρως of Daphnis and Chloe gives rise to the enduring musical beauty that is Longus' μῦθος. Bruce MacQueen has argued for a similar interpretation; but for MacQueen the myth of Chloe which is offered

[34] For antiquarian interest in traditional work-music cf. 4.38.3 with Bowie 2019g *ad loc.*; for heavy emphasis on rusticity cf. the expression τῆς ἀμούσου βοῆς, 2.2.3.

by Book 4 is her abduction by Lampis, and her recovery (4.27–32).[35] This brief episode seems to me hardly to match up to the expectations raised by Pan's phrase 'a maiden out of whom Eros wishes to make a μῦθος', and there is no hint in Longus' narration of that episode that it is to be classed as a μῦθος despite the part it plays as an event in his own story. It seems to me more likely that if, as I believe, Book 4 does offer a μῦθος to be seen alongside those in Books 1, 2 and 3, it is the successful culmination of the ἔρως of Daphnis and Chloe, not the failed ἔρως of Lampis for Chloe. That culmination necessarily implies all the stages through which their ἔρως has developed, so that the closing episode of Book 4 becomes a metonomy for the progress of their ἔρως as a whole, and thereby for the μῦθος that Longus has spread over four books.

If this is a sequence the reader is to observe, then it further establishes the difference between Chloe and Pitys, Syrinx and Echo precisely by asking the reader to compare them. But it also puts back on the reader's agenda the issue of whether this tale is history or myth. The interpretation of the tale of Chloe as a μῦθος had been prescribed by Pan in a context where the miraculous perhaps pulled in the direction of myth, but the Thucydidean description of the Methymnans' naval expedition pulled in the direction of history. The bulk of the narrative of Books 3 and 4, drawing increasingly on New Comedy and on stereotypes of Greek city life, had read much more like history. Now at the close of Book 4 the very absence of an inset tale of the sort that has earlier established a distance between the world of myth and of Daphnis and Chloe returns readers to a state of uncertainty, so that, like the couple listening to Philetas at 2.7.1, they may wonder if they are 'listening to a μῦθος, not to a λόγος'.

[35] MacQueen 1985, 1990.

27 Metaphor in *Daphnis and Chloe* (2005)

1 Introduction

Metaphor is a slippery term. It may seem cowardly to offer a plain man's working definition without some theoretical underpinning, but other papers in the collection where this chapter first appeared have offered helpful definitions, and it seems to me that a substantial discussion here would yield limited returns and would not materially advance our understanding of the phenomena in the text of Longus' *Daphnis and Chloe* that I want to consider. Let me say simply, then, that by metaphor (on a micro-level) I understand taking a word (or occasionally a small group of related words) with a widely or universally accepted meaning in relation to one sphere or category of discourse and using it or them to refer more or less meaningfully to a different sphere or category of discourse.[1]

Different genres vary markedly in their uses of metaphor, and so too within any one genre do different authors. Within the Greek novelists my impression has been that Heliodorus is richest in metaphor. By contrast large proportions of narrative and description in *Daphnis and Chloe* proceed with only rare recourse to metaphor. What metaphor we do find falls chiefly into three main groups, with a fourth which is less well represented, and may even be seen as a sub-species of the third. There are also a few cases that belong to no one of these four groups: these I have gathered together in an Appendix. The four categories are:

Terms which describe the psychosomatic symptoms and concomitants of desire and a social aspect of desire.

Terms which attribute to animals, to plants and even to inanimate nature responses one might expect only from humans or other anthropomorphs, or to the relations of humans to animals or to plants a relation

[1] For collections of essays on metaphor in Greek and Latin writing see Boys-Stones 2003, particularly his introduction and the chapters by Doreen Innes and Michael Silk, and that in which this chapter appeared, in Harrison, Paschalis, and Frangoulidis 2005. Of earlier literature Silk 1974 and Padel 1992 remain important. Stanford 1936, though bearing many marks of its date, still offers some useful insights.

one might expect only between humans, and to humans features that one might expect only in plants.

Terms which can be argued to bear not only a literal meaning within the story but also to bear a meta-poetic meaning, directing a reader's attention to the literary qualities of the text or to the literary activity of its author.

Terms which allude to the world of learning inhabited by the writer and his readers.

2 Concomitants of Desire

Symptoms and Concomitants of Desire

The terms used by Longus to describe the psychosomatic symptoms and concomitants of desire have a history going back to Greek poetry of the archaic period: not surprisingly in an author who has chosen to set his story on Lesbos and to make it one of ἔρως, 'desire', the majority leads us back to Sappho, but there are a few examples traceable by us – and presumably by both Longus and the πεπαιδευμένοι, 'educated men', who were his readers – to Archilochus, Hesiod and even Homer. There are bound to be intertexts we cannot detect because we no longer have access to canonical works still read in the second and third centuries AD – a prime example of which I would argue to be the *Cypria*.

The most prominent group draws on the vocabulary of heat, fire, and burning (with occasional appearances of its opposite, cold): here for ancient readers, as for us, the point of reference is the poem of Sappho cited almost complete by Ps.-Longinus, referred to three times by Plutarch,[2] and known from papyri, fr. 31. Such terms are so closely interwoven with ones denoting physical pain that although it is clear that they are formally different I shall attempt to treat them together. Occasionally the intertext is the poetry of Theocritus instead of, or as well as, that of Sappho.

Pain and Fire

On occasion pain is experienced but not attributed to fire: the association of pain with love begins in the preface, when the writer expresses the wish that his work λυπούμενον παραμυθήσεται, 'will console him who feels pain'

[2] On Plu.'s citations of Sappho see Bowie 2008c, 150–2 (Chapter 21 in Volume 3).

(*pr*. 3). In Book 1 Daphnis ἤλγει τὴν καρδίαν ὡς ἐσθιομένην ὑπὸ φαρμάκων, 'felt pain in his heart as if it were being eaten by poisons' (1.32.4); in Book 4 Astylus is said by litotes to be οὐκ ἄπειρος ἐρωτικῆς λύπης, 'not unfamiliar with the pain of desire' (4.17.1). More often, however, terms for pain are tied in with terms for fire and burning.

One sequence runs from 1.13 to 1.17. After Chloe has been smitten by Daphnis, whom she has now seen naked, her ψυχή, 'soul', is gripped by ἄση, 'love-pain' (1.13.5),[3] and she claims physical pain that is related to burning: ἀλγῶ, 'I ache',[4] λυποῦμαι ('I feel pain'), and καίομαι, each begin one of a sequence of three short sentences. She is mystified that she has pain but no ἕλκος, 'wound' (1.14.1).[5] Then she contrasts her pain with that caused by bramble-scratches and bee-stings: τουτὶ δὲ τὸ νύττον μου τὴν καρδίαν, 'this thing that jabs at my heart', is πάντων ἐκείνων πικρότερον, 'more stinging than all these things' (1.14.2). Soon after this monologue the cowherd Dorcon in turn begins to desire Chloe; over a number of days μᾶλλον τὴν ψύχην ἐξεπυρσεύθη, 'his soul becomes more inflamed' (1.15.1). Then Chloe gives Daphnis the fateful kiss πάνυ … ψύχην θερμᾶναι δυνάμενον, 'fully capable of heating up a soul' (1.17.1).[6] The consequence is that Daphnis, as if not kissed but δηχθείς, 'bitten', often ἐψύχετο, 'would feel cold',[7] and is unable to control τὴν καρδίαν παλλομένην. 'his palpitating heart' (1.17.2).[8]

After this point fire-imagery recurs from time to time until 3.13. When summer comes, it too inflames the couple: ἐξέκαε δὲ αὐτοὺς καὶ ἡ ὥρα τοῦ ἔτους, 'and the season of the year also stoked their fire' (1.23.1). θαλπόμενος, 'heated up', by summer's manifestations of nature's fecundity, Daphnis leaps into rivers and drinks their water ὡς τὸ ἔνδοθεν καῦμα σβέσων, 'so as to quench the fire inside him' (1.23.2).[9] An unusual variant on the image is found when Dorcon, dying, is presented as ὀλίγον ἐκ τοῦ πρότερον ἔρωτος

[3] Longus probably draws the term from Sappho fr. 1.3, though it may also have stood in fr. 96.17; Longus will also know its use at Eur. *Med.* 245.

[4] Theoc. 3.52 ἀλγέω τὰν κεφαλάν, 'my head aches'.

[5] This is the nearest that Longus or any novelist gets to the not uncommon metaphor of ἕλκος for the 'wound' of desire, for which cf. Eur. *Hipp.* 530, Call. *AP* 12.134 (= *HE* 1103–8), Theoc. 11.15, 30.10. For Longus' use of Callimachus see Bowie 2019i (Chapter 45 in this volume).

[6] θερμαίνειν, 'to heat up', is much less commonly used of the fire of desire than καίειν, 'to burn', and its compounds: our first case is P. *O.* 10.87.

[7] Sappho 31.13, Theoc. 2.106.

[8] A throbbing heart (to recur at 2.7.5) has no poetic model, but is already in Ach. Tat. 2.37.10, 5.27.1. Like Daphnis' symptoms as enumerated in his following monologue – ἐκπηδᾶι μοι τὸ πνεῦμα, ἐξάλλεται ἡ καρδία, 'my breath leaps out, my heart jumps up' (1.18.1) – it should probably be treated as literal and not metaphorical.

[9] Longus may recall Hesiod's lines on the aphrodisiac effect of summer heat, *Op.* 582, as he had shortly before done with his mention of σκόλυμοι at 1.20.3: see Bowie 2019g, 141–2.

ἐμπύρευμα λαβών, 'recovering a small ember from his former desire' (1.29.1).[10] A similar set of symptoms recurs when Philetas describes his desire for Amaryllis (the similarity is crucial to Philetas' aim of explaining ἔρως, 'desire', to the young couple): psychological pain, ἤλγουν τὴν ψυχήν, 'my soul ached', τὴν καρδίαν ἐπαλλόμην, 'my heart was palpitating', τὸ σῶμα ἐψυχόμην, 'my body felt cold' – but it was also hot, since εἰς ποταμοὺς ἐνέβαινον ὡς καόμενος, 'I went into rivers thinking I was burning up' (2.7.5). The couple then reflect that they have similar symptoms: ἀλγοῦσιν οἱ ἐρῶντες … καὶ ἡμεῖς … κάεσθαι δοκοῦσι … καὶ παρ' ἡμῖν τὸ πῦρ, 'those who feel desire ache … so do we … they think they are burning up … we too experience fire' (2.8.2): they make a plausible leap in their metaphorical inference – what they experience can be called πῦρ, 'fire'. At this point we may recall, or even re-read, the phrase just used to describe the god Eros as ξανθὸς ὡς πῦρ, 'blond like fire' (2.4.1). Since fire-metaphor has been recurrent we may decide that this comparison with fire goes far beyond hair-colour. So too later, when the winter households of herding folk have to be warmed by πῦρ … μέγα, 'a huge fire' (3.3.3), we are encouraged to think of the 'fire' of Book 2 that is now consuming the separated lovers. Metaphorical uses are adding resonance to literal uses.

At the end of Book 2 the time that the couple can once more spend together makes them 'hotter': τούτοις ἅπασι θερμότεροι γενόμενοι καὶ θρασύτεροι, 'because of all this they became hotter and bolder' (2.39.1). Later, Chloe's reassurance to Daphnis that the hot sun will melt the snows of winter that part them brings the response 'οὕτως γένοιτο θερμός, ὡς τὸ καῖον πῦρ τὴν καρδίαν τὴν ἐμήν', '"if only it could be so hot as the fire that is burning my heart"' (3.10.4). Then in the second spring the sexual activities of goats excite them: ἐξεκάοντο πρὸς τὰ ἀκούσματα καὶ ἐτήκοντο πρὸς τὰ θεάματα, 'they were set on fire in response to the sounds and wasted away in response to the sights' (3.13.3): the parallel with Book 1's description of summer (1.23.1–2) prompts us to give the goats' sexual activities a similar place in Longus' universe to the inanimate erotic catalysts of 1.23.1–2.

This use of fire-imagery at 3.13.3 is Longus' last exploitation of it in his presentation of Daphnis and Chloe. It is as if Daphnis' sexual experience with Lycaenion extinguishes the fire, or at least dampens it down. It

[10] In Greek the metaphorical use of ἐμπύρευμα, 'ember', has no parallel known to me in erotic literature – rather it has a philosophical use, of vestiges of life in the body, perhaps already in Democritus, cf. Proclus *In R.* ii 113.6 Kroll. The closeness of Vergil's phrase (*Aen.*4.23) *veteris vestigia flammae*, 'traces of an old flame', needs to be weighed in considering whether Longus knew any Latin literature, the case for which has now been well made by Hubbard 2006; Jolowicz 2021.

reappears only once, of Gnathon's desire for Daphnis, προσεκκαυθείς, 'further inflamed' (4.16.1), by his failed assault on Daphnis (4.12).[11]

Other Images of Desire

Four other groups of images are used to describe the psychological effects of desire. One of these has only a single but important example: in an image derived from Plato's *Phaedrus*, Eros, says Philetas, τὰς ψυχὰς ἀναπτεροῖ, 'gives wings to souls' (2.7.1).[12] Here the Platonic allusion points the reader to the similarity between Philetas' λόγος and a Platonic μῦθος.

Each of the other three groups is represented by several examples. We found ἐτήκοντο, 'they began to waste away', linked with burning-imagery at 3.13.3; τήκεσθαι, 'I waste away', is earlier used in author-narrative of the emotions of Chloe – ἐτήκετο, 'she wasted away' (1.24.1) – and of Daphnis – τήκεται ἡ ψυχή, 'his soul wastes away' (1.18.1).[13] Daphnis himself says δέδοικα μὴ ἐγὼ πρὸ ταύτης τακῶ, 'I am afraid I may melt away before it' (sc. the winter snow) (3.10.3). Only once does Longus use the alternative metaphor from a related field μαραίνεται, 'he withers', when Daphnis describes his own state at 1.18.2: here the idea is drawn from the life-cycle of the blooming violets and hyacinths with which he contrasts himself.[14]

Another group transfers imagery from the language of war.[15] Both Daphnis and Chloe finds themselves prisoners of their mutual gaze – ἐγίνετο ἤδη τῶν ὀφθαλμῶν ἅλωσις, 'it was at this point that capture through their eyes happened' (1.24.1).[16] Then at the end of the book, after the literal capture of Daphnis by pirates, the love-sick Daphnis imagines he has left his soul with the pirates, ἔτι ἀγνοῶν τὸ Ἔρωτος ληιστήριον, 'being as yet ignorant of the piracy of Eros' (1.32.4).[17] We are invited to ponder the analogy between losing one's physical freedom to predatory pirates and losing one's psychological freedom to an object of desire.

[11] In a parallel sub-plot Lampis wants Chloe for his wife (4.7.1), but we are never told he 'desires' her.

[12] Cf. Pl. *Phdr.* 246a1 ff., 249d4 ff., and esp. 255c.

[13] For τήκεσθαι of supposed physical wasting cf. Theoc. 1.66, 82, 2.82. It is unusual with ψυχή, 'soul', as its subject.

[14] μαραίνεται, only here in Longus, is not used with a personal subject by other novelists: X.Eph. uses it of κάλλος, 'beauty', 1.5.6, 2.6.3; Ach. Tat. of the ἀκμή, 'prime' (of a young man), 1.8.9.

[15] As far as I know our earliest example is Archil. fr. 23.17–21.

[16] Although the verb is common of erotic captivation (cf. X.Eph. 1.3.1. etc.), only Longus here and *Anacreont.* 26.3 West seem to use the noun ἅλωσις in this way.

[17] Cf. the description of prostitutes by (?)Asclepiades as τὰ ληιστρικὰ τῆς Ἀφροδίτης, 'the pirate fleet of Aphrodite', *AP* 5.161.5 = *HE* 40.5 = 40.5 Sens, and by Maccius of Eros as ληιστὰ λογισμοῦ, 'robber of reason', *APl.* 198.3 = *GP* 11.3.

A final group of metaphors relates to consumption and repletion. One person can fill another with an emotion: so Daphnis on his worryingly late return home is described as τοὺς ἀμφὶ τὸν Λάμωνα … εὐφροσύνης ἐμπλήσας, 'having filled Lamon and his family with rejoicing' (2.24.4); at the end of Book 2 Daphnis and Chloe ἐνέπλησαν ἕως νυκτὸς ἀλλήλους, 'gave each other full measure (literally 'filled each other') until nightfall' (2.38.2). In earlier writers ἀπλήστως, 'insatiably', soon moved out from its presumably original use of food and drink, but Longus may be the first to use it of sexual desire:[18] Daphnis gazes ἀπλήστως, 'insatiably', at Chloe when she has begun to snooze (1.25.1), and when kissing Daphnis and Chloe γευσάμενοι τῆς ἐν φιλήματι τέρψεως ἀπλήστως ἐνεφοροῦντο τῆς ἡδόνης, 'after tasting the delight that lies in a kiss, they began to take their fill of pleasure insatiably' (2.11.1). Here γευσάμενοι, 'after tasting', complements the terms ἀπλήστως and ἐνεφοροῦντο, 'they filled themselves with'.[19] Tasting is also used of Daphnis' first experience of ἔρως, 'desire', in the form of Chloe's kiss, and of his verbal reaction to it: οἷα πρῶτον γευόμενος τῶν ἔρωτος καὶ ἔργων καὶ λόγων, 'as might be expected since he was for the first time tasting the acts and words of desire' (1.19.1): that this 'taste' is an oral experience might be argued to make the use only just metaphorical.

So too with Longus' uses of γλυκύς, 'sweet'. When he uses it of kisses, having Daphnis say Chloe's mouth is κηρίων γλυκύτερον, 'sweeter than honeycombs' (1.18.1), and Gnathon talk of γλυκέα φιλήματα, 'sweet kisses' (4.17.6), I am tempted to take it as literally of the kisses' taste, just as a φίλημα, 'kiss', is μελιτώδης, 'honey-like' (2.18.1). A similar argument might be made for γλυκεῖα … τῆς ὀπώρας ὀδμή, the 'sweet smell of ripe fruit' (1.23.1): here the scent suggests the sweetness that can be tasted. Other cases, however, are more clearly metaphorical, as when Lamon's story of Syrinx is μῦθον ᾠδῆς γλυκύτερον, 'a tale sweeter than a song' (2.35.1); when rustics' leisure in winter makes it seem καὶ μετοπώρου καὶ ἦρος αὐτοῦ γλυκύτερον, 'sweeter both than autumn and than spring itself' (3.4.1); or when Daphnis, after finding the 3,000 drachmas that will enable him to marry Chloe, τὴν θάλασσαν ἐνόμιζε τῆς γῆς γλυκύτερον 'thought the sea sweeter than land' (3.28.3).

[18] Neither the adjective ἄπληστος, 'insatiable', nor the adverb ἀπλήστως, 'insatiably', appears in any other place in Longus or the other novelists, though ἀπλήστως is very common in D.C. (twenty-five times). Most classical uses relate to food or money, but cf. Xen. *Cyr.* 4.1.14–15 where it relates to ἡδονή, 'pleasure'.

[19] For this use of ἐμφορεῖσθαι cf. already Hdt. 1.55.1, and, in a contemporary writer, Lucian *Philopseudes* 39.

The two remaining cases might at first sight be taken as equally metaphorical. Daphnis notes that for sheep and goats γλυκύ τι ὡς ἔοικέν ἐστι τὸ ἔργον καὶ νικᾶι τοῦ ἔρωτος τὸ πικρόν, 'the (sexual) act is something sweet, it seems, and it conquers the bitterness of desire' (3.14.3). Then, very shortly after this, Lycaenion differentiates the sexual act in which she is about to initiate Daphnis from a kiss, an embrace, and what rams and billy-goats do: ἄλλα ταῦτα πηδήματα καὶ τῶν ἐκεῖ γλυκύτερα, 'these leapings are different and sweeter than those others' (3.17.2). The two passages are so close that they must be read together, and Lycaenion's comparison with kissing connects them in turn with the earlier passages where kisses have been described as 'sweet'. Longus thus presents his readers with a view of the sexual act as sweet in a sense that is almost literal.

Desire in Society

Another aspect of desire is brought out by two of Longus' three uses of the term μισθός, 'payment'.

What I take to be the literal use appears at 2.33.3: Lamon tells the story of Syrinx that he persuaded a Sicilian goatherd to sing for the μισθός of a goat and a syrinx – exchangeable goods are offered as the price either of other goods or, as here, of a service. I pass over the interesting implication for Longus' view of the marketability of literary products of this allusion to the sometimes mercenary poet Theocritus (though cf. in Section 3 on κτῆμα, 'possession').

Longus' two other uses, quite close together, relate to sex. Lycaenion says to Daphnis that another man (other than …?) taught her how to have sex, taking her virginity as a μισθός, 'payment' (3.19.2). A few chapters later Daphnis, now equipped with the concept 'payment' and word μισθός, promises to tell Chloe the tale of Echo for a μισθός of ten kisses (3.22.4). We may briefly wonder why Daphnis does not ask for Chloe's virginity as a μισθός, and thus take the chance to teach her about rather more than the story of Echo: but Longus has given reasons for Daphnis' hesitation, and, more important, he intends to present their consummation at the end of Book 4 as entirely reciprocal, and indeed as near to symmetrical as Daphnis' greater experience will allow. So the element of μισθός in Lycaenion's autobiography helps to mark off her approach to sex from that of the couple.

3 Anthropomorphisation

Anthropomorphisation of the Inanimate

In the vintage that opens Book 2 the manufacture of wine is assimilated to human and animal reproduction by the term γένεσις, 'generation',[20] in the phrase οἷον ἐν ἑορτῆι Διονύσου καὶ οἴνου γενέσει, 'as one might expect in a festival of Dionysus and the generation of wine' (2.2.1), complementing Longus' explicit descriptions here of the couple's sexual attractiveness. The hint reappears in the second vintage, that of Book 4: ordinary grapes are taken off for pressing, but the rustics are described as τῶν βοτρύων τοὺς ἡβῶντας ἐπὶ κλημάτων ἀφαιροῦντες, ὡς εἴη καὶ τοῖς ἐκ τῆς πόλεως ἐλθοῦσιν ἐν εἰκόνι καὶ ἡδονῆι γενέσθαι τρυγητοῦ, 'taking grapes in their prime, stalk and all, so that it might be possible for the party which came from the city also to have the image and pleasure of the vintage' (4.5.3). Longus' use of the term εἰκών, 'image', prompts the reader to be alert to symbolism, and the metaphorical ἡβῶντας, 'in their prime' – almost 'adolescent' – leaves little doubt as to how to read the signs: the plump grapes are, like Daphnis and Chloe, ready for plucking, and the city toffs might well expect to have first refusal.

Like grapes, cheese acquires anthropomorphic features. The cheeses presented by Dorcon to Chloe's father Dryas are γεννικῶν 'noble' or 'of good stock' (1.19.1) – perhaps reminding us that Chloe is, but Dorcon is not.[21] In the first spring scene the joints of reeds used to make a syrinx are γόνατα, 'knees' (1.10.1). The metaphor is attested as early as Herodotus (3.98),[22] and might be thought to be no metaphor at all, but it is at the least intriguing that it is used by the Lesbian writer Theophrastus of the joints that develop in wheat plants as spring succeeds winter and the plants are no longer green shoots, or 'in blade', for which his term is χλόη.[23] Ivy too acquires animal features: the thicket where Daphnis was found has κιττὸς ἐπιπλανώμενος, 'ivy straying across it' (1.2.1).[24] Pines can be competitors with Daphnis' syrinx-playing: ὁ μὲν ἐσύριζεν ἁμιλλώμενος πρὸς τὰς πίτυς, ἡ δὲ ἦιδε ταῖς ἀηδόσιν ἐρίζουσα, 'he would pipe in competition with the pine-trees, she would sing vying with the nightingales' (3.24.2).

20 Inevitably many cases in the category of anthropomorphisation of the inanimate might be claimed rather to be 'personification'. Even if that term is sometimes appropriate, these cases must still be seen against Longus' whole metaphorical system.

21 The extension from humans to objects starts with Old Comedy, Antiph. fr. 47 K–A (of a λεπαστή, 'limpet-shaped drinking cup').

22 Hdt. 3.98.3 23 Thphr. *HP* 8.2.4.

24 ἐπιπλανᾶσθαι is very rare: it may be Longus' use that caught the eye of Hld. 3.5.6, 7.17.1.

Like the couple, the earth sheds clothes – the clothing of snow it has had in winter: τῆς δὲ γῆς γυμνουμένης, 'when the earth began to be laid bare' (3.12.1): Longus uses the verb only in two other places, of Daphnis (1.24.2) and Chloe (3.24.3), and it is not far-fetched to propose that the nakedness of the earth here reminds us of the couple's recurrent, albeit ineffectual, nakedness. The idea is complementary to that whereby Longus suggests (in a formula chiefly found in *ecphraseis* of works of art) that εἴκασεν ἄν τις, 'one might have imagined', that the sun, being φιλόκαλον, 'a lover of beauty', was stripping the young people naked so as to admire them, part of a sequence where inanimate rivers and winds are made to join the chorus of animal noises elicited by the first spring and where the apples that fall to the ground do so through ἔρως:

> ἡδεῖα μὲν τεττίγων ἠχή, γλυκεῖα δὲ ὀπώρας ὀδμή, τερπνὴ δὲ ποιμνίων βληχή. εἴκασεν ἄν τις καὶ τοὺς ποτάμους ᾄδειν ἠρέμα ῥέοντας καὶ τοὺς ἀνέμους συρίττειν ταῖς πίτυσιν ἐμπνέοντας καὶ τὰ μῆλα ἐρῶντα πίπτειν χαμαὶ καὶ τὸν ἥλιον φιλόκαλον ὄντα πάντας ἀποδύειν.
>
> Pleasing was the voice of the crickets, sweet was the scent of ripe fruit, delightful was the bleating of flocks. One might have imagined that the rivers were singing as they flowed gently, and that the winds were piping as they blew upon the pine-trees, and that the apples were falling to the ground out of desire, and that because the sun was a lover of beauty he was stripping everyone.
>
> Longus, *Daphnis and Chloe* 1.23.1

By similar anthropomorphism heat can tire – κοπάσαντος τοῦ καύματος, 'when the heat grew weary' (1.8.2): although this verb is almost always used of natural phenomena, etymology suggests a primary and literal sense of animate subjects. The sea too is anthropomorphised: βαλάντιον … ὑπὸ τοῦ κύματος ἀπεπτύσθη, 'the wallet (whose contents will allow Daphnis to marry Chloe) was spat out by the waves' (3.27.4).[25] Sounds too acquire life-force: so the rowers' songs are 'cast' ashore: σαφῆ δὲ ἐξέπιπτεν εἰς τὴν γῆν τὰ τῶν κελευστῶν ᾄσματα, 'and the songs of the coxes were thrown clearly to land' (3.21.3) – the verb is one used elsewhere of sailors being cast ashore. This is appropriate when we are about to be introduced to the intertwined physics and mythology of Echo.

[25] Longus may recall the simile of Il. 4.426 where the stormy sea ἀποπτύει ἁλὸς ἄχνην, 'spits out the salty foam' (i.e. onto the shore).

Anthropomorphisation of Animals

The animal kingdom is assimilated to humanity in several ways. Cicadas are λάλοι, 'garrulous' (1.14.4: cf. 1.25.3), as are grasshoppers (3.24.2).[26] One effect of this can be seen when a cicada flies into Chloe's bosom for shelter: when Daphnis has delicately – or indelicately – used his hand to extract it, Chloe kissed it and αὖθις ἐνέβαλε τῶι κόλπωι λαλοῦντα, 'put it back chattering into her bosom' (1.26.3). Since we have recently read that the love-struck Daphnis used to be a greater chatter-box than grasshoppers (1.17.4), we are prompted to notice that Daphnis has not yet emulated the cicadas to the extent of chatting with Chloe with his head resting on Chloe's breasts.

In a description that activates the work's recurrent focus on issues of learning, rams are implied to be ἀμαθεῖς, 'bad learners' when Daphnis is called κριῶν ἀμαθέστερος, 'a worse learner than rams' (3.14.5). By a similar trope one billy-goat's possible sexual relations with another's nanny-goats is termed adultery: καὶ ἕκαστος εἶχε ἰδίας καὶ ἐφύλαττε μή τις αὐτὰς μοιχεύσηι λαθών, 'each billy-goat had his own nanny-goats and kept an eye on them to make sure some goat did not secretly commit adultery with them' (3.13.3). This is the only use of either the verb or the noun from the root μοιχ- in the work, and is to be found strikingly close to the passage where Daphnis covertly (i.e. λαθών, though Longus does not use that term) has adulterous sex with Chromis' wife Lycaenion, observed by neither Chromis nor Chloe (3.17–18).

Less striking, perhaps, is the use of the term αἰχμάλωτος, 'prisoner of war', for the sheep and goats which, like Chloe, have been captured by the Methymnans (2.22.4). Although the term had been used in earlier writers for things (e.g. οἰκήματα, 'houses', χρήματα, 'things', νῆες, 'ships', cf. LSJ *s.v.*) its use of animals further tightens the bond between the couple and their animal kingdom. The closeness between human and animal actors is also visible in the way that many characters are compared to animals.[27] One such case is a denigratory metaphor: Chloe's mother tells Daphnis that Chloe would rather sleep with a handsome pauper than with a 'rich ape', πιθήκωι πλουσίωι (3.26.4).

[26] For grasshoppers' chatter cf. Theoc. 5.34 καὶ ἀκρίδες ὧδε λαλεῦντι, 'and here the grasshoppers chatter'.

[27] For a fuller discussion of the relation between humans and animals in Longus, including comparisons, see Bowie 2005a and 2019b (Chapter 43 in this volume).

Anthropomorphs as Plants

Echo's physical and sexual prime is described as her ἄνθος, 'flower' (3.24.3): this is so common a term for the phenomenon in other writers[28] that it might almost be dismissed as a dead metaphor. But in a text where parallels between nature and humanity are constantly drawn (note especially Daphnis' self-comparison with ἄνθη, 'flowers', 1.18.2), and shortly before a voluptuous description of an apple that symbolises Chloe (3.33–4) it makes a significant contribution to the network of terms linking the natural world with that of anthropomorphs.

Body-Parts with a Mind of Their Own

It is part of the same slippage that parts of the body can be treated as having volition: when Chloe is woken by the cicada τοὺς … ὀφθαλμοὺς ἀπέματτεν ἔτι καθεύδειν θέλοντας, 'she rubbed her eyes which wanted to go on sleeping' (1.26.2). If the body-parts of one of the lovers are autonomous, what will happen to Longus' careful delay of their consummation? The threat is not realised, except in so far as nature takes over in Daphnis' encounter with Lycaenion.[29] It is an unsurprising extension of this conceit that seasons too can have volition, ἐπείγοντος τοῦ τρυγητοῦ, 'when the harvest demanded immediate attention' (2.1.1).[30] The verb reinforces our impression that the cycle of the seasons plays almost as an important part as Eros himself in shaping the progress of the couple's shallow learning-curve.

All these images contribute to what was arguably a major part of Longus' literary agenda, to present a world in which the element of φύσις, 'nature', in Daphnis and Chloe's discovery of Eros is reinforced and symbolised by a recurrent invitation to see humans, animals and even inanimate nature as all functioning on similar principles.

[28] Though its only other conjunction with the root παρθέν- is in Archil. fr. 196a.27. First of physical prime in Il. 13.484, in its other early erotic uses (Mimn. fr. 4.1, Sol. fr. 25.1) ἥβης ἄνθεα means 'the delights of youth'.

[29] αὐτὴ γὰρ ἡ φύσις λοιπὸν ἐπαίδευε τὸ πρακτέον, 'for nature herself taught what had to be done thereafter', 3.18.4. For the attribution of volition to body-parts at 1.26.2 cf. 2.22.3 ποίοις ποσίν …; 'with what steps?', and Arr. *Epict.* 2.6.10. καὶ γὰρ ὁ πούς, εἰ φρένας εἶχεν, ὥρμα ἂν ἐπὶ τὸ πηλοῦσθαι, 'for if my leg had intelligence it would have been taking steps to become muddy'.

[30] It must be admitted that several other writers in the first and second centuries AD have the non-classical use of a non-personal subject and the sense 'was pressing': cf. LSJ IV.2 and 3.

4 Literary and Meta-Literary Activity

Possession

Metaphors relating to writing and reading literary works begin with the preface's claim that the work is both an ἀνάθημα, 'dedication', and a κτῆμα τερπνὸν πᾶσιν ἀνθρώποις, 'a pleasing possession for all men' (*pr.* 3). The intertextuality with Thucydides (1.22.4) may blunt our sense that here the term κτῆμα, 'possession', is a metaphor,[31] but in both Thucydides and Longus it arguably is, and one that here contributes to the elision of the boundary between that which represents (Longus' literary work) and that which is represented (the painting): a fine painting can be a κτῆμα, 'possession', which its owner can treasure, show to his friends, and contemplate selling in a time of crisis, but in the ancient world few if any single books acquired that status. A further contribution to the issue of 'possession' is made later in Book 1 by the phrase used of Daphnis when he first admires Chloe's hair, eyes and complexion ὥσπερ τότε πρῶτον ὀφθαλμοὺς κτησάμενος, 'as if he had acquired eyes for the first time' (1.17.3). Eyes, like texts, can be viewed as possessions, but they are beneficial possessions only if they are used.[32]

These two cases of metaphorical possession may prepare the reader to question the appropriateness of the term in a third case: possession is the relationship Lycaenion wishes to establish between herself and her prospective lover, Daphnis – ἐπεθύμησεν ἐραστὴν κτήσασθαι, 'she conceived a desire to acquire him as her lover' (3.15.2) – but it is not a relationship we are ever told that either Daphnis or Chloe wish to establish *vis-à-vis* the other.

The last of the four uses of κτήσασθαι by Longus is 'straightforwardly' literal, when the couple is described at the narrative's closure as ἀγέλας … προβάτων καὶ αἰγῶν πλείστας κτησάμενοι, 'having acquired very many flocks of sheep and goats' (4.39.1): but even this instance may be seen as re-opening the issue of what can and cannot be a κτῆμα, 'possession'.

Creation

A different set of terms draws attention to the author's creative skills. The meadow in front of the Nymphs' cave is γλαφυρός (1.4.3): perhaps in the sense 'hollow' or 'concave', so that McCail's translation 'sunken' is more

[31] For an important discussion of this and other terms in the proem see Hunter 1983, 49–52.

[32] Philetas' words at 2.6.2 εἰ δὲ μή … ματαιοτέρας τὰς φρένας ἐκτησάμην, 'if I have not acquired too feeble a mind', might suggest ἐκτησάμην to be a dead or dormant metaphor when used of human attributes: but even a dormant metaphor can be reactivated by context.

likely than Lindsay's 'neatly flourishing'. But neither is very apt, and the epithet was surely chosen because it evokes a particular 'polished' or 'elegant' literary style.[33] A little later in Book 1 Eros' creation of a plot within the narrative (which can also be read as the creation of a plot-component by the author) is described as 'moulding' or 'devising': τοίανδε σπουδὴν Ἔρως ἀνέπλασε, 'Eros devised the following serious incident' (1.11.1).[34] This act of creativity re-emerges in Philetas' garden in Book 2: τὰ ἄνθη πάντα Ἔρωτος ἔργα, τὰ φυτὰ πάντα τούτου ποιήματα, 'all the flowers and plants are the works of Eros, all the plants are his creations' (2.7.3). True, this is no longer a metaphor: but given that the other, and much more common, sense of ποιήματα is what we find in Longus' only other use of this word, viz. 'poems' (2.31.2), its deployment here invites us to pursue the parallel between Eros and his beautiful but natural rustic ποιήματα, 'creations', on one hand and Longus and his elegantly crafted ποίημα, '(prose-)poem', on the other.[35]

A further aspect of Longus' creativity comes out in the work's sole use of the term σοφιστής, 'sophist', when Astylus wryly comments on Gnathon's eloquence in justifying his desire for Daphnis: μεγάλους ὁ Ἔρως ποιεῖ σοφιστάς, 'Eros produces great sophists' (4.18.1). Astylus here displays his own, and assumes Gnathon's, literary culture by adapting a famous line of Euripides,[36] but at this late stage in the work this is also an invitation to Longus' readers to assess how accomplished an erotic work has been composed by the writer whom some modern scholars think was clearly a sophist.

Neglect

A rather different issue which straddles the world of the creator and the world created by Longus is ἀμέλεια, 'neglect'. The presence of Pan in the paintings of the temple of Dionysus is referred to the lack of neglect on the part of the painter: οὐδὲ ὁ Πὰν ἠμέλητο, 'nor had Pan been neglected' (4.3.2). This is presumably metaphor, or at least a trope, in so far as the

33 Cf. LSJ *s.v.* γλαφυρός III.4: Gill's 'smooth' and Henderson's 'silky' are better still.

34 For ἀνέπλασε see Bowie 2019g, 117.

35 Longus' style has many poetic features, and some have seen it as so poetic as to justify setting out a translation as verse, most recently Cikán and Danek 2018. See Bowie 2019g, 7, and for poetic elements in the vocabulary of the novels Bowie 2017a (Chapter 40 in this volume).

36 ποιητὴν δ' ἄρα | Ἔρως διδάσκει, κἂν ἄμουσος ᾖι τὸ πρίν, 'Desire instructs a man to be a poet, even if he did not know the Muse before', Eur. fr. 663 Kannicht, also re-worked by Theocritus' friend Nicias of Miletus (*SH* 566), and much quoted by Plutarch: see further Bowie 2019g, 284.

painter's neglect or otherwise is not to be taken as the actual reason for Pan's appearance or non-appearance in his paintings; but Longus' choice of an oblique mode of expression is arguably the result of his recurrent interest in ἀμέλεια, an idea he uses in situations ranging between those in which literal 'neglect' is involved to others where it a very extended idea of 'neglect' is at stake, extended to the point where it becomes metaphorical.

Our first meeting with ἀμέλεια is when Lamon feels concern that a kid is ἀμέλουμενον, 'being neglected' by its mother-goat (1.2.2). The immediately following suggestion that he himself contemplated ἀμελῆσαι, 'neglecting' (1.3.1), the exposed child reminds us that its parents had shown an extreme form of ἀμέλεια in deciding to expose it. In the first spring the couple's still innocent foreplay causes Chloe to neglect her sheep (1.10.2), then as a consequence of Chloe's desire she τροφῆς ἠμέλει, 'neglected food' (1.13.6) – but is not eating 'neglecting food'? Then as a consequence of Daphnis' desire ἠμέλητο καὶ ἡ ἀγέλη, 'even his flock was neglected' (1.17.4). That neglect can also have a part in erotic relationships has just been shown by the fact that Dorcon τοῦ μὲν Δάφνιδος ἠμέλει, 'neglected Daphnis', in order to press his suit with Chloe (1.15.3). These instances of culpable or understandable ἀμέλεια culminate in Book 1 in the ἀμέλεια, 'neglect', shown by Chloe once again for her sheep when she discovers that Daphnis has been captured by pirates (1.28.3).

Similar neglect of flocks marks the couple's mutual help in the vintage (2.1.3); but when they are there described as ἀμελήσαντες … τῶν αἰγῶν καὶ τῶν προβάτων, 'neglecting … their goats and sheep', we are not entitled to imagine they made no alternative arrangements for tending them. A little later neglect of food as a symptom of a desire is pondered by the couple (2.8.2, twice). Neglect then vanishes from Book 2 until, in the couple's pantomime, Chloe mimes Syrinx ἀμελοῦσα, 'ignoring', her suitor: we are suddenly confronted with the possibility that one partner in this couple will start to 'neglect' the other, primarily in the sense of not reciprocating a sexual overture. That is the basis of Chloe's extraction of an oath from Daphnis at the end of the book, and her fear of ἀμέλεια comes out in her language when she discounts an oath Daphnis might swear by the god Pan: Pan's erotic inclinations make him untrustworthy, and, she says, Pan ἀμεληθεὶς ἐν τοῖς ὅρκοις ἀμελήσει σε κολάσαι, 'neglected in your oaths will neglect to punish you' (2.39.3).

The possible consequences of even apparently trivial ἀμέλεια are then explored early in Book 3. It is the escape of one of Dryas' sheepdogs with a piece of meat – having ἀμέλειαν φυλάξας, 'watched for a moment of inattention' – that enables Daphnis to make contact with Chloe in deep midwinter

(3.7.1). That this phrase is neither casual nor inattentive becomes clear when ἀμέλεια reappears *fortissimo* at the end of Book 3:[37] the apple plucked (with heavy symbolism) by Daphnis is there because a(nother) plucker ἠμέλησε καθελεῖν, 'had neglected to bring it down' (3.33.4). Daphnis' decision to pluck it against Chloe's wishes is perceived as ἀμέλεια of Chloe both by her and by the narrator – Χλόης κωλυούσης ἠμέλησεν. ἡ μὲν οὖν ἀμεληθεῖσα ..., 'when Chloe tried to prevent him he ignored her. So she, ignored, ...' (3.34.1) – and she runs off in anger to her sheep.

It is against this background that in Book 4 the reader approaches οὐδὲ ὁ Πὰν ἠμέλητο, 'nor had Pan been neglected' (4.3.2). First, this resurrects the earlier cases of ἀμέλεια and their sometimes unpredictable contributions to the advancement of the plot; second, it recalls the pivotal case of Pan's miraculous assistance to the couple in Book 2 despite their neglect of him hitherto – we realise that, though neither Pan nor Longus had specifically called this ἀμέλεια, it clearly was a flagrant case of culpable inattention; finally the artistic context of this (lack of) ἀμέλεια invites us to contrast Longus' own scrupulous attention to detail in his literary work with the variety of forms of ἀμέλεια displayed by his characters. That this ἀμέλεια has not run its course is shown late in Book 4 when Daphnis, rediscovered by his real parents, has almost forgotten Chloe, something he perceives as ἀμέλεια, 'neglect', when he apologises to her (4.29.5).

Image and Imitation

Two other, related terms also tie together the writer and the written. These are the noun εἰκών, 'image', and various forms of the verb μιμεῖσθαι, 'imitate'. The noun εἰκών is stretched to mean anything that stands in a mimetic relationship to something else. When Daphnis and Chloe fall to the ground while kissing they recognise their posture as τῶν ὀνείρων τὴν εἰκόνα, 'the figure of their dreams' (2.11.2); earlier the surface of the wolf-trap had been landscaped so as to be τῆς πρότερον γῆς εἰκόνα, 'a replica of the earth that had been there before' (1.11.2). In each case Longus seeks to remind us of the issue of *mimesis* central to the themes of his work, *mimesis* of which his preface insists his own writing is an example. Hence some of his uses of μιμεῖσθαι, 'to imitate', extend it too into the realm of metaphor. In this same wolf-trap scene the sense of τῆς πρότερον γῆς εἰκόνα is immediately

[37] I have some doubt that ἐς καμάτων ἀμέλειαν, perhaps 'to take their attention off their labours', is the correct text at 3.21.2: but if it is it can be seen as further extending the range of the operation of ἀμέλεια in Longus' world.

refashioned in the sentence γῆ οὐκ ἦν ἀλλὰ ἐμίμητο γῆν, 'it was not earth but it imitated earth' (1.11.2). Inanimate earth cannot be imitative, even if its landscapers aim at imitation. Nor can an unconscious body be imitative, but in the attack of Pan on the Methymnans σχῆμά τις ἐκεῖτο νεκροῦ μιμούμενος, 'one lay imitating the posture of a corpse' (2.25.4), while in Dionysophanes' garden ὁ κόρυμβος αὐτοῦ μέγας ὢν καὶ μελαίνομενος βότρυν ἐμιμεῖτο, 'the cluster of ivy berries in their size and darkening colour imitated grapes' (4.2.3). These cases where the inanimate is described as 'imitating' reinforce those where Daphnis and Chloe learn by imitation (e.g. 1.9.2), and the whole *assemblage* keeps reminding us of the literary work's claimed imitation of a (mimetic) painting.

Prizes and Play

Two remaining instances are more open to debate. First νικητήριον, 'a prize for victory'. When Daphnis has plucked the apple so manifestly symbolic of Chloe and presented it to her, he compares it to the golden apple awarded to Aphrodite and himself to Paris, saying τοῦτο ἐγώ σοι δίδωμι νικητήριον, 'I give this to you as a victory-prize' (3.34.2). But it is a recognition only of excellence, not of victory, since as far as Daphnis is concerned Chloe has not been in competition with any other girl. Given the not uncommon use of νικητήριον in contexts of artistic competition,[38] I am tempted to see the apple as a prize awarded by Longus to his own creation of the novel *Chloe*.[39]

Finally, Longus' last word. On her wedding night Chloe learns that what had happened in the woods had been ποιμένων παίγνια, 'shepherds' games' (4.40.3).[40] Now Longus does indeed use the verb παίζειν, 'to play', in several different contexts. He uses it of some of the couple's innocent activities, e.g. at 1.11.1; of Eros' behaviour in his garden Philetas says that ἔπαιζεν, 'he was playing' (2.4.1); Syrinx συνέπαιζεν, 'would play with', Nymphs (2.34.1); Chloe says to Daphnis παίζεις ἀπατῶν με, 'You are pulling my leg', when he claims that a fire burns his heart (3.10.4); and in Book 4 Gnathon refers to Astylus' habit of calling him Gnatharion as παίζων, 'teasing' (4.16.1). None of these numerous cases of 'play' is explicitly sexual, even if it is Eros in person who 'plays' at 2.4.1. The idea that the lovers lying down together

[38] Cf. LSJ *s.v.* νικητήριος II. *Chloe* is, of course, competing with other novels.

[39] The original titles of the Greek novels are uncertain (for a good discussion see Whitmarsh 2005b) but in the case of Longus Pan's statement that Chloe is παρθένον ἐξ ἧς Ἔρως μῦθον ποιῆσαι θέλει, 'a maiden out of whom Eros wants to make a myth' (2.27.2) supports the view that *Chloe* was his preferred title.

[40] For the text see Bowie 2019g, 308.

naked is to be seen as 'play' is thus new and metaphorical. At the time they do this they are deadly serious. That Longus chooses his last words to put the principal action of his four books into this metaphorical perspective is to be explained partly as the diminuendo of closure, partly, no doubt, as one way of saying that now, and only now, do the couple have serious, adult sexual relations. But the apparently technical literary term παίγνιον for a light-weight work (e.g. it was one category in the oeuvre of the Hellenistic poet Philetas)[41] gives the phrase a meta-literary thrust: 'this work, gentle reader, has been a shepherds' romp'.

5 The World of Learning

Terms for 'teaching' might be seen as a sub-set of 'the world of literature', but they probably deserve a separate category. In his preface Longus proclaims his work as one which will give preliminary instruction to τὸν οὐκ ἐρασθέντα προπαιδεύσει, 'the person who has not felt desire' (*pr.* 3). Perhaps this is not a strictly a metaphor, but this is not παιδεία, 'instruction' or 'education', in the sense that predominated in the literary and sophistic world of the late second or early third centuries AD (and which is found at 1.8.1, γράμματα ἐπαίδευον, 'they taught them letters'). Throughout his work Longus continues to play with the idea that instruction in ἔρως, 'desire', is a form of παιδεία. The most striking and important cases are:

(i) when, after Lycaenion's foreplay and manoeuvring, Daphnis is guided by his φύσις, 'nature': αὐτὴ γὰρ ἡ φύσις λοιπὸν ἐπαίδευε τὸ πρακτέον, 'for after that point nature herself instructed him what had to be done' (3.18.4)
(ii) when, once completed, Lycaenion's instruction is termed ἐρωτικὴ παιδαγωγία, 'an erotic tutorial' (3.19.1). This echoes the couple's night of pondering Philetas' exegesis in Book 2, an exegesis Longus later describes as παιδεύματα, 'lessons' (3.14.1): this pondering is termed a 'nocturnal tutorial', νυκτερινὸν παιδευτήριον (2.9.1).

It is characteristic of Longus that these central cases are set off by others which on their own would seem peripheral and trivial, and which also belong with the material discussed above ('Anthropomorphisation of Animals'). So Longus writes that the couple's animals ἐπεπαίδευντο, 'had been taught',

[41] Cf. Philetas *CA* frr. 10 and 11 = fr. 23 Spanoudakis, and the discussion in Spanoudakis 2002: 327–8.

to respond to their voice, to their panpipes, or to hand-clapping (1.22.2). Similarly he calls the way that Dorcon's cows had been taught to respond to music, τὸ παίδευμα τῶν βοῶν, 'the cows' instruction' (1.31.2); and his character Daphnis calls the Methymnans' dogs κακῶς πεπαιδευμένους, 'badly trained' (2.16.2). Like so much else in Longus, the world of παιδεία too affects the actions of animals as well as humans.

6 Conclusions

What emerges from these varied but interwoven exploitations of metaphorical language? The chief role of 'Symptoms and Concomitants of Desire' may be to locate Longus' writing ostentatiously and mimetically in the Greek literature of ἔρως, 'desire'. That may be complemented by a possible function of 'Literary and Meta-Literary Activity', i.e. to underline the literary origins and texture of the world that Longus offers his readers: he is a self-conscious narrator who never wants them to forget that everything on the page is his novelistic creation.

The part played by 'Anthropomorphisation' may be rather different. On a philosophical level it sets human ἔρως, 'desire', in the wider context of animal and even plant life, putting Longus in a tradition that goes back to Hesiod and Empedocles and appearing to offer a profounder λόγος, 'account', of ἔρως than do his novelistic intertexts, in which its operation had been examined almost wholly in a human context. But it also presents to a readership whose social and political world was emphatically hierarchical a universe in which such a hierarchy can be seen to break down. The Aristotelian hierarchy which placed human souls above animal souls, and these above vegetable souls, is challenged. So too is the hierarchy of the Greek πόλις that was endorsed by and was integral to the Roman imperial administration: the superiority of the city elites, οἱ πρῶτοι τῆς πολέως, 'the first men of the city', to the δῆμος, 'the people', and of both to δοῦλοι or οἰκέται, 'slaves', is called into question. This may be seen as complementing other features of *Daphnis and Chloe* that I have argued elsewhere raise questions about Roman control of the Greek world.[42] As some nine hundred years of Greek literary artists before Longus had shown, metaphor is good to think with.

[42] See Bowie 2019b (Chapter 43 in this volume).

Appendix

I gather in this appendix the few cases of metaphor in Longus that do not seem to fall into the above categories.

διαντλᾶν. In the phrase, ἡμέρας διήντλει μοχθηράς, 'she drained toilsome days' (4.9.1), the verb is used to give tragic colour to the reactions of Chloe when she fears Daphnis will be punished for Lampis' destruction of the master's garden: LSJ notes only metaphorical uses of the verb.

ἔνθεος. When the couple have had their lesson from Philetas, have failed to apply it, and have had a night of erotic dreams, they get up and go off to herd ἐνθεώτεροι (2.10.2). On one level this is metaphorical, like the English 'enthusiastic', but on another, and (in Longus) more important, level it is literal: the god Eros is working within them.[43]

ἐπιρρωνύναι. The verb is used not of physical but of psychological strengthening, ἐπιρρωνύουσα (2.23.2), as in many classical instances (cf. LSJ *s.v.*).

καθαρός. Daphnis postpones kissing Chloe until he has kissed all other members of her family ἵνα τὸ ἐκείνης καθαρὸν μείνῃ φίλημα, 'so that her kiss may remain untainted' (3.11.3). This may not be the most obvious choice of phrase, but it reminds the reader that the maintenance of Chloe's 'purity', in the sense of virginity, is an issue throughout the work (cf. especially Dionysophanes' question to Daphnis at 4.31.3).

καταφέρειν. In the phrase εἰς βάθυν ὕπνον κατενεχθέντος, 'borne down into a deep slumber' (4.34.1), the metaphor is paralleled in imperial (though not classical) writing (e.g. Luc. *DMeretr.* 2.4) and may be unremarkable; but it might perhaps be here to remind us of the surprising turn of events towards the end of Book 1 where (in Longus' only other use of the verb) the pirates drowned because τὰ ὅπλα κατήνεγκεν ἐς βυθόν, 'their weaponry pulled them down to sea-bed' (1.30.4).

μαλθάσσειν. Gnathon is described as μαλθάσσων, 'softening up' (4.11.4), Daphnis by praising his goats and offering to secure his freedom. The metaphor's pedigree in Attic tragedy (cf. Soph. *Ant* 1194, Eur. *HF* 298), immediately after Gnathon has been termed a θεατής, 'spectator', not of his performing goats but of Daphnis himself, suggests that Longus is underlining the generic oddity of this tragic spectacle.[44]

[43] Cf. Xen. *Smp.* 1.10.

[44] For the bearing of this scene on Longus' take on tragedy see Bowie 2007c (Chapter 31 in this volume).

ὀνειροπολεῖν. The verb, ὀνειροπολῶ, 'I have dreams', is once used literally (3.9.5) but three times of waking fantasy or speculation (3.32.3, 4.6.3, 30.3). The ontological status of such fantasising is cast into doubt by the recurrence and importance of real dreams in the work.

ὄχημα. Daphis' fall into the wolf-trap is cushioned by his having a goat as his ὄχημα, 'vehicle' (1.12.2). This borders on the cluster of metaphors that relates the animal and the human world, but does not quite fall within that cluster. It does, however, make a contribution to the recurrent contrast between ways of the city (where an ὄχημα is an ὄχημα) and of the country. Later in Book 1 Daphnis swims ashore effortlessly between two cows ὥσπερ ἐλαύνων ἅμαξαν, 'as if driving a wagon' (1.30.5), but none of the rural community is said to have, or indeed would be likely to have, a wagon or access to one. By contrast, though we are not told exactly how Dionysophanes and Clearistē come from the city (4.13), it must be with the ἵπποις καὶ ζεύγεσι καὶ τρυφῆι πολλῆι, 'horses, wagons, and much luxury', with which they returned to it (4.33.2).

28 The Construction of the Classical Past in the Ancient Greek Novels (2006)

1 Introduction

In *Daphnis and Chloe* the two eponymous children are taught γράμματα, 'letters', in a way that Longus suggests is not characteristic of rural life.[1] He does not tell us anything about what is involved in this basic education, but let us imagine – *per impossibile* – that their instruction was based exclusively on the Greek novels that we now know: what sort of conception of history would they have acquired from these texts? How would they see the periods of history of which they were given glimpses as relating to the world in which they or their master Dionysophanes lived?

2 The World According to Chariton

The Olympian gods have ruled the world from time immemorial – there is no mention of Giants or Titans. History, or myth, begins with the story of Amphion and Zethus (2.9.5). It acquires more substance in the generation before the Trojan war with Medea (2.9.3–4), whom Chariton presents as Scythian, and with Ariadne, who figures frequently as an example of a woman abandoned by her lover (1.6.2, 3.3.5, 4.1.7, 8.1.2). In the same generation Thetis (6.3.4) marries Peleus (1.1.16, 3.3.6), and their son Achilles appears early in the novel as a type of masculine beauty (1.1.3) and as an emblem of constancy to his partner Patroclus (1.5.2). Further glimpses of the Trojan war come when Callirhoe is compared to Helen (2.6.1, 5.2.8, 5.9) and Dionysius of Miletus sees himself as a Menelaus (5.2.8). The very short roll-call of heroes of the Trojan war is completed by Protesilaus (5.10). However the world of the Trojan war is repeatedly evoked by Chariton's frequent citations of hexameters from the Homeric poems, more from the *Iliad*, but quite a few from the *Odyssey*.

[1] τροφαῖς ἁβροτέραις ἔτρεφον καὶ γράμματα ἐπαίδευον καὶ πάντα ὅσα καλὰ ἦν ἐπ' ἀγροικίας, 'they fed them on more delicate foods and they taught them writing and all the things that were admired in the countryside', Longus 1.8.1.

Thereafter Chariton's time-line is a blank until the sixth century BC, from which he offers two fleeting references to Cyrus the Great (2.9.5, 6.8.7). By contrast the period in which the novel's action is set, some time after the end of the Peloponnesian War and the accession of Artaxerxes II to the Persian throne, is filled out with much convincing detail, not all of it accurate. Syracuse is a democracy in which Hermocrates, father of the heroine Callirhoe, still has a leading role; his rival, father of the hero Chaereas, has the name Ariston, which Chariton may also have drawn from the historians' accounts of the Athenian expedition of 415–413 BC, but there it is the name of a Corinthian ally[2] – if Chariton has got it from his reading of the events of 415–413, it was a careless reading. It suits the plot to have Hermocrates insist that Syracusan democracy is one in which the law is supreme (3.4.16) – a man who participated in Callirhoe's abduction must be put to death, following a court-judgement, and not be questioned further so that Chaereas and the Syracusans can discover where Callirhoe is likely to be. It also suits the colour Chariton wants to give this scene that the assembly should include women as well as men: this is a move from the world of reality to the world of adventure – it is not simply an anachronism, because even if women played a major part as benefactors in the Greek cities of Asia Minor in the Roman period, they did not take part in meetings of βουλαί, 'councils', or of ἐκκλησίαι, 'assemblies'.[3]

Syracuse's old enemy Athens is also represented as large, rich and under the rule of law, but there trials are conducted by the Areopagus (1.11.6–7), a detail more likely to reflect imperial practice than to be a simple distortion of the state of affairs in early-fourth-century Athens – though Chariton may have encountered the ascription to the Areopagus of a duty to νομοφυλακεῖν, 'safeguard the laws', either by the author of *Ath.* 8.4 or in some similar tradition. That apart, the Athenians are garrulous busybodies hell-bent on litigation,[4] a caricature of classical Athens that is also found later in Lucian.[5] Sparta comes into the story only tangentially: the Laconian in Chaereas' band of mercenaries who proposed that the band return to Greece is by happy coincidence a relative of Brasidas (8.2.12).

2 Th. 7.39.2. On Chariton's presentation of fifth-century history see Billault 1989; Connors 2002; Smith 2007; on mythology Billault 2019.

3 See van Bremen 1996, esp. 55–6.

4 τὴν πολυπραγμοσύνην τῶν Ἀθηναίων ... δῆμος λάλος καὶ φιλόδικος, 'the Athenians who are natural busybodies ... a loquacious and litigious people', Ch. 1.11.6.

5 E.g. Luc. *Icar.* 16.

Two other areas of the Greek world are added to the chronotope. Ionia, where Callirhoe is sold to an agent of the rich Dionysius of Miletus and then marries Dionysius, has the cities Miletus and Priene: not a hint of Ephesus, Clazomenae or Smyrna, and when Callirhoe is compared to Artemis it is manifestly to the lean huntress and not to the cult-statue of the Artemisium (4.7.5, 6.4.6). But then the only citizen of Miletus whose name we learn is Dionysius himself. The Hellenic credentials of Dionysius are stressed more than once, and his marriage to Callirhoe is emphatically under Greek law (3.2.2).

Chariton's Ionia has two features we might want to call anachronisms. One is the temple at Miletus of Ὁμόνοια, '*Concord*', where Dionysius and Callirhoe are married according to what is said to be traditional Milesian practice.[6] Cults of *Homonoia* may be getting going early in the fourth century, when we have a cult of the Ὁμόνοια of the Hellenes attested at Plataea.[7] But we have none attested for Miletus then or later, and marriages in a temple of Ὁμόνοια can hardly have been traditional in the early fourth century BC. It is most likely that Chariton's conception of Ὁμόνοια is a fusion of its prominence in the Greek city and inter-city politics of the Hellenistic and Roman periods – well attested by coins and by Plutarch, Dio, and Aristides[8] – and the very important temple of *Concordia* in Rome, re-dedicated by the future emperor Tiberius in AD 10.

The other 'anachronism' is the ruler of Priene; a στρατηγός (*stratēgos*) with the name Bias. Chariton never flags this Bias as the σοφός, 'sage',[9] and we are left wondering if he has collapsed his archaic and classical worlds, so that a seventh-century figure is transplanted to the fourth century BC, or if he is just playing with the name, and tempting his readers to see in

[6] ὅπου πάτριον ἦν τοῖς γαμοῦσι τὰς νύμφας παραλαμβάνειν, 'where it was the ancestral custom for bridegrooms to receive their brides', Ch. 3.3.16.

[7] Cf. Étienne and Piérart 1975, discussing a text of the third century BC, *SEG* 40.412.

[8] See D. Chr. *Or.* 38, Plu. *Prae. reip. ger.*, Aristid. *Orr.* 23 and 24 Keil: cf. Pera 1984; Sheppard 1984–6; Shapiro 1990; Kienast 1995. For a temple of *Homonoia* at Stratonicea in 39 BC see *IStr.* 11.5; at Cyme, *SEG* 33.1041.viii.8; a statue of *Homonoia Sebastē* in the theatre of Ephesus in AD 104, *IEph.* 27F.440, 27G.471; priests at Mylasa, *IMyl.* 903.18, Priene, *IPri.* 111.199, and Blaundus, *SEG* 46.1491 (where a propylon is dedicated jointly to *Homonoia* and Athena); of *Homonoia Sebastē* at Perge, *IPerge* 58.5 etc.

[9] Bias was commemorated on coins of Priene in the imperial period, see *RPC* iv.2 1364 and 2415, which also show that the city's chief magistrate in this period was not a στρατηγός but an ἄρχων, *RPC* ii 1144–5. Like fifth-century Athens, Hellenistic Priene had a college of στρατηγοί, cf. *IPriene* 113.114. By the 80s BC Priene had a public building suitable for entertainment of the council and magistrates called the Βιαντιεῖον, *IPriene* 111.245, 113.73, 117 B ii 34.

this στρατηγός a descendant of the famous Bias of Priene.[10] The temptation to do the former might have been all the greater if Chariton knew the Plutarchan dialogue *Symposium of the Seven Sages*,[11] but if I am right to date Chariton as early as the 50s AD[12] such knowledge is impossible.

The other extension of Chariton's world beyond the cities in which its action is actually set is in the West. In Sicily Acragas and Messene, in South Italy Rhegium and Thurii: the suitors of Callirhoe include the son of a tyrant of Rhegium and a tyrant from Acragas (1.2.2 and 4), the bandit Theron knows potential accomplices from Messene and Thurii (1.7.2). Again we have either inaccuracy or insouciant collapsing. By the early fourth century BC neither Acragas nor Rhegium had tyrants – indeed after being sacked by the Carthaginians in 406 BC Acragas was unlikely to produce an eminent suitor of any sort – but the model of Penelope's suitors in the *Odyssey* and the suitors of Agariste in Herodotus (6.126ff.) pushed Chariton to have tyrants in these cities too, and Pindaric *epinicia* (*Olympians* 2 and 3 for Theron), whose reading in the first and second centuries AD was not confined to the very learned, made tyrants of Acragas especially colourful. Messene and Thurii are not in themselves problematic: but later Chariton also seems to suppose a Sybaris that was still flourishing, despite the original city's destruction in 510 BC and its refounding as Thurii. We might take refuge in the fact that Sybaris figures only in a false tale,[13] but Chariton may not have been so scrupulous. Sybaris is a well-known name from archaic Greek history that gives Chariton's South Italy plausible local colour.

Chariton's historical geography of Asia Minor is a little more complex. The terms Phrygia, Lydia and Caria all fit an Asia Minor administered by Persian satraps,[14] and a Pharnaces who is satrap of Lydia and Ionia[15] might be deemed a fictional successor, with a decent Persian name, to the

[10] Such evocation of great men of the classical past was not uncommon. From Ephesus early in the third century AD we know a Ti. Claudius Themistocles (*ILS* 883 = *IEph* 655; *PIR*^{2} C 1040; Campanile 1994, 80–1 no. 68a) whose name passed to his grandson Q. Statius Themistocles. *IG* ii^2 3704. A different family in Ephesus has an Aurelius Themistocles (*IGR* i 798; Campanile 1994,128 no. 143). A distant relative of the sophist Varus of Perge was given the name Pericles: P. Plancius Magnianus Aelianus Arrius Pericles, honoured at Selge, see *PIR*^{2} P 440, *ISelge* 15. In Priene a prominent citizen in the third century BC was called Bias (*IPriene* 23.10), and in the first century BC a large public building was called the Biantieion (*IPriene* 113.88), but no imperial cases of the personal name Bias are yet known.

[11] *Mor*. 146b–64d.

[12] Bowie 2002a (Chapter 25 in this volume): cf. Tilg 2010; Henrichs 2011, both accepting a Neronian date.

[13] Ch. 1.12.8, 2.1.9, 5.5. [14] Ch. 2.4 etc. [15] Ch. 4.1.7 etc.

historical Tissaphernes who had been based in Sardis. However the satrap who falls in love with Callirhoe, Mithridates, has Caria as his fief. Chariton never specifies Mithridates' headquarters, but the implications of his movements[16] put them surprisingly near the great city of Aphrodisias in Caria, from which the author Chariton claims to come. I take it that readers are meant to perceive this, to be well aware that Aphrodisias itself was nothing at all in the early fourth century BC, but to feel a twinge of *campanilismo* when Mithridates, satrap of Caria, is given a major role in the story. That Mithridates is sympathetically presented may be argued to relate to the presence in first-century Aphrodisias of a prominent citizen who bore the name Mithradates, and who happens to be the son of an Athenagoras, the name borne by the *rhetor* to whom Chariton claims to be secretary.[17]

There are some other contaminations from Chariton's contemporary world.[18] Greek is spoken as far East as the Euphrates, in Cilicia and Syria;[19] it is the Euphrates that is seen as the boundary between Greek and barbarian territory. Less important, perhaps, are details such a Chinese bow and quiver,[20] the situation of Paphus by the sea,[21] whereas the classical site was inland, and the name Hyginus given to a man who seems to be Persian working for the satrap Mithridates[22] – a name whose use in the Greek world does not seem to antedate the first century BC. Perhaps it would be right to dismiss this material, like the temple of Ὁμόνοια, and to say that Chariton may not have realised that these were anachronisms, and if he had done, he would not have cared. They might have seemed part of the long and relatively unchanging fabric of Greek culture, like competitive games, of which those at Olympia are twice picked out,[23] the mysteries at Eleusis,[24] the monetary use of talents, and the social phenomenon of banquets and *symposia*.[25]

But that is not the only way of explaining these phenomena. In his first sentence Chariton identifies himself as the secretary of a *rhetor* from Aphrodisias. The implied reader is a person to whom those terms make sense, and the recurrent intrusions of the authorial person in the narrative remind the reader that all this *is* being told by a man from early imperial Aphrodisias. If dissonances are detectable by such a reader, he may

[16] Especially Ch. 3.7.
[17] *IAph2007* 12.410: cf. Reynolds 1999; Ch. 1.1.1.
[18] For some further cases see Alvares 2001–2.
[19] Ch. 5.1.3. [20] Ch. 6.4.2. [21] Ch. 8.2.7. [22] Ch. 4.5.1–3, 7.1.
[23] Games, Ch. 4.4; Olympia Ch. 5.4.4, 6.2.1. [24] Ch. 5.4.4.
[25] Talents, Ch. 1.14.5; banquets and *symposia*, Ch. 4.3.7.

be inclined to read them against the proclaimed identity of the author. Mithridates' Carian location is one such detail. Perhaps the name Hyginus is too. Some readers are likely to know of the prolific Augustan writer C. Iulius Hyginus,[26] pupil of the even more prolific Alexander Polyhistor, a man from one of Chariton's two Ionian cities, Miletus, captured and brought to Rome in Rome's wars against none other than the great Mithridates. Another allusion to a contemporary figure has been suggested by Christopher Jones – to the great sophist from Miletus, Ti. Flavius Claudianus Dionysius, whose eminence earned him one of Philostratus' *Lives of the sophists*.[27] The sort of allusion to a contemporary that Jones supposes seems to me to be provocatively risky, and I would indeed see the important role given to a Dionysius of Miletus in the novel as a support for the earlier date for Chariton for which I have argued on other grounds.[28]

If there is anything at all here, it is chiefly that Chariton is teasing the reader with the oddity of this name Hyginus being attached to an agent of a man Mithridates. Another such game may be his choice of the name Polycharmus. This is not a very common name, but it was well known in Athens of the first half of the first century AD, the only Athens Chariton is likely personally to have known. There it was borne by one of the brothers of the Herodes who was great-grandfather of Herodes Atticus. This Polycharmus of Marathon was priest of a Drusus in the year of the latter's consulate (perhaps Drusus the son of Tiberius in the year AD 21) and later, between AD 30 and 37, priest of Tiberius, as attested at Eleusis.[29]

But something more is at least conceivable. By lacing his mainly consistent presentation of a classical Greek setting with occasional features that may strike a reader as contemporary, not classical, Chariton may ask them to bring these worlds closer to each other than they were. That collapse is aided by his silence on the intervening periods. Of course if the narrative is set in the very early fourth century BC we should not expect authorial references to the political developments of the 450 or so years between then and 'now'. But if some of these 'anachronisms' suggest the 'here and now', and if Chariton's opening sentence explicitly takes us to the 'here and now', then in some sense we must notice the gap. We form the impression that the immediate antecedent of the world of Chariton of Aphrodisias and his readers is not the

[26] On Hyginus and his role as librarian in Rome see Bowie 2013e (Chapter 32 in Volume 3).

[27] Philostr. *VS* 1.22: see Puech 2002, 229–32; Jones 1992a.

[28] Bowie 2002a (Chapter 25 in this volume).

[29] Drusus, *IG* ii^2 1730; Tiberius, *IEleusis* 344 = *IG* ii^2 3530. See further *PIR*^{2} P 559.

later fourth century BC – we hear of no Philip, no Alexander[30] – nor is it the Hellenistic period: it is the period of Hermocrates, Chaereas and Callirhoe.

Chariton's temporal scheme thus has three blocks: the Trojan war, the era of Chaereas and Callirhoe, and the readers' own world. Not much seems to separate the first and the second, and even less separates the second and the third.

3 The World According to Achilles Tatius

Achilles Tatius' readers are confronted with a world in some ways similar to those of Chariton, but also perceptibly different. The state of affairs before the rule of the Olympian gods is twice implied by references to the Prometheus myth (2.21.1–2, 3.6.3–8.7). Of the Olympians, Aphrodite and her son Eros predictably figure very frequently (1.10.2–3 etc., 1.1.13 etc.) but others too are much more in evidence than in Chariton: Zeus (1.8.2 and eleven other places); Artemis (from 4.1.4 onwards), though many of her appearances are concerned with her cult at Ephesus and its part in the concluding books. Less frequent are Poseidon (3.5.4, 3.6.4, 5.16.5), Apollo (1.5.5, 7, 3.6.1), Athena (2.14.1, 5–6, 8.6.6), Hephaestus (2.14.1, 5–6), and Dionysus (2.2.1, 3–5, 2.3.1, 3.3, 8.4.2). Hera (2.37.3), Hermes (2.6.3), and Selene (1.4.3) are each mentioned only once.

Myths are told at length or are alluded to much more often than in Chariton. The reader learns that Thebes was founded from Sidon (1.1.1), that Tithonus was loved by Eos (1.15.8), Alcmena, Danae, Ganymede and Europa by Zeus,[31] Arethusa by Alpheus (1.18.2). Myths whose setting antedates the Trojan war include those of Andromeda (3.6.3–7.9), Marsyas (3.15.4); Niobe (3.15.6); Omphale (2.6.2); Phaedra and Hippolytus (1.8); Stheneboea, Eriphyle, and Aerope (1.8.4); and Tereus, Philomela and Procne (esp. 5.5.2–3, 7–9). The generation of the Trojan war itself is represented by Achilles (1.8.5, 6.1.3), Agamemnon (1.8.5–7), Briseis (1.8.5), Chryseis (1.8.5), Helen (1.8.6), and Penelope (1.8.6); the following generation by Orestes and Iphigeneia (8.2).[32]

[30] There is, of course, an allusion to the campaigns of Alexander in the obstinacy of the besieged Tyrians in 7.2–4: Chaereas' success in capturing Tyre reworks and upstages that of Alexander after a seven-month siege in 332 BC.

[31] Alcmena 2.36.4, 37.4, Danae 2.36.4, 37.4; Ganymede 2.37.3; Europa 1.1.2, 2.15.4.

[32] They are not named, but the reader must think of them when picking up the allusion to Eur. *IT* 617–21 at 8.2.3. For an important investigation of the novelists' reworking of several of these mythological patterns see Lefteratou 2018.

The overlap between Chariton's mythology and that of Achilles Tatius is not great. Partly, perhaps, this is due to the latter's interest in paintings, and it might be fanciful to see a conscious avoidance of duplication. But some absences clearly have a literary purpose: no Homeric Menelaus – that name is needed by Achilles Tatius for a young Egyptian who plays a major role as a companion and friend of Cleitophon from 2.33 to 5.15. And, by contrast with Chariton's numerous hexameter quotations, Achilles quotes very little. In the case of two references in his authorial voice to the *Iliad* (2.1.1 to the simile of a lion fighting a boar at 16.823–6; 2.15.3 to the horses of Rhesus at 10.436–7), and two lines actually quoted (by the character Menelaus, 20.234–5 at 2.36.3), Homer each time is mentioned by name. Two lines (57–8) are cited from the *Works and Days* by Cleinias at 1.8.2, without attribution to Hesiod. So these two archaic poets are present in Achilles Tatius' *imaginaire*. But this quotation of Homer is nugatory by comparison with that in Chariton, and one might wonder if his decision to quote two lines of Hesiod as well as *only* two of Homer – and these about a character so peripheral to the Iliad and so congenial to Achilles Tatius as Ganymede – is asking us to question the literary merit of Chariton's recurrent quotations from *Iliad* and *Odyssey*.

Between the generation after the Trojan war and the Hellenistic period there is a striking desert. The archaic period, well-evoked by the author of *Metiochus and Parthenope*, might as well not have existed. There are fleeting allusions to Candaules and his wife (1.8.5) and to the cup crafted by Glaucus of Chios (2.3.1), both likely to be familiar to Achilles and his readers from Herodotus (1.12 and 25 respectively).

The classical period, about which much can be learned by readers of Chariton, is also shadowy, and again it is texts and not historical events that offer what details there are. A reference to Taurian practices (8.2.3) alludes to Euripides' *Iphigeneia in Tauris* (617–21); the priest of Artemis resorts to abuse (8.9.1) on the grounds of which the narrator says of him that τὴν Ἀριστοφάνους ἐζήλωκει κωμωιδίαν, 'he emulated the comedy of Aristophanes'. These canonical authors are the nearest we are taken to classical Athens, unless we see the fact that the presidency of the Ephesian court falls to a man who is τοῦ βασιλικοῦ γένους, 'of royal descent', as some sort of transference to Ephesus of the role of the ἄρχων βασιλεύς, 'royal archon', in Athens.

By contrast many references show the action to be later than Alexander. The cities of Alexandria (2.31 etc.) and probably Berytus (2.31.5–6); the cults of Zeus Sarapis (5.2.1) and perhaps of Zeus Casius (3.6.1). But how much later? Egypt is governed by a man whom Achilles Tatius calls a σατράπης, 'satrap' (4.11.1), perhaps a classicising way of referring to the Roman *praefectus Aegypti*, 'prefect of Egypt'. The description μητρόπολις used of Alexandria or Heliopolis (4.18.1) fits imperial practice.[33] But the war fought by the city of Byzantium against Thracians (1.3.6, 2.24.2–3) prevents a simple location of the action in the Roman Empire. No help is given by references to many places or phenomena that could be either Hellenistic or Roman – Olympic games (1.18.2), commerce with India (3.7.5), the temple of Artemis and associated asylum and festivals at Ephesus (7.13.2ff.). One explanation might be that Achilles Tatius does not himself care, or even prefers us (his readers) to be unable to decide between Hellenistic and Roman contexts. Another is that for him and his readers Alexander is the only important dividing line: before Alexander some canonical texts and a clutch of myths known from such texts and from the visual arts (myths we associate with the Bronze Age), after Alexander a 'modern world' where the difference between the third century BC and Achilles Tatius' own time is of no consequence. To some extent I would support the latter explanation. But the exclusion of Romans or anything manifestly Roman is a problem. Not, then, a careless, but a careful and premeditated, elision of the Hellenistic and Roman periods.

4 The World According to Xenophon

Xenophon's world is quite different from that of the other four 'ideal' novels. Like Achilles Tatius, he offers a setting that has the flavour both of the Hellenistic and of the Roman periods. Stray hints might point to location in a pre-Alexandrian world: the inhabitants of Tyre are βάρβαροι, 'non-Greeks' (2.2); Syria is adjacent to Phoenicia but somehow different from it (2.3); the old Aegialeus who fled from Sparta as a young man (5.1) seems to be a throw-back to Sparta of the classical period. But none of this can be pressed, and clear markers set the action after Alexander. Most obvious among these are the cities of Alexandria itself (3.8, 10), of Antioch (2.9), and of Laodicea in Syria (4.1, 5). Mazaca (3.1), by Xenophon's time Caesarea Mazaca, is Hellenistic too, but that might not strike a reader so forcefully. Other details point in the same direction, even if they are not compelling: the cult of Isis (1.6, 5.13), the formal organisation of ephebes (1.2, 5.1), firmly documented in Athens of the 330s BC, but becoming a widespread institution in the Hellenistic period.[34] As in Achilles Tatius,

[33] For the early first century AD see from Egypt *IGR* iv 1163–4. But the term (and competition for it) was much commoner in Asia Minor, especially *provincia Asia*, with almost 500 epigraphic cases.

[34] For the ephebic system in Hellenistic and Roman Egypt see Legras 1999.

some details point to a Roman imperial time-frame: Egypt is governed not by a king but by an ἄρχων, 'ruler', though it turns out that this ἄρχων has a relation called Polyidus (5.3.1 etc.); ostriches from Nabataea stride into the text (1.8.2). Some ancient readers may have known that the office of εἰρηνάρχης, 'commissioner of the peace', was not documented before the end of the first century AD, but they may have been less inclined to make much of this than modern scholars have been.[35] More influential on their perceptions may have been the fact that Habrocomes, the hero, is taken by the story as far west as Nuceria in south-central Italy (5.8, 10).[36] For a reader of the first or second centuries AD this might well impart a contemporary flavour. But again, as we have already seen in Achilles Tatius, there seems to be an amalgam of the Hellenistic and Roman worlds, with nothing absolutely demanding the latter to be taken as the historical context, far less an explicit mention of Rome or of Romans (the nearest being the perhaps teasing introduction of Nuceria).

Unlike Achilles Tatius, however, Xenophon gives his half-modern world no past. There is not a single reference to a Greek myth, nor to the archaic or classical periods of Greek history. Xenophon's world might, in theory, have been created during the conquests of Alexander and have existed for no more than two or three hundred years. This presents a remarkable contrast with Xenophon's broad geographical sweep – his narrative introduces many more parts of the Mediterranean world than that of Chariton or Achilles Tatius – but that is a different, albeit related, issue. In the matter of his construction of the past, Xenophon knows only one block of time, an imprecise fusion of the Hellenistic and contemporary worlds.

5 The World According to Longus

Yet a different temporal vision is presented by Longus. Like Achilles Tatius and Xenophon, and unlike Chariton and Heliodorus, Longus does not point his readers to a specific era as the context of his chiefly pastoral story. Many features could be taken to mark any one of the classical, the Hellenistic or the Roman periods: the prosperous and beautiful city of

[35] Perilaus ἄρχειν μὲν ἐχειροτονήθη τῆς εἰρήνης τῆς ἐν Κιλικίαι, 'had been elected to be in charge of peace in Cilicia', 3.9.5. For discussions see Bowie 2002a (Chapter 25 in this volume, 521); Rife 2002.

[36] Coleman 2011 argues persuasively that Xenophon's choice of Nuceria (which Xenophon's MS F spells Μουκέριον) points to a date after Stabiae's destruction by Vesuvius' eruption in 79 and before Stabiae's resurgence as a port in the reign of Pius. For an isolated testimony to a Greek γραμματικός, '*grammaticus*', in Nuceria see *SEG* 54.960.

Mytilene (1.1); the government of Mytilene and of Methymna by a δῆμος that elects στρατηγοί[37] and expects its elite to disburse its riches generously on liturgies;[38] and that elite's ownership of large estates, where the couple grows up as a goatherd and a shepherdess in a simple rustic environment. The two young people's elite fathers, Dionysophanes and Megacles, could also fit almost any period, though the name Dionysophanes matches a pattern of Mytilenean nomenclature known from the first century BC and later,[39] while the name Megacles is only specifically attested for Mytilene for the archaic period.[40] The narrator's visit to a shrine of the Nymphs which opens the novel and allegedly furnishes its plot well fits the cultural tourism of the imperial period but could be imagined at any epoch in pagan Greek culture.[41]

But some details do not fit the context of the Roman Empire. Pirates in the north-eastern Aegean are anomalous after the thirties BC.[42] The apparently total autonomy of Methymna and Mytilene, empowered to go to war with each other, and to deploy respectively ten ships[43] and 3000 hoplites and 500 cavalry under a general Hippasus,[44] can hardly be imagined after the creation of *provincia Asia* in 129 BC, and seems to suggest that the story took place in the classical or the Hellenistic period, but certainly not later.

The time-frame is to some extent vague, then. Moreover this world lacks temporal depth. Whereas Achilles Tatius mentions the foundation of a city (that of Thebes from Phoenician Sidon),[45] we are given no hint how

[37] Longus 3.1. An ἐκκλησία, 'assembly', is explicitly attributed to Methymna (2.19.1), whereas for Mytilene the official designation in Longus is always (οἱ) Μυτιληναῖοι, '(the) Mytileneans', not ὁ δῆμος τῶν Μυτιληναίων, 'the people of the Mytileneans'. But the term κεχειροτονημένος, 'elected' (3.1.4), and the parallel with Methymna, together strongly suggest an actively participating δῆμος.

[38] Longus 4.35.3. For the role of liturgies in Greek cities cf. Davies 1967; Veyne 1978; van Bremen 1996.

[39] Especially the historian Theophanes, whose *patronus* was Pompey, and whose descendants included the *consul suffectus* of AD 115, M. Pompeius Macrinus (*PIR*² P 628), honoured in some epigraphic texts as νέος Θεοφάνης, 'the new Theophanes': cf. Morgan 2004, 1; Mason 2018, 140–1; Bowie 2019g, 274–5.

[40] Arist. *Pol.* 1311b27; Bowie 2019g, 301.

[41] For nymphs see Larson 2001; Bowie 2015c (Chapter 39 in this volume); at Mytilene, Mason 2018, 138–44.

[42] 1.28.1. These pirates, probably Tyrian (Τύριοι) as they are described by MS V (a reading for which Morgan 2004, 173 *ad loc.* offers good arguments), have of course an important literary function, linking Longus' story with earlier Greek novels by exploitation of a recurrent motif: cf. Bowie 2019g, 155–6.

[43] Methymna, 2.19.3. [44] Mytilene, 3.1.2. [45] Ach. Tat. 1.1.1.

Methymna or Mytilene came to be where they are. We may be prompted to recall Mytilene's history in archaic Greece by the name given to Chloe's real father, Megacles (cf. n.40), and by several allusions to Sappho and Alcaeus, or we may be tempted to recall Mytilene's revolt from the Athenian empire in 428 BC by repeated echoes of Thucydides in the account of the war between Methymna and Mytilene at the end of Book 2 and the beginning of Book 3, where the narrative has a strong 'historiographical flavour',[46] one that is indeed particularly Thucydidean.[47] But these are data drawn upon by the narrating 'I' whom Longus creates – a figure from outside the world of Daphnis and Chloe, perhaps indeed from outside Lesbos. They are not features of which characters in the narrative can be seen to be aware. Likewise it is the narrator's touch to evoke *Odyssey* Book 19 and Penelope's dream of her geese being attacked by an eagle when he has the concupiscent Lycaenion lure Daphnis into the woods by pretending that an eagle has taken one of her geese.[48] Unlike characters in Chariton, Achilles Tatius and Heliodorus, the *dramatis personae* of Longus either do not know, or certainly do not show that they know, Homer.

There is, admittedly, some knowledge shown of other mythology. Eros presents himself as older than Cronus; Daphnis, surprisingly, knows that Zeus was suckled by a goat, alludes to the myth of Pan and Pitys, and tells the myth of Echo and an otherwise unattested myth about a cowgirl metamorphosed into a φάττα, 'dove'.[49] Lamon knows the stories of Pan and Syrinx, and of Marsyas.[50] The narrator refers to myths which led to wide diffusion of the name Bosporus, but offers no details,[51] and compares Daphnis to Apollo when he herded cattle for Laomedon, alluding to lines of the *Iliad*.[52] The narrator also tells us that Gnathon, Astylus' parasite from the city, is well-versed in ἐρωτικὴ μυθολογία, 'myths about love', which he has learned in συμπόσια, 'symposia', of the dissolute, and indeed Gnathon then adduces myths of Anchises and Aphrodite, Branchus and Apollo, and Ganymede and Zeus.[53]

[46] Morgan 2004, 186. [47] Cf. Cueva 1998; Trzaskoma 2005; Bowie 2019g, 221.
[48] 3.16, cf. Od. 19.536ff.; Bowie 2019g, 238.
[49] Cronus, 2.5.2; Zeus, 1.16.3; Pitys 1.27.2; Echo 3.23; the φάττα 1.27.
[50] Syrinx 2.34; Marsyas 4.8.4. [51] 1.30.6, cf. Bowie 2019g, 160–1.
[52] 4.10.2, cf. Il. 21.444ff.
[53] 4.17.3–7. Likewise it is the city couple Dionysophanes and Cleariste who utter the only exclamations ὦ Ζεῦ δέσποτα, 'O lord Zeus', and φίλαι Μοῖραι, 'Dear Fates', respectively, at 4.21.2–3.

This is much more than Xenophon offers his readers, but it is a very selective set of glimpses of traditional mythology by comparison with the other three novelists. Its bias towards myths involving herding is natural, given the plot of *Daphnis and Chloe*, but that bias simply reinforces our impression of a world in the Mytilenean χώρα, 'countryside', that has constructed for itself a Greek mythological past quite different from that current in the city cultures of the eastern Empire.

There is a related idiosyncrasy. Daphnis is given the name Daphnis, we are told, so that it might *seem* pastoral.[54] That implies, without explicitly stating, the existence of a previous Daphnis who was also a herdsman – and for readers of the second or third centuries AD that Daphnis will inevitably be identified with the quasi-mythical Daphnis who was the subject of the song of Thyrsis in Theocritus 1 (and who is also alluded to by Lycidas in his song in Theocritus 7).[55] Of course as readers proceed further into Longus' work they discover how closely dependent his pastoral landscape is on that of Theocritean poetry, and indeed in Book 2 they are given a carefully worked allusion to the song of Thyrsis in Theocritus 1.[56]

The paucity of allusion to standard mythology in the mouths of the country-folk therefore has a purpose. The urban readers are to understand that these people do have a μυθολογία, 'a telling of myths', but that it is different from theirs: it already has a figure called Daphnis, it knows a metamorphosis of a cowgirl into a bird that is nowhere to be found in our very ample collections of stories of metamorphosis, and its main strand of story-telling, μυθολογία, centres on Pan[57] – as, of course, does the narrator's own tale. This rural mythology cannot therefore be fitted into the genealogical time-line and kinship networks that had provided a framework for πόλις-centred and (very often)

[54] ὡς δ' ἂν καὶ τοὔνομα τοῦ παιδίου ποιμενικὸν δοκοίη, Δάφνιν αὐτὸν ἔγνωσαν καλεῖν, 'and so that the child's name might also seem pastoral, they decided to call him "Daphnis"', 1.3.2.

[55] Theoc. 1.19, 64–137; 7.73–7. Daphnis also appears as a young cowherd engaged in a singing context with another cowherd, Damoetas, in Theoc. 6, and is mentioned in poems 5, [8] and 27 in the Theocritean corpus, but these appearances do not give him the quasi-mythical character Daphnis has in 1 and 7. There do indeed seem to have been Sicilian myths about Daphnis before Theocritus (see the commentaries of Gow, Dover and Hunter on Theoc. 1), and the Sicilian poet Stesichorus of Himera is credited by Ael. *VH* 10.18 with a poem about Daphnis which editors tend incautiously to deem a misattribution, e.g. Stesich. fr.279 *PMGF* = 323 Finglass. On these see Bowie 2012b (Chapter 23 in Volume 1).

[56] μῦθον, ὃν αὐτῶι Σικελὸς αἰπόλος ᾖισεν ἐπὶ μισθῶι τράγωι καὶ σύριγγι, 'a tale, which a Sicilian goatherd sang to him for the payment of a he-goat and a panpipe', 2.33.3, reworks Theoc. 1.23–61, where an unnamed Sicilian αἰπόλος offers Thyrsis a marvellous cup and the opportunity to milk his best she-goat in exchange for Thyrsis singing τὰ Δάφνιδος ἄλγεα, and [Theoc.] 8.85ff., where payment takes the form of a goat and of a panpipe just won in a contest. See further Bowie 2019g, 212; 2021b.

[57] 2.34–5, 3.23, and at one remove in 1.27.2.

aristocratic mythology since the Hesiodic *Catalogue of women* and Hecataeus, and that were still being much exploited by the civic elites of the eastern Roman empire.[58] The timelessness of the story of Daphnis in Theocritus 1 is matched by the timelessness of the story of Daphnis (Jr.) and Chloe.

It is far from surprising, then, that, like the other novelists, Longus seems not to introduce Romans, and that by his staging of a war between Mytilene and Methymna he seems to set his action before Roman control of the Eastern Aegean. That is not to say that Longus might not invite his readers to compare his timeless universe (never-never-land) with that presided over (ever-ever-land) by the power of Rome that was claimed to be temporally unbounded. Some details repay attention.

First, the young couple's suckling by a goat and by a sheep. The Roman foundation myth, well known to educated Greeks, had the twins Romulus and Remus suckled by the pastoral animals' perpetual enemy, the wolf. We should ask if Longus wants to offer an alternative and more peaceful foundation legend for the pastoral household of Daphnis and Chloe and one that is manifestly more gentle and sympathetic than that claimed by Rome.

Secondly, the role of wolves in Longus' narrative. They are certainly important – it is a predatory she-wolf that causes the rustics to dig a wolf-trap into which Daphnis falls, thus needing to bathe in Chloe's presence, with the result (intended by the god Eros) that she begins to feel sexual desire for him.[59] This incident also lays the foundation for a reader's perception of wolves as dangerous to Daphnis and Chloe's way of life. Soon after, Dorcon dresses in a wolf-skin to try to rape Chloe – and gets badly bitten by the sheep-dogs for his pains.[60] Then, climactically, in Book 3 it is a young city woman with the name Lycaenion, 'Little she-wolf', who introduces Daphnis to the sexual act.[61] Lycaenion is not portrayed unsympathetically, and her action is as necessary to the forward movement of the erotic plot as Daphnis' tumble into the wolf-trap is necessary to set it in motion. But Lycaenion's mendacity (she is cheating on her ageing husband as well as persuading Daphnis to cheat on Chloe) is not wholly commendable, and readers might well feel a frisson of concern that she might decide to keep Daphnis for herself – we are told explicitly that she formed the desire to have him as her lover.[62]

[58] For this huge topic cf. Strubbe 1984–6; Jones 1999; Spawforth and Walker 1985, 1986; Newby 2003.
[59] 1.11–13.2. [60] 1.20.2–21.4. [61] 3.16–18.
[62] ἐπεθύμησεν ἐραστὴν κτήσασθαι, 'she formed the desire to possess him as her lover', 3.15.2.

Taken together with the story of Daphnis and Chloe being suckled by a goat and a sheep, this bad press for wolves *might* be seen as poking fun at Rome.[63] I would be inclined to discount these wolves, however, were it not for a third detail. When Daphnis and Chloe have a boy child and a girl child they give the boy the name Philopoemen.[64] The name is not entirely unfitting, though it has no known antecedent in pastoral poetry, and its meaning 'fond of shepherd' might seem a more suitable name for a sheep or for an estate-owner than for an actual shepherd or goatherd. But this is a name that has a clear resonance for any Greek with a knowledge of history: it was borne by the Arcadian who led resistance to Rome in the second century BC, and whom an unnamed Roman is quoted by Plutarch as having called 'the last of the Greeks, on the ground that after him Greece produced no man who was great or was worthy of herself.'[65]

Perhaps, then, the fact that Longus' time-line seems to extend no further than the Hellenistic period is significant. He does not wish to anchor it explicitly in the classical period like Chariton and Heliodorus, but he *is* concerned to give us clear indications that the absence of Rome and of Romans is not accidental, and to make his readers reflect on what it was to live in a world before Rome.[66] Like Xenophon, furthermore, Longus turns out to have only one block of time, pre-Roman time. Unlike Xenophon's characters, however, those of Longus seem to know scraps of myth, above all the city-slicker Gnathon: but the earlier world from which these scraps are ostensibly drawn does not play the significant part as a recurrent frame of reference that it does in Chariton and Achilles Tatius.

6 The World According to Heliodorus

I shall be much briefer in my discussion of Heliodorus. This is partly because some scholars have argued firmly that he belongs to the second half of the fourth century AD. If that were so (and I regard the matter as still open) then he would reflect a different *mentalité* from the other four novelists,

[63] For the way the presence and imagery of wolves in *Daphnis and Chloe* relate to Longus' treatment of other animals cf. Bowie 2005a and 2019b (Chapter 43 in this volume).

[64] 4.39.2.

[65] Ῥωμαίων δέ τις ἐπαινῶν ἔσχατον αὐτὸν Ἑλλήνων προσεῖπεν, ὡς οὐδένα μέγαν μετὰ τοῦτον ἔτι τῆς Ἑλλάδος ἄνδρα γειναμένης οὐδ' αὐτῆς ἄξιον, Plu. *Phil.* 1.7.

[66] For a further argument that Longus wants readers to ask questions about Roman power, based on his use of metaphor to undermine the hierarchy human masters – human slaves – animals – plants, see Bowie 2005b and 2019b (Chapters 27 and 43 in this volume).

whom I take it to be writing between AD 50 and (say) AD 220.[67] But another reason for relative brevity is that the picture offered by Heliodorus is more clear-cut than that of any of the others except Chariton: this follows from the fact that, like Chariton, Heliodorus sets his narrative in a fairly clearly documented historical context – the Greek world of the early fifth century BC when the Persians are still masters of Egypt.[68]

This is a world that knows the name Cronus (*Kronos*),[69] and in which Zeus and other Olympians are frequently mentioned.[70] Heroic myth starts with Hellen son of Deucalion[71] and is presented both as a self-standing set of data and as a product of the genius of Homer, a poet whom the most important narrator within the text, Calasiris, claims to be Egyptian.[72] The foregrounding of the poetic activity of Homer helps readers to perceive the gap between the Trojan war – many of whose heroes are mentioned[73] – and the date at which Heliodorus' story is set: within that seven-hundred-year gap only one historical figure is located, the Spartan Lycurgus.[74] As to events before the Trojan war, the reader is made aware of the battle between Eteocles and Polynices over Thebes by its evocation in the scene where Thyamis and Petosiris fight in front of the walls of Memphis;[75] the myth of Hippolytus as treated by Euripides is introduced *nominatim* in Cnemon's story and alluded to in the death of Arsace.[76]

Many vividly presented scenes bring Heliodorus' early classical world to life. But they are not without 'anachronisms'. Athens' celebration of the Panathenaea and a meeting of the ἐκκλησία, 'assembly', have the appearance of authentic classical décor, but the formal organisation of Athenian ephebes that seems to be associated with their participation in the Panathenaea and the use of the ἐκκλησία as a court (in which 2700 votes are cast) are at the least anachronistic.[77] Manifestly so (to us at least) is the mention of a

[67] For Longus' date see Bowie 2019g, 19–20.

[68] Cf. the Great King and his satraps, Hld. 2.24, 5.8–9.

[69] Hld. 2.24.6: but the use here of the adjective Κρόνιον, 'of Kronos', to refer to the evil influence of the planet Saturn need not imply knowledge by the speaker (Calasiris) of the whole story of Uranus, Cronus and Zeus.

[70] E.g. Athena, Hld. 3.3.5; Poseidon, 5.20.2; Apollo 2.27.2ff., 3.11.5, 4.18.6; Artemis 2.35.3ff., 3.4.1, 11.5, 4.18.6; Aphrodite 4.18.6, cf. 3.2.4; Ares 3.2.4; Dionysus 2.23.5, 5.15.3, 16.4; Thetis 2.34.5, 3.2.4; Hermes 3.14.2, 5.16.4; Helios 1.1.1 (?), 2.1.1, 4.12, 10.41.4; Proteus 2.24.4. Note also a Gorgon at 3.3.5, 4.7.11.

[71] 2.34.2. [72] 3.14.

[73] Odysseus is evoked *passim*, and appears to Calasiris in a dream at 5.22; Achilles, Neoptolemus, Orestes, Agamemnon, Spercheius, Polydora and Menesthios are at 2.34, the last three drawn from Il. 16.173–8. Note too Lapiths and Centaurs at 3.3.5.

[74] 2.27.1. [75] 7.6. [76] 1.10.2, 8.14.2.

[77] 1.10.1, 13.1–14.1. The status of the Areopagus (1.9.1) may also be intended as classicising décor, but that body also had an important part in the constitution of Roman Athens.

'monument of the Epicureans'[78] and of trading relations with India.[79] These seem likely simply to be slips, but just once or twice Heliodorus may want to tease us into imagining the world as it developed later than the events of his plot, as he certainly does in his self-identifying closure at the end of Book 10. So the scene on the beach with which the novel opens is marked by association with the Heracleotic mouth of the Nile as near the site of future Alexandria, and amethysts from Britain are mentioned by the narrator (but not by any character in the text).[80] These few and somewhat diverse cases apart, Heliodorus manages to maintain over ten books a world that is pre-Hellenistic. We might, most of the time, be reading a text completed in the middle of the fifth century BC – or rather, we might be reading such a text until we reach the very last sentence. There we are told:

> τοιόνδε πέρας ἔσχε τὸ σύνταγμα τῶν περὶ Θεαγένην καὶ Χαρίκλειαν Αἰθιοπικῶν, ὃ συνέταξεν ἀνὴρ Φοῖνιξ Ἐμισηνός, τῶν ἀφ' Ἡλίου γένος, Θεοδοσίου παῖς Ἡλιόδωρος.
>
> so concludes the book of the Ethiopian tales about Theagenes and Charicleia, the work of a Phoenician from the city of Emesa, one of the families of the descendants of the sun, Theodosius' son, Heliodorus.[81]

Like Chariton's signature at the beginning of his novel, this σφραγίς, 'seal', modifies our reading of the text; but since it is placed at the end it does so to very different effect. Like Odysseus in *Odyssey* Book 23 we rapidly review the events of the last ten books and refocus them in the light of this new information. At this point we know (or have every reason to think that we know) that the narrative we have just read was written when Emesa had become a Greek city, producing πεπαιδευμένοι, 'educated men', who could write in Greek and who chose to do so. That in turn may prompt readers' reflections on the very large number of features of the classical world that Heliodorus has created that are still present in the contemporary world of writer and first readers, and may invite the conclusion that at least the Greek world of the fifth century BC is broadly, perhaps even essentially, similar to that of the Roman Empire.

Heliodorus, then, has two major blocks of time: mythological time, encompassing the Trojan war and a generation or two before; and historical time, which is almost entirely taken up by the fifth-century world in which the narrative is set. But his concluding σφραγίς draws our attention

[78] 1.16.5. [79] 5.14.1. [80] 1.1.1, 5.13.3. [81] 10.41.4.

to the insignificance of the gap between that world and the world in which Heliodorus and his first readers lived. In this he turns out to be very close to Chariton.

7 Conclusion

It seems that the five fall into two groups: one containing Xenophon and Longus, each of whom offers very little antecedent myth or history before the period of the events they narrate; and one containing Chariton, Achilles Tatius and Heliodorus, who not only use much plausible circumstantial detail to build up a classical or (in Achilles Tatius' case) Hellenistic world in which their characters live, but also give that world temporal depth by much exploitation of Trojan war and other mythology, and very occasionally by introduction of events or persons from earlier Greek history. The way these worlds are presented by Xenophon and Achilles Tatius is such that their similarity with that of writer and readers can almost be taken for granted, and I detect little incentive to readers to ask in what way and with what effect these worlds are to any degree different from their own. The cases of Chariton and Heliodorus are different: the more or less determinable historical setting combines with the decidedly contemporary σφραγίς to give readers both a strong sense of Greek cultural continuity and at the same time alertness to the possibility of identifying features where their contemporary Greek world might be significantly different. That the most important element of difference is to be found in Roman control of the Greek world is also strongly hinted at by Longus, though his choice of a timeless, predominantly non-urban context entails his achieving this by different means.

29 Viewing and Listening on the Novelist's Page (2006)

1 Introduction

This paper explores the different ways in which the five surviving 'ideal' Greek novels approached the problem of conveying to their readers the aural elements of the scenes and events they described and narrated.* I take it that the typical mode of 'consumption' of an imperial Greek novel was reading – sometimes aloud, sometimes silently, often or almost always by a solitary reader, closeted with a papyrus roll or with a codex in some room, courtyard or *hortus conclusus*, 'enclosed garden', or perhaps occasionally in some outdoor *locus amoenus*, 'pleasant place'. Modern readers of our extant novels will recall that only in Achilles Tatius do we have a scene in which a book is being read, and that there the reader, Cleitophon, does so while perambulating the courtyard off which the doorway to Leucippe's room leads.[1] There may have been occasions when an individual or a small group was read to by a slave, and perhaps there were even reading circles in communities where literacy was low,[2] though we have no firm evidence for this phenomenon. Whereas audiences of longer-standing performance genres – rhapsodic performances of hexameter poetry, solo and choral performances of melic poetry, sympotic recitations of elegy, *iambi* and epigrams, and of course the various dramatic genres – could be prompted to re-create in their imagination sound effects in the performances that they heard, an imperial Greek reader had to work entirely from lines of letters in

* A preliminary version of this paper was delivered to a conference on 'Viewing and listening' at the University of Crete, Rethymnon, in May 2004. I am grateful to Lucia Athanassaki and Anastasia-Erasmia Peponi for inviting me to that conference, and to them and other participants for helpful discussion. A revised version was delivered at a panel in honour of Gareth Schmeling at *CAMWS* in Gainesville in 2005; again I profited much from the discussion.

[1] Ach. Tat. 1.6.

[2] For arguments in favour of this practice see Hägg 1994; for some arguments against, Bowie 1996c, 95–100 (Chapter 23, 481–5 in this volume); for a good defence of Hägg's position, and the suggestion that the earliest novel was written to replace oral story-telling as an entertainment for women engaged in domestic tasks like spinning, see West 2003.

columns on a roll or codex – lines in which words were not divided and in which there was usually little or no punctuation.

The reader's task will not necessarily have be facilitated by the fact that some of writers and readers of the novels will have been trained in an oral performance medium – that of epideictic and symbouleutic rhetoric – and indeed may themselves have actually performed as epideictic sophists. For in doing this they will have been trained to privilege the re-creation of the visual, deploying well-honed techniques of *ecphrasis*. Imperial Greek handbooks of rhetoric clearly identify the purpose of an *ecphrasis*. It is a λόγος περιηγηματικὸς ἐναργῶς ὑπ' ὄψιν ἄγων τὸ δηλούμενον, 'descriptive account bringing what is shown vividly before one's vision'.[3] The whole issue was well discussed by Shadi Bartsch.[4] She compared the remark of the late-second-century rhetor Hermogenes δεῖ γὰρ τὴν ἑρμηνείαν διὰ τῆς ἀκοῆς σχέδον τὴν ὄψιν μηχανᾶσθαι, 'for putting thoughts into words ought virtually to contrive the effect of vision though the medium of hearing',[5] and that of Nicolaus of Myra that *ecphrasis* ought to make the audience into spectators.[6] Alongside vividity is set the ability to move the audience. Despite this focus in rhetorical education upon recreating in words what the audience is asked to visualise, we can also see how in different ways novelists developed a corresponding procedure of re-creation for their readers of what – if they had been actors in the narrative – they would have been able to hear.

2 Chariton

The earliest of our extant novelists, Chariton, handles lively scenes involving spectacle and sound in a way that does not depart significantly from the narrative tradition that descends through historiography from Homer. The hetero-diegetic narrative is regularly punctuated by speeches, and less often by monologues, and the reader of an ancient book was at liberty to imagine in silent reading, or to represent in reading aloud, the various tones that might appropriately and conventionally match the characters' emotions, arguments and words. But there are no signals to suggest that the aural quality of such speeches was a feature to which Chariton expected his readers to give *special* emphasis.

[3] Theon 118.6 = p. 66 Patillon.

[4] Bartsch 1989, chapter 4 entitled 'Spectacles'.

[5] Hermog. ii 16 Spengel. For early discussions of the closely linked quality of ἐνάργεια cf. Pl. *Ion* 535b–c, Arist. *Rh.* 1411b–13b, D.H. *Lys.* 7, Demetr. *Eloc.* 209–20.

[6] iii 491 Spengel.

So too with descriptions of spectacle where there is a distinct sonic or aural component. Chariton offers us several such spectacles, all or most of which ancient rhetoric would have classified as an *ecphrasis*. His recipe regularly involves drawing attention briefly to sounds but not taking any special steps to re-create them for our viewing ears. Thus in the first assembly at Syracuse, where Hermocrates is brought under pressure to agree to the marriage of his daughter Callirhoe to Chaereas, Chariton quotes (*verbatim*, we are to understand) what the *demos* shouted (ἐβόα):

> 'καλὸς Ἑρμοκράτης, μέγας στρατηγός, σῶζε Χαιρέαν· τοῦτο πρῶτον τῶν τροπαίων. ἡ πόλις μνηστεύεται τοὺς γάμους σήμερον· ἀλλήλων ἄξιοι.'
>
> 'Handsome is Hermocrates! Great is our general! Save Chaereas! This will be the chief among your spoils of victory! The city requests their wedding today: they are worthy of each other.'
>
> Chariton 1.1.11

We find similar acclamations later, for example at Callirhoe's wedding to the Milesian nabob Dionysius:

> πάντες οὖν ἀνεβόησαν· 'ἡ Ἀφροδίτη γαμεῖ'.
>
> So all shouted out: 'The bride is Aphrodite'.
>
> Chariton 3.2.17

Such brief descriptions of sounds are, understandably, especially prominent in Chariton's accounts of processions. Thus at Callirhoe's first wedding (to Chaereas) we read that the wedding hymn was sung throughout the city:

> ὑμέναιος ᾔδετο κατὰ πᾶσαν τὴν πόλιν· μεσταὶ δὲ αἱ ῥῦμαι στεφάνων, λαμπάδων· ἐρραίνετο τὰ πρόθυρα οἴνωι καὶ μύροις.
>
> The wedding hymn was sung across the whole city; the alleys were filled with garlands, with torches; the porches were sprinkled with wine and perfumes.
>
> Chariton 1.1.13

The pendant scene of Callirhoe's funeral has corresponding sound effects:

> τούτων δὲ θρηνούντων μάλιστα Χαιρέας ἠκούετο.
>
> and when these lamented Chaereas' voice was heard loudest.
>
> Chariton 1.6.5

Likewise, when a crowd accompanies Callirhoe to the temple of Aphrodite and Dionysius has prayed to the goddess, ἐπευφήμησε τὸ πλῆθος τῶν περιεστηκότων, 'the crowd of bystanders followed it up with pious utterances' (3.8.5).[7]

Another context in which Chariton punctuates his narrative with crowd noises is that of the trial in Book 6 which must decide whether Callirhoe is to go to Dionysius or Chaereas. The supporters of each shout 'σὺ κρείττων, σὺ νικᾷς', 'You are the better man, you are the victor' (6.2.2). This is followed up by a description of a thirty-day period of public festivity in which the role of music is picked out:

> αὐλὸς ἤχει καὶ σῦριγξ ἐκελάδει καὶ ᾄδοντος ἠκούετο μέλος·
>
> A pipe rang out and a panpipe trilled and there was heard the music of somebody singing.
>
> Chariton 6.2.4

Earlier too, at the party which Dionysius has thrown to entertain leading citizens in a characteristic act of euergetism, and at which Chaereas' letter to Callirhoe is produced, we get a bare descriptive hint that music was just beginning:

> ἤδη δέ που καὶ αὐλὸς ἐφθέγγετο καὶ δι' ᾠδῆς ἠκούετο μέλος.
>
> And it was now perhaps that a pipe began to raise its voice and a song could be heard being chanted.
>
> Chariton 4.5.7

Of course this is only a selection of passages where readers encounter spoken or sung words, or music produced by instruments. In all cases, however, Chariton communicates these phenomena with considerable economy. This contrasts with a much less restrained presentation of visual aspects. To take an extreme case – Chariton's only extended *ecphrasis* of material objects[8] – consider his account of the Persian king setting off to hunt in the hope of distracting himself from his passion for Callirhoe:

> πάντων δὲ ὄντων ἀξιοθεάτων διαπρεπέστατος ἦν αὐτὸς ὁ βασιλεύς. καθῆστο γὰρ ἵππωι Νισαίωι καλλίστωι καὶ μεγίστωι χρύσεον ἔχοντι χαλινόν, χρύσεα δὲ φάλαρα καὶ προμετωπίδια καὶ προστερνίδια· πορφύραν δὲ ἠμφίεστο Τυρίαν (τὸ δὲ ὕφασμα Βαβυλώνιον) καὶ τιάραν ὑακινθινοβαφῆ· χρύσεον δὲ

[7] For crowds in Chariton cf. Billault 1996, 116; Kaimio 1996, 60.

[8] In 7.2 there is a shorter description of the island city of Tyre.

> ἀκινάκην ὑπεζωσμένος δύο ἄκοντας ἐκράτει, καὶ φαρέτρα καὶ τόξον αὐτῶι παρήρτητο, Σηρῶν ἔργον πολυτελέστατον. καθῆστο δὲ σοβαρός· ἔστι γὰρ ἴδιον ἔρωτος <τὸ> φιλόκοσμον· ἤθελε δὲ μέσος ὑπὸ Καλλιρόης ὁραθῆναι, καὶ διὰ τῆς πόλεως ἁπάσης ἐξιὼν περιέβλεπεν εἴ που κἀκείνη θεᾶται τὴν πομπήν. ταχέως δὲ ἐνεπλήσθη τὰ ὄρη βοώντων, θεόντων, κυνῶν ὑλασσόντων, ἵππων χρεμετιζόντων, θηρῶν ἐλαυνομένων.
>
> Whereas they were all a sight worth seeing, the most striking of them was the King. For he was seated on the biggest and most handsome Nisaean horse, which had a golden bit, and golden cheek-pieces and frontlets and breastplates. He was dressed in a cloak of Tyrian purple – the cloth had been woven in Babylon – and a turban dyed the colour of hyacinth; he had a short golden sword in his belt and two spears in his hand, and slung at his side were a quiver and bow, a most extravagant piece of Chinese craftsmanship. He sat proudly on his mount, for love of ornament is a special feature of Eros. He wanted to be seen by Callirhoe surrounded by his retinue, and as he made his way out through the whole city he looked around to see if by chance she too was watching the procession. Soon the mountains were filled with people shouting, running, dogs barking, horses neighing, beasts being pursued.
>
> Chariton 6.4.1–3

Chariton's attention to magnificent and costly armour falls into a tradition again going back to Homer, but here it is combined with some lexicographically signalled intertextuality[9] and exotic name-dropping. If we ask why here he has gone beyond his practice in the novel hitherto, he may give us the answer in a phrase that can be read self-reflexively: ἔστι γὰρ ἴδιον ἔρωτος <τὸ> φιλόκοσμον, 'for κόσμος is a characteristic of Eros', that is, of this erotic narrative, one strand of whose pedigree Chariton here allusively traces back to Xenophon's *Cyropaedeia*, albeit he is pioneering the form of the novel into which he has drawn it.[10] Within this ornamentation,

[9] The repetition of the epithet χρύσεον, 'golden', the προμετωπίδια καὶ προστερνίδια, 'frontlets and breastplates', and the epithets ἀξιοθεάτων, 'worth seeing', and ὑακινθινοβαφῆ, 'dyed the colour of hyacinth', all evoke a single passage in Xenophon's account of the love of Abradatas and Pantheia, *Cyr.* 6.4.1–4: here it is the helmet-plume of Abradatas that is ὑακινθινοβαφῆ, 'dyed the colour of hyacinth'. For the strong presence of Xenophon in Chariton see Trzaskoma 2018, and for his wider impact in imperial Greek literature Bowie 2016g (Chapter 39 in Volume 3).

[10] This too recalls but reworks *Cyr.* 6.4.4, where Abradatas asks Pantheia if she has cut up her κόσμον, 'finery', in order to make his armour, to which she replies: 'μὰ Δί'', ἔφη ἡ Πάνθεια, 'οὔκουν τόν γε πλείστου ἄξιον· σὺ γὰρ ἔμοιγε … μέγιστος κόσμος ἔσηι', 'not my most valuable adornment, to be sure … for you will be my greatest adornment'. For other Xenophontic intertextuality in Ch. see Trzaskoma 2018.

however, attention to the visual greatly outbalances representation of the aural, so that what might be heard is conveyed in just a few words: βοώντων ... ὑλασσόντων ... χρεμετιζόντων, 'shouting ... barking ... neighing'.

3 Xenophon of Ephesus

Xenophon of Ephesus merits less discussion. His look-alike narrative opening of his *Anthia and Habrocomes* does indeed have a full-scale πομπή, 'procession', from the city to the temple of Artemis. The procession is described in detail to paint an opulent backdrop for the handsome Habrocomes, who leads the ephebes, and the dazzling Anthia, who leads the παρθένοι:

> παρῄεσαν δὲ κατὰ στίχον οἱ πομπεύοντες· πρῶτα μὲν τὰ ἱερὰ καὶ δᾶιδες καὶ κανᾶ καὶ θυμιάματα· ἐπὶ τούτοις ἵπποι καὶ κύνες καὶ σκεύη κυνηγετικὰ ... ὧν <τὰ μὲν> πολεμικά, τὰ δὲ πλεῖστα εἰρηνικά ... ἑκάστη δὲ αὐτῶν οὕτως ὡς πρὸς ἐραστὴν ἐκεκόσμητο. ἦρχε δὲ τῆς τῶν παρθένων τάξεως Ἀνθία ... ἦν δὲ τὸ κάλλος τῆς Ἀνθίας οἷον θαυμάσαι καὶ πολὺ τὰς ἄλλας ὑπερεβάλλετο παρθένους. ἔτη μὲν τεσσαρεσκαίδεκα ἐγεγόνει, ἤνθει δὲ αὐτῆς τὸ σῶμα ἐπ' εὐμορφίαι, καὶ ὁ τοῦ σχήματος κόσμος πολὺς εἰς ὥραν συνεβάλλετο· κόμη ξανθή, ἡ πολλὴ καθειμένη, ὀλίγη πεπλεγμένη, πρὸς τὴν τῶν ἀνέμων φορὰν κινουμένη· ὀφθαλμοὶ γοργοί, φαιδροὶ μὲν ὡς κόρης, φοβεροὶ δὲ ὡς σώφρονος· ἐσθὴς χιτὼν ἁλουργής, ζωστὸς εἰς γόνυ, μέχρι βραχιόνων καθειμένος, νεβρὶς περικειμένη, γωρυτὸς ἀνημμένος, τόξα, [ὅπλα], ἄκοντες φερόμενοι, κύνες ἑπόμενοι ... καὶ τότ' οὖν ὀφθείσης ἀνεβόησε τὸ πλῆθος, καὶ ἦσαν ποικίλαι παρὰ τῶν θεωμένων φωναί, τῶν μὲν ὑπ' ἐκπλήξεως τὴν θεὸν εἶναι λεγόντων, τῶν δὲ ἄλλην τινὰ ὑπὸ τῆς θεοῦ περιποιημένην· προσηύχοντο δὲ πάντες καὶ προσεκύνουν καὶ τοὺς γονεῖς αὐτῆς ἐμακάριζον· ἦν δὲ διαβόητος τοῖς θεωμένοις ἅπασιν 'Ἀνθία ἡ καλή'. ὡς δὲ παρῆλθε τὸ τῶν παρθένων πλῆθος, οὐδεὶς ἄλλο τι ἢ Ἀνθίαν ἔλεγεν· ὡς δὲ Ἁβροκόμης μετὰ τῶν ἐφήβων ἐπέστη, τοὐνθένδε, καίτοι καλοῦ ὄντος τοῦ κατὰ τὰς παρθένους θεάματος, πάντες ἰδόντες Ἁβροκόμην ἐκείνων ἐπελάθοντο, ἔτρεψαν δὲ τὰς ὄψεις ἐπ' αὐτὸν βοῶντες ὑπὸ τῆς θέας ἐκπεπληγμένοι, 'καλὸς Ἁβροκόμης' λέγοντες, 'καὶ οἷος οὐδὲ εἷς καλοῦ μίμημα θεοῦ'. ἤδη δέ τινες καὶ τοῦτο προσέθεσαν· 'οἷος ἂν γάμος γένοιτο Ἁβροκόμου καὶ Ἀνθίας'.
>
> So the procession filed past line by line – first the sacred objects, the torches, the baskets and the incense; then horses, dogs, hunting equipment ... some for war, most for peace. And each of the girls was dressed as if for a lover. Anthias led the line of maidens ... Anthia's beauty was something wonderful, far surpassing the other girls'. She was fourteen, her shapely body was blossoming, and the adornment of her dress was a great addition to her attractiveness. Her hair was golden – most hanging loose, a little of

it plaited, all blowing in the wind. Her eyes were quick; she had the bright glance of a young girl yet the bashful look of chastity. Her garment was a purple tunic, girdled to reach her knee, falling down from her shoulders over her arms, with a fawnskin worn over it, a quiver attached, and arrows [for weapons]; she carried javelins and was followed by dogs ... And so on this occasion too the crowd gave a cheer when they saw her, and there were many different exclamations from the spectators: some were amazed and said she was the goddess, others that she had been fashioned as her own by the goddess. All prayed and prostrated themselves and congratulated her parents. 'Anthia the beauty!' was the cry shouted out by all the spectators. When the group of maidens came past, no one said anything but 'Anthia!' But when Habrocomes came into sight with the ephebes, then, although the spectacle of the maidens had been a beautiful sight, everyone forgot about them and turned their gaze to him, shouting out, astounded at the spectacle: 'Beautiful Habrocomes!' they said, 'Peerless image of a beautiful god!' And at this point some added 'What a marriage would be that of Habrocomes and Anthia!'.

Xenophon 1.2.4–8

Here Xenophon makes similar moves to Chariton in picking out *verbatim* the exclamations of the spectating crowd (cf. Ch. 1.1.11, discussed above).[11] But whereas Chariton was describing a civic assembly, Xenophon describes a religious ceremony, yet gives no hint that in this seven-stade procession a single musical note was sounded – the participants in the procession itself seem to be imprisoned in a silent film. This is at first sight surprising: if Xenophon had been intent on recreating a classical procession, one would have expected him to have it sing a *paean* or προσόδιον, 'processional song', or at least a something more broadly described as a ὕμνος, 'hymn'. If he was drawing on his personal knowledge of Ephesus in the first century AD, he should have known of the ὑμνωιδοί who seem to have been attached to the cult of Artemis from at least as early as the reign of Tiberius.[12] On the other hand it is possible that these ὑμνωιδοί sang only inside the temple precinct, and it does indeed seem that the elaborate procession set up by C. Vibius Salutaris in AD 104 involved the carrying of statues around the city without any accompanying singing.[13] Perhaps Ephesian readers would, after all, think Xenophon was getting it right. I am more inclined to think, however, that Xenophon simply displays less imagination in recreating festive

[11] The signature exclamation Ἀνθία, 'Anthia', is uttered again by Habrocomes himself in the final scene of the couple's reunion at 5.15.2. Less vivid is Xenophon's description, without quotation, of bustle and shouting at 1.10.4.

[12] Picard 1922; Rogers 1991, 55: cf. Bowie 1989a, 221, n.27 (Chapter 12, 229, n.46 in this volume).

[13] See Rogers 1991.

situations than Chariton.[14] True, elsewhere he does note the singing of the ὑμέναιος, 'wedding-song', at Anthia's much-desired wedding to Habrocomes – ἦγον τὴν κόρην εἰς τὸν θάλαμον μετὰ λαμπάδων, τὸν ὑμέναιον ᾄδοντες, ἐπευφημοῦντες, 'they led the girl into the bedchamber with torches, singing the wedding-song, and adding their blessings' (1.8.1, recalled at 3.6.2) – and again at her forced marriage to Perilaus – ἀνευφήμησαν τὸν ὑμέναιον, 'they sang the blessing of the wedding song' (3.6.1: cf. 3.5.3). But the wedding-song (ὑμέναιος) is so central a part of a Greek wedding that it demands to be mentioned (and is sometimes metonymic for the whole ceremony): it is not surprising that once introduced it leads Xenophon to convey its singing with the terms ᾄδοντες and ἀνευφήμησαν.

4 Achilles Tatius

Achilles Tatius plays more creatively with this *topos* of the ὑμέναιος, 'wedding-song'. In Melite's fantasies of her union at sea with Clitophon she exclaims:

> λιγυρὸν δὲ συρίζει περὶ τοὺς κάλως καὶ τὸ πνεῦμα· ἐμοὶ μὲν ὑμέναιον ᾄδειν δοκεῖ τὰ τῶν ἀνέμων αὐλήματα.
>
> the wind plays like a panpipe in the rigging: to my ears the piping of the winds are singing a wedding-song.
>
> Achilles Tatius 5.16.5

This passage in itself shows Achilles' eye for new twists in old rope.[15] So too do his two scenes of citharodic song: in reading these we must remember that in the first and second centuries AD the citharode was the most highly regarded of all performing artists, being rewarded more highly with money and statues by cities and emperors and receiving the highest level of monetary prizes at ἀγῶνες μουσικοί. Achilles describes two such performances, in both cases leaving his reader quite uncertain about the nature either of the tune or the actual words of the song.[16]

14 We may also observe the oddity that the ferocious dogs with whom Anthia is imprisoned in a trench at 4.6 seem at no point to bark. Contrast the barking dogs at Ch. 6.4.2 (quoted in Section 2), Longus 2.13.4.

15 Ach. Tat. also plays with the *topos* of the θρῆνος, 'lament', being sung instead of the ὑμέναιος 'wedding song': 1.13.5, 3.10.5, 5.11.2.

16 On citharodes see the important and wide-ranging study of Power 2010; for the two songs see Whitmarsh 2020, 142–3, 185 (suggesting the second might be imagined to be *Anacreontea* 55 West).

First, during the dinner and symposium at which Cleitophon's passion for Leucippe develops, one of his father's young slaves sang to the accompaniment of a lyre:

> παῖς ἔρχεται κιθάραν ἁρμοσάμενος, τοῦ πατρὸς οἰκέτης, καὶ ψιλαῖς τὸ πρῶτον διατινάξας ταῖς χερσὶ τὰς χορδὰς ἔκρουε· καί τι κρουμάτιον ὑπολιγήνας ὑποψιθυρίζουσι τοῖς δακτύλοις, μετὰ τοῦτο ἤδη τῶι πλήκτρωι τὰς χορδὰς ἔκρουε καὶ ὀλίγον ὅσον κιθαρίσας συνῆιδε τοῖς κρούμασι. τὸ δὲ ἆισμα ἦν Ἀπόλλων μεμφόμενος τὴν Δάφνην φεύγουσαν καὶ διώκων ἅμα καὶ μέλλων καταλαμβάνειν, καὶ γινομένη φυτὸν ἡ κόρη, καὶ Ἀπόλλων τὸ φυτὸν στεφανούμενος.
>
> a boy came in with a tuned lyre, one of his father's house-slaves. At first he simply strummed its strings, vibrating them with his bare hands; then, after outlining a short melody by his whispering fingers, he began to pluck the strings with a plectrum, and after just a little lyre-playing he began to sing to the notes. The song was Apollo reproaching Daphne for running away from him, him pursuing and on the point of capturing her, and the girl becoming a tree, and Apollo weaving himself a wreath from the tree.
>
> Achilles Tatius 1.5.4–6

Achilles Tatius presents us with different types of sound, and when describing the movement of the boy's fingers and the notes they generate he teasingly uses a regular term for a vocal sound, ὑποψιθυρίζουσι, 'whispering'. The writer's close attention to several details in the performance helps a reader to re-create a sense of the musical event that cannot be transmitted in writing.

Second, we hear (or rather we may think we hear, but in fact as readers we do not hear) Leucippe herself singing in a sequence prominently placed at the beginning of Book 2:

> ἡ δὲ πρῶτον μὲν ἦισεν Ὁμήρου τὴν πρὸς τὸν λέοντα τοῦ συὸς μάχην, ἔπειτά τι καὶ τῆς ἁπαλῆς μούσης ἐλίγαινε· ῥόδον γὰρ ἐπήινει τὸ ἆισμα. εἴ τις τὰς καμπὰς τῆς ὠιδῆς περιελὼν ψιλὸν ἔλεγεν ἁρμονίας τὸν λόγον, οὕτως ἂν εἶχεν ὁ λόγος· 'εἰ τοῖς ἄνθεσιν ἤθελεν ὁ Ζεὺς ἐπιθεῖναι βασιλέα, τὸ ῥόδον ἂν τῶν ἀνθέων ἐβασίλευε. γῆς ἐστι κόσμος, φυτῶν ἀγλάϊσμα, ὀφθαλμὸς ἀνθέων, λειμῶνος ἐρύθημα, κάλλος ἀστράπτον· ἔρωτος πνέει, Ἀφροδίτην προξενεῖ, εὐώδεσι φύλλοις κομᾶι, εὐκινήτοις πετάλοις τρυφᾶι· τὸ πέταλον τῶι Ζεφύρωι γελᾶι'. ἡ μὲν ταῦτα ἦιδεν· ἐγὼ δὲ ἐδόκουν τὸ ῥόδον ἐπὶ τῶν χειλέων αὐτῆς <ὁρᾶν>, ὡς εἴ τις τῆς κάλυκος τὸ περιφερὲς εἰς τὴν τοῦ στόματος ἔκλεισε μορφήν.

> First she sang Homer's account of the boar's fight with lion,[17] then she trilled too a piece of the tender Muse. Her song praised the rose. If one took away the modulations of the song and one were speaking the plain words of the composition, the words would be as follows: 'If Zeus had wanted to set a king over the flowers, the rose would be king of the flowers: adornment of the earth, a jewel among plants, the cynosure of flowers, the meadow's blush, a lightning-flash of beauty: it exudes scent of Eros, it plays chamberlain to Aphrodite, it has a *coiffure* of fragrant leaves, it luxuriates in delicate petals: the petal laughs in the West wind.' That is what she sang; and I imagine I could see the rose on her lips, as if one were to compress the circle of its head into the shape of her mouth.
>
> Achilles Tatius 2.1.1–3

In this virtuoso sequence Achilles Tatius produces a snappy sophistic ἔπαινος, 'encomium', of a rose, while at the same time he parodies the style of his near-contemporary the poet and citharode Mesomedes.[18] He explicitly draws our attention to his text's inability to reproduce the music, and in compensation moves from the highly metaphorical and therefore mostly non-visual language of the ἔπαινος – ἀγλάϊσμα, 'adornment', ὀφθαλμός, 'jewel' (literally 'eye'), ἐρύθημα, 'blush'; and πνέει, 'breathes', κομᾶι, 'has a *coiffure*', τρυφᾶι, 'luxuriates', γελᾶι, 'laughs' – to an intensely visual and sexually charged close-up of Leucippe's rose-like and (we must assume) constantly moving mouth.[19] Achilles Tatius has displayed how powerfully the words on the page can evoke the object of the gaze, while conceding their inability to convey the quality of sounds.

5 Longus

The varying levels of alertness to sound prompted by Longus' text are well brought out by its different handling of the σῦριγξ, 'panpipe' – the instrument whose inventor, Pan, and whose paradigmatic players, herdsfolk, are central to the story, and whose imagined music is used to underscore various aspects of the couple's relation to their universe.[20] Panpipes first appear as soundless dedications in the cave of the nymphs (1.4.3). Next,

[17] Il. 16.823–6.

[18] On Mesomedes, active in the reigns of Hadrian and Pius, see Horna 1928; Pöhlmann 1970: Bowie 1990b (Chapter 14 in this volume); Whitmarsh 2004; Regenauer 2016.

[19] For Ach. Tat.'s powers of visualisation see Morales 2004, section 6(a).

[20] For the importance of music in *Daphnis and Chloe*, and different interpretations of that importance, see Maritz 1991; Morgan 1994; Montiglio 2012; Schlapbach 2015.

whereas Chloe's childish games include making a grasshopper-cage, those of Daphnis include making a panpipe by cutting, boring and sticking together reeds, and then playing it until nightfall (1.10.2): noise that we, like Daphnis, take for granted. Soon Chloe, in love, wonders if Daphnis' panpipe is the cause of his attractiveness, plays them herself in the hope of becoming attractive too, and wishes she could become Daphnis' panpipe so that he would blow into her (1.13.4; 14.2–3). Here the power of the panpipe's music is hinted at, but since we know that Chloe's diagnosis is wrong, the precise quality of that music matters little. This is also true of Dorcon's gift of a panpipe to Daphnis (1.15.2), of Daphnis' abandonment of his panpipe when smitten by desire (1.17.4, 18.2), and of Daphnis' giving Chloe a music lesson in playing the panpipe with the aim of transmitting a kiss to her *via* the instrument (1.24.4). The next chapter reminds us that panpiping is a constant background to the couple's play (1.25.1), but reflection on the different *sounds* a panpipe might make comes only when pirates have kidnapped Daphnis and beaten up Dorcon: Dorcon has trained his cows to respond to his panpipe's music, and if Chloe uses the panpipe he now gives her to play the tune that Dorcon once taught Daphnis, and he taught her, his cows will react – as indeed they do, capsizing the pirate boat when Chloe plays the panpipe as loudly as she can (1.29.2–30.2).

Book 1, then, has introduced the notions that panpipes can make their player attractive (false), and that they can be played especially loudly, and can evoke responses from herded animals (true). These ideas are re-run early in Book 2. Philetas' panpiping, like Dorcon's, was able to control his cattle (2.3.2), but was unable to win him Amaryllis (2.7.6, cf. 2.5.3). Longus now adds the important idea that the σῦριγξ, 'panpipe', is specially linked to Pan: it is to Pan that Philetas used to play (2.3.2). After the couple's encounter with Philetas we read nothing of panpipes for almost half the book: kissing has replaced playing the panpipe as the couple's mode of communication. They reappear in a major role when the Methymnaeans abduct Chloe: Daphnis finds her abandoned panpipe (2.21.2) and mentions her dedication of a panpipe (Dorcon's?) in his angry outburst to the Nymphs (2.22.1). The Nymphs assure him of Pan's aid (2.23.2–5), and that by the next day they will again be herding and panpiping together – their shared musical activity is paired with and given equal importance in their lives with herding: καὶ νεμήσετε κοινῆι καὶ συρίσετε κοινῆι, 'you will graze your flocks together and play your panpipes together'. When Daphnis runs to pray to Pan and vows to sacrifice a billy-goat we read (for the first time) that the cult-statue of Pan represents him holding a panpipe (2.24.2).

This sets the scene for the terror inflicted by Pan on the Methymnan admiral and his men. They hear strange nocturnal noises – κτύπος δὲ ἠκούετο ῥόθιος κωπῶν, 'a thud could be heard of oars upon waves' (2.25.4) – and then the next day an eery and apparently invisible panpipe is heard:

> ἠκούετό τις καὶ ἀπὸ τῆς ὀρθίου πέτρας τῆς ὑπὲρ τὴν ἄκραν σύριγγος ἦχος, ἀλλὰ οὐκ ἔτερπεν ὡς σῦριγξ, ἐφόβει δὲ τοὺς ἀκούοντας ὡς σάλπιγξ.
>
> and there began also to be heard, from the beetling crag beyond the headland, a sort of panpipe noise; but it did not create pleasure like a panpipe, but created panic in those who heard it, like a war-trumpet.
>
> Longus 2.26.3

Pan appears to the admiral in a dream, assuring him he will not escape τὴν σύριγγα τὴν ὑμᾶς ταράξασαν, 'the pan-pipe that caused your panic', with Chloe and her flock on his ship (2.27.2). Ultimately, once Chloe is released and back on land, the terrifying panpipe is succeeded by one that is peaceful and pastoral, that leads Chloe's flock from the ships, and that then guides both them and Chloe home:

> σύριγγος ἦχος ἀκούεται πάλιν ἐκ τῆς πέτρας, οὐκέτι πολεμικὸς καὶ φοβερός, ἀλλὰ ποιμενικὸς καὶ οἷος εἰς νομὴν ἡγεῖται ποιμνίων
>
> the noise of a panpipe again began to be heard from the crag, no longer martial and terrifying, but pastoral and of the sort that leads flocks to their grazing.
>
> Longus 2.28.3

> τῶν δὲ αἰγῶν καὶ τῶν προβάτων ἡγεῖτο σύριγγος ἦχος ἥδιστος καὶ τὸν συρίττοντα ἔβλεπεν οὐδείς, ὥστε τὰ ποίμνια καὶ αἱ αἶγες προήιεσαν ἅμα καὶ ἐνέμοντο τερπόμεναι τῶι μέλει.
>
> The goats and the sheep were led by a most sweet noise of a panpipe, and the piper was seen by nobody, so that the sheep and the goats moved forward and grazed together, taking pleasure in the tune.
>
> Longus 2.29.3

Chloe's account of her adventure to Daphnis includes mention of τὰ συρίσματα ἀμφότερα, τὸ πολεμικὸν καὶ τὸ εἰρηνικόν, 'both kinds of pan-piping, the warlike and the peaceful' (2.30.3). We now know, then, that panpipes' music may differ not only in loudness but in ethos. Longus soon encourages us to form more precise ideas. At the party celebrating Chloe's rescue Philetas boasts that he is second only to Pan in piping (2.32.3);

encouraged to play at Pan's feast the instrument Pan likes (2.33.1), Philetas finds Daphnis' boy-size panpipe inadequate to his great art, and sends his son Tityrus off for his own. During this interlude Lamon tells the myth of Pan and Syrinx, to some extent 'explaining' the element of violence in one mode of pan-piping. Tityrus returns with Philetas' μέγα ὄργανον καὶ αὐλῶν μεγάλων <κρεῖττον> 'mighty instrument, more powerful than mighty pipes' (2.35.1). The party can now enjoy a performance by old Philetas on his mighty panpipe, and in describing *this* performance Longus does indeed zoom in on sound-quality:

> αὐλῶν τις ἂν ᾠήθη συναυλούντων ἀκούειν· τοσοῦτον ἤχει τὸ σύριγμα. κατ' ὀλίγον δὲ τῆς βίας ἀφαιρῶν εἰς τὸ τερπνότερον μετέβαλλε τὸ μέλος καὶ πᾶσαν τέχνην ἐπιδεικνύμενος εὐνομίας μουσικῆς ἐσύριττεν οἷον βοῶν ἀγέληι πρέπον, οἷον αἰπολίωι πρόσφορον, οἷον ποίμναις φίλον. τερπνὸν ἦν τὸ ποιμνίων, μέγα τὸ βοῶν, ὀξὺ τὸ αἰγῶν· ὅλως πάσας σύριγγας μία σῦριγξ ἐμιμήσατο.
>
> you might think you were listening to several pipes piping together, so strong was the sound of his panpipe. Gradually reducing his force, Philetas changed the tune to a more pleasing sound and displayed every kind of skill in musical herdsmanship: he played panpipe music of the sort that befits a herd of cows, of the sort that suits a herd of goats, of the sort that flocks of sheep like. Pleasing was the one for flocks of sheep, loud was the one for cows, shrill was the one for goats. Altogether that single panpipe imitated all the panpipes in the world.
>
> Longus 2.35.3–4

This passage develops the idea that the panpipe can produce different sorts of music, and encourages us to speculate (perhaps using our own experience of panpipes to cash-out the bare epithets τερπνόν … μέγα … ὀξύ) what these different types 'really' sound like. A few lines later Longus takes us through a similar exercise when the couple mime the story of Syrinx in a ballet: when Chloe, miming Syrinx, flees to the woodland,

> Δάφνις δὲ λαβὼν τὴν Φιλητᾶ σύριγγα τὴν μεγάλην ἐσύρισε γοερὸν ὡς ἐρῶν, ἐρωτικὸν ὡς πείθων, ἀνακλητικὸν ὡς ἐπιζητῶν.
>
> Daphnis took Philetas' mighty pan-pipe and piped a tune of lament like one experiencing desire, a tune of desire like one coaxing, a tune of recalling like one repeatedly seeking.
>
> Longus 2.37.3

We emerge from these two performances with an awareness that panpipe music has different tunes with different effects, and that a set of tunes to command animals is balanced by a set addressed to human objects of desire. The remaining chapters re-emphasise that dual role of music in the couple's daily life, guiding their animals and (like kisses) expressing their feelings for each other (2.38).

The winter near the start of Book 3 silences the panpipes just as it separates the couple (3.4.3), so that their resumption of piping in spring symbolises their return to a shared life (3.12.4). That makes Lycaenion's gift of a panpipe to Daphnis especially underhand (3.15.3), but we are reassured when Daphnis, once again at Chloe's side, gives his panpiping an important place in their shared life in the scene preceding the tale of Echo (3.21–2). Here Longus uses a different device to invite us to concentrate on the quality of musical sounds – Chloe is puzzled by the bay's echo of sailors' songs (hence Daphnis' tale of Echo); Daphnis on the other hand tries to remember how the songs went so as to rework them as tunes for his panpipe:

> ἐπειρᾶτό τινα διασώσασθαι τῶν ᾀσμάτων, ὡς γένοιτο τῆς σύριγγος μέλη.
>
> he tried to retain some of the songs, so that they might become tunes for his panpipe.
>
> Longus 3.22.1

Daphnis' effort to remember what readers have not even been allowed to hear forces our attention on their inaccessibility. It may also be a *mis-en-abyme* for the claimed activity of the Longan narrator, who had to remember (we must assume) the exposition of the painting in the grove of the Nymphs in order that his labour might turn it into a four-book narrative (*pr.* 3).

The panpipe reverts from a minor role in Book 3 to a major role in Book 4, and its first appearance re-opens the issue of how the reader is to interpret brief and imprecise clues to the quality of sounds. That is surely the point of Longus' phraseology in his description of Pan playing his panpipes that figures in one of the Dionysiac paintings in the temple of Dionysus in Dionysophanes' luxurious park:

> οὐδὲ ὁ Πὰν ἠμέλητο· ἐκαθέζετο δὲ καὶ αὐτὸς συρίζων ἐπὶ πέτρας, ὅμοιος ἐνδιδόντι κοινὸν μέλος καὶ τοῖς πατοῦσι καὶ ταῖς χορευούσαις.
>
> Nor was Pan neglected, but he too sat playing his panpipes on a rock, like somebody providing a common tune both for the grape-tramplers and for the dancers.
>
> Longus 4.3.2

In this description of a painting – which uniquely in Longus' narrative might in principle be *exactly* what the narrator saw in the paintings in the Nymphs' grove – Longus is circumspect: Pan's piping was *like* (ὅμοιος) that of somebody using his music to help the two groups to leap and dance in time.[21] We as readers are left to decide whether that interpretation of 4.3.2 is the right one. Equally, this phraseology reminds us that when we encountered other sounds in the text that were not so circumspectly described, we should conclude (given our knowledge of the preface) that much of the narrative as a whole must have been supplied by the narrator.

That is surely the case for a passage later in Book 4 which reworks on the plane of actions what 4.3.2 has introduced on the plane of artistic representation, at the same time echoing elements in the performances of Philetas at 2.35 and of Daphnis on Philetas' panpipe at 2.37.3. Daphnis' real mother wants to test the claim of his foster-father Lamon that Daphnis has made his goats μουσικάς, 'musical', so Daphnis arranges his audience as if in a theatre and

> στὰς ὑπὸ τῆι φηγῶι καὶ ἐκ τῆς πήρας τὴν σύριγγα προκομίσας πρῶτα μὲν ὀλίγον ἐνέπνευσε, καὶ αἱ αἶγες ἔστησαν τὰς κεφαλὰς ἀράμεναι· εἶτα ἐνέπνευσε τὸ νόμιον, καὶ αἱ αἶγες ἐνέμοντο νεύσασαι κάτω· αὖθις λιγυρὸν ἐνέδωκε, καὶ ἀθρόαι κατεκλίθησαν· ἐσύρισέ τι καὶ ὀξὺ μέλος, αἱ δὲ ὥσπερ λύκου προσιόντος εἰς τὴν ὕλην κατέφυγον· μετ᾽ ὀλίγον ἀνακλητικὸν ἐφθέγξατο, καὶ ἐξελθοῦσαι τῆς ὕλης πλησίον αὐτοῦ τῶν ποδῶν συνέδραμον.
>
> standing beneath the oak tree, and taking his panpipes out from his wallet, first of all he blew into them gently, and the she-goats lifted up their heads and stood still; then he blew into them the 'grazing tune', and the she-goats put their heads down and began to graze; then again he gave them a clear, pure note, and all together they lay down; and he also piped some sort of shrill tune, and as if a wolf were approaching they fled into the woodland; after a little while he sounded the 'recall tune', and they came out of the woodland and ran together close him by his feet.
>
> Longus 4.15.2–3

Mention of the ἀνακλητικὸν, 'recall tune', ties this description to that of Daphnis' piping during the pantomime of Syrinx. Readers can now perform a διαίρεσις, 'taxonomy', and construct a stemma of panpipe music. Pan's own intervention established a broad division between the πολεμικός and ποιμενικὸς, 'polemical' and 'pastoral' (2.28.3). Within the pastoral there are tunes for humans and tunes for animals. Tunes for humans can be

[21] For the verb cf. 4.15.2, Hld. 5.14.

contributions to the success and pleasure of group activity – grape-pressing or dancing – or can be a lover's reactions to an individual (desiring, persuading, recalling). Tunes for animals are not simply sub-divided, as Philetas' playing might have suggested, into tunes for different types of beast: a sub-division similar to that in the lover's tunes also classifies different types of command to cows (1.30.1–2) or goats (4.15.2–3). This taxonomy may well induce readers to imagine that by 4.15 they have a good understanding of the complexities of panpipe music: yet as 4.3.2 warned them, the few descriptive terms offered by the text leave them to make a huge leap of faith.

In reaching any overall interpretation of that text a reader is likely (and certainly well-advised) to revert to the preface, where it is claimed that the whole narrative is based on the explication of a painting offered to the narrator by an ἐξηγητής, 'interpreter': a painting must inevitably fail to convey sounds, and any interpretation or narrative based on a painting would be more likely to privilege the visual over the aural than would a narrative based on autopsy or imagination. The few places where Longus *does* offer his readers some detail on sounds therefore raise epistemological issues: those elements in Longus' narrative that are such as could be *depicted* can be supposed to rest on the secure evidence of the painting, whereas details concerning the quality or intensity of sounds must have been supplied either by the 'interpreter' or by the narrator. Longus will have been well aware of the tradition of *ecphrasis* of works of art (going back to the Homeric description of Achilles' shield in Il. 18.483–602) and of the games that might be played by an artist in words when conveying – or refusing to convey – musical and other sounds implied by a scene depicted.

The remaining panpiping of Daphnis and Chloe is almost in parenthesis: Gnathon fantasises about listening to Daphnis' panpipe and being herded by him (he has elided its erotic and herding modes, 4.16.3); Daphnis and Chloe each plays his/her panpipe for the last time before dedicating it respectively to Pan (4.26.3) and to the Nymphs (4.32.3–4). Finally we read of Philetas' piping at the rustic wedding-party and unnamed panpipers escorting the couple to their bed-chamber as part of a sequence of noise effects in which Longus seems to be challenging the reader to reconstruct his sound-track:

> ὁ μὲν ἦιδεν οἷα ἄιδουσι θερίζοντες, ὁ δὲ ἔσκωπτε τὰ ἐπὶ ληνοῖς σκώμματα· Φιλητᾶς ἐσύρισε, Λάμπις ηὔλησε, Δρύας καὶ Λάμων ὠρχήσαντο …
>
> One man began to sing the sorts of thing reapers sing, another began to utter the taunts that are taunted at grape-pressings. Philetas played the panpipe, Lampis played the pipe, Dryas and Lamon danced …
>
> Longus 4.38.3

Our reading of early iambic texts may help us to guess at the 'taunts that are taunted at the grape-pressings', and scholars contemporary with Longus were interested in reaping songs:[22] but again the music of the panpipe remains elusive. So too the last noise we hear in the work, the bizarrely described wedding-song: in the climactic scene at the end of Book 4 we are offered a ὑμέναιος, 'wedding-song' – as we are by all our other novelists – but one in which Longus stresses that the music is harsh and rustic:

> πάντες αὐτοὺς παρέπεμπον εἰς τὸν θάλαμον, οἱ μὲν συρίττοντες, οἱ δὲ αὐλοῦντες, οἱ δὲ δᾶιδας μεγάλας ἀνίσχοντες. καὶ ἐπεὶ πλησίον ἦσαν τῶν θυρῶν, ἦιδον σκληρᾶι καὶ ἀπηνεῖ τῆι φωνῆι, καθάπερ τριαίναις γῆν ἀναρρηγνύντες, οὐχ ὑμέναιον ᾄιδοντες.
>
> Everyone escorted them to the bed-chamber, some playing panpipes, others playing pipes, and others holding huge torches aloft; and when they were near the door they began to sing in a harsh and relentless voice, as if breaking up the ground with tridents, not singing a wedding song.
>
> Longus 4.40.1–2

This is not the place to argue about this scene's contribution to our interpretation of the novel. For my purposes, however, it stands alongside several other scenes where the close attention to aural effects, contrasting with the 'white' sound of much of Longus' text, prompts readers to ask questions about the quality of the sounds described by the text they are reading. The comparison with 'people breaking up the ground with tridents', which as a simile might be expected to illuminate, of course sheds no light at all.

6 Heliodorus

There are several places in Heliodorus where his handling of scenes involving both sounds and spectacle falls within the spectrum we have already encountered in earlier novels – for example the wedding of his couple Charicleia and Theagenes in Book 10. But one scene is strikingly and interestingly different from anything before. During Calasiris' long narrative to Cnemon setting out for him (and for the novel's readers) the story of who Charicleia and Theagenes are, how they met, and why they are now

[22] Longus' near contemporary Pollux was interested in a reaping song called Lityerses (Poll. 4.54) named after a Lityerses son of Midas: cf. Apollod. *FGrH* 244 F149 (quoted by Σ Theoc. 10.41–2d). See further Bowie 2019g, 304.

in Egypt, Heliodorus offers us an extended and vivid description of the four-yearly θεωρία, 'religious pilgrimage', of Aenianes, Thessalians from Hypata, to Delphi in order to offer sacrifice at the tomb of Neoptolemus (cf. 2.34). Their arrival interrupts the story that Calasiris himself has been hearing from Charicles (Charicleia's foster-father at Delphi) of how it happened that he brought Charicleia from the frontier of Ethiopia to Delphi. When Charicleia's two surrogate fathers make their way to the precinct to observe the arrival of the θεωρία Heliodorus serves us two tasters of what is shortly to come: first we are offered a close-up of the handsome Theagenes

> Ἀχίλλειόν τι τῶι ὄντι πνέων καὶ πρὸς ἐκεῖνον τὸ βλέμμα καὶ τὸ φρόνημα ἀνεφέρων· ὀρθὸς τὸν αὐχένα καὶ ἀπὸ τοῦ μετώπου τὴν κόμην πρὸς τὸ ὄρθιον ἀναχαιτίζων, ἡ ῥὶς ἐν ἐπαγγελίαι θυμοῦ καὶ οἱ μυκτῆρες ἐλευθέρως τὸν ἀέρα εἰσπνέοντες, ὀφθαλμὸς οὔπω μὲν χαροπός, χαροπώτερον δὲ μελαινόμενος, σοβαρόν τε ἅμα καὶ οὐκ ἀνέραστον βλέπων, οἷον θαλάσσης ἀπὸ κύματος εἰς γαλήνην ἄρτι λεαινομένης.
>
> who really did exude something of Achilles, recalling his expression and his pride. He carried his head erect, and his mane of hair swept up and back from his forehead, his nose proclaimed his spirit, as did his nostrils breathing the air self-assertively; his eyes were not quite slate blue but verging on black tinged with blue, with a gaze that was haughty and not unattractive, as when the sea moves from turbulence to calm as it has just become smooth.
>
> Heliodorus 2.35.1

Second, the great set-piece description of the procession in the festival at Delphi, narrated by Calasiris to Cnemon, also stresses the visual, as we might expect of a subject which was noted as suitable for *ecphrasis* by the rhetor Nicolaus of Myra.[23] Heliodorus gives us clear guidance on how we should react. In the opening words of Book 3 Calasiris makes a brief allusion to a procession: ἐπεὶ δὲ ἡ πομπὴ καὶ ἡ συμπᾶς ἐναγισμὸς ἐτελέσθη, 'when the procession and the whole sacrificial ceremony had been completed'. Cnemon stops him excitedly, saying:

> 'καὶ μὴν οὐκ ἐτελέσθη, πάτερ', ὑπέλαβεν ὁ Κνήμων. 'ἐμὲ γοῦν οὔπω θεατὴν ὁ σὸς ἐπέστησε λόγος ἀλλ' εἰς πᾶσαν ὑπερβολὴν ἡττημένον τῆς ἀκροάσεως καὶ αὐτοπτῆσαι σπεύδοντα τὴν πανήγυριν, ὥσπερ κατόπιν ἑορτῆς ἥκοντα, τὸ τοῦ λόγου, παρατρέχεις ὁμοῦ τε ἀνοίξας καὶ λύσας τὸ θέατρον.'

[23] *Rh.* iii 492 Spengel.

> 'But in fact it has not been completed, father', interrupted Cnemon. 'Your account has not yet made me, for one, a spectator. I am utterly in the grip of your recitation and am eager to see the festival with my own eyes, but you rush on past me as if I were a late arrival at a feast, lifting and dropping the curtain at the same time.'
>
> Heliodorus 3.1.1

Thus prompted, Calasiris duly describes the procession. Shortly he describes two choruses of Thessalian girls, one of which sings a hymn to Peleus and Thetis (3.2.1–2). He is about to move his narrative on when Cnemon again interrupts, demanding to hear the hymn and criticising Calasiris as having given *only* a visual picture:

> 'τί "Κνήμων"', ἔφη ὁ Κνήμων, 'πάλιν γάρ με τῶν βελτίστων ἀποστερεῖς, ὦ πάτερ, αὐτόν μοι τὸν ὕμνον οὐ διερχόμενος, ὥσπερ θεατὴν μόνον τῶν κατὰ τὴν πομπὴν ἀλλ' οὐχὶ ἀκροατὴν καθίσας.'
>
> 'What do you mean "Cnemon"?', interrupted Cnemon. 'Again, father, you are depriving me of the best bits by not taking me through the hymn itself – as if you had seated me where I could only be a spectator of what happened in the procession, but not an auditor.'
>
> Heliodorus 3.2.3

Not only is Heliodorus focusing our attention on the virtuosity of his own hymnic composition, which he now proceeds to give us (3.2.4), but he is playing a complicit game with his rhetorically trained readers. They will have observed, as have modern scholars, that Heliodorus' technique, much more often than that of his predecessors, is to present his readers with visual images.[24] They know too that the goal of *ecphrasis* is traditionally the more difficult one of rendering a visual image in words, and that what Cnemon asks for is a *prima facie* easier task, simply rendering sung words on a written page. But *is* it an easier task? Only if 'the details of the hymn' are limited to the text, but not if they are to be extended to include its musical setting. As is inevitable, of course, what follows in Heliodorus' manuscripts, and presumably in his own autograph copy, when Calasiris agrees to let Cnemon 'hear' the hymn, is no more than the following text:

[24] Cf. the succinct assessment of Morgan 1996a, 441: 'In general terms, there is a movement away from telling to showing, from diegesis to mimesis; this is one aspect of the work's explicit theatricality. The omniscient author abstracts himself from most of the text, and the reader is often presented with a visual description of what an observer of an imaginary scene might have seen.'

'Ἀκούοις ἄν', ἔφη ὁ Καλάσιρις, 'ἐπειδήπερ οὕτω σοι φίλον· εἶχε γὰρ ὧδέ πως ἡ ὠιδή·
τὰν Θέτιν ἀείδω, χρυσοέθειρα Θέτιν,
Νηρέος ἀθανάταν εἰναλίοιο κόραν
τὰν Διὸς ἐννεσίηι Πηλέϊ γημαμέναν
τὰν ἁλὸς ἀγλαΐαν ἁμετέραν Παφίην,
ἃ τὸν δουρομανῆ τόν τ' Ἄρεα πτολέμων
Ἑλλάδος ἀστεροπὰν ἐξέτεκεν λαγόνων
δῖον Ἀχιλλῆα, τοῦ κλέος οὐράνιον,
τῶι ὕπο Πύρρα τέκεν παῖδα Νεοπτόλεμον,
περσέπολιν Τρώων, ῥυσίπολιν Δαναῶν.
ἱλήκοις ἥρως ἄμμι Νεοπτόλεμε,
ὄλβιε Πυθιάδι νῦν χθονὶ κευθόμενε,
δέχνυσο δ' εὐμενέων τάνδε θυηπολίην,
πᾶν δ' ἀπέρυκε δέος ἁμετέρας πόλιος.
τὰν Θέτιν ἀείδω, χρυσοέθειρα Θέτιν.'

'You may hear, since that is what you want. The song went something like this:
Of Thetis I sing, golden-locked Thetis,
immortal daughter of Nereus, lord of the brine,
who married Peleus at the behest of Zeus,
the glory of the brine, our own Paphian goddess.
He of the mad spear, the War-god of wars,
the lightning bolt of Hellas, was born from her loins,
Godlike Achilles, whose renown reached heaven,
to whom Pyrrha bore their son Neoptolemus,
city-sacker for the Trojans, city-saver for the Greeks.
be gracious to us, hero Neoptolemus,
blessed one now buried in Pythian soil,
and receive with favour this sacrifice,
and ward off all fear from our city.
Of Thetis I sing, golden-locked Thetis.'

Heliodorus 3.2.4

This gambit of Heliodorus places him ahead of his novelistic predecessors, at least so far as is known to us. No earlier novelist had so explicitly drawn attention to the problems of communicating a musical performance through the medium of a written text, and certainly none had adopted Heliodorus' solution – full quotation. Is it, then, simply one of the many sophisticated ways in which his multifarious originality tweaks the tradition? Perhaps not: for we can be almost certain where he is getting the idea from – Philostratus' *Heroicus*, a work of ca. AD 214 on which Heliodorus' brief *ecphrasis* of Theagenes in Book 2 had also drawn.[25] There the vintner in the Thracian Chersonese, who is telling the temporarily landbound Phoenician about the afterlife of Trojan heroes, reports a hymn sung to Thetis by pilgrims to the dwelling-place and hero-cult of Achilles on White Island in the Black Sea:[26]

> Θέτι κυανέα, Θέτι Πηλεία,
> τὸν μέγαν ἃ τέκες υἱὸν Ἀχιλλέα,
> τοῦ θνατὰ μὲν ὅσον φύσις ἤνεγκε,
> Τροία λάχε· σᾶς δ' ὅσον ἀθανάτου
> γενεᾶς πάις ἔσπασε, Πόντος ἔχει.
> βαῖνε πρὸς αἰπὺν τόνδε κολωνὸν
> μετ' Ἀχιλλέως ἔμπυρα,
> βαῖν' ἀδάκρυτος μετὰ Θεσσαλίας,
> Θέτι κυανέα, Θέτι Πηλεία.
>
> Dark blue Thetis, Thetis wife of Peleus,
> who gave birth to your mighty son, Achilles,
> whose portion that mortal nature produced
> was allotted to Troy, but the portion which your son
> drew from your immortal ancestry, that the Black Sea has.
> Come to this steep hill
> to the burnt offerings for Achilles,
> come without tears together with Thessaly,
> dark blue Thetis, Thetis wife of Peleus.
>
> Philostratus *Heroicus* 53.10 = 68.1–9 De Lannoy

It is ironic that the very author who was the first we know to have uttered a depreciatory comment on the novels[27] provided the genre with new way of handling 'listening' and of blending its treatment with that of 'viewing'.

7 Conclusions

The ways in which the five novels diverge one from another are not surprising when compared with the ways in which modern scholarship has found their other techniques to differ. Chariton seems well aware of what can be

[25] Compare Hld. 2.35.1 with Philostr. *Her.* 19.5: for this Morgan 1989a, 408 n.75 suggests that both texts 'reflect a well-known work of art'; but even if this were so, the verbal proximity seems to me to point to the use of one author by the other.

[26] On the hymn see further Bowie 1989a (Chapter 12 in this volume); on the Thessalian *theoria* Rutherford 2009; on *theoriae* in general Rutherford 2013.

[27] *Ep.* 66, to Chariton: cf. Bowie 1996c, 102 (Chapter 23, 488 in this volume).

achieved by briefly-sketched sound effects: but such brief sketches are all we get, with no hint of problematisation. Xenophon seems almost wholly unconcerned to communicate sound effects at all. In Achilles Tatius elaborate rhetoric and sometimes striking imagery is offered in compensation for what seems to be conceded as the incapacity of words to render sound on the page. Both Longus and Heliodorus in different ways force their readers to perpend the problem, and each offers them a different solution – that of Heliodorus a striking advance on anything in the earlier novels. It looks like a story of technical progress. I have not discussed surviving fragmentary texts, but nothing I have found in them would suggest a different story. Of course a new papyrus of a novel might require a different reconstruction, but unless or until such a papyrus is published the sort of technical progress I have been claiming seems to fit the phenomena.

30 Direct Speech in Longus' *Daphnis and Chloe* (2006)

1 Introduction

This paper does not set out to argue for any new, grand or ambitious hypothesis. It is, rather, a set of low-key reflections on the way that Longus uses direct speech in *Daphnis and Chloe*. I embarked on this investigation with no very clear idea of what I would find; and much of what has emerged has been for me, at least, more surprising and more interesting than I expected.[1]

There are fifty-one blocks of direct speech of varying length in the four books of the novel. Overall they add up to 4528 words, ca. 23% of the whole text (19,858 words). That is a lower figure than one finds in Longus' poetic ancestors and intertexts: 45% of the *Iliad* consists of direct speech;[2] in many poems of Theocritus inset songs, whether framed by narrative or dialogue, exceed 50% of the whole;[3] and several songs of Sappho embed direct speech, though the fragmentary nature of most impedes quantification.[4] While higher than the proportion of direct speech in Herodotus (14.5%),[5] Longus' proportion is (unsurprisingly) quite close to that in Thucydides (20.7%).[6] Of earlier novelists, Xenophon stands closest to Longus (with 28.8%): on the other hand Chariton (with 42.5%), and Achilles Tatius (with 46.1% within the narrative of his secondary narrator Cleitophon) have strikingly higher proportions.[7]

[1] For a nuanced and narratologically sophisticated analysis of speech in Longus see Morgan 2021. For discussion of the speeches of Eros, the Nymphs and Pan, and of characters' soliloquy-like reflections, Cusset 2006.

[2] The figure of 66% for the *Odyssey* is skewed by the *Apologoi*.

[3] Examples of dialogue frame: of *Idyll* 1's 152 lines 78 (51%) are song; of *Idyll* 15's 149 lines 45 (30%) are song. Examples of narrative frame: of *Idyll* 7's 157 lines 45 (28%) are speeches and 70 (45%) songs (i.e. a total of 73%); of *Idyll* 6's 46 lines 34 (74%) are song; of *Idyll* 11's 81 lines 61 (75%) are song. But, like Longus, Theoc. can surprise: in the 75 narrative lines of *Idyll* 13 only one (52) is direct speech; in the 25 lines of *Idyll* 28 only one and a half (24–5).

[4] For example 7 of fr. 1's 28 lines are direct speech (25%); 7 of fr. 44's extant 34 lines (21%); 3 of fr. 44A's extant 12 lines (25%); and 26 of fr. 94's extant 29 lines (90%).

[5] de Bakker 2021, 200: 'Herodotus presents 441 speeches in DD, which amounts to 14.5% of the entire text ...': but as he also notes (p. 202) Hdt. has more speeches in indirect than in direct discourse.

[6] Hess and Corien 2020, 559–60. I am grateful to Tim Rood for directing me to this article. For Thucydidean features in Longus see Cueva 1998, Luginbill 2001–2, Trzaskoma 2005.

[7] De Temmerman 2021a, 636; 2021b, 673.

2 The Speakers

It is clear, however, that Longus has not simply thought of an appropriate proportion and written to a dry formula. It is striking, for a start, how the proportion of direct speech builds up from book to book. The data are set out below: seven pieces of direct speech in Book 1, then ten or eleven in Book 2, fifteen in Book 3, and finally nineteen in Book 4.[8]

(1) The number of pieces of direct speech in each book.
Book 1. Seven pieces of direct speech: Daphnis four; Dorcon two; Chloe one.

1.14.1 Chloe to herself
1.16.1 Dorcon to Daphnis and Chloe
1.16.3 Daphnis to Dorcon and Chloe
1.18.1 Daphnis to himself
1.25.2 Daphnis to himself
1.27.2 Daphnis to Chloe
1.29.1 Dorcon to Chloe

Book 2. Ten pieces of direct speech: Daphnis, and Daphnis and Chloe, each two; Philetas, the Methymnan youths, a Nymph, Pan, Lamon, and Chloe each one: Eros' speech embedded in that of Philetas might be claimed to be an eleventh.

2.3.2 Philetas to Daphnis and Chloe (including Eros' speech to Philetas at 2.5.1)
2.8.2 Daphnis and Chloe to themselves
2.9.2 Daphnis and Chloe to themselves
2.15.2 νέοι Μηθυμναῖοι, 'Methymnan youths'
2.16.1 Daphnis to the rustic court
2.22.1 Daphnis to the Nymphs
2.23.2 A Nymph to Daphnis
2.27.1 Pan to Bryaxis
2.34.1 Lamon to Daphnis and Chloe
2.39.2 Chloe to Daphnis

Book 3. Fifteen pieces of direct speech: Daphnis six; Lycaenion three; Dryas, Daphnis and Chloe, Chloe, Myrtale, Lamon, and a Nymph each one.

[8] Taking Eros' embedded speech as one of Book 2's speeches yields an even progression from seven in Book 1 to nineteen in Book 4, with each book adding four. For the number of words per sentence in all four books see Table 30.1 at the end of this chapter.

3.6.3 Daphnis to Dryas (imagined)
3.7.3 Dryas to Daphnis
3.10.3 Daphnis and Chloe to each other
3.14.2 Daphnis to Chloe
3.14.4 Chloe to Daphnis
3.16.2 Lycaenion to Daphnis
3.17.1 Lycaenion to Daphnis
3.19.2 Lycaenion to Daphnis
3.23.1 Daphnis to Chloe
3.26.4 Myrtale to Daphnis
3.27.2 A Nymph to Daphnis
3.29.2 Daphnis to Dryas
3.31.1 Lamon to Daphnis
3.32.2 Daphnis to himself
3.34.2 Daphnis to Chloe

Book 4. Nineteen pieces of direct speech: Lamon and Dionysophanes each four; Gnathon, Astylus, Daphnis, and Megacles each two; Clearisté, Chloe and Dryas each one.

4.8.3 Lamon to himself
4.14.2 Lamon to Dionysophanes
4.16.2 Gnathon to Astylus
4.17.3 Gnathon to Astylus
4.18.3 Lamon to Myrtale
4.19.3 Lamon to Dionysophanes
4.20.2 Dionysophanes to himself
4.21.2 Dionysophanes to all (a three-word exclamation)
4.21.3 Cleariste to all
4.22.2 Astylus to Daphnis (a one-word exclamation)
4.22.3 Astylus to Daphnis
4.24.1 Dionysophanes to all
4.25.1 Daphnis to Dionysophanes
4.27.1 Chloe to herself
4.28.3 Daphnis to himself
4.30.2 Dryas to Dionysophanes and Cleariste
4.35.1 Megacles to all
4.35.2 Megacles to all
4.36.1 Dionysophanes to all

(2) The number of speakers

The number of speakers in each book also rises, though not so evenly. Only three characters speak in Book 1 (Daphnis, Chloe, Dorcon); then seven in Book 2 (Daphnis, Chloe, Philetas, the Methymnan youths, a Nymph, Pan, Lamon: Eros would be an eighth); seven in Book 3 (Daphnis, Lycaenion, Dryas, Chloe, Myrtale, a Nymph, Lamon); and finally nine in Book 4 (Lamon, Dionysophanes, Gnathon, Astylus, Chloe, Megacles, Cleariste, Daphnis, Dryas). This to some extent mirrors the extension of the couple's world. In Book 1 they interact with each other and with Dorcon. Daphnis and Dorcon also, of course, interact with the pirates, but these are not allowed direct speech; nor, more surprisingly, are the rustic foster-parents. This allows some nice effects.

Prima facie Book 1 is very much Daphnis' book, as far as speaking goes (four out of seven blocks of direct speech): he bears out his description as ὁ πρότερον τῶν ἀκρίδων λαλίστερος, 'who was previously more garrulous than grasshoppers' (1.17.4). But Daphnis is not the first person to speak in the novel: that honour is given to Chloe, and her words are the emblematic outburst νῦν ἐγὼ νοσῶ μέν, τί δὲ ἡ νόσος ἀγνοῶ, 'now I am sick, but I do not know what the sickness is' (1.14.1). Her verbalised reflections are not merely her own longest speech by some way, but the fourth longest by any character in the novel: 143 words, closer to Dionysophanes' 146 at 4.24 than to Daphnis' 165 at 3.23.1, though well behind Philetas' 461 at 2.3.2. The impact of Chloe's words is enhanced by the fact that this piece of direct speech comes so late in Book 1 – seven Teubner pages into the novel: about eleven per cent of the story has already been told before *any* character is given direct speech.

In Book 2 Daphnis maintains his vocal lead – two speeches in mid-Book, and at the Book's beginning two occasions when we hear what are both his and Chloe's reactions to their symptoms of ἔρως, 'love' or 'desire'. By contrast, Chloe is given only one speech of her own, the last of the book (2.39.2), providing symmetry with her allocation of the first speech in Book 1. It might also be seen to balance the penultimate block of direct speech in Book 2, Lamon's tale of Syrinx. Other characters also get only one each, again seemingly in pairs: Philetas and the youths from Methymna; the Nymphs and Pan. But this pairing cannot be pressed: the speech of Philetas which opens the Book is by some way the longest in the novel – 461 words[9] – and is very important both for the work's major theme and for its literary ancestry.

[9] The second longest is that of Daphnis to Chloe (3.23.1–5) after his tutorial from Lycaenion – 165 words. Lycaenion's three successive speeches totalling 260 words (3.16–19) can be seen as a pendant to Philetas' long speech in Book 2.

The dominance of Daphnis in Book 1 is replayed in Book 3: six speeches, three of them to Chloe; two to Chloe's father Dryas (first one that Daphnis merely imagined, then one that he actually makes); and one to himself. Significantly, perhaps, he is given no direct speech in his encounter with Lycaenion. That is marked by three speeches in succession from Lycaenion – the only character to be presented as so forward: Daphnis' responses are described but never voiced. Again Chloe has only one speech of her own (3.14.4), though in the stichomythia of 3.10.3 we hear thoughts voiced equally by both Daphnis and Chloe. Her father Dryas gets one speech, Daphnis' mother Myrtale and father Lamon each get one, and the senior Nymph who spoke in Book 2 again utters.

Book 4 greatly reduces Daphnis' spoken contribution: he is at the mercy of other actors and speakers. These are dominated by his foster-father and his real father, Lamon and Dionysophanes, each with four speeches. Whereas Chloe, her mother Cleariste and her foster-father Dryas each get only one speech, her real father Megacles gets two, as do Daphnis' brother Astylus (even if one is but a single-word exclamation) and Astylus' parasite Gnathon. Likewise Daphnis in this book has only two speeches, though like Chloe's opening utterance in Book 1 one is of considerable significance: Dionysophanes' promise that from the property to be left to Daphnis and Astylus he will set aside for Daphnis, and Daphnis alone, his pastureland, flocks and foster-parents reminds Daphnis that he ought to be getting back to take his goats to drink (4.25.1). Despite all that has happened Daphnis is still an αἰπόλος, 'goatherd', at heart.

One effect of the greater number of speeches and speaking characters in Book 4 is that it reads or sounds much closer to New Comedy, the genre from which so many features marking Dionysophanes, Astylus, and Gnathon – and their relations with each other – are drawn. This hubbub of city life – some of it, admittedly, city life transposed into the country by Dionysophanes' tour of inspection – contrasts markedly with the much less vocal texture of the rural scene-setting in Book 1.

This rather mechanical review of course neglects many features which add much complication to the picture. Either a character or an incident, or both, can be illuminated by the length of his or her speech or by elements of its style – average sentence-length; variation of sentence-length within a speech; the proportion of statements, questions and imperatives; the relative proportion of co-ordination and subordination, of *tricola* and doublets; the frequency of metaphors and similes; prose rhythm. Of these features I now examine only some.

3 The Length of Speeches

Most speeches are between 62 and 144 words long. Those in Book 1, for instance, in the order in which we read them, are speeches respectively of 143, 74, 105, 117, 62, 133 and 107 words; those in Book 2, after that of Philetas, are speeches respectively of 127, 24, 89, 97, 109, 132, 109, 115 and 83 words. That makes the first speech of Book 2, Philetas' *erotodidaxis*, especially striking at 572 words, even if 199 of them are the words of Eros he transmits. By contrast, the first words actually uttered in Book 3 – since the first conversation is simply imagined by Daphnis – are few but full of resonance: Χαῖρε, ὦ παῖ, 'Welcome, my boy' (3.7.3), says Dryas to Daphnis when he finds him hanging around outside his snowbound cottage. Dryas does not yet know that Daphnis will indeed become his son-in-law, in a sense his παῖς, far less that by Book 4 he will be addressed by his real father. The three words have a cledonomantic role. Book 4's predominance of longer speeches also gives immense power to Astylus' first utterance to his newly-rediscovered brother: the single word Δάφνι, 'Daphnis' (4.22.1). None of that power is lost when, immediately after this, Astylus, in his second and final speech, communicates the key facts about the discovery of Daphnis' identity in an extremely economical 42 words.

A similar divergence from mean length picks out in Book 2 not only Philetas' speech, as already observed, but the unusually short sequence of the couple's second set of reflections on its bearing on their condition at 2.9.2 – 24 words – and the unusually long speech of the senior Nymph at 2.23.2–5 – 132 words communicating an important message for Daphnis and for readers. In Book 3 the length of the myth of Echo – 165 words (3.23.1–5), much longer than the inset tales of Book 1 (133 words) and Book 2 (115 words) – gives it greater importance than these, while its sentence-length diverges from Daphnis' habit in his other speeches. Elsewhere Daphnis displays great variety in sentence-length, from 4 or 5 words (e.g. 1.18.1, 2.16.1, 3.29.2) to 27 (1.16.3) or 29 (2.16.1), and even (opening his address to Chloe accompanying his gift of the symbolic apple at 3.34.2–3) 43: in telling the story of Echo, however, his sentences are never shorter than 14 nor longer than 28 words, offering a sense of discipline quite at variance with the uncontrolled violence of Pan in the myth.

Evenness of sentence-length may also, however, have a negative impact. Dorcon's self-praise at 1.16.1–2 has three 12-word sentences, one of 14 and one of 17, offset by only one short sentence of 7. Daphnis follows on with a speech which has two short sentences, of 6 and 5 words, contrasting with five between 10 and 16 and one long sentence of 27. His ability to vary the length of his sentences comes out again in his speech to the rustic court at 2.16.1, to the Nymphs at 2.22.1, and to Dryas at 3.29.2–4 (see Table 30.1).

4 Stichomythia

A phenomenon connected with that of length is the replacement of continuous speech by stichomythia-like conversation. This is a trope deployed by Longus early in Book 3. We have become accustomed to set-piece speeches, and so we are surprised and perhaps impressed when at 3.6.3–4 Daphnis thinks through various excuses he might give for knocking on the door of Chloe's snowbound cottage: each of his excuses, in three- or four-word phrases, is followed immediately by Dryas' imagined reply, invariably rather longer. That perhaps slightly reduces the impact of Dryas' three-worder mentioned above (Χαῖρε, ὦ παῖ, 3.7.3) – but only slightly. It also in a sense prepares us for the next oral communication between Daphnis and Chloe: not, this time (3.10.3–4) a pair of set speeches, but another mimesis of dramatic stichomythia.

So far as I can recall the three earlier novelistic texts we know only once play either of the games with which Longus entertains his readers at 3.6.3 and 3.10.3–4: that of Chariton, presenting the debate between Chaereas and Dionysius at 5.7.5–6. But again an unusual passage of Thucydides may have caught Longus' eye – the stichomythic exchange after the Ambraciot disaster at 3.113.4.[10] Like contemporary epideictic performers, Longus is alert to catching his reader unawares.

5 Vocatives

Longus may also expect his readers to admire the artistry with which his passages of direct speech are marked by vocatives It is no surprise that the first speech, Chloe's soliloquy at 1.14.1, has no vocative addressing herself (although of course some soliloquies in literature do use such a vocative). The pair of competitive speeches that follow shortly in the mouths of Dorcon and Daphnis both address Chloe: not, however, by her name, but by her status, παρθένε, 'maiden': and Longus carefully balances the position of these vocatives – Dorcon places his in his first sentence as its second word

[10] Cf. also (in an erotic context!) Philostr. *Ep.* 5.

(1.16.1), Daphnis places his in his last sentence, as its third word (1.16.5). Like Chloe's soliloquy, the first and second soliloquies of Daphnis (1.18.1, 25.2) have no vocatives. Daphnis' next utterance, telling Chloe the tale of Phatta, makes the same vocative choice as (guided by Dorcon) he had made at 1.16.5: παρθένε – a choice that well suits this tale about a παρθένος, as indeed the juxtaposition of the two cases underlines, ἦν παρθένος, παρθένε, 'There was a maiden, maiden' (1.27.2). This repeated avoidance of Chloe's name makes it all the more effective when the dying Dorcon addresses her by it at 1.29.1: Χλόη, 'Chloe'. His use of her name reinforces his appeal and draws attention to their closeness, at least in Dorcon's eyes, and it might be thought to contribute to her allowing him a first and last kiss.

Address by status resumes in Book 2. Philetas' *erotodidaxis* both begins and ends ὦ παῖδες, 'children' (2.3.2, 6.2) – a vocative that reminds us, if we need reminding, of their adolescent innocence. That is followed by two sequences in which Daphnis and Chloe think aloud to themselves: like their earlier soliloquies, these have no vocatives (2.8.2, 9.2).

More surprising, perhaps, is the absence of vocatives from the speeches of the νέοι Μηθυμναῖοι and of Daphnis to the rustic tribunal: perhaps even Longus felt that ὦ ἄνδρες αἰπόλοι, 'O goatherding men', or ὦ οἰκέται Μυτιληναῖοι, 'O Mytilenean slaves', would strain readers' credulity! But the combination of these speeches' lack of any vocative with its even more remarkable absence from Daphnis' complaint addressed to the Nymphs (2.22.1) highlights the two vocatives that we do get in this sequence: during that complaint Daphnis begins to address the absent Chloe – indeed the first time that he does address her by name: ἆρα καὶ σύ, Χλόη, τοιαῦτα πάσχεις; 'Are you too, Chloe, suffering this sort of experience?' (2.22.4). A few lines later the Nymphs reply to Daphnis, and are the first speakers in the novel to address him by name: μηδὲν ἡμᾶς μέμφου, Δάφνι, 'Do not blame us for anything, Daphnis' (2.23.2). It is a *coup-de-theatre* not uncharacteristic of Longus that Daphnis' first address to Chloe by name is in her absence, and that it is not Chloe but the Nymphs who first address Daphnis by name.

The second vocative address to Daphnis is in words we have already encountered: the words of Dryas mentioned above – χαῖρε, ὦ παῖ (3.7.3). His use of ὦ παῖ links this address with that of Philetas to the couple at roughly the same stage in Book 2, ὦ παῖδες (2.3.2, 6.2), and like that it reminds us of his adolescence. By contrast the mutual addresses of Daphnis and Chloe a few chapters later, the first time either had addressed the other by name in the other's presence, and the first time either has reciprocated the other's address, offers us a signal that emotionally, at least, the couple are getting closer and closer: 'διὰ σὲ ἦλθον, Χλόη', 'It is because of you I have come, Chloe' – 'οἶδα, Δάφνι', 'I know, Daphnis' (3.10.3). In the following dialogue Daphnis again uses the vocative Χλόη twice, and Chloe the vocative Δάφνι once. That imbalance is redressed when at 3.14 Daphnis explains how animals manifestly enjoy the sexual act without his using the vocative Χλόη, whereas she replies marking her sharp observations with ὦ Δάφνι.

Chloe's regular use of the vocative in addressing Daphnis is, *inter alia*, a mark of her feeling that he now belongs to her. If that is so, then when Lycaenion uses the vocative in each of her three speeches to Daphnis this augments the reader's concern that Lycaenion's intervention may turn out to be a threat to the couple's relationship. Such concern may be increased and not allayed when Daphnis, in telling Chloe the tale of Echo, addresses her not by the vocative Χλόη but the vocative ὦ κόρη, 'Girl' (3.23.1). The suppression of the couple's names in the vocative continues to the end of the book. When Myrtale addresses Daphnis she uses ὦ παῖ, 'My boy' (3.26.4), when the Nymphs address him they use no vocative at all (3.27.3–5), just as Daphnis himself uses no vocative in approaching Dryas (3.29.2–4). The last vocative name in the book is that of Dryas, so addressed by Lamon at the end of his speech (3.31.4). Daphnis, as we have come to expect, does not address himself by name in his soliloquy at 3.32.1–2. More strikingly, he does not use Chloe's name when giving her the apple he has plucked, but instead addresses her with ὦ παρθένε (3.34.1). That of course draws attention to the function of the apple as a symbol of Chloe's virginity, but it may suggest to the reader that by now they are further apart and not nearer to each other than they were when each used the other's name so generously in the vocative at 3.10.3–4. It could also remind us that the last woman to address Daphnis by name in this book was Lycaenion, three times.

The fourth book has a quite different pattern of vocative use. Of thirteen vocatives only three are proper names – Astylus' two addresses to Daphnis as Δάφνι (4.22.1, 22.3) which we have already noted, and Megacles' address of a part of his speech at 4.35.1–2 to Dionysophanes. With one exception the rest are, like the first part of Megacles' speech here, terms of relationship or status. Here Megacles' outburst begins by addressing his newly-found θυγάτριον, 'dear daughter' (4.35.1), just as earlier Lamon has addressed Myrtale with ὦ γύναι (4.18.3), Dionysophanes had addressed his two sons with the phrase already familiar in addresses to the couple, ὦ παῖδες (4.24.1), and Daphnis had at last addressed his father as πάτερ, 'father' (4.25.1), momentously sealing the newly-discovered relationship.

But the vocatives that open the book are the most significant in their contribution to directing our attention to matters of status. After Lamon has, predictably, been given a soliloquy with no vocative, there follow three identical vocatives, δέσποτα, 'master': Lamon to Dionysophanes (4.14.2) and Gnathon twice to Astylus (4.16.2, 17.3). These are followed by Lamon's ὦ γύναι, 'wife' (4.18.2), and then again by the vocative δέσποτα, this time used by Lamon to Dionysophanes (4.19.3). The pattern forces upon our attention the ways in which Lamon and Gnathon are both subservient.[11] But the next vocative adds a further layer. After reflections in which he uses no vocative (4.20.2) Dionysophanes exclaims to the company ὦ Ζεῦ δέσποτα, 'O master Zeus' (4.21.2); and when his wife sees the tokens he has summoned her to scrutinise she exclaims ὦ φίλαι Μοῖραι, 'O dear Fates' (4.21.3). Only here do the Μοῖραι, 'Fates' appear in Longus; they were absent from Chariton and Xenophon, and were exploited only once by Achilles Tatius (1.3.2) when his narrator Cleitophon invokes their role in his matrimonial fate. Whether or not that passage in Achilles Tatius is an intertext for this outburst by Cleariste (as I suspect it is), its close conjunction with Dionysophanes' ὦ Ζεῦ δέσποτα asks us to re-examine the implications of the slaves' repeated use of ὦ δέσποτα. All the participants in this story, as we have been reminded from time to time, are acting within limits imposed by higher powers.

The last two speeches in the work, by Megacles and by Dionysophanes to the assembled company (4.35.3, 36.1), have no vocatives. In the latter case this may be so that a vocative should not distract from the other proper names' role in these few lapidary lines – Daphnis twice, then Pan, the Nymphs and Eros. But its effect is also to leave the last vocatives we remember as those of Megacles to the two mortals who, along with himself and Daphnis, are the key participants: θυγάτριον, 'dear daughter', and Διονυσόφανες (4.35.1–2).

6 Comparison and Subordination

What, then, of metaphor, simile and other sorts of comparison; of subordination *versus* parataxis; of questions *versus* statements? To illustrate Longus' ποικιλία, 'variety', I present an analysis only of Books 1 and 2.

In Book 1 each speaker displays slightly different tendencies. Chloe's opening outburst – I am tempted to call it an *aria* – progresses chiefly by metaphor and comparison. In Book 1 only this speech of Chloe (1.14.1) and the pendant speech of Daphnis (1.18.1) use metaphors – the long-established, perhaps even hackneyed, metaphor of desire as a disease: νῦν

[11] On Gnathon's status see Bowie 2019b, 120 (Chapter 43, 878 in this volume).

ἐγὼ νοσῶ μέν, τί δὲ ἡ νόσος ἀγνοῶ, 'now I am sick, but I do not know what the sickness is' (1.14.1); τήκεται ἡ ψυχή, 'My soul melts away' (1.18.1). Both Chloe and Daphnis resort to questions: Chloe at least twice (more if the phrases introduced by πόσοι,'how many', are questions rather than exclamations), Daphnis three times. They also exploit many comparisons. Chloe's comparisons are not mere similes – she notes that brambles and bees have caused her pain by their scratches and stings, and contrasts this pain with the pain of desire which is πικρότερον, 'harsher' (1.14.2). Daphnis also uses comparative adjectives to set up some of his five comparisons: χείλη μὲν ῥόδων ἁπαλώτερα καὶ στόμα κηρίων γλυκύτερον, τὸ δὲ φίλημα κέντρου μελίττης πικρότερον, 'her lips are more delicate than roses and her mouth sweeter than honeycombs, but her kiss is more painful than a bee's sting' (1.18.1). He goes on to compare kissing Chloe to kissing young animals, and ends by contrasting his condition with that of flowers: ἀλλὰ τὰ μὲν ἴα καὶ ὁ ὑάκινθος ἀνθεῖ, Δάφνις δὲ μαραίνεται, 'but the violets and hyacinth bloom, but Daphnis withers away' (1.18.2). Questioning, comparison, and contrast are of course the way we should expect Chloe and Daphnis to speak at this point: they are trying to locate a totally unfamiliar phenomenon in the geography of their existing rural experience. But it is interesting that Daphnis' inclination to exploit comparisons persists into his telling of the Phatta myth at 1.27.2.

But some features distinguish one from the other. Chloe uses a vocative exclamation ὦ πονηρὸν ὕδωρ, 'O evil water!' (1.14.3), whereas Daphnis uses two successive genitives of exclamation: ὢ νίκης κακῆς, ὢ νόσου καινῆς, 'O bad victory!' (1.18.2). That is followed by the only subordinate clause in Daphnis' 117 words: ἧς οὐδὲ εἰπεῖν οἶδα τὸ ὄνομα, 'whose name I do not even know how to utter'. By contrast Chloe was allowed four subordinate clauses in her 144 words, and Daphnis certainly knows how to use subordinate clauses: there are two in his beauty-competition speech at 1.16.3, and two in his telling of the Phatta myth at 1.27.2. So Daphnis' musings on his love-sick condition at 1.18 stand out – and are presumably meant to stand out – as different both from his other speeches in Book 1, and from Chloe's similar *cris-de-coeur*, as unusually paratactic, even for Longus.

Book 2's grand opening speech by Philetas differs from these speeches in Book 1 in several ways. Even allowing for its length, it has a very high number of participles (twenty-four) and various sorts of subordination (twenty-six). It also has a high total of comparisons (fourteen). It is also the only speech to have a speech within a speech – the speech of Eros to Philetas (2.5.1–5). By contrast it has neither a single direct question nor a single metaphor. The ensuing speeches revert in varying degrees to the patterns of Book 1. The two speeches in which Daphnis and Chloe reflect to themselves on their symptoms each use once the metaphor of φάρμακον, 'remedy', the first after re-introducing the idea that love causes pain ἀλγοῦσιν ... ἀλγοῦμεν, 'they feel pain ... we feel pain' (2.8.2 and 4). That first speech's five subordinations are somewhat few for its length, but its five questions rather above average. That it has only two participles, οὐκ εἰδότες, 'not knowing', and ἐρῶντα, 'when he felt desire for', is remarkable, but is partly a corollary of its high proportion of short paratactic sentences.

Daphnis' speech in reply to the Methymnans has a different balance, and we can see why. The Methymnans (2.15.2) used four participles, two subordinations, one comparison and one question. Daphnis follows suit in his reply, using three participles, two subordinations, one comparison and one question. The pattern changes in his complaint to the Nymphs (2.22.1): here he uses six participles, two comparisons, only one subordination, and – not surprisingly in his situation – three questions. In reply the Nymphs have seven participles, five subordinations, but no comparison, and certainly no questions. Pan's castigation of Bryaxis is closely similar: six participles, three subordinations, no comparison, and no questions. With Lamon's telling of the tale of Syrinx (2.34.1) we revert to the very high proportion of participles found in Philetas' narrative – ten, with only three subordinations, one comparison, and no question. This can be set against the final speech of the book, that of Chloe (2.39.2): two comparisons, three participles, and – like her opening speech in Book 1 – an unusually high frequency of subordination, five. Of all ten speeches in Book 2 it is only the second and third, the reflections of Daphnis and Chloe on their condition, that employ any sort of metaphor.

Most of these differences can perhaps better be attributed to the purposes of the speech and the situation of the speaker than to the latter's character, though I am tempted to see something more in Chloe's greater readiness to use syntactical subordination. That Longus – of course within his chosen stylistic parameters – should be seen to mould the style of speeches to situation rather than to character is of course what we might expect from our knowledge of sophistic *epideixis* and rhetorical training in this period.

7 Conclusion

Longus' uses of direct speech display the delicate artistry and the attention to telling detail that marks the whole of his work. Several other aspects of that artistry could be pursued – for example the variation in sentence-length within these speeches, a variation that a glance at Table 30.1 will immediately observe. Different issues have been very illuminatingly explored by John Morgan in his most recent of many contributions to our better understand of Longus.[12] I hope that some contribution has also been made by this chapter.

[12] Morgan 2021.

Table 30.1 *Number of words in each speech and in each sentence in speeches*

The total of words in 51 speeches is 3956 (i.e. average 78). Without the exclamations at 3.7.3, 4.21.2 and 4.22.2 (7 words in all) the total is 3949 and the average is 82.

Book 1							
Average length 106 words							
Speakers (7)	1.14.1 C to herself	1.16.1 Dorcon to C	1.16.3 D to C	1.18.1 D to himself	1.25.2 D to himself	1.27.2 D to C	1.29.1 Dorcon to C
Words per sentence in sequence (total 741)	9–6–7–6–8–8–10–7–9–5–13–11–13–5–5–16–11	12–7–17–12–14–12	27–14–65–10–16–16–11	7–14–14–4–15–12–7–4–9–7–8–11–6	8–7–3–12–7–3–6–8–8	12–12–26–37–20–26	12–12–26–37–20–26
Words in speech	143	74	105	117	62	133	107
Words in sentence							
3	–	–	–	–	2	–	
4	–	–	–	2	–	–	
5	3		1	–	–		–
6	2		1	2	1		
7	2	1		2	2		
8	2	–	–	1	3		
9	3	–	–	1	–		
10	–	–	1	–	–		

Table 30.1 (*Cont.*)

Book 1							
Average length 106 words							
Speakers (7)	1.14.1 C to herself	1.16.1 Dorcon to C	1.16.3 D to C	1.18.1 D to himself	1.25.2 D to himself	1.27.2 D to C	1.29.1 Dorcon to C
11	2		1	1	–		1
12	–	3	–	1	1	2	
13	1	–	–	1	–		
14	1	1	1	1	–		
15	–	–	–	1	–		2
16	1		2	–	–		
17		1					
19							2
20						1	
26						2	
27			1				
28							1
37						1	

Book 2										
Average length 146 words										
Speakers (10)	2.3.2 Philetas to D & C	2.8.2 D & C to themselves	2.9.2 D & C to themselves	2.15.2 Methymnans	2.16.1 D to the court	2.22.1 D to the Nymphs	2.23.2 Senior Nymph to D	2.27.1 Pan to Bryaxis	2.34.1 Lamon to D & C	2.39.2 C to D
Words per sentence in sequence (total 1457)	26–9–24–25–17–8–8–30–4–5–18–20–14–8–24–23–33–17 [Eros 8–24–15–13–17–33–13–32–13–21–10] 20–18–22	3–2–2–2–3–5–2–4–3–7–10–10–5–4–5–18–5–4–6–4–6–8–6–7–7	4–4–6–3–7	7–19–17–10–11–8–17	5–16–29–4–10–10–6–5–12	25–28–16–5–8–6–10–11	4–7–15–20–20–20–6–15–18–7	10–39–41–19	15–7–18–15–6–9–8–28–9	9–16–20–22–16
Words in speech	572	127	24	89	97	109	132	109	115	83
Words in sentence										
2	–	4								
3			1							
4	1	2	2	6	1		1			
5	1		–	1	2	1				
6		2	1	1	1	1	1		1	
7		3	1	2			2		1	
8	8	1	–	2	–	1			1	

Table 30.1 (*Cont.*)

Book 2										
Average length 146 words										
Speakers (10)	2.3.2 Philetas to D & C	2.8.2 D & C to themselves	2.9.2 D & C to themselves	2.15.2 Methymnans	2.16.1 D to the court	2.22.1 D to the Nymphs	2.23.2 Senior Nymph to D	2.27.1 Pan to Bryaxis	2.34.1 Lamon to D & C	2.39.2 C to D
9	1	–	–	2	–				2	1
10	1	2	–	–	2	1	–	1		
11		–	–	–	–	1				
12			–	–	1			–		
13	3		–	–		–		–		
14	1		–	–	–	–		–		
15	1		–	–	–	–	2	–	2	
16					1	1				2
17	3									
18	2	1					1		1	
19								1		
20	2						3			1
21	1									
22	1									
24	2									
25	1					1				
26	1									
28						1			1	

29							1								
32		1													
33		2													
39											1				
41											1				

Book 3

Average length 79 words

Speakers (15)

	3.6.3–4 D to self, quasi-stichomythia	3.7.3 Dryasto D	3.10.3–4 D & C stichomythia	3.14.2–3 D to C	3.14.5–5 C to D	3.16.2–4 Lycaenion to D	3.171–3 Lycaenion to D	3.19.2–3 Lycaenion to D	3.23.1–5 D to C	3.26.4 Myrtale to D	3.27.2–5 Senior Nymph to D	3.29.2–4 D to DryasNB short cola	3.31.1–4 Lamon to Dryas	3.32.1–3 Dryas to himself	3.34.2–3D to C
Words per sentence in sequence (total 1178)	3–7–3–5–2–6–3–6–4–5–3–8–13		4–2–6–4–2–21–11–6–14–3–9	12–22–12	31–8–6	5–37–42–6–8	29–13–7–6–24	7–17–15–33–9	14–17–18–23–20–18–28–27	10–7–14–15	15–38–36–9–12	4–11–8–6–5–12–15–6–21–9	14–9–9–25–11–15–7–10–5–6–5–5	18–10–7–8–9–24	43–5–5–4–5
Words in speech	68	3	82	46	45	98	79	81	165	46	110	97	121	76	61
Words in sentence															
2	1		2												

Table 30.1 (*Cont.*)

Book 3

Average length 79 words

Speakers (15)

	3.6.3–4 D to self, quasi-stichomythia	3.7.3 Dryasto D	3.10.3–4 D & C stichomythia	3.14.2–3 D to C	3.14.5–5 C to D	3.16.2–4 Lycaenion to D	3.171–3 Lycaenion to D	3.19.2–3 Lycaenion to D	3.23.1–5 D to C	3.26.4 Myrtale to D	3.27.2–5 Senior Nymph to D	3.29.2–4 D to DryasNB short cola	3.31.1–4 Lamon to Dryas	3.32.1–3 Dryas to himself	3.34.2–3D to C
3	4	1	1												
4	1		2									1			1
5	2		–			1	-					1	2		3
6	2		2		1	1	1					2	1		
7	1		–		–		1	1		1				1	
8	1	–	–		1	1						1		1	
9		–	1		–			1			1	1	1	1	
10		–	–	–	–		–			1				1	
11		–	1	–	–							1			
12			–	2	–			–			1	1			
13	1	–	–	–	–	–	1	–							
14	–	–	1	–	–	–	–	–	1	1			1		

15	–	–	–	–	–			1		1	1	1			
17								1	1						
18									2					1	
20									1						
21			1									1			
22				1											
23									1				1		
24							1							1	
26													1		
27									1						
28															
29							1		1						
31					1										
33								1							
34													1		
36											1				
37						1									
38											1				
39								1							
42						1									
43															1

Table 30.1 (*Cont.*)

Book 4

Average length 61 words

Speakers (19)

	4.8.3–4 Lamon to D and Myrtale	4.14.2–3 Lamon to Dionysophanes	4.16 2–4 Gnathon to Astylus	4.17.3–7 Gnathon to Astylus	4.18.3 Lamon to Myrtale	4.19.3–5 Lamon to Dionysophanes	4.20.2 Dionysophanes to himself	4.21.2 Dionysophanes to all	4.21.3 Clearişte to Dionysophanes	4.22.2 Astylus to D	4.22.3–4 Astylus to D	4.24 Dionysophanes to D and Astylus	4.25.1 D to Dionysophanes	4.27 C to herself	4.28.2–3 D to himself	4.30.3–4 Dryas to Dionysophanes	4.35.1–2 Megacles to all	4.35.3–5 Megacles to all	4.36.1–2 Dionysophanes to Megacles
Words per sentence in sequence (total 1152)	5–5–11–7–7–6–18–7–4–17	6–17–11–5–5	4–33–33–11–30	15–10–11–9–33–9–6–7–7–10–24	3–5–15–38–8–6	8–10–10–32–9–8–30	11–7–15	3	2–6–8–7–6–8	1	2–2–9–9–8–4–7	14–11–20–6–23–39–16–17	4–19	3–3–10–5–10–8–1–4	3–5–5–7–12–13	11–17–9–19–13	3–4–11–4–5–7	7–8–6–18–20–24	4–12–11–11
Words in speech	87	44	111	131	75	107	33	3	37	1	41	146	23	44	45	69	34	83	38
Words in sentence																			
1	–		–							1				1					
2									1		2								
3					1			1						2	1		1		
4	1		1								1		1	1			2		1
5	2	2	–		1		-							1	2		1		

6	1	1	–	1	1				2		1						1	
7	3		–	2			1		1	1				1		1	1	
8		–	–		1	2			2	1			1				1	
9		–		2		1				2					1			
10		–	–	1		2	–						2					
11	1	1	1	1	–		1				1				1	1		2
12			–		–			–						1				1
13		–	–		–	–		–						1	1			
14	–	–			–	–		–			1							
15	–	–	–	1	1		15	–										
16											1							
17	1	1									1				1			
18	1																1	
19												1			1			
20									1		1						1	
23									1		1							
24				1													1	
25								1										
27									1									
30			1			1												
32						1												
33			2	1				1										
36																		
37						1												
38					1													
39								1			1							
43																1		
45									1									

31 | Pulling the Other? Longus on Tragedy (2007)

1 Introduction

The five 'ideal' Greek novels that have been transmitted complete in a continuous manuscript tradition present as their major theme heterosexual desire, one sense of the term 'pulling the other' which my title (unashamedly intertextual) exploits. All five novels also include Attic tragedies of the classical period among the canonical texts that they evoke to achieve their own literary goals: this is most insistent and self-conscious in Heliodorus' *Theagenes and Charicleia*,[1] but the technique is already visible in our earliest novel, Chariton's *Chaereas and Callirhoe*. This paper explores to what extent and with what possible purpose Attic tragedy is exploited by Longus in his miniature and pastoral novel, *Daphnis and Chloe*, and argues that a major objective is to stress how different is the presentation of ἔρως in *Daphnis and Chloe* and in its novelistic predecessors from that in Attic tragedy. I contribute it in the hope that its focus on generic boundaries, on tragedy, and on the novel will match our honorand's interests.

At first glance tragedy is not the most prominent among the archaic and classical genres evoked by *Daphnis and Chloe*. That work's resonances are much more with historiography, Attic comedy, pastoral poetry and archaic lyric poetry.[2]

After Thucydides' claims for his work have been teased in the preface (*pr.* 3), and a typically historiographic description of a city has been fleetingly displayed in the opening lines of the narrative itself (1.1.1), historiography fades into the background until the war between Mytilene and Methymna that Chloe's abduction has provoked allows the writer to indulge in a twenty-three-line vignette flecked with Thucydidean detail (3.1.1–3.1).[3] Chloe's abduction itself gives Longus the opportunity for a reworking of the striking Herodotean passage in which Philippides conveys to the Athenians Pan's

[1] Cf. Paulsen 1992; Lefteratou 2018.

[2] The discussion of Hunter 1983, 9–83 remains fundamental. For further work see the excellent commentary of Morgan 2004, now an essential point of departure; Pattoni 2005; Bowie 2019g, 2–5 and *passim* in that commentary, whose indices offer guidance on links with individual poets.

message that they had hitherto been neglecting him: the Nymphs point out to the distraught Daphnis that he and Chloe had hitherto failed to honour, even with garlands, the statue of Pan erected beneath their pine-tree.[4]

Attic New Comedy also makes its debut in the preface. The cave of the Nymphs is immediately revealed to be connected with Pan (*pr.* 3), a *mise-en-scène* that to many readers would evoke Menander's Δύσκολος, '*Bad-tempered man*'. A New Comedy motif is immediately presented in the exposure of the two babies of city families (1.2–4). New Comedy characters emerge first with the pleasure cruise of the rich young Methymnans (2.12–18), then in greater strength in Book 4 – the elite parents of the exposed couple, the son of one of these families, playing a role that matches his name Astylus, and his loathsome parasite, Gnathon.

The constant backcloth is of course a pastoral world meticulously constructed from the hexameter poetry of the Hellenistic poet Theocritus. Detail after evocative detail takes readers back to Theocritus; some lead them further back to Sappho and Alcaeus, palmary intertexts for a novel exploring ἔρως, 'desire', and set on Lesbos.[5] Thus archaic Aeolic lyric poetry becomes the fourth genre to make an important contribution to the texture of *Daphnis and Chloe*.

It is only after these four genres that tragedy can be claimed as an intertext. Given that there are other poetic genres also occasionally exploited – for example, early hexameter epic and Hellenistic epigram – the relatively low profile of tragic intertextuality is remarkable.

In what follows I first set out cases where a tragic intertext might be argued for on grounds of language or (less often) content; then I offer a possible explanation of the phenomena.

2 Tragic Intertexts?

(a) Language That May Evoke Two or More Tragedians

1.9.2 τοσαύτης δὴ πάντα κατεχούσης εὐωρίας, 'with everything in the spell of so fine a spring'. εὐωρία, 'fineness of season', appears only here in extant literature before Libanius *Ep.* 434.4 (though it is also found in a document,

[3] For the preface cf. Hunter 1983; Luginbill 2001–2; Thucydidean vocabulary also marks the opening of the cruise by rich *νέοι* which precipitates the abduction. i.e. προσκώπους at 2.12.1: cf. Th. 1.10.3; Hunter 1983, 85 with n.6; Cueva 1998; Trzaskoma 2005.

[4] 2.23.4: cf. Hdt. 6.105.3, Paus. 1.28.4.

[5] See Bowie 2013d (Chapter 37 in this volume); Bowie 2019g *passim*; Bowie 2021a and 2021b.

Sammelbuch 4324.7); but its existence is perhaps implied by the verb εὐωριάζειν in Soph. fr. 561, and it was conjectured by Porson at [Aes.] *Pr.* 17 (Longus will have imagined the *Prometheus* to be by Aeschylus), though this verb seems to mean 'to be negligent'. Note too εὔωρος γάμος, 'marriage at time of ripeness', Soph. fr. 200 Radt.

1.20.2 The stately phrase ἀνδρὸς ὁπλίτου, 'hoplite man' (instead of simply ὁπλίτου, 'hoplite') is poetical (Aes. *Th.* 717, Eur. *Supp.* 585). It is never used by Th., and only once, for effect, by Hdt., writing of the phantom at Marathon (6.117.3). κράνος, 'helmet', is also poetical, e.g. Aes. *Th.* 385. Of claimed prose usages Xen. *Cyr.* 1.51 is interpolated, Plu. *An seni* 10 (= *Mor.* 789d) is perhaps consciously poetical. It may be relevant that ἀνδρὸς ὁπλίτου κράνος could form the second limb of an iambic trimeter.

1.23.2 θαλπόμενος τούτοις ἅπασιν, 'heated up by all these things'. The metaphorical sense of θάλπειν is only found here in the novelists, although other metaphorical terms from the language of fire are common.[6] Almost all earlier metaphorical uses in the context of passion are in tragedy: [Aes.] *Pr.* 590, 650; Soph. *Tr.* 102, *El.* 888, fr. 474 Radt. Herodas' use at 2.81 is formally an exception, but can be argued itself to be allusive; Alciphron's use at 2.2, probably later than Longus, is in a related but not identical context.

2.1.2 κατεξασμένης (from καταξείνειν) 'pounded to shreds' is a word whose classical attestations are chiefly in tragedy, e.g. Aes. *Ag.* 197, fr. 132 c Radt; Soph. *Aj.* 728; Eur. *Med.* 1030, *Hipp.* 274, *HF* 285, *Ion* 1267, *Tro.* 509, *Ph.* 1145, *Supp.* 503. Ar.'s use at *Ach.* 320 is arguably paratragic. Its use by Longus elevates the humble function of the *agnus castus* that has been shredded to make a rustic torch.

2.14.1 κλυδώνιον of (slightly) rough water is chiefly tragic, whether literally in Eur. (*Hec.* 48, *Hel.* 1209), or metaphorically in Aes. (*Th.* 795, *Cho.* 183). Although it also appears as a *varia lectio* at Th. 2.84.3 and Arr. *Peripl.M.Eux.* 3, it seems most likely that for Longus it had a tragic resonance.

3.4.1 In classical Greek the noun οἰκουρία, 'the act of staying at home', is found only in Eur. (*HF* 1373); most cognate words (οἰκουρεῖν, 'to stay at home', οἰκούρημα, 'the act of staying at home', οἰκούριος, 'staying at home') are found only in tragedy (although οἰκουρός, 'staying at home' is more widely attested). However οἰκουρία is common in imperial prose (e.g. Plu. *Quaest. Rom.* 30 = *Mor.* 271e, *Cor.* 35.2, Ael. *NA* 1.15, Alciphr. 3.22.2) so it is unclear whether for Longus it had a tragic ring.

3.12.4 τὸν Ἴτυν … ἠκρίβουν, 'perfected their song of Itys'. Explanation of the nightingale's song as a lament for Itys is found as early as Od. 19.522,

[6] For metaphor in Longus see Bowie 2005c (Chapter 27 in this volume).

but there the form of his name is Ἴτυλος. It is chiefly in tragedy that Ἴτυς is the name-form that signals the myth: Aes. *Ag.* 1144 with Fraenkel *ad loc.*, Soph. *El.* 148–9, Eur. fr. 773 Kannicht. Although there are of course other places Longus could find the name Itys used to evoke the whole myth (e.g. Ar. *Av.* 212), and although his predecessor Ach. Tat. tells the myth twice (but without using the name Itys: 5.3.4–5.9), the link here with a story of family violence might support a claim that Longus draws Itys from tragedy.

4.21.2 πόρπην χρυσήλατον, 'a clasp of beaten gold': at 1.2.3 this clasp was simply termed χρυσῆ, 'gold', but the higher emotional register of this scene may have induced Longus to choose a grand compound adjective which may evoke Attic tragedy. It is found at Aes. *Th.* 644 and Soph. *OT* 1268, and, most strikingly, of πόρπαι by Euripides at *Ph.* 62 (χρυσηλάτοις πόρπαισιν, 'clasps of beaten gold').[7] Though it also found in some other imperial Greek texts (e.g. Plu. *Dem.* 53.2, Luc. *Sat.* 8), a tragic and especially Euripidean intertextuality seems likely.

4.24.3 κρεῖττον γὰρ τοῖς εὖ φρονοῦσιν ἀδελφοῦ κτῆμα οὐδέν, 'for there is no possession better than a brother for those who think aright': this high value set on brothers might recall Soph. *Ant.* 905–20.[8] The intertextuality is made more probable by the formulation, which is reminiscent of tragic γνῶμαι, 'maxims', e.g. Eur. *Andr.* 896 οὐκ ἔστιν οὐδὲν κρεῖσσον οἰκείου φίλου, 'There is nothing better than a friend that is one's own'; *Or.* 1155 οὐκ ἔστιν οὐδὲν κρεῖσσον ἢ φίλος σαφής, 'There is nothing better than a sure friend'. There are of course similar formulations in other gnomic poetry, e.g. the *Theognidea*, though in that collection all are positive and lack οὐδέν, e.g. Thgn. 1074 κρεῖσσόν τοι σοφίη καὶ μεγάλης ἀρετῆς, 'Better, I tell you, is wisdom even than great excellence' (cf. also 218, 618, 1173).

(b) Aeschylus

2.22.3 λιπεργάτης ἐσόμενος, 'destined to abandon my work'. In λιπεργάτης Longus uses a word otherwise unattested to convey Daphnis' tragic vision of himself. The model is perhaps Agamemnon imagining himself as λιπόναυς at Aes. *Ag.* 212, picked up by λιποναύταν at Theoc. 13.73.

2.27.1 μαινομέναις φρεσίν, 'with maddened minds', maintains the high poetic style of the preceding superlatives and seems to recall Aes. *Th.* 484 μαινομέναι φρενί, 'with maddened mind'. The context – intervention by a

7 For the popularity of Eur. *Ph.* in the imperial period see Bowie 2022a.

8 So Morgan 2004, 240 *ad loc.* The notoriously related passage at Hdt. 3.119.6 is less likely to be evoked here by Longus.

wrathful divinity – is as near as Longus' main narrative ever comes to the mad, bad world of Attic tragedy.

2.27.3 βορὰν ἰχθύων, 'a meal for the fish', might recall the self-imprecation of Io at [Aes.] *Pr.* 582–3 ἢ ποντίοις δάκεσι δὸς βοράν, 'or give me to sea monsters as fodder'. But the threat of being βορά, 'food', for fish is already in Ach. Tat. 3.5.4 εἰ δὲ καὶ θηρίων ἡμᾶς βορὰν πέπρωται γενέσθαι, εἷς ἡμᾶς ἰχθὺς ἀναλωσάτω, 'but if it is in fact fated that we should be the fodder of wild creatures, let a single fish consume us'; and the idea goes right back to Il. 19.268, where βόσιν ἰχθύων, 'a meal for the fish', characterises a sacrifice thrown into the sea.

(c) Sophocles

pr. 4 πάντως γὰρ οὐδεὶς ἔρωτα ἔφυγεν ἢ φεύξεται, 'for by no means has anybody escaped desire, nor shall escape it'. Morgan 2004, 150 persuasively suggests that this alludes to the well-known song in Soph. *Ant.* 787 where it is said of Eros καί σ' οὔτ' ἀθανάτων φύξιμος οὐδεὶς | οὔθ' ἁμερίων σέ γ' ἀν|θρώπων, 'and neither is any of the immortals able to escape you, nor, certainly, any among ephemeral mortals'. As he goes on to observe: 'The allusion points L's innovation: Love in this novel is wholly positive, if properly conducted'.

2.22.3 ποίοις ποσὶν ἄπειμι παρὰ τὸν πατέρα καὶ τὴν μητέρα, 'with what sort of gait shall I go back to my father and mother', has been convincingly argued by Pattoni to recall Ajax's words in Soph. *Aj.* 462–4:[9]

> καὶ ποῖον ὄμμα πατρὶ δηλώσω φανεὶς
> Τελαμῶνι; πῶς με τλήσεταί ποτ' εἰσιδεῖν
> γυμνὸν φανέντα τῶν ἀριστείων ἄτερ ...
>
> And what sort of expression shall I display to my father when I appear,
> to my father Telamon? How will he bring himself ever to look at me
> when I have appeared unarmed, without prizes of excellence?

Pattoni shows how a number of details in Longus' phraseology remodel this passage with what she argues to be parodic intent (e.g. the replacement of the high-style ὄμμα, 'eye', with the down-to-earth ποσίν, 'feet', though she misses the possible Aeschylean allusion in λιπεργάτης (cf. above). It seems to me that the contrast Pattoni observes between the expected response of Ajax's father Telamon (adducing also 1010–21) and the sympathetic

[9] Pattoni 2004, 84–9.

distress of Daphnis' parents (οἳ καὶ αὐτοὶ κεῖνται χαμαί, 'who themselves are also lying prostrate', 2.23.5) offers less support to an explanation in terms of parody than to the advertisement of generic difference for which I am arguing.

3.6.2 ὡς οὐκ αἰσίοις ὄρνισιν ἐλθών, 'as having coming with birds not of good omen': Di Virgilio 1991, 232–3 suggests that these words allude to Soph. *OT* 52 ὄρνιθι … αἰσίωι, 'with a bird of good omen'. If there is such an allusion it is hard to gauge its effect in a context where, as is seen by Morgan 2004, 203, the reference to augury in connection with a bird-hunt is playful; but the collocation is not rare enough to support an allusion (cf. e.g. Pi. *N.* 9.18).

3.28.2 μυδῶν 'rotting' or 'clammy' describes the body of Polynices at Soph. *Ant.* 410, and its use in that play again at 1008, and at *OT* 1298, might mark it as a particularly Sophoclean word. But it is also found in Plb. and medical writers (e.g. Hp. *VC* 15, *Ulc.* 10, Dsc. 1.71,72). Evocation here of Polynices in *Antigone* might be thought far-fetched, were it not that in his preface (see above on *pr.* 4) Longus had given readers such a clear pointer to that play.

(d) Euripides

pr. 4 The prayer ἡμῖν δ' ὁ θεὸς παράσχοι σωφρονοῦσι τὰ τῶν ἄλλων γράφειν, 'but to us may the god grant that we write the deeds of others with self-control',[10] may recall the prayer to Ἔρως of the chorus in Eur. *Hipp.* 528–9: μή μοί ποτε σὺν κακῶι φανείης | μήδ' ἄρρυθμος ἔλθοις, 'may you never appear to me accompanied by evil, and may you not come disruptively'.

1.9.1 κατῆιδον, 'filled with song'. The verb appears only twice in classical texts, at Eur. *IT* 1337 and Hdt. 7.191.2. Longus could have known the word from either passage, but his phraseology is also influenced by Ar. *Av.* 224 οἷον κατεμελίτωσε τὴν λόχμην ὅλην, 'how she has filled the whole grove with honey'.

1.13.5 ἄση, 'heart-ache', appears first in Sappho's prayer to Aphrodite, fr. 1.3, perhaps also at fr. 96.17, then at Eur. *Med.* 245. Although found in medical writing its rarity, and the influence of Sappho fr. 31 elsewhere in this passage, together suggest that Longus draws directly on Sappho, and that the word's appearance at *Med.* 245 is not enough to support a claim that this is a Euripidean intertext.

[10] For the (as often) complex connotations of σωφροσύνη here and its implications for our reading of Longus' text see the very perceptive discussion by Morgan 2004, 148.

1.13.6 Chloe's inability to eat (cf. 1.17.4, 2.7.4) may be drawn from that of Phaedra in Eur. *Hipp.* 135–7, 275; her restlessness from *Hipp.* 181–5; the term οἶστρος, 'gadfly', from *Hipp.* 1300.

1.14.1 For love as a νόσος, 'disease', cf. Eur. *Hipp.* 131–40. *Prima facie* this is too widespread a perception of ἔρως to allow us to infer a Euripidean intertext, cf. Pl. *Phdr.* 255d, Theoc. 2.85, X.Eph. 1.5, 6, Ach. Tat.1.6. However its appearance close to the metaphor ἕλκος, 'wound', for which cf. Eur. *Hipp.* 530, greatly strengthens the case: ἕλκος is found only here in Longus, and indeed only here in the novelists for the metaphorical wound of love (Achilles Tatius uses ἕλκος metaphorically, but not of love, at 2.29.3, 5, 5.8.2). Longus could, admittedly, have drawn it from Call. *AP* 12.134 (= *HE* 1103–8);[11] or (more probably) from Theoc. 11.15, a poem he certainly reworks shortly after this passage (1.17.3); or from Theoc. 30.10.

1.15.2: The νεβρὶς βακχική, 'bacchant's fawnskin', that Dorcon gives to Chloe may be known to readers from Eur. *Ba.* 676: but there could be many other literary sources, e.g. *AP* 6.172 (= *FGE* 1124–9, possibly Hellenistic), [Theoc.], *AP* 6.177 (= *HE* 3398–3401) and indeed artistic representations, cf. Merkelbach 1988.

1.20.2 Dorcon's trick of dressing himself in a wolf-skin could recall its wearing in the Doloneia, Il. 10.334, or its use for disguise at [Eur.] *Rh.* 208–9. The way his donning it is described (κατανωτισάμενος … τὸ χάσμα, 'after tossing it over his back … its gaping jaws') recalls the description of Heracles at Eur. *HF* 361–3: πυρσῶι δ' ἀμφεκαλύφθη | ξανθὸν κρᾶτ' ἐπινωτίσας | δεινοῦ χάσματι θηρός, 'and he enveloped his blond head in the red jaws of the fearsome beast, throwing it upon his back'.

1.20.3 The verb ἐκθηριῶ, 'I transform into a beast', occurs only once in a classical author, at Eur. *Ba.* 1331 (of Agave's fate).

1.21.5 τολμημάτων, 'reckless acts', here those of lovers. τόλμημα is common (especially in the plural) in Eur., but so too in Josephus and Plu., and occurs twice elsewhere in the novelists (Ch. 4.2.9, Hld. 6.13.5).

1.22.3 φάρμακον, 'remedy', is a well-established metaphor in an erotic context: cf. Morgan 2004, 183 on 2.7.7. Its earliest such use is at Eur. *Hipp.* 516 (though cf. ἴησιν, 'cure', at Archil. fr. 67.2). But Longus may know it chiefly from Theoc. 11.1 and 17 (where, as here, amelioration and not cure is meant): this is a poem that Longus has already evoked in his use of νόσος, 'disease' (1.14.1, see above).

[11] For this and other possible Callimachean intertexts see Bowie 2019i (Chapter 45 in this volume).

1.27.1 τὰ θρυλούμενα, 'the oft-told events': cf. τὸ θρυλούμενον, 'the oft-told event' in Eur. fr. 285.1 Kannicht; but θρυλεῖσθαι is also used of stories at Pl. *Phd.* 65b, Isoc. 12.237.

2.5.1 οὔτε κύκνος ὅμοιος ἐμοὶ γέρων γενόμενος, 'nor a swan when like me it grows old'. The legend that the swan sings shortly before death first appears at Aes. *Ag.* 1444 (cf. Fraenkel 1950 *ad loc.*). The chorus of *HF* compares itself to a swan at 110–11, γέρων ἀοιδὸς ὥστε πολιὸς ὄρνις, 'an aged singer, like the white-haired bird', and commentators dispute whether this is an allusion to the legend (see Bond 1981 *ad loc.*). The chorus figures itself later as γέρων ἀοιδός, 'aged singer' (678, 692), and at 692 the comparison is explicitly with a swan, κύκνος ὣς γέρων ἀοιδός, 'like the swan an aged singer'. Although the legend is known from later texts (the next being Pl. *Phd.* 84e), the collocation κύκνος … γέρων seems very likely to have come to Longus from Eur. *HF.*

2.7.7 Ἔρωτος γὰρ οὐδὲν φάρμακον, οὐ πινόμενον, οὐκ ἐσθιόμενον, οὐκ ἐν ᾠδαῖς λαλούμενον …, 'for there is no remedy for Desire, not one drunk, not one eaten, not one uttered in songs …', might perhaps recall Eur. *Hipp.* 516 πότερα δὲ χριστὸν ἢ ποτὸν τὸ φάρμακον; 'Is the remedy an ointment or something drunk?' But, as for φάρμακον at 1.22.3 (cf. above), the immediate inspiration is most likely Theoc. 11.1–2 οὐδὲν ποττὸν ἔρωτα πεφύκει φάρμακον ἄλλο,| Νικία, οὔτ' ἔγχριστον, ἐμὶν δοκεῖ, οὔτ' ἐπίπαστον, 'There is no other remedy in the world for desire, Nicias, neither an ointment, I believe, nor something to be sprinkled': cf. Hunter 1999 on 11.1–6.

2.11.2 κατὰ τὴν τῶν χειλῶν προσβολήν, 'to match the impact of their lips'. Jackson emended the reading of F and V, χειρῶν, 'hands' or 'arms', to χειλῶν, 'lips'. If that emendation is correct, it may recall προσβολαί of kisses at Eur. *Supp.* 138, προσβολὰς προσώπων, 'impacts of faces', and προσβολαί is used on its own to mean 'embraces' at *Med.* 1074. Ach. Tat. 5.8.3, however, had already adapted the first of these phrases in τὰς προσβολὰς τῶν ἀσπασμάτων, 'the impacts of his greetings', where these 'greetings' are kisses.

2.25.3ff. The combination of fire and noise in these portents is also found at Eur. *Ba.* 622–3, and that may be one, but only one, of many sources drawn upon by Longus for his depiction of Pan's miracles: others include Dionysus' capture by Tyrrhenian pirates in *h.Bacch.*, esp. 38–41, and *h.Ap.* 399–441.

3.4.5 ἀμήχανος, 'helpless', is found only here in Longus, and here alone of persons in the novelists. It picks out women's 'helplessness' at Eur. *Med.* 408 and *Hipp.* 643; but the word itself is not uncommon, and in the sense 'helpless' is also used by Eurycleia to describe herself at Od. 19.363.

3.20.2 ἀρτιμαθής, 'novice', is used of Daphnis' recent acquisition of sexual experience. The word appears only once in classical poetry, at Eur. *Hec.* 687, βακχεῖον … ἀρτιμαθῆ νόμον, 'a Bacchic tune that I have just learned', of Hecuba's response to recent acquaintance with misfortune. It reappears in second-century medical and philosophical contexts that might be thought closer to the situation of Daphnis here (Sor. 1.4, Gal. xi 466 Kühn, Clem. Al. *Quis dives salvetur* 20.5): Longus might know it from one of these.

3.21.2 The sense of ἀμέλειαν, 'distraction', in the phrase ἐς καμάτων ἀμέλειαν, 'as a distraction from their labours' is hard to parallel. Valley 1926, 69 compared ἀμελίαι δός in the sense 'apportion to what does not cause you concern' at Eur. *IA* 850 (where L and P read, unmetrically, ἀμελεία, but the sense is not close enough to suggest that Longus had Eur. in mind.

κελευστὴς ναυτικὰς ᾖδεν ᾠδάς, 'the time-caller sang sailors' shanties'. The 'time-caller', important to keeping the rowers of a classical trireme in time, could be known to Longus from Eur. *Hel.* 1576; but it is just as likely he knew the term from one of the several prose texts in which it is found, e.g. Th. 2.84.3.

4.17.2 μυσάττεσθαι, 'to feel revulsion at', is not common in classical writing, and Eur. *Med.* 1149 with the form μυσαχθείς, 'feeling revulsion at', is one place Longus might have found it. But he could also know it (in the participial form μυσαττόμενον) from Xen. *Cyr.* 1.3.5; and he is not the only second sophistic writer to use it, cf. Luc. *Somn.* 8, *Prom.Es.* 4, *DMeretr.* 11.3.

4.18.1 μεγάλους ὁ Ἔρως ποιεῖ σοφιστάς, 'Love creates mighty sophists'. The speaker Astylus here surely alludes to the well-known line from Eur. *Sthen.* (fr. 663 Kannicht): ποιητὴν δ' ἄρα | Ἔρως διδάσκει, κἂν ἄμουσος ᾖι τὸ πρίν, 'Love, it seems, instructs a man to be a poet, even if he did not know the Muse before'. The lines are much quoted by Plu. and picked up in two hexameters (*SH* 566) which the scholiast on Theocritus claims to be a response by Nicias of Miletus to Theoc. 11: ἦν ἄρ' ἀληθὲς τοῦτο, Θεόκριτε· οἱ γὰρ Ἔρωτες | ποιητὰς πολλοὺς ἐδίδαξαν τοὺς πρὶν ἀμούσους, 'So after all this was true, Theocritus: the Loves | have taught many to be poets who did not know the Muse before'.[12] Assessment of Longus' strategy is complicated by a further probable intertext, Xen. *Cyr.* 6.1.41, where the words νῦν τοῦτο πεφιλοσόφηκα μετὰ τοῦ ἀδίκου σοφιστοῦ τοῦ Ἔρωτος, 'now I have formulated this philosophical thought with the aid of the unjust sophist Love', are spoken by Araspas in Xenophon's famous tale of his love for Pantheia – a story reworked in the second century AD, whether by the sophist Dionysius of Miletus or by the imperial secretary Celer (cf. Philostr. *VS* 1.22.524).

[12] See Hunter 1999, 221 on Theoc. 11.

Given the other Euripidean intertexts that have seemed possible or even probable it should be allowed that here Longus does indeed evoke Euripides, especially since the aphorism was clearly well-known.

4.35.4 πλοῦτος ἐπέρρει, 'wealth kept flowing in'. The phrase may recall Eur. *Med.* 1229 ὄλβου ἐπιρρυέντος, 'when prosperity had flowed in', though Xen. *Apol.* 27 has ἀγαθῶν ἐπιρρεόντων, 'while good things are pouring in', and Ch. had already written πλοῦτος … βασιλικὸς … ἐπιρρέων, 'royal … wealth … flowing in' (1.11.7). Longus himself a little earlier had used ἐπιρρεῖ, 'surges up', of a πλῆθος … θεραπόντων, 'crowd of servants' (4.23.1: cf. Xen. *Cyr.* 7.5.39, Pl. *Phdr.* 229d7, Theoc. 15.59). *Non liquet.*

3 An Explanation?

As I have already said, the above set of possible intertexts seems to me remarkably small in an author so richly intertextual as Longus. But it is not negligible. Two different sorts of explanation might be offered for the presence of tragic intertexts:

(a) Longus might be using words that he saw as classical, poetic or elevated, but that he did not associate either with the genre tragedy in general or with tragic poets or any of their individual plays in particular. This explanation might indeed be correct for some cases (e.g. the phrase ἀνδρὸς ὁπλίτου at 1.20.2, discussed in Section 2); and it must be borne in mind that some tragic vocabulary appears in most of the ambitious writers of the period and that a word's appearance in tragedy is cited by some lexicographers as a support for its Attic pedigree.[13] Even if this were how the phenomenon in Longus should be understood, it can still be argued that some tragic colour is bound to remain attached to words chosen as both high style and Attic if the guarantee of those registers is their presence in an Attic tragedy. But in fact the apparent verbal intertextuality with one or two particular passages in tragedy, together with arguable intertextuality of content (e.g. the combination of fire and noise in the portents at 2.25.3, also found at Eur. *Ba.* 622–3), suggests that a more purposeful game is being played.

(b) Longus' game may be to highlight important features of his own work by contrast with tragedy. The opening intertexts with Soph. *Ant.* and Eur. *Hipp.* are crucial for this effect.

[13] Though not by Moeris, as Dr Claudia Strobel has pointed out to me.

The penultimate sentence of *pr.* 4, beginning πάντως γὰρ οὐδεὶς ἔρωτα ἔφυγεν ἢ φεύξεται, 'for by no means has anybody escaped desire, nor shall escape it', takes readers to a hymn to Ἔρως, 'Love' or 'Desire', in a play (and in a genre) in which fraternal conflict destroys a whole family and where a young couple's ἔρως simply draws in yet another victim. Longus' own story, we shall discover, is of fruitful, not destructive, ἔρως, and is one in which the relations between Astylus and Daphnis are marked not by any fraternal conflict or jealousy but by solicitude and harmony. If we learn this lesson from the preface, it may be to remind us of it that Longus' use of μυδῶν, 'rotting', at 3.28.2 to describe the body of the dolphin takes us to Soph. *Ant.* 410 and 1008. The lesson is hammered home by the evocation of *Antigone* 905ff. in Dionysophanes' words at 4.24.3: κρεῖττον γὰρ τοῖς εὖ φρονοῦσιν ἀδελφοῦ κτῆμα οὐδέν.

The preface's next and final sentence takes readers to another hymn to Ἔρως, that of Eur. *Hipp.* 525–64, where the young women of Trozen pray for the *sophrosyne* that is denied in different ways to Hippolytus and Phaedra. It focuses our attention on the issue of how ἔρως can be appropriately managed, and prepares us to see differences in its handling by Longus and by tragedians.

When the symptoms of desire are first described (1.13.5–14.1), a cluster of terms seems to evoke Eur. *Med.* and *Hipp.*: other intertexts may also be claimed at 2.1.1, 3.4.5, 4.17.2 (see further below) and 4.35.4. That the principle point of contrast in the latter play is the chain of destructive consequences of Phaedra's ἔρως seems likely if my reading of the preface is correct: note the destructive power of Ἔρως which the chorus of *Hipp.* picks out at 541–3, and which greatly outweighs its gentler qualities in the stasimon as a whole. It might be confirmed by the *Hipp.* intertext of φάρμακον at 1.22.3 and 2.7.7. The contrast is again brought out in the virtually certain intertext with Eur. *Sthen.* at 4.18.1, where Astylus' comment on Gnathon's speech also invites us to compare different genres' application of the motif. But *Hipp.* also displays brutal and uncaring treatment of a child by a parent: that too is a story-pattern which is developed by *Daphnis and Chloe* (as it is by Comedy), in such a way that fathers make potentially destructive decisions, but that these decisions are not irreversible, and a happy reunion of parent and child is somehow achieved. The destruction of children by a divinely-maddened parent is of course a central theme of Eur. *HF* and *Ba.*: the contrast with the judicious and (by and large) controlled behaviour of the parents of Daphnis and Chloe in Book 4 may then be one of the reasons for the certain intertexts with *HF* at 2.5.1 and *Ba.* at 2.25.3 and for those that can be argued for at 1.20.2 (*HF*) and 1.15.2, 20.3 (*Ba.*).

What can be adduced in favour of this line of interpretation? In a piece written a decade ago but only published in 2003 I argued for an analogous function for the three inset tales (at 1.27, 2.34 and 3.23).[14] I was to some extent concerned to challenge the view of Jack Winkler[15] that the sexual violence perpetrated by Pan against Nymphs in the second and third of the inset tales (and alluded to in the song sung by the cow-girl in the first) is in some way a warning of violence that Chloe will herself experience when she loses her virginity: instead I proposed that the inset tales' pattern of domination of females by males is contrasted with the behaviour of Daphnis and Chloe at all stages in Longus' story, and at no point is imitated by them.[16] This argument can now be taken further. The mythological world of the inset tales – divine lust leading to destruction or metamorphosis of a girl who is not herself immortal – is part of a nexus of tales drawn upon by Attic tragedy (e.g. the story of Semele) and more generally by archaic, classical and Hellenistic narrative poetry, even if the particular myths of Syrinx and Echo were probably first developed in Hellenistic poetry,[17] while the origins of the Pitys story are uncertain. In confining destructive consequences of sexual attraction to his inset tales, firmly described as μῦθοι, 'myths',[18] Longus contrasts the characteristic actions of gods and sufferings of mortals in traditional Greek mythology with their handling in his own sort of story.

This is not to say that Longus does not also engage in other intertextual games. For example, the use of *Sthen.* fr. 663 Kannicht (see in Section 2(d) on 4.18.1) has been seen to draw in – by its change of the word ποιητήν, 'poet', to the word σοφιστάς, 'sophists' – one of the Greek novel's classical models, Xenophon's *Cyropaedeia*. We are thus invited to speculate whether the writer of our text is himself a practising σοφιστής, 'sophist', and even whether he too owes his sophistic skill to his subject Eros. Our readerly reaction to the words may be further modulated by our awareness of their relation to the opening and theme of Theoc. 11, a poem evoked repeatedly in *Daphnis and Chloe*. On this assessment, the exploitation of Euripidean tragedy in Longus' work can on occasion significantly modify its impact by fusing it with other, more novelistic genres.

A further detail in Longus' narrative might seem to confirm the above nexus of hypotheses – that a number of intertexts with Attic tragedy function as pointers to contrasts between the texture of tragedy and that of Longus'

[14] Bowie 2003b (Chapter 26 in this volume).
[15] Winkler 1990.
[16] Bowie 2003b, esp. 372 (Chapter 26, 540–1 in this volume).
[17] So persuasively Morgan 2004, 196, 215.
[18] See Bowie 2003b, 365 (Chapter 26, 532–3 in this volume).

narrative, and that the inset tales likewise point up a contrast between novelistic narrative and traditional mythological narrative. When the parasite Gnathon pleads with his young master Astylus to be given Daphnis, his two highly emotional, over-the-top speeches are separated by Astylus' response to the first: Astylus promises to ask his father to give Daphnis to Gnathon, but then ἐπυνθάνετο μειδιῶν εἰ οὐκ αἰσχύνεται Λάμωνος υἱὸν φιλῶν, ἀλλὰ καὶ σπουδάζει συγκατακλιθῆναι νέμοντι αἶγας μειρακίωι, 'asked with a smile if he felt no embarrassment kissing Lamon's son, but was actually keen to lie down with a lad who tended goats' (4.17.2). Longus then gives a stage direction: καὶ ἅμα ὑπεκρίνετο τὴν τραγικὴν δυσωδίαν μυσάττεσθαι. How should this be understood? On the surface it seems to mean what all translators have decided it must mean: 'and at the same time he acted out revulsion at the foul smell of goats'. But the term ὑπεκρίνετο, 'he acted out', should give us pause. It is of course the regular term for an actor playing a stage role (cf. LSJ *s.v.* ὑποκρίνω B.II.1), and once we are taken on stage our reading of τραγικὴν has to be re-examined. In by far the greatest number of cases in literary texts τραγικός means 'tragic' (cf. LSJ *s.v.* τραγικός II). Among the very few instances where it means 'goatish' is a passage in Plato's *Cratylus* (408c7) where it seems at the same time to mean 'tragic' *and* 'goatish'. Here too, in Longus, I suggest we are invited to read the text on two levels: alongside revulsion at the foul smell of goats Astylus is 'acting out' revulsion at tragedy. The revulsion is occasioned by the rhetoric of Gnathon's total domination by ἔρως, culminating in his threat to seize a dagger and kill himself (4.16.4) – rhetoric which reworks, albeit in a parodic and comic register, the despair of a tragic lover. It is perhaps a deliberate tactic by Longus to have held back the ambiguous adjective τραγικός for use in this *coup de théâtre*: it is surely surprising that in a novel so heavily populated by goats the writer has somehow had no occasion to use the adjective earlier.[19]

That such a reading is appropriate may be supported by further points.

First, the register of Gnathon's emotional and exaggerated outburst is what some writers of the second and third centuries AD call τραγωιδία, 'uncontrolled rant',[20] or for which they use the verb τραγωιδεῖν, 'to rant theatrically'.[21] The use is one which can be traced back to a passage in Plato's *Cratylus* (414c4), a few pages after that which puns on the senses 'tragic' and 'goatish' for τραγικός. It is true that a male lover is rare in tragedy and very common

[19] This point was made to me (along with other helpful suggestions) in a discussion following delivery of a version of this paper at a Kyknos conference at Gregynog on 19 May 2005.

[20] Plu. *De Pyth. Or.* 12 = *Mor.* 400c, *Adv. Col.* 22 =1119c.

[21] Plu. *Dem.* 21.2, Arr. *Epict.* 4.7.15, Hld. 2.11.2 (and ἐπιτραγωιδεῖν at 1.3).

in New Comedy,[22] and that as I noted in my introduction Gnathon is very much a character evocative of New Comedy. But it is not beyond Longus' skill in fusing intertextualities to offer us a character who both recalls a comic stereotype and reminds of us tragedy by his flowery, paratragic rhetoric.[23]

Secondly, Astylus' reaction to Gnathon's second speech suggests that he hears in it the tones of τραγωιδία: it is precisely in this reaction (4.18.1) that he unambiguously evokes Eur. *Sthen.* in his wry exclamation μεγάλους ὁ Ἔρως ποιεῖ σοφιστάς, 'Love creates mighty sophists'.

Thirdly, there may also be a pun lurking in δυσωδίαν. The element -ωδία is one that in this period would be chiefly familiar from the technical terms of artistic performances – αὐλωιδία, 'singing to the pipe', ἱλαρωιδία, 'singing of joyous songs', κιθαρωιδία, 'singing to the *cithara*', κωμωιδία, 'comedy', and, of course, the granny of them all, τραγωιδία, 'tragedy'. So τραγωιδία can be read as 'the foul singing of tragedy' as well as 'the foul smell of goats'. It is important to bear in mind that in most documents of this period, as in not a few literary papyri,[24] *iota* adscript is not written.

4 Conclusions

Astylus' response to Gnathon's emoting matches the game the narrator plays with tragic intertexts and with the destructive erotic myths of the inset tales. Longus wants us to contrast the type of story about ἔρως, 'desire', that he and his novelistic predecessors tell from that preponderant in classical mythology in general and in tragedy in particular. As far as we can tell Attic tragedy never explores stories of mutual and symmetrical desire nor does it present a positive image of female desire (i.e. one that does not lead to destruction). Both symmetrical desire and a positive image of female ἔρως are crucial to the discourse of the novel. The clue that Longus plants in Astylus' speech of course stretches our readerly credulity: is he pulling our leg? When we recall the 'learned' and internally inconsistent digressions of 1.30.6 and 2.1.4, parodying the recurrent exploitation of this trope by Achilles Tatius,[25] we can see that there Longus is surely pulling our leg. Why not concede, then, that at 4.17.2 he is pulling the other?

[22] I am grateful to Helene Foley for drawing my attention to this point.

[23] We should recall that a male comic version of female tragic ἔρως goes back as far as Philocleon in Ar. *V.*

[24] E.g. *P.Oxy.* 2301 fr. 4(b) 8 (Alc.); *P.Oxy.* 4760 fr. 2.4 (Antonius Diogenes).

[25] See Bowie 2019g, 160, 167.

32 Links between Antonius Diogenes and Petronius (2007)

1 Introduction

In this paper I make a proposal of whose speculative nature I am well aware. I have long been struck by some features shared between the Τὰ ὑπὲρ Θούλην ἄπιστα, '*The incredible things beyond Thule*', of Antonius Diogenes and the *Satyrica* of Petronius, and want belatedly to see how far a hypothesis of some knowledge of one author by the other can be taken, and in what direction such a hypothesis would carry us.

2 Shared Features

What are these shared features?

(1) First, the size and articulation of the work: we do not know for certain the size and articulation of the *Satyrica*, but many suppose that the narrative from whose Books 14, 15 and 16 our fragments come was a work in twenty-four books. Photius is explicit that Antonius Diogenes' Τὰ ὑπὲρ Θούλην ἄπιστα, *The incredible things beyond Thule*, was a twenty-four-book work;[1] and although he is unhelpful on how the narrative of the first twenty-three books was divided, he does say explicitly what fell in Book 24. That contained the narrative of a character perhaps not previously named, Azulis, the release of the siblings Dercyllis and Mantinias from their spell,[2] their return to Tyre where they resuscitated their bewitched parents, the paradoxical further travels of Deinias, his miraculous falling asleep on or near the moon, and his waking up in the temple of Heracles at Tyre.[3] Finally there was a coda of *Beglaubigungsapparat*. None of our other ancient prose

[1] Phot. *Cod.* 166, 109a6. For a comprehensive discussion see now the excellent text, introduction and commentary of Schmedt 2020.

[2] I retain the name Mantinias which is that given in thirteen places by the MSS of Photius, despite Mantias (three times in the MSS of Photius) being the name offered by *P.Oxy.* 4760 and (probably Antonius Diogenes) 4761, published by Parsons 2006a. For good discussions see Ruiz Montero 2018, 117; Schmedt 2020, 143–4.

[3] Phot. *Cod.* 166, 110b20–11a19.

narrative texts is known to have had twenty-four books, and several are known not to – the Greek famous five (ranging between four and ten books), Apuleius (with eleven or, on van Mal Maeder's suggestion, twelve), Iamblichus (sixteen according to Photius, thirty-nine according to manuscripts of the Suda).

(2) Second, both texts have an element of comedy. The comic aspects of the *Satyrica* are too well-known to need discussion. In the Τὰ ὑπὲρ Θούλην ἄπιστα of Antonius Diogenes there is much weird and wonderful teratology, and the tone of its presentation is not easy to evaluate on the basis of Photius' summary: for example, what was the register of the scene in which the wizard Paapis cast a spell on Dercyllis and Mantinias by spitting openly in their faces?

> καὶ τὸ πάθος ἐκεῖνο τέχνηι μαγικῆι ἐπέθηκε θνήισκειν μὲν ἡμέρας, ἀναβιώσκειν δὲ νυκτὸς ἐπιγινομένης. καὶ τὸ πάθος ἐνέθηκεν ἐμπτύσας αὐτῶν κατὰ τὸ ἐμφανὲς τοῖν προσωποῖν.
>
> And he inflicted upon them by his magic art the following condition, that they were dead during the day, but that they revived at the arrival of night. And he implanted this condition by spitting in full view of all onto the faces of the two of them.[4]

The consequences are dire, but the actual casting of the spell could have a *Monty Python* or *Blackadder* flavour, or could be wannabe-serious Grand Guignol in a *Dracula* or *Raiders of the Lost Ark* mode.[5]

I do not think we can decide on the basis of the texts we have, but any decision must take into account Antonius Diogenes' claim ὅτι ποιητής ἐστι κωμωιδίας παλαιᾶς, 'that he is a poet of old comedy' (111a35).[6] Photius goes on immediately to report Antonius Diogenes as having written that εἰ καὶ ἄπιστα καὶ ψευδῆ πλάττοι, ἀλλ' οὖν ἔχει περὶ τῶν πλείστων αὐτῶι μυθολογηθέντων ἀρχαιοτέρων μαρτυρίας 'even if he is fabricating things incredible and fictitious, nevertheless he has the testimonies of older writers for the majority of the stories he has told' (111a35–7). I am inclined to take κωμωιδίας παλαιᾶς, 'old comedy' to mean fifth-century Attic Comedy, technically κωμωιδία ἀρχαία, and so to see this as generic self-affiliation with plays which had uproarious humour and, like *Peace* and *Frogs*, both

[4] Phot. *Cod.* 166, 110b1–5.

[5] For the issue of humour in the 'ideal' novels see Anderson 1982. Another case hard to judge is that of the fabulous bean-plant that after ninety days turns into a child's head or a woman's genitals in Ant. Diog. fr. 1(b) Stephens and Winkler 1995 = Lyd. *Mens.* 4.42.

[6] Misleading rendered as 'that he is the author of an ancient story' by Sandy in Reardon 1989, 781.

aerial journeys and potentially frightening καταβάσεις, 'descents to the underworld'.[7]

(3) Third, location (see Appendix). Again we are hampered by deficient material, in this case our ignorance about the territory traversed by Petronius' principal characters in the many missing books. The narrative that we have starts in the Bay of Naples, and involves a sea-voyage (99–115) that ends in shipwreck between Italy and Sicily (114.3) and in the drowning of the evil Lichas of Tarentum (115); it goes on to take Encolpius, Eumolpus and Giton to Croton (124–5). An earlier episode, Encolpius' seduction of Lichas' wife Tryphaena, seems to have been set in a portico of Heracles (106.2), perhaps at Lichas' *origo* Tarentum. There is no hint of any place further north than Capua (62.1) or further east than the Ionian Sea, though the origin of Trimalchio himself (75.10) and of one of his guests, Ganymedes (44.4), is '*Asia*' which I take to be *provincia Asia*, whither Eumolpus also claims to have gone in the *cohors amicorum* of a *quaestor* (85.1). Knowledge of the other books could change our perception radically, but in what we have the axis of action is the bay of Naples, the Gulf of Taranto and the cities of the Roman province Asia.

The extent of the travels of Antonius Diogenes' characters is vastly greater: the peregrinations of its main narrator, an Arcadian Deinias (109b3–4), include the Black Sea, the Caspian Sea and sources of the river Tanais, i.e. the Don (109a15), Thule itself, and places even further north. Its main characters are the Arcadian Deinias and a brother and sister from Tyre, Mant(in)ias and Dercyllis, but no action (at least involving any of them) seems to be set in Arcadia, and as in Achilles Tatius only small sections of the adventures of Mant(in)ias and Dercyllis, and the denouement of all three characters' travels, are set in Phoenicia.

Dercyllis' route seems to have been as follows: Rhodes, Crete, Etruria, the Bay of Naples, Spain, Gaul, Aquitania, again Spain, Sicilian Eryx and Leontini, Rhegium, Metapontum, Massagetic or Getic territory, and penultimately Thule: here Dercyllis narrates all these travels to Deinias, who has fallen in love with her (109a26), and here her brother Mant(in)ias also has one or more amorous encounters: τοὺς ἔρωτας Μαντινίου, καὶ ὅσα διὰ τοῦτο συνέβη, 'the love affairs of Mantinias, and what took place as a result' (110b13–14). It is striking that a writer whose writing medium and presumably whose chief imagined audience is Greek should have given such prominence to travels in Gaul, Spain, Italy and Sicily. Within these it is also noteworthy how significant the action in the Bay of Naples seems

[7] For further discussion of this issue see Bowie 2007e (Chapter 15 in Volume 3).

to have been: after Crete, Dercyllis and her brother Mant(in)ias went εἰς Τυρρηνούς, 'to the Etruscans' (109a38): at the dramatic date of these adventures – ca. 490 BC to judge from the identification of Aenesidemus as tyrant of Leontini (110a6–7)[8] – that could even mean territory south of Rome, though it is more likely, perhaps, that Antonius Diogenes imagined Etruria. From there Dercyllis came 'to the so-called Cimmerians', εἰς Κιμμερίους οὕτω καλουμένους (109a39): there τὰ ἐν Ἅιδου παρ' αὐτοῖς ἴδοι καὶ πολλὰ τῶν ἐκεῖσε μάθοι, 'she saw what was in Hades and learned much about goings-on there', from her long dead servant Myrto (109a39–40).[9] The next stop after these so-called Cimmerians turns out to be the tomb of the Siren: ὅπως μετὰ τὴν ἐξ Ἅιδου αὐτῆς ἀναχώρησιν σὺν Κηρύλλωι καὶ Ἀστραίωι … ἐπὶ τὸν Σειρήνης ἀφίκοντο τάφον, 'how, after her return from Hades, with Ceryllus and Astraeus … they arrived at the tomb of the Siren' (109b11–12). The tomb of the Siren fixes the location in the Bay of Naples, so the entrance to Hades is most probably that at *lacus Avernus*, Lago d'Averno. The description of the local population as Κιμμέριοι, 'Cimmerians', is mysterious, but the name presumably alludes, perhaps *inter alia*, to the location of Odysseus' κατάβασις, 'descent to the underworld', at Od. 11.13–15:[10]

> ἡ δ' ἐς πείραθ' ἵκανε βαθυρρόου Ὠκεανοῖο.
> ἔνθα δὲ Κιμμερίων ἀνδρῶν δῆμός τε πόλις τε
> ἠέρι καὶ νεφέλῃ κεκαλυμμένοι.

> and she (sc. the ship) came to the limits of the deep-flowing Ocean.
> There is the people and city of the Cimmerians
> wrapped in mist and cloud.

The journey to the Bay of Naples just mentioned offers a transition to my next feature.

(4) Types of incident.

(a) The infernal communication by the servant Myrto concerning Hades has an analogy in our surviving parts of the *Satyrica*, i.e. the

[8] For complexities see however Schmedt 2020, 16–17.

[9] That the goings-on in Hades should be of interest either to Dercyllis or to readers is perfectly understandable, cf. what we are offered by the poet of Od. 11. But it is worth asking whether ἐκεῖσε is a mistake (by the scribe or by Photius in his apparently hasty activity of summarising) for ὄπισθε 'thereafter': in this case (again with Od. 11 as a precedent) Dercyllis would be discovering something about her later travels.

[10] See Heubeck's long and useful note *ad loc.* in Heubeck-Russo-West 1988–92. Ephorus put the *Odyssey*'s Cimmerians near Avernus: cf. *FGrH* 70 F134.

prophecy delivered by Hades himself, precisely at *lacus Avernus*, in Eumolpus' 120-line poem of which it occupies one-sixth (lines 79–99). The location suggests that the *Aeneid* should be seen as one intertext for Eumolpus' account; in that case we should ask if, as well as the *Odyssey*, suggested by the location among the Κιμμέριοι, the *Aeneid* was also known to and drawn upon by Antonius Diogenes. The use of a prophecy delivered by a dead person recurs in our novelistic corpus only once, in Heliodorus (6.14-15), on any chronology much later than Antonius Diogenes and certainly very differently handled.[11]

(b) The death of the arch-villain is another feature common to the *Satyrica* and Τὰ ὑπὲρ Θούλην ἄπιστα. In the *Satyrica* it is the death of Lichas by drowning (115); in Τὰ ὑπὲρ Θούλην ἄπιστα we have first the murder of Astraeus, which is presented by the narrator as just retribution for his early crimes (110a1–3), and which offers a foretaste of the ultimate death of the arch-villain, the priest Paapis (110b7–9). The death of a villain or arch-villain is not a common *topos* in the surviving Greek novels. At the end of *Leucippe and Clitophon* Achilles Tatius' nasty character Thersander simply fades away (8.19). In Xenophon a walk-on character, the brigand Anchialus, who tries to satisfy his lust for Anthia, is stabbed and killed by her during his attempt (4.5), but the initially darker figure of Hippothous becomes a goody. In Chariton the pirate Theron is eventually caught, tried and condemned to death by crucifixion (3.4, cf. 8.7); but he never has the major role apparently played by Lichas and Paapis, any more than have the two Phaedra-figures in Heliodorus' *Aethiopica*, Demaenete (cf. 6.2) and Arsace, both of whom meet a death presented as richly deserved.

(c) The central linking feature of at least one of the story-lines in both works is the wrath of a powerful being: more than that, the name given by Antonius Diogenes to his persecuting Egyptian priest, Paapis, is remarkably similar to the name borne by the divinity whose wrath some act of Encolpius has excited, Priapus.

(d) One might wonder whether the spell laid by Paapis upon Dercyllis and Mant(in)ias, that they sleep by day but wake up at night (110b1–2, quoted above), has some analogy with Encolpius'

[11] Somewhat different is the information about his own and an unidentified girl's place of burial imparted to Glaucetes by (it seems) a phantom (which disappears once the message has been conveyed) in the Oxyrhynchus fragment (*P.Oxy.* 1368 col. ii 1–15) of Lollianus' *Phoenicica*, best read in Stephens and Winkler 1995, 326. Also different is the exotic Zatchlas in Apul. *Met.* 2.28–9.

repeated situations of arousal which then reach their climax only in humiliating sexual 'death'.

(e) The text encapsulates a multitude of inserted stories told by characters both major and minor. Inserted stories are of course, in varying degrees, a feature of all the Greek prose fiction of the period, but the *Satyrica* and Antonius Diogenes are extreme cases, closer to Heliodorus and to Apuleius' version of the ass-story than to our other earlier writers Chariton, Xenophon or even Achilles Tatius.

(5) Finally, two small details:

(a) The outlandishness of Gauls: *Satyrica* 102.14 presents Gauls as having pale faces; for Antonius Diogenes (109b23) they are ὠμοὶ καὶ ἠλίθιοι, 'cruel and feeble-minded'.[12]

(b) At the banquet of Trimalchio one guest is called C. Pompeius Diogenes (38.10), now very rich (but he has not always been so). It is worth at least toying with the idea that this Diogenes is a version of the successful Diogenes from Aphrodisias: a version, no more, since clearly the writer's *gentilicium*, Antonius, which as argued above points to early acquisition of the *civitas Romana*, has been replaced by another *gentilicium* also frequently found as a marker of an Eastern family's early capture of Roman patronage, Pompeius. Petronius was in a position to observe the senatorial progress in Rome, generation after generation, of the descendants of Theophanes of Mytilene, proud bearers of the *gentilicium* Pompeius.[13]

If the guess that the character C. Pompeius Diogenes is meant to bring Antonius Diogenes (*inter alios*) to the reader's mind, then of the hypotheses set out below (2) will be decidedly preferable to (1).

3 Where Does This Take Us?

The features to which I have drawn attention certainly do not prove knowledge by one author of the other's work. But to me, as I said, they do raise the question. If the similarities are thought to be significant, what are the possible ways of explaining them? There seem to be three:

[12] Such a perception of Gauls is easier to imagine in a text of the mid-first century AD than one written significantly later. For the paleness implied by *increta facies*, 'a face whitened with chalk', see Schmeling 2011 *ad loc.*

[13] On Theophanes see Bowie 2011b (Chapter 26 in Volume 3); on his son Pompeius Macer Bowie 2013e (Chapter 32 in Volume 3).

(a) Antonius Diogenes knows the *Satyrica*.
(b) The author of the *Satyrica* knows Antonius Diogenes.
(c) The author of the *Satyrica* and Antonius Diogenes draw on a common source.

(a) Antonius Diogenes Knows the Satyrica

Setting aside for the moment chronological issues, the hypothesis that Antonius Diogenes knows the *Satyrica* would entail two *prima facie* improbabilities: first, that a Greek writer knew and choose to be influenced by a work written in Latin; second, that a work that seems overall to aim at a middle-brow rather than a low register should draw on a work which aggressively presented itself as 'low'.

The first of these apparent improbabilities is hard to assess. The *communis opinio*, which I have certainly tended to share and reinforce, has been that the works of high literature written by Greeks of the later first to the early third centuries AD were written by authors who had little or no knowledge of Latin literature for readers who had even less. But there are clearly exceptions. Plutarch the philosopher, as he would have preferred to be classified, read much Varro for his *Roman Questions* and even more Cicero and Livy for his *Lives*; and he cites the poet Horace. My colleague Stephen Heyworth is sure that Chariton knew some Latin elegy; Thomas Hubbard has argued for Longus' knowledge of Vergil, Stefan Tilg for Chariton's;[14] and Daniel Jolowicz argues persuasively for considerable knowledge of Vergil and of Latin love elegy by Greek novelists.[15] Argentarius' epigrams in the first century AD and Ammianus' satirical epigrams directed at Polemo of Laodicea around AD 140 have bilingual puns,[16] and the *conversazioni* reworked in the *Attic Nights* of Aulus Gellius suggest an Athenian society that was in some respects bilingual. Knowledge of Latin must have varied greatly from place to place and person to person. Of the Greek cities of *provincia Asia* Ephesus must have heard most Latin spoken, above all in official communications or exchanges; but Aphrodisias, as is becoming clearer with the last few decades' excavations, maintained close contacts with Rome and could deploy a number of prominent citizens to whom Rome and Italy were familiar. Unlike Ephesus, Aphrodisias has not yet yielded Latin inscriptions from the

[14] Hubbard 2006; Tilg 2010. On the whole question see Rochette 1997.

[15] Jolowicz 2015; Jolowicz 2021. [16] See Nisbet 2003.

first two centuries AD.[17] If, as Bowersock argued,[18] the combination of the *nomen* Antonius and the *cognomen* Diogenes point to an Aphrodisian origin for our writer, then a man whose family got citizenship at an early stage – already perhaps in the 30s BC as the *nomen* Antonius might suggest – could well have made visits, even prolonged visits, to Rome, and, if there in the 60s and 70s AD, might have been aware of Petronius' adaptation of a genre of prose fiction that was not simply a very recent development in the Greek world but might even have been developed precisely by a fellow-citizen of Antonius Diogenes, that is, by Chariton of Aphrodisias.

Chronology can no longer be evaded. The model just suggested would work best if Τὰ ὑπὲρ Θούλην ἄπιστα of Antonius Diogenes were responding both to Chariton and to Petronius. Chariton will have given him some ideas for the erotic plots which seem not to have dominated Τὰ ὑπὲρ Θούλην ἄπιστα (though Photius, *pace* Rohde, is hardly a reliable guide on this, and it certainly seems as if the love affair between Deinias and Dercyllis provided one overarching framework for the work's complicated nexus of plots); Petronius could have given him some ideas for a massive and complex serio-comic work. One might also wonder if Pliny's *Natural History* encouraged him in the idea of prefacing each book with a list of authors whose testimony he claimed for far-fetched phenomena. All this would cohere with an Antonius Diogenes writing shortly after Agricola's circumnavigation of Britain ca. AD 80 had brought Thule into the Roman public eye and, as Stramaglia suggested following Bowersock (himself reviving an idea of Hallström), an Antonius Diogenes dedicating his work to a Faustinus who is also the dedicatee of poems by Martial.[19]

(b) *The Author of the* **Satyrica** *Knows Antonius Diogenes*

Prima facie this hypothesis might seem more probable than (a): any Latin writer knows Greek texts, and Petronius' range of allusion to both Greek and Latin texts is impressively wide-ranging. Encounters with both an example of the ideal Greek romance such as Chariton – or perhaps *precisely* with Chariton – and the curious and arguably overblown cousin of the ideal Greek romance that was written by Antonius Diogenes – might have

[17] Joyce Reynolds in a private communication. [18] Bowersock 1994, 38–40.

[19] For arguments for this chronology, and for evidence of a Faustinus at Aphrodisias published since Bowersock and Stramaglia wrote, see Bowie 2002a (Chapter 25 in this volume) n.65.

contributed to suggesting to Petronius his schema of a sexually intertwined trio, one of whose members is a victim of the wrath of the god Priapus.

This sequence has one slight argument in its favour over that which postulates that Antonius Diogenes knows the *Satyrica* (as well as the hypothesis about C. Pompeius Diogenes suggested above). Petronius notoriously makes recurrent and effective use of verse – as, of course, very differently, does Chariton. There is, however, no hint at all in Photius or in our few scraps of papyri that Antonius Diogenes did so.[20] Of course Photius may have been too keen to sketch out the baffling plot to spare any attention for poetic passages, and our papyri may just happen to have missed them. It is true that in one of our quoted fragments, fr. 2a, 16–17 in Stephens and Winkler 1995 (= Porph. *VP* 16–17), Pythagoras is said by Antonius Diogenes to have composed epigrams for 'Apollo's tomb' at Delphi (an elegiac couplet, not quoted by Porphyry) and a hexameter for a 'tomb of Zeus' on Mount Ida in Crete.[21] But such citation of epigrams (with a pedigree going back to Hdt. 7.228) is found in a number of novelists (Xenophon and Heliodorus) and is quite different from the exploitation of verse by Petronius. On present evidence, at least, Τὰ ὑπὲρ Θούλην ἄπιστα was not prosimetric. Yet could a reader inspired by Petronius have abstained from recurrent play with poetic passages?

The main problem with the sequence Τὰ ὑπὲρ Θούλην ἄπιστα → Petronius might be that it requires a very tight chronology. If we retain the identification of Petronius with the Neronian consul, as I believe we should, then Antonius Diogenes has to write and publish before, say, AD 60. That requires him to be detached from Martial's Faustinus; it requires his attention to Thule to be a response not to Agricola's circumnavigation of Britain in the 80s but perhaps merely to geographical intelligence-gathering associated with Claudius' invasion in AD 43 and its aftermath; and Pliny's first book listing sources for the *Natural History* can no longer be invoked as a possible springboard for Antonius Diogenes' list prefaced to each book. But as our knowledge stands, nothing actually prevents us supposing a publication date of ca. AD 55 for Τὰ ὑπὲρ Θούλην ἄπιστα: if published at this date it would follow Chariton's *Callirhoe* by a just a few years, and it would point both to close links between literary circles in Rome and Aphrodisias,[22] and

[20] For the various categories of evidence see Stephens and Winkler 1995, 101–72.

[21] Quoted by Porph. *VP* 17 as ὧδε θανὼν κεῖται Ζεὺς ὃν Δία κικλήσκουσιν, 'Here, dead, lies Zeus, whom they call "Dia"' (i.e. the accusative of 'Zeus').

[22] For an argument that Ant. Diog.'s idea of Greeks travelling far and wide in pursuit of knowledge is in part a response to the reliefs of Julio-Claudian Sebasteion at Aphrodisias portraying Rome's extensive conquests see Bowie 2017c (Chapter 42 in Volume 3).

to a greater interest being shown by Greek Aphrodisian novelists – and by their hanger-on Xenophon of Ephesus[23] – in the Latin-speaking West than is later shown by the Greek novelists of the second and early third centuries Achilles Tatius, Iamblichus and Longus.[24]

*(c) The **Satyrica** and Antonius Diogenes Draw on a Common Source*

The recent work of Jensson has offered powerful arguments in favour of the view that the *Satyrica* is based on a lost Greek predecessor.[25] If these are accepted (as for example they are by Dowden 2007) then the problems and opportunities raised by either (a) or (b) above may be thought to dissolve. The elements of similarity between the *Satyrica* and the work of Antonius Diogenes can be argued to be derived by both these texts from the postulated lost Greek original of the former; if that is the case, nothing can then be inferred about the one's direct knowledge of or chronological relation to the other. Two points, however, suggest to me that my explorations above have not been pointless. First, the hypothesis of a lost Greek original for the *Satyrica* remains just that, a hypothesis. Persuasive as many of Jensson's points are, I am still inclined to suspend judgement; and it will be an unusual hypothesis in which sceptical scholars over the years do not manage to pick holes. Second, even if the hypothesis of a Greek original for the *Satyrica* is accepted, it need not explain all or even any of the elements common to Petronius and Antonius Diogenes: that it does so is a further, supplementary hypothesis.

How likely is it, then, that in an extended Milesian-tale narrative there were to be found any of the common features for which I have set out the case above? On the one hand some general features might derive from a Milesian creation – complexity of structure, abundance of narration by characters in the narrative,[26] humour. On the other hand the pursuit of the hero and his companion by a powerful and vengeful force, the

[23] For an explanation of why X.Eph. brought his hero Habrocomes to Nuceria, not far from the bay of Naples, and not to the usual port Stabiae see Coleman 2011.

[24] In the Appendix I have tabulated the occurrence of place-names in the Western Mediterranean in Petronius, Antonius Diogenes, *Metiochus and Parthenope*, Chariton and Xenophon, and Greek place-names from the eastern Mediterranean found in the first three of those (i.e. Eastern Mediterranean toponyms in Ch., and X.Eph. are only registered if they also appear in one or more of the first three).

[25] Jensson 2002, 2004.

[26] On the importance of character-narration in Milesian tales see Bowie 2013c (Chapter 38 in this volume).

death of the arch-villain, and the location in the Bay of Naples and South Italy have no parallel in any extant Greek 'low' narratives – e.g. the title of Lollianus' Φοινικικά, '*Phoenician Tales*', suggests very strongly that the action is anchored in the Eastern Mediterranean, though not necessarily all in Phoenicia (cf. Achilles Tatius).[27]

Proof, were it to emerge, that Petronius drew on a lost Greek original would therefore indeed add complexity to the calculation: but we would still be left to make a judgement whether either (a) or (b) above was a scenario supported by the phenomena, and whether in either case the issue of literary influence should be supposed to be further complicated by allowing that both Petronius and Antonius Diogenes might have drawn some (though hardly all) common features from the former's lost original.

Appendix: Toponyms and Ethnics in Petronius, Antonius Diogenes and Three Early Greek Novels

Place	Petronius	Antonius Diogenes	*Metiochus and Parthenope*	Chariton	Xenophon
Acragas				1.2.4 etc.	
Aphrodisias				1.1.1	
Apulia	77.3				
Aquitanians		109b25			
Arcadia		109b4			
Athens	2.7, 5.9, 38.3	fr. 2a.34 (=*VP*) (Hymettus)		1.1.2, 11.5	
Baiae	53.10, 104.2				
Capua	62.1				
Caspian Sea		109a15			
Celts		109b23			
Cimmerians		109a39			
Crete		109a38			
Croton	116.2, 124.2, 125.1	fr. 2a.54–5 (=*VP*)			
Cumae	48.8, 53.2				
Delos		fr. 2a.15 (=*VP*)			
Delphi		fr. 21.16, 41 (=*VP*)			
Ephesus	111.1 etc.				1.1.1 etc.
Eryx		110a5			

[27] It must be admitted that the part of the world in which the *Iolaus*-story was set is wholly obscure.

Place	Petronius	Antonius Diogenes	*Metiochus and Parthenope*	Chariton	Xenophon
Getae		110a24, etc.			
Hyrcania	134.12	109a16			
Iberia	66.3, 121.112	109b19			
Imbros		fr. 2a.10 (=*VP*)			
Ionia/*provincia Asia*	2.7, 44.4, 75.10, 85.1			1.11.8 etc.	
Italy	114.3, 116.2	110a4			5.6
Lemnos		fr. 2a.10 (=*VP*)			
Leontini		110a6			
Lesbos	133.3				5.15
Lycia				1.13.6	5.6, 10
Messana				1.7.4	
Metapontum		110a20			
Miletus		fr. 2a.11		1.7.5 etc.	
Naples	*Sirenum domus* 5.11, Parthenope 120.68, fr. 16 *crypta Neapolitana*	Σειρήνης τάφος 109b13	*via* Parthenope? Cf. Σ on Dionysius Periegetes 358		
Nuceria					5.8
Numantia	141.11				
Petelia	141.10				
Persia, Persians				1.13.1 etc.	
Pontus	123.241	109a15			
Puteoli	120.68				
Rhipaean mountains		109a16			
Rhegium		110a20	(? *via* Ibycus)	1.2.2	
Rhodes		109a36			5.6 etc.
Samos		fr. 2a.10, 15, 16	cols. i and ii		
Scyros		fr. 2a.10 (=*VP*)			
Scythian sea		109a18			
Sicily		110a4 etc.		1.1.3 etc.	5.6 etc.
Sybaris				1.12.8, 2.1.9, 2.5.5	
Syracuse				1.1.1 etc.	5.1, 6
Tanais/Don		109a17			
Tarentum	5.10 etc.				5.5
Tauromenium					5.6

Place	Petronius	Antonius Diogenes	*Metiochus and Parthenope*	Chariton	Xenophon
Thrace, Thracians	5.4	110a22, fr. 2a.14 (=*VP*)			
Thurii				1.7.2	
Thule		109a24 etc.			
Tyre	30.11	109a27 etc.			
Tyrrhenians		109a38, fr. 2a.10 (=*VP*)			

33 | Literary Milieux (2008)

1 Introduction

'Am I always to be a listener? Am I never to get my own back?' With these words the Latin poet Juvenal in the early second century AD opened the first of his *Satires*, purporting to give his readers a reason for his taking up writing at all. He goes on to give 'reasons' for his choice of satire. These can only be some of the factors we might want to see as contributing to an explanation for his writing what he did, but his opening offers us a good way into the issues relevant to why, in the literary world of the high Roman Empire, somebody might choose to write poetry or prose at all, and into the factors that might have influenced a would-be-writer either to choose an unusual genre or even to develop one that could be seen as in all or many respects new. Some of these factors are different in the Greek and the Latin worlds, and the greater part of the following exploration of the place of novels in the literature of the Roman Empire will focus on the setting of the Greek novels within Greek literary production and consumption.

My discussion of the Greek novels will attempt to set each of four surviving 'ideal' novels in the context of the Greek literature that had recently been written.[1] For each period I shall ask what sort of literature was already prevalent when a choice to write a novel was made; what features in that literature might have encouraged or contributed to the novelist's project; and in assessing the subsequent period will ask whether there are any traces of the novel impinging on literature in other genres. This procedure will involve the heuristic device of artificial periodisation – roughly, 31 BC–AD 50; AD 50–160; AD 160–220; AD 220–270 – which should not be taken to imply that these divisions are important for anything other than this investigation. It will also require careful distinction between features that might be claimed as specifically 'novelistic' – in the sense 'characteristic of the five ideal novels' – and others which may be generally associable with other sorts of erotic writing – e.g. types of short story, *novelle*/*Novellen*, including *Milesian Tales*.

[1] Xenophon's *Ephesiaca* will only be mentioned *en passant*. His date remains controversial, his work's closeness to that of Chariton undoubted, and many of the questions and answers sparked by Chariton would apply to Xenophon too.

First, however, the general issue of consumption must be addressed. Wherever in the Roman Empire Greek was the language of πεπαιδευμένοι, 'cultivated men', i.e. the educated elite, the vast majority of the texts read were poetry and prose of the classical period. This was not least because such texts were studied and used at all levels of education,[2] from the learning of the alphabet to training by a *rhetor* or sophist in the skills of forensic, political and epideictic rhetoric: they thus became both the texts that were widely known and the texts of which knowledge had to be displayed in order to establish a claim to παιδεία, 'culture', the defining characteristic of the πεπαιδευμένος 'cultivated person'. Quotations in authors with substantial surviving *oeuvres* – e.g. Dio of Prusa, Plutarch, Aelius Aristides, Lucian and Philostratus – and the distribution of papyri found in the rubbish dumps of (admittedly bookish) Oxyrhynchus suggest a broadly similar range of reading in the years from AD 50 to AD 250. Only occasionally does any of these authors earlier than Philostratus mention a Greek writer of the imperial period, and even more rarely offer any citation from one. Correspondingly only a very low proportion of papyri have yielded texts of imperial Greek writers, though among these texts novels bulk large.

The message to anyone who contemplated embarking upon a literary work was mixed. On the one hand those literary works that were read often enjoyed great authority; on the other hand the authority accorded to works from the archaic and classical past was much greater than could be expected by a work composed more recently: even if a new work succeeded in achieving distribution by *samizdat* and by the book trade, it was very unlikely ever to join the canon of those cited with reverence, far less those used in the educational system.[3] At the same time it is clear that to be known as a writer had a cachet that could give an individual worthwhile leverage among those who were attempting to join, or to rise within, the constantly competitive society of Greco-Roman civic elites. In picking out participants in his Συμποσιακά, '*Sympotic questions*', as 'the philosopher', 'the *rhetor*', or 'the poet', Plutarch was recognising a claim to status that was significant, however ephemeral their writings might turn out to be. One of our most telling documents is from a slightly later generation. A text inscribed in Aphrodisias preserves two decisions taken to honour C. Iulius Longianus, one by the Council and People of Halicarnassus, the

[2] Morgan 1998; Cribiore 1996, 2001b. For visual evidence of the prestige of learning cf. Zanker 1995.

[3] Note, however, that the crash-course in elevated reading suggested by D. Chr. *Or.* 18 does at least allow some attention to more recent writers.

other (taken on 27 March AD 127) by the synod of Dionysiac artists. This synod's decree identifies Longianus as a tragic poet and resolves to honour him with an εἰκὼν γραπτή, 'a painted likeness' – presumably a painting – in whichever part of his native city he preferred; the Halicarnassians gave him citizenship and resolved to honour him with bronze statues, one to be set up next to that of 'old Herodotus'. Longianus was commended for ἐπιδείξεις, 'displays', of every sort of poetry, which entertained the old and improved the young: hence it was also decided that his books should be lodged in the libraries so that the young might learn from them as from the classics.[4]

About the same time an aspiring poet from Side, known to us only by his Roman *cognomen* Marcellus, succeeded in bringing his voluminous medical poem in hexameters, loftily entitled Χειρωνίδες, '*Daughters of Chiron*', to the attention of the emperor Hadrian, with the outcome (as an epigram presumably composed by Marcellus himself claims) that its forty-two-book text was lodged in official libraries in Rome by Hadrian and then by Pius.[5] No later than AD 128/9 an Athenian decree honoured Q. Pompeius Capito of Pergamum with a statue in the theatre of Dionysus and Athenian citizenship 'on account of his poetic virtuosity, demonstrated in impromptu performances in every rhythm and metre'.[6] Similarly, at some date in the second century, Rhodiapolis in Lycia honoured its poet Heraclitus as the ἰατρικῶν ποιημάτων Ὅμηρον, 'Homer of medical poetry', with statues in its theatre – a gilded statue of Heraclitus himself and a statue of Παιδεία, 'Education' or 'Culture'.[7] Heraclitus was also honoured at Athens by the Epicureans and by the Areopagus – presumably also by the erection of statues.

An aspiring writer, then, might dream of recognition. However it may not be accidental that all the above honours were conferred for the production of poetry. Some writers of prose did indeed achieve great prestige and significant honours, above all sophists: but in this last case it was for their epideictic performances before live audiences and for their contribution

[4] *MAMA* viii 418(a), (b) and (c), re-edited Roueche 1993, 223–7 no. 88, *IAph2007* 12.27(i), (ii) and (iii). See further Bowie 1989b, 202 (Chapter 13 in this volume, 277).

[5] *AP* 7.158: cf. Bowie 1990b, 66–7 (Chapter 14 in this volume, 296).

[6] *IG* ii^2 3800. Ath. 8.350c cites an ἐποποιός, 'epic poet', Capito who dedicated ὑπομνήματα, '*Commentaries*' or '*Essays*', to a Philopappus – the item reported from the fourth book of these '*Commentaries*' is a *bon mot* of the Hellenistic citharist Stratonicus. *RE*, perhaps inferring from the fact that this *bon mot* was directed at a Ptolemy, judged that Capito was an Alexandrian. That is at best a guess. He might well be the same as this Q. Pompeius Capito, and his dedicatee may be the Antiochus Philopappus known from Plutarch and from his monument of the Hill of the Muses in Athens, cf. *PIR*^{2} I 151.

[7] *TAM* ii 910 = *IGR* iii 733: cf. Robert 1980b, 14 and the temple of Asclepius dedicated by Heraclitus *TAM* ii 906 = *IGR* iii 732.

to teaching that they seem to have been honoured.[8] As far as can be seen it is also true of philosophers that they were accorded the title φιλόσοφος, 'philosopher' without reference to specific written works.[9] Public honour of a historian as such is rare,[10] though it was manifestly for historical research at some level concerning the claims to kinship between his own Cilician city Aegeae and Argos that the sophist P. Anteius Antiochus was honoured by Argos,[11] and predictably the historian of an emperor's military achievements might expect imperial recognition.

In what follows one further qualification applies. The short account of a love-affair that ended disastrously can be found in Greek literature of almost any generation, beginning with the classical period.[12] It is tempting but perhaps mistaken to register these as elements in the Greek literature of my various artificial periods that might be seen as important for illuminating the place of the novels. Such stories are indeed introduced as sub-plots in many novels, often to offer a stark contrast with the main narrative. But they can turn up in almost any literary genre, and they differ crucially from the narratives of the novels in lacking a happy ending (to say nothing of a teenage, mutually attracted couple). I have decided therefore neither to flag their presence in writers of any of these periods nor to adduce that presence as an explanation of a novelist's choice of theme. Thus I am not inclined to see the stories of Zarinaea and Stryangaeus in Nicolaus of Damascus (*FGrH* 90 F5), or of Rhadinē and Leontichus,[13] both anecdotes of ill-fated lovers who kill themselves,[14] as important for the context of Chariton's writing, nor Plutarch's similar stories of Cammas and Sinatus in his work *On the virtues of women*,[15] and of Epona and Sabinus in his Ἐρωτικός, '*On desire*',[16] as important for the context of that of Achilles Tatius. The same applies to

[8] For a comprehensive analysis of the inscriptions in which sophists and *rhetors* figure see now Puech 2002.

[9] E.g. the statue base honouring Arrian as φιλόσοφον, 'philosopher', *SEG* 30.159, cf. Stadter 1980, 189 n.5 and 198 n.89.

[10] The statue honouring Dexippus as a *rhetor* and historian was erected by his children, *IG* ii^2 3669 = Puech 2002, 220 no. 95 line 5.

[11] Cf. Puech 2002, 68–74 no. 10.

[12] Cf. Trenkner 1958.

[13] A version of the Rhadinē story is quoted from Stesich. (fr. 278 *PMGF* = 327 Finglass) by Str. 8.347; the name of the cousin who fell in love with her, Leontichus, appears only in Paus. 8.5.13.

[14] For discussion and further bibliography see Pignataro and Di Giglio in Stramaglia 2000, 299–304 and 263–6.

[15] *De mul. vir.* 20 = *Mor.* 257e–8c with Stadter 1965, 103–6: for further bibliography see Romani in Stramaglia 2000, 97–103.

[16] 24, 770c–25, 771c: for further bibliography see Romani in Stramaglia 2000, 147–54.

the ghost story of ill-fated love of Machatus and the deceased Philinnion that opens the surviving text of the *On things miraculous* by a freedman of Hadrian, Phlegon of Tralles, apparently written early in the 140s AD:[17] in itself it does not seem to me to have great importance for the context in which Achilles Tatius or Iamblichus wrote. Nor, finally, does the Milesian tale of Ps.-Aeschines *Letter* 10, probably composed in the later second century AD,[18] help our understanding of Longus.

2 31 BC–AD 50

What, then, might have been the calculations of a citizen of Aphrodisias in the forties or fifties AD, Chariton the *soi-disant* secretary of a *rhetor* Athenagoras, when he decided to embark upon an eight-book work of romantic prose fiction, thereby either following some writer of the recent past who had developed this genre or, as I judge more likely on the evidence currently available, actually 'inventing' a new genre?[19]

In the forties AD the Roman province Asia may have begun to respond culturally to the two generations of peace and economic prosperity that had passed since Octavian's victory at Actium ended the Roman civil wars in 31 BC. But the figure whom Philostratus picked out as the first sophist after Aeschines to merit a biography, Ti. Claudius Nicetes of Smyrna, may only have been at the very beginning of his career, and Scopelianus of Clazomenae not even that. The most recent works to have made their mark in Greek literature had been produced by Greeks of Asia Minor who seem to have spent some time in Rome – perhaps most of his life, in the case of Dionysius from Halicarnassus, author both of a historical work, *Roman Antiquities*, and of several rhetorical monographs, including one evaluating the classical Attic orators; and significant parts of their lives in the case of Strabo from Pontic Amaseia, author of a *History* (now lost) and of a historically sensitive *Geography*, and of Nicolaus of Damascus, whose historical writing included an account of Augustus' reign. A naturalised Athenian, C. Iulius Nicanor, had composed poetry in Augustus' reign that earned him the flattering soubriquet νέος Ὅμηρος, 'new Homer' on several honorific

[17] Text in *FGrH* 257; Giannini 1965; translation and commentary Hansen 1996. For further bibliography see Stramaglia in Stramaglia 2000, 167–84.

[18] For discussion and bibliography see Mignogna in Stramaglia 2000, 85–96.

[19] For the dating of Chariton, absolutely and relatively to other novelists, see Bowie 2002a (Chapter 25 in this volume), where I argue that the *Ninus* was composed slightly later than Chariton's *Callirhoe*. For Chariton as inventor of the genre see Tilg 2010.

statue-bases,[20] but not a line of his poetry survives, and we cannot tell if it made any impact in the Roman province of Syria even though its city Hierapolis seems to be his origin.

The works we still have may be seen to some degree as responding to the new situation. From Dionysius came a version of Roman history that often tried to assimilate Rome to a Greek city,[21] and an attempt to offer elite Greeks and Hellenophone Romans a rhetoric that might appeal to Roman taste and at the same time highlight the contribution to sound rhetorical technique of classical Athens;[22] about the same time Caecilius of Caleacte initiated a genre later to be expanded by Plutarch, comparison of a great Greek orator – Demosthenes – and a great Roman orator – Cicero. From Strabo came a geography that expounded to elite Greeks the vast Roman Empire within which they all had to operate and in which some of them would try to lever their careers onto an international level.[23] From Nicolaus came a work explaining the rise and rule of the man now most powerful in the Greek world. Traces of other historical work – e.g. by the philosopher Athenodorus of Tarsus[24] – remind us how much has been lost, and it must be allowed that if we had a complete set of Greek works produced in the period 31 BC to AD 54 we might well discern a different pattern.[25]

Literature composed principally for entertainment, however, might be thought to have been thinner on the ground. Greek epigrams indeed flourished, but some, such as most surviving poems of Crinagoras, were calculated to maintain good relations with Rome and the Julio-Claudian household.[26] A lighter touch is evident in some other epigrammatists, for example Argentarius, and by the reign of Nero satirical epigram had made a splash with the poetry of Nicarchus and Lucilius.[27] But another type of epigram is of especial relevance to the novel. Erotic epigram, well established

[20] *IG* ii^2 3786–9, cf. *PIR* ^{2} I 440; for Nicanor's date and honours see Jones 2011 (with earlier bibliography).

[21] See Gabba 1991.

[22] See Hidber 1996.

[23] See Clarke 1999; Dueck 2000; Dueck, Lindsay, and Pothecary 2006.

[24] Athenodorus *FGrH* 746.

[25] This brief examination excludes from its category 'Greek literature' the many technical works on grammar, metre and other sorts of scholarship that can be assigned to this period, more or less technical philosophical work such as that of Musonius Rufus or the work of Thrasyllus on the Platonic corpus, and the voluminous output of the Hellenising Jew Philo of Alexandria.

[26] The classic study remains Cichorius 1922. For commentary *GP*; Ypsilanti 2018. Further discussion Bowie 2012e (Chapter 17 in this volume); Mayer forthcoming.

[27] For texts and commentary of Argentarius and Nicarchus see *GP*; of Nicarchus, Schatzmann 2012; of Lucilius, Floridi 2014; for assessment of all these, Nisbet 2003. Lucilius' place in his contemporary world was the subject of a masterly essay by Robert 1968.

since the third century BC, attracted an especially elegant exponent who seems to belong around AD 40–60 and whose activity is suggested by one epigram to have been near but not in the city of Ephesus, Rufinus.[28] It is vexing that we cannot date Rufinus more precisely: did his handling of the *loci communes* of love give a cue to Chariton in nearby Aphrodisias, or was the influence the reverse, or even mutual? It is certainly tempting to think that the production in the same area of western Asia Minor of a slim volume of (heterosexual) erotic epigrams and of a work of prose fiction centred on the adventures of a teenage (heterosexual) couple was not wholly accidental.

3 AD 50–160

Between the composition by Chariton of his *Callirhoe* (which I have argued to be in the fifties AD)[29] and by Achilles Tatius, probably from Alexandria, of his *Leucippe and Cleitophon* (perhaps written nearer AD 120 than AD 150) the landscape of contemporary Greek literature changed radically. The sophist and (after what he himself claimed as a conversion) philosopher Dio of Prusa (ca. AD 40 – ca. 115) had not only circulated speeches purporting to have been delivered to Greek cities concerning their politics and to the Roman emperor (supposedly Trajan) concerning the characteristics of a good king. He had also composed essays addressing philosophical and literary-critical issues on a relatively vulgarising, unprofessional level, and he had composed two 'What if …' works, exploiting literary fictionality in different ways. One was a long lecture, probably first delivered at Troy, in which he argued that Homer had misrepresented the outcome of the Trojan war – it had in fact been a victory for the Trojans. This may be a version chosen for its commendability to the contemporary descendants of Aeneas ruling from Rome, as well as to citizens of the Roman *colonia* of Alexandria Troas, but the engine which keeps the speech in motion is the enjoyment of speaker and audience in clever reversals of the Homeric story argued on the basis of the text of Homer's *Iliad* itself.[30] The second of Dio's excursions into entertaining prose fiction is a narrative of his shipwreck on the East coast of Euboea and his encounter there with the family of a virtuous hunter.

[28] For his date Cameron 1982. For commentary, Page 1978 and (much more sympathetic) Höschele 2006. For proximity to Ephesus see *AP* 5.9 = Rufinus 1 Page, though Page's belief that the location of Rufinus' home as Samos is confirmed by *AP* 5.44 = Rufinus 17 Page was rightly questioned by Robert 1982b.

[29] Bowie 2002a (Chapter 25 in this volume).

[30] For good discussions see Kim 2010, 85–139; Trapp 2016.

His family's virtues are opposed to the corrupt practices in the city on the margins of whose territory he, his cousin and their families live by hunting. Several features locate this *Euboean oration* (*Or.* 7) of Dio not very far from the Greek novels: themes of travel, the protagonist's encounter with a culture different from that of the Greco-Roman *polis* (also found in his *Borysthenite oration*, *Or.* 36) and a love-interest, albeit here involving minor characters – the hunter's son falls in love with, and marries, his cousin's daughter (very much the girl next door).[31]

Another philosopher, Plutarch of Chaeronea, also showed great skill and interest in using absorbing narrative to construct tense situations, lively dialogue and sympathetic characters. The overall objective of his parallel *Lives* may have been moral education and not mere entertainment,[32] but his 'heroes' are often found in cliff-hanging situations comparable to those in novels (e.g. Marius hiding in the marshes, *Marius* 37–38), and love affairs play an important part in several *Lives*, notably the *Antonius*, albeit they never provide their dominant framework, nor are they teen romances. Adventure and sexual passion also surface from time to time in his *Essays*, but in some cases, for example in his work *On the virtues of women*, with unhappy consequences (see the *caveat* already voiced p. 658). Another of these essays, the Ἐρωτικός, '*Tale of Desire*', has a decidedly novelistic plot: in the city of Thespiae, which alone had a major cult of Eros, a wealthy widow kidnaps and carries off to her home a handsome young man for whom she lusts. Interlocutors propose different reactions, but she is allowed to keep him.

We cannot judge whether Chariton was read more in mainland Greece, in the Roman province Asia, and in Rome, than Dio or Plutarch (as he certainly seems to have been in Oxyrhynchus): but both these philosophers acquired a high reputation for the production of edifying literature, and that their varied oeuvre included themes and modes of writing contiguous with those of Chariton and Xenophon may well have helped some πεπαιδευμένοι, 'cultivated men', to be readier to extend their reading to novels. It is a corollary, of course, that these other writers' awareness of the success of *Callirhoe* and the like may have encouraged them to include amatory subjects. In general there is rather more evidence of writing on erotic themes between the reigns of Nero (AD 54–68) and Pius (AD 138–61). Philostratus reports a work he describes as 'Araspas in love with Pantheia', a reworking of a tale of faithful love immortalised by Xenophon in his *Cyropaedeia*: some attributed this to the sophist Dionysius of Miletus,

[31] D.Chr. *Or.* 7.67 ff.: excellent commentary by Russell 1992.
[32] Cf. e.g. Duff 1999.

but Philostratus judges it alien to his style and pronounces his enemy Celer, perhaps the imperial secretary Caninius Celer, to have been its author.[33] Whether a declamation or a properly novelistic book-text (on whatever scale), it attests romantic themes enticing a writer at the highest social level. A book of homoerotic epigrams by Strato of Sardis can plausibly be dated to the reign of that emperor most sympathetic to its subject matter, Hadrian.[34] Finally Antoninus Liberalis' collection of forty-one *Metamorphoses*, many of them brought about by amatory misadventures, seems to belong in this period.

Alongside such works, which accommodated *erotica* somewhere on their canvas, there were indeed many more in the years between AD 50 and AD 160 that addressed subjects less hospitable to *eros*. In this context a mere list must suffice, but it will show their range and number. In moral philosophy Musonius Rufus and Arrian's version of the lectures of Epictetus; in more technical philosophy Favorinus; in historiography with a global sweep Arrian of Nicomedia (most famously his *Anabasis of Alexander*), Claudius Charax of Pergamum, Amyntianus, Appian of Alexandria;[35] in geography and astronomy Ptolemy; in physiognomonics Bryson and the sophist Polemo of Laodicea; in literary criticism the work *On the sublime* attributed to a Longinus. As to poetry, we know of epics and tragedies, some by sophists, all almost entirely lost, and some surviving lyric poems by Hadrian's freedman P. Aelius Mesomedes.[36]

Finally we should take note of some often loosely structured collections that catered either to the appetite for bizarre or unusual stories or simply for scientific, literary or linguistic knowledge. Between Pliny's *Historia Naturalis*, in Latin, from the sixties and seventies AD and the Praenestine Claudius Aelianus' Ποικίλη ἱστορία, *Varied history*, in Greek, from the 220s AD, no straightforward examples survive, unless we admit Phlegon's *On things miraculous*.[37] But such material was exploited by Plutarch in several

[33] Philostr. *VS* 1.22.524. Stramaglia 2000 suggests that the title given by Philostratus counts against the view of Perry 1967, 168–9 and Bowie 1994a, 445 (Chapter 20, 433 in this volume) that this could have been a novel: but is the phrase Ἀράσπας ὁ Πανθείας ἐρῶν, 'Araspas in love with Pantheia', a title? We may note how Philostratus rewrites the title of Pollux's *Onomasticon* as simply τὰ ὀνόματα, *VS* 2.12.592.

[34] See Cameron 1982; Bowie 1990b, 56–7 (Chapter 14, 286–7 in this volume); Floridi 2007.

[35] Note, however, his careful telling of the story of Stratonice's infatuation with Antiochus, *Syr.* 308–28, earlier narrated in Plu. *Demetr.* 38, later in Luc. *Syr.D.* 17–18: cf. Lightfoot 2003 *ad loc.*; Romani in Stramaglia 2000, 271–81.

[36] For the Greek poetry of this period see Bowie 1989a, 1989b, 1990b (Chapters 12–14 in this volume). That Mesomedes (on whom see now Regenauer 2016) was not insensitive to the possibilities of erotic writing is clear from his poem on a sponge (9 Heitsch = 6 Horna).

[37] See above n.17.

essays, and was adapted to more elegant presentation in dialogue form in his afore-mentioned *Sympotic questions* (written between AD 99 and 116). It was similarly dressed up by Aulus Gellius in his (largely) Latin *Attic Nights*. Less artistic presentation of similar material seems to have characterised the Σύμμεικτα ἱστορικὰ ὑπομνήματα, '*Miscellaneous historical essays*', of the Epidaurian lady Pamphila[38] and the Παντοδαπὴ ἱστορία, '*Varied history*', and Ἀπομνημονεύματα, '*Memoirs*', of Favorinus of Arelate.

This is how we moderns might see the world of letters in which Achilles Tatius chose to follow Chariton, Xenophon, the author of *Metiochus and Parthenope*, and doubtless other early 'ideal' novelists unknown to us, and to write his eight-book *Leucippe and Cleitophon*. Achilles Tatius and his local bookseller might well have known a quite different selection of recently published Greek literature and consequently have formed a different perspective. It must be admitted that nothing in what we know prepares us for what recent scholarship has brought out in *Leucippe and Cleitophon* – sophisticated handling of erotic and other commonplaces, occasional play with the game of fiction, and persistent inversion of Platonic dialogue.[39] Apparently writing in a much more active Greek literary world than that of Chariton, Achilles very probably turned down a wider range of literary opportunities than his predecessor, and may have done so because in Roman Egypt, at least, he saw that the novel had come to stay. Not that he put all his eggs in one basket. He is one of only two of our novelists to whom ancient evidence (in each case the Suda) ascribes other works:[40] Ἐτυμολογίαι, '*Etymologies*', a Ἱστορία σύμμικτος, '*Miscellaneous history*', and a work Περὶ σφαίρας, *On the sphere*, which might possibly be identical with a surviving commentary on Aratus ascribed to an Achilles.[41] These works (if correctly assigned to Achilles Tatius) suggest a mind with several strands of interest – scientific and philological – and make it easier to understand why *Leucippe and Cleitophon* so often presents to its readers 'scientific' digressions which *prima facie* make unsatisfying contributions to the narrative. But it is also relevant to their interpretation how much ποικίλη ἱστορία, 'varied history', was being written, as we have seen, in diverse literary forms. So too the discussion of the respective advantages of homoerotic and heterosexual sexual activity (2.35–8) might have particular appeal for readers in the time of Hadrian's

[38] Cf. Phot. *Cod.* 175.

[39] Goldhill 1995, 66–111; Most 1989; Bartsch 1989; Morales 2004; Repath 2005; Laplace 2007; Whitmarsh 2020.

[40] Suda α 4695 *s.n.* Ἀχιλλεὺς Στάτιος. The other is Xenophon, to whom the Suda ξ 50 *s.n.* Ξενοφῶν (perhaps conflating two different writers) gives a work Περὶ τῆς πόλεως Ἐφεσίων, '*On the city of Ephesus*'.

[41] For the problem see Stramaglia 2000, 10–11; Whitmarsh 2020, 3–4.

infatuation with Antinous. Achilles' extensive scene-setting in Egypt and his glittering *ecphrasis* of Alexandria can also be seen to fit respectively into a widespread Hellenic interest in things and creatures Egyptian, going back to Hecataeus and Herodotus and tapped in a long speech (*Or.* 36) ca. AD 147–9 by the sophist Aelius Aristides, and into one of the basic tasks assigned during rhetorical training, the 'praise of a city'.

It might be argued tentatively, then, both that Achilles Tatius' novel shows some responses to the literary tendencies of the decades since Chariton, and (less confidently) that the non-novelistic literature of that period might have been different had it not been for Chariton's impact.

4 AD 160–220

What of our next novel, Iamblichus' Βαβυλωνιακά, '*Babylonian Histories*'. Its author's claim to have predicted the successful outcome of Rome's war against Parthia (AD 161–5), reinforced by his story that he had been tutored by a captive in the earlier Parthian war of Trajan (AD 114–17), not only gives us an unusually secure date (surely shortly after AD 165), but also shows that its author was quick to exploit an interest in the world Rome claimed to have conquered (just as Lucian assures us that many historians jumped onto the bandwagon of writing up the war itself, *On how to write history* 2). In other respects too the Βαβυλωνιακά seem to draw closer to history and mythography. Iamblichus' narrative ran to at least sixteen books,[42] so its bulk alone might have helped its ambiguous title to lead a reader or purchaser to expect a historical rather than novelistic work. The names of some of its chief characters – Euphrates, Tigris and Mesopotamia[43] – might also induce a reader brought up on poetic Αἴτια, '*Origins*', and on local prose historiography (which seems to have flourished in the second century AD),[44] to see the Βαβυλωνιακά as an exploration of mythical traditions about the Euphrates valley – and indeed the writer claimed to draw his material from indigenous sources.[45] The work seems also (to judge from

[42] So Phot. *Cod.* 94: the Suda entry, more probably corrupt (but see Bianchi 2016), gives thirty-nine books.

[43] Photius *Cod.* 94, 75a40–1.

[44] See cursorily Bowie 1970, 19–22 (Chapter 1 in Volume 3). The dates of some authors (e.g. Telephus of Pergamum) remain uncertain, as does the identity of the Xenophon to whom the Suda ξ 50 gives *On the city of Ephesus*: cf. above n.40 and Strubbe 1984–6.

[45] Cf. the scholion in manuscript A (*Marcianus gr.* 450) on Phot. *Cod.* 94 (p. 2 Habrich), which seems, like Photius' summary, to have been written by somebody with access to a full text of Iamblichus.

Photius' summary) to have had a higher proportion of bizarre and even miraculous events than the three preceding ideal novels; but that this component is unlikely to be a function of the time of writing (though we might note Lucian's near-contemporary use of such material in his Φιλοψευδής, '*Lover of lies*') is clear from a comparable mixture in Antonius Diogenes' Τὰ ὑπὲρ Θούλην ἄπιστα, '*The unbelievable things beyond Thule*', written at least two generations earlier.[46]

The delayed entry of Lucian to this plot should not be taken as a low evaluation of his importance. Of all Greek authors of the first and second centuries AD he shows most signs of writing in a literary environment where prose fiction was a significant player. Fictionality of various sorts and on differing scales can be found in almost all parts of Lucian's oeuvre – produced between the 150s and early 180s AD, although few works can be precisely dated. Many pieces need owe little to the now established genre of extended prose fiction: for example, the *Dialogues of the gods* are miniature transpositions from epic, the *Dialogues of courtesans* from New Comedy and from Machon's iambic Χρεῖαι, '*Aphorisms*'; the fictionality of the *Nigrinus* reworks that of Platonic dialogue, that of the *Dream* owes much to Plato's *Apology*. But *Toxaris*, with its parallel Greek and Scythian tales of friendship, and the tall stories in his Φιλοψευδής, '*Lover of lies*', share the novels' exploitation of exotic locations. Moreover, as has been recently argued, *Toxaris* offers its readers a coded commentary on the novels so that it becomes not merely comic fantasy, moralistic rhetoric, or something indefinable in between, but also a practical exposition of the theory of reading and writing fiction.[47] Other aspects of the reading and writing of fiction are explored in Lucian's *True histories*, and even if the most important targets of his parody are the classical authors Homer, Ctesias and Herodotus, with some admixture of Iambulus, Photius may have been right to assert some dependence on Antonius Diogenes' Τὰ ὑπὲρ Θούλην ἄπιστα.[48] More imponderably, the narrator in Lucian's *On the Syrian goddess* expounds to Greek readers an exotic cult of the sort that sometimes catches novelists' eyes in a tone and voice that is less plausibly interpreted as that of a real, pious pilgrim than that of a fictive, quasi-Herodotean narrator and ironic parodist.[49]

[46] For a dating of Antonius Diogenes in or around the 90s AD see Stramaglia 1999; Bowie 2002a (Chapter 25 in this volume). A case for an earlier date, ca. AD 60, is made in Bowie 2007d (Chapter 32 in this volume).

[47] Ní Mheallaigh 2014, 39–71.

[48] *Contra* Morgan 1985.

[49] On the problem see Lightfoot 2003, 161–221.

That Lucian should have read and reacted to the ideal novels and expected his own readers to appreciate his engagement with their codes of fiction is all the more intelligible if, as seems likely, he was also the author of a version of the *Ass* story. There seem to have been at least three Greek versions of the story that Apuleius took up and ran with in his Latin *Metamorphoses*: a work in some thirty pages (fifty-six chapters) transmitted with other works of Lucian in Byzantine manuscripts in which the narrating 'I' claims to be Lucius of Patrae; a work summarised by Photius (*Cod.* 129) which he supposed to be written *by* a Lucius of Patrae; and a prosimetric version different in at least some details, a papyrus fragment of which has recently been published.[50] The Greek of the first of these is in a much lower register than found elsewhere in the Lucianic corpus, and on present evidence it seems most likely (as was argued by Perry) that the version summarised by Photius is to be credited to Lucian. If that is so, or indeed if any one of the versions is by Lucian, then we find him both reacting in some writing, above all the *Toxaris*, to prose fiction which includes the ideal novels, and deciding to make a contribution of his own to those other strands of prose fiction which may in different ways be represented by Antonius Diogenes and by the papyrus fragments of the Iolaus story and of Lollianus' Φοινικικά, '*Phoenician histories*'.

Lucian is not the only late-second-century Greek writer who shows some interaction with the novels. The decades between Iamblichus and Longus – it is uncertain how many these were, but one guess would put Longus between AD 190 and AD 220 – are ones from which fewer works have survived than from the previous half-century:[51] but one of the four, Pausanias' Ἑλλάδος περιήγησις, '*Tour of Greece*', can be claimed to have influenced Longus and perhaps to show novelistic influence and another, Philostratus' *Heroicus*, to have been influenced by the novels.[52] A fifth work,

[50] On *P.Oxy.* 4762, published by Obbink 2006b, see May 2010.

[51] Again I omit declamations and technical works, e.g. Hermogenes' Περὶ ἰδεῶν, '*On styles*', ca. AD 184, the two lexica of Phrynichus, and the *Onomasticon* of Pollux (the latter, and one of the former, chiefly works of the 180s).

[52] The other two works are Aristides' Ἱεροὶ λόγοι, '*Sacred Tales*', and Athenaeus' Δειπνοσοφισταί, '*Experts in banqueting*'. I take Aristides' preoccupation with his salvation and his readiness to seek and accept divine advice, not least through dreams, to be features that his *Sacred Tales* share with the general *mentalité* of his age rather than their showing any link with the use of broadly similar motifs by novelists. Although we have particular testimony to an interest in dream-interpretation in the later second and early third century both in the Ὀνειροκριτικά, '*How to interpret dreams*', of Artemidorus and in their important place in Cassius Dio's first historical work, sadly lost, on Septimius Severus' rise to power, this is an on-going preoccupation throughout the ancient world, and there is little to suggest particular cross-fertilisation with the novels.

the collection of letters purporting to be by the Attic orator Aeschines, might also belong in this period, and likewise has a novelistic feature.

Pausanias' composition of his work in fact seems to straddle the point at which Iamblichus is likely to have been writing (ca. AD 165–70) with Book 1 of the *Tour of Greece* composed perhaps as early as the early 160s AD, and Book 10 as late as the late 170s.[53] An interest in local αἴτια, 'origins', noted above as a feature shared by Iamblichus and local Greek historians, is also of course prominent in Pausanias. Moreover at least two of these prompt him to tell a brief erotic tale in explanation of a religious custom – the story of Comaetho and Melanippus (7.19.1–5) – or of a toponym – that told shortly after, of Callirhoe and Coresus (7.21.1–5).[54] Like the stories told by Nicolaus and Strabo (see above with nn.13–14) these end with the death of one or both lovers. But Pausanias rounds off that of Comaetho and Melanippus with a vehement insistence on the power of Eros: while stating that the annual sacrifice of a boy and a girl to Artemis Laphria ordered by Delphi was a most pitiable fate for them and for their parents, Pausanias says he does not see the sacrifice of the furtive lovers Comaetho and Melanippus themselves as a disaster:

> παίδων δὲ καὶ παρθένων ὁπόσοι μὲν ἐς τὴν θεὸν οὐδὲν εἰργασμένοι Μελανίππου καὶ Κομαιθοῦς ἕνεκα ἀπώλλυντο, αὐτοί τε οἰκτρότατα καὶ οἱ προσήκοντές σφισιν ἔπασχον, Μελάνιππον δὲ καὶ Κομαιθὼ συμφορᾶς ἐκτὸς γενέσθαι τίθεμαι· μόνον γὰρ δὴ ἀνθρώπωι ψυχῆς ἐστιν ἀντάξιον κατορθῶσαί τινα ἐρασθέντα.
>
> As for all the young men and maidens who died because of Melanippus and Comaetho although they had perpetrated nothing against the goddess, their fate and that of their families was most pitiable. But Melanippus and Comaetho I reckon to have been outside disaster: for the only thing that for a human being is of equal value to life is for someone who has fallen in love to attain its object.
>
> Pausanias 7.19.5

This uncompromising claim for the value of the object of ἔρως, 'desire', sets Pausanias apart from earlier writers in whom similar *Novellen* have been noted.[55] It may also be relevant that it is only in Book 7, on Achaea, that we find such erotic *Novellen*, together with a brief reference at 7.5.13 to the tomb of Rhadinē and Leontichus (whose story was told in full, but

[53] For these dates see Bowie 2001c (Chapter 12 in Volume 3).
[54] For discussion and further bibliography see Stramaglia 2000, 81–4, 129–33.
[55] Cf. pp. 658–9 with nn.12–17.

without naming its hero, by Strabo, see above with n.14). Some have suspected that for his account of Achaea Pausanias has drawn on a source with greater interest in *erotica* than those used for other books,[56] but the extent of Pausanias' mechanical dependence on his sources now seems to be less than judged by older scholarship. Wherever he got the stories, his asseveration about ἔρως reveals a πεπαιδευμένος, 'cultivated man', responsive to the values esteemed in the ideal novels, and perhaps one who had recently been reading one or more such books.

As for Athenaeus' Δειπνοσοφισταί, '*Experts in banqueting*', probably written ca. AD 193,[57] the absence of any direct reference to Greek novels is more probably due to the scant material that these might have yielded on things and texts sympotic or meta-sympotic than to their generic unpretentiousness or recent composition: after all, Athenaeus cited the Hadrianic poet Pancrates – though Pancrates could be seen as an exception, being as he was from Naucratis, and admittedly composing some version of a higher genre, epic.[58] But Athenaeus does cite at least one striking *Novelle*, the story of Zariadres and Odatis, which shares more features with the ideal romances than do most *Novellen*.[59] Zariadres and Odatis are not only of outstanding beauty and high birth (he a king, she a princess); after falling in love not by meeting but by dreaming of each other, Zariadres abducts Odatis just when, at a specially convened symposium (from which Zariadres is of course absent) her father has told her to marry whomever she chooses. Allegedly the couple lived happily ever after, and so renowned was their ἔρως in Asia that it figured in public and private painting and parents named their daughters Odatis.[60] Athenaeus introduces the story, which he found in the Alexander-historian Chares of Mytilene, to support the claim that sometimes people fall in love with a person they know only by reputation. To some extent, perhaps, his choice of this excerpt reflects his sense of contemporary interest in love-plots with happy endings, but since his source is a historian of the late fourth century BC that argument cannot be pressed.

[56] Already Kalkmann 1886, 132–3. For 7.19.1–5 Reinach 1925, 138 suggested the Ἀχαϊκά, '*Achaean history*', of the Hellenistic poet Rhianus of Bene. For further bibliography see Dorati in Stramaglia 2000, 132.

[57] As argued by Zecchini 1989.

[58] For the poem of Pancrates see Bowie 1990b, 2002e (Chapters 14 and 15 in this volume); Höschele 2018.

[59] Ath. 13.575a–f = Chares *FGrH* 125 F5; for other uses of Chares by Ath. cf. esp. 12.538a–539b = F2, on the mass cross-cultural wedding at Susa, with Zecchini 1989, 60–68.

[60] This detail receives no support from epigraphy.

The strongest case can be made for Philostratus' Ἡρωικός, '*On heroes*', a work whose bearing upon the development of Greek prose fiction and on religious ideas of the period has justly begun to attract much recent attention.[61] Of course it offers a very different brand of fiction from that of the ideal novels. It is a dialogue between a vintner in the Thracian Chersonnese and a Phoenician sailor delayed by winds (neither is named). Although slightly longer than *Daphnis and Chloe*, it is not divided into books; its psychological progression is not to do with ἔρως, 'desire', but with belief – the vintner's belief in the continued if ghostly existence of the heroes who fell in the Trojan war, to which he ultimately converts the Phoenician. Overall, then, it is a work more reminiscent of Dio's *Euboean oration* than of the novels. But within it is a panel which strongly recalls them. The love of Achilles and Helen on the White Island,[62] which started not when they saw each other (since Helen was in Egypt while Achilles fought at Troy) but on the basis of what they heard about each other's beauty. Philostratus' account picks up the novelistic theme of passion between the most handsome youth and the most beautiful young woman, and he resolves the doubts that must have struck some readers of ideal novels about what happened after their end: *did* the couple live happily ever after (as claimed at X.Eph. 5.15.3 and Longus 4.39.1)? What happened when they grew old? Since Achilles and Helen are divinised, or divine, *they* at least never grow old, but perpetually sing of their mutual ἔρως.[63]

So three authors of the period AD 170–220, Pausanias, Athenaeus and Philostratus, arguably make some of their choices in a way they would not have done in a world without novels. What of the choice made by the novelist Longus? On the one hand (as argued for Achilles Tatius and Iamblichus) his decision to compose a novel might reflect a sense that the genre was well established. On the other hand, his decision to fuse an 'ideal' novel and Theocritean pastoral poetry (with a dash of Hellenistic pastoral epigram) could be argued with equal plausibility to reflect a sense that the genre was tired and needed to take a new direction, or that it was so vigorous that even drastic modification could be applied without endangering its survival. In either case the direction in which he decided to go can only in part be explained by the Greek literary climate of his time. Rural scenarios are also chosen by Aelian for his Ἐπιστολαὶ ἀγροικικαί, '*Rustic epistles*', but a

[61] Editions: de Lannoy 1977; Maclean and Aitken 2001; Rossi 1997; Beschorner 1999; Grossardt 2006. Of other discussions the best is Hodkinson 2011; see also Bowie 1994b (Chapter 21 in this volume); Aitken and Maclean 2004; Rutherford 2009; Kim 2010, 175–215; Grossardt 2018.

[62] Philostr., *Her.* 54.

[63] Philostr., *Her.* 54.12.

precise date for these is wanting – around the AD 220s or 230s would fit what we know from Philostratus of Aelian's career – as it is for Longus; so it is unclear which writer made the first move (and even less clear is the relative chronology of Alciphron and Aelian). The exploitation of Theocritus is not matched by any other evidence that he was especially in fashion in this period (the commentary activity of Munatius of Tralles seems to be rather earlier). The interest in religion and local cults (in Longus' case ostentatiously rural, not urban cults) is indeed comparable to what we find in Pausanias and Philostratus' *Heroicus*, but it is also well-documented in earlier imperial Greek literature, notably in Plutarch's presentation of Delphi in the late first and early second centuries.[64] All in all, it is very difficult to pin down elements in Longus that can be confidently explained as reactions to contemporary literary trends.

5 AD 220–70

The artificiality of my periodisation (in this case hanging upon a supposed date for Longus) becomes even more blatant for this last section. On the one hand the year AD 220 bisects the important literary career of Philostratus. On the other, the place of a single work, Heliodorus' Αἰθιοπικά, '*Ethiopian histories*', remains to be assessed, yet on its date there is as yet no consensus, and one view would put it a century later than AD 270. Three different stories will be offered in the awareness that only one (if that) can be true.

(a) Heliodorus of Emesa (as the end of the work claims its author to be) may be writing about the same time as Philostratus composed his later works, the 220s and 230s. His Ethiopian council of Gymnosophists and details of his description of the phoenix[65] seem to draw upon Philostratus eight-book work on Apollonius of Tyana, and his magisterial plot-creator and internal narrator Calasiris may also owe something to

[64] Such interests probably also figured in Arrian's history of his own part of western Asia Minor, his Βιθυνι(α)κά, '*Bithynian history*', which mentioned his priesthood of Demeter and Kore (Phot. *Bibl. Cod.* 93, 73b2).

[65] The φροντιστήριον, 'academy', of Gymnosophists in Philostr. *VA* 6.6.1 seems to be taken over by Hld. (2.31.1 etc.) for Ethiopian gymnosophists who speak Greek (9.25.3) and act as a Council for king Hydaspes (10.2.1 etc.). The phoenix's attribution to India *or* Ethiopia (Hld. 6.3.3) may reflect its claim for India at Philostr. *VA* 3.49 (an alternative tradition already known to Luc. *Peregr.* 28) combined with its allocation to Ethiopia at Ach. Tat. 3.25 and Alex. Aphr. *Fat.* 28, p. 199.17 Bruns = *SVF* iii p. 165 no. 658. The apotropaic qualities of the magical stone called παντάρβη, 'Fear-all' (Hld. 8.11), may owe something to *VA* 3.46.

[66] Cf. Bowie 1989a, 228–9 (Chapter 12, 237–8 in this volume).

Philostratus' Apollonius. The hymn to Thetis sung by the Thessalian religious delegation to Delphi seems to be a clever upstaging of a closely similar hymn to Achilles in Philostratus' work of ca. AD 214, the Ἡρωικός, '*On heroes*'.[66] In some details, then, Heliodorus seems to react to the oeuvre of a major literary figure of the period 200–240 AD. His presentation of religion also shares the seriousness of Philostratus' *In honour of Apollonius*, and although his plot centres on the mutual attraction of two young people, Charicleia and Theagenes, their relationship is soon moved onto a spiritual plane, and in the Αἰθιοπικά physical sexuality characterises 'bad' minor characters, such as the promiscuous young Thisbe and the older women Demaenete and Arsace. There can be little doubt that Heliodorus knows some earlier novels, since he repeatedly plays with and upstages their conventions; and direct knowledge of Achilles Tatius and of Longus' *Daphnis and Chloe* has been claimed.[67] But among the many ways in which he reworks the novelistic tradition is a shift towards a more spiritual texture – something that might be seen as showing the influence of the *In honour of Apollonius*, if the Αἰθιοπικά indeed belongs around AD 240.

(b) An alternative chronology has set the writing of the *Ethiopian histories* around AD 270–75.[68] Our knowledge of literary activity in that period is sketchier than for the earlier third century, but nothing that we know can be construed as a text to which Heliodorus seems to be responding. Sophistic rhetoric of course continued to be a dominant cultural form, but nothing we know of Nicagoras (himself proud to be a descendant of Plutarch and Sextus of Chaeronea)[69] or that we read in Menander Rhetor differs from earlier recipes in a way that might be used to explain features of Heliodorus' unusual style. Nor is there any obvious point of contact with the (largely lost) histories of the Athenian P. Herennius Dexippus. Much more neo-Platonic writing was available to be read by the later third century, some of it from Heliodorus' own part of the Greek world, e.g. the work of the philosopher Iamblichus. That would indeed chime with the neo-Platonic ideas that have been observed in Heliodorus, but is not strictly a *literary* influence, and it is anyway clear that neo-Platonic thought was already being disseminated by the 230s and 240s AD.

[67] For Ach. Tat. see Rohde 1914: 503–4; Szepessy 1957, 1978; for Longus, Bowie 1995b (Chapter 22 in this volume).

[68] Rohde 1914, 496–7, arguing from the emperor Aurelian's promotion of the cult of Sol/Ἥλιος, 'the Sun'.

[69] *Syll.*^{3} 845 = *IG* ii^2 3814: cf. Puech 2002, 357–60.

(c) An influential body of scholarly opinion now sets the *Ethiopian histories* in the later fourth century, based partly on the argument that Heliodorus' account of the siege of Syene (9.3–8) draws significantly from Julian's account of the siege of Nisibis in his *First* and *Third Orations* (of ca. AD 353).[70] As in the case of the later third-century dating, it is hard to see to what in contemporary Greek literature Heliodorus might be reacting, though our knowledge of this Greek literary scene is rather better. Neither Julian's own speeches, even if one or two might have suggested details for the siege of Syene, nor his intense and satirical *Caesars* or *Beard-hater* seem likely stimuli, unless in the limited sense that they might have encouraged Heliodorus to take Hellenic paganism seriously and totally to ignore Christianity. That too might have been the consequence if Heliodorus has spent time reading speeches or letters of Libanius, but despite the huge volume of Libanius' surviving works nothing, so far as I know, has been spotted that might be linked to anything in the *Ethiopian histories*. Paradoxically, the writing that stands closest to that of Heliodorus is Christian, whether the discourses of Cappadocian fathers on the merits of virtue and chastity, martyr acts with tortures and burnings, or saints' lives like Athanasius' influential life of St. Antony. It is possible, but in my view unlikely, that such texts impinged on Heliodorus, but if so he has muffled their impact. His response to Homer, Herodotus and some Attic drama is much clearer than any reaction to such contemporary writing.

Moreover some writers from the Greek-speaking world were now choosing Latin as their medium – Claudian and Ammianus Marcellinus – and it seems that the Latin West was a more lively literary forum: among the works it generated were two with novelistic links: the occasionally fraudulent, always mischievous *Augustan History*, and a Latin translation of Philostratus' *Apollonius*. It would be entertaining to suppose, with Bowersock, that the former drew inspiration for its description of the triumph of Aurelian in AD 274 from Heliodorus' account of Blemmyes and Seres in Hydaspes' army when he defeated the Persians (9.17) and of Blemmyes, Seres and Auxumitae among the embassies to the victor (10.25–7), with a giraffe among their gifts (10.27).[71] But neither the giraffe neither these exotic nations are unique to these texts.

Whichever of the dates proves correct, then, it seems that Heliodorus' work made no impact on other Greek writing that we can now discern.

[70] Good statements of the arguments in Bowersock 1994; Morgan 1996a, 418–19.

[71] Bowersock 1994, 149–60.

Only if Heliodorus was writing shortly after Philostratus' *Apollonius* can some reaction to contemporary Greek literature be claimed (which is not in itself, of course, an argument in favour of this date). Moreover it is the reaction to a single work of a single author. If such a Heliodorus was also writing shortly after the publication of the contemporary history of Herodian or the massive (80-book) Roman history of Cassius Dio, he either did not read these works or had almost no use in his novel for what he read.[72]

6 Conclusions

It has been possible to suggest some respects in which Greek novels show affinity with some other Greek writing of their time or an awareness of the tastes that this writing implies. That such affinities are clearest for writers of the period ca. 120–240 AD, Achilles Tatius, Iamblichus, Longus and (perhaps) Heliodorus, the period from which a much higher volume of Greek literature survives, should be a ground for caution. I suggested that Chariton was partly responding to a world in which Greek literary activity was more constricted: but perhaps the constriction is simply in our own knowledge. Equally, if Heliodorus *were* writing ca. 270 or ca. 370, a fuller understanding of Greek pagan literature of the time *might* allow us to see affinities that currently elude us.

As to influence on other writing, the case is strongest for the impact of novels upon Lucian and Philostratus. The former has enjoyed a high reputation, albeit not principally for his narrative fictions, since the Renaissance, and the latter's high standing in the Renaissance is now beginning to be re-established. If by dreadful misfortune the *codex unicus* of Chariton and Xenophon had perished it is perhaps comforting to think that the presence of the novel in the literature of the second sophistic would not have been charted only by the works of Achilles Tatius, Longus and Heliodorus, but also by those of Lucian, Pausanias and Philostratus.

[72] A single exception might be his account of Phoenician dancing 'Assyrian style' at 4.17.1 which is strikingly similar to Herodian's unsympathetic account of Elagabalus' performances when sacrificing: Hdn. 5.38, cf. again 5.5.9, 6.1, 7.4, 7.6.

34 | The Uses of Bookishness (2009)

1 Introduction

This paper addresses some of the different ways in which the surviving texts of Greek novels recognise and make play with their textuality, their status as a book to be read, and it directs its focus particularly upon *The incredible things beyond Thule* of Antonius Diogenes and upon Longus' *Daphnis and Chloe*. It does so because these two texts appear to be much more interested than the others in flaunting their textuality. Of these other novels (which I briefly discuss first) those of Xenophon and Achilles give their readers no overt nudge to remind them that they are engaged in an act of reading, while that of Heliodorus does so only very late in his work: Chariton occupies an interesting, intermediate position.

The openings of Xenophon and of Achilles Tatius plunge the reader *in medias res* without any gesture towards the reading process:

> ἦν ἐν Ἐφέσωι ἀνὴρ τῶν τὰ πρῶτα ἐκεῖ δυναμένων, Λυκομήδης ὄνομα. τούτωι τῶι Λυκομήδει ἐκ γυναικὸς ἐπιχωρίας Θεμιστοῦς γίνεται παῖς Ἁβροκόμης …
>
> There was in Ephesus a man among those who had the greatest power there, Lycomedes by name. To this Lycomedes was born, by a wife from that area, Themisto, a son Habrocomes …
>
> Xenophon of Ephesus 1.1.1

> Σιδὼν ἐπὶ θαλάττηι πόλις· Συρίων ἡ θάλασσα· μήτηρ Φοινίκων ἡ πόλις· Θηβαίων ὁ δῆμος πατήρ …
>
> Sidon is a city on the sea; the sea that of the Syrians; the city the mother-city of the Phoenicians; its people the father of the Thebans …
>
> Achilles Tatius 1.1.1

The same technique is adopted by Heliodorus in his famous opening ἡμέρας ἄρτι διαγελώσης καὶ ἡλίου τὰς ἀκρωρείας καταυγάζοντος …, 'As day was just spreading its smile and the sun was casting its beams down upon the ridges …': only after ten books does Heliodorus imprecisely describe his work as τὸ σύνταγμα … ὃ συνέταξεν ἀνὴρ Φοῖνιξ Ἐμισηνός … Ἡλιόδωρος, 'the composition … which a Phoenician man from Emesa composed, Heliodorus'.[1]

Chariton's opening creates for the reader a narrator, but a narrator with features of the oral, as suggested by his verb 'I shall narrate', as well as of the written, hinted at by his self-description as ὑπογραφεύς, 'secretary': Χαρίτων Ἀφροδισιεύς, Ἀθηναγόρου τοῦ ῥήτορος ὑπογραφεύς, πάθος ἐρωτικὸν ἐν Συρακούσαις γενόμενον διηγήσομαι, 'I, Chariton of Aphrodisias, secretary to the rhetor Athenagoras, shall narrate an amatory affair that happened in Syracuse'.[2] There is no clear marker of textuality in his recapitulations, at the opening either of Book 5, ὡς μὲν ἐγαμήθη Καλλιρόη Χαιρέαι … ταῦτα ἐν τῶι πρόσθεν λόγωι δεδήλωται· τὰ δὲ ἑξῆς νῦν διηγήσομαι, 'How Callirhoe was married to Chaereas … this was set out in my earlier account; and what followed I shall now narrate', or of Book 8, ὡς μὲν οὖν Χαιρέας ὑποπτεύσας Καλλιρόην Διονυσίωι παραδεδόσθαι … ἐν τῶι πρόσθεν λόγωι δεδήλωται, 'How Chaereas, suspecting that Callirhoe had been given to Dionysius, … was set out in my earlier account.'[3] Interestingly, however, we find Chariton introducing a term indicating textuality a few lines later: νομίζω δὲ καὶ τὸ τελευταῖον τοῦτο σύγγραμμα τοῖς ἀναγινώσκουσιν ἥδιστον γενήσεσθαι, 'and I think that in fact this last piece of writing will be most pleasurable to my readers.'[4] This presentation of the work at Book 8's opening as a written composition is ultimately endorsed in Chariton's *envoi* at its end: τοσάδε περὶ Καλλιρόης συνέγραψα, 'This much is what I have written up about Callirhoe.'[5] The movement of Chariton's terminology from words which are poised between orality and textuality to a word which is definitively textual, συνέγραψα, 'I have *written* up', may reflect the author's own awareness of moving from a mode of story-telling which had strong affinities with oral narration to a para-Thucydidean written text. It would require the eye of faith to see here some impact of the work of Antonius Diogenes, which I have argued might after all have been written as early as the fifties or early sixties AD.[6] But I would like to retain the idea of some such impact during Chariton's period of composition as at least a formal possibility.

Quite independently of that or of any other hypothesis about the date of Antonius Diogenes, however, let me now turn to the ways his work plays off orality against textuality.

[1] Hld. 1.1.1, 10.41.4. For the term σύνταγμα cf. D.S. 1.3, Plu. *De Sto. rep.* 10 = *Mor.* 1036c.
[2] Ch. 1.1.1. [3] Ch. 5.1.1–2, 8.1.1. [4] Ch. 8.1.4. [5] Ch. 8.8.16.
[6] Bowie 2007d (Chapter 32 in this volume).

2 Textuality and Orality in Antonius Diogenes

Diogenes (as he is almost always named by Photius, our chief source for the content and structure of *The incredible things beyond Thule*) offers a recurrent tension between the textual and the oral. This is true in whatever way we reconstruct his written work from Photius' summary, though of course the particular effects will be different if we think that Photius has altered the order in which a reader acquires information.

The reconstruction that seems to be most widely accepted has a preface consisting of two epistles:[7] in one of these Diogenes addressed a Faustinus; called himself a poet of Old Comedy (which, we should recall, was a performance genre);[8] claimed the testimony of his predecessors for most of what he told; and set out, apparently at the beginning of each book, the names of the men who had published such material earlier. It is worth noting that although he later insists on the bookishness of his own product, we do not know from Photius that Diogenes referred explicitly to *books* written by his predecessors, and the sentence ἀλλ' οὖν ἔχει περὶ τῶν πλείστων αὐτῶι μυθολογηθέντων ἀρχαιοτέρων μαρτυρίας, 'but at any rate he has the testimonies of older people about the majority of the tales he has spun', allows for either oral or written sources – with the term τῶν … μυθολογηθέντων, 'the tales he has spun', conjuring up intimations of orality.[9]

Books, reading and writing, however, dominate his second epistle, a dedication of his συγγράμματα, 'written works', to Faustinus' sister Isidora: Photius is explicit that this was to be found κατ' ἀρχὰς τοῦ βιβλίου, 'at the beginning of the book'.[10] In it he first adduces the intermediary Balagrus (whose name is spelled Balacrus in other sources) writing to his wife Phila, daughter of Antipater, about the discovery of the burial inscriptions of Deinias, Dercyllis, Mantinias and family after Alexander's siege of Tyre, then the discovery of cypress-wood tablets on which (as we have been told earlier by Phot. *Bibl.* 111a20–5) the Athenian Erasinides had, on Deinias' instructions, written out the whole story which Deinias διεμυθολόγησε, 'had told', in Tyre to an Arcadian called Cymbas.[11]

[7] Stephens and Winkler 1995, 101–18 (and for a translation of Phot.'s summary, 121–9). For a new text, commentary, German translation and full discussion see Schmedt 2020. For the elaborate *Beglaubigungsapparat* see Ní Mheallaigh 2008.

[8] For some ways in which Diogenes does indeed appear to exploit Old Comedy see Bowie 2007e (Chapter 15 in Volume 3).

[9] Phot. *Bibl.* 111a36–7: the translation of Stephens and Winkler 1995, 127 'he has a library of ancient testimonials' imports a bookishness not explicitly present in the Greek.

[10] Phot. *Bibl.* 111a41.

[11] 'With διεμυθολόγησε cf. διηγεῖσθαι, 'to narrate' and διηγούμενος, 'narrating', 109b3 and 7. It is not at all clear from Photius where in Diogenes' text this information was to be found.

The version of the genesis of the *The incredible things beyond Thule* that Isidora, and any like-minded reader, is encourage to adopt, then, is that the multi-volume written text of Diogenes, with its prefatory, written epistles, is a faithful replica of a similar written text, whose transcription was commissioned by Balagrus: Photius' participle in the middle voice, μεταγραψάμενος, 'he had the tablets transcribed', does not of course imply that this Hellenistic war-lord executed the transcription with his own hand and eye. This written text that lay behind the written narrative of Diogenes was, he claimed, preserved on cypress-wood tablets (he might expect an alert reader to begin calculating how many tablets such a voluminous story would occupy!) but was a version of the explicitly oral narrative of Deinias; and of course this oral narrative in turn encapsulated the orally communicated narratives of Dercyllis and Azulis.[12]

If, as usually held, not just one but both of those letters stood before the main body of Diogenes' work, then it seems overwhelmingly probable that at the outset he announced that it was to be a work in twenty-four books. This would certainly help to explain why Photius himself assigns it twenty-four books at the start of his summary: ἀνεγνώσθη Ἀντωνίου Διογένους τῶν ὑπὲρ Θούλην ἀπίστων λόγοι κδ', 'Read: twenty-four books of Antonius Diogenes' *The incredible things beyond Thule*.'[13] It also quite probable, on this scenario, that his list of authorities for each book was assembled in a section prefatory to the whole work, presumably (to judge from the phraseology of 111a39–40) in the epistle addressed to Faustinus.[14]

This highlighting of the difference between oral narrative, μυθολογηθέντα, 'tales that are told', and the power of written texts to preserve such a narrative may have been reflected in at least one more of the work's details.

At 110a16–17 we read for the first time in Photius' summary about two items in Paapis' magic weaponry of mass destruction, a bag of books and a box of herbs: ἔπειτα ὡς λαβόντες Μαντινίας καὶ Δερκυλλὶς ἐκ Λεοντίνων τὸ

[12] Deinias ἀναμανθάνει, 'interrogates', Dercyllis (109a29); μυθολογούσης Δερκυλλίδος, 'when Dercyllis was telling the story' (109b15); cf. Azulis διηγούμενον, 'narrating' (110b21).

[13] Phot. *Bibl.* 109a6. Does the use of the singular verb ἀνεγνώσθη imply that Photius initially expected its subject to be the neuter plural τὰ ἄπιστα, '*The incredible things* …', and at some stage modified his sentence to include the number of λόγοι, 'books'?

[14] I am far from confident that this widely accepted reading of Phot.'s report is correct. It seems possible, for example, that the letter to Faustinus was incorporated in Book 24 at the conclusion of the whole work (i.e. roughly where we find it in Phot.'s summary) and that only the letter dedicating the work to Isidora and setting out the *Beglaubigungsapparat* of the discovery of the cypress-wood tablets in coffins was located at the opening of the work (a location that is inescapable given the phrase κατ' ἀρχὰς τοῦ βιβλίου, 'at the beginning of the book', Phot. *Bibl.* 111a41). But this would not affect the central elements in my argument, and cannot be pursued here.

Παάπιδος πηρίδιον μετὰ τῶν ἐν αὐτῶι βιβλίων καὶ τῶν βοτανῶν τὸ κιβώτιον, 'next how Mantinias and Dercyllis took from Leontini Paapis' little bag, with the books in it, and the little box of herbs'. Paapis must have recovered these by the time he bewitched Mantinias and Dercyllis after catching up with them on Thule (110a42–b4). Once Paapis has been killed by Thruscanus of Thule, ἐραστὴς διάπυρος Δερκυλλίδος, 'passionately in love with Dercyllis', near the end of Book 23 (110b5–8), the following Book 24 εἰσάγει Ἄζουλιν διηγούμενον, 'introduces Azulis narrating' (110b20–1). Azulis is a new narrator, and presumably, like Paapis, an Egyptian: he is able to discover ἐκ τοῦ πηριδίου ... τοῦ Παάπιδος, 'from Paapis' bag of books' (110b27), how to cure both the trance of Mantinias and Dercyllis and the death-like condition of their parents.

This 'little bag', πηρίδιον, has now appeared in another context, in fragmentary texts preserved on a papyrus roll from Oxyrhynchus, *P.Oxy.* 4760.[15] The attribution of these fragments to the work of Antonius Diogenes is virtually assured by its reference both to Paapis (in fr. 1) and (in fr. 2) to a 'little bag', πηρίδιον, and soon after to a κιβώτιον, 'box', which is very probably the box of herbs:

fr. 1

. .	
κ . [	
Πάαπις [	Paapis
ηξιουϲ . [	'she asking' or 'they ask'
. .	

2–3 Πάαπις ... ἠξίου *vel* Πάαπις ... ἠξίουσ'? Parsons.

fr. 2

] . επα . [	
]ευων καὶ π . .	
] .σ.αυρω τὸ δὲ πη-	] to the cross(?): but the li-
ρίδιον τ]ῶν βιβλίων περι-	[ttle box] of books
ήψατο] . αὐτοῦ τῷ τραχή-	[he attached] around his neck
λῳ]ν συγκαταφλεχθείη	might (?not) be burned together with
. τὸ δὲ κι]βώτιον παρεθή-	b]ox 'he put next to' or 'was cast aside'
κατο] . ὁ Μαντίας	[ ] Mantias
]ν τοῖς ἄρχου-	[ ] to the authorities
σι] . [	] . . [

[15] Parsons 2006a; Schmedt 2020, 291–310.

The details of the action here are far from clear, but they show that the duo of the πηρίδιον, 'little bag', and κιβώτιον, 'box', had already been highlighted at some point earlier in the story than their important part in the events on Thule, perhaps indeed before they were annexed by Mantinias and Dercyllis in Leontinoi. As Parsons noted, there is another little box in the work, the κιβώτιον, 'box', which was found in Tyre to contain the cypress-wood tablets on which the whole story was written. I suggest that the pairing of books and κιβώτιον, 'box', in both places is not due to mere chance. Their use as Paapis' stage-props, which turn out to be crucial to the resurrection of his victims, reminds the reader, both when reading whatever book contained the Leontini episode, and then later when reading the opening of Book 24, that the literary resurrection of the whole story depended on a κιβώτιον, 'little box', whose existence was a pre-condition for the survival of the cypress-wood tablets on which the story of the twenty-four books of Antonius Diogenes had been written. It would perhaps be going too far to claim this as a *mise-en-abyme*, but, in a narrative within which we are insistently being asked to attend to the role of oral narrators,[16] it reminds us that without the magical effect of writing and of books we readers cannot expect access to oral narratives, μυθολογηθέντα, 'tales that are told'.

I have deliberately avoided discussion of the epistles within the story (*PSI* 1177, *P.Oxy*. 3012) since these have recently been discussed by Hans Bernsdorff.[17] But of course they too, as noted already by Stephens and Winkler, display 'a self-consciousness about writing and about the physical media', and emphasise within the story the importance to communication of γράμματα, 'letters', in a way that mirrors the writing down of the story on tablets that readers encounter in a frame which was itself epistolary.[18]

Before leaving Antonius Diogenes let me draw attention to two other details in the first of which, at least, it may be thought that the narrator is playing with modes of transmitting information, while in the second he is revealed as highly conscious of the character of the narrative.

First, the name of his envoy from Arcadia to Tyre whose mission is presented as the catalyst for the recording of the adventures of Deinias

[16] Cf. the well-formulated judgement of Stephens and Winkler 1995, 116: 'In a fairly strong sense, we may say that this is a novel in which many things happened but nothing happens: the only present-time events are acts of narrating and listening. The lovers Deinias and Dercyllis do not have adventures together, they do not woo, they narrate.'

[17] Bernsdorff 2009; Schmedt 2020, 206–70.

[18] Stephens and Winkler 1995, 149.

and Dercyllis on the cypress-wood tablets: Κύμβας, 'Cymbas'.[19] This is an unusual name, and I guess it would have struck an imperial Greek reader as unusual.[20] But I note that among the range of meanings registered by Hesychius κ 4541 Latte *s.v.* κύμβη is to be found the meaning 'knapsack' or 'bag': κύμβη· νεὼς εἶδος. καὶ ὀξύβαφον. καὶ πήρα, 'κύμβη (*kymbē*): a type of ship; and a vinegar jar; and a bag'. Is Diogenes playing with the idea that the vehicle for the transportation to Arcadia of the cypress-tablets bearing the narrative of Deinias' adventures is a Bag, just as it was a bag that carried round the indispensable magic books of Paapis?[21] Note that, at least in Photius' summary, the bag and Cymbas are juxtaposed.[22]

Second, a detail in the other 2006 Oxyrhynchus fragment.[23] My point relates only to column ii 20–4, where Mantias (found as the hero's name in *P.Oxy.* 4760 fr.2.9, just discussed, and already as an alternative form of the hero's name in the manuscripts of Photius), is being pursued by παρθένοι, 'maidens', for reasons which are obscure:

P.Oxy. 4761 col. ii

… διώκουσα̣ι̣ [δὲ	… but pursuing (them)
ἡμέραν ὅλην καὶ νύκτα ἑπόμες-	for a whole day and a night, by their
ναι ἠνώχλουν. ἀλλ' ὁ Μαντία[ς κατ'	chase harassed them. But Mantias by
ἄλλας καὶ ἄλλας σκολιὰς ὁδ[οὺς	one set of twisting paths after another
ὑ̣π̣εξα̣γ̣αγὼν̣ ἔ̣λ̣αθεν ἀφι[κόμενος	getting away from them, arrived undetected
] . […] … . [	[ ]

[19] Phot. *Bibl.* 109b3, 111b27.

[20] The *LGPN* registers Κυμβάδεια, 'Cymbadeia', for Laconia in the third century BC (*SEG* 11.677b); Κύμβαλος 'Cymbalos' for Arcadia in the fourth and third centuries BC (*SEG* 11.1070; *IG* v.2 38.52). No other epigraphic attestation is registered for volumes i–v. It is likely that Κύμβαλος, 'Cymbalos', and certain that Lucian's name Κυμβάλιον, 'Cymbalion' at *DMeretr.* 12.1 and 14.4 (in the first case certainly, and in the second probably, for an *auletris*, 'pipe-player') derive from the Greek word for 'cymbal' (κύμβαλον) and not from κύμβα or κύμβος meaning 'cup' etc.

[21] Against this interpretation, and linking the name with κυμβίον 'drinking-vessel', cf. Hsch. κ 4542 *s.v.* κυμβίον· εἶδος ποτηρίου, καὶ πλοίου, 'κυμβίον: a sort of drinking-vessel; and a sort of ship', see Ruiz Montero 2013, 2017.

[22] ἅπερ αὐτὸς συνείρων εἰσάγεται διηγούμενος τῶι Ἀρκάδι Κύμβαι. ἔπειτα ὡς λαβόντες Μαντινίας καὶ Δερκυλλὶς ἐκ Λεοντίνων τὸ Παάπιδος πηρίδιον …, 'he (sc. Deinias) put these tales together himself and is introduced telling them to the Arcadian Cymbas. Then (he told) how Mantinias and Dercyllis brought Paapi's little bag from Leontini …', 110a15–17.

[23] *P.Oxy.* 4761 = Parsons 2006b; suggestions for supplement and interpretation by Bernsdorff 2006; Schmedt 2020, 310–43.

The strategy adopted by Mantias to secure his escape from this mysterious group of young women is rational and predictable enough in a real situation. But this rapidly narrated episode of Mantias' escape is a *mise-en-abyme* of the deceptive skills shown in the author's own elusive narrative. Any reader hoping for a close encounter with *The incredible things beyond Thule* advertised by the work's title has to wait until Book 24, and is taken on many sets of twisting paths on the way. The chase in *P.Oxy.* 4761 might therefore have as one of its functions the metaliterary role also played by the labyrinthine cave in which Heliodorus has Charicleia secreted and Thisbe killed, a place of darkness and complexity that precipitates confusion and misunderstanding.[24]

3 Textuality and Orality in Longus

As in the novels of Chariton and Antonius Diogenes, so too in *Daphnis and Chloe* there is a clear opposition between stories orally told and the writing down of the text which is the vehicle for conveying these stories to the reader. In some ways the unnamed ἐξηγητὴς τῆς εἰκόνος, 'interpreter of the painting' (*pr.* 3) plays a role like that of Deinias in Antonius Diogenes, while the similarly unnamed narrator who boasts τέτταρας βίβλους ἐξεπονησάμην, 'I have elaborated four books', has the role played in *The incredible things beyond Thule* by the Athenian λόγων τεχνίτης, 'craftsman in words' (i.e. presumably a *rhetor*), Erasinides.[25] But Deinias is narrating his own and others' adventures, while the unnamed 'interpreter of the painting' is working with his eye on a material object which in other ways is like the cypress-wood tablets written in duplicate. Moreover the redundant description of the painting as an εἰκόνος γραφή, 'depiction of a painting', allows Longus to call it simply ἡ γραφή, 'the depiction', in his narrator's mission statement: ἰδόντα με … πόθος ἔσχεν ἀντιγράψαι τῆι γραφῆι, 'a longing seized me when I saw it … to write a pendant to the depiction', giving a *trompe l'oeil* impression of exact correspondence between his highly pictorial narrative and the picture in the cave.[26] The narrating figure of the ἐξηγητής, 'interpreter', thus risks becoming little more than an interface between two forms of γραφή, 'depicting/writing'.

[24] Hld. 1.28–9.

[25] For the phrase used of Erasinides at Phot. *Bibl.* 111a22, 'λόγων τεχνίτης', 'craftsman in words', cf. X.Eph. 3.2.8, where it is used of the profession fraudulently claimed by the rich Byzantine Aristomachus who falls in love with Hyperanthes.

[26] Cf. Philippides 1983.

Once warmed up by this tension in the preface the reader encounters instance after instance of μυθολογήματα, 'tales told'. This particular term μυθολόγημα, 'a tale told', is used only once (2.35.1), where it is applied to story of Syrinx that Lamon tells the company: but the verb μυθολογεῖν, 'to tell a tale', is used of the two other inset tales, those of those of the cow-girl who is turned into a φάττα, 'woodpigeon', in Book 1, and of Echo in Book 3;[27] and the simple noun μῦθος, 'tale', is applied to the stories of Syrinx and of Echo.[28] The couple's response to the oral exposition of Philetas at 2.7.1 is also compared to responses to a μῦθος, 'tale', showing both that 'tales' were reckoned to give pleasure and that what Philetas has been saying is not in all respects, in Longus' terms, a μῦθος, 'tale', however much it may recall a Platonic μῦθος, 'tale'. It is not surprising to find the collective term μυθολογία, 'tales told', used (4.17.3) of Gnathon's learned repertoire, acquired in the symposia of *roués*, i.e. in a context of live story-telling, when he makes a sophistic speech proving that a love-object can well be of a lower status than his or her lover, and cites the cases of Aphrodite's desire for Anchises, Apollo's for Branchus and that of Zeus for Ganymede.

What is, perhaps, surprising is that Pan castigates the impious Methymnan admiral on the grounds that Eros wants to create a μῦθος, 'tale', from Chloe (2.27.2). Coming before the two μῦθοι, 'tales', that illustrate the erotic violence of Pan, but after the use of μῦθος, 'tale', for the story of the metamorphosed cow-girl (1.27.1), this divinely authorised generic classification forces the reader to re-examine the terminology offered by the preface: what the 'interpreter' has told to the writer, and what the painter of the εἰκόνος γραφή, 'depiction of a painting', had previously painted, are to be seen as a μῦθος, 'tale' – and just like the μῦθοι, 'tales' of the cow-girl, Syrinx and Echo, it is an aetiological μῦθος, 'tale', explaining why there is a cult in that particular place that takes that particular form.[29]

That the whole story is a μῦθος, 'tale', albeit a μῦθος, 'tale', in which Eros operates under very different rules from those obtaining in 'classical' μῦθοι, 'tales',[30] may be one of the reasons that Longus has devoted so much πόνος, 'labour', as asserted by his verb ἐξεπονησάμην, 'I have elaborated', to creating a world that exists entirely without texts. Admittedly Longus teases us with the detail that Lamon and Dryas have Daphnis and Chloe taught γράμματα, 'letters' (1.8.1), and he prompts us to see this as fishy by twinning γράμματα,

[27] 1.27.1, 3.22.4, 23.5; cf. 3.9.4. [28] 2.33.3, 35.1, 3.22.4.

[29] For the possible influence of Call. *Aitia* on this aetiological element in *Daphnis and Chloe*, and on other features, see Bowie 2019i (Chapter 45 in this volume).

[30] For the differences see Bowie 2007c (Chapter 31 in this volume).

'letters', with πάντα ὅσα καλὰ ἦν ἐπ' ἀγροικίας, 'all that is reckoned fine in the countryside'. But this knowledge of γράμματα, 'letters', turns out to be superfluous not simply in the country but even in Longus' city, Mytilene. No epistles are sent; no amorous graffiti are carved; no inscriptions identify the paintings or the statue of Eros Ποιμήν, 'Eros the Shepherd', in the cave of the Nymphs, the new temple of Pan Στρατιώτης, 'Pan the Soldier', or even the temple of Dionysus in the garden of Dionysophanes. This is a very different world from the inscription-populated cityscapes in which Longus himself and his (presumably) city-dwelling readers lived. Even the urban members of the cast never resort to writing. The nearest we come to a textually inscribed object is the νεβρὶς βακχική, 'bacchic fawnskin', given by Dorcon to Chloe (1.15.2): καὶ αὐτῆι τὸ χρῶμα ὥσπερ γεγραμμένον χρώμασιν, 'and its colour was as if it was sketched/inscribed with colours'. This non-textual use of γεγραμμένον 'sketched/inscribed', takes us back to the εἰκόνος γραφή of the preface and warns us that within the story the γράμματα, 'letters', taught to Daphnis and Chloe at 1.8.1 will never be realised as an act of writing.

Is Longus' elimination of textuality simply a predictable and logical consequence of his thought-experiment? Perhaps. But Longus constantly reworks the tropes of earlier novelists, and I suggest that in this play with orality and textuality he is also doing this. Just as the pair of digressions parading pseudo-scientific nonsense (1.30.6, 2.1.4) poke fun at such digressions in Achilles Tatius (and, it may be, in Antonius Diogenes and Iamblichus),[31] so too the sharp and scrupulous division between the oral and textual worlds may be there partly to remind us of Antonius Diogenes, to endorse Diogenes' distinction between the orally narrated and the written in his frame, but perhaps also to question the appropriateness of his reliance on a satchel of books and on several written epistles in a fictional world which is so predominantly one of oral narrators. The clue is given in the phrase τέτταρας βίβλους, 'four books' (*pr.* 3). Enumeration of books had become common enough in the prefaces of long histories, sometimes, as in Diodorus Siculus,[32] to help the reader understand how these books were apportioned. Its migration to a fictional work is first attested in the case of Antonius Diogenes, where part of its effect was of course to assimilate the written work to historiography. But a preface proclaiming twenty-four books and announcing that ἀρχαιοτέρων μαρτυρίαι, 'testimonies

[31] Cf. Bowie 2019g, 160. [32] D.S. 1.4–5.

of older people', for τὰ … μυθολογηθέντα, 'the tales told', would be offered for each book was so outrageous as to be a tempting target. Of course, whether Longus is aiming at this target or not, his advertisement of four books, for a reader in whose hands either a codex or a roll would manifestly be the bearer of quite a short work, would be likely to be read as somewhat parodic. Is it any surprise, then, that when Longus surprisingly and incredibly introduces Tyrian pirates (as I believe they indeed are) in the north-eastern Aegean, they resort to a Carian ship to assist their piracy, a ship whose claimed Carian origins[33] takes the connoisseur reader to Caria's greatest city during the empire, Aphrodisias, and to its two founders of imperial Greek fictional narratives, Chariton and Antonius Diogenes?[34]

4 Conclusions

Both Antonius Diogenes and Longus present their narratives in ways that draw attention to the differences between oral story-telling to be heard and the writing down of texts to be read. In each case this ploy may to some extent be prompted by the writers' awareness that their written work stands close to an oral genre or genres likely to be familiar to readers, and it may have as one of its aims the direction of readers' minds to reflect on the way this genre of prose fiction is pioneering a different relation to oral narratives from any exemplified in previous writing, whether poetry or prose. In the case of Antonius Diogenes this interest may be partly explained by his own time of writing being so near to that of the birth of Greek prose fiction. In the case of Longus the explanation may partly be sought in the writer's decision to adopt an entirely new recipe for a novel, drawing on Theocritean bucolic poetry as well as on earlier novels;[35] but some details, particularly Longus' specification of the number of books into which his miniature work is divided, raise the possibility that this focus is also attributable to the influence of Antonius Diogenes.

[33] Τύριοι λῃσταὶ Καρικὴν ἔχοντες ἡμιολίαν, 'Tyrian pirates with a Carian light ship', 1.28.1.

[34] For arguments in favour of Chariton's priority in developing the Greek ideal novel see Bowie 2002a (Chapter 25 in this volume); a full and persuasive case is made by Tilg 2010. For arguments for a similarly early (i.e. mid-first century AD) date for Antonius Diogenes see Bowie 2007d (Chapter 32 in this volume); for an endorsement of the proposal made by Bowersock 1994 that Antonius Diogenes' place of origin was also Aphrodisias, see Bowie 2002a.

[35] For exploration of this recipe see Bowie 2013d (Chapter 38 in this volume), 2021b.

35 Country Virtues, City Vices in Longus, *Daphnis and Chloe*? (2009)

1 Introduction

One often finds comparisons made between Longus' *Daphnis* and *Chloe* and the *Euboean Tale* of Dio of Prusa (*Or.* 7). Both are works in which the virtues of the countryside are paraded and the city is presented as less virtuous. In this respect, however, as in many others, the two works are very different. There is no doubting the predominance of vice in the Euboean city of Dio, nor the predominance of virtue in Dio's Euboean countryside. Longus' world is more complex. Certainly, the virtues of the country-folk are drawn to the reader's attention throughout the novel, and the space given to displaying the virtues of the city-dwellers is much less. But they do have virtues, in many cases the same or similar virtues to those of the country-folk, and although they have vices, they are neither numerous nor predominant. The country-folk have vices too, in some cases corresponding to a city vice, and we should not forget that of the three individuals who behave distinctly badly – Dorcon, Lampis and Gnathon – two are from the country, and one of these, Lampis, is the only one of the three who is not redeemed by a good action. He is indeed present at the wedding at 4.38.2, not because he has done anything to deserve it, but simply because everybody wants to be happy and he is συγγνώμης ἀξιωθείς, 'thought worthy of pardon'.

That pardon has implicitly been granted both by the ἀστικοί, 'city-folk', and the country people involved in the wedding. This brings out what seems to me an important objective of Longus in his representation of virtues and vices: he presents the rural system of morality as parallel and similar to that of the city, not as essentially different. The consequence is not, therefore, that, as in Dio's *Euboean Tale*, we form sharply different evaluations of city and country morality, but that we, urban readers as we surely are, build up a picture of the rural system of values that becomes increasingly recognisable as a variant upon that with which we are familiar in our cities, and that may occasionally help us to understand better how that civic system operates.

The most important component of this paper is Tables 35.1 and 35.2, in which I have attempted to set out the virtues and vices displayed and the places in the text they are encountered. It has not been straightforward. The division between virtues of ἦθος, 'character',[1] and of πρᾶξις, 'action', could be objected to in principle, and may not have been correctly made in every case. Under the category 'virtues of πρᾶξις' are a number of activities which are admired in the country and whose performance brings social credit, such as singing and dancing, but we may not all be ready to agree that the ability to sing or to dance is a 'virtue'. The ability and commitment to look after a herd of sheep or goats, to ensure that it grows in number (see Table 35.2 under 'εὖ *νέμειν*'), and to do other farming tasks,[2] certainly constitute the ἀρετή, 'excellence', of the herdsman and farmer respectively – they are what mark out an αἰπόλος ἀγαθός, 'good goatherd', from an αἰπόλος κακός, 'bad goatherd': but they do not constitute a moral virtue. They do, however, play their part in prompting reflection on the comparison between the rural and city economy. We know fairly well by the end of the novel what must be done in the country to generate a surplus. We also know that in the city Megacles turned out to be much more successful financially than he expected he would be when he exposed Chloe, 4.35.2–4, but we are not told what he did to bring about this financial success. Perhaps we should simply infer that he was lucky to have good αἰπόλοι, 'goatherds', and ποιμένες, 'shepherds', and simply watched the profits coming in.

Another respect in which the construction of the table has not been straightforward is that some πράξεις, 'actions', performed either by country-folk or by city people, are presented as praised or at least approved of by both. In those cases I have entered the *locus* in both the country and the city columns.

2 Piety and Impiety

The most obvious feature of my tables is the large number of entries that I have grouped under εὐσέβεια, 'piety', though that term does not itself appear in Longus. Human recognition of gods, offering of regular cult and obedience to divine commands (invariably communicated in dreams), and consequent divine aid to human beings, constitute the novel's most important

[1] For Longus' drawing of character see De Temmerman 2014, 207–45. For less generous but well-argued views of his presentation of city-dwellers see Saïd 1987; Whitmarsh 2008a, 76–9.

[2] For agricultural tasks see 3.29.2–3, 4.1.3.

theme after that of young people's discovery of ἔρως, 'sexual desire'.[3] It is as a part of this fully-functional religious system that we read of Daphnis, Chloe and the other members of the rural community making regular offerings and occasional sacrifices. Daphnis and Chloe have a temporary and it seems venial lapse from εὐσέβεια when they initially fail to honour the image of Pan which they pass every day (2.23.4, remedied at 2.31.2–3). But the only perpetrators of ἀσέβεια, 'impiety', are the Methymnans, who dragged off Chloe from the cave of the Nymphs where she had sought refuge as a suppliant (2.20.3). For this reason they are addressed by Pan, appearing in a dream to their general Bryaxis, as πάντων ἀνοσιώτατοι καὶ ἀσεβέστατοι, 'of all men the most unholy and impious'. Indeed in his account of what they have done he heightens their sacrilege by saying they have dragged Chloe from altars (2.27.2). This is the first and last we read of altars to the Nymphs in their cave: Pan may be suspected of elevating the scene by assimilating it to the famous incident when the lesser Ajax dragged Cassandra from the altar of Athena during the sack of Troy.

Dorcon also calls the pirates who kill him ἀσεβεῖς, 'impious', in his dying speech at 1.29.1, likewise elevated by an epic allusion, κατέκοψαν ὡς βοῦν, 'they cut me down like an ox'.[4] Such imprecision is not surprising in moments of stress,[5] and here it may be seen as some sort of *prolepsis* of what will follow in Book 2.

The ἀσεβέστατοι Methymnans are an exception to the general pattern to which Longus' city-dwellers also conform. As well as having built an altar and *tempietto* to Dionysus in his rural παράδεισος, 'formal garden' or 'park' (4.3), Daphnis' real father Dionysophanes sacrifices to the gods of the countryside on his arrival at his country estate (4.13.3), adding Demeter and Dionysus to those already well-known to the reader, Pan and the Nymphs; to Zeus Soter, when Daphnis' identification as his son is celebrated by a symposium (4.25.2); and again to the country gods at 4.26.1 and at the party celebrating Chloe's identification as Megacles' daughter (4.32.3). The final party at 4.38 presumably includes sacrifices, but these are not mentioned.

Megacles too, Chloe's real father, is presented as εὐσέβης, 'pious'. When he decided he must expose Chloe he entrusted her to the Nymphs (4.35.4); to the Nymphs he dedicated her γνωρίσματα when she was returned to him by them (4.37.2); and in their presence he formally gave Chloe to her husband (4.37.2).

3 For a sketch see Bowie 2019g, 8–11.

4 Cf. Od. 4.535 (= 11.411) of Agamemnon's murder ὥς τίς τε κατέκτανε βοῦν ἐπὶ φάτνῃ, 'like someone who slaughters an ox by its manger'.

5 Cf. Ch. 1.5.5, 4.3.6, Ach. Tat. 7.5.4.

3 Deception

Another respect in which country and city march in step is in the moral acceptance of what in English is called a 'white lie', a lie told by a good person for a good τέλος, 'end'. There are many precedents in Greek literature for such *suppressio veri* or *suggestio falsi*. The sum of human happiness is increased, not reduced, by Chloe's silence about Dorcon's dying kiss (1.31.2), silence which she observes impelled by the good quality αἰδώς, 'sense of shame', displayed only by country-folk, even indeed by Dorcon (1.21.3), and spectacularly ignored by the ἀσεβέστατοι Methymnans (2.27.3). Chloe's silence makes it easier for the reader not to condemn Daphnis' silence concerning his sexual initiation by Lycaenion, or indeed Lycaenion's elaborate charade to deceive Daphnis, Chloe and her husband Chromis. Earlier in Book 1 we are not expected, I think, to condemn Daphnis and Chloe for deciding to pretend that wolves had taken the billy-goat who fell into the wolf-trap and was given to Dorcon in reward for his assistance (1.12.5), and indeed to bathe Daphnis carefully so that the whole incident would never be known to his parents (1.12.5–13).[6]

Of course these lies are necessary to the forward movement of the story, not just to the tranquillity of its characters. Indeed the whole plot depends on the initial deception perpetrated by Lamon and Myrtale, and by Dryas and Nape, in pretending that the babies they found exposed were in fact their own. Deception continues to play a role in Daphnis' attempt to see Chloe in winter (3.4.5ff), in their parents' negotiations with each other over the marriage, and in the final book in Astylus' readiness to conceal from his father the correct explanation for the vandalising of his rural παράδεισος (4.10.2). It might be added that in Book 4 it is implicit, although never stated, that Dionysophanes, Cleariste, Megacles and Rhodē have been deceiving their fellow city aristocrats for some fifteen years by concealing their exposure of Daphnis and Chloe.

4 τέχνη

The matter of deception is related to that of τέχναι, 'tricks' and τέχνη, 'artifice'. On the one hand rustic naivety is presented as admirable, if on occasion somewhat ridiculous. Chloe's passing on of Dorcon's gifts to Daphnis (1.15.3) betrays her charming unawareness of lovers' manoeuvres, just as in Book 4.12.2 does Daphnis' slowness to realise what Gnathon is proposing;

[6] In fact Daphnis had never lost a single she-goat to a wolf, 4.4.3.

but the kiss Chloe gives Daphnis at 1.17.1 is in no way lacking in erotic power for being ἀδίδακτον μὲν καὶ ἄτεχνον. Famously, when Daphnis learns the ἔργα ἔρωτος from Lycaenion (3.18.4), it is a combination of the experienced woman acting ἐντέχνως,[7] 'with accomplished skill', and the mobilisation of φύσις, 'nature', which leads to the desired result.

These instances of human behaviour are part of the larger web of contrasts and complementarities between φύσις and τέχνη which embraces both the couple's sexual activity – or the lack of it – and the complementarity of art and nature in the creation of *loci amoeni* like the cave of the Nymphs, the garden of Philetas, and the παράδεισος of Dionysophanes.[8] In the matter of products of τέχνη it is almost exclusively those produced in the country that are on display: the cave and gardens just mentioned; the pan-pipe; tunes for managing cows (Dorcon, 1.30.1) and goats (Daphnis, 4.15.2–4); the meticulously constructed wolf-trap; singing, dancing and even (as it were) story-telling. Almost the only urban products of τέχνη introduced into the main narrative are the luxurious villas and spas on the coast along which the holidaying Methymnans travel. We see them through their eyes (2.12.2): τὰ μὲν φύσεως ἔργα, τὰ δὲ ἀνθρώπων τέχνη. The narrator had told us at 1.1.1 of the marble splendours of the city of Mytilene: we might expect that when Daphnis and Chloe are taken there we will be given their perspective (cf. the opening of Achilles Tatius' Book 5 on Alexandria): but we hear nothing more of the city, nor any detail of Dionysophanes' mansion, a deliberate silence from which we are slightly distracted by the narrator's observation that the party arrived in Mytilene during the night (4.33.3).

At a rather lower level of culture the presentation of *haute cuisine* is ambivalent. At 4.15.4 we read of Daphnis enjoying the new taste of ἀστικὴ ὀψαρτυσία, 'fine urban cuisine': it seems to be neutral. In the next paragraph Gnathon characterises himself as having hitherto been more interested in τοὺς σοὺς ὀψαρτυτάς, 'your chefs', than in the ephebes of Mytilene, and we form a view of *haute cuisine* as part of an urban life-style that is not admirable. Perhaps Longus is having his patisserie and eating it.

Similarly, excessive drinking by the urban Gnathon seems to be bad (4.11.2, 12.3), whereas when old rustics get a bit tipsy it is simply charming (2.32.2). Gnathon's activity of λαγνεύειν, 'fornication' (4.11.2) is disturbingly close to what Daphnis and Chloe try to do for four books of the novel, but perhaps its combination with his inebriation and his preference for young male partners differentiates it.

[7] On ἐντέχνως see Bowie 2019g, 240 *ad loc.*

[8] For φύσις and τέχνη in Longus see Teske 1991; Whitmarsh 2001, 82–3; Bowie 2019g, 12–14.

5 Fear and Boldness

There is also ambiguity in presentation of the range of behaviour between φόβος, 'fear', and τόλμα, 'boldness'. The two cases in which fear is certainly represented as good both concern fathers who fear that they may make a move that is not the best for their daughter or daughter-in-law, in each case Chloe: Dryas δείσας, 'fearing' (1.19.3), Dionysophanes δεδοικώς, 'feeling fear' (4.31.1). In this context 'fear' is 'a concern lest something undesirable may happen'. What is important is that Longus offers us closely similar cases in the person of the rustic step-father and of the urban father-in-law-to-be of Chloe. Less obviously laudable is the ὄκνος, 'hesitation', about raising a daughter in πενία, 'poverty', that persuaded Megacles to expose Chloe as a baby (4.35.3). In a sense Megacles made the wrong decision, because he became rich again soon.

There are other cases where fear is to some degree laudable. It is φόβωι τῶν ἀγερώχων ποιμένων, 'from fear of the self-assertive shepherds', that Chloe goes out later to the pastures than Daphnis (1.28.2), and this is a reasonable emotion in an attractive young girl: it distinguishes her from τις τῶν θρασυτέρων, 'one of the bolder women', who kisses Daphnis during the vintage (2.2.1). When Chloe exhibits sudden panic as her face is brushed by the swallow's wings (1.26.2) we are invited to laugh with Daphnis at her δέος/φόβος, 'fear', because it is groundless. But we are laughing because she misclassified the situation, not because fear at a touch on the cheek is always inappropriate. It could have been a wolf's tail. And of course, like the departure for the pastures, it builds up a picture of the girl Chloe as gentler and less self-assertive than the boy Daphnis. Thus, on the arrival of Dionysophanes' entourage (4.13), Chloe takes refuge in the woods ὄχλον τοσοῦτον αἰδεσθεῖσα καὶ φοβηθεῖσα, 'embarrassed and afraid at so large a crowd' (4.14.1). Earlier, however, both felt anxiety and fear at the prospect of their unfamiliar master's visit to his estates: ὁ Δάφνις ἀγωνιῶν τῆι Χλόηι συνένεμεν. εἶχε δὲ κἀκείνη πολὺ δέος, 'It was with anxiety that Daphnis grazed alongside Chloe: and she too felt great fear' (4.6.2), compare καθάπερ ἤδη παρόντα τὸν δεσπότην φοβουμένων ἢ λανθανόντων, 'as if they were afraid of or hiding from a master who was already there'.[9]

Shortly after this, when Lampis has vandalised the παράδεισος, the whole family, Lamon, Myrtale and Daphnis, justifiably feel fear at the consequences – especially justifiable in Lamon's case since he expects to be hung (4.8, esp. 4.8.1).

[9] 4.6.3. For the fear marking the relationship of Longus' slaves to their masters see Bowie 2019b (Chapter 43 in this volume).

In a number of situations it is clear that fear is not an appropriate reaction for a male. Daphnis himself is told by Lycaenion that he must not be afraid if Chloe bleeds when he deflowers her (3.19.3); he has to be told by Astylus not to be afraid when he is being pursued by the congratulatory crowd (4.22.3). We know that Daphnis overcomes fear in both cases. We are not told how Gnathon overcame the fear that led him to take refuge in the temple of Dionysus (4.25.2), but that he stayed there a night and a day presents him as excessively vulnerable to fear: compare his remark καίτοι τίς οὐκ ἂν ἐραστὴν ἠλέησεν, ὃν ἔδει φοβεῖσθαι τὸν ἐρώμενον, 'but who would have felt no pity for a lover who had to be afraid of his beloved?' (4.17.4).

The Methymnans' reactions to Pan's miracles are quite a different matter: gods are at work, and men have no control. That Bryaxis is τεθορηβημένος, 'in a confused state' (2.28.1), after the dream that orders Chloe's release is inevitable: it does not reflect on his general character.

Overall, more questions can be asked about the fear displayed by city- than by country-folk, but a fairer division would put Gnathon in one category, that of the δειλός,[10] 'coward', and all the rest in another.

The same perhaps applies to displays of θρασύτης, 'boldness' or 'confidence'. Gnathon is described as θρασυνομένου, 'blustering', and threatening to beat Lamon up when he makes his revelation about Daphnis' exposure (4.20.1): this behaviour is presented as bad. By contrast, the θρασύτης which makes Daphnis more forward than Chloe is a sign that he is entering ἥβη, 'adolescence': οἷα γοῦν ἐφηβήσας τῆι κατὰ τὸν χειμῶνα οἰκουρίαι ..., 'indeed since he had entered adolescence in the time spent at home during the winter ...' (3.13.4).

6 A Conclusion

It should be clear by now why a question mark is placed at the end of my title. Longus' novel does not assign virtues to the country and vices to the city, but in his portrayal of the countryside he offers a moral world parallel to that of the city. Upright people and good actions outnumber base people and bad actions in both; and on occasion extremely reprehensible behaviour – that of Dorcon, of the young Methymnans, of Gnathon, and of Lampis – contributes to throwing into relief the overall pattern of praiseworthy conduct. The country's vices prompt readers to reflection as much as do its virtues.

[10] Cf. Arist. *EN* 1115b33.

Table 35.1 *Virtues of ἦθος in country and city in Longus, Daphnis and Chloe*

Virtue: ἦθος	Country	City	Vice	Country	City
ἀγαθὸς εἶναι	3.31.3; 4.19.5	4.18.1, 19.5			
ἀγερωχία	2.32.1		ἀγερωχία	1.28.2; 4.7.1	
αἰδώς	1.3.1–2, 21.2(?), 25.1, 31.2; (2.10.3); 4.14.1, 3		ἀναιδεία	2.27.2	
			ἀμαθία	3.14.5	
ἀπειρία	1.21.5				
τὸ ἄτεχνον	1.15.3, 17.1; (4.12.2)	4.20.2			
			δειλία	1.25.3	
δικαιοσύνη	1.27.1; 3.31.1	2.19.3			
ἔλεος	1.6.1; 2.23.2			4.17.4	
εὐνομία	1.5.1				
εὐσέβεια	*pr.*; 1.6.1; 2.2.4–6, 22.1, 23.4, 24.2, 30.5, 31, 38.1, 3; 3.9.2, 12.2–4, 17.3, 27.1; 4.(10.3), 26.2–4, 32.3–4, 39.1–2	4.3.1–2, 13.3, 25.2, 26.1, 32.3, 33.4, 35.4, 37.2	ἀσέβεια	2.39.6?	1.29.1; 2.20.3, 27.1
θρασύτης	3.13.4 (26.1)			4.20.1	
καρτερία	2.8.5; 4.28.2				
μεγαλοφροσύνη		4.17.1			
οἶκτος	1.2.1; 2.17.1; 3.6.5; 4.10.1–2				
			ὀργή	1.12.2; 2.34.3; 3.(8.2), 23.3, 34.2; 4.10.1	
πίστις	2.39.4, 6; 3.32.3				
σωφροσύνη		(3.1–2)			
τόλμα	2.10.3, (16.1); 3.26.1–3, 34.2; 4.18.2, 28.2				
φιλανθρωπία	1.3.1				
φιλία	1.6.1, 3, 8.3, (12.3–4); 3.30.3; 4.(6.2), (18.3), 19.4, 24.3	4.18.1. 19.4. 24.3	ἔχθρα	4.7.5	
φιλοτιμία	(1.16, 27.4)				

Table 35.2 *Virtues of πρᾶξις in country and city in Longus, Daphnis and Chloe*

Virtue: πρᾶξις	Country	City	Vice	Country	City
ἄιδειν	2.2.6, 3.2, 31.2; 3.9.4, 11.2, 21.2, 23.2, 24.2; 4.38.3, 40.2				
ἀκρίβεια	1.12.2; 3.12.4, 16.1	4.31.1			
ἀληθεύειν	4.19.3, 22.4	4.19.3, 22.4			
ἀποκερδαίνειν	3.25.3				
αὐτάρκεια/εὐτέλεια	(1.16.4; 4.39.1)		τρυφᾶν	4.28.3	
βιάζεσθαι		4.29.2		(1.15.1, 20.1); 2.34.2 (×2); 4.28.1	4.12.3
γείτων εἶναι ἀγαθός	3.29.3, 31.1				
διδάσκειν	*pr.* 3; 1.6.1; 3.17.2–3				
δῶρα δοῦναι/ ἀφθονία	1.19.2; 2.8.1; 3.15.3, 17.2–3, 27.2; 4.6.1, 14.3, 25.3	4.33.2, (35.3), 37.2			
ἐνεργεῖν	3.8.2, 18.4				
ἐπιμελεῖσθαι/μέλειν	2.31.1; (4.4.3, 39.1)	4.31.1	ἀμελεῖν	1.15.3; 2.39.3; 3.7.1, 34.2; 4.25.1, (27), 29.5, 36.2	
εὖ νέμειν, cf. εὐνομία	1.8.2, 12.5, 13.4; 3.29.2–3; 4.4.(3), 4, 14.3				
εὐνοεῖν		4.9.3			
κάμνειν	1.14.4, (17.4), 22.2, 23.3, 30.4; 2.4.3				
καταφρονεῖν	2.16.1			1.15.1; 2.34.2	4.17.6
κλαίειν τὸν ἀποθανόντα	1.29.3; (4.32.4)				
			κλέπτειν	(2.13.1)	
κοινωνεῖν	1.10.3; 4.4.5, 9.3, 18.2, (38.4)			4.26.1	
			λαγνεύειν		4.11.2
			λοιδορεῖν	3.26.3	

Virtue: πρᾶξις	Country	City	Vice	Country	City
μεθύειν	(2.32.2)				4.11.2, 12.3
μιμεῖσθαι	1.9.2; 2.35.4			3.14.5, 16.1	4.17.6
			μιαρία		4.18.3
			μνησικακεῖν	4.24.3, 29.4	4.24.3, 29.4
μυθολογεῖν	(*pr.*) 1.27.1; 2.33.3; 3.9.4, 22.4				
ὀρχεῖσθαι	2.36–7; 3.23.2; 4.3.2, 38.3				
ὀψαρτυσία				4.15.4	4.16.2
παραμυθεῖσθαι	1.21.5; 3.30.3				
πολυτέλεια		2.12.2; 4.23.2, 38.2			4.16.3?
πονεῖν	*pr.* 3; 2.4.3				
σοφίζεσθαι/σόφισμα/τέχναι	1.11.2, 12.3–4, 30.5; 3.4.5, 15.3, 18.4; (4.2–3)	4.32.1	ἐπιτεχνᾶσθαι	1.15.3, 20.1; 4.7.2	
συγγνώμης ἀξιοῦν τινα	4.38.2	4.38.2			
τιμᾶν τὸν εὐεργέτην	1.31.1				
			φθονεῖν	1.27.2?; 3.23.3	4.35.2
φιλοφρονεῖσθαι	3.31.4				
φοβεῖσθαι/δεδοικέναι/ὀκνεῖν	1.19.3, 28.2	4.31.1, (35.3)		1.26.2; 3.19.3; 4.6.(2), 3, 8.1, 14.1, 24.3	4.17.4, 22.3, 25.2
χαρίζεσθαι (cf. δῶρα δοῦναι)	1.15.3, 29.3; 2.37.3; 3.17.3	4.12.4, 15.1–4			
ψεύδεσθαι/ἀπατᾶν		4.10.2	ψεύδεσθαι/ἀπατᾶν	1.12.5–6, 31.2; 3.10.4, 20.2, 23.5.(31)	
ὠφελεῖν	2.1.3				

36 Socrates' Cock and Daphnis' Goats: The Rarity of Vows in the Religious Practice of the Greek Novels (2012)

1 Introduction

Our five surviving Greek pagan novels, often termed 'ideal novels', are in many ways highly realistic. The world they present is of men, women, children, animals, cities, countrysides, mountains, rivers, seas and ships comfortably within the experience of their first readers, whether direct experiences from their own lives in the Greek cities of the eastern Mediterranean or the vicarious experiences derived from reading historical, geographical, or periegetic texts. We are often tempted to think we are reading about something which might 'actually' have happened, but which simply fell outside the brief of a historian such as Thucydides or Philistus.[1] The extent and manner of the novelists' challenges to our belief in the 'reality' of their narratives vary in interesting ways,[2] but overall these challenges are outweighed by the provision of apparently convincing detail. Upon the interpreter of the Greek novels as an important phenomenon in Western European literature, therefore, there presses the recurrent question of how some detail resembles or differs from 'real' life, and what such resemblances or differences mean for our understanding of the text. For the historian of culture and society, on the other hand, there is a constant temptation to draw upon the novels to supplement the lacunose reconstruction of the procedures and habits of imperial Greek society that we can attempt on the basis of other literary texts and of archaeology, epigraphy and numismatics.[3]

[1] Parts of this chapter were presented to an Apuleius conference in Rostock in 2008 organised by Christiane Reitz and Wytse Keulen; to the 2009 meeting of the biennial 'Colloque roman' organised in Tours by Bernard Pouderon and Cécile Bost-Pouderon; and to audiences in Ohio State and Notre Dame Universities in spring 2010. I am grateful to the audiences on these occasions for valuable discussion.

[2] See Morgan 1993; Whitmarsh 2011.

[3] I discussed some of these issues, and drew attention to some details concerning which the novels seemed to offer material valuable for historians, in Bowie 1977 (Chapter 19 in this volume). This chapter attempts to some extent to make amends for the fact that a full text of that paper was never published. Millar 1981 exploited Apuleius' *Metamorphoses* very effectively for historical information on Roman Greece; Thomas 1995 has used the Greek novels to cast some light on Ephesus. For earlier work on *Realien* in Longus see Morgan 1998, 2243–7. Mason 1979, 1995 and 2019 publish some of the important work he has done in establishing Lesbian

One area in which one might expect information that might supplement contemporary documents of other sorts is religion. All five novels present a world in which religion is of great importance[4] – so much so that, notoriously, Kerényi, Chalk, and Merkelbach argued that they were (in different ways) mystery texts. Not many other scholars have been persuaded of their theses, and several might acquiesce in the view that the novelists, writing in a world where traditional Greek religion remained central to the lives of the inhabitants of Greek cities, albeit now competing with Mithraism, Christianity and (on a different level) the imperial cult, represented their characters in a wholly realistic way – convinced of the existence and intervention of divine powers, and of the importance of securing their support and benevolence by worship and dedications. Within those holding this sort of view there remains plenty of room for disagreement as to whether the writer manipulates the mode of divinities' control and interventions (and of his characters' awareness and reaction to these) to the point where a reader might conclude that 'fate' means little more than 'the plot as constructed by the author' (as argued by Morgan for Heliodorus) or whether we should see a serious attempt by the author to render the complexity of humans' views of the divine.[5]

It does not seem to me that the representation of religion in Chariton, Xenophon, Achilles Tatius and Heliodorus gives it less importance than it had in Greek civic societies of the imperial period as we can reconstruct them from literary texts, epigraphy and archaeology. But it does seem that many of the constituent acts of religious ritual are presented incompletely, even defectively: these authors' divine chariot is firing on at least one cylinder less than it should. How this should be explained will have to wait until we have looked at some of the evidence. In Longus, on the other hand, it seems to me that we have what is almost hyper-religion – a rural society that is scrupulous in the extreme in following the traditional praxis of polytheistic paganism, that hardly omits a conventional act, and that in this respect, as in some others, is contrasted with some less attractive examples of urban practice on Lesbos.[6] I am uncertain whether this should be seen chiefly as a thought-experiment – what would it be like for religion

Realien in *Daphnis and Chloe*: for important unpublished work see https://utoronto.academia.edu/HughMason. But so far as I know no thorough and comprehensive work has been done on *Realien* in the Greek novels overall. I have not seen Avaert 1948.

[4] For a concise but rich, nuanced, and very stimulating essay on religion in the novels see Zeitlin 2008. For a systematic analysis of many features see Alperowitz 1992.

[5] So Dowden 1996; Dowden 2010.

[6] See Bowie 2009b (of which Chapter 35 in this volume is an English version).

to be practised by ἄγροικοι, 'rustics', uncorrupted by city *mores*? If it were, it would be an experiment that the author was running in parallel with his thought-experiment with naïve young people's discovery of sex. Or does it in some way reflect the attribution to ἄγροικοι, *pagani*, of a purer form of traditional Greek religion that pleases the pious narrator constructed by the author right from the preface.

Whichever of these explanations comes nearer the truth, the presence in *Daphnis and Chloe* of an apparently fully-functional religious system makes it best to begin there and then move on to see in what ways religion's representation in Chariton, Xenophon, Achilles Tatius and Heliodorus can be claimed to be defective. I shall examine a range of constituents of religious practice, but I omit priests, which have been the subject of a recent and authoritative study by Jan Bremmer.[7]

2 Religion in Longus, *Daphnis and Chloe*

Gods in Longus, who are of course predominantly the gods of the country, are regularly the recipients of worship and offerings, made especially, but not only, by Daphnis and Chloe, who on occasion show their gratitude for these offerings. Early in Book 1 we read that in the Nymphs' cave there were πρεσβυτέρων ποιμένων ἀναθήματα, 'offerings by shepherds of earlier generations' (1.4.3), and a little later that the teen couple regularly offer στεφανίσκους, 'little garlands', to the Nymphs (1.9.2: cf. 1.13.4). An explicit statement of the couple's piety and its rewards is made early in Book 2:

> καὶ μάλα χαίροντες τὰς Νύμφας προσεκύνουν, βότρυς αὐταῖς κομίζοντες ἐπὶ κλημάτων, ἀπαρχὰς τοῦ τρυγητοῦ. οὐδὲ τὸν πρότερον χρόνον ἀμελῶς ποτε παρῆλθον, ἀλλ' ἀεί τε ἀρχόμενοι νομῆς προσήδρευον καὶ ἐκ νομῆς ἀνιόντες προσεκύνουν, καὶ πάντως τι ἐπέφερον, ἢ ἄνθος ἢ ὀπώραν ἢ φυλλάδα χλωρὰν ἢ γάλακτος σπονδήν. καὶ τούτου μὲν ὕστερον ἀμοιβὰς ἐκομίσαντο παρὰ τῶν θεῶν.

> And (sc. after the vintage) they joyfully saluted the Nymphs, bringing them grapes on their stalks as first-fruits of the vintage. Nor indeed on previous occasions had they ever neglected them when they passed, but always when beginning their grazing they would attend them and

[7] Bremmer 2012; for priests in the imperial period see Bremmer 2011 (which I was very grateful for the opportunity to read before publication). For the absence of priests from *Daphnis and Chloe* see Bowie 2015c (Chapter 39 in this volume).

> returning from their grazing they would salute them and would make some offering whatever the situation, either a flower or a piece of fruit or a green shoot or a libation of milk:[8] and for this they later got rewards from the gods.
>
> Longus, *Daphnis and Chloe* 2.2.4–5

Again in Book 3, on the arrival of spring, the couple ran to the Nymphs' cave, to Pan and to his pine, garlanded their ἀγάλματα, 'statues', poured libations, and ἀπήρξαντο καὶ τῆς σύριγγος, 'made a musical first-offering with the panpipe' (3.12.4).[9] This helps us understand Philetas' earlier statement: 'πολλὰ μὲν ταῖσδε ταῖς Νύμφαις ἦισα, πολλὰ δὲ τῶι Πανὶ ἐκείνωι ἐσύρισα', 'I have often sung to these Nymphs, I have often piped to Pan over there' (2.3.2) – these musical performances are offerings to the Nymphs and to Pan.[10] Similarly in Book 4 we read that Lamon had often garlanded Dionysus in Dionysophanes' elaborate garden with its flowers:

> οὐδὲ σύ, δέσποτα Διόνυσε, τὰ ἄθλια ταῦτα ἠλέησας ἄνθη, οἷς παρώικεις, ἃ ἔβλεπες, ἀφ' ὧν ἐστεφάνωσά σε πολλάκις;
>
> Did not even you, lord Dionysus, take pity on these wretched flowers beside which you dwelt, upon which you gazed, from which I often made garlands for you?
>
> Longus, *Daphnis and Chloe* 4.8.4

These offerings and acts of worship are performed in the clear general expectation that the gods reward piety. Particular acts of divine assistance are recognised in various ways. At entry level, as it were, on the morning after the Nymphs have told Daphnis in a dream where to find a purse containing 3000 drachmae, he goes to the beach only after greeting them,[11] and when he duly finds the purse he is said to have acknowledged the help of both the Nymphs and the sea:

[8] A simplification of normal practice, in which milk might be offered mixed with honey (μελίκρατον, cf. LSJ *s.v.*) or along with libations of wine, water or honey (cf. Eur. *IT* 159–68, Aes. *Pers.* 611–17): see Graf 1980 (I am grateful to Jan Bremmer for drawing my attention to this article).

[9] On libations cf. 'Apollonius' in Philostr. *VA* 4.20.

[10] For the great importance of music in *Daphnis and Chloe* see Maritz 1991; Morgan 1994; Montiglio 2012.

[11] Compare how at 2.38.3, on the day after the party celebrating Chloe's recovery, it is only after προσαγορεύσαντες, 'saluting', the Nymphs and then Pan that the couple indulging in music and kissing.

καὶ τὰς Νύμφας προσκυνήσας κατῆλθεν ἐπὶ θάλασσαν … οὐ πρόσθεν ἀπῆλθε, πρὶν τὰς Νύμφας εὐφημῆσαι καὶ αὐτὴν τὴν θάλασσαν.

And after greeting the Nymphs he (sc. Daphnis) went down to the sea … and he did not depart before he had ritually praised the Nymphs and the sea itself.

Longus, *Daphnis and Chloe* 3.28.2–3

The addition here of αὐτὴν τὴν θάλασσαν, 'the sea itself', is a rhetorical trope which must be admitted slightly to dilute the cocktail of piety: we shall encounter such hype more prominently in the other four novelists. At the opposite end of the scale of thanksgiving are the actions of Daphnis and Chloe near the end of the narrative:

καὶ τὸ ἄντρον ἐκόσμησαν καὶ εἰκόνας ἀνέθεσαν καὶ βωμὸν εἵσαντο Ποιμένος Ἔρωτος· καὶ τῶι Πανὶ δὲ ἔδοσαν ἀντὶ τῆς πίτυος οἰκεῖν *νεών*, Πανὸς Στρατιώτου ὀνομάσαντες.

And they beautified the cave and dedicated images and established an altar of Eros the Shepherd; and to Pan too they gave a temple to dwell in instead of his pine-tree, giving him the title 'Pan the Soldier'.

Longus, *Daphnis and Chloe* 4.39.2

A more frequent mode of recognition is sacrifice and associated banqueting. Like offerings, sacrifices can be part of a regular, usually annual, calendar, and in Longus they usually have all the traditional elements. Thus in Book 3 Dryas' mid-winter festival of Dionysus involves sacrifice, libations, ivy-garlands, and ritual cries:

καὶ ἀπαρξάμενοι τῶι Διονύσωι κρατῆρος ἤσθιον κιττῶι τὰς κεφαλὰς ἐστεφανωμένοι. καὶ ἐπεὶ καιρὸς ἦν, ἰακχάσαντες καὶ εὐάσαντες προέπεμπον τὸν Δάφνιν …

and after making an offering to Dionysus of the first wine from the mixing bowl they ate, their heads garlanded with ivy; and when the time came they sent Daphnis off with cried of 'Iacchus!' and 'Euhoe!' …

Longus, *Daphnis and Chloe* 3.11.1–2

Again in Book 4 Dionysophanes, on the first day of his tour of the estate on which Daphnis and Chloe are his slaves, gives priority to sacrifices and ritual banqueting:

οὗτος ἐλθὼν τῆι πρώτηι μὲν ἡμέραι θεοῖς ἔθυσεν, ὅσοι προεστᾶσιν ἀγροικίας, Δήμητρι καὶ Διονύσωι καὶ Πανὶ καὶ Νύμφαις, καὶ κοινὸν πᾶσι τοῖς παροῦσιν ἔστησε κρατῆρα …

He (sc. Dionysophanes) arrived and on the first day sacrificed to the gods who preside over the countryside, Demeter and Dionysus and Pan and Nymphs, and he set up a mixing bowl for all those who were present to share.

Longus, *Daphnis and Chloe* 4.13.3

This expression ἔστησε κρατῆρα, 'he set up a mixing bowl' (cf. 4.32.3), seems to refer to the provision of wine for festivity and may be assumed to include libations,[12] though Longus does not specify these here. Again, later in Book 4, when Daphnis has been recognised as the son of Dionysophanes, there is a sacrifice and a lavish feast:

οἱ δὲ θύσαντες Διὶ Σωτῆρι συμπόσιον συνεκρότουν … ἅμα ἕωι συνέτρεχον ἄλλος ἀλλαχόθεν … ὁ δὲ Διονυσοφάνης κατεῖχε πάντας κοινωνοὺς μετὰ τὴν εὐφροσύνην καὶ τῆς ἑορτῆς ἐσομένους. παρεσκεύαστο δὲ πολὺς μὲν οἶνος, πολλὰ δὲ ἄλευρα, ὄρνιθες ἕλειοι, χοῖροι γαλαθηνοί, μελιτώματα ποικίλα· καὶ ἱερεῖα δὲ πολλὰ τοῖς ἐπιχωρίοις θεοῖς ἐθύετο.

And they sacrificed to Zeus Soter and knocked together a symposium … at dawn people hurried there from every direction … and Dionysophanes kept them all there to share not just in his good cheer but in a banquet too. And much wine was prepared, much wheat-bread, marsh birds, sucking pigs, various sorts of honey cakes; and many sacrificial animals were offered to the local gods.

Longus, *Daphnis and Chloe* 4.25.2–26

Immediately after this elaborate ceremony Daphnis dedicates his pastoral gear to the gods who have watched over him:

ἐνταῦθα ὁ Δάφνις συναθροίσας πάντα τὰ ποιμενικὰ κτήματα διένειμεν ἀναθήματα τοῖς θεοῖς. τῶι Διονύσωι μὲν ἀνέθηκε τὴν πήραν καὶ τὸ δέρμα, τῶι Πανὶ τὴν σύριγγα καὶ τὸν πλάγιον αὐλόν, τὴν καλαύροπα ταῖς Νύμφαις καὶ τοὺς γαυλοὺς οὓς αὐτὸς ἐτεκτήνατο.

Then Daphnis gathered together all his pastoral possessions and apportioned them as offerings to the gods: to Dionysus he dedicated his bag and goatskin, to Pan his panpipe and transverse *aulos*, to the Nymphs his staff and the milk-pails which he had himself crafted.

Longus, *Daphnis and Chloe* 4.26.2

The sacrifices and mixing bowls are repeated on successive days, and Chloe (not as yet recognised for who she is) also dedicates her rustic kit, upstages

[12] Cf. ὁ κρατὴρ ἐξ οὗ σπένδουσιν Ἑρμῆι, 'the mixing bowl from which they pour libations to Hermes', 4.34.3.

urban libations by mixing spring water from the cave with wine, and garlands the grave of the ewe that fostered her: she then utters a prayer, to find parents worthy of her marriage to Daphnis:

> πάλιν οὖν ταῖς ἑξῆς ἡμέραις ἐθύετο ἱερεῖα καὶ κρατῆρες ἵσταντο καὶ ἀνετίθει καὶ Χλόη τὰ ἑαυτῆς, τὴν σύριγγα, τὴν πήραν, τὸ δέρμα, τοὺς γαυλούς· ἐκέρασε δὲ καὶ τὴν πηγὴν οἴνωι τὴν ἐν τῶι ἄντρωι, ὅτι καὶ ἐτράφη παρ' αὐτῆι, καὶ ἐλούσατο πολλάκις ἐν αὐτῆι· ἐστεφάνωσε καὶ τὸν τάφον τῆς ὄϊος, δείξαντος Δρύαντος, καὶ ἐσύρισέ τι καὶ αὐτὴ τῆι ποίμνηι. καὶ συρίσασα ταῖς θεαῖς ηὔξατο τοὺς ἐκθέντας εὑρεῖν ἀξίους τῶν Δάφνιδος γάμων.
>
> So again on the following days sacrificial animals were offered and mixing bowls were set up. And Chloe too dedicated her own things, her panpipe, her bag, her goatskin, her pails; and with wine she mixed the spring water from the cave, because she had been reared beside it and had often bathed in it. She also garlanded the ewe's grave (Dryas showed her where it was) and played something on her pipe to the flock itself; and after piping she prayed to the goddesses to discover those who had exposed her worthy of her marriage to Daphnis.
>
> Longus, *Daphnis and Chloe* 4.32.3–4

Finally, back in the city, the Nymphs tell Dionysophanes in a dream to entertain the best of the Mytileneans and at the feast to display Chloe's tokens: he arranges an ἑστίασις, 'banquet', involving rich food and libations to Hermes at which Chloe is eventually recognised (4.34.2).

In almost all these descriptions of feasting the religious element is prominent. One possible exception is in the first description of Dryas' winter banquet (3.7.1–8.2): no ritual is specified in Longus' description of *this* part of Dryas' eating and drinking, but it is perhaps implied by the subsequent mention of 'setting up a second mixing bowl' (δεύτερος κρατὴρ ἵστατο, 3.9.3). A more significant exception, which in fact proves the rule, is the Methymnan expedition's 'victory feast' (ἐπινίκιος ἑορτή), apparently devoid of any religious element (2.25.3): but the Methymnans are being constructed as impious, and they will be punished.

Within this well-tempered religious system, prayers and oaths are not infrequent, and there is one, crucially important, vow. This is in Book 2, where Daphnis vows to sacrifice a nanny-goat to Nymphs and a billy-goat to Pan if Chloe is rescued:

> τοιαῦτα ἰδὼν καὶ ἀκούσας Δάφνις ἀναπηδήσας τῶν ὕπνων καὶ κοινῆι ὑφ' ἡδονῆς καὶ λύπης δακρύων τὰ ἀγάλματα τῶν Νυμφῶν προσεκύνει καὶ ἐπηγγέλλετο σωθείσης Χλόης θύσειν τῶν αἰγῶν τὴν ἀρίστην. δραμὼν δὲ καὶ ἐπὶ τὴν πίτυν, ἔνθα τὸ τοῦ Πανὸς ἄγαλμα ἵδρυτο ... κἀκεῖνον προσεκύνει καὶ ηὔχετο ὑπὲρ τῆς Χλόης καὶ τράγον θύσειν ἐπηγγέλλετο ...

> That was what Daphnis saw and heard. He leapt up from his sleep and, weeping at the same time from joy and grief, saluted the statues of the Nymphs and promised that if Chloe were saved he would sacrifice the best of his nanny-goats. And running to the pine-tree where the statue of Pan was set up … he greeted him too, and made a vow, and promised also to sacrifice a billy-goat for Chloe …
>
> Longus, *Daphnis and Chloe* 2.24.1–2

But whereas this is the only vow, prayers abound. In the preface the narrator says that many come to pray to Nymphs as ἱκέται, 'suppliants', as well as to look at the picture in the cave. In Book 2 Daphnis prays to see the Nymphs again in a dream (2.24.4); again in Book 3 he calls on them αὖθις, 'once more', as βοηθούς, 'helpers' (3.27.1, cf. 2.8.5). Shortly after this Dryas prays 'ὦ δεσπότα Πᾶν καὶ Νύμφαι φίλαι', 'O lord Pan and dear Nymphs' (3.32.2), a prayer that Daphnis too may be discovered to have been exposed.

Complementary to prayers, but perhaps more rhetorical than realistic, is castigation of gods:[13] in Book 1 Chloe castigates the Nymphs for not 'saving' her from her erotic torment (1.13.3), in Book 2 Daphnis castigates them for not protecting Chloe despite her provision of garlands and libations and her offering of her panpipe (2.22.1). Also in Book 2 Philetas, recalling his youthful passion for Amaryllis, says that he invoked Pan, but in vain (2.7.6); and in Book 4 Lamon chides Dionysus for not protecting the flowers with which he had garlanded him (4.8.4, already quoted p. 699).

Gods can be castigated in this way because it is unquestioned that they have the power to intervene. Thus the narrative of Book 1 presents Eros as potentially interventionist when the fathers dream that the Nymphs hand over the couple to a winged boy (1.7.2), and when, shortly after, we read that for the couple absorbed in play Eros fashioned τοιάνδε σπουδήν, 'the following serious matter' (1.11.1). In Book 2 Philetas claims to have seen him in his orchard (2.4.1) and narrates that Eros in person had asserted that he was now shepherding the couple, an assertion Philetas endorses (2.6.2) before explaining Eros' power, giving the example of his own desire for Amaryllis (2.7.1–7). When in Book 3 the Nymphs say 'γάμου μὲν μέλει τῆς Χλόης ἄλλωι θεῶι', 'another god cares for Chloe's marriage' (3.27.2), the reader knows by now that this other god is Eros.

The Nymphs themselves also intervene, always in dreams. First, early in Book 1, the fathers dream that the Nymphs hand over the couple to a boy,

[13] Verbal castigation may be related to, but is different from, rituals of beating cult statues or otherwise demonstrating anger against them, for which see Gow on Theoc. 7.108; Borgeaud 1979, 107–17 (I owe this reference to Jan Bremmer).

surely to be read as a dream sent by Nymphs (to whom the fathers then sacrifice) rather than sent by Eros (1.7.2). That the Nymphs might be seen in waking life is suggested by Daphnis' belief later in Book 1 that Chloe wearing a fawn-skin and garland is a Nymph (1.24.1). In Book 2 the couple think of seeking help from Nymphs for their recently diagnosed ἔρως, 'desire' (2.8.5, cf. 3.27.1 mentioned above). Later in the same book the Nymphs appear to Daphnis in dream and assure him that they care for Chloe, and that they have asked Pan, whom the couple never honoured, to aid her (2.23). Again in Book 3 the Nymphs appear to Daphnis in dream, tell him that another god cares for Chloe (cf. above), and themselves tell him about the 3000 drachma purse that will put him back in the running as a suitor for Chloe (3.27.2).

Pan appears less often in the narrative, and as we have seen he had been invoked in vain by Philetas (2.7.6). But his recovery of Chloe is crucial in the sequence late in Book 2, from the moment he is asked by the Nymphs to aid Chloe, through his miracles that panic the Methymnans, to his castigation of them for their impious kidnapping of Chloe (2.23.4–27).[14]

With all this information the reader can flesh out Dryas' belief registered early in Book 1 that his finding Chloe is θεῖον, 'due to the gods' (1.6.1), and can correct the corresponding belief of Dionysophanes late in Book 4 that Daphnis' siblings' death and his own survival is due to Τύχη, 'Fortune' and to πρόνοια θεῶν, 'divine providence' (4.24.2). If Dionysophanes thinks simply that Fortune was at work, he is in the wrong novel; we readers know that his second phrase 'πρόνοια θεῶν', is correct – we first find this phrase in the narrator's account of the fathers' actions early in Book 1 (1.8.2) and again in Dionysophanes' own account of Chloe's survival late in Book 4 (4.36.1); but, like Dionysophanes in this last passage, we can at all points, ever since our reading of the preface, specify these gods as Pan, the Nymphs and Eros.

More could be said about the religious fabric of Longus' narrative, e.g. the place of oaths sworn by the gods. But this would not modify the overall pattern.

3 Religion in Chariton, *Chaereas and Callirhoe*

Some, but not all, the features found in Longus had earlier appeared in Chariton's presentation of religion in *Chaereas and Callirhoe*, but there are some revealing inconcinnities and omissions.

[14] On this central episode and its relation to the religiosity of Longus' novel see Whitmarsh 2011, 97–8.

(a) Prayers

All three of Chariton's major characters pray to the novel's dominant divinity, Aphrodite. The greatest devotion to her is displayed by the rich and highly educated Dionysius of Miletus: his steward's wife Plangon tells Callirhoe of Aphrodite's importance in the locality and of her favour to her regular worshipper, Dionysius:

> 'ἐλθὲ πρὸς τὴν Ἀφροδίτην καὶ εὖξαι περὶ σεαυτῆς· ἐπιφανὴς δέ ἐστιν ἐνθάδε ἡ θεός, καὶ οὐ μόνον οἱ γείτονες, ἀλλὰ καὶ οἱ ἐξ ἄστεος παραγινόμενοι θύουσιν αὐτῆι. μάλιστα δὲ ἐπήκοος Διονυσίωι· ἐκεῖνος οὐδέποτε παρῆλθεν αὐτήν.'
>
> 'Go to Aphrodite and pray concerning yourself: she is a goddess who manifests herself here, and not only people in this neighbourhood but even those who come from the city sacrifice to her. And Aphrodite listens especially to Dionysius: he is someone who has never passed her by.'
>
> Chariton, *Chaereas and Callirhoe*, 2.2.5

That Dionysius had himself built this temple and that he too sacrificed there we learn later when he expostulates to Aphrodite that these pious acts are not being rewarded:[15]

> 'δέσποινα Ἀφροδίτη, σύ με ἐνήδρευσας, ἣν ἐν τοῖς ἐμοῖς ἱδρυσάμην, ἧι θύω πολλάκις. τί γὰρ ἔδειξάς μοι Καλλιρόην, ἣν φυλάττειν οὐκ ἔμελλες; τί δὲ πατέρα ἐποίεις τὸν οὐδὲ ἄνδρα ὄντα;'
>
> 'Lady Aphrodite, you have ambushed me, you whose temple I set up on my land, to whom I often sacrifice. For why have you shown me Callirhoe, when you were not going to keep her mine? And why did you make a father a man who was not even her husband?'
>
> Chariton, *Chaereas and Callirhoe* 5.10.1

This chimes with Dionysius' own view of his piety in Book 2: in an Odyssean moment of self-confidence he introduces himself grandiloquently: 'Διονύσιός εἰμι, Μιλησίων πρῶτος, σχεδὸν δὲ καὶ τῆς ὅλης Ἰωνίας, ἐπ' εὐσεβείαι καὶ φιλανθρωπίαι διαβόητος', 'I am Dionysius, first of the Milesians, and virtually of the whole of Ionia, renowned for his piety and kindness' (2.5.4). So pious is Dionysius that when he first encounters Callirhoe in this temple he greets her as Aphrodite and begins to offer *proskynesis*, a misperception that

[15] That the priestly function in this temple is performed by an old woman (3.9.1 and 4) seemed to Bremmer 2012, n.8 unlikely to reflect cult practice 'in the area of Miletus, where most priests of Aphrodite were male and in fact, in Miletus itself a female priesthood is attested only once in inscriptions, but not before the late second century'.

does not in itself diminish his piety: 'ἵλεως εἴης, ὦ Ἀφροδίτη, καὶ ἐπ' ἀγαθῶι μοι φανείης', 'Be gracious, Aphrodite, and appear to me with a good outcome' (2.3.6). When Callirhoe's son is born and the city celebrates, Dionysius fills temples with offerings and lays on banquets involving sacrifice:

> κἀκεῖνος ὑπὸ τῆς χαρᾶς πάντων παρεχώρησε τῆι γυναικὶ καὶ δέσποιναν αὐτὴν ἀπέδειξε τῆς οἰκίας. ἀναθημάτων ἐνέπλησε τοὺς ναούς, πανδημεὶ τὴν πόλιν εἱστία θυσίαις.
>
> And in his joy he (sc. Dionysius) withdrew from all his control in favour of his wife and appointed her the mistress of the household. He filled the temples with offerings,[16] and he entertained the whole city to sacrificial banquets.
>
> Chariton, *Chaereas and Callirhoe* 3.7.7

At the sacrifice that Chariton picks out for detailed description Dionysius addresses Aphrodite, implicitly but not explicitly thanking her, and asks her to secure the safety of Callirhoe and the child he believes to be his son. It is surprising that he makes no vow at this point, even though he does see the need to back up his prayer to Aphrodite with one to Nemesis: καὶ ἡσυχῆ τὴν Νέμεσιν προσεκύνησε, 'he unobtrusively saluted Nemesis' (3.8.6). Perhaps Dionysius takes the view – or Chariton expects his reader to take the view – that his lavish expenditure on the temple, offerings and sacrifices has established a huge credit balance in his favour. But I suggest that a character so pious as this in Longus, and so pious a citizen of the 'real' imperial Greek world, would surely make a vow.

But Dionysius' failure to make any vow is part of a broader pattern in *Chaereas and Callirhoe*. Callirhoe addresses many prayers to Aphrodite. At the beginning of her story she impulsively asks Aphrodite for Chaereas: ἡ δὲ παρθένος τῆς Ἀφροδίτης τοῖς ποσὶ προσέπεσε καὶ καταφιλοῦσα, 'σύ μοι, δέσποινα', εἶπε, 'δὸς ἄνδρα τοῦτον ὃν ἔδειξας, 'and the maiden threw herself at Aphrodite's feet and kissed them and said "To me, mistress, give this man whom you have shown me"' (1.1.7).[17] In Book 2 Callirhoe prays

[16] Reardon 1989, 61 translated ἀναθημάτων 'votive gifts': many ἀναθήματα are of course votives, but not all, and it is important that here Chariton does not specify that they are.

[17] With τοῦτον ὃν ἔδειξας, 'this man whom you have shown me', cf. 'σύ μοι' φησὶ 'πρώτη Χαιρέαν ἔδειξας', '"You it was", she said, "who first showed me Chaereas"' (2.2.7) and 'ἐμοὶ δὲ οὐκ ἔδειξας αὐτὸν ἐλθόντα', '"But you did not show him to me when he came"' (3.10.6); also Chaereas' pendant 'σύ μοι, δέσποινα … πρώτη Καλλιρόην ἔδειξας', '"It was you, lady, … who first showed me Callirhoe"' (3.6.3), and Dionysius' symmetrical complaint at 5.10.1, 'τί γάρ ἔδειξάς μοι Καλλιρόην', '"So why did you show me Callirhoe?"', cited above, and finally Callirhoe's own closural 'πάλιν γάρ μοι Χαιρέαν ἐν Συρακούσαις ἔδειξας', '"For once again you have shown me Chaereas in Syracuse"', 8.8.15–16, cited below.

not to attract another man after Chaereas: 'μίαν αἰτοῦμαι παρὰ σοῦ χάριν· μηδενί με ποιήσῃς μετ' ἐκεῖνον ἀρέσαι', '"I ask you for a single favour: do not make me please any man after him"' (2.2.7). A little later she is once more praying to Aphrodite when (as we have just seen) Dionysius prays to *her* as Aphrodite: ἡ δὲ Καλλιρόη τῆς νυκτὸς ἐκείνης θεασαμένη τὴν Ἀφροδίτην ἠβουλήθη καὶ πάλιν αὐτὴν προσκυνῆσαι, καὶ ἡ μὲν ἑστῶσα ηὔχετο, 'and that night Callirhoe saw Aphrodite and wanted yet again to salute her; and she was standing and praying' (2.3.5). Early in Book 3 she prays to Aphrodite not to betray her deception of Dionysius: 'ἱκετεύω δέ σε', φησὶν, 'οὐχ ὑπὲρ ἐμαυτῆς, ἀλλ' ὑπὲρ τούτου. ποίησόν μου λαθεῖν τὴν τέχνην', '"I beg you", she said, "not on my own behalf, but on behalf of this child: keep my strategem a secret"' (3.2.13). Later in the same book she prays to Aphrodite to preserve her child: 'ἀλλὰ μίαν ἀντὶ πάντων αἰτοῦμαι χάριν παρὰ σοῦ καὶ διὰ σοῦ παρὰ τῶν ἄλλων θεῶν· σῶζέ μοι τὸν ὀρφανόν', '"But I request one favour above all others from you,[18] and through you from the other gods: keep my fatherless child safe"' (3.8.9). Finally in the last words of Book 8 Callirhoe thanks Aphrodite at Syracuse and prays for herself and Chaereas to have a happy life together:

> εἰς τὸ τῆς Ἀφροδίτης ἱερὸν ἀφίκετο. λαβομένη δὲ αὐτῆς τῶν ποδῶν καὶ ἐπιθεῖσα τὸ πρόσωπον καὶ λύσασα τὰς κόμας, καταφιλοῦσα 'χάρις σοι', φησίν, 'Ἀφροδίτη· πάλιν γάρ μοι Χαιρέαν ἐν Συρακούσαις ἔδειξας, ὅπου καὶ παρθένος εἶδον αὐτὸν σοῦ θελούσης. οὐ μέμφομαί σοι, δέσποινα, περὶ ὧν πέπονθα· ταῦτα εἵμαρτό μοι. δέομαί σου, μηκέτι με Χαιρέου διαζεύξῃς, ἀλλὰ καὶ βίον μακάριον καὶ θάνατον κοινὸν κατάνευσον ἡμῖν'.
>
> She went to the sanctuary of Aphrodite, and clasping her feet, and pressing her face against them, and untying her hair, kissing them, she said 'Thank you, Aphrodite: for you have again shown me Chaereas in Syracuse, where I also saw him when I was a maiden, by your wish. I do not blame you, mistress, concerning what has happened to me: that was my destiny. I beg you, do not unyoke me from Chaereas again, but agree that we shall have a blessed life and a common death'.
>
> Chariton, *Chaereas and Callirhoe* 8.8.15–16

Yet at no point in all these prayers does Callirhoe offer to do anything for Aphrodite or explicitly claim to have done anything for her. We are perhaps to understand that she has in time past made offerings, but they are not

[18] Reardon 1989, 62 translates ἀντὶ πάντων 'in requital of all', and Trzaskoma 2010, 52 'to make up for all of it': if these were correct Callirhoe would indeed be using her earlier worship in a *dedi ut dares* negotiation, but the sense 'above all others' seems to me more likely.

mentioned in Chariton's narrative, so Callirhoe has much less ground for expecting to be listened to than Dionysius. Moreover, it is clear from the passage where Callirhoe deceptively asks the gods to reward Theron that she knows the divine reward-and-punishment system:

> καὶ 'χάριν σοι', φησὶν, 'ἔχω, πάτερ, ὑπὲρ τῆς εἰς ἐμὲ φιλανθρωπίας· ἀποδοῖεν δέ', ἔφη, 'πᾶσιν ὑμῖν οἱ θεοὶ τὰς ἀξίας ἀμοιβάς'.

> And 'I thank you, father', she said, 'for your kindness towards me'. 'And may the gods', she said, 'give you all of you the rewards that you deserve'.
>
> Chariton, *Chaereas and Callirhoe* 1.13.10

In Book 3, indeed, Callirhoe seems to go so far as to negotiate with Aphrodite, suggesting that she has had so much misery that it is now time for Aphrodite to be kind to her and also to preserve her son:

> στᾶσα πλησίον τῆς Ἀφροδίτης καὶ ἀνατείνασα χερσὶ τὸ βρέφος 'ὑπὲρ τούτου σοι', φησίν, 'ὦ δέσποινα, γινώσκω τὴν χάριν· ὑπὲρ ἐμαυτῆς γὰρ οὐκ οἶδα. τότ' ἂν σοι καὶ περὶ ἐμαυτῆς ἠπιστάμην χάριν, εἴ μοι Χαιρέαν ἐτήρησας. πλὴν εἰκόνα μοι δέδωκας ἀνδρὸς φιλτάτου καὶ ὅλον οὐκ ἀφεῖλω μου Χαιρέαν. δὸς δή μοι γενέσθαι τὸν υἱὸν εὐτυχέστερον μὲν τῶν γονέων, ὅμοιον δὲ τῶι πάππωι· πλεύσειε δὲ καὶ οὗτος ἐπὶ τριήρους στρατηγικῆς, καί τις εἴποι, ναυμαχοῦντος αὐτοῦ, "κρείττων Ἑρμοκράτους ὁ ἔκγονος"· ἡσθήσεται μὲν γὰρ καὶ ὁ πάππος ἔχων τῆς ἀρετῆς διάδοχον, ἡσθησόμεθα δὲ οἱ γονεῖς αὐτοῦ καὶ τεθνεῶτες. ἱκετεύω σε, δέσποινα, διαλλάγηθί μοι λοιπόν· ἱκανῶς γάρ μοι δεδυστύχηται. τέθνηκα, ἀνέζηκα, λελῄστευμαι, πέφευγα, πέπραμαι, δεδούλευκα· τίθημι δὲ καὶ τὸν δεύτερον γάμον ἔτι μοι τούτων βαρύτερον. ἀλλὰ μίαν ἀντὶ πάντων αἰτοῦμαι χάριν παρὰ σοῦ καὶ διὰ σοῦ παρὰ τῶν ἄλλων θεῶν· σῶζέ μοι τὸν ὀρφανόν'.

> Standing close to Aphrodite and holding up the baby in her arms 'For him', she said, 'I acknowledge my thanks; for myself, I don't know. I would have felt gratitude on my own behalf too if you had watched over Chaereas for me. But you have given me an image of my dearest husband and you have not robbed me of Chaereas entirely. Grant me that our son will be more fortunate than his parents, and like his grandfather; may he too sail upon the admiral's trireme, and when he fights a sea battle may somebody say "Hermocrates' grandson is greater than he was". For his grandfather will be happy to have a successor to his valour, and we his parents will be happy even when dead.[19] I beg you, mistress, from now on observe a truce with me: for I have had enough misfortune. I have died, I have been resurrected, I have been taken by pirates, I have escaped, I have been sold, I

[19] A challenge to Arist. *EN* 1100a19ff. and to the Aristotelian philosophers of Aphrodisias?

have become a slave – but I regard my second marriage as worse still than all this. But I request one favour above all others from you,[20] and through you from the other gods: keep my fatherless child safe'.

Chariton, *Chaereas and Callirhoe* 3.8.7–9

This sort of bargaining is par for the course in a woman who will shortly castigate Aphrodite for the recent fate of Chaereas:

ἄδικε Ἀφροδίτη, σὺ μόνη Χαιρέαν εἶδες, ἐμοὶ δὲ οὐκ ἔδειξας αὐτὸν ἐλθόντα· λῃστῶν χερσὶ παρέδωκας τὸ σῶμα τὸ καλόν· οὐκ ἠλέησας τὸν πλεύσαντα διὰ σέ. τοιαύτηι θεῶι τίς ἂν προσεύχοιτο, ἥτις τὸν ἴδιον ἱκέτην ἀπέκτεινας; οὐκ ἐβοήθησας ἐν νυκτὶ φοβερᾶι φονευόμενον ἰδοῦσα πλησίον σου μειράκιον καλόν, ἐρωτικόν· ἀφείλω μου τὸν ἡλικιώτην, τὸν πολίτην, τὸν ἐραστήν, τὸν ἐρώμενον, τὸν νυμφίον. ἀπόδος αὐτοῦ μοι κἂν τὸν νεκρόν.

Unjust Aphrodite, you alone saw Chaereas, and you did not show me him when he came; you betrayed his beautiful body to the hands of pirates; you did not pity the man who sailed because of you. Who would pray to a goddess like this, who has killed her own suppliant? You did not go to the help of a beautiful young man, a lover, whom you saw being murdered beside you in the terrifying darkness of night. You took from me my age-mate, my fellow citizen, my lover, my beloved, my bridegroom. Give me him back, even if it is his corpse.

Chariton, *Chaereas and Callirhoe* 3.10.6–8

In Book 7 she again castigates Aphrodite in her shrine at Aradus:

θεασαμένη δὲ Καλλιρόη τὴν Ἀφροδίτην, στᾶσα καταντικρὺ τὸ μὲν πρῶτον ἐσιώπα καὶ ἔκλαιεν, ὀνειδίζουσα τῆι θεῶι τὰ δάκρυα· μόλις δὲ ὑπεφθέγξατο 'ἰδοὺ καὶ Ἄραδος, μικρὰ νῆσος ἀντὶ τῆς μεγάλης Σικελίας καὶ οὐδεὶς ἐνταῦθα ἐμός. ἀρκεῖ, δέσποινα. μέχρι ποῦ με πολεμεῖς; εἰ καὶ ὅλως σοι προσέκρουσα, τετιμώρησαί με ...'

When Callirhoe saw Aphrodite she stood in front of her and at first wept in silence, blaming the goddess for her tears; then with difficulty she said quietly. 'Look, there is Arados, a small island instead of mighty Sicily, and nobody here is one of mine. Enough, mistress! How far will you go in your war with me? Even if I have utterly offended you, you have punished me ...'

Chariton, *Chaereas and Callirhoe* 7.5.2–3

Admittedly even the pious Dionysius castigates Aphrodite, as we have seen (5.10.1, already cited p. 705), for bringing Chaereas back into the frame, and

[20] For this translation see above n.18.

in his summary at the opening of Book 8 the narrator presents Chaereas' miseries as Aphrodite's punishment and the reunion to follow as the result of her relenting: but nothing of this longer perspective has been offered to the reader in the narrative of Book 1 or indeed of later books.

Chaereas is the least frequent of the three major characters to pray to Aphrodite – only once, when he prays to her in Dionysius' temple to restore Callirhoe:

> μεταξὺ δὲ ἀλύοντες περιέπεσον τῶι νεῶι τῆς Ἀφροδίτης. ἔδοξεν οὖν αὐτοῖς προσκυνῆσαι τὴν θεόν, καὶ προσπεσὼν τοῖς γόνασιν αὐτῆς Χαιρέας 'σύ μοι, δέσποινα' <φησί>, 'πρώτη Καλλιρόην ἔδειξας ἐν τῆι σῆι ἑορτῆι· σὺ καὶ νῦν ἀπόδος, ἣν ἐχαρίσω'.
>
> And while they were ranging around they encountered the temple of Aphrodite. So they decided to salute the goddess, and Chaereas threw himself upon her knees and said 'You, mistress, were the first to show me Callirhoe in your festival: now too return the woman with whom you favoured me'.
>
> Chariton, *Chaereas and Callirhoe* 3.6.3

The reader should perhaps assume that Chaereas prayed to Aphrodite again near the end of the work when, putting in at Paphos, ἀναθήμασι τὴν Ἀφροδίτην ἐτίμησε· πολλῶν δὲ ἱερείων συναχθέντων εἰστίασε τὴν στρατιάν, 'he honoured Aphrodite with offerings, and gathering together many animals for sacrifice he feasted his army' (8.2.7–8). But Chariton does not pick out prayer for mention, and the way he narrates the ἑστίασις links it to Chaereas' management of his army rather than to his joy at recovering Callirhoe. Nothing is said about its being a thank-offering, nor is there any hint that vows were made. It is thus rather different from the festivity that celebrated the capture of Tyre in Book 7, a celebration in which only Chaereas did not sacrifice or wear a garland (οἱ μὲν ἄλλοι πάντες ἑώρταζον, μόνος δὲ Χαιρέας οὔτε ἔθυσεν οὔτε ἐστεφανώσατο), pleading the emptiness of the achievement for him without Callirhoe (7.4.10).

The readiness of Dionysius and Callirhoe to castigate Aphrodite suggests that rhetoric rather than real life may be guiding the writer's hand. That is perhaps supported by such cases as that in Book 3 where Chaereas, in the posture of prayer, asks which of the gods has taken Callirhoe:

> Χαιρέας δὲ ἀναβλέψας εἰς τὸν οὐρανὸν καὶ τὰς χεῖρας ἀνατείνας 'τίς ἄρα θεῶν ἀντεραστής μου γενόμενος Καλλιρόην ἀπενήνοχε καὶ νῦν ἔχει μεθ' αὑτοῦ μὴ θέλουσαν, ἀλλὰ βιαζομένην ὑπὸ κρείττονος μοίρας;'

> Chaereas looked up at the heavens and stretched up his arms, saying ‘So which of the gods has become my rival in love for Callirhoe, and has carried her off, and now retains her with him against her will, constrained by a more powerful destiny?’
>
> Chariton, *Chaereas and Callirhoe* 3.3.4

Rhetoric also hijacks religion a little later when Chaereas orders the sea, and prays to Poseidon, to reunite him with Callirhoe (3.5.9), and a little earlier when Callirhoe had asked Dionysius to swear by the sea, Aphrodite and Eros that he would make her his full wife:[21]

> ‘ὄμοσόν μοι’ φησὶ ‘τὴν θάλασσαν τὴν κομίσασάν με πρός σε καὶ τὴν Ἀφροδίτην τὴν δείξασάν μέ σοι καὶ τὸν Ἔρωτα τὸν νυμφαγωγόν.’
>
> ‘Swear for me’, she said, ‘by the sea which brought me to you and by Aphrodite who showed me to you and by Eros who makes me your bride.’
>
> Chariton, *Chaereas and Callirhoe* 3.2.5

Similarly rhetorical is the passage in Book 8 where Callirhoe prays that gods not make her so mad as to have Stateira as her slave (8.3.2).

(b) Festivals

I adduce some more features which seem to me to point to a more secular ‘take’ on the world than that of Longus. I have touched briefly on three festivals where some religious content is indeed prominent (3.7.7, 7.4.10, 8.2.7–8). In other, more numerous festivals the religious element is not foregrounded. In Book 5 the Persian king postpones his hearing for thirty days because of festive ceremonies (5.3.11), and again in Book 6 he orders a second thirty-day festival, claiming that the gods in a dream had told him to do so (6.2.2–3): we know the claim to be false, and we hear nothing about the actual performance of religious rituals. Even at the festival of Aphrodite near the beginning of Book 1 there is minimal reference to ritual acts: Chariton narrates only that women go to Aphrodite’s temple, and then, it seems (but there is a lacuna in our *codex unicus*), Callirhoe is told by her mother (and perhaps by her father) to join them and salute Aphrodite: τοῦ πατρὸς (?) > κελεύσαντος προσκυνῆσαι τὴν θεόν, ‘<since her father had told

[21] Cf. Hermog. 333 Rabe, noting that Hdt. 7.35 achieved γλυκύτης, ‘sweetness’, in his description of Xerxes’ admonition and whipping of the Hellespont. That the notion is not confined, however, to rhetorical imagination is shown by the oath from Cretan Dreros where ephebes swear not only by gods and heroes but also by κράνας καὶ ποταμούς, ‘springs and rivers’, *ICret.* I ix 1.34–5 (ca. 200 BC).

her> to salute the goddess' (1.1.5). Thus, when the Olympic Games and Eleusinian Mysteries are mentioned, it is as no more than paradigmatic occasions of great public attention (5.4.4),[22] just as the way the two rivals for Callirhoe arrive escorted by crowd of supporters is compared to competitors arriving at Olympia with no hint of that festival's religious element (6.2.1).

(c) *Weddings and Funerals*

Minimal attention to any religious component also marks weddings and funerals. Only the wedding of Dionysius and Callirhoe in Book 3 is said to involve sacrifices: ἅμα δὲ τῆι ἕωι πᾶσα ἦν ἡ πόλις ἐστεφανωμένη. ἔθυεν ἕκαστος πρὸ τῆς ἰδίας οἰκίας, οὐκ ἐν μόνοις τοῖς ἱεροῖς, 'At dawn the whole city was wearing garlands. Each individual sacrificed in front of his own house, not only in the temples' (3.2.14–15). The wedding of Chaereas and Callirhoe is described without any mention of prayers or sacrifices (1.1.13–16), as are the weddings dreamt about by Dionysius (2.1.2) and Callirhoe (5.5.5).[23]

As for tombs and funerals, Callirhoe asks who will pour libations at Chaereas' tomb when she goes east to Babylon (5.1.7), but we are not told that she has actually done so. Chaereas himself had come with στεφάνους καὶ χοάς, 'wreaths and libations', to Callirhoe's tomb, though we are told this is merely a front for his plan to kill himself there (3.3.1). Again no religious element is to be found in the extensive descriptions of Callirhoe's funeral in Syracuse (1.6.3–5) or of Callirhoe's construction of a tomb and the ensuing funeral for the supposedly dead Chaereas (4.1.6–12).

4 Religion in Xenophon, *Anthia and Habrocomes*

As in many other respects, Xenophon stands quite close to Chariton, though his world is one in which on two occasions gods are seen responding much more directly to prayer than in Chariton's.[24]

[22] For the continuing importance of Eleusis in the imperial period see Clinton 1999; Bremmer 2011, 229–30 (with references to earlier scholarship). For Olympia in the second century AD Hitzl and Kropp 2013.

[23] The singing of the ὑμέναιος, 'wedding song', mentioned in the first two cases, is a regular symbol of a wedding rather than an invitation to contemplate its religious dimension. See below on X.Eph. 3.6.1–3.

[24] Cf., with a focus on somewhat different issues, Dowden 2010, 369–70; Whitmarsh 2011, 47–8.

(a) Prayers

The first of these two occasions on which a divine response is immediate comes when Habrocomes, nailed to a cross on the banks of the Nile, looks at the sun and then at the Nile and prays:

> 'ὦ θεῶν', φησί, 'φιλανθρωπότατε, ὃς Αἴγυπτον ἔχεις, δι' ὃν καὶ γῆ καὶ θάλασσα πᾶσιν ἀνθρώποις πέφηνεν, εἰ μέν τι Ἁβροκόμης ἀδικεῖ, καὶ ἀπολοίμην οἰκτρῶς καὶ μείζονα τιμωρίαν εἴ τις ἐστὶ ταύτης ὑπόσχοιμι· εἰ δὲ ὑπὸ γυναικὸς προδέδομαι πονηρᾶς, μήτε τὸ Νείλου ῥεῦμα μιανθείη ποτε ἀδίκως ἀπολομένου σώματι, μήτε σὺ τοιοῦτον ἴδοις θέαμα, ἄνθρωπον οὐδὲν ἀδικήσαντα ἀπολλύμενον ἐπὶ τῆς σῆς ἐνταῦθα.'
>
> 'Kindest of gods, ruler of Egypt, revealer of land and sea to all men: if I, Habrocomes, have done anything wrong, may I perish miserably and incur an even greater penalty if there is one; but if I have been betrayed by a wicked woman (sc. Cyno), I pray that the waters of the Nile should never be polluted by the body of a man unjustly killed; nor should you look on such a sight, a man who has done no wrong being murdered here on your territory.'
>
> Xenophon, *Anthia and Habrocomes* 4.2.4–5

Like Callirhoe (Ch. 3.8.7–9), Habrocomes is negotiating, partly on the basis of his innocence and partly by claiming an issue of potential pollution. The negotiation seems to be successful: αὐτὸν ὁ θεὸς οἰκτείρει, 'the god pities him', and a gust of wind blows the cross and its victim into the Nile. After he has been carried downstream, recaptured and put on a pyre to be burned another prayer causes the Nile to rise and extinguish the flames. Like the *archon* of Egypt in Xenophon's narrative, the reader must accept that Habrocomes is under divine protection. Unlike Dionysius in Chariton (5.10.1), however, Habrocomes can point to no earlier acts of worship; and, unlike Daphnis in Longus (2.24.1–2), he makes no vows to be fulfilled if he is saved.

In this Habrocomes aligns himself with all the other characters to pray in Chariton and Xenophon. He has already prayed to Eros to give him Anthia and not punish him (1.4.5); Anthia has prayed to the gods and to Artemis Ephesia to reward the kind goatherd Lampon (2.11.8); shortly after the Nile miracle Anthia's voices a long prayer to Isis in front of her temple at Memphis, hinting that her success in remaining chaste as a result of claiming to be dedicated to Isis makes a case for Isis now to secure either her return to Habrocomes or her death unviolated (4.3.3–4); later she makes a similar case in a prayer to Isis to save her from the attentions of Polyidus (5.4.6). In Book 5 Habrocomes sails to Rhodes εὐξάμενος τῆι πατρίωι Κυπρίων θεῶι, 'after he had prayed to the ancestral goddess of Cyprus' (5.10.3), the closest that Aphrodite comes to a significant divine role in Xenophon, though at the couple's wedding she and Erotes are represented on the luxurious fabric of their bed's canopy (1.8.2). In none of these cases is a vow made; and only in the case of the goatherd Lampon is the good behaviour of the potential beneficiary explicitly cited.

The second case of immediate divine response is when Anthia prays to Apis for a prophecy about the fate of Habrocomes (5.4.10–11). Children singing outside the temple immediately answer her prayer.

So Xenophon presents a world in which gods can respond even more rapidly than those in Longus, whereas the impact of prayer in Chariton is much less immediate, if detectable at all. None of Xenophon's characters castigates gods in quite the way that Chariton's do, though Habrocomes on the cross may be obliquely reminding a divinity of his presumed commitment to justice. It is perhaps also significant that Xenophon offers two cases of characters' concern that they may be the object of an unidentified evil power's spite: we lived together happily ἕως δαίμων τις ἡμῖν ἐνεμέσησε, 'until some divine power expressed his anger against us' (3.2.5), narrates Hippothous; ἐνεμέσησε δέ τις ἄρα θεῶν, 'but it seems that one of the gods was angry with us' (5.1.6), tells Aegialeus. This realistic uncertainty about the precise source of divine malice is expressed only once by a character in Chariton, Chaereas at Babylon (6.2.11), though the device is also twice used by the otherwise omniscient narrator (1.1.16, 3.2.17) and on three occasions Callirhoe expostulates against Τύχη βάσκανε, 'malicious Fortune' (1.14.7, 4.1.12, 5.1.4), a fortune she elsewhere takes to be managed by Aphrodite.[25]

(b) *Festivals and Other Rituals*

The supporting cast of religious practices is also strongly represented in Xenophon. Early in the novel we learn that Anthia regularly worshipped in the temple of Artemis: ἤιει δὲ ἡ παρθένος ἐπὶ τὴν ἐξ ἔθους θρησκείαν τῆς θεοῦ, 'the maiden was going to her habitual worship of the goddess' (1.5.1). It is there too that the smitten Habrocomes seems to pray (1.5.5). The families of the couple seek religious assistance of various sorts for the couple's malady – diviners, soothsayers, prayers, sacrifices (1.5.6–6.12):

> εἰς τέλος εἰσάγουσι παρὰ τὴν Ἀνθίαν μάντεις καὶ ἱερέας, ὡς εὑρήσοντας λύσιν τοῦ δεινοῦ. οἱ δὲ ἐλθόντες ἔθυόν τε ἱερεῖα καὶ ποικίλα ἐπέσπενδον καὶ

[25] On the evil eye in imperial Greek literature see Dickie 1991.

> ἐπέλεγον φωνὰς βαρβαρικάς, ἐξιλάσκεσθαί τινας λέγοντες δαίμονας, καὶ προσεποίουν ὡς εἴη τὸ δεινὸν ἐκ τῶν ὑποχθονίων θεῶν. πολλὰ δὲ καὶ ὑπὲρ Ἁβροκόμου οἱ περὶ τὸν Λυκομήδην ἔθυόν τε καὶ ηὔχοντο. λύσις δὲ οὐδεμία τοῦ δεινοῦ οὐδὲ ἑτέρωι αὐτῶν ἐγίνετο, ἀλλὰ καὶ ἔτι μᾶλλον ὁ ἔρως ἀνεκαίετο.
>
> Eventually they brought prophets and priests to see Anthia, so that they might discover a remedy for her terrible condition. They came and made sacrifices and poured many sorts of libation and recited in accompaniment non-Greek words, saying they were placating some divine powers, and they claimed that her terrible condition was caused by the gods of the underworld. And Lycomedes' family made many sacrifices and prayers on behalf of Habrocomes. But no remedy was achieved for either of their terrible conditions, but their desire became even more inflamed.
>
> Xenophon, *Anthia and Habrocomes* 1.5.6–8

Eventually they turn to the oracle at Claros (called Colophon by Xenophon) and when that has pronounced they take its command so seriously as to set the perilous travels of the couple, once married, in motion (1.6–7, 1.10).[26] The couple's departure from Ephesus (1.10.9–10) involves prayers, people carrying torches,[27] and sacrifices on departure: vows, however, are not specified. It may be implicit that such an elaborate send-off involved vows, but our text suppresses them. Indeed, as we have once seen in Chariton, rhetoric, or narrative guile, plays a role in detaching the narrative from reality in the pattern given to Megamedes' prayer:

> μελλούσης δὲ τῆς νεὼς ἐπανάξασθαι, πᾶν μὲν τὸ Ἐφεσίων <πλῆθος> παρῆν παραπεμπόντων, πολλαὶ δὲ καὶ τῶν <…> μετὰ λαμπάδων καὶ θυσιῶν …
>
> (10) ὁ δὲ Μεγαμήδης φιάλην λαβὼν καὶ ἐπισπένδων ηὔχετο ὡς ἐξάκουστον εἶναι τοῖς ἐν τῆι νηὶ 'ὦ παῖδες' λέγων 'μάλιστα μὲν εὐτυχοῖτε καὶ φύγοιτε τὰ σκληρὰ τῶν μαντευμάτων, καὶ ὑμᾶς ἀνασωθέντας ὑποδέξαιντο Ἐφέσιοι, καὶ τὴν φιλτάτην ἀπολάβοιτε πατρίδα· εἰ δὲ ἄλλο <τι> συμβαίη, τοῦτο μὲν ἴστε οὐδὲ ἡμᾶς ἔτι ζησομένους· προΐεμεν δὲ ὑμᾶς ὁδὸν δυστυχῆ μὲν ἀλλ' ἀναγκαίαν.'
>
> And when the boat was about to set sail, the whole populace of Ephesus came escorting them, and there were many <…> with torches and sacrifices …

[26] For the importance of the oracle at Claros see Parke 1985; J. and L. Robert 1989; Oesterheld 2008; Ferrary 2014. For oracles in the novels see Said 1977.

[27] The term in the lacuna at 1.10.6 was suggested by Hemsterhuys to have been ἱερειῶν, 'priestesses', or ἱερῶν παρθένων, 'sacred maidens'; by Cobet ξένων, 'visitors'.

> (10) Megamedes took a cup and as he made a libation uttered a prayer such as could be heard by those on the boat: 'Children', he said, 'may you be happy in every way and escape the harsh predictions of the oracles, and may the Ephesians welcome you back again safe and sound, and may you regain your own dear country. But if anything else should happen, know one thing, that we will not go on living; we are sending you off on a journey that is ill-fated but inevitable.'
>
> Xenophon, *Anthia and Habrocomes* 1.10.6 and 10

Pious behaviour continues when the seafaring couple reaches Rhodes: Anthia and Habrocomes dedicated (ἀνέθεσαν) a gold panoply (πανοπλίαν χρυσῆν) to Helios (1.12.2). The choice of a panoply is as puzzling as the absence from the dedicatory epigram ('quoted' by Xenophon) and from the surrounding narrative of any indication whether the dedication is in thanks for their safe travels so far or to support a request for future protection. The same must be said of later sacrifices and dedications. The *stele* put up by Leucon and Rhode on Rhodes 'on behalf of Habrocomes and Anthia' may be read as a move to secure the couple's salvation, but the narrator does not make wholly this clear:

> ἐν Ῥόδωι ἀναθήματα ἀνατεθείκεσαν ἐν τῶι τοῦ Ἡλίου ἱερῶι παρὰ τὴν χρυσῆν πανοπλίαν, ἣν Ἀνθία καὶ Ἀβροκόμης ἀνατεθείκεσαν· ἀνέθεσαν στήλην γράμμασι χρυσοῖς γεγραμμένην ὑπὲρ Ἀβροκόμου καὶ Ἀνθίας, ἀνεγέγραπτο δὲ καὶ τῶν ἀναθέντων τὰ ὀνόματα, ὅ τε Λεύκων καὶ ἡ Ῥόδη.
>
> At Rhodes they had dedicated dedications in the sanctuary of Helios alongside the golden panoply which Anthia and Habrocomes had dedicated: they dedicated a *stele* inscribed with golden letters on behalf of Habrocomes and Anthia; and there were also inscribed on it the name of the dedicators, Leucon and Rhode.
>
> Xenophon, *Anthia and Habrocomes* 5.10.6

The narrator's lack of explicitness is perhaps partly to be explained because he is more interested in the dedication as a device to hasten ἀναγνώρισις, 'recognition'. The same may be claimed about Anthia's dedication a little later of a lock of her hair:

> δεῖται τοῦ Ἱπποθόου ἐπιτρέψαι αὐτῆι τῆς κόμης ἀφελεῖν τῆς αὑτῆς καὶ ἀναθεῖναι τῶι Ἡλίωι καὶ εὔξασθαί τι περὶ Ἀβροκόμου. συγχωρεῖ ὁ Ἱππόθοος· καὶ ἀποτεμοῦσα τῶν πλοκάμων ὅσα ἐδύνατο καὶ ἐπιτηδείου καιροῦ λαβομένη, πάντων ἀπηλλαγμένων, ἀνατίθησιν ἐπιγράψασα 'ὑπὲρ τοῦ ἀνδρὸς Ἀβροκόμου Ἀνθία τὴν κόμην τῶι θεῶι ἀνέθηκε'. ταῦτα ποιήσασα καὶ εὐξαμένη ἀπήιει μετὰ τοῦ Ἱπποθόου.

She implored Hippothous to allow her to take some of her own hair, to dedicate it to Helios, and to offer some prayer concerning Habrocomes. Hippothous agreed; and she cut off as many of her tresses as she could and, seizing a suitable moment when everybody had gone, dedicated them with an inscription 'On behalf of her husband, Habrocomes, Anthia dedicated her hair to the god'. When she had done this and offered a prayer she went away with Hippothous.

Xenophon, *Anthia and Habrocomes* 5.11.5–6

The phrase used by Leucon and Rhode, 'on behalf of Habrocomes and Anthia', and Anthia's own words 'on behalf of Habrocomes', perhaps justify seeing these dedications as properly votive, i.e. as part of vows: but if so they are the only clearly identifiable vows in Xenophon's novel, and the translation generally given for εὐξαμένη, 'having offered a prayer' or 'having prayed', here seems more likely to be right than 'having made a vow'.

The same blend of manifest piety and lack of specificity on worshippers' intent recurs. At the end of the story we do indeed learn that Anthia and Habrocomes make thank-offerings to Artemis at Ephesus as well as prayers and sacrifices:

ὡς δὲ ἐξέβησαν, εὐθὺς ὡς εἶχον ἐπὶ τὸ ἱερὸν τῆς Ἀρτέμιδος ἤιεσαν καὶ πολλὰ ηὔχοντο καὶ θύσαντες ἄλλα <τε> ἐνέθεσαν ἀναθήματα καὶ δὴ καὶ [τὴν] γραφὴν τῆι θεῶι ἀνέθεσαν πάντα ὅσα τε ἔπαθον καὶ ὅσα ἔδρασαν.

When they disembarked they immediately went to the sanctuary of Artemis, just as they were, and offered many prayers and made a sacrifice, and dedicated dedications, and in particular dedicated to the goddess an inscription telling of all that had happened to them and all that they had done.

Xenophon, *Anthia and Habrocomes* 5.15.2

Xenophon does not bring out explicitly the χάρις, 'gratitude', that links their safe return from their adventures and their prayer, sacrifice, and dedication: he is more interested in drawing attention to what might seem to be a documentation of these adventures. Similarly, a little earlier, in Rhodes, when the couple has been reunited and indeed goes to thank Isis in her temple there, neither they nor the narrator make specific reference to any offering made in recognition of divine help:

οἱ δὲ ἀναλαβόντες ἑαυτούς, διαναστάντες εἰς τὸ τῆς Ἴσιδος ἱερὸν εἰσῆλθον 'σοί', λέγοντες, 'ὦ μεγίστη θεά, τὴν ὑπὲρ τῆς σωτηρίας ἡμῶν χάριν οἴδαμεν· διὰ σέ, ὦ πάντων ἡμῖν τιμιωτάτη, ἑαυτοὺς ἀπειλήφαμεν'· προεκυλίοντό τε τοῦ τεμένους καὶ τῶι βωμῶι προσέπιπτον.

> They recovered, and stood up, and went into the sanctuary of Isis, saying 'We are grateful to you, most mighty goddess, for our safety; it is through you, o goddess whom we honour most, that we have recovered each other'. And they paid homage in front of her precinct and prostrated themselves at her altar.
>
> Xenophon, *Anthia and Habrocomes* 5.13.4

Then, when a few lines and a day later they sacrifice and feast – ὡς δὲ ἔθυσαν ἐκείνης τῆς ἡμέρας καὶ εὐωχήθησαν, 'when that day they had sacrificed and feasted' (5.13.5) – none of these celebrations is specifically linked with Isis, Helios, or Artemis. The same imprecision had been exhibited in their visit to Samos in Book 1:

> εἰς Σάμον κατήντησαν τὴν τῆς Ἥρας ἱερὰν νῆσον· κἀνταῦθα θύσαντες καὶ δειπνοποιησάμενοι, πολλὰ εὐξάμενοι τῆς νυκτὸς ἐπιγινομένης ἐπανήγοντο.
>
> they arrived at Samos, the island sacred to Hera. There they sacrificed and banqueted, and after many prayers they put out to sea as night was falling.
>
> Xenophon, *Anthia and Habrocomes* 1.11.2

Perhaps these religious acts are to be imagined as having been performed in the famous sanctuary of Hera, but Xenophon does not tell us so. Occasionally, indeed, Xenophon seems to represent a festival without much attention to its religious content at all. Thus, in Book 1 we visualise the procession and its many people and objects (1.2.4–9), but at this point we read nothing concerning prayers, sacrifices, or music (a sacrifice follows shortly at 1.3.1). In Book 1 the remark that ἑορτὴ δὲ ἦν ἅπας ὁ βίος αὐτοῖς, 'their whole life was a festival, (1.10.2), echoed at 5.15.3,[28] foregrounds the fun and not the ritual of religious festivals, as do Aegialeus' brief reference to a *pannychis* at Sparta (5.1.5)[29] and Anthia's fictional account of how (she claims) she became epileptic (5.7.7).

Other practices which in the 'real world' usually involve a religious element do not do so in Xenophon's narrative. No religious ritual is mentioned when Hippothous buries Hyperanthes (3.2.13), nor any other than the singing of the ὑμέναιος, 'wedding song', when Perilaus is about to marry Anthia (3.6.1–4). It is perhaps part of the same 'thin' account of religious practice that when Habrocomes dreams that he and Anthia have escaped safely from a burning ship there is no suggestion that they then expressed thanks to the gods (1.12.4).

[28] On this trope see Whitmarsh 2011, 49 n.120.

[29] For *pannychides* in the real and literary worlds see Bravo 1997.

But these are perhaps unimportant exceptions. Overall prayers, sacrifices, and offerings *are* an integral part of Xenophon's world: even brigands perform sacrifices, to Ares, as Anthia discovers to her cost (2.13.1–2), and one, Amphinomus, in love with Anthia, swears oaths by the Sun and by the Egyptian gods to respect her chastity (5.2.5). Here, as we have seen in Longus and Chariton, the rhetoric of the novelist can extend and therefore dilute what might be expected in 'real life'. Similarly in Book 1 Habrocomes and Anthia swear oaths of mutual fidelity by Artemis, by the sea, and by Eros (1.11.5); a little later they plead with the pirate Corymbus μὴ πρὸς αὐτῆς θαλάσσης, μὴ πρὸς δεξιᾶς τῆς σῆς, 'by the sea itself, by your own right hand', not to separate them (1.13.6). But despite such literary flourishes religiosity is spread more evenly in Xenophon's world and balanced by less 'secularity' than in that of Chariton.[30] As in Chariton, however, the traditional procedure of vows, uttered in prayers or formulated in dedications, and of offerings made in explicit recognition of divine assistance, have been only very faintly adumbrated.

5 Religion in Achilles Tatius, *Leucippe and Cleitophon*

In Achilles Tatius we find a universe that is not very different, but the indications of what I have called 'secularity' are more numerous. Again I begin with prayers.

(a) Prayers

Cleitophon prays to a wide range of gods. His first prayer to Aphrodite comes remarkably late in his narrative, during his retrospective account in Book 8, when he asks her not to be insulted by the fact that he and Leucippe have postponed having sex – indeed, it is more of an apostrophe than a prayer:

> 'δέσποινα Ἀφροδίτη, μὴ νεμεσήσῃς ἡμῖν ὡς ὑβρισμένη. οὐκ ἠθέλομεν ἀπάτορα γενέσθαι τὸν γάμον. πάρεστιν οὖν ὁ πατήρ· ἧκε καὶ σύ· εὐμενὴς ἡμῖν ἤδη γενοῦ.'
>
> 'Mistress Aphrodite, do not be angry with us in the belief that we had insulted you. We did not want to wed without a father present. The father is here now. Come to us too, and now be benign to us.'
>
> Achilles Tatius, *Leucippe and Cleitophon* 8.5.8

At this stage and in this context it might be surprising to find a vow as well as a prayer. But a vow might well have been expected in some earlier prayers, either when in Book 3 Cleitophon asks Poseidon let him and Leucippe die together if they are indeed fated to die (3.5.4); or when he prays ineffectively to Zeus Serapis not to add to their adventures (shortly followed by a reference to the gymnasium of Τύχη, 'Fortune', 5.2.3); or, right at the end of the novel, when Cleitophon and Leucippe attend Callisthenes' wedding εὐξόμενοι, 'so as to pray', that both their own marriages and his may prosper (8.19.3).

Gods can be appealed to straightforwardly, as Satyrus entreats Menelaus, Δία Ξένιον καλῶν, 'invoking Zeus, god of hospitality' (3.21.6). But, as in Chariton, a prayer can also be exploited to castigate a deity: Cleitophon's address to unnamed θεοὶ καὶ δαίμονες, 'gods and divine powers' (3.10.1–6), is little more than a handle on which to hang a string of complaints, and by its termination Cleitophon is upbraiding the sea and not his initial addressees:

> 'μάτην σοι, ὦ θάλασσα, τὴν χάριν ὡμολογήσαμεν. μέμφομαί σου τῆι φιλανθρωπίαι· χρηστοτέρα γέγονας πρὸς οὓς ἀπέκτεινας, ἡμᾶς δὲ σώσασα μᾶλλον ἀπέκτεινας. ἐφθόνησας ἡμῖν ἀληιστεύτοις ἀποθανεῖν.'
>
> 'It was in vain, O sea, that we expressed our thanks to you. I blame your kindness. You behaved better to those whose you killed, but in saving us you killed us more. You have grudged us an unpirated death.'
>
> Achilles Tatius, *Leucippe and Cleitophon* 3.10.6

For a similar hijacking of religion by Cleitophon's rhetoric compare the scene where (in his narrative) Leucippe asks Thersander if he was not deterred from his attempt to seduce her by the city's goddess Artemis, concluding with δέσποινα, ποῦ σου τὰ τόξα; 'Mistress, where are your arrows?' (6.21.2). Rhetoric also dominates her father Sostratus' castigation of Artemis:

> 'ἐπὶ τούτωι με, δέσποινα, ἤγαγες ἐνταῦθα; τοιαῦτά σου τῶν ἐνυπνίων τὰ μαντεύματα; κἀγὼ μὲν ἐπίστευόν σου τοῖς ὀνείροις καὶ εὑρήσειν παρὰ σοὶ προσεδόκων τὴν θυγατέρα. καλὸν δέ μοι δῶρον δέδωκας· εὗρον τὸν ἀνδροφόνον αὐτῆς παρὰ σοί.'
>
> 'Is this the basis, mistress, on which you brought me here? Are these the prophecies of my dreams? And I trusted the dreams you sent me and expected to find my daughter in your city – it is a fine gift you have given me: I have found her murderer in your city.'
>
> Achilles Tatius, *Leucippe and Cleitophon* 7.14.5

A comparably rhetorical twist, this time applied to a curse, is found in Melite's prayer to Eros to punish Cleitophon: 'εὐνοῦχε καὶ ἀνδρόγυνε καὶ κάλλους βάσκανε, ἐπαρῶμαί σοι δικαιοτάτην ἀράν· οὕτως σε ἀμύναιτο ὁ Ἔρως εἰς τὰ σά', 'Eunuch! Effeminate! Beauty-grudger! I curse you with a most just curse; may Eros punish you in this way in your life!' (5.25.8).

That curse, of course, is not implemented. But at least two cases display the divine machinery working according to the textbook. At Pelusium Cleitophon and Leucippe tour the temple of Zeus Casius προσευξάμενοι ... τῶι θεῶι καὶ περὶ τοῦ Κλεινίου καὶ τοῦ Σατύρου σύμβολον ἐξαιτήσαντες, 'after praying to the god and asking for a sign concerning Cleinias and Satyrus' (3.6.2). Guidance, if it is guidance, comes in the form of paintings of Prometheus and Andromeda that they next see in the *opisthodomos* of the temple. Then in Book 5, on asking Zeus to clarify the message he has apparently sent by the possible portent of a hawk pursuing a swallow and striking Leucippe's head with its wing, Cleitophon immediately spots a painting of Tereus' rape of Philomela (5.3.3–8). In both cases we may conclude that Zeus had indeed responded, or at least that the narrator Cleitophon believed that he had.[31] Similarly in Book 7 we learn that 'Artemis had appeared' to the Byzantines (τῆς Ἀρτέμιδος ἐπιφανείσης) and aided them in their war with Thracians;[32] she had also νύκτωρ ... ἐπιστᾶσα, 'stood at night', beside Sostratus in a dream, telling him he would find Leucippe and Cleitophon in Ephesus (7.12.4). In thanks for her help a *theoria* is sent by Byzantium to Artemis of Ephesus, as one had also earlier been sent (in obedience to a hexameter oracle) to Heracles of Tyre (2.14–15): its arrival at Ephesus and Sostratus' participation in it play important roles in the development of the plot.

In these cases we are encouraged to be confident that the divine appearances have been beneficent and veridical. Earlier in the novel, however, when Artemis appeared in a dream to Leucippe promising she would remain a virgin until Cleitophon married her (4.1.3–4), and when Aphrodite told Cleitophon in a dream that he could not enter her temple now, but would

[30] I agree with Dowden 2010, 374: 'Xenophon in particular may be more pious than is generally supposed'.

[31] On the ways in which Achilles Tatius plays with characters' interpretations of paintings Bartsch 1989 remains important.

[32] This may be a reworking of or (as suggested by Bremmer 2013, 146) allusion to the tradition that in a siege of Byzantium by Philip of Macedon Hecate saved the city by displaying the besiegers' torches, and hence received cult as Hecate *Phosphoros*, found in St. Byz. β 130 *s.v.* Βόσπορος and Hsch. Mil. *FGrH* 390 F1.27.

soon be her archpriest (4.1.6–7), neither characters nor readers can be so sure the divine messages are reliable.[33]

Other respects in which religion plays an important part in the world according to Cleitophon are as follows.

(b) Sacrifices

Sacrifices are described in some detail. The offering at a prenuptial sacrifice (προτέλεια τῶν γάμων) by Cleitophon's father is snatched away by an eagle, and on priestly advice another is then made to Zeus, god of hospitality (2.12.1–3). The sacrifice performed at Tyre by the *theoria* to Heracles is described in great detail: this description, however, shows more interest in *ecphrasis* of flowers and exotic animals than of the sacrifice itself (2.14–16). The sacrifice described in most loving detail, however, is that by the *boukoloi* of the girl whom Cleitophon supposes to be Leucippe (3.12, 15 and 19). This has little to do with traditional Greek polytheism: the gods in whose name or honour the ritual is performed are not even named, and Achilles Tatius is playing the Herodotean Greek abroad who can report bongo-bongo type anthropology for the astonishment and self-congratulation of cultivated Greek readers.[34] The same move is being made in his description of the bizarre Egyptian ritual performed at Heliopolis when the fabled phoenix arrives (3.25.5–7).[35]

(c) Oaths

A regular feature of the relationship of couples in the novels, oaths are reported in a way that has them match those in the real world. Thus, Cleitophon and Melite exchange oaths in Iseum at Alexandria ἐπὶ μάρτυρι τῆι θεῶι, 'with the goddess as a witness': ὠμνύομεν, ἐγὼ μὲν ἀγαπήσειν ἀδόλως, ἡ δὲ ἄνδρα ποιήσασθαι καὶ πάντων ἀποφῆναι δεσπότην, 'we swore oaths, I that I would cherish her without deception, she that she would

[33] Bremmer 2013, 145 observes that, on the basis of the dreams analysed by van Straten, where Aphrodite is not mentioned at all in 300 dream dedications (van Straten 1976, 14), Cleitophon's dream is unlikely to correspond to reality.

[34] Bremmer 2013, 143 judges the scene to be 'a *bricolage* of Greek sacrificial elements (libation, flute, circumambulation) and Egyptian hymns'.

[35] Even in the details of the ordeal Leucippe undergoes in Ephesus it seems that Ach. Tat., in having it supervised by a virgin priestess, is presenting 'a construction that Achilles Tatius has developed from several different elements that did not exist as a whole in historical reality' (Bremmer 2013, 143).

make me her husband and would declare me the master of all her estate' (5.14.2). Soon after this Cleitophon, aware that Leucippe is alive and near, deceptively claims to be sick but nevertheless to reciprocate Melite's excited desire, reinforcing the claim by saying 'ὄμνυμί σοι, φιλτάτη, τοὺς πατρῴους θεούς', 'I swear to you, my dearest, by my ancestral gods' (5.21.6). In his retrospective narrative in Book 8 Cleitophon again swears 'μὰ ταύτην τὴν Ἄρτεμιν', 'by Artemis who is here' (8.5.2), that his relationship with Melite during their voyage to Ephesus had been chaste – an economical version of the truth (he is silent about their later intercourse). Neither of Cleitophon's abuses of the oath is punished, and I am tempted to see in them little more than a literary manoeuvre similar to the initial plea made to Cleitophon himself by the anonymous narrator to divulge his story 'πρὸς τοῦ Διὸς καὶ τοῦ Ἔρωτος αὐτοῦ', 'in the name of Zeus and Eros himself' (1.2.2).

(d) Festivals and Other Rituals

There are also some descriptions of religious festivals which would be expected to have involved a sacrifice but where nothing is written of this. In the festival of Serapis at Alexandria only the procession is picked out for mention: ἦν δὲ καὶ πυρὸς δαιδουχία, 'there was also a torchlight procession' (5.2.1). In the description of the *Artemisia* at Ephesus the narrator's focus is on inebriation: ἦν δὲ τῆς Ἀρτέμιδος ἱερομηνία καὶ μεθυόντων πάντα μεστά, 'it was the month marked by the festival of Artemis and everywhere was packed with people who were drunk' (6.3.2); he adds the detail that festivities continued throughout the night (6.4.4).

Other social rituals are described without reference to a religious aspect. When the mangled body of the dead Charicles is carried in Cleitophon gives a full report of the competitive lamentations of his father and lover, but the burial itself is elided (1.13–15.1). A little earlier Cleinias' astringent vignette of wedding ceremonies picked out ritual with no religious colour, βόμβος αὐλῶν, δικλίδων κτύπος, πυρσῶν δαιδουχία, 'the booming of pipes, the banging of double-doors, the carrying of torches' (1.8.3). Symposia are conducted without libations (1.5, 2.2–3), even though ἦν ... ἑορτὴ προτρυγαίου Διονύσου τότε, 'at that time there was a festival of Dionysus of the Vintage' (2.2.1).

More religiosity is displayed in offering thanks to the gods. Thus, when Leucippe is found ὁ μὲν δὴ Κλεινίας ἀνεκρότησε παιανίσας, 'Cleinias clapped his hands and sang a paean' (7.15.3) – perhaps an exclamation of praise rather than a paean proper, and more probably for Artemis than Apollo.

Immediately after this those present εὐφήμουν … τὴν Ἄρτεμιν, 'ritually praised Artemis' (7.16.1): i.e. we are to imagine they shouted the well-documented cry 'Great is Artemis'. It must be noted, however, that at no point in the description of thank-offerings to gods is there mention of vows, from the opening of the novel where the narrator says that he σῶστρα ἔθυον ἐμαυτοῦ, 'I offered sacrifice for my safe escape', (1.1.2) to the place in Book 7 where the Byzantines send a θυσίαν … ἐπινίκιον, 'victory sacrifice', to Ephesian Artemis for her epiphany and her help to them in their war against Thracians (7.12.3). Perhaps we are to imagine that she appeared only when they had made a vow, but there is no hint of this. A sacrifice or the erection of an altar to express gratitude is apparently the furthest that dealings with the gods go, as when Melite contrasts the ingratitude of Cleitophon with the finder of a treasure who typically τὸν τόπον τῆς εὑρέσεως ἐτίμησε, βωμὸν ἤγειρε, θυσίαν προσήνεγκεν, ἐστεφάνωσε τὴν γῆν, 'honours the findspot, erects an altar, offers a sacrifice and garlands the ground' (5.26.9).

In contrast to these cases of manifest but perhaps somewhat deficient religiosity there are some striking silences.

During a terrible storm described at great length (3.2–4) no prayers or vows are voiced: only after the ship has broken apart does Cleitophon eventually pray to Poseidon, and there (as we have often seen) the novelist uses the prayer as a vehicle for slick rhetorical pyrotechnics:

> ἀνοιμώξας οὖν, 'ἐλέησον', ἔφην, 'δέσποτα Πόσειδον, καὶ σπεῖσαι πρὸς τὰ τῆς ναυαγίας σου λείψανα. πολλοὺς ἤδη τῶι φόβωι θανάτους ὑπεμείναμεν· εἰ δὲ ἡμᾶς ἀποκτεῖναι θέλεις, μὴ διαστήσηις ἡμῶν τὴν τελευτήν. ἓν ἡμᾶς κῦμα καλυψάτω. εἰ δὲ καὶ θηρίων ἡμᾶς βορὰν πέπρωται γενέσθαι, εἷς ἡμᾶς ἰχθὺς ἀναλωσάτω, μία γαστὴρ χωρησάτω, ἵνα καὶ ἐν ἰχθύσι κοινῆι ταφῶμεν'.
>
> So with a wail 'Show pity', I said, 'lord Poseidon, and make the libations of a truce with the remnants of your shipwreck. We have already undergone many deaths in our fears: if you wish to kill us, do not separate our end. May one wave engulf us. And if it is in fact fated that we shall be the food of beasts, let one fish consume us, one belly find space for us, so that even among fishes we may have a common tomb'.
>
> Achilles Tatius, *Leucippe and Cleitophon* 3.5.4

Again, Cleitophon addresses no prayer or vow to a god when he takes the great risk of administering an alleged healing drug to Leucippe: instead we hear a melodramatic 'prayer' to the drug itself:

> ἐπεὶ οὖν καιρὸς ἦν πιεῖν αὐτὴν τὸ φάρμακον, ἐγχέας προσηυχόμην αὐτῶι· 'ὦ γῆς τέκνον, φάρμακον, ὦ δῶρον Ἀσκληπιοῦ, ἀληθεύσειάν σου τὰ

ἐπαγγέλματα, εὐτυχέστερόν μου γενοῦ καὶ σῶζέ μοι τὴν φιλτάτην. νίκησον τὸ βάρβαρον ἐκεῖνο καὶ ἄγριον φάρμακον'.

So when the time came for her to drink the drug, I poured it out and addressed it with a prayer: 'O child of the earth, drug, o gift of Asclepius, may your promised capacities be realised. Be more successful than me, and save the girl who is dearest to me. Vanquish that other non-Greek and savage drug'.

Achilles Tatius, *Leucippe and Cleitophon* 4.17.1

Nor does Cleitophon voice any expression of thanks, far less make a thank-offering, when Leucippe indeed wakes up cured (4.17.4–6).

Similarly, when Cleinias tells of his survival in the storm, he says nothing of any thanks or thank-offerings (5.9–10); nor, perhaps even more surprisingly, do Cleitophon and Melite make any such offering when they have arrived safely in Ephesus (5.17.1). This is in contrast with the opening of the novel, where the narrator may not make any vows, but at least he makes a sacrifice to Astarte in Sidon for his safe escape from shipwreck. Later it is suggested by the repugnant Sosthenes that such survival demonstrates the gods' favour, when he describes Thersander as a man ὃν οὕτω φιλοῦσιν οἱ θεοί, ὡς αὐτὸν καὶ ἐκ μέσων τῶν τοῦ θανάτου πυλῶν ἀγαγεῖν, 'whom the gods love so much as to bring him back even from the midst of the gates of death' (6.13.2).

A comparable but different sort of evidence is offered by the extended presentation of Callisthenes' moral rehabilitation (8.17): all sorts of good qualities are attributed to him, but they are exclusively secular, and Sostratus makes no reference at all to piety.

Alongside these cases there are others where Achilles Tatius' narrative might be thought to establish him as the novelist with the least investment in religion.

First, gods are frequently used as hypostatisations of natural forces. Aphrodite and Eros are often simply *façons de parler* for sex.[36] Achilles also makes a similar, albeit trite, play with Ares figuring war and Aphrodite love: Ἀφροδίτη με πρὸς Ἄρεα ἀποστειλάτω, 'Let Aphrodite despatch me to Ares' (4.7.5). By the same token Dionysus stands for alcoholic drink, as too Eros does for desire (2.3.3), cf. τοῦ Διονύσου κατὰ μικρὸν ἐξιλασκομένου τὴν αἰδῶ (ἐλευθερίας γὰρ οὗτος πατήρ), 'as Dionysus gradually placated shame (for

[36] E.g. 1.7, 8, 10 (*autodidact*), 11 and 17; 2.3, 5, 19, 38 (three times); 4.7; 5.16, 25, 26, 27; 8.10 (facilitating a clever play with temples of Artemis and Aphrodite) and 11.

he is the father of freedom)' (8.4.2). In none of the other three novelists so far discussed are the gods' names used in quite this way.

There are also more cases in Achilles Tatius where gods are presented as actors in a myth rather than either as powers controlling characters' destinies or as the recipients of cult.[37] Most of these myths are not integral to the message of the narrative (as are, for example, Longus' mythological treatments of Pan in his inset tales);[38] but Achilles' myth about Pan in Book 8 is closely integrated and not mere décor.

6 Religion in Heliodorus, *Aethiopica*

I mention only in passing Heliodorus' exuberant accounts of grand festivals and rituals – the *theoria* of the Aenianes at Delphi, the *Nilōa*, the grid-iron test, and the great sacrificial ceremony at Meroe. Heliodorus' representations of Egyptian or Ethiopian religious practices, creating as they do a largely imaginary world which has a complex relationship to that of Greek religion, can only with difficulty be used to assess how realistic a representation we encounter of Greek religion itself. The Aenianes at Delphi (2.34ff.) are of course a different matter, and have been much discussed:[39] suffice here to say that Heliodorus incorporates many details that would ring true for Greeks familiar with the quadrennial Pythian games or with the irregular dispatch of a *Pythais* from Athens, and he cleverly builds in a device to protect his account of the *theoria* of the Aenianes from scholarly or historiographical criticism as a practice contrary to known reality: the Delphians abolish the *theoria* of the Aenianes after Theagenes' supposed abduction of Charicleia (4.20).

What I wish rather to examine, as in my discussion of the earlier novels, are smaller-scale elements of religious practice: prayers, vows, libations, offerings or sacrifices made in thanks for divine services rendered. At first sight we seem here to encounter the full religious apparatus of pagan practice, but, as in all the other novels except that of Longus, there are some puzzling omissions and inconcinnities.

[37] Eros at 1.1–2; 2.34; 8.12; Apollo at 1.5; Zeus at 1.8; 2.1, 6, 36 (Ganymede); 3.8 (Prometheus and Heracles); Aphrodite, Poseidon and the Nereids at 5.16; Aphrodite and Artemis at 8.12.

[38] For the bearing of these tales on the narrative see Winkler 1990; Wouters 1994; Bowie 2003b, 2019g; Montiglio 2012.

[39] Pouilloux 1983; Rougemont 1992; Rutherford 2013, 351–4; Nobili 2020.

(a) *Prayers*

There are many examples of prayers offered by several characters (though never by the evil Demaenete or the wicked Arsace!). What interests me particularly here is that only once does it seem possible that Heliodorus wants us to understand that a *vow* as well as a prayer is made. So Charicles is represented as πολλὰ τὸν θεὸν ἱκετεύων, 'often praying to the god in supplication', presumably to Apollo at Delphi, and duly getting a child (2.29). Charicleia goes to Nausicles' thanksgiving sacrifice to Hermes to use it εἰς τὰς ὑπὲρ Θεαγένους εὐχάς, 'for her prayers for Theagenes' (5.13.1), and does indeed do so (5.15.3, quoted in full shortly p. 729). But there is no hint that vows are involved, and indeed when Calasiris finds Charicleia clinging to the cult-statue (that of Hermes: cf. 5.13.3) she has fallen asleep after a long εὐχή which, from its length, must be a 'prayer' not a 'vow':

> καταλαμβάνει τοῖς ἴχνεσι τοῦ ἀγάλματος προσπεφυκυῖαν καὶ εὐχῆς τε μακρᾶι παρολκῆι καὶ λύπης προσβολῆι πρὸς ὕπνον βαθὺν ὀλισθήσασαν.
>
> He found her clinging to the feet of the cult-statue – she had slipped into a deep sleep as a result of her long protraction of her prayer and her attack of distress.
>
> Heliodorus, *Aethiopica* 5.34.1

After Calasiris' last supper we read that he σπεῖσαί τε καὶ πολλὰ ἐπεύξασθαι τῆι θεῶι, 'poured libations and offered many prayers to the goddess' (7.11.3): it is in theory possible that we are to understand him a making vows to Isis, but prayers that gave thanks and wished for his sons' felicity seem to be more probably what the reader is expected to understand.

The most elaborate prayer is that offered by Charicleia on her pyre:

> '"Ηλιε', ἀνεβόησε, 'καὶ Γῆ καὶ δαίμονες ἐπὶ γῆς τε καὶ ὑπὸ γῆν ἀνθρώπων ἀθεμίτων ἔφοροί τε καὶ τιμωροί, καθαρὰν μὲν εἶναί με τῶν ἐπιφερομένων ὑμεῖς ἐστε μάρτυρες ἑκοῦσαν δὲ ὑπομένουσαν τὸν θάνατον διὰ τὰς ἀφορήτους τῆς τύχης ἐπηρείας· ἐμὲ μὲν <οὖν> σὺν εὐμενείαι προσδέξασθε, τὴν δὲ ἀλάστορα καὶ ἀθεμιτουργὸν καὶ μοιχαλίδα καὶ ἐπ' ἀποστερήσει νυμφίου τοῦ ἐμοῦ ταῦτα δρῶσαν Ἀρσάκην ὡς ὅτι τάχιστα τιμωρήσασθε'.
>
> 'Sun', she cried in a loud voice, 'and Earth, and divine powers who are watchers over and punishers of men who transgress what is right on earth and beneath the earth, be witnesses that I am innocent of what is being brought against me and that I am willingly enduring death because of the unbearable grudges of fortune against me. Receive me benignly, but as for the she-devil, the sinner, the adulteress, the woman who is doing this to deprive me of my bridegroom, Arsace, punish her as swiftly as possible'.
>
> Heliodorus, *Aethiopica* 8.9.12

This prayer falls into the age-old Greek category of praying for punishment of one's enemies. The corollary is found when Oroondates prays that if anything befalls him the gods may reward Hydaspes:

> 'θεοὶ τῶν εἰς ἐμὲ καλῶν Ὑδάσπην τε καὶ οἶκον τὸν Ὑδάσπου καὶ γένος ἀμείβοιντο.'
>
> 'May the gods reward Hydaspes, and the household and family of Hydaspes, for his good treatment of me.'
>
> Heliodorus, *Aethiopica* 9.27.3

We also hear prayers for divine benevolence in cases where gods might be angry: Hydaspes himself prays for forgiveness if he has uttered anything impious:

> 'ὑμεῖς δὲ ἱλήκοιτε, ὦ θεοί, τῶν εἰρημένων [καὶ] εἰ δή τι πρὸς τοῦ πάθους νικώμενος οὐκ εὐαγὲς ἐφθεγξάμην ὁ τέκνον ὁμοῦ καλεσάμενος καὶ τεκνοκτόνος γινόμενος'.
>
> 'And may you, o gods, be forgiving for what has been said, if in fact overcome by what is happening I have uttered something that is not holy, I who have at the same moment have called her my child and become a child-killer'.
>
> Heliodorus, *Aethiopica* 10.16.10

Likewise, immediately afterwards the people of Meroe pray: 'ἱλήκοιεν οἱ θεοὶ τῆς δοκούσης παρανομίας', 'May the gods be forgiving to his apparent law-breaking' (10.17.2).

Alongside these many cases of simple prayer there remains one where a vow might indeed be involved: Calasiris narrates that on entering the Delphic temple 'προσεκύνουν καί τι καὶ κατ' ἐμαυτὸν ηὐχόμην' (2.26.5). This was translated by John Morgan 'I entered the temple, and as I knelt in private prayer'.[40] It is possible that a vow is meant – in that case κατ' ἐμαυτόν would not refer to privacy or interiority but to relevance or commitment 'I made a vow relating to myself'. But however appropriate it may be for Calasiris to have made a vow at this juncture, it does not seem to me, any more than it has seemed to other scholars, that the text invites this interpretation.

[40] Morgan 1989a, 400. Similar translations are offered by Maillon 1934, 'je formulai à part moi une prière', and Colonna 1987, 167, 'formulai una pregiera dentro di me'.

(b) Offerings or Sacrifices Made in Thanks for Divine Services Rendered

The situation is similar with regard to offerings or sacrifices made in thanks for divine services rendered. These are numerous, and help to build up an overall picture of a world in which piety and cultic observances are a widespread and well-established practice; and of course they prepare the ground for the apparently unavoidable sacrifice of Charicleia and Theagenes at Meroe towards the end of Book 10.

But there seem to be varieties of piety. Charicles is unusual in that, after taking custody of the infant Charicleia, he looked after her simply, we are told by Calasiris, 'πολλὴν τοῖς θεοῖς ὁμολογῶν χάριν', 'expressing much gratitude to the gods' (2.32.1). In comparable situations other characters make a sacrifice. So Nausicles announces 'θύειν ... μέλλω χαριστήρια τοῖς θεοῖς', 'I am going to offer a thanksgiving sacrifice to the gods' (5.12.3). At the ensuing feast,

> οἱ μὲν ἄνδρες ἐμβατήρια τῶι Διονύσωι καὶ ἦιδον καὶ ἔσπενδον, αἱ δὲ γυναῖκες ὕμνον τῇ Δήμητρι χαριστήριον ἐχόρευον· ἡ Χαρίκλεια δὲ χωρισθεῖσα τὸ ἑαυτῆς ἔπραττεν· ηὔχετο Θεαγένει σώιζεσθαι κἀκεῖνον ἑαυτῆι φυλάττεσθαι.
>
> The men danced departure-songs to Dionysus and poured libations, the women danced a thanksgiving hymn to Demeter. But Charicleia left them and attended to her own concern: she prayed that she might be saved for Theagenes, and that he might be preserved for her.
>
> Heliodorus, *Aethiopica* 5.15.3

It is not clear whether the participants are predominantly Greek, but his mention of Dionysus and Demeter shows that Heliodorus conceives of this as a description of Greek ritual.

Shortly thereafter we read in Calasiris' narrative that on reaching Egypt even Trachinus and his pirates 'χαριστήρια δῆθεν Ποσειδῶνι θύειν βούλεσθαι', 'wanted to offer a thanksgiving sacrifice to Poseidon' (5.27.9) – a sacrifice to which is linked a sumptuous εὐωχία, 'banquet', of which Calasiris gives a detailed *ecphrasis*, and which he later calls an 'ἀσώτωι συμποσίωι', 'profligate symposium' (5.29.2).

Some form of thanksgiving also seems to be implied when the populace of Memphis conducts Calasiris, now restored to his city and priesthood, ceremonially to the temple of Isis: Arsace, wanting to be part of the show and to be able to ogle Theagenes, ὅρμους καὶ πολὺν χρυσὸν ἐνέβαλεν εἰς τὸ Ἰσεῖον, 'cast jewellery and much gold into the Iseum' (7.8.6).

A more straightforward case is found when we read of Hydaspes' piety at Syene after defeating Oroondates:

> ὁ μὲν αὐτίκα πρὸς ἱεροῖς ἦν καὶ θεραπείαις τῶν κρειττόνων χαριστηρίοις.
>
> He immediately busied himself with religious matters and with thankful tendance of the higher powers.[41]
>
> Heliodorus, *Aethiopica* 9.22.2

In all these there is only one case where a vow made earlier might be involved: after Hydaspes' victory the Gymnosophists offer εὐχάς:

> κἀπειδὴ προσπεσόντες τοὺς θεοὺς προσεκύνησαν καὶ τὰς χαριστηρίους εὐχὰς ὑπέρ τε τῆς νίκης καὶ σωτηρίας ἐτέλεσαν, ἐκτὸς περιβόλων ἐλθόντες ἐπὶ τὴν δημοτελῆ θυσίαν ἐτρέποντο.
>
> And when they had prostrated themselves and saluted the gods and had completed the *euchai* of thanksgiving for his victory and safe return, they went outside the walls and addressed themselves to the public sacrifice.
>
> Heliodorus, *Aethiopica* 10.6.2

Morgan translated 'discharging their vows of thanksgiving for his victory and safe return'; Colonna rendered εὐχὰς 'preghiere di ringraziamento'.[42] Which is right? On the evidence of the practice in the rest of the text, these might more probably be 'prayers'. But the Gymnosophists of Meroe are paragons of religiosity – if anybody in Heliodorus' novel were allowed to make a vow, it would be them that he would choose.

(c) Libations

Libations are encountered both in public ceremonies and in private *symposia*. The most important case of the former is at Delphi, when the ceremonial lighting of the fire on the altar is accompanied by a libation:

> 'κατάρχειν τῆς σπονδῆς τὸν ἱερέα τοῦ Πυθίου καὶ τὸν βωμὸν ἀνάπτειν ἠξίουν· ὁ δὲ Χαρικλῆς τὴν μὲν σπονδὴν αὐτῶι προσήκειν ἔλεγε "τὸν βωμὸν

[41] Note the similarity of phrasing to the self-description of the Syenians' own religiosity, 'καὶ ὡς πρὸς θεραπείαν τῶν κρειττόνων ὄντας καὶ πρὸς τῆς εὐωχίας ἀφυπνωμένους, 'both being absorbed in their cult of the gods and having fallen asleep as a result of their feasting' (9.12.2). Against the suggestion of Dowden 2006, 255–8 that the term οἱ κρείττονες, 'the more powerful ones', is not found referring to the gods earlier than the fourth century AD see (e.g.) Luc. *Symp.* 7, *Demon.* 11.

[42] Morgan 1989a, 561; Colonna 1987, 537. Maillon 1943, 80 is ambiguous: 'lui firent des actions de grâce'.

δὲ ὁ τῆς θεωρίας ἄρχων ἁπτέτω παρὰ τῆς ζακόρου τὴν δᾶιδα κομισάμενος, τοῦτο γὰρ ἔθος ὁ πάτριος διαγινώσκει νόμος". ταῦτα εἶπε, καὶ ὁ μὲν ἔσπενδε, τὸ πῦρ δὲ Θεαγένης ἐλάμβανεν ...'

'They asked the priest of the Pythian to begin the libation and to light the altar: and Charicles said that the libation was his own concern, "but let the leader of the *theoria* set light to the altar, receiving the torch from temple attendant, for this is the custom that the ancestral law determines". These were his words, and he began to pour the libation, and Theagenes began to take the fire ...'

Heliodorus, *Aethiopica* 3.5.3–4

A second set of libations in a public ceremony is implied by Hydaspes' question to his now recognised daughter Charicleia concerning her male companion:

'ἀλλ' οὑτοσὶ τίς ποτέ ἐστιν, ὁ σοὶ μὲν ἅμα συλληφθεὶς καὶ εἰς τὰς ἐπινικίους σπονδὰς τοῖς θεοῖς φυλαχθείς, νυνί τε τοῖς βωμοῖς εἰς τὴν ἱερουργίαν προσιδρυμένος;'

'But who is this man here, who was captured together with you and has been kept for the victory libations to the gods, and is now located by the altars for his sacrifice?'

Heliodorus, *Aethiopica* 10.18.1

In the event, of course, Theagenes is not sacrificed. But Hydaspes' metonymy suggests that the sacrificial procedure would have included libations had it been initiated.

As to libations in private parties, it is remarkable that we witness only Calasiris explicitly pouring them. He does so at the start of the first meal with Cnemon at Chemmis:

'σπένδωμεν', ἔλεγε, 'θεοῖς ἐγχωρίοις τε καὶ Ἑλληνικοῖς', καὶ αὐτῶι γε Ἀπόλλωνι Πυθίωι καὶ προσέτι Θεαγένει καὶ Χαρικλείαι τοῖς καλοῖς τε καὶ ἀγαθοῖς, ἐπειδὴ καὶ τούτους εἰς θεοὺς ἀναγράφω.' καὶ ἅμα ἐδάκρυσεν, ὥσπερ ἑτέραν αὐτοῖς σπονδὴν ἐπιφέρων τοὺς θρήνους.

'Let us pour libations', he said, 'to the gods of this country and of the Greeks, and indeed to Pythian Apollo himself, and also to Theagenes and Charicleia the fair and noble, since I inscribe them too in the number of the gods.' And at the same time he shed a tear, as if contributing his lamentations as another libation to them.

Heliodorus, *Aethiopica* 2.23.1

The religious correctness of this act is somewhat undermined by Calasiris pouring libations to Theagenes and Charicleia on grounds that for him they are gods, and that Heliodorus is playing literary games with the practice of libations is made clear by his move to the trope of the libation of tears. He must also, of course, create a reason for Calasiris mentioning the couple in Cnemon's presence. For Heliodorus, building up a picture of Calasiris' protective closeness to Charicleia and Theagenes is more important than getting religious practices right, and the subordination of theology to literary effect is further displayed a few moments later when Calasiris declares that he will think even Cnemon 'θεοῖς ἰσοστάσιον', 'on a par with the gods' (2.23.3), if he can tell him where Charicleia and Theagenes are.

Later, on the same occasion, during his narrative to Cnemon, Calasiris proposes interrupting the narrative to pour the last libation of the day, 'τὰ κοιταῖα τοῖς νυχίοις θεοῖς ἐπεσπείσαντες', 'pouring a bedtime libation to the gods of the night' (3.4.11). In the description that follows only Calasiris pours a libation, to other gods and finally to Hermes.[43]

Again when the Tyrians set up a νικητήριος εὐωχία, 'victory banquet', to Heracles at Delphi (to celebrate their unnamed compatriot's wrestling-victory in the *Pythia*), Calasiris offers a sacrifice of λιβανωτός, 'frankincense', and pours a libation of water (4.16.4): the reader is perhaps to assume that the Tyrians had poured the customary libations of wine before Calasiris' arrival, but they do not do so in our text, even though Calasiris says (in a ploy to discover more about his impromptu hosts):

> 'δημῶδες γὰρ οἶμαι καὶ τῶν ἀγροικοτέρων σπονδῶν καὶ τραπέζης κοινωνήσαντας μὴ οὐχὶ καὶ τὴν περὶ ἀλλήλων γνῶσιν ἔχοντας ἀπελθεῖν, φιλίας ἀρχὴν ἱεροὺς ἅλας ποιησαμένους.'
>
> 'For I think it plebeian and a feature of more rustic folk to share libations and the table and to leave without also acquiring some knowledge of each other, making sacred salt the beginning of friendship.'
>
> Heliodorus, *Aethiopica* 4.16.5

Again, at the end of Nausicles' thanksgiving feast, Calasiris says: 'μνήμη τοῦ δαιμονίου γινέσθω, καὶ τὰς λυτηρίους τις σπονδὰς περιαγέτω', 'Let us take thought for the divine power, and let somebody bring round the concluding libations' (5.34.5);[44] and libations are duly poured. In Memphis, at the end of his last meal, as we have already seen, Calasiris is said to σπεῖσαί τε καὶ πολλὰ ἐπεύξασθαι τῆι θεῶι, 'pour libations and with them offer many prayers to the goddess' (7.11.3).

[43] An echo of the Phaeacians libations at Od. 7.137ff., as pointed out by Morgan 1989a, 414.

[44] Meineke printed περιαγέτω, later editors περιαγέσθω.

When Calasiris is not there, however, we rarely hear of libations. One exception is the omniscient narrator's *ecphrasis* of the perverted banquet at the start of the novel, where the opposites inappropriately conjoined include (for alliteration) σπονδὰς καὶ σφαγάς, 'libations and assassinations' (1.1.6) – libations that are assumed to have been poured, because there was a symposium, but not libations that occur during the time of the narrative.

Another pair of exceptions that are only apparent are two of Charicleia's frenzied outbursts. The first is in her bedroom during the celebrations for the wedding of Nausicleia and Cnemon, when she apostrophises the missing, perhaps dead Theagenes:

> 'τὸ παρὸν δέ σοι τάσδε ἐπιφέρω χοάς', καὶ ἅμα ἔτιλλε τὰς τρίχας καὶ τῆι κλίνηι ἐπέβαλλε. 'καὶ τάσδε ἐπιχέω τὰς σπονδὰς ἐκ τῶν σοι φίλων ὀφθαλμῶν', καὶ αὐτίκα διάβροχος ἦν ἡ στρωμνὴ τοῖς δάκρυσιν.
>
> 'For the moment I pour you these offerings', and she at once began to tear out her hair and throw it on the bed; 'and I also pour you these libations from those eyes that are dear to you', and at once the bedding was soaked with her tears.
>
> Heliodorus, *Aethiopica* 6.8.6

The second apparent exception presents Charicleia, deeming herself prevented by Calasiris' religious position from performing a ritual lamentation and professing instead to offer libations and offerings drawn from her own body:

> οὐδὲ θρηνῆσαι τὰ νενομισμένα ἔτι κειμένωι τῶι πτώματι πρὸς τοῦ προφητικοῦ συγκεχώρημαι. ἀλλ' ἰδού σοι, τροφεῦ καὶ σῶτερ, προσθήσω δὲ καὶ πάτερ κἂν ὁ δαίμων μὴ βούληται, ἔνθα γοῦν ἔξεστι καὶ ὡς ἔξεστιν ἀποσπένδω τῶν ἐμαυτῆς δακρύων καὶ ἐπιφέρω χοὰς ἐκ τῶν ἐμαυτῆς πλοκάμων.' καὶ ἅμα ἀπεσπάραττεν ὡς ὅτι πλείστας τῶν ἑαυτῆς τριχῶν.
>
> 'Nor am I allowed by his status as a prophet to perform the customary lamentations over his fallen body as it still lies there. But behold, guardian and saviour – and I shall add the name "father" too even if the heaven power does not wish it – at least in a place that I am permitted and a manner I am permitted I shed a libation from my own tears and I pour offerings from my own locks.'[45] And she at once began to tear out as many as she could of her own tresses.
>
> Heliodorus, *Aethiopica* 7.14.6

[45] For a comparison of tears to libations see also the description of Charicleia's and Theagenes emotional preparation for separation at 5.5.3: ἐπὶ τούτοις αὖθις περιέβαλλον ἀλλήλους καὶ αὖθις ἔκλαιον ὥσπερ οἶμαι σπονδῶν τῶν δακρύων ἀπάρχοντες καὶ ὅρκια τὰ φιλήματα ποιούμενοι, 'Thereupon they again began to embrace each other and again to weep, as if, I suppose, pouring libations of their tears and making their kisses oaths'.

One is tempted to wonder if Heliodorus knows of χοαί, 'libations', only from undiagnostic uses of the word in Attic tragedies, or from such titles as Χοηφόροι, '*Libation-bearers*', and does not realise that χοαί must be liquid.

At private *symposia*, however, where we might expect real, not metaphorical, libations, they do not happen. In his victory party in Delphi Theagenes προέπινεν ... ἑκάστωι φιλοτησίαν, 'proposed toasts of friendship to each (symposiast)', but libations are not mentioned (3.11.2). Nor when Theagenes plays *sommelier* for Arsace (7.27.3) and when Arsace in her last moments entertains Charicleia (8.7.7) are libations mentioned either, despite Arsace's alleged philhellenism. Part of Heliodorus' purpose is doubtless to portray Calasiris as extremely pious and ultra-ritualistic, and Arsace as religiously challenged. But in doing so he has Theagenes' victory party at Delphi fall short of Greek religious practice, practice that to judge from Plutarch and Athenaeus was alive and well at the beginning and end of the second century AD.

(d) Vows Made before Critical Actions

If we interrogate the text to see whether vows are made before critical actions we also have a negative result. In real life vows were made before sea journeys (cf. Aelius Aristides 26.1 Keil). The Tyrian victor at Delphi, Calasiris narrates, about to undertake a long sea voyage, regards his party at Delphi as 'νικητήριόν τε καὶ χαριστήριον, ἅμα δὲ καὶ ἐμβατήριον', 'a celebration and thanksgiving for his victory, and at the same time an embarcation-sacrifice' (4.16.8): but no mention is made of vows. When Nausicles is about to depart, Calasiris prays elaborately 'σοὶ μὲν ἐπ' αἰσίοις ὁ ἔκπλους στέλλοιτο', 'may your departure may be accompanied by good omens' (6.7.1) and escorted by Hermes, Κερδῷος, 'god of profit', and Poseidon Ἀσφάλειος, 'god of security': but here even he makes no vows.

At two points during the voyage from Delphi we might expect vows. Calasiris asks the fisherman Tyrrhenus to sacrifice on his behalf to Odysseus:

> 'θῦε διαπλεύσας εἰς Ἰθάκην ὑπερ ἡμῶν Ὀδυσσεῖ, καὶ αἴτει τῆς μήνιδος ἀνεῖναι τῆς καθ' ἡμῶν ἣν ἀγανακτεῖν, ὡς παρεωραμένος, τῆσδέ μοι τῆς νυκτὸς ἐπιφανεὶς ἐξηγόρευσεν.'
>
> 'Sail over to Ithaca and sacrifice on our behalf to Odysseus, and ask him to relent from his wrath against us which, appearing to me this very night, he has proclaimed, wrath that he nurses because he has been overlooked.'
>
> Heliodorus, *Aethiopica* 5.22.5

Perhaps Calasiris is right to think a sacrifice will be enough, but a reader would expect most Greeks so religiously sensitive as Calasiris also to have made a vow. Shortly after this there is a huge storm – a prime occasion for making vows – but again no vow is mentioned in Calasiris' narrative (5.27). When the couple is planning for their departure from the bandits' island Theagenes says that their survival to live with each other is something for which ἡμεῖς τε εὐχόμεθα θεοί τε Ἑλλήνιοι παρέχοιεν, 'we pray and may the Greek gods provide' (5.4.6). So too in Syene when part of their wall collapses the people θεοὺς ἐπεβοῶντο σωτῆρας, 'called upon the gods to save them' (9.5.1). In neither case does the party in such a life-threatening situation make a vow. Finally neither Persians nor pious Ethiopians make vows or even engage in any religious ritual when they join battle (9.16.1).

Before concluding let me mention another oddity where the problem seems to be of excess rather than of deficiency. Twice we read of hymns offered to a god in response to a critical situation. At Delphi Charicles ὕμνον ἀποθύει τῶι θεῶι, τεταραγμένος τι κατὰ τοὺς ὕπνους, 'makes a sacrifice of a hymn to the god, since he had been troubled in some way during his sleep' (3.18.1). Charicles is of course a priest, but for an individual to arrange for the performance of a ὕμνος, 'hymn', after having a bad dream seems like over-kill. Aristides, of course, set up choruses of boys in Pergamum to sing hymns, but that was a response to quite explicit instructions from Asclepius.[46] Then at Chemmis the women ὕμνον τῆι Δήμητρι χαριστήριον ἐχόρευον, 'danced a thanksgiving hymn to Demeter' (5.15.3): again a response that perhaps exceeds what would be expected in a private matter. I have not found any parallels from 'real life'.[47]

(e) Theology

One point can be made on the basis of these hymnic performances, and that is that Heliodorus presents a world in which all but the worst characters esteem piety and regard the gods as important agents in their lives.

[46] Aristid. *Or.* 50.38 Keil, cf. Bowie 1989a, 215. It is possible that Heliodorus is influenced by (and wants his reader to think of?) Socrates' composition of τὸ εἰς τὸν Ἀπόλλω προοίμιον, 'the hymn to Apollo', when awaiting death in prison, Pl. *Phd.* 60d2.

[47] For choral performances in the cult of Zeus at Panamara and Apollo at Claros in the imperial period see Bowie 2006c (Chapter 16 in Volume 3) at nn. 25–30, Bowie 2022b; for publication and discussion of the voluminous epigraphic evidence from Claros, Ferrary 2014. For a hymn to Antinous sung at Curium on Cyprus see Bowie 1990b (Chapter 14 in this volume). For a hymn commanded by the oracle at Claros and sung by six youths and six maidens in the proconsulate of P. Iuventius Celsus (AD 128–9) on the initiative of P. Aelius Glycon of Laodicea ad Lycum, *prophetes* of Apollo Pythius, see Ferrary 2014, i 256-9 no. 31. An elegiac poem was later sung by Athenian ephebes to welcome Herodes Atticus in his return from exile, *IG* ii^2 3606.

This can be said without delving deep into the complex theology of the author and his characters, who at various points attribute responsibility for what is happening to them to divine or universal powers that are differently named – most frequently to θεοί or οἱ θεοί, 'gods' or 'the gods', but also to οἱ κρείττονες, 'the higher powers', ὁ δαίμων, 'the divine spirit', Μοῖραι, 'Fates', τὰ εἱμαρμένα, 'what is allotted', τὰ πεπρωμένα, 'what is fated', or Τύχη, 'Chance'. It may be significant for characterisation that whereas Charicleia (7.14.5–6), Theagenes (2.1.6, 2.6.2), and Cnemon (2.17.2) blame ὁ δαίμων for their situation, and whereas the author once attributes a situation to ὁ δαίμων (1.1.6) and once to δαιμονία ἐπικουρεία, 'divine assistance' (9.8.2), Calasiris, despite the extent of his narrative, only does so twice. Once concerns his sexual feelings for Rhodopis, where he describes himself as συνεὶς ὡς τῶν πεπρωμένων ἐστὶν ὑπόκρισις καὶ ὡς ὁ τότε εἰληχὼς δαίμων οἱονεὶ προσωπεῖον αὐτὴν ὑπῆλθε, 'realising that this was a staging of what was fated, and that the divine spirit who at that time had been allotted me had crept into her as if she were his mask' (2.25.3). The second occasion is where he sums up the trio's dire situation after capture by the infatuated Trachinus: πρὸς τοῦτο ὁ δαίμων ἀντέπραξεν, 'this outcome has been blocked by the divine spirit' (5.29.6). It may also be significant for characterisation that neither Calasiris nor Charicleia ever attributes the characters' situation to Τύχη, 'Fortune': it is not a real exception when the use of the Phoenician traders' luxurious goods for the pirates' banquet is presented by Calasiris as narrator as something that came about since 'ἀσώτωι συμποσίωι τῆς τύχης ἐνυβρίσαι παραδούσης', 'Fortune had abandoned them to be humiliated in a profligate drinking party' (5.29.2). All these diverse stances, and even the several cases where the same character attributes the events to a combination or disjunction of these forces, are wholly compatible with reality, and they could not be used in an argument that attempted to cast doubt on the realism of Heliodorus' representation. Nor does this diversity settle the question whether in Heliodorus' novel 'fate' means little more than 'the plot as constructed by the author', or is part of a serious attempt by the author to render the complexity of humans' views of the divine.[48]

7 Conclusions

In Heliodorus we found a similar incomplete presentation of traditional pagan ritual to that in three of the other four novels: the exception remains Longus, in whose *Daphnis and Chloe* a vow is indeed explicitly made by

[48] For the latter view Dowden 1996, 2010.

Daphnis (2.24.1–2), and only the victory feast of the impious Methymnans (2.25.3) unambiguously proceeds without libations and associated prayers..

What is happening? Has pagan practice in the Greek world of the Roman Empire 'declined' so that vows and libations are no longer integral to communication with the gods? That is certainly not so in many aspects of religious practice.[49] Nor is it the case for vows. Many epigraphic texts from Asia Minor and Syria specify that the dedicator has made the dedication εὐξάμενος, 'having made a vow'. The practice can be observed uninterruptedly from the archaic and classical periods to the third century AD. I have put a small selection of instances in the Appendix, divided into cases known from epigraphy and others found in literary texts, though it is an artificial distinction (and inscribed epigram, which I have allocated to 'literary texts', is of course *optimo iure* epigraphic). Very many more examples could be added. I mention just two from Athens that will have been well known to many Greek readers of the imperial period. First, the fact that the annual Athenian *theoria* to Delos was said to be in fulfilment of a vow made by the Athenians when Theseus and the δὶς ἑπτά, 'twice seven', returned safely from Crete.[50] Second, the end of Plato's dialogue *Phaedo* that refers to this *theoria* presents Socrates' last words as a reminder to Crito that a cock must be offered to Asclepius in fulfilment of a vow.[51]

It seems, then, that the novelists are giving a less than fully realistic reflection of religion as they can know it from their own times. In this their portrayal of religion chimes with that of some other aspects of either the world of the Roman Empire or the world of late-fifth-century Greece apparently chosen as his setting by Chariton, e.g. the way their cities functioned, or the impact of Persia. The world of the novel may often look like that of historiography, but the genre cannot be treated as an identical twin – indeed from time to time we would have to suppose that the twin we call the novel has been taken over by an alien. In some cases we might wish to argue that the differences between the world as known to readers (whether a classical or contemporary world, i.e. of the fifth or fourth centuries BC or of the first to third centuries AD) and the world presented by a novelist are there to provoke re-assessment of the latter, a case easiest to argue in the case of Longus. Stephen Trzaskoma has argued eloquently for the creation by Chariton of an 'uchronic' world whose details deliberately do not fit what he and his readers could have known about the politics of Syracuse and of

[49] See e.g. Lane Fox 1986; for priests Bremmer 2011.

[50] Pl. *Phd.* 58a–b.

[51] Pl. *Phd.* 118a.

the eastern Mediterranean in the years after Hermocrates' victory over the Athenians, a world which invites us to speculate 'what if ...' concerning the subsequent course of history.[52]

The novelists' failure to have their characters make vows, despite often being trapped in critical situations of just the sort in which vows were made in the 'real' world, may be part of a wider strategy of this sort. Or it may just be an acquiescence in offering a 'thin', less than full account of certain aspects of their characters' world on which their literary attention is not primarily focused – whatever else, the novelists are not historians of Greek religion. But another explanation deserves consideration. The vow is a part of the *do ut des* religious system in which a pious worshipper can expect his or her chosen god to deliver the divine side of the bargain at least some of the time: our epigraphic dedications document cases which were held to be just such a contractual delivery. The possibility of an Anthia or a Callirhoe, of a Cleitophon or a Charicles, resorting to a vow would greatly reduce the anxiety and distress of readers contemplating the character in cliff-hanging peril. Given that the novelists' gods are ultimately benevolent, even if characters have to ensure many vicissitudes from which these gods seem unwilling to protect or release them, a high-value vow made by an otherwise pious character would give the novelist the choice between two unwelcome alternatives: either the god is to take no action, which would undermine the ascription to that god of general, albeit often deferred, benevolence, or the character's request is to be granted, thereby short-circuiting the protraction of the characters' gruelling adventures which are the very stuff of the genre.

Appendix: A Selection of 'Real' Vows Attested by Epigraphy and Literature

Epigraphically Documented Vows

(1) ἐπὶ ὑπάτων Οὐεσπασιανοῦ Καί-
σαρος τὸ ἔνατον καὶ Τίτου Κα-
ίσαρος τὸ ζʹ, Σεξτιλία Ποπλί-
ου θυγάτηρ Ἡδονὴ ὑπὲρ τῶν
Σεβαστῶν καὶ ὑπὲρ Τίτου Φλα̣-
βίου Ἡλίου εἰρηνοφύλακος τῆς
ἐπαρχείας υἱοῦ Γλύκωνος Ἀ-
γροστεανοῦ Τειμαίου τοῦ ἑ-
αυτῆς ἀνδρὸς καὶ ὑπὲρ Τίτου

[52] In a talk given at Corpus Christi College, Oxford on 22 May 2012.

Φλαβίου Σεξτιλιανοῦ υἱοῦ ἰδίου Δι-
ὶ Βεννίωι Ἀγροστεων καὶ Ζβου-
ρηας καὶ θεοῖς πατρίοις τοῖς
Ἡλίου τοῦ ἑαυτῆς ἀνδρὸς εὐ-
ξαμένη ἀνέθηκεν.

In the consulships of Vespasian Cae|sar for the ninth time and Titus Ca|esar for the sixth time Sextilia Hedone, daughter of Publi|us, on behalf of the| Augusti and of Titus Fla|vius Helius, warden-of-the-peace of the| province, son of Glycon A|grosteanus Timaeus, h|er own husband, and on behalf of Titus| Flavius Sextilianus, their own son, to Z|eus Bennius of the Agrostes and Zbu|rea, and to the ancestral gods of her husband Helius, after making a vow dedicated (this).

SEG 40.1233: from Kirkpinar in Phrygia, Upper Tembris Valley, dated to AD 79, cf. *ANRW* ii 18.3 (1990) 1977, 16

(2) Ἡλίωι Μίθ̣ρ̣[αι]
Μᾶρκος Λούκκιος Κρίσπος
ὑπὲρ τῆς ἱερᾶς βουλῆς καὶ δήμου Περγα[ίων]
εὐξάμενο̣[ς] καθιέρωσεν μετὰ τῶν τέ[κνων]

To Helios Mithras | Marcus Luccius Crispus | on behalf of the sacred council and people of Perge | after making a vow consecrated (this) along with his children.

IPerge 248 (AD 150–200)

(3) ἀγαθῆι τύχηι.
Ἀκρίσιος Ἀμύντου
καὶ Διογένης καὶ Ἀμύν-
τας υἱοὶ ἀρχιβωμισταὶ
Ἀπόλλωνος καὶ Κόρης
καὶ τῶν συννάων θεῶν
εὐξάμενοι τῆι Κυρίαι Οὐρανίαι
Ἀρτέμιδι τὸν ἀκμάζοντα
Καιρὸν ἐκ τῶν ἰδίων
ἀνέθηκα̣ν.

May good fortune attend! | Acrisius son of Amyntas | and his sons Diogenes and Amyn|tas, chief altar-tenders| of Apollo and the Maiden | and of the gods that dwell with them,| after making a vow to the Heavenly Lady | Artemis dedicated the (statue of) 'Timeliness in his prime' with their own funds.

SEG 38.1652 Gerasa, Arabia, second century AD

(4) ὑπὲρ διαμονῆς τοῦ εὐσεβεστάτου Αὐτοκράτορος Ἀντωνίνου·
Παπίνιος ὁ φιλόσοφος ἐγκατοχήσας τῶι κυρίωι Σαράπιδι
παρὰ ταῖς Νεμέσεσιν, εὐξάμενος αὐξῆσαι τὸ Νεμέσειον,
τὸν παρατεθέντ<α> οἶκον ταῖς Νεμέσεσιν ἀνιέρωσεν, ὡς
εἶναι ἐν ἱερῶι τῶν κυρίων Νεμέσεων τὸ ὅλον.
ὁ τόπος συνεχωρήθη ὑπὸ τοῦ Αὐτοκράτορος Ἀντωνίνου,
Γεντι{νι}ανῶι καὶ Βάσσωι ὑπάτοις, πρὸ *νωνῶν* Ὀκτωβρίων.

For the long life of the most pious emperor Antoninus:| Papinius the philosopher, after having been possessed by the lord Sarapis | beside the Nemeseis, made a vow to extend the Nemeseion,| and dedicated the adjacent house to the Nemeseis, so| that the whole (complex) should be in the sacred space of the Lady Nemeseis.| The ground was granted by the emperor Antoninus, in the consulship of Gentianus and Bassus, on the 6th October.

Building/dedicatory inscription for *Nemeseion* by Papinius the philosopher; AD 211/212, Smyrna (*CIG* 3163= *IGRR* iv 1403 = Vidman, *Syll.* 306 = *ỊSmyrna* 725)

(5) Διὶ Ὀλυμπίωι | Μαρ̣η[-]λλη | [Ἀν]τώνιος | Δομιττιανὸς | οὐετρανὸς | [ε]ὐξάμεν̣[ος] | ἀνέστησα.

To Zeus Olympius | Mare[-]lles | I, Antonius | Domittianus, | a veteran, | after making a vow| set (this) up.

SEG 41.1420 from Til(li) (Çattepe) ca. AD 200

(6) θε<ὲ>ς {θεαῖς} ἐπη-
κόοις Καρπεῖ-
να εὐξαμέν-
η κὲ ἐπακουσ-
θῖσα ἀνέθηκε

To gods {and goddesses}(?) who list|en Carpi|na after making a vow | and having been listen|ed to dedicated (this).

IGLS iv 1262 Syria, Laodicea

Literary Presentation of Vows

(a) τὴν δ' αὖ Τηλέμαχος πεπνυμένος ἀντίον ηὔδα·
'μῆτερ ἐμή, μή μοι γόον ὄρνυθι μηδέ μοι ἦτορ
ἐν στήθεσσιν ὄρινε φυγόντι περ αἰπὺν ὄλεθρον·
ἀλλ' ὑδρηναμένη, καθαρὰ χροῒ εἵμαθ' ἑλοῦσα,
[εἰς ὑπερῶι' ἀναβᾶσα σὺν ἀμφιπόλοισι γυναιξὶν]
εὔχεο πᾶσι θεοῖσι τεληέσσας ἑκατόμβας
ῥέξειν, αἴ κέ ποθι Ζεὺς ἄντιτα ἔργα τελέσσηι'.

To her in turn sound-thinking Telemachus voiced in reply:
'Dear mother, do not rouse grief in me, nor make my heart
turn over in my breast, escaped as I have from sheer destruction.
But bathe yourself, and pick out clean clothes for your body,
[and go up to the upstairs rooms with your attendant women]
and vow in prayer to all the gods that complete hecatombs are what
you will sacrifice to them, if ever Zeus brings acts of requital to
completion'.

Homer, Od. 17.45–51

(b) Δημοκύδης τόδ' ἄγαλμα Τε|λεστοδίκη τ' ἀπὸ κοινῶν |
εὐξάμενοι στῆσαν παρ|θένωι Ἀρτέμιδι |
σεμνῶι ἐπὶ δαπέδωι κό|ρηι Διὸς αἰγιόχοιο·
τῶν γενέην βίοτόν τ' α|ὖχσ' ἐν ἀπημοσύνηι.

Democydes and Telestodice, having vowed this object of delight,
set it up from their common resources to the maiden Artemis
in her solemn precinct, the daughter of Zeus the aegis-bearer:
may she augment their family and livelihood without them suffering any
loss

IG xii.5 215 =*CEG* 414, Paros, ca. 500 BC

(c) πότν', ἀπαρχὲν τένδε Μένανδρο[ς – ⏑ ⏑ – –] |
εὐχολὲν τελέσας σοὶ χάριν ἀντ[ιδιδός] |
Αἰγιλιεὺς hυιὸς Δεμετρίο hὸ[ν ⏑ ⏑ – –] |
σδιζε, Διὸς θύγατερ, τõνδε χάρ[ιν θεμένε].

Lady, this first fruit did Menander [... ... .]
bringing to completion his vow and requiting you with thanks –
a man from Aigialus, the son of Demetrius, whom [... .]
please save, daughter of Zeus, giving requital for these things.

IG i^3 872 = *CEG* 275, Attica 450–25 BC

(d) ἐπειδὴ δὲ αἱ νῆες πληρεῖς ἦσαν καὶ ἐσέκειτο πάντα ἤδη ὅσα ἔχοντες ἔμελλον ἀνάξεσθαι, τῆι μὲν σάλπιγγι σιωπὴ ὑπεσημάνθη, εὐχὰς δὲ τὰς νομιζομένας πρὸ τῆς ἀναγωγῆς οὐ κατὰ ναῦν ἑκάστην, ξύμπαντες δὲ ὑπὸ κήρυκος ἐποιοῦντο, κρατῆράς τε κεράσαντες παρ' ἅπαν το στράτευμα καὶ ἐκπώμασι χρυσοῖς τε καὶ ἀργυροῖς οἵ τε ἐπιβάται καὶ οἱ ἄρχοντες σπένδοντες …

And when the boats were full and everything had at last been loaded which the Athenians were to take when they sailed, silence was commanded by a trumpet-call, and they made the vows that are customary before putting to sea, not ship by ship, but all together as directed by the herald, with both the marines and the officers mixing mixing-bowls throughout the whole fleet and making libations with gold and silver drinking vessels...

Thucydides 6.32.1

(e) Ἰναχίηι ἕστηκεν ἐν Ἴσιδος ἡ Θαλέω παῖς
Αἰσχυλὶς Εἰρήνης μητρὸς ὑποσχεσίηι.

Aeschylis, daughter of Thales, stands in the temple of Inachian Isis, because of the promise of her mother Eirene.

Callimachus, *Epigram* 18 *HE*/Asper = 57 Pfeiffer = *AP* 6.150

(f) Δήμητρι τῆι Πυλαίηι
τῆι τοῦτον οὐκ Πελασγῶν
Ἀκρίσιος τὸν νηὸν ἐδείματο, ταῦθ' ὁ Ναυκρατίτης
καὶ τῆι κάτω θυγατρί
τὰ δῶρα Τιμόδημος
εἵσατο τῶν κερδέων δεκατεύματα – καὶ γὰρ εὔξαθ' οὕτως.

To Demeter of the Gates, for whom Acrisius descended from the Pelasgi built this temple, and to her daughter below, Timodemus of Naucratis set up these gifts as tithes of his gains: for indeed that is how he vowed.

Callimachus, *Epigram* 19 *HE*/Asper = 39 Pfeiffer = *AP* 13.25

(g) ὅμως δὲ πειρατέον τήν γε πρόσρησιν ἐκτελέσαι, ἄλλως τε καὶ εὐχὴν ἀποπληροῦντας, ἐπειδήπερ ἐσώθημεν.

Nevertheless an attempt must be made to accomplish this address, especially since we are fulfilling a vow, since we have indeed been saved.[53]

Aelius Aristides *Or.* 45 (*To Sarapis*).13 Keil (AD 142)

(h) ηὐξάμην γάρ, ὁπότε ὁ πόλεμος μάλιστα ἐφλέγμαινε, καὶ μυηθῆναι, εἴη δὲ καὶ σοῦ μυσταγωγοῦντος.

for I vowed, when the war was raging at its height, that I should also be initiated, and may it happen with you as my initiator in the mysteries.

Marcus Aurelius quoted by Philostr., *VS* 2.1.563

[53] Aristides had apparently made a vow to Sarapis during a storm as he was sailing back from Egypt: cf. *Or.* 45.33 Keil and the introduction to that speech in Behr 1981, 419–20.

37 Caging Grasshoppers: Longus' Materials for Weaving 'Reality' (2013)

1 Introduction

The other papers in the volume entitled *Real and Ideal in the Ancient Novel* have operated, explicitly or implicitly, with a number of different definitions of 'the real' and 'the ideal'.[1] I had better make it clear how *I* mean to use these terms. By 'ideal' I understand a presentation of action and character that emphasises praiseworthy qualities or actions, on occasion by eliminating or obscuring motives or choices that might be expected in 'ordinary', 'real' people. The resulting characters are like those attributed by Aristotle to tragedy, βελτίους ἢ καθ' ἡμᾶς, 'better than in our world'.[2] By 'real' I understand situations and behaviour which seem to a reader to correspond more or less closely with what he or she has encountered or expects to encounter in the world in which he or she lives. It is immediately apparent that on this understanding 'real' and 'ideal' are not opposites. 'Real' and the 'ideal' may indeed be opposite when they apply to behaviour, but my concept of the 'ideal' has no simple relation to 'situation'. On my terminology, then, the gang of four other Greek novels – those of Chariton, Xenophon, Achilles Tatius and Heliodorus – earn their frequently given epithet 'ideal' by reason of their characters' behaviour, but their settings are in general as 'real' as those of historians, ethnographers, geographers or letter-writers. Indeed in an early paper, delivered at the first conference on the ancient novel, ICAN, in Bangor 1976, I argued that for this reason the Greek novels could and should be taken, albeit with caution, as evidence for the society of the Greek world in the Roman Empire.[3]

I still think that for the gang of four this is broadly the case. Chariton, for example, builds up a readily recognisable universe in which what is familiar to him and his readers from their contemporary world – cities,

[1] Paschalis, Panayotakis, and Schmeling 2013.

[2] *Po.* 1448a4. Translations such as 'better than ourselves' (Halliwell 1987) or 'better than we are' (Janko 1987) do not fully catch the sense of the phrase, explained correctly by Lucas 1968, 64 as comparable to 'people now' (τῶν νῦν, at 1448a18).

[3] Summarised in Bowie 1977 (Chapter 19 in this volume).

meetings of an assembly, sea-journeys, country villas, local aristocrats, reasoned discussions of possible courses of action and, of course, the whole gamut of emotions including ἔρως, 'desire' – are blended with data about the early-fourth-century Mediterranean world that can be acquired by reading historians like Thucydides, Philistus and Ephorus, or geographers like Poseidonius and Strabo, spiced up with some features like pirates that may owe more to declamation than to historiography. Declamation and New Comedy are perhaps the closest to fictional sources that we can postulate for Chariton's *inventio*, though of course he draws on Attic tragedy for patterns of plot, and on Homer both for these and for carefully calibrated inter-textuality in the form of telling citations of single lines.[4]

With Longus, however, things are different. Many of the general features and details of the pastoral world in which Daphnis and Chloe are located for most of their story seem to derive neither from personal observation, nor from the descriptions of a political or socio-economic historian of Lesbos, but from literary texts *that are themselves presenting fiction*: chief amongst these are Homer, Theocritus and post-Theocritean bucolic poetry.[5] Other poetic texts on which Longus drew were not, perhaps, overtly presenting a fictional world: I think here of the poets of the sixth century BC, Sappho and Alcaeus, both of whose Mytilenean connections recommended them as intertexts for Longus' project; perhaps of Ibycus; and of Philetas in the third century BC. But the poetic universe presented by these melic poets of archaic Greece or even by the Hellenistic elegy of Philetas was arguably by the second and third centuries AD a world much more distant from readers than the worlds of Thucydides and Ephorus and shared more with the fictional worlds of Homer and Theocritus. Moreover, at an early stage in his miniature novel, Longus gives his readers very clear indications that the universe of Daphnis and Chloe has as its principal point of origin not the real world but that of artistic creations, above all literary creations.

In looking at the debt of Longus to Theocritus and Sappho I am of course revisiting well-trodden territory, and I shall be repeating points found in the excellent discussions of Hunter and of Pattoni as well as plundering ideas from other scholars.[6] But I hope that approaching these issues with different questions will still yield some new and worthwhile perspectives.

[4] For the novelists' exploitation of canonical Greek mythology, especially as mediated by Attic tragedy, see now Lefteratou 2018.

[5] For Homer as fiction see Bowie 1993a (Chapter 4 in Volume 1). For Theocritus as an 'inventor' of fiction see Payne 2007.

[6] Hunter 1983; Pattoni 2004. For the contribution of the pastoral tradition to Longus' construction see also Cresci 1999; Effe 1999. For that of Sappho and Theocritus Bowie 2019g, 2021a, and 2021b.

2 The Country

Longus' pointers to intertextuality with Theocritus start with his preface. On the one hand it presents crucial details evocative of Theocritus' pastoral world. Its description of a *locus amoenus* with a πηγή, 'spring', and of a painting depicting ποίμνια, 'grazing beasts', and ποιμένες, 'shepherds', and a story given over entirely to desire (πάντα ἐρωτικά), points strongly to pastoral.[7] The word πηγή, 'spring', of course prompts a reader also to think of (literary) sources.[8] Shortly after the preface we read that the goatherd who found an abandoned baby being suckled by one of his goats decided, with his wife, to call this child Daphnis, ὡς … ἂν καὶ τὸ ὄνομα τοῦ παιδίου ποιμενικὸν δοκοίη, 'so that the name of the child might also seem pastoral' (1.3.2). Given that some traditions about Daphnis preceded Theocritus this cannot be conclusive,[9] but surely the best known Daphnis is that of Theoc. 1 – perhaps the same as the one who makes a cameo appearance in Theoc. 7.73, but less easy to conceive as identical with the homo-erotic Daphnis of Theoc. 6.[10] It becomes progressively more certain that the constituents of Longus' pastoral landscape are to be seen as drawing on that of Theocritus, and that *Idyll* 1 is of primary importance. At 1.10.2 Longus describes Daphnis and Chloe's spring pastimes: while Daphnis made a panpipe, Chloe gathered some rushes and began to weave a grasshopper cage or trap. The passage evokes the boy depicted weaving a grasshopper cage or trap on the cup in (once again) Theoc. 1.52–4, likewise totally absorbed in his artistic activity: both texts even have the same disagreement in the manuscript tradition – is this an ἀκριδοθήραν, 'grasshopper trap', or an ἀκριδοθήκην, 'grasshopper cage'?[11]

7 Above all to the opening of the poem that stood first in at least some ancient editions of Theoc., Ἁδύ τι τὸ ψιθύρισμα καὶ ἁ πίτυς, αἰπόλε, τήνα, | ἁ ποτὶ ταῖς παγαῖσι, μελίσδεται, ἁδὺ δὲ καὶ τύ | συρίσδες …, 'A sweet sort of whispering does that pine-tree, goatherd, over there | the one by the springs, make as its music, and sweetly too do you play the rustic pipe …', Theoc. 1.1–3. Of course Theocritus' *locus amoenus* itself exploits earlier well-known intertexts: the cave of Calypso at Od. 5.55–74, perhaps Sappho fr. 2 and Ibycus fr. 286 *PMGF* – all of these with erotic associations.

8 Cf. LSJ *s.v.* πηγή II.2.

9 Notably the poem ascribed to Stesich. by Ael. *VH* 10.18 = fr. 279 *PMGF* = 323 Finglass. On this see Bowie 2012c (Chapter 23 in Volume 1).

10 On the Daphnis of Theoc. 6 see Bowie 1996a (Chapter 9 in this volume).

11 The identity of the *variae lectiones* itself raises questions: are the two readings of Longus' MSS, ἀκριδοθήραν, 'grasshopper trap', in V and ἀκριδοθήκην, 'grasshopper cage', in F, the same as the two of those of Theocritus by chance, or because Longus himself circulated two editions with variants, as once argued by Young 1968 and 1971? Or has an ancient or Byzantine reader of Longus been sent to his text of Theocritus by the signals to which I have drawn attention and corrected his text?

But as well as such details the opening sequence of *Daphnis and Chloe* flashes a different sort of signal. By a provocative pleonasm Longus calls the painting in the cave εἰκόνος γραφήν, 'the sketch of a painting', and proposes ἀντιγράψαι τῆι γραφῆι, 'to sketch in emulation of the sketch', having sought out an ἐξηγητής, 'expounder', who can explain its contents. We are thus taken on a vertiginous journey that brings us several steps from the real world: the work we are asked to imagine is itself the γραφή, 'representation', of an εἰκών, 'painting', – itself a representation, we imagine, of events in some sort of universe: the exposition of the ἐξηγητής takes us one further step from reality, and in the narrator's version – the one *we* are reading – even by arithmetic progression, and not the geometric progression on which a Platonist reader might insist, we are already four steps from the real world.

This gap from the real world is important to remember when we encounter some further, clearly signalled Theocritean intertexts: I pick out three, each of which is very familiar.

(1) For my first case I move forward to a scene late in Book 2. Chloe, abducted by the naval task-force from Methymna, has been rescued through the intervention of Pan, whose capacity for anger is known to readers from *Idyll* 1.[12] A party is held to celebrate Chloe's safe return. The couple and their families celebrate by sacrificing their best she-goat to the nymphs; the next day they sacrifice their leading he-goat to Pan. Philetas joins the ensuing celebration, accompanied by his son Tityrus, πυρρὸν παιδίον καὶ γλαυκόν, 'a young boy with red hair and bright eyes' (2.32.1). The reader who has Theocritus in mind could well be puzzled: the suitor of Amaryllis in *Idyll* 3 also had a young Tityrus to do his bidding, in his case to watch his goats during his wooing; but the description given to that Tityrus suggested a younger fellow-shepherd with whom the singer had a sexual relationship, not a son: the diagnostic phrase is Τίτυρ' ἐμὶν τὸ καλὸν πεφιλημένε, βόσκε τὰς αἶγας, 'Tityrus, my lovely darling, graze the goats' (*Idyll* 3.3). Is Longus simply playing randomly, or at least carelessly, with pastoral names? Or is he asking his reader to revisit the opening of *Idyll* 3 and to ponder whether the Tityrus there is perhaps a beloved son and not a beloved ἐρώμενος?[13]

[12] οὐ θέμις, ὦ ποιμήν, τὸ μεσαμβρινὸν οὐ θέμις ἄμμιν | συρίσδεν. τὸν Πᾶνα δεδοίκαμες· ἦ γὰρ ἀπ' ἄγρας | τανίκα κεκμακὼς ἀμπαύεται· ἔστι δὲ πικρός, | καί οἱ ἀεὶ δριμεῖα χολὰ ποτὶ ῥινὶ κάθηται, 'It is not allowed, shepherd, at midday, it is not allowed for us | to play the pipe. Pan it is that we fear: for indeed from his chase | at that time he is tired, and rests; and he is sharp-tempered, | and pungent bile is always seated at his nose', Theoc. 1.15–18.

[13] There might also have been such an ancient scholarly debate on the relation to Sappho of her πάις, 'girl', Cleis, frr. 132 and 98b: cf. the claim that Sappho had a daughter Cleis made in *P.Oxy.* 1800 and Suda σ 107 *s.v.* Σαπφώ.

If this inclines the reader to detach Longus' pastoral universe from that of Theocritus, she soon encounters a deterrent. Philetas sends off his son Tityrus to fetch his full-size panpipe so that he can demonstrate his skill, second only to Pan's.[14] Meanwhile Daphnis' father Lamon expounds the μῦθος, 'tale' of syrinx (panpipe). Lamon presents this μῦθος as one ὃν αὐτῶι Σικελὸς αἰπόλος ᾖισεν ἐπὶ μισθῶι τράγωι καὶ σύριγγι, 'which a Sicilian goatherd sang to him for the fee of a goat and a panpipe'. Sicilian goatherds are as out of place in Lesbos as the Tyrian pirates who in Book 1 carried off Daphnis (to whom I shall return), and Longus' unusual breach of verisimilitude flags up a literary allusion, chiefly if not wholly to the poetry of Theocritus. We are not indeed to understand the goatherd to be Theocritus himself:[15] Theocritus was, after all, no goatherd. Rather this αἰπόλος is the fictional Pan-fearing and mysteriously unnamed goatherd of *Idyll* 1.23–63, domiciled on the slopes of Sicilian Etna, who persuaded the fictional shepherd Thyrsis to sing *his* myth of Daphnis for the reward of a splendid cup and three milkings of a goat. The panpipe with which Longus here replaces the Theocritean cup is a payment thematically appropriate to both texts, and it too has a model within Thyrsis' song in *Idyll* 1, when the dying Daphnis hands his panpipe to Pan.[16] Lamon's μῦθος, 'tale', about Pan's erotic self-assertiveness, then, has a similar sort of plausible pastoral aetiology to the song of Theocritus' fictional character Thyrsis about the erotic misadventures of a mythical Daphnis, and this similarity reminds the reader always to be alert to read Longus' text against that of Theocritus.

(2) For my second case I move back to Book 1. Here Longus blends the fictional world of Theocritus with the less demonstrably fictional world of Sappho, whose poetry is naturally an important model for a story of desire set on Lesbos. The first distinct allusion is at 1.17.3: after having had his life's first kiss from Chloe, Daphnis, for the first time, begins to marvel at her blonde hair, her eyes and her complexion.

> τότε πρῶτον καὶ τὴν κόμην αὐτῆς ἐθαύμασεν ὅτι ξανθή, καὶ τοὺς ὀφθαλμοὺς ὅτι μεγάλοι καθάπερ βοός, καὶ τὸ πρόσωπον ὅτι λευκότερον ἀληθῶς καὶ τοῦ τῶν αἰγῶν γάλακτος, ὥσπερ τότε πρῶτον ὀφθαλμοὺς κτησάμενος, τὸν δὲ πρότερον χρόνον πεπηρωμένος.

[14] Cf. μετὰ Πᾶνα τὸ δεύτερον ἆθλον ἀποισῆι, 'after Pan you will carry off the second prize', Theoc. 1.3.

[15] Morgan 2004, 195 surprisingly identifies the Σικελὸς αἰπόλος as 'implicitly Theokritos of Syracuse'.

[16] Theoc. 1.128–30. This moment is also exploited by Longus for the scene in which the dying Dorcon gives Chloe his panpipe, 1.29.3. The fee that combines a goat and a panpipe is also found in Ps.-Theoc. 8.85: Morgan 2004, 195 is right to suggest that this (too) is drawn upon by Longus; but it seems to me that Theoc. 1 remains the primary intertext.

> Then for the first time he marvelled at her hair, that it was blonde, and her eyes, that they were large like a cow's, and her face, that it was really whiter even than goats' milk – as if it was then for the first time he had acquired eyes, and had previously been bereft of sight.
>
> Longus 1.17.3

Longus' comparison of Chloe's complexion to milk seems certainly to have its ultimate origin in early Greek love poetry, since it is shortly followed by a comparison of her lips to roses, χείλη ῥόδων ἁπαλώτερα, 'lips more tender than roses' (1.18.1), and we read in the late writer Gregory of Corinth:

> οἷον τὰ Ἀνακρέοντος, τὰ Σαπφοῦς, οἷον γάλακτος λευκοτέρα, ὕδατος ἁπαλωτέρα, πηκτίδων ἐμμελεστέρα, ἵππου γαυροτέρα, ῥόδων ἁβροτέρα, ἱματίου ἑανοῦ μαλακωτέρα, χρυσοῦ τιμιωτέρα.[17]
>
> Such as the phrases of Anacreon, the phrases of Sappho, such as 'more white than milk', 'more gentle than water', 'more tuneful than lyres', 'more spirited than a mare', 'more delicate than roses', 'more soft than a fine robe', 'more precious than gold'.

Milk is an obvious standard of whiteness, but the pastoral context which is very unlikely to have been that in Sappho or Anacreon makes the comparison especially appropriate in *Daphnis and Chloe*. Longus, however, is not simply picking out a phrase from the poetry of a canonical poet, well known to some in the second century AD;[18] his game is more complicated. Theocritus had already drawn on the Sapphic or Anacreontic comparisons in *Idyll* 11,[19] where he has his young, love-sick Polyphemus open his song with the following address to a nymph whose name Galatea makes her complexion's comparison to milk especially witty:

> Ὦ λευκὰ Γαλάτεια, τί τὸν φιλέοντ' ἀποβάλλῃ,
> λευκοτέρα πακτᾶς ποτιδεῖν, ἁπαλωτέρα ἀρνός,
> μόσχω γαυροτέρα, φιαρωτέρα ὄμφακος ὠμᾶς;
>
> O white Galatea, why do you reject him who loves you,
> whiter than curd-cheese to look upon, gentler than a lamb,
> more spirited than a calf, plumper than an unripe grape.
>
> Theocritus 11.19–21

17 Greg. Cor. (commenting on Hermog. *Meth.* 13 = *Rh.* vii 1236 Walz, giving, with Demetr. *Eloc.* 162, Sappho fr. 156.

18 The clearest witnesses are the rubbish dumps of Oxyrhynchus which have yielded so much Sappho: see most recently Bierl and Lardinois 2016. But note also quotations by Plu. (cf. Bowie 2004b, 2008c, Chapters 15 and 21 in Volume 3), Max. Tyr., and Ath.: cf. Bowie 2021a.

19 Given Theoc.'s telling use of Sappho elsewhere it is more likely that, of the two poets named by Greg. Cor., Sappho and not Anacr. is his intertext. For a fuller treatment of this passage see Bowie 2019g, 134–6.

Longus expects his reader to know this poem of Theocritus, and ups the ante by insisting that in the case of Chloe her face was *really*, ἀληθῶς, whiter than goat's milk. 'Really'. *Really*? In what level of 'reality' is Longus' reader now located? Or rather, how many steps away from reality is she? The whole issue of fictionality has been thrown open by the carefully chosen word ἀληθῶς. Longus and his readers are quite likely to have taken the girls addressed or recalled in Sappho's poems to have been 'real' people, but they know that the worlds both of Theocritus' pastoral poetry and of *Daphnis and Chloe* are not real but fictional. They know too that the mythical Polyphemus of Homer's *Odyssey*, developed by Theocritus in this poem (and in *Idyll* 6), as it had also earlier been by Philoxenus of Cythera, was a character introduced to the Greek world by Homer's Odysseus in his *apologoi*, for ancient readers a stronger candidate for classification as fiction than the Greeks and Trojans of Homer's author-narrative.

That the issue of fictionality is intended to continue to occupy at least a part of the reader's mind is suggested by its re-introduction by Longus only a page later.[20] When Dorcon bestialises himself in a wolf-skin and hides to ambush Chloe, we read of the thick bushes and undergrowth in which he secretes himself: ῥαιδίως ἂν ἐκεῖ καὶ λύκος ἀληθινὸς ἔλαθε λοχῶν, 'there even a real wolf could easily have hid in ambush' (1.20.3).

One of Longus' only two other uses of the adverb ἀληθῶς, 'really', and one of his only two other uses of the adjective ἀληθινός, 'real', also relate to procedures of creating verisimilitude in a work of τέχνη, 'craft', comparable to those in which he is engaged himself.[21]

At 2.36.2 the contribution of Chloe's father Dryas to the *fête champêtre* is a pantomime in which his dance mimes a worker at different stages in the vintage:

> ταῦτα πάντα οὕτως εὐσχημόνως ὠρχήσατο Δρύας καὶ ἐναργῶς, ὥστε ἐδόκουν βλέπειν καὶ τὰς ἀμπέλους καὶ τὴν ληνὸν καὶ τοὺς πίθους καὶ ἀληθῶς Δρύαντα πίνοντα.
>
> All this Dryas danced so elegantly and vividly that they thought they were looking at the grapes and the grape-press and the wine-vats and Dryas *really* drinking.

[20] Forty-two lines of Teubner text, or a few columns on a papyrus roll (though our remarkable lack of any fragment of a roll or codex of Longus from Egypt prevents us knowing the formats in which his text circulated).

[21] Longus' other uses of ἀληθῶς (3.18.2) and ἀληθινούς (3.25.3), like his other uses of ἀληθής, seem not to raise so insistently issues relating to Longus' own creation of fiction: but after sensitisation by the cases in Book 2 a reader will at least be reminded of the fictionality of the narrative in which they appear.

By selecting for this rustic version of one of Greek middlebrow culture's most popular art-forms in the Roman imperial period a subject of which he had himself offered a virtuoso ecphrastic treatment at the beginning of this book (2.1),[22] Longus invites his readers to consider whether he too has been telling his rural story εὐσχημόνως ... καὶ ἐναργῶς, 'elegantly and vividly', to the point that they too think they have 'reality' before their eyes (i.e. with the sort of ἐνάργεια, 'vividness', commended in *ecphrasis*). That such an invitation is indeed made seems to me to be corroborated by the narrator's comment on the pantomime that immediately follows Dryas' performance, this time a pantomime danced by Daphnis and Chloe themselves: they dance the myth of Syrinx that has just been narrated by Lamon (2.34) Although, as I have argued elsewhere,[23] they bowdlerise and soften the traditionally brutal myth, their performance too 'captures' reality: Daphnis kisses Chloe ὡς ἐκ φυγῆς ἀληθινῆς εὑρεθεῖσαν τὴν Χλόην, 'as if it was after a real flight that he had found her again' (2.38.1).

(3) My next case explores how Longus can engage in elaborate weaving of strands without moving outside the corpus of a single author. At 3.33.4 he returns to the great love poet of Lesbos, Sappho: it is autumn, abundant crops of fruit have been harvested, and Daphnis, now assured that his marriage to Chloe is secure and will take place soon, τῶι μετοπώρωι, 'in late autumn' (3.32.3), rushes to her with the good tidings and is keen to pluck the one remaining and apparently unattainable apple to present to her as a gift, manifestly a plucking and presentation that symbolise his imminent taking of her as his bride:

> μία μηλέα τετρύγητο καὶ οὔτε καρπὸν εἶχεν οὔτε φύλλον· γυμνοὶ πάντες ἦσαν οἱ κλάδοι· καὶ ἓν μῆλον ἐπέττετο ἐπ' αὐτοῖς ἄκροις ἀκρότατον, μέγα καὶ καλὸν καὶ τῶν πολλῶν τὴν εὐανθίαν ἐνίκα μόνον· ἔδεισεν ὁ τρυγῶν ἀνελθεῖν, ἠμέλησε καθελεῖν· τάχα δὲ καὶ ἐφυλάττετο τὸ καλὸν μῆλον ἐρωτικῶι ποιμένι. τοῦτο τὸ μῆλον ὡς εἶδεν ὁ Δάφνις, ὥρμα τρυγᾶν ἀνελθὼν καὶ Χλόης κωλυούσης ἠμέλησεν· ἡ μὲν ἀμεληθεῖσα, ὀργισθεῖσα πρὸς τὰς ἀγέλας ἀπῆλθε· Δάφνις δὲ ἀναδραμὼν ἐξίκετο τρυγῆσαι καὶ κομίσαι δῶρον Χλόηι καὶ λόγον τοιόνδε εἶπεν ὠργισμένηι· 'ὦ παρθένε, τοῦτο τὸ μῆλον ἔφυσαν Ὧραι καλαὶ καὶ φυτὸν καλὸν ἔθρεψε πεπαίνοντος Ἡλίου, καὶ ἐτήρησε Τύχη. καὶ οὐκ ἔμελλον αὐτὸ καταλιπεῖν ὀφθαλμοὺς ἔχων, ἵνα πέσηι χαμαὶ καὶ ἢ ποίμνιον αὐτὸ πατήσηι νεμόμενον ἢ ἑρπετὸν φαρμάξηι συρόμενον ἢ χρόνος δαπανήσηι κείμενον, βλεπόμενον, ἐπαινούμενον. τοῦτο

[22] For the importance of pantomime in this period see Robert 1930; Lada Richards 2007; Hall and Wyles 2008; Webb 2008.

[23] Bowie 2003b (Chapter 26 in this volume); further suggestions in Bowie 2007c (Chapter 31 in this volume).

Ἀφροδίτη κάλλους ἔλαβεν ἆθλον· τοῦτο ἐγὼ σοὶ δίδωμι νικητήριον. ὁμοίους ἔχετε τοὺς μάρτυρας· ἐκεῖνος ἦν ποιμήν, αἰπόλος ἐγώ.' ταῦτα εἰπὼν ἐντίθησι τοῖς κόλποις· ἡ δὲ ἐγγὺς γενόμενον κατεφίλησεν, ὥστε ὁ Δάφνις οὐ μετέγνω τολμήσας ἀνελθεῖν εἰς τοσοῦτον ὕψος· ἔλαβε γὰρ κρεῖττον καὶ χρυσοῦ μήλου φίλημα.

One apple-tree had been harvested, and had neither fruit nor foliage; all its branches were bare; and one apple was ripening, on the very topmost branches the topmost, large and fair, and on its own it surpassed the fineness of the bloom of many. The harvester had been afraid to climb up, had paid no attention to bringing it down; and perhaps the fair apple was in fact being saved for a shepherd in the power of Desire. When Daphnis saw this apple he was keen to climb up and harvest it and paid no attention to Chloe when she tried to stop him. When he paid no attention she became angry and went off to the flocks. But Daphnis shinned up and reached and harvested it, and brought it as a gift to Chloe, and delivered this speech to her in her anger: 'Maiden, this apple the fair Seasons have created, and a fair tree has nurtured as the sun ripened it, and Fortune has kept it safe. And I who have eyes was not going to abandon it, so that it might fall to the ground and either a sheep might trample it as it grazed or a creeping thing might poison it as it slithered or time might wither it as it lay, as it was seen, as it was praised. This is what Aphrodite got as the prize for beauty; this is what I give to you as your victory prize. You two have similar witnesses: that man was a shepherd, I am a goat-herd.' With these words he placed the apple in her bosom: and she kissed him as he came close to her, so that Daphnis did not repent that he had dared to climb up to such a height, for he got a kiss better even than a golden apple.

Longus 3.33.3–34.3

With the phrase καὶ ἓν μῆλον ἐπέττετο ἐπ' αὐτοῖς ἄκροις ἀκρότατον, 'one apple was ripening, on the very topmost branches the topmost', Longus begins a complex refashioning of two sequences from Sappho's *Epithalamia*, preserved for us by Demetrius *On Style*, and Syrianus commenting on Hermogenes,[24] but doubtless familiar to Longus and to some of his readership in the context of a complete poem, a poem which may also have included fr. 107 ἦρ' ἔτι παρθενίας ἐπιβάλλομαι;, 'So then do I still yearn for my virginity?'[25]

[24] Demetr. *Eloc.* 106 = fr. 105(c), Syrian. *in Hermog.* Id. 1.1 = fr. 105(a).

[25] Known to us from A.D. *Conj.* 490. Its dactylic metre suggests that it came from either the same hexametric poem as frr. 105(a) and (c) or from one in a similar genre and presumably found in the same section of editions of Sappho. If 104(a), known from Demetr. *Eloc.* 141, was also hexametric, and hence likewise in this same section, then its reference to sheep and goats may have caught Longus' pastoral eye: Ἔσπερε πάντα φέρων ὄσα φαίνολις ἐσκέδασ'

In the first sequence Sappho fr. 105(a) compares a bride to an unplucked apple, a comparison also alluded to by Himerius:[26]

> οἶον τὸ γλυκύμαλον ἐρεύθεται ἄκρωι ἐπ᾽ ὔσδωι,
> ἄκρον ἐπ᾽ ἀκροτάτωι, λελάθοντο δὲ μαλοδρόπηες,
> οὐ μὰν ἐκλελάθοντ᾽, ἀλλ᾽ οὐκ ἐδύναντ᾽ ἐπίκεσθαι.
>
> As the sweet-apple reddens upon the high bough,
> high on the highest, and the apple-pickers have forgotten it –
> no, it is not that they have quite forgotten it, but they could not reach it.

In the second sequence Sappho fr. 105(c) compares a bride to a hyacinth trampled by shepherds:

> οἴαν τὰν ὐάκινθον ἐν ὤρεσι ποίμενες ἄνδρες
> πόσσι καταστείβοισι, χάμαι δέ τε πόρφυρον ἄνθος …
>
> like the hyacinth that in the mountains shepherd men
> trample down with their feet, and on the ground its dark-red flower …

Longus takes his καὶ ἓν μῆλον … ἐπ᾽ αὐτοῖς ἄκροις ἀκρότατον, 'one apple … on the very topmost branches the topmost', from Sappho fr. 105(a) but offers a different pair of explanations for the apple's survival: instead of λελάθοντο δὲ μαλοδρόπηες, | οὐ μὰν ἐκλελάθοντ᾽, ἀλλ᾽ οὐκ ἐδύναντ᾽ ἐπίκεσθαι, 'the apple-pickers have forgotten it – | no, it is not that they have wholly forgotten it, but they could not reach it', Longus writes: ἔδεισεν ὁ τρυγῶν ἀνελθεῖν, ἠμέλησε καθελεῖν, 'The harvester had been afraid to climb up, had paid no attention to bringing it down'. His characteristic asyndeton here leaves the reader uncertain which of the two explanations to prefer. Then Longus offers a third explanation which relocates ποίμενες, 'shepherds', from Sappho fr. 105(c): τάχα δὲ καὶ ἐφυλάττετο τὸ καλὸν μῆλον ἐρωτικῶι ποιμένι, 'and perhaps the fair apple was in fact being saved for a shepherd in the power of Desire'. Longus' ποιμένι, 'shepherd', now significantly singular,

Αὔως, |†φέρεις ὄιν, φέρεις αἶγα, φέρεις ἄπυ† μάτερι παῖδα, 'Evening star, bringing everything that luminous dawn has scattered, you bring the sheep, you bring the goat, you bring the child back to its mother'. But it is not certain that the apparently corrupt first half of the second line was originally dactylic. Did the hexametric fr. 106 (from Demetr. *Eloc.* 146) also belong here with its reference to the superiority of Lesbian singers: πέρροχος, ὠς ὄτ᾽ ἄοιδος ὀ Λέσβιος ἀλλοδάποισιν, 'outstanding, as when a singer from Lesbos (competes with?) singers from other places'?

26 Fr. 105(b) Σαπφοῦς ἦν ἄρα μήλωι μὲν εἰκάσαι τὴν κόρην … τὸν νύμφιόν τε Ἀχιλλεῖ παρομοιῶσαι καὶ εἰς ταὐτὸν ἀγαγεῖν τῶι ἥρωι τὸν νεανίσκον ταῖς πράξεσι, 'so Sappho was able to compare the girl to an apple … and to liken the bridegroom to Achilles and to place the youth on the same level as the hero in his achievements', Him. *Or.* 1.16.

is marked out by his attribute ἐρωτικῶι, 'in the power of desire', as (at least potentially) Daphnis (who is ἐρωτικῶι, 'in the power of desire') by contrast with Sappho's plural ποίμενες, 'shepherds' – plural as Daphnis' pastoral rivals for Chloe are plural, and ἄνδρες, 'grown men', by contrast with the still ephebic Daphnis.

Longus then re-exploits Sappho fr. 105(c) at 3.34.2 to adumbrate one of the fates from which Daphnis wishes to save the unique apple, trampling by a sheep: ἵνα πέσηι χαμαὶ καὶ ἢ ποίμνιον αὐτὸ πατήσηι νεμόμενον ..., 'it might fall to the ground and either a sheep might trample it as it grazed ....' It is also possible, though no more, that the poem from which fr. 105(c) is drawn also contributed to Daphnis' description of the apple as τοῦτο τὸ μῆλον ἔφυσαν Ὧραι καλαὶ καὶ φυτὸν καλὸν ἔθρεψε πεπαίνοντος Ἡλίου, καὶ ἐτήρησε Τύχη, 'This apple the fair Seasons have created, and a fair tree has nurtured as the sun ripened it, and Fortune has kept it safe'. The case for Sappho's contribution here rests on Catullus 62.39–42, arguably also drawing on Sappho fr. 105(c), in its comparison of a bride to a flower:

Ut flos in saeptis secretus nascitur hortis
ignotus pecori, nullo convolsus aratro,
quem mulcent aurae, firmat sol, educat imber;
multi illum pueri, multae optavere puellae.

As a flower grows hidden away in a walled garden
unknown to the flock, torn up by no plough,
which the breezes soften, the sun strengthens, the rain rears;
many are the lads that have desired it, many the lasses.

But if Longus here recalls Sappho, he very probably also recalls Theocritus 28.7, where in a non-pastoral (i.e. non-fictional) context the poet praises his friend Nicias as Νικίαν, Χαρίτων ἰμεροφώνων ἴερον φύτον, 'Nicias, holy tree of the Graces with their voices of longing', a phrase itself calqued on that of another love poet of the archaic period:

Εὐρύαλε γλαυκέων Χαρίτων θάλος, < Ὡρᾶν >
καλλικόμων μελέδημα, σὲ μὲν Κύπρις
ἅ τ' ἀγανοβλέφαρος Πει-
θὼ ῥοδέοισιν ἐν ἄνθεσι θρέψαν

Euryalus, sapling of the blue-eyed Graces,
darling of the fair-tressed Seasons, you are one whom the Cyprian
and Persuasion with her soft eyelids
have nurtured amid rose flowers

Ibycus fr. 288 *PMGF*

Here of course both the addressee of Theocritus and that of Ibycus, Nicias and Euryalus, will have been taken by audiences or readers of their poems to have been real people.

So Longus has created a sequence that complicates and deepens the fictional texture of his pastoral landscape, enhancing its ποικιλία, 'complexity', by weaving together details that come from different parts of the same poem of Sappho, or perhaps from different poems of Sappho in Sappho's book of *Epithalamia*, and in at least one detail drawing yet again on Theocritus, and through him on another celebrated love poet of the archaic period, Ibycus. The fictionality of Longus' world is brought out by the fact that this time the Theocritean text, like its Ibycan intertext, introduces a 'real' and not a fictional character.

3 The City

The world of the city, which we encounter much less in *Daphnis and Chloe*, works with a different set of intertexts, some of which will have pulled a contemporary reader closer to τὸ καθ' ἡμᾶς, 'reality', whether immediate or mediated. The civic aristocrat, who owned large estates worked by slaves and himself lived chiefly in an urban landscape beautified by white marble, while enjoying ready access to opulent coastal villas, was very familiar to imperial Greek πεπαιδευμένοι, 'educated men', some of whom were precisely such aristocrats. Some scholars may also be right to see Daphnis' 'real' father Dionysophanes as a fictional version of a 'real' descendant of Pompey's friend and historian the great Theophanes of Mytilene.[27] But once again literary texts play a prominent role. The name of Chloe's father, Megacles, disclosed to the reader only late in the narrative (4.35.1) in a significantly sympotic context in Mytilene, evokes both the seventh-century Mytilenean warlord known to Aristotle (probably from the συμποτικά, 'sympotic songs', of Alcaeus)[28] and the many Athenian Alcmaeonids of that name, among them the early fifth-century Athenian victor in the chariot race at Delphi celebrated by Pindar in *Pythian* 7.[29] These men called

[27] See e.g. Morgan 2004; Mason 2018. Pompeius Theophanes of Mytilene was a *cliens*, 'client', of Pompey: his grandson Q. Pompeius Macer reached the praetorship in Rome in AD 15, and his descendants included M. Pompeius Macrinus Neos Theophanes, *cos. suff.* AD 115 (*PIR*² P 628) and that man's son M. Pompeius Macrinus Theophanes (*PIR*² P 629), grandfather of Cornelia Cethegilla (*PIR*² G 118) honoured as benefactor by Mytilene in (probably) the 170s, cf. *IG* xii.2 237 = *ILS* 8824. For a stemma see *PIR*² P p.274. On Theophanes see Bowie 2011b (Chapter 26 in Volume 3).

[28] οἷον ἐν Μυτιλήνῃ τοὺς Πενθιλίδας Μεγακλῆς περιιόντας καὶ τύπτοντας ταῖς κορύναις ἐπιθέμενος μετὰ τῶν φίλων ἀνεῖλεν, Ar. *Pol.* 1311b26–28.

[29] On Megacles the Pythian victor see Athanassaki 2011, 2013.

Megacles were 'real' people, but were distanced from second-century readers by their appearance only in canonical literary texts – Alcaeus, Pindar, Aristotle. But the migration of the name Megacles into fiction begins no later than Aristophanes' *Clouds* 46–8, where Strepsiades, an ἄγροικος, 'rustic', identifies his hyper-urban wife as the niece of a Megacles, son of Megacles. Daphnis – apparently (but not, as we know, 'really') an ἄγροικος, 'rustic', goes one better than Strepsiades by marrying a girl who is 'really' the daughter of a Megacles. The fictions of Comedy, but chiefly New Comedy, are also important as sources of Longus' exposure- and recognition-themes, and of the name and status of Astylus' parasite Gnathon, but such New Comedy intertexts are ones that Longus shares with novelists both earlier (e.g. Chariton) and later (Heliodorus).

4 The Sea

Longus makes a similar move in his abrupt and unselfconscious introduction at 1.28.1 of Tyrian pirates who kill Dorcon and briefly kidnap Daphnis – abrupt even though a λῃστῶν καταδρομή, 'a piratical incursion', has been advertised in his preface (*pr.* 2): Τύριοι λῃσταὶ Καρικὴν ἔχοντες ἡμιολίαν ὡς ἂν δοκοῖεν βάρβαροι προσέσχον τοῖς ἀγροῖς …, 'Tyrian pirates with a light Carian cutter so that they might seem to be non-Greeks put into the estate …'.[30] Admittedly these pirates' Tyrian ethnicity is in question, since the two important manuscripts F and V offer different readings: F has Πύρριοι, V Τύριοι. Πύρριοι cannot stand, and if we accept Reeve's conjecture Πυρραῖοι, 'from Pyrrha', Longus confines even the novelistic commonplace of pirates to the island of Lesbos. If we are to imagine the action as taking place in the classical period, Pyrrha was then an independent Greek city on the large gulf running far into the south-west coast of Lesbos, now the gulf of Kalloni, where theoretically pirates might indeed be based. But Pyrrha is never attested as a pirates' nest, as were (ever since the *Odyssey*) the Phoenician cities; and if Pyrrha did harbour pirates, why did Longus' Mytileneans not take some action against it as they later do against Methymna?

Prima facie against the reading Τύριοι, 'from Tyre', is the phrase offered by both manuscripts: ὡς ἂν δοκοῖεν βάρβαροι, 'so that they might seem to be non-Greeks', apparently explaining why these pirates were in a Carian boat. But it is no explanation, since Tyrians were already βάρβαροι, 'non-Greeks', anyway. The conjecture made by one of the correctors of V, ὡς μὴ

[30] For the suitability of such a craft for piracy cf. Arr. *An.* 3.24.

δοκοῖεν βάρβαροι, 'so that they might not seem to be non-Greeks', was presumably made to solve this problem. Reeve objected that Carians too were barbarians;[31] but although this was the case in the classical period, it may not have been the perception of Longus, writing when all Caria was an integral part of the Roman province Asia and boasted many Greek cities. If, as I believe we should, we accept the reading Τύριοι, Longus' Tyrian pirates take us to the pirates of earlier novels, and his combination of Tyrians and Carians recalls their association as piratical inhabitants of the Aegean in Thucydides (1.8.1, cf. 1.4.1). But a more particular and meaningful allusion is possible. The reference to Caria may also be calculated to trigger thoughts of the greatest city of Caria, Aphrodisias, as a cradle of the novels, home of Chariton (as he himself wrote in his opening sentence) and, it seems likely, of both Antonius Diogenes and the author of the Ninus romance.[32]

Longus thus impresses upon his reader that his very unusual novel, dominated by a Theocritean pastoral landscape, is nevertheless to be read as a variant within the genre created by Chariton of Aphrodisias,[33] and that its construction weaves together materials drawn from both traditions.

5 'Reality' (?)

Alongside such predominantly fictional intertexts one writer professedly committed to τὸ ... ἀληθέστερον, 'what is more true', stands out: Thucydides. In this context there is neither space nor need for a detailed analysis: briefly, Longus' account of the war between Mytilene and Methymna (2.19–3.3.1) presents a parodic version of Thucydidean war-narrative, glancing repeatedly at the Mytilene episode in Book 3 of Thucydides and exploiting many details of his language. One point of this sequence is to show those readers who know the Thucydidean features of Chariton's novel, especially his opening, that Longus can play the Thucydides game too; another is to invite readers to compare the different ontological status of fictions woven from fictions and fictions woven from 'history'. But although it is only in 2.19–3.3.1 that extended comparison with Thucydides is proposed to the reader, Thucydides' importance for reading *Daphnis and Chloe* had already been

[31] Reeve 1982, apparatus *ad loc.*

[32] For Aphrodisias as the probable origin of Antonius Diogenes see Bowersock 1994; as also the possible origin of the author of the Ninus romance see Stephens and Winkler 1995, 26; Bowie 2002a (Chapter 25 in this volume) and 2004c (Chapter 14 in Volume 3).

[33] For a strong case for seeing Chariton as the inventor of the genre see Tilg 2010.

advertised unambiguously in the preface.[34] There the key phrase is κτῆμα δὲ τερπνὸν πᾶσιν ἀνθρώποις, 'a pleasing possession for all men', which many have seen to pick up Thucydides' arguments at 1.21–22, presenting poets and λογογράφοι, 'prose-writers', as unreliable and as more interested in achieving τὸ προσαγωγότερον τῆι ἀκροάσει ἢ ἀληθέστερον, 'what is more attractive to listen to than what is nearer the truth' (1.21.1), whereas Thucydides himself has produced κτῆμά τε ἐς αἰεὶ μᾶλλον ἢ ἀγώνισμα ἐς τὸ παραχρῆμα ἀκούειν, 'a possession for ever rather than a competitive piece with an eye on immediate listening' – a κτῆμα, 'possession', which he expects to be judged ὠφέλιμα, 'useful', by whoever wants a clear account, even if avoidance of τὸ μυθῶδες, 'that which is like myth', has tied his hands in the production of τέρψις, 'pleasure' (1.22.4). In his preface Longus is picking up key words both from Thucydides' historiographical programme in this section of his first book and from Theocritus' self-presentation as laborious creator of pastoral τέρψις, 'pleasure', and he is claiming to be successful on both sets of criteria.

I have tried to set out the key elements in a table (printed as Table 37.1). Longus' prose emulates the careful elaboration of Theocritus' poetry. His term ἐξεπονησάμην, 'I have laboured to create', used again by Philetas in 2.3.3 of his garden that is a *mis-en-abyme* of the whole book, just as Philetas the ἐρωτοδιδάσκαλος, 'instructor in love', is a poetic representative of Longus' narrator in his text, varies the term ἐξεπόνασα, 'I laboured to create', used by Lycidas of his own song at Theoc. 7.51 – a song that was significantly about a journey to Mytilene. Like Theocritus, Longus hopes his work will be τερπνόν, 'pleasing'. But alongside this quality, only implicitly acknowledged as a goal by Thucydides, he expects, like Thucydides, that it will be ὠφέλιμον, 'useful', despite, as we discover later, moving towards τὸ μυθῶδες, 'that which is like myth'.[35] In his quest for his material Longus is both like and unlike Thucydides: ζήτησις, 'enquiry', is involved, but it is ζήτησις of

[34] The full text of the relevant sentences of Thucydides, essential to an understanding of its parts, runs as follows: καὶ ἐς μὲν ἀκρόασιν ἴσως τὸ μὴ μυθῶδες αὐτῶν ἀτερπέστερον φανεῖται· ὅσοι δὲ βουλήσονται τῶν τε γενομένων τὸ σαφὲς σκοπεῖν καὶ τῶν μελλόντων ποτὲ αὖθις κατὰ τὸ ἀνθρώπινον τοιούτων καὶ παραπλησίων ἔσεσθαι, ὠφέλιμα κρίνειν αὐτὰ ἀρκούντως ἕξει. κτῆμά τε ἐς αἰεὶ μᾶλλον ἢ ἀγώνισμα ἐς τὸ παραχρῆμα ἀκούειν ξύγκειται, 'and for something to listen to perhaps their lack of myth-like content will seem to diminish pleasure: but it will be sufficient if they are judged useful by all those who shall wish to examine that which is secure in what has happened and what is going to happen of a similar sort and along similar lines at some point again given human nature. And it has been composed as a possession for ever rather than as a competitive piece with an eye on immediate listening', Th. 1.22.4. For the bearing of these sentences on Longus' preface see Hunter 1983; Luginbill 2001–2; for Longus' use of Th. Cueva 1998, Trzaskoma 2005.

[35] Most explicitly when Pan classifies the story that will be told about Chloe as a μῦθος, 2.27.2.

an expounder or interpreter, suspiciously like ὁ παρατυχών, 'the man who (conveniently) happened to be present (at the time)', the sort of testimony Thucydides rejects in his phrase οὐκ ἐκ τοῦ παρατυχόντος, 'not from a man who happened to be present' (1.22.2). But this intermediary is not the weak link he would be in Thucydides' chain because Longus' ultimate goal is not τὸ ἀληθέστερον, 'what is more true': τὸ ἀληθές, 'what is true', has indeed an important part to play, as we have seen, but the word's introduction is as often as not to remind the reader of the narrative's exuberant fictionality.

6 Conclusion

Was my title misleading, then, with its phrase 'weaving "reality"'? Not so. The inverted commas around 'reality' are crucial. Longus knows that the universe he creates is, like that of earlier novelists, a fictional universe. Like them he works hard, if not entirely consistently, to create a universe that might well have existed. But he expects not simply to be compared to them in respect of his success in the production of verisimilitude, but to be seen to outstrip them by the infrequency of his resort to 'the real world' as basket-work material and by his predominant mode of reworking and reweaving earlier literary and chiefly fictional texts. It is my stress on the fictionality, rather than on the poetic status, of the majority of these texts that differentiates what I have been arguing for from the positions taken by Richard Hunter and Maria Pia Pattoni. If we are to read the grasshopper cage being woven by Chloe at 1.10.2 as a symbol of Longus' own meticulously crafted construction, then we should also reflect that we, the grasshoppers confined pleasurably within that miniature cage, are separated from the outside world by no more than fictional barriers.

Table 37.1 *πόνος, τὸ ἀληθές, τὸ ὠφέλιμον and τὸ τερπνόν in pre-Thucydidean writers, Thucydides, Theocritus and Longus*

	πόνος in εὕρεσις / ζήτησις τῆς ἀληθείας	πόνος in ἀπόδειξις	The result is ἀληθέστερον	The result is τερπνόν / προαγωγόν	The result is ὠφέλιμον	The result is μυθῶδες
Pre-Thucydides ποιηταί	No: cf. Th. 1.20.3–21.1	?	No	?✓	?	✓
Pre-Thucydides λογογράφοι	No, cf. Th. 1,20.3–21.1	?	No	✓	?	✓
Thucydides	✓ 1.22.3 ἐπιπόνως δὲ ηὑρίσκετο	?✓	✓ 1.21.1 with 1.22.4 τὸ σαφές	? ✓ in 1.22.4 note the force of ἴσως and φανεῖται	✓ 1.22.4 ὠφέλιμα κρίνειν αὐτὰ ἀρκούντως ἕξει	No, cf. 1.21.1
Theocritus	?	✓ cf. 7.51 ἐξεπόνασα, 1.52 ἀκριδοθήραν/ ἀκριδοθήκην	? cf. 7.13–14 ἐπεὶ αἰπόλωι ἔξοχ' ἐώικει	✓ cf. e.g. 1.146 πλῆρές τοι μέλιτος τὸ καλὸν στόμα	Sometimes, cf. 11.1 ff. φάρμακον … κοῦφον δέ τι τοῦτο καὶ ἁδύ	✓ cf. 1.64–145 Thyrsis' song about Daphnis
Longus	✓some: *pr.* 3 ἀναζητησάμενος ἐξηγητήν	✓ *pr.* 3 ἐξεπονησάμην, cf. Philetas 2.3.3 ἐξεπονησάμην, Chloe 1.10.2 ἀκριδοθήραν/ ἀκριδοθήκην	**?**	✓ *pr.* 3 κτῆμα δὲ τερπνὸν πᾶσιν ἀνθρώποις	✓ *pr.* 3 ὃ καὶ νοσοῦντα ἰάσεται …	✓ 2.27.2 (Chloe) ἐξ ἧς Ἔρως μῦθον ποιῆσαι θέλει

38 | ‘Milesian Tales’ (2013)

iunxit Aristides Milesia crimina secum,
        pulsus Aristides nec tamen urbe sua est.
nec qui descripsit corrumpi semina matrum,
        Eubius, impurae conditor historiae,
nec qui composuit nuper Sybaritica fugit,
        nec qui concubitus non tacuere suos.

Aristides linked the charges against Miletus to his own person,
        yet Aristides was not driven out of his own city.
Nor did the man who described how mothers’ offspring were destroyed,
        Eubius, establisher of an immoral account,
nor did the man who recently composed Sybaritic tales go into exile,
        nor the ones who did not keep silent about their own liaisons.

Ovid, *Tristia* 2.413–18

vertit Aristiden Sisenna, nec obfuit illi
        historiae turpis inseruisse iocos.

Sisenna translated Aristides, and it was not a problem for him
        to have woven filthy pranks into a narrative.

Ovid, *Tristia* 2.443–4

τὴν δὲ γερουσίαν τῶν Σελευκέων ἀθροίσας, εἰσήνεγκεν ἀκόλαστα βιβλία τῶν Ἀριστείδου Μιλησιακῶν, οὔτι ταῦτά γε καταψευσάμενος· εὑρέθη γὰρ ἐν τοῖς Ῥουστίου σκευοφόροις, καὶ παρέσχε τῶι Σουρήναι καθυβρίσαι πολλὰ καὶ κατασκῶψαι τοὺς Ῥωμαίους, εἰ μηδὲ πολεμοῦντες ἀπέχεσθαι πραγμάτων καὶ γραμμάτων δύνανται τοιούτων. τοῖς μέντοι Σελευκεῦσιν ἐδόκει σοφὸς ἀνὴρ ὁ Αἴσωπος εἶναι, τὸν Σουρήναν ὁρῶσι τὴν μὲν τῶν Μιλησιακῶν ἀκολαστημάτων πήραν ἐξηρτημένον πρόσθεν, ὄπισθεν δὲ Παρθικὴν Σύβαριν ἐφελκόμενον ἐν τοσαῖσδε παλλακίδων ἁμάξαις ... ψεκτὸς μὲν γὰρ ὁ Ῥούστιος, ἀναιδεῖς δὲ Πάρθοι τὰ Μιλησιακὰ ψέγοντες, ὧν πολλοὶ βεβασιλεύκασιν ἐκ Μιλησίων καὶ Ἰωνίδων ἑταιρῶν γεγονότες Ἀρσακίδαι.

Gathering together the *Gerousia* of Seleuceia he brought before them the licentious books of Aristides' *Milesiaca*, and in this at any rate he was not perpetrating a falsehood; for they had been found in Rustius' baggage train, and they gave Surenas the opportunity to hurl many insults and taunts against the Romans, unable even when at war to abstain from such acts and writings. But the Seleuceians reflected that Aesop was a wise man, when they saw Surenas with the bag containing the Milesian licence slung over his shoulder in front of him, but followed behind by a Parthian Sybaris in so many waggons full of his concubines ... Rustius was indeed to be criticised, but the Parthians were shameless to criticise Milesian tales, since many Arsacids had held the royal throne despite having been born from Milesian and Ionian *hetaerae*.

Plutarch, *Crassus* 32.4–6

1 Introduction

The above passages are among our few clues to the nature of narratives that in Greek were apparently called Μιλησιακά, 'Milesian tales'. In 1996 I aligned myself with those scholars who held the defining characteristic of these narratives to have been that they were told about characters and/or events set in Miletus, and that this might be their only connection with Miletus or indeed with Ionia.[1]

What has happened since then? In a paper published in 1998 Stephen Harrison revived a moderate form of the thesis argued by Bürger in 1892.[2] Bürger's suggestion had been that the *Milesian Tales* were a novel in which Aristides was both the protagonist and a first-person narrator. Harrison suggested that Aristides' *Milesian Tales* were rather 'a collection of salacious stories not unconnected with the purer tradition of the Greek erotic novel, stories by a non-Milesian writing a prurient exposé in a pseudo-ethnographical manner of a notorious foreign location'.[3] He rightly stressed the importance of the Lucianic Ἔρωτες, '*Love affairs*',[4] where the interlocutor Lycinus compares himself to Aristides being charmed by Milesian tales,

[1] Bowie 1996b. [2] Bürger 1892b. [3] Harrison 1998, 64.

[4] For arguments in favour of the ascription of the Ἔρωτες to Lucian see Jope 2011. Most scholars have questioned this work's attribution to Lucian in the manuscript tradition or left the matter open (e.g. Mossman 2007).

for the conclusion that 'Aristides' work was in some sense a first-person narrative with Aristides reporting tales that had been told to him'.[5] The passage is important enough for our understanding of Milesian Tales to merit citation in full:

> ἐρωτικῆς παιδιᾶς, ἑταῖρέ μοι Θεόμνηστε, ἐξ ἑωθινοῦ πεπλήρωκας ἡμῶν τὰ κεκμηκότα πρὸς τὰς συνεχεῖς σπουδὰς ὦτα, καί μοι σφόδρα διψῶντι τοιαύτης ἀνέσεως εὔκαιρος ἡ τῶν ἱλαρῶν σου λόγων ἐρρύη χάρις· ἀσθενὴς γὰρ ἡ ψυχὴ διηνεκοῦς σπουδῆς ἀνέχεσθαι, ποθοῦσι δ' οἱ φιλότιμοι πόνοι μικρὰ τῶν ἐπαχθῶν φροντίδων χαλασθέντες εἰς ἡδονὰς ἀνίεσθαι. πάνυ δή με ὑπὸ τὸν ὄρθρον ἡ τῶν ἀκολάστων σου διηγημάτων αἱμύλη καὶ γλυκεῖα πειθὼ κατεύφραγκεν, ὥστ' ὀλίγου δεῖν Ἀριστείδης ἐνόμιζον εἶναι τοῖς Μιλησιακοῖς λόγοις ὑπερκηλούμενος, ἄχθομαί τε νὴ τοὺς σοὺς ἔρωτας, οἷς πλατὺς εὑρέθης σκοπός, ὅτι πέπαυσαι διηγούμενος.
>
> With amorous sport, my friend Theomnestus, you have since dawn filled my ears which were exhausted by continuous attention to labour, and for my intense thirst for such relaxation the charm of your hilarious stories flowed out at just the right time. For the mind is feeble in its tolerance of continuous labour, and toils that aim at distinction hanker for short periods of release from burdensome cares and for pleasurable relaxation. So at the break of day the seductive and sweet persuasion of your licentious narratives wholly overcame me with delight, so that I almost thought I was Aristides being entranced by Milesian tales, and I am aggrieved, I swear by your *Loves*, by which you have been identified as a wide-open target, that you have stopped narrating.
>
> Lucian (?), Ἔρωτες, '*Love affairs*' 1

Harrison also discussed the second passage in Ovid's *Tristia*,[6] and while leaving it open whether *historiae turpis inseruisse iocos* (2.444) referred to writing both *Milesiaca* and a serious *historia*, 'history',[7] or to the insertion of lewd tales in a narrative framework, the whole constituting Milesian tales, he strongly favoured the latter interpretation.[8] He supported this choice by a discussion of two well-known inserted tales in the *Satyrica*, the Pergamene boy (85–7) and the widow of Ephesus (111–12), and by Apuleius' reference in the opening of his *Metamorphoses* to Milesian *sermo*, by the Milesian origin of his character Thelyphron (2.2.1), and by his self-description as *Milesiae conditor*, 'the founder of the Milesian', in the tale of Cupid and

[5] That Aristides' work also included events that he claimed himself to have witnessed (as suggested e.g. by Ruiz Montero 1996, 62) has less support from our testimonia.

[6] Harrison 1998, 65. [7] The view of Walsh 1970, 10–18. [8] Harrison 1998, 65–7.

Psyche (4.32). I find almost all of his argumentation persuasive, though given the paucity of our evidence any reconstruction is inevitably fragile. It is attractive, as he suggests, to suppose that Milesian tales were in some way taking off serious ethnographic writing, and that they involved a narrating character reporting stories he claimed to have heard concerning events and *mores* in Miletus. But the idea that this character represented himself as a traveller[9] is largely dependent on retrojection from traveller-listeners in Petronius and Apuleius: the scenario imagined by Walsh (largely following Schissel)[10] in which the framework was a symposium cannot be rejected quite as confidently as it was by Harrison on the ground either of absence of evidence for a sympotic frame or that a work exceeding thirteen books in length would be too long for such a structure.

Two under-exploited straws may be added to the few already used.

First, the emphasis in the Ἔρωτες, '*Love affairs*', on the χάρις, 'charm', of the narrator's tales (εὔκαιρος ἡ τῶν ἱλαρῶν σου λόγων ἐρρύη χάρις ... τοῖς Μιλησιακοῖς λόγοις ὑπερκηλούμενος) might be taken to support Walsh's proposed sympotic frame, since self-reflexive praise of their charm is a feature of sympotic works.[11] But it is certainly not unique to them, and cannot shift the weight of argument far.

Second, and perhaps more telling, the early history of prose ethnographic writing starts with a figure not mentioned by Harrison: Hecataeus, precisely of Miletus. We should ask whether the perhaps pseudo-ethnographic Milesian tales of Aristides were in some way cleverly inverting the pattern of one of Miletus' few non-philosophical candidates for literary fame in the archaic and classical periods. If so, it may be worth registering that although the numerous if mostly exiguous fragments of Hecataeus' two-book Περίοδος γῆς, '*Travel about the world*', nowhere explicitly introduce the author as an eye-witness or as hearing an account from another witness, unlike poetic predecessors such as characters in the *Odyssey*, Mimnermus (fr.13), and Aristeas of Proconnesus,[12] and unlike his (in some sense)

[9] Harrison 1998, esp. 71. [10] Schissel von Fleschenberg 1913, 94–105.

[11] E.g. Dionysius Chalcus fr. 1.3.

[12] For Aristeas' citation of a witness see fr. 5.1–2 Bernabe: καὶ φάσ<αν> ἀνθρώπους εἶναι καθύπερθεν ὁμούρους | πρὸς Βορέω, 'and they said that there were men beyond them with whom they shared a boundary, to the north'. For possible characterisation of his own response as a *soi-disant* eyewitness see fr. 11.1–2 Bernabe: θαῦμ' ἡμῖν καὶ τοῦτο μέγα φρεσὶν ἡμετέρῃσιν.| ἄνδρες ὕδωρ ναίουσιν ἀπὸ χθονὸς ἐν πελάγεσσι, 'and this too is a great source of wonder for our minds: men inhabit water, away from land in the oceans'. Proconnesus was an offshoot of the Milesian colony Cyzicus: the extent to which first the hexameter travel narrative of Aristeas and then the encyclopaedic gazetteer of Hecataeus were stimulated and facilitated by a network of Milesian colonies is a topic that cannot be pursued here.

successor Herodotus, it seems very probable from Herodotus' account of Hecataeus offering his genealogy to the priests at Egyptian Thebes (and getting his come-uppance) that his presentation of Egypt included at least one incident in which he was a listening character.[13] And even if he visited only some of the places that his work catalogued he must have travelled widely, as is indicated by his characterisation as ἀνὴρ πολυπλανής, 'a much-travelled man', by Agathemerus.[14] Thus it can very tentatively be claimed that if Aristides' intertexts included the Milesian Hecataeus' Περίοδος γῆς, '*Travel about the world*', then this offers some support for the hypothesis that his Milesian tales exploited the figure of an eagerly (or perhaps sometimes sceptically) listening traveller.

In 2004 Jensson returned to a position near to that of Bürger, arguing for a close similarity between Encolpius' narrative *in personis* and the sort of narrative which is described as *heard* by the character Aristides in the Ἔρωτες ascribed to Lucian. To me he seems to exaggerate the closeness of these two texts. The narrative of Encolpius has many incidents in which he is a major player: by contrast the narrative offered to Theomnestus by Lycinus is no more than a frame – a sophisticated frame, as Simon Goldhill has expounded,[15] but a frame in which Lycinus himself is never actually the protagonist of a story. This leads me to conclude that if there was a 'Greek original' for Petronius' *Satyrica* it was not straightforwardly a Milesian tale or collection of Milesian tales such as the work entitled Ἔρωτες, '*Love affairs*', evokes.[16]

Our understanding of this family of genres was slightly advanced by the publication in 2006 of an Oxyrhynchus papyrus offering a fragmentary prosimetric narrative of a sexual encounter between a woman and an ass. The question naturally arose whether this fragment was part either of the *Metamorphoses* summarised by Photius and ascribed to Lucius of Patrae, or of the ass-tale, Λούκιος ἢ Ὄνος, '*Lucius* or *The ass*', transmitted in the Lucianic corpus. Regine May has argued that it is not, chiefly on the ground

[13] πρότερον δὲ Ἑκαταίωι τῶι λογοποιῶι ἐν Θήβῃσι γενεηλογήσαντί [τε] ἑωυτὸν καὶ ἀναδήσαντι τὴν πατριὴν ἐς ἑκκαιδέκατον θεὸν ἐποίησαν οἱ ἱρέες τοῦ Διὸς οἷόν τι καὶ ἐμοὶ οὐ γενεηλογήσαντι ἐμεωυτόν, 'and on an earlier occasion the priests did to Hecataeus the prose-writer – who in Thebes told them his genealogy and traced his paternal line back to a god in the sixteenth generation – much what they also did to me (though I did not tell the my genealogy)', Hdt. 2.143. It is of course possible that the work Herodotus uses here was not Hecataeus' Περίοδος γῆς, '*Travel about the world*', but his Γενεαλογίαι, '*Genealogies*'. On Hdt.'s presentation of Hecataeus see West 1991.

[14] *Geog.* 1.1 = Hecataeus *FGrH* 1 T12a (=T12 *EGM*). [15] Goldhill 1995, 102–9.

[16] Bowie 2007d (Chapter 32 in this volume) explores the possibility that Antonius Diogenes preceded and influenced the *Satyrica*.

that in the Lucianic *Ass* (as in the related narrative of Apul. *Met.* 10.22) the ass seems to be represented as hesitant about his penetration of the woman, whereas in the Oxyrhynchus papyrus text it is the woman who, albeit excited, seems to be more hesitant.[17] May proposed that the papyrus actually gives us a part of Aristides' *Milesian tales*, corresponding to fr. 10 Bücheler of his Latin translator, Sisenna, *ut eum paenitus utero suo recepit*, 'when she had received him deep into her womb', often seen as an intertext with Apuleius' *totum me prorsus, sed totum recepit*, '(she) admitted me absolutely all the way' (*Met.* 10.22: cf. εἴσω ὅλον παρεδέξατο, 'she admitted me in my entirety', *Lucius* or *The ass* 51).[18]

If either Jensson or May is right, these Μιλησιακοὶ λόγοι, '*Milesian Tales*', now appear to have been in at least some cases prosimetric. With only one fragment of Aristides' Greek text so far identified[19] and only ten fragments of Sisenna surviving, it is not easy to control this hypothesis. Two of the Sisenna fragments could be from the end of a hexameter: fr. 1 *nocte vagatrix*, 'night-wanderer' (feminine), and fr. 3, *eamus ad ipsam*, 'let us go to the lady herself'. But if Aristides' collection *was* prosimetric then we must concede that no hint of this emerges either in Ovid's mentions of Aristides (cited above) or in the Lucianic Ἔρωτες, '*Love affairs*' – nor, for that matter, in the *Metamorphoses* ascribed to Lucius of Patrae or in the Lucianic Ὄνος, '*Ass*'.

The possibility that Milesian tales were prosimetric re-opens the question of the classification of the Iolaus narrative published in 1971.[20] Is this too part of a Milesian tale? Its crude presentation of sex (well reflected in Stephens and Winkler's translation of δόλωι ... βινεῖν as 'crafty fuck')[21] would support such a categorisation. The location of the incident described

[17] May 2010 on *P.Oxy.* 4762.

[18] Tim Whitmarsh points out to me that the fact that the scene in *P.Oxy.* 4762 is described in the third person rather than the first lends further support to May's claim that it is not directly related to the *Ass* traditions (fundamentally built on the paradox of a first-person narrative delivered by a (one-time) dumb beast).

[19] *FGrH* 495 F1, quoted by Harp. δ 23 *s.v.* δερμηστής· Λυσίας ἐν τῶι πρὸς Εὐπείθην. Δίδυμος μὲν ἀποδίδωσι τὸν σκώληκα οὕτω λέγεσθαι τῶι Σοφοκλεῖ ἐν Νιόβηι, ἐν ζʹ τῆς ἀπορουμένης λέξεως, Ἀρίσταρχος δὲ τὸ Σοφόκλειον ἐξηγούμενος τὸν ὄφιν ἀπέδωκε. μήποτε δὲ μᾶλλον ἂν εἴη ὅστις τὰ δέρματα ἐσθίει δερμηστής, ὡς ὑποσημαίνεται καὶ ἐν ςʹ Μιλησιακῶν Ἀριστείδου, 'skinner: Lysias in his speech *To Eupeithes* (*Or.* 61, fr. 122 Carey). Didymus explains that the worm is so termed by Sophocles in his *Niobe* (fr. 449 Radt) in Book 7 of his work *Puzzling language*, but Aristarchus when interpreting the Sophoclean passage explains it as "snake". Perhaps it is more likely that "skinner" is the one who eats skins, as is the meaning also in Book 6 of Aristides' *Milesian Tales*'.

[20] Parsons 1971, definitive publication Parsons 1974a; text, trans. and discussion Stephens and Winkler 1995, 358–74 (with an important discussion of the implications of its prosimetric form, now needing revision after publication of the ass-papyrus, at 363–6); trans. and brief discussion Sandy 1989b.

[21] Stephens and Winkler 1995, 371.

in our papyrus fragment is sadly unclear. It may be noted that the name Iolaus is twice attested in Miletus, once in Colophon and once in Teos,[22] and Nico once in Miletus:[23] but the name Iolaus is not distinctively rare, and Nico is relatively common.

2 The Impact on Greek and Latin Novels

The impact of Milesian tales on the Latin novels has already been apparent in the course of my attempt to pin down the characteristics of the genre. A major problem in reaching any conclusion on either of these problems remains our uncertainty on how far either Petronius or Apuleius was unconsciously or (more probably) consciously departing from what each knew to be the pattern of Milesian tales. The prominence of magic and the supernatural in Apuleius' tale of Thelyphron of Miletus, for example, has encouraged Harrison to see these as generic markers: but they are not appropriately categorised as ἀκολασία, 'obscenity', and it may be that Apuleius is leading his reader to expect a sexually entertaining story by giving Thelyphron Miletus as his origin and then defeating such expectations by diverting along a different generic path.

Petronius' Ephesian widow had been a less substantial modification. As is often noted,[24] Ionia seems to have had a reputation for sexual laxity, and we sometimes encounter slippage from Miletus to Ionia as a whole, which may at an early date have acquired a dubious reputation for sexual licence. The sexually explicit poetry of Hipponax of Ephesus, certainly known in late fifth-century Athens (cf. Ar. *Ra.* 661) could well have contributed to such a reputation. Likewise in the late fifth century we hear Aristophanes' Agathon saying:

σκέψαι δ' ὅτι
Ἴβυκος ἐκεῖνος κἀνακρέων ὁ Τήιος
κἀλκαῖος, οἵπερ ἁρμονίαν ἐχύμισαν,
ἐμιτροφόρουν τε καὶ διεκλῶντ' Ἰωνικῶς.[25]

[22] Record of a grant of citizenship to Iolaus of Adramytteion and Seleuceia; 188/7 BC: *Milet* i 3, 49; *SEG* 37.985; record of a grant of citizenship to Habrotera of Euromos, daughter of Iolaus, 57/6 BC: *Milet* i 3, 59; with the Ionian spelling Ἰόλεως, 'Ioleos'; at Colophon, *Corpus Inscriptionum Regni Bosporani* 248; a list of names at Teos includes an Ἰόλας Νικοστράτου, 'Iola(u)s son of Nicostratus', *SEG* 2.581 col. 2.18.

[23] As στεφανηφόρος, 'crown-bearer', i.e. the city's chief magistrate: *Milet* i 3 111.

[24] E.g. Trenkner 1958; Harrison 1998; and Tagliabue 2013.

[25] διεκλῶντ', 'ponced around', is a conjecture by Toup: R (*Ravennas* 409) reads διεκίνων, the *Suda* διεκίνουν at ε 989, ι 495.

> That famous Ibycus and Anacreon of Teos
> and Alcaeus, who gave their harmony taste,
> wore headbands and ponced around in the Ionian style.
>
> Aristophanes, *Thesmophoriazousae* 160–3

The reputation persists into the Hellenistic and Roman periods. At Herodas *Mimiambus* 7.86 the month Taureon points to Ionia as the setting for the ladies' dildo-buying expedition. Indecent dancing is still associated with Ionia in the late first century BC,[26] and Plutarch's account of the discovery of a copy of Aristides' *Milesiaca* in the Roman baggage train at Carrhae slips from that to the issue of *hetaerae*, 'courtesans', from Ionia. The association resurfaces in the late-second-century authors Lucian, Pollux and Athenaeus.[27]

So Petronius' relocation of the central character and the incident from Miletus to Ephesus may be an almost trivial *variatio* (though of course it remains possible that the Milesian tales of Aristides already moved their action beyond Miletus itself). It is, at the same time, an interesting *variatio*, since the shift involves a Romanisation of the incident (a microcosm of the *Satyrica*'s Romanisation of Greek genres as a whole), moving it from a city with a long Hellenic pedigree and a lesser role in the Roman province Asia, Miletus, to one that was now the province's capital, residence of the Roman *proconsul* who was its governor, and that had a social mix in which the descendants of Italian settlers bulked large (and where of course Roman soldiers would be more often visible).[28]

More blurring of boundaries may be involved in the tale of the Pergamene boy. Pergamum was not in Ionia,[29] and it was only the Roman provincial structure after the area had been bequeathed to Rome in 133 BC by the last Attalid (ruling precisely in Mysian Pergamum) that might seem to give Pergamum a similar profile to Ephesus and Miletus. Thus, despite the Greek

[26] Nisbet and Rudd 2004, 106 on Hor. *Carm.* 3.6.21–2 *motus doceri gaudet Ionicos | matura virgo*, 'the maiden who is already an adult takes pleasure in being taught Ionian dance-routines'.

[27] ἦν δέ τις καὶ Ἰωνικὴ ὄρχησις παροίνιος, 'And there used to be a 'Drunken' Ionian dance', Ath. 14.629e. The Ἰωνικόν, 'the Ionian', was danced by Sicilian Greeks according to Poll 4.103: τὸ δ' Ἰωνικὸν Ἀρτέμιδι ὠρχοῦντο Σικελιῶται μάλιστα, 'It was especially the Greeks of Sicily who would dance "the Ionian" in honour of Artemis'. Luc. *Salt.* 34, however, takes the παροίνιος, 'Drunken dance', to be Phrygian: ἐκεῖνο τὸ Φρύγιον τῆς ὀρχήσεως εἶδος, τὸ παροίνιον καὶ συμποτικόν, μετὰ μέθης γιγνόμενον ἀγροίκων πολλάκις πρὸς αὔλημα γυναικεῖον ὀρχουμένων σφοδρὰ καὶ καματηρὰ πηδήματα, καὶ νῦν ἔτι ταῖς ἀγροικίαις ἐπιπολάζοντα, 'that Phrygian type of dance, the one for drinking and symposia, which is performed amid inebriation, in which rustics often dance to the accompaniment of female pipe-playing with intense and exhausting leaps that are still widespread in rural areas'.

[28] On Italians in imperial Ephesus see Kirbihler 2016.

[29] *Pace* Harrison in Morgan and Harrison 2008, 233.

names and apparent ethnic identity of narrator and character, the tale of the boy to some degree Romanises the Greek genre.[30]

Similar apparently conscious adaptations of Milesian tales (and perhaps of their congeners) may be proposed for some Greek 'ideal' novels.

A palmary case is that of Dionysius of Miletus in Chariton. Handsome, rich, noble, pious, educated, generous – he has all the qualities we might expect to be lacking in figures in Milesian tales. Similarly the heroine Callirhoe, albeit coming near to a Milesian-tale fate when the robbers decide to sell her, conducts herself throughout her Milesian adventure with dignity and good judgement. That good judgement leads her to accede to Dionysius' insistence that she marry him, but her decision-making and its outcome are given an entirely different colour from those of Petronius' Ephesian widow.[31]

Another species of discreditable tale is evoked by the false identity claimed for Callirhoe by the robber Theron – she is alleged to have been the slave of a Sybarite woman whose jealousy her beauty aroused (1.12.8). Readers know as well as Callirhoe herself that she is no character in a Sybaritic tale, and the claim that she is, despite an anachronism puzzling even in the mouth of an uneducated robber, may be partly calculated to let us measure the distance between Chariton's narrative and a Sybaritic tale.

Xenophon's opening of his story in Ephesus might raise expectations in some readers that they would encounter a narrative tinged with Ionian licence. But we soon discover Ephesus and its citizens to be moral and pious, even if Habrocomes is fatally haughty in a Hippolytean vein, a piety that is confirmed when the oracle at 'Colophon', i.e. Clarus, is consulted and its commands are executed.[32] That Clarus is chosen, not the oracle at Didyma controlled by Miletus, might signal the writer's rejection of a Milesian narrative texture.

Two other Greek cities were also traduced in irresponsible fictional writing – Rhodes (in the Ῥοδιακά, '*Rhodian affairs*', of Philip of Amphipolis),[33] and Tarentum (to judge from Juvenal, who links it with Sybaris, Rhodes, and Miletus).[34] Rhodes plays a key role in Xenophon's story of his couple's

[30] For a possible precedent for a Mysian/Pergamene Milesian tale see below.

[31] For a good assessment of Callirhoe's character, taking account of earlier discussions, see De Temmerman 2014.

[32] X.Eph. 1.6.1–7.2.

[33] Φίλιππος, Ἀμφιπολίτης, ἱστορικός. Ῥοδιακὰ βιβλία ιθ΄· ἔστι δὲ τῶν πάνυ αἰσχρῶν· Κωιακὰ βιβλία β΄, Θασιακὰ βιβλία β΄· καὶ ἄλλα, 'Philip, of Amphipolis, a historian. *Rhodian affairs*, nineteen books (they are extremely lewd); *Coan affairs*, two books; *Thasian affairs*, two books; and other works', Suda φ 351 *s.v.* Φίλιππος.

[34] *nullum crimen abest facinusque libidinis ex quo | paupertas Romana perit. hinc fluxit ad istos | et Sybaris colles, hinc et Rhodos et Miletus | atque coronatum et petulans madidumque Tarentum*, 'no crime or lustful deed is undocumented since Roman poverty has perished: from that point Sybaris has surged onto those hills you live on, from that point Rhodes, and Miletus, and garland-wearing, provocative, inebriated Tarentum', Juv. 6.294–7.

travels and reunion, but like his Ephesus it is a place of religious cult, not of immorality. Tarentum has also an important place in Anthia's adventures: it is here that she is sold by Rhēnaea's slave Clytus to a brothel-keeper and risks subjection to a life of prostitution.[35] Did Xenophon expect his readers to recognise an inverted 'Tarentine tale'?[36]

A self-styled widow from Ephesus, Melitē, reappears in Achilles Tatius. Despite her passion for the hero Cleitophon and the lengths to which it drives her, she is a much more complex and sympathetic character than Petronius' widow. By contrast her returning husband Thersander is unrestrained in the violence of his actions and of his invective, while his own early life is alleged by the priest of Artemis (a man with a developed skill in Aristophanic rhetoric)[37] to have been devoted to serial affairs with older men. Miletus is nowhere mentioned in Achilles Tatius' novel: but the defamatory and abusive rhetoric provoked by the debate over the behaviour of Melitē and Cleitophon evokes a world and a discourse familiar to some readers (certainly some in second-century Oxyrhychus) from the seamy iambic poetry of the sixth-century BC Ephesian Hipponax. If *Milesiaca* exploited a broader landscape of a sexually self-indulgent Ionia, we might suppose that the concentration of these features in the Ephesian denouement of Achilles Book 8 is an author's re-configuration of the Milesian tale's generic features.

One might expect none of this in Heliodorus, whose characters' adventures never take them into, or even very near, Ionia, and whose narrative's principal intertexts are epic and tragedy.[38] But both false and 'true' stories in Heliodorus introduce Ionia. First, in Book 1, we encounter a false tale told by Charicleia to her captor Thyamis: she and Theagenes, she alleges, are brother and sister from a noble family in Ephesus, she a priestess of Artemis, he a priest of Apollo.[39] This is several removes from a Milesian tale, but that the Ionian link makes some literary contribution is suggested by its second appearance. In Book 7 the two pre-pubescent slaves whom Arsace has assigned to minister to Theagenes and Charicleia are Ionians

35 X.Eph. 5.5.7; Anthia remains in Tarentum until 5.11.1.

36 I am reluctant to extend the boundaries of Milesian tales to include any *anilis fabula* / γραώδης μῦθος, 'old wives' tale', as suggested by Ruiz Montero 1996, 63, adducing particularly the Tarsian tale of Anthia told by Chrysion at X.Eph. 3.9.8.

37 ἦν δὲ εἰπεῖν οὐκ ἀδύνατος, μάλιστα δὲ τὴν Ἀριστοφάνους ἐζηλωκὼς κωμῳδίαν, 'and he was not incapable of making a speech, having modelled his discourse especially on the comedy of Aristophanes', Ach. Tat. 8.9.1.

38 But for importance of New Comedy for Cnemon's name, character and narrative see Bowie 1995b (Chapter 22 in this volume).

39 Hld. 1.22.2.

(Hld. 7.19, 8.9); of these two the girl nobly takes the blame for Arsace's poisoning in an attempt to save Charicleia (Hld. 8.9). A reader familiar with the Ionia of Milesian tales and of the rhetoric in Achilles Tatius Book 8 might see that here, as in so many other ways, Heliodorus is elevating the character and behaviour of types encountered in earlier prose fiction, both ideal and 'Milesian'.

3 Beginnings

How early can Milesian tales be traced back? In the 1990s I suggested that Aristides put together his work shortly before the Latin translation of Sisenna,[40] and hence around 100 BC. But there is really no evidence for Aristides' date, just as there is no evidence concerning where he was writing. It might well be Athens. Recent studies of the population of Athens in the first century BC and the first two centuries AD show that there was a strikingly high percentage of Milesians there from around 100 BC.[41] It is just as likely that Aristides was writing there, or in the largest and most prosperous of the cities of the area that from 129 BC had been the Roman province 'Asia', Ephesus, as that he was writing in the smaller city of Miletus. But even we were able to determine the date of Aristides' work or the place of its composition, there are hints that the tales he assembled might well have had a generic existence long before he exploited them to create his literary work.

Some help can be sought from the apparently related genre of Συβαριτικοὶ λόγοι, 'Sybaritic tales'. These are explicitly linked with Milesian tales by Ovid *Tristia* 2.413–18, and perhaps implicitly by Plutarch's mention of Sybaris in his *Crassus* 32.5–6 (both cited at the beginning of this chapter). 'Sybaritic tales' can be traced back as far as Aristophanes' comedy *Wasps*, first performed in Athens in early spring 422 BC (at the *Lenaea* of the archon year 423/422). But since the South Italian city of Sybaris was destroyed in 510 BC it is virtually certain that the genre goes back at least a century before that. To judge from utterances by Aristophanes' characters, in the 420s these tales were defined by being *about* somebody from Sybaris. Thus after Bdelycleon, instructing his pro-Cleon father how to conduct himself appropriately in an upper-class symposium, has very ill-advisedly told him to handle complaints by telling ἀστεῖοι λόγοι, 'witty stories', whether Aesopic or Sybaritic (1259–60), the drunken Philocleon tries to see off a citizen who

[40] Bowie 1996b. [41] Vestergaard 2000, 81–110.

wants to charge him with ὕβρις, 'aggressive violence', by beating him up and telling two appropriate Sybaritic stories:

Κατήγορος: σὺ λέγε. δικῶν γὰρ οὐ δέομ' οὐδὲ πραγμάτων.
Φιλοκλέων: ἀνὴρ Συβαρίτης ἐξέπεσεν ἐξ ἅρματος,
καί πως κατεάγη τῆς κεφαλῆς μέγα σφόδρα·
ἐτύγχανεν γὰρ οὐ τρίβων ὢν ἱππικῆς.
κἄπειτ' ἐπιστὰς εἶπ' ἀνὴρ αὐτῶι φίλος·
'ἔρδοι τις ἣν ἕκαστος εἰδείη τέχνην'.
οὕτω δὲ καὶ σὺ παράτρεχ' εἰς τὰ Πιττάλου.
Βδελυκλέων: ὅμοιά σου καὶ ταῦτα τοῖς ἄλλοις τρόποις.
Κατήγορος: ἀλλ' οὖν σὺ μέμνησ' οὗτος ἀπεκρίνατο.
Φιλοκλέων: ἄκουε, μὴ φεῦγ'. ἐν Συβάρει γυνή ποτε
κατέαξ' ἐχῖνον.
Κατήγορος: ταῦτ' ἐγὼ μαρτύρομαι. 1436bis
Φιλοκλέων: ούχῖνος οὖν ἔχων τιν' ἐπεμαρτύρατο· 1437
εἶθ' ἡ Συβαρῖτις εἶπεν, 'αἰ ναὶ τὰν κόραν
τὰν μαρτυρίαν ταύταν ἐάσας ἐν τάχει
ἐπίδεσμον ἐπρίω, νοῦν ἂν εἶχες πλείονα'.

Plaintiff: Tell me: for I have no wish for court cases or trouble.
Philocleon: A Sybarite fell from his chariot,
and somehow sustained a great crack on his head –
for he happened to be no expert in horsemanship.
And then a friend came up to him and said
'Each man should practise the trade he understands'.
And so you too should run along to Pittalus' clinic.
Bedycleon: This too is just like your other behaviour.
Plaintiff: Whatever, will you please remember what this man's answer was.
Philocleon: Listen, don't run away. In Sybaris a woman once
cracked her little pot.
Plaintiff: I ask you to bear witness to this.
Philocleon: So her little pot kept asking somebody to bear witness to it.[42]
Then the Sybarite woman said 'If, by the Daughter goddess,
you had abandoned this attempt to get a witness and had quickly
bought a bandage, you would have had more sense'.

Aristophanes, *Wasps* 1426–40

[42] I have offered a translation of a line that seems to make little sense: more probably the text should read τὸν ἐχῖνον οὖν οὔχων τιν' ἐπεμαρτύρατο, 'so the man who owned the little pot asked somebody to bear witness'.

The tales both concern Sybarites. The first is about an ἀνὴρ Συβαρίτης, 'Sybarite man' (1427–31), the second about a woman located in Sybaris who must surely also be supposed to be from Sybaris (1435–40). Each tale seems to have a punch-line, meant to be funny, which Philocleon adapts to his objective of seeing off his accuser. The first has no apparent sexual content; the second does so only if one takes the ἐχῖνος, 'little pot', which the woman in Sybaris breaks to be an obscene sexual double entendre – an interpretation I have often toyed with but by which I am not wholly convinced.[43] Of course it may not have been an essential feature of what Aristophanes' audience and later Greeks took to be Sybaritic stories that there should be a punch-line – this could be a twist or selection by Aristophanes to suit his own dramatic purpose. Certainly the stories of the bizarre and self-indulgent behaviour of Sybarites told by Aelian do not in the same way depend on a verbal punch-line, at least as he transmits them.[44] But if there *was* usually a punch-line, then both in this respect, and in the fact that a sexual theme was apparently *not* obligatory, Sybaritic stories seem to have had a different texture from Milesian.

It seems probable that, unlike *Milesiaca*, Sybaritic stories were not collected until shortly before Ovid composed *Tristia* 2.417–18:

[43] For the frequent use of the names of containers of various shapes as *double entendres* for female genitals, and for the possible place of ἐχῖνος, 'little pot', in this category, see Henderson 1975, 142 under his no. 161. Another possible case is Archil. fr. 201: cf. Corrêa 2001 and 2010.

[44] Aelian's two stories are (a) Σμινδυρίδης ὁ Συβαρίτης ἐς τοσοῦτον τρυφῆς ἐξώκειλε (καὶ γάρ τοι Συβαρίταις πᾶσιν ἔργον ἦν τρυφᾶν καὶ τῶι βίωι διαρρεῖν, ὁ δὲ Σμινδυρίδης καὶ πλέον)· φύλλοις ῥόδων γοῦν ἐπαναπεσὼν καὶ κοιμηθεὶς ἐπ' αὐτῶν ἐξανέστη λέγων φλυκταίνας ἐκ τῆς εὐνῆς ἔχειν. σχολῆι γ' ἂν οὗτος ἐπὶ χαμεύνης κατεκλίθη ἢ στιβάδος ἢ πόας ἐν προσάντει πεφυκυίας ἢ ταύρου δορᾶς, ὡς ὁ Διομήδης, πρεπούσης στρατιώτηι σκληρῶι καὶ γενναίωι 'ὑπὸ δ' ἔστρωτο ῥινὸν βοὸς ἀγραύλοιο', 'Smindyrides of Sybaris ended up with extremely luxurious habits (for all Sybarites were intent on living luxuriously and extravagantly, and Smindyrides more than most): for example, he threw himself down on rose petals, and after sleeping on them he got up and said his bed had given him blisters. He would scarcely have been able to lie on a camp bed, a straw mattress, grassy growing on a slope, or, like Diomedes, on a bull's hide, as befitted a tough and noble warrior (Il. 10.155): "Beneath him was spread the skin of an ox from the farm"', Ael. *VH* 9.24. Smindyrides is otherwise known as a suitor of Cleisthenes' daughter Agariste from Hdt. 6.127.1, saying of him ὃς ἐπὶ πλεῖστον δὴ χλιδῆς εἷς ἀνὴρ ἀπίκετο, 'who of all men had developed the most self-indulgent habits'; (b) Συβαρίτης ἀνὴρ παιδαγωγὸς (καὶ γὰρ οὖν μετὰ τῶν ἄλλων Συβαριτῶν καὶ αὐτοὶ ἐτρύφων) τοῦ παιδός, ὃν ἦγε διὰ τῆς ὁδοῦ, ἰσχάδι περιτυχόντος καὶ ἀνελομένου, ἐπέπληξεν αὐτῶι ἰσχυρότατα· γελοιότατα δὲ αὐτὸς τὸ εὕρημα παρὰ τοῦ παιδὸς ἁρπάσας κατέτραγεν. ὅτε τοῦτο ἀνελεξάμην ἐν ἱστορίαις Συβαριτικαῖς, ἐγέλασα· ἔδωκα δὲ αὐτὸ ἐς μνήμην, μὴ βασκήνας διὰ φιλανθρωπίαν γελάσαι καὶ ἄλλον, 'A boy-minder at Sybaris – they too indulged in luxury with the other Sybarites – gave a very severe beating to the boy he was leading along the road who had found a fig and picked it up; but then, quite ridiculously, he snatched it from the child and ate it. When I read of this in stories about Sybaris, I laughed; but I put it on record, since out of kindness I do not grudge others a laugh', Ael. *VH* 14.20.

Nec qui composuit nuper Sybaritica fugit,
nec qui concubitus non tacuere suos.

Nor did the man who recently composed Sybaritic tales go into exile,
Nor the ones who did not keep silent about their own liaisons.

The way Ovid tries to use this datum also suggests that by the Roman imperial period Sybaritic stores had acquired a marked sexual orientation that they may not already have had in the fifth century BC.

If Sybaritic stories can be traced back in some form to the fifth or even sixth century BC, might this also have been true of Milesian tales? Two very slight indications may suggest that this could have been so.

First, Aristophanes twice picks out Miletus as the principal source of dildos for Athenian ladies, in *Lysistrata* and in a fragment from an unknown play:

ἀλλ᾽ οὐδὲ μοιχοῦ καταλέλειπται φεψάλυξ.
ἐξ οὗ γὰρ ἡμᾶς προὔδοσαν Μιλήσιοι,
οὐκ εἶδον οὐδ᾽ ὄλισβον ὀκτωδάκτυλον.

But not even a glimmer of an adulterer has been left behind.
And indeed from the moment the Milesians abandoned us,
I have not set eyes even on an eight-finger dildo.[45]

Aristophanes, *Lysistrata* 108–110

τί ἐστι τοῦθ᾽ ὃ λέγουσι τ[ὰς Μιλησίας]
παίζειν ἐχούσας, ἀντιβολῶ, [τὸ σκύτινον;]

What is that thing that they say the [women of Miletus]
have in their hands when playing around, please tell me [the leather thing?].

Aristophanes, fr. 592.16–17 K–A[46]

The second of these texts seems explicitly to represents the women of *Miletus* as indulging in recreational sex with dildos – I say 'seems', because Μιλησίας, 'women of Miletus', is a supplement, albeit one that has been widely accepted.

Second, there is the matter of Pericles' non-citizen partner, Aspasia, who was of course from Miletus. What we find in such acts of mockery

[45] Henderson 1971, 81 *ad loc.* expresses surprise at the shortness of 'eight-finger' dildos. Lateral thinking suggests that the thickness, not the length of the device may be in question.

[46] Grenfell and Hunt 1899, no. 212 = Page 1941, no. 44.

as Dicaeopolis' speech in Aristophanes *Acharnians*, where two of Aspasia's πόρναι, 'prostitutes', are claimed to be responsible for the outbreak of the Peloponnesian war, can only be a small sample of what was being said or sung about Aspasia in the symposia and other private gatherings in Athens of the 430s and 420s:

> κἆιθ' οἱ Μεγαρῆς ὀδύναις πεφυσιγγωμένοι
> ἀντεξέκλεψαν Ἀσπασίας πόρνας δύο·
> κἀντεῦθεν ἀρχὴ τοῦ πολέμου κατερράγη ...
>
> And next the Megarians, garlicked up in agony,
> stole in reprisal two of Aspasia's prostitutes:
> and it was from this that the beginning of the war burst forth ...
>
> Aristophanes, *Acharnians* 525–7

So far as I can discover no extant testimony links Aspasia and dildos. But of course Aspasia had her pick of Athenian elite men, so perhaps she never resorted to a dildo. Taken together, however, I suggest that these two sets of data make it quite likely that Milesian tales, in which some sexual element was part of the laws of the genre, *scritti* or *non scritti*, were already circulating in the last three decades of the fifth century. One might even guess that the mention of Aspasia and her (perhaps) Milesian prostitutes might for some members of the audience have marked Dicaeopolis' account of the war's outbreak as a comic variation on a Milesian tale.

4 Conclusions

It remains the case that very little about Milesian tales can be said with certainty. There was a Greek genre with that name, and the work of its most famous exponent, claiming the name Aristides, was circulating by the early first century BC in time to be translated into Latin by the historian and *praetor* of 78 BC Sisenna; it was in the headlines quarter of a century later when discovered by Parthians in the Roman baggage-train after the battle of Carrhae in 53 BC. The content could be described as ἀκόλαστος or *turpis*, 'lascivious' or 'lewd'. Both Aristides' work and Sisenna's translation could be assumed by Ovid to be known to some of the readers of his *Tristia* (between AD 9 and 12), and the former was among the wide range of texts cited by the mid-second-century lexicographer Valerius Harpocration in his *Lexicon of the Ten Orators*, albeit only once, but attesting at least three books.[47] Fragments of Sisenna show that his translation ran to at least thirteen books.

Thereafter all is speculative reconstruction. I have argued that Milesian tales were most probably a collection of short narratives about people or incidents set in, or linked to, Miletus, perhaps extending more widely into adjacent parts of Ionia. Their attraction was their amusing rendering of disreputable sexual behaviour, and they may well not have regularly ended with a verbal punch-line, such as was perhaps a feature of the related genre of Sybaritic tales. In his work Aristides probably presented himself as a narrator passing on stories he had heard from others, and, although he may have represented himself travelling to Miletus or more widely in Ionia, he need not have done, nor have we any indication that he represented himself as a protagonist in any of his stories. That is not to say this posture can be confidently excluded, any more than the suggestion that these tales were marked by a proclivity towards magic and the supernatural. But whereas it is clear that Milesian tales had important influence on aspects of the form and content of both Petronius' *Satyrica* and Apuleius' *Metamorphoses*, the ideas that Milesian tales already exploited a narrating protagonist (as argued by Jensson) or displayed a sensationalist interest in magic (as argued by Harrison) should not be treated as more than possibilities. Nor is my suggestion that any pseudo-ethnographic features in Aristides evoked the Περίοδος γῆς, '*Travel about the earth*', of Hecataeus of Miletus anything more than a possibility.

It also now seems to be a possibility, following the publication in 2006 of the papyrus with an apparently prosimetric ass-tale, similar to that found in the *Lucius or the ass* and used by Apuleius, but different in some details, that some Milesian tales were prosimetric; and that in turn re-opens the question of the genre of the Iolaus narrative first published in 1971. Did it (too?) come from a collection of Milesian tales?

I have drawn attention to some details of the Greek ideal novels which might be seen as predicated on a readership's knowledge of a genre of Milesian tales, details which most often show the novelist drawing attention to his distance from their literary level. Much more could be done, but the traps are numerous.

[47] ἐν γ′ Μιλησιακῶν Ἀριστείδου, 'in Book 3 of Aristeides' *Milesiaca*', Harpocration δ 23 *s.v.* δερμηστής Keaney.

I have also put forward a hypothesis about the earlier history of Milesian tales, suggesting that they may already have circulated in later fifth-century Athens, as Sybaritic tales certainly did, and that Aristophanes allows us to infer their exploitation of Milesian dildoes and of the high-class *hetaera* Aspasia of Miletus. Whereas papyri may be hoped to resolve some of our many uncertainties about Milesian tales in the Hellenistic and Roman periods, my hypothesis about their fifth-century prehistory is almost certain never to be confirmed.

39 A Land without Priests? Religious Authority in Longus, *Daphnis and Chloe* (2015)

1 The Other Novels

One of the many ways in which the universe created by Longus in *Daphnis and Chloe* differs from those offered by the other four 'ideal' Greek novels is the absence of institutionalised community religion – and with that absence goes the absence of priests, whether honest or fraudulent.[1] All four of the other 'ideal novels' involve priests or priestesses at some point.

Thus, in Chariton the temple of Aphrodite built and dedicated by Dionysius has attached to it a ἱέρεια, 'priestess'.[2] Again in Chariton's last book priests are involved in Chaereas' dedications and banquet in honour of Aphrodite on Cyprus:

> δεξαμένων δὲ αὐτῶν ἐξεβίβασε τὴν δύναμιν ἅπασαν εἰς γῆν καὶ ἀναθήμασι τὴν Ἀφροδίτην ἐτίμησε· πολλῶν δὲ ἱερείων συναχθέντων εἱστίασε τὴν στρατιάν. σκεπτομένου δὲ αὐτοῦ περὶ τῶν ἑξῆς ἀπήγγειλαν οἱ ἱερεῖς (οἱ αὐτοὶ δέ εἰσι καὶ μάντεις) ὅτι καλὰ γέγονε τὰ ἱερά.
>
> When they (sc. the Cypriots) had welcomed him, he disembarked his whole force and honoured Aphrodite with dedications; and gathering together many animals for sacrifice he feasted the army. And when he enquired about what was going to happen the priests (who are also prophets) reported that the sacrifice had been propitious.
>
> Chariton 8.2.9

This chapter was first given as a paper to RICAN 6, 30–31 May 2011, on holy men/women and charlatans in the Ancient Novel, published as Panayotakis, Schmeling, and Paschalis 2015; then in Harvard in November 2013. I am grateful for points made by both audiences. On the issues addressed cf. Bremmer 2013, esp. 153.

1 On some definitions the sacrifices and feasts set up at 2.30.3–37 to celebrate Chloe's return, at 4.3. to mark Dionysophanes' visits to his estates, and at 4.6 to celebrate Daphnis' recovery of his identity might be counted as 'institutionalised religion', as indeed might the symposia at 4.5. and 4.34–6. But all of these are one-off responses to a particular situation, and seem not to imply regular, institutionalised cult.

2 Ch. 3.9.1 μικρὸν οὖν διαλιποῦσα καλεῖ τὴν ἱέρειαν· ἡ δὲ πρεσβῦτις ὑπακούσασα ..., 'so after a short interval she summoned the priestess: and the old lady did as she asked ...'; 3.9.4 τοῦτο μόνον εἶπεν, ὅπερ ἤκουσε παρὰ τῆς ἱερείας, 'he only said what he had heard from the priestess'.

It is likewise in Xenophon. Anthia's parents seek help from priests and prophets to solve the mystery of their daughter's malady:

> εἰς τέλος εἰσάγουσι παρὰ τὴν Ἀνθίαν μάντεις καὶ ἱερέας, ὡς εὑρήσοντας λύσιν τοῦ δεινοῦ. οἱ δὲ ἐλθόντες ἔθυόν τε ἱερεῖα καὶ ποικίλα ἐπέσπενδον καὶ ἐπέλεγον φωνὰς βαρβαρικάς, ἐξιλάσκεσθαί τινας λέγοντες δαίμονας, καὶ προσεποίουν ὡς εἴη τὸ δεινὸν ἐκ τῶν ὑποχθονίων θεῶν.
>
> In the end they brought prophets and priests to Anthia to discover a solution for the crisis. And when they came they slaughtered sacrificial beasts, accompanying this by various libations and by non-Greek utterances, saying that they were trying to propitiate certain divinities, and they claimed that the crisis had been caused by the gods of the underworld.
>
> Xenophon 1.5.6–8

Later in the same book, in Xenophon's description of Anthia's and Habrocomes' departure from Ephesus (1.10.7–8), the addition of the words ἱερειῶν, 'priestesses', or ἱερῶν παρθένων, 'holy virgins', was proposed by Hemsterhuys to give syntax and sense to the manuscript reading.[3]

In Achilles Tatius the priest of Artemis at Ephesus appears garlanded with laurel (7.12.2–3), signalling the arrival of a θεωρία, 'sacred embassy', that requires a suspension of Cleitophon's trial, and that then plays an important part in the story's denouement in Book 8.

Heliodorus offers his readers two styles of priest: the relatively straightforward, pious and wholly Hellenic Charicles, who engages in such traditional ritual action as arranging for the performance of a ὕμνος, 'hymn', at Delphi (3.18); and the ambiguous Calasiris, about whom much has been written.

2 Longus

In the world of Longus' *Daphnis and Chloe* the religious structures (like much else) are very different. Why? Part of the explanation may be that in Longus' day, and indeed apparently ever since the archaic and classical periods, some Greek rural cults virtually ran themselves: caves and other natural features that were regarded as holy could attract regular worshippers and be graced with frequent offerings, but they might not be expected

[3] πολλαὶ δὲ καὶ τῶν <ἱερειῶν> or τῶν <ἱερῶν παρθένων>, 'many of the priestesses' or 'many of the holy virgins', Hemsterhuys 1732. There are other possibilities: Cobet 1858 proposed simply ξένων, 'foreign women', and Zagoiannis 1897 γυναικῶν, 'women'.

to have any established priest or priestess in charge. Almost all the places discussed as the locations of cults of Nymphs by Jennifer Larsen are in this category.[4] The only exception I have discovered is the unusually elaborate cult of the Nymphs at Aquae Calidae, near the Greek colony of Anchialus on the Black Sea, north of Salmydessus. In the first centuries BC and AD this cult is documented as attracting worshippers from Asia Minor as well as from Thrace, Macedonia and the Black Sea; by the Severan period there are dedications to these *Nymphai Anchialiae*; they are also commemorated on coins. This place sounds like Bath, Baden Baden and Loutraki all rolled into one, and is very different from the vast majority of cults of Nymphs.[5]

It is also worth noting that even so well established a cult as that of Amphiaraus at Oropus did not have a full-time priest. Surviving regulations from the fourth century BC require its priest to be there only from the end of winter until the first ploughing, and not continuously even during that period. But in this case it is also clear that the day-to-day needs of worshippers are handled by a resident νεωκόρος, 'temple-attendant':

> θεοί. τὸν ἱερέα τοῦ Ἀμφιαράου φοιτᾶν εἰς τὸ ἱερόν, ἐπειδὰν χειμὼν παρέλθει μέχρι ἀρότου ὥρης, μὴ πλέον διαλείποντα ἢ τρεῖς ἡμέρας καὶ μένειν ἐν τοῖ ἱεροῖ μὴ ἔλαττον ἢ δέκα ἡμέρας τοῦ μηνὸς ἑκ<ά>στο : καὶ ἐπαναγκάζειν τὸν νεωκόρον τοῦ τε ἱεροῦ ἐπιμελεῖσθαι κατὰ τὸν νόμον καὶ τῶν ἀφικνεμένων εἰς τὸ ἱερόν ...
>
> (To) the gods. The priest of Amphiaraus is to come regularly to the sanctuary when winter passes until the season of ploughing, not omitting to do so for more than three days, and he is to remain in the sanctuary for no fewer than ten days in each month. And he is to ensure that the temple-attendant cares for the sanctuary according to the law and for those who visit the sanctuary ...
>
> *IG* vii 235 = *Syll.*^{3} 1004= *SEG* 31.416= *IOrop.* 277 (ca. 387–77 BC)

It is of course very relevant that the majority of the action of *Daphnis and Chloe* takes place in the countryside, where there appears to be no nucleated settlement so large even as one of the smaller classical Attic demes. It

4 Larson 2001.

5 For the cult of *Nymphai Anchialiae* at *Aquae Calidae* see Larson 2001, 174; for sculpted reliefs with dedicatory texts see *IGBulg.* i^2 380 (above relief 1) [κυ]ρίες Νύφες (i.e. κυρίαις Νύμφαις), 'to the lady Nymphs', and (below relief 2) Ζωπᾶς Ἰουλίου| εὐχαριστôν (i.e. εὐχαριστῶν) ἀνέ|θηκεν, 'Zopas son of Iulius dedicated [sc. this relief] in gratitude', and *IGBulg.* i^2 381 (above relief 1) Μ̣(ᾶρκος) Ἰούλιọς Μίκκαλος [– – –] | Νύμφαις Ἀνχιαλ[είαις – – – – – –], 'Marcus Iulius Miccalus ... to the Nymphs of Anchialus'. For a priest see *IGBulg.* i^2 382 [– – – – ω]ν̣ Τίτου εὐχαρισ|[τήριον ἱ]ερατεύοντος β̣ʹ|[– – – – – –]ς Σαλου, '... a thank-offering of Titus during the second priesthood of [... . .] Salus). For coins see Robert 1959, 223–5.

would be reasonable to suppose that Longus saw institutionalised religion as a feature of Greek *polis* life, where the city elites controlled and provided officials for cults not only in the urban centres but also in many extra-urban shrines that were located in the territory of a *polis*. One of his objectives might be to display how rural religion might be imagined to operate when such control from the centre was *not* being exercised. I think there is something in this supposition. But, as I have argued elsewhere,[6] Longus does not set out to allocate all virtues to the country and all vices to the city, and it would have been open to him to have a figure like Dionysophanes actively involved not merely in the cult of Dionysus but in some cult of Eros or Pan as well – all cults which could in principle have either an urban or a rural location.

What Longus does instead is subtle and interesting. The city magnate Dionysophanes is the nearest person in *Daphnis and Chloe* to a historical priest from the urban elite. But, despite his ostentatiously theophoric name, Dionysophanes is neither a holy man nor even a priest. He has indeed dedicated a temple to Dionysus in the elaborate παράδεισος, 'park', or *hortus conclusus*, 'walled garden', on his rural estate outside Mytilene – a *villa rustica* whose actual *villa* is never described by Longus, but is simply referred to once by the term καταγωγή, 'residence' (4.1.2).[7] However, although arrangements have been made for tending the παράδεισος, 'park' – this is clearly one of Lamon's duties (4.1.1–3), and so in some sense he is a νεωκόρος, 'temple-attendant', though never so described – Longus gives no hint of any provision for recurrent festivals or sacrifices, nor indeed does he indicate that there was any regular form of worship at the temple itself. It has something of the air of a museum temple of the sort represented by the small *tholos* temple of Cnidian Aphrodite at Hadrian's villa at Tivoli – a *mimesis* of a temple. But that it is something more than that is shown by Gnathon's flight there as a ἱκέτης, 'suppliant' (4.25.2). It is, then, a sacred space, but it is one without cult. Dionysophanes does indeed offer sacrifices to the country deities on the first day of his visit to his estate, but they are to Demeter, Dionysus, Pan and the Nymphs, not just to Dionysus, and they are not said to happen in association with Dionysus' temple (4.13.3).

In this respect Dionysophanes is quite different from his distant but recognisable literary ancestor, Chariton's Dionysius of Miletus. The priestess

[6] Bowie 2009b (Chapter 35 in this volume).

[7] The choice of the word καταγωγή, used of inns or modest public rooms (cf. *IGR* iv 1209) may be made to tease the reader with a comparison between Dionysophanes' trip into the country and that of Socrates in Pl. *Phdr.*, where at 230b he uses it of the *locus amoenus* where they have halted.

who has been mentioned above as associated by Chariton with the temple of Aphrodite that is close to Dionysius' house, that he frequents, and that we later discover he actually built,[8] must be supposed to have been provided for in a foundation set up when the temple was built and dedicated. In the real world of an historical Greek city a figure like Dionysius, acting through the city's governing bodies – whether the *demos*, 'people', or the *boule*, 'council', or both – would have made financial arrangements for the appointment and maintenance of a priestess and for the performance of rituals at regular intervals.[9]

In *Daphnis and Chloe* we might imagine that Dionysophanes was indeed a priest of Dionysus, holding that office, as so many did in the imperial period, διὰ βίου, 'for life',[10] but Longus does nothing to nudge our imagination in that direction. Rather, I think, we are asked to see the temple and its set of paintings that narrate episodes from the deeds of Dionysus (more succinctly than such poets as Nonnus) as part and parcel of Dionysophanes' limited and inadequate understanding of the world. This is an understanding that allows him to expose his son because he thinks that his three older children make up a large enough family to inherit his wealth, and that they will always be there to do so; and an understanding that has him create a παράδεισος, 'park', in which art exploits and dominates rather than complements nature – as so well interpreted by John Morgan[11] – and which anyway Dionysophanes visits only rarely. For a man like this a temple decorated with the clichés of Dionysiac myth are enough to publicise the special relationship with Dionysus that we are to presume he felt on the basis of his name Dionysophanes. Longus gives us no hint that this relationship had any religious far less spiritual importance for him. Dionysophanes twice acknowledges that Daphnis and Chloe were saved προνοίαι θεῶν, 'by the providence of the gods', 4.24.2, 36.1), but he does not specify which gods these were; and when he sets up his rustic feast to celebrate Daphnis' discovery, its sacrifices are to ἐπιχώριοι θεοί, 'gods of the locality', in general, and there is no special mention of Dionysus. Indeed it is Daphnis, not Dionysophanes, who is mentioned as making a dedication to Dionysus – τῶι Διονύσωι μὲν ἀνέθηκε τὴν πήραν καὶ τὸ δέρμα, 'to Dionysus he dedicated his leather bag and his animal skin' (4.26.2) – as well as to Pan and the Nymphs.

[8] Priestess 3.9.1 and 4; location 2.2.5, 5.10.1; built by Dionysius 5.10.1.

[9] For arrangements for the performance of elaborate rituals (though in this case not associated with a temple), see the foundation of C. Vibius Salutaris at Ephesus, with Rogers 1991.

[10] As did many of the priests of the civic imperial cult catalogued and discussed by Frija 2010a and 2010b.

[11] Morgan 2004, 224–5.

Again, when the gods in a dream tell Dionysophanes to throw a party in his opulent house in Mytilene (4.34.1), a party at which it turns out that Chloe's paternity will be discovered, these gods of whom he dreams are Eros and the Nymphs, not Dionysus. The rustic gods who assiduously watched over Daphnis and Chloe seem to have moved into the religious vacuum left by Dionysophanes' hollow and formal attachment to Dionysus.

It seems clear, then, that Dionysophanes is no holy man. He is not even a regular worshipper like Chariton's Dionysius of Miletus, who prays repeatedly and with some success to Aphrodite, never simply passing her temple near his house (2.2.5), and who on his supposed son's birth fills temples with offerings and lays on banquets that involve sacrifice (3.7–8). But Dionysophanes' negative role is itself important. His presentation makes it clear to readers that they must look outside the city limits for holiness.

Another of Longus' characters has a much stronger claim to be a holy man, Philetas. Philetas' relationship with Eros is the closest that any mortal has with a divinity in any of the novels. Just as in other novels gods communicate with mortals through dreams, so too in *Daphnis and Chloe* the Nymphs appear to several characters in a dream – once to both Dryas and Lamon (1.7.2), twice to Daphnis (2.23.1, 3.27.2), and together with Eros to Dionysophanes, as has just been noted (4.34.1). They probably also appear to Megacles (at 4.35.5).[12] Similarly Pan communicates angrily with the Methymnaean commander Bryaxis in a deep midday sleep (2.26–7), following upon a series of miraculous phenomena that have no detectable anthropomorphic involvement. But Philetas is in a class by himself. He is privileged, not simply to have had a life in which Eros was watching over him ever since in his youth he fell in love with Amaryllis (2.5.3), but actually in old age to see Eros in his well-tempered garden and to receive from him a λόγος, 'account', of ἔρως, 'desire'/Eros, which he passes on to Daphnis and Chloe (2.4–6). Its blend of elements drawn from early cosmogonic poetry, from Anacreon, from Empedocles, from Plato's *Phaedrus* and from the figure of Diotima in his *Symposium*, spiced up with allusions to Hellenistic love-poetry triggered by the name Philetas, mixes a powerful cocktail that ensures that this particular scene's impact is as forceful as its

[12] Megacles is unspecific: ἀλλ' ὥσπερ οἱ θεοὶ γέλωτά με ποιούμενοι νύκτωρ ὀνείρους μοι ἐπιπέμπουσι δηλοῦντες ὅτι με πατέρα με ποιήσει ποίμνιον, 'but as if the gods were making me a laughing-stock they have been sending me dreams in the night indicating that a sheep will make me a father'. But the reader is likely to take the gods who have sent these dreams to be, as in all other cases but one in the novel, the Nymphs. I exclude Lycaenion's fraudulent claim (3.17.2) that the Nymphs have appeared to her in a dream, discussed shortly, though that claim reinforces the general expectation that in Longus' world dreams come from Nymphs. When writing this chapter I had not seen Carlisle 2009.

content is important for the novel as a whole.[13] It is not surprising that it was a scene that caught the eye of the Brazilian painter Rodolfo Amoedo.[14]

Although the only individual act of worship we read of Philetas performing is when he comes στεφανίσκους τινὰς τῶι Πανὶ κομίζων καὶ βότρυς ἔτι ἐν φύλλοις καὶ κλήμασι, 'bringing little garlands, and grapes still with their leaves and stalks, to Pan' (2.32.1), he is the sort of numinous figure who has, or claims to have, a special relation to divinity that we find in many Greek texts of this period, some dismissively sceptical, like Lucian's quasi-biography of Alexander of Abonouteichos, other adopting at least a posture of reverence, like Philostratus' *In honour of Apollonius*. Another analogue, cocooned like Longus' characters in layers of narrative authentication, is the provocatively unnamed vintner of Philostratus' *Heroicus* who, he tells his wind-delayed Phoenician interlocutor, has regular encounters with the epic hero Protesilaus.[15]

As this case of the vintner in Philostratus' *Heroicus* shows, what makes a mortal holy is not simply a close relationship with a divinity and some expectation of special protection by that divinity, but the capacity to draw upon that relationship to expound the nature of the divine, whether particular or general. I have suggested that such a capacity was certainly not evident in Dionysophanes, whereas equally evidently it is present in Philetas. But it is also to some extent evident in some other characters in *Daphnis and Chloe*, and I shall briefly assess their claims to being holy men, or holy women.

First, a character who can swiftly be dismissed as a charlatan, Gnathon. This urban parasite, who behaves as might be expected οἷα πᾶσαν ἐρωτικὴν ἐν τοῖς τῶν ἀσώτων συμποσίοις πεπαιδευμένος, 'since he had been educated in the whole range of erotic mythology in the symposia of roués' (4.17.3),[16] glibly adduces precedents from gods' sexual misbehaviour to support his own lecherous inclinations and has no divine truths to offer the pastoral world. His pseudo-didactic role is that of a foil to narrators who have stronger claims to understand the gods.

One of these narrators is Daphnis himself. But the two myths he tells involving Pan (1.27.2–4, 3.23) lack authority. The reader is not told where Daphnis learned these myths, and we have some reason to suspect he does

[13] For an excellent discussion see Morgan 2004, 179–80, proposing a more systematic set of associations than Hunter 1983, 35f.

[14] See the oil-painting of Philetas' lesson, now in the Museu Nacional de Belas Artes, Rio de Janeiro, by Rodolfo Amoedo (b. December 11, 1857 in Salvador, Bahia–d. May 31, 1941 in Rio de Janeiro).

[15] The most subtle and illuminating analysis of Philostr.'s *Her.* is Hodkinson 2011.

not understand them. For us readers they briefly conjure up the spectre that Daphnis, like Pan in the cow-girl's song of 1.27 and in the story of Echo at 3.23, may find that the power of ἔρως, 'sexual desire', will drive him into a destructive relationship with Chloe that replaces symmetry and consensuality with patriarchal male domination and her subjection to sexual violence. That indeed was the interpretation offered by Winkler in a classic chapter.[17] But as I have argued elsewhere, the reader does not need long to see how improbable this outcome would be, and is guided to interpret these μῦθοι, 'myths' or 'tales', both as testimonies to Pan's overall power, exemplified in the Methymnaean episode and in the cult-title he is given by the couple at the end of the book, Πὰν Στρατιώτης, 'Pan the Soldier'(4.39.2), and as markers of the generic difference between novelistic, happy-end story-telling and traditional, disaster-prone Greek mythology.[18]

Daphnis is undoubtedly pious (as also is Chloe). After the serious mistake of omitting Pan from their worship (2.22.4) the couple continue worshipping Pan, the Nymphs and Eros not simply for the rest of the novel but for the rest of their lives: καὶ οὐ τότε μόνον ἀλλ' ἔστε ἔζων τὸν πλεῖστον χρόνον βίον ποιμενικὸν εἶχον, θεοὺς σέβοντες Νύμφας καὶ Πᾶνα καὶ Ἔρωτα, 'and not only then, but so long as they lived, they had the life of herdsfolk for most of the time, honouring as their gods the Nymphs, and Pan, and Eros' (4.39.1). Their make-over of the Nymphs' cave (τὸ ἄντρον ἐκόσμησαν, 'they beautified the cave'),[19] their dedication of εἰκόνες, 'images', and their erection of an altar to Ἔρως Ποιμήν, 'Eros the Shepherd', and of a temple for Pan the Soldier (all at 4.39.2) are marks of a heartfelt gratitude to the gods that totally outclass the ostentatious but less meaningful edifice of Dionysophanes. We are also encouraged to imagine that the truths about Eros that Daphnis and Chloe had learned from Philetas are truths that they in turn pass on to their (almost) look-alike children. But even if all this is so, nothing in it elevates them to theologically authoritative figures.

Daphnis' father Lamon may have a slightly stronger claim. Like Daphnis, he too tells a myth about Pan, and purports to guarantee its provenance: a

16 If, as seems very possible, Longus is writing around AD 200, it is tempting to see this compact description as a snipe at the *paideia*, much of it to do with *eros* and *erotica*, offered by Ath. in his distended *Deipnosophistae*, probably written in the 190s.

17 'The education of Chloe: hidden injuries of sex', in Winkler 1990, 102–26.

18 See Bowie 2003b (Chapter 26 in this volume), 2007c (Chapter 31 in this volume); Kossaifi 2012.

19 For a remarkable fifth-century BC case of an individual at Vari in Attica building a cave of the Nymphs in response to their commands see *IG* i^3 977–80, especially 980 = *CEG* 321: Ἀρχέδημος ὁ Θ|ηραῖος ὁ νυμφ| όληπτος φραδ|αῖσι Νυμφôν τ|ἄντρον ἐξηργ|άξατο, 'Archedemos of Thera, nymph-possessed, at the behest of the Nymphs constructed the cave', discussed by Larson 2001, 14–16, 242–5.

Sicilian αἰπόλος, 'goatherd' (2.33.3). That reference is not, on this fictional version of Lesbos, to the historical Syracusan poet Theocritus, but to the fictional and mysteriously unnamed αἰπόλος, 'goatherd', of the first poem of Theocritus in modern and in some ancient editions, ἁδύ τι τὸ ψιθύρισμα καὶ ἁ πίτυς, αἰπόλε, τήνα | ἁ ποτὶ ταῖς παγαῖσι, μελίσδεται ..., 'Sweet is the whispering that that pine too, goatherd, | the one beside the springs, sings ....' The reference prompts the reader to link Lamon and his pastoral world with the Theocritean pastoral tradition, which is such an important intertext for *Daphnis and Chloe*, and to attempt connect Lamon's foster-son Daphnis in some way with the mythical Daphnis of Theocritus 1.[20] Lamon is thus, like Philetas, 'poetically enfranchised' (to borrow a term used by Morgan of Philetas).[21] But this literary genealogy claimed by Lamon for his μῦθος, 'myth' (2.33.3), takes us to the erotic fictions of a Hellenistic poet, Theocritus, whose presentation of the incurable nature of sexual desire in another of his works, *Idyll* 11, had been revised if not refuted by Philetas earlier in that same Book 2 of *Daphnis and Chloe*. Nothing that Lamon says or does, either at this celebration or elsewhere in the novel, makes him a serious candidate for the title of 'holy man'.

Is Philetas, then, left holding the cup of Bathycles? One more candidate within the story needs to be considered, even if also to be dismissed. That is Lycaenion. In some sense Lycaenion might be seen as a missionary of Eros, and her instruction in the ἔργα, 'acts', of Eros manifestly complements Philetas' theoretical exposition. But Lycaenion has many bad marks that might be seen as obstacles to holiness: her lupine name ('Little Wolf'), her urban origin, the fact that it is her own sexual desire that first prompts her to seduce Daphnis, her spying on the couple to confirm her hunch that they are enamoured, her deception both of her husband and of Daphnis in achieving her sexual objective. Indeed her deception of Daphnis is double: she first pretends that an eagle has snatched one of her twenty geese (3.16.2) – despite learning γράμματα, 'letters' (1.8.2), Daphnis does not have the literary schooling to spot that this is a calque on a move made in the *Odyssey* by the ever-astute Penelope –[22] and then she claims that the Nymphs have appeared to her in a dream and told her to teach Daphnis the ἔργα, 'acts', of Eros (3.16–17). The narrative makes it clear to the reader that this is a fraudulent claim, and to point up the fraud in Lycaenion's self-presentation

[20] For Longus' use of Theoc. and the pastoral tradition to construct his own pastoral world see Hunter 1983; Cresci 1999; Effe 1999; Bowie 2013d (Chapter 38 in this volume), 2021b. A link between Longus' Daphnis and that of pastoral poetry had already been hinted at earlier, at 1.3.2.

[21] Morgan 2004, 179. [22] Od. 19.536 ff.

[23] On hunting images in Longus see Paschalis 2005; Kossaifi 2012, 585.

as a divine agent Longus uses the pregnant term καταμαντευομένη, 'divining' (3.15.3), to describe Lycaenion's entirely unsupernatural thought-processes in concluding that Daphnis and Chloe are in love. So, like Gnathon in the next book, Lycaenion has something of the charlatan about her, but like Gnathon she also unwittingly plays an important role in the divine purpose.

The cup of Bathycles, then, seems secure in the hands of Philetas. But I have so far failed to introduce a figure who has been lurking, like Lycaenion, in the wooded landscape near the cottages of Daphnis and Chloe. The narrator created by Longus notoriously turns to an ἐξηγητής, 'expounder', to interpret the painting he has discovered in the cave of the Nymphs (*pr.* 3), and he represents his own narrative as an account based on that of the ἐξηγητής. At this point the preface deserves to be quoted in full:

> 1. Ἐν Λέσβωι θηρῶν ἐν ἄλσει Νυμφῶν θέαμα εἶδον κάλλιστον ὧν εἶδον· εἰκόνος γραφήν, ἱστορίαν ἔρωτος. καλὸν μὲν καὶ τὸ ἄλσος, πολύδενδρον, ἀνθηρόν, κατάρρυτον· μία πηγὴ πάντα ἔτρεφε, καὶ τὰ ἄνθη καὶ τὰ δένδρα· ἀλλ' ἡ γραφὴ τερπνοτέρα καὶ τέχνην ἔχουσα περιττὴν καὶ τύχην ἐρωτικήν, ὥστε πολλοὶ καὶ τῶν ξένων κατὰ φήμην ἤιεσαν, τῶν μὲν Νυμφῶν ἱκέται, τῆς δὲ εἰκόνος θεαταί. 2. γυναῖκες ἐπ' αὐτῆς τίκτουσαι καὶ ἄλλαι σπαργάνοις κοσμοῦσαι, παιδία ἐκκείμενα, ποίμνια τρέφοντα, ποιμένες ἀναιρούμενοι, νέοι συντιθέμενοι, ληιστῶν καταδρομή, πολεμίων ἐμβολή, πολλὰ ἄλλα καὶ πάντα ἐρωτικά. 3. ἰδόντα με καὶ θαυμάσαντα πόθος ἔσχεν ἀντιγράψαι τῆι γραφῆι, καὶ ἀναζητησάμενος ἐξηγητὴν τῆς εἰκόνος τέτταρας βίβλους ἐξεπονησάμην, ἀνάθημα μὲν Ἔρωτι καὶ Νύμφαις καὶ Πανί, κτῆμα δὲ τερπνὸν πᾶσιν ἀνθρώποις, ὃ καὶ νοσοῦντα ἰάσεται, καὶ λυπούμενον παραμυθήσεται, τὸν ἐρασθέντα ἀναμνήσει, τὸν οὐκ ἐρασθέντα προπαιδεύσει. 4. πάντως γὰρ οὐδεὶς ἔρωτα ἔφυγεν ἢ φεύξεται, μέχρις ἂν κάλλος ἦι καὶ ὀφθαλμοὶ βλέπωσιν. ἡμῖν δ' ὁ θεὸς παράσχοι σωφρονοῦσι τὰ τῶν ἄλλων γράφειν.

> 1. On Lesbos, while hunting, in a grove of the Nymphs I saw a spectacle, the most beautiful I have seen, the painting of a picture, a story of desire. Beautiful too was the grove, with many trees, flowery, well watered: a single spring nourished everything, both the flowers and the trees. But the painting was more delightful, since it displayed outstanding craftsmanship and the fortunes of desire, so that because of its fame many, even strangers, came as suppliants of the Nymphs, as spectators of the image. 2. In it were women giving birth and others dressing babies in swaddling clothes, babies exposed and grazing beasts feeding them, shepherds taking them into their care, youngsters plighting their troth, a pirate incursion, an enemy invasion, and much more, all of it amorous. 3. I looked and wondered, and a longing seized me to vie with the painting in writing; I sought out an expounder of the image and have laboured to create four books, an offering to Love and the Nymphs and Pan, a delightful possession for all

mankind that will heal the sick and console the distressed, that will stir recollections in one who has experienced desire, and will offer instruction beforehand to one who has not experienced desire. 4. For neither has anybody at all escaped desire nor ever shall, as long as beauty exists and eyes see. But to us may the god grant to write chastely of the experiences of others.

Longus, preface

Together, then, Longus and his narrator have created a four-book work which purports to deliver a fundamental message about Eros. It is sometimes suggested that Philetas is an *alter ego* for Longus, or for the narrator created by Longus: it is a corollary that a reader is invited to scrutinise the narrator's credentials just as she scrutinises the credentials of Philetas. The narrator claims to be someone ἐν Λέσβωι θηρῶν, 'hunting on Lesbos' – but hunting what?[23] *Prima facie* more probably wild beasts, as we are to imagine Dionysophanes sometimes did on his ὄρη θηροτρόφα, 'beast-breeding mountains' (1.1.2), than grasshoppers, like Chloe (1.10.2), birds, like Daphnis (3.5.3), or Nymphs, like Pan.[24] But that early in the preface we learn that the paintings represented τύχην ἐρωτικήν, 'amorous adventure',[25] may suggest that the narrator's hunting was more to do with ἔρως, 'desire', than with wild beasts. Hunting imagery is sometimes used of sexual pursuit,[26] though Longus never uses it of the mutual attraction of Daphnis and Chloe. Hunting terms are also used to refer to a thinker's pursuit of ideas. Thus the chorus of Aristophanes' *Clouds* addresses Socrates as θηρατὰ λόγων φιλομούσων, 'hunter of Muse-loving words' (358), and in philosophy a hunt can be a hunt for truth.[27] Within the story the most important hunt of this sort is the quest of Daphnis and Chloe for sexual knowledge, and this idea is foregrounded during Philetas' encounter with Eros, where Eros is described by Philetas as χρῆμα … ἀθήρατον, 'something impossible to catch' (2.4.3), and calls himself δυσθήρατος, 'difficult to catch' (2.5.2), even for a swift bird of prey. But parallel to this quest we are asked to contemplate

[24] Pan's sexual pursuit of Nymphs is a common theme in classical vase-painting and in Hellenistic and Greco-Roman epigram, and plays a part in all three inset tales (1.27, 2.34, 3.23), though in the first only in a *mis-en-abyme*.

[25] The translation of Morgan 2004.

[26] Xen. *Mem.* 1.2.24 (Alcibiades) διὰ κάλλος ὑπὸ γυναικῶν θηρώμενος, 'hunted by women because of his beauty'; cf. Ath. 5.219c κυνηγεῖ οὖν ὁ καλὸς Σωκράτης ἐρωτοδιδάσκαλον ἔχων τὴν Μιλησίαν, ἀλλ᾽ οὐκ αὐτὸς θηρεύεται, ὡς ὁ Πλάτων ἔφη, λινοστατούμενος ὑπὸ Ἀλκιβιάδου, 'So the fine figure of Socrates goes hunting, with the woman from Miletus as his tutor in erotics, and is not himself hunted, as Plato asserts, netted by Alcibiades'.

[27] Pl. *Tht.* 200a, cf. Plu. *Per.* 13.16. See further Edwards 1997.

the reader's own quest for knowledge, not generally, concerning the meaning of life at large, as suggested by Morgan,[28] but particularly concerning ἔρως, 'desire'.

The preface, then, can be read as presenting us with a questing figure, keen to hear λόγοι, 'stories', and to be told what they mean, and with an encounter between that figure and a shadowy ἐξηγητής, 'expounder'. This narrator can be credited with an enthusiasm for the power of ἔρως, 'desire', that shines through the preface, with confidence in his own literary creation's didactic and healing powers, but with a wish himself to tread a path of σωφροσύνη, 'chastity' or 'self-control'.[29] To that extent he presents himself as a holy man, a would-be disinterested evangelist of the kingdom of desire.

But how has the narrator discovered that this kingdom is as he presents it? The succinctness of his own account of the painted scenes leaves much room for interpretation and elaboration by his ἐξηγητής. Despite his much-discussed echoes of Thucydides,[30] the narrator does precisely what Thucydides denies that he himself did – he seeks information ἐκ τοῦ παρατυχόντος, 'from whoever happened to be at hand' (Th. 1.22.2). But the credentials of this exegetic informant are never validated by the narrator as are those of Philetas (validated, that is, within the ἐξηγητής-generated narrative!), or as are those of the vintner in Philostratus' *Heroicus*.

Perhaps we should acquiesce in the narrator's decision to accept the story of the ἐξηγητής without question. But if we do so we shall be traitors to Longus' persistent cause of nuanced, sometimes multiple readings. We must take away with us another possibility: that we are to suppose that the ἐξηγητής was a charlatan. I note the scepticism and criticisms often voiced by Pausanias concerning the stories offered to him by the ἐξηγηταί, 'expounders', at several shrines in mainland Greece. Thus of Argos he says: οὐ μὴν οὐδὲ αὐτῶν λέληθεν Ἀργείων τοὺς ἐξηγητὰς ὅτι μὴ πάντα ἐπ' ἀληθείαι

[28] That the narrator's hunt is for the 'meaning of life' (Morgan 2004, 148) seems to me to take us beyond any hints offered in the preface.

[29] This proposal is similar to, but does not go so far as, that of Paschalis 2005, who notes analogies between the narrator's attraction to the painting and that of his characters to objects of sexual desire (Daphnis, Dorcon and Daphnis to Chloe; Gnathon to Daphnis) and between his expectation of rural pleasure in hunting and that of Daphnis, the Methymnans, and Astylus, and concludes 'The metaphor of the narrator as hunter is a manifestation of this general pressure towards enjoyment and possession of the desired object, intended to render the process of devising and writing a pastoral novel the very plot of which underlies this very same mechanism of desire' (Paschalis 2005, 65). Acceptance of this enticing interpretation would still leave room for the question I raise concerning the imagined sources of this enthused narrator's story of desire and possession.

[30] Cf. Hunter 1983, 47–52; Philippides 1983, 32–35; Pandiri 1985, 117–18; Cueva 1998; Teske 1991, 2–7; Wouters 1994, 142–3; Luginbill 2002, 233–47; Trzaskoma 2005.

λέγεταί σφισι, λέγουσι δὲ ὅμως· οὐ γάρ τι ἕτοιμον μεταπεῖσαι τοὺς πολλοὺς ἐναντία ὧν δοξάζουσιν, 'indeed the Argive guides themselves are aware that not all the stories they tell are true; yet they tell them all the same; for it is not at all straightforward to persuade ordinary people to adopt opinions contrary to their beliefs' (2.23.6).[31] We may also recall the arguments I have offered in favour of the view that Longus had read Pausanias.[32] It is possible, then, that we should imagine that nothing like this story had ever happened on Lesbos, even in the narrator's fictional world, and that the narrator's enthusiasm and pious naivety have allowed him to be deceived by one of the many ἱεροὶ λόγοι, 'sacred tales', circulating in the space between Bethlehem and Berga. A universe in which teenagers know nothing about ἔρως, 'desire', in which they learn about it implausibly slowly from a maudlin old man and a lecherous young housewife, in which their learning about ἔρως, 'desire', and their being discovered themselves to be the exposed children of city magnates does not (*pace* Winkler) destroy the symmetry of a relationship that has developed in a natural, rural environment – all this is to be credited to an unnamed and undescribed ἐξηγητής, 'expounder', and is thus one remove from the masterly narrator who takes us through the story, and two removes from the historical person who wrote or dictated the four books.

The ἐξηγητής is a perilously weak link in the 'chains of multimedia transmission'[33] by which we are told the story reaches us. Whereas in Plato's *Phaedrus* the numinous *locus amoenus* is presented as some sort of validation of the accounts of ἔρως, 'desire', that are presented, here in a preface that evokes that Phaedran scene the excitement created in the narrator by the grove and its paintings leads him to accept the account of an ἐξηγητής, 'expounder', that nothing supports.[34] However much we admire the narrative skill that this innovative master of fiction deploys, we should never forget that the vision of ἔρως, 'desire', as a religious force to whose power the paintings have sensitised the narrator is a vision whose theology and anthropology that narrator is careful to delegate to another voice – a

[31] On Pausanias' ἐξηγηταί see Jones 2001a; for a list of Pausanias' references to them Whitmarsh 2011, 99 n.148. The Latin term is *monstrator*, Lucan 9.979.

[32] Bowie 2001c. [33] The expression used in the important discussion of Whitmarsh 2011, 100.

[34] It might even be suggested that the conclusion of that account (4.39.2), involving dedication of εἰκόνες, 'images', and a βωμός, 'altar', that seem not to match the single εἰκόνος γραφήν, 'representation of a painting', of the preface (where there is no word of an altar) is intended to warn the reader that it comes from an ἐξηγητής who is not even careful to match his exposition to the site he purports to explain. For other ways of interpreting Longus' relation to Plato, especially the *Phaedrus*, see Blanchard 1975, Danek and Wallisch 1993, Hunter 1997, Repath 2011.

voice whose identity, like Philetas' anthropomorphic Ἔρως, is so presented as to be utterly elusive, and whose authority must always remain open to question.

This is perhaps to be related to the apparent fact that the version of the interaction between mortal and gods presented in Longus stands at one end of the spectrum we find in the novels, i.e. it offers a world in which gods and mortals interact much more closely than in our other examples of the genre. Thus the account of Pan's intervention to save Chloe goes much further in ascribing supernatural events to a specific god than the miracle that comes nearest to it, Habrocomes' repeated escape from crucifixion in Egypt (X.Eph. 4.2); and Philetas' close encounter with Eros (admittedly resting on his own narrated testimony) is unparalleled in the Greek novels, just as Daphnis' sacrifice of a goat to Pan in fulfilment of his vow is surprisingly the only novelistic case of a vow explicitly made and then fulfilled by a mortal.[35] But, by introducing the sort of ἐξηγητής he does, Longus carefully removes any testimony which might persuade his readers that there ever was such a world. In this his use of *Beglaubigungsapparat* is diametrically opposed to that of Antonius Diogenes, Dictys and Iamblichus. These writers offer their readers tempting grounds for thinking the events in the story might 'really' have happened. Longus' reversal of the novelistic trope has the consequence that readers will suspect that the entire basis of his narrator's enthusiasm for the power of Eros is of 'such stuff as dreams are made on'.[36]

[35] See Bowie 2012f (Chapter 36 in this volume).
[36] Shakespeare, *The Tempest*, Act iv Scene 1.

40 Poetic Elements in the Greek Novelists' Prose (2017)

1 Introduction

The focus of this paper is strictly the vocabulary of the Greek novels – not the syntax, nor indeed the choice of metaphors which may be demonstrably poetic, a subject that has been given attention elsewhere.[1] So far as I have been able to discover, remarkably little analytic work has been done specifically on the vocabulary of the novelists, despite the availability of the *Lessico dei romanzieri greci*, the fourth and last volume since 1997.[2] That vocabulary has not been wholly neglected, but most of the scholars who have given it their attention have done so in order to establish a particular intertextual relation between a part of a novelistic text and an earlier poetic text (or texts), whether the earlier text(s) in question be Homeric epic, Attic tragedy, New Comedy, Hellenistic pastoral or some other poetic genre. Investigations of such intertextuality have been numerous and fruitful throughout the modern history of scholarship on the novel, and I do not attempt to register them here. It may be that I have missed a discussion of poetic usage in the Greek novels that addressed the issue independently of an attempt to establish some specific intertextuality, but so far as I can discover only the lexicon of Longus has been systematically studied, by Gunnar Valley in 1926.[3] No close discussion of the lexicon of Heliodorus can be found, for example, in Feuillâtre,[4] despite his acknowledging help from Chantraine in his preface, nor in Paulsen.[5] For Chariton there is nothing on poetic usage comparable to Hernández Lara on Chariton's supposed Atticism.[6]

[1] E.g. in Harrison, Paschalis and Frangoulidis 2005, and by several of the papers in Biraud and Briand 2017, where this chapter first appeared, based on a paper delivered at a colloquium organised at Nice, 21–22 March 2013: I am grateful for the audience's comments on that occasion. For a discussion of Longus' lexicon from a different perspective see Bowie 2019c (Chapter 42 in this volume); for fuller discussion of some of the words here considered, Bowie 2019g *ad locc.*

[2] Conca, De Carli and Zanetto 1963–97. [3] Valley 1926. [4] Feuillâtre 1966.

[5] Paulsen 1992. [6] Hernández Lara 1994.

What is needed, indeed, is thorough study of the linguistic texture of each of the novelists, a study that would require years and that would fill at least a substantial volume, or perhaps better an electronic database. What I offer here is something much less ambitious and hence much less satisfactory. I present a number of preliminary *sondages* which I hope may help determine how much poetic vocabulary there is in three of our five complete Greek texts, which may give some indication of the classical and Hellenistic ancestry of that vocabulary, and which will also take account of words' use by some poets who were near contemporaries of the novelists. These *sondages*, represented by my eight tables, are not all of the same kind. The first five tabulate words in three novelists: Longus, Achilles Tatius, and Heliodorus. I begin with Longus – my Tables 40.1, 40.2 and 40.3 – because for Longus one has the systematic study by Valley as a starting point. Thus my Table 40.1 presents words in Longus listed by Valley 1926, 56–8, as poetic in the classical period but as also found in prose of the Hellenistic and imperial periods; my Table 40.2 presents words listed by Valley 1926, 58–9, as poetic without qualification ('Poetische Ausdrücke'); my Table 40.3 presents some words in Longus that seem to me to have a claim to be 'poetic', but which are not in Valley's two lists.

My Tables 40.4 and 40.5 are far from systematic: they offer simply an indication of the classical, Hellenistic and contemporary poetic uses of words that have a *prima facie* claim to be poetic in the opening chapters of Achilles Tatius and of Heliodorus. I have attempted nothing similar for Chariton and Xenophon.

All these first five tables take the text of a novel as the main axis of investigation. Tables 40.6, 40.7, and 40.8 start from contemporary poetry. Table 40.6 lists the eighteen words with interesting poetic ancestry that are also used by at least one of the five novelists in the lexicon of one of Marcellus' poems on Regilla from the Via Appia, Rome, the fifty-nine lines on *stele* A. Table 40.7 assembles some hopefully diagnostic words in the lexicon of the poet or poets who composed five elegiac epigrams for the tomb-obelisk of Sacerdos of Nicaea, ca. AD 130, *AP* 15.4–8, thirty-six lines in all. Finally Table 40.8 takes a small number of poetic words from the *index verborum* of Ps.-Oppian's *Cynegetica* and tabulates their use by the novelists, but does not attempt to sketch their earlier poetic appearances.

As I have said, these *sondages* are heterogeneous, but this heterogeneity may be a strength as well as a weakness. If different types of data seem to point to the same conclusion, then that conclusion has a stronger claim to credibility. Nevertheless they are only *sondages*, and systematic study might lead to different results.

Table 40.1 *Words in Longus listed by Valley 1926, 56–8 as poetic in the classical period but as also found in prose of the Hellenistic and imperial periods*

I exclude instances of usage: e.g. λοιπόν, 'thereafter', without the article (said by Valley 1926, 57 to be poetic until Plb.); or κόλπος/κόλποι, in the sense 'lap' (Longus 1.26.1, 31.1; 3.34.3; 4.36.3). None of the words listed appears in Aratus, so he is not included in this table.

Longus	Homer	Hes./ *h.Hom.*	Melic/ tragic	A.R.	Call. / Theoc.	Nic.	*AP*	D.P.	Opp. *H.*	Opp. *C.*	Q.S.	Other novels
ἀγέρωχος 1.28.2, 2.32.1, 4.7.1	*Il.* 2.654, 3.36, 5.623, 7.343, 10.430 Od. 11. 286	fr. 33a.12 fr. 150.30	Alc. fr. 402				7.425, 9.365, 15.28, 16.127, 16.211					Hld. 5.14.3, 7.8.5, 19.7, 9.19.4, 10.17.4
ἄδακρυς 2.24.4			Eur. × 3 (and ἀδάκρυτ- × 2)		Theoc. 24.31		7.229				4.16, 13.421	ἀδάκρυτος Hld. × 2 ἀδακρυτί Ch. × 2
ἀκρεμών 3.5.1			Eur. *Cyc.* 455	2.1101, 1145, 3.931, 4.1158	Theoc. 16.96 *Ep.* 1.6	*Ther.* 391, 891	× 18		2.122, 4.295, 4.387	2.304, 3.181		Hld. 6.14.4
ἀντιφωνῶ 3.11, 22			Aes. *Eu.* 303 Soph. × 5									

Table 40.1 (*Cont.*)

Longus	Homer	Hes./ *h.Hom.*	Melic/ tragic	A.R.	Call. / Theoc.	Nic.	*AP*	D.P.	Opp. *H.*	Opp. *C.*	Q.S.	Other novels
ἀπηνής 4.40.2 (common in later prose: cf. LSJ)	Il. × 2 Od. × 2	*h.Hom.* × 1	Never in tragedy	1.87, 2.76, 3.492	Theoc. 22.169 Ps-Theoc. 23.1, 23.48 Call. fr. 194.61		9.361, 9.471, 11.298	768	× 9	2. 251, 3.211	3.120, 11.163	Hld. × 9
ἄσχετος 2.14. 2	Il. 16.549 ἀάσχετος 5.892, 24.708 Od. × 5	*Th.* 832	Alc. fr. 364 Aes. fr. 461.6	1.1334, 3.606, 3.1048, 4.622, 4.742, 4.1087, 1738			*AP* 9.285, 16. 110	474	× 8	1.266, 2.60, 2.135, 2.472, 4.176	× 23	
βληχή 2.23.1	Od. 12.266			4.968			9.430, 9.823		4.316	2.365, 4.96		
γοερός 2.37.3			Aes. *Ag.* 1186 Eur. × 3	4.19	Call. *h.* 5.94 *Hec.* fr. 323.1	*Alex.*301	× 10				13.542	

δρεπάνη 2.1.2 (LSJ *s.v.*: 'rare in prose')	Il. 18.551	*Sc.* 292		4.990 as a name		6.21 6.41 6.104, 7.225, 9.383, 9.384, 11.37	5.257, 5.653	1.63, 92	5.58	Hld. 2.4.1, 5.2.6, 7.7.5
ἐκθηριῶ 1.20.3			Eur. *Ba.* 1331							
ἔνθεος 2.10.2			Aes. × 3 Soph. *Ant.* 963 Eur. × 2			× 5				
ἐνορμίζομαι 2.12.3			*Thgn.* 1274				3.409			
εὐάζω 3.11.2 (εὔασμα E *Ba* 129, 151)			Soph. *Ant.* 1135 Eur. *Ba.* 68, 1034			9.363, 16.289				
εὐλίμενος 2.12.2		Εὐλιμένη *Th.* 247	Eur. *Hel.* 1463							Hld. 6.7.1
θέλγω 1.19.3, 22.2, 27.3, 2.4.4, 7.6, 3.25.3, 27.2	Il. 12.255, 15.494, 24.343 Od. × 10	*h.Ap.* 161	Aes. × 2 Eur. *Hipp.* 1274, fr. 724, [Eur.] *Rh.* 554	× 9	*Ther.* 556	× 15	4.114, 141		1.136, 3.500	Hld. 4.4.3 (name Θελξινόη, X.Eph. 5.1.5)
καλαῦροψ 1.8.3, 12.1, 27.2, 3.17.1 4.26.2	Il. 23.845			2.33, 4.974		6.106, 16.74				

Table 40.1 (*Cont.*)

Longus	Homer	Hes./ *h.Hom.*	Melic/ tragic	A.R.	Call. / Theoc.	Nic.	*AP*	D.P.	Opp. *H.*	Opp. *C.*	Q.S.	Other novels
κεράστης 2.8.1			Eur. *Cyc.* 52 Soph. *El.* 568 fr. 314.307			*Ther.* × 4 *Alex.* 150	15.21					
κερασφόρος 2.24.2			Eur. × 2 Soph. × 2									
νεβρίς 1.15.2, 23.3, 24.1			Aes. fr. 64 Eur. *Ba.* × 5 *Ph.* × 2		Theoc. *Ep.* 2		6.87, 172, 292, 16.185		703, 946, 1155	4.245		
παρθενία 3.19.2, 23.2 (× 2), 25.2	Od. 11.245		Sapph. frr. 107,114 [Aes.] *PV* 898 Eur. *Ph.* 1487	× 7	Call. *h.* 3.6 frr. 75.45, 110.77		× 15					Ch. 3.7.5 X.Eph. 2.5.7 Ach. Tat. × 8 Hld. × 4
περκάζω 4.2.2					Call *h.* 5.76							
πόρπη 1.2.3, 4.21.2	Il. 18.401	*h.Ap.* 163	Eur. *El.* 318, *Ph.* 62, *Hec.* 1170				16.253					
πτοοῦμαι 1.22.2			Sapph. fr. 22.14, 31.6 Eur. *Ba.* 1268		Call. *h.* 3.191	*Alex.* 243	7.214					Hld. 6.1.4
πυροφόρος 1.1.2	Il. 12.314, 14.123, 21.602	*Op.* 549 fr. 180		1.628, 1.796	Theoc. 25.30		7.176, 16.200			2.85		

ῥινηλατῶ 2.13.3		Soph. fr. 314.94							
ῥόθιος 2.25.3	Od. 5.412	Aes. *Th.* 362 [Aes.]*PV* 1048 Soph. *Ph.* 688 Eur.× 14	1.370, 1.541, 2.1109		× 7	× 15	7.283		Hld. 1.31.3, 5.17.5, 9.15.5
σκίρτημα 1.9.1		[Aes.] *PV* 599, 675 Eur. × 3			4.39, 4.217, 4.543				Hld. 5.14.3. 9.19.4
στεφανίσκος 1.9.2, 2.32.1, 3.20.2		Anacr. fr. 410 *PMG* *Anacreont.* × 2							
τρυφερός 1.13.2		Eur. *Ba.* 150 Ar *V.* 551, 1169 *Ec.* 901		Theoc. 20.7		× 19			Ch. 2.2.2
ὑλακή 2.13.4			3.749, 3.1040, 3.1217		6.167 (Agath), 7.69 (Iulianus)	5.437		14.286	
χρυσήλατος 4.21.2		Aes. × 3 Soph. × 2 Eur. × 5			6.342, 15.5				Ch. × 4 X.Eph. × 1

Table 40.2 *Words listed by Valley 1926, 58–9 as poetic ('Poetische Ausdrücke')*. I exclude items of syntax (such as θέλγω, 'I charm', with the infinitive, 2.4.4; μέλεσθαι τινί τι, 'that something should be a concern to someone', 2.27.1); figures of speech (πτερόν, 'feather', in the sense 'bird', 3.5.2, 22.1); or phraseology (ἁπαλὸν γελῶ, 'I laugh lightly', 2.4.4). None of the words listed appears in Aratus, so he is not included in this table.

Longus	Homer	*h.Hom.* / Pi.	Tragedy	A.R.	Call. / Theoc.	Nic.	AP	D.P	Opp. *H.*	Opp. *C.*	Q.S.	Other novels
οὐκ ἀθεεί 2.26.5	Od. 18.353											
διαντλῶ 4.9.1		Pi. *P.* 4.293	Eur. *Andr.* 17 *HF* 1373				7.127					
θηροτρόφος 4.1.2			Eur. *Ph.* 820 *Ba.* 102, 556	4.1561		fr. 32.3	7.332					
μεσαιπόλιος 4.13.2	Il. 13.361						5.234					
οἰκουρία 3.4.1, 8.1, 13.4			Eur. *HF* 1373									
πρωθήβης 2.5.3	Il. 8.518 Od. 1.431, 8.283	*h.Ap.* 430 *h.Ba.* 4		1.132		*Ther.* 905	7.438					
στιλπνός 2.4.1	Il. 14.351											
συφεός 3.3.4	Od. × 5											
ταρσός of a cheese-basket 3.33.2, 4.4.4	Od. 9.219		(cf. Ar. *Nu.* 226)		Theoc. 11.37							
χθιζός 3.11.1, 17.2	Il. × 5, Od. × 5	*h.Merc.* 376		4.1397, 1436	Call × 3 Theoc. 25.56		× 9				× 6	

Table 40.3 *Some words in Longus with a claim to be 'poetic' but not in Valley's lists*

None of the words listed appears in Hesiod, Aratus, Callimachus, Nicander, the *Greek Anthology*, Dionysius Periegetes, the two Oppians or Quintus, so they have not been included in this table.

Longus	Homer	Tragedy / melic poetry	A.R.	Theoc.	Other novels
ἐνδινεύω 1.23.2 (*hapax*: δινεύω in poets)	Il. × 4 Od. 18.67	Eur. *Or.* 837	3.310	ἐνδινεῦντι 15.82	
εὔμορφος 1.18.2, 4.32.1 (comp., as in Sapph. fr. 82a)		Aes. × 3 Soph. fr. 88.10 Sapph. frr. 82(a) and (b)			Ch. × 6 X.Eph. × 3 Ach. Tat. × 6
κράνος 1.20.2		Aes. *Th.* 385, 459 Eur. *El.* 470 *Supp.* 318			Hld. × 5
οἴχομαι ('I am lost') 1.14.3, 4.16.2, 18.2		*passim*			Ch. × 2 Ach. Tat. × 1 Hld. × 5

One generalisation does, however, seem to be permitted: just as in the archaic and classical period, as is shown by a particular case observed by a speaker in Plato's *Cratylus* in the fourth century BC,[7] so too in this period some words are found only, or predominantly, in poetry, others only, or predominantly, in prose. That seems to follow both from the large proportion of the words in the poetic texts tabulated in Tables 40.6, 40.7, and 40.8 that do not appear in the novels and from the low proportion of apparently poetic words in the admittedly small samples of the writing of Achilles Tatius and Heliodorus.

But these are, indeed, small samples. What emerges concerning the lexicon of Longus from the two lists of words drawn up by Valley and from the further information I present about their use in earlier and in contemporary poetry? I begin with two general points. First, the number of poetic words identified by Valley might be thought surprisingly small for a text that runs to sixty-five Teubner pages. Secondly, many of these words – and

[7] οἱ ποιηταὶ τὰ πνεύματα ἀήτας καλοῦσι, 'the poets call winds "breezes"', Pl. *Cra.* 410b: cf. Phryn. *Ecl.* 294 on χθιζός, 'of yesterday', and Poll. 2.9 πρωθήβης, 'in first adolescence', both cited later in my discussion of these words.

other words not registered by Valley, like ἀκριδοθήρα, 'grasshopper trap', or ἀκριδοθήκη, 'grasshopper cage', at 1.10.2 – do indeed seem to be used to trigger a reader's awareness of a particular intertextuality, in the case of ἀκριδοθήρα or ἀκριδοθήκη with Theoc. 1.45–54. Given how much we have lost of the Greek literature written before AD 200 and still available to readers of the high Roman empire, it is quite possible, perhaps even likely, that some of the words we can simply identify as 'poetic' were expected by Longus to guide his readers to a particular earlier text that is unidentifiable by us.

Bearing this *caveat* in mind, I now explore the question whether there are nevertheless cases where Longus' apparently poetic words might be seen as used to evoke not particular texts, but genres. The outcome of this exploration will be largely negative – i.e. in only a very few cases may we be at all confident that Longus is aiming to give a general poetic colour or to evoke a particular genre: the vast majority of cases do seem to be best explained as modes of intertextuality with specific poets or even with specific passages in their works.

One further *caveat* is needed. Many of Valley's words, in both my Table 40.1 and my Table 40.2, have a very weak claim to be seen as poetic. Thus I exclude ἐνορμίζομαι, 'I anchor in', at 2.12.3, which is hardly poetic, *pace* Valley 1926: before D.H. 1.36 it appears only in *Theognidea* 1274 (if indeed *Theognidea* 1274 precedes D.H.), and Poll. 1.102 seems to treat it as a prose word. Similarly the single use of εὐλίμενος, 'offering a good harbour', at Eur. *Hel.* 1463 does not suffice to show as poetic a word that Poll. 1.100 includes in his list of terms of praise for a harbour. I also exclude οἰκουρία, 'staying at home': its claim to be a poetic word rests on Eur. *HF* 1373, where indeed its conjunction with διαντλῶ, 'I drain to the dregs' (used by Longus 4.9.1), might point to Longus' recalling that line of Euripides.[8] But οἰκουρία is much used by Plutarch, which counts against it being perceived by Longus or his readers as poetic.[9] Similarly the claim of οὐκ ἀθεεί, 'not without the gods' (2.26.5), to be poetic is fragile – a single appearance in the *Odyssey* (18.353). Soon after Longus, Philostratus uses οὐκ ἀθεεί or μὴ ἀθεεί six times.[10] I also exclude the verb ὑπερηφανῶ, 'I scorn' or 'I am too proud for …' (Longus 3.30.5, 4.19.5) which is found often in late prose, including e.g.

[8] μακρὰς διαντλοῦσ' ἐν δόμοις οἰκουρίας, 'draining to the end long periods spent at home'.

[9] *Ant.* 10.5; *Cic.* 41.6; *Cor.* 35.2; *Prae. coniug.* 142d7; *Quaest. Graec.* 271b5, 271e11; *De Is. et Os.* 381e4; *An seni* 784a6, 788f10.

[10] *Her.* 35.7, 43.6; *VA* 2.40, 3.36; *VS* 1.21.516, 25.533.

Luc. *Nigr.* 31 (though never in Aelius Aristides), and in the other novelists at X.Eph. 1.4.5, 16.5, 2.5.5 and Ach. Tat. 5.11.6. Its only poetic use seems to be at *Iliad* 11.694.

2 Terms Evoking Epic?

Epic colour might be thought especially to be conveyed by ἀγέρωχος, 'proud' or 'self-assertive', ἀπηνής, 'harsh' or 'relentless', ἄσχετος, 'irresistible', δρεπάνη, 'pruning knife', καλαῦροψ, 'herdsman's stick', πόρπη, 'brooch', and πυροφόρος, 'wheat-producing', in my Table 40.1; by μεσαιπόλιος, 'slightly grey', πρωθήβης, 'adolescent', τάρσος, 'cheese-basket', and χθιζός, 'of yesterday', in my Table 40.2; and perhaps by ἐνδινεύοντα, 'going in circles', in my Table 40.3. But many of these cases seem to justify a different conclusion when subjected to close scrutiny.

(1) The epithet ἀγέρωχος, 'proud' or 'self-assertive', is well established as epic by its appearances in Homer and Hesiod, and is certainly not tragic: but we know from Eustathius that it was used by Archilochus, Alcman and Alcaeus.[11] Perhaps its use by the Mytilenean Alcaeus suggested to Longus that he should use it of his Mytilenean characters: unnamed shepherd-lads at 1.28.2; Philetas' feisty son Tityrus at 2.32.1; the self-assertive Lampis at 4.7.1. One might argue that each of these bearers of the term ἀγέρωχος is being presented by Longus as readier to act self-assertively than Daphnis, and that this presentation is meant to recall the conflicted worlds of epic and of Alcaeus from which, as from Attic tragedy, Longus seeks to distance his own work.[12] One might also argue that, in applying it twice negatively and once positively, Longus is picking up a contemporary philological debate about its use in early poetry, a debate we know was already under way by the time of Suetonius' Περὶ βλασφημιῶν, '*On terms of abuse*'. But such arguments might be quite erroneous: if we had the whole poem of Alcaeus from which the single word that constitutes fr. 402 comes, we might reach a quite different interpretation.

ἀπηνής, 'harsh' or 'relentless', is also clearly an epic word – found not only in Homer, but also in Apollonius, Oppian, Ps.-Oppian and Quintus

[11] Eust. *Comm. in Hom. Iliad.* i 489.3–7 van der Valk, citing also Alcm. (the adjective appears at both fr. 5, fr. 1 (b) 4 and 10 (b) 15 *PMGF*); Archil. fr. 261 (cf. *Et. Gud.* 1.10.13 de Stefani; Suet. *De blasph.* p.56 Taillardat); Alc. fr. 402.

[12] For Longus' techniques of contrasting his world with that of Attic tragedy see Bowie 2007c (Chapter 31 in this volume).

of Smyrna.[13] The lexicon of Liddell and Scott (Tenth edition) notes that ἀπηνής is also frequent in 'later prose': but it is never used by the careful Atticist Aelius Aristides, nor indeed by the novelists Chariton, Xenophon or Achilles Tatius. On the other hand the epithet ἀπηνής is much favoured by Heliodorus, who uses it nine times. Might Heliodorus be influenced by Longus' decision to use it? The issue is complicated by the problem of interpreting the sentence in which it appears in *Daphnis and Chloe*: the wedding guests sing σκληρᾶι καὶ ἀπηνεῖ τῆι φωνῆι καθάπερ τριαίναις γῆν ἀναρρηγνύντες οὐχ ὑμέναιον ἄιδοντες, 'with a harsh and unrelenting voice, as if breaking up earth with tridents, not singing a wedding song' (4.40.2.). Winkler notoriously argued that this 'amazing detail of attendant discord, unexplained roughness in the song', together with the mention of Lycaenion (4.40.3), recalls Lycaenion's 'careful description of defloration as trauma' (3.19.2–3), and he invites us to read Chloe's imminent matrimonial defloration as painful and traumatic.[14] That I doubt; and the matter is further complicated by the fact that the combination of σκληρός, 'harsh', and ἀπηνής is found in Ps-Aristides, *Ars rhetorica* 2.3.1.6: ἀλλὰ καὶ κατὰ τὸ ἐναντίον τούτου, οἷον σκληρότερον καὶ ἀπηνῆ περιθεῖναι λόγον, ὅταν τοιοῦτόν τι ὑποτεθῆι, 'but also the opposite of this, such as using somewhat harsh and unrelenting discourse, when something of this sort is proposed'. For the moment I believe that Longus is doing something particular by using the word ἀπηνής, but I don't know what that something is.

What about the epithet ἄσχετος, 'irresistible', used by Longus of the speed with which the boat of the Methymnan elite tourists is carried away by wind and wave at 2.14.2? Again the word is very clearly epic, with Homer and Hesiod reinforced by Apollonius, the two Oppians, Quintus, and even Dionysius Periegetes.[15] But like ἀγέρωχος, ἄσχετος is also attested as having been used by Alcaeus, in this case in fr. 364.1. This seems to have been in a quite different context, an aphorism preserved in Stobaeus linking Πενία, 'Poverty', with Ἀμαχανία, 'Helplessness': ἀργάλεον Πενία κακὸν ἄσχετον, ἃ μέγαν | δάμνα λᾶον Ἀμαχανίαι σὺν ἀδελφέαι, 'Poverty is a harsh thing, an irresistible evil, which conquers a mighty people together with her sister Helplessness'. Does Longus expect his readers to know this aphorism from Alcaeus and to reflect on the contrast between the wealth

[13] Also in some epigrams, as registered in Table 40.1 (from which I exclude, as being later, *AP* 7.568, by Agathias).

[14] Winkler 1990, 124–6.

[15] Its currency in imperial Greek poetry is also established by the two *Anthology* poems in which it appears: *AP* 11.285 (Philip); 16.110 (the only surviving epigram of Philostratus).

of the Methymnan *jeunesse dorée* and the πενία, 'poverty', and ἀμαχανία, 'helplessness', of Daphnis, a πενία and ἀμαχανία that will be resolved by the purse of 3000 drachmas washed ashore precisely from this pleasure boat (3.27.4)? Or is the Odyssean paternity of ἄσχετος the key,[16] and are we meant to contrast the miniature seaborne adventures of the Methymnan youths with the serious, large-scale epic voyages and shipwreck of Odysseus? And does the closeness of Longus' phrase to ἀσχέτωι ὁρμῆι, 'with unstoppable impetus', in Opp. *Hal.* 1.492 show that Oppian has been reading Longus, or that Longus has been reading Oppian, or neither of these things?[17]

δρεπάνη, 'pruning knife', at 2.2.2, however, may be meant to lead us to a single passage: Homer's *Shield of Achilles*, where it first appears (at Il. 18.551). Longus may have chosen the poetic form δρεπάνη, rather than the prose δρέπανον (twice used by Achilles Tatius),[18] to take us precisely to that part of the *Iliad* where, some lines later, Greek poetry presented one of its earliest surviving images of sheep and shepherds (18.587–9). Or has Longus simply been reading the *Garland of Philip* and been reminded of the poetic form δρεπάνη by its appearance in *AP* 11.37,[19] a poem by Antipater of Thessalonica circulating in the *Garland of Philip* and depicting the autumn vintage shortly to be followed by winter (a sequence that chimes with Longus' attention to the succession of the seasons), as well as in a poem by the *Garland*'s creator, Philip of Thessalonica, *AP* 6.104?[20] In all this, however, caution is counselled: Poll. 1.245 and 10.128 give no indication that δρεπάνη has a different colour from δρέπανον.

Perhaps the frequent use of καλαῦροψ, 'herdsman's stick', has a similar purpose. καλαῦροψ is used only once in the *Iliad* (23.845), but that one use suffices to establish it as the epic *vox propria* for a stick thrown by herdsmen, partly to head off their cattle. Theocritus equipped his herdsmen not with a καλαῦροψ but with a λαγωβόλον, 'hare-hitter',[21] a term that Longus never uses. Leonidas also chose the term λαγωβόλον in a dedication to Pan, *AP* 6.188,[22] whereas Diodorus Zonas opted for καλαῦροψ, *AP* 6.106.[23] Longus

[16] E.g. Od. 3.104.

[17] The date of the *H.* seems to be AD 177–80, and Book 2 may perhaps be tied down to AD 178: cf. Fajen 1999, viii. Note also ἀκατάσχετος οὖν ὁρμὴ κατειλήφει τὴν πόλιν, 'So an unstoppable movement took hold of the city' (Hld. 10.4.6). The context of *H.* 1.492 is maritime, but the unstoppable surge is not that of waves but of female pursuing male fish to mate.

[18] 3.7.8; 4.12.1. [19] Antipater *GP* 96. [20] Philip *GP* 19.

[21] Theoc. 4.49 (with Gow *ad loc.*); 7.128. [22] Leonidas *HE* 4. [23] Zonas *GP* 3.

may of course choose this term because it and λαγωβόλον are the only *voces propriae*, and he simply has to opt for one: but in choosing καλαῦροψ he may be taking sides in a dispute about poetic pedigree and reminding us that Homer's *Iliad* uses only καλαῦροψ.

One cannot, however, suggest that Longus' choice of the predominantly poetic term πόρπη, brooch', for the pin found among Daphnis' tokens (1.2.3) – rather than περόνη, 'pin', found in prose as well as poetry – has much to do with its Iliadic attestation, since the *Iliad* has both πόρπη and περόνη.[24] But that the appearance of πόρπη in the *Iliad* is again, like δρεπάνη, in the scene where Hephaestus makes Achilles' shield (Il. 18.401), may be relevant to Longus' choice. That *Shield*, after all, was the earliest and most influential extended description of a work of art in Greek literature: it was thus a significant literary ancestor of the painting Longus describes in his *proem* and that he professed to be the source of his whole narrative.

(2) Of the epic words in my Table 40.2 πρωθήβης, 'adolescent', is explicitly pronounced by the lexicographer Pollux to be poetic.[25] We are perhaps expected to notice that Longus' only use of πρωθήβης, at 2.5.3, is in the mouth of Eros addressing Philetas at a time when Philetas himself is already a γέρων, 'old man', whereas the *Iliad*'s only use, at 8.518 (Hector is speaking), couples it in the same hexameter with γέροντας, 'old men'. But equally we might be expected to think of the only place where the *Odyssey* uses it of young men, the virtuoso Phaeacian dancers on Scherie (8.263), whom we are perhaps again meant to recall when Dryas dances his ballet at 2.36.[26] It is in quoting these lines that Pollux's compatriot Athenaeus offers his only use of πρωθήβης (1.15a).[27] Whether we adopt either of these explanations, or neither, the epithet πρωθήβης confers on Philetas an epic stature.

The same can be claimed of Longus' only use of μεσαιπόλιος, 'slightly grey', at 4.13.2. This gives Dionysophanes a general epic patina rather than likening him in any specific way to the Cretan hero Idomeneus, who is termed μεσαιπόλιος in the *Iliad*'s only use of the word (13.361). That μεσαιπόλιος still had a poetic colour in the second century is indicated by its appearance in

[24] But it may be relevant too that these accessories have a different function: ὁ δὲ σχιστὸς χιτὼν περόναις κατὰ τοὺς ὤμους διεῖρτο καὶ πόρπηι κατὰ τὰ στέρνα ἐνῆπτο, 'the divided dress would be held together by pins at the shoulder and drawn together by a clasp at the breasts', Poll. 7.54.

[25] τὸ γὰρ πρωθήβης ποιητικόν, 'for the word πρωθήβης is poetic', Poll. 2.9.

[26] The other of the word's only two appearances in Od. is at 1.431 of the young, nubile Eurycleia.

[27] A rarity even in poetry from Hom. to Nicander, πρωθήβης is even rarer in the imperial period: not in poets, nor in D. Chr., Plu., Aristid., Paus., or Philostr.; in Luc. only *Syr.D.* 35, *D.Mort.* 15.2.

Mesomedes (6.2 Heitsch = 3.2 Horna) and Triphiodorus (168): Philostratus' two uses in his *Lives of the sophists* may perhaps also be seen as poetic.[28]

ταρσός, 'cheese-basket', invites a quite different explanation. The word's only use in Homeric epic is at Od. 9.219, of the Cyclops' cheese-baskets. That use is picked up by the love-sick Cyclops of Theoc. 11.37: Longus is surely picking up both, and in using Theoc. 11 he evokes a poem he exploits many times (e.g. 1.17.3).[29] It is perhaps no accident that we first encounter Daphnis' ταρσοί at 3.33.2, when he has just been assured that he will be allowed to marry Chloe, and that their second appearance, at 4.4.4, is when he is making preparations for Dionysophanes' tour of inspection, a tour that will result first in Daphnis' recognition by his true parents and then in turn in his marriage to Chloe. The window-allusion to the brutish Cyclops of Od. Book 9, the first closely observed herdsman in Greek poetry, *via* the love-sick Cyclops of Theoc. 11 who is never going to get his Galateia, prompts us to reflect how much more satisfying a species of young herdsfolk Longus has created. But this is inevitably speculative. It remains possible that ταρσός is not a specifically poetic term at all: Pollux thrice includes it in a list of items related to cheese-making (1.231, 7.173, 10.130).

χθιζός, 'of yesterday', may take a reader in a similar direction. Its second use, at 3.17.2, is in the mouth of Lycaenion, who has just impudently played a Penelope figure in fabricating a false tale about her twenty geese (3.16.1–2). It is fitting that an inverted Penelope should now use epic language when she has lured Daphnis into the woods with his likewise Homeric καλαῦροψ (3.17.1); but at the same time these epic terms may draw our attention to how un-Penelope-like is Lycaenion, how un-Odysseus-like is Daphnis. If this is how 3.17.1–2 should be taken, then it helps us see the point of the earlier use of χθιζός at 3.11.1, when it is used by the narrator to contrast the couple's substantial catch on the second day of Daphnis' winter hunting with the small game he got on the first – a catch whose trapping allowed Daphnis and Chloe to talk and kiss.

But again, that χθιζός is poetic at all may be questioned. For the lexicographer Moeris it is simply Attic: χθές καὶ χθιζόν Ἀττικοί· ἐχθές καὶ ἐχθεσινόν Ἕλληνες 'Attic speakers use χθές and χθιζόν· Hellenes ἐχθές and ἐχθεσινόν', Moeris χ 6. Poll. 1.66 recommends it without any hint that it has poetic colour.[30] Only Phrynichus in his *Ecloga* dismisses it as poetic: χθιζόν

[28] *VS* 2.3.568, 18.599.

[29] For Longus' systematic and careful reworking of Theoc. see Bowie 2013d (Chapter 37 in this volume), 2021b.

[30] Note too Hdn. *De orthographia* iii 2.574.23 Lenz *s.v.* πρωιζόν. In fact χθιζός is also used by Hdt. 1.126.5.

ἀποβλητέον ὅτι ποιητικόν, ἀντὶ δὲ τοῦ χθιζὸν ἐροῦμεν χθεσινόν, 'χθιζόν is to be rejected because it is poetic, and instead of χθιζόν we shall say χθεσινόν', *Ecl.* 294. In *Praeparatio sophistica* he also offers χθιζινός and notes the Homeric colour of χθιζός (τὸ δὲ χθιζόν Ὅμηρος, 'Homer uses χθιζόν', *PS* 127.9–10 de Borries). But of Phrynichus' preferred terms χθεσινός and (in *PS*) χθιζινός, the former seems to be *koinē* Greek: only χθιζινός is supported by Aristophanes and used by Atticists such as Aelius Aristides and Alciphron.[31] Contrary to Phrynichus' (later) recommendation, χθιζός is used without any hint of poetic colour by Plutarch and Lucian.[32] Whether one believes that Longus' use of χθιζός involves sophisticated intertextuality with Homer, or is simply his use of a word he takes to be regular in prose, its appearance does not constitute a case of a word being employed to give general or generic poetic colour.

If most of the suggestions made above are accepted, then the number of cases of epic poetic terms used by Longus *simply* to give epic colour is very drastically reduced.

3 Terms Evoking Early Melic Poetry

We have already seen that part of the explanation of ἀγέρωχος and ἄσχετος may lie in their use by Alcaeus. It seems likely that εὔμορφος, 'handsome' or 'beautiful', used in the comparative εὐμορφότερος of Dorcon at 1.18.2 and of Chloe at 4.32.1, in each case focalised through Daphnis, is picking up its comparative use in a line of Sappho, fr. 82(a),[33] quoted by the second-century metrical writer Hephaestion – i.e. a line that was known to at least some second-century readers – rather than its uses at Aes. *Ag.* 416 and 454 or *Ch.* 490. But the fact that εὔμορφος had already been used several times by Chariton, Xenophon and Achilles Tatius may mean that Longus did not see it as either markedly poetic in general, or as Sapphic in particular.[34]

Another term that perhaps evokes Sappho is πτοοῦμαι, 'I am excited', used at 1.22.2 of goats. Its first known uses are in two fragments of the poetry of Lesbos' great poet Sappho, whose songs (like those of Alcaeus)

[31] χθιζινός, Ar. *V.* 281, *Ra.* 987; Aristid. *Or.* 28.2; Alciphr. 3.61.

[32] Plu. *De prof. virt.* 75e5; *Quaest. conv.* 688b10, 696e6; *De soll. an.* 975c9; Luc. *Herm.* 1: note also [Plu.], *De lib. ed.* 13f2.

[33] εὐμορφωτέρα Μνασιδίκα τὰς ἀπάλας Γυρίννως, 'Mnasidica is more shapely than delicate Gyrinno'. The reference to the name Gyrinna by Max.Tyr. 18.9 suggests that this line was known to him too (perhaps with the variant Γυρίννας).

[34] Further discussion at Bowie 2019g, 138.

are exploited by Longus to construct *his* Lesbos:[35] there, of course (frr. 22.14, 31.6), the term refers to the sexual or sexually-related excitement of young women. If Longus indeed expects Sapphic bells to ring – and fr. 31 was a poem well known in antiquity as it is now – he is perhaps aiming partly at humour (giddy goats, not giddy girls) and partly offering one of several suggestions that in the pastoral world humans and animals are closer to each other than urban readers might expect. But the word could also be familiar to him from Callimachus' *Hymn to Artemis* 191, from Nicander's *Alexipharmaca* 243, or from a poem of Archias in the *Garland of Philip*.[36] And once again, its use by Pollux does not hint at any poetic colour at all.[37]

4 The Impact of Epigram

Some terms found especially in ecphrastic epigrams transmitted by the Palatine Anthology suggest that Longus admires the genre's handling of the *locus amoenus*, perhaps because, like him, the poets were creating miniatures.

The case of ἀκρεμών, 'bough' (Table 40.1), is striking. Longus uses ἀκρεμών just once, in his *ecphrasis* of the myrtle-trees and ivy intertwined outside Dryas' cottage (3.5.1). For us the term comes into Greek literature in Eur. *Cyc.* 455, used of the olive branch which Odysseus might sharpen to blind the Cyclops. Again, perhaps, a reader of Longus may be asked to contrast his shepherd Daphnis with the mythical shepherd Polyphemus. But ἀκρεμών then reappears in an idyllic scene along with shepherds and cicadas at Theoc. 16.96, and is used of the foliage nibbled by a goat about to be sacrificed to Apollo Pythius in Theoc. *Ep.* 1.6 Gow. Thereafter ἀκρεμών reappears in a host of ecphrastic epigrams, many of them in the *Garland of Philip*.[38] I think it is this plethora of appearances in poetic *loci amoeni* that moved Longus to choose this term for a branch rather than, for example, the Sapphic term ὅρπαξ (chosen by Theoc. 7.146).

Another term much found in epigrams preserved in the Anthology is γοερός, 'mournful', though unsurprisingly it is well established in Attic tragedy. In this case origin may be less relevant than the special effect at which

[35] See Bowie 2013d (Chapter 37 in this volume). [36] *AP* 7.214 = Archias *GP* 22.

[37] ἐπτοημένος, 'excited', ἐπτόημαι, 'I am excited', Poll. 5.123; πτοούμενος, 'being excited', Poll. 1.197.

[38] Including *AP* 7.24, 'Simonides', an epitaph for Anacreon = *HE* 3 = *FGE* 66 = 100 Sider; *AP* 7.385 (on Protesilaus' tomb) = Philip *GP* 33; *AP* 9.3 (on a walnut-tree) = Antipater *GP* 106; *AP* 9.71 (shelter from mid-day sun) = Antiphilus *GP* 33; *AP* 9.220 (love under a plane-tree) = Thallus *GP* 5; *AP* 9.256 (a caterpillar eats an apple) = Antiphanes *GP* 4.

Longus aims in 2.37.3: here Daphnis' playing of different sorts of tune on Philetas' panpipe includes one where he created a sound that was γοερὸν ὡς ἐρῶν, 'the mournful sound like a lover makes', expressing the feelings of Pan pursuing Syrinx. As I have argued elsewhere, the inset tale of Syrinx offers a world of sexual violence endemic in traditional myth and Attic tragedy to which Longus contrasts both his own particular fiction and overall his own genre:[39] the use of the tragic term γοερόν points up this contrast, but at the same time Longus' encounters with the word may have been as much in epigram as in Attic tragedy. But there may be no intertextuality at all: we know from Poll. 5.87 that one type of tune played on the αὐλός, 'pipe, was called γοερόν – Pollux offers no hint that this term of musical classification was in any sense poetic.

Erotic epigram was very probably the main poetic site of Longus' and his readers' encounters with τρυφερός in its physical sense of 'soft' or 'tender', though it should be kept in mind that τρυφερός is common in second-century AD prose in a moral sense.[40] Eighteen of the twenty appearances of τρυφερός in the *Greek Anthology* are in erotic epigrams, many composed by grand masters of the genre: from the Hellenistic period Meleager and Dioscorides,[41] from more recent times Philodemus, Rufinus and Strato.[42] Both Meleager and Rufinus use τρυφερός of χρώς, 'skin', the latter in his splendid parody of the judgement of Paris in which the speaker narrates and describes his assessment of the buttocks of three girls who are presumably *hetaerae*.[43] A single pederastic epigram whose author was unclear to the compiler of the *Anthology* uses it, like Longus 1.13.2, of σάρξ, 'flesh'.[44] It is tempting to think that Rufinus' poem, perhaps little more than a century old when Longus wrote, was known to him and might even have suggested some of the themes associated with the judgement of Paris he deploys (Chloe's κρίσις,

39 Bowie 2007c (Chapter 31 in this volume).

40 D. Chr. *Or.* 2.47, 55; 4.22, 84, 112; 6.15; 32.67; 33.15; 66.25; 70.8; Plu. *Alex.* 22.10; *Dem.* 4.6; *Per.* 27.4; *Phoc.* 2.4; *Sert.* 13.1; *De aud.* 41f; *De Pyth. or.* 397b; *De tranq. an.* 466b (quoting Men.); *De vit. pud.* 528e; Arr. *Epict.* 2.24.28; 3.1.27. Plu. uses the comparative at *De cap. ex inim.* 89e; τρυφερός has a clearly physical sense at *Cat. Ma.* 4.5 and *De sera* 560c (ἐν σαρκὶ τρυφερᾷ, 'in delicate flesh').

41 *AP* 5.151, 154, 174, 190, 198, 12.109 = Meleager *HE* 33, 63, 36, 64, 24, 61; *AP* 5.193 = Dioscorides *HE* 4.

42 *AP* 7.222 = Philodemus *GP* 26; *AP* 5.35 and 66 by Rufinus; *AP* 12.10 and 208 by Strato. *AP* 9.232 = Philip *GP* 42 uses τρυφερός but not in an erotic context.

43 *AP* 5.35.

44 *AP* 12.136: ὄρνιθες ψίθυροι, τί κεκράγατε; μή μ' ἀνιᾶτε | τὸν τρυφερῆι παιδὸς σαρκὶ χλιαινόμενον, | ἑζόμεναι πετάλοισιν ἀηδόνες· εἰ δὲ λάληθρον | θῆλυ γένος, δέομαι, μείνατ' ἐφ' ἡσυχίης, 'Chattering birds, why are you screaming? Do not distress me, | who am being warmed by the tender flesh of a boy, you nightingales perched on leaves! If you belong to the talkative female gender, please, keep quiet!'

'judgement', of Daphnis and Dorcon at 1.15.4–17.1; the apple at 3.34.1–2). Even if it was not, the association of τρυφερός with erotic epigram in which an experienced poet applies the epithet to the skin of urban and sometimes professional sexual objects, female and male, adds a frisson to Chloe's action at 1.13.2: in touching herself to see if Daphnis' skin is τρυφερώτερος, 'softer', than hers, the forever naïve Chloe is presented to the knowing reader as slipping into the sexual thought-world of sophisticated urban lovers.

5 Bacchic Terms

At least two of the terms in Table 40.1, i.e. νεβρίς, 'fawn-skin', and εὐάζω, 'I cry "euoi"', have a special place in the terminology of Dionysiac cult, and should probably be regarded as having not a poetic but rather a cultic colour. Such a cultic colour would be well known to a writer who gave so prominent a place to Dionysus and to the civic leader Dionysophanes in his fourth book. But of the two, νεβρίς may be regarded simply as the correct and only term for a garment made from a deer's skin.[45]

6 Other Technical Terms?

One might, of course, object that at least one term I have discussed above, ἀκρεμών, belongs in category of words which were virtually technical terms in special areas – terms for hunting, herding and botany: ῥινηλατῶ, 'track by scent',[46] βληχή, 'bleating',[47] κερασφόρος and κεράστης, both 'horned',[48] συφεός, 'pig-sty',[49] σκίρτημα, 'gambolling' or 'leaping',[50] and περκάζω, 'I turn

[45] Cf. Poll. 4.117, 118; 5.16.

[46] In poetry ῥινηλατῶ seems only to be found in Soph. *Ichn.* fr. 314.94 Radt, one of the places Longus may also have encountered κεράστης (fr. 314.307 Radt). Poll. 2.74 offers it as the correct term for τὸ τὰς ὀσμὰς ἕλκειν, 'following up scents'.

[47] βληχή is taken by Poll. 5.87 to be the correct term for the sound made by sheep.

[48] Poll. 5.76 seems to offer both as terms acceptable in prose: ὁ δ' ἄρρην κερωφόρος ἢ κερασφόρος ἢ κεράστης, 'the masculine is "horn-bearing" or "horn-bearing" or "horned"'.

[49] Despite its frequent use in the Od., συφεός does not appear in any of the later poetic texts in my table: it is used in imperial prose by D. Chr. not only (predictably) in his *Euboean* (7.74) but also in 8.25 and 30.33.

[50] The epigrams in which σκίρτημα is found include two from Philip's *Garland*, which seems likely to have been known to Longus: *AP* 7.217 = Scaevola *GP* 1; 9.543 = Philip *GP* 54. But the term is clearly also the *vox propria* for animal movements in prose of this period, e.g. Plu. *Art.* 7.5, *Quaest. conv.* 706e; Luc. *Alex.* 40, *Bacch.* 5, *Asin.* 40. When used of humans it can retain some animal overtones, e.g. Philostr. *VA* 8.7.23.

dark'.[51] If these were the only terms he could properly use for the thing or action he wanted to convey, can their use correctly be seen as poetical? ὑλακή, 'barking', constitutes a similar case. Its poetic use is limited – thrice in Apollonius Rhodius, once each in the *Halieutica* and in Quintus.[52] Several instances show that it remains the *vox propria* for the barking of dogs in second-century AD prose.[53]

The same sort of argument might be offered for Longus' very frequent use of θέλγω, 'I charm', and παρθενία, 'virginity'. I suspect παρθενία does not merit its place in Valley's list. In prose writing παρθενία was already well established; it had appeared in Parthenius, *Erotopathemata* 26.2, and in previous novelists. Its centrality to the sexual ideology of the novels would make it hard to avoid, which is also one of the reasons for its frequency in erotic epigram.[54]

But note that θέλγω is different. As Table 40.1 shows, θέλγω has wide poetic attestation, including very many Anthology epigrams, but is not used at all by Chariton, Xenophon and Achilles Tatius, and appears only once in Heliodorus. Longus may be using θέλγω in awareness of its role in the *Odyssey*, and then more prominently in Apollonius of Rhodes and in Hellenistic epigram: but his decision to use it so often as he does must also be a function of the concept's importance for his narrative of ἔρως, 'desire'.

7 A Poetic Residue?

There remain a few words for which no special explanation under my above categories seems appropriate. These include ἔνθεος, 'divinely inspired', found in tragedy and in epigram;[55] πυροφόρος, 'wheat-bearing', found in hexameter poetry from Homer to the *Cynegetica*;[56] and ῥόθιος, 'splashing' (of a

51 περκάζω is a botanic *terminus technicus* in Theophr. and *Gp*.

52 The two cases in the *Anthology* are later than Longus: *AP* 6.167 (Agathias), 7.69 (Iulianus).

53 D. Chr. 7.3, 20.16; Plu. *Cim.* 18.2; Luc. *Nec.*10.2, *VH* 1.32: cf. Poll. 5.86 φωναὶ ζώιων. κυνῶν μὲν ὑλακή, 'animal noises: of dogs, barking …'.

54 Including *AP* 5.8 = Asclepiades *HE* 2; 6.276 = Antipater *HE* 51; 7.164 = Antipater *HE* 21; 7.182 = Meleager *HE* 123; 7.183 = Parmenion *GP* 3; 7.351 = Dioscorides *HE* 17; 7.352 = Meleager *HE* 132; 7.352 = Mnasalcas *HE* 10; 7.491 = Pamphilus *HE* 2.

55 Of the five pre-Byzantine epigrammatic uses one might expect Longus especially to know *AP* 9.64 = Asclepiades *HE* 45, on Hesiod and the Muses; 16.133 = Antipater *GP* 87; 16.226 = Alcaeus *HE* 20, on Pan, his panpipe and Nymphs: ἔνθεος is used seven times by Aristid.

56 Its two uses in epigram are in poems Longus might well have known: *AP* 16.200 = Moschus *HE* 1; 7.176 = Antiphilus *GP* 25. Cf. the epigram for a statue at Eleusis of Isidote, daughter of Isaeus, *IG* ii^2 3632.2 (AD 176–92), where it qualifies Demeter.

noise), used by Heliodorus but not by Longus' predecessors, and well established, both in its adjectival and nominal form (ῥόθιον), in several genres of poetry, though it is worth noting that Pollux treats it as a word to be used in prose.[57] Each of these should perhaps be admitted to be a 'poetic' word that might add some 'poetic' colour to Longus' prose, though the frequency with which Pollux has ἔνθεος (and four times the adverb ἐνθέως) may suggest that by the late second century AD it is simply a prose word.[58] στεφανίσκος, 'little garland', however, has a very different profile, found only in Longus among the novelists, present in Anacreon (fr. 410 *PMG*) and the *Anacreontea*, but absent from other poetry. It should perhaps not be seen as 'poetic' at all. That as a diminutive term it is suitable for Longus' miniaturising world is arguably more important than its appearance in Anacreontic sympotic contexts.

8 Conclusions Concerning Longus

Where has this circuitous path taken me? As my analysis of several cases has tried to show, there may be many terms in Valley's lists which are not 'simply' poetic but which may rather be chosen to trigger some intertextuality, whether with a particular earlier text or more broadly and loosely with an earlier genre. There are others which have no strong claim to be 'poetic'. The remaining 'poetic words' that cannot so be explained are not numerous. Longus may be writing a poetic sort of prose in terms of his Theocritean subject, of his rhythmical sentences, and of his preference for coordination over subordination: but the actual language he uses to do this is predominantly the language of prose.

9 Achilles Tatius

Very few words in Achilles Tatius' opening chapter seem to have a claim to be poetic, and not one of these few is used by Homer, Hesiod or Pindar.[59]

Only θερίζω, 'I harvest', is used by the tragedians, and thereafter it is used literally both in prose (as by Longus) and in poetry, but metaphorically only

[57] Of a river, Poll. 3.103; a rainstorm, 1.116; metaphorically, 4.69, 72; 5.79; 6.147.

[58] ἔνθεος Poll. 1.8, 15, 20, 23; 3.59; 4.52, 82; ἐνθέως 1.16, 22; 3.68; 4.52.

[59] For Achilles' use of short cola, rhythm and rhyme as aiming at a 'prose-poetic' effect see Whitmarsh 2020, 36–8.

Table 40.4 *Words with a claim to be 'poetic' in Achilles Tatius 1.1*

I exclude e.g. ἐπικάθημαι, six times in Achilles Tatius and found in Herodotus, Attic and later prose. None of the words listed appears in Homer, Hesiod, Aratus, or Dionysius Periegetes, so they are not included in this table.

Achilles Tatius 1.1	Tragedy	A.R.	Call. / Theoc.	Nic.	AP	Opp. *H.*	Opp. *C.*	Q.S.	Other novels
ἐπινήχομαι			Call. *h.* 4.21, 193 Theoc. 23.61		9.568	2.46			
ἠρέμα		3.170, 4.1314	Theoc. 21.50, 56	*Alex.* 206, fr. 68	7.22, 71, 356, 476, 9.556, 10.6		2.558, 4.344		Ch. × 6 Longus × 2 Hld. × 16
θερίζω	Aes. × 2 Soph. × 2 Eur. × 4				4.2, 9.451, 9.561				Longus 3.29.2, 4.33.2, 4.38.3
κοιλαίνω			Theoc. 23.43 transitive			5.214		9.382	Hld. 1.28.2, 1.31.2, 9.4.1

in poetry. The particular sense in which it is used by Achilles Tatius, 'to summer', is also found in Xenophon.[60]

Like θερίζω, ἐπινήχομαι, 'I swim on the surface', is found in the *Anthology*, though only once: but the poem is one by Dioscorides on the disastrous effects on a peasant of the Nile flood,[61] a poem that the apparently Alexandrian Achilles Tatius might well have known, as he could also have known its two uses in Callimachus' *Hymn to Delos* and that at Theoc. 23.61. That might be enough to make him see ἐπινήχομαι as a poetic word, as too Oppian may have done at *H.* 2.46.

Prima facie ἠρέμα might seem to have an even stronger claim to be 'poetic', with two appearances in each of Apollonius, Theocritus and Nicander, six in the *Anthology* and two in the *Cynegetica*. But it is frequent in Plato, a prose writer with whose works Achilles plays in various ways, and even used occasionally by Aristotle. Its frequent uses by Achilles himself,[62] and by Chariton and Heliodorus, together with a couple of appearances in Longus (1.23.2, 25.1), suggest that it was not perceived as a specifically poetic word.

The same probably holds for κοιλαίνεται, 'is hollowed out' or 'curves round': found in Achilles Tatius both here and at 3.25.4, its few poetic appearances (in Choerilus fr. 10, as well as its use once each by Theocritus, Oppian and Quintus) have to be set against its employment by Herodotus and Thucydides.

Of the four words with some claim to be seen as poetic, therefore, only in the case of ἐπινήχομαι might that claim be pressed.

10 Heliodorus

A brief glance at the opening chapter of Heliodorus' *Aethiopica* may provisionally point to a similar conclusion. The words I have picked out and included in Table 40.4 as apparently having *some* claim to be poetic have acquired that status in five cases because of their use in Attic tragedy: but most are little used by the poets which this table shares with Tables 40.1 to 40.3.

Thus ἄρδην, 'utterly', is much used in tragedy, but in my other diagnostic poets only in the *Anthology*, and there only thrice.[63] It is used by Xen., Pl. and Dem. in the fourth century BC, and eight times by Aristid. in the second century AD.

[60] *An.* 3.5.15; *Oec.* 5.9.3. [61] *AP* 9.568 = Dioscorides *HE* 34.

[62] 1.1.1, 1.4, 1.11; 10.5; 12.2; 2.21.5; 3.7.3; 4.19.2; 6.7.1; 8.7.5.

[63] 15.37, 40; 16.387b (a palindrome).

Table 40.5 *Words with a claim to be 'poetic' in Heliodorus,* Aethiopica *1.1*

None of these words appears in Hesiod, Pindar, Aratus, Dionysius Periegetes or Quintus, so these poets have not been included in this table.

Heliodorus 1.1	Homer	Tragedy	A.R.	Call. / Theoc.	Nic.	*AP*	Opp. *H.*	Opp. *C.*	Other novels
ἀκρωρεία				Call. *h.* 3.224		7.626			
ἄρδην (also εἰς ἄρδην 9.2.3)		Aes. fr. 73b.5 [Aes.] *PV* 451 Soph. × 3 Eur. × 7				1.94, 15.37, 15.40, 16.387b (all late)			
διαγελῶ		Soph. fr. 171 Eur. *Ba.* 272, 286, 322							
ἔδεσμα				Call *h.* 3.148	*fr.* 80.2				
καταυγάζω			4.1248			9.58			
λείψανον			2.193			× 30	5.674	2.250, 288	X.Eph. × 3 Ach. Tat. × 6
νεοσφαγής		Aes. fr. 298.1 Soph. × 3, Eur. *Hec.* 894			*Ther.* 101, fr. 68				
ῥαχία		[Aes.] *PV* 715 Soph. fr. 1088.1				7.393			
σαλεύω		[Aes.] *PV* 1081 Soph. × 2, [Eur.] *Rh.* 248				× 10			Ach. Tat. 4.14.2
χηρεύω	Od. 9.124	Soph. *OT* 479 Eur. *Cyc.* 440, *Alc.* 1089				16.159, 270			Ach. Tat 4.1.2

διαγελῶ, here 'I smile' (of sunrise), appears in its literal sense in Soph. fr. 171 Radt and Eur. *Ba.* 272 and 322, but not in my later poets. It has a respectable pedigree in prose (e.g. Xen. *An.* 2.6.26) and we know that for Phrynichus and his readers, at any rate, it was a normal locution for daybreak, precisely Heliodorus' use.[64]

The compound *νεοσφαγής*, 'freshly slaughtered', used by Hld. at 1.1.2 and 6.12.1, has some marks of a poetic word – five uses in Attic tragedy, two in Nicander: but it seems to be treated by Ps.-Herodian as a prose term.[65]

ῥαχία, 'rocky shore', appears twice in tragedy, and only one of these uses is in the sense 'shore' that we find in Hld.[66] It makes a single appearance in the *Anthology*.[67] But it is also much employed in prose – e.g. by Th., Plb., Str. and Aristid., *Orr.* 1 Lenz-Behr (*Panathenaic*) and 25 Keil (*Rhodian*).

σαλεύω, 'I am tossed', is certainly used in poetry – five appearances in tragedy. But it is also used by Plato and in later prose, including *koine*, both in its literal and its metaphorical sense (e.g. each once in Aristid.). Its use in the novels begins with Ach. Tat. 4.14.2: it becomes a favourite of Hld.[68]

χηρεύω, 'I lack' or 'I am deprived of', is different: used by Heliodorus at 6.8.4 as well as at 1.1.2, it is the only one of the words in this table to appear in Homer – once, at *Odyssey* 9.124 – and it has three appearance in tragedy as well as two in the *Anthology*. Again in the novels it was used once before Hld., by Ach. Tat. 4.1.1, and Ps.-Herodian thinks it unusual enough to need glossing.[69] Perhaps here indeed there is a poetic word.

Only four words in the table have a life in Hellenistic poetry outside epigram. ἀκρωρεία, 'mountain peak' or 'ridge', is used at Call. *Dian.* 224 and in an epigram ascribed by Cichorius to Antipater.[70] But ἀκρωρεία is much used in military contexts by Xen. in his *Hellenica* and by Plb. I doubt if a reader of Hld. would have perceived it as poetic: Poll. certainly seems not to have done (2.161).[71]

[64] ὄρθρος μὲν γάρ ἐστιν ἡ ὥρα τῆς νυκτός, καθ' ἣν <οἱ> ἀλεκτρυόνες ᾄδουσιν. ἄρχεται δὲ ἐνάτης ὥρας καὶ τελευτᾶι εἰς διαγελῶσαν ἡμέραν ... ἕως δὲ τὸ ἀπὸ διαγελώσης ἡμέρας ἄχρις ἡλίου ἐξέχοντος διάστημα, 'early morning is the hour of the night at which nightingales sing. It begins with the ninth hour and ends with the smile of daybreak ... dawn is the interval between the smile of daybreak until the sunrise', Phryn. *PS* 93–4 de Borries.

[65] Hdn. *Epim.* 100.12 ὠμοβόειον δέρμα, τὸ ἀπὸ νεοσφαγοῦς βοός, 'a raw oxhide, one from a freshly-slaughtered ox'.

[66] [Aes.] *PV* 713. In Soph. fr. 1088 Radt its sense is 'ridge'. [67] Diocles *GP* 1.

[68] 1.1.7 and 9, 8.13, 26.3; 2.22.1, 26.3, 33.3; 3.10.5; 6.1.2; 9.6.4, 7.2; 10.4.6.

[69] χηρεύω, τὸ στερίσκομαι, 'I am bereft of', i.e. 'I am deprived of', *Epim.* 100.1.

[70] *AP* 7.626.7: *contra GP* on their lines 3494–501. Ἀκρώρεια also appears as a toponym at Theoc. 25.31.

[71] Cf. Hdn. *De pros. cath.* iii 1.277.18 Lentz: ἀκρώρεια ἄκρον ὄρους.

Another of the four words, ἔδεσμα, 'food(stuff)', is used in the same Call. hymn (*Dian.* 48) and in a fragment of Nicander (fr. 80.2): again the evidence of several cases in prose writing,[72] augmented by that of Poll., who uses it seven times to mean 'foodstuff', counts against any poetic colour.[73]

A word whose poetic attestation starts with Apollonius Rhodius in the third century BC, λείψανον, 'remnant', is indeed much exploited by epigram, almost entirely (and predictably) sepulchral epigram,[74] and is quite a favourite of Hld.[75] But it is clear from its use in prose writers that it is in no sense a poetic word.[76]

There remains καταυγάζω, 'I shine down upon', once in A.R. (4.1248), once in epigram (*AP* 9.58).[77] The Homeric uses of the simple verb αὐγάζω (noted by Livrea commenting on A.R. 4.1248) may strengthen the case for seeing Hld.'s recurrent uses of the compound verb as poetic.[78]

11 Two (or Three?) Epigraphic Poets

The corollary – which I have no space to pursue at length here – is that very few poetic words used by Marcellus, by the Sacerdos poet or poets, or found in my small sample of the *Cynegetica*, also appear either in Longus or in the other novelists.

Table 40.6 sets out some of the poetic pedigree of the eighteen terms (out of seventy-one in all that I have analysed) in the lexicon of the first of Marcellus' poems on Regilla from the Via Appia, Rome (the fifty-nine lines on *stele* A) which are also used by at least one of the five novelists.[79] Of these eighteen, three are in fact quotations from the Homeric poems,[80] leaving only around twenty per cent of Marcellus' poetic vocabulary as words also

[72] E.g. Xen. *Hier.* 1.23.1; *Cyr.* 1.1.3; and other prose including Call. fr. 407.48.

[73] Poll. 6.32, 38, 48, 57, 58, 182; 10.87.

[74] To the thirty instances in the *Greek Anthology* can be added, e.g., the epigram preserved by Paus. 5.20.7.

[75] 1.1.4, 22.5; 2.1.3, 3.3; 5.22.1; 6.7.6; 7.4.3, 18.1.

[76] For the second century AD see e.g. Poll. 6.94; 9.129.

[77] Antipater *GP* 91. [78] 1.1.1; 2.1.1; 5.7.3, 31.2; 6.14.2; 7.7.7, 26.1; 9.22.4.

[79] I hope to publish elsewhere the evidence for the poetic pedigree of the other fifty-three words analysed, evidence that is not strictly relevant to the argument of this paper.

[80] ἀνηρείψαντο, 'snatched away', Il. 20.324–5, cited by Ach. Tat. 2.36.3; ἴκελος in Ἀρτέμιδι ἰκέλη ἢ χρυσείηι Ἀφροδίτηι, 'like Artemis or golden Aphrodite', Od. 17.37 and 19.54, quoted by Ch. 4.7.5, and in ὄμματα καὶ κεφαλὴν ἴκελος Διὶ τερπικεραύνωι, 'in his eyes and head like Zeus who rejoices in his thunderbolt', Il. 2.478, quoted by Ach. Tat. 1.8.7; the epithet καλλίσφυρος, 'with beautiful ankles', quoted by Ch. 4.1.8.

Table 40.6 *The lexicon of Marcellus' poem on Regilla from the Via Appia, Rome:* IG *xiv 1389 stele A* (= IGUR *iii 1155 A, cf.* SEG *29.999) ca. AD 161*

Of seventy-one words with varying degrees of poetic pedigree only the following eighteen are also found in the novelists.

Marcellus	Homer	Hes.	Aratus	A.R.	Call.	Nic.	*AP*	D.P.	Opp. *H.*	Opp. *C.*	Q.S.	Novels
ἄγαλμα	Il. × 1 Od. × 7		1.197, 1.453		*h.* 4.307, 5.39 *ep.* 33.1	fr. 69.1		*Lith.* 4			1.627, 13.427	All five, Ch. only metaphorical
ἀγνώς	Od. × 1		ἄγνωτοι, 1.401		fr. 620		*pass.* 7.468	ἀγνώσσοντι 173				Ch. 1.4.5
ἀνηρείψαντο/ ἀνηρέψαντο	Il. 20.324 Od. × 4						9.187				× 6	Ach.Tat 2.36.3 citing Il. 20.324
ἄπυστος	Od. × 3				*h.* 4.215, 6.9 frr. 228.45, 611.1, 680.2				2.232	1.236		Ch. 7.2.4
ἄρουρα	Il. × 27 Od. × 17	*Op* × 6, fr. 59	× 5	× 8	*h.* 3.130 fr. 24.7	*Alex.* × 2 *Ther.* × 2	× 25	× 3	× 3	× 5	× 9	Hld. 2.28.4
αὔρα		*Op.* × 1 *Th.* × 1		× 4	*h.* 3.94 fr. 228.41		× 16		4.415	4.65, 75	× 3	Longus × 1 Hld. × 3
γέρας	Il. × 2 Od. × 1				fr. 384.28		× 74	374				Ch. × 1 Hld. × 2
γηραιός		*Op* × 1		× 1			× 4					Hld. × 3
ἕδος					*h.* 3.57, 4.11, fr. 100.4		× 17					Hld. 9.11.4

Table 40.6 (*Cont.*)

Marcellus	Homer	Hes.	Aratus	A.R.	Call.	Nic.	*AP*	D.P.	Opp. *H.*	Opp. *C.*	Q.S.	Novels
ἠυγενής							× 8					(εὐ- Ch., Ach. Tat., Hld.)
εὔζωνος	Il. × 3 Od. × 4	*Sc.* 31 *fr* × 2									10. 143	Ch. 7.4.12, 8.3.12
θαλερός	Il. 3.53	× 15					× 18					Ach. Tat. 6.7.4
ἴκελος	Il. × 10 Od. × 7	*Th.* 572 *Op.* × 2 *Sc.* × 6	1.296	× 15	*h.* 4.232 fr. 523.1	*Ther.* 719, 764	× 9	287	1.662, 3. 566, 5.4	× 7		Od. 17.37, 19.54 cited Ch. 4.7.5 Il. 2.478 cited Ach. Tat 1.8.7
καλλίσφυρος	Il. × 3 Od. × 2	*Th.* × 3 fr. × 6					13.30			2.1		Od. 5.333/11.603 cited Ch. 4.1.8
κεχαρισμένος	Il. × 6 Od. × 4	*Op.* 683			*h.* 5.37				×2	2.41		Hld. × 3
παρορῶ							× 2					Ch. × 1 Hld. × 4
περικείμενος	Il. 19.4		1.812									Ch. × 1 X.Eph. × 1
πρόγονος	Od. 9.221						× 8					Ch. × 1 Hld. × 3
σφυρόν	Il. × 3			× 2	*h.* 3.128 fr. 75.46, 384.33	*Ther.* × 3	× 8	557		× 3		Hld. × 2

found in the novelists: among these may be a word, παρορῶ, 'I overlook', more common in prose than in poetry.[81]

Table 40.7 traces the uses of terms that seem to be poetic in five elegiac epigrams for the tomb of Sacerdos of Nicaea, probably composed around AD 130, and preserved as *AP* 15.4–8.[82] Two words that seem to be poetic have been excluded since they occur neither in my selected poets nor in the novels – ἀποικεσίη, 'living apart', and ἀρχέγονος, 'origin of my stock'. Another term, ὀργιοφάντας, 'mystery-displayer', has been set aside from the assessment as being technical, though its poetic use is not limited to the Sacerdos poems.[83] Of the remaining fourteen words with various claims to be seen as poetic,[84] only six are used by the novelists, or only five if one excludes the used of ἀντωπῶ, 'I look in the eye', by Hld. 1.21.3 (whereas *AP* 15.6.3 has ἀντωπός, 'facing' or 'face to face with').

Five poetic words used by the novelists out of a list of eighteen is not a negligible proportion (twenty-eight per cent): but even of these five, two have only slender claims to be poetic: βεβοαμένος, 'celebrated' with two appearances (in the form βεβοημένος) in the *Anthology*; ζάκορος, 'temple-attendant', with one in Nic.'s *Alexipharmaca*. Only three are left that have a broadly based poetic pedigree, κλαρόνομος, 'heir, νεαζόμενος,

[81] In poetry it is found at Ar. *Av.* 454. For elevated prose cf. *IGLSyr* i 47 col. 1.17 (Antiochus of Commagene) ὅ]σ[α] γε [κ]αιρὸς παρεῖδε[ν χρ]όνοις [προτέρ]ο[ι]ς, 'things which opportunity has overlooked in times past'.

[82] See Bowie 2014d (Chapter 36 in Volume 3), and for the possibility that two poets were involved 2016f (Chapter 18 in this volume).

[83] It also appears in *AP* 9.688, a poem inscribed on a gate of Argos (according to J in the *codex Palatinus*) by its erector Cleadas sometime in the second or third century AD: τήνδε πύλην λάεσσιν ἐυξέστοις ἀραρυῖαν, | ἀμφότερον κόσμον τε πάτρηι καὶ θάμβος ὁδίταις, | τεῦξε Κλέης Κλεάδας ἀγανῆς πόσις εὐπατερείης,| Λερναίων ἀδύτων περιώσιος ὀργιοφάντης, | τερπόμενος δώροισιν ἀγασθενέων βασιλήων, 'This gate, built by the close-fitting of polished stones, both as an adornment to his native country and an object of wonder to travellers, Cleadas built, the husband of gentle, nobly-born Clea: he was the outstanding hierophant of the Lernaean temple, rejoicing in gifts from greatly-powerful kings'. Cleadas was also the erector and perhaps poet of *IG* ii^2 3674 from Attica: Δηοῦς καὶ κούρης θεοΐκελον ἱεροφάντην | κυδαίνων πατέρα στῆσε δόμοις Κλεάδας, |[Κ]εκροπίης σοφὸν ἔρνος Ἐρώτιον· ὧι ῥα καὶ αὐτός | Λερναίων ἀδύτων ἶσον ἔδεκτο γέρας, 'Cleadas set up in their house the statue of his father, honouring him, the god-like hierophant of Demeter and Kore, the wise offspring of Cecrops' land, Erotium: by whom, after all, he himself also received the same honour in the Lernaean temples'.

[84] E.g. οὐρανομήκης, as well as appearing at Aes. *Ag.* 92, is used by Ar. *Nu.* 357 and 459 (neither Fraenkel on *Ag.* nor Dover on *Nu.* comments) and also in prose, e.g. Hdt. 2.138.4 (δένδρεα), Lys. fr. 47 Carey (a στήλη, exaggerating). ἀοιδότατος and ἀοιδότερος are entirely poetic: as well as Eur., Call., and *AP* note *IG* xii.2 443 (on Alcibiades, a poet from Byzantium who died in Mytilene); *IK* 33.144.

[85] Aes. *Supp.* 1055. *Ag.* 764, fr. 458 Radt; Soph. *Tr.* 144; Eur. *Ph.* 713, 1619. It is also found in Men. and Epicur. *Ep.* 3, 59.

Table 40.7 *The lexicon of the poets who composed five elegiac epigrams for the tomb-obelisk of Sacerdos of Nicaea, ca. AD 130,* AP *15.4–8 =* GVI *1999, some examples*

Sacerdos' poet	Homer	Hes. / tragic	Aratus	A.R.	Call	Nic.	*AP*	D.P.	Op *H.*	'O' C.	Q.S.	Novels
ἀοιδότερος or ἀοιδότατος		Eur. *Hel.* 1109			*h.* 4.252		× 4					
ἀντωπόν				ἀντώπιον 4.729			× 4		5.7			ἀντωπεῖν Hld. 1.21.3
βεβοημένος							7.138, 9.20					Hld. 6.1.3
γειτονῶ					fr. 194.104		× 5					—
δηρίσαντο/ δηρίσασθαι (only here in the PHI database)	Od. 8.76			1.1343, 4.1767					2. 627	δηρίσα- ιντο × 2, σθαι × 4		—
ἐριποῦσ(α)/ ἐριπών etc.	Il. × 6	*Sc.* 423		3.1310							× 3	
ζάκορος						*Alex.* 217						Ch. × 2, Hld. × 7
ἠρίον	Il. 23.126			1.1165, 2.658	fr. 43.4, 254.7, 262.1		× 19					—
κεκλιμένος/ κεκλιμένη etc.	*Il.* × 3 Od. × 3	Soph. fr. 314.125	1. 161, 356	× 4	*h.* 3.254		× 23	847 1003	× 21		8.132	

κλαρονόμος						× 6			Ch. × 1, Longus × 1, Hld. × 2
νεαζόμενον	-	Aes. *Supp.* 105, *A.* 765, fr. 458 Soph. *Tr.* 144, *OC* 374 Eur. *Ph.* 713, 1619				11.256, 9.261, 16. 383			active Ach. Tat. 4.10.1 1
οὐρανομάκεα[a]	Od. 5.139	Aes. *A.* 92				7.84			—
περίσαμος/ περίσημος		Eur. *Her.* 1017		fr. 228	*Ther.* 19	× 3	556		—
ῥυσάμενος etc.	Il. × 4 Od. × 3	Aes. *Eu.* 232, 300 Soph. *OT* 312–3 Eur. × 5	× 4			× 10		ῥύσαιτο 4.621	Ch. × 1, Hld. × 3

[a] Add Simon. *fr. el.* 11.27 and Dareius' letter in Plu. *De coh. ira* 455d.

'being renewed', and ῥυσάμενος, 'having saved'. Forms of νεάζω/νεαζόμαι, 'I renew/I am being renewed' are well represented in Attic tragedy,[85] as are forms of ῥυσάμενος;[86] νεάζω appears twice in pre-Byzantine *Anthology* epigrams,[87] while forms of ῥυσάμενος are frequent in the *Anthology*.[88] Finally κλαρόνομος in its Doric form appears in other poetry only in a text that has not otherwise been included in my searches, [Mosch.], *Epitaph. Bionis* 3.96 (in the phrase κλαρονόμος Μοίσας τᾶς Δωρίδος); but there are several cases of κληρονόμος in the *Anthology*.[89] Unlike νεαζόμενος and ῥυσάμενος it seems to be absent from archaic and classical poetry.

The evidence of Marcellus and the Sacerdos poet or poets may point to a slightly greater permeability of the frontier between prose and poetic vocabulary than the evidence from the novelists themselves, or it may point to the novelists other than Xenophon (who appears only once in the final column of Table 40.6 and does not appear in the final column of Table 40.7 at all) being ready to use poetic terms. Further close analysis would be needed to establish which explanation should be favoured.

The small sample of words from Ps.-Oppian, *Cynegetica* in Table 40.8 seems to confirm that some poetic words seep into the novelists, with the highest uptake in Heliodorus. Of course the claim of some to be poetic can be questioned: ἀγάλλομαι, 'I take pride in', is much used by poets, but also by Herodotus, Thucydides, Plato and Xenophon; alongside its 'poetic' uses ἄγρη/ἄγρα, 'prey', is also found in Herodotus and Plato; αἰθήρ, 'upper air', appears in philosophical prose as well as in poetry. Only a careful examination of Heliodorus' use of each term, comparable to that offered above for Longus, would be able to establish the modes and possible objectives of such apparently 'poetic' vocabulary.

12 Conclusions

Scrutiny of the 'poetic' words listed by Valley for Longus has suggested that only a small proportion of these words seemed likely to be employed to give a generally 'poetic' colour or even to evoke a particular poetic genre. Many

[86] Aes. *Eum.* 300; Soph. *OT* 312, 313; Eur. *Andr.* 575, *Ion* 165, *Hyps.* fr. 60.28, *Hel.* 925, 1086.

[87] 11.256 (Lucill.), 261 (Epig.); 16.383 (late).

[88] 6.125 (Mnasalc.), 141 ('Anacr.'), 231 (Philip); 7.72 (Men.), 74 (Diod.), 195 (Mel.), 250 'Simonides' (*FGE* 'Simonides' 12, also quoted by Plu. *De Hdt. mal.* 39 and Aristid. *Or.* 28.66), 286 (Antip.); 9.40 (Zos.), 71 (Antiphil.), 178 (Antiphil.), 496 (Ath.).

[89] 7.607 (Pall.); 9.50 (*incertus*); 11.166 (*incertus*), 171 (Lucill.), 294 (Luc.), 384 (Agath.).

Table 40.8 *Ps.-Oppian* Cynegetica: *some of Ps.-Oppian's words that do appear in the novelists*

[Oppian] *Cynegetica*	Chariton	Xenophon	Achilles Tatius	Longus	Heliodorus
ἀγάλλομαι 3.192	5.9.2	1.1.4			
ἄγαμαι 3.96	2.5.11				3.4.3, 5.18.2, 10.9.4
ἀγκλίνω 1.192, 2.95, 227, 4.117			1.5.2, 2.15.4		
ἀγλαΐη/ἀγλαΐα 1.337, 2.209					3.2.4 (hymn, pentameters)
ἄγονος 1.260					4.7.13, 12.3, 10.16.8
ἄγρη/ἄγρα × 14			× 11	2.12.4, 3.7. 2, 8.1	1.1.1, 8.17.4
ἀδάκρυτος 1.39					2.8.1, 33.8
ἀδαμάντινος 3.240 (literal)					4.4.3, 7.9.5 (metaphorical)
ἀδρανῶ 2.106			(ἀδρανής 5.13.3)		
ἀήτης × 5		3.2.13			1.22.14
ἀθήρητος 1.524 (hares)				2.4.3 (Eros)	
ἀθλεύω 2.76, 110			2.38.4, 3.6.4 (ἀθλῶ)		4.3.1, 9.9.3 (ἀθλῶ)
ἄθυρμα 1.33				1.10.1	
ἀίδηλος 2.324, 496		1.6.2 in a hexameter			
αἰθήρ × 8					10.16.3
αἱμάσσω 2.175			2.11.6, 7, 8.2.3	1.12.5, 6, 2.18.1, 3.19.3, 20.1	
ἀίσσω × 5			5.19.1		
αἰχμή × 7			× 6		× 4
αἶψα × 17					2.26.5
ἀλῶμαι 2.253, 312					5.11.4, 6.15.4, 10.34.3

were arguably chosen to trigger intertextuality with particular passages in earlier poetry, and some seem to have no good claim to be 'poetic' at all. A brief overview of a small selection of potentially 'poetic' words in Achilles Tatius and Heliodorus has supported the view that, in their writing too, only a low proportion of 'poetic' words was to be found, a view that might be thought to be corroborated by the small number of predominantly 'poetic' words in Marcellus, the Sacerdos poet or poets and my sample from the *Cynegetica* that are also found in the novelists. Overall, although much more work remains to be done, my investigation suggests that poets and writers of novelistic prose are still drawing their vocabulary from two different linguistic pools.

41 Captured Moments: Illustrating Longus' Prose (2018)

1 Introduction

It is a great pleasure as well as an honour to be part of a volume arising from the conference organised to honour the work of Tomas Hägg. This chapter explores illustrations of printed translations of Longus, *Daphnis and Chloe*, a subject to which Tomas himself made a very illuminating contribution in the English edition of his influential book *The Novel in Antiquity*.[1] Unlike the text of Longus, this is not a subject that can readily be confined within a small compass, and in many respects the following discussion is necessarily selective. Thus, whereas I have tried to offer an outline history of the illustrated editions known to me that were published between 1626 and 2014, I have picked out just ten illustrators for more detailed documentation in Table 41.1. I initially expected that such a table would enable me to point to certain scenes as favourites with visual artists, and that this would make a perhaps predictable contribution to our understanding of the modern reception of the work. To some extent this has turned out to be the case. But the number of scenes chosen for illustration by just one or two artists forms a far higher proportion than I had expected. That has reinforced my confidence in my decision to tabulate only a small number of editions; and the fact that one artist in the period on which I concentrate, Pierre Bonnard, did no fewer than 151 illustrations, made me decide to exclude him from my table. As it is, a review of the illustrations of my ten chosen volumes has required the tabulation of some 150 scenes.

My illustrators are all European, and the dates of birth of those represented in the table range from 13 March 1848 (Champollion) to the year 1901 (Eva Schwimmer). The editions of Longus that they illustrated were printed between 1890 (Collin and Champollion) and 1961 (Marc Chagall). They are thus witnesses to the European taste of the last decade of the nineteenth and the first six decades of the twentieth century. A much wider

[1] Hägg 1983, 214–27 'Pictorial supplement. Daphnis and Chloe in the mirror of art'. His illustrations include Aristide Maillol's 'cicada' (221 fig. 72) and 'piggy back' (224 fig. 76), and Yngve Berg's 'Daphnis teaches Chloe to play the syrinx' (219 fig. 69).

chronological span is offered by the magisterial treatment of Giles Barber (son of the Oxford editor of Propertius, E. A. Barber) in his 1988 Panizzi lectures,[2] and in his coverage of the nineteenth and twentieth centuries he takes account of two illustrated editions that I have regretfully excluded from my table, those of Charles Ricketts and Charles Shannon (1893) and of Gwen Raverat (1931).

Of my eleven artists two, out of consideration for this volume's honorand, are Scandinavian: the Swede Yngve Berg and the Dane Ebbe Sadolin. Three are German, Paul Scheurich, Eva Schwimmer and Renée Sintenis; two are English, John Austen and William Ellis; three are French, Raphaël Collin, Eugène-André Champollion and Aristide Maillol; and one is a Russian Jew who chose France as his place of residence, Marc Chagall.

I have so far made no systematic attempt to trace illustrations of *Daphnis and Chloe* in the form of paintings or sculptures, but my impression is that there has been nothing on the scale of the two cycles of paintings of scenes from Heliodorus, those done by Ambroise Dubois at Fontainebleau for the wedding of Henri IV and Maria de' Medici in 1600 and the cycle of ten paintings from later in the seventeenth century of which nine now hang in the Landgrafenmuseum in Kassel[3] – unless one admits Chagall's murals for the foyer of the Metropolitan Opera House, New York, which recycle some of his 1961 illustrations. In the Appendix I present a very preliminary inventory of the paintings known to me.

Before some remarks on the ten editions in my table, however, I offer a broad-brush sketch of the illustrators of *Daphnis and Chloe* since the first book that I know, published in 1626 – a sketch that at many points, especially for the earlier centuries, is heavily dependent on Barber 1989. To exclude those illustrated editions which had been discussed at some length by Barber would have made my own account extremely unbalanced.

2 Illustrators from 1626 to 1983

The first illustrated printed edition was the 1626 French translation of Pierre Marcassus (1584–1664), who himself wrote pastoral novels and plays and was professor at the Collège de la Marche. Marcassus' translation, published

[2] Barber 1989. I do not know whether his father's edition of an elegist for whom the Hellenistic poet Philetas was important contributed to Barber's interest in the novel which gives a significant role to a character Philetas.

[3] See Stechow 1953; Hägg 1983, 207–9.

by Toussaint du Bray, was illustrated by a title page and four engravings (one for each book) by Crispin de Passe the Younger (1593–1660), each combining several scenes: he chose ones that depicted the young couple's adventures, not their slow discovery of ἔρως, 'love' or 'desire'.[4]

Almost a century later the French Regent, Philippe d'Orléans, painted ('*inv. et pinxit*') twenty-eight illustrations which were then engraved by Benoit II Audran. They were first published without attribution in an edition of 1714 that used Amyot's translation.[5] They were again printed in 1716 for a corrected edition of that translation (including passages Amyot had omitted) published in both Paris and Amsterdam. Finally, in 1718, an octavo Paris edition appeared which acknowledged the Regent's contribution and whose title page was drawn by Antoine Coypel (1661–1722) and engraved by Audran.[6] The subjects of many of the twenty-eight plates (of which thirteen were double-page size and fifteen single-page size) are discussed briefly by Barber, who suggests that they set the agenda for later artists' choice of scenes to illustrate.[7] That is certainly not the case for all the illustrators discussed in this chapter. In a further twist to the story of the Regent's illustrations, in 1728 the Comte de Caylus produced a plate also based on one of his sketches, depicting the final scene of the novel and often referred to as '*Les petits pieds*'.

Meanwhile in London in 1719 James Craggs the Younger (1686–1721) published an English translation with the title *The Pastoral Amours of Daphnis and Chloe* and six illustrations by Michael van der Gucht (1660–16 October 1725), all of which had subjects already found in the Regent's sequence: Daphnis extracted from the pit, Chloe asleep, the vintage, Philetas and Eros, Daphnis bird-catching, the wedding dance. There was a second edition in 1720,[8] and 'fourth' editions in London in 1746, and London and Dublin in 1763, some with the title *The Power of Love*. Of these some include '*Les petits pieds*'.

It was again in Paris that Jacques Guérin, who had married the widow of Antoine-Urbain I Coustelier, published in 1731 Amyot's translation with eight plates by Gérard Scotin, all based on the Regent's edition: in 1734 this

[4] See Barber 1989, 19–20, with a reproduction of the title page on p. 21 (Barber's fig. 1).

[5] Barber 1989, 31 doubts the reliability of this title page.

[6] See Barber 1989, 32–6, with a reproduction of the title page on p. 33 (Barber's fig. 5). Barber thought the publisher was Antoine-Urbain I Coustelier and noted that a 1730s source asserts that only 250 copies were printed.

[7] Barber 1989, 34–5.

[8] *The pastoral amours of Daphnis and Chloe. Written originally in Greek by Longus, and translated into English. Adorn'd with cuts*: available in *Eighteenth Century Collections Online*.

edition was copied by François Changouin in an Amsterdam edition with reversed plates. A reissue, using Amyot's translation as supplemented by Courier, was published in 1947 by Aux Horizons de France, Paris.

A quarter of a century later, in 1754, Charles Antoine Coypel (1694–1752), son of the Regent's collaborator Antoine Coypel, published a quarto edition presenting a Greek text with a Latin translation by Moll, notes by J. S. Bernard (1718–93), and touched-up plates of the Regent's illustrations with frames by Simon Fokke (1712–84), headpieces by Fokke and Charles-Dominique-Joseph Eisen (17 August 1720–4 January 1778), and tailpieces by (probably) Charles Nicolas Cochin the Elder (1688–1754).[9] The same illustrations were used again in 1757 in an edition which printed Amyot's translation together with a modernised version by Antoine Le Camus (1722–72).

The next flurry of activity coincides with the turbulent close of the 1780s. In 1787 – the year in which he achieved membership of the Académie on the basis of his painting *The Death of Agis* – Nicolas-André Monsiau (1754–31 May 1837) illustrated a duodecimo edition published by Didot: between then and 1793 another edition was illustrated with engravings by L. Binet. In 1793 a larger edition was commissioned from Jean-Jacques-François Le Barbier (b. Rouen November 11 1738, d. Paris May 7 1826) but never published.

It was also in 1793 that Didot commissioned illustrations from Pierre-Paul Prud'hon: what appeared, just after 1800, was a folio edition with plates by Prud'hon and François Gérard (b. Rome 5 April 1770, d. Paris 2 November 1837), entitled *Amours pastorales de Daphnis et Chloé*. The earlier scenes were done by Prud'hon and the later by Gérard.[10] Gérard had recently illustrated a Didot edition of *Amours de Psyché et de Cupidon* by Jean de La Fontaine (1797) and was shortly (1806) to illustrate another of *Paul et Virginie* by Bernardin de Saint-Pierre.[11] Much later, in 1824, François Gérard painted a Chloe kneeling with her head on the lap of Daphnis (see the Appendix).

From the middle of the nineteenth century I know two illustrated editions, both published in 1863. One was a reprint with illustrations in 1863 of Annibale Caro's translation *Gli amori pastorali di Daphni e Chloe,*

[9] See Barber 1989, 38–41, with reproductions of Chloe saving Daphnis by playing on Dorcon's syrinx (depicted as a recorder-like pipe), Barber's fig. 6; and of a head and tailpiece each showing the couple enraptured with each other, Barber's fig. 7.

[10] See Barber 1989, 48–9, with a reproduction of Gérard's illustration of the three Nymphs appearing to Daphnis in a dream (his fig. 9, p. 50).

[11] See the illustrated biography by Lenormant 1847.

volgarizzati da Annibale Caro, nuova e corretta edizione (Milano: Daelli). The second was yet another reprint of Amyot's translation, iv + eighty pages, accompanied by forty-three illustrations by Léopold Burthe (Louisiana 1823–Paris 1860), published by J. Hetzel, Paris: an introduction was written by Burthe's teacher Eugène Emmanuel Amaury-Duval, who soon after showed an oil painting of *Daphnis and Chloe* in the *Salon* of 1865 (see the Appendix). Burthe was already known for his oil paintings *Alphée et Aréthuse* (1846), *Sappho joue de la lyre* (1848: now in the Musée des Beaux-Arts, Carcassonne) and *Ophélia* (1862), all offering opportunities for depiction of naked or partly-clothed young women.

The end of the nineteenth century saw illustrated editions in both London and Paris. In London in 1893 Longus, *Daphnis and Chloe*, illustrated by Charles de Sousy Ricketts (b. Geneva, Switzerland 2 October 1866, d. 7 October 1931) and Charles Haslewood Shannon (b. Sleaford, Lincolnshire 26 April 1863, d. 18 March 1937), was published by The Bodley Head (i.e. Elkin Matthews and John Lane). The illustrations were drawn on the wood by Ricketts and then cut by Shannon: it took them about eleven months to finish the job.[12]

A little later there were two Paris editions with illustrations by Raphaël Collin (b. Brionne, Eure, 17 June 1850, d. Paris 20 or 21 October 1916). The first, an octavo edition running to xviii + 186 pages, was published in 1890 by Jules Tallandier in the Collection '*Les Chefs-d'oeuvre de l'Esprit*'. There was a preface by Jules Claretie, and the translation itself was followed by Paul-Louis Courier's letter to M. Renouard (pp. 153–86): twenty-nine etchings in the text were by Raphaël Collin and twelve etchings, each on its own page '*hors-texte*', were by Eugène-André Champollion (b. Embrun, Hautes Alpes, 30 March 1848, d. Lettret 1901). The second was a duodecimo edition published in 1899 by Charavay and Martin in their collection '*Ma bibliothèque*', 138 pages, with illustrations by Collin alone.

The next, in 1902, was the most extensive and luxurious illustrated edition so far, that with 156 lithographs by Pierre Bonnard, painter, printmaker and book illustrator (b. near Paris in 1867, d. 1947 in the south of France). He originally studied law before attending the École des Beaux-Arts and the Académie Julian, where he met Vuillard, Sérusier and Denis. He produced his first poster in 1889 and after a short period of military service took a Paris studio with Vuillard.

From 1891 Bonnard exhibited regularly at the *Salon des Indépendants* and produced designs for Paris theatres. He became a member of 'Les

[12] Cf. Barber 1989, 70–1.

Nabis', a group that chose to work on posters, theatre designs, book illustrations, screens and tapestries and was influenced by Gauguin, the Post-Impressionists and Japanese prints. Bonnard became known as 'Le Nabi-Japonard' and was especially successful in lithography. In 1895 Bonnard met the sixteen-year-old Maria Boursin, then using the name Marthe de Méligny: she became his mistress, model, and later, in 1926, his wife. She is probably the model for some of his illustrations of Longus. In 1926 he also bought a small villa, 'Le Bosquet', at Le Cannet on the Côte d'Azur, near his friend in Nice, Henri Matisse: this was his residence until his death in 1947.

In 1894, the year before he met Maria Boursin, Bonnard was introduced to Ambroise Vollard, who commissioned his lithographs for *Quelques Aspects de la Vie de Paris* (1895) and Paul Verlaine's *Parallèlement* (1900). These were followed by Bonnard's 156 lithographs for Vollard's sumptuous 1902 edition of Amyot's translation of Longus:[13] Vollard had chosen Bonnard in preference to Maurice Denis.[14] Their execution gave Bonnard great pleasure.[15] Some but not all were reprinted in a limited edition (3000 copies) published by Mermod in Lausanne in 1948,[16] and in 1961 Piper Verlag (Munich) published forty-eight of the lithographs in a small octavo edition (sixty-five pages), followed by a summary of the novel and a discussion of Bonnard's illustrations by Günther Busch: no translation of the novel itself was printed. In or after 1979 a larger format East German edition (18.5 × 28.5 cm) was published illustrating the translation of Arno Mauersberger (Leipzig 1960) with forty-eight of Bonnard's lithographs; there is a *Nachwort* by Mauersberger.

In 1914 H. S. Ciolkowski together with Charles-Georges Maylander illustrated a duodecimo volume which yet again used Amyot's translation of

[13] Pierre Bonnard, *Daphnis et Chloe*, x + 294 pp, quarto. Barber 1989, 71–5 has an excellent discussion, and illustrates (p. 74, fig. 13) Bonnard's version of the young couple in winter (Bonnard p. 156): he also discusses the spring (p. 169), the summer (p. 215), and Chloe's preparation for her marriage (p. 277), but only illustrates the first (p. 74).

[14] For a painting by Maurice Denis illustrating *Daphnis and Chloe* that may belong to this time see the Appendix.

[15] 'I started the lithographs for *Daphnis and Chloe*, of a more classical inspiration. I worked rapidly and with enjoyment; Daphnis was able to appear in 1902. On each page I evoked the shepherd of Lesbos with a sort of happy intoxication that quite carried me away …' (Pierre Bonnard to Marguette Bouvier).

[16] 'Ce livre, le sixième de la collection LES AMOUREUSES, édité par H.-L. Mermod, à Lausanne, imprimé par la Concorde, à Lausanne, dessins reproduits par Héliographie, S.A., à Lausanne, a été tiré à trois mille exemplaires numérotés de 1 à 3000. Les numéros 1 à 500 sont réservés exclusivement aux membres du Club des lecteurs de la Gazette de Paris, octobre 1948.' My copy is n° 1307.

Longus and was published in Paris by Georges Crès et Compagnie in their collection '*Les Maîtres du livre*': it ran to xi + 306 pages and at least some copies were numbered. Ciolkowski had been exhibiting his drawings, stylistically related to those of Aubrey Beardsley, at the *Salon des Indépendants* since 1907.

At just this time another classy edition was in preparation with illustrations by Charles Émile Egli, who used the name Carlègle (b. Aigle, Vaud, Switzerland 30 May 1877, d. Paris in 1937). Carlègle's woodcuts for Longus *Daphnis et Chloé* had been displayed at the Paris *Salon d'Automne* of 1913. Six years later, in 1919, thirty-nine woodcuts were published with Amyot's translation in an octavo edition by Léon Pichon, Paris. Its 395 numbered copies (of which 200 were printed on *vélin d'Arches*) had twenty-two illustrations, six ornamental initial letters, five headpieces and six tailpieces. Carlègle was an engraver and designer whose range extended from children's books to the classical *Aurore et Phébus*.[17]

The year before, 1918, a reprint of Jacob's 1832 translation of Longus had appeared in Munich and Leipzig with illustrations by Paul Scheurich.[18] Scheurich was born in New York on 10 October 1883, studied in Berlin from 1900 to 1902, and had the rest of his career in Germany, where he died on 18 November 1945. He not only illustrated and did stage designs but also created figures for the Meissen porcelain factory, in whose school he held the rank of Professor. His illustrations for Longus were shortly followed by a portfolio of illustrations of *Der Rosenkavalier* (1920). Before the war he had been producing *Art Nouveau* work, including a poster for a dog show in 1911.

Four years later, in 1923, a quarto *Daphnis and Chloe* was published in Munich, its 197 pages illustrated by ninety-three lithographs by Otto Hettner, a painter and drawer from Dresden, where he was born on 27 January 1875 and died on 19 April 1931.

In the same year the Rarity Press, New York, published an edition with 'decorations' by John Archibald Austen (b. Dover, Kent, on 5 January 1886, d. Hythe, Kent, on 27 October 1948). He made his career as a book illustrator. Early works, including a *Hamlet*, were Beardsley-esque in style, but he was later influenced by the *Art Deco* movement, and it is in this style that he illustrated the *Daphnis and Chloe* whose London publication in

[17] One illustration of this work can be found in *The Studio* 1910.

[18] *Longus / Hirtengeschichten von Daphnis und Chloe*. Überzetzt von Friedrich Jacob (1832). Neubearbeitet von Hanns Floerke / Einband nach Entwürfen von Paul Renner. München und Leipzig (1918). Verlegt bei Georg Müller. Illustrationen von Paul Scheurich.

1925 was followed by a New York edition in 1931.[19] The translation used was the old one of George Thornley (1657), which had also been used for the first Loeb edition of Longus in 1916. Austen used several techniques in his illustrations, including wood-engraving and scraperboard. He was a friend of Alan Odle and Harry Clarke and in 1925 exhibited with them at the St George's Gallery.[20]

The next illustrator is the first of my Scandinavians, Yngve Berg. Berg was born in Stockholm on 23 December 1887 and died there on 19 July 1963. From 1906 to 1907 he studied at the *Göteborgs Musei-, Rit- och Målarskola*, then continued his artistic studies in Paris from 1908 to 1913, with visits to Spain in 1910 and 1913. His book illustrations include *Kleopatra* (twenty-six plates, 1913) and Ovid's *Ars amatoria* (1925, reprinted 1957). It was shortly after these Ovid illustrations were published that he was commissioned to illustrate a Swedish translation of Longus by the scholar Gunnar Valley, published in 1928.[21] Later in his career he illustrated Goethe's *Römische Elegien* (1929) and Bo Bergman's *Stockholmsdikter* (1947) and was involved in the interior decoration of the Villa Bonnier i Diplomstaden, Stockholm.

In 1930 Konstantin Somov painted, in a mixture of styles, four brightly coloured scenes that are described as illustrations:[22] they represent (1) Daphnis, Chloe and a third young pastoral figure (?Dorcon) surrounded by numerous sheep and goats in a green sward leading down to the sea; (2) Daphnis and a clothed Lycaenion; (3) the abduction of Chloe, wearing a short νεβρίς, 'fawnskin'; and (4) Daphnis gazing at a sleeping Chloe, partly clothed in her νεβρίς. I have failed to discover for which edition they were meant, and it is possible they were not intended to be book illustrations.

The next year, 1931, saw a Longus illustrated by Gwen Raverat (26 August 1885–11 February 1957, grand-daughter of Charles Darwin),[23] first printed by the Ashendene Press, Chelsea (iv + 163 pages). The translation was that

[19] *Daphnis and Chloe* Translated out of the Greek of Longus by George Thornley (1657), with decorations by John Austen. New York 1931. Privately printed for Rarity Press, New York, NY. The 1925 London edition was published by Geoffrey Bles. For one of Austen's illustrations see the cover of this volume.

[20] Issue 27 of The Imaginative Book Illustration Society's *Studies in Illustration* contains a full bibliography by Martin Steenson.

[21] *Longos Daphnis och Chloe en Herderoman* översatt från Grekiskan av Gunnar Valley, försedd med teckningar av Yngve Berg. Stockholm. Albert Bonniers Förlag (1928). Valley's Uppsala doctoral thesis was Valley 1926.

[22] See www.wikiart.org/en/konstantin-somov/illustration-to-the-novel-daphnis-and-chloe-1, -2, -3 and -4.

[23] The classic account of her place in her family remains her autobiographical *Period Piece. A Cambridge Childhood* (London 1956).

of Amyot, edited and corrected by Courier: its title was thus *Les amours pastorals de Daphnis et Chloé*. Owing to a problem with ink all but ten copies of the 1931 printing were destroyed, and the book was only finally published in 1933 with a run of 290 copies, of which 250 were for sale, printed on Batchelor hand-made paper, and twenty copies printed on vellum. It was set in Ptolemy type.[24]

Four years later, in 1935, a translation was published in Hamburg with thirty-one woodcuts by Renée Sintenis (b. Glatz/Kłodzko in Silesia, 20 March 1888, d. Berlin 22 April 1965). She studied from 1908 to 1911 at the *Hochschule für angewandte Kunst*, Berlin, under the painter L. von Koenig and the sculptor Haverkamp. Her forte was engraving and sculpting, above all (working from animals in Berlin Zoo) small bronzes and terracottas of young animals at play (she later designed the Berlin bear emblem), but also statuettes of male and female athletes: in 1928 she won an Olympic bronze medal for her *Footballeur* (1927).[25] She was encouraged by Rilke and by the painter and engraver E. R. Weiss, whom she married. As early as 1921 she illustrated a *Sappho* with etchings, and her focus on animals made her an obvious choice to do woodcuts for an illustrated *Daphnis and Chloe*. These were initially to be used by Count Kessler for a Cranach Press edition, but in the end they illustrated a translation by Ludwig Wolde published in 1935 by Verlag Dr. Ernst Hauswedell and Co, Hamburg. Four year later, in 1939, Hauswedell used them again for a reprint of Friedrich Jacobs' 1832 translation.[26] The text was set up and printed by Haag-Drugulin, Leipzig; a second (corrected) edition appeared in 1940; a third edition (an unchanged reprint of the second) in 1941, and a sixth in 1946. Sintenis was a member of the Prussian Academy of Arts from 1929 (its first female sculptor) until expelled by the Nazis in 1934. Her studio and home were destroyed in an air raid in 1944. After the war she was appointed (in 1947) to a position at the *Hochschule der Künste*, and became a full professor at the Berlin Art Academy in 1955.[27]

[24] Barber 1989, 76 illustrates 'Winter'. Many of Raverat's wood-engravings, some dated as early as 1928, are to be found in www.gwenraverat.com/collection/4137/daphnis-et-chloe.

[25] Now in the Kunsthalle, Hamburg. The entry in the Art Directory under www.renee-sintenis.com/ ('Sintenis' success grew during the 1920s, culminating in the 1926 bronze "Der Läufer von Nurmi" ["The Runner from Nurmi"], for which she was awarded the 1932 Olympia Prize') misdescribes her sculpture of the Finnish multiple-gold-medallist Paavo Nurmi.

[26] *Des Longus Hirtengeschichten von Daphnis und Chloe, mit 31 Abbildungen nach Holzschnitten von Renée Sintenis*: see Barber 1989, 79–80.

[27] For illustrations of her work up to (1949) see Jannasch 1949 and with later objects Kiel and Sintenis 1956 (a revised edition of their 1935 book cataloguing Sintenis' work). For a biography see Kettelhake 2010.

Only two years later, in 1937, Maillol's woodcuts were published. Aristide Maillol was born on 8 December, 1861, at Banyuls-sur-Mer, Roussillon, and died there on September 27, 1944. His forty-six woodcut illustrations and fifteen woodcut initial letters had originally been commissioned by Count Harry Kessler (d. 1937) for his Cranach press in Weimar in 1927. In 1937 they were ultimately published in French and English editions simultaneously. The English edition was published by A. Zwemmer, London. The woodcuts are discussed by Barber and noticed by Hägg.[28] The illustrations were later (1974) used by Reclam in Leipzig for a translation with notes by Arno Mauersberger and 'afterwords' by Reimar Müller and Verena Zinserling-Paul. This was reprinted by Verlag Fourier and Fertig, Wiesbaden in 1977, with no reference to the 1974 edition.[29]

While in Germany reprint of Sintenis succeeded reprint, in occupied Denmark Ebbe Sadolin did illustrations for a Danish translation of Longus that appeared in 1941.[30] Sadolin (b. 1900, d. 1982) had already illustrated an English book, published in London.[31] Later he was commissioned to make the Bodil Danish film prize, a white porcelain statuette named after actor and director Bodil Ipsen and modelled on the American Oscar: the prize was established in 1948 by the Film Employees Association in Copenhagen.

1948 was also the year in which William Lionel Ellis did fourteen woodcuts to illustrate a translation of Longus by Jack Lindsay, published by the Daimon Press, London. Ellis (b. Plymouth, Devon, 1903, d. 1988) was both a painter and a wood-engraver, who studied at the Plymouth School of Art from 1917 to 1922 and the Royal College of Art from 1922 to 1925. He was in his forties when he was asked to do the Longus woodcuts, which are sombre and heavy, and have none of the rural exuberance of his 1936 oil painting *Nudes and musicians in a landscape*.[32]

It was also in 1948 that Mieczysław Jurgielewicz (b. Warsaw 4 February 1900, d. Warsaw 18 May 1983) illustrated a Polish translation of Longus by Jan Parandowski (1895–1978). The book was published in Warsaw.

[28] Barber 1989, 77–9, illustrating 'Chloe bathing', fig. 15 p. 78; Hägg 1983, 211, fig. 72, 'the cicada', and 224, fig. 76, 'piggy back'.

[29] *Longos Daphnis und Chloe. Mit Holzschnitten von Aristide Maillol.* Wiesbaden (1977). Verlag Fourier und Fertig. *Aus dem Griechischen Übersetzung und Anmerkungen von Arno Mauersberger. Mit Nachworten von Reimar Müller und Verena Zinserling-Paul.*

[30] *Longos Daphnis og Chloe, oversat fra Graesk af A. Kragelund, Tegninger af Ebbe Sadolin.* Copenhagen. Nyt Nordisk Forlag. Arnold Busck (1941).

[31] Eric Dancy, *Hyde Park*, London, Methuen (1937).

[32] Height thirty-two inches, width fifty-four inches, sold in September 2012 by Ewbank auctioneers, Woking, Surrey for £950.

A second edition of Parandowski's translation, published in Czytelnik 1962, was illustrated by Jerzy Jaworowski.

Eva Schwimmer was born Eva Götze in 1901 in Gut Kalkstein, East Prussia, and died in 1986 in Berlin. She had a career as a painter, drawer, and illustrator after studying at the *Staatliche Akademie für graphische Künste* in Leipzig. In 1933 she married Max Schwimmer, also a graphic artist (1895–1960).[33] She was not allowed to work under the Nazi regime, but in 1947 she became Professor at the *Hochschule für angewandte Kunst Berlin-Weißensee*, a position she lost in 1951 in a dispute over Formalism: she then settled in West Berlin. Her illustrations to a translation of Longus by Ernst Lehmann appeared in 1959.[34] Her paintings still sell well at auction.

Marc Chagall is perhaps the most famous of Longus' illustrators. Born on 7 July 1887 in Vitebsk, now in Belarus, he lived most of his life in France. He was commissioned early in the nineteen-fifties to illustrate *Daphnis and Chloe* by a Greek who had also become a French resident, Tériade, i.e. Stratis Eleftheriadis (Στρατής Ελευθεριάδης). Tériade was himself from Lesbos – he was born on 2 May 1897 at Varia (Βαρειά) just south of Mytilene – and this was the major impulse for his project. To remind himself of Greek landscapes Chagall visited Greece in 1954 (his first visit had been immediately after his second marriage) and stayed (*inter alia*) in Poros: he may not have got as far as Lesbos.

The outcome, published by Tériade in 1961, was a handsome edition in two volumes, 42.4 by 33 cm. The text, Amyot's translation, was typed by hand in the font '*romain de l'université*'. There were forty-two coloured off-the-text original lithographs, printed on '*vélin d'Arches*' paper. 250 numbered copies were printed for sale, and twenty further copies were made but not released on the market (numbered I–XX) as well as forty additional suites, which included all the lithographs, numbered XXI–LX. There was a New York edition by Braziller in 1977: here the translation used was that of George Moore. There was also a reduced-format edition of the illustrations together with Paul Turner's 1956 translation by Prestel, New York, in the Pegasus library, ca. 1994, with a reprint in 2000.[35] The 1961 edition is discussed at some length by Barber,[36] who notes that the illustrations started off as gouaches and took several years to evolve into lithographs. Many

[33] I have not been able to consult the biography of Max Schwimmer by Stuhr 2010.

[34] *Daphnis und Chloe. Longos. Ins Deutsche übertragen von Ernst R. Lehmann. Mit 27 Illustrationen von Eva Schwimmer.* Vollmer Verlag, Wiesbaden and Berlin 1959.

[35] The frontispiece of the 1990s Prestel edition bears no date.

[36] Barber 1989, 80–2: a very good discussion, but without illustrations.

figures that had already appeared, often more than once, in earlier works, were reworked into Chagall's illustrations,[37] and some were to be used yet again in the murals at the Lincoln Centre, which are only a little later. Like Bonnard, Chagall's favourite part of France was the Côte d'Azur: he died on 28 March 1985, at Saint-Paul-de-Vence, some twenty-five kilometres from Le Cannet, where Bonnard had spent his last years.[38]

Equally ambitious and successful is the illustrated edition privately printed in London in 1982 by Susan Allix – fifty-five copies of a translation by her husband Andrew Burnett, illustrated by twenty colour plates which, like the book's binding, were her own work.[39]

The last two editions known to me both reprinted Jacobs 1832 translation. In 1983 Artemis Verlag in Zürich and Munich published a duodecimo volume with a colour image on the cover and four etchings in the text, all by Salomon Gessner (1730–88): of these the first two (two ladies in a country setting, demure apart from their exposed breasts; Pan and Daphnis) are, unlike the third and fourth (a huge herm of Pan; Chloe alone), not at all related to the text.

A new approach was adopted by Karl Lagerfeld in 2014. In an exhibition in the Hamburg *Kunsthalle* (21 February–15 June 2014), devoted to Anselm Feuerbach and Karl Lagerfeld and entitled 'Feuerbach's Musen – Lagerfeld's Models', Lagerfeld displayed photographs of some of his fashion models posed and dressed (or not) as characters in *Daphnis and Chloe*, mostly shot in a wooded landscape (though Daphnis swims with just one cow in a lake or the sea). In association with the exhibition two books were published. One was a duodecimo reprint of Jacobs' 1832 translation with twenty-six photographs by Lagerfeld, all quite small, placed at points in the narrative that they illustrate, with a shot of a tree as a frontispiece and three portrait studies of his models at the end. The depiction of Daphnis and Chloe lying together naked after he has had his tutorial from Lycaenion (p. 97) is also printed on the dust cover.[40] The second book, also published in 2014 by

[37] He did a water-colour of a scene from *Daphnis and Chloe* in 1911: see www.wikiart.org/en/marc-chagall/daphnis-and-chloe-1911.

[38] For a juxtaposition of the two artists in the Phillips Gallery, Washington DC, see https://blog.phillipscollection.org/2012/12/17/congenial-spirits-chagall-bonnard-off-walls/.

[39] One illustration is reproduced in *Susan Allix: three decades of creative achievement: Artists' books: Calligraphy, poetry, letterforms, pop-ups: Modern fine bindings by living masters of the craft: Fine printing and private press books; printing on vellum*, Catalogue twenty-nine, Summer (2004), published by Joshua Heller Rare Books, Washington DC, 2004, in which 1–10 are devoted to Susan Allix.

[40] *Longus. Hirtengeschichten von Daphnis und Chloe.* Mit Fotografien von Karl Lagerfeld. Göttingen, Lagerfeld, Steidl, Druckerei Verlag, 2014. 152 pages.

Steidl, Göttingen, is a large-format collection of the photographs with a few snippets of text,[41] again in Jacobs' translation, entitled *Moderne Mythologie*: ninety-four (unnumbered) pages have thirty-five photographs: the first two, illustrating a 'prologue' entitled 'Der perfekte Körper is die Seele selbst', are portraits of Lagerfeld's model for Daphnis, while the last five (illustrating an 'epilogue' entitled 'Die Antike ist die Jugend der Welt') follow portraits of his models for Chloe and Lycaenion with three shots of woodland (one with an owl: cf. Longus 4.40.3).[42] Longus, whose narrator makes much of his narrative being based on a painting and of the importance of *mimesis* in learning skills, would have been amused that his own *mimesis* of a *mimesis* had been illustrated by photographs of real people in a real landscape.

3 The Table

The ten volumes tabulated (involving eleven artists, since Collin and Champollion both contributed to the 1890 Paris edition) do indeed have a number of favourite subjects for illustration, though as I earlier remarked there is a much greater diversity in their overall choices than I had expected. Not surprisingly, perhaps, elements in the story of Daphnis' lesson in love-making from Lycaenion tops the list (seven artists, nine depictions) – though not always the same elements. That is followed by Chloe bathing Daphnis and herself, their wedding night and Philetas' garden, each with six illustrations. The tally of high-scorers is as follows:

Daphnis and Lycaenion	seven (nine if depiction twice by two artists is counted)
Chloe bathes Daphnis and herself	six
Wedding night	six
Philetas' garden	six (if two depictions of Eros in the garden are included)
The vintage	five (six if both of Schwimmer's pictures are counted)
Echo	five or six
The second spring	five

[41] On pp. 11, 15, 33, 43, 47, 67 (Lycaenion's lesson), 71, 77 (the last chapter).

[42] Karl Lagerfeld, *Moderne Mythologie*. Göttingen, Steidle / Hamburger Kunsthalle, 2014. 94 pages, 38 × 30 cm.

Table 41.1 *Scenes chosen for illustration by Austen, Berg, Chagall, Collin and Champollion, Ellis, Maillol, Sadolin, Scheurich, Schwimmer, and Sintenis*

	Austen	Berg	Chagall	Collin/ Champollion[a]	Ellis	Maillol	Sadolin	Scheurich	Schwimmer	Sintenis
A youth lies reading				✓						
D and C lie (?) embracing				✓						
A syrinx[b]							✓			
D and C experiment					✓[c]					
D man-handles goat					✓[d]					
Book 1										
Nymphs						✓				
'Grove of Pan'	✓ bis									
A hilly landscape							✓			
A she-goat and D										✓
Lamon finds D		✓	✓					✓		
Lamon returns with D (?)				✓			✓			
Dryas finds C			✓	✓						
Lamon's and Dryas' dream			✓		✓?[e]			✓		
The first spring			✓		✓[f]				✓	
D and C cut reeds and asphodel						✓				
D and C bring the Nymphs garlands										✓
D pipes						✓				
D rides a goat	✓									
D and C stand embracing				✓						

The wolf-trap		✓	✓							
D gives C his *chitoniskos*										x
C bathes D and herself	✓?		✓			✓[g]	✓	✓	✓	
Dorcon courts C									✓	
A goat				✓						
C kisses D			✓	✓ (Ch)					✓[h]	
D after C's kiss							✓			
Dorcon's ploy										✓
Summer noon		✓?	✓							
D swims						✓				
D herds goats					✓					
D drinks milk gazing at C wearing a *nebris* and garlanded				✓ (Ch)[i]						✓
C garlands D?						✓				
D teaches C to play syrinx[j]		✓		✓ (Ch)	✓	✓				✓
D gazes at sleeping C		✓				✓	✓[k]			
Sleeping C					✓					
Swallow/cicada	✓?[l]		✓			✓			✓?	
Pirates abduct D										
Dorcon's death			✓							
C kisses Dorcon				✓						
C plays to sink the ship				✓						
D holds cow-horn and swims										✓
D and C bathe in nymphs' cave		✓	✓			✓	✓		✓	
D with a dog					✓					

Table 41.1 *(Cont.)*

	Austen	Berg	Chagall	Collin/ Champollion[a]	Ellis	Maillol	Sadolin	Scheurich	Schwimmer	Sintenis
Book 2										
D and C lie kissing				✓						
Vintage	✓	✓	✓						✓ *bis*	✓
Pithoi and altar							✓			
D and C cuddle after vintage	✓									
Philetas' garden		✓	✓					✓	✓	
Eros in Philetas' garden				✓						✓
D and C experiment						✓[m]		✓		
Philetas' lesson			✓	✓ (Ch)		✓				
Eros and bow										✓
Kid and lamb						✓				✓
D and C kiss/experiment						✓ *bis*[n]	✓	✓[o]		
Methymnan νέοι			✓						✓	
Goats and dog						✓				
D and Lycaenion?			✓			✓[p]				
D and C walk naked						✓				
Lamb nuzzles ewe				✓						
C pipes to D					✓					
D piping			✓							
C abducted	✓		✓			✓				✓
D distraught		✓		✓			✓			

Nymphs in D's dream			✓						
Methymnan boats anchored							✓	✓	
Methymnan armed men	✓[q]				✓[r]				
Bryaxis' dream			✓		✓[s]				✓
D and C reunited				✓		✓			
Sacrifice to Nymphs			✓						
Sacrifice to Pan				✓ (Ch)		✓	✓	✓	✓
Philetas and Tityrus									✓
Pan chases Syrinx			✓			✓			✓
Dryas' dance								✓	
D and C's ballet	✓	✓		✓					
D plays syrinx				✓					
D and goats in wood						✓	✓[t]		
D swears holding a he- and she-goat									✓
A syrinx							✓[u]		
C sleeps naked				✓					
Book 3									
D and C kiss					✓	✓			
D's winter walk				✓			✓	✓	✓ (D runs!)
D with cages	✓								
Bird-snaring		✓ *bis*	✓	✓					
Dryas' meal			✓			x			
Dog escapes with meat									✓

Table 41.1 *(Cont.)*

	Austen	Berg	Chagall	Collin/ Champollion[a]	Ellis	Maillol	Sadolin	Scheurich	Schwimmer	Sintenis
Second spring		✓	✓				✓*bis*		✓?	✓ *bis* (a foal and a he-goat!)
D and C kiss									✓	
Lycaenion snoops				✓						
D and Lycaenion		✓ *bis*	✓	✓ (Ch)		✓*bis*[v]	✓		✓	✓
Echo	✓?	✓?	✓			✓?			✓?	
Second summer			✓							
C naked by waterfall							✓			
C naked steps into stream				✓ (Ch)						
D and C embrace	✓[w]					✓				
D sits with a scythe, C stands					✓					
Goats						✓				
D and Dryas					✓?					
Dolphin and purse			✓							
D gives 3000 drachmae									✓	
Plougher with two oxen										✓
Gift of apple			✓[x]	✓ (Ch)		✓	✓			
D gropes C						✓				
D and C recumbent				✓	✓[y]					
C with a goat									✓	
C with rod				✓						

Book 4									
C naked			✓[z]						
D presents kid to master and mistress				✓					
D supplicates naked C				✓ (Ch)					
Nymph and satyr dance, a satyr plays on *auloi*	✓								
A royal garden			✓				✓		
Three Nymphs[aa]	✓								
Temple/altar of Dionysus			✓				✓		
Goats/a kid									✓
Lampis' aggression							✓	✓	
Trampled flowers			✓						
A calf									✓
Lamon distraught				✓					
C gives D piggy-back						✓			
Preparing for inspection						✓			
Astylus riding					✓?				✓
5 goat heads									✓
Dionysophanes arrives			✓						
Dionysophanes and Astylus				✓?[bb]					
Lamon and D receive Cleariste/ Dionysophanes		✓							
Gnathon and Astylus					✓				
Gnathon embraces D			✓		✓			✓	✓
D pipes to goats for Cleariste						✓		✓	

Table 41.1 *(Cont.)*

	Austen	Berg	Chagall	Collin/ Champollion[a]	Ellis	Maillol	Sadolin	Scheurich	Schwimmer	Sintenis
D recognised				✓					✓	
D runs away from Astylus				✓ (Ch)						
C herds alone				✓			✓			✓
C, Lampis and Gnathon (?)		✓							✓	
Megacles recognises C			✓							
Cleariste dresses and coiffes C			✓			✓?				
Wedding party by nymphaeum			✓		✓	✓?				✓
A goat										x
Wedding night		✓ to-rches	✓	✓ (Ch)		✓*bis*	✓[cc]		✓	
Three Nymphs				✓						

[a] In this column C indicates that the work is Collin's, Ch that it is Champollion's.
[b] Both frontispiece and end of preface.
[c] Before 'foreword' (i.e. preface).
[d] At end of foreword a goat sacrifice?
[e] But placed beside opening of Book 3.
[f] D with goat.
[g] C bathing is reproduced by Barber 1989, 78.
[h] Frontispiece.
[i] Placed between pp. 32 and 33, after Dorcon's death.
[j] Several illustrators represent the instrument as the double αὐλός, 'pipe', not the syrinx.
[k] C asleep near a sheep, focalised through D.

[l] Frontispiece (illustrated on this volume's front cover).
[m] Why here (p. 46)?
[n] Chosen as his front-cover picture by Barber 1989.
[o] At 2.37, but perhaps intended for 3.17? No illustrations are printed for Books 3 and 4.
[p] Why here (p. 64)?
[q] At the beginning of Book 2.
[r] One on a horse, so perhaps rather Astylus? But the placing suggests a Methymnan.
[s] Placed at start of Book 3.
[t] D and C looking from a wood at grazing beasts (mainly goats).
[u] As colophon.
[v] Pp. 100 and 104.
[w] Perhaps the frontispiece, with Daphnis and Chloe entwined in front of Pan's cult-image.
[x] Frontispiece.
[y] Focus on C's breasts: cf. 3.34.3.
[z] It is not clear why this illustration of a naked, recumbent Chloe was put here.
[aa] Title from list of illustrations (p. 19): placed opposite the description of the *paradeisos*.
[bb] A tall bearded older man flanked by a beardless youth, printed beside Dionysophanes' sacrifice. Perhaps an out of place Philetas?
cc Symbolised by musical instruments and stars.

Daphnis and Chloe bathe in a cave	five
Daphnis teaches Chloe to play the syrinx	five
The sacrifice to Pan	five
The wedding party by the Nymphs' cave	five
The swallow and cicada	four (if this is the subject of Austen's frontispiece)
Chloe's abduction	four
Daphnis' winter walk	four
Daphnis gives Chloe the apple	four
Gnathon and Daphnis	four

Many scenes are chosen by three of the ten illustrators in my table: Lamon finds Daphnis, Lamon's and Dryas' dream, the first spring, Chloe kisses Daphnis, Daphnis gazes at a sleeping Chloe, Philetas' lesson, Daphnis and Chloe kiss, Daphnis distraught, Daphnis and Chloe's ballet, Pan chases Syrinx, Dryas' winter meal, Chloe alone, Cleariste dresses and coiffes Chloe.

A few general observations may be made. First, Paris is by far and away the pre-eminent location for the production of illustrated editions, with London *longo, sed proximus, intervallo*. I realise that this perception may to some extent a result of a bias in the sources at which Barber, and I following Barber, have looked (and have known where to look). But Paris, especially in the nineteenth century, was undoubtedly the city in which both publishing and the visual arts flourished as in no other, so although I may have failed to dig up editions in Germany, Italy, Russia or Spain, I would be surprised to discover they were so numerous as to unseat Paris from its primacy.

Secondly, unlike Crispin de Passe the Younger in his illustrations for Marcassus' 1626 translation, these later artists choose subjects bearing upon the development of the couple's understanding of ἔρως much more than ones depicting their adventures. Moreover, unsurprisingly, the male artists are drawn to depictions of Chloe's adolescent or young adult body, often naked, whereas Daphnis is partly clothed: alongside Chloe bathing herself and Daphnis and the couple bathing in a cave there are several depictions of a sleeping Chloe less than fully clothed, and on occasion

Chloe's pose strikes the knowing viewer as sexually provocative in a manner and to a degree at variance with Longus' own representation of the couple's naivety.[43]

Again it is no surprise that these choices are made less often by Renée Sintenis, or that Sintenis, already known for her drawing and sculptures of animals and athletes, should scatter drawings of animals throughout the text and, departing from the French tradition, offer an athletic naked Eros (p. 38 of the 1941 edition) and some images of a naked Daphnis. In her woodcut of Daphnis drinking while gazing at a garlanded Chloe attention is as much on Daphnis and his clearly represented genitalia as on the demure and dignified Chloe who has only one breast exposed (1941 edn, p. 25); Sintenis alone depicts a naked Gnathon attempting to embrace a naked Daphnis (1941 edn, p. 105). Eva Schwimmer too prefers stylised and sometimes comic depictions of the female body (e.g. the woman at the vintage, p. 30) and her two largest figures are a naked and an almost naked Daphnis (pp. 15 and 91 respectively).

It is hard to determine what part gender, nation and period played in these differences, but it may be said that there was a French tradition, starting with Philippe d'Orléans, that found in *Daphnis and Chloe* a convenient text for sexually suggestive illustrations which offered artists yet another opportunity for depicting the young female body. Even Maillol was to some extent influenced by that tradition. Although he too has some woodcuts in which Daphnis is naked (p. 19, Chloe bathes Daphnis; p. 42, Daphnis and Chloe bathing; p. 67, a naked Daphnis strides behind a naked Chloe; p. 144, a depiction of a naked Daphnis fondled by another half-naked figure),[44] naked females, mostly Chloe, are more numerous; the image of Daphnis approaching a naked Lycaenion (as it seems) from behind and touching her left breast (p. 100) is both sexually suggestive and little related to anything in Longus' text.

A related phenomenon is the production of sets of images without any accompanying text at all. In Vollard's 1902 edition the majority of Bonnard's lithographs shared pages with at least a few lines of the text of Amyot's

[43] E.g. Champollion's (1890) etching (facing p. 32) of Daphnis drinking while gazing at a garlanded Chloe whose νεβρίς has fallen to her waist; Bonnard's 1902 lithograph of a Chloe who has just disrobed to bathe (illustrating 3.24.1 ἡ δὲ ἐν ταῖς πηγαῖς ἐλούετο, 'and she bathed in the springs'), on p. 67 of the (?1979) Mauersberger/Koch edition.

[44] The page references are to the 1977 Wiesbaden edition. The figure fondling Daphnis at p. 144 looks female, but its placing near the discovery of Daphnis' identity suggests it might be Clearisté (unless its small breasts mark it as a corpulent Gnathon?).

translation,[45] so a reader *had* to take account of both. But the 1961 Munich edition by Piper Verlag prints no text, only forty-eight of Bonnard's 151 lithographs, and Tériade's Chagall edition in the same year was so produced that sets of the forty-two lithographs could be bought and sold separately – as indeed they have been, e.g. at a Sotheby's sale on Tuesday 26 June 1990.[46] In the exhibition of Lagerfeld's photographs in the Hamburg *Kunsthalle* only short excerpts of text were offered to the viewer, as to the reader in his large-format *Moderne Mythologie*. As in the case of the paintings noted in the Appendix, the power of Longus' prose abides even when, like a Marxist Utopian vision of the state, the prose itself has withered away.

Appendix: Drawings and Paintings

Drawings

Four drawings, perhaps by Ambroise Dubois (1542–1614), and possibly first intended for the Cabinet de la Volière in Fontainebleau,[47] are now dispersed in four different museums:

1. Lamon hands the baby Daphnis over to his wife Myrtale, in the Art Institute, Chicago.
2. Dryas discovers Chloe in the cave of the Nymphs, in the Kestner Museum, Hanover.
3. Daphnis and Chloe sacrifice to Pan, in the Musée du Louvre, Paris.
4. Daphnis and Chloe spied on by Lycaenion, in the Musée Bonnat, Bayonne.

Paintings

1. Paris Bordone (Treviso 5 July 1500–19 January 1571), 'Daphnis and Lycaenion', oil on canvas, painted between 1555 and 1560. Height 139.1 cm, width 122 cm, in the National Gallery, London. Barber doubts that Bordone's painting represents this scene.[48]

[45] Not, admittedly, very many lines. E.g. the drawing of the pirate ship sinking as the cows career to one side shares p. 63 with '*épées au côté, leurs corselets aux dos, leurs bottines à mi-jambe, tandis que Daphnis étoit tout déchaux, comme celui qui ne menoit ses chèvres que dans la plaine, et quasi nu au demeurant; car il faisoit encore chaud. Eux donc, après avoir …*'.

[46] Copies of the catalogue are available from several bookshops.

[47] Cf. Béguin 1971, 35; Barber, 1989, 10. Barber seems to err in saying the fourth is in a private collection.

[48] Barber 1989, 10.

2. Adriaen van der Werff (Kralingen 21 January 1659–Rotterdam 12 November 1722), 'Daphnis and Chloe in a wooded landscape', oil on panel, ca. 1713. Height 40.4 cm, width 33.4 cm, in a private collection.
3. François Boucher (Paris 29 September 1703–Paris 30 May 1770), a half-naked Chloe reclines on Daphnis, with them five sheep and a dog, in the background an Italianate tower-building, oil on canvas, 1743. Height 110, width 155 cm, in the Wallace Collection, London.
4. Louis Jean François Lagrenée (Paris 30 December 1724–Paris 19 June 1805), Chloe, holding an apple, distances herself from a contemplative Daphnis, oil on panel, 1784. In a private collection.
5. Louis Hersent (Paris 10 March 1777–Paris 2 October 1860), (a) Daphnis extracting a thorn from Chloe's foot in a cave, shown in the *Salon* of 1817. The incident does not occur in *Daphnis and Chloe*, but has been grafted onto it from the well-known sculpture of a boy extracting a thorn from his foot (*Lo Spinario*), (b) Daphnis teaches Chloe to play the double *aulos* (not, as in Longus, a syrinx), a dog at his feet and two goats behind, against a wooded and mountainous background, in the Musée du Louvre.
6. François Gérard (Rome 5 April 1770–Paris 2 November 1837), Chloe kneeling with her head on the lap of Daphnis, who holds a garland; in the background are water and trees, oil on canvas, 1824. Height 204 cm, width 228 cm, 1824, shown in the *Salon* of 1825, in the Musée du Louvre.[49]
7. Eugène Emmanuel Amaury-Duval (Montrouge, Hauts-de-Seine, 1808–Paris 1885), an early pupil of Ingres. An oil painting of *Daphnis and Chloe* now in the Musée des Beaux Arts, Saint-Étienne, shown in the *Salon* of 1865. He also wrote the preface for an edition of the Amyot translation accompanied by forty-three illustrations by Léopold Burthe, J. Hetzel, Paris, 1863 (see above p. 829).
8. Jean-François Millet (Gruchy, Gréville-Hague 4 October 1814–Barbizon 20 January 1875), 'Le Printemps (Daphnis et Chloé)', a half-naked Chloe, kneeling, feeds nestlings in a nest held by on his knees by a seated Daphnis,[50] a huge herm of Pan behind them, oil on canvas, 1865. Height 235.5 cm, width 134.5 cm, in the National Museum of Western Art, Tokyo.

[49] See Barber 1989, 60–62, Moulin 1983. Gérard had earlier, in the 1790s, worked on illustrations for a translation of Longus, see p. 828.

[50] Presumably the nestlings from the hills that were among Dorcon's courtship gifts to Chloe, 1.15.3.

9. Jules Joseph Lefebvre (14 March 1836–24 February 1911), a naked girl by a pool, entitled *Chloe*, done in Paris in 1875: the model was a 19-year-old baker's daughter, Marie. *Chloe* was exhibited in the Paris *Salon* that year and Lefebvre was awarded the Gold Medal of Honour. It then went on exhibition to Australia in 1880, and was bought at auction in 1882 by Thomas Fitzgerald, who sold it to Henry Young in 1908. It now hangs in Young and Jackson's bar in Melbourne, Victoria. That Lefebvre had Longus' Chloe in mind is probable, given the number of other visual representation of Longus' novel at the time, but far from certain.
10. Jean-Eugène Buland (1852–1926), Daphnis and Lycaenion, oil on canvas, 1880. Height 140.3 cm, width 99.7 cm, in private ownership.[51]
11. Pierre Bonnard (1867–1947), a naked young woman (Chloe or Lycaenion?) against a wooded background, presumably done when he was working on the lithographs for his illustrated edition ca. 1900–1901 (see p. 829–30), oil on cradled canvas. Height 38.4 cm, width 37.5 cm, in private ownership.[52]
12. Maurice Denis (Granville November 25, 1870–Paris November 1943), Chloe bathes naked in a river, Daphnis watches, perched on an overhanging branch of a tree, ca. 1900.[53] Location unknown.
13. Rodolfo Amoedo (Salvador, Bahia, December 11, 1857–Rio de Janeiro May 31, 1941), Philetas instructing Daphnis and Chloe, oil on canvas. Museu Nacional de Belas Artes, Rio de Janeiro.
14. Marc Chagall, a pastoral painting of a scene from *Daphnis and Chloe*, water colour, 1911. Height 16.5. cm, width 21 cm: see www.wikiart.org/en/marc-chagall/daphnis-and-chloe-1911. In private ownership.

[51] Suggested date 1880.
[52] It is oil on cradled panel, height 38.4 cm and width 37.5 cm.
[53] The model may be Marthe Meurier, whom he married in 1893.

42 Λέξεις Λόγγου (2019)

1 Introduction

This paper has two principal objectives. The first is to give a flavour of the post-classical vocabulary in Longus' artistic prose and to see at what literary level the range of authors with whom he shares such vocabulary locates him. The second is to see whether any of his choices of words might help us to get nearer to determining the date at which he was writing. This second objective is perhaps unattainable, for reasons that I shall address when I reach that part of the chapter, but it seemed to me worth trying to see what could be done.

The first objective cannot be achieved by attention to vocabulary alone, or even to vocabulary considered with some attention to a word's syntactical behaviour, as I shall sometimes be offering. A much wider investigation would be needed, taking in forms of verbs, declension of nouns, the uses of cases and of prepositions, etc. An investigation on that scale, which would vastly exceed the space available, was last conducted for Longus by G. Valley, in his Inaugural Dissertation.[1] This paper builds upon Valley, and hopes to be more useful than his work in at least one respect: Valley very rarely gives precise references for the places in other texts in which he found words or grammatical and syntactical features also found in Longus. That makes it maddeningly difficult to check whether modern editions of these authors do indeed have the word or usage also found in Longus, and whether it is indeed closely parallel, or rather involves differences that could be significant.

The issue of modern editions also affects the Longan end of our calculations. Valley justly complained that his work on Longus was hampered by the absence of a reliable critical edition. Since Reeve's Teubner that complaint cannot be voiced.[2] But problems and choices still remain for anybody conducting an investigation like this. Thus, although Morgan 2004 generally accepts Reeve's text in his excellent edition and commentary, Henderson 2009 sometimes makes different decisions, as do I in Bowie 2019g.

[1] Valley 1926. [2] Reeve 1982.

I take just one example. Valley 1926, 15, notes that at 2.29.3 Longus uses the nominative δελφίν instead of the classical form δελφίς. δελφίν is indeed the MS reading in the *Laurentianus*, **F**; but **V** has δελφίς, as do both MSS of Longus at 3.28.2, and Reeve is surely right to print δελφίς at 2.29.3. This is one of very many cases where the scribe of the *Laurentianus* shows himself – or his source – to be slovenly, imprecise and apparently quite ready to write down what was in his head rather than what he saw. That should alert us to the possibility that some, perhaps many, post-classical forms in our manuscripts have come into the tradition by corruption.

2 The Literary Level of Longus' Prose

The first main section of this chapter assembles some lexical evidence for Longus' literary aspirations. It says nothing of the many respects in which he succeeds in writing Attic Greek, sometimes making choices which were also approved by Atticist lexicographers: but it documents, albeit selectively, his use of words that he almost certainly could not have found in a classical Attic author, or even in Homer or Herodotus, but that may have been known to him from post-classical literary texts, from non-literary texts, or from the spoken Greek of his time.

A Some Words That Are **Hapax Legomena**, *or Are Not Found in Extant Literary Texts before Longus*

1. ἀλωνοτριβεῖν, 'work on the threshing floor', 3.29.1: only here and in the *Suda* α 1385. The word may well have been current in spoken Greek: cf. ἀλωνοφυλακεῖν, 'to guard a threshing floor', *P.Cair.Zen.* 745.86 (third century BC), and ἀλωνευόμενος, 'threshing', *Suda* α 1383 (documenting its use by App. *Mac.* 13).
2. ἐγκόμβωμα, 'jacket', 2.33.3: a term first found not in a literary text but in Poll. 4.119, who explains it as an outer garment worn by slaves over an ἐξωμίς, 'one-sleeved tunic', to keep it clean. It is found later in Basil of Caesarea, *Enarratio in prophetam Isaiam* 3.125 (on *Isaiah* 3.20) and in Hsch. *s.vv.* κοσύμβη κ 3774 and κοσσύμβη/κόσσυμβος κ 3780, 'shepherd's cloak'.
3. ἐμπαροίνημα, 'object of drunken lust', 4.18.1: the word appears again only again only in Nicetas Choniates, *Man. 1* p. 171 line 22 and Joannes

Cinnamus, *Epitome* p. 183 line 3 (cf. πρωτοφορήματα, 3.12.2, below no. 5). But the use of the verb ἐμπαροινεῖν, 'to behave drunkenly', in J. *Ap*. 1.8, *AJ* 6.12.7, Luc. *DDeor*. 8.4, *Tim*. 14 cautions against concluding the noun to be a neologism by Longus, or emending to παροίνημα, the MSS reading at 4.19.5 (which Jungermann wanted to emend to ἐμπαροίνημα on the basis of its use at 4.18.1).

4. κυνόδεσμος, apparently 'dog-leash', 2.14.3: the masculine κυνόδεσμος appears only here in Greek literature, but the existence of the slang terms κυνοδέσμη (Phryn. *PS* 85 de Borries) and κυνοδέσμιον (*v.l.* in Poll. 2.171) – for a cord used by human males, particularly athletes, to tie up the foreskin or penis – suggests that the literal sense 'dog-leash' may well have been current at some level. As often, a reader is uncertain whether Longus saw (and perhaps welcomed) the likelihood of the slang usage competing with a literal reading here.
5. πρωτοφόρημα, 'first product', 3.12.2: only here before the twelfth century, when it is used by Constantine Manasses, *Breviarium Chronicum* 79, and by Nicetas Choniates, *Or*. 12.114 (cf. no. 3 ἐμπαροίνημα); but Ath. 13.565f has the verb πρωτοφορεῖν.

It seems likely, but is not demonstrable, that all the above words were known to Longus from spoken Greek or from non-literary Greek texts. The same is perhaps true for the form ὁμογάλακτος.

6. ὁμογάλακτος, 'one nursed at the same breast', 4.9.3. It is unclear whence Longus gets this nominative singular form ὁμογάλακτος, since in its other appearances (Arist. *Pol*. 1252b18, Philoch. *FGrH* 328 F35a and b, and several others) the accusative plural is ὁμογάλακτας. Perhaps Longus encountered the word in a lexicographer and mis-formed the nominative singular; or perhaps this form was current in the *koinē*, since it appears as a gloss in Hsch. *s.v.* ἀγάλακτες α 260 and in the Byzantine legal text Βασιλικά 25.5.20 and 48.2.11. It is also possible that Longus in fact wrote ὡς <ἐφ'> ὁμογάλακτος, using the correct Attic genitive.

Likewise Longus' literal use of the term χειραγωγία, 'leading by the hand', may be drawn from spoken Greek.

7. χειραγωγία, 4.12.3: this is our first literal use of χειραγωγία in literature; it is already used metaphorically in Max. Tyr. 9.4 Trapp (if indeed Maximus writes earlier than Longus). It is also found in a documentary text *BGU* 1768.1, and in Σ Eur. *Or*. 663. The noun χειραγωγός, 'guide', 4.24.2, is first used literally by *Act.Ap*. 13.11 or Plu. *An seni* 21 = *Mor*.

794d,[3] cf. Philostr. *Her.* 51.5; and first metaphorically by Plu. *De fort.* 3 = *Mor.* 98b.[4] The verb χειραγωγεῖν, 'lead by the hand', 1.21.5, appears only in post-classical Greek (first in the *Septuagint*), usually metaphorically, of physical or spiritual guidance. Longus seems to play with this metaphor in his unusual literal use (cf. his game with ἐκθηριώσας, 'turned himself into a wild beast', 1.20.3), for which the closest parallel is *Anacreont.* 1.9–10 West: τρέμοντα δ' αὐτὸν ἤδη |Ἔρως ἐχειραγώγει, 'And since he was by now unsteady (sc. an aged Anacreon) Eros was leading him by the hand'.

There are some other words in this category which it may be more likely that Longus knew from a literary text now lost to us.

8. εὐωρία, 'joys of spring' (Morgan 2004), 'letizia della stagione' (Pattoni 2005), 1.9.2: first here in extant literature, then in Lib. *Ep.* 434.4, though its existence is perhaps implied by the verb εὐωριάζειν ([A.] *Pr.* 17 conj. Porson, Soph. fr. 561). The sense 'freedom from care' is the only one noted by the *Suda* ε 3628 *s.v.*, whereas Hsch. ε 7319 glosses it ὀλιγωρία, ἀμέλεια: Photius' lexicon gives both the senses τὸ μὴ πάνυ φροντίζειν, 'not to give any thought to', ε 2382, and ὀλιγωρία, 'neglect' or 'negligence', ε 2381; εὐωρία also appears with the sense 'freedom from care' in a magical papyrus, *Sammelbuch* 4324.7.
9. κορυμβοφόρος, 'berry-bearing', 2.26.1: first here in extant literature, but its use by Nonnus in Dionysiac contexts (e.g. *D.* 14.311; 24.102) may well draw on a lost Hellenistic hexameter or elegiac poet.
10. παταγή, 'clap', 1.22.2: **V** has χειρὸς παταγῆι, 'cracking of the hand', which is printed by Vieillefond 1987 and Pattoni 2005; **F** has χειροπλαταγῆι, 'handclapping'; Cobet proposed χειρὸς πλαταγῆι, 'clapping of the hand', which is printed by Reeve 1982, but with the note that **V**'s χειρὸς παταγῆι might be right. παταγή is found at D.P. 574 (in a maritime context: note the proximity of τῆς θαλάσσης in Longus 1.22.2).
11. προσκαταγέλαστος, 'ridiculed besides', 2.19.2: Ath. 11.508b and Jul. *Or.* 6.182b (conj.) have the verb προσκαταγελᾶν, 'to ridicule besides'. Reeve 1982 retains the verbal adjective προσκαταγέλαστοι, which appears nowhere else in Greek literature; Cobet had proposed reading πρὸς καταγέλαστοι, 'in addition, ridiculed'.

[3] I take the *Acts of the Apostles* to be the earlier of these two texts, but some might think differently.

[4] Against the authenticity of Philemon fr. 127 Kock, cited by LSJ, see K-A VII p.317.

12. ῥινηλασία, 'hunting by scent', 1.21.2: found in *Anon. Lond.* ἰατρικά 33 and 34, then in a late paraphrase, perhaps by Eutecnius, of [Opp.] *C.* 9.3. The *Suda* ῥ 173 offers it as a gloss on ῥινολαβίς, 'nose-gripper'. But ῥινηλατεῖν, 'to track by scent', used by Longus 2.13.3, is already in Aes. *Ag.* 1185, cf. Soph. *Ichn.* 88; ῥινηλάτης Poll. 2.74, Opp. *H.* 2.290.
13. ὠρυγμός, 'howling', 2.26.1, 30.3: in Poll. 5.86, Ael. *NA* 5.51 (and *v.l.* at Theoc. 25.227). But Maccius 8 *GP* = *AP* 6.233 could coin (?) the form ὤρυγμα.

B *Words and Usages First Found in Post-Classical Literary Texts*

A large number of words and usages are post-classical, and, if Longus knew roughly the same range of texts known to us, would be likely to carry for him and for his more educated readers the flavour of philosophical or historiographic writing of the Hellenistic and Greco-Roman periods with few or no aspirations to Atticism. I arrange these in the chronological order of the authors in which we first find them, partly because those that appear only at the end of the chronological sequence might be argued to have some bearing on my second question, Longus' date.

1. *Words first in Epicurus*
   ἐξολισθαίνειν, 'slip and slide', 2.28.3: a post-classical form (first in Epicur. *Ep.* 2 p. 45 Usener) for the classical ἐξολισθάνειν. Cf. ἀπωλίσθαινε, Plu. *Alc.* 6.1.
2. *Words first in (?) Chrysippus*
   ἀνατροφή, 'nurture', 1.11.1: post-classical, always of rearing young. Perhaps in Chrysipp. *Stoic.* fr. 234, quoted by Origen *Cels.* 3.69, and fr. 1139, quoted by Gal. *UP* 1.14.4; but first securely in D.S. 32.15.2, then Plu. *TG* 8.4, etc., Arr. *Cyn.* 29, Artem. 1.16 (p. 25.15 Pack), and often in Soranus. Longus may use it because he does not want to repeat τροφή, 'nurture', a fifth time.
3. *Words first in Callixeinus of Rhodes*
   ἁλιτενής, 'projecting into the sea' 2.12.3: the word appears first in Callix. *FGrH* 627 F1, applied to a ship, in the sense 'of shallow draught'; then in this sense in Posidon. *FGrH* 87 F73 (= Str. 17.827), D.S. 3.44.
   ἐπιλήνιος, 'of the vintage', 2.36.1: Callix. *ap.* Ath. = *FGrH* 627 F2, p.170.11 Jacoby.
4. *Words first in Aristophanes of Byzantium*
   ἀρτιγέννητος, 'new-born', 1.9.1: a favourite word of Longus (also 1.18.1, 2.4.3; probably 1.15.3), and, after a first appearance in Arist. Byz. fr. 204

Slater, found only in post-classical Greek: 1 *Peter* 2.2, (later quoted by Clem. Al. and Origen), Luc. *Alex.* 13, 14, *DMar.* 12.1.

5. *Words first in Polybius*
ἀγερωχία, 'boisterousness', 2.4.2: Plb. 10.35.8, later D. Chr. *Or.* 32.9 (the Alexandrian oration, of the insolent self-assertiveness of Cynics), Philostr. *VA* 2.28 (in the plural, meaning 'acts of bravado').[5]
ἀσκόπως, 'aimlessly' 4.31.1: Plb. 4.14.6, and with a negative (as here) first at J. *BJ* 3.53 (later *AJ* 2.2.3); then from the second century onwards in technical writing (e.g. Cleom. *De mot. circ.* 190.14), but not in high literature.
ναυαρχίς, 'flagship', 2.28.2: Plb. 1.51.1.
6. *Uses first in Polybius*
ἀλύειν 1.28.2, in the sense of purposeless wandering: Plb. 26.1.1, D. Chr. *Or.* 7.79, Plu. *TG* 21.6, Luc. *DMar.* 13.1, Philostr. *Her.* 6.2. (though here there is possibly an echo of Achilles at Il. 24.12).
βάλλεσθαι, 'construct', of fortifications, 3.2.4: Plb. 3.105.10.
βαστάζειν, in the sense 'purloin', 1.3.1: Plb. 32.15.4.
ὡς ἔνι μάλιστα, 'to the best of his ability', 1.20.3: Plb. 21.4.14; later Luc. *Prom.es* 6, Hld. 7.11.14 etc.
ἀνακτᾶσθαι in the sense 'cause to recover', 2.18.1: first in Plb. 3.60.7, cf. D.Chr. *Or.* 7.7, Arr. *Epict.* 3.25.4.
λοιπόν (without the article), 'henceforth', 1.7.2 etc., is poetic (e.g. Pi. *P.* 1.37) until Plb.
ξενίζειν 4.26.3 in the sense 'be strange or unfamiliar': Plb. 3.114.3, Gal. xvii.1 162 Kühn, Luc. *Anach.* 16, *Merc.cond.* 24, *Hist.conscr.* 25.
7. *Uses first in the Septuagint*
ποίμνιον, of a single beast, *pr.* 2; 1.8.3 etc.: 1 *Kings* 25.2, 1 *Ep.Pet.* 5.2; cf. *IGSK* 33.120 (fourth century AD).
8. *Words first in Philodemus*
προσεκκαίειν, 'further inflame', 4.161: a post-classical compound, cf. Phld. *Lib.* p. 21 O., J. *BJ* 3.9.6, Plu. *Quomodo adulat.* 19 = *Mor.* 60e περὶ τοὺς ἔρωτας, 'concerning (their) love-affairs'.
9. *Uses first in Parthenius*
προσρεῖν, 'rush towards' (in form of aor. part. pass. προσρυείς) with a personal subject, 4.19.1: Parth. *Erotopath.* 7.1 (Lightfoot 1999 does not discuss). This use continues in imperial writers: Plu. *Brut.* 16.2, cf. *Amat.* 16 = *Mor.* 760a, Philostr. *VS* 2.30, Luc. (?) *Am.* 8, perhaps taking authority from the absolute use at Men. *Dysc.* 225 προσερρύη.

[5] Note however the long poetic pedigree of ἀγέρωχος, discussed by Bowie 2017a (Chapter 40 in this volume, 801).

10. *Words first in Cicero*
παλιγγενεσία, 'rebirth', 3.4.2: Cic. *Ad Att.* 6.6.4; then (if he is later) Memnon of Heracleia *FGrH* 434 F40.2.

11. *Words first in Nicolaus of Damascus*
τυροποιεῖν, 'make cheese', 3.33.1: *FGrH* 90 F104 (unless Str. 3.169 was written earlier).

12. *Words first in Diodorus Siculus*
ἀνατροφή: see 2 under Chrysippus.
παιδευτήριον, in the sense '(source of) school(ing)', 2.9.1: first in D.S. 13.27.1, cf. Str. 4.181 (both writers alluding to παίδευσιν 'school', at Th. 2.41.1); later Jul. *Or.* 9.182b Bidez. The sense of παιδευτήριον at 2.9.1 is nearer to 'lesson' than to 'school'.
περίκηπος, 'adjacent garden', 4.19.4, 28.2, 29.4: this sense is first found in literature in D.S. 34/35.2.13 (whose content, but not necessarily vocabulary, comes from Posidon., cf. *FGrH* 87 F108), though it appears earlier in documents (e.g. *P.Cair.Zen.* 193.8, third c. BC); cf. later D.L. 9.36.
διορμίζειν, 'moor', 2.25.2: D.S. 20.88, then Hierocl. p.56 von Arnim.

13. *Phrases and forms first in Diodorus Siculus*
ἡμέρας γενομένης, 'at daybreak', 4.9.3: D.S 20.86,109, Jos. *BJ* 6.141, Plu. *Agis* 31.1, etc.
ξυρᾶν, 'shave', 4.10.1: ξυρᾶν (here ξυρώμενος, a participle found elsewhere before the third century only once in Plu.; then in Origen) replaces Attic ξυρεῖν in later Greek, cf. D.S. 1.84, Artem. 122, Luc. *Cyn.* 14, *v.l* at [Plu.] *Reg. et imp. apophth., Alex.* 10 = *Mor.* 180b.
πεφρόντισται, 'it has been decided', 2.23.3: πεφρόντισται as the passive of φροντίζειν is a post-classical use, always as here in the perf.; cf. D.S. 15.78, 16.32, Ael. *NA* 7.9, Philostr. *VS* 1.11.496 and for the adverb πεφροντισμένως, D.S. 12.40.

14. *Words first in Dionysius of Halicarnassus*
ἀνακλητικός, of a tune used by a goatherd to recall his flock, and for different types of syrinx music, 2.37.3; 4.15.3: this sense is classical for the verb ἀνακαλεῖν, cf. Pl. *R.* 440d3, but the adjective is not attested until post-classical Greek, where ἀνακλητικὸν σημαίνειν in a military context means 'to sound a retreat', D.H. 8.65.6, Ch. 8.2.6, and (of a hunt) Ch. 6.4.9; cf. metaphorically Lucill., *AP* 11.136.5 σάλπιγξον ταχέως ἀνακλητικόν, 'quickly sound the call for retreat'. Longus may have constructed his use by analogy with such instances rather than on the basis of any knowledge of herders' tunes specific to recalling goats.

δεξίωσις, 'greeting', 4.5.2: D.H. 5.7.4, then often in Philo and Plutarch.

15. *Words first in Strabo (?)*
    ὁμοφώνως, 'in unison', 3.21.2: first securely Str. 9.411, later Plu. *Galb.* 5.
    ὀψήματα, 'honeyed cakes', 3.5.3: ὀψήματα (and not, as our MSS of Plato read, ἑψήματα), may have been in Longus' text of Pl. *R.* 372c7 (the diet of primitive citizens reclining on στιβάδες, 'beds of straw'); cf. ὀψίματα in the MSS of Plu. *Quaest. conv.* 4.1.3 = *Mor.* 664a. If not, then its first appearance is at Str. 7.311, in the sense 'delicacy'.
    κρημνοβατεῖν, 'cliff-walk', 2.28.3: Valley 1926, 65, asserts that the word appears first in Str. (i.e. 15.710), but apparently it was in Ctes., *FGrH* 688 F63 (*ap.* Lyd. *Mens.* 4.14); the noun κρημνοβάταν, 'cliff walker', describes Pan in *AP* 9.142.1 (= *FGE* 1424, anon.).
16. *Words first in Philo*
    ἀγελάρχης, 'leader of the flock', 2.31.2.[6] ἀγελάρχης and cognates are frequent in Philo, twenty-three instances in all (e.g. ἀγελάρχης, *Leg. ad Gaium* 20, 76; ἀγελαρχεῖν, 'to lead a group', *De somniis* 1.255, 2.153). All these uses are metaphors or comparisons, as are those of ἀγελάρχης at Plu. *Rom.* 6.4, *Milet* vi.2 596 ('imperial'), ἀγελαρχεῖν (at Plu. *Galb.* 17.7), and ἀγελαρχία, 'leadership of a group' (*IGR* iii 648.14–16 = *TAM* ii 838.14–16, ca. AD 134), the equivalent at Idabessus to ἐφηβαρχία, 'leadership of the ephebes'.

    Although this evidence points to the metaphorical use of ἀγελάρχ- terms gaining currency in the first century AD, the first use of the image may have been that by the Pythagorean writer Hippodamus p. 101.10–11 Thesleff = Stob. 4.1.95.18, excerpted from Ἱπποδάμου Πυθαγορείου ἐκ τοῦ Περὶ πολιτείας, 'the work of Hippodamus the Pythagorean *On government*': διὸ δεῖ τὼς νομοθέτας καὶ τὼς ἀγελάρχας ἐπιμελῶς παρατηρεῖν …, 'so legislators and leaders of communities should attentively watch …'. The date of Hippodamus, however, remains uncertain: he might be Hellenistic or early imperial.

    Literal uses are rare, e.g. Luc. *Am.* 22, of a ταῦρος, 'bull' (the *Suda* α 183 *s.v.* ἀγελάρχης also specifies bovines); but ΔΙΕΛΑΡΥ may be read as <ἀ>γέλαρ<χ>(ος) (or ἀγελάρχης) on the Nile mosaic at Praeneste, ca. 140–120 BC, see *SEG* 45.1452.

    Longus' literal, pastoral use of a word more often used metaphorically is a humorous touch.

[6] In Bowie 2019c, 108 it is wrongly stated that ἀγελάρχης was a term first found in Plutarch, an error repeated at Bowie 2019g, 209; in both places it is also wrongly said that at [Luc.] *Am.* 22 its use was metaphorical.

ἀθήρατος, 'impossible to catch', 2.4.3: only here in the novelists, and not found before Ph. *Spec.* 3.44, *Virt.* 40.1; cf. [Opp.] *C.* 1.514, Ael. *NA* 1.4; 5.6 in the sense 'not caught'.

ἐνθαλαττεύειν, 'stay at sea', 2.12.5: Ph. *Immutat.* 98 (= 1.287), later Poll. 1.137, Clem. Al. *Paed.* 2.22, Ael. *NA* 9.63.

17. *Words first in Josephus*
ἐκπυρσεύειν, 'inflame', 1.15.1: literally in J. *BJ* 4.10.5, 5.169.3, 7.8.5, etc.; metaphorically (as here) in S.E. *M.* 11.179.
προσστερνίζεσθαι, 'clasp to one's breast', 4.23.2: not found before J. *AJ* 2.9.7, cf. Sor. 1.106, Poll. 2.162, Σ Theoc. 3.48, *SEG* 34.1259 (a flowery lament preserved on stone at Claudiopolis, Bithynia, first century AD).

18. *Forms first in Josephus*
γαληνότερος, 'calmer' (comp. of γαληνός), 2.25.2: γαληνός is poetical (esp. Eur.) until Pl. *Ax.* 370d. It appears in the novels only here and Hld. 3.3.7; its comp. first appears in J. *BJ* 1.28.2.

19. *Uses first in Josephus*
ἀνευφημεῖν, 'proclaim (Pan's) power', 2.29.2: a late use of the verb, cf. of gods X.Eph. 5.13.3, Ach. Tat. 3.5.6, Hld. 2.27.1; of men J. *BJ* 4.2.5, Ch. 7.3.11, Hdn. 6.4.1.
οὐκ ἀσκόπως, 'not aimlessly', 4.31.1: positive first in Plb. 4.14.6 (see on Plb., 5), but the first use with a negative is at J. *AJ* 2.2.3.
The expression (μιᾶς) χρόνον ἡμέρας, 'space of a (single) day', 2.39.1: cf. J. *AJ* 9.22; *BJ* 2.39.1.
ὑπερηφανεῖν, 'scorn', with acc. and inf., 4.19.5: first J. *AJ* 4.8.23. Apart from the participle ὑπερηφανέοντες at Il. 11.694, the verb (also at 3.30.5) is post-classical: LXX *Ne.* 9.10, Plb. 6.10.

20. *Uses first in Cornutus*
ἀποκοσμεῖν, 'disfigure', 4.7.2: Corn. *ND* 30; later J. *AJ* 16.8.5, Aristid. *Or.* 43.39 Keil, Paus. 7.26.9, D.C. fr. 102.9.

21. *Words first in either Philip of Thessalonica or [Apollodorus Mythogr.]*
ἐπισκέπειν, 'cover over', 1.21.3: *AP* 6.62 (= Philip 11 *GP*), [Apollod.] 1.6.2.

22. *Uses first in Chariton*
δέησις, 'request', 2.33.1: the use with προσφέρειν is late; cf. Ch. 7.6.9, Ach.Tat 7.13, and (with ποιεῖσθαι) Luke 5.33.

23. *Uses first in [Apollodorus]*
μνηστεύεσθαι, 'court', with man as the subject, 3.25.4: [Apollodorus] 2.5.12, J. *AJ* 4.8.23, [Plu.] *Narr.am.* 4.1 = *Mor.* 774e. Condemned by

Luc. *Sol.* 9, but used by him at *Merc.cond.* 23, *Tox.* 27; also in [Luc.] *Asin.* 26.

24. *Uses first in Leonides of Alexandria*
περιττότερος, in the sense 'more than': a favourite usage of Longus, e.g. περιττότερα τῶν αἰγῶν κινούμενος 'who used to be more restless than his goats', 1.17.4, cf. 2.12.4; 3.11.1, 13.3, 20.1, 21.1, 31.2. The nearest I can find elsewhere is in the mid-first century AD poet Leonides of Alexandria, *AP* 6.321 (= *FGE* 1867) θύσει τοῦδε περισσότερα, 'will sacrifice more than he': but cf. already Pl. *Ap.* 20c τῶν ἄλλων περιττότερον πραγματευομένου, 'being more busy than the rest'.

25. *Words first in Plutarch*
γόμφωμα, of a structure (here a boat) fastened by γόμφοι, 'pegs', 2.26.2: a late word, Plu. *Marc.* 15.6, *De fort.Rom.* 9 = *Mor.* 321d, Vett.Val. 334.11.
ἡμιθωράκιον 'half-cuirass', 1.28.1, 30.3: a light armour said by Poll. 1.134 to have been developed by the fourth-century tyrant Jason of Pherae. *IG* ix.1^2 1.3.40 = *Syll.*[3] 421.40, however, shows the term already in use in Aetolia in the third century BC, cf. *SEG* 40.524 B.1.7 from Amphipolis ca. 200 BC. It is not attested in literary texts, however, before Plu. *De gen.Soc.* 30 = *Mor.* 596d (then Polyaen. 4.3.13).
προσλιπαρεῖν, 'keep close to', 1.10.1: e.g. Plu. *Aem.* 23 7, *De mul.virt.* 3 = *Mor.* 245b–c.

26. *Uses first in Plutarch*
αἰφνίδιον, 'suddenly', 2.25.3: this adverbial use of the neuter appears first in Plu. *Num.* 15.1, though the adjective αἰφνίδιος is Thucydidean (2.61.3, 8.14.1).
ἐπείγειν, of an activity or season that is pressing or imminent, 2.1.1: [Plu.] *Consol. ad Apoll.* 14 = *Mor.* 108 f.
εὐτυχεῖν, 'have the good fortune to', with inf., 1.11.2, 4.19.4, 35.5: Plu. *De Alex.fort.* 1 = *Mor.* 333d.

27. *Forms first in Plutarch*
δεδηιωμένον, 'devastated', 4.7.5: the verb is used by classical historians (e.g. Th. 1.81.1), but only here in the novels; the perfect participle passive is found only in imperial Greek: here, Plu. *Arist.* 10.6, Luc. *DMort.* 20.11, Hdn. 8.5.4, Lib. *Or.* 17.19, Theodoret *Interpr. in xii prophetas minores*, lxxxi 1641.51 Migne, and in scholia and lexica.

28. *Words first in the New Testament*
νεκρούμενος, 'becoming a corpse', 2.7.5: first in *Epist. Rom.* 4.19, cf. Gal. xi 265 Kühn, xviii.1 156 Kühn, M. Ant. 7.2, and the aorist νεκρωθείς,

IG xiv 1976 = *GVI* 1169 = Kaibel 642 = *IGUR* iii 1321 (Rome, third or fourth century AD).

29. *Uses first in the New Testament*
σεσοφισμένος, in passive sense, 'cleverly devised', 1.11.2: *2nd Ep.Pet.* 1.16.
30. *Words first in Babrius*
ἐφαπλοῦν, 'unfold over', 1.20.2: Babr. 95.2, Sor. 2.11, Orph. *A.* 457, 1336, Hierocl. *in CA* 21 p. 467, Nonn. *D.* 15.9.
31. *Uses first in Dio of Prusa*
στεφανοῦσθαι, 'be crowned with', with gen., 2.26.2: D. Chr. *Or.* 9.10, cf. Philostr. *Her.* 35.9.
32. *Words first in Galen*
πρωτόρρυτος, 'first-flowing', 3.18.2: Gal. xiii 626 Kühn, [Opp.] *C.* 4.238.
33. *Forms first in Pausanias*
εὐαγγελίζετο, 'he brought good news', 3.33.1. Other tenses in middle and passive are found in several imperial texts, e.g. Ch. 2.1.1, and often in Hld. The imperfect middle appears here and in Paus. 4.19.5.
34. *Some words shared with Lucian*
ἀποβάθρα, 'a gangplank', 2.28.3: rare, but found at Hdt. 9.98.2 and Th. 4.12.1, a passage picked out for comment by Demetr. *Eloc.* 65 and paraphrased by Plu. *De glor. Ath.* 3 = *Mor.* 347b (where ἀποβάθρα is conjectured); according to lexicographers (e.g. Hsch. α 6250) in Soph. (fr. 415 Radt). Then Ach. Tat. 3.3.1; Polyaen. 4.6.8; Paus. 10.25.3; nine times in Luc. (e.g. *DMort.* 20). Listed by Poll. 1.93 and used by him at 10.134, it is prescribed as Attic by Phryn. *PS* 1.9 de Borries; later Hld. 1.18.3. Perhaps an Attic term that caught the attention of later-second-century Atticisers.
ξενίζειν, 'be strange', 4.26.3: cf. under 6, Polybius; perhaps a *Lieblingswort* of Lucian noticed by Longus.
τραγοσκελής, κερασφόρος, 'goat-legged, horn-bearing', 2.24.2 (of the cult-statue of Pan): these are regular attributes of Pan in the visual arts, cf. Borgeaud 1979, *LIMC*; τραγοσκελής is already found at Hdt. 2.46.2 αἰγοπρόσωπον καὶ τραγοσκελέα; the epithets appear together at Luc. *DDeor.* 2.2, κερασφόρος at *Bis acc.* 9.
35. *Words first in Sextus*
σεμνολόγημα, 'boast', 2.32.3: S.E. *P.* 3.200; Hld. 9.22.7; D.C. 50.27.2, 53.7.4, 72.4.4; Lib. *Decl.* 15.1.8; widespread in late antique and Byzantine Christian texts.

36. *Uses first in Sextus*
 ὀνειροπολεῖσθαι, 'dream', in the middle (the active is classical) 3.9.5: S.E. *M.* 8.57.
37. *Words first in Athenaeus*
 λινοστατεῖν 2.13.3: Ath. 4.219d (metaphorical), referring to Pl. *Smp.* 219d, where the word is not in fact used; then [Opp.] *C.* 4.64. The noun λινοστασία appears first in Leonidas, *AP* 7.448.2 (= *HE* 12.2), then Archias, *AP* 6.16.2 and 179.2 (= *GP* 4.2 and 5.2), 9.76.6 (Antipater Thess.); later Agathias (*AP* 9.766.6), Iulius Diocles (6.186.6).
38. *Words first in Philostratus*
 ὑπανθεῖν, 'begin to bloom', 3.12.1,[7] 4.8.1: its first use in another literary text is by Philostr. *Imag.* 1.31.2 (ὑπηνθηκέναι). Poll. 1.60 and 2.10 show its currency at some level: Poll. 1.60 specifically relates it to spring (ἦρος ὑπανθούσης, 'when spring begins to bloom'), the context of Longus 3.12.1. Perhaps both Poll. and Longus knew a literary text (or texts) in which it had already appeared, but to my mind the constellation of appearances in Poll., Longus and Philostr. *Imag.* suggests that it might be a word coming into vogue late in the second century AD.
39. *Words shared with Cassius Dio*
 μόλις ποτέ, 'only just', 2.24.3: Eur. *Ion* 383, *Hel.* 396; Th. 7.40.3; Men. *Dys.* 684, *Sam.* 493; Plu. *Pel.* 8.5, 11.6; D.Chr. 7.56; 11.107; Luc. *Nec.* 12, *Rh.Pr.* 5 (ποτὲ μόλις); D.C. 5.18.11, 36.30.2, 40.17.2, 48.41.6, 48.43.6, 54.16.6, 57.4.3, 63.25.2, 65.5.3; Hdn. 3.15.2 Aristid. *Or.* 48.6 Keil (= *Sacred Tales* 2.6). Cf. μόγις ποτέ Pl. *Prt.* 314e2, *Lg.* 798a5. μόλις is naturally much used for cliff-hanging scenes by the novelists: twenty-three times by Ch., four by X.Eph. (adept at missing tricks), thirteen by Ach. Tat., and twelve by Hld.
40. *Words shared with Heliodorus alone among the novelists*
 ἀνεύρεσις, 'recovery', 4.28.3: Hld. five times (4.5.7, 33.3, 6.4.2, 7.2, 9.24.4).
 λυμαίνεσθαι, 'damage', 4.1.1: Hld. ten times (3.8.2, 18.2, 4.10.3, 11.3, 7.3.4, 8.1.4, 9.13, 9.6.5, 18.2, 10.16.7).
41. *Uses first in Himerius* (!)
 προξενεῖν, in the sense of 'find a bride for', 3.26.3: Him. *Or.* 1.11.

[7] ὑπανθούσης **V**: ἐπανθούσης **F**. At 2.30.3 both MSS have ἐπανθήσασαν.

C Some Conclusions about the Literary Level of Longus' Prose

What I have set out above constitutes only a sub-class of the much more numerous cases of vocabulary and usage that Longus shares with authors of the Hellenistic and Greco-Roman periods, most of whose attention is directed to their content and not to their style. Longus does himself often Atticise, but much less consistently than other Atticising writers of the late second and early third centuries. What Valley wrote about his literary models can also be said of his linguistic choices:[8]

> Longus ist ein Eklektiker. Wie eine emsige Biene sammelt er seinen Honig aus den Werken der älteren Dichter und Prosaiker. Mit einer sophistischen Kunst, wie sie wohl nie höher gestiegen ist, fügt er das verschiedene zusammen ...

In some respects, then, Longus' linguistic behaviour can be seen as analogous to that of Chariton. As Ruiz Montero and Hernández Lara have shown,[9] Chariton's vocabulary matches that of several writers of the first century AD; but though writing in a period when Atticism was gaining strength, and may well have been prominent in some places and for some individual writers, Chariton himself does not follow this path. A century and a half later Longus is writing in a world where some lexicographers and sophists both preached and attempted to practise hard-core Atticism; but Longus blends Atticist and Hellenistic usage without apparent concern.

3 Language and Date

Can any arguments about the date at which Longus was writing be constructed on the basis of the words he uses that first appear (above **2** B32, 34, 35, 37, perhaps 38) in late second- and early third-century authors? I must admit that the hard-headed answer is 'no!' These words may have appeared earlier in literary texts that have not survived; and even if they did not, we cannot tell whether (a) their first use was by Galen/Lucian/Pausanias/Athenaeus/Philostratus, and Longus derived the word in question from them, or (b) it was indeed Longus who got there first. If Longus is writing after Pausanias, as I have once argued,[10] then it is only in the case of **2** B38 and perhaps 37 that Longus might be the first to use the word in a literary text; and even there we have seen that for 38, ὑπανθεῖν, its appearance in

[8] Valley 1926, 79. [9] Ruiz Montero 1991; Hernández Lara 1994.
[10] Bowie 2001c (Chapter 12 in Volume 3).

Pollux may be due to his knowing it from an earlier literary text. But an impressionistic response to these data might be different. The presence of a cluster of words attested for the first time, together with the great enthusiasm for μόλις ποτέ shown by Cassius Dio, and the absence (so far as I have been able to determine) of words in Longus that are first attested in later third-century writing (e.g. in Iamblichus or Porphyry) suggest to me that Longus' lexicon points to his time of writing as having been the 220s or 230s AD.

43 Animals, Slaves and Masters in Longus' *Daphnis and Chloe* (2019)

1 Introduction

This chapter examines the presentation of animals, slaves and masters in Longus, *Daphnis and Chloe*.[1] As has often been observed, Longus miniaturises the scenario familiar from the other four 'ideal' novels in a number of ways. He shrinks the geographical frame to the island of Lesbos, and indeed most of the action takes place on a rich man's estate some twenty-four miles north of Mytilene, with Chloe briefly carried off a few more miles north by a Methymnan fleet. It is a corollary that the effects achieved by other novelists through exploitation of spatial change are replaced by the impact of time: the reader encounters the couple as new-born babies, and is asked to contemplate how their maturation in an unsophisticated environment affects their slow and naïve discovery of sex. Longus also shrinks the cast: for most of the action the couple encounter only each other, their foster-parents, and five other members of the small rural community where they grow up (Dorcon, Philetas, Tityrus, Lycaenion, Lampis). At the same time he moves his cast's social centre of gravity. In the other novels the hero and heroine know that they are from an elite, and most people they encounter are also in varying degrees wealthy or powerful, whereas slaves or servants play only a supporting role, albeit sometimes an important one. But until, in Longus' last book, Daphnis and Chloe discover that each is the child of a Mytilenean aristocrat, exposed at birth and brought up by a goat-herding and shepherding family respectively, their rural society is (with only one clear exception) a society of slaves. Finally, and for this paper fundamentally, into the vacuum left by the kaleidoscopic range of human characters who populate the other four novels Longus introduces animals.

[1] I am grateful for the comments and suggestions made by audiences who heard an oral version of this chapter – first in Rethymno at RICAN 2013; then at Brown University, Providence, RI; the Classical Association of South Africa at Cape Town; the University of Leeds; the University of Illinois at Urbana-Champaign; Florida State University; and the classical seminar at Corpus Christi College, Oxford. I am also very grateful to the organiser of that seminar, Daniel Jolowicz, for discussing many points and for letting me see chapters of his excellent doctoral thesis (Jolowicz 2015, now Jolowicz 2021), which puts the issues I raise in a much wider context. This paper develops my shorter paper 2005a, which is accordingly not printed in this volume.

2 Animals

This introduction of animals is partly attributable to a generic crossing that Longus' work implements:[2] with the prose narrative romance of adventure he has blended Theocritean pastoral poetry,[3] where the central characters are shepherds and goatherds, with the occasional cowherd, and their animals are always there and a focal point of their day-to-day lives.

Of course animals had played a part in Greek literature ever since the earliest texts that survive. In Homeric epic their relation to the main action can be threefold:

(a) Animals can be actors in the poem, like the other two major classes of animate beings, men and gods. The most common such animal is the horse, essential to the style of chariot-warfare Homer depicts, but on one memorable occasion exploited, contrary to nature, to predict Achilles' death (Il. 19.404–18). But in the *Iliad* birds of prey have a part too, both as omens and as the threatened devourers of slain warriors, as do dogs, who are likewise scavengers (e.g. 22.68; 24.411), but are also guards and table-companions (22.69). Fish eat corpses too (Il. 21.203–4, 222–3; Od. 14.135, 24.291). The different milieus of the *Odyssey* reduce the role of horses and advance that of dogs. Odysseus' faithful hound Argos has a cameo scene, and Eumaeus' dogs help construct a realistic picture of an animal-rearing economy in which we naturally find pigs, cattle, sheep and goats. The *Odyssey* also has a place for predatory, wild animals – wolves which attack flocks, and the boar which gored the macho young Odysseus (Od. 19.447–51).

(b) In the *Iliad* we find a much wider range of animals used for comparison than as actors in the poem. These comparisons are mostly similes, in which warriors are compared to lions, boars or wolves, and their destined victim is compared to these animals' prey. Occasionally the comparison is oblique: Achilles insults Agamemnon by saying he has 'the eyes of a dog and the heart of a deer' (κυνὸς ὄμματ' ἔχων, κραδίην δ' ἐλάφοιο, Il. 1.225).

(c) Animals may appear neither as real actors nor as objects of comparison but simply in the imagination, as when Penelope dreams that an eagle has killed her twenty geese (Od. 19.535–53).

The predominance of domesticated animals in the *Odyssey* is matched in Hesiod's *Works and days*, where animals also have a fourth role, as actors

[2] For aspects of this crossing see Bowie 2013d (Chapter 37 in this volume).

[3] For Longus' use of Theocritus see Bowie 2021b.

in an animal fable, that of the hawk and the nightingale (202–12). Such morally instructive tales in which animals can be seen to stand for humans were also part of the archaic sympotic repertoire: we find this story-form, the *ainos*, being exploited by Archilochus,[4] and later in Attic *skolia*,[5] and it is clear that a corpus of such fables was already attached to the name of Aesop by the fifth century. Meanwhile the possibilities of explicit comparison of humans to animals had been devastatingly exploited, also in a sympotic context, by Semonides in his character-assassination of various types of wife (fr. 7).[6]

So brief a sketch is bound to distort, and any generalisation is likely to be in some way false: but overall the predominant role of animals in these texts is as comparisons or as allegories of human behaviour, and their appearance as actors is much less common.

Fifth-century Attica adds an important variant: animal-choruses in Old Comedy, like animal fable, present us with animals playing human roles, but also offer the poets an opportunity to develop at length colourful details of the chosen creatures' physiognomy or habits.

With Theocritus we find a crucial shift which is taken further by Longus. In his pastoral poetry humans remain centre-stage, but since that stage is not simply rustic but usually pastoral, the poet augments the realism of his picture by a recurrent focus on animals (as well, of course, as on flora). So, although in Theocritus the Homeric animal simile is still deployed (e.g. 7.41, a frog competing against grasshoppers), animals who appear in their own right are more numerous, e.g. those mourning Daphnis in the song of Thyrsis (1.71–5).

Longus, and probably his target readership, knew all these texts I have mentioned, and doubtless many others lost to us. In setting out the landscape in which the story of Daphnis and Chloe is set, and in exploiting various types of intertextuality with canonical authors, Longus' choice of animals and of the parts they are called upon to play makes an important contribution to guiding the reader's interpretation of his work.

Not surprisingly, there is a long list of animal characters: forty-six terms describe animals, covering forty species.[7] Although several are not to be found in Homer, almost all are somewhere in archaic elegy, iambic or melic, with a few names of birds added by Aristophanes.

[4] The fox and the eagle, frr. 172–81, the fox and the ape, fr. 185–7.

[5] E.g. *carmina convivalia* 892 *PMG*: cf. Ar. *V.* 1289.

[6] For the sympotic context see Osborne 2001.

[7] See the table in Bowie 2005a. As rightly pointed out by Kossaifi 2012, 575 n.12, both discussion and table unaccountably omitted the φάττα, 'wood-dove', into which the defeated cow-girl is metamorphosed in the *mythos* told at 1.27.

The most common animals, those that are constant companions to Daphnis and Chloe, and that can always be imagined in their pastoral landscape even when not specifically mentioned, are sheep and goats. In Longus' preface (*pr.* 2) they are simply termed ποίμνια, 'grazing animals', but thereafter they are specified time and again as sheep and goats, beginning with the points at which Lamon and Dryas find Daphnis and Chloe respectively. The dominant model here, as so often, is Theocritus, whose first *Idyll*, probably the opening of a collection Longus knew, introduced a ποιμήν, 'shepherd', and an αἰπόλος, 'goatherd', together with their flocks. Homer had occasionally paired goats and sheep: Il. 1.66 (though here the sheep are ἄρνες, 'lambs'), 10.486, 23.383. But more often he linked one of these two species with other animals (e.g. bulls, Il. 1.41; pigs 11.678). Longus' choice of almost symmetrical presentation of sheep and goats of course suits his almost symmetrical presentation of Daphnis and Chloe, but it also underlines his use of Theocritus.

Longus mentions cattle almost as frequently as sheep and goats. We first discover that they too are herded on Dionysophanes' estate when Chloe summons a βουκόλος, 'cowherd', initially unnamed, to help her rescue Daphnis from the pit dug to trap a predatory wolf (1.12.3). Dorcon's entry prompts readers to reflect that Longus' Daphnis differs from the Daphnis of Theocritus in *not* being a cowherd but a goatherd, and that Longus has diverged from the dominant Theocritean pattern in locating his cowherds, goatherds and shepherds in the same chronological frame.[8] By contrast, in Theocritus it seems from *Idylls* 1 and 7 as if Daphnis and the cows he herds belong to a time that for the main characters is the distant past. That impression is not contradicted by the two young cowherds in poem 6, Daphnis and Damoetas, who seem to inhabit world that is timeless.

This is not, however, the most important function of cows or cowherds in Longus. The cowherd Dorcon's greatest contribution is to offer a pattern of conventional sexual pursuit, including courtship, that throws into relief the untutored mutual feelings of Daphnis and Chloe, and that encourages readers to worry that further erotic threats may await Chloe. The greatest contribution of Dorcon's cows is to save Daphnis when he is captured by pirates (1.30–31). This passage late in Book 1 revives the impression of its opening chapters that in this work animals will not just be background décor: they will make important contributions to the development of the plot.

[8] On Longus' demotion of the cowherd from his high status in Theocritus see Bowie 2019h (Chapter 44 in this volume).

That had also been made clear in the middle of Book 1, the point at which Eros gives the maturing children's playtime a serious twist, 1.11.1:

> τοιαῦτα δὲ αὐτῶν παιζόντων τοιάνδε σπουδὴν Ἔρως ἀνέπλασε. λύκαινα τρέφουσα σκύμνους νέους ἐκ τῶν πλησίον ἀγρῶν ἐξ ἄλλων ποιμνίων πολλὰ ἥρπαζε, πολλῆς τροφῆς ἐς ἀνατροφὴν τῶν σκύμνων δεομένη ...
>
> And as they played in this way Eros fashioned the following serious turn: a she-wolf, nursing young cubs, was snatching many animals from other flocks in neighbouring fields, since she needed lots of food to feed her cubs ...

The key figure, placed prominently at the start of the first, asyndetic narrative sentence, is a λύκαινα, 'she-wolf'. She comes as a shock. The pastoral background so far has been dominantly Theocritean, even if its animals are familiar from many earlier texts. That was also true of the description of spring at 1.9, to which I shall return. The λύκαινα breaks this pattern. Whereas λύκοι, 'male wolves', are well established in all classes of text, a λύκαινα is a rarity. Only later will the reader perceive one reason for this choice: this λύκαινα, a threat to Daphnis and Chloe's herds, is a forerunner of the sexually predatory Lycaenion, whose long-term contribution to the couple's sexual fulfilment is vital, as is that of the λύκαινα, but who for a short time seems a possible threat to their future happiness.

But at 1.11.1 that is still to come. At this point Longus may be playing two games with his introduction of a λύκαινα. One is that of casual and opportunistic parody. The greatest of epic stories, the Trojan War, was often seen as having its start in the misdemeanour of Helen, sometimes simply described as ἡ Λάκαινα, 'the Laconian woman'.[9] Longus asks us (as in some other places) to set his erotic narrative alongside that of the Trojan war. But the she-wolf also raises other spectres. Some readers may have known the story of the child Miletus raised by a she-wolf, a story told near to Longus' time by Antoninus Liberalis.[10] But many more surely know the story of Romulus and Remus suckled by a she-wolf,[11] and may indeed have thought of it when Longus began his story with the animal fostering of Daphnis and Chloe. If they had decided then that Longus himself had not thought of this Roman myth, the she-wolf of 1.11 might encourage them to think again. This is a point to which I shall return.

Less threatening, it would seem, is the next animal to advance the plot: the τέττιξ, 'cicada'. The τέττιξ first appears as part of the tableau of the first

[9] E.g. Eur. *Tr.* 34, 869. [10] Ant. Lib. 30.1, according to the manchette taken from Nicander.

[11] See below p. 881.

summer at 1.23. In a vivid picture that ranges through trees, crops, apples, rivers and winds, the flocks and the τέττιγες are the only real *animals*, however animated these other entities may be in Longus' presentation. He might have been tempted to include the τέττιξ in his picture of spring (1.9), but he will have known that it is only prominent in the heat of later months, so instead he has reserved it for an important summer-season performance. In a scene often chosen by artists in illustrated translations of Longus a τέττιξ, trying to escape from a pursuing swallow, takes refuge in Chloe's bosom, and thus gives the no longer quite innocent Daphnis a reason to plunge his hand between her breasts to extract it. Longus does not comment on the implication for the advance of the couple's sexual awareness, but he does include this in the 'pleasures' of summer,[12] and the knowing reader can see this as a further step in the couple's slow discovery of Eros. A sexual reading of the incident is encouraged by the probable literary ancestry of Longus' summer-singing τέττιξ. Whereas in Homer and Pratinas the τέττιγες had been figures for human beings,[13] and in Callimachus and Theocritus they were either palmary singers against whom humans might be matched or decorative background noise,[14] Longus' summer scene set in the Mytilenean *chora* with an active τέττιξ will recall to educated readers two passages in a different tradition – a very well-known poem of Alcaeus in which he reworks Hesiod, *Works and days* 582–96.[15] Outbidding Hesiod's characterisation of women as μαχλόταται, 'most wanton' (586), in the summer heat, Alcaeus describes them as μιαρώταται, 'dirtiest' – his men, by contrast, are λέπτοι, 'delicate', and Hesiod's ἀφαυρότατοι, 'weakest' (586). The reader schooled in Hesiod and Alcaeus will observe that by contrast here, as often, Chloe is the more passive and Daphnis the more active partner. We are reminded of this scene later when Longus mentions catching τέττιγες among the pleasures of the second summer (3.24.2). The active role accorded to τέττιγες by Longus puts them discernibly in a Hesiodic and Alcaic tradition.

[12] τέρψεις, 'pleasures', 1.28.1; cf. ἔτερψεν '(sc. a wood-dove) pleased them', 1.27.1.

[13] Il. 3.151; Pratinas fr. 709 *PMG*.

[14] Singers against whom humans might be matched, Call. *Aet.* fr.1.30, Theoc. 1.148; as decorative background, Theoc 7.139.

[15] τέγγε πλεύμονας οἴνῳ, τὸ γὰρ ἄστρον περιτέλλεται, | ἀ δ' ὤρα χαλέπα, πάντα δὲ δίψαισ' ὐπὰ καύματος, | ἄχει δ' ἐκ πετάλων ἄδεα τέττιξ ... | ἄνθει δὲ σκόλυμος, νῦν δὲ γύναικες μιαρώταται | λέπτοι δ' ἄνδρες, ἐπεὶ < > κεφάλαν καὶ γόνα Σείριος | ἄσδει, 'Wet your lungs with wine, for the star is coming round, and the season is hard, and everything is thirsty because of the heat, and the cicada sings sweet songs from the leaves ... and the artichoke is in flower; and now the women are most dirty and the men are delicate, since Sirius parches their heads and knees ...', fr. 347(a). For discussion of the possible location of this poem's first performance see Bowie 2009a, 118–19 (Chapter 13 in Volume 1, 298–9).

By comparison Longus' use of the ἀκρίς, 'cricket' or 'grasshopper', is more conventional. An ἀκρίς is first introduced in Chloe's despairing monologue at 1.14: she will die of her undiagnosed disease, and then who will look after the ἀκρίς which she had caught with great effort and whose song now lulled her to sleep (1.14.4)? ἀκρίδες then reappear shortly in the matching description of Daphnis' symptoms – he who had been more voluble than ἀκρίδες was now taciturn (1.17.4). That these ἀκρίδες are chiefly there as part of the Theocritean pastoral furniture had already been made clear at 1.10.2, when Chloe's spring amusements include making a cricket trap or cage, recalling that being constructed intently by the boy on the cup in Theocritus 1.52.[16] The couple's hunting of a ἀκρίδες again contribute to their innocent play in the second summer (3.24.2). Although ἀκρίδες are there linked with τέττιγες their role in the novel is much less significant.

Longus' next important animal actor is the dolphin. When Pan moves against the Methymnans who have abducted Chloe, a night of terror is followed by a day even more fearful (3.26.1): the miracles include dolphins πηδῶντες ἐξ ἁλός, 'leaping out of the sea', striking the ships with their tails, and shivering their timbers (3.26.2). Then, when Chloe is released, the Methymnan fleet begins to sail back to Methymna before the anchors have been weighed, the leading ship guided by a dolphin πηδῶν ἐξ ἁλός, 'leaping out of the sea' (3.29.3). Part of Longus' strategy is to construct a miracle that in several respects recalls that in the *Homeric hymn to Dionysus*. It is also true that there were many dolphin stories in canonical texts,[17] so that unlike several of Longus' animals the dolphin was just as familiar to readers as an agent it was as a *comparandum*. That said, the dolphin must join the she-wolf, cows and cicadas as participants with an important role.

A reader is likely to embark on Book 3 with the expectation that again animals will play an important part. Longus meets that expectation in a surprising way. When Longus brings in an older woman to educate Daphnis in the ἔργα ἔρωτος, 'acts of love', we discover her name to be Λυκάινιον, Lycaenion (3.15.1). For a moment we wonder if the she-wolf of 1.11 has reappeared, then we realise that this female is wholly human.[18] But animals are important here too. In a passage that recalls Penelope's dream of an eagle

[16] In both places the MSS offer the alternatives ἀκριδοθήρα, 'grasshopper trap', and ἀκριδοθήκη, 'grasshopper cage'. For a reason for preferring ἀκριδοθήκη see Bowie 2019g, 115 on 1.10.2.

[17] E.g. Archil. fr. 192 (Coeranus), Hdt. 1.23–4 (Arion, precisely of Methymna!). For the relation between dolphins and Dionysiac cults in the archaic and classical periods see Kowalzig 2013.

[18] We may also wonder whether the name Lycaenion has anything to do with the comic mask called λυκαίνιον noted by Longus' near-contemporary, the sophist and lexicographer Pollux 4.150. For a full discussion of wolves, animal and human, in Longus see Epstein 1995.

killing her twenty geese (Od. 19.535–53), Lycaenion pretends to Daphnis that an eagle has carried off the finest of *her* twenty geese and has been forced by its weight to come down in the adjacent wood (3.16.2–3). Like Penelope's eagle, this αἰετός, 'eagle', is imaginary, but a fiction rather than a dream. Again, as so often in Longus, a creature most familiar to readers in similes (though it also figured in omens) has been represented as an agent.

The second half of Book 3 again hinges on animal intervention, this time once more a real animal. But as if to show his capacity for ποικιλία, 'variety', Longus now presents not a live but a dead animal, once again a dolphin. Like the previous dolphins, this too has a connection with the Nymphs. In danger of losing Chloe to richer suitors, Daphnis dreams that the Nymphs appear to him and tell him that a purse containing 3000 drachmae is to be found on the shore near the rotting corpse of a dolphin (3.27.2–5). The stink of the rotting animal makes his task easy, and he rushes first to Chloe and then to her father Dryas with the god-sent silver (3.28.1–3).

The book's close switches back to imagined animals. In an eloquent speech to Chloe in which he praises the apple that is both a symbol for Chloe herself and a gift to her, Daphnis explains that he could not leave it to fall to the ground where it might be destroyed: ἵνα πέσηι χαμαὶ καὶ ἢ ποίμνιον αὐτὸ πατήσηι νεμόμενον ἢ ἑρπετὸν φαρμάξηι συρόμενον ἢ χρόνος δαπανήσηι, 'so that it (sc. the apple) might fall on the ground and either a grazing beast might trample it or a slithering monster might poison it or time might waste it' (3.34.2). In this densely allusive passage the ποιμένες ἄνδρες, 'shepherd men', that trample the hyacinth in one of the lines of Sappho which Longus evokes have become grazing animals, ποίμνια;[19] the unspecified monster with which Sappho once compared erotic desire[20] has by its slithering movement, συρόμενον, become identifiable as a potentially phallic snake.[21] That Daphnis imagines his rivals for Chloe, for whom the apple stands, not as humans but as animals tells us something about Daphnis. We may recall that one of the couple's failed attempts at the sexual act involved imitation of the position taken up by their animals (3.14.5),[22] and we shall later hear Daphnis rejecting the homo-erotic advances of

[19] οἵαν τὰν ὐάκινθον ἐν ὤρεσι ποίμενες ἄνδρες | πόσσι καταστείβοισι, χάμαι δέ τε πόρφυρον ἄνθος …, 'like the hyacinth that shepherd men trample with their feet, and on the ground the dark red flower …', Sapph. fr. 105(c). For Sappho's wider impact on imperial Greek literature see Bowie 2021a.

[20] γλυκύπικρον ἀμάχανον ὄρπετον, 'bitter-sweet, uncontrollable monster', Sapph. fr. 130.2.

[21] For fuller discussion of the intertextualities in this important passage see Bowie 2013d, 187–91 (Chapter 37 in this volume, 750–4), 2019g, 256–9.

[22] Cf. Gnathon's point at 4.17.7.

Gnathon partly on the grounds that animals' behaviour shows this to be unnatural (4.12.2). But that animals and humans walk on the same stage also coheres with the overall texture of Longus' work.

That texture changes a little in Book 4. Its first animal seems to relocate Longus' writing in the mainstream Greek tradition: Lampis, attempting to wreck the prospects of Daphnis' marriage to Chloe, vandalises the carefully-ordered garden of Dionysophanes which is in Lamon's care, and in doing so is compared to an animal often found in earlier similes, a boar: τὰ δὲ κατεπάτησεν ὥσπερ σῦς, 'he trampled it down like a pig' (4.7.3). This is one of Longus' very few conventional animal similes introduced by ὥσπερ, 'just as', or a similar word, and like his earlier comparison of humans with ψᾶρες ἢ κολοιοί, 'starlings or jackdaws' (2.17.3), refashioning Il. 16.583,[23] it invites us to contrast the rustic events in his miniature work with those on an epic battlefield.

Book 4's next animal is also an intruder: both Astylus and his parasite Gnathon visit the estate on horse-back (4.10.1). Horses have only appeared once so far, not in the countryside but in Mytilene, when a force of ἵππων πεντακοσίων, '500 cavalry', is called up alongside ἀσπίδα τρισχιλίαν, '3000 infantry', and sent out against Methymna under the command of the significantly named Hippasus. In both places the horse symbolises male aristocratic ostentation and the power of the πόλις, and the evocation of Sappho's contrast of cavalry and infantry with the object of one's desire nudges us to compare what is important to Dionysophanes with what is important to Daphnis and Chloe.[24] We hear of horses once more, when Dionysophanes and his retinue return to the city ἵπποις καὶ ζεύγεσι καῖ τρυφῆι πολλῆι, 'with horses and carriages and much luxury' (4.33.2).

But just as Daphnis and Chloe's visit to the city is merely temporary, and their attachment to their country abode is reasserted, so too the epic and city animals give way once more to sheep and goats. In a remarkable scene Daphnis demonstrates to Cleariste the musical skill of his goats, who can respond to different tunes on his panpipe (4.15.2–3). Longus stresses the animals' anthropoid behaviour by saying in his authorial voice that οὐδὲ ἀνθρώπους οἰκέτας εἶδεν ἄν τις οὕτω πειθομένους προστάγματι δεσπότου, 'not even human slaves could be observed to be so obedient to their masters'

[23] Achilles is compared to a falcon routing κολοιούς τε ψῆράς τε, 'jackdaws and starlings'. Homer's use of the form ψῆρας here but the genitive ψαρῶν at Il. 17.755 attracted the attention of Hellenistic scholars, cf. A. Gell. *NA* 13.21.

[24] οἰ μὲν ἰππήων στρότον, οἰ δὲ πέσδων | οἰ δὲ νάων φαῖσ' ἐπὶ γᾶν μέλαιναν | ἔμμεναι κάλλιστον, ἔγω δὲ κῆν' ὄτ|τω τις ἔραται, 'some say a force of cavalry, some of infantry, and some of ships is the fairest thing across the black earth, but I say it is that which one desires', fr. 16.1–4.

(4.15.4).[25] Here again animals are given a role as important a human beings, and one that prompts the reader to reflect on the servile relation between Daphnis and Chloe and the other members of their pastoral community on the one hand and their urban master Dionysophanes on the other. We may remember that at 3.26.4 Myrtale, Daphnis' mother, had encouraged him to think that Chloe would rather sleep with a handsome but poor Daphnis than with a πιθήκωι πλουσίωι, 'a rich ape'.

The permeable boundary between humans and goats resurfaces in the very next chapter. The former glutton Gnathon confesses he no longer takes pleasure in expensive food: ἡδέως δ' ἂν αἲξ γενόμενος πόαν ἐσθίοιμι καὶ φύλλα τὰ Δάφνιδος ἀκούων σύριγγος καὶ ὑπ' ἐκείνου νεμόμενος, 'but I would rather be a goat eating grass and leaves if it meant listening to Daphnis' panpipe and being tended by him' (4.16.3). Even the city *flaneur* has succumbed to the idea of imitating animal behaviour.

The closing chapters once more set goats on an equal footing with humans. They are pastured close to the wedding party – something not welcome to the city guests – and Daphnis calls them by their names, feeds them and even kisses them (4.38.4). The swapping of roles between men and goats continues in Longus' vignette of the happy future awaiting Daphnis and Chloe: they will have children who will also be suckled by a goat and a sheep, and ἐκάλεσαν τὸν μὲν Φιλοποίμενα, τὴν δὲ Ἀγέλην, 'they called the boy Philopoemen and the girl Agelē' (4.39.2). Both these names perpetuate the obliteration of the boundary between herdsfolk and their animals. Agelē, 'flock', is a good name for an animal, less so for a girl;[26] Philopoemen, 'loving the shepherd', picks out the quality of an animal, not of its ποιμήν, though unlike Agelē it is well established as a personal name, especially in the Peloponnese.

3 Slaves and Masters

The servile shepherds have been shown to be obedient to their masters; the relationship of the animals to their goatherd, Daphnis, has emerged as analogous to that of Daphnis and his fellow-slaves to their masters. How are these slaves and masters presented?

[25] The most common use of πρόσταγμα, 'command', in the imperial period is of divine commands executed by erecting an altar etc., κατὰ πρόσταγμα θεοῦ, 'by the command of the god': but it is also used of commands issued by mortal superiors, cf. e.g. *IGBulg* iv 2236.67 for προστάγματα of imperial commands (Pautalia/Scaptopara, Thrace, AD 238).

[26] But Agelē does appear as a name: *FdD* iii 6.8 (servile, Delphi, 20–46 AD); *SEG* 37.454.23 (servile, Thessaly, second–third century AD); *ISmyrn.* 505 (status unclear, Smyrna, imperial);

Longus uses three terms for slave: οἰκέτης, 'house-servant', a more polite term, glossing over servile status, than the unambiguous term δοῦλος, 'slave'; and θεράπων, 'attendant' (with the feminine θεράπαινα, also 'attendant'). The sense of οἰκέτης, 'house-servant', overlaps with that of θεράπων, 'attendant', though θεράπων could in theory refer to non-servile servants. The term οἰκέτης appears only once before Book 4, at 2.12.1, where it refers to the Methymnan youths' slaves who row their pleasure boat – more an illustration of how οἰκέτης had long functioned as a primary term for a slave in an urban context than a game played by Longus with the idea that house-servants are rowing a boat. The appearance of the term θεράπων is delayed until 4.23.1, where θεράποντες, 'attendants', are among the crowd that rushes up to congratulate Daphnis on his recovery of his elite identity: these are surely the same people, or some of the same people, who were called οἰκέται, 'house-servants', at 4.13.1. So too the θεράπων, 'attendant', who passes round Chloe's tokens at 4.34.3, is hardly distinguishable in status from an οἰκέτης, 'house-servant' – though his description as θεράπων, 'attendant', may stem from his function at this point. Perhaps οἰκέτης, 'house-servant', yields in Book 4 to the term θεράπων, 'attendant', because in this Book, especially in the latter half, the key issues of what it is to be servile are focused closely upon Daphnis and Chloe themselves. The ending of that servile status is pointed up by Dionysophanes' statement that he will bestow on both Astylus and Daphnis much land, many οἰκέται, 'house-servants', gold, silver and all the other possessions that the prosperous have. Here οἰκέται, 'house-servants', are emphatically included among κτήματα, 'possessions' (4.24.4).

The term δοῦλος appears only once in the first three Books (at 3.31.3), then five times in Book 4; and only there does ὁμόδουλος, 'fellow slave', appear.[27] This distribution of the terms δοῦλος and ὁμόδουλος is partly because it is only in Book 4 that the non-servile status of Daphnis and Chloe becomes a dominant issue, complicated at 4.19.5 by the possibility of Daphnis becoming a slave of Gnathon:

> Ἀστύλου μὲν οὖν εἶναι δοῦλον αὐτὸν οὐχ ὑπερηφανῶ, καλὸν οἰκέτην καλοῦ καὶ ἀγαθοῦ δεσπότου· παροίνημα δὲ Γνάθωνος οὐ δύναμαι περιιδεῖν γενόμενον, ὃς ἐς Μιτυλήνην αὐτὸν ἄγειν ἐπὶ γυναικῶν ἔργα σπουδάζει.

SEG 2.621 (status unclear, Teos, no date); *MAMA* v 256 (status unclear, Nacoleia in Phrygia, no date); *IPerge* 238 (not servile, Perge, first–second century AD); *SEG* 26.1539 (status unclear, Seleuceia/Zeugma, no date); *IGUR* iii 1144 = *GVI* 181 (status unclear, Rome, first century AD).

27 δοῦλος 4.17.1; 17.4; 19.5; 28.3; 29.4; ὁμόδουλος at 4.1.1; 19.3. The verb δουλεύω also appears twice, in neither case simply of the activity of the rustics as slaves: at 2.23.3 it refers to the sort of slavery facing Chloe if she were to be taken as a war-captive to Methymna, and at 3.12.1 it refers to the couple's domination by Eros.

> I do not underrate his being a slave of Astylus, a fine house-servant of a fine master: but I cannot stand by and let him become the object of the drunken behaviour of Gnathon, who is keen to take him to Mytilene to play a woman's roles.

But this factor only partly explains the distribution. It seems to me that Longus has carefully minimised the extent to which Daphnis and Chloe might be perceived by the reader as slaves until the matter of Chloe's marriage has to be addressed. Note that neither in the purportedly explanatory painting of the preface, nor in the description of Dionysophanes' estate (1.2.1), is any reference at all made to their servile condition.[28]

I have said 'Daphnis and Chloe' because I am not persuaded, as some are, that Longus gives us evidence that Dryas and his family are *not* slaves. On the one hand it is true that, whereas Lamon claims he cannot make decisions about Daphnis' marriage without reference to his master,[29] Dryas does not say the same in relation to Chloe. But there may be literary reasons for this. Does Longus want to compress into his lean and economical narrative some reference to the frequency or infrequency of Dryas' master's visits to *his* estates? Is that master Megacles? Will too much have to be revealed too soon? In many respects, of course, Daphnis and Chloe are handled symmetrically by Longus, but *sometimes* we are told about an activity of one that we should assume was also pursued by the other. I take Longus' failure to make Dryas refer to his servile status as part of this asymmetry.

The second piece of evidence deployed in this debate is the speech of the Nymphs to Daphnis in his dream in which they insist that their agenda includes preventing Chloe being taken to be a slave in Methymna (2.23.3):

> 'καὶ νῦν δὲ ἡμῖν πεφρόντισται τὸ κατ' ἐκείνην, ὡς μήτε εἰς τὴν Μήθυμναν κομισθεῖσα δουλεύοι μήτε μέρος γένοιτο λείας πολεμικῆς.'

> 'and now too her situation has been in our plans, so that neither should she be taken to Methymna and be a slave, nor should she become a part of enemy booty.'

To me this reads as reassurance that Chloe will not be the sort of female captive-become-slave that is depicted in Greek literature from the *Iliad*'s

[28] ἐν τῷδε τῷι ἀγρῶι νέμων αἰπόλος, Λάμων τοὔνομα, παιδίον εὗρεν ὑπὸ μιᾶς τῶν αἰγῶν τρεφόμενον, 'On this estate a goatherd pasturing his flock, Lamon by name, discovered a baby being nursed by one of his goats', 1.2.1.

[29] δοῦλος δὲ ὢν οὐδενός εἰμι τῶν ἐμῶν κύριος, ἀλλὰ δεῖ τὸν δεσπότην μανθάνοντα ταῦτα συγχωρεῖν, 'but since I am a slave I have no power over any of what is mine, but my master must be told about this and give his consent', 3.31.3.

Andromache onwards, a slave that had a firm expectation of an imposed sexual relation with her new master. That is very different from the sort of land-tied servitude enjoyed – and to some extent I do mean 'enjoyed' – by Lamon, Myrtale and Daphnis and (in my view) by Dryas, Nape and Chloe. Moreover this argument can be turned round: if Daphnis is servile and Chloe is indeed not, why is this card never played at the time Dryas is asked to consider Chloe's marriage to Daphnis? The prolonged silence concerning the status of Daphnis and the persistent uncertainty concerning that of Chloe is mirrored, and perhaps reinforced, by uncertainty concerning the other inhabitants of the island within an island that is the two families' home. When Longus brings into the picture the cowherd Dorcon (at 1.5.1) and Philetas (at 2.3.2) he tells us nothing of their status, nor *a fortiori* of the status of Philetas' son Tityrus (at 2.32.1). I believe that we are meant to assume that, since they too are herdsfolk, they share the unambiguously servile status of Lamon and Dryas. That would explain, for example, why Dorcon does not take the obvious step of accusing Daphnis of being a slave in their beauty competition (1.15.4–16): the reason for this is that Dorcon himself is a slave. He is one who has become, as some slaves did,[30] extremely prosperous, to judge from the bridal gifts he can offer for Chloe (1.19.2) – a pair of plough oxen, four hives of bees, fifty apple trees, the skin of a bull to make leather goods, and a young cow who never runs out of milk – but a slave nevertheless.

As to Philetas, however, I admit it is perhaps surprising that, if he is a slave, once Daphnis has regained his free status and become the owner of the land and its servile inhabitants he makes no suggestion that Philetas, to whom he and Chloe owe so much, should be freed. But Longus never makes it clear that Philetas lives on the same estate as Daphnis: if he does not, Daphnis cannot free him in the way he frees his foster-parents (4.33.2), just as no move can be made by the family of Dionysophanes to free Chloe's parents at that point.

One exception to Longus' vagueness is Chromis, the ageing husband of Lycaenion, who is γεωργὸς γῆς ἰδίας ... παρηβῶν ἤδη τὸ σῶμα, 'a farmer of his own land ... already past his physical prime' (1.15.1). That precision concerning Chromis' ownership of his land seems to me to count against exempting Dorcon, Dryas, or Philetas from the servile community.

What then of Lycaenion? She too is marked out as different, but only in the sense that she is ἐξ ἄστεος, 'from the town', and ἀγροικίας ἁβρότερον, 'too fancy for a country life'. She is Chromis' γύναιον, 'woman', which is not

[30] See Bradley 1994.

to say she is his γυνή, 'wife'. Her Penelope-*mimesis* might hint that she is indeed his wife, and is free, but we are given no clear indication, and that Penelope-*mimesis* is seriously flawed.[31]

The case of Astylus' parasite Gnathon is also unclear. In New Comedy, from which Gnathon seems to have stepped into Longus' plot on a short-term contract, parasites are usually free. When Gnathon enters at 4.10.1, it is simply as Astylus' 'parasite', παράσιτος, that he is introduced. But later he refers to himself unambiguously as Astylus' 'slave', δοῦλος, the last use of the term δοῦλος in the novel (4.29.4):

> καὶ δεῖται μηδὲν ἔτι μνησικακοῦντα δοῦλον ἔχειν οὐκ ἄχρηστον.

> and he begged him not to harbour any bad feelings, but to have him as a slave who would not be useless.

It is possible that here Astylus uses the term 'slave', δοῦλος, metaphorically, to express his readiness to be subservient to his benefactor. If so, it prepares the reader looking back over the narrative as a whole to reflect that, just as the rustics may be technically slaves but rarely feel the limitations of servitude, so too a city-dweller may be technically free but operate under servile constraints.

I now move to uses of the term for 'master', δεσπότης, thirty-one in all:[32] none of them comes before the last part of Book 3.

δεσπότης is the only term used for 'master'. Only once does Longus use the word κύριος, not with the meaning 'master', but in the sense of being in control of one's own life-choices: the speaker is Lamon, explaining to Dryas why he cannot simply agree to his proposal that Daphnis marry Chloe (3.31.3), and what he says well illustrates what is at stake in servitude:

> δοῦλος γὰρ ὢν οὐδενός εἰμι τῶν ἐμῶν κύριος, ἀλλὰ δεῖ τὸν δεσπότην μανθάνοντα ταῦτα συγχωρεῖν

> For since I am a slave I have no power over anything that is mine, but my master must be told about this and give his consent.

The term δεσπότης, then, is the only term for 'master', almost always used of human masters in a master-slave relationship – twenty-eight times in all. But it is also used three times in invocations to gods: ὦ δεσπότα Πάν, 'O master Pan', by Dryas (3.32.2); δεσπότα Διόνυσε, 'Master Dionysus', by

[31] See above pp. 871–2 on 3.16.

[32] 3.26.3, 31.3, 32.2; 4.1.1, 4.2, 5.1, 6.2 (twice), 6.3 (twice), 7.2 (twice), 8.1, 8.4 (twice), 9.1, 9.2, 9.3, 14.2, 15.4 (twice), 16.2, 17.3, 19.3, 19.5 (twice), 21.2, 22.3, 25.2, 25.3.

Lamon (4.8.4); and ὦ Ζεῦ δεσπότα, 'O master Zeus', by Dionysophanes (4.21.2). I have resisted the temptation to translate δεσπότα here as 'Lord' since it is important that the same term is used for both human and divine 'masters'.

What is striking is that Longus avoids even that use of gods until late in Book 3 (3.32.2) – were there no occasions earlier when a character might be made to exclaim in this way that many literary genres show to have been common?[33] Indeed the very idea of a master/slave, δεσπότης/δοῦλος, relationship is also suppressed by Longus' postponement of his only use of the feminine equivalent δέσποινα, 'mistress', until the chapter immediately before the first appearance of δεσπότης (3.25.2). Thus the first appearance of each term is closely linked with independence and control of property. We first encounter δέσποινα, 'mistress', when Nape urges marrying Chloe to one of her suitors to forestall her losing her virginity while shepherding – better that she should be the δέσποινα, 'mistress', of a household and that they should acquire substantial bridal gifts (3.25.2). It is only a few lines later that δεσπότης, 'master', first appears, where Lamon rejects the idea of Daphnis marrying the daughter of a mere shepherd because his tokens suggest that he is someone ὃς αὐτοὺς εὑρὼν τοὺς οἰκείους καὶ ἐλευθέρους θήσει καὶ δεσπότας ἀγρῶν μειζόνων, 'who would, once he found his own parents, both free them (sc. his foster-parents) and make them masters of a larger estate' (3.26.3).

Once in play, at 3.26.3, the term δεσπότης becomes common in the rest of the novel, especially in the first twelve chapters of Book 4, where it is repeatedly used to refer to Dionysophanes. That is largely because at this point in the narrative Dionysophanes has become a central figure, but Longus carefully withholds his revelatory name from his readers until it can be disclosed with maximum effect on his actual arrival at the estate (4.13.1).

The emotional relationship between the rustic slaves and their masters is characterised by φόβος, 'fear'. Thus when Lampis has trashed Dionysophanes' garden Lamon and Daphnis φοβούμενοι τὸν δεσπότην ἔκλαον, 'began to lament in fear of their master' (4.8.1), and Gnathon (who may or may not be a slave) absents himself from the party celebrating Daphnis' identification and hides in the temple φοβούμενος, 'in fear' (4.25.2).[34] Such fear may

[33] Cf. Myrtale's exclamation φίλαι Μοῖραι, 'Dear Fates', at 4.21.3, complementing Dionysophanes' ὦ Ζεῦ δεσπότα at 4.21.2, and for the phenomenon as a whole (though missing both these instances in Longus) Dickey 1996.

[34] οὐχ ἧκε Γνάθων ἀλλὰ φοβούμενος ἐν τῶι νεὼι τοῦ Διονύσου καὶ τὴν ἡμέραν ἔμεινε καὶ τὴν νύκτα ὥσπερ ἱκέτης, 'Gnathon did not come, but in fear remained in the temple of Dionysus as a suppliant both day and night' (4.25.2).

be felt even if the characters have every reason to believe their masters to be kind and reasonable people.

The postponement until late in Book 3 of the terms δέσποινα, δεσπότης, and δοῦλος reflects the fact that it is there and in Book 4 that Daphnis and Chloe's servile status and its implications for their life-choices become important. I suggest, however, that their frequency after 3.25.2 (the first use of δέσποινα) is at least partly intended to encourage readers to think about the broader question of freedom and servitude.[35] The three uses of δεσπότης in addresses to gods draw attention to an important parallel between the relations of humans to gods and human slaves to human masters. The human masters themselves, like the slaves, are at the mercy of higher powers, gods. That is brought out explicitly when we read that Daphnis and Chloe were the first to lead their flocks out to pasture in spring οἷα μείζονι δουλεύοντες ποιμένι, 'since they were slaves to a more powerful shepherd' (i.e. Eros, 3.12.1).[36]

4 The Bigger Picture

Are these gods the only higher power to whom the elite of Mytilene is subordinate?

This observation, οἷα μείζονι δουλεύοντες ποιμένι, 'since they were slaves to a more powerful shepherd', and some other hints, suggest to me that Longus invites his readers to ponder the meaning of the relation between sheep and goats and their masters. *Daphnis and Chloe*, as we have seen, presents a world in which the boundaries between herdsfolk and their animals are repeatedly blurred: goats dance to music, feel affection, and in some instances even display better moral qualities than their shepherds – e.g. as early as the moment when Lamon initially contemplates snitching the tokens and abandoning the baby Daphnis to his fate, but then changes his mind αἰδεσθεὶς εἰ μηδὲ αἰγὸς φιλανθρωπίαν μιμήσεται, 'in shame that he would not imitate even a goat's philanthropy' (1.3.1). The stratum the novel

[35] Other interpretations can of course be offered. Owen Hodkinson has suggested to me that the suppression of the servile status of the couple and their foster-parents could be an authorial strategy to enable readers more easily to empathise with the protagonists, or more simply a consequence of them not interacting with characters from the outside world who are not δοῦλοι, 'slaves', and in some cases are δεσπόται, 'masters'. Both these factors may be in play, and do not necessarily exclude the further explanation that I offer.

[36] Cf. Eros' revelation to Philetas νῦν δὲ Δάφνιν ποιμαίνω καὶ Χλόην, 'I am now shepherding Daphnis and Chloe' (2.5.4), and the couple's dedication at the end of the story of an altar to Ἔρως Ποιμήν, 'Eros the Shepherd' (4.39.2).

presents above the shepherds, the members of the Mytilenean city elite, at least one of whom, Dionysophanes, owns fields, flocks and the shepherds themselves, turn out to display rather more bad moral qualities than the shepherds and goatherds.[37] All this may have little bearing on the real world of Longus' readership, arguably members of these very city elites. But there are hints in Daphnis and Chloe that encourage readers to think further. What lies outside the closed garden, the quasi-*paradeisos* that is the island of Lesbos, whose world's insulated and enclosed situation is reflected and emphasised in the *mise-en-abyme* of Dionysophanes' enclosed *paradeisos* at the beginning of Book 4? Are the readers invited to recall that outside Lesbos there was, in the real Roman world in which they lived, yet another stratum above the city elites of Mytilene and Methymna? Should the reader feel a frisson of Hellenic pride when Mytilene and Methymna go to war in the classical manner with ships, hoplites and cavalry, narrated in a markedly Thucydidean style that is very different from that used in the rest of the novel? Is the reader expected to feel still more pride in his or her Hellenic identity when a peaceful solution to the conflict is achieved by rational negotiation? Does any thought enter a reader's head of the very different political situation of the Greek world in the second and third centuries AD, any thought of the controlling role of Rome and Roman power?

At least two details seem to me to prompt thoughts of Rome. First, the way in which Daphnis and Chloe, exposed by their elite parents, are saved and suckled by a goat and a sheep respectively. Chloe's father is called Dryas, which may prompt us to contemplate what it is to be a true ποιμένα λαῶν, 'shepherd of the people', since the best known use of the name in earlier Greek literature was that in the *Iliad* of the Lapith Dryas, described metaphorically as ποιμένα λαῶν, 'shepherd of the people', at Il. 1.263. Though there were many such tales of suckling of human children by animals, that told of how Romulus and Remus were suckled by a she-wolf was the best known in the first three centuries AD.[38] Indeed there is continuous documentation of knowledge of this tradition from the second century BC onwards, when in the nearby East Greek island of Chios a politician whose name is not preserved was honoured because

> [ἐποίησεν ἐκ τῶν] | ἰδίων ἀνάθημα τῆι Ῥώμηι ἀπὸ δραχμῶν Ἀλεξ[ανδρείων χιλίων ἱστορίαμ πε]| ριέχον τῆς γενέσεως τοῦ κτίστου τῆς Ῥώ[μης Ῥωμύλου καὶ τοῦ ἀδελφοῦ] | αὐτοῦ Ῥέμου· vac καθ' ἣν συμβέβηκεν αὐτού[ς ὑπ' αὐτοῦ τοῦ Ἄρεος γεννηθῆναι] | …

[37] See Bowie 2009b (in English as Chapter 35 in this volume).
[38] Cf. p. 869 with n.11.

> from his own funds he made a dedication to Rome, costing 1000 Alexandrian drachmas, comprising the story of the birth of Rome's founder Romulus and his brother Remus, according to which it came about that they were fathered by Ares himself ...[39]

Around 20 BC an epigram of Diodorus of Sardis refers to Rome as the city of Remus,[40] and about a decade later a Greek reader could find the legend in Dionysius of Halicarnassus' *Roman Antiquities* (1.79). The story was depicted on one of the mid-first-century reliefs on the Sebasteion at Aphrodisias.[41] From the early second century AD it was also available in Plutarch's *Life of Romulus* (3–4),[42] and a little later Favorinus expected a Hellenophone audience to pick up the story from a brief allusion to Fortune sending shepherds to the kings of Rome.[43] We are perhaps asked, then, to contrast Longus' predominantly virtuous pastoral community with one whose founding myths notoriously involved in the first instance predatory wolves, and a little later robbers and asylum-seeking malefactors.[44] There is no doubt that on Longus' Lesbos wolves are to be perceived as predatory: it is the depredations of a she-wolf that sets the love-story in motion (1.11, already discussed); it is in a wolf-skin that the concupiscent cowherd Dorcon dresses himself in his attempt to rape or abduct Chloe (1.20–21); and in Book 3 it is a city woman with the wolfish name Lycaenion who seduces Daphnis.

The second detail is the name I have already noted as given to the son of Daphnis and Chloe in the penultimate sequence of the novel (4.39): Philopoemen. This name too prompts comparisons between Greek culture and Rome. Philopoemen was one of the latest in Plutarch's *Lives* of Greek heroes, and his valiant resistance to Rome earned him an ominous compliment from an unnamed Roman: Ῥωμαίων δέ τις ἐπαινῶν ἔσχατον αὐτὸν Ἑλλήνων προσεῖπεν, 'and a Roman praising him called him the last of the Greeks'.[45]

Two further points may be added. First, the scene earlier in Book 4 where Daphnis uses music to make his goats perform their obedience that is compared to that of οἰκέται, 'house slaves', to their masters.[46] This comparison becomes especially significant if we recall the readiness of at least

[39] *SEG* 30.1073.24–7: for discussion see Salvo 2013.

[40] ἄστυ Ῥέμοιο, Diodorus 1 *GP* = *AP* 9.219.3 (on Tiberius, ca. 20 BC): on Diodorus see Bowie 2012e (Chapter 17 in this volume).

[41] See Smith 1987, 9; full publication Smith 2013.

[42] For a full discussion see Wiseman 1995.

[43] [D.Chr.] 64.23, perhaps but not certainly delivered in Naples.

[44] For this way of presenting Rome's early history see Fuchs 1938.

[45] Plu. *Phil.* 1.7.

[46] 4.15.2–4, discussed at pp. 873–4 with n.25.

one Roman emperor to see provincial taxpayers as sheep. Suetonius in the early second century AD and Cassius Dio in the third concur in attributing this perspective to Tiberius:[47] *boni pastoris esse tondere pecus, non deglubere*, 'it is the mark of a good shepherd to shear sheep, not to skin them'; κείρεσθαί μου τὰ πρόβατα, ἀλλ᾽ οὐκ ἀποξύρεσθαι βούλομαι, 'I want my sheep sheared, not shaved'.

As Longus' camera swings back to Daphnis and Chloe's marriage bed (4.40) we are left pondering whether the sort of power and control exercised by shepherds and goatherds over their sheep and goats, and by elite Greeks both over their slaves and over others lower than themselves in the socio-economic scale, has an analogy in the power exercised by a Roman emperor and his administration over the elites of Greek cities – even over the elite of a city like Mytilene for which Theophanes, the historical literary ancestor of the fictitious Dionysophanes, had regained the status of *civitas libera* almost three centuries before.[48] Would a world without the predatory Roman wolf have been a better world? Was the Greeks' self-definition as sheep inevitable? The work's last sentence describes Daphnis and Chloe spending their wedding night together ἀγρυπνήσαντες τῆς νυκτὸς ὅσον οὐδὲ γλαῦκες, 'more wakefully even than owls' (4.40.3). Must readers of Longus' carefully crafted Attic Greek be alert as an Attic owl to conclude that one among the many things Longus does with his novel is to question the impact on the Greek world of Roman power?

[47] Suet. *Tib.* 32.3; D.C. 57.10.5.

[48] For the political role and literary activities of Theophanes see Bowie 2011b (Chapter 26 in Volume 3). The case for seeing Dionysophanes as a literary descendant of Theophanes was well put by Hugh Mason in his paper to ICAN V at Houston TX (2015) 'Longus' Mytilenean readers', of which he has very generously shown me a text.

44 | The Demotion of the Literary Cowherd (2019)

Much of Longus' refashioning of his principal model, the imaginary world of Theocritus' pastoral poems, hinges on his decision to give to the child reared by a goatherd the pastoral name 'Daphnis'. That this is to be read as a significantly pastoral name is flagged for the reader by his authorial comment ὡς δ' ἂν καὶ τοὔνομα τοῦ παιδίου ποιμενικὸν δοκοίη, Δάφνιν αὐτὸν ἔγνωσαν καλεῖν, 'and, so that the baby's name should also seem pastoral they decided to call him Daphnis' (2.3.2). But although Daphnis had been sung about by the ποιμήν, 'shepherd', Thyrsis in Theocritus 1, and by Tityrus within the song of the αἰπόλος, 'goatherd', Lycidas in Theocritus 7, in both Theocritus 1 and 7 Daphnis is himself a βουκόλος or βούτας, 'cowherd', and Longus' change involves promoting an αἰπόλος, 'goatherd', to be the bearer of the privileged name Daphnis and transferring his canonical role of βουκόλος, 'cowherd', to other pastoral characters.[1] This promotion is not difficult, since one of the Theocritean Daphnis' accomplishments is excellence in playing the panpipe (Theoc. 1.128–30), an instrument also regularly played by an αἰπόλος, 'goatherd', for example the unnamed αἰπόλος of Theocritus 1 (1.1–6). But one Theocritean characteristic of a goatherd or a shepherd seems to be discarded by Longus, and that is the gift of mellifluous song, an almost defining feature of the unnamed first-person αἰπόλος of Theocritus 3, of the goatherd Lycidas in Theocritus 7, and also of the ποιμήν, 'shepherd', Thyrsis in Theocritus 1 and the shepherd Polyphemus in 11. Only in Theocritus 6 do two young βουκόλοι or βοῦται, 'cowherds', (6.1, 44) sing, and one of these two is indeed called Daphnis, though it is unclear how he is supposed to relate to the dying Daphnis of Theocritus 1, or to the Daphnis who loves Xenea at Theocritus 7.73, if at all. But neither in Theocritus 1 nor in Theocritus 7 is it stated or hinted that Daphnis is himself a singer.

Promoting an αἰπόλος, 'goatherd', to be bearer of the marked cowherd-name Daphnis, then, may be partly responsible for relieving or robbing him of a feature we might expect in a goatherd, distinction in singing.

[1] For the notion of a hierarchy of pastoral characters implied by my terms 'demotion' and 'promoting' see Schmidt 1969, Hodkinson 2012.

Thus although Daphnis is sometimes said to sing together with Chloe,[2] or it is implied that he sings as a member of a larger group, when one of the couple sings solo it is always Chloe, e.g. at 3.24.2 (cf. 2.31.3):

> ὁ μὲν γὰρ ἐνήχετο ἐν τοῖς ποταμοῖς, ἡ δὲ ἐν ταῖς πηγαῖς ἐλούετο· ὁ μὲν ἐσύριζεν ἁμιλλώμενος πρὸς τὰς πίτυς, ἡ δὲ ᾖδε ταῖς ἀηδόσιν ἐρίζουσα.
>
> For he would swim in the rivers, and she would bathe herself in the springs; he would play the panpipe, competing with the pine-trees, and she would sing, vying with the nightingales.

What the goatherd Daphnis and his goatherd father Lamon do is not sing but tell μῦθοι, 'myths',[3] an action which is set alongside playing the panpipe and pantomime dancing in the party recounted at 2.32–7, a party at which (unlike the earlier celebration at 2.31.2) there is no singing. So although there is group singing at that celebration (2.31.2) and of a ὑμέναιον, 'wedding song', at the couple's wedding (4.40.2), and although Chloe, as mentioned, sings solo, no male sings solo in the *hic et nunc* of the narrative either.

That silence makes all the more striking the two exceptions to the absence from *Daphnis and Chloe* of male solo singing. One exception is Philetas. In an *analepsis* from his youth as a working βουκόλος, 'cowherd', he recalls how he often sang to the Nymphs, 2.3.2:

> 'Φιλητᾶς', ὦ παῖδες, 'ὁ πρεσβύτης ἐγώ, ὃς πολλὰ μὲν ταῖσδε ταῖς Νύμφαις ᾖισα, πολλὰ δὲ τῶι Πανὶ ἐκείνωι ἐσύρισα, βοῶν δὲ πολλῆς ἀγέλης ἡγησάμην μόνηι μουσικῆι.'
>
> I am old Philetas, children, who sang many times to these Nymphs here, and who played the panpipe many times to Pan over there, and who led a large herd by music alone.

Not only is this an exception to the absence from the action of *Daphnis and Chloe* of male solo singing, it ascribes to Philetas the cowherd a capacity or habit that the cowherd Daphnis of Theocritus 1 and 7 seems not himself to have had.

The other exception is the unnamed cowherd of Daphnis' first μῦθος, the story of the cow-girl who was metamorphosed into a φάττα, 'wood-dove'

[2] Daphnis and Chloe sing imitating birds at 1.9.2; expressing their joy at their release from the vintage, 2.2.6; and (perhaps along with the other participants) in the party celebrating Chloe's release, 2.31.2.

[3] Daphnis 1.27, 3.23; Lamon 2.34.

(1.27). The competitive cowherd of Daphnis' story charmed eight of the girl's cattle into his herd by his singing, and in her distress she prayed successfully to be turned into a bird (1.27.3–4). Like the case recalled by Philetas from his youth, this solo singing by a cowherd is not part of the world in which the young Daphnis and Chloe live: even more remote than Philetas' youthful singing, it is set in mythical time. What is Longus' game here?

One objective may be to avoid having *any* song in his prose text. Longus may have seen that there was a general problem about having words imagined or represented as sung to music in a prose text designed for reading, whether silently or aloud, and may not have been happy with the solution of Achilles Tatius, which was to paraphrase rather than reproduce the song (Ach. Tat. 1.5.5, 2.1). Moreover one detail in Philetas' long speech may suggest that Longus had a particular agenda in the matter of songs expressing *eros*, love-songs: Philetas denies that a φάρμακον ('remedy') for Eros can be found ἐν ᾠδαῖς λαλούμενον, 'uttered in songs', and thus seems directly to question the concluding two lines (80–1) of Theocritus 11:

> οὕτω τοι Πολύφαμος ἐποίμαινεν τὸν ἔρωτα
> μουσίσδων, ῥᾷον δὲ διᾶγ' ἢ εἰ χρυσὸν ἔδωκεν.
>
> Thus, you see, did Polyphemus shepherd his desire,
> by making music, and he endured it more easily than if he had paid gold.

If we put this alongside Longus' ambition, declared in his preface, to produce a κτῆμα τερπνὸν πᾶσιν ἀνθρώποις, ὃ καὶ νοσοῦντα ἰάσεται καὶ λυπούμενον παραμυθήσεται, 'a pleasing possession for all men, which will both cure the one who is ill and console the one who is grieving' (*pr.* 3), we may conclude that he sees his own, often poetic, prose as achieving what song had done for Polyphemus, and that the elimination of male solo song from his narrative is part of his broader programme of creating a prose refashioning of Sappho and Theocritus.

A second function of Philetas' mention of the songs that he once sang may be to contribute to the distinction Longus draws between good and bad βουκόλοι, 'cowherds'. To that distinction I now turn, and in the second part of this paper I address the following question: what does Longus do with the part of the cowherd that he has in a sense taken away from Daphnis?

In place of a protagonist cowherd such as the Daphnis in Thyrsis' song in Theocritus 1 we are given three minor characters, all identified as βουκόλοι, 'cowherds', each with an important role in advancing the plot.

The first of these cowherds is Dorcon, introduced at first unnamed, simply as a βουκόλος, 'cowherd', called to help by Chloe at 1.12.3–4 when Daphnis falls into the wolf-trap. He is explicitly said to be ἐκ τῶν ἀγρῶν τῶν πλησίον, 'from the neighbouring fields', and is not from Dionysophanes' estate, whose brief description at 1.1.2 in fact says nothing of grazing for cattle. Dorcon helps Chloe to winch Daphnis out of the pit, using her ταινία, 'bra', that she has taken off for this purpose. We are not told if this has been her own idea, or if it has been suggested by Dorcon; but when he reappears, named, at 1.15, it is as a youth who knows the ὄνομα, 'name', and ἔργα, 'acts', of Eros, and whose desire for Chloe, sparked off by that fateful encounter, has grown daily, to the point where he is determined to get Chloe either by giving her gifts or by force. The name Dorcon, perhaps related to the verb δέρκομαι, 'I look', may suggest that he is above all a 'gazer',[4] and that Chloe's stripping had indeed been his idea; but Dorcon is a relatively well-attested name in all regions so far covered by the published volumes of the *Lexicon of Greek Personal Names*,[5] and it is debateable whether Longus offers it as a speaking name.

But Dorcon not only gazes, he can also act, and he successively attempts (and fails) to get Chloe by bringing her gifts, by giving her father Dryas gifts and thus seeking her hand in marriage, and by unconvincingly disguising himself as a wolf and ambushing the couple. These manoeuvres by a Dorcon who knows what he wants and how it might be achieved are narrated in parallel to, and as a foil to, the young couple's own growing feelings of mutual desire which they are quite unable to diagnose, Chloe's feelings fired by seeing Daphnis bathe naked after his misadventure (1.13), Daphnis' feelings by the kiss given him by Chloe as winner of the verbal beauty competition with Dorcon (1.17.2) – a competition in self-praise in prose that replaces the competing or complementary *songs* of Theocritean pastoral.

At this point Dorcon's role as a foil is more important than as a contributor to advancing the couple's knowledge of Eros. Chloe seems to be unaware of what is driving Dorcon, or of what his gifts mean, and her own desire for Daphnis would have been aroused even if Dorcon had not been introduced into the plot. To be sure, without Dorcon there would have been no beauty competition, and Chloe would have had to wait longer for an excuse to kiss Daphnis, but she would surely have found one. Moreover, nothing in Dorcon's behaviour seems to lead either Daphnis or Chloe to a better understanding of Eros. Unlike some other people, animals and things in the novel, Dorcon is at no point held up as an object of *mimesis*.

[4] Cf. Morgan 2004, 163. [5] Bowie 2019g, 126.

Dorcon's part in the last episode in which he appears is of crucial importance, but he is important for saving Daphnis from pirates rather than for saving the couple from their erotic ignorance. When Dorcon has been savagely beaten up by the pirates and his cattle, together with Daphnis, are being carried off on their ship, Dorcon tells Chloe to play on his panpipe a tune he had taught Daphnis, and Daphnis had then taught her (1.29.2). This causes Dorcon's cattle to leap into the sea, thus capsizing the ship, and allowing Daphnis to swim ashore with two of them supporting him by their horns (1.30). Meanwhile Dorcon has died, giving his panpipe to Chloe and in exchange asking, this time successfully, for a kiss (1.29.3). Chloe's awareness of the games of Eros has indeed increased, since in her account to Daphnis of how Dorcon died she says nothing of this kiss (αἰδεσθεῖσα, 'out of embarrassment', 1.31.2); but we do not read that the kiss was a factor in their decision that Daphnis should bathe Chloe, a bath that raises his desire to a new intensity when he sees her naked (1.32).

Overall, then, this first cowherd in Longus' narrative is important in twice saving Daphnis, and is perhaps crucial in setting up a situation where Chloe kisses Daphnis for the first time. He is potentially an example of how a less naïve and more sexually knowledgeable herdsman might be imagined to behave, but that knowledgeable example is not followed. His attempts to get Chloe for himself might have made him a villain had they been successful, but they are not, and they elicit less condemnation than his death elicits sympathy. That sympathy is all the greater because his gift to Chloe of his σῦριγξ, 'panpipe', recalls how the dying Daphnis of Theocritus 1 gave *his* σῦριγξ to Pan (1.128–30). Like the first poem of at least one Hellenistic collection of Theocritus, the first book of Longus' novel ends with the death of a cowherd who has suffered the pangs of Eros, but the name of Theocritus' cowherd has been transferred to an αἰπόλος, 'goatherd', who does not die, and whose entanglement with Eros he is beginning to find as overwhelming as that of Theocritus' Daphnis.

The second of the minor characters identified as βουκόλοι, 'cowherds', and one who makes a more important contribution, is Philetas. Admittedly, as we have seen, he is a *retired* βουκόλος, now almost wholly concerned with his garden (2.3.3), even if he still dresses like a herdsman (2.3.1). Like herdsmen of all types he has been a panpipe-player, and unlike the Daphnis of both Theocritus and Longus he has sung songs to the Nymphs (2.3.2, quoted above), as does the celebratory group at 2.31.2. Like the goatherd of Theocritus 3 he once wooed an Amaryllis, but unlike that goatherd he won her, with the help of Eros (2.5.3), and they now have sons who herd cattle and farm land. There is no hint that Philetas himself or any of his sons was ever a goatherd, and the wooing of an Amaryllis is the only element in Longus' picture that might compromise its presentation of him as a herder of cattle who thereby stands higher in the hierarchy than herders of goats and sheep. In his exposition to the young couple of the nature of Eros and his prescription of the only φάρμακον, 'remedy', for it – φίλημα καὶ περιβολὴ καὶ συγκατακλιθῆναι γυμνοῖς σώμασι, 'kissing and embracing and lying down together naked', 2.7.7 – the old Philetas' sharing of his recent and past experiences raises the prospect that Daphnis and Chloe too will soon indeed be able to engage in the ἔργα ἔρωτος, 'acts of love'. As in the later scene in which he acts as a judge in the dispute between Daphnis and the angry Methymnans (2.15), Philetas comes across as both wise and level-headed – a safe pair of hands.

The third cowherd, Lampis, re-establishes an image of young cowherds as hot-headed and easily driven by Eros (as Philetas too may well have been in his youth). Like Dorcon, Lampis woos Chloe by offering her father many gifts; and, like Dorcon, he fails (4.7.1). The imminent possibility of Daphnis being given his master's permission to marry Chloe precipitates Lampis' extreme measures to get Lamon and Daphnis into trouble with that master, vandalising the παράδεισος, 'enclosed garden' or 'park', that is in Lamon's charge (4.7.1–3). Later, when Daphnis' recognition as Dionysophanes' son is being celebrated, Lampis assembles some farmers and abducts Chloe, thinking that Daphnis will no longer want her (4.28.1), and she is only rescued by a counter-raid on Lampis' cottage, master-minded by the parasite Gnathon (4.29.2–5).

Lampis comes out as the least likeable character in the novel, and when he is listed as a participant in the rustic wedding he is catalogued last, with the authorial explanation that he had been forgiven (4.38.2), though he does participate in the celebrations to the extent of playing the αὐλός, 'pipe', an instrument played by each of the βουκόλοι, 'cowherds', in Theocritus 6 (6.43–4) but only marginal to the world of shepherds and goatherds.[6]

What has Longus achieved? Where does he leave his reader? Despite the profound and helpful advice of the old and experienced ex-cowherd Philetas, the actions of Dorcon and Lampis taken together leave us with the impression that Theocritus may have been wrong to seek so much sympathy for βουκόλοι, 'cowherds', who in Longus' novel tend to be boisterous

[6] Cf. the dedications of 1.4.3.

and self-assertive,[7] and that a society in which cowherds were allowed to have their way would be a rougher and crueller society than one in which the standards of behaviour were set by αἰπόλοι, 'goatherds', and ποιμένες, 'shepherds'. One telling detail in Longus' representation of ποιμένες, 'shepherds', as more inclined to be gentle than cowherds or even goatherds is his adaptation of Sappho's comparison of a bride to a hyacinth trampled by shepherds, Sappho fr. 105(c):

> οἴαν τὰν ὐάκινθον ἐν ὤρεσι ποίμενες ἄνδρες
> πόσσι καταστείβοισι, χάμαι δέ τε πόρφυρον ἄνθος ...
>
> like the hyacinth that in the mountains shepherd men
> trample down with their feet, and on the ground its dark-red flower ...

Longus' reworking of this image replaces Sappho's ποιμήν, 'shepherd', with a ποίμνιον, 'grazing beast', which Daphnis fears may trample the apple that symbolises Chloe – he is afraid that if he leaves the apple on the tree it might πέσηι χαμαὶ καὶ ἢ ποίμνιον αὐτὸ πατήσηι νεμόμενον ..., 'fall to the ground and either a sheep might trample it as it grazed ...', (3.34.2).[8]

Longus has to some extent, then, elevated the role of the Theocritean shepherd, while, like the shepherd Thyrsis in Theocritus 1, his shepherds are still allowed to compose songs (2.31.2) and his shepherdess, Chloe, to sing (2.31.3, 3.24.2). But at the same time Longus has dethroned Daphnis the Theocritean βουκόλος or βούτας, 'cowherd', who is the fabled subject of songs (Theoc. 1, 7.73), and is sometimes heard singing (Theoc. 6), and has replaced him with a goatherd who never sings solo, whose cultural gifts are for telling μῦθοι, 'myths', in prose, and who will himself achieve through the prose of Longus the mythical status that his Pan predicts for Chloe (2.27.3).

[7] The epithet ἀγέρωχος, 'self-assertive', first appears applied to older shepherd lads, of whom Chloe is afraid, at 1.28.2: there, as when used to describe the cowherd Lampis at 4.7.1, it is clearly negative. That is less clear when it is used of Philetas' son Tityrus (perhaps, as his father had once been, a cowherd) at 2.32.1, or when Philetas at 2.4.2 describes Eros' behaviour in his garden as ἀγερωχία, better rendered 'boisterousness' (so Morgan 2004, 53) than 'naughtiness' (so Gill 1989, 305).

[8] On Longus' complex reworking of different pieces of Sappho in this sequence see Bowie 2013d (Chapter 37 in this volume), 2019g, 257–9; Segers 2017; Nagy 2019.

45 Callimachus and Longus (2019)

1 Introduction

Most of the five Greek novels to be transmitted as complete texts in a manuscript tradition seem not to include Callimachus in their wide range of intertexts – not even Achilles Tatius, despite his supposed origin in Alexandria and his enthusiastic *ecphrasis* of that city at the opening of his fifth book (5.1), nor Heliodorus, despite his locating much of his narrative in Egypt. I say 'seem' because I may not have been so thorough as I should have been in my explorations: but so far neither I nor scholars expert in the novels whom I have consulted have anything to suggest.[1]

Longus' *Daphnis and Chloe* is quite different in this matter, as indeed it differs in many respects from the other novels both complete and fragmentary. Longus seems to know and to use Callimachus' *Aitia*, his *Hymns*, his *Epigrams*, his *Branchus* or perhaps his *Iambi*. Such knowledge of Callimachus is not *a priori* surprising in a careful writer who draws much of his description of a pastoral setting and habits from Callimachus' contemporary Theocritus and – I have suggested and would still maintain – from Philitas in the generation before Theocritus, and whose exploitation of erotic epigram seems to reveal him as a reader of Asclepiades and Dioscorides. But this exploitation of Callimachus does set Longus apart not simply from the novelists but from many other Greek writers of the second and third centuries AD.

On what, then, do I base this claim?

2 ἀρτιγένειος and the *Aitia*

I begin with a lexical item: ἀρτιγένειος (1.15.1, 4.10.1). Longus uses this adjective twice, first of Daphnis' potential rival for Chloe, Dorcon, at 1.15.1; Δόρκων δὲ ὁ βουκόλος, ὁ τὸν Δάφνιν ἐκ τοῦ σιροῦ καὶ τὸν τράγον ἀνιμησάμενος,

[1] I am grateful to the participants in the Hellenistic workshop held at Groningen in September 2017 for helpful questions and interventions, and to Christiaan Caspers for his carefully thought-out response, some aspects of which I address in my conclusions (Section 8).

ἀρτιγένειος μειρακίσκος καὶ εἰδὼς ἔρωτος καὶ τὰ ἔργα καὶ τὰ ὀνόματα, 'But Dorcon the cowherd, who had winched Daphnis out of the pit, and also the billy-goat, a young man whose beard had just begun to grow, and who knew both the deeds and the words of desire'. He uses it again in Book 4 (4.10.1) of Astylus, the young son of the estate-owner Dionysophanes, a son who turns out to be Daphnis' brother: ἧκε μὲν ὁ Ἄστυλος ἐφ' ἵππου καὶ παράσιτος αὐτοῦ, καὶ οὗτος ἐφ' ἵππου· ὁ μὲν ἀρτιγένειος, ὁ δὲ Γνάθων (τουτὶ γὰρ ἐκαλεῖτο) τὸν πώγωνα ξυρώμενος πάλαι, 'Astylus arrived on horseback together with his parasite, and he too was on horseback – the former was just growing his first beard, while Gnathon (for this was his name) had long had his beard shaven'.

ἀρτιγένειος is used nowhere else in the novels. It is almost certain that the adjective ἀρτιγένειος was in the *Aitia*: see Σ Flor. on fr. 2.17 Pfeiffer = fr. 2d Harder, and we may compare the phrase ἄρτι γένεια | περκάζων, 'whose chin was just beginning to darken', at Callimachus, *Hymn* 5.75–6, to which I return later. Longus may also have noticed the choice epithet ἀρτιγένειος in the Augustan epigrammatist Diodorus, *GP* 1 = *AP* 9.219, a poem whose subject is probably Augustus' stepson Tiberius when he was aged seventeen or eighteen:

αἰγιβότου Σκύροιο λιπὼν πέδον Ἴλιον ἔπλω
οἷος Ἀχιλλείδης πρόσθε μενεπτόλεμος,
τοῖος ἐν Αἰνεάδῃσι Νέρων ἀγὸς ἄστυ Ῥέμοιο
νεῖται ἐπ' ὠκυρόην Θύβριν ἀμειψάμενος,
κοῦρος ἔτ' ἀρτιγένειον ἔχων χνόον. ἀλλ' ὁ μὲν ἔγχει
θῦεν, ὁ δ' ἀμφοτέροις, καὶ δορὶ καὶ σοφίῃ.

As was Achilles' son in olden days, steadfast in war, when he left the plain of goat-grazing Scyros and sailed to Ilium, such was Nero, prince among the descendants of Aeneas, when he changed his abode to the city of Remus and headed for the swift-flowing Tiber, a youth who still had the down of a freshly grown beard. But whereas the former dominated with his spear, the latter did so with both lance and wisdom.

Longus may well know all these poetic texts, but it is very likely that he was also, and perhaps especially, drawn to deploy the epithet ἀρτιγένειος by a different intertext – the participial phrase ἄρτι γενειάζων, 'just growing a beard', describing Polyphemus at Theoc. 11.7–9,[2] where, to quote Richard Hunter's 1999 commentary, 'the first beard marks the transition to young

[2] Cf. ἡμιγένειος, 'with his beard half-grown', of Damoetas at Theoc. 6.3.

manhood or from *eromenos* to *erastes*, when thoughts may turn to marriage' (Hunter 1999 *ad loc.*);

> οὕτω γοῦν ῥάιστα διᾶγ' ὁ Κύκλωψ ὁ παρ' ἁμῖν,
> ὡρχαῖος Πολύφαμος, ὅκ' ἤρατο τᾶς Γαλατείας,
> ἄρτι γενειάσδων περὶ τὸ στόμα τὼς κροτάφως τε.
>
> It was in the way, at any rate, that the Cyclops from our land kept going most easily, Polyphemus of old, when he was in love with Galatea, just growing a beard around his mouth and his temples.

It is also not unlikely, given the considerable influence of Xenophon's *Cyropaedia* on the novels, that the phrase ἄρτι γενειάσκοντα, 'just growing a beard', used there by Gobryas of his murdered son (*Cyr.* 4.6.5), could have caught Longus' eye. But the two chief intertexts for Longus' use of ἀρτιγένειος of Dorcon are Call. *Aet.* and Theoc. 11, the former of which offered precisely that adjective in the nominative (as it is in both instances in Longus), while the latter associated the physical condition described by the participial phrase ἄρτι γενειάζων with the psychological condition of erotic desire, the emotion that is driving Longus' cowherd Dorcon at 1.15.1, and that a reader of 4.10.1 may worry might impel the handsome young Astylus to make a move that would disrupt Daphnis' relationship with Chloe.

3 Epigram

My inclination to see Callimachus' *Aitia* as the main source for the epithet ἀρτιγένειος is strengthened by Longus' use of ἕλκος, 'wound', at 1.14.1, very shortly before his first use of ἀρτιγένειος. Here Longus has his lovesick Chloe say: *νῦν ἐγὼ νοσῶ μέν, τί δὲ ἡ νόσος ἀγνοῶ· ἀλγῶ, καὶ ἕλκος οὐκ ἔστι μοι*, 'Now I am sick, but what the sickness is, I do not know; I feel pain, but I have no wound'. That Chloe diagnoses her erotic pain as similar to that which she might have expected to come from a ἕλκος, 'wound', plays with the idea that ἔρως, 'love' or 'desire', is itself a wound – an idea not found in the other novelists.[3] This idea, like many in the lexicon of ἔρως, is already there in Eur. *Hipp.* (530); and it reappears at Theoc. 11.15–16, where Polyphemus is described as follows:

> ἔχθιστον ἔχων ὑποκάρδιον ἕλκος,
> Κύπριδος ἐκ μεγάλας τό οἱ ἥπατι πᾶξε βέλεμνον.

[3] A.T. uses ἕλκος, 'wound', metaphorically, but not of love, 2.29.3, 5, 5.8.2.

with a most hateful wound beneath his heart
which a dart from mighty Cypris had fixed in his liver.

It appears again at Theocritus 30.10–11:

εἰς οἶκον δ' ἀπέβαν ἔλκος ἔχων καῖνο<ν ἐν ἤπατι>.
πόλλα δ' εἰσκαλέσαις θῦμον ἐμαύτωι διελεξάμαν.

and I went off home with a new wound <in my liver>
and calling my soul into action, I had a dialogue with myself.

But alongside these two Theocritean uses stands that by Callimachus in *AP* 12.134 = 43 Pfeiffer = *HE* 1103–8, a justly admired epigram:

ἕλκος ἔχων ὁ ξεῖνος ἐλάνθανεν· ὡς ἀνιηρὸν
  πνεῦμα διὰ στηθέων – εἶδες; – ἀνηγάγετο,
τὸ τρίτον ἡνίκ' ἔπινε, τὰ δὲ ῥόδα φυλλοβολεῦντα
  τὠνδρὸς ἀπὸ στεφάνων πάντ' ἐγένοντο χαμαί·
ὤπτηται μέγα δή τι, μὰ δαίμονας· οὐκ ἀπὸ ῥυσμοῦ
  εἰκάζω, φωρὸς δ' ἴχνια φὼρ ἔμαθον.

Our guest has a wound and we did not notice. How painfully he heaved his breath up from his chest – did you see him? – when he was drinking the third cup? And the roses, casting their petals from the man's wreaths, all fell on the ground. He is being roasted by some great fire, by the gods: I am not guessing wildly – as a thief, I have recognised the tracks of a thief.

That this epigram made some contribution to Longus' play with ἕλκος is supported by his re-exploitation of it a few chapters later, when Daphnis describes his symptoms of love that are parallel to those of Chloe: his description ἐκπηδᾶι μου τὸ πνεῦμα, 'my breath leaps out', 1.18.1) recalls the exclamation ὡς ἀνιηρὸν | πνεῦμα διὰ στηθέων – εἶδες; – ἀνηγάγετο, 'with what pain he drew the breath – did you see? – up through his chest' (*AP* 12.134.1–2).

So far, then, I think there is a reasonable case for Longus' knowledge of the *Aitia* and a comparably strong case for his knowledge of the *Epigrams*.

Let me add two further possible intertexts in Callimachus' *Epigrams*. The first is Longus' use of ἀνέραστον, 'without love', at 3.11.3, where Longus sums up the happy outcome of Daphnis' attempts to visit Chloe despite the winter snow:

καὶ ἄλλας δὲ πολλὰς ἦλθεν ὁδοὺς ἐπ' ἄλλαις τέχναις, ὥστε μὴ παντάπασιν αὐτοῖς γενέσθαι τὸν χειμῶνα ἀνέραστον.

And he made many other journeys on the basis of other strategems, so that the winter might not be entirely loveless for them.

The adjective ἀνέραστος is found first in Hellenistic poetry, and even there it is rare. Its debut is in Callimachus, *AP* 12.148 = 32.4 Pfeiffer = *HE* 1071–4:

> οἶδ' ὅτι μευ πλούτου κενεαὶ χέρες· ἀλλά, Μένιππε,
> μὴ λέγε πρὸς Χαρίτων τοὐμὸν ὄνειρον ἐμοί.
> ἀλγέω τὴν διὰ παντὸς ἔπος τόδε πικρὸν ἀκούων·
> ναὶ φίλε, τῶν παρὰ σεῦ τοῦτ' ἀνεραστότατον.

> I know my hands are empty of wealth; but, I beseech you, Menippus, by the Graces, do not tell me my own dream. I feel constant pain when I hear this bitter phrase. Yes, my dear, this is the most loveless thing in your dealings with me.

ἀνέραστος is then used by Moschus, fr. 2.7 and Bion, fr. 9.3, and it is common in imperial Greek prose.[4] But in the novelists before Heliodorus it is found only here and once in Xenophon of Ephesus (1.2.9). Longus could know ἀνέραστος from any one or more of these or a number of other texts – among them Dio of Prusa's *Euboean Oration* (7.133), which anticipates his treatment of love between two innocent rustics and with which he seems to be familiar. But the appearance of ἀνέραστος in an epigram of Callimachus about the obstacle of poverty – an obstacle that at one point in *Daphnis and Chloe* seems likely to prevent the couple's marriage – together with the other Callimachean intertexts discussed points to the probability that Longus first found it in Callimachus' epigram.

My other suggested intertext in the *Epigrams* is based not on similarity not of words but of theme. At 4.24.2 Dionysophanes explains why he had decided to expose the baby Daphnis: he already had three children when Daphnis was born, and three children seemed enough. But after Daphnis' exposure both Dionysophanes' older son and his only daughter died from the same disease on the same day, leaving only one child, Astylus. Such things can happen in real life – e.g. in Panticapaeum in the second or first century BC a mother and three children were killed on a single καιρός, 'occasion'.[5] And the simultaneous death of two children is the theme of epigrams by Apollonides, *AP* 7.378 (= *GP* 1149–52 = *GVI* 1718), and by the unidentified poet of *AP* 7.323 (= *FGE* 1276–7 = *GVI* 1716). But the most memorable handling of the theme is by Callimachus, in *AP* 7.517 (= 20 Pfeiffer = *HE* 1193–8), where the simultaneous deaths are those of a son and a daughter, apparently historical figures in Cyrene:

> ἠῷοι Μελάνιππον ἐθάπτομεν, ἠελίου δὲ
> δυομένου Βασιλὼ κάτθανε παρθενικὴ

[4] D. Chr. *Or.* 7.133, Plu. *De Pyth. or.* 23 = *Mor.* 406a, Luc., Philostr., etc. [5] *GVI* 845.

αὐτοχερί· ζώειν γὰρ ἀδελφεὸν ἐν πυρὶ θεῖσα
οὐκ ἔτλη. δίδυμον δ' οἶκος ἐσεῖδε κακὸν
πατρὸς Ἀριστίπποιο· κατήφησεν δὲ Κυρήνη
πᾶσα τὸν εὔτεκνον χῆρον ἰδοῦσα δόμον.

At dawn we buried Melanippus: and as the sun set the maiden Basilo died by her own hand; for she could not bear to live after placing her brother on the pyre. The house of their father Aristippus saw a twin woe, and all Cyrene was downcast when they saw the home of fine children bereft.

Before returning to the *Aitia* let me make some tentative suggestions concerning the *Hymns.*

4 The *Hymns*

At 2.18.1, after the rustics have routed the complaining Methymnans, Chloe takes Daphnis off to the Nymphs' grove to bathe his face, bloodstained from a broken nose. This is done κατὰ πολλὴν ἡσυχίαν, 'in considerable tranquillity', contrasting with the τάραχος, 'uproar', of the rustics' hot pursuit. The phrase πολλὴ ἡσυχία appears in Longus alone of the novelists, and although it is not uncommon in classical and imperial texts,[6] the context in *Daphnis and Chloe*, which is of bathing and Nymphs, might indicate that Longus drew it from Call. *Lav.Pall.* 74, where Callimachus emphasises, by repetition of ἁσυχία, the tranquillity in which Artemis and her Nymphs bathed:

μεσαμβρινὰ δ' εἶχ' ὄρος ἁσυχία.
ἀμφότεραι λώοντο, μεσαμβριναὶ δ' ἔσαν ὧραι,
πολλὰ δ' ἁσυχία τῆνο κατεῖχεν ὄρος.
Τειρεσίας δ' ἔτι μῶνος ἁμᾶ κυσὶν ἄρτι γένεια
περκάζων ἱερὸν χῶρον ἀνεστρέφετο

midday tranquillity held the mountain. Both were bathing, and the hour was that of midday, and great tranquillity held that mountain in its grasp. Teiresias still, alone with his dogs, his chin just beginning to darken, was ranging through the sacred space.

That ἄρτι γένεια περκάζων may also be seen as one of the intertexts of ἀρτιγένειος at 1.15.1 and 4.10.2 may give some support to the case for seeing this part of the *Bath of Pallas* as relevant to our reading of 2.18.1 – perhaps,

[6] Cf. D. 8.12, 24.29, Isoc. *Pac.* 137, *Areop.* 80, Plu. *Arat.* 27.3, *Cat. Mi.* 70.7, *Aem.* 39.2, D. Chr. *Or.* 7.23, 12.51, Aristid. *Or.* 51.56 Keil.

like some of Longus' tragic intertexts, pointing up how his pastoral world is one where the gods are a threat only to the impious, not, as in the traditional mythology treated by tragedy and Hellenistic poetry, to the merely inadvertent.

There is also some similarity of content, though not of phraseology, between 2.20.3, where the Methymnans drag Chloe off πολλὰ τῶν ἀγαλμάτων κατακερτομήσαντες ('uttering much abuse against the cult-statues') and Erysichthon's impious outburst in Call. *Cer.* 53–5:

> 'χάζευ', ἔφα, 'μή τοι πέλεκυν μέγαν ἐν χροΐ πάξω.
> ταῦτα δ' ἐμὸν θησεῖ στεγανὸν δόμον, ᾧι ἔνι δαῖτας
> αἰὲν ἐμοῖς ἑτάροισιν ἅδην θυμαρέας ἀξῶ'.

> 'Get back!', he said, 'lest I plant my great axe in your flesh. But these will make me a well-protected banqueting hall, in which forever shall I unceasingly hold heart- warming feasts for my companions'.

That similarity might add to our evidence for Longus' familiarity with Callimachus' *Hymns.* Similarly ἐπτοηθεῖσαι at 1.22.2 may have been noticed by Longus in Call. *Dian.* 190–1:

> ἧς ποτε Μίνως
> πτοιηθεὶς ὑπ' ἔρωτι κατέδραμεν οὔρεα Κρήτης

> for whom Minos' desire was set a-flutter so that he ran all over the mountains of Crete

But πτοιεῖσθαι is a word first known from Sappho,[7] and far from rare.[8] So this is not a strong case.

An even less strong case is the suggestion by Morgan in his excellent Longus commentary that at 1.9.1 Longus alludes to Callimachus' use of bees at *Ap.* 110 as a symbol for the poet.[9] Longus' phraseology does not seem to me to point in this direction:

> βόμβος ἦν ἤδη μελιττῶν, ἦχος ὀρνίθων μουσικῶν, σκιρτήματα ποιμνίων ἀρτιγεννήτων· ἄρνες ἐσκίρτων ἐν τοῖς ὄρεσιν, ἐβόμβουν ἐν τοῖς λειμῶσιν αἱ μέλιτται, τὰς λόχμας κατῇδον ὄρνιθες.

> Now there was a buzzing of bees, the music of tuneful birds, the gambols of new-born sheep; lambs gambolled in the hills, the bees buzzed in the meadows, birds filled the thickets with song.

7 Frr. 22.14 and 31.6.

8 Cf. e.g. πτοιήσεις, Archias, *AP* 7.214 = *GP* 3724–31; ἐπτοημένος and ἐπτόημαι, Poll. 5.123; πτοούμενος, Poll.1.197; πτοιητόν, Nic. *Alex.* 243.

9 Morgan 2004, 157.

5 The *Iambi* and *Branchus*

From the *Hymns* I turn briefly to the *Iambi* and *Branchus*.

At *Daphnis and Chloe* 4.17.6 Gnathon cites Apollo's love for Branchus in his list of precedents for his passion for Daphnis: αἶγας ἔνεμε Βράγχος, καὶ Ἀπόλλων αὐτὸν ἐφίλησε, 'Branchus was herding goats, and Apollo kissed him'. The somewhat recondite myth of Branchus was mentioned by Callimachus in his *Iambi* (fr. 194.28 Pfeiffer) and was the subject of his poem entitled *Branchus* (fr. 229 Pfeiffer) where, as we know from Hephaestion (30.18 Consbruch), Callimachus told the story of Branchus in choriambic pentameters. The myth is mentioned in several places in the first four centuries AD,[10] so Callimachus need not be Longus' source for the myth. But it is tempting to me, at least, to think that Longus' readers were expected to see Gnathon, οἷα πᾶσαν ἐρωτικὴν μυθολογίαν ἐν τοῖς τῶν ἀσώτων συμποσίοις πεπαιδευμένος, 'since he had been taught the whole of amatory mythology in the symposia of the dissolute' (4.17.3), as having supplemented that teaching by a reading of such metrically unusual poems as Callimachus' *Branchus*. This suggestion may receive support from the fact that it is only in this sequence (4.14.2, 17.6) that Longus mentions that especially Callimachean god, Apollo, a rare exception to his general exclusion of Olympians.[11]

6 The *Aitia* Again

Let me now return to the *Aitia*, where I began in Section 2 with the word ἀρτιγένειος.

First, Longus 2.7.6: the old herdsman Philetas recalls how nothing assuaged his desire for Amaryllis:

> ἐκάλουν τὸν Πᾶνα βοηθόν, ὡς καὶ αὐτὸν τῆς Πίτυος ἐρασθέντα· ἐπῄνουν τὴν Ἠχὼ τὸ Ἀμαρυλλίδος ὄνομα μετ' ἐμὲ καλοῦσαν
>
> I would call on Pan to come to my aid, since he himself had desired Pitys; I would praise Echo when she called the name of Amaryllis after I did.

[10] Str. 9.421, Luc. *Dom.* 24, *DDeor.* 6.2, D.L. 1.72, Clem. Al. *Strom.* 5.8.48 (observing that Branchus' foundation of Didyma is found in Call. *Iamb.*), Philostr. *Ep.* 5 and 8, Q.S. 1.283, Him. *Or.* 8.210.

[11] Demeter is mentioned at 4.13.3, Hermes at 4.34.3, Zeus and Dionysus several times, but Athena, Artemis, Hera and Poseidon not at all.

This has long been seen to be close to a passage in Propertius, 1.18.19–32, of which the key lines are as follows:[12]

> uos eritis testes, si quos habet arbor amores,
>   fagus et Arcadio pinus amica deo.
> ah quotiens uestras resonant mea uerba sub umbras,
>   scribitur et teneris 'Cynthia' corticibus! …
> sed qualiscumque's, resonent mihi 'Cynthia' silvae,
>   nec deserta tuo nomine saxa uacent.

> You will be witnesses, if a tree experiences any desire, you, beech, and pine dear to the Arcadian god. Ah! How often do my words echo beneath your shade, and 'Cynthia' is written in your tender bark … But however you behave, the woods will echo my cry 'Cynthia', nor will the deserted rocks be without your name.

This passage in turn (on the basis of similarities in Aristaenetus 1.10) has been argued to relate to Callimachus, *Acontius and Cydippe*. In his discussion almost four decades ago Richard Hunter tentatively concluded that both *Acontius and Cydippe* and Longus might echo the Hellenistic poet Philitas.[13] I suggest that Longus may echo both Philitas and Callimachus, though the view that Chariton and Longus knew Latin poetry has been much more forcefully argued recently than it was in 1983.[14]

But if Longus knew Callimachus' *Acontius and Cydippe*, then his use of the term ἱστορία in his *prooemion* must be re-assessed. His opening sentence runs:

> ἐν Λέσβωι θηρῶν ἐν ἄλσει Νυμφῶν θέαμα εἶδον κάλλιστον ὧν εἶδον· εἰκόνα γραπτήν, ἱστορίαν ἔρωτος.

> In Lesbos, hunting, in a grove of the Nymphs I saw a spectacle that was the fairest I ever saw: an image that was painted, a story of desire.

The term ἱστορία appears elsewhere in the novels only at Heliodorus 2.29.5 (an ostentatiously Herodotean use, in the sense 'enquiry'),[15] and it might be thought to be an unexpected term for what will become Longus' narrative. But significantly it is used by Callimachus, *Aitia*, fr. 75.6–7 Pfeiffer

[12] 2.13.3–8 have also been brought into the discussion.

[13] Hunter 1983, 79–81.

[14] See Tilg 2010, Jolowicz 2015 and forthcoming.

[15] ἦλθον δὴ καὶ εἰς τὴν σὴν Αἴγυπτον καὶ Καταδούπους αὐτοὺς καθ' ἱστορίαν τῶν καταρρακτῶν τοῦ Νείλου, 'Indeed I even came to your country Egypt and the Catadoupi themselves in pursuit of knowledge about the Nile's cataracts'.

of another tale of ἔρως, 'desire', that of Acontius and Cydippe, though as is pointed out by Harder its meaning here 'must be "information" or "knowledge" obtained by scholarly inquiries (see LSJ s.v. I 2) rather than just "story" as suggested by e.g. Hopkinson ad loc. and d'Alessio's translation':[16]

> ὤναο κ̣άρτ̣' ἕνεκ' οὔ τι θεῆς ἴδες ἱερὰ φρικτῆς,
> ἐξ ἂν ἐπεὶ καὶ τῶν ἤρυγες ἱστ̣ορίην.

> You have benefited greatly that you did not see the rites of the dreadful goddess, since forth you would have spewed information even about them.

Whether Longus, if he knew this couplet, understood ἱστ̣ορίη to mean 'information' or (like Hopkinson, d'Alessio and others) 'story', we cannot tell.

If I seem to have made some case for Longus knowing the *Aitia*, then let me add two long shots. Longus' animals are confined to pens in winter, 3.3.4:

> τότε βοῶν ἐπὶ φάτναις φροντὶς ἦν ἄχυρον ἐσθιόντων, αἰγῶν καὶ προβάτων ἐν τοῖς σηκοῖς φυλλάδας, ὑῶν ἐν τοῖς συφεοῖς ἄκυλον καὶ βαλάνους.

> then attention was given to the cattle beside their mangers, eating bran, to goats and sheep eating shoots in their pens, to pigs eating mast and acorns in their pig-sties.

Does this confinement recall that of Molorcus' animals – which include a goat – penned in because of the depredations of the Nemean lion, as Molorcus describes at *Aitia* fr. 54b27–32?

An even longer shot, which I can claim to be no more than a suspicion, is that the term νικητήριον, 'prize of victory', with which Longus stamps the last triumphant speech of Daphnis at the very end of his Book 3 (3.34.2) is deployed partly to recall the prominence of the *Victoria Berenices* in Book 3 of the *Aitia*.

7 Some More Key Words

Now three further lexical throws. The opening word of the *Aitia*, πολλάκις, 'often', occurs sixteen times in Longus, from its application to the frequent disappearance of the nanny-goat that suckles Daphnis (1.2.1) to its

[16] Harder 2012, 590.

retrospective use of Chloe's frequent baths in the spring of the Nymphs (4.32.3). This frequency is much higher than that of πολλάκις in any of the other three earlier novels: it averages four per book, as against 1.375 per book in Chariton, 1.8 per book in Xenophon of Ephesus, 2.625 per book in Achilles Tatius. Heliodorus, admittedly, has proportionately even more uses of πολλάκις, 4.9 per book.

Longus' use of λεπτός, 'slender', is also of interest. In it he outstrips all the other novelists: one instance in each book, as opposed to an average of 0.625 per book in Chariton and Achilles Tatius, 0.4 per book in Xenophon, and 0.3 per book in Heliodorus.

Longus' first and last uses of λεπτός are especially striking. In the first, at 1.10.2, Daphnis is described cutting slender reeds to make a syrinx, his main creator of music:

> ὁ δὲ καλάμους ἐκτεμὼν λεπτοὺς καὶ τρήσας τὰς τῶν γονάτων διαφυάς, ἀλλήλοις τε κηρῶι μαλθακῶι συναρτήσας, μέχρι νυκτὸς συρίττειν ἐμελέτα.

> And he would cut slender reeds and after piercing their knobbly joints and fixing them to each other with soft beeswax would practise syrinx-playing until nightfall.

Daphnis never composes songs or poems, though at the party celebrating Chloe's recovery he does, along with others, sing ὠιδὰς εἰς τὰς Νύμφας, παλαιῶν ποιμένων ποιήματα,'songs to the Nymphs, the creations of shepherds of old' (2.31.2); so the music of the syrinx is for Daphnis what poetry is for Callimachus, and the epithet λεπτός given to the reeds from which his syrinx is fashioned becomes significantly Callimachean.

Longus' fourth and last use of λεπτός is of the αἱμασιά, 'dry-stone wall', that surrounds the παράδεισος, 'formal garden', of Dionysophanes at 4.2.4:[17] καὶ ταῦτα μέντοι λεπτῆς αἱμασιᾶς περιέθει περίβολος, 'and around them (sc. the outer circle of non-fruiting trees) in turn ran a slender perimeter-wall of dry stones'. Why does Longus choose to describe the wall as λεπτῆς, 'slender', when its protecting function would be better achieved if it were sturdy? The παράδεισος, like Philetas' garden in Book 2, is (amongst other things) a *mis-en-abyme* of Longus' work as a whole, as many scholars have seen: early in Book 4, which we know from his *prooemion* will be his last,[18] he uses this *mis-en-abyme* to ask us to contemplate his work's combination of smallness of scale with superlative τέχνη:

[17] The two other uses are at 2.12.3 (of the Methymnan pleasure-cruisers' fishing lines) and 3.26.2 (of Daphnis' slim hope of marrying Chloe given his foster-father's poverty).

[18] τέτταρας βίβλους, 'four books', *pr.* 3.

> τέτμητο καὶ διακέκριτο πάντα καὶ στέλεχος στελέχους ἀφειστήκει, ἐν μετεώρωι δὲ οἱ κλάδοι συνέπιπτον ἀλλήλοις καὶ ἐπήλλαττον τὰς κόμας· ἐδόκει μέντοι καὶ ἡ τούτων φύσις εἶναι τέχνης. ἦσαν καὶ ἀνθῶν πρασιαί, ὧν τὰ μὲν ἔφερεν ἡ γῆ, τὰ δὲ ἐποίει τέχνη.
>
> Everything was divided and kept distinct, and tree-trunk stood apart from tree-trunk, whereas up in the air the branches hung close to each other and interwove their foliage: it seemed, however, that even their natural shape was the product of art. There were also beds of flowers, some of which the earth produced, whereas others were created by art.
>
> Longus, *Daphnis and Chloe* 4.2.5–6

It is to that small scale associated with extreme τέχνη, 'art', that Longus' epithet λεπτός points, inviting readers to measure his Persian παράδεισος, and his work as a whole, not by the Persian chain, thus heeding the prescription of *Ait.* fr.1.17–18: αὖθι δὲ τέχνηι | κρίνετε, μὴ σχοίνωι Περσίδι τὴν σοφίην, 'and hereafter judge skill by art, not by the Persian chain'.[19]

It is no surprise, then, that Longus also makes much more frequent use of the word τέχνη than the other novelists: they average 3.25 instances per book, beginning with the τέχνην περιττήν, 'outstanding art', in the second sentence of his *prooemion* (where it is used of the painting with which his literary work competes), as opposed to 1.5 per book in Chariton, 1.4 in Xenophon, 1.75 in Achilles Tatius and 2.3 in Heliodorus.

It may be held that no one of these suggestions on its own, even that concerning ἀρτιγένειος, goes very far towards showing that Longus knew and exploited Callimachus' *Aitia*. But taken together they make a case that must at least be considered. And if Longus did know and decide to exploit the *Aitia*, a further question arises: was the rather unusual four-book structure of Longus' ἱστορία ἔρωτος, 'story of desire', also a tribute to Callimachus, as well as a general catalyst of readerly reflection on where Longus stands in relation to his many literary predecessors? And if his choice of four books is significant, what relation should we see between *Daphnis and Chloe* and Callimachus' theme and title *Aitia*? Should we read as a tribute to the *Aitia* Longus' inclusion in each of his first three books of a short μῦθος, 'myth', which in every case offers an αἴτιον, 'explanation' or 'origin' – the tale of Phatta (1.27), the myth of Syrinx (2.34), the myth of Echo (3.23) – corresponding to which in his fourth book we are given the answers to our hitherto unanswered questions about the origins of Chloe and about the *aition*, 'origin', of the nymphs' sanctuary and its paintings which opened

[19] For the 'Persian chain' see Harder 2012, 52–3.

Book 1? The number of features of the *Aitia* which are shared with *Daphnis and* Chloe is not small, and which of these was the first to catch Longus' eye cannot even be guessed. It may, indeed, have been none of those already examined, but the image of Hesiod μῆλα νέμοντι, 'herding his sheep', early in *Aitia* Book 1 (fr. 2.1–2).

8 Conclusions

In my discussion above I began my examination of instances of possible intertextuality of *Daphnis and Chloe* with Callimachus with what seemed to me the one for which the strongest case could be made, and then I grouped further instances broadly by genre. In conclusion I want to revisit some of these instances in the order in which a reader of Longus encounters them, and ask what can be inferred about Longus' agenda.

Longus' proem immediately presents a concentration of Callimachean elements which may be noticed by a second-time reader (a reader who has been alerted by ἀρτιγένειος, see above Section 2) and even by some first-time readers: the very existence of a preface, absent from our four other extant novels unless we include the rather different, albeit related, introductory sequence of Achilles Tatius 1.1–2; the highlighting of τέχνη, 'skill'; the announcement that the work will be divided into four books; and the description of its content as ἱστορία ἔρωτος, 'a story of desire'.

Longus' account of the exposed babies' discovery, naming and upbringing (1.1–10) establishes Theocritean pastoral poetry as his chief intertext, but that sequence concludes (1.10.2) with Daphnis' syrinx-making from reeds that are λεπτοί, 'slender' (see above Section 7); only a few chapters later Chloe compares her love-sickness to a ἕλκος, 'wound' (1.14.1), and Dorcon is introduced as ἀρτιγένειος (1.15.1).

After that concentration of possible Callimachean intertexts it is only in Book 2 that they reappear, with Philetas' recollections of his desire for Amaryllis (2.7.6, see above Section 6) and Chloe's bathing of Daphnis κατὰ πολλὴν ἡσυχίαν, 'in great tranquillity' (2.18.1, see above Section 4).

Book 3 has only two, less certain intertexts: the penned-in animals of 3.3.4 (see above Section 6) and the description of winter as potentially ἀνέραστον at 3.11.3 (see above Section 3).

Book 4 has a much greater frequency. It opens with a further evocation of Callimachean τέχνη, 'skill', in its *ecphrasis* of Dionysophanes' garden at 4.2.5–6 (see above Section 7), then introduces Astylus as another youth who is ἀρτιγένειος (4.10.1); continues with Gnathon's appeal to the myth of

Apollo and Branchus (4.17.6, see above Section 5) and with Dionysophanes' account of his son and daughter dying on the same day (4.24.2, see above Section 3). The final Callimachean touch in *Daphnis and Chloe* may be the recapitulory remark at 4.32.3 that Chloe had πολλάκις, 'often', bathed in the πηγή, 'spring', where readers had encountered her bathing Daphnis κατὰ πολλὴν ἡσυχίαν 'in great tranquillity' (2.18.1), reminding them that Longus' *Chloe* has repeatedly drawn upon Callimachus as its πηγή, 'source'.[20]

What is the nature of this intertextuality? On the one hand Longus is not reworking an earlier classic work or *oeuvre* to create something new that stands firmly in the same tradition, in the way that Quintus of Smyrna, for example, perhaps in the same century, hangs his *Posthomerica* predominantly upon the *Iliad* and the *Odyssey*. The two traditions in which *Daphnis and Chloe* stands are those of pastoral poetry and the novels, and other intertexts, such as Sappho, Callimachus, and Hellenistic epigram play a subordinate albeit important role.[21]

Nor, however, are these subordinate intertexts simply random demonstrations of Longus' wide reading. Many of them invite his reader to add something from the text evoked to their response to a passage in *Daphnis and Chloe* – the hint at the erotic proclivities of an ἀρτιγένειος (which admittedly comes from the Theocritean, not the Callimachean intertext); the *aura* of Nymphs' divine presence that is imparted by the phrase κατὰ πολλὴν ἡσυχίαν; the wide range of mythological knowledge that can be expected in urban πεπαιδευμένοι, 'educated men', as exemplified even in one of their lesser members, Gnathon, and that adds to our understanding of the society from which Dionysophanes and Megacles come; the profound grief that Dionysophanes must have felt, even if he does not now express it in his narrative, when his two children died. Such intertexts offer a subtle and economical enrichment of Longus' slender work.

[20] For the privileging of Chloe as the work's subject cf. Pan's description of her at 2.27.2 as παρθένον ἐξ ἧς Ἔρως μῦθον ποιῆσαι θέλει, 'a maiden of whom Eros wants to create a myth'.

[21] Cf. Bowie 2019g, 2–6.

46 Silence in Chariton, Xenophon, Achilles Tatius and Longus (2020)

1 Introduction

In this paper I explore some of the important roles that silences play in our first four extant Greek novels.[1] Silence is a topic that has received little attention from scholars working on the novels, and Silvia Montiglio's classic study of 2000 stopped short of later Greek literature.[2] In what follows I limit my discussion to silences that involve the absence of speech. There are of course other sorts of silence – e.g. the puzzling absence of any reference to music in Xenophon's account of the processions to the Ephesian temple of Artemis (1.2.2–3) and to the couple's wedding chamber (1.8.2–3) – which fall outside my focus.

2 Authorial Revelation

I begin on a macro-level, and suggest that the novelist's writing of his text itself constitutes a breaking of silence. This breaking is never more than implicit, but in two of our novels a narrator is introduced in such a way as to draw readers' attention to the replacement of silence by the authorial voice. In the opening of Achilles Tatius the unnamed first-person narrator, himself a self-declared ἐρωτικός, 'man susceptible to desire', moves silently from the temple of Astarte in Sidon to tour the city: that silence is broken in front of the sexually provocative painting of Europa, first by his exclamation at the power of Eros, then by the stranger Cleitophon's sudden disclosure of his tribulations:[3]

[1] Like most scholars who have worked on the Greek novels since papyri demonstrated the mistakes in Rohde's chronology, I am persuaded that Heliodorus wrote after Longus, but at a Heliodorus conference in Cambridge in December 2018 Georg Danek assembled a list of similar passages where one of the two writers may be argued to be influenced by the other, and proposed that this evidence pointed rather to the priority of Heliodorus. For the chronology of the earlier novels see Bowie 2002a (Chapter 25 in this volume); Henrichs 2011.

[2] Montiglio 2000; Montiglio 2020a discusses Heliodorus.

[3] For the important contribution made by this scene to the characterisation of Cleitophon see De Temmerman 2014, 152–61; Whitmarsh 2020 *ad loc.*

ἐγὼ δὲ καὶ τἄλλα μὲν ἐπῄνουν τῆς γραφῆς, ἅτε δὲ ὢν ἐρωτικὸς περιεργότερον ἔβλεπον τὸν ἄγοντα τὸν βοῦν Ἔρωτα, καὶ 'οἷον', εἶπον, 'ἄρχει βρέφος οὐρανοῦ καὶ γῆς καὶ θαλάσσης'. ταῦτά μου λέγοντος, νεανίσκος καὶ αὐτὸς παρεστώς, 'ἐγὼ ταῦτ' ἂν ἐδείκνυν',[4] ἔφη, 'τοσαύτας ὕβρεις ἐξ ἔρωτος παθών'. 'καὶ τί πέπονθας', εἶπον, 'ὦγαθέ; καὶ γὰρ ὁρῶ σου τὴν ὄψιν οὐ μακρὰν τῆς τοῦ θεοῦ τελετῆς'. 'σμῆνος ἀνεγείρεις', εἶπε, 'λόγων· τὰ γὰρ ἐμὰ μύθοις ἔοικε'.

I was admiring the whole picture, but – being susceptible to desire myself – paid more particular attention to that part of it where Eros was leading the bull; and 'Look', I said, 'how that baby controls sky and land and sea!' As I was speaking, a young man who was also standing by the painting broke in: 'I could have demonstrated that', he said, 'since I am one who has suffered many humiliations at the hands of love'. 'What have your sufferings been, my friend?', I asked: 'I can see by your looks that it is not long since you became one of the god's initiates'. 'You are stirring up a whole swarm of stories', he said, 'my experiences are like myths'.

Achilles Tatius 1.2.1–2[5]

This scene prompts readers to see the novel's text as a whole as breaking silence, an outpouring of the novelist's ear-catching λόγοι, 'words', into what could otherwise be readerly tranquillity.

The relation between a silent image and audible λόγοι is revisited by Achilles Tatius in Book 5 when he narrates Cleitophon's telling of (as Cleitophon has it) Philomela's trick of revealing her rape by weaving her story into a πέπλος, 'robe':

'ἡ γὰρ Φιλομήλας τέχνη σιωπῶσαν εὕρηκε φωνήν. ὑφαίνει γὰρ πέπλον ἄγγελον καὶ τὸ δρᾶμα πλέκει ταῖς κρόκαις, καὶ μιμεῖται τὴν γλῶτταν ἡ χείρ ...'

'Philomela's art invented a silent voice. For she weaves a tapestry that is a messenger, working her drama into its threads, and her hand imitates her tongue ...'

Achilles Tatius 5.5.4–5

A comparable decision to present speech in place of silence is made by Longus' first-person narrator who (like that of Achilles Tatius) is never named. This narrator chooses not simply to admire the painting in the

[4] ἐδείκνυν is the reading of **F** (i.e. the far from reliable *Laurentianus Conv. Soppr.* 627) accepted by Gaselee 1917. The other manuscripts read εἰδείην, printed by Vilborg 1955 and Garnaud 1991.

[5] The translations of Chariton, Xenophon, Achilles Tatius and Longus are based on those of the Loeb Classical Library editions by Goold, Henderson, Gaselee and Henderson, respectively, but adapted.

Nymphs' grove in silent awe, but to seek out an ἐξηγητής, a *cicerone*, who will expound its story, thus admitting readers to a world from which either party's silence would have excluded them:

> ἰδόντα με καὶ θαυμάσαντα πόθος ἔσχεν ἀντιγράψαι τῆι γραφῆι· καὶ ἀναζητησάμενος ἐξηγητὴν τῆς εἰκόνος τέτταρας βίβλους ἐξεπονησάμην.
>
> I looked and marvelled, and a longing seized me to rival the painting in writing; I sought out an expounder of the image and have carefully fashioned four books.
>
> Longus *pr.* 3

Nothing similar is found in the openings of the earlier works of Chariton or Xenophon, but a related move is made by Chariton almost at his novel's close. Late in Book 8, Hermocrates urges Chaereas, inclined to excise from his narration episodes that might be distressing, rather to tell all:[6]

> Ἑρμοκράτης δὲ ἔφη 'μηδὲν αἰδεσθῆις, ὦ τέκνον, κἂν λέγης τι λυπηρότερον ἢ πικρότερον ἡμῖν· τὸ γὰρ τέλος λαμπρὸν γενόμενον ἐπισκοτεῖ τοῖς προτέροις ἅπασι, τὸ δὲ μὴ ῥηθὲν ὑπόνοιαν ἔχει χαλεπωτέραν ἐξ αὐτῆς τῆς σιωπῆς'.
>
> Hermocrates said: 'My son, do not be embarrassed, even if you have something rather painful or distressing to tell us. The brilliant conclusion overshadows all that has gone before, but saying nothing means that we will suspect worse from your very silence'.
>
> Chariton 8.7.4

Shortly thereafter Chaereas indeed asks to be allowed to omit the later, allegedly more distressing part of his narrative to the Syracusans:

> θρῆνον ἐξέρρηξεν ἐπὶ τούτοις τὸ πλῆθος, εἶπε δὲ Χαιρέας 'ἐπιτρέψατέ μοι τὰ ἑξῆς σιωπᾶν, σκυθρωπότερα γάρ ἐστι τῶν πρώτων'· ὁ δὲ δῆμος ἐξεβόησε 'λέγε πάντα'. καὶ ὃς ἔλεγεν …
>
> At this a groan burst forth from the crowd, and Chaereas said: 'Let me pass over in silence what came next, for it is grimmer than what happened at the start'. But the people shouted: 'Tell us everything!' And he began to tell …
>
> Chariton 8.8.2

On the surface it seems that Chaereas, and his puppet-master Chariton, have given both the Syracusans within the text and readers outside the text

[6] For the importance of Chaereas' narrative here for establishing the mature and decisive character he has developed as a result of the novel's tribulations see Whitmarsh 2011, 63–4.

a narrative in which all has been told. But this repeated reference to omission, as well as drawing attention to the omissions and distortions that can be detected in Chaereas' narrative,[7] may perhaps be intended to tempt readers into thinking that both tales – that of Chaereas and the encapsulating narrative of Chariton – might well be incomplete and selective accounts.

3 Characters' Choices between Speech and Silence

This instance has taken my discussion down to the level of characters' silences in the novelists' narratives, and I now examine a range of situations where their choice between speech and silence is crucial to the plot's development. One such situation, whose analysis would carry my argument too far from my core themes, is when the nature or degree of a protagonist's romantic involvement with a third party is crucially suppressed in communications between the couple or to third parties. This pattern, traceable ultimately to Odysseus' censored account of his wanderings to Penelope, is found in Chariton, Achilles Tatius and Longus, but eschewed by Xenophon. In the following pages I examine some other cases in Chariton and Longus, together with a single, ephemeral case in Xenophon.

(a) Chariton

In Chariton the choice between speech and silence repeatedly affects how the plot develops. Thus the motif of concealing a protagonist's sexual involvement with a third party mentioned above is implied and inverted when, in Book 1, Chariton has the lackey of his villain from Agrigento claim to Chaereas he can no longer keep silent about Callirhoe's infidelity, a disclosure of 'fake news' that is momentous for the plot:[8]

> 'ἀηδῶς μέν,' εἶπεν, 'ὦ Χαιρέα, σκυθρωπόν σοι πρᾶγμα μηνύω καὶ πάλαι βουλόμενος εἰπεῖν ὤκνουν· ἐπεὶ δὲ ἤδη φανερῶς ὑβρίζῃ καὶ θρυλλεῖται πανταχοῦ τὸ δεινόν, οὐχ ὑπομένω σιωπᾶν· φύσει τε γὰρ μισοπόνηρός εἰμι καὶ σοὶ μάλιστα εὔνους'.
>
> 'Chaereas, it is with distress that I report to you a grim matter; I have long wanted to speak, but I hesitated. Since, however, the point has been reached

[7] On these distortions and omissions see De Temmerman 2014, 100–5.
[8] On this and related episodes of manipulation see De Temmerman 2014, 81.

> when you are being publicly humiliated and the scandal is being discussed everywhere, I cannot remain silent. It is my nature to hate wrong, and I have good will to you in particular'.
>
> Chariton 1.4.5

Chariton's remaining cases involve the suppression of facts whose revelation would almost certainly have given the story a quite different turn – above all concealment of the speaker's identity, another motif that goes back as far as the *Odyssey*. Thus in Book 2 Callirhoe reveals her name, but is initially reticent about her origins, and asks Dionysius of Miletus to let her remain so:

> 'Καλλιρόη', φησίν (ἤρεσε Διονυσίωι καὶ τὸ ὄνομα), τὰ δὲ λοιπὰ ἐσιώπα. πυνθανομένου δὲ λιπαρῶς 'δέομαί σου' φησίν, 'ὦ δέσποτα, συγχώρησόν μοι τὴν ἐμαυτῆς τύχην σιωπᾶν.'
>
> 'Callirhoe', she said, and the very name delighted Dionysius. On the rest of her story, however, she remained silent; and when he questioned her insistently, she said, 'Master, I beg you, allow me to remain silent about my fortunes'.
>
> Chariton 2.5.6

In the event Callirhoe does not persist in her silence, and what she says about the contrast between her present servile and previous elite status touches on the theme of the instability of fortune important in all the novels.[9]

In Chariton's third Book, three cases cluster between 3.9 and 3.11, their close sequence forcing readers to contemplate the respective narrative dividends of silence and revelation.

In the first, the aged priestess of Aphrodite initially resists Callirhoe's demand to be told more about the two young men whom she has observed visiting her temple – had she persisted in this silence, the story would have developed quite differently. But she gives in, and once Callirhoe realises that one of these men was Chaereas she decides that they must start looking for him, but that they must not reveal they are doing so:

> δείσασα δὲ ἡ πρεσβῦτις τὸ μὲν πρῶτον ἄφωνος εἱστήκει, μόλις δὲ ἐφθέγξατο 'μόνον εἶδον αὐτούς, οὐδὲν ἤκουσα'. 'ποδαποὺς τὸ εἶδος; ἀναμνήσθητι τὸν χαρακτῆρα αὐτῶν'. ἔφρασεν ἡ γραῦς οὐκ ἀκριβῶς μέν, ὑπώπτευσε δὲ ὅμως ἐκείνη τὴν ἀλήθειαν. ὃ γὰρ βούλεται, τοῦθ' ἕκαστος καὶ οἴεται. βλέψασα δὲ πρὸς Πλαγγόνα, 'δύναται', φησίν, 'ὁ δυστυχὴς Χαιρέας πλανώμενος ἐνθάδε παρεῖναι. τί οὖν ἐγένετο; ζητήσωμεν αὐτόν, ἀλλὰ σιγῶσαι'.

[9] On this and on the Odyssean motif of concealing identity see Whitmarsh 2011, 215–16.

> At first the old woman stood there speechless with fright, but eventually she managed to say, 'I only saw them. I heard nothing'. 'What did they look like? Try to remember their features'. Though the old woman's account was imprecise, still Callirhoe suspected the truth, for people are apt to believe what they want to. Looking at Plangon she said, 'It is possible that ill-fated Chaereas has come here in his wanderings. What can have happened to him? Let us look for him; but let us keep quiet about it'.
>
> Chariton 3.9.2–3

Here the adverb μόλις, 'eventually', pinpoints the moment at which the character's decision might go either way – the old woman almost decided *not* to speak. And if she had remained silent …? In this passage Chariton, like other novelists elsewhere,[10] uses the single but powerful word μόλις to zoom in on a cliff-hanging situation.

Very soon after this, the estate-manager Phocas, realising that he will be in trouble whether he speaks or is silent, agrees to tell Dionysius – but *only* Dionysius – what he knows:

> αἰσθόμενος δὲ Φωκᾶς οἷ καθέστηκε δεινοῦ καὶ λέγων καὶ σιωπῶν 'σοί,' φησί, 'δέσποτα, ἐρῶ μόνωι τὴν ἀλήθειαν'.
>
> But realising what a tight spot he had got into, whether he spoke or remained silent, Phocas said, 'Master, I will tell you the truth in private'.
>
> Chariton 3.9.7

Only a page or so later Dionysius himself insists on the suppression of information, namely two crucial facts about the burning of Chaereas' trireme:

> προστάξας δὲ Φωκᾶι τὰ μὲν ἄλλα τῶν γεγονότων φανερῶς διηγεῖσθαι, δύο δὲ ταῦτα σιγᾶν, τὸ ἴδιον στρατήγημα καὶ ὅτι ἐκ τῆς τριήρους τινὲς ἔτι ζῶσι …
>
> He instructed Phocas to speak freely of all else that had happened, but to keep silent on two matters: first, the stratagem that he had himself employed, and, second, the fact that some of the men on the trireme were still alive …
>
> Chariton 3.10.1

(b) Xenophon

The single and less momentous Xenophontic case of such silence is when the noble bandit Hippothous recognises that the girl offered for sale by the

[10] E.g. Longus 4.23.1.

brothel-keeper in Taranto is Habrocomes' bride Anthia: *she* does not recognise Hippothous, but he buys her, and for the moment keeps quiet. The reader may be allowed to imagine that this silence is chosen so as not to incite the brothel-keeper to up his price for Anthia; but the narrator has the further objective of postponing, albeit momentarily, her recognition of Hippothous:

> τότε μὲν ἡσυχίαν ἤγαγεν, ὠνησάμενος δὲ αὐτὴν παρὰ τοῦ πορνοβοσκοῦ ἄγει πρὸς ἑαυτὸν καὶ θαρρεῖν παρεκελεύετο καὶ ὅστις ἦν λέγει.
>
> For the moment he kept quiet, but once he had bought her from the brothel-keeper he took her to his house, encouraged her to keep her spirits up, and told her who he was.
>
> Xenophon 5.9.9

(c) Longus

The most far-reaching instance in Longus where the choice between speech and silence is crucial for the development of the plot is where (as later less protractedly in the case of Charicleia in Heliodorus), the couple's foundling origins must be concealed for some four fifths of the narrative in order to allow them to grow up as simple herdsfolk. In Longus both sets of herding foster-parents initially keep the origins of their babies secret: ultimately in Book 4 first Lamon's decision to break silence (4.18.3), then Dryas' resolve to do likewise (4.30.1), create turning-points in the plot that release Longus' readers from suspense.

Equally significant for Longus' plot-development is the moment late in Book 3 when Lamon thinks very carefully before replying to Dryas' request that he let Daphnis marry Chloe: if at this point Lamon had given the 'wrong' answer, the story might have had a quite different ending:

> ὁ μὲν ταῦτα καὶ ἔτι πλείω <τούτων> ἔλεγεν, οἷα τοῦ πεῖσαι λέγων ἆθλον ἔχων τὰς τρισχιλίας· ὁ δὲ Λάμων μήτε πενίαν ἔτι προβάλλεσθαι δυνάμενος (αὐτοὶ γὰρ οὐχ ὑπερηφάνουν) μήτε ἡλικίαν Δάφνιδος (ἤδη γὰρ μειράκιον ἦν) τὸ μὲν ἀληθὲς οὐδ' ὣς ἐξηγόρευσεν, ὅτι κρείττων ἐστὶ τοιούτου γάμου, χρόνον δὲ σιωπήσας ὀλίγον οὕτως ἀπεκρίνατο.
>
> He said this and more <than this>, as was natural for one whose prize for speaking persuasively was the three thousand drachmas. As an excuse Lamon could no longer plead poverty, since the other couple were not looking down on them, nor Daphnis' age, since he was now a young man.

Even so, he did not speak out with the truth, that Daphnis was too good for such a marriage; but after a brief silence he gave this answer.

Longus 3.30.5

The 'silence' card is played slightly differently when, near the end of Book 4, Dryas reveals Chloe's real status to Dionysophanes: here the silence is not his, but like a good servant Dryas waits for his masters to stop conversing:

καὶ γενομένης ἡμέρας ἔχων ἐν τῆι πήραι τὰ γνωρίσματα πρόσεισι τῶι Διονυσοφάνει καὶ τῆι Κλεαρίστηι καθημένοις ἐν τῶι παραδείσωι (παρῆν δὲ καὶ ὁ Ἄστυλος καὶ αὐτὸς ὁ Δάφνις) καὶ σιωπῆς γενομένης ἤρξατο λέγειν ...

At daybreak he packed the tokens in his knapsack and visited Dionysophanes and Cleariste as they sat in the park; Astylus was present, as was Daphnis himself. When silence fell he began his speech ...

Longus 4.30.2

This pattern is related to the *topos* 'all others were silent, and X began to speak', which I shall discuss shortly.

Earlier in Book 3 Daphnis himself makes a different choice between speech and silence. His decision to give up his mid-winter attempt to see Chloe and instead to return home in silence almost deprives *him* of quality time with *her* and the reader of an entertaining episode:[11]

'ἄμεινον ἄρα σιγᾶν. Χλόην δὲ ἦρος ὄψομαι, ἐπεὶ μὴ εἵμαρτο, ὡς ἔοικε, χειμῶνός με ταύτην ἰδεῖν'. τοιαῦτα δή τινα διανοηθεὶς καὶ σιωπῆι τὰ θηραθέντα συλλαβὼν ὥρμητο ἀπιέναι· καὶ ὥσπερ αὐτὸν οἰκτείραντος τοῦ Ἔρωτος τάδε γίνεται.

'So better to say nothing. I will see Chloe in the spring, since I'm apparently not fated to see her during the winter'. With ideas of this sort he silently collected what he had caught and set off on the way back: and, as if Love had taken pity on him, the following happened.

Longus 3.6.4–5

In the event one of Dryas' dogs scampers off with a piece of meat it has stolen and Dryas, in hot pursuit, spots Daphnis and invites him to join the family meal. The choice Daphnis had made was all set to short-circuit the description of his winter canoodling with Chloe, and the turn taken by events is attributed to a dog's exploitation of human ἀμέλεια, 'negligence', not to Daphnis having made a bold decision.

Another form of silence is that which is a product of fear.

[11] Note that winter itself is later figured as a μακρὰ σιωπά, 'long silence', Longus 3.10.4.

4 The Silence of Fear

In Book 1 of Chariton his pirate Theron reckons that while being sold Callirhoe will keep quiet about her identity out of fear:

> 'ἐγὼ δὲ ἀποδώσομαι τὴν γυναῖκα μᾶλλον ἢ ἀπολέσω· πωλουμένη μὲν γὰρ σιγήσει διὰ τὸν φόβον, πραθεῖσα δὲ κατηγορείτω τῶν μὴ παρόντων'.
>
> 'I will sell the girl rather than kill her. While she is being sold she will be silent out of fear; once sold let her accuse us, when we are no longer there'.
>
> Chariton 1.10.8

Another case in Chariton exemplifying the silence of fear is found in the silence of the litigants entering the courtroom when the Persian king is about to hear the claims of Mithridates and Dionysius to Callirhoe:

> παράγονται δὲ οἱ δικαζόμενοι μετὰ σιγῆς καὶ δέους …
>
> Those summoned to judgment are brought forward in silence and trepidation …
>
> Chariton 5.4.7

Longus too has a scene in Book 4 displaying the silence of a fearful inferior. When Lamon ends *his* speech of disclosure (ἐσιώπησε, 'he fell silent') and the parasite Gnathon threatens him, Dionysophanes is peremptory in his handling of Gnathon:

> ὁ μὲν Λάμων ταῦτα εἰπὼν ἐσιώπησε καὶ πολλὰ ἀφῆκε δάκρυα· τοῦ δὲ Γνάθωνος θρασυνομένου καὶ πληγὰς ἀπειλοῦντος ὁ Διονυσοφάνης τοῖς εἰρημένοις ἐκπλαγεὶς τὸν μὲν Γνάθωνα σιωπᾶν ἐκέλευσε, σφόδρα τὴν ὀφρὺν εἰς αὐτὸν τοξοποιήσας.
>
> With this Lamon fell silent and wept copious tears, while Gnathon kept up a bold front and threatened to beat him. Dionysophanes was astonished by what he had heard and with a severe frown told Gnathon to be quiet.
>
> Longus 4.20.1

Needless to say, Gnathon is now totally silent.

Longus offers a different take on fearful silence in Book 1: the cowherd Dorcon, attempting to ambush Chloe, initially puts up in silence with the couple's dogs' biting because he is desperate not to be discovered:

> τέως μὲν οὖν τὸν ἔλεγχον φοβούμενος καὶ ὑπὸ τοῦ δέρματος ἐπισκέποντος φρουρούμενος ἔκειτο σιωπῶν ἐν τῆι λόχμηι.

> For a while, fearful at the prospect of exposure and protected by the skin that covered him, he lay silent in the thicket.
>
> Longus 1.21.3

5 Silence and ἔρως

Next I address four other types of silence that relate specifically, and often closely, to the novels' central theme of ἔρως, 'sexual desire'.

First, silence in somebody usually voluble is a symptom of ἔρως, a motif that goes back to Sappho fr. 31. In Chariton we see it in Dionysius when in Book 2 he has fallen for Callirhoe; he tries to conceal his lovesickness, but his silence betrays it:

> Διονύσιος δὲ ἐτέτρωτο μέν, τὸ δὲ τραῦμα περιστέλλειν ἐπειρᾶτο, οἷα δὴ πεπαιδευμένος ἀνὴρ καὶ ἐξαιρέτως ἀρετῆς ἀντιποιούμενος. μήτε δὲ τοῖς οἰκέταις θέλων εὐκαταφρόνητος δοκεῖν μήτε μειρακιώδης τοῖς φίλοις, διεκαρτέρει παρ' ὅλην τὴν ἑσπέραν, οἰόμενος μὲν λανθάνειν, κατάδηλος δὲ γινόμενος μᾶλλον ἐκ τῆς σιωπῆς.
>
> Dionysius was wounded, but tried to keep the wound under wraps, as became an educated man who made especial claims to excellence. Not wanting his servants to look down on him, or his friends to think him immature, he kept a tight rein on himself throughout the evening, thinking he was not noticed, but making himself more noticeable by his very silence.
>
> Chariton 2.4.1

In Longus this sort of silence appears first in Book 1's description of Daphnis' condition:

> σιωπηλὸς ἦν ὁ πρότερον τῶν ἀκρίδων λαλίστερος.
>
> He who before had been more voluble than a grass-hopper was now taciturn.
>
> Longus 1.17.4

The same *topos* is then re-run in Book 2 when Philetas recalls the symptoms of his own desire for Amaryllis:

> ἐβόων ὡς παιόμενος, ἐσιώπων ὡς νεκρούμενος, εἰς ποταμοὺς ἐνέβαινον ὡς καόμενος.
>
> I would scream as if beaten, I was as silent as if becoming a corpse, I plunged into rivers as if on fire.
>
> Longus 2.7.5

Second, being constrained to remain silent about one's ἔρως makes it less bearable. Thus a παρθένος, 'maiden', like Callirhoe suffers from her passion more acutely because she feels she cannot disclose it:[12]

> νὺξ ἐπῆλθεν ἀμφοτέροις δεινή· τὸ γὰρ πῦρ ἐξεκάετο. δεινότερον δ' ἔπασχεν ἡ παρθένος διὰ τὴν σιωπήν, αἰδουμένη κατάφωρος γενέσθαι.
>
> The ensuing night brought torment to both, for love's fire was raging. But the girl's suffering was worse because she had to keep silent, since she was ashamed of being discovered.
>
> Chariton 1.1.8

A similar maxim to that in Chariton, though not specifically about ἔρως, is attributed by the narrating Cleitophon to Leucippe in Achilles Tatius Book 2 – being able to respond to wounding accusations, he suggests, would make them more bearable:

> ἂν δέ τις ἀνάγκηι τοῦ κρείττονος σιγήσηι τὴν ἄμυναν, ἀλγεινότερα γίνεται τὰ ἕλκη τῆι σιωπηι· αἱ γὰρ ὠδῖνες τῶν ἐκ τοῦ λόγου κυμάτων, οὐκ ἀποπτύσασαι τὸν ἀφρόν, οἰδοῦσι περὶ ἑαυτὰς πεφυσημέναι.
>
> If the fact that one is dealing with a superior silences such a riposte, the wound grows more painful by reason of the silence thus enjoined. For the pains which are the result of these stormy waves of speech, if they cannot cast off their foam, swell up and become distended in their own world.
>
> Achilles Tatius 2.29.5

That it is Cleitophon, not Leucippe, who formulates these thoughts goes together with the relative silence and general inaccessibility of Leucippe after the end of Book 2.[13]

Silence about one's desire is also seen as problematic for different reasons by Cleitophon when he reproaches himself for not telling Leucippe that he desires her:

> ταῦτα εἰπὼν ἐχώρησεν ἔξω τῶν θυρῶν. ἐγὼ δὲ κατ' ἐμαυτὸν γενόμενος καὶ ὑπὸ τοῦ Σατύρου παροξυνθεὶς ἤσκουν ἐμαυτὸν εἰς εὐτολμίαν ἐπὶ τὴν παρθένον· 'μέχρι τίνος, ἄνανδρε, σιγᾷς; τί δὲ δειλὸς εἶ στρατιώτης ἀνδρείου θεοῦ; τὴν κόρην προσελθεῖν σοὶ περιμένεις;'

[12] On Callirhoe's 'self-isolating behaviour', of which this is one example, see De Temmerman 2014, 85.

[13] See Morales 2004, 201 on Leucippe's 'relative voicelessness'; De Temmerman 2014, 189; and Leucippe's remark at 3.11.2 discussed later p. 926.

> This said, he (sc. Satyrus) left the room. And when I was by myself, stimulated by Satyrus' words, I began to brace myself for making a bold approach to the maiden. 'How long', said I, 'do you mean to keep silent, you coward? Why are you so fearful a soldier of so brave a god? Do you expect the maiden to make an advance to you?'[14]
>
> Achilles Tatius 2.5.1

Third, and very different, Achilles Tatius' Cleitophon is advised by the more experienced Cleinias to conduct *in silence* his first physical advances to Leucippe and his attempts to kiss her:

> 'σὺ μηδὲν μὲν εἴπῃς πρὸς τὴν παρθένον Ἀφροδίσιον, τὸ δὲ ἔργον ζήτει πῶς γένηται σιωπῆι. παῖς γὰρ καὶ παρθένος ὅμοιοι μέν εἰσιν εἰς αἰδῶ· πρὸς δὲ τὴν τῆς Ἀφροδίτης χάριν κἂν γνώμης ἔχωσιν, ἃ πάσχουσιν ἀκούειν οὐ θέλουσι· τὴν γὰρ αἰσχύνην κεῖσθαι νομίζουσιν ἐν τοῖς ῥήμασι ...'
>
> 'ἐὰν δέ, τὴν πεῖραν προσάγων τὴν ἄλλην καὶ εὐάγωγον αὐτὴν κατασκευάσας, ἡδέως ἤδη προσέρχηι, σιώπα μὲν οὖν τὰ πολλὰ ὡς ἐν μυστηρίοις, φίλησον δὲ προσελθὼν ἠρέμα· τὸ γὰρ ἐραστοῦ φίλημα πρὸς ἐρωμένην θέλουσαν μὲν παρέχειν αἴτησίς ἐστι σιωπῆι, πρὸς ἀπειθοῦσαν δέ, ἱκετηρία.'
>
> 'Now say nothing to the maiden of the sexual act, rather look for a means whereby it may come about in silence: boys and maidens are alike bashful, however much they may be inclined towards the pleasures that Aphrodite can afford, they do not care to be told what is happening to them. For they think that shame lies in talking about it ...'[15]
>
> 'If, however, you act upon the other tack, gradually moulding her to your wishes and gaining easy access to her, be as silent as in mystery rituals, but approach her gently and kiss her: if the beloved is compliant, the lover's kiss is an invitation to her to accord him all her favours; if reluctant, it is a supplication.'
>
> Achilles Tatius 1.10.2–5

This is what Cleitophon indeed does in the next Book, avoiding not just speech but even any noise:

> ἡ δὲ παῖς προσελθοῦσα εἷλκε τὴν χεῖρα καὶ ἐπυνθάνετο ποῖ παταχθείην. κἀγώ, 'κατὰ τοῦ χείλους,' ἔφην. 'ἀλλὰ τί οὐκ ἐπάιδεις, φιλτάτη;' ἡ δὲ προσῆλθέ τε καὶ ἐνέθηκεν ὡς ἐπάισουσα τὸ στόμα, καί τι ἐψιθύριζεν, ἐπιπολῆς ψαύουσά μου τῶν χειλέων. κἀγὼ κατεφίλουν σιωπῆι, κλέπτων τῶν φιλημάτων τὸν ψόφον, ἡ δὲ ἀνοίγουσα καὶ κλείουσα τῶν χειλέων τὴν συμβολὴν τῶι τῆς ἐπωιδῆς ψιθυρίσματι φιλήματα ἐποίει.

[14] On the military imagery and the *topos* of *militia amoris* see Goldhill 1995, 75–76, De Temmerman 2014, 162–64.

[15] For the reluctance of παῖδες, 'boys', and παρθένοι (as opposed to mature γυναῖκες, 'women') to talk about sex, i.e. their preference for suppressive silence, see Morales 2004, 208– 9.

The girl came close to me, drew my hand away, and asked me where I had been stung: 'On my lip', said I: 'Will you not utter the charm, my dearest?' She came close to me and put her mouth beside mine, so as to utter the charm, and murmured something while she touched the surface of my lips; and I kissed her silently, concealing the noise of kissing, until, in the successive opening and shutting of her contiguous lips, she converted the whispering of the charm into kisses.

Achilles Tatius 2.7.4

Fourth, and again quite different, is the silent awe which a protagonist's dazzling beauty catalyses. This phenomenon is first found in Chariton when Dionysius, meeting Callirhoe in the temple of Aphrodite, reacts with stunned silence, a silence that is broken by the *topos* ὀψέ ποτε καὶ μόλις ἐφθέγξατο, 'at last and with great difficulty he spoke' (other cases of which are reviewed later):

ἐπεὶ δὲ ἧκεν, ἔτι μᾶλλον αὐτὴν ἐθαύμασαν ἅπαντες. καταπλαγεὶς οὖν ὁ Διονύσιος ἄφωνος ἦν. οὔσης δὲ ἐπὶ πλεῖστον σιωπῆς ὀψέ ποτε καὶ μόλις ἐφθέγξατο· 'τὰ μὲν ἐμὰ δῆλά σοι, γύναι, πάντα. Διονύσιός εἰμι, Μιλησίων πρῶτος, σχεδὸν δὲ καὶ τῆς ὅλης Ἰωνίας, ἐπ' εὐσεβείαι καὶ φιλανθρωπίαι διαβόητος.'

When she arrived, all admired her still more; Dionysius was speechless with amazement. After a prolonged silence, at last and with great difficulty he spoke: 'My entire situation, lady, is known to you. I am Dionysius, the foremost citizen of Miletus and virtually all Ionia, well known for his piety and kindness.'

Chariton 2.5.4

The reaction of the satrap Mithidrates when he first sets eyes on Callirhoe is even more extreme:

Μιθριδάτης δέ, ὁ Καρίας ὕπαρχος, ἀχανὴς κατέπεσεν, ὥσπερ τις ἐξ ἀπροσδοκήτου σφενδόνηι βληθείς, καὶ μόλις αὐτὸν οἱ θεραπευτῆρες ὑποβαστάζοντες ἔφερον.

And Mithridates, the governor of Caria, fell to the ground speechless, like somebody struck unexpectedly by a slingshot, and it was with difficulty that his attendants lifted him up and carried him.

Chariton 4.1.9

A similar stunned silence, but differently described, descends on the court room in Babylon when Callirhoe makes her entrance:

> εἰσῆλθεν οὖν εἰς τὸ δικαστήριον, οἵαν ὁ θεῖος ποιητὴς τὴν Ἑλένην ἐπιστῆναί φησι
>
> τοῖς ἀμφὶ Πρίαμον <καὶ> Πάνθοον ἠδὲ Θυμοίτην
> δημογέρουσιν·
> ὀφθεῖσα δὲ θάμβος ἐποίησε καὶ σιωπήν,
> πάντες δ' ἠρήσαντο παραὶ λεχέεσσι κλιθῆναι·
>
> So when she entered the courtroom she looked just as the divine poet describes Helen when she appeared 'to those that were with Priam and Panthous and Thymoetes, elders of the people'. The sight of her brought astonishment and silence, 'and they all prayed to lie beside her in bed'.
>
> Chariton 5.9.9

Chariton goes on to remark (again 5.9.9) that if Mithridates had been obliged to plead his case immediately he would have been quite unable to do so.

A similar stunned reaction is described by Longus, albeit without specifying silence, when Chloe, now for the first time dressed and coiffed to urban standards, astonishes the Mytilenean company:[16]

> ἐξέπλησσε γὰρ κἀκείνας ἡ Χλόη κάλλος ἐκφέρουσα παρευδοκιμηθῆναι μὴ δυνάμενον
>
> for Chloe's display of unsurpassable beauty stunned even them.
>
> Longus 4.33.4

A fifth type of silence related to ἔρως is that which strikes a character when confronted with news of his or her partner's infidelity or risk of seduction. It is first found in Chariton when Chaereas is told (falsely) that Callirhoe is unfaithful:

> ἐπὶ πολὺ μὲν οὖν ἀχανὴς ἔκειτο, μήτε τὸ στόμα μήτε τοὺς ὀφθαλμοὺς ἐπᾶραι δυνάμενος· ἐπεὶ δὲ φωνὴν οὐχ ὁμοίαν μὲν ὀλίγην δὲ συνελέξατο, 'δυστυχῆ μὲν' εἶπεν 'αἰτῶ παρὰ σοῦ χάριν αὐτόπτης γενέσθαι τῶν ἐμῶν κακῶν'.
>
> So for a long time he lay speechless, unable to lift his mouth or his eyes; and when he had summoned up a voice that was feeble and unlike his own 'I request from you', he said 'the unhappy favour of being an eye-witness of my misfortunes'.
>
> Chariton 1.4.7

This pattern is exploited twice by Xenophon. The first occasion is in Book 1, when Habrocomes, told by Euxeinus that the pirate chief Corymbus has fallen in love with him, is initially silent, but then begs for time:

[16] But cf. the reverse at X.Eph. 1.12.1, discussed below p. 922.

ἀκούσας ὁ Ἁβροκόμης εὐθὺς μὲν ἀχανὴς ἦν καὶ οὔτε τι ἀποκρίνεσθαι ηὕρισκεν, ἐδάκρυσε δέ, καὶ ἀνέστενε πρὸς αὑτὸν ἀφορῶν, εἰς οἷα ἄρα ἐλήλυθε· καὶ δὴ λέγει πρὸς τὸν Εὔξεινον 'ἐπίτρεψον, δέσποτα, βουλεύσασθαι βραχύ, καὶ πρὸς πάντα ἀποκρινοῦμαί σοι τὰ ῥηθέντα.'

When Habrocomes heard this he was immediately speechless and could find no words to answer him, but wept, and lamented inwardly as he contemplated the sort of situation he had apparently landed in. So he said to Euxeinus: 'Allow me, master, to ponder for a while, and I shall reply to everything that has been said'.

Xenophon 1.16.6

Shortly thereafter, in Book 2, Anthia reacts similarly to the news of Manto's determination to seduce Habrocomes – and here Xenophon uses the ὀψὲ δὲ καὶ μόλις formula:[17]

ὁ μὲν ταῦτα ἔλεγεν, ἡ δὲ Ἀνθία ὑπὸ συμφορᾶς ἔκειτο ἀχανής, οὐδὲ προσφθέγξασθαί τι δυναμένη· ὀψὲ δὲ καὶ μόλις αὑτὴν ἐγείρασα 'ἔχω μέν', φησίν, "Ἁβροκόμη, τὴν εὔνοιαν τὴν σήν …'

This was what he (sc. Habrocomes) said. But Anthia lay speechless at the disaster, and was unable to say a word to him. Eventually, and with difficulty, she pulled herself together and said 'I have your affection, Habrocomes …'

Xenophon 2.4.5

These five types of silence are all more or less closely related to the novels' central theme of ἔρως.

Another astonished silence is the product of the intersection of the novels' ἔρως-driven plot with some of their other *leitmotifs*, adventure and disguise. Such is the silence of Xenophon's Habrocomes when the prefect of Egypt summarily orders his crucifixion:

ὁ δὲ ἀπὸ μὲν τῶν κακῶν ἀχανὴς ἦν, παρεμυθεῖτο δὲ αὐτὸν τῆς τελευτῆς ὅτι ἐδόκει καὶ Ἀνθίαν τεθνηκέναι.

He was speechless at his misfortunes, but he was consoled concerning his death by the belief that Anthia too was dead.

Xenophon 4.2.2

A less momentous instance is that in Achilles Tatius of Cleitophon's jailor when he discovers Melite in Cleitophon's clothes when *he* has escaped in hers:

[17] I discuss other cases of the ὀψὲ δὲ καὶ μόλις trope shortly.

> θέαμα ἰδὼν παραδοξότατον τῆς κατὰ τὴν ἔλαφον ἀντὶ παρθένου παροιμίας, ἐξεπλάγη καὶ ἔστη σιωπῆι.
>
> when he saw this extraordinary substitution, like that of the deer for the maiden in the fable, he stood still, struck dumb.
>
> Achilles Tatius 6.2.1

A distant relation of these cases is found in the astonished silence of the Persian eunuch when Callirhoe rejects the proposition of his king Artaxerxes:

> καὶ ἡ μὲν ἀπέδραμεν, ἔστη δὲ ὁ εὐνοῦχος ἀχανής· οἷα γὰρ ἐν μεγάληι τυραννίδι τεθραμμένος οὐδὲν ἀδύνατον ὑπελάμβανεν, οὐ βασιλεῖ μόνον, ἀλλ᾽ οὐδ᾽ ἑαυτῶι.
>
> She (sc. Callirhoe) ran off, but the eunuch stood speechless: for as one brought up in a powerful tyranny he imagined nothing was impossible, not simply for the king, but even for himself.
>
> Chariton 6.5.10

6 Cases Shared with Other Genres

I conclude with some cases which are shared with other genres, beginning with the *topos* one form of which has already been encountered[18] 'everybody else was silent, but X began to speak', and then examining the related *topos* 'For a long time X was silent, but eventually began to speak'.

(a) Everybody Else Was Silent, but X Began to Speak

Chariton has two related instances of this *topos* in the military contexts of Books 7 and 8. The first of these derives much of its effect from the exploitation of the *topos* in the *Iliad*, first in Book 3:

> ὣς ἔφαθ᾽, οἳ δ᾽ ἄρα πάντες ἀκὴν ἐγένοντο σιωπῆι·
> τοῖσι δὲ καὶ μετέειπε βοὴν ἀγαθὸς Μενέλαος …
>
> So he spoke, and all the others were silent; and then Menelaus, good at the war-cry, addressed them …
>
> *Iliad* 3.95–6

[18] Longus 4.30.2 noted already p. 912.

The most important Iliadic intertext, however, is in Book 9, when Diomedes rejects Agamemnon's proposal that the Achaeans should abandon their siege of Troy:[19]

> ὣς ἔφαθ', οἳ δ' ἄρα πάντες ἀκὴν ἐγένοντο σιωπῇ.
> δὴν δ' ἄνεῳ ἦσαν τετιηότες υἷες Ἀχαιῶν·
> ὀψὲ δὲ δὴ μετέειπε βοὴν ἀγαθὸς Διομήδης·
> 'Ἀτρεΐδη, σοὶ πρῶτα μαχήσομαι ἀφραδέοντι ...'
>
> So he spoke, and all the others were silent: and long did the sons of the Achaeans remain in quiet distress; then at long last Diomedes, good at the war-cry, spoke: 'Son of Atreus, with you shall I first contest, since you have no sense ...'
>
> *Iliad* 9.29–32

As well argued by De Temmerman, this intertext guides a reader's interpretation of the scene where Chaereas alone replies to Egyptian king's proposal to withdraw, whereas all others are despondently silent, establishing that Chaereas is a 'non Agamemnon':[20]

> ταῦτα εἰπόντος λίαν εὐλαβῶς σιωπὴ πάντων ἐγένετο καὶ κατήφεια· μόνος δὲ Χαιρέας ἐτόλμησεν εἰπεῖν.
>
> At these overcautious words, all sat silent and dejected. Chaereas alone dared to speak.
>
> Chariton 7.3.3

This pattern is replayed in Book 8, again in a context of military decision-making, when Chaereas' own assessment of his special forces' critical situation is received in silence, eventually broken by a Spartan who is a relative of Brasidas and has been exiled from Sparta:

> σιωπῆς ἐπὶ τούτοις γενομένης Λακεδαιμόνιος ἀνήρ, Βρασίδου συγγενής, κατὰ μεγάλην ἀνάγκην τῆς Σπάρτης ἐκπεσών, πρῶτος ἐτόλμησεν εἰπεῖν.
>
> In the ensuing silence, a man from Lacedaemon, a relative of Brasidas, whom a very serious situation had caused to be exiled from Sparta, was the first who was bold enough to speak.
>
> Chariton 8.2.12

The 'all were silent' *topos* is used only in an inverted form by Xenophon, who overall has different preferences from the other novelists for key

[19] The *topos* is also found at Il. 7.92 and 398, 8.28, 9.430, 693, 10.218, 313, 23.676.

'silence' words. He frequently uses ἀχανής – five times, as against only three cases in the longer novel of Chariton, and none in Achilles Tatius or Longus – and he never uses the words σιγή or σιγῶ. Only once does he use σιωπῶν, 'in silence' (1.12.1) and once the imperative σιώπα, 'keep quiet' (2.3.8). Each of these two cases, however, is of interest. In Book 1 Xenophon inverts the more common reaction to the beauty of the couple discussed above, a reaction of stunned silence, and instead presents the Rhodians as *not* maintaining silence, but complimenting the couple as godlike:

> συνήεσαν δὲ πάντες οἱ Ῥόδιοι τὸ κάλλος τῶν παίδων καταπεπληγότες καὶ οὐκ ἔστιν ὅστις τῶν ἰδόντων παρῆλθε σιωπῶν· ἀλλ' οἱ μὲν ἔλεγον ἐπιδημίαν θεῶν, οἱ δὲ προσεκύνουν καὶ προσεπιτνοῦντο.
>
> All the Rhodians gathered round, thunderstruck at the young people's beauty, and not one of those who saw them passed by in silence: some said they were gods visiting earth, others worshipped and bowed before them.
>
> Xenophon 1.12.1

The second case (2.3.8) I discuss shortly.

The 'all were silent' *topos* is not exploited at all by Achilles Tatius (surprisingly, given the wide range of his refashioning of *topoi* from various genres) and it resurfaces only once in Longus. There its single appearance is low key – the moment late in Book 2 when (at the party celebrating Chloe's safe return) after the admiring silence provoked by the aged cowherd Philetas' performance on his panpipe Dryas takes the floor:[21]

> οἱ μὲν οὖν ἄλλοι σιωπῆι κατέκειντο τερπόμενοι· Δρύας δὲ ἀναστὰς καὶ κελεύσας συρίζειν Διονυσιακὸν μέλος, ἐπιλήνιον αὐτοῖς ὄρχησιν ὠρχήσατο.
>
> The others reclined in silent enjoyment, but Dryas got up, and asked him to play a Dionysiac tune on his syrinx, and danced them a dance of the vintage.
>
> Longus 2.36.1

This is one of many places in *Daphnis and Chloe* where an idea or word familiar to readers from high literary genres (above all epic) is transposed by Longus into his humble rural *mise-en-scène* – and in this case

[20] De Temmerman 2014, 95–8.

[21] The contrast between the actions of others and those of Daphnis and Chloe is deployed twice elsewhere with the οἱ μὲν ἄλλοι … formula: at 3.4.1 (other rustics were glad to be spared their usual tasks by winter, but Daphnis and Chloe …) and differently at 3.12.1 (the other herdsfolk led their flocks out in spring, and *before* the others Daphnis and Chloe).

is transferred from hesitation to speak at a tense council of military leaders in *Iliad* Book 9 to the tranquil rural contentment induced by virtuoso panpipe-playing.[22]

(b) For a Long Time X Was Silent, but Eventually Began to Speak

Two cases of this pattern in Chariton, that of Chaereas in Book 1 and of Plangon in Book 3, have already been discussed under different headings.[23] A third, in Book 2, also involves Plangon, when she asks Callirhoe what she has decided about marrying Dionysius, apparently her only hope of saving her child by Chaereas: both Callirhoe and Plangon are silent for a long time, until Plangon asks outright her about her decision:

> τῆς δὲ ὑστεραίας ἐλθοῦσα ἡ Πλαγγὼν πρῶτον μὲν καθῆστο σκυθρωπὴ καὶ σχῆμα συμπαθὲς ἐπεδείξατο, σιγὴ δὲ ἦν ἀμφοτέρων. ἐπεὶ δὲ μακρὸς ἐγίνετο χρόνος, ἡ Πλαγγὼν ἐπύθετο 'τί σοι δέδοκται; τί ποιοῦμεν; καιρὸς γὰρ οὐκ ἔστι τοῦ μέλλειν.' Καλλιρόη δὲ ἀποκρίνασθαι μὲν ταχέως οὐκ ἐδύνατο κλαίουσα καὶ συνεχομένη, μόλις δὲ εἶπε 'τὸ τέκνον με προδίδωσιν ἀκούσης ἐμοῦ.'
>
> The next day Plangon came back, and first sat down beside her, looking sad and presenting a sympathetic figure; both remained silent. After a long time had passed Plangon inquired, 'What have you decided? What shall we do? This is no time for delay'. Callirhoe could not answer immediately because of her tears and distress, but at length she said, 'The child betrays me, against my will.'
>
> Chariton 2.11.4–5

The same *topos* is deployed by Xenophon in Book 2, when the couple's man-servant Leucon, overwhelmed by what he hears from his partner Rhode (also servile), is apparently silent for some time. Xenophon, however, does not *describe* that silence, but instead implies it with the ὀψὲ δὲ formula, then re-applies the sigma-word to Leucon's instruction to Rhode: 'keep quiet about this ....'

> Λεύκων δακρύων ἐνεπλήσθη, μεγάλας ἐκ τούτων συμφορὰς προσδοκῶν· ὀψὲ δὲ ἀνενεγκὼν 'σιώπα', ἔφη, "Ρόδη, ἐγὼ γὰρ ἕκαστα διοικήσω'.

[22] For the τέρψις, 'enjoyment', generated by playing the panpipe, see De Temmerman 2014, 211 with n.23.

[23] 1.4.7, p. 918, and 3.9.2–3, p. 910.

> Leucon listened and was overwhelmed with tears, as he expected this would result in great calamities. But at last he pulled himself together and said, 'Keep quiet, Rhode, I'll take care of everything'.
>
> Xenophon 2.3.8

Another case is found in Book 3, when the old woman Chrysion tells a false tale of a girl's death by poison and Hippothous remarks that this girl was surely Anthia. Habrocomes is totally distraught while listening to the tale, but nevertheless does so in silence, and is only pushed to speech by Hippothous' remark:

> παρεῖτο δὲ ὑπὸ ἀθυμίας· ὀψὲ δὲ καὶ <μόλις> ἀναθορὼν ἐκ τῆς τοῦ Ἱπποθόου φωνῆς 'ἀλλὰ νῦν μὲν σαφῶς τέθνηκεν Ἀνθία ...'
>
> but in despondency Habrocomes ignored it, until at length and with difficulty he leapt up at Hippothous' utterance: 'Now Anthia is manifestly dead ...'
>
> Xenophon 3.9.7

A trio of instances are found towards the denouement of the novel in Book 5, all imbricated in recognition scenes. First Leucon and Rhode fall into astonished silence when they recognise Habrocomes in Rhodes:

> ἀκούσαντες οἱ περὶ τὸν Λεύκωνα εὐθὺς μὲν ἀχανεῖς ἐγένοντο, ἀνενεγκόντες δὲ κατὰ μικρὸν ἐγνώριζον ἐκ τοῦ σχήματος. ἐκ τῆς φωνῆς, ἐξ ὧν ἔλεγεν, ἐξ ὧν Ἀνθίας ἐμέμνητο, καὶ πίπτουσι πρὸ τῶν ποδῶν αὐτοῦ καὶ τὰ καθ' αὑτοὺς διηγοῦνται ...
>
> When Leucon and Rhode heard this they were immediately speechless, but gradually they recovered and recognised him by his appearance, by his voice, by what he said, by his mention of Anthia, and they fell at his feet and told their own story ...
>
> Xenophon 5.10.11

Soon after, Leucon and Rhode lie prostrate in silence when they recognise Anthia:

> οὕτως κατὰ βραχὺ ἐγνώριζον αὐτήν· προσπεσόντες δὲ τοῖς γόνασιν ἔκειντο ἀχανεῖς· ἡ δὲ ἐτεθαυμάκει τίνες τε εἴησαν καὶ τί βούλοιντο· οὐ γὰρ ἄν ποτε Λεύκωνα καὶ Ῥόδην <ἰδεῖν> ἤλπισεν ... οἱ δὲ ἐν ἑαυτοῖς γενόμενοι 'ὦ δέσποινα' ἔφασαν 'Ἀνθία, ἡμεῖς οἰκέται σοί ...'
>
> So little by little they recognised her: and falling at her knees they lay speechless. And she was astonished at who they might be and what they

wanted – for she would never have expected to see Leucon and Rhode ... When they recovered themselves, 'Mistress Anthia', they said, 'we are your servants ...'

Xenophon 5.12.4–5

Immediately thereafter Anthia herself is described as reacting in a similar way when she in turn discovers Leucon's and Rhode's identities and hears from them that Habrocomes is alive and close to her in Rhodes:

ἀκούσασα ἡ Ἀνθία ἐξεπλάγη τοῦ λόγου, μόγις δὲ ἀνενεγκοῦσα καὶ γνωρίσασα περιβάλλει τε αὐτοὺς καὶ ἀσπάζεται καὶ σαφέστατα τὰ κατὰ Ἁβροκόμην μανθάνει ...

Anthia was astounded to hear this news, but when with an effort she recovered herself and recognized them, she threw her arms around them, kissed them, and learned in great detail what had happened to Habrocomes ...

Xenophon 5.12.6

The case of Lamon late in Longus Book 3 has already been discussed.[24]

(c) One Character's Silence Provokes Another to Ask for an Explanation

We find a related silence, that of one character which provokes another to seek an explanation, in Achilles Tatius Book 1, when Cleinias expresses frustration at Charicles' silence concerning the reason for his distress:

ἄρτι δὲ λέγοντος αὐτοῦ Χαρικλῆς εἰστρέχει (τοῦτο γὰρ ἦν ὄνομα τῶι μειρακίωι) τεθορυβημένος, 'οἴχομαί σοι', λέγων, 'Κλεινία'. καὶ συνεστέναξεν ὁ Κλεινίας, ὥσπερ ἐκ τῆς ἐκείνου ψυχῆς κρεμάμενος· καὶ τῆι φωνῆι τρέμων, 'ἀποκτενεῖς', εἶπε, 'σιωπῶν· τί σε λυπεῖ; τίνι δεῖ μάχεσθαι;' καὶ ὁ Χαρικλῆς, 'γάμον', εἶπεν, 'ὁ πατήρ μοι προξενεῖ, καὶ γάμον ἀμόρφου κόρης, ἵνα διπλῶι συνοικῶ τῶι κακῶι'.

He was still speaking, when Charicles (that was the youth's name) burst in, greatly disordered, crying: 'I'm done for, Cleinias'. Cleinias gave a deep groan, as though his life hung on his friend's, and murmured with a trembling voice: 'You will kill me if you do not tell me at once; what is distressing you? What have we to fight against?' 'Marriage', Charicles answered, 'which my father is arranging for me, and marriage with an ugly girl, so that I may be wedded to a double evil'.

Achilles Tatius 1.7.3–4

[24] 3.30.5, p. 912.

A similar sequence appears in Book 3, where, after Cleitophon has been lamenting their capture by bandits in silence (ταῦτα μὲν οὖν ἐθρήνουν ἡσυχῆι, 'so I quietly lamented this situation', 3.11.1) Leucippe explains *her* silence to him:

> λέγω οὖν πρὸς τὴν Λευκίππην πάντα σιγῶσαν· 'τί σιγᾷς, φιλτάτη, καὶ οὐδέν μοι λαλεῖς;' 'ὅτι μοι,' ἔφη, 'πρὸ τῆς ψυχῆς, Κλειτοφῶν, τέθνηκεν ἡ φωνή.'
>
> So I said to Leucippe, who lay totally speechless, 'Why are you silent, my darling, and say nothing to me?'; 'Because, Clitophon', she said, 'my voice is dead, even before my soul.'
>
> Achilles Tatius 3.11.2

This is perhaps a subtle reworking of Sappho fr. 1, a poem very well known in the imperial period, and one which readers have every right to expect a girl like Leucippe from an elite household to know.[25] The passage is one of a sequence which De Temmerman persuasively argues 'thematises' Leucippe's 'cognitive inaccessibility' after the end of Book 2, an inaccessibility brought about by the sparseness of information concerning her thoughts offered by Cleitophon's narrative.[26]

7 A Brief Conclusion

The four writers display different preferences in their exploitations of silence. Achilles Tatius, and he alone, relates silence closely to techniques of seduction, and he has no case either of the *topos* 'All were silent, until …' or of the related *topos* 'X was long silent, until …': perhaps a product of his choice of a homodiegetic narrator, and certainly one of many details that contribute to that narrator's characterisation. Both these *topoi*, however, which are devices ideal for creating suspense, are found in some form in Chariton (predictably exploiting the former's Homeric ancestry) and Xenophon, who prefers both in these contexts and elsewhere to use the term ἀχανής, 'speechless', to the otherwise commoner σιωπ- or σιγ- words for silence. Longus too employs both these *topoi*, albeit his one case of 'All were silent, until …' refashions it for the low-key context of Dryas' decision to dance. Silences of characters concerning facts (or fictions) whose disclosure is crucial to the plot are most prominent in Chariton and Longus,

[25] For the interest in Sappho manifest in imperial Greek literature see Bowie 2021a.

[26] De Temmerman 2014, 189.

though an analogous narratorial silence plays an important part in readers' deception concerning Leucippe's 'false deaths' in Achilles Tatius. Overall the various deployments of silence reveal it, and the terms used for it, as meaningful and often important elements in the creation of a narrative well-calculated to engage readers: of the four novelists only Longus has an 'unmarked' use of σιωπ- to mean little more than 'he/she stopped speaking' (4.20.1).

Bibliography

This bibliography does not include the many illustrated editions referred to in Chapter 40.

Adams, J. N. 2003. *Bilingualism and the Latin Language*. Cambridge.

Adams, J. N., Janse, M. and Swain, S. C. R. (eds.) 2002. *Bilingualism in Ancient Society: Language Contact and the Written Text*. Oxford.

Agosta, G. 2009. *Ricerche sui Cynegetica di Oppiano*. Amsterdam.

Aitken, E. B. and Maclean, J. K. B. (eds.) 2004. *Philostratus' Heroikos: Religion and Cultural Identity in the Third Century CE*. Atlanta.

Alcock, S., Cherry, J. and Elsner, J. (eds.) 2001. *Pausanias. Travel and Memory in Roman Greece*. Oxford and New York.

Alperowitz, M. 1992. *Das Wirken und Walten der Götter im griechischen Roman*. Heidelberg.

Alvares, J. 2001–2. 'Some political and ideological dimensions of Chariton's *Chaireas and Callirhoe*', *CJ* 97: 113–44.

Alvares, J. and Renner, T. 2001. 'A new fragment of the Metiochus and Parthenope romance?', in I. Andorlini, G. Bastianini, M. Manfredi and G. Menci (eds.), *Atti del XXII Congresso Internazionale di Papirologia*. Florence: i 35–40.

Amato, E. 1995. *Studi su Favorino: le orazioni pseudo-crisostomiche*. Salerno.

Amato, E. 2005. *Dionisio di Alessandria. Descrizione della terra abitata*. Milano.

Ameling, W. W. 1983. *Herodes Atticus*. 2 vols. Subsidia Epigraphica 11. Hildesheim.

Anderson, G. 1976a. *Lucian. Theme and Variation in the Second Sophistic*. Mnemosyne Suppl. 41. Leiden.

Anderson, G. 1976b. 'Lucian's classics: some short cuts to culture', *BICS* 23: 59–68.

Anderson, G. 1976c. *Studies in Lucian's Comic Fiction*. Mnemosyne Suppl. 43. Leiden.

Anderson, G. 1982. *Eros sophistes. Ancient Novelists at Play*. Chico, CA.

Anderson, G. 1986. *Philostratus*. London.

Anderson, J. K. 1985. *Hunting in the Ancient World*. Berkeley, Los Angeles and London.

Anderson, R. D., Parsons, P. J. and Nisbet, R. G. M. 1979. 'Elegiacs by Gallus from Qasr Ibrîm', *JRS* 69: 125–55.

Aneziri, S. 2003. *Die Vereine der dionysischen Techniten im Kontext der hellenistischen Gesellschaft: Untersuchungen zur Geschichte, Organisation und Wirkung der hellenistischen Technitenvereine*. Stuttgart.

Arena, G. and Cassia, M. 2015. *Marcello di Side: Gli imperatori adottivi e il potere della medicina*. Roma.

Argentieri, L. 2003. *Gli epigrammi degli Antipatri*. Bari.

Argentieri, L. 2007. 'Meleager and Philip as epigram collectors', in Bing and Bruss (eds.): 147–64.

Aricò, G. 1972. '*Diviso vertice flammae*', *RFIC* 100: 312–22.

Arnott, W. G. 1965. 'Ὥσπερ λαμπάδιον δράματος', *Hermes* 93: 253–5.

Arnott, W. G. 1979. '*The Mound of Brasilas in Theocritus' Seventh* Idyll', *QUCC* n.s. 3: 99–106.

Arnott, W. G. 2002. 'Some orthographical variants in the papyri of later Greek comedy', in Willi (ed.): 191–217.

Athanassaki, L. 2011. 'Song, politics and cultural memory: Pindar's *Pythian* 7 and the Alcmeonid temple of Apollo', in Athanassaki and Bowie (eds.): 235–68.

Athanassaki, L. 2013. 'Rekindling the memory of the alleged treason of the Alcmaeonids at Marathon: from Megacles to Alcibiades', in K. Buraselis and E. Koulakiotis (eds.), *Marathon: The Day After*. Athens: 95–111.

Athanassaki, L. 2018. 'The cult of peace in the Athenian theatre during the Peloponnesian War: from Euripides' *Cresphontes* to Aristophanes' *Peace* and beyond', *ICS* 43: 1–24.

Athanassaki, L. and Bowie, E. L. (eds.) 2011. *Archaic and Classical Choral Song: Performance, Politics and Dissemination*. Berlin.

Austin, N. 1994. *Helen of Troy and Her Shameless Phantom*. Ithaca and London.

Avaert, P. 1948. *Éléments de réalité chez Xénophon d'Ephèse*. Thèse pour la licence, Louvain.

Aymard, J. 1951. *Essai sur les chasses romaines, des origines à la fin du siècle des Antonins (Cynegetica)*. Paris.

Bachmann, C. 2018. *Bilder einer Ausstellung*. Wiesbaden.

Bady, C. 2021. *La Rome des pepaideumenoi: mobilité, patronage et sociabilité des élites intellectuelles hellénophones dans la Rome du Haut-Empire (31 av. J.-C.–235 ap. J.-C.)*. DPhil thesis, Université Paris Nanterre.

Bär, S. 2009. *Quintus Smyrnaeus, Posthomerica 1: die Wiedergeburt des Epos aus dem Geiste der Amazonomachie: mit einem Kommentar zu den Versen 1–219*. Göttingen.

Baillet, J. 1920–6. *Inscriptions grecques et latines des tombeaux des rois ou Syringes à Thèbes*. Cairo.

Bakola, E. 2010. *Cratinus and the Art of Comedy*. Oxford.

Baldwin, B. 1975. 'The epigrams of Lucian', *Phoenix* 29: 311–35.

Baldwin, B. 1988. 'Demetrius "Aetolicus"', *Hermes* 116: 116–17.

Baragwanath, E. and de Bakker, M. (eds.) 2012. *Myth, Truth, and Narrative in Herodotus*. Oxford.

Barber, G. 1989. *Daphnis and Chloe: The Markets and Metamorphoses of an Unknown Bestseller*. London.

Barchiesi, A. 1996. 'Poetry, praise, and patronage: Simonides in Book 4 of Horace's "Odes"', *CA* 15: 5–47.

Bardon, H. 1956. *La littérature latine inconnue*, Vol. ii. Paris.

Barigazzi, A. 1966. *Favorino di Arelate. Opere*. Firenze.

Barker, A. D. 2002. *Euterpe: ricerche sulla musica greca e romana*, eds. F. Perusino and E. Rocconi. Pisa.

Barringer, J. M. 1981. *The Hunt in Ancient Greece*. Baltimore.

Bartley, A. N. 2003. *Stories from the Mountains, Stories from the Sea: The Digressions and Similes of Oppian's Halieutica and the Cynegetica*. Göttingen.

Bartol, K. 1993. *Greek Elegy and Iambus: Studies in Ancient Literary Sources*. Poznań.

Bartsch, S. 1989. *Decoding the Ancient Novel*. Princeton.

Baslez, M.-F. 1992a. 'La famille de Philopappos de Commagène, un prince entre deux mondes', *DHA* 18: 89–101.

Baslez, M.-F. 1992b. 'De l'histoire au roman: la Perse de Chariton', in Baslez, Hoffmann and Trédé (eds.): 199–212.

Baslez, M.-F., Hoffmann, P. and Trédé, M. (eds.) 1992. *Le monde du roman grec. Études de littérature ancienne*. Paris.

Bastianini, G. 2010. '*PSI* XIII 1305, *Romanzo di Nino*', in Bastianini and Casanova: 279–88.

Bastianini, G. and Casanova, A. (eds.) 2010. *I papiri del romanzo antico. Atti del convegno internazionale di studi, Firenze, 11–12 giugno 2009*. Firenze.

Baumann, M. 2011. *Bilder Schreiben: Virtuose Ekphrasis in Philostrats "Eikones"*. Berlin.

Baumbach, M., Bär, S. and Dümmler, N. (eds.) 2007. *Quintus Smyrnaeus: Transforming Homer in Second Sophistic Epic*. Berlin.

Bean, G. E. 1965. *The Inscriptions of Side*. Türk tarıh kurumu yayınlarından 5.20. Ankara.

Bean, G. E. and Mitford, T. B. 1970. *Journeys in Rough Cilicia 1964–1968*. Denkschriften der Österreichische Akademie der Wissenschaften. Philosophisch-Historische Klasse 102. Ergänzungsbände zu den Tituli Asiae Minoris 3. Wien.

Beaton, R. 1989. *The Medieval Greek Romance*. Cambridge.

Béguin, S. 1971. 'Quelques nouveaux dessins d'Ambroise Dubois', *Revue de l'art* 14: 31–8.

Behr, C. A. 1968. *Aelius Aristides and the Sacred Tales*. Amsterdam.

Behr, C. A. 1981. *P. Aelius Aristides. The Complete Works. Volume II. Orations xvii–liii* (transl. into English). Leiden.

Bejarano, V. 1975. 'El emperador Adriano ante la tradición romana', *Pyrenae* 11: 81–98.

Bekker-Nielsen, T. 2008. *Urban Life and Local Politics in Roman Bithynia*. Aarhus and Oakville, CT.

Bélis, A. 1988. 'A proposito degli "inni delfici" ad Apollo', in B. Gentili and R. Pretagostini (eds.), *La musica in Grecia*. Bari: 205–18.

Bélis, A. 1992. *Les Hymnes à Apollon. Corpus des inscriptions de Delphes*. Paris.

Bélis, A. 2001. 'Esthétique musicale du péan à travers l'exemple des Hymnes delphiques à Apollon', in P. Brulé et C. Vendries (eds.), *Chanter les dieux: musique et religion dans l'antiquité grecque et romaine. Actes du colloque des 16, 17 et 18 décembre 1999, Rennes et Lorient)*. Rennes: 97–114.

Beltran Fortes, J. 1992. 'Arriano de Nicomedia y la Bética, de nuevo', *Habis* 23: 171–96.
Benaissa, A. 2018. *Dionysius: The Epic Fragments*. Cambridge.
Benjamin, A. S. 1963. 'The altars of Hadrian in Athens and Hadrian's Panhellenic program', *Hesperia* 32: 57–86.
Benner, A. R. and Fobes, F. H. 1949. *The Letters of Alciphron, Aelian and Philostratus*. Cambridge, MA and London.
Bergquist, B. 1990. 'Sympotic space: a functional aspect of Greek dining-rooms', in Murray (ed.): 38–65.
Bernand, A. and Bernand, E. 1960. *Les inscriptions du Colosse de Memnon*. Paris.
Bernays, U. 1905. *Studien zu Dionysius Periegetes*. Heidelberg.
Bernhardy, G. 1847. *De scriptoribus historiae Augustae: prooemia duo scholis Universitatis Fridericianae indicendis*. Halle.
Bernsdorff, H. 2006. 'Zur Handlung von P.Oxy. 4761 (Antonios Diogenes?)', *GFA* 9: 7–12.
Bernsdorff, H. 2009. 'Antonios-Diogenes-Interpretationen', in *Studien zur Philologie und zur Musikwissenschaft. Akademie der Wissenschaften in Göttingen. Philologisch-Historische Klasse*. Berlin: 1–52.
Bertazzoli, V. 2009. 'Il peana di Filodamo Scarfea per Dioniso', *Paideia* 64: 437–75.
Bertrand, J.-M. 1988. 'Les Boukoloi ou le monde à envers', *REA* 90: 139–49.
Beschorner, A. 1999. *Helden und Heroen, Homer und Caracalla: Übersetzung, Kommentar und Interpretationen zum Heroikos des Flavios Philostratos*. Bari.
Bianchi, N. 2016. 'The number of books of Iamblichus' *Babyloniaca* (On Photius *Bibl.* 94, 78b3)', *Prometheus* 42: 219–25.
Bidez, J. 1960. *L'Empereur Julien. Œuvres complètes. i 2. Lettres et fragments. 2me éd.* Paris.
Bieber, M. 1911. 'Die Medaillons am Konstantinsbogen', *MDAI(R)* 26: 214–37.
Bierl, A. and Lardinois, A. (eds.) 2016. *The Newest Sappho. P. Sapph. Obbink and P. GC inv. 105, Frs.* 1–4. Leiden and Boston.
Billault, A. 1989. 'De l'histoire au roman: Hermocrate de Syracuse', *REG* 102: 540–8.
Billault, A. 1996. 'Characterization in the ancient novel', in Schmeling (ed.): 115–29.
Billault, A. (ed.) 2001. *'ΟΠΩΡΑ: la belle saison de l'hellénisme: études de littérature antique offertes au Recteur Jacques Bompaire*. Paris.
Billault, A. 2019. 'Histoire, mythologie, rhétorique et récit dans le roman de Chariton', in Chew, Morgan and Trzaskoma (eds.): 51–64.
Bing, P. and Bruss, J. (eds.) 2007. *Brill's Companion to Hellenistic Epigram*. Leiden.
Biraud, M. and Briand, M. (eds.) 2017. *Roman grec et poésie. Dialogue des genres et nouveaux enjeux du poétique*. CMO 56. Lyon.
Birley, A. R. 1994. 'Hadrian's farewell to life', *Laverna* 5: 176–205.
Birley, A. R. 1997. *Hadrian. The Restless Emperor*. London.
Birley, A. R. 2000. *Marcus Aurelius: A Biography*, revised ed. (1st ed. 1966). London.
Blanchard, J. M. 1975. 'Daphnis et Chloé: histoire de la mimesis', *QUCC* 20: 19–62.
Boatwright, M. T. 2000. *Hadrian and the Cities of the Roman Empire*. Princeton.

Boedeker, D. and Sider, D. (eds.) 2001. *The New Simonides. Contexts of Praise and Desire*. Oxford and New York.

Bomer, F. 1976. *P. Ovidius Naso Metamorphosen: Kommentar. ii*. Heidelberg.

Bonanno, M. G. 1980. 'Nomi e suprannomi archilochei', *MH* 37: 65–88.

Bond, G. W. 1981. *Euripides Heracles with Introduction and Commentary*. Oxford.

Borg, B. (ed.) 2004. *Paideia: The World of the Second Sophistic*. Berlin and New York.

Borgeaud, P. 1979. *Recherches sur le dieu Pan*. Roma (transl. by K. Atlass and J. Redfield as *The Cult of Pan in Ancient Greece*, Chicago and London 1988).

Borthwick, E. K. 1971. 'Emendations and interpretations in the Greek Anthology', *CQ* 21: 426–36.

Borthwick, E. K. 1972. 'Nicetes the rhetorician and Vergil's "plena deo"', *Mnemosyne* 25: 408–12.

Bosch, E. 1967. *Quellen zur Geschichte der Stadt Ankara im Altertum*. Ankara.

Bossi, F. 1990. *Studi su Archiloco*, 2nd ed. Bari.

Bosworth, A. B. 1993. 'Arrian and Rome: the minor works', *ANRW* ii 34.1: 226–75.

Boter, G. 2015. 'The title of Philostratus' *Life of Apollonius of Tyana*', *JHS* 135: 1–7.

Bouchon, R., Brillet-Dubois, P. and Le Meur Weissman, N. (eds.) 2012. *Hymnes de la Grèce Antique. Approches littéraires et historiques. Actes du colloque international de Lyon, 19–21 juin 2008*. Lyon.

Bougot, A. and Lissarrague, F. 1991. *Philostrate, La Galerie de Tableaux, traduit par A. Bougot; révisé et annoté par F. Lissarrague; préface de P. Hadot*. Paris.

Boulanger, A. 1923. *Aelius Aristide et la sophistique dans la province d'Asie au IIe siècle de notre ère*. Paris.

Bouquiaux-Simone, O. 1968. *Les lectures Homériques de Lucien*. Académie royale de Belgique, Classe des lettres. Mémoires, 2nd ser. 59.2. Bruxelles.

Bousquet, J. 1959. 'Inscriptions de Delphes', *BCH* 83: 146–92.

Bowersock, G. W. 1965. *Augustus and the Greek World*. Oxford.

Bowersock, G. W. 1969. *Greek Sophists in the Roman Empire*. Oxford.

Bowersock, G. W. (ed.) 1974. *Approaches to the Second Sophistic*. University Park, PA.

Bowersock, G. W. 1985. 'Poetry', in P. E. Easterling and B. M. W. Knox (eds.), *The Cambridge History of Classical Literature, Vol. i*. Cambridge: 659–64 (pb. i 4, 1989: 89–94).

Bowersock, G. W. 1994. *Fiction as History: Nero to Julian*. Berkeley and Los Angeles.

Bowie, E. L. 1970. 'Greeks and their past in the second sophistic', *P&P* 46: 3–41 (repr. in M. I. Finley (ed.), *Studies in Ancient Society*. London: 166–209).

Bowie, E. L. 1977. 'The novels and the real world', summary of a paper delivered to the International Conference on the Ancient Novel, in B. P. Reardon (ed.), *Erotica Antiqua*. Bangor: 91–6.

Bowie, E. L. 1978. 'Apollonius of Tyana: tradition and reality', in H. Temporini and W. Haase (eds.), *ANRW* ii.16.2. Berlin and New York: 1652–99.

Bowie, E. L. 1982. 'The importance of sophists', *YClS* 27: 29–59.

Bowie, E. L. 1985a. 'Theocritus' seventh *Idyll*, Philetas and Longus', *CQ* 35: 67–91.

Bowie, E. L. 1985b. 'The Greek novel', in P. E. Easterling and B. M. W. Knox (eds.), *The Cambridge History of Classical Literature, Vol. i Part 4*. Cambridge: 669–99, 703–9 (pb. 1989: 123–39, 243–52).

Bowie, E. L. 1986a. 'Early Greek elegy, symposium and public festival', *JHS* 106: 13–35 (repr. in Rutherford [ed.] 2019: 110–49).

Bowie, E. L. 1988. 'Who is Dicaeopolis?', *JHS* 108: 189–91.

Bowie, E. L. 1989a. 'Greek sophists and Greek poetry in the Second Sophistic', in *ANRW* ii 33.1: 209–58.

Bowie, E. L. 1989b. 'Greek poetry in Asia and Achaea', in S. Walker and A. Cameron (eds.), *The Greek Renaissance in the Roman empire*, Papers from the Tenth British Museum Classical Colloquium (December 1986), *BICS Suppl.* 55: 198–205.

Bowie, E. L. 1990b. 'Greek poetry in the Antonine Age', in D. A. Russell (ed.), *Antonine Literature*. Oxford: 53–90.

Bowie, E. L. 1990c. '*Marginalia Obsceniora*: some problems in Aristophanes' *Wasps*', in E. M. Craik (ed.), *Owls to Athens. Essays on Classical Subjects for Sir Kenneth Dover*. Oxford: 31–8.

Bowie, E. L. 1992. 'Les lecteurs du roman grec', in Baslez, Hoffmann and Trédé (eds.): 55–61.

Bowie, E. L. 1993a. 'Lies, fiction and slander in early Greek poetry', in C. Gill and T. P. Wiseman (eds.), *Lies and Fiction in the Ancient World*. Exeter: 1–37.

Bowie, E. L. 1993b. 'Greek table-talk before Plato', *Rhetorica* 11.4: 355–73.

Bowie, E. L. 1994a. 'The readership of Greek novels in the ancient world', in J. Tatum (ed.), *The Search for the Ancient Novel*. Baltimore and London: 435–59.

Bowie, E. L. 1994b. 'Philostratus: writer of fiction', in R. Stoneman and J. R. Morgan (eds.), *Greek Fiction*. London: 181–99.

Bowie, E. L. 1995a. 'Wine in Old Comedy', in Murray and Tecuşan (eds.): 113–25.

Bowie, E. L. 1995b. 'Names and a gem: aspects of allusion in the *Aethiopica* of Heliodorus', in D. C. Innes, H. M. Hine and C. B. R. Pelling (eds.), *Ethics and Rhetoric. Classical Essays for Donald Russell on His Seventy-Fifth Birthday*. Oxford: 269–80.

Bowie, E. L. 1996a. 'Frame and framed in Theocritus poems 6 and 7', *Hellenistica Groningana* 2: 91–100.

Bowie, E. L. 1996b. 'Aristides (2)', in *The Oxford Classical Dictionary*, 3rd ed. Oxford: 160.

Bowie, E. L. 1996c. 'The ancient readers of the Greek novels', in Schmeling (ed.): 87–106.

Bowie, E. L. 1997c. 'Hadrian, Favorinus, and Plutarch', in J. Mossman (ed.), *Plutarch and His Intellectual World*. London: 1–15.

Bowie, E. L. 1998a. 'Le portrait de Socrate dans les *Nuées* d'Aristophane', in M. Trédé and P. Hoffmann (eds.), *Le rire des anciens*. Paris: 53–66.

Bowie, E. L. 1998b. 'Phoenician games in Heliodorus' *Aethiopica*', in Hunter (ed.): 1–18.

Bowie, E. L. 2000a. 'The reception of Apollonius Rhodius in imperial Greek literature', *Hellenistica Groningana* 4: 1–10.

Bowie, E. L. 2001a. 'Ancestors of historiography in early Greek elegiac and iambic poetry', in N. Luraghi (ed.), *The Historian's Craft in the Age of Herodotus*. Oxford: 45–66.

Bowie, E. L. 2001c. 'Pausanias: inspiration and aspiration', in Alcock, Cherry and Elsner (eds.): 21–32.

Bowie, E. L. 2002a. 'The chronology of the earlier Greek novels since B. E. Perry: revisions and precisions', *AN* 2: 47–63.

Bowie, E. L. 2002c. 'Ionian *iambus* and Old Attic Comedy', in A. Willi (ed.), *The Language of Old Comedy*. Oxford: 33–50.

Bowie, E. L. 2002d. 'Plutarch and literary activity in Achaea: AD 107–117', in P. A. Stadter and L. Van der Stockt (eds.), *Sage and Emperor. Plutarch, Greek Intellectuals and Roman Power in the Time of Trajan (98–117 AD)*. Leuven: 41–56.

Bowie, E. L. 2002e. 'Hadrian and Greek poetry', in E. Ostenfeld, K. Blomqvist and L. C. Nevett (eds.), *Greek Romans, Roman Greeks*. Aarhus: 172–97.

Bowie, E. L. 2003b. 'The function of mythology in Longus' *Daphnis and Chloe*', in J.-A. López Férez (ed.), *Mitos en la literatura griega helenística e imperial*. Madrid: 361–76.

Bowie, E. L. 2004a. 'Denys d'Alexandrie: un poète grec dans l'empire romain', *REA* 106: 177–85.

Bowie, E. L. 2004b. 'Poetry and music in the Life of Plutarch's *Statesman*', in L. de Blois, J. Bons, T. Kessels and D. M. Schenkeveld (eds.), *The Statesman in Plutarch's Works, Vol. 1*. Mnemosyne Suppl. 250. Leiden: 115–23.

Bowie, E. L. 2004c. 'The geography of the Second Sophistic: cultural variations', in Borg (ed.): 65–83.

Bowie, E. L. 2005a. 'Les animaux dans le *Daphnis and Chloé* de Longus', in B. Pouderon (ed.), *Lieux, décors et paysages de l'ancien roman des origines à Byzance*. Lyon: 75–85.

Bowie, E. L. 2005b. 'Metaphor in Longus, *Daphnis and Chloe*', in S. J. Harrison, M. Paschalis and S. Frangoulidis (eds.), *Metaphor and the Ancient Novel*. ANS 4. Groningen: 68–86.

Bowie, E. L. 2006a. 'The construction of the classical past in the ancient Greek novels', in S. Eklund (ed.), *Συγχάρματα: Studies in Honour of Jan Fredrik Kindstrand, Acta Universitatis Upsaliensis*. Studia Graeca Upsaliensia 21. Uppsala: 1–20.

Bowie, E. L. 2006b. 'Le discours direct dans le Daphnis et Chloé de Longus', in B. Pouderon and J. Peigney (eds.), *Discours et débats dans l'ancien roman*. Lyon: 27–39.

Bowie, E. L. 2006c. 'Choral performances', in D. Konstan and S. Saïd (eds.), *Greeks on Greekness*. Supplement to the Proceedings of the Cambridge Philological Society. Cambridge: 61–92.

Bowie, E. L. 2006d. 'Viewing and listening on the novelist's page', in S. N. Byrne, E. P. Cueva and J. Alvares (eds.), *Authors, Authority and Interpreters in the Ancient Novel. Essays in Honor of Gareth L. Schmeling*. ANS 5. Groningen: 60–82.

Bowie, E. L. 2007a. 'Early expatriates: displacement and exile in archaic poetry', in J.-F. Gaertner (ed.), *Writing Exile. The Discourse of Displacement in Greco-Roman Antiquity and Beyond*. Leiden: 21–49.

Bowie, E. L. 2007c. 'Pulling the other: Longus on tragedy', in J. Elsner, H. P. Foley, S. Goldhill and C. Kraus (eds.), *Visualizing the Tragic: Drama Myth and Ritual in Greek Art and Literature*. Oxford and New York: 338–52.

Bowie, E. L. 2007d. 'Links between Antonius Diogenes and Petronius', in M. Paschalis, S. Frangoulidis, S. J. Harrison and M. Zimmerman (eds.), *The Greek and the Roman Novel: Parallel Readings*. ANS 8. Groningen: 121–32.

Bowie, E. L. 2007e. 'The ups and downs of Aristophanic travel', in E. Hall and A. Wrigley (eds.), *Aristophanes in Performance*. Oxford: 32–51.

Bowie, E. L. 2007f. 'Socrates in Aristophanes' Clouds and the Audience of Attic Comedy', lecture at the European Cultural Centre of Delphi.

Bowie, E. L. 2008a. 'Aristides and early Greek lyric, elegiac and iambic poetry', in W. V. Harris and B. Holmes (eds.), *Aelius Aristides between Greece, Rome and the Gods*. CSCT 33. Leiden and Boston: 9–29.

Bowie, E. L. 2008c. 'Plutarch's habits of citation: aspects of difference', in A. Nikolaidis (ed.), *The Unity of Plutarch's Work: 'Moralia' Themes in the 'Lives', Features of the 'Lives' in the 'Moralia'*. Berlin and New York: 143–57.

Bowie, E. L. 2008d. 'Literary milieux', in Whitmarsh (ed.): 17–38.

Bowie, E. L. 2009a. 'Wandering poets, archaic style', in R. L. Hunter and I. C. Rutherford (eds.), *Wandering Poets*. Cambridge: 105–36.

Bowie, E. L. 2009b. 'Vertus de la campagne, vices de la cité dans Daphnis et Chloé de Longus', in B. Pouderon and C. Bost-Pouderon (eds.), *Passions, vertus, vices dans l'ancien roman*. Lyon: 13–22.

Bowie, E. L. 2009c. 'The uses of bookishness', in M. Paschalis, S. Panyotakis and G. Schmeling (eds.), *Readers and Writers in the Ancient Novel*. ANS 12. Groningen: 115–26.

Bowie, E. L. 2009d. 'Quotation of earlier texts in τὰ ἐς τὸν Τυανέα Ἀπολλώνιον', in K. Demoen and D. Pratt (eds.), *Theios Sophistes. Essays on Flavius Philostratus' 'Vita Apollonii'*. Mnemosyne Suppl. 305. Leiden and Boston: 57–73.

Bowie, E. L. 2010b. 'Historical narrative in archaic and early classical Greek elegy', in D. Konstan and K. A. Raaflaub (eds.), *Epic and History*. Malden, MA and Oxford: 145–66.

Bowie, E. L. 2010c. 'Stobaeus and Early Greek Melic, Elegiac and Iambic Poetry', in M. Horster and C. Reitz (eds.), *Condensing Texts – Condensed Texts*. Stuttgart: 587–617.

Bowie, E. L. 2010d. 'Marathon in fifth-century epigram', in K. Buraselis and K. Meidani (eds.), *Marathon: The Ancient Deme and the Battle*. Athens: 203–19.

Bowie, E. L. 2011b. 'Men from Mytilene', in T. Schmitz and N. Wiater (eds.), *The Struggle for Identity. Greeks and Their Past in the First Century BCE*. Stuttgart: 49–63.

Bowie, E. L. 2012a. 'An early chapter in the history of the Theognidea', in X. Riu and J. Pòrtulas (eds.), *Approaches to Archaic Greek Poetry*. Orione 5. Messina: 121–48.

Bowie, E. L. 2012c. 'Stesichorus and Ibycus: plain tales from the western front', in J. Marincola, L. Llewelyn-Jones and C. Maciver (eds.), *Greek Notions of the Past in the Archaic and Classical Eras: History without Historians*. Edinburgh Leventis Studies 6. Edinburgh: 83–94.

Bowie, E. L. 2012d. 'Epinicians and "patrons"', in P. Agocs, C. Carey and R. Rawles (eds.), *Reading the Victory Ode*. Cambridge: 83–92.

Bowie, E. L. 2012e. 'Luxury cruisers? Philip's epigrammatists between Greece and Rome', *Aevum Antiquum* 8: 223–58.

Bowie, E. L. 2012f. 'Socrates' cock and Daphnis' goats. The rarity of vows in the religious practice of the Greek novels', *Trends in Classics* 4.2: 225–73.

Bowie, E. L. 2012g. 'Hadrien et Smyrne', in A. Hostein and S. Lalanne (eds.), *Les voyages des empereurs dans l'orient romain. Époques Antonine et Sévérienne*. Paris: 247–61.

Bowie, E. L. 2012h. 'Hadrien et Éphèse', in A. Hostein and S. Lalanne (eds.), *Les voyages des empereurs dans l'orient romain. Époques Antonine et Sévérienne*. Paris: 263–96.

Bowie, E. L. 2013c. 'Milesian tales', in T. Whitmarsh and S. Thomson (eds.), *The Romance between Greece and the East*. Cambridge: 243–57.

Bowie, E. L. 2013d. 'Caging grasshoppers: Longus' materials for plaiting "reality"', in Paschalis, Panyotakis and Schmeling (eds.): 179–97.

Bowie, E. L. 2013e. 'Libraries for the Caesars', in J. Koenig, K. Oikonomopoulou and G. Woolf (eds.), *Ancient Libraries*. Cambridge: 237–60.

Bowie, E. L. 2014a. 'Rediscovering Sacadas', in A. Moreno and R. Thomas (eds.), *Patterns of the Past: Epitēdeumata in the Greek Tradition*. Oxford: 39–55.

Bowie, E. L. 2014c. 'Becoming wolf, staying sheep', in R. Rees and J. Madsen (eds.), *Roman Rule in Greek and Latin Writing*. Leiden and Boston: 39–78.

Bowie, E. L. 2014d. 'Greek culture in Arrian's Bithynia', in S. Lalanne and A. Hostein (eds.), *Le monde d'Arrien de Nicomédie*. Ktèma 39: 37–49.

Bowie, E. L. 2015a. 'Stesichorus at Athens', in Finglass and Kelly (eds.): 111–24.

Bowie, E. L. 2015b. 'Aristophanes *Clouds*: an agonistic note', in C. Fernández, J. Nápoli and G. Zecchin (eds.), *ΑΓΩΝ: Competencia y cooperación de la antigua Grecia a la actualidad. Homenaje a Ana María González de Tobia*. La Plata: 95–109.

Bowie, E. L. 2015c. 'Land without priests? Religious Authority in Longus, *Daphnis and Chloe*', in Panayotakis, Schmeling and Paschalis : 67–84.

Bowie, E. L. 2015d. 'Time and place, narrative and speech in Philicus, Philodamus and Limenius', in A. Faulkner and O. Hodkinson (eds.), *Hymnic Narrative and the Narratology of Greek Hymns*. Leiden and Boston: 87–118.

Bowie, E. L. 2016a. 'Cultic contexts for elegiac performance', in L. Swift and C. Carey (eds.), *Iambus and Elegy. New Approaches*. Oxford: 15–32.

Bowie, E. L. 2016b. '*Quo usque tandem*? How long were sympotic songs?', in V. Cazzato, D. Obbink and E. E. Prodi (eds.), *The Cup of Song: Studies on Poetry and the Symposium*. Oxford: 28–41.

Bowie, E. L. 2016f. 'Doing Doric', in E. Sistakou and A. Rengakos (eds.), *Dialect, Diction, and Style in Greek Literary and Inscribed Epigram*. Trends in Classics Supplementary Volume 43. Berlin and New York: 3–22.

Bowie, E. L. 2016g. 'Xenophon's influence in imperial Greece', in M. Flower (ed.), *The Cambridge Companion to Xenophon*. Cambridge: 403–14.

Bowie, E. L. 2016h. 'Gymnosophists', in *OCD* online.

Bowie, E. L. 2016i. 'Literary criticism of archaic lyric, elegiac and iambic poetry in Dio of Prusa', in E. Amato, C. Bost-Pouderon, T. Grandjean, L. Thévenet, and G. Ventrella (eds.), *'Dion de Pruse: l'homme, son œuvre et sa postérité' (Actes du colloque Nantes, 21–23 mai 2015). Spoudasmata* 169. Hildesheim 2016, 365–72.

Bowie, E. L. 2017a. 'Poetic elements in the vocabulary of the Greek novelists', in M. Biraud and M. Briand (eds.), *Roman grec et poésie. Dialogue des genres et nouveaux enjeux du poétique*. CMO 56. Lyon: 97–133.

Bowie, E. L. 2017c. 'The view from Aphrodisias and Hadrianoutherae', in M. R. Niehoff (ed.), *Journeys in the Roman East: Imagined and Real*. Tübingen: 23–51.

Bowie, E. L. 2018a. 'The Lesson of Book 2', in Harrison and Irwin (eds.): 53–74.

Bowie, E.L. 2018c. 'Captured moments: illustrating Longus' prose', in T. S. Thorsen and S. J. Harrison (eds.), *The Dynamics of Ancient Prose*. Trends in Classics Supplementary Volume 62. Berlin and New York: 195–222.

Bowie, E. L. (ed.) 2018d. *Herodotus. Narrator Scientist Historian*. Berlin and New York.

Bowie, E. L. 2019b. 'Animals, slaves and masters in Longus' *Daphnis and Chloe*', in M. Paschalis, S. Panayotakis and C. Panayotakis (eds.), *Masters and Slaves*. ANS 23: 107–25.

Bowie, E. L. 2019c. 'Λέξεις Λόγγου', in Chew, Morgan and Trzaskoma (eds.): 99–114.

Bowie, E. L. 2019d. 'Marcus Aurelius, Greek poets, and Greek sophists: friends or foes?', in P. R. Bosman (ed.), *Intellectual and Empire in Greco-Roman Antiquity*. London: 142–59.

Bowie, E. L. 2019e. 'The marginalisation of women in Philostratus' *Lives of the sophists*', in S. Lalanne (ed.), *Femmes grecques de l'Orient romain*, DHA Suppl. 18: 207–19.

Bowie, E. L. 2019f. 'Poetic and prose oral performance in the Greek world of the Roman Empire', in C. Ruiz Montero (ed.), *Aspects of Orality and Greek Literature in the Roman Empire*. Newcastle: 50–81.

Bowie, E. L. 2019g. *Longus: Daphnis and Chloe*. Cambridge.

Bowie, E. L. 2019h. 'The demotion of the literary cowherd', in J. Bastick, C. Cusset and C. Vieilleville (eds.), *Aitia 9.1. Le bouvier dans la poésie hellénistique et le roman grec*. Lyon: no pagination.

Bowie, E. L. 2019i. 'Callimachus and Longus', in J. Klooster, M. Cuyper, R. Regtuit and G. C. Wakker (eds.), *Callimachus Revisited. New Perspectives in Callimachean Scholarship. Hellenistica Groningana* 24. Groningen: 51–64.

Bowie, E. L. 2020b. 'Silence in Chariton, Xenophon, Achilles Tatius and Longus', in E. Papadodima (ed.), *Faces of Silence in Ancient Greek Literature*. Trends in Classics Supplementary Volume 100. Berlin and Boston: 51–72.

Bowie, E. L. 2021a. 'Sappho in imperial Greek literature', in P. Finglass and A. Kelly (eds.), *The Cambridge Companion to Sappho*. Cambridge: 313–29.

Bowie, E. L. 2021b. 'Theocritus and Longus', in E. Sistakou, P. Kyriakou and A. Rengakos (eds.), *Brill's Companion to Theocritus*. Leiden and Boston: 747–68.

Bowie, E. L. 2022a. 'Theatre and autocracy in the Greek world of the High Roman Empire', in E. Csapo, J. R. Green, B. Le Guen, E. Paillard, J. Stoop and P. Wilson (eds.), *Theatre and Autocracy in the Ancient World*. Berlin and Boston: 163–79.

Bowie, E. L. 2022b. 'Singing Rome', in B. Delignon, N. Le Meur and O. Thévenaz (eds.), *Performance et mimesis: variations sur la lyrique cultuelle de la Grèce archaïque au Haut Empire romain*. Actes du colloque international organisé les 5–7 novembre 2015 par l'ENS de Lyon, HiSoMA (UMR 5189) et l'Université de Lausanne, Supplément de Kernos. Liège: 147–60.

Bowie, E. L. 2022c. 'Greek culture in Hellenistic and early imperial Bithynia', *Mnemosyne* 75: 73–112.

Bowie, E. L. 2022d. 'Tradition and authority in Philostratus' *Lives of the sophists*', in K. Scarlett Kingsley, G. Monti and T. Rood (eds.), *The Authoritative Historian: Tradition and Innovation in Ancient Historiography*. Cambridge: 292–312.

Bowie, E. L. 2022e. 'Greek Grammatici in the Roman Empire', in A.-M. Favreau-Linder, S. Lalanne, J.-L. Vix (eds.), *Passeurs de culture. Recherches sur les Rhétoriques Religieuses* 32. Turnhout: 17–32.

Bowie, E. L. forthcoming. 'Philicus' Demeter: not a hymn?', in B. Cartlidge, J. Kwapisz and M. Perale (eds.), *Hellenistic Poetry before Callimachus*. Cambridge.

Bowie, E. L. and Harrison, S. J. 1993. 'The romance of the novel', *JRS* 83: 159–78.

Bowie, E. L. and Elsner, J. (eds.) 2009. *Philostratus*. Cambridge.

Bowman, A. 1986. *Egypt after the Pharaohs*. London.

Boys-Stones, G. R. (ed.) 2003. *Metaphor, Allegory, and the Classical Tradition: Ancient Thought and Modern Revisions*. Oxford.

Bradley, K. R. 1994. *Slavery and Society at Rome*. Cambridge.

Bravo, B. 1997. *Pannychis e simposio: feste private notturne di donne e uomini nei testi letterari e nel culto*. Pisa.

Bréchet, C., Videau, A. and Webb, R. (eds.) 2013. *Théories et pratiques de la fiction à l'époque impériale*. Paris.

Bremer, J. M. 1975. 'The meadow of love and two passages in Euripides' *Hippolytus*', *Mnemosyne* 28: 268–80.

Bremer, J. M. 1996. 'A purposeful manipulation of myth: Philodamus' paian to Dionysus', in D. Aristodemo, C. Maeder and R. de Rooy (eds.), *Studi di Teoria e Storia letteraria, in onore di Pieter de Meijer*. Firenze: 81–92.

Bremer, J. M., van Erp Taalman Kip, A. M. and Slings, S. R. 1987. *Some Recently Found Greek Poems*. Mnemosyne Suppl. 99. Leiden.

Bremer, J. M. and Handley, E. W. (eds.) 1993. *Aristophane: Sept exposés suivis de discussions*. Entretiens Hardt 38. Vandœuvres–Genève.

Bremer, J. M. and Furley, W. 2001. *Greek Hymns*. Tübingen.

Bremmer, J. N. 1998. 'The novel and the Apocryphal Acts: place, time and readership', in H. Hofmann and M. Zimmerman (eds.), *Groningen Colloquia on the Novel IX*. Groningen: 157–80.

Bremmer, J. N. 2012. 'Athenian civic priests from classical times to late antiquity: some considerations', in M. Horster and A. Klöckner (eds.), *Civic Priests. Cult Personnel in Athens from the Hellenistic Period to Late Antiquity*: Berlin and New York: 219–35.

Bremmer, J. N. 2013. 'The representation of priests and priestesses in the pagan and Christian Greek novel', in B. Dignas, R. Parker and G. Stroumsa (eds.), *Priests and Prophets among Pagans, Jews and Christians*. Leuven: 136–61.

Bremmer, J. N. and Roodenburg, H. (eds.) 1991. *A Cultural History of Gesture*. Cambridge.

Brennan, T. C. 1998. 'The poets Julia Balbilla and Damo at the Colossus of Memnon', *CW* 91: 215–34.

Brioso Sánchez, M. 1989. 'Caritone III 5 y sus modelos', *Minerva* 3: 205–8.

Brodersen, K. 1994. *Dionysius von Alexandria, Das Lied von der Welt. Zweisprachige Ausgabe*. Hildesheim, Zürich and New York.

Brommer, F. 1973. *Vasenlisten zur griechischen Heldensage*, 3rd ed. Marburg.

Brown, C. G. 1983. 'From rags to riches: Anacreon's Artemon', *Phoenix* 37: 1–15.

Brown, C. G. 1990. 'Honouring the goddess: Philicus' Hymn to Demeter', *Aegyptus* 70: 173–89.

Brown, E. L. 1981. 'The Lycidas of Theocritus' *Idyll* 7', *HSPh* 86: 59–100.

Buchheit, V. 1962. *Studien zum corpus Priapeorum*. Zetemata 28. Munich.

Buffière, F. 1970. *Anthologie grecque: Anthologie palatine, XII, livres XIII–XV*. Paris.

Bühler, W. 1978. 'Ein unbekanntes, Kaiser Hadrian zugeschriebenes Epigramm (Mitteilungen aus griechischen Handschriften, 6)', *ZPE* 31: 55–60.

Bulloch, A. W. 1985. *Callimachus: The Fifth Hymn*. Cambridge.

Bürger, K. 1892a. 'Zu Xenophon von Ephesus', *Hermes* 27: 36–67.

Bürger, K. 1892b. 'Der antike Roman vor Petronius', *Hermes* 27: 345–458.

Burgess, T. C. 1902. *Epideictic Literature*. Chicago Studies in Classical Philology. Chicago.

Burkert, W. 1972. *Lore and Science in Ancient Pythagoreanism*. Cambridge, MA (transl. by E. L. Minar of *Weisheit und Wissenschaft. Studien zu Pythagoras, Philolaos und Platon*. Nürnberg 1962).

Burnet, J. 1911. *Plato's Phaedo*. Oxford.
Burton, J. B. 2012. 'From Theocritean to Longan bucolic: Eugenianus' *Drosilla and Charicles*', *GRBS* 52: 684–713.
Byrne, S. 2003. *Roman Citizens of Athens*. Studia Hellenistica 40. Leuven and Dudley, MA.
Cabanes, P. 1976. *L'Épire de la mort de Pyrrhos à la conquête romaine, 272–167 av. J.C.* Paris.
Cairns, F. 1963. 'Propertius 1.18 and Callimachus', *CR* 19: 131–4.
Cairns, F. 1972. *Generic Composition in Greek and Latin Poetry*. Edinburgh.
Cairns, F. 1979. *Tibullus*. Cambridge.
Calame, C. 2009. 'Apollo in Delphi and in Delos: poetic performances between paean and dithyramb', in L. Athanassaki, R. P. Martin and J. Miller (eds.), *Apolline Politics and Poetics*. Athens: 169–97.
Calder, W. M. III 1970. 'Aristophanes *Vespae* 68–69. An unnoticed obscenity', *CPh* 65: 257.
Calder, W. M. III 1983. 'Longus 1.2: the she-goat nurse', *CPh* 78: 50–1.
Calza, G., Becatti, G., Gismondi, I., De Angelis D'Ossat, G. and Bloch, H. 1953. *Scavi di Ostia i. Topografia Generale*. Roma.
Cameron, A. 1980a. 'The *Garland* of Philip', *GRBS* 21: 43–62.
Cameron, A. 1980b. 'Two notes on the Anthology', *CPh* 75: 140–1.
Cameron, A. 1980c. '*Poetae novelli*', *HSPh* 84: 127–75.
Cameron, A. 1980d. 'Crinagoras and the elder Julia. *A.P.* 6.345 = *GP* 6', *LCM* 5: 129–30.
Cameron, A. 1982. 'Strato and Rufinus', *CQ* 32: 162–73.
Cameron, A. 1993. *The Greek Anthology from Meleager to Planudes*. Oxford.
Cameron, A. 1995. *Callimachus and His Critics*. Princeton.
Campanile, M. D. 1994. *I sacerdoti del koinon d'Asia*. Pisa.
Cantarelli, L. 1898. 'Gli scritti latini di Adriano imperatore', *Studi e documenti di storia e diritto* 19: 113–70.
Carden, R. J. D. 1969. 'P. Schubart 7: a fragment of Euphorion?', *BICS* 16: 29–37.
Carey, C. 1986. 'Archilochus and Lycambes', *CQ* 36: 60–7.
Carlisle, D. P. C. 2009. *Καὶ ὄναρ καὶ ὕπαρ: Dreaming in the Ancient Novel*. Dissertation, University of North Carolina at Chapel Hill.
Carvounis, K. 2019. *A commentary on Quintus of Smyrna*, Posthomerica *14*. Oxford.
Cassio, A. C. 1977. *Aristofane. I Banchettanti*. Pisa.
Cassio, A. C. 1981. 'Attico "volgare" e ioni in Atene alla fine del 5 secolo a.c.', *AION (filol.)* 3: 79–93.
Cassio, A. C. 1985. *Commedia e partecipazione: La Pace di Aristofane*. Napoli.
Casson, L. 1992. 'The nautical imagery in *Anthologia Graeca* 10.23', *CQ* 42: 555–7.
Cavallo, G. 1996. 'Veicoli materiali della letteratura di consumo: maniere di scrivere e maniere di leggere', in Pecere and Stramaglia (eds.): 11–46 (repr. in Cavallo 2005: 213–33).

Cavallo, G. 2005. *Il calamo e il papiro: la scrittura greca dall'età ellenistica ai primi secoli di Bisanzio*. Firenze.

Chalk, H. H. O. 1960. 'Eros and the Lesbian pastorals of Longus', *JHS* 80: 32–51.

Champlin, E. 1980. *Fronto and Antonine Rome*. Cambridge, MA.

Champlin, E. 2003. 'Nero, Apollo, and the poets', *Phoenix* 57: 276–83.

Chantraine, P. 1968–80. *Dictionnaire étymologique de la langue grecque*. 4 vols. Paris.

Charitonidis, S. 1960. *Αἱ Ἐπιγραφαὶ τῆς Λέσβου. Συμπλήρωμα*. Αθήνα.

Chaumont, M.-L. 1992. 'Échos de la campagne de Tibère en Arménie (20 av. J.-C.) dans une épigramme de Krinagoras (*Anthologia Palatina* IX, 430)', *AC* 61: 178–91.

Chew, K., Morgan, J. R. and Trzaskoma, S. (eds.) 2019. *Literary Currents and Romantic Forms. Essays in Memory of Bryan Reardon*. ANS 26. Groningen.

Christesen, P. 2007. *Olympic Victor Lists and Ancient Greek History*. Cambridge.

Christian, J. 1984. 'Dédale géographe: Regard et voyages aériens en Grèce', *LALIES* 3: 147–64.

Chuvin, P. 1991. *Chronique des derniers païens: la disparition du paganisme dans l'Empire romain, du règne de Constantin à celui de Justinien (2e édition revue et corrigée)*. Paris.

Cikán, O. and Danek, G. 2018. *Longos, Daphnis und Chloë*. Vienna and Prague.

Cichorius, C. 1888. *Rom und Mytilene*. Leipzig.

Cichorius, C. 1922. *Römische Studien*. Leipzig.

Cioffi, R. L. 2013. 'Seeing Gods: epiphany and narrative in the Greek novels', *AN* 11: 1–42.

Clarke, K. J. 1999. *Between Geography and History: Hellenistic Constructions of the Roman World*. Oxford.

Clausen, W. V. 1994. *Virgil Eclogues*. Oxford.

Clinton, K. 1972. 'A verse inscription from Eleusis concerning Herodes Atticus', *Ἀρχ. Ἐφημ*: 182–3 with pl. 72.

Clinton, K. 1974. 'The sacred officials of the Eleusinian mysteries', *Trans. Am. Philosophical Soc.* 64.3: 1–143.

Clinton, K. 1999. 'Eleusis from Augustus to the Antonines: progress and problems', in *Atti XI Congresso Internazionale di Epigrafia Greca e Latina*. Roma: ii 93–102.

Cole, S. G. 1981. 'Could Greek women read and write?', in H. P. Foley (ed.), *Reflections of Women in Antiquity*. New York: 219–45.

Coleman, K. M. 1988. *Statius: Silvae IV*. Oxford.

Coleman, K. M. 2011. 'Sailing to Nuceria: evidence for the date of Xenophon of Ephesus', *AClass* 54: 27–42.

Coleman, R. G. G. 1977. *Vergil, Eclogues*. Cambridge.

Colonna, A. 1957. 'Dionysii Periegetae *Vita Chisiana*', *BollClass* 5: 9–12.

Colonna, A. (ed.) 1987. *Eliodoro. Le etiopiche*. Torino.

Conca, F. 1969. 'I papiri di Achille Tazio', *RIL* 103: 649–77.

Conca, F., De Carli, E. and Zanetto, G. 1963–97. *Lessico dei Romanzieri Greci* (Vol. i Milano 1963, Vols. ii–iv Hildesheim, Zürich and New York 1989–97).

Connelly, J. B. 2007. *Portrait of a Priestess: Women and Ritual in Ancient Greece*. Princeton.

Connors, C. 2002. 'Chariton's Syracuse and the histories of empire', in M. Paschalis and S. Frangoulidis (eds.), *Space in the Ancient Novel*. ANS 1. Groningen: 12–26.

Conti, G. 1970. *Decorazione architettonica della Piazza d'oro a Villa Adriana*. Roma.

Corrêa, P. da Cunha 2001. 'The fox and the hedgehog', *Phaos* 1: 81–92.

Corrêa, P. da Cunha 2010. *Um Bestiário Arcaico. Fábulas e imagens de animais na poesía de Arquíloco*. Campinas.

Counillon, P. 1981. 'Un autre acrostiche dans la périégèse de Denys', *REG* 94: 514–22.

Cresci, L. R. 1981. 'Il romanzo di Longo sofista e la tradizione bucolica', *A&R* 26: 1–25 (repr. as 'The novel of Longus the sophist and the pastoral tradition', in Swain (ed.) 1999: 210–42).

Cribiore, R. 1996. *Writing, Teachers, and Students in Graeco-Roman Egypt*. Atlanta.

Cribiore, R. 2001a. 'The grammarian's choice: the popularity of Euripides' *Phoenissae* in Hellenistic and Roman education', in Too (ed.): 241–59.

Cribiore, R. 2001b. *Gymnastics of the Mind: Greek Education in Hellenistic and Roman Egypt*. Princeton.

Crismani, D. 1994. *Il teatro nel romanzo ellenistico d'amore e di avventure*. Alessandria.

Crum, W. E. 1902. *Coptic Ostraka from the Collections of the Egypt Exploration Fund, the Cairo Museum and Others*. London.

Csapo, E. 2007. 'The men who built the theatres: *Theatropolitai*, *Theatronai* and *Arkhitektones*', in Wilson (ed.): 85–105.

Cueva, E. P. 1994. '*Anth. Pal.* 14.34 and Achilles Tatius 2.14', *GRBS* 35: 281–6.

Cueva, E. P. 1996. 'Plutarch's Ariadne in Chariton's *Chaereas and Callirhoe*', *AJPh* 117: 473–84.

Cueva, E. P. 1998. 'Longus and Thucydides: a new interpretation', *GRBS* 39: 429–40.

Cueva, E. P. 2000. 'The date of Chariton's *Chaereas and Callirhoe* revisited', *C&M* 51: 197–208.

Cueva, E. P. 2004. *The Myths of Fiction: Studies in the Canonical Greek Novels*. Ann Arbor.

Cueva, E. P. and Byrne, S. N. (eds.) 2014. *A Companion to the Ancient Novel*. Oxford and Malden, MA.

Currie, B. and Rutherford, I. C. (eds.) 2019. *The Reception of Greek Lyric Poetry in the Ancient World: Transmission, Canonization and Paratext*. Studies in Archaic and Classical Greek Song 5, Mnemosyne Suppl. 430. Leiden and Boston.

Curty, O. 1995. *Les parentés légendaires entre cités grecques: catalogue raisonné des inscriptions contenant le terme ΣΥΓΓΕΝΕΙΑ et analyse critique*. Genève.

Cusset, C. 2006. 'Discours divins et débats intérieurs dans les Pastorales de Longus', in B. Pouderon and J. Peigney (eds.), *Discours et débats dans l'ancien roman*. CMO 36. Lyon: 231–48.

Danek, G. and Wallisch, R. 1993. 'Notizen zu Longus Daphnis und Chloe', *WS* 106: 45–60.

Davies, J. K. 1967. 'Demosthenes on liturgies: a note', *JHS* 87: 33–40.

Davies, M. and Pomeroy, S. B. 2012. 'Marcellus of Side's epitaph on Regilla (*IG* XIV 1389): an historical and literary commentary', *Prometheus* 38: 3–34.

Dawson, S. 1997. 'The theatrical audience in fifth-century Athens: numbers and status', *Prudentia* 29: 1–14.

De Bakker, M. 2021. 'Herodotus', in M. de Bakker and I. de Jong (eds.), *Studies in Ancient Greek Narrative, Volume 5*. Mnemosyne Suppl. 448. Leiden and Boston: 197–222.

Degani, E. 1993. 'Aristofane e la tradizione dell' invettiva personale in Grecia', in Bremer and Handley (eds.): 1–36.

Del Corso, L. 2006. 'Lo "stile severo" nei P.Oxy. Una lista', *Aegyptus* 86: 81–106.

Del Corso, L. 2010. 'Il romanzo greco a Ossirinco e i suoi lettori. Osservazioni paleografiche, bibliogiche, storio-culturali', in Bastianini and Casanova (eds.): 247–77.

de Lannoy, L. 1977. *Flavii Philostrati Heroicus*. Leipzig.

de Romilly, J. 1985. *A Short History of Greek Literature*. Chicago and London.

De Temmerman, K. 2014. *Crafting Characters: Heroes and Heroines in the Ancient Greek Novel*. Oxford.

De Temmerman, K. 2021a. 'Chariton', in M. de Bakker and I. de Jong (eds.), *Studies in Ancient Greek Narrative, Volume 5*. Mnemosyne Suppl. 448. Leiden and Boston: 635–53.

De Temmerman, K. 2021b. 'Achilles Tatius', in M. de Bakker and I. de Jong (eds.), *Studies in Ancient Greek Narrative, Volume 5*. Mnemosyne Suppl. 448. Leiden and Boston: 673–91.

de Vries, G. 1970. 'Notes on Greek epigrams', *Mnemosyne iv* 23: 22–32.

Demoen, K. 1988. 'The date of the Cyzicene epigrams. An analysis of the vocabulary and metrical technique of AP, III', *AC* 57: 231–48.

Dickey, E. 1996. *Greek Forms of Address: From Herodotus to Lucian*. Oxford.

Dickie, M. W. 1991. 'Heliodorus and Plutarch on the evil eye', *CPh* 86: 17–29.

Dickie, M. W. 1998. 'Poets as Initiates in the Mysteries. Euphorion, Philicus and Posidippus', *Antike und Abendland* 44: 49–77.

Dihle, A. 1978. 'Zur Datierung des Metiochos-Romans', *WJA* 4: 47–55.

Dihle, A. 1989. *Der griechische und lateinische Literatur der Kaiserzeit*. München.

Dillery, J. 2018. 'Making *logoi*', in Harrison and Irwin (eds.): 17–52.

Di Maria, G. 1996. *Achillis quae feruntur Astronomica et in Aratum Opuscula: De Universo; De Arati Vita; De Phaenomenorum Interpretatione*. Palermo.

Di Marzio, M. 2019. 'L'Epigramma 31 Bernand di Giulia Balbilla e l'acrostico con la voce di Phamenoth/Memnone', *QUCC* 123: 105–30.

Di Virgilio, R. 1991. *Longo Sofista. Dafni e Cloe*. Milano.

Dougherty, C. 1994. 'Archaic Greek foundation poetry: questions of genre and occasion', *JHS* 114: 35–46.

Dover, K. J. 1964. 'The poetry of Archilochos', in *Archiloque. Entretiens Hardt 10*. Vandœuvres-Genève: 181–222 (repr. in Dover 1988: 97–121).

Dover, K. J. 1968. *Aristophanes Clouds. Edited with an Introduction and Commentary*. Oxford.

Dover, K. J. 1971. *Theocritus. Select Poems*. Basingstoke and London.

Dover, K. J. 1972. *Aristophanic Comedy*. London.

Dover, K. J. 1976. 'The freedom of the intellectual in Greek society', *Talanta* 7: 24–74 (repr. in Dover 1988: 135–58).

Dover, K. J. 1978. *Greek Homosexuality*. London.

Dover, K. J. 1988. *The Greeks and Their Legacy. Collected Papers II: Prose Literature, History, Society, Transmission, Influence*. Oxford.

Dover, K. J. 1993a. *Aristophanes Frogs. Edited with an Introduction and Commentary*. Oxford.

Dover, K. J. 1993b. 'The chorus of initiates in Aristophanes' *Frogs*', in Bremer and Handley (eds.): 173–93.

Dover, K. J., West, M. L., Griffin, J. and Bowie, E. L. 1980. *Ancient Greek Literature*. Oxford.

Dowden, K. 1996. 'Heliodoros: serious intentions', *CQ* 46: 267–85.

Dowden, K. 2006. 'Pouvoir divin, discours humain chez Héliodore', in B. Pouderon and J. Peigney (eds.), *Discours et débats dans l'ancien roman*. CMO 36. Lyon: 249–61.

Dowden, K. 2007. 'A lengthy sentence: judging the prolixity of the Greek novels', in M. Paschalis, S. Frangoulidis, S. J. Harrison and M. Zimmerman (eds.), *The Greek and Roman Novel. Parallel Readings*. ANS 8. Groningen: 133–50.

Dowden, K. 2010. 'The gods in the Greek novel', in J. Bremmer, A. Erskine and C. Auffarth (eds.), *The Gods of Ancient Greece: Identities and Transformations*. Edinburgh: 362–74.

Downie, J. 2013. *At the Limits of Art: A Literary Study of Aelius Aristides' Hieroi logoi*. Oxford.

Downie, J. 2017. 'The geography of empire in Dionysius' *Periegesis*: a view from the Aegean', *CW* 110: 163–86.

Drago, A. and Hodkinson, O. 2023. *Ancient Love Letters: Form, Themes, Approaches*. Berlin.

Drews, R. 1970. 'Herodotus' other *logoi*', *AJP* 91: 181–91.

Dubel, S. 1990. 'La description d'objets d'art dans les Éthiopiques', *Pallas* 36: 101–15.

Dueck, D. 2000. *Strabo of Amasia: A Greek Man of Letters in Augustan Rome*. London.

Dueck, D., Lindsay, H. and Pothecary, S. (eds.) 2006. *Strabo's Cultural Geography. The Making of a Kolossourgia*. Cambridge.

Duff, T. 1999. *Plutarch's Lives. Exploring Virtue and Vice*. Oxford.

Duncan-Jones, R. 1977. 'Age-rounding, illiteracy, and social differentiation in the Roman Empire', *Chiron* 7: 333–53.

DuQuesnay, I. M. LeM. 1981. 'Vergil's First Eclogue', in F. Cairns (ed.), *Papers of the Liverpool Latin Seminar* 3. Liverpool: 29–182.

Dümmler, N. N. 2012. 'Musaeus, *Hero and Leander*: between epic and novel', in M. Baumbach and S. Bär (eds.), *Brill's Companion to Greek and Latin Epyllion and Its Reception*. Leiden: 411–46.

Dyck, A. R. 1986. *Michael Psellus. The Essays on Euripides and George of Pisidia and on Heliodorus and Achilles Tatius*. Byz. Vindobon. 16. Wien.

Dzielska, M. 1986. *Apollonius of Tyana in Legend and History*. Roma.

Eck, W. 1983. 'Jahres- und Provinzialfasten der senatorischen Statthalter von 69/70 bis 138–139. 2 Teil', *Chiron* 13: 147–237.

Edmunds, L. 1985. 'Aristophanes' Socrates', in *Proceedings of the Boston Area Colloquium in Ancient Philosophy*. Volume I. Lanham: 209–30.

Edwards, M. J. 1991. 'Damis the Epicurean', *CQ* 41: 563–6.

Edwards, M. J. 1997. 'The art of love and love of art in Longus', *AC* 66: 239–48.

Effe, B. 1977. *Dichtung und Lehre. Untersuchungen zur Typologie des antiken Lehrgedichts*. Zetemata 69. München.

Effe, B. 1982. 'Longos. Zur Funktionsgeschichte der Bukolik in der römischen Kaiserzeit', *Hermes* 110: 65–84 (repr. as 'Longus: towards a history of bucolic and its function in the Roman Empire', in Swain (ed.) 1999: 189–209).

Egger, B. 1988. 'Zu den Frauenrollen im griechischen Roman: Die Frau als Heldin and Leserin', *GCN* 1: 33–66.

Elsner, J. 2000. 'From the culture of spolia to the cult of relics: the Arch of Constantine and the genesis of late antique forms', *PBSR* 68: 149–84.

Elsner, J. and Squire, M. forthcoming. *The Art of Looking in the Roman World: Painting and Description in the Imagines of the Elder Philostratus*. Cambridge.

Epstein, S. J. 1995. 'Longus' werewolves', *CPh* 90: 58–73.

Erim, K. 1986. *Aphrodisias: City of Venus-Aphrodite*. New York.

Étienne, R. and Piérart, M. 1975. 'Un décret du Koinon des Hellènes à Platées en l'honneur de Glaucon, fils d'Étéoclès d'Athènes', *BCH* 99: 51–75.

Fajen, F. 1999, *Oppianus Halieutica. Einführung, Text, Übersetzung in deutscher Sprache, Auführliche Kataloge der Meeresfauna*. Stuttgart.

Fantuzzi, M. 2007. 'Mescolare il ludicro al serio: la poetica del Corcirese Filico e l'edonismo dei Feaci (SH 980)', in G. Lozza and S. M. Tempesta (eds.), *L'epigramma Greco: problemi e prospettive: atti del Congresso della Consulta Universitaria del Greco, Milano, 21 ottobre 2005*. Milano: 53–68.

Faraone, C. A. 2008. *The Stanzaic Architecture of Early Greek Elegy*. New York.

Fehling, D. 1971. *Die Quellenangaben bei Herodot: Studien zur Erzählkunst Herodots*. Berlin and New York (transl. by J. G. Howie as *Herodotus and His 'Sources': Citation, Invention, and Narrative Art*. Leeds 1989).

Fein, S. 1994. *Die Beziehungen der Kaiser Trajan und Hadrian zu den Litterati*. Stuttgart and Leipzig.

Fellmann, B. 1972. *Die antiken Darstellungen des Polyphemabenteuers*. München.

Fernandez, C. and Zecchin de Fasano, G. (eds.) 2015. *Agon. Studies in Honor of Ana-María González de Tobia*. La Plata.

Fernandez-Garrido, R. 2021. 'Ninus and Metiochus in the school of rhetoric: the first Greek novels', *AN* 18: 57–75.

Ferrary, J.-L. 2014. *Les mémoriaux de délégations du sanctuaire oraculaire de Claros, d'après la documentation conservée dans le Fonds Louis Robert*. 2 vols. Paris.

Feuillâtre, E. 1966. *Études sur les Éthiopiques d'Héliodore*. Paris.

Finglass, P. J. and Kelly, A. (eds.) 2015. *Stesichorus in Context*. Cambridge.

Fisher, E. 1982. 'Greek translations of Latin literature in the fourth century AD', *YClS* 27: 173–215.

Flacelière, R. 1951. 'Le poète stoïcien Sarapion d'Athènes, ami de Plutarque', *REG* 64: 323–7.

Flinterman, J.-J. 1993. *Politiek, Paideia & Pythagorisme*. Groningen.

Flinterman, J.-J. 1995. *Power, Paideia and Pythagoreanism: Greek Identity, Conceptions of the Relationship between Philosophers and Monarchs and Political Ideas in Philostratus' Life of Apollonius*. Amsterdam.

Floridi, L. 2007. *Stratone di Sardi; introduzione, testo critico, traduzione e commento; foreword di Kathryn Gutzwiller*. Alessandria.

Floridi, L. 2014. *Lucillio, Epigrammi: Introduzione, Testo Critico, Traduzione e Commento*. Berlin and New York.

Foerster, R. and Richtsteig, E. 1929. *Choricius*. Leipzig (repr. Stuttgart 1972).

Foley, H. P. 1988. 'Tragedy and politics in Aristophanes' *Acharnians*', *JHS* 108: 33–47.

Follet, S. 1968. 'Hadrien en Égypte et en Judée', *RPh* 42: 53–77.

Follet, S. 1976. *Athènes au iie et au iiie siècle*. Paris.

Follet, S. 1977. 'La datation de l'archonte Dionysios (*IG* ii^{2}3968)', *REG* 90: 47–54.

Follet, S. 2001. 'Un ami de Plutarch: l'orateur Athénien Glaukias', in Billault (ed.): 85–96.

Fornara, C. 1971. *Herodotus: An Interpretation*. Oxford.

Fowler, R. L. 1996. 'Herodotus and his contemporaries', *JHS* 116: 62–87.

Fraenkel, E. 1950. *Aeschylus Agamemnon*. Oxford.

Fraenkel, E. 1962. *Beobachtungen zu Aristophanes*. Roma.

Fraser, P. M. 1959. 'An agonistic dedication from Roman Egypt', *JEA* 45: 79–80.

Frija, G. 2010a. *Les prêtres des empereurs: le culte impérial civique dans la province romaine d'Asie*. Rennes.

Frija, G. 2010b. *Prosopographie des prêtres du culte impérial dans les cités de la province romaine d'Asie*. www.pretres-civiques.org/.

Frijhoff, W. 1991. 'The kiss, sacred and profane', in Bremmer and Rodenburg: 210–36.

Frost, F. J. 1968. 'Scyllias: diving in antiquity', *G&R* 15: 180–5.

Fuchs, H. 1938. *Der geistige Widerstand gegen Rom in der antiken Welt*. Berlin.

Furley, W. D. 2009. 'Philikos' Hymn to Demeter', *Paideia* 64: 483–507.

Furley, W. D. and Bremer, J. M. 2001. *Greek Hymns. Selected Cult Songs from the Archaic to the Hellenistic Period*. 2 vols. Tübingen.

Fusillo, M. 1990a. 'Il Testo nel testo: la citazione nel romanzo Greco', *MD* 25: 27–48.

Fusillo, M. 1990b. *Antonio Diogene. Le Incredibili Avventure al di là di Tule*. Palermo.

Gabba, E. 1991. *Dionysius and the History of Archaic Rome*. Berkeley, Los Angeles and London.

Gärtner, H. 1967. 'Xenophon von Ephesos', *RE* IX A 2, 2055–89.

Gärtner, T. 2006. 'Zu den erotischen Epigrammen des Rufinus', *Eos* 93: 251–65.

Gagné, R. and Höschele, R. 2009. 'Works and nights: Marcus Argentarius (*A.P.* 9.161)', *Cambridge Classical Journal* 55: 59–70.

Galli, M. 2002. *Die Lebenswelt eines Sophisten: Untersuchungen zu den Bauten und Stiftungen des Herodes Atticus*. Mainz.

Gallavotti, C. 1931. 'Inno a Demetra di Filico', *SIFC* 9: 37–60.

Gallavotti, C. 1951. 'Philico, inno a Demetra', *PSI* 1282: 140–9.

Gamberale, L. 1993. 'L'epigramma dell'imperatore Adriano all'Eros di Tespie', in Pretagostini (ed.): iii 1089–1110.

Garnaud, J.-P. 1991. *Achille Tatius d'Alexandrie, Le roman de Leucippé et Clitophon*. Paris.

Garnett, J. 1895. 'On the date of the Ἀποτελεσματικά of Manetho', *Journal of Philology* 23: 238–40.

Garzya, A. 1955–7. 'Paraphrasis Dionysii poematis De aucupio', *Byzantion* 25–7: 195–240.

Garzya, A. 1957. 'Sull'autore e il titolo del perduto poema Sull'aucupio attribuito ad Oppiano', *GFI* 10: 156–60.

Garzya, A. 1963. *Dionysii ixeuticon seu de aucupio*. Leipzig.

Geagan, D. J. 1964. 'A new Herodes epigram from Marathon', *MDAI(A)* 79: 149–56.

Geagan, D. J. 1967. *The Athenian Constitution after Sulla*. Hesperia Suppl. 12. Princeton.

Geagan, D. J. 1991. 'The Sarapion monument and the quest for status in Roman Athens', *ZPE* 85: 145–65.

Geiger, J. 2021. 'Varro and Pompey: some more (multiple) *hebdomads*?', *CQ* 71: 1–6.

Geissen, A. 2005. 'The nome coins of Roman Egypt', in Howgego, Heuchert and Burnett (eds.): 167–70.

Georgiadou, A. and Larmour, D. H. J. 1998. *Lucian's Science Fiction Novel, True Histories: Interpretation and Commentary*. Leiden and Boston.

Gera, D. L. 1993. *Xenophon's Cyropaedia: Style, Genre and Literary Technique*. Oxford.

Gerber, D. E. 1999a. *Greek Elegiac Poetry*. Cambridge, MA and London.

Giangrande, G. 1968. 'Théocrite, Simichidas et les Thalysies', *AC* 37: 491–533.

Giangrande, G. 1975. 'Fifteen Hellenistic epigrams', *JHS* 95: 31–44.

Giangrande, G. 1990. 'Ein Epigramm des Bianor Gow-Page, Garl. Phil., 1731 ff.', *AC* 59: 179–80.

Giannini, A. 1965. *Paradoxographorum Graecorum reliquiae*. Milano.

Giannuzzi, M. E. 2007. *Stratone di Sardi. Epigrammi. Introduzione, traduzione e commento*. Lecce.

Gill, C. 1989. 'Longus', in Reardon (ed.): 285–348.

Giuseppetti, M. 2011. 'Miti e culti tra Attica e Argolide nell' Ecale di Callimaco', in A. Mortira, A.-T. Cozzoli and M. Giuseppetti (eds.), *Callimachea II. Atti della seconda giornata di studi su Callimaco*. Roma: 129–56.

Giuseppetti, M. 2012. 'Two poets for a goddess: Callimachus' and Philicus' hymns to Demeter', in M. A. Harder, R. F. Regtuit and G. C. Wakker (eds.), *Gods and Religion in Hellenistic Poetry*. Hellenistica Groningana 16. Leuven, Paris and Walpole, MA: 103–29.

Gkourogiannis, T. K. 1999. *Pindaric Quotations in Aelius Aristides*. PhD thesis, University College London.

Gleason, M. W. 2010. 'Making space for bicultural identity: Herodes Atticus commemorates Regilla', in T. Whitmarsh (ed.), *Local Knowledge and Microidentities in the Imperial Greek World*. Cambridge: 125–62.

Goette, H. R. 2007. 'The men who built the theatres: an archaeological appendix', in Wilson (ed.): 116–21.

Goggin, M. G. 1951. 'Rhythm in the prose of Favorinus', *YClS* 12: 149–201.

Gold, B. K. (ed.) 1982. *Literary and Artistic Patronage in Ancient Rome*. Austin.

Goldhill, S. 1995. *Foucault's Virginity*. Cambridge.

Goldhill, S. 2009. 'Constructing identity in Philostratus' Love Letters', in Bowie and Elsner (eds.): 287–308.

Gómez Cárdo, P. 2008. 'A propósito de algunos epigramas atribuidos a Luciano', *Synthesis* 15: 37–57.

Gomme, A. W. 1927. 'The Athenian hoplite force in 431 BC', *CQ* 2: 142–50.

Gomme, A. W. 1933. *The Population of Athens in the Fifth and Fourth Centuries BC*. Oxford.

Gomme, A. W. 1956. *A Historical Commentary on Thucydides ii*. Oxford.

Gomme, A. W. 1959. 'The population of Athens again', *JHS* 79: 61–8.

Gonis, N. 1997. '4418. Apollonius Rhodius Argonautica I 623-33', in *The Oxyrhynchus Papyri. Vol. 64*. London.

González Ponce, F. J. 1993. 'El periplo griego antiguo', *Habis* 24: 69–76.

González Rincón, M. 1996. *Estratón de Sardes. Epigramas. Introducción, edición revisada, traducción y comentario*. Sevilla.

Gordon, R. L. 2020. '(Re-)modelling religious experience', in V. Gasparini, M. Patzelt, R. Raja, A.-K. Rieger, J. Rüpke and E. Rubens Urciuoli, *Lived Religion in the Ancient Mediterranean World*. Berlin: 23–48.

Gosetti-Murrayjohn, A. 2006. 'Sappho as the tenth Muse in Hellenistic epigram', *Arethusa* 39: 21–45.

Gould, J. 1980. 'Law, custom and myth: aspects of the social position of women in classical Athens', *JHS* 100: 43–59.

Gow, A. S. F. 1952. *Theocritus*. 2 vols, 2nd ed. Cambridge.

Graf, F. 1980. 'Milch, Honig und Wein. Zum Verständnis der Libation im griechischen Ritual', in *Perennitas. Studi in onore di Angelo Brelich*. Rome: 209–21.

Green, P. 1982. 'Longus, Antiphon and the topography of Lesbos', *JHS* 102: 210–14.

Greifenhagen, A. 1975. 'Philopotes', *Gymnasium* 82: 26–32.

Gren, E. 1941. *Kleinasien und Ostbalkan in der wirtschaftlichen Entwicklung der römischen Kaiserzeit*. Uppsala.

Grenfell, B. and Hunt, A. S. 1899. *The Oxyrhynchus Papyri. Vol. 2*. London.

Grenfell, B. and Hunt, A. S. 1908. *The Oxyrhynchus Papyri. Vol. 6*. London.

Greenwood, E. 2018. 'Surveying greatness and magnitude in Herodotus', in Harrison and Irwin (eds.): 163–86.

Greensmith, E. 2020. *The Resurrection of Homer in Imperial Greek Epic*. Cambridge.

Grethlein, J. 2007. 'Diomedes Redivivus. A new reading of Mimnermus fr. 14 W2', *Mnemosyne* 60: 102–11.

Grethlein, J. 2010. *The Greeks and their Past. Poetry, Oratory, and History in the Fifth-Century BCE*. Cambridge.

Griffith, J. G. 1988. *Festinat Senex. Essays in Greek and Latin Literature and Archaeology*. Oxford.

Griffiths, A. H. 1970. 'Six passages in Callimachus and the Anthology', *BICS* 17: 32–43.

Grimal, P. 1969. *Les jardins romains*, 2nd ed. Paris.

Grintser, N. P. 2018. 'Herodotus as a literary critic', in Bowie (ed.): 157–73.

Groag, E. 1902. 'Cn. Claudius Severus und der Sophist Hadrian', *WS* 24: 261–4.

Gronewald, M. 1977. 'Ein neues Fragment aus dem Metiochos-Parthenope Roman (*Ostracon Bodl.* 2175 = P2 2782)', *ZPE* 24: 21–2.

Gronewald, M. 1979. 'Ein Fragment aus den *Aithiopica* des Heliodor', *ZPE* 34: 19–21.

Grossardt, P. 2006. *Einführung, Übersetzung und Kommentar zum Heroikos von Flavius Philostrat*. 2 vols. Basel.

Grossardt, P. 2018. 'Der Heroikos des Flavius Philostrat - eine Nachlese', *WS* 131: 13–75.

Gruen, E. S. 1993. 'The Polis in the Hellenistic world', in R. M. Rosen and J. Farrell (eds.), *Nomodeiktes: Greek Studies in Honor of Martin Ostwald*. Ann Arbor: 339–54.

Guidorizzi, G. 1979. 'La pesca miracolosa (Isidoro, *AP* 9.94)', *RIL* 113: 277–84.

Gurd, S. A. 2007. 'Meaning and material presence: four epigrams on Timomachus's unfinished *Medea*', *TAPhA* 137: 305–31.

Guthrie, W. K. C. 1971a. *The Sophists*. Cambridge (= *History of Greek Philosophy* iii 1, Cambridge 1969).

Guthrie, W. K. C. 1971b. *Socrates*. Cambridge (= *History of Greek Philosophy* iii 2, Cambridge 1969).

Gutzwiller, K. 1991. *Theocritus' Pastoral Analogies*. Madison.

Gutzwiller, K. 2004. 'Seeing thought: Timomachus' *Medea* and ecphrastic epigram', *AJP* 125: 339–86.

Gyselinck, W. and Demoen, K. 2009. 'Fiction and metafiction in Philostratus' *Vita Apollonii*', in K. Demoen and D. Pratt (eds.), *Theios Sophistes. Essays on Flavius Philostratus' Vita Apollonii*. Mnemosyne Suppl. 305. Leiden and Boston: 95–127.

Habicht, C. 1969. *Die Inschriften des Asklepieions. Deutsches Archäologisches Institut*. Altertümer von Pergamon viii 3. Berlin.

Habicht, C. 1985. *Pausanias' Guide to Ancient Greece*. Berkeley, Los Angeles and London.

Hadjimichael, T. A. 2019. *The Emergence of the Lyric Canon*. Oxford.

Haeberlin, K. 1887. *Carmina figurata Graeca*. Hannover.

Hagel, S. and Harrauer, C. (eds.) 2005. *Ancient Greek Music in Performance. Symposion Wien 29.9–1.10. 2003 VÖAW*. Wiener Studien Beihefte. Wien.

Hägg, T. 1971. *Narrative Technique in Ancient Greek Romances. Studies of Chariton, Xenophon Ephesius, and Achilles Tatius*. Stockholm.

Hägg, T. 1980. *Den antika romanen*. Uppsala.

Hägg, T. 1983. *The Novel in Antiquity*. Oxford.

Hägg, T. 1994. 'Orality, literacy, and the "readership" of the early Greek novel', in R. Eriksen (ed.), *Contexts of Pre-Novel Narrative: the European Tradition*. Berlin and New York: 47–81.

Halfmann, H. 1979. *Die Senatoren aus dem östlichen Teil des Imperium Romanum bis zum Ende des 2. Jh. n.Chr*. Hypomnemata 58. Göttingen.

Halfmann, H. 1986. *Itinera Principum: Geschichte und Typologie der Kaiserreisen im Römischen Reich*. Stuttgart.

Hall, E. and Wyles, R. (eds.) 2008. *New Directions in Ancient Pantomime*. Oxford.

Halliwell, S. 1987. *The Poetics of Aristotle: Translation and Commentary*. London.

Hallström, A. 1910. 'De aetate Antonii Diogenis', *Eranos* 10: 200–1.

Halperin, D. 1983. *Pastoral before Theocritus*. New Haven.

Handley, E. 1982. 'Aristophanes' rivals', *Proceedings of the Classical Association* 79: 23–5.

Hansen, M. H. 1981. 'The number of Athenian hoplites in 431 BC', *SO* 56: 19–32 (repr. in Hansen 1988).

Hansen, M. H. 1988. *Three Studies in Athenian Demography*. Copenhagen.

Hansen, W. 1996. *Phlegon of Tralles' Book of Marvels. Translated with an Introduction and Commentary*. Exeter.

Harder, M. A. 2012. *Callimachus Aetia. Introduction, Text, Translation and Commentary*. Oxford.

Hardie, A. 1983. *Statius and the Silvae. Poets, Patrons and Epideixis in the Graeco-Roman World*. Liverpool.

Hardie, A. 1997. 'Philitas and the plane tree', *ZPE* 119: 21–36.
Harris, W. V. 1983. 'Literacy and Epigraphy I', *ZPE* 52: 87–111.
Harris, W. V. 1989. *Ancient Literacy*. Cambridge, MA.
Harrison, S. J. 1998. 'The Milesian Tales and the Roman Novel', *GCN* 9: 61–73.
Harrison, S. J. 2000. *Apuleius: A Latin Sophist*. Oxford.
Harrison, S. J., Paschalis M. and Frangoulidis S. (eds.) 2005. *Metaphor and the Ancient Novel*. ANS 4. Groningen.
Harrison, T. and Irwin, E. K. (eds.) 2018. *Interpreting Herodotus*. Oxford and New York.
Havelock, E. A. 1968. 'The Socratic self as it is parodied in Aristophanes' *Clouds*', *YClS* 22: 1–18.
Hawes, G. 2014. *Rationalizing Myth in Antiquity*. Oxford.
Heberdey, R. and Wilhelm, G. A. 1896. *Reisen in Kilikien ausgeführt 1891 und 1892 von R. Heberdey und A. Wilhelm*. Denkschrift K. Akad. d. Wiss., phil.-hist. Kl., Bd. 44. Wien.
Hefti, V. 1950. *Zur Erzählungstechnik in Heliodors Aethiopika*. Wien.
Heiserman, A. 1977. *The Novel before the Novel*. Chicago.
Heitsch, E. 1963–4. *Die griechischen Dichterfragmente der römischen Kaiserzeit*. 2 vols. Göttingen.
Heitsch, E. 1963. 'Überlieferungsgeschichtliche Untersuchungen zu Andromachos, Markellos von Side und zum Carmen de viribus herbarum', *NGAW* 1963.2: 23–50.
Helmbold, W. C. and O'Neil, E. N. 1959. *Plutarch's Quotations*. Baltimore.
Henderson, J. 1975. *The Maculate Muse*. New Haven (repr. Oxford 1991).
Henderson, J. 1987. *Aristophanes Lysistrata. Edited with an Introduction and Commentary*. Oxford.
Henderson, J. 2008. *Aristophanes Fragments, Vol. v*. Cambridge, MA.
Henderson, J. 2009. *Longus: Daphnis and Chloe. Xenophon of Ephesus: Anthia and Habrocomes*. Cambridge, MA and London.
Henrichs, A. 1976. 'The atheism of Prodicus', *CErc* 6: 15–21.
Henrichs, A. 2011. 'Missing pages: papyrology, genre, and the Greek novel', in D. Obbink and R. B. Rutherford (eds.), *Culture in Pieces: Essays on Ancient Texts in Honour of Peter Parsons*. Oxford: 302–22.
Hepding, H. 1910. 'Die Arbeiten zu Pergamon, 1908–1909: II. Die Inschriften', *AM* 35: 401–93.
Hernández Lara, C. 1994. *Estudios sobre el Aticismo de Caritón de Afrodisias*. Amsterdam.
Herrmann, L. 1950. 'La réplique d'Hadrien à Florus', *Latomus* 9: 385–7.
Herrmann, L. 1951. 'Anthologie palatine VII, 233 et 234', *AC* 20: 101–2.
Herzog, R. 1934. 'Ein Asklepios-Hymnos des Aristeides von Smyrna', *Sitzungsb. Preuss. A. Wiss., phil.-hist. Kl.* 31: 734–69.
Herzog, R. 1941. 'ap. K. Gerth', *Bursians Jahresb.* 272: 99.

Hess, L. and Corien, B. 2020. 'Narrator language and character language in Thucydides: A quantitative study of narrative perspective', *Digital Scholarship in the Humanities* 35.3: 557–86.

Heubeck, A., Russo, J. and West S. R. 1988–92. *A Commentary on the Odyssey*. Oxford.

Hidber, T. 1996. *Das klassizistische Manifest des Dionys von Halikarnass. Die praefatio zu De oratoribus veteribus*. Stuttgart and Leipzig.

Highet, G. 1949. *The Classical Tradition*. Oxford.

Hitzl, K. and Kropp, A. J. M. 2013. 'Das Heiligtum von Olympia im 2. Jh. n.Chr.', *Boreas* 36: 53–89.

Hodkinson, O. 2011. *Authority and Tradition in Philostratus' Heroikos*. Lecce.

Hodkinson, O. 2012. 'Attic idylls: hierarchies of herdsmen and social status in Alciphron and Longus', *JHS* 132: 41–53.

Hodkinson, O. 2013. 'Aelian's Rustic Epistles in the context of his corpus: a reassessment of Aelian's literary programme and qualities', in O. Vox (ed.), *Lettere, mimesi, retorica: Studi sull'epistolografia letteraria greca di età imperiale e tardo antica*. Lecce: 257–310.

Hodot, R. 1990. *Le dialecte éolien d'Asie. La langue des inscriptions VIIe a.C.–IVe p.C.* Paris.

Hoffa, W. 1912. 'Die Löwenjagd des Kaisers Hadrians', *MDAI(R)* 27: 97–100.

Hogarth, D. G., Edgar, C.C. and Gutch, C. 1898–9. 'Excavations at Naucratis', *ABSA* 5: 26–97.

Holford-Strevens, L. 1993. *Aulus Gellius: An Antonine Scholar and His Achievement*. London (1st ed. 1988).

Holzberg, N. 1986. *Der antike Roman: Eine Einführung*. Munich.

Holzberg, N. 1988. 'Ovids "Babyloniaka" (*Met.* 4,55–166)', *WS* 101: 265–77.

Holzberg, N. 1995. *The Ancient Novel: An Introduction*. London.

Hornblower, N. S. and Spawforth, A. (eds.) 2003. *The Oxford Classical Dictionary*, 3rd ed. revised. Oxford.

Horna, K. 1928. *Die Hymnen des Mesomedes*. SAWW 207.1. Wien and Leipzig.

Höschele, R. 2006. *Verrückt nach Frauen. Der Epigrammatiker Rufin*. Classica Monacensia 31. Tübingen.

Höschele, R. 2007. 'Journeys through ancient epigram books', *TAPhA* 137: 333–69.

Höschele, R. 2018. 'Two lovers and a lion: Pankrates' poem on Hadrian's royal hunt', *Philologus* 162: 1–23.

Householder, F. W. 1941. *Literary Quotation and Allusion in Lucian*. New York.

Howgego, C. J., Heuchert, V. and Burnett, A. (eds.) 2005. *Coinage and Identity in the Roman Provinces*. Oxford.

Hubaux, J. and Leroy, M. 1939. *Le mythe du phénix dans les littératures grecque et latine*. Liège and Paris.

Hubaux, J. 1953. 'Le dieu Amor chez Properce et chez Longus', *Acad. Roy. de Belgique (Bull. Cl. des lettres et des sc. mor. et pol.)* 5.39: 263–70.

Hubbard, T. K. 1991. *The Mask of Comedy: Aristophanes and the Intertextual Parabasis*. Ithaca and London.
Hubbard, T. K. 1998. *The Pipes of Pan: Intertextuality and Literary Filiation in the Pastoral Tradition from Theocritus to Milton*. Ann Arbor.
Hubbard, T. K. 2006. 'Virgil, Longus and the Pipes of Pan', in M. Fantuzzi and T. Papanghelis (eds.), *Brill's Companion to Greek and Latin Pastoral*. Leiden and Boston: 499–513.
Humphrey, J. H. (ed.) 1991. *Literacy in the Roman World*. JRA Suppl. 3. Ann Arbor.
Humphreys, S. C. 2007. 'Notes on Attic prosopography', *ZPE* 160: 65–75.
Hunter, R. L. 1983. *A Study of Daphnis & Chloe*. Cambridge.
Hunter, R. L. 1993. 'One party or two? Simonides 22 W^2', *ZPE* 99: 11–14.
Hunter, R. L. 1994. 'History and historicity in the romance of Chariton', in *ANRW* ii 34.2: 1055–86.
Hunter, R. L. 1997. 'Longus and Plato', in M. Picone and B. Zimmermann (eds.), *Der antike Roman und seine mittelalterliche Rezeption*. Basel: 15–28 (repr. in Hunter 2008: 775–89).
Hunter, R. L. (ed.) 1998. *Studies in Heliodorus*. Cambridge Philological Society Supplementary Vol. 21. Cambridge.
Hunter, R. L. 1999. *Theocritus. A Selection. Idylls 1, 3, 4, 6, 7, 10, 11 and 13*. Cambridge.
Hunter, R. L. 2003. 'Aspects of technique and style in the "Periegesis" of Dionysius', in D. Accorinti and P. Chuvin (eds.), *Des géants à Dionysos: mélanges de mythologie et de poésie grecques offerts à Francis Vian*. Alessandria: 343–56 (repr. in Hunter 2008: 700–17).
Hunter, R. L. 2004. 'The Periegesis of Dionysius and the traditions of Hellenistic poetry', *REA* 106: 217–31 (repr. in Hunter 2008: 718–36).
Hunter, R. L. 2008. *On Coming After: Studies in Post-Classical Literature and Its Reception*. Berlin.
Hunter, R. L. 2022. *Greek Epitaphic Poetry. A Selection*. Cambridge.
Hutchinson, G. O. 1988. *Hellenistic Poetry*. Oxford.
Inan, J. and Alföldi-Rosenbaum, E., 1979. *Römische und frühbyzantinische Portratplastik aus der Turkei. Neue Funde*. Mainz.
İplikçioğlu, B. 2014. 'Heraklit von Rhodiapolis, ein gefeierter Arzt der trajanischen Zeit', in J. Fischer (ed.), *Der Beitrag Kleinasiens zur Kultur-und Geistesgeschichte der griechisch-römischen Antike*. Denkschriften der österreichischen Akademie der Wissenschaften, philosophisch-historischen Klasse 469. Wien: 231–56.
Irigoin, H., Waltz, P., Laurens, P. and Soury, G. (eds.) 1974. *Anthologie Grecque* ix. Paris.
Irwin, E. K. 2014. 'Ethnography and empire: Homer and the Hippocratics in Herodotus' Ethiopian logos, 3.17–26', *Histos* 8: 25–75.
Irwin, E. K. 2018. 'The end of the *Histories* and the end of the Atheno-Peloponnesian wars', in Harrison and Irwin (eds.): 279–334.

Irwin, E. K. and Greenwood, E. (eds.) 2007. *Reading Herodotus. A Study of the Logoi in Book 5 of Herodotus' Histories*. Cambridge.
Israelowich, I. 2012. *Society, Medicine and Religion in the Sacred Tales of Aelius Aristides*. Leiden and Boston.
Jacob, C. 1981. 'L'œil et la mémoire: sur la Périégèse de la terre habitée de Denys', in C. Jacob and F. Lestringant (eds.), *Arts et légendes d'espaces*. Paris: 23–97.
Jacob, C. 1990. *La Description de la terre habitée de Denys d'Alexandrie, ou, la leçon de géographie*. Paris.
Jacobs, F. 1813–17. *Anthologia Graeca ad fidem codicis olim Palatini nunc Parisini ex apographo Gothano edita*. Leipzig.
Jacoby, F. 1913. 'Herodot', in Pauly-Wissowa-Kroll, *RE* Suppl. 2: 205–520.
Jamot, P. 1895. 'Fouilles de Thespies', *BCH* 19: 311–85.
Janko, R. 1987. *Aristotle Poetics, with the Tractatus Coislinianus, Reconstruction of Poetics II, and the Fragments of the On Poets, Translated with Notes*. Indianapolis and Cambridge.
Jannasch. A. 1949. *Kunst der Gegenwart. Renée Sintenis. Achtundvierzig Bilder*. Potsdam.
Jansen, K. 2008. *Herodes Atticus und seine Trophimoi*. 2 vols. Münster.
Jensson, G. 2002. 'The *Satyrica* of Petronius as Roman palimpsest', *AN* 2: 86–122.
Jensson, G. 2004. *The Recollections of Petronius: The Satyrica of Petronius as Milesian Fiction*. ANS 2. Groningen.
Jocelyn, H. D. 1967. *The Tragedies of Ennius: The Fragments*. Cambridge.
Jolowicz, D. 2015. *Latin Poetry and the Idea of Rome in the Greek Novel*. DPhil thesis, University of Oxford.
Jolowicz, D. 2021. *Latin Poetry in the Ancient Greek Novels*. Oxford.
Jones, A. H. M. 1952. 'The economic basis of Athenian democracy', *Past and Present* 1: 13–31 (repr. in Jones 1957: 3–21).
Jones, A. H. M. 1957. *Athenian Democracy*. Oxford.
Jones, C. P. 1968. 'A leading family of Roman Thespiae', *HSPh* 74: 223–55.
Jones, C. P. 1974. 'The reliability of Philostratus', in G. W. Bowersock (ed.), *Approaches to the Second Sophistic*. University Park, PA: 11–16.
Jones, C. P. 1980. 'Apuleius' *Metamorphoses* and Lollianos' *Phoinikika*', *Phoenix* 34: 243–54.
Jones, C. P. 1992a. 'La personnalité de Chariton', in Baslez, Hoffmann and Trédé (eds.): 161–7.
Jones, C. P. 1992b. 'Hellenistic history in Chariton of Aphrodisias', *Chiron* 22: 91–102.
Jones, C. P. 1993. 'Greek drama in the Roman Empire', in Scodel (ed.): 9–52.
Jones, C. P. 1996. 'The Panhellenion', *Chiron* 26: 29–56.
Jones, C. P. 1997. Review of J. M. Mossman, *Plutarch and His Intellectual World*, London 1997, *EMC* 1997: 527–30.
Jones, C. P. 1998. 'The pancratiasts Helix and Alexander on an Ostian mosaic', *JRA* 11: 293–8.
Jones, C. P. 1999. *Kinship Diplomacy in the Ancient World*. Cambridge, MA.

Jones, C. P. 2001a. 'Pausanias and his guides', in Alcock, Cherry and Elsner (eds.): 33–9.

Jones, C. P. 2001b. 'Time and place in Philostratus' *Heroicus*', *JHS* 121: 141–9.

Jones, C. P. 2004. '*Epigraphica VIII–IX*', *ZPE* 146: 93–8.

Jones, C. P. 2011. 'Julius Nicanor again', *ZPE* 178: 79–83.

Jones, C. P. and Smith, R. R. R. 1994. 'Two inscribed monuments of Aphrodisias', *Archaeologischer Anzeiger* 3: 455–72.

Jong, I. de, 2012. 'The Helen logos and Herodotus' fingerprint', in Baragwanath and de Bakker (eds.): 127–42.

Jope, J. 2011. 'The authenticity of the Lucianic *Erotes*', *Helios* 38: 103–20.

Kahane, A. and Laird A. (eds.) 2002. *A Companion to the Prologue to Apuleius' Metamorphoses*. Oxford.

Kaimio, M. 1996. 'How to enjoy a Greek novel: Chariton guiding his audience', *Arctos* 30: 49–73.

Kalinka, E. and Schönberger, O. 1968. *Philostratos: Die Bilder*. München.

Kalkmann, A. 1886. *Pausanias der Perieget*. Berlin.

Käppel, L. 1992. *Paian. Studien zur Geschichte einer Gattung*. Berlin.

Kannicht, R. 1969. *Euripides: Helena*. 2 vols. Heidelberg.

Kapetanopoulos, E. A. 1994. 'The Sarapion monument at Athens', *Prometheus* 20: 234–42.

Karageorghis, V. 1981. *Ancient Cyprus: 7,000 Years of Art and Archaeology*. Baton Rouge.

Karydis, D. N. and Kiel, M. 2000. *Μυτιλήνης Αστυγραφία και Λέσβου Χωρογραφία*. Athens.

Kazanskaya, M. 2019. 'Indirect tradition on Sappho's *kertomia*', in Currie and Rutherford (eds.): 257–76.

Keil, J. 1930. 'Vorläufiger Bericht über die Ausgrabungen in Ephesos', *JÖAI* 26 *Beiblatt*: 57–8.

Keil, J. 1953. 'Vertreter der zweiten Sophistik in Ephesos', *JÖAI* 40: 5–26.

Kennedy, D. F. 1987. '"Arcades ambo": Virgil, Gallus and Arcadia', *Hermathena* 143: 47–59.

Kettelhake, S. 2010. *Renée Sintenis. Berlin, Boheme und Ringelnatz*. Berlin.

Keydell, R. 1941. 'Die griechische Dichtung der Kaiserzeit', *Bursians Jahresbericht* 272. Leipzig.

Keydell, R. 1982. *Kleine Schriften*. Leipzig.

Kiel, H. 1956. *Renée Sintenis*. Berlin.

Kienast, D. 1995. 'Zu den Homonoia-Vereinbarungen in der römischen Kaiserzeit', *ZPE* 109: 267–82.

Killeen, J. F. 1971. 'The comic costume controversy', *CQ* 21: 51–4.

Kim, L. 2010. *Homer between History and Fiction in Imperial Greek Literature*. Cambridge.

Kim, L. 2017. 'The trouble with Calasiris: duplicity and autobiographical narrative in Heliodorus and Galen', *Mnemosyne* 72: 229–49.

Kindstrand, J. J. 1973. *Homer in der Zweiten Sophistik*. Uppsala.
Kindt, J. 2012. *Rethinking Greek Religion*. Cambridge.
Kirbihler, F. 2009. 'Territoire civique et population d'Éphèse (ve siècle av. J.-C.–iiie siècle apr. J.-C.)', in H. Bru, F. Kirbihler and S. Lebreton (eds.), *L'Asie Mineure dans l'Antiquité: échanges, populations et territoires: regards actuels sur une péninsule. Actes du colloque de Tours, 21–22 octobre 2005*. Rennes: 301–33.
Kirbihler, F. 2016. *Des Grecs et des Italiens à Ephèse: histoire d'une intégration croisée: 133 a.C.–48 p.C.* Bordeaux.
Kleiner, D. E. E. 1983. *The Monument of Philopappos in Athens*. Rome.
Kleve, K. 1983. 'Anti-Dover or Socrates in the *Clouds*', *SO* 58: 23–37.
Klotz, A. 1909. 'Zu Dionysius Periegetes', *RhM* 64: 476–7.
Klotz, F. and Oikonomopoulou, K. 2011. *The Philosopher's Banquet: Plutarch's Table Talk in the Intellectual Culture of the Roman Empire*. Oxford.
Kneebone, E. 2008. 'ΤΟΣΣ' ΕΔΑΗΝ: The Poetics of Knowledge in Oppian's *Halieutica*', *Ramus* 37: 32–59.
Kneebone, E. 2017. 'The limits of enquiry in imperial Greek didactic poetry', in J. König and G. Woolf (eds.), *Authority and Expertise in Ancient Scientific Culture*, Cambridge: 203–30.
Kneebone, E. 2020. *Oppian's Halieutica: Charting a Didactic Epic*. Cambridge.
Knoepfler, D. 1992. 'Sept années de recherches sur l'épigraphie de la Béotie (1985–1991)', *Chiron* 22: 411–503.
Knoepfler, D. 1996. 'La réorganisation du concours des Mouseia à l'époque hellénistique: esquisse d'une solution nouvelle', in A. Hurst and A. Schachter, *La montagne des Muses*. Genève: 141–67.
Knox, P. E. 1989. 'Pyramus and Thisbe in Cyprus', *HSPh* 92: 315–28.
Koechly, H. 1858. *Manethonis Apotelesmaticorum qui feruntur libri VI*. Leipzig.
Körte, A. 1931. 'Der Demeter-Hymnos des Philikos', *Hermes* 66: 442–54.
Kondis, J. K. 1978. *Λέσβος καὶ ἡ Μικρασιατική της Περιοχή*. Αθήνα.
Kondoleon, C. 1994. *Domestic and Divine: Roman Mosaics in the House of Dionysos*. Ithaca.
Konstan, D. 1994. *Sexual Symmetry: Love in the Ancient Novel and Related Genres*. Princeton.
Konstan, D. 2008. 'Antiphilus' erotic epigrams: two notes', *Mnemosyne* 61: 290–7.
Konstan, D. 2009. 'Le courage dans le roman grec: de Chariton à Xénophon d'Éphèse, avec une référence a Philon d'Alexandrie', in B. Pouderon and C. Bost-Pouderon (eds.), *Passions, vertus et vices dans l'ancien roman*. Lyon: 117–26.
Korres, M. 2002. 'Modell des Dionysos-Theaters', in *Die griechische Klassik: Idee oder Wirklichkeit*. Exhibition March 1st–June 2nd, 2002, Berlin. Mainz: 540–1.
Kossaifi, C. 2012. 'The legend of Phatta in Longus' Daphnis and Chloe', *AJPh* 133: 573–600.
Kost, K. 1971. *Musaios, Hero und Leander*. Bonn.

Kowalzig, B. 2013. 'Dancing dolphins on the wine-dark sea', in Kowalzig and Wilson (eds.): 31–58.

Kowalzig, B. and P. Wilson (eds.). 2013. *Dithyramb in Context*. Oxford.

Kowerski, L. M. 2005. *Simonides on the Persian Wars. A Study of the Elegiac Verses of the 'New Simonides'*. New York and London.

Krausse, D. 1996. *Hochdorf. 3: Das Trink- und Speiseservice aus dem späthallstattzeitlichen Fürstengrab von Eberdingen-Hochdorf (Kr. Ludwigsburg)*. Stuttgart.

Kruchió, B. 2017. 'What Charicles knew: fragmentary narration and ambiguity in Heliodorus' *Aethiopica*', *AN* 14: 175–94.

Kuchenmüller, G. 1928. *Philitae Coi reliquiae*. Berlin.

Kühn, J.-H. 1958. 'Die Thalysien Theokrits', *Hermes* 86: 40–79.

Kuttner, A. L. 1999. 'Culture and history at Pompey's museum', *TAPhA* 129: 343–73.

Kwapisz, J. 2013. *The Greek Figure Poems*. Hellenistica Groningana 19. Leuven.

Lada Richards, I. 2007. *Silent Eloquence: Lucian and Pantomime Dancing*. London.

Lane Fox, R. L. 1986. *Pagans and Christians*. London.

Laplace, M. 2007. *Le roman d'Achille Tatios: 'discours panégyrique' et imaginaire romanesque*. Bern and Oxford.

Larson, J. 2001. *Greek Nymphs: Myth, Cult, Lore*. Oxford.

Lasserre, F. 1959. 'Aux origines de l'Anthologie: II. Les Thalysies de Théocrite', *RhM* 102: 307–30.

Lateiner, D. 1986. 'The empirical element in the methods of early Greek medical writers and Herodotus: a shared epistemological response', *Antichthon* 20: 1–20.

Lateiner, D. 1989. *The Historical Method of Herodotus*. Toronto and London.

Laurens, P. 1965. 'Martial et l'épigramme grecque du 1er siècle après J.-C.', *REL* 43: 315–41.

Latte, K. 1954. 'Der Demeterhymnos des Philikos', *MH* 11: 1–19 (repr. in his *Kleine Schriften zu Religion, Recht, Literatur und Sprache der Griechen und Röme*, eds. O. Gigon, W. Buchwald and W. Kunkel. München 1968: 539–58).

Lambert, R. 1984. *Beloved and God*. London.

Lawall, G. 1967. *Theocritus' Coan Pastorals*. Cambridge, MA.

Lebek, W. 1973. 'Ein Hymnus auf Antinoos (Mitford, the Inscriptions of Kourion No. 104)', *ZPE* 12: 101–37.

Lefkowitz, M. R. and Fant, M. B. 1992. *Women's Life in Greece and Rome: A Source Book in Translation* (1st ed. 1982). London.

Lefteratou, A. 2018. *Mythological Narratives: The Bold and Faithful Heroines of the Greek Novel*. Berlin.

Legras, B. 1999. *Néotês: recherches sur les jeunes Grecs dans l'Egypte ptolémaïque et romaine*. Genève.

Le Guen, B. 2001. *Les associations de technites dionysiaques à l'époque hellénistique*. 2 vols. Nancy.

Lehmann, W. 1910. *De Achillis Tatii aetate. Accedit corollarium De Achillis Tatii studiis Lucianeis*. Dissertation, Wroclaw.
Lehnus, L. 1975. 'Note Stesicoree: I poemetti "minori"', *SCO* 24: 191–6.
Lenormant, C. 1847. *François Gérard, peintre d'histoire: essai de biographie et de critique*, 2nd ed. Paris.
Leo, F. 1903. 'Virgils erste und neunte Ecloge', *Hermes* 38: 1–18 (repr. in *Ausgewählte kleine Schriften*, 2 vols. Roma 1960).
Lesky, A. 1966. *A History of Greek Literature* (= *Geschichte der Griechischen Literatur*, transl. by J. Willis and C. de Heer). London.
Leue, C. 1884. 'Zeit und Heimat des Periegeten Dionysios', *Philologus* 42: 175–8.
Leue, C. 1925. 'Noch einmal die Akrostichen in der Periegese des Dionysios', *Hermes* 60: 367–80.
LeVen, P. 2014. *The Many-Headed Muse: Tradition and Innovation in Late Classical Greek Poetry*. Cambridge.
Levi, D. 1944. 'The novel of Ninus and Semiramis', *PAPhS* 87: 420–8.
Levi, D. 1947. *Antioch Mosaic Pavements*. 2 vols. Princeton.
Levin, D. N. 1977. 'To whom did the ancient novelists address themselves?', *Rivista di studi classici* 25: 18–29.
Lewis, D. M. 1955. 'Notes on Attic Inscriptions (II). XXIII Who was Lysistrata?', *ABSA* 50: 1–12.
Lidov, J. B. 2002. 'Sappho, Herodotus, and the *hetaira*', *CPh* 97: 203–37.
Lightfoot, C. S. 1988. 'Facts and fiction – the third siege of Nisibis (AD 350)', *Historia* 37: 107–25.
Lightfoot, J. L. 1999. *Parthenius of Nicaea*. Oxford.
Lightfoot, J. L. 2003. *Lucian. On the Syrian Goddess*. Oxford.
Lightfoot, J. L. 2014. *Dionysius Periegetes, Description of the Known World. With Introduction, Text, Translation, and Commentary*. Oxford.
Lissarrague, F. 1990. *The Aesthetics of the Greek Banquet*. Princeton.
Livrea, E. 1973. *Dionysii Bassarika*. Rome.
Lloyd, A. B. 1988. *Herodotus: Book II. Commentary 99–182*. Leiden and Boston.
Lloyd-Jones, P. H. J. and Parsons, P. J. 1983. *Supplementum Hellenisticum*. Berlin.
Lohse, G. 1966, 'Die Kunstauffassung im VII Idyll Theokrits und das Programm des Kallimachos', *Hermes* 94: 413–25.
López Martínez, M. P. 2019. 'The *Ninus* romance: new textual and contextual studies', *Archiv für Papyrusforschung und verwandte Gebiete* 65.1: 20–44.
Lopilato, R. 1998. *The Apotelesmatika of Manetho*. PhD thesis, Brown University.
L'Orange, H.-P. and van Gerkan, A. 1939. *Der spätantike Bildschmuck des Konstantinbogens*. Studien zur Spätantiken Kunstgeschichte 10. Berlin.
Lowe, J. C. B. 1962. 'The manuscript evidence for changes of speaker in Aristophanes', *BICS* 9: 27–42.
Lucas, D. W. 1968. *Aristotle Poetics*. Oxford.
Luginbill, R. D. 2001–2. 'A delightful possession: Longus' Prologue and Thucydides', *CJ* 97: 233–47.

Lulli, L. 2011. *Narrare in distichi. L'elegia greca arcaica e classica di argomento storico-mitico*. Seminari romani di cultura greca, Quaderni 13. Rome.

Luz, C. 2010. *Technopaignia. Formspiele in der griechischen Dichtung*. Leiden and Boston.

Ma, J. 2007. 'The worlds of Nestor the poet', in S. C. R. Swain, S. J. Harrison and J. Elsner (eds.), *Severan Culture*. Cambridge: 83–133.

Maass, E. 1898. *Commentariorum in Aratum reliquiae*. Berlin.

MacDowell, D. M. 1971. *Aristophanes Wasps. Edited with an Introduction and Commentary*. Oxford.

Maciver, C. A. 2012. *Quintus Smyrnaeus' Posthomerica: Engaging Homer in Late Antiquity*. Mnemosyne Suppl. 343. Leiden.

Maclean, J. K. B. and Aitken, E. B. 2001. *Flavius Philostratus: Heroikos*. Atlanta.

Macleod, M. D. 1967. *Lucian, with an English translation. Vol. viii*. London and Cambridge, MA.

Macleod, M. D. 1987. *Luciani Opera. Vol. iv*. Oxford.

MacMullen, R. 1982. 'Roman attitudes to Greek love', *Historia* 31: 484–502.

MacQueen, B. D. 1985. 'Longus and the myth of Chloe', *ICS* 10: 119–34.

MacQueen, B. D. 1990. *Myth, Rhetoric and Fiction: a Reading of Longus's Daphnis and Chloe*. Lincoln, NE and London.

Maehler, H. 1976. 'Der Metiochos-Parthenope-Roman', *ZPE* 23: 1–20.

Magie, D. 1950. *Roman Rule in Asia Minor*. 2 vols. Princeton.

Magnelli, E. 2007a. 'Meter and diction: from refinement to mannerism', in Bing and Bruss (eds.): 165–83.

Magnelli, E. 2007b. 'Notes on four Greek verse inscriptions', *ZPE* 160: 37–40.

Mai, A. 1823. *M. Cornelii Frontonis et M. Avrelii imperatoris epistvlae. L. Veri et Antonini Pii et Appiani epistvlarvm reliqviae. Fragmenta Frontonis et scripta grammatica. Editio prima romana plvs centvm epistvlis avcta ex codice rescripto Bibliothecae pontificiae Vaticanae cvrante Angelo Maio bibliothecae eivsdem praefecto*. Roma.

Manieri, A. (ed.) 2009. *Agoni poetico musicali nella Grecia antica. 1. Beozia*. Testi e commenti 25; Certamina musica graeca 1. Pisa/Roma.

Männlein-Robert, I. 2004. 'Griechische Kunst und römischer Stil: Zum Eurotas-Epigramm des Philipp von Thessalonike (AP 9.709 = GP I 63)', *WJA* N.F. 28a: 35–48.

Mantero, T. 1966. *Ricerche sull' Heroikos di Filostrato*. Genova.

Marcos Macedo, J. 2010. *A palavra ofertada*. Campinas.

Marcovich, M. 1975. 'Philodamus' Delphic hymn to Dionysus', *ZPE* 17: 167–8.

Maritz, J. 1991. 'The role of music in Daphnis and Chloe', *GCN* 4: 57–67.

Maróth, M. 1979. 'Le siège de Nisibe en 350 ap. J.C. d'après les sources syriennes', *AAntHung* 27: 239–43.

Martin, F. 1982. *La documentación griega de la cancillería del emperador Adriano*. Pamplona.

Martin, L. H. 1994. 'The anti-individualistic ideology of Hellenistic culture', *Numen* 41: 117–40.

Martin, R. P. 1989. *The Language of Heroes*. Ithaca and London.
Mason, H. J. 1978. 'Fabula Graecanica: Apuleius and his Greek sources', in B. L. Hijmans and R. T. van der Paardt (eds.), *Aspects of the Golden Ass*. Groningen: 1–15 (repr. in S. J. Harrison (ed.), *Oxford Readings in the Roman Novel*. Oxford 1999: 217–36).
Mason, H. J. 1979. 'Longus and the topography of Lesbos', *TAPhA* 109: 149–63.
Mason, H. J. 1995. 'Romance in a limestone landscape', *CPh* 90: 263–6.
Mason, H. J. 2004. 'Sappho's apples', in M. Zimmerman and R. van der Paardt (eds.), *Metamorphic Reflections: Essays Presented to Ben Hijmans at His Seventy-Fifth Birthday*. Leuven and Dudley, MA: 243–53.
Mason, H. J. 2018. 'Hunters' dedications: Longus and Lesbos', in Chew, Morgan and Trzaskoma (eds.): 137–47.
Massimilla, G. 2016. 'Nel laboratorio del parafraste: i richiami alla poesia ellenistica nella Parafrasi del Vangelo di San Giovanni di Nonno di Panopoli', *Prometheus* 42: 249–79.
Matthews, V. J. (ed.) 1996. *Antimachus of Colophon: Text and Commentary*. Mnemosyne Suppl. 155. Leiden and Boston.
Maull, I. 1955. 'Hadrians Jagddenkmal', *JÖAI* 42: 53–67.
Maxwell-Stuart, P. G. 1972. 'Strato and the *Musa puerilis*', *Hermes* 100: 215–40.
May, R. 2010. 'An Ass from Oxyrhynchus: *P.Oxy*. LXX.4762, Loukios of Patrae and the Milesian Tales', *AN* 8: 59–84.
Mayer, R. G. forthcoming. 'Crinagoras of Mytilene and Octavia', in B. Acosta-Hughes, J. Arthur-Montagne and P. Vasunia (eds.) *Hellenistic Literature and Culture: Studies in Honor of Susan A. Stephens*. London.
Mazal, O. 1971. *Aristaeneti Epistularum Libri II*. Stuttgart.
Mayor, H. B. 1939. 'The strategi at Athens in the fifth century. When did they enter on office?', *JHS* 59: 45–64.
Melfi, M. 2010. 'Ritual spaces and performances in the Asklepieia of Roman Greece', *ABSA* 105: 317–38.
Merkelbach, R. 1962. *Roman und Mysterium in der Antike*. München.
Merkelbach, R. 1987. *Nikaia in der römischen Kaiserzeit*. Opladen.
Merkelbach, R. 1988. *Die Hirten des Dionysos: die Dionysos-Mysterien der römischen Kaiserzeit und der bukolische Roman des Longus*. Stuttgart.
Merkelbach, R. and Stauber, J. (eds.) 1998–2004. *Steinepigramme aus dem griechischen Osten*. 5 vols. Stuttgart. 2001 vol. ii. Stuttgart.
Mesk, J. 1927. 'Zu den Prosa und Vershymnen des Aelius Aristides', in A. Gemelli (ed.) *Raccolta di scritti in onore di F. Ramorino*. Milan: 660–72.
Mignogna, E. 1996a. 'Narrativa greca e mimo: il romanzo di Achille Tazio', *SIFC iii* 14: 232–42.
Mignogna, E. 1996b. 'Il mimo Leucippe: un' ipotesi su PBerol inv. 13927 [Pack2 2437]', *RCCM* 38: 161–6.
Miguelez-Cavero, L. 2013. *Triphiodorus, The Sack of Troy: A General Study and a Commentary*. Berlin and New York.

Miguélez-Cavero, L. 2016. 'Nonnus and the novel', in D. Accorinti (ed.), *Brill's Companion to Nonnus of Panopolis*. Leiden and Boston: 549–73.
Miles, G. 2017. *Philostratus: Interpreters and Interpretation*. London.
Millar, F. G. B. 1981. 'The world of *The Golden Ass*', *JRS* 71: 63–75.
Millis, B. W. and Olson, S. D. 2012. *Inscriptional Records for the Dramatic Festivals in Athens: IG II² 2318–2325 and Related Texts*. Leiden.
Milne, J. G. 1933. *University of Oxford. Ashmolean Museum. Catalogue of Alexandrian Coins*. Oxford and London.
Mitchell, S. 1990. 'Festivals, games, and civic life in Roman Asia Minor', a review of Wörrle 1998 in *JRS* 80: 183–93.
Mitchell, S. 1993. *Anatolia. Men and Gods in Asia Minor.* 2 vols. Oxford.
Mitford, T. B. 1971. *The Inscriptions of Kourion*. Memoirs of the American Philosophical Society 83. Philadelphia.
Möller, A. 2000. *Naukratis: Trade in Archaic Greece*. Oxford.
Molinié, G. 1979. *Chariton. Le roman de Chaireas et Callirhoé*. Paris.
Molyneux, J. H. 1992. *Simonides: A Historical Study*. Wauconda.
Montiglio, S. 2000. *Silence in the Land of Logos*. Princeton.
Montiglio, S. 2012. 'The (cultural) harmony of nature: music, love, and order in *Daphnis and Chloe*', *TAPhA* 142: 133–56.
Montiglio, S. 2020a. 'The silences of Chariclea in Heliodorus' Aethiopica: from cunning to shame', in Papadodima (ed.): 73–83.
Montiglio, S. 2020b. *Musaeus' Hero and Leander. Introduction, Greek Text, Translation and Commentary*. London.
Morales, H. 2004. *Vision and Narrative in Achilles Tatius' Leucippe and Clitophon*. Cambridge.
Moretti, J.-C. 1999–2000. 'The theatre of the sanctuary of Dionysos Eleuthereus in late 5th century Athens', *ICS* 24–5: 377–98.
Moretti, L. 1978. 'Frammento di inno tardo-stoico sulla creazione', in L. Gasperini (ed.), *Scritti storico-epigrafici in memoria di M. Zambelli*. Roma: 251–6.
Moretti, L. 1981. 'Iscrizioni di Tespie della prima età imperiale', *Athenaeum* 59: 71–7.
Morgan, J. R. 1978. *A Commentary on the Ninth and Tenth Books of the Aithiopica of Heliodoros*. DPhil thesis, University of Oxford.
Morgan, J. R. 1982. 'History, romance and realism in Heliodorus', *ClAnt* 1: 221–65.
Morgan, J. R. 1985. 'Lucian's *True Histories* and the *Wonders beyond Thule* of Antonios Diogenes', *CQ* 35: 475–90.
Morgan, J. R. 1989a. 'Heliodorus', in Reardon (ed.): 349–588.
Morgan, J. R. 1989b. 'The story of Knemon in Heliodorus' *Aithiopika*', *JHS* 109: 99–113 (repr. in Swain 1999: 259–85).
Morgan, J. R. 1993. 'Make-believe and make believe: the fictionality of the Greek novels', in C. Gill and T. P. Wiseman (eds.), *Lies and Fiction in the Ancient World*. Exeter: 175–229.

Morgan, J. R. 1994. 'Daphnis and Chloe: love's own sweet story', in Morgan and Stoneman (eds.): 64–79.

Morgan, J. R. 1996a. 'Heliodorus', in Schmeling (ed.): 417–456.

Morgan, J. R. 1996b. Review of O'Sullivan 1995, *JHS* 116: 199–200.

Morgan, J. R. 2004. *Longus Daphnis and Chloe, with an Introduction, Translation and Notes*. Oxford.

Morgan, J. R. 2021. 'Longus', in M. de Bakker and I. de Jong (eds.), *Studies in Ancient Greek Narrative, Volume 5*. Mnemosyne Suppl. 448. Leiden and Boston: 692–714.

Morgan, J. R. and Harrison, S. J. 2008. 'Intertextuality', in T. Whitmarsh (ed.), *The Cambridge Companion to the Greek and Roman Novel*. Cambridge: 218–36.

Morgan, J. R. and Stoneman, R. (eds.) 1994. *Greek Fiction: The Greek Novel in Context*. London.

Morgan, T. 1998. *Literate Education in the Hellenistic and Roman Worlds*. Cambridge.

Mori, A. 2008. *The Politics of Apollonius Rhodius' Argonautica*. Cambridge and New York.

Morrison, J. S. 1941. 'The place of Protagoras in Athenian public life', *CQ* 25: 1–16.

Morrison, J. S. 1958. 'The origins of Plato's philosopher-statesman', *CQ* 8: 198–218.

Mossman, J. M. 1996. 'Chains of imagery in *Prometheus Bound*', *CQ* 46: 58–67.

Mossman, J. M. 2007. 'Heracles, Prometheus, and the play of genres in [Lucian]'s *Amores*', in Swain, Elsner and Harrison (eds.): 146–59.

Most, G. W. 1989. 'The stranger's stratagem: self-disclosure and self-sufficiency in Greek culture', *JHS* 109: 114–33.

Moulin, M. 1983. 'Daphnis et Chloé dans l'œuvre de François Gérard (1770–1837)', *Revue du Louvre et des Musées de France* 2: 100–9.

Müller, C. 1861. *Geographi Graeci Minores*. 2 vols. Paris.

Müller, C. W. 1981. 'Der griechische Roman', in E. Vogt (ed.), *Neues Handbuch der Literaturwissenschaft ii, Griechische Literatur*. Wiesbaden: 377–412.

Münscher, K. 1907. *Die Philostrate*. Philologus Suppl. 10. Leipzig: 469–558.

Münscher, K. 1920. *Xenophon in der griechisch-römischen Literatur*. Philologus Suppl. 13.2. Leipzig.

Munson, R. V. 2001. *Telling Wonders: Ethnographic and Political Discourse in the Work of Herodotus*. Ann Arbor.

Murphy, C. T. 1938. 'Aristophanes and the art of rhetoric', *HSPh* 1938: 69–113.

Murray, O. 1983a. 'The Greek *symposion* in history', in E. Gabba (ed.), *Tria Corda: scritti in onore di Arnaldo Momigilano*. Como: 257–72 (repr. in Murray 2018).

Murray, O. 1983b. 'The symposion as social organisation', in R. Hägg (ed.), *The Greek Renaissance of the Eighth Century BC: Tradition and Innovation*. Stockholm: 195–9 (repr. in Murray 2018).

Murray, O. 1985. 'Symposium and genre in the poetry of Horace', *JRS* 75: 39–50 (repr. in Murray 2018).

Murray, O. (ed.) 1990, *Sympotica. A Symposium on the Symposion*. Oxford.

Murray, O. 1993. *Early Greece*. London (1st ed. Hassocks 1980).

Murray, O. and Tecuşan, M. (eds.) 1995. *In Vino Veritas*. London.

Murray, O. 1996. 'Hellenistic royal symposia', in P. Bilde, T. Engberg-Pedersen, L. Hannestad and J. Zahn (eds.), *Aspects of Hellenistic Kingship*. Aarhus: 15–27 (repr. in Murray 2018).

Murray, O. 2018. *The Symposion: Drinking Greek Style*. Oxford.

Nagy, G. 2015. 'Herodotus and a courtesan from Naucratis', *Classical Inquiries* 2015.07.01: http://classical-inquiries.chs.harvard.edu/herodotus-and-a-courtesan-from-naucratis/.

Nagy, G. 2018. 'Herodotus on queens and courtesans of Egypt', in Bowie (ed.): 109–22.

Nagy, G. 2019. 'Homo ludens at play with the songs of Sappho: experiments in comparative reception theory, Part Two', *Classical Inquiries* 2019.01.16: https://classical-inquiries.chs.harvard.edu/homo-ludens-at-play-with-the-songs-of-sappho-experiments-in-comparative-reception-theory-part-two/.

Nannini, S. 1982. 'Alcm. fr. 50b P. ῏ΙΝΩ ΣΑΛΑΣΣΟΜΈΔΟΙΣ' ῞ΑΝ ἈΠΟ ΜΑΣΔΩΝ', *Sileno* 7: 49–51.

Nauck, A. 1889. 'Zu Dionysios Periegetes', *Hermes* 24: 325.

Nauta, R. R. 2002. *Poetry for Patrons. Literary Communication in the Age of Domitian*. Mnemosyne Suppl. 206. Leiden.

Neppi Modona, A. 1933. *L'isola di Coo nell'Antichità classica: delineazione storica in base alle fonti letterarie e ai documenti archeologici ed epigrafici*. Mem. ist. storico-arch. di Rodi 1. Rodi.

Nesselrath, H.-G. 1996. 'Herodot und der griechische Mythos', *Poetica* 28: 275–96.

Neugebauer, O. and van Hosen, H. B. 1959. *Greek Horoscopes*. Mem. Amer. Philos. Soc. 48. Philadelphia.

Neutsch, B. 1938. 'Bildbeschreibungen des Antiphilos von Byzans', *MDAI(R)* 53: 175–88.

Newby, Z. 2003. 'Art and identity in Asia Minor' in S. Scott and J. Webster (eds.), *Roman Imperialism and Provincial Art*. Cambridge: 192–213.

Newiger, H.-J. 1957. *Metapher und Allegorie: Studien zu Aristophanes*. München.

Newiger, H.-J. 1980. 'War and peace in the comedies of Aristophanes', *YClS* 26: 219–37 (repr. in E. Segal (ed.), *Oxford Readings in Aristophanes*. Oxford 1997: 143–61).

Nikolaou, K. 1963. 'The mosaics from Kato Paphos, the House of Dionysos', *RDAC* 56–72.

Nikolaou, K. 1967. 'Excavations at Nea Paphos, the House of Dionysos: outline of the campaigns 1964–1965', *RDAC* 100–25.

Ní Mheallaigh, K. 2005. *Lucian's Self-Conscious Fiction. Theory in Practice*. PhD thesis, Trinity College Dublin.

Ní Mheallaigh, K. 2008. 'Pseudo-documentarism and the limits of ancient fiction', *AJPh* 129: 403–31.

Ní Mheallaigh, K. 2014. *Reading Fiction with Lucian: Fakes, Freaks and Hyperreality*. Cambridge.

Nisbet, G. 2003. *Greek Epigram in the Roman Empire. Martial's Forgotten Rivals*. Oxford.

Nisbet, R. G. M. 1978. '*Felicitas* at Surrentum (Statius, *Silvae* II. 2)', *JRS* 68: 1–11.

Nisbet, R. G. M. and Hubbard, M. 1970. *Horace Odes Book 1*. Oxford.

Nisbet, R. G. M. and Rudd, N. 2004. *A Commentary on Horace, Odes, Book III*. Oxford.

Nobili, C. 2009. 'Tra epos ed elegia: il nuovo Archiloco', *Maia* 61: 229–49.

Nobili, C. 2020. 'The sanctuary of Delphi in Heliodorus' *Aethiopica*: between material culture and intertextuality', *AN* 16: 15–36.

Norden, E. 1898. *Die antike Kunstprosa*. 2 vols. Stuttgart.

Norden, E. 1913. *Agnostos Theos: Untersuchungen zur Formengeschichte religiöser Rede*. Leipzig.

Norsa, M. 1927. 'Frammenti di un inno di Philiskos', *SIFC* 5: 87–92.

North, H. 1952. 'The use of poetry in the training of the ancient orator', *Traditio* 8: 1–33.

Nussbaum, M. 1982. 'Aristophanes and Socrates on learning practical wisdom', *YClS* 26: 43–97.

Obbink, D. 2005. '4708. Archilochus, elegies (more of VI 854 and XXX 2507)', *The Oxyrhynchus Papyri. Vol. 69*. London: 19–42.

Obbink, D. 2006a. 'A new Archilochus poem', *ZPE* 156, 1–9.

Obbink, D. 2006b. '4762: Narrative Romance', *The Oxyrhynchus Papyri. Vol. 70*. London: 22–9.

Obbink, D. 2014. 'Two new poems by Sappho', *ZPE* 189, 32–49.

Obbink, D. and Trnka-Amrhein, Y. 2009. '4948. Achilles Tatius, Leucippe and Clitophon ii 37.8–10, 38.4', *The Oxyrhynchus Papyri. Vol. 73*. London: 119–22.

Oesterheld, C. 2008. *Göttliche Botschaften für zweifelnde Menschen: Pragmatik und Orientierungsleistung der Apollon-Orakel von Klaros und Didyma in hellenistisch-römischer Zeit*. Göttingen.

Ogden, D. 2004. 'The Apprentice's Sorcerer: Pancrates and his powers in context (Lucian, *Philopseudes* 33–36)', *AClass* 47: 101–26.

Ogden, D. 2007. *In Search of the Sorcerer's Apprentice*. Swansea.

Oikonomopoulou, K. 2007. *The Symposia in the Greek and Roman World of the High Empire: Literary Forms and Intellectual Realities*. DPhil thesis, University of Oxford.

Oliver, J. H. 1936. 'The Sarapion monument and the Paean of Sophocles', *Hesperia* 5: 91–122.

Oliver, J. H. 1949. 'Two Athenian poets', *Hesperia Suppl.* 8: 223–58.

Oliver, J. H. 1967. '*The Sacred Gerusia* and the Emperor's *Consilium*', *Hesperia* 36: 329–35.

Oliver, J. H. 1970. *Marcus Aurelius. Aspects of Civic and Cultural Policy in the East*. Hesperia Suppl. 15. Princeton.

Oliver, J. H. 1989. *Greek Constitutions of Early Roman Emperors from Inscriptions and Papyri*. Philadelphia.

Olson, S. D. 2006. *Athenaeus. The Learned Banqueters. Books iii.106e–v*. Cambridge, MA and London.

Orsini, P. 1968. *Musée, Héro et Léandre*. Paris.

Osborne, R. G. 2001. 'The use of abuse: Semonides 7', *PCPhS* 47: 47–64.

O'Sullivan, J. N. 1995. *Xenophon of Ephesus. His Compositional Technique and the Birth of the Novel*. Berlin and New York.

O'Sullivan, J. N. 2014. 'Xenophon, The Ephesian Tales', in Cueva and Byrne (eds.): 43–61.

Ott, U. 1969. *Die Kunst des Gegensatzes in Theokrits Hirtengedichten*. Spudasmata 22. Hildesheim.

Overduin, F. 2018. 'The didactic aesthetics of Marcellus' *De piscibus* (GDRK 63)', *AJP* 139: 31–57.

Pack, R. A. 1965. *The Greek and Latin Literary Texts from Greco-Roman Egypt*, 2nd ed. Ann Arbor.

Padel, R. S. 1992. *In and Out of the Mind: Greek Images of the Tragic Self*. Princeton.

Paga, J. 2010. 'Deme theaters in Attica and the trittys system', *Hesperia* 79: 351–84.

Page, D. L. 1941. *Greek Literary Papyri*. Cambridge, MA and London.

Page, D. L. 1955. *Sappho and Alcaeus*. Oxford.

Page, D. L. 1976. 'Five Hellenistic epitaphs in mixed metres', *WS* 10: 165–76.

Page, D. L. 1978. *The Epigrams of Rufinus*. Cambridge.

Panayotakis, S., Schmeling, G. and Paschalis, M. (eds.), 2015. *Holy Men and Charlatans in the Ancient Novel*. ANS 19. Groningen.

Pandiri, T. A. 1985. 'Daphnis and Chloe: the art of pastoral play', *Ramus* 14: 116–41.

Papadodima, E. 2020. *Faces of Silence in Ancient Greek Literature*. Berlin and Boston.

Papanikolaou, A. D. 1973. *Chariton-Studien*. Göttingen.

Papastamati-von Moock, C. 2014. 'The theatre of Dionysus Eleuthereus in Athens: new data and observations on its "Lycurgan' phase", in E. Csapo, H. R. Goette, J. R. Green and P. Wilson (eds.), *The Greek Theatre in the Fourth Century BC*. Berlin and Boston: 15–76.

Papastamati-von Moock, C. 2015. 'The wooden theatre of Dionysos Eleuthereus in Athens: old issues, new research', in R. Frederiksen, E. R. Gebhard and A. Sokolicek (eds.), *The Architecture of the Ancient Greek Theatre: Acts of an International Conference at the Danish Institute at Athens 27–30 January 2012*. Aarhus: 39–73.

Papathomopoulos, M. 1976. *Ἀνωνύμου Παράφρασις εἰς τα Διονισίου Ἰξευτικά*. Ioannina.

Papathamopoulos, M. 2003. *Oppianus Apameensis. Cynegetica*. München.

Paraskevaidis, M. 1963. 'Pyrrha', *RE* xxiv: 1403–20.

Parke, H. W. 1985. *The Oracles of Apollo in Asia Minor*. London.

Parke, H. W. and Wormell, D. E. W. 1956. *The Delphic Oracle*. 2 vols. Oxford.
Parsons, P. J. 1971. 'A Greek *Satyricon*?', *BICS* 18: 53–68.
Parsons, P. J. 1974a. 'P.Oxy. 3010. Narrative about Iolaus', *The Oxyrhynchus Papyri. Vol. 42*. London: 34–41.
Parsons, P. J. 1974b. '3012. Romance (Antonius Diogenes?)', *The Oxyrhynchus Papyri. Vol. 42*. London: 43–6.
Parsons, P. J. 1989a. '3836. Achilles Tatius 3.21–3', *The Oxyrhynchus Papyri. Vol. 56*. London: 62–6.
Parsons, P. J. 1989b. '3837. Achilles Tatius 8.6.14–8.7.6', *The Oxyrhynchus Papyri. Vol. 56*. London: 66–9.
Parsons, P. J. 1992. '3965. Simonides, Elegies', *The Oxyrhynchus Papyri. Vol. 59*. London: 4–50.
Parsons, P. J. 2006a. '4760. Antonius Diogenes', *The Oxyrhynchus Papyri. Vol. 70*. London: 9–15.
Parsons, P. J. 2006b. '4761 Novel. (Antonius Diogenes?)', *The Oxyrhynchus Papyri. Vol. 70*. London: 15–22.
Parsons, P. J. 2007. '4811. Novel ("Panionis")', *The Oxyrhynchus Papyri. Vol. 71*. London: 47–53.
Parsons, P. J. 2010. 'Panionis and the culture of culture (P.Oxy. LXXI 4811)', in Bastianini and Casanova (eds.): 43–9.
Parsons, P. J. 2018. '5354. Antonius Diogenes', *The Oxyrhynchus Papyri. Vol. 83*. London: 54–63.
Paschalis, M. 2005. 'The narrator as hunter: Longus, Virgil and Theocritus', in S. J. Harrison, M. Paschalis, and S. Frangoulidis (eds.), *Metaphor and the Ancient Novel*. ANS 4. Groningen: 50–67.
Paschalis, M., Panayotakis, S. and Schmeling, G. (eds.) 2013. *Real and Ideal in the Ancient Novel*. ANS 17. Groningen.
Paton, W. R. and Hicks, E. L. 1891. *The Inscriptions of Cos*. Oxford.
Pattoni, M. P. 2004. 'I Pastoralia di Longo e la contaminazione dei generi. Alcune proposte interpretative', *MD* 53: 83–123.
Pattoni, M. P. 2005. *Longo Sofista: Dafni e Cloe*. Milano.
Paulsen, T. 1992. *Inszenierung des Schicksals: Tragödie und Komödie im Roman des Heliodor*. Bochumer Altertumswissenschaftscolloquium 10. Trier.
Payne, M. 2007. *Theocritus and the Invention of Fiction*. Cambridge.
Pearce, T. E. V. 1987. 'The function of the *locus amoenus* in Theocritus' seventh poem', *RhM* 131: 276–304.
Pecere, O. and Stramaglia, A. 1996. *La letteratura di consumo: atti del convegno internazionale, Cassino, 14–17 settembre 1994*. Cassino.
Peek, W. 1942 [1951]. 'Attische Inschriften', *MDAI(A)* 67: 1–231.
Peek, W. 1960. *Griechische Grabgedichte*. Berlin.
Peek, W. 1974. 'ANTH. PLAN. 322', *ZPE* 15: 142.
Peek, W. 1979. 'Zu den Gedichten des Marcellus von Side auf Regilla und das Triopion des Herodes Atticus', *ZPE* 33: 76–84.

Peek, W. 1980. *Attische Versinschriften*. ASAW lxix.2. Berlin.

Pekáry, T. 1970. 'Das Grab des Pompeius', *BHAC* 1970: 195–8.

Penella, R. 1974. 'Scopelianus and the Eretrians in Cissia', *Athenaeum* 52: 295–300.

Penzel, J. 2006. *Variation und Imitation. Ein literarischer Kommentar zu den Epigrammen des Antipater von Sidon und des Archias von Antiocheia*. Trier.

Pera, R. 1984. *Homonoia sulle monete da Augusto agli Antonini. Studio storico-tipoligico*. Genova.

Perry, B. E. 1930. 'Chariton and his romance from a literary-historical point of view', *AJPh* 51: 93–134.

Perry, B. E. 1965. *Babrius and Phaedrus*. Cambridge, MA and London.

Perry, B. E. 1967. *The Ancient Romances*. Berkeley and Los Angeles.

Petrovic, A. 2009. 'Epigrammatic contests, *poeti vaganti* and local history', in R. Hunter and I. Rutherford (eds.), *Wandering Poets in Ancient Greek Culture: Travel, Locality and Panhellenism*. Cambridge: 195–216.

Perusino, F. 1989. *Platonio: la commedia greca. Edizione critica, traduzione e commento*. Urbino.

Petsalis-Diomidis, A. 2010. *Truly beyond Wonders: Aelius Aristides and the Cult of Asklepios*. Oxford.

Petzke, G. 1970. *Die Traditionen über Apollonius von Tyana und das Neue Testament*. Leiden.

Pfeiffer, R. 1968. *A History of Classical Scholarship. Vol. 1*. Oxford.

Pflaum, H.-G. 1960–1. *Les carrières procuratoriennes équestres sous le Haut-Empire romain*. 3 vols. Paris.

Philippides, M. 1983. 'The prooemium in Longus's *Lesbiaka*', *CB* 59: 32–5.

Picard, C. 1922. *Éphèse et Claros*. Paris.

Pickard-Cambridge, A. W. 1946. *The Theatre of Dionysus in Athens*. Oxford.

Pickard-Cambridge, A. W. 1988. *The Dramatic Festivals of Athens*, 2nd ed. revised by J. Gould and D. M. Lewis 1968 with addenda 1988. Oxford.

Pingree, D. 1976. *Dorotheus Sidonius: carmen astrologicum*. Leipzig.

Pirenne-Delforge, V. and Pironti, G. 2014. 'Héra et Zeus à Lesbos: Entre poésie lyrique et décret civique', *ZPE* 191: 27–31.

Pithou, P. 1590. *Epigrammata et poematia vetera ex codicibus et lapidibus collecta*, i. Paris.

Plassart, A. 1926. 'Fouilles de Thespies et de l'Hiéron des Muses de l'Hélicon: inscriptions', *BCH* 50: 383–462.

Plastira, M. P. 1982. 'An epigram by Antipater of Thessalonica', *CL* 2: 161–4.

Pleket, H. W. 1965. 'An aspect of the emperor cult: imperial mysteries', *HThR* 58: 331–64.

Pöhlmann, E. 1970. *Denkmäler der altgriechischen Musik*. Nürnberg.

Pöhlmann, E. 2019. 'The Hymn of Mesomedes on Antinous (Inscriptions of Courion, Mitford No. 104)', *GRMS* 7: 128–39.

Poignault, R. and Schneider, C. (eds.) 2016. *Fabrique de la déclamation antique: (controverses et suasoires)*. Lyon.

Pomeroy, S. B. 1977. 'Technikai kai mousikai', *AJAH* 2: 51–68.
Pomeroy, S. B. 1981. 'Women in Roman Egypt', in H. P. Foley (ed.), *Reflections of Women in Antiquity*. New York: 303–22.
Pomeroy, S. B. 2007. *The Murder of Regilla: A Case of Domestic Violence in Antiquity*. Cambridge, MA.
Pouilloux, J. 1983. 'Delphes dans les Éthiopiques d'Héliodore; la réalité dans la fiction', *JS* 4: 259–86.
Powell, J. E. 1936. *The Rendel Harris Papyri*. Cambridge.
Power, T. C. 2010. *The Culture of Kitharôidia*. Lanham.
Prauscello, Lucia. 2011. 'Μελίβοια: the Chthonia of Hermione and Kore's lost epithet in Lasus fr. 702 PMG', *CQ* 61: 19–27.
Prauscello, L. 2013. 'Demeter and Dionysos in the sixth-century Argolid: Lasos of Hermione, the cult of Demeter Chthonia and the origins of dithyramb', in Kowalzig and Wilson (eds.): 76–92.
Préaux, C. 1929.'Lettres privées grecques d'Égypte relatives à l'éducation', *RBPh* 8: 757–800.
Pretagostini, R. (ed.) 1993. *Tradizione e innovazione nella cultura greco da Omero all'età ellenistica: scritti in onore di Bruno Gentili*. 3 vols. Roma.
Provenzale, F. 2009. *Filico di Corcira: testimonianze e frammenti. Introduzione, testo critico, traduzione e commento*. PhD dissertation, Università degli studi "Roma Tre", https://core.ac.uk/display/41157713.
Puech, B. 2002. *Orateurs et sophistes grecs dans les inscriptions d'époque impériale. Avec préface de L. Pernot*. Paris.
Puelma, M. 1960. 'Die Dichterbegegnung in Theokrits "Thalysien"', *MH* 17: 144–64.
Quet, M. H. 1992. 'Romans grecs, mosaïques romaines', in Baslez, Hoffmann and Trédé (eds.): 125–60.
Radermacher, L. 1916. 'Der Dichter Pankrates', *Berliner Philologische Wochenschrift* 883–4.
Radt, W. 1988. *Pergamon. Geschichte und Bauten, Funde und Erforschung einer antiken Metropole*. Berlin.
Rattenbury, R. M., Lumb, T. W. and Maillon J. 1960. *Héliodore. Les Éthiopiques (Théagène et Chariclée)*, 2nd ed. Paris.
Rawles, R. 2018. *Simonides the Poet: Intertextuality and Reception*. Cambridge.
Raynor, D. H. 1984. 'Moeragenes and Philostratus: two views of Apollonius of Tyana', *CQ* 34: 223–8.
Rea, J. R. 1972. '2946. Triphiodorus, Fall of Troy, 391–402', *The Oxyrhynchus Papyri. Vol. 41*. London.
Reardon, B. P. 1971. *Courants littéraires grecs des iième et iiième siècles après J.-C.* Paris.
Reardon, B. P. (ed.). 1977. *Erotica Antiqua*. Bangor, Wales.
Reardon, B. P. 1982. 'Theme, structure, and narrative in Chariton', *YClS* 27: 1–27.
Reardon, B. P. (ed.) 1989. *Collected Ancient Greek Novels*. Berkeley, Los Angeles and London.

Reardon, B. P. 1991. *The Form of Greek Romance*. Princeton.

Reardon, B. P. 1996. 'Chariton', in Schmeling 1996a: 309–35.

Reardon, B. P. 2004. *Chariton Aphrodisiensis. De Callirhoe narrationes amatoriae*. München and Leipzig.

Reeve, M. D. 1971. 'Hiatus in the Greek novelists', *CQ* 21: 514–39.

Reeve, M. D. 1982. *Longus, Daphnis & Chloe* (1st ed. 1982, 2nd ed. 1986, 3rd ed. 1994). Leipzig.

Regenauer, J. 2016. *Mesomedes: Übersetzung und Kommentar*. Studien zur klassischen Philologie. Frankfurt.

Reinach, S. 1925. 'Un mythe de sacrifice', *RHR* 91: 137–52.

Reitzenstein, R. 1893. *Epigramm und Skolion*. Giessen.

Repath, I. 2005. 'Achilles Tatius' *Leucippe and Clitophon*: what happened next?', *CQ* 55: 250–65.

Repath, I. 2011. 'Platonic love and erotic education in Longus' Daphnis and Chloe', in K. Doulamis (ed.), *Echoing Narratives: Studies of Intertextuality in Greek and Roman Prose Fiction*. ANS 13. Groningen: 99–122.

Revermann, M. 2006. *Comic Business: Theatricality, Dramatic Technique, and Performance Contexts of Aristophanic Comedy*. Oxford.

Reyhl, K. 1969. *Antonios Diogenes: Untersuchungen zu den Romanfragmenten der Wunder jenseits von Thule und zu den Wahren Geschichten des Lukian*. Tübingen.

Reynolds, J. 1999. 'The first known Aphrodisian to hold a procuratorship', in P. Scherrer, H. Taueber and H. Thür (eds.), *Steine und Wege. Festschrift für Dieter Knibbe zum 65. Geburtstag*. Wien: 327–34.

Rice, E. E. 1983. *The Grand Procession of Ptolemy Philadelphus*. Oxford.

Richardson, N. J. 1974. *The Homeric Hymn to Demeter*. Oxford.

Ricks, D. 1991, '*A. P.* 5.63', *Hermes* 119: 494–5.

Rife, J. R. 2002. 'Officials of the Roman provinces in Xenophon's *Ephesiaca*', *ZPE* 138: 93–108.

Rife, J. R. 2008. 'The burial of Herodes Atticus: élite identity, urban society, and public memory in Roman Greece', *JHS* 128: 92–127.

Rigsby, K. J. 1985. 'On the high priest of Egypt', *BASP* 22: 279–89.

Robert, L. 1930. 'Pantomimen im griechischen Orient', *Hermes* 65: 106–22.

Robert, L. 1937. *Études Anatoliennes*. Paris.

Robert, L. 1938. *Études épigraphiques et philologiques*. Paris.

Robert, L. 1959. 'Les inscriptions grecques de Bulgarie', *RPh* 33: 11–236.

Robert, L. 1960. 'Recherches épigraphiques iv–ix', *REA* 62: 276–361 (repr. in *Opera Minora Selecta* ii, Amsterdam 1969: 792–877).

Robert, L. 1968. 'L'épigrammes satiriques de Lucilius sur les athlètes', in *L'épigramme grec*. Entretiens Hardt 14. Vandoeuvres-Genève: 179–295.

Robert, L. 1977. 'Documents d'Asie Mineure', *BCH* 101: 43–132.

Robert, L. 1978a. 'Malédictions funéraires grecques', *CRAI* 122: 241–89.

Robert, L. 1978b. 'Documents d'Asie Mineure V–XVII', *BCH* 102: 395–543 (repr. in *Opera Minora Selecta* vi, Amsterdam 1987: 91–239).

Robert, L. 1979. 'Un voyage d'Antiphilos de Byzance, Anthologie Palatine X, 17, géographie antique et byzantine', *JS*: 257–94.

Robert, L. 1980a. *A travers l'Asie Mineure: poètes et prosateurs, monnaies grecques, voyageurs et géographie*. Paris.

Robert, L. 1980b. 'Deux poètes grecs à l'époque impériale', in *ΣΤΗΛΗ. Τόμος εἰς μνήμην τοῦ Νικόλαου Κοντολέοντος*. Αθήνα: 1–20.

Robert, L. 1981. 'Une épigramme satirique d'Automédon et Athènes au début de l'empire', *REG* 94: 338–61.

Robert, L. 1982. 'La date de l'épigrammatiste Rufinus. Philologie et réalité', *CRAI* 126: 50–63.

Robert, J. and L. 1948. 'Inscriptions de la vallée du Haut Caïque', *Hellenica* 6: 80–8.

Robert, J. and L. 1989. *Claros i. Décrets hellénistiques 1*. Paris.

Roberts, C. H. 1956. *Greek Literary Hands, 350 BC–AD 400*. Oxford.

Robiano, P. 2020. 'Nommer les personnages perses dans le roman grec: les choix de Chariton, *Callirhoé*, et d'Héliodore, *les Éthiopiques*', *AN* 17: 63–89.

Robinson, B. 2012. 'Helikon and the Valley of the Muses. The production of a sacred space', *JRA* 25: 227–58.

Rochette, B. 1997. *Le latin dans le monde grec*. Brussels.

Roesch, P. 2007–9. *Les Inscriptions de Thespies (IThesp), Fasc. I–XII, Concordances. Édition électronique mise en forme par Gilbert Argoud, Albert Schachter et Guy Vottéro, et publiée sous l'égide de l'UMR 5189 – HiSoMA (Histoire et Sources des Mondes Antiques)*. Maison de l'Orient et de la Méditerranée Jean Pouilloux, Lyon. www.hisoma.mom.fr/production-scientifique/les-inscriptions-de-thespies.

Rogers, G. M. 1991. *The Sacred Identity of Ephesos: Foundation Myths of a Roman City*. London.

Rohde, E. 1894. 'Zum griechischem Roman', *RhM* 28: 110–39.

Rohde, E. 1914. *Der griechische Roman und seine Vorläufer*, 3rd ed. Leipzig.

Rommel, H. 1923. *Die naturwissenschaftlich-paradoxographischen Exkurse bei Philostratos, Heliodoros und Achilleus Tatios*. Stuttgart.

Roos, A. G. 1912. *Studia Arrianea*. Leipzig.

Roos, A. G. 1968. *Arriani quae exstant omnia, II: Scripta minora et fragmenta*, 2nd ed. Addenda et corrigenda adiecit G. Wirth. Leipzig.

Rosen, R. M. 1988. *Old Comedy and the Iambographic Tradition*. American Classical Studies 19. Atlanta.

Rosenmeyer, P. A. 1992. *The Poetics of Imitation: Anacreon and the Anacreontic Tradition*. Cambridge.

Rosenmeyer, P. A. 2001. *Ancient Epistolary Fictions: The Letter in Greek Literature*. Cambridge.

Rosenmeyer, P. A. 2008. 'Greek verse inscriptions in Roman Egypt: Julia Balbilla's Sapphic voice', *ClAnt* 27: 334–58.

Rosenmeyer, P. A. 2018a. *The Language of Ruins: Greek and Latin Inscriptions on the Memnon Colossus*. Oxford.

Rosenmeyer, P. A. 2018b. 'Sapphic Memnon', in Rosenmeyer 2018a: 141–68.

Rosenmeyer, T. G. 1969. *The Green Cabinet*. Berkeley, Los Angeles and London.

Rossi, V. 1997. *Filostrato: Eroico*. Venezia.

Roueche, C. M. 1993. *Performers and Partisans at Aphrodisias in the Roman and Late Roman Periods: A Study Based on Inscriptions from the Current Excavations at Aphrodisias in Caria*. Journal of Roman Studies Monographs 6. London.

Rougemont, G. 1992. 'Delphes chez Héliodore', in Baslez, Hoffmann and Trédé (eds.): 93–9.

Ruiz Montero, C. 1991. 'Aspects of the vocabulary of Chariton of Aphrodisias', *CQ* 41: 484–9.

Ruiz Montero, C. 1994. 'Chariton von Aphrodisias: Ein Überblick', *ANRW* ii 34.2: 1006–54.

Ruiz Montero, C. 1996. 'The rise of the Greek novel', in Schmeling 1996a: 29–85.

Ruiz Montero, C. 2013. 'Antonio Diogenes autór de comedia? Observaciónes sobre la recepción de la comedia en epoca imperial', in L. M. Pino Campos, G. Santana Henriquez and J. A. López Férez (eds.), *Καλὸς καὶ ἀγαθὸς ἀνήρ· διδασκάλου παράδειγμα*. Madrid: 749–56.

Ruiz Montero, C. 2018. 'Personal names in Antonius Diogenes' *Incredible Things beyond Thule*', in A. Papaioannou, A. N. Michalopoulos and A. Zissos (eds.), *Dicite, Pierides: Classical Studies in Honour of Stratis Kyriakides*. Newcastle: 107–23.

Russell, D. A. 1983. *Greek Declamation*. Cambridge.

Russell, D. A. 1990a. 'Aristides and the prose hymn', in Russell 1990b: 199–219.

Russell, D. A. (ed.) 1990b. *Antonine Literature*. Oxford.

Russell, D. A. 1992. *Dio Chrysostom Orations VII, XII, and XXXVI*. Cambridge.

Russell, D. A. and Wilson, N. G. 1981. *Menander Rhetor*. Oxford.

Rutherford, I. C. 2000. 'The genealogy of the *boukoloi*: how Greek literature appropriated an Egyptian narrative motif', *JHS* 120: 106–21.

Rutherford, I. C. 2004. 'χορὸς ἐκ τῆσδε τῆς πόλεως (Xen. *Mem*. 3.3.12): song-dance and state-pilgrimage at Athens', in P. Murray and P. Wilson (eds.), *Music and the Muses: The Culture of "Mousike" in the Classical Athenian City*. Oxford: 67–90.

Rutherford, I. C. 2009. 'Black sails to Achilles. Pilgrimage and initiation in Philostratus' *Heroicus*', in Bowie and Elsner (eds.): 230–47.

Rutherford, I. C. 2013. *State Pilgrims and Sacred Observers in Ancient Greece. A Study of Theōriā and Theōroi*. Cambridge.

Rutherford, I. C. 2015. 'Stesichorus the romantic', in Finglass and Kelly (eds.): 98–108.

Rutherford, I. C. 2019. *Oxford Readings in Greek Lyric Poetry*. Oxford.

Saïd, S. 1977. 'Oracles et devins dans le roman grec', in J. G. Heintz (ed.), *Oracles et prophéties dans l'antiquité*. Paris: 367–403.

Sajdak, J. 1914–15. 'Spór o Hadrianowe żegnanie się ze światem', *Eos* 20: 147–58 (repr. in J. Sajdak, *Pod urokiem literatury patrystycznej i bizantyńskiej*. Poznań 2009: 192–207).

Sakolowski, P. 1893. *De Anthologia Palatina quaestiones*. Dissertation, Leipzig.

Saller, R. P. 1982. *Personal Patronage under the Early Empire*. Cambridge.

Saller, R. P. 1989. 'Patronage and friendship in early imperial Rome: drawing the distinction', in A. F. Wallace-Hadrill (ed.), *Patronage in Ancient Society*. London: 49–62.

Salvo, I. 2013. 'Romulus and Remus at Chios revisited: a re-examination of *SEG* XXX 1073', in P. Martzavou and N. Papazarkadas (eds.), *Epigraphical Approaches to the Post-Classical Polis: Fourth Century BC to Second Century AD*. Oxford: 125–37.

Sandy, G. 1982. *Heliodorus*. Boston, MA.

Sandy, G. 1989a. 'Ninus', in Reardon (ed.): 803–8.

Sandy, G. 1989b. 'Iolaus', in Reardon (ed.): 816–18.

Scarcella, A. M. 1968. *La Lesbo di Longo Sofista*. Roma.

Scarcella, A. M. 1977. 'Les structures socio-économiques du roman de Xénophon d'Éphèse', *REG* 90: 249–62.

Scarcella, A. M. 1981. 'Metastasi narratologica del dato storico nel romanzo erotico greco', *Materiali e contributi per la storia della narrativa greco-latina* 3: 341–67.

Schachter, A. 1981. *Cults of Boiotia, fasc. 1 Acheloos to Hera*. BICS Suppl. 38.1. London.

Schachter, A. 1986. *Cults of Boiotia, fasc. 2 Herakles to Poseidon*. BICS Suppl. 38.2. London.

Schanz, M. and Hosius, C. 1922[1969]. *Geschichte der römischen Literatur, bis zum Gesetzgebungswerk des Kaisers Justinian. III. Die Zeit von Hadrian 117 bis auf Constantin 324. Neuarb. Auf. von C. Hosius und G. Kruger*. München.

Schatzmann, A. 2012. *Nikarchos II: Epigrammata. Einleitung, Texte, Kommentar.* Hypomnemata 188. Göttingen.

Scheibner, G. 1965. 'Ein Unbekanntes Philitasfragment in der Berliner Papyrussammlung', in F. Zucker (ed.), *Menanders Dyskolos als Zeugnis seiner Epoche*. Berlin: 103–14.

Schissel von Fleschenberg, O. 1913. *Die griechische Novelle, Rekonstruktion ihrer literarischen Form*. Halle.

Schizzerotto, G. 1968. 'Uguccione e l'epigrafe per il cavallo di Adriano', *Maia* 20: 276–83.

Schlapbach, K. 2015. 'Music and meaning in Longus' Daphnis and Chloe: the inset tales in their performative settings', *Phoenix* 69.1/2: 79–99.

Schmedt, H. 2020. *Antonius Diogenes, Die unglaublichen Dinge jenseits von Thule. Edition, Übersetzung, Kommentar*. Berlin and New York.

Schmeling, G. 1974. *Chariton*. New York.

Schmeling, G. 1980. *Xenophon of Ephesus*. New York.

Schmeling, G. 1996a. *The Novel in the Ancient World*. Leiden, New York and Köln.

Schmeling, G. 1996b. Review of O'Sullivan 1995, *AJP* 117: 660–3.

Schmeling, G. 2011. *A Commentary on the Satyrica of Petronius*. Oxford.

Schmid, W. 1887–96. *Der Atticismus in seinen Hauptvertretern von Dionysius von Halikarnass bis auf den zweiten Philostratus*. 5 vols. Stuttgart.

Schmid, W. 1932. 'Das Socratesbild der Wolken', *RhM* 81: 30–8.

Schmid, W. and Stählin, O. 1920–6. *Geschichte der griechischen Literatur ii. 2.* München.

Schmidt, E. A. 1969. 'Hirtenhierarchie in der antiken Bukolik', *Philologus* 113: 183–200.

Schmitz, T. 1997. *Bildung und Macht. Zur sozialen und politischen Funktion der zweiten Sophistik in der griechischen Welt der Kaiserzeit.* Zetemata 97. München.

Schmitz, T. 2017. 'The rhetoric of desire in Philostratus' *Letters*', *Arethusa* 50, 257–82.

Schönberger, O. 1989. *Longos. Hirtengeschichten von Daphnis und Chloe.* Darmstadt (1st ed. Berlin 1960).

Schröder, S. 1999. *Geschichte und Theorie der Gattung Paian: eine Kritische Untersuchung mit einem Ausblick auf Behandlung und Auffassung der lyrischen Gattungen bei den alexandrinischen Philologen.* Stuttgart.

Schulte, H. 2004. *Die Epigramme des Ammianos. Text, Übersetzung, Kommentar.* Trier.

Schwartz, J. 1967. 'Quelques observations sur des romans grecs', *AC* 36: 536–52.

Scobie, A. 1973. *More Essays on the Ancient Romance and Its Heritage.* Meisenheim am Glan.

Scobie, A. 1983. *Apuleius and Folklore.* London.

Scodel, R. (ed.) 1993. *Theater and Society in the Classical World.* Ann Arbor.

Segal, C. 1974. 'Theocritus' Seventh Idyll and Lycidas', *WS* 8: 20–76 (repr. in Segal 1981, 110–66).

Segal, C. 1981. *Poetry and Myth in Ancient Pastoral.* Princeton.

Segers, H. 2017. 'The apple in Longus' Lesvos: Sapphic imagery in the poetic space of *Daphnis and Chloe*', in *Classics@16: Seven Essays on Sappho.* Center for Hellenic Studies. Washington, DC. http://nrs.harvard.edu/urn-3:hlnc.essay:SegersH.The_Apple_in_Longus_Lesvos.2017

Sens, A. 2004. 'Doricisms in the New and Old Posidippus', in B. Acosta-Hughes, E. Kosmetatou and M. Baumbach (eds.), *Labored in Papyrus Leaves. Perspectives on an Epigram Collection attributed to Posidippus (P. Mil. Vogl. VIII 309).* Washington, DC: 65–83.

Sens, A. 2007. 'One thing leads (back) to another', in Bing and Bruss (eds.): 373–90.

Sens, A. 2011. *Asclepiades of Samos: Epigrams and Fragments.* Oxford.

Shapiro, H. A. 1990. 'Homonoia', in *LIMC* 1: 476–9.

Sharples, R. W. 1983. *Alexander of Aphrodisias on Fate.* London.

Shear, J. 2013. 'Choruses and tripods. The politics of the choregia in Roman Athens', in B. Kowalzig and P. Wilson (eds.): 389–408.

Sheppard, A. R. R. 1984–6. 'Homonoia in the Greek cities of the Roman Empire', *AncSoc* 15–17: 229–53.

Sherwin-White, S. M. 1978. *Ancient Cos.* Hypomnemata 51. Göttingen.

Sider, D. 1997. *The Epigrams of Philodemus.* New York.

Sider, D. 2006. 'The new Simonides and the question of historical elegy', *AJPh* 127: 327–46.

Sider, D. 2020. *Simonides. Epigrams and Elegies: Edited with an Introduction, Translation and Commentary*. Oxford.

Sidwell, K. 1994. 'Aristophanes' Acharnians and Eupolis', *C&M* 45: 71–115.

Sidwell, K. 2009. *Aristophanes the Democrat: The Politics of Satirical Comedy during the Peloponnesian War*. Cambridge and New York.

Sijpesteijn, P. J. 1969. 'A new document concerning Hadrian's visit to Egypt', *Historia* 18: 107–18.

Silk, M. S. 1974. *Interaction in Poetic Imagery with Special Reference to Early Greek Poetry*. Cambridge.

Sittl, C. 1890. *Die Gebärden der Griechen und Römer*. Leipzig.

Skenteri, F. 2005. *Herodes Atticus Reflected in Occasional Poetry of Antonine Athens*. Stockholm.

Slater, W. J. 1971. 'Pindar's house', *GRBS* 12: 141–52.

Small, S. G. 1951. 'Marcus Argentarius: a poet of the Greek Anthology', *YClS* 12: 65–145.

Smith, R. R. R. 1987. 'The imperial reliefs from the Sebasteion at Aphrodisias', *JRS* 77: 88–138.

Smith, R. R. R. 1988. 'The *Ethne* from the Sebasteion at Aphrodisias', *JRS* 78: 50–77.

Smith, R. R. R. 1993. *The Monument of C. Iulius Zoilos*. New York.

Smith, R. R. R. 2013. *The Marble Reliefs from the Julio-Claudian Sebasteion: Aphrodisias VI*. Darmstadt.

Smith, S. D. 2007. *Greek Identity and the Athenian Past in Chariton: The Romance of Empire*. ANS 9. Groningen.

Smith, S. D. 2014. *Man and Animal in Severan Rome: The Literary Imagination of Claudius Aelianus*. Cambridge.

Snyder, J. M. 1989. *The Woman and the Lyre: Women Writers in Classical Greece and Rome*. Carbondale.

Sokolowski, F. 1936.'Sur le péan de Philodamos', *BCH* 60: 135–43.

Solmsen, F. 1940. 'Some works of Philostratus the Elder', *TAPhA* 71: 556–72 (repr. in *Kleine Schriften* ii. Hildesheim 1968: 74–90).

Solmsen, F. 1941. 'Philostratos (9)–(12)', in *RE* xx.1. Stuttgart: cols. 124–34.

Sommerstein, A. H., Halliwell, S., Henderson, J. and Zimmermann, B. (eds.) 1993. *Tragedy, Comedy and the Polis: Papers from the Greek Drama Conference, Nottingham, 18–20 July 1990*. Bari.

Sommerstein, A. H. 1997. 'The theatre audience, the *Demos* and the *Suppliants* of Aeschylus', in C. B. R. Pelling (ed.), *Greek Tragedy and the Historian*. Oxford: 63–79.

Sourvinou-Inwood, C. 1991. *'Reading' Greek Culture: Texts and Images, Rituals and Myths*. Oxford.

Spanoudakis, K. 2002. *Philetas of Cos*. Mnemosyne Suppl. 221. Leiden and Boston.

Spawforth, A. J. and Walker, S. 1985. 'The world of the Panhellenion. I. Athens and Eleusis', *JRS* 75: 78–104.

Spawforth, A. J. and Walker, S. 1986. 'The World of the Panhellenion. II. Three Dorian Cities', *JRS* 76: 88–105.
Spawforth, A. J. 2011. *Greece and the Augustan Cultural Revolution*. Cambridge.
Spoerri, W. 1975. 'Lykos no. 12', *KP* iii 818.
Stadter, P. A. 1965. *Plutarch's Historical Methods. An Analysis of the De Mulierum Virtutibus*. Cambridge, MA.
Stadtmüller, H. 1894–1906. *Anthologia Graeca epigrammatum Palatina cum Planudea*. Leipzig.
Stadter, P. A. 1980. *Arrian of Nicomedia*. Chapel Hill.
Stanford, W. B. 1936. *Greek Metaphor: Studies in Theory and Practice*. Oxford.
Stechow, W. 1953. 'Heliodorus' *Aethiopica* in art', *JWI* 16: 144–52.
Stefanis, I. K. 1988. *Διονυσιακοὶ τεχνῖται*. Heraklion.
Stein, H. 1869–71. *Herodoti historiae*. Berlin.
Steinbichler, W. 1998. *Die Epigramme des Dichters Straton von Sardes. Ein Beitrag zum griechischen paiderotischen Epigramm*. Berlin, Bern and Frankfurt.
Steinmetz, P. 1982. *Untersuchungen zur römischen Literatur des zweiten Jahrhunderts nach Christi Geburt*. Wiesbaden.
Steinmetz, P. 1989. 'Lyrische Dichtung im 2. Jahrhundert n. Chr.', *ANRW* ii 33.1: 259–302.
Stella, L. A. 1956. 'Gli dei di Lesbo in Alceo fr. 129 LP', *PP* 11: 321–34.
Stephens, S. A. 1994. 'Who read ancient novels?', in J. Tatum (ed.), *The Search for the Ancient Novel*. Baltimore and London: 405–18.
Stephens, S. A. and Winkler, J. J. 1995. *Ancient Greek Novels: The Fragments*. Princeton.
Stone, L. M. 1978. 'The obscene use of μέγας in Aristophanes', *AJP* 99: 427–32.
Storey, I. C. 2003. *Eupolis, Poet of Old Comedy*. Oxford.
Storey, I. C. 2014. 'The first poets of Old Comedy', in M. Fontaine and A. C. Scafuro (eds.), *The Oxford Handbook of Old Comedy*. Oxford: 95–112.
Stewart, A. F. 1982. 'Dionysos at Delphi. The pediments of the sixth temple of Apollo and the religious reform in the age of Alexander', in B. Barr-Sharrar and E. N. Borza (eds.), *Macedonia and Greece in Late Classical and Early Hellenistic Times*. Washington, DC: 205–27.
Stramaglia, A. 1996. 'Fra "consume" e "impegno": usi didattici della narrativa nel mondo antico', in Pecere and Stramaglia (eds.): 99–166.
Stramaglia, A. 1999. *Res inauditae, incredulae. Storie di fantasmi nel mondo Greco-latino*. Bari.
Stramaglia, A. 2000.*Ἔρως. Antiche trame greche d'amore*. Bari.
Strauss, L. 1965. *Socrates and Aristophanes*. Chicago.
Strauss Clay, J. 1996. 'Fusing the boundaries: Apollo and Dionysos at Delphi', *Metis* 11: 83–100.
Strazdins, E. 2022. 'Herodes Atticus and the sanctuaries of Achaea: reinterpreting the Roman present via the Greek past', in A. Kouremenos (ed.), *The Province of Achaea in the 2nd Century CE*. London: 166–90.

Strazdins, E. 2023. *Fashioning the Future in Roman Greece: Memory, Monuments, Texts*. Oxford.

Strohmaier, G. 1976. 'Übersehenes zur Biographie Lukians', *Philologus* 120: 117–22.

Strubbe, J. 1984–6. 'Gründer kleinasiatischer Städte: Fiktion und Realität', *AncSoc* 15–17: 253–304.

Sullivan, J. P. 1993. *Martial: The Unexpected Classic. A Literary and Historical Study*. London and New York.

Svensson, N. 1926. 'Réception solennel d'Hérode Atticus', *BCH* 50: 527–35.

Swain, S. C. R. 1991. 'The reliability of Philostratus' *Lives of the Sophists*', *ClAnt* 10: 148–63.

Swain, S. C. R. 1992. 'Novel and Pantomime in Plutarch's *Antony*', *Hermes* 120: 76–82.

Swain, S. C. R. 1996. *Hellenism and Empire. Language, Classicism and Power in the Greek World AD 50–250*. Oxford.

Swain, S. C. R. (ed.) 1999. *Oxford Readings in the Greek Novel*. Oxford and New York.

Swain, S. C. R., Harrison, S. J. and Elsner, J. (eds.) 2007. *Severan Culture*. Cambridge.

Syme, R. 1968. 'The Ummidii', *Historia* 17: 72–105 (repr. in *Roman Papers* ii. Oxford 1979: 659–93).

Syme, R. 1986. *The Augustan Aristocracy*. Oxford.

Syme, R. 1987. 'M. Bibulus and four sons', *HSPh* 91: 185–98.

Szepessy, T. 1957. 'Die Aithiopika des Heliodoros und der griechische sophistische Liebesroman', *AAntHung* 5: 241–59.

Szepessy, T. 1976. 'Le siège de Nisibe et la chronologie d'Héliodore', *AAntHung* 24: 247–76.

Szepessy, T. 1978. 'Zur Interpretation einer neu entdeckten Liebesroman', *AAntHung* 26: 29–36.

Tagliabue, A. 2013. 'The victory of Greek Ionia in Xenophon's *Ephesiaca*', in Whitmarsh and Thomson (eds.): 225–42.

Tagliabue, A. 2017. *Xenophon's Ephesiaca: A Paraliterary Love-Story from the Ancient World*. ANS 22. Groningen.

Taillardat, J. 1962. *Les images d'Aristophane: études de langue et de style*. Paris.

Taplin, O. P. 1993. *Comic Angels*. Oxford.

Tatum, J. 1989. *Xenophon's Imperial Fiction*. Princeton.

Tatum, W. J. 1997. 'Friendship, politics and literature in Catullus', *CQ* 47: 482–500.

Taylor, A. E. 1911. 'The Phrontisterion', in *Varia Socratica*. Oxford: 129–77.

Taylor, C. C. W. 1983. 'The arguments in the *Phaedo* concerning the thesis that the soul is *harmonia*', in J. P. Anton and A. Preus, *Essays in Ancient Greek Philosophy*, vol. ii. Albany: 217–31 (repr. in C. C. W. Taylor, *Pleasure, Mind, and Soul: Selected Papers in Ancient Philosophy*. Oxford 2008: 74–90).

Teske, D. 1991. *Der Roman des Longos als Werk der Kunst: Untersuchungen zum Verhältnis von Physis und Techne in Daphnis und Chloe*. Münster.

Thesleff, H. 1965. *The Pythagorean Texts of the Hellenistic Period*. Åbo.

Thomas, C. 1995. 'At home in the city of Artemis. Religion in Ephesos in the literary imagination of the Roman period', in H. Koestler (ed.), *Ephesos. Metropolis of Asia*. Valley Forge (repr. in *Harvard Theological Studies* 2004: 81–117).

Thomas, R. 2000. *Herodotus in Context: Ethnography, Science and the Art of Persuasion*. Cambridge.

Thyresson, I. L. 1964. 'Quatre lettres de Claude Élien inspirées par le Dyscolos de Ménandre', *Eranos* 62: 7–25.

Tilg, S. 2010. *Chariton of Aphrodisias and the Invention of the Greek Love Novel*. Oxford.

Tobin, J. 1993. 'Some new thoughts on Herodes Atticus' tomb, his stadium of 143/4, and Philostratus *VS* 2.550', *AJA* 97: 81–9.

Tobin, J. 1997. *Herodes Attikos and the City of Athens: Patronage and Conflict under the Antonines*. Amsterdam.

Too, Y. L. (ed.) 2001. *Education in Greek and Roman Antiquity*. Leiden and Boston.

Tovar, A. 1971. 'Un nuevo epigrama griego de Córdoba: Arriano de Nicomedia, Procónsul de Bética?', in P. Laín Entralgo (ed.), *Estudios sobre la obra de Américo Castro*. Madrid: 403–12.

Trapp, M. B. 1986. *Studies in Maximus of Tyre*. DPhil thesis, University of Oxford.

Trapp, M. B. 1990. 'Plato's *Phaedrus* in second-century Greek literature', in Russell 1990b: 141–73.

Trapp, M. B. 2016. 'Philostratus, Aristides and the geography of declamation', in Poignault and Schneider (eds.): 197–210.

Trendall, A. D. and Webster, T. B. L. 1971. *Illustrations of Greek Drama*. London.

Trenkner, S. 1958. *The Greek Novella in the Classical Period*, Cambridge.

Treu, K. 1989. 'Der antike Roman und sein Publikum', in H. Kuch (ed.), *Der antike Roman. Untersuchungen zur literarischen Kommunikation und Gattungsgeschichte*. Berlin: 178–97.

Trzaskoma, S. 2005. 'A novelist writing "history": Longus' Thucydides again', *GRBS* 45: 75–90.

Trzaskoma, S. 2010. *Two Novels from Ancient Greece: Chariton's Callirhoe and Xenophon of Ephesus' An Ephesian Story: Anthia and Habrocomes*. Indianapolis.

Trzaskoma, S. 2011. 'The Anabasis of Chaereas and Callirhoe', *AN* 9: 1–35.

Trzaskoma, S. 2018. 'Citations of Xenophon in Chariton', in Chew, Morgan and Trzaskoma (eds.): 65–79.

Tsavari, I. 1990. *Διονυσίου Ἀλεξανδρέως οἰκουμένης περιήγησις. Κριτική Εκδοσή*. Ioannina.

Ubsdell, S. 1983. *Herodotus on Human Nature: Studies in Herodotean Thought, Method and Exposition*. DPhil thesis, University of Oxford.

Vaio, J. 1971. 'Aristophanes' *Wasps*. The relevance of the final scenes', *GRBS* 14: 335–51.

Valley, G. 1926. *Über den Sprachgebrauch des Longus*. Inaugural-Dissertation, Uppsala.

Valley, G. 1928. *Longos. Daphnis och Chloe. En Herderoman, Översatt från Grekiskan av Gunnar Valley, Försedd med Teckningar av Yngve Berg.* Stockholm.

Vallois, R. 1931. 'Les strophes mutilées du péan de Philodamos', *BCH* 55: 241–364.

Vamvouri, M. 1998. 'Fiction poétique et realité historique à propos du *Péan* de Limenios', *Gaia* 3: 37–57.

Vamvouri Ruffy, M. 2004. *La fabrique du divin. Les Hymnes de Callimaque à la lumière des Hymnes homériques et des hymnes épigraphiques.* Kernos, suppl. 14. Liège.

van Bremen, R. 1996. *The Limits of Participation. Women and Civic Life in the Greek East in the Hellenistic and Roman Periods.* Amsterdam.

van Groningen, B. 1958. 'Quelques problèmes de la poésie bucolique grecque', *Mnemosyne* 11: 293–317.

Van Nijf, O. 1997. *The Civic World of Professional Associations in the Roman East.* Amsterdam.

van Straten, F. T. 1976. 'Daikrates' Dream. A votive relief from Kos, and some other kat'onar dedications', *BABesch* 51: 1–38.

van Thiel, H. 1971. *Der Eselsroman. I, Untersuchungen.* Zetemata 54. München.

Vetta, M. 1976–7. 'Un capitolo di storia di poesia simposiale (per l'esegesi di Aristofane, "Vespe" 1222–1284)', *DArch* 9–10: 243–66 (repr. in Vetta (ed.) 1983: 119–31).

Vetta, M. (ed.) 1983. *Poesia e simposio nella Grecia antica: Guida storica e critica.* Roma and Bari.

Veyne, P. 1978. *Le pain et le cirque. Sociologie historique d'un pluralisme politique.* Paris.

Vestergaard, T. 2000. 'Milesian immigrants in late Hellenistic and Roman Athens', in G. J. Oliver (ed.), *The Epigraphy of Death.* Liverpool: 81–110.

Vian, F. 1954. 'Les comparaisons de Quintus de Smyrne', *RPh* 28: 30–51, 235–54.

Vian, F. 1959. *Recherches sur les 'Posthomerica' de Quintus de Smyrne.* Paris.

Vian, F. 1974. *Argonautiques. Tome I: Chants I–II.* Paris.

Vian, F. 1980. *Argonautiques. Tome II: Chant III.* Paris.

Vian, F. 2001. 'Echoes and imitations of Apollonius in late Greek epic', in A. D. Papanghelis and T. Rengakos (eds.), *A Companion to Apollonius Rhodius.* Leiden 387–411.

Vian, F. 1986. 'L'épopée grecque de Quintus de Smyrne à Nonnos de Panopolis', *Bulletin de l'Association Guillaume Budé*: 333–43.

Vieillefond, J.-R. 1987. *Longus, Pastorales (Daphnis et Chloé).* Paris.

Vinchesi, M. A. 1988. 'L'epitafio di Adriano per il cavallo Boristene (CE 1522 Bücheler)', in V. Tandoi (ed.), *Disiecti membra poetae. Studi di poesia latina in frammenti.* Foggia: 180–93.

Vogliano, A. 1938. 'Un papiro di Achille Tazio', *SIFC* 15: 121–30.

Vogliano, A. and Cumont, F. 1933. 'La grande iscrizione Bacchica del Metropolitan Museum / La grande inscription Bachique du Metropolitan Museum', *AJA* 37: 215–70.

Vollgraff, W. 1926. 'Le péan delphique à Dionysos', *BCH* 50: 263–304.
Walden, J. W. H. 1894. 'Stage terms in Heliodorus' Aethiopica', *HSPh* 5: 1–43.
Walker, A. 1992. '*Erōs* and the eye in the *Love-letters* of Philostratus', *PCPhS* 38: 132–48.
Walsh, P. G. 1970. *The Roman Novel*. Cambridge.
Waltz, P., Soury, G., Irigoin, J. and Laurens P. 1974. *Anthologie grecque. Anthologie palatine, t. VIII, livre IX, épigr. 359–827*. Paris.
Warden, P. and Bagnall, R. 1988. 'The forty thousand citizens of Ephesus', *CPh* 83: 220–3.
Wartenberg, U. 1997. 'Papyri of Apollonius Rhodius nos. 4414–17, 4419', in *The Oxyrhynchus Papyri. Vol. 64*. London.
Webb, R. 2008. *Demons and Dancers: Performance in Late Antiquity*. Cambridge, MA and London.
Webb, R. 2013. 'Mime and romance', in T. Whitmarsh and S. Thomson (eds.), *The Romance between Greece and the East*. Cambridge: 285–99.
Weber, W. 1907. *Untersuchungen zur Geschichte des Kaisers Hadrianus*. Leipzig.
Weil, H. 1895. 'Un péan delphique à Dionysos', *BCH* 19: 343–418.
Weil, H. 1897. 'Le péan delphique à Dionysos', *BCH* 21: 510–13.
Weil, H. and Reinach, T. 1909–13. 'Hymnes avec notes musicales', *FdD* iii 2: 147–59.
Weitzmann, K. 1959. *Ancient Book Illumination*. Cambridge, MA.
Wellmann, M. 1934. *Marcellus von Side als Arzt und die Koiranides des Hermes Trismegistos*. Philologus Suppl. 27.2. Leipzig.
Wesseling, B. 1988. 'The audience of the ancient novels', *GCN* 1: 67–79.
West, M. L. 1970. 'Melica', *CQ* 20: 205–15.
West, M. L. 1974. *Studies in Greek Elegy and Iambus*. Berlin and New York.
West, M. L. 1977. 'Balbilla did not save Memnon's soul', *ZPE*: 120.
West, M. L. 1978. 'Die griechische Dichterinnen der Kaiserzeit', in H. G. Beck, A. Kambylis and P. Moraux (eds.), *Kyklos: Griechisches und Byzantinisches: Rudolf Keydell zum 90. Geburtstag*. Berlin: 106–8.
West, M. L. 1982. *Greek Metre*. Oxford.
West, M. L. 2013. *Hellenica. Volume III: Philosophy, Music and Metre, Literary Byways, Varia*. Oxford.
West, S. 1991. 'Herodotus' portrait of Hecataeus', *JHS* 111: 144–69.
West, S. 2003. 'κερκίδος παραμυθία? For whom did Chariton write?', *ZPE* 143: 63–9.
Whitby, J. M. 2007. 'The *Cynegetica* attributed to Oppian', in Swain, Harrison and Elsner (eds.): 125–34.
Whitehead, D. M. 1986. *The Demes of Attica, 508/7–ca. 250 BC*. Princeton.
Whitmarsh, T. 2001. *Greek Literature and the Roman Empire*. Oxford.
Whitmarsh, T. 2004. 'The Cretan lyre paradox: Mesomedes, Hadrian and the poetics of patronage', in Borg (ed.): 377–402.
Whitmarsh, T. 2005a. 'The lexicon of love: Longus and Philetas *GRAMMATIKOS*', *JHS* 125: 145–8.
Whitmarsh, T. 2005b. 'The Greek novel: titles and genre', *AJPh* 126: 587–611.

Whitmarsh, T. 2008a. 'Class', in Whitmarsh (ed.): 72–87.

Whitmarsh, T. (ed.) 2008b. *The Cambridge Companion to the Greek and Roman Novel*. Cambridge.

Whitmarsh, T. 2011. *Narrative and Identity in the Greek Novel: Returning Romance* Cambridge.

Whitmarsh, T. 2013. *Beyond the Second Sophistic: Adventures in Greek Postclassicism*. Berkeley, Los Angeles and London.

Whitmarsh, T. 2018. *Dirty Love: The Genealogy of the Ancient Greek Novel*. Oxford.

Whitmarsh, T. 2020. *Achilles Tatius' Leucippe and Cleitophon*. Cambridge.

Whittaker, M. 1982. *Tatian. Oratio ad Graecos and fragments*. Oxford.

Wiegand, T. 1904. 'Reisen in Mysien', *MDAI(A)* 29: 254–339.

Wifstrand, A. 1933. *Von Kallimachos zu Nonnos*. Lund.

Wilamowitz-Moellendorf, U. von 1880. *Aus Kydathen. Philologische Untersuchungen* i. Berlin.

Wilamowitz-Moellendorf, U. von 1906. *Textgeschichte der griechischen Bukoliker*. Berlin.

Wilamowitz-Moellendorf, U. von 1913. *Sappho und Simonides*. Berlin.

Wilamowitz-Moellendorf, U. von 1921. *Griechische Verskunst*. Berlin.

Wilamowitz-Moellendorf, U. von 1928. Marcellus von Side. *Sitzungsb. der Preuss. Ak. Wiss., Phil. Hist. Kl.* 1982: 3–30 (repr. in *Kleine Schriften* ii. ed. R. Pfeiffer *et al.*, Berlin 1941 (repr. 1960): 192–228).

Wilamowitz-Moellendorf, U. von 1889. 'Commentariolum Grammaticum III', *Index scholarum publice et privatim in Academia Georgia Augusta per semester aestivum*. Göttingen: 3–30 (repr. in *Kleine Schriften* iv ed. K. Latte, Berlin 1962: 619–59).

Willi, A. (ed.), 2002. *The Language of Greek Comedy*. Oxford.

Williams, F. 1971. 'A Theophany in Theocritus', *CQ* 21: 137–45.

Williams, G. W. 1978. *Change and Decline*. Berkeley, Los Angeles and London.

Willis, W. H. 1968. 'A census of the literary papyri from Egypt', *GRBS* 9: 205–41.

Wilson, N. G. 2007. *Aristophanis fabulae*. 2 vols. Oxford.

Wilson, N. G. 2015. *Herodoti Historiae*. 2 vols. Oxford.

Wilson, P. 2000. *The Athenian Institution of the Khoregia*. Cambridge.

Wilson, P. (ed.) 2007. *The Greek Theatre and Festivals. Documentary Studies*. Oxford Studies in Ancient Documents. Oxford.

Winkler, J. J. 1980. 'Lollianos and the Desperadoes', *JHS* 100: 155–81.

Winkler, J. J. 1982. 'The mendacity of Calasiris and the narrative strategy of Heliodoros' *Aithiopika*', *YClS* 27: 93–158.

Winkler, J. J. 1990. *The Constraints of Desire. The Anthropology of Sex and Gender in Ancient Greece*. London and New York.

Wiseman, T. P. 1995. *Remus: A Roman Myth*. Cambridge.

Wörrle, M. 1988. *Stadt und Fest im kaiserzeitlichen Kleinasien: Studien zu einer agonistischen Stiftung aus Oinoanda*. München.

Wouters, A. 1994. 'Longus, Daphnis et Chloé: le prooemion et les histoires enchâssées, à la lumière de la critique récente', *LEC* 62: 131–67.

Wyss, B. 1936. *Antimachi Colophonii reliquiae*. Berlin.

Young, D. C. C. 1968. 'Author's variants in the manuscript tradition of Longus', *PCPhS* 194: 65–74.

Young, D. C. C. 1971. 'Second thoughts on Longus' second thoughts', *PCPhS* 197: 91–107.

Ypsilanti, M. 2018. *The Epigrams of Crinagoras of Mytilene: Introduction, Text, Commentary*. Oxford.

Zanetto, G. 1990. 'La lingua dei romanzieri greci', *GIF* 42: 233–42.

Zanetto, G. 2001. 'Iambic Models in Aristophanic Comedy', in A. Cavarzere, A. Barchiesi and A. Aloni (eds.), *Iambic Ideas: Essays on a Poetic Tradition from Archaic Greece to the Late Roman Empire*. Lanham: 65–76.

Zanker, G. 1980. 'Simichidas' walk and the locality of Bourina', *CQ* 30: 373–7.

Zanker, P. 1995. *Die Maske des Sokrates. Das Bild des Intellektuellen in der antiken Kunst*. München (transl. in English as *The Mask of Socrates*. Berkeley and Los Angeles 1997).

Zecchini, G. 1989. *La cultura storica di Ateneo*. Milano.

Zeitlin, F. 2008. 'Religion', in Whitmarsh (ed.): 91–108.

Ziebarth, E. 1913. *Aus der antiken Schule. Sammlung griechischer Texte auf Papyrus, Holztafeln, Ostraka, ausgewählt und erklärt*, 2nd ed. Bonn.

Zimmermann, B. 1993. 'Aristophanes und die Intellektuellen', in Bremer and Handley (eds.): 255–86.

Index Locorum

This index does not register the numerous *loci* that are no more than recorded in the tables in Chapter 40.

Index of Greek Terms

General Index

www.ingramcontent.com/pod-product-compliance
Ingram Content Group UK Ltd.
Pitfield, Milton Keynes, MK11 3LW, UK
UKHW052044090325
455831UK00005B/10

9 781107 058125